This book follows Daniel's last, *The Crown and Completion of All*
more thorough treatment of the sa

The Servant of God Luisa Piccarreta was a 19th and 20th centu
Jesus (encompassing thousands of pages of material) reveal a new, definitive gift of sanctity for the
Church — *the Gift of Living in the Divine Will* — and trumpet its impending universal reign. **Here you**
will find an introduction to just what this Gift entails (after a foundation for this introduction has
been laid in accord with Church doctrine), an explanation of how to receive this Gift yourself, a
description of the nature of its universal reign (along with how you can hasten this reign), and a
theological analysis of the orthodoxy of these revelations as perfectly and beautifully harmonious
and compatible with Catholic faith and morals.

The top cover image shows the mystery of the Annunciation — the greatest event in history — because
the essence of Living in the Divine Will is contained within this most sublime moment. Though
countless renditions exist, I have chosen the painting by Leonardo da Vinci because it is among the few
that rightly depicts Our Lady as higher than the Archangel Gabriel — who, though referred to as an
Archangel, nevertheless belongs to the highest (Seraphic) choir, and even still is immeasurably below
the Immaculate Queen. The middle cover image is an actual photograph from NASA (with color
optimization) of the sun rising over the earth. The rear cover image is the original [Vilnius] Divine
Mercy Image Jesus gave to St. Faustina along with the promise that whoever venerates it, "will not
perish."

In this book you will see that from Our Lady's Fiat, and our own modeled after it, the Reign of the
Divine Will shall dawn first in our own hearts, and then over the whole world, in fulfillment of what
was both the greatest prayer and greatest prophecy, for it was uttered by the Son of God Himself: *Thy*
Kingdom come, Thy Will be done, on earth as it is in Heaven, **and the total fulfillment of what Pope St.**
Pius X foretold as both a prophecy and a Magisterial teaching in his Encyclical *E Supreme* — **The**
Restoration of All Things in Christ.

Moratorium Notice: As of the publication of this book, the official Church-approved and footnoted Critical Edition of Luisa's Volumes is not yet published, and as such a temporary Moratorium continues to exist, limiting the open publication of the unofficial manuscript translations of Luisa's works, but not preventing the dissemination of these translations among prayer groups dedicated to Luisa's spirituality. (It is important to note, however, that at least two of Luisa's works may already licitly be openly published in their entirety: "The Hours of the Passion" and "The B.V.M. in the Kingdom of the Divine Will.") Despite several false claims to the contrary found scattered about the internet (including on some otherwise trustworthy websites), this Moratorium does not prohibit lay people from writing and speaking on Luisa's writings, nor does it prohibit individual excerpts of the writings from being used in publications with great theological care for Catholic orthodoxy (which Daniel has painstakingly ensured in each case throughout this book);

indeed, such publication has already been done many times (fully licitly) to date since the Moratorium's issuing, sometimes even with full Ecclesiastical approbation. Daniel's last book used only quotes from Luisa's writings found in Fr. Iannuzzi's Doctoral Thesis only because he wished to provide a resource for even the most overly cautious of Catholics; not because this approach was in any way in itself necessary. Nor does this Moratorium imply any form of reservation or "unapproved status" from the Church regarding Luisa's writings; in fact, every relevant consideration points to the opposite conclusion: that Ecclesiastical Authority earnestly desires that these revelations be believed and promulgated (this conclusion is definitively demonstrated within the pages of this book; for now, suffice it to say that the very Archbishop from whom this Moratorium came was — he has since died — an avid Divine Will devotee and zealously promoted Luisa, her cause, and her revelations). More details on this matter can be found in the corresponding Appendix.

Published March 4, 2019

© Daniel O'Connor

ISBN 9781795766197

To the four women of my life: The Blessed Virgin Mary, my heavenly mother; my dear wife, Regina, whose support and help made this book possible; my daughter, Mary Faustina; and my own earthly mother, Eileen.

Readers of my first book may remember its own dedication page, in which I shared that my mother had just been diagnosed with malignant Pleural Mesothelioma, a particularly lethal cancer of the lungs with a prognosis generally allowing for only 6-12 months to live, even with aggressive treatment (although in my mother's case, the doctors thought she might even have 1-3 years).

That was over 4 years ago. Since then, we have been praying nightly for her healing through the intercession of Luisa Piccarreta.

According to my mother's last CT Scan, she is completely cancer free.

ALL FOR THE SACRED HEART OF JESUS, THROUGH THE IMMACULATE HEART OF MARY, UNDER THE PROTECTION OF ST. JOSEPH, TERROR OF DEMONS AND PATRON OF THE UNIVERSAL CHURCH.

1) __Brief Contents__

__Pages to Read for a Quick Introduction to Luisa's Revelations__

Table of Contents

2) Preface: My Journey in the Divine Will

I begin by sharing some history of my own life's journey in the Divine Will in hopes that readers will pause and, upon reflection, come to realize that their own lives, too, have truly been journeys in the Will of God. But I hasten to add that there is no need for anyone to read this preface; it is not important for understanding anything in this book, for it pertains only to its unworthy author. I include this preface, also, recognizing that some readers may wish to understand the inspiration and motivation of the authors of books they read (a justifiable wish in these days of rampant ulterior motives), and this motivation will be made clear in the following few pages.

My journey began in the Year of Our Lord 1986, on the Feast of St. Francis of Assisi, when I came forth from my mother's womb—or, rather, it began nine months earlier, for as Jesus says to Luisa, "*as soon as a baby is conceived, My Conception goes around the conception of the baby, to form him and keep him defended.*"[1] But I have no memories to share until around my 3rd birthday, when my first memory was formed as I stood at my deeply repentant uncle's death bed, moments before his particular Judgment, as he prayerfully clutched Rosary beads in his hand and succumbed to the AIDS that he contracted from his former wayward lifestyle. Though my 3-year-old understanding could not grasp it at the time, imprinted upon my soul nevertheless was the potency of a clear impression: the ugliness of life apart from the Will of God, and the beauty of a return to the same, no matter what had transpired in the ugly time.

But sadly, the spiritual seeds sown in me by that event took many years to sprout, for, although I indeed grew up a believing and mostly practicing Catholic, I was lukewarm, and in the behavior of my youth I blended in quite well with the average promiscuous, intemperate, wild partying teenager of the day. While living that lifestyle, I began studying Mechanical Engineering at RPI, for I was dead-set on saving the world through my ideas for inventions relating to better energy generation and transportation technology that I had already begun designing.

Upon entering I did not know that it would ironically be at this institution—which, in its very motto, urges its students to "change the world"—that I would discover that the change this world needs has nothing to do with technology. For it was there, at RPI of all places, that I realized no invention would save the world, but only something much simpler. My path to this recognition began when, shortly after enrolling, I finally saw that my sins were tearing my soul to shreds, and vowed to radically change my life forever. I still remember the precise moment of incredible clarity dawning upon my mind like the rising sun; it presented itself without invitation as I was merely amid my ordinary daily endeavors, and seared into my soul forever the recognition of one simple fact that took no heed of the rationalizations I had hitherto concocted: I knew the Will of God (for I did at least know the basics from my Confirmation classes), and I was not doing it; thus, there was absolutely nothing left to wait for. It was I who had to change, not God, and no delay could be justified. The vow followed immediately in the very spot I was standing.

The foundation of my awakening to a genuine life of Faith now being laid, I nevertheless wandered about for some time in affairs far below my calling as a Catholic. At that time, what bothered me most about my fellow students was their slothfulness and obsession with video games. So, along with two friends, I started the "RPI Up Sluggards,"[2] essentially an adventure club of sorts. If some endeavor was painful, embarrassing, fearful, exertion-requiring, or disgusting, we pursued it and encouraged all in the group to do the same; jumping into iced-over ponds in January, doing "tough mudders" and triathlons, scaling mountains, cliffs, and caves, hunting for wild rattlesnakes to eat for dinner while camping, and the list goes on with plenty of absurdities (I will be sure to leave our "embarrassing" endeavors to the imagination). Although I soon thereafter realized that much of what we did lacked the virtue of prudence, a noble theme did at least exist in our

---

[1] March 6, 1932

[2] A take on the Benjamin Franklin quote, "Up, sluggard, and waste not life; in the grave will be sleeping enough."

inspiration: leading a life dedicated to satiating the self-will is one doomed to failure, therefore that which the self-will universally tends towards (comfort, pleasure, safety, and the like) must be zealously opposed by deliberately and regularly engaging in activities opposite them.

Thankfully God continued guiding me and I realized that video game obsession—and the vice of sloth in general—though lamentable, was only one small part of a much bigger battle that could only be won by Christ. I received the grace of this recognition thanks to the apartment I moved into before my junior year, or rather, its proximity to a perpetual adoration chapel and daily Mass (located only one block away). I began to frequent both—and as a student at a University known for its enormous workload for engineering undergraduates, I was used to getting little sleep, and thus became a go-to sub to call for the nocturnal adoration hours. This precious time with Jesus in the Blessed Sacrament made me realize that, ultimately, all that matters is becoming a saint.

Pursuant to this new end to which I decided I must dedicate my life, I attended World Youth Day in Australia the following summer and, deeply impacted by an exhibit there on the life of Bl. Pier Giorgio Frassati and by praying next to his incorrupt body, I had another moment of great clarity; one that, though it did not result in a vow, did result in a firm decision. I recognized that God certainly deserved at least one hour of each of my remaining days' twenty-four, and I then took on as a commitment those two great gifts that have ever since served as the foundation of my daily life (and will, please God, until the day I die); daily Mass and daily Rosary.

Now, in this time I was devouring knowledge of the Faith. I can relate to the many conversion stories one often hears of Protestants coming into the Catholic Church and then, being blown away by the Sacred Tradition we are blessed with, proceeding to bury themselves in books. From this era of my life I recall most fondly my time reading the Imitation of Christ and the works of St. Louis de Montfort, St Francis de Sales, and St. Alphonsus Liguori (books I still love and strive to live by; long before I knew anything of Luisa, God lead me to St. Alphonsus' *Uniformity with God's Will* and convicted me that it above all contained the ultimate key to sanctity). But I also stumbled upon many other works; some found through my lengthy perusal of Traditionalist websites, which did not leave such holy impressions upon my heart, but instead inclined me to a servile fear in the spiritual life due to the "fewness of those saved." I became obsessed with avoiding the possibility of damnation, and my preferred methods of combating this possibility were mortification and scrupulosity.

I spent years of my life around this time sleeping each night on a wooden board, taking only full-blast cold showers, taking little or no pleasure in food, and sometimes wearing a cilice all day (although I had earlier undertaken some of these practices for other reasons, their continuation was due to this newfound servile fear). More problematic,[3] I became afraid of approaching Jesus in the Eucharist thanks to the scrupulosity which accompanies this servile fear.

You see, I had already poured over as many readings as I could find on the matter of the number of the elect, but nothing satisfied me, for all the apologists and theologians I read had themselves spoken only with human authority (and I did not know of any Magisterium broaching the issue). How can human words heal a wound seemingly inflicted by Divine Words? (As it then wrongly seemed to me that the near impossibility of my being among the elect was a consequence of the words of Scripture). They cannot. But it dawned on me that there was another authority to consult: Heaven itself. Thus, I asked God for my first ever sign; and, although I will spare you the details, suffice it to say that He gave me "neon lights," and in this incredibly clear sign, my scrupulosity and

---

[3] I should add that I do not intend to imply that I now reject the notion of mortification, or that I've since "grown out" of my "overzealous early days when I thought the flesh should be forcefully opposed," as some self-proclaimed "experienced Catholics" assert, in a thinly veiled attempt to clothe their lukewarmness in pious looking attire. Rather, I now know – as will be discussed in this book – that mortification must be undertaken for the right reasons (out of love for God and a desire to suffer redemptively with Christ, not out of a servile fear of Him), and if it is done for the right reasons it will naturally be done in accord with the virtue of prudence (for indeed, prudence, being a virtue, has the same *form* as all the virtues: charity).

servile fear finally began to die (although the process still took time).[4] If my life thus far had been a journey in the Divine Will, this was the point I realized that there is nothing formulaic about such a journey, as if one could merely discover a few dogmas to live by and rest assured of the sufficiency thereof; rather, it is more personal than even a marriage, and requires constant Communion with the Holy Spirit to hear His voice speaking to you, directly, in everything, and a corresponding commitment to heed that voice, come what may.

Immediately after graduating the next year, I began working as an engineer for GE Global Research. One day there, I became a "world record holder;" having successfully run a test resulting in the greatest quantum emission of electrons off a carbon nanotube surface yet achieved. It also so happened that the same evening, after work, I accepted an invitation to participate in a local radio show with a friend to defend the Right to Life in a debate on abortion. At the end of the day came the epiphany that I had done incomparably more good for the world by simply speaking up for our unborn brothers and sisters than I did by contributing to further the technological advancement of our technology-obsessed culture. Furthermore, around that same time, what I already had grown to understand in the preceding year (in my moments of honesty at least) became abundantly obvious to me in this job: the corporate engineering world was simply not my calling, and I was delaying obedience to the Divine Will by remaining in it. I realized at that moment in my life that, no matter how many "experienced Catholics" told me I really *had to* remain in it for at least five years given my circumstances, I simply knew it was not where God wanted me.

This knowledge tore at me and rendered me unbearably restless. But, thankfully, I now had a new weapon in my arsenal for precisely such times: asking God for His direct and clear guidance. One morning, when my restlessness was extreme, I went to the adoration chapel early in the morning before work, and I suddenly found myself asking

Our Lord in the Blessed Sacrament to simply remove me from this job somehow if remaining in it not be His Will. That very day at work, I was told by my boss' boss that I needed to "promise to never again talk about religion at work if I were to keep my job." Knowing that was a promise I could not in good conscience make, I quit on the spot. (At that time, I was the Outreach Coordinator for the local 40 Days for Life campaign and had been zealous in both praying and sidewalk counseling outside Planned Parenthood and going door-to-door in nearby neighborhoods to spread word. I decided to distribute invitations at work as well, which is what GE found intolerable, along with a pro-life comment I made on their online employee portal).

Later that year, on the Vigil of the Solemnity of All Saints, I was sitting in the basement of St. Mary's Church in New Haven, Connecticut, listening attentively to the great scholar, Dr. Scott Hahn, sharing his wisdom with a group of eager ears. Incidentally, I did not then know that I would marry my wife in that very Church less than four years later; indeed, I did not even know her then, nor would I meet her for two more years, for on that day I thought I had merely driven hours from my home in order to visit a parish I had never before been to or heard of, but that I had coincidentally been told was hosting a great speaker, and this simply was an opportunity I did not want to miss.

Most ingrained in my memory from these talks was one astounding observation in particular that Dr. Hahn made: what if, he pondered, just as Satan has always tried to squelch God's greatest plans by slaughtering innocent children—seeking to eradicate Moses through inciting Pharaoh's murderous rage against the newborns in Egypt, and doing the same for Our Lord through Herod—so too today, through the greatest slaughter of innocents in history (indeed, the greatest evil in general, namely, abortion) Satan is trying again to prevent some new great Divine Intervention? This observation could not possibly have been more pertinent to the calling that God would send my way in mere minutes.

For during a break after one of Dr. Hahn's talks, I

---

[4] I later discovered that every trustworthy private revelation that has addressed the issue teaches squarely – either explicitly or implicitly – that, although damnation is the greatest tragedy imaginable and indeed countless souls are now falling into hell, nevertheless most are saved—albeit only thanks to Purgatory. The only private "revelation" that I know of which says otherwise is that of "Maria Divine Mercy," in which Jesus said that 33 times as many people go to hell as go to Heaven. This "revelation" is now condemned by the Church.

was approached by a fellow attendee of the event—an older man I also did not know at the time, but whom I now know to be very pious and devout. I soon learned that his intention was not to make small talk, but to share an important message with me. *"There is something big coming your way, and you need to be open to it,"* he relayed to me with conviction. Though he did not know what exactly "it" was, he assured me, as confused by the mystery as he was certain of its reality, that there was *"something special here"* that he had *"never seen before."* Somehow I knew, and never once forgot, that this message was not of human origin, but rather truly constituted a Divine Message to which I had no choice but to humbly submit.

***

Exactly one year later, I moved out to the old, dilapidated, and abandoned St. George's rectory in Utica, New York, to begin a new apostolate and job living there alone while working with several others during the day to convert it into a transitional home for homeless young men (it was to be called the John Bosco House, and once we had it ready, I served there as the live-in house father or big brother to the residents we welcomed). Friday of that same initial week was a particularly grueling day of manual labor spent preparing the house's floors, and I was eager to take a break from work and head off to daily Mass at the nearby parish that I was blessed to live an easy five-minute walk from; a Church in which I could not only attend daily Mass but also visit Our Lord in the Blessed Sacrament any time, night or day, in its Perpetual Adoration chapel. As God would have it (as I learned much later on), my wife's family, too, had lived in Utica several years before, and she frequented this very chapel which was so instrumental to my journey.

So off I was, as I thought, to attend daily Mass as I did each ordinary, uneventful day. But as I entered the Church, instead of seeing the usual priest, I saw whom I now know to be Fr. Joseph Iannuzzi in the Sanctuary. After an announcement was made, I realized that I had come not to the ordinary Friday evening Mass, but had rather stumbled upon the beginning of a weekend-long retreat on a topic I had never formerly heard of: *the Gift of Living in the Divine Will in the writings of the Servant of God Luisa Piccarreta.* What followed were two days of utter holy amazement as I had never before experienced.

"Something big" that I "needed to be open to" could not have been more accurate a prophecy—indeed, there is nothing greater, nothing more essential that we be open to—than the Divine Will.

The adventure of life went on, and I continued to both study the Gift of Living in the Divine Will and strive to receive this Gift myself. About ten months later, I embarked upon another rather epic journey that God had placed on my heart: to purchase a 60-day unlimited ride Greyhound Bus pass and, with only a small backpack on my person, travel from one corner of the country to the other and back; making of it a true road-trip-pilgrimage. My goals were three-fold: to discern my vocation, to visit holy sites throughout the country, and to listen to an audiobook of all of Luisa's revelations as I spent hundreds of hours sitting on buses, waiting at bus stops (often overnight in some less than inviting places), and walking. In the midst of this pilgrimage—between sleeping on the wood floor and waking at midnight to pray the Divine Office with a holy Franciscan order in Indiana, stumbling upon moose while trekking through the remote Sangre de Cristo mountains of New Mexico, and participating in a Eucharistic Procession outside a Planned Parenthood in Albuquerque—I received amazingly clear guidance of Providence, through the intercession of St. Francis on the Feast of the Portiuncula, that I was to begin studying as a seminarian at Holy Apostles College & Seminary in Cromwell, CT—even though God had made it equally clear that He was not yet revealing my ultimate vocation to me at that time. Alas, knowing at least the next step is enough.

Though it was technically too late in the game for such a large move so quickly to go forward "by the book," I knew I was called to at least try—and try I did. Faithful as He always is when we follow His guidance, God opened the door, and that same month I found myself at this Institute, in the midst of hundreds of wonderful seminarians, priests, religious brothers and sisters, and lay students. (I later discovered that my wife, too, as a completely last-minute maneuver, had felt called to totally change her preexisting plans to the contrary and instead apply to Holy Apostles. And although her application should not have been feasible to accommodate either, God intervened, and she began studying there the same semester.)

Now, one day each month at Holy Apostles was set

aside as a "Day of Recollection," in which the seminarians kept total silence as they prayed and attended a retreat given by a priest. It was my first day of recollection as a seminarian, and I entered the Chapel that morning eager to receive whatever edification it might be God's Will to impart through the priest's lips, though I was entirely uninformed as to whom it would be or what would be the topic. As I looked towards the sanctuary, I saw to my great surprise a familiar face. I immediately knew I would not be disappointed, for the holy amazement on the Divine Will that I had received from this priest ten months earlier was alive and well.

I left the Chapel knowing that there was no way to deny God had called me to dive head first into these most sublime revelations on His Most Holy Will, given to the Servant of God Luisa Piccarreta, and to do my humble best to introduce others to the same. Ever since then it has been the overarching passion of my life, and I pray it may become the same for yours as well.

God's clear guidance to me did not end that day, and He revealed that—as blessed and grace-filled a time as my one semester as a seminarian was—His Will for me was not priesthood, but marriage. I continued studying at Holy Apostles as a lay student, proposed to my wife on the Feast of the Immaculate Conception the following year in that same Chapel at Holy Apostles after we together re-consecrated ourselves to Mary, and I received my

Diploma for a master's in theology in this chapel as well the year after that. Two months after graduation—on the 96th anniversary of Our Lady's promise at Fatima that her Heart would Triumph, and an Era of Peace would be granted to the world—my wife and I were married. We moved into a 400 square-foot plumbing-free pond house (which my father and I had built several years earlier) before embarking upon our honeymoon road-trip-pilgrimage around the holy sites of the country.

In the years that have followed, the Will of God has led me still, in many ways: founding an apostolate (the Divine Will Missionaries of Mercy—DWMoM.org), buying and renovating a 100-year-old broken down house, a run for U.S. Congress, becoming a Philosophy Professor, beginning my doctoral studies in Philosophy, and many other things. Above all, the Will of God has blessed me and my wife with three beautiful children (with a fourth who departed for Heaven after a brief time in the womb) and, we hope, will bless us with many more. Amid all this, I've learned that if there's one thing the Divine Will is *not*, that one thing would be *boring*. I remain as dedicated as ever to doing my small part in helping to make the Divine Will known and loved, that it may reign on earth as It does in Heaven.

Please join me in this Greatest of All Missions and read on to learn more about it.

3) Foreword by Mark Mallett

There is a mysterious passage in the Book of Daniel that speaks of a time to come that will be unsurpassed in distress. He is given visions of beasts and battles, trials and triumphs. But an angelic messenger then says to him: *"As for you, Daniel, keep secret the message and seal the book until the end time; many shall wander aimlessly and evil shall increase"* (Dan 12:4).

Several hundred years later, St. John would pen his "Apocalypse" using remarkably similar symbolic language. But now the Christian community would be beneficiaries of not only hindsight, but the Divine prism of the New Covenant through which the writings of the prophets and patriarchs could pass. Christ, the "light of the world", would illuminate that which was written in *shadows* and *types* of things to come. The "secret" was beginning to unfold.

Still, the early Church's understanding of the eschaton was limited, evidenced by the imminent expectation by some of Christ's return in glory. St. Paul, like St. John, was given glimpses of the travails that would assail the Church and the appearance of Christ in judgment. Still, he admitted; *"At present we see indistinctly, as in a mirror... At present I know partially; then I shall know fully..."* (1 Corinthians 13:12)

Now, as the Church crosses the threshold of the third millennium, *we* are the beneficiaries of 2000 years of hindsight, doctrinal development, and prophetic revelations that enable us to "see" more clearly. And this especially, as Pope St. Paul VI attested, with "signs of the end" clearly emerging. And yet, few scholars have undertaken a proper study of the Book of Revelation that isn't restricted to a mere allegorical sense, or that edits out (as rationalists tend to do) those "private" revelations or Marian apparitions that, in fact, do not threaten or correct the "deposit of faith" but further illuminate it.

The word "apocalypse" means "unveiling," which is a reference, in part, to the *unveiling of a bride.* Just as a bride's face is partially hidden, as her veil begins to lift, her beauty comes more into focus. In a word, St. John's Apocalypse (the Book of Revelation) is not so much about the persecution of the Church by her infernal enemy, the "red dragon" and "the beast." Rather, it is about the purification and unveiling of a new and internal beauty and holiness of the Bride of Christ, the Church. *"Let us rejoice and exult and give him the glory, for the marriage of the Lamb has come, and his Bride has made herself ready; it was granted her to be clothed with fine linen, bright and pure."* (Revelation 19:7-8) This affirms the teaching of St. Paul who compared Christ and the Church to a husband and wife, *"that he might present the Church to himself in splendor, without spot or wrinkle or any such thing, that she might be holy and without blemish"* (Ephesians 5:27).

Clearly, a brief examination of the "signs of the times" reveals a Bride who is anything *but* spotless and unblemished, anything *but* prepared for Christ's return. Who could have envisioned the kind of scandals that have made the Church's bridal garments so filthy? Nonetheless, the prophet Daniel and Saints Paul and John all foretold a future period when apostasy would cause a massive falling away from the Faith and "abomination" would enter her sanctuary. The reason God permits the "son of perdition" or "Antichrist" comes into view: he is the instrument the Lord permits to humble and purify the mystical Body of Christ.

But clearly, according to a straight forward reading of Revelation 19 and 20 (and how the Early Church Fathers read it), this persecution of Antichrist is *not* the end of the world. After the destruction of the beast and its followers, there ensues a period of what St. John calls a "thousand years" (Rev 20:6) and what the Fathers would affirm as being the "Day of the Lord." Says Lactantius, "**...this day of ours, which is bounded by the rising and the setting of the sun, is a representation of that great day to which the circuit of a thousand years affixes its limits.** *(Fathers of the Church: The Divine Institutes, Book VII, Chapter 14, Catholic Encyclopedia;* www.newadvent.org*).* And again, **"Behold, the Day of the Lord shall be a thousand years."** (Letter of Barnabas, *The Fathers of the Church,* Ch. 15) It is a day of both judgment and vindication, but most especially, of *preparation for the Wedding Feast of the Lamb.*

If indeed the mysteries of Daniel's vision would be "unsealed" toward the end times, then *The Crown of Sanctity in The Revelations of Jesus to Luisa Piccarreta* is unquestionably lifting the veil higher. This may, in fact, be one of the most important books in recent times. For within its pages are explained, in a precise, orthodox, and practical manner, what exactly the "thousand years" entail and how we can and must prepare for the Day of the Lord. But unlike other "end times" literature that are rife with speculations, wild conspiracies, myopic interpretations, and even heresies, Daniel O'Connor has merely unpacked for the reader what was taught from the beginning (even if the "father of lies" has tried his best to distort those teachings).

The main protagonist of this work is Servant of God Luisa Piccarreta to whom Christ "unveiled" the theological framework of precisely *how* God is going to restore and purify the Bride of Christ. As Daniel masterfully weaves Sacred Scripture, private revelation, philosophy, apologetics, and careful theology throughout the book, something begins to emerge from between the lines that will startle and even overwhelm the reader: *Hope*. At a time when the Church is suffering under the weight of her sin and all signs point toward the imminence of her own Passion, this book has the potential to bring supernatural encouragement, joy and strength. It has for me.

At one point, Jesus gives Luisa and us a hint as to when these times might come: "***The time in which these writings will be made known is relative to and dependent on the disposition of souls who wish to receive so great a good, as well as on the effort of those who must apply themselves in being its trumpet-bearers by offering up the sacrifice of heralding in the new era of peace...***" (Jesus to Luisa, *The Gift of Living in the Divine Will in the Writings of Luisa Piccarreta*, n. 1.11.6, Rev. Joseph Iannuzzi). Daniel O'Connor is one of the privileged few among Christ's flock to be the herald of so great a triumph that lies beyond this present Storm. As you read each page, then, and dispose your soul to God's plan, you too will be hastening the coming of the Christ's Kingdom that we pray for each day: "Thy Kingdom come and Thy will be done *on earth as it is in heaven.*"

When St. John Paul II prophetically called the youth to "**be the watchmen of the morning who announce the coming of the sun who is the Risen Christ!** *(Message of the Holy Father to the Youth of the World,* XVII World Youth Day, n. 3) he added that "**The young have shown themselves to be** *for Rome* **and** *for the Church* **a special gift of the Spirit of God...** (*Novo Millennio Inuente*, n.9). Daniel O'Connor is such a soul. He is not only completely faithful to the Church's magisterium through his rare gift of theological clarity that is both deep and yet accessible; he is also a true servant to his students, family, and friends. Those who know him respect Daniel not only for this authenticity but for his zeal and bravery. I am reminded of St. John Paul II's words that "**holy people alone can renew humanity.**" (World Youth Day Message for 2005, Vatican City, Aug. 27th, 2004)

In that regard, Daniel and this work form an integral part of the "signs of a new springtime" that continue to unexpectedly appear in the midst of this present Winter.

Mark Mallett

Author of *The Final Confrontation* and "The Now Word" blog

www.MarkMallett.com

4) This Book's Viewpoint

100% Catholic

Let there be no confusion at all: I write this book as, above all else, a 100% faithful, orthodox, and obedient Roman Catholic. I absolutely submit—without question, reservation, or hesitation—to every single one of the teachings of the Church, and I always will. Rest assured that each word in this book is coming from one who would rather shed every drop of his blood than deny a teaching of the Catholic Church. And I wish to state from the onset, without any hesitation or ambiguity: **I submit the entire contents of this book, unconditionally, to the judgment of Holy Mother Church.**

Furthermore, I write this book as one fully cognizant of the fact that Public Revelation is already complete, and that Jesus' revelations to Luisa are *private* **revelations.** As such, they have no right to add to, much less correct, anything contained in the Deposit of Faith. Rather, their role is to further explicate this Deposit of Faith, as the Catechism of the Catholic Church, paragraph 66-7, teaches is its role.

And yet I write this, as well, as a Catholic fully committed to Luisa's revelations, completely convinced that they are thoroughly authentic, and deeply convicted that they constitute the greatest mission in history and the greatest private revelation that ever has been given or ever will be given (while not in the least detracting from the enormous importance of the many other private revelations Heaven has blessed us with, especially in the past two centuries).

Therefore, we must begin by considering that much (if not most) error which infects our minds arises from either failing to see a contradiction where one exists, or insisting upon seeing a contradiction where none exists. While the former trap especially ensnares the worldly (i.e. the Dictatorship of Relativism), it is the latter trap that is most dangerous for religious people; especially those who are subtly proud or too sure of themselves—that is, those whose sense of security comes not primarily from trust in the Divine Mercy, but from a vain confidence in their own intellectual grasp of Doctrine. It is by this latter error that the Pharisees condemned Our Lord; for they refused to see how the words of Jesus Christ in no way contradicted God's Revelation to Moses. And it is this same trap that a faithful Catholic must be zealously on guard against in learning about Luisa's revelations. Be assured that there is not a single contradiction between them and Catholic Faith and Morals. This has already been settled by multiple theologians appointed by the Vatican to this very task. But just as it can sometimes require patience and prayer to see how—to give another example—there is no contradiction between the Documents of the Second Vatican Council and the older Magisterial Documents, so too it will no doubt require the same to see how some more astounding teachings in Luisa's writings are fully orthodox.

Likewise here, it is important to commit to remaining patient, prayerful, and humble; otherwise there is no point in continuing, and you might as well put this book down—but first, do at least ask yourself this question: *"When, in His infinite wisdom, God decrees that the time has come to bless the world with the Greatest Private Revelation, will it not perhaps be more than a mere confirmation of all of my opinions and current understandings? Will it not, rather, at once confirm the essence of my Faith and all its true teachings while also correcting my own limitations I have placed upon it, revealing its full glory like the rising sun, when previously I searched about with only a lamp?"* If you have prayed sincerely for humility before asking that question, you will easily find the grace to answer it in the affirmative immediately after it is posed.

"There are more things in Heaven and earth, Horatio, than are dreamt of in your philosophy" – Shakespeare

Abbreviations, formatting, style, etc.

As with all books, the best way to read this one is from cover to cover, as I have carefully and deliberately laid out the order of the various chapters and sections. But there is no strict necessity to read it so thoroughly; this book may simply be used as a reference to answer individual questions when the need arises. For the latter use, **I have made the Table of Contents particularly detailed and comprehensive, and I encourage any reader to jump freely to whatever section he**

wishes to know more about. Those who do read this book from cover to cover will need to forgive a small bit of repetitiveness, as I needed to resort to this style at times in order to ensure that certain sections could reasonably stand on their own; however, my repetition, where it is found, is only for this single intent, and you can be confident you will not find in this book that patronizing form of repetition wherein authors refuse to trust their readers to remember and take note of important things the first time they are presented, and consequently say the same thing over and over again.

Miscellaneous points:

- Whenever a footnote contains only a date (Month, Day, Year), or a quotation is attributed only to a date, this is a reference to the entry that corresponds to that date in Luisa's Diary.
- For the sake of brevity, I will regularly use the phrase **"Luisa's revelations"** in this text. It must be understood that **what I mean by this is "the private revelations given by Jesus and Mary to the Servant of God Luisa Piccarreta."**
- With respect to the quotes themselves from Luisa's Revelations, emphasis may be added (by way of bolding, italicizing, or underlining), but **understand that all such emphasis has been added by me and was not found in the original, unless otherwise noted.** This is true for all quotes in this book; not just those from Luisa's writings.
- Please note that **"CCC"** is a reference to the Catechism of the Catholic Church.
- Most Bible quotations will be taken from the Revised Standard Version: Catholic Edition; although other translations will be used, including the Douay Rheims and the New American Bible.
- Whether you are reading this book as a PDF (on a computer or printed out) or as a purchased paperback, its dimensions are the same in order to ensure that page numbers may be referenced identically, no matter what version is being used.
- Footnotes may include information which is particularly important to the content they correspond to, so whenever time allows, they should be read. Needless to say, **if any confusion or concern arises after reading a sentence in this book, be** *sure* **to read the footnote if the sentence has one; as the footnote will hopefully address the concern.** Relevant information which is important but somewhat less urgent is placed in Appendices.

***

For the sake of brevity, I make heavy use of ellipses (that is, the abridging "…") when quoting Luisa's revelations. I do this in order to not give anyone the impression that this book's brief sample of Jesus' words to Luisa is sufficient. No, it really is necessary to dive headfirst into the writings themselves; hence the quotes I do provide are generally carefully picked through so that only the gist of the teaching is presented—this way, I hope, no one will be even tempted to suppose that I think this unworthy book I have written, which is nothing but an introduction, is actually any sort of substitute for the Book of Heaven itself; the actual 36 Volumes (and other writings) Jesus gave to Luisa.

Some veterans in Divine Will spirituality may criticize this book as inadequate; especially when it comes to the highest and greatest modes of Living in the Divine Will. **I completely agree with them;** this book is *radically* inadequate. I often refer to my task with this book as to "introduce," but a better way of looking at this book is perhaps to consider it as nothing but an invitation or a preview, just like a movie preview is only an invitation to watch the film. And just as no one begrudges a preview for only giving glimpses, I hope no one will be offended that I do the same in this book, now that my intention with it is clear. Luisa's writings themselves contain the necessary truths for real growth in continuously living and acting in the very center of the Divine Will in the highest degree. In this book, on the other hand, all you will find is the heartfelt plea of Luisa's weakest and most unworthy follower beseeching others to at least begin to take the first steps. Tasks beyond these first steps are far beyond my meager talents. I would much rather merely invite people in from the highways and byways, so that, upon entering, they may learn these truths from Luisa's writings themselves, but also—if they seek additional commentary—from teachers far worthier than myself. And there are many of them: I think of Fr. Joseph Iannuzzi, Fr. Robert Young, Thomas Fahy, Hugh Owen, Fr. Gabriel Barrera, Mother Gabrielle, Fr. John Brown, Robert Lozano, Robert Hart, Tony Hickey, and many others. If these teachers of the

Divine Will and others like them are the main act, then I am not even a warm-up act. Quite the contrary; I am just a man out in the streets going up to as many souls as I can find and begging them to come inside.

Scattered throughout this book is material that I have previously published: much of my previous book, *The Crown and Completion of All Sanctity*, is republished here in the corresponding sections. I have also republished here and added to some of my own material from several of my blog posts (at www.DSDOConnor.com), my Divine Will Missionaries of Mercy website (www.DWMoM.org), and my evangelization website (www. PrepareToSeeHim.org). Finally, I wrote some of Part Three of this book (on the Era of Peace) originally as a research paper for a graduate theology course on Eschatology in 2017. Needless to say, any and all work created by others is presented and cited clearly as such. However, if reading this book as an "ebook," one should be careful to ensure that it is appropriately displayed with the block-quote formatting, as the absence of such formatting would mean that quotations from other authors might not appear to be quotes. (Formatting can be verified by checking other versions of the book which can be found through DSDOConnor.com)

My last book

A stack of books in my office

5) Introduction

I have a confession to make. Having read many spiritual, theological, and philosophical books over many years, I have observed a common theme in these situations. My reaction after putting them down is often:

"Oh, what wonderful things I have just read! I have just learned hundreds of excellent pieces of advice that I should really live my life by … but **how on earth am I to even begin to do this? I could scarcely at this moment pass a pop-quiz on the contents of these pieces of advice, much less succeed in, first, remembering them all; second, holding them all continually before my mind; third, realizing when I am in a situation that they apply to; and, fourth, succeeding in applying them to these situations!"**

Perhaps you sympathize with my sentiments, in which case you will be relieved to hear that Living in the Divine Will is the answer to all such anxieties. It is the simplest thing you will ever learn about the spiritual life, while also being the most endless, beautiful, deep, wide, and intricate a thing you will ever learn about the same. And the truly great thing is that the simplicity enfolds within itself the intricacy, while the intricacy is permeated throughout by the simplicity. What this means for you, practically, is that after you have read this one single page which follows, you can rise to the same height as one who has spent his whole life studying Luisa's writings. And if at any point during your journey in the Divine Will the greatness and diversity of what you are exploring overwhelms you, you can always return to the following page to be reminded of the great simplicity of the journey you have embarked upon, and thus be reassured that you have nothing to fear and nothing to even suffer the slightest anxiety about. You are already where you need to be. For it is as simple as this:

The Essence of the Message in One Page

At this unique moment in the history of the world, the fitting time has at long last arrived in which God wishes to give us His Own Will—the Gift that contains every imaginable gift—the true Crown and Completion of all Sanctity both in Heaven and on earth. This Gift entails not only the grace to do God's Will perfectly but also the total immersion of your human will within His Will, so that this Divine Will becomes the life principle of your soul even as your soul is the life principle of your body.

Within this Gift is all love, invincible joy, and perfect peace. Within It is absolute assurance of salvation. Within It is total deliverance from Purgatory. Within It is God's infinite pleasure. Within It is the complete victory of every noble mission in one simple principle. Within It alone is the full realization of man's creation in the Image *and Likeness* of God. Within It is the Culmination of Deification, the fruitfulness of Mystical Marriage, the aspiration of the Unification of Wills, and the essence of Marian Consecration. Within It is the Triumph of the Immaculate Heart of Mary promised at Fatima.

You cannot earn this Gift or merit It—you can only allow God to give It to you, and in exchange for His Divine Will, He asks only for your loving and trusting relinquishing of the tiny pebble of your own human will.

Whoever you are, no matter what, it is easy to allow Him to give His Will to you: simply say with sincerity, "*Jesus, I Trust in You. Thy Will be Done. I give you my will, and in return I want to live only in Your Will.*" If you strive to converse with Him continually in this manner, then rest assured that He has given you His Will. Though your journey is not yet over, the victory already permeates your every step.

God wishes also to give this Gift to the whole world. Pray unceasingly, therefore, for the Coming of the Kingdom of the Divine Will, by way of which God's Original Design for the world and for mankind will at last be realized. Pray with the joy and confidence that comes from knowing that the arrival of this reign is a guarantee, for it is nothing other than the full realization of the *Fiat Voluntas Tua* of the Lord's Prayer, which Jesus Himself prayed, and thus bears the absolute certainty of being fulfilled. Its arrival is only a question of time, but you can—and now are called to—hasten this time.

Entrust yourself completely to Our Lady, who lived more perfectly in the Divine Will than any other creature ever has or ever will, and she, who loves you—her dear child—will ensure that you Live in the Will of her Son. Especially let her sorrows and the Passion of her Son be always before your mind.

Finally, rejoice always in the invincible and continuous peace that will inevitably inundate the soul of anyone who really believes these truths.

"Do you want that My Will Reigns and Lives in you as Life? If you truly want it, everything is done... not too much is needed to Live of My Will... if [your volition] decides and strongly and perseveringly wants it, already [you have] conquered Mine and made It [yours]." —Jesus to Luisa. Solemnity of St. Joseph, 1935.

"See then, how easy it is to live in Our Will: the creature does not have to do new things, but whatever she does—that is, to carry out her life as We gave it to her, in Our Will." —Jesus to Luisa. May 17, 1938.

"O! how I would Love everyone to know that if they want to Live in My Will, they have a Queen and a Powerful Mother who will compensate for all they lack. She will raise them on Her Maternal lap ... " —Jesus to Luisa, from the very last paragraph of Luisa's writings, the Fourth Day of Christmas, 1938.

The Greatest Story Ever Told

Let the preceding page stand as a perennial reminder of the essence of this message, and what the essence of our response must be.

And now, we proceed to consider more deeply what God is doing in these amazing revelations, and let us begin—where else—at the *very* beginning.

All Christians know how it all began, and even Pagan religions usually teach the main thrust of the nature of creation somewhat correctly: The Universe, the World, and most importantly *man himself* came out of God's Creative Hands perfect in every way. Whatever was essential to the nature of man was not lacking in man as God created him, for if it were lacking then God would have created an evil,[5] which could never be. But what is essential to the nature of man? Certainly, his perfect happiness, perfect health, and perfect safety are all essential… **but, above all else, his perfect *holiness* is that which is truly called for by man's nature itself; made in the image and likeness of God.**[6] And if one now were to behold how creation was issued forth from God, one word would ring out: *beauty*.

But beauty, the Angelic Doctor[7] rightly teaches, "consists in due proportion."[8] Therefore, we call something "beautiful" if it contains within itself the symmetry necessary for the recognition of its proportionality. For example, a beautiful sanctuary never contains an off-center altar with a collection of only icons on the right side, and a collection of only statues on the left side. The greatest thing—the altar (and tabernacle)—must be in the center, and both sides of it must be symmetric, though not identical. This symmetry, as an essential characteristic of beauty, applies not only to spatial considerations but, of utmost importance, to chronological ones. **The greatest authors all know that to write a great story, they must begin writing it knowing that they will, after the story's trial has been endured and conquered, return the setting in some manner to where it began.** *The Lord of the Rings*, written by the devout Catholic scholar J.R.R. Tolkien, and often considered the greatest novel of modern times, gives a prime example of this symmetry. It begins in the green and peaceful land of the Shire, only to return to this same setting after the great adventure, the tremendous trial, and the vanquishing of the evil antagonist. Likewise, Alexander Dumas' *The Count of Monte Cristo* begins with the blissful life of the betrothed Edmond Dantès and Mercédès, only to return to this bliss after enormous trials, with the final words of the book reminding us that *"all human wisdom is summed up in these two words, 'Wait and Hope.'"*

Nothing could be more germane to the question at hand, for in reading this book you will see that **God, as the Greatest Author, will not fail to ensure that His own story contains this symmetry** between its beginning and ending. This story—the greatest one ever told—is history itself; therefore, if we wish to understand how God will ensure that it returns to Himself at the end of time, we need only look to its noble beginning. In the Mass, the priest prays:

> **… you call human nature back to its original holiness** … [9]

This, indeed, as the Church teaches in her liturgy—and as Jesus repeatedly tells Luisa—is a call: that is, an invitation to which we must respond; not an acknowledgement of some achievement already finished (in which case the prayer would instead say "you *have*, through Redemption, *placed* our human nature back in the position of its original holiness"). The revelations Jesus has given to Luisa constitute the instructions of that response.

"[Man] must enter once again the Divine Fiat from which he came. There are no ways in the middle; not even my very Redemption is sufficient to make man return to the beginning of the happy era of his creation. Redemption is means, way, light, help—but not the end. The end is my Will, because my Will was the beginning and, by justice, one who is the beginning must also be the end. Therefore, humanity must be enclosed in my Divine Volition to be given back

---

[5] The traditional (and most theologically and philosophically accurate) definition of evil is simply "the absence of a due perfection."
[6] Cf. Genesis 1:27. The question of exactly what is essential to the nature of man will be treated with more theological detail in a later section

[7] St. Thomas Aquinas
[8] *Summa Theologica*, I, q. 5 a.4
[9] Preface of Virgins. The Roman Missal

her noble origin, her happiness, and to place the marriage with her Creator in force once again ... True love never contents itself; only then is it content, when it can say: 'I have nothing else to give him."

-Jesus to Luisa. June 16, 1928

"...just as Creation started in an Outpouring of Love, in the same way, we will close it with Our children-in an Outpouring of Love."

—Jesus to Luisa. March 22, 1938

But before we set out to read and heed these instructions, I propose that we first take a moment to remind ourselves of just how very sure our footing is now, as we begin this task, by examining again our Faith's "Certain Logical Foundations." After examining these foundations, we may proceed to consider the nature of private revelation, and how any alleged private revelation is to be properly discerned in light of the Deposit of Faith. Then we will apply these Church-sanctioned methods of discernment to the case of the private revelations Jesus and Mary have given to Luisa, after which we will see that there is simply no room for any reasonable doubt as to their validity. Once this has been settled, we will be ready to do what we have come for: delve into the revelations themselves that Jesus gave to Luisa to receive the Gift contained within them.

Part I: The Gift

Luisa

"... if [your will] wants the life of Our Will into its own — [which is] wanted, commanded by Us with such great longing ... it will have the great good of possessing Our Will as life. And if it were not so, the sanctity of living in my Will would be a difficult sanctity, and almost impossible, while neither do I know how to teach difficult things, nor do I want impossible things. On the contrary, it is my usual way to make easy, as much as it is possible for the creature, the most difficult things and the hardest sacrifices...

And my love is so great, that in order to facilitate her even more, I whisper to the ear of her heart: 'If you really want to do this good, I Myself will do it together with you, I will not leave you alone, I will place at your disposal my grace, my strength, my light, my sanctity; it will be the two of us doing the good you want to possess.' Therefore, it does not take too much to live of my Will; the 'too much' is in wanting it, but if the creature makes up her mind and wants it, firmly and perseveringly, she has already won my Will and has made It her own...

The human will possesses, with indelible characters, everything it does and wants to do; and if the memory forgets, the will loses nothing, it contains the deposit of all of its acts, unable to disperse anything. Therefore it can be said that the whole of man is in his will: if the will is holy, even the most indifferent things are holy for him; but if it is evil, maybe even good itself changes for him into a perverted act. So, if you truly want my Divine Will as life, it does not take too much; more so, since united to yours there is Mine that wants it, there is a power that can do anything; and on your part it will show by deeds if in all things you will conduct yourself as the possessor of a Divine Will."

-Jesus to Luisa. March 19, 1935.

6) The Certain Logical Foundations

Before proceeding to construct a sturdy house, which we will do throughout this book, let us first, as Jesus teaches in the Gospel,[10] dig down deep and lay the foundations upon the bedrock itself. Let us not fret that we will be spending some time reviewing what we already know; for these essentials undergird our every belief in the Faith and, consequently, every action that follows from them. A worthier thing to review cannot be imagined.

Therefore, three rock-solid pillars must be set down on this bedrock first. But before examining the three pillars, let us first acknowledge why we must say that there is indeed a truth which demands that we seek and follow it once we have found it, no matter what.

Why do we know there *is* a truth? Because to even attempt to contradict the existence of truth (whether through Relativism, Subjectivism, Radical Skepticism, Agnosticism, or any other popular "-ism" that has made its way into pop pseudo-philosophy since the dawn of Modernism) is immediately and utterly self-refuting. For to attack the notion of truth is to make a truth claim; to attack objective reality is to attempt an objectively real assertion; to insist upon radical skepticism is to fail to be skeptical toward that insistence. We simply cannot avoid the fact that there are facts; that there is a real difference between a lie and a truth. And even if we spend ourselves in a life dedicated to comical intellectual acrobatics to strive to escape this clear either/or, our hearts know better than our minds. For our hearts know with unshakeable certainty that when someone lies to us, a real injustice has been done, for truth has been neglected.

Why do we know we must *seek* the truth? Because our existence itself thrusts this demand upon us so powerfully that no one human can dare claim exemption. That "all men by nature desire to know" was the first observation, in the first line, of history's greatest philosopher, Aristotle, in his most fundamental treatise, *Metaphysics*. Our rationality, which separates us from the beasts (who needn't seek truth—not because it is irrelevant to them, but

because they are constrained to follow the truth automatically), drives us on to this end with such compulsion that, if it were capable of envy, the sun itself would wish it had similar power over the earth. It takes a true mad man, a true mental delinquent, a true sad and sorry excuse for a human, to say along with Nietzsche *"why not truth? Why not, rather, untruth?"* That "philosopher" showed the world, with his own life, what it is to reject knowingly the duty to seek truth: it is to become insane, to declare oneself the antichrist, and to die alone in superlative misery in an insane asylum; all of which, in fact, Nietzsche did.

Why do we know we must *follow* the truth once we have found it? Because just as clearly as every integer is either even or odd, so also two and only two options present themselves to us: *Follow known truth or live a lie.* Given these options, the one we must follow is at once obvious to anyone. One who is content with living a lie has condemned himself, and we need not bother addressing such a person in this text, for writing a book to achieve what only a Divine Intervention can solve would be like treating a hewn-off leg with a small band aid. But since any man worthy of the name will refuse to live a lie, we can rely on this refusal, with the following three pillars of truth, to see clearly what we *must* do. **So, let us go forward now and consider the Three Pillars.**

I) The Certainty of God's Existence

First. God exists. Of the truths—the very existence of which we have settled in the previous section—which demand our assent, the Existence of God is foremost.

Although His existence is confirmed and known with certainty by supernatural Faith, which is a gift from God Himself and not a product of human effort, this Faith is not needed to know that He exists, for reason alone tells any serious thinker, in many ways, that there is no possible way to escape the rational necessity of a Being whose essence is existence itself; a Being who created the universe, a Being who designed all the order we see in living

---

10 cf. Matthew 7:24

things, a Being who imbues with transcendent meaning all of those things that we simply intuitively *know* are more than mere matter.

But I have told you that reason demonstrates these conclusions with clarity, and I do not want to leave to a poem what is the proper job of a good argument. Therefore, let us briefly consider only a few of the many ways that God's existence can be quickly and easily known, with reason and with certainty, by anyone who has the courage and the honesty to follow his intellect wherever it leads.

Life

There is simply no other way to explain the *functional* order that all forms of life contain without acknowledging the existence of a Divine Author of that order. Although most atheists seek to explain this order away by appealing to the Theory of Evolution, the fact is that even if we grant the validity of all the claims of the evolutionists, this still says nothing about how life came to be in the first place. For under their own premises, the starting point of evolution (which, then, obviously cannot itself be explained by evolution) is a single cell with DNA capable of reproduction: a masterpiece of design that never has been matched by even the most impressive feats of human innovation.

Even the recently published and authoritative *Encyclopedia of Evolution* from Oxford University Press has the honesty to admit "…how the ancestral cell[11] originated, some 3.5 to 3.8 billion years ago, remains an issue of intense speculation…"[12] before proceeding to dedicate a whopping *one* page (of its overall 1,326) to pondering how this may have happened—in this one page, giving a meditation which would qualify as a nice fairy tale if it were not so utterly scientifically and *logically* absurd (for the author of a fairy tale can justify including some scientific absurdities, but not logical absurdities).

I note the incredible brevity with which they treat this matter of the so-called "ancestral cell"—totaling less than 0.08% of the entire encyclopedia—because **precisely this question of its origin must be settled in order to give the atheistic evolutionary hypothesis any credence whatsoever; yet, it is systematically the most ignored question in all evolutionary biology.** An atheist might protest that the treatment is minuscule in the encyclopedia only because there isn't yet enough of substance to summarize. But this protestation only proves the point even more clearly, for Darwinism has had well over 100 years to explain the "origin of the ancestral cell," devouring entire careers of generations of countless scientists—not to mention mountains of money—in the process. If, after all this monumental effort, there has not been enough substantial progress on the question to merit more than one page of summary in the Encyclopedia of Evolution, then what conclusion any reasonable person should draw from this categorical failure of progress is too obvious to be worth stating. For these efforts make those of a little boy trying to jump up and touch the moon look rather reasonable and even achievable. Realizing he must simply despair of ever giving a rational, scientific account of the origin of the "ancestral cell," an atheist may then resort to platitude and assert *"Ah, but given enough time, it is still bound to come into existence by chance,"* followed with the remark, *"even a monkey smashing away at a typewriter would eventually create Shakespeare, you know,"* as if merely conjuring up such an image proves its validity.

Of course, mere illustrations of a point never by themselves prove what they depict; they are only useful in helping one understand a point he already grants—therefore, the monkey-typewriter hypothesis is one that requires testing against reason, which we will presently commence. Let us suppose only one work of Shakespeare's need be completed[13] in order to validate the monkey-

---

[11] Also referred to by evolutionary biologists as the LUCA (Last Universal Common Ancestor); it is the alleged "starting point of evolution."
[12] The Oxford Encyclopedia of Evolution. Edited by Mark Pagel. 2012 Oxford University Press, Inc. Page 138.
[13] An American computer programmer, in the year 2011, triumphantly asserted that his "computer monkeys" already succeeded in typing out Shakespeare at random. Though many news outlets reported on this, I could not find even one

that bothered to clearly report that his claim was a lie. For his erroneous personal criteria with which he measured his "victory" was merely that all the *individual words* in Shakespeare be successfully typed out by these computational pseudo monkeys. This is nearly as ridiculous as saying that once all 26 letters have been successfully punched at random (which any monkey would likely accomplish over the course of a few minutes), Shakespeare's

typewriter theory: *Hamlet*. *Hamlet* consists of over 150,000 characters in their proper configuration. When these 150,000 characters have been properly arranged, *viola*, there you have *Hamlet* in front of you. An easy task for a Monkey and a typewriter with several billion years, one might suppose.

Well, let us give the monkey-typewriter hypothesis every benefit of the doubt; for our opponents' arguments deserve no less. Let us suppose that even only *half* of the characters (75,000) being chosen correctly will be sufficient for successfully creating the work in question. Thus, even if the monkey produces a work in which *every other character* is a blatant typo, we will still grant that it has succeeded in producing Shakespeare. To give the hypothesis even more undeserved benefit of the doubt, let us also ignore capital letters and punctuation, as getting these correct would make the monkey's task vastly more difficult.

Given these extremely generous criteria, we can now proceed with a simple calculation: each character has only 26 options: the letters from "a" to "z." The chance of choosing the first letter correctly at random, therefore, is 1/26. The chance of choosing the second letter after that correctly as well is $(1/26)^2$. The chance of choosing the third letter after that one correctly again is $(1/26)^3$, and so on. Therefore, we need only do a simple calculation to know the probability of *Hamlet* being typed at random: $(1/26)^{75,000}$.

I urge you at this moment to type that calculation into the first calculator you can find; it is important that you see the results for yourself and not merely take my word for it. **Your calculator will tell you, rightly, that this probability you have calculated is *equal to zero*. That's right—there isn't even a mathematical possibility for something so relatively simple as *Hamlet* to come to be from mere chance.** But a single strand of DNA (itself contained within the single cell that is needed as the starting point of the theory of evolution) dwarfs *Hamlet* in its detailed complexity—containing not a mere 150,000 pieces of information but, rather, **billions** in a precisely necessary configuration.

Now, the most ardent atheists will still protest that, although minuscule, the probability is not literally the exact same thing as zero. And this mathematical fact we must indeed grant; but the calculation can easily be continued to show that even if we give the monkey-typewriter argument every possible, imaginable benefit of the doubt and suppose that each atom in the universe is a monkey with his own typewriter, ferociously pecking away at the keys at a rate only achievable by an expert typist, and having had the entire history of the universe to execute this task, **the probability still works out to zero.**[14] When an argument has been given every possible benefit of the doubt and still falls flat on its face, only a fool can continue to hold it. (This benefit we have given here, mind you, is infinitely more generous than any conceivable "*primordial-soup-bubbles-collisions-causing-RNA on the surface of the earth billions of years ago*" scenario could ever be.) Here an anecdote is necessary. I still recall vividly when, as an undergraduate engineering student in a top engineering University (which also happens to be the oldest technical University in the Western Hemisphere and was founded 25 years before Darwin published his famous *On the Origin of Species*), I sat down for an "Origins of Life" class which I had signed up for because I was curious to see what the supposed best and brightest scientific minds of the modern world had to say about the matter. In the midst of all manner of convoluted theories swirling about during the class, the actual crux of the matter was conveniently glossed over and written off as "emergence." We were hurriedly told that just as one may sometimes observe a pretty pattern of ripples emerge on the sands of a

---

works have successfully been typed, for they are essentially nothing but a large conglomeration of such letters. For a story is in the configuration of the words and therein lies the essence of its design.

[14] There are approximately 10^{80} atoms in the universe. If there were 10^{80} monkeys with typewriters, each typing 100 words per minute, then each would have completed approximately 24,178 billion (about twenty-four-thousand-billion) attempts at pounding out *Hamlet* over the course of 13.8 billion years (the number physicists often cite as the approximate age of the universe). With each of the 10^{80} monkeys completing 24,178 billion attempts, we have a total of approximately 2.4 times 10^{93} attempts made. Take the previously calculated probability $(1/26^{75000})$ of a given attempt succeeding, and multiply it by that number of attempts, and you will *still* calculate a *zero* percent chance of success. We cannot possibly be more generous to the argument that chance can create order, and we still have arrived at a zero percent chance of this happening. Bear in mind that, despite some referring to this as the "infinite monkey theorem," the simple fact is that we are not dealing with infinite monkeys or typewriters; at the very minimum, we can say that we must limit ourselves to deal with the actual hypothetical maximum constraints which the actual universe gives.

beach, so too that first cell necessary to initiate the process of evolution "emerged" out of the primordial soup that, hypothetically, was the surface of the earth billions of years ago. I then recognized openly what I in fact already knew before signing up for the course: the so-called scientific geniuses heralded by today's atheists and agnostics hadn't themselves even the faintest clue how it is possible to reconcile their views with the fact of the existence of life. For emergence, which is all they can appeal to, was just tested against real reason in the preceding paragraphs and was demonstrated to be a total failure in explaining what it proposes to explain.

Let us remind ourselves of the inescapable mathematical facts. Absurdly generous benefits of the doubt always give even the most basically impossible but perhaps conceivable scenarios a virtual statistical guarantee of occurring. For example, the notion of a small toddler who has never even seen a gun nevertheless outperforming an expert marksman in a target shooting competition is ridiculous. And yet, if we take any reasonable estimate of the probability of that occurring (let's say one in a million—that is, .0001%), and give it a billion-trillion attempts, it has now become an utter guarantee; rising from a .0001% chance of occurring to essentially a 100% chance. Similarly, all computer scientists agree that 128-bit encryption is *logically unbreakable*. As the name implies, this method of encrypting (or "coding") data entails scrambling it by means of a key of 128 pieces of information (it is as if your ordinary house key, instead of having several distinct notches, had 128). If somebody succeeds in decrypting data that was encrypted in this manner, you can be certain he had access to the encryption key and did not merely guess it correctly with the help of a "brute force" software attack; as the world's greatest supercomputers are utterly powerless against 128-bit encryption.[15] Nevertheless, if we give the would-be-breakers of this *unbreakable* situation the same absurd benefit of the doubt we just gave the monkey-typewriter-

Shakespeare argument, this impossibility also becomes a veritable *guarantee*.[16]

Now, the chance-producing-Shakespeare argument has not merely been given an absurdly generous benefit of the doubt; no, we have gone much farther and have given it *every imaginable, conceivable* benefit of the doubt. It makes the billion-trillion chances given to the child sharpshooter look like a downright miser's benefit of the doubt. You see, a billion-trillion is *nothing* compared to the number of chances we gave the order-from-randomness scenario to work. These givens, therefore, as shown, should turn any mere possibility into a veritable guarantee. Not only have they failed to do that, but they have failed to make it even likely ... not only have they failed to make it likely; no, indeed, the probability is still *zero*. In brief: The most absurdly generous, greatest imaginable benefit of the doubt, instead of rendering the practically impossible scenario a guarantee, as such concessions are supposed to do in all cases, still gives the scenario a zero percent chance of happening. Briefer still: even given every imaginable chance, functional order without God remains categorically impossible; even when applied to an ordered thing nowhere near the complexity of that which is required, such as the alleged *starting point* of evolution.

It is now obvious that there is no possible way for life to exist without a God Who made it.

"But Who Made God?" Won't Work

Once any conclusion—no matter how certain—has been definitively demonstrated by reason or science, anybody (even a toddler, or a parrot for that matter) can always mindlessly retort "But why?"

And this, indeed, usually is the atheist's recourse: "*Okay, fine: God made life. But who made God, then?*" While superficially similar to the believer's response when the Big Bang Theory is given as an explanation for the existence of the Universe (that is, the believer asking, in response to being told that

---

[15] The world's most powerful computer (named "Summit," it is a joint venture of the US DoE and IBM capable of executing 200,000 trillion calculations per second) would need about 100 trillion years of continuous operation solely dedicated to the task in order to have a good chance at breaking a single 128-bit encryption key.

[16] $(1/2^{128})$ [the probability of guessing the encryption key in each attempt] x 10^{80} x 24,178 billion attempts each (which is

the same number of attempts that still gives a *zero* statistical probability of Shakespeare's Hamlet arising from randomness) yields a statistical certainty of success more than a trillion trillion trillion trillion times over.

the Big Bang "made" the universe: "Well, who caused the Big Bang?"), it in fact is radically divergent.

Recall, first, that the "Big Bang Theory" itself was created by a Catholic priest,[17] and even if true, says nothing about how the Big Bang itself happened; it only speaks of what would have happened immediately after and since. Consequently, believers have long appealed to the existence of *something* rather than *nothing* as a clear proof of a Creator, with atheists responding, *"Well, then who created God? If you can say that He just exists, then we can say that the Universe just exists."* The atheists proceed to insist that this is just another question that science is still working on and eventually will answer.

But the plain truth is that the existence of something rather than nothing—how anything at all came to be—is simply a mystery radically beyond the capability of the human mind to grasp. Continuing the tit-for-tat, the atheist says that he is allowed to appeal to mystery if the believer is. But this is not the case. **Any believer can authentically proclaim, without undermining his own premises, "I don't know how God can simply exist. I don't know how He can be uncreated, and I could not possibly ever understand." An atheist cannot.** For this response is perfectly acceptable with regard to God (the argument against Him by atheists that reference His inherent intangibility allow for it), but this is the one response that empirical science and materialist mindsets do not have the authority to give.

Nothing that pertains to the merely physical (which, by definition, is all that an atheist believes in) could be inherently unknowable. Though some areas remain to be discovered, **there is no room for mystery in mechanics**. Without God, "it is unknowable" is simultaneously the only possible response to the universe's creation and the existence of life, and an impossible response. This paradox then can only be solved by the introduction of a non-, or super- natural, element, or in other words, God.

We return to the issue with which we began the section. Any atheist could easily and cheaply pretend he has rebutted any argument for God by simply responding "Well, what _____ God, then?" (putting "created," "caused," "ordered," or whatever else, in that blank); similar to how a criminal who knows he is guilty of a certain offense invariably responds to any accusation with the words "where's your proof!?" even when he knows full well that what has been presented already constitutes proof.

But when one has succumbed to such obstinacy that he employs methods that could just as easily be undertaken by a two-year-old or a parrot—arbitrarily and thoughtlessly continuing to say "why?" or "how?" even when the question has already been answered—he should consider what brought him to such a lamentable state. For no believer in God pretends that he has an answer as to how exactly God can be a *Cause Who Himself Needs No Cause* or a *Designer Who Himself Needs No Designer*; believers simply realize that such a Being is necessary given the hard data; that is, given what we already know with certainty about the brute facts of the universe.

For just as no story explains itself, but rather its existence can only be explained by an author who himself is outside of the story, so too *matter* can only be explained by something *outside of* material being—at the very minimum as its first cause and designer. Now "outside of" matter simply means extra-material; or, better put, "super-natural," which is simply a reference to God.

The point here is that the whole material, natural universe—that is, the entirety of the domain of empirical science and the entirety of that which an atheist believes in—is categorically incapable of giving answers to questions which the material, natural universe *itself* demands that we answer, including: how did it begin, and how did the functional order we see in it come to be? It is only possible to answer those questions by appealing to the existence of some Being Who radically transcends corporeality itself; that is, existing in a realm in which "it is a mystery" is a legitimate answer to a question pertaining to, as opposed to any question pertaining to the material universe, for which "it is a mystery" is never licit, and whenever it is given it automatically undercuts materialism itself.

The Errors of Today's Most Famous

---

[17] Fr. Georges Lemaitre

Atheist

We turn now to address the arguments of perhaps the most appealed to giant of atheistic science today: the recently deceased Stephen Hawking. For if the best methods of the best mind in support of a given thesis are shown to be absurd, this speaks volumes to any earnestly inquiring seeker of truth about the thesis itself.

In his posthumous work, *Brief Answers to the Big Questions* (a magnum opus in brief of Hawking's *"most profound"*[18] reflections, carefully extracted from *"half a million"* words from his writings and speeches), Hawking began his argument against God by repeating the slander Christians are used to hearing: "Science is increasingly answering questions that used to be the province of religion,"[19] which in turn is reminiscent of the tired "God of the gaps" argument against God's existence. One wonders if Hawking and the other atheists who promote this old know-nothing view have ever bothered to open a Bible—which, of its tens-of-thousands of verses, has scarcely a handful that concern themselves with matters overlapping with the proper domain of modern empirical science, thus rendering the attack of these atheists about as meritorious as that of a frustrated High School student who, not wanting to learn the laws of Geometry, complains that Euclid and Pythagoras have been increasingly shown incorrect in their medical, political, or religious views, and thus should be ignored, abandoned, and rejected. Just as any teacher would see straight through this complaint, so too should we all see through the "gaps" attack against God.

Knowing that he could not back up that statement as it pertains to Christianity (which was clearly the primary object of his attack), Hawking diverts the reader's attention with irrelevant examples, bringing up an ancient Greek astronomer, Aristarchus, who argued well that eclipses were not the direct effects of gods (and later, bringing up an African creation myth wherein a god named Bumba vomited out the world after a stomach ache). Confident that he has assured his readers that the time has come for science to replace religion, he proceeds to attempt to explain scientifically what, in fact, only religion can address; namely, the existence of the Universe. He said, " ... I think that actually you can get a whole universe for free."[20]

In seeking to justify the manifest absurdity, Hawking refers to a man creating a hill with the dirt he excavates from a hole. This, Hawking teaches, is all the Big Bang was; an explosion of "positive energy" (the hill) along with an equal and opposite precipitation of "negative energy" (the hole); thus, since these amounts allegedly negate each other perfectly, no further explanation need be given for their existence and separation.

(How stupid I feel even bothering to refute in this book an argument that no four-year-old would fall for! Nevertheless, I must, for this type of "argument" is what passes for logical discourse today.) We must first acknowledge that Hawking was speaking here of science fiction—or at best little more than conjecture—not of empirical science properly so-called, which has yet to even produce a consistent and convincing theory about "negative energy," much less has it ever observed or proven it. Though such inadequacy should be more than sufficient to reject a scientific hypothesis, we needn't limit ourselves to pointing it out, for the theory itself is absurd even as it is stated and reminds me of the various "Free Energy" scams I analyzed as an engineer.[21]

Hawking is of course only using an analogy, but his analogy is in fact perfectly chosen to refute his very own argument. For a hole cannot be dug unless there already is a substrate in which to dig it. A hole—or, in this case, "negative energy"—as a privation, can only be spoken of, or even have any existence whatsoever, in relation to the already existing reality to which it is opposed (a "hole" can only be a hole *in something*). One, for example, cannot identify or speak of a shadow without referring to the boundary of light to which this

---

18 Cf. Phys.org
19 *Brief Answers to the Big Questions*. Stephen Hawking, 2018. Chapter 1.
20 ibid
21 Wherein, for example, one supposes he can use the heat produced in a thermodynamic cycle (e.g. a refrigerator) to in turn power a heat engine (e.g. a steam turbine) hooked up to a generator, which then powers the same thermodynamic cycle to continue the process and generate abundant free heat and electricity. This can never work because the excess heat from the thermodynamic cycle can never possibly exceed the inherent (Carnot) inefficiency of the heat engine.

shadow is adjacent. In other words, in striving to prove the Big Bang came from nothing, Hawking appeals to an already-existing something from which it came. Is there anybody who finds this argument of his even remotely insightful, much less convincing?

But perhaps Hawking does not realize the emptiness of his own words; like many other popular atheists, he sneered at good philosophy, once claiming "philosophy is dead" (Richard Dawkins also, for example, admits he has no idea what an *essence* is[22] — a basic philosophical teaching that one should not even need any formal training in philosophy to grasp[23]); which is unfortunate for Hawking, because it could have saved him much effort, just as knowledge of the laws of algebra could save those who play the lottery much money. (In his defense, Hawking went through school long after good logic and philosophy became unpopular).

Studiously and sincerely, dear reader, consider well what we have seen here. A scientist lauded by the world like no other, a veritable intellectual giant, dedicating much of his career to answering these questions of origins, can come up with nothing better, even in the final work of his life, for an atheistic explanation of the existence of the Universe, than an argument that has already manifestly refuted itself before one has even finished reading it.

The absurdity of this text does not end there. In one breath, Hawking says that his beliefs boil down to nothing more than the assertion that there are laws of nature, and that these laws are absolute and immutable. Shortly after, he says that particles can *randomly* pop into existence for no reason (which is precisely, he says, what the Universe conveniently did in accord with the aforementioned hole-hill principle). It doesn't even occur to him that he has just asserted blatant contradictions: if something can happen randomly, then either there are not laws of nature, or they are not immutable and absolute; for an event cannot be both by a "law" and by "randomness," as these predicates are contraries, and therefore cannot be said of the same

thing.

Hawking ventures further in his babbling, arguing that because time did not exist before the Big Bang, it does not even "make sense" to ponder if God caused it, because there was no time before it in which there could have been a God to cause it. Here he continues to reveal his baffling ignorance of the most basic teachings of philosophy and theology. For anyone who has graduated from Catechism 101 knows that God is *timeless*; to argue that there wasn't a *time* in which God could cause the Big Bang to try to prove God couldn't have caused the Big Bang is to beg the question:[24] to assume that there is no timeless Being in striving to prove there is no timeless Being.

And what have we seen here in the "scientific" atheism of Hawking? Nothing but contradiction, theories that neglect the axioms on which they are built, straw men, ignorance, and fallacy. Behold, dear reader, the hero of the atheists. A man whose best arguments would flunk if used in an essay written by a middle school student.

The Nature of Today's Most Common Fallacy

It seems there is one fallacy that defines virtually all the common attacks made against Faith and the faithful: **the Fallacy of Conflated Premises**.

By this fallacy, one proceeds from his own premises to condemn the actions of somebody else, and this condemnation takes the form of pointing out how very absurd the other's behavior is if compared to the premises that the condemner himself holds. But this approach, of course, is just as foolish as a morbidly obese man who rebukes a man of a healthier weight for buying a shirt made to fit an ordinary body. Certainly, this shirt will not fit the large man, but that is irrelevant to the one buying it.

This fallacy is, of course, rarely employed in so explicit a fashion; rather, it is as subtle and unrecognized as it is pervasive. In its common use, the errant attackers condemn someone simply for being consistent with his own premises; whereas in

---

[22] *The God Delusion.* Page 43.
[23] Indeed, over years of teaching introductory philosophy to hundreds of students, I have found that all of them have a fairly solid intuitive grasp of this concept which Dr. Dawkins admits he cannot fathom. If this does not show his lack of

intelligence, it should at least demonstrate his utter cluelessness regarding how ordinary people actually operate and understand the world.
[24] That is, to commit the logical fallacy of circular reasoning.

their condemnation all they have accomplished is the highlighting of the virtue of their chosen object of scorn! When it is pointed out, the nature of this fallacy is obvious; but it is almost never pointed out, hence people everywhere constantly fall into it.

Consider, for example, what is often said about Saudi Arabia. In that country, the practice of all its citizens dropping everything five times a day to pray is institutionalized and carefully observed. But the practice is certainly a burden, and many are therefore quick to condemn: they point out how difficult it is for traffic and business to stop five times a day, and how much of an economic impact there is, how much more money could be made each day without this frequent stopping of trade; and on the list goes. But all these complaints are themselves absurd and irrelevant. If Muhammad is a true prophet, and if the Quran[25] is truly God's word, and if the Hadith[26] truly bears the same authority, and if the Hadith truly commands this practice, then the only absurd thing would be to *fail* to implement it as diligently as Saudi Arabia does. If one wishes to take issue with this practice, then he ought not waste his breath bringing up economic considerations, or anything of the sort, but should instead argue either that the Quran is not from God, that Muhammad is not a true prophet, or that the Hadith is not of sufficient authority to command in the name of Muhammad or the Quran. Any other argument completely misses the point.

Similarly, the whole point of Faith in God is that believers hold that He is giving us this very small window of time; wherein there is suffering, there is sin, and there is a veil obscuring the clarity of His presence, in order to allow us to merit by our faith; that this is *not* how it will be for the vast, vast, vast majority of our existence (almost all of which will be in either Heaven or Hell where there will be no more possibility for doubt), and that we are only given a relatively brief few moments before our deaths to take advantage of this once-in-an-eternity opportunity.

Returning to the Fallacy of Conflated Premises, we can now clearly see how it is succumbed to. The most common "arguments" one hears against the life of Faith have nothing to do with carefully constructed attempts to show that life or the universe could exist without God; nor do they make any serious attempt to refute any of the various clear proofs of His existence. Rather, they usually amount to nothing but an application of this very fallacy, lamenting how ridiculous the faithful are if there is no God, usually sounding something like this:

1. *"Look at this miserable sheep, going about submitting to the arbitrary commands of a 2,000-year-old book instead of doing as he pleases."*
2. *"Look at those parrots, mouthing prayers every day and going to Church; taking up so much time that could be better spent enjoying life."*
3. *"These ridiculous believers; every time something good happens, they thank God for it, but they never blame the bad things on God!"*
4. *"Stop wasting your life thinking about where you're going to wind up after you die! Live your life now!"*
5. *"What fools! They won't even think for themselves; with all their subjecting themselves to myths."*
6. *"How convenient! Their 'God' won't work miracles to make His existence clearer, and they say He has a reason for that without thinking that this is just what it would look like if there wasn't a God!"*
7. *"Imagine no religion! No God to fight over, no afterlife to worry about, no man in the sky to obey…"*
8. *"We should believe in science above all! Why resort to old outdated myths used by primitive peoples to explain things when we now have a better way? Why not get rid of all that and let hard science be our sole guide?"*
9. *"Faith is an intellectually bankrupt cop-out; it's very assertion demonstrates the emptiness of its object, for one would not appeal to Faith if he were supporting something reasonable."*
10. *"Foolish believers! They have just made-up a God in their own image, and in so doing have only revealed their anthropocentrism."*
11. *"Blindly trusting masses! They always credit God with their answered-prayers, but they never bother to consider that their not-answered prayers indicate the opposite."*
12. *"Most people are already atheists with respect to Zeus and Thor and all such other gods — we atheists just go one God further than most and do not believe in **any** God!"*

Few, I think, will deny that the statements listed

---

[25] The primary Islamic sacred text

[26] The secondary Islamic sacred text

above are drastically more common than attempts at reasonable refutations of the proofs for God's existence, or reasonable attempts at positive proofs against the same. Frankly, atheists know that they don't have much of a chance in that arena and they realize that they are way out of their league when they try to wade into it, so it is almost always these shallow soundbites that they rely on and promulgate—tweeting them, posting them on billboards, and the like.

And yet, when we understand the nature of the Fallacy of Conflated Premises, we see how absurd all these soundbites are; how, in its own way, each one castigates believers with admonishments that are totally irrelevant if the believer's premises (premises ignored by these soundbites) are true.

1) If the Bible really is the Word of God, then its age has nothing to do with whether it should be obeyed; for if God exists, He is all-knowing, and cannot be so ignorant as to give commandments and teachings which would have an expiration date due to future and unanticipated advancements of human knowledge.

2) If there really is an all-powerful Being, then it is difficult to imagine a better use of one's time than speaking to Him and worshipping Him.

3) If there really is an all-good and all-powerful God, then it does not take a genius philosopher to conclude that whatever happens can only be according to His Will, which is always ultimately for the best, and that all that happens is part of His perfect plan which will in time be seen.

4) If we really are going to live forever either in Heaven or in Hell, then it is difficult to imagine a worthier consideration than pondering which of these two places one will wind up in, and, in accordance with this consideration, to direct one's actions towards attaining the former and avoiding the latter.[27]

5) Even the most arrogant of men usually will admit they do not have it all figured out; if there really is an all-knowing God who occasionally reveals a few glimpses of His Truth to His creatures, then it would obviously be absurd to contradict these revelations merely because our flimsy attempts at reason have trouble at first understanding them.

6) A reality being "convenient" is not a mark against its validity. If there really is a God then it is easy to imagine Him allowing a period of time during which, only for the eternal benefit of His creatures, He largely veils His presence from them. The whole fundamental premise of most religions is precisely that we are in this time right now; merely acknowledging that and condemning it as "convenient" does not refute its truth.

7) Children play pretend, and that is okay, because they are children. Adults are expected to do their best to discover the truth and act in accord with their discovery, no matter how much they might enjoy imagining things being another way.

8) If there really is a God—Who created us and gave us our intellects by virtue of which we undertake scientific investigation—then we should of course zealously use the tools He gave us, but we should also never be so stupid as to suppose that the effect can refute the cause (in other words, that science—the tool to discover truths empirically—can refute other Truths directly revealed by the very One Who made the tool and therefore already knows everything it can, and cannot, do).

9) No believer worthy of the name supposes that Faith replaces reason; rather, believers understand that it is a God-given gift which confirms and fortifies their knowledge of the truth: a truth already confirmed (or, at the minimum lead to) by reason. If indeed there is a God, and if many are constantly arguing against Him and striving to get others to reject Him as well, then it only makes sense that, if one indeed understands by reason also that He exists, then one would benefit greatly from a supernatural gift (Faith) directly from God, both confirming the fact of His existence (and thus safeguarding the benefits of this belief against the inevitable fluctuations and doubts in ordinary human knowledge), and revealing, with certainty, truths about Himself and His creation that reason alone would not be capable of discovering.

10) If indeed there is a God Who made man in His own image, then the likeness between man and

---

[27] This, of course, is not to mention that believers almost always do live more full and happier lives than unbelievers, rendering the "live now; don't let concerns of the afterlife ruin this life!" argument ridiculous from the very outset.

God cannot be merely arbitrarily accused of an anthropocentric formation of the latter by the former. As usual—as with all 12 of these points—the atheist here is purely looking at how absurd the believer's creed and practice is compared to the atheist's own premises; furthermore, the atheist erroneously supposes that the believer uses arguments for God that, in fact, almost never have been used in this fashion: no believer claims he believes in God because of God's similarity to man (for obviously if one were to invent a religion, he would do just that). But if there was a God; why *wouldn't* He make creatures like Himself? And if indeed He did so, these creatures would be perfectly capable of, upon observing this similarity, accuse the Creator of being a creation of the creature; just as even now a flat-earther who observes a photograph of the earth from orbit would accuse it of being Photoshopped in the image of a fiction.

11) In moments of honesty, most believers readily admit that their prayers of petition are often more or less self-centered, and they do not hold it against God for not answering them exactly in the way, and in the time, they wanted them answered; they are sorely aware of their own weaknesses (both moral and intellectual) in contrast to God's perfection, and they rightly recognize that, given such a stark contrast, the whims of the weaker would often fail to correspond to the Providential Will of the Perfect. Even this aside, it is only reasonable (especially considering point number 6 above) that, given what has already been demonstrated about the nature of God and the nature of this brief time in which we now live, that God would choose to act in a usually hidden, subtle, and mysterious (but no less real) way in answering prayers. Nevertheless, most believers have clear examples of their prayers being answered in a way that is difficult if not impossible to chalk up to any reason other than God's intervention: all it takes is one such example to prove the believer's point, notwithstanding any number of supposed "not answered" prayers which, wrongly, are considered by atheists and agnostics as reasons to not believe in Him.

12) The vast majority of believers in the world hold that there must be *one* Supreme Being above all others; in stark contrast to a few brands of ancient pagan polytheism which held that there were many such Beings (but even most brands of paganism themselves hold that the many 'gods' are really all inferior beings to some other absolute, supreme, transcendent One). To suppose that this monotheism can be refuted merely by accusing it of lacking sufficient boldness to take its own quest of rejecting pagan gods "one step further" is as absurd as saying a good husband must become celibate, since his monogamy is nothing but a tepid and arbitrary stopping point foisted upon his endeavor to be celibate with respect to all women other than his wife. *One* is a completely unique and exalted reality, radically distinct from both the *many* and the *none* between which it stands. This will be readily attested to by any mathematician worth his salt (many of whom admirably, to distinguish *one* as not merely another number among equally important numbers, refer to it as "unity" in the more advanced mathematical textbooks they produce). Judaism, Christianity, and Islam in particular were distinguished from the start by their zealous rejection of pagan 'gods,' and it would even today be laughable for any atheist to suppose that he has been bolder in this rejection "merely by going on god further."

Therefore, these twelve attacks—and the many others like them—should simply be given up on by anyone who wishes to act in accordance with reason. Such a person must, instead, simply strive to discover—as honestly as he can—through the rigorous application of his intellect, whether God exists; a question which has nothing to do with these twelve protestations. And if there is any doubt about God's existence aside from these twelve soundbites, please simply re-read this chapter.

In brief: Dear atheist, if you wish to criticize someone's conclusions, you must either refute his premises or reveal the fallacy in his logic. For you are only making a fool of yourself if you undertake this criticism by merely complaining about those conclusions of his which do clearly follow from his premises, and are instead only questionable under your own premises, succumbing as you are to the Fallacy of Conflated Premises.

The Ultimate Question for the Atheist

I conclude the philosophical and logical portion of

this section with a simple question to the atheist:

So you are firm in your disbelief. Well and good. What would it take for you to change your mind?

If you just answered, "*Nothing – there is nothing that would change my mind,*" then you have just shown your true hand: you have just revealed yourself as an unscientific and prejudiced fanatical ideologue. For any scientific view to even begin to qualify as such, it must at least be falsifiable. That is, there must be a conceivable scenario in which what actually transpires proves it to be wrong. To assert anything as scientific in nature but declare it to be unfalsifiable (which is implied in saying that you will always hold a view, no matter what), is to succumb to pseudoscience by rejecting the cornerstone of science itself. And how tragic it would be to, in an attempt at a heroic effort of rising above old, mythical faith, only succeed in falling into pseudoscience!

But, if you gave a different answer: if you did give some criteria under which you would revise your unbelief and choose Faith instead, then I in turn have a different response for you. And perhaps you are now wincing in anticipation since you are used to others castigating you for this very thing; perhaps some believers have rebuked you for putting conditions on your response to God. And although there is merit in this rebuke, that is not what I wish to do now. Instead, I have a radically different message for you: God will give you that. Yes, He truly will. He will eliminate any excuse; He will leave your doubt with no more recourse.

He may, however, wait until the moment of your death to do that; hoping beyond hope that, in His delay, you will finally listen to the countless invitations He has already given you. Because you lose *so* much—incalculably much—by waiting so long for the satisfaction of the arbitrary prerequisites you have placed on Faith. You miss the entire purpose of life. You turn your whole earthly existence, with which God wanted to write an amazing story to tell all of Heaven about for all of eternity, into a long, drawn out, boring preface to a story that turned out to be nothing but a sentence or two. You turn your whole life into one of those miserable jokes that meanders about agonizingly as the clock ticks loudly and guest after guest sneaks out of the room, only to give a half-hearted punchline, seeming like centuries after it should have been given. In a word, you render the object of that glorious prayer useless in your case: **"Lord, save me at death from the agonizing memory of a wasted life."**

Dear brother, dear sister: do not waste your life.

***

To end this section, let us leave aside the logical arguments and instead simply be honest and open about what all humans *just know*—what they always have known, and always will know about the most important experiences they have had—experiences of transcendent and spiritual love, beauty, truth, and goodness.

For truly there can be no love for an atheist, only neuron firings. No music, only noise. No beauty, only varying light wavelengths. Would you allow your eye to command your nose to deny an aroma since it knows it not? Neither then should you allow the tempests of your mind, even if you find them doubting God, to insist the heart deny what it knows to be true; meaning, music, beauty, love…and the source of all these: God.

And so, I have a personal message for all atheists: I know that you have loved—looking into the eyes of a spouse. Embracing a child. Forgiving and seeking forgiveness. Do you really believe that was nothing but chemical reactions? True atheists do. Surely you have enjoyed true beauty- a symphony beyond description. A movie that leaves you speechless. A landscape that took your breath away. Do you really believe that was no more than the triggering of a certain part of your brain via sensory input? True atheists do. There must have been many times when you helped another person and felt God's presence in you with a happy conscience—a time when you rejected selfishness and gave up something you had a right to for the sake of a friend. When you cared for someone who was suffering. When you gave without expecting anything in return. Do you really believe that was nothing but the evolutionary herd-instinct? True atheists do.

To remain in the truth, we often need only to refuse to forget those moments when we knew we were closest to it; when we were at the heights of reason *confirmed* by the highest emotions. Whoever you are, you have had times when you knew that God exists. The only reason you do not even now believe is because you have permitted yourself to forget those moments like a bride forgetting her wedding vows. When we permit ourselves to forget, mindless drifting dictates the direction in which we travel, and when we wake up after a time of doing this, we far too often scramble to justify our position instead of coming back home. If you, dear atheist, review your life, you will find this is true. You did not simply sit down one day to conclude rationally there is no God, and then go about living a life free from the chains of His non-existent tyranny. On the contrary, one day you found yourself living a life without God, and then sought to convince yourself it was OK, because He does not exist. Consider this, therefore, an invitation to be governed by reason instead of drifting.

***

Finally, as a brief endnote, understand that this section has refuted all forms of agnosticism just as thoroughly as atheism. For here, we have not simply refuted an argument against God's existence (as one would do, for example, by refuting the "problem of evil"[28]); rather, we have positively demonstrated God's existence in these pages. Appealing to agnosticism is a common tactic of a lukewarm soul once he realizes that atheism has been thoroughly refuted, but this appeal cannot work. The evidence is conclusive and one who refuses to align his own beliefs in accord with that conclusion is not being wise, cautious, or humble; he is, rather, being just as obstinate as one who flatly denies what the evidence conclusively indicates.

II) The Fact that God Became Man

Second. Almost 2,000 years ago, this very same God entered into the universe He created. He became Man: Jesus Christ.

The easiest (and cheapest) way one may try to evade this particular certainty is by pretending that the whole thing—the entire New Testament of the Bible and above all Jesus Himself—is just a matter of fiction: whether a deliberate conspiracy or an elaborate myth which was later misinterpreted (or some mixture of the two), so we begin by pointing out Jesus' historicity.

Undeniable Historicity

When it comes to the study of historical events that extend back to time periods before the modern era, there are two fundamental options: either believe what is reasonable to believe about them in proportion to the reliable evidence we have, or else categorically reject it all as uncertain (or perhaps even conspiracy). Those who choose the latter may also be interested in Flat Earth Theory. Indeed, **if one is going to believe anything whatsoever about history, he must at least believe that the New Testament says what it is known to say.** Whether what it says is true (that is, whether it recounts events that actually happened), is a question we will discuss next. But not even a fool could deny that it is a real historical document and that we know its contents. For these contents are verified by more manuscripts (tens of thousands) than any other document in ancient history and have furthermore been cross-examined with more rigor than any document in any era of history, resulting in astonishing consistency. Of course, most of these manuscripts were made several centuries after Christ, but even the earliest manuscripts alone easily succeed in demonstrating the validity and agreement of their content.

Now, to what wild conspiracy theory masquerading as historical scholarship can one flee? To what species of obstinacy masquerading as reasonable doubt can one turn?

Shall one flee to so-called "mythicism," which holds that Jesus is a mere myth invented by the authors of the New Testament? Even professor Bart Ehrman, a world-renowned scholar who is an agnostic and skeptic (who in his own words is "not a Christian" and has "no interest in promoting the Christian cause"), and who has spent most of his professional career attacking traditional Christian views, and is beloved by the so-called "nones" (those who do not identify with any particular religion), nevertheless has the honesty to write of the "mythicist" view:

> ... none of this [mythicist] literature is written by scholars [on Scripture or early Christianity who teach at schools dedicated to the same] ... Of the thousands of [these qualified scholars] none of

---

28 The answer to which is the essence of the remainder of this book; so read on.

them, to my knowledge, has any doubts that Jesus existed. … Those who do not think Jesus existed are frequently militant in their views and remarkably adept at countering evidence that to the rest of the civilized world seems compelling and even unanswerable. But … the reality is that whatever else you may think about Jesus, he certainly did exist … **It is striking that virtually everyone who has spent all the years needed to attain [scholarly early Christian/New Testament] qualifications is convinced that Jesus of Nazareth was a real historical figure** … [but, unfortunately] as is clear from the avalanche of sometimes outraged postings on all the relevant Internet sites, there is simply no way to convince conspiracy theorists that the evidence for their position is too thin to be convincing and that the evidence for a traditional view is thoroughly persuasive. Anyone who chooses to believe something contrary to evidence that an overwhelming majority of people find overwhelmingly convincing … simply will not be convinced.[29]

Living in a fantasy world of pseudo-history like the one portrayed in Dan Brown's fictional novels is only palatable for one who does not care about truth. But then again, all *must* care about truth— and I refer anyone who says otherwise to the introductory remarks of this chapter. Within the same excerpt quoted above, Professor Ehrman writes that *"Some of [the mythicists] rival The Da Vinci Code in their passion for conspiracy and the shallowness of their historical knowledge, not just of the New Testament and early Christianity, but of ancient religions generally and, even more broadly, the ancient world."*[30]

Dr. Ehrman is right: mountains of overwhelmingly compelling evidence exist in support of Jesus' existence as a real person Who literally, physically walked the earth 2,000 years ago, and there is precisely zero evidence that He did not exist—only fantasy and conjecture. Remember that Dr. Ehrman is one of today's most popular critics of traditional Christianity; he of all people has everything to gain from the "Jesus is a myth" conspiracy, for this would justify his own errant, heretical views that pertain to Christianity (for why bother with orthodoxy if Christianity is just based on a myth?).

Unfortunately, this is where the wisdom of Professor Ehrman ends, for he lacks either the authenticity or the courage to realize that this Jesus (Whom he has proven well did indeed exist) places demands upon us all that cannot be safely treated as mere scholarly matters of history at a nice, comfortable distance—**because Jesus claimed to be God.**

Clear Divinity

We need not denigrate other religions or their founders to see why none of them suffice; we can simply take an honest look at the undisputed claims of each. A few minutes of careful research into the question will allow anyone to easily see that Jesus is the only one who even claims to literally be God Himself. Muhammad only claimed to be a prophet. The Buddha only claimed to be an "awakened" one. Confucius claimed to be a mere teacher. Abraham and Moses claimed only to be men to whom the Lord spoke, with nothing definitive about either of their own places in the history of Judaism. And Hinduism does not even have a clear founder, as it is a distillation of ancient Indian culture into a loose set of beliefs, worship, and way of life. Find your way to any one of those religions—Islam, Buddhism, Confucianism, Judaism, Hinduism (or any other non-Christian religion)- **and each of them will have much to say to you *about* God. But none of them even proposes to show you God Himself. Only one religion does that: Christianity.** (Words directly from Jesus below are bolded.)

- Luke 22: 70- "And they all said, 'Are You the Son of God, then?' And He said to them, '**Yes, I am.**'"
- John 14:6- "**I am the way, the truth, and the life. No one comes to the Father except by me.**"
- John 14:9- "**Whoever has seen me has seen the Father**"
- John 10:30-33- "'**I and the Father are One.**' The Jews took up stones again to stone him … [saying] 'We stone you for no good work but for blasphemy; because you, being a man, make yourself God.'"
- Matthew 3:17- "…and behold, a voice out of the heavens said, 'This is My beloved Son, in whom I am well-pleased.'"
- Colossians 2:9- "For in Christ all the fullness of Deity lives in bodily form … "

---

[29] Bart Ehrman. *Did Jesus Exist?: The Historical Argument for Jesus of Nazareth.* Pages 2-5.

[30] Ibid.

Dozens, if not hundreds, more Scripture verses could easily be appealed to in demonstrating beyond any doubt that Jesus claimed Divinity. Only a small number is presented here. But even this sample shows that Christ's claims to Divinity cannot be compartmentalized into one area of Scripture; for some try to argue such claims only exist in the Gospel of John,[31] and yet we clearly see them here in the Synoptic Gospels and Pauline Letters. The few who try to deny Christ's own claims to Divinity (e.g. Unitarians, Jehovah's Witnesses, Mormons) invariably resort to systematically distorted translations of Scripture. But even such quasi-Christians who rely on demonstrably dishonest Scriptural translations to back their claims should pause to ponder: *"Even the Scriptures I read acknowledge that the Pharisees had Jesus killed … but why? Why would they go **so far** and succeed? **Why did they kill Jesus?!"***

One and only one answer rings out clearly: **Because He claimed to be God. Nothing else Jesus was** *even* **accused of saying or doing could have possibly merited death under Jewish law.** Healing on the Sabbath, criticizing the Pharisees, cleansing the temple with a whip, eating with unwashed hands, etc., were all things that the Pharisees hated him for, but even they knew that none of that was even remotely close to a reason to seek His death. Rather, during His trial before the Sanhedrin, in the midst of all manner of chaos and contradictory accusations levied against Jesus, it was only when He finally openly responded to the question of who He was with the words, "I AM," that everything changed. For in so doing all present knew well that He appropriated for Himself Yahweh's Sovereign "I AM" (EGO EIMI),[32] asserting His own *essence as existence itself* just as the Father revealed Himself to Moses in the desert. And in that moment, the farce of a trial immediately changed from an event that would have been merely another failed nefarious plot of the Pharisees, to a dead-set mission by them to ensure that Jesus was put to death.

But the next thing we must do is to consider what such a claim to Divinity implies. There simply is no possibility for lukewarmness here. It doesn't take a psychologist to realize that **someone who claims to** *be* **God either** *is* **God or is a madman.** One making such a claim certainly is not a mere wise teacher, a mere philosopher, a mere spiritual guide, a mere Jewish preacher from Galilea.

Granted, Jesus Christ is not alone in His claims to Divinity. Some today make the same claim and some others in the past have done likewise — there are plenty of television shows and documentaries made about them which are always fun to watch for a good laugh and a recognition that **Jesus** *is* **the only one who has ever made this claim and who, at the same time, is not obviously insane.** Those who would give Jesus the credit of being a "good teacher" while rejecting His claims to Divinity are confronted with quite a task. Knowing that humans are all made of the same stuff and tend towards similarity; a perfectly reasonable expectation would be to find similar people often throughout history. Or at the *very* minimum, we would expect to find at least *some*; at least one in each generation from each culture or nation. That is, other moral teachers who dispensed of impeccable wisdom throughout a spotless life and had the courage to die for it, never recanting under any pressure, but also the whole time claiming divine status as the only truth. Such an inquiry will find none but Jesus Christ. Even if one insists upon closing his eyes to mountains of evidence in support of Christ's resurrection and miracles, he is still confronted with the question of why Jesus is so immeasurably unlike any other who has walked the earth, even with respect to those facts that the very skeptics themselves cannot manage to doubt.

Therefore, anyone who strives to evade the duty to become a Christian by fretting *"I cannot just go bowing down before every teacher who claims to be God; I'd have no time left to do anything else!"* is conjuring up excuses without any substance, like a rich miser who will not even lend a small sum to a relative in dire need the first time the relative asks, for fear of this "generosity consuming all his wealth." In other words, there is no "slippery slope" involved in worshipping men who claim Divinity and appear by all accounts trustworthy. There is only a staircase with just one step, and only a truly paranoid and sorry excuse for a man would refuse to take that step out of fear.

Now, although what has hitherto been shown should suffice in convincing one to become a Christian, we still have not even touched on the most obvious reason. For we are not dealing purely with a historically reliable account of a man

---

[31] A false claim which, even if true, would prove nothing   [32] Luke 22:70

who merely was trustworthy and merely *claimed* Divinity. Instead, we are dealing with a man who claimed it *and* proved it through miracles; above all, His own Resurrection.

So much evidence for the reliability of the Resurrection and demonstration of its soundness has been accumulated that it would be far too lengthy to try to summarize it here. Instead I will refer you to the works of Dr. Peter Kreeft (e.g. "Evidence for the Resurrection of Christ," posted freely on his website[33]), and the works of Lee Strobel, as well as *The Resurrection of the Son of God* by N.T. Wright, and *Did Jesus Really Rise from the Dead?* By Carl Olson.

Beyond encouraging these works, I simply exhort you to consider as honestly, thoroughly, and logically as you possibly can, just those truths which few if any of the qualified scholars deny (for while there is no doubt that anyone who looks at all the details honestly will also easily conclude that the Resurrection did in fact occur, few people will have enough time to comprehensively study the matter).

The Nature of Evidence

And in considering these agreed-upon truths, we also must address a claim made by the skeptics which they resort to so often that it has become a veritable reflex of theirs. There is indeed extraordinary evidence for the Resurrection of Christ. But even if there were not, this would say nothing. It is a tired old lie and a fallacy that **"extraordinary claims require extraordinary evidence."** First of all, that itself is an extraordinary claim, and it has precisely *no* evidence. But beyond it being simply without evidence, it is also absurd, for everybody knows that **all claims require** *reasonable* **evidence.** If one conclusion is more evident and reasonable than another contradictory one, then it should be believed despite one's prejudiced (and itself unreasonable and unproven) claim that it is "extraordinary." The degree of evidence required for a claim is meted out solely on the grounds of how much evidence exists for other claims which contradict it.

If, for example, one wanted to argue the earth was flat, then he would need extraordinary evidence simply because there already is great evidence that it is round. Likewise, **the only case wherein extraordinary evidence would be demanded in the present scenario is if one were to *deny* the Resurrection of Jesus;** for in so doing he is contradicting what great evidence already points to, whereas one who believes in the Resurrection is not thereby believing anything that is contrary to evidence. In addition to all the documents of the New Testament (which we have already settled is at the minimum a solid historical document) boldly asserting the Resurrection of Christ, it is also true (looking beyond the pages of the Bible for other relevant evidence that virtually no one denies) that:

- We have no historical record of *anyone* seeing the dead body of Jesus after Easter Sunday.
- We have no record—historical or current—of *anyone ever* finding the dead body of anyone who could reasonably have been Jesus, even though archeologists have had 2,000 years to do so and still regularly find corpses even older, and have no problem discerning to whom they belonged.
- We do *not* have *any* record of *anyone* who claimed to have seen the resurrected Jesus later retracting this claim.
- We *do* have records of many people—and most importantly, each Apostle[34]—being willing to die for their belief in the Resurrection, and this is not only recounted in the Bible, but in other extra-Biblical ancient documents from the same time period.[35] And if the Apostles were lying, it must be considered that we have no record of any other comparable scenario ever occurring at any time, in any place, in all history: that is, a group of people proclaiming a certain verifiable and falsifiable claim about an actual observable, objective event for many years (going so far as to die rather than deny it), without a single one recanting, only to have the whole matter later revealed as fraudulent.[36]

---

[33] At www.PeterKreeft.com
[34] Even though St. John was not killed, they did try to kill him, and he still did not recant.
[35] It is only natural that far more direct accounts would exist of the Apostles' death than of Jesus', since, first of all, there were more of them; and secondly, over the course of their preaching, Christianity grew to be a more significant

movement which in turn caused the happenings pertaining to it to be written down by more authors.
[36] Contrast this to the alleged miracle of the founder of Mormonism, Joseph Smith, whose "miraculous" tablets that revealed the Book of Mormon are only even said to have been seen by three people, each of whom faced no serious tests of

- We have no historical record of anyone *ever* surviving a Roman Crucifixion the likes of which Jesus endured (thus rendering completely absurd the so-called "swoon hypothesis," wherein the Resurrection apparently occurred but was actually a fraud)
- We have *no* historical *or* contemporary record of *any* so-called "mass hysteria," "collective hallucination," or "collective delusion" wherein many people falsely believe that *precisely the same objective and external event* occurred. In fact, there is not any scientific evidence that there even *is any such thing* as "collective hallucination."[37]

To summarize the list above: even if we restrict our considerations to only those facts which no one denies, we have extraordinary evidence for the Resurrection, and we do not have a single piece of evidence contradicting Jesus' Resurrection other than the atheistic prejudice that it couldn't possibly have happened because this would mean atheists themselves are wrong. (And why does anyone lend an ear to an argument which boils down to nothing but *"That cannot be right, because if that were right, my own presuppositions would be wrong."*?)

Consider some other illustrations. For a friend you know you can trust, it should require no additional proof for you to believe him when he tells you about a newsworthy fifty car pile-up he witnessed on his drive to work, than when he tells you he saw someone get pulled over for speeding. One is an ordinary claim, one an extraordinary claim, and both should be believed since they have reasonable evidence: namely, trustworthy eyewitness testimony that is not contradicted by any other definitive evidence.

A father's plea of *"Jump! Just do it! I know I can catch you!"* as his son stands on the edge of some drop-off which the son cannot see due to his angle as he looks through the fog, should compel the son just as readily as when this father gives the child a glass of milk to drink. For if the father is unworthy of trust and had evil plans for his son, he could have

easily poisoned the milk. Why bother leading his son to some cliff on the edge of a foggy abyss perfectly suited for an act of faith on the part of the son leading to death? The implicit claims in each scenario (namely, "this milk is safe to drink," and "this unknown abyss you cannot see is safe to jump into") are of course ordinary and extraordinary claims, respectively. And yet, this distinction would be absurd for the son to use as the criteria for decision making.

We can see that deciding an ordinary issue based on minimal evidence, it is more likely to be detrimental if those who put forth the evidence are unworthy of trust, than deciding an extraordinary issue based on reasonable evidence is; even though this risk is the very thing that the "extraordinary claims require extraordinary evidence" crowd is trying to do away with. The only question that matters, then, is not the irrelevant one ("Is this ordinary or extraordinary?"), but rather it is the essential one: "Is this reasonable?" That is, "is this the clear claim of one I know is trustworthy, on a matter-of-fact that he is merely relaying to me as opposed to giving his own interpretation of events, and pertaining to a scenario which is not prone to being mistaken about?" If an affirmative answer is given to that question, the truly reasoning man no longer doubts the proper course of action.

The converse is true as well. In a serial line of reasoning leading to the conviction of a man, each piece of this logical chain, no matter how seemingly ordinary, must be given the same scrutiny as if it was the sole convicting piece. Only the most evil prosecutor and the most gullible jury would convict a man of murder if the whole argument which supposedly demonstrates his guilt requires (for its validity) the admission of some "ordinary" claim (perhaps the defendant's being at Walmart at 6pm on Tuesday, October 30th) which nevertheless has no "evidence" other than that he was not at his job at that time. And only the most duplicitous of defenders and the most obstinate of juries would fail to convict a man of murder solely because of some "extraordinary" claim (perhaps the victim's murder being the result of expert marksmanship) if

---

his genuineness (e.g. through martyrdom), and one of whom essentially recanted by later admitting he only saw the tablets with the "eyes of Faith," with all three at some point leaving the Mormon religion.

[37] The only type of scientifically well-documented mass hysteria that is even remotely comparable is the case where a

large number of people are deluded to think they have the same (non-existent) disease. But this is obviously not relevant to the discussion at hand, for when many people are self-diagnosing, they are only describing a subjective phenomenon. This is not the case when people describe what they actually *see*.

there is sufficient evidence to prove beyond a reasonable doubt that it nevertheless occurred, even if one does not classify the evidence as "extraordinary."

Like Nothing Else in World History

Let us take a step back, because there is only so much even the best presentation of the most relevant evidence can do. One who is dead-set on believing a conspiracy theory will, tragically, continue to do so until reality itself comes and wallops him over the head like a 2 by 4. And indeed, the hardened conspiracy theorists will stick to their conspiracies despite the evidence that has been shown here.

So instead of presenting more evidence—which easily could be done—I conclude this section by imploring even the most hardened conspiracy theorist to simply take a cursory glance at the most fundamental facts of history—and of the world as it now is—that not even the most eccentric of such theorists deny.

There is a religion called Christianity. It has existed for 2,000 years. From its very founding, it exploded in numbers of adherents—across nations and cultures—like no other phenomenon in history. Centuries upon centuries have passed and its demise has not been seen—nor (and even the most anti-Christian will admit this), will its demise ever be seen. It is not some comfortable platitude or self-help system whose wildfire spread would not be surprising due to its lack of any demands or difficulty involved. No, rather, it is an all-consuming fire that any Christian acknowledges must be the absolute principle of his entire life; demanding the entirety of his very self.

Recall, next, that we have already settled God exists. Feel free to consult again the preceding section if you need to be reminded of this fact.

If you really think that God would allow such an utter farce—but far worse, a categorically diabolical lie (which is what Christianity is if it is not true)—to exercise unrivaled dominion over the religions of the world for two-thousand years ... **then I do not think that you actually *do* believe in God.** For given these premises, what you believe in is some sort of semi-powerful being who cannot even succeed in reigning over the world he made; not the Omnipotent Creator and Master of the Universe Who is the one and only true God. There is no use arguing that this criticism works against Christianity too, due to the existence of other religions with large followings (e.g. Islam and Hinduism); for, as we settled in the beginning of this section, the very claims of those religions are not anything like the claims of Christianity. So what if Islam has almost two billion adherents? Its founder did not claim to be God, and therefore its spread cannot be said to be the spread of such a diabolical lie as Christianity would be if it were false. Muhammad claimed to be a prophet, and whether he was a true prophet or a false prophet does not change the fact that much of his message overlaps that of Christianity, and it is perfectly reasonable to consider God, with His permissive Will, allowing Islam to remain the dominant religion of a relatively small geographic area and a relative few cultures (even if not small in adherents) until these people are ready for the Gospel. It is not similarly reasonable to consider God allowing Christianity to have **such dominion** for **such a long period of time** over **such a vast expanse** of the world if its fundamental claims (e.g. the Divinity of Christ and His Resurrection) are not true. Instead—as is clear to anyone who has honestly taken stock of even just those historical (and present day) facts which no one denies—**it simply isn't possible to acknowledge God's existence, power, and goodness and at the same time say of Christianity what must be said of it (explicitly or implicitly) in order to not follow it.**

But perhaps there is still one final and desperate plea—lingering sheepishly in the recesses of the mind like a stubborn child who does not want to complete his chores—to escape the duty to follow the God-Man. *"Can't I just be a good person!? Isn't that enough?"* Well, let us suppose it is enough; let us grant, for the sake of argument at least, that as long as you really are a good person, you are "all set" as far as God, Judgment Day, and the afterlife are concerned. Even granting this, have those who resort to this plea ever bothered to consider what they mean by "good"? Do they really think that someone who ignores or rejects what he knows is true is a "good" person? Is a duplicitous, hypocritical liar a "good" person? Does a duplicitous, hypocritical liar become a "good" person if he occasionally volunteers at a soup kitchen, isn't a criminal, and isn't usually blatantly mean to people? Is a man a "good" spouse simply because he pays the bills and doesn't cheat, even if he responds to his wife's every "I love you" with his own "no you don't," even when she has given him every proof of this love and never acted against it? This may be a popular definition of "good," but it is surely a pathetic one.

The hard and naked truth must now be stated clearly: one who has come to realize that Jesus is God—and if you have read this far, you certainly should have come to that realization—and refuses to acknowledge Him as such (both in word and in deed), is *not* a good person.

III) The Fact that this Man Founded the Catholic Church

Third. That same man, Jesus Christ, Whom we have seen can only be reasonably regarded as God Himself, founded a Church on St. Peter, and this Church truly persists to this day.

Peter, the Rock with the Keys

All Christians acknowledge that Jesus did indeed say to Peter: **"Thou art Peter; and upon this rock I will build my church, and the gates of hell shall not prevail against it."** —Matthew 16:18

But there are two basic types of interpretation of this verse. One interpretation holds that it means the following: "*Thou art Peter; and upon this rock I will build my church, and the gates of hell shall not prevail against it.*"

All other interpretations in one way or another wager that Jesus was engaging in semantic acrobatics here and didn't even mean anything close to what He said. Some, for example, believe that by "*this rock*," Jesus wasn't referring to *Peter* at all, but perhaps was making an oblique and vague reference merely to the *faith* of Peter (however one goes about building a Church merely on that is anyone's guess).

Other attempts within this second class of interpretations recognize that this first attempt was perhaps not the most honest, so they seek in looking at the Greek word used for "rock" to insist that this can only be understood as a reference to Jesus Himself, not to Peter. But this attempt is equally bizarre. If Jesus was speaking only about Himself why on earth would He have begun that same sentence with "Thou art Peter ... "? That is the kind of speech one would expect from a schizophrenic or an otherwise mentally disabled person—or at best from a small toddler who does not yet understand how sentences work—not from Wisdom Incarnate. This interpretation furthermore makes no sense when considering the very next verse, in which Jesus says, **"I will give <u>you</u> the keys of the kingdom of heaven, and whatever <u>you</u> bind on earth shall be bound in heaven ... ,"** reminding us that He is still speaking about Peter, the man standing before Him, in no vague terms.

This, of course, is all besides the fact that any Catholic will readily grant that Jesus Himself *is* indeed the only true rock upon Whom the Church is built; for all Catholics look to Peter—and to any Pope following him—as only a vicarious stand-in for Christ after His Ascension (hence the well-known title for any Pope, the *Vicar* of Christ). Popes, just like all Christians, are sinners; and just like all Christians, they must stand before Jesus Christ on Judgment Day to give an account of their lives. Therefore, it is not illicit to refer to "the rock of Peter's Faith," as even the Catholic Catechism does,[38] but this cannot possibly be interpreted as the only thing that Christ meant. (Note that the same Catechism goes on to clearly state that Peter *himself* is also the "unshakeable rock of the Church."[39])

Jesus did not simply give Peter a blessing or a mandate, in which case even some sincere seekers of truth might suppose that this task of being the Vicarious Head of the Church on earth died along with Peter; rather, **Jesus gave Peter "*keys*" because keys are something that can, and indeed must, be handed on to the next steward**, just as one tenant of a house must always surrender the keys to whomever moves in afterward.

And although the debate is not entirely over (for there are a relative few who claim genuine Apostolic Succession lies elsewhere), it is a settled fact that the one who always has held the same keys which Jesus gave to Peter is the one who sits enthroned as the Bishop of Rome[40]—Pope Francis,

---

[38] Cf. Paragraph 424
[39] CCC 552
[40] Excepting of course relatively brief periods like the Avignon Papacy; for what makes a Pope the head of the Church is his being the valid successor of the last valid Pope (not necessarily the Bishop of a certain city), who is almost always in Rome, but can be elsewhere.

as of this writing. And before him, Pope Benedict XVI, then Pope St. John Paul II, and so on.

Do you have doubts? Here is a simple task anyone can easily complete in about 15 minutes. Go now to the nearest computer with internet access. Navigate to the current Pope's page[41] in any online encyclopedia. Click "preceded by" to be taken to the pope's predecessor's page. Now click the same link on the page you find yourself and repeat this process again. Do this about 265 times,[42] and you will suddenly be at the page of St. Peter himself, whose installation date as Pope will be rightly listed as 30 A.D., which is approximately when Jesus spoke the aforementioned words to Peter and handed him the keys.

Now, I have encouraged this simple task merely to give a clear illustration of the proper line of Apostolic Succession; this alone does not prove my point, just as, one could argue, following one branch of a tree all the way back to its trunk does not prove anything definitive about that particular branch from which the process began. Let us, therefore, proceed to consider the other branches so that we may see if any of them show evidence of being connected to the trunk.

No Viable Alternatives

Next, we must ask: **Who other than the Catholic Church can even with a straight face claim this Succession all the way back to Jesus Himself, as the same Church that He founded?**

The Church of England (or any member of the Anglican Communion)? Does anyone seriously wish to convert to become a member of a Church founded by a King (Henry VIII) who was so wrathful that the Catholic Church would not grant him a divorce that he founded a *new* Church and exalted *himself* to be its head, in order to create a Church which did not get in the way of his lusts and ambitions? That this is the history of the Church of England is not difficult to discover, nor is it disputed by serious historians—the many English Catholic martyrs, seeing clearly the utter absurdity of the situation, shed their blood because they would not go along with this blasphemous attempt of a secular power to usurp Divine Authority, and they will never be able to be forgotten. It is no accident that perhaps the greatest Christian Apologist of the 20th Century, C. S. Lewis, was an Anglican who could not even bring himself to evangelize for his own denomination, writing, for example:

> ... in this book I am not trying to convert anyone [to the Church of England] ... ever since I became a Christian I have thought that the best, **perhaps the only,** service I could do for my unbelieving neighbours was to explain and defend the belief that has been common to nearly all Christians ... [43]

Here Lewis strongly implies (if not explicitly asserts) that striving to bring souls into the fold of his own particular Church would not even be a "service" for unbelievers.

The Orthodox Church? We cannot even speak of "an" orthodox Church, for there are many and they are not in Communion even with each other (whereas *all* Catholic rites are in Communion with the Successor of Peter). So let us instead look to the largest Orthodox Church: the particular autocephalous church governed by the Patriarch of Constantinople[44]—as of this writing, Bartholomew I. One need only follow Bartholomew's lineage back briefly, to the early 20th century, to find such splintering and fracturing as to indicate that it is clearly an institution of the world, not of Heaven, with which we are dealing, for at this point we find Joachim III (a freemason) and the turmoil which immediately preceded him.

Even more splintering occurred shortly before that when four separate Eastern Churches declared themselves "autocephalous" in the late 19th century (consider that to declare autocephaly is little more than a euphemism for "schism.") And now, yet

---

[41] As of this writing, Pope Francis

[42] This process is smooth, easy, and clear, at all but one point: the Papacies of Pope Benedict IX, who held the office on three separate occasions and who is considered a disgrace to the Chair of Peter. Despite his dissolute lifestyle and his horrendous practices regarding the papacy itself (e.g. selling the office itself in one of the terms), the Church persevered, and God did not allow Benedict to Magisterially teach any heresies; thus fulfilling, as always, the promise Jesus made to Peter, that the Gates of Hell shall not prevail against the Church that He founded on St. Peter. It is worth noting that Benedict IX himself died repentant of his sins.

[43] Preface to Mere Christianity

[44] Who, as of this writing, recently had Communal Relations broken off with the Russian Orthodox Church, thus further splintering Eastern Orthodoxy and demonstrating that it simply cannot be considered to be the true Church founded by Jesus Christ.

another splinter can be added: the "Moscow-Constantinople schism" or the "Orthodox Church Schism of 2018," which is already making its way into the history books of the scholars now authoring them. **If it were not previously clear, it now is: Orthodoxy is no refuge for a Christian seeking that** *One*, **Holy, Apostolic Church founded by God Incarnate when He walked on earth 2,000 years ago.**[45]

Even if we grant the claims to succession of the Ecumenical Patriarchate of Constantinople, we are still left only with **a** Church founded **by** St. *Andrew*; not with **the** Church founded by Jesus **on** St. *Peter*. For the Orthodox centered in Constantinople themselves only claim that they trace their authority back to a Church in Byzantium allegedly (but probably not actually) founded by this apostle—a founding which, even if true, is mentioned nowhere in Scripture and had nothing to do with Jesus' direct intervention. Why, then, even if we grant all the dubious claims of the founding of the Orthodox Church at Constantinople, would you choose a Church founded by St. Andrew over the Church founded by Jesus Christ?

Recall that it is *repeatedly* made clear in Scripture that Peter is the foremost among the Apostles. Besides being the one upon whom Jesus clearly founded his Church in the aforementioned Matthew 16:18, we also see that:

- Peter is the one Jesus directed to "feed my sheep" after His resurrection and before departing to Heaven (John 21:15).
- Peter alone is spoken of as *declaring* with *authority* at the Council of Jerusalem depicted in Acts Chapter 15.
- Only Peter has the faith to walk on water in Matthew 14.
- In Matthew 16, Mark 8, and John 6, Peter is the first of the apostles to confess the Divinity of Christ.
- In Matthew 19, Mark 10, Mark 11, and other places, Peter asks Jesus questions on behalf of all the Apostles.
- Peter's boat, a metaphor for the Church, is the chosen vessel in which Jesus instructs in Luke 5.
- Jesus tells Peter, also in Luke 5, to lower the nets for the catch.
- Virtually every time in the New Testament when multiple apostles are listed, Peter is listed first, even when John (the "one whom Jesus loved") is included.
- Peter's name in the New Testament is, in fact, mentioned more times than all the other apostles' names added together.

Now, no one denies that Peter governed the Church at Rome during his lifetime; and no one denies that the Catholic Church alone lays proper claim to being the Christian Church of Rome. Even if we try to use exegetical acrobatics to wiggle out of the clear words of Jesus in founding his Church on Peter, no other apostle, given the basic data of Scripture, even comes remotely close to being the one we could identify as the legitimate head of the Church.

Can we then simply reject Apostolic Authority entirely and turn to Protestantism? These Christians, whether they class themselves Evangelicals, Baptists, Methodists, Pentecostals, Lutherans, Presbyterians, or what have you, usually do not claim Apostolic Succession. But they do each claim something special for themselves, and this is proven by deeds at least: for all of them seek converts (and any Protestant who does not seek converts should ask himself why he remains in a denomination for which he cannot even muster up sufficient enthusiasm to desire to invite others into).

In joining any one of these Protestant churches, you are becoming a member of a religion founded no

---

[45] This is not to dispute the validity of the Sacraments of the Orthodox; they do indeed have an Apostolic Succession – a lineage of valid bishops who can validly ordain priests who, in turn, can validly consecrate, absolve, etc. (unlike the various Protestant denominations, who only have valid marriage and baptism). But it is not the clear succession of one Head of the Church, to the next, all the way back to Jesus Himself, that the Catholic Church has. Therefore, one cannot suppose that Orthodoxy is a safe refuge for his soul: **there is much more to salvation and sanctification than valid sacraments.** Indeed, the Orthodox have already succumbed to a number of heresies; some pertaining to Faith (e.g. the Immaculate Conception and the Filioque), and others to morals (e.g. to marriage and contraception), for the promise of Christ to Peter—that the gates of hell shall not prevail—does not apply to those who have separated themselves from Communion with the Successor of Peter, as the Orthodox have.

earlier than 1521 A.D. **Where was the Church for those 1,500 years since God Incarnate founded it?** Did the One Who came to earth and Who said to Peter of His Church "the gates of hell shall not prevail against it," in fact lie because that is precisely what happened for the following 1,500 years? (Or at least for 1,200 years after its alleged "Romanization"?). To assert this—which is required in order to adhere to Protestantism of any flavor—is to deny either the goodness or the Omnipotence of Christ. But either denial is blasphemy.

Do you really wish to be a member of a church whose impetus was a man like Martin Luther? For although Lutheranism is the denomination founded by him directly, all Protestant denominations are his spiritual children. Luther: a man who rejected the absolute and unconditional vows which he offered freely as an adult; a man who exhibited all the qualities of a psychotic individual, who then proceeded to blame the Catholic Church for his own spiritual problems and start a new religion of his own, which was little more than a futile attempt to self-medicate his neurotic temperament (by way of pretending that "faith alone," a phrase found **nowhere** in Scripture, is all that matters for the Christian, so any Christian might as well "sin mightily")? By his own admission, he had no idea what this thing called an "indulgence," which is what he is most known for rebelling against, even was. His so-called "conversion" after allegedly being repulsed at the sight of the Faith in a trip to Rome was a convenient afterthought published years after the journey as it proved a helpful weapon with which to lash out at Rome after his excommunication, like an angry 19-year-old writing an autobiographical rant against his parents only after he is kicked out of the house for some perfectly just cause.

But besides considering what the biographical facts of Luther's life point to, **how can one take the teachings of a man seriously who denies the existence of the very truth which every single reasonable human being knows with absolute** certainty: *that we have free will*? Free Will is God's greatest gift to man as well as the most obvious (for everyone *knows* he has free will). That a few mad men masquerading as academics here and there throughout the history of philosophy pretend this fact isn't true is not surprising. The tragic thing is that there is even a single follower to be found for such mad men; much less the countless millions Luther had and has. As we now stand 500 years later, with a great opportunity for wisdom in hindsight by seeing what has become of Protestantism, it is long overdue that those who follow Luther—whether Lutherans in particular or Protestants in general, who see him as the "first reformer"—wake up and see the plain truth regarding the man himself and the Protestant movement he started.[46]

Shall we then resort to so-called "non-denominationalism," as so many millions today are doing, seeing the obvious weakness among all the churches of Protestantism and Orthodoxy? (Bearing in mind that "Pentecostalism" often winds up being little but a movement, as opposed to a religion, and therefore it, too, can often be rightly classed as a certain strand of "non-denominationalism." This sometimes goes for some versions of "Evangelicalism" as well.) For indeed, there ought not even be denominations, as Jesus prayed that "all may be one,"[47] so there is admittedly something noble in the inspiration for this movement. But it, too, entirely misses the point. For "non-denominationalism" has become nothing other than another denomination; but one with even *more* weaknesses and evils than many of the denominations who are not afraid of admitting they are denominations.

There is no such thing as a religion of "mere Christianity." Although that is the title of a wonderful book, its author, C. S. Lewis, insisted that no one dare suppose that "his Christianity is 'mere Christianity.'"

> I hope no reader will suppose that "mere" Christianity is here put forward as an alternative to the creeds of the existing communions—as if a

---

[46] I have no desire to denigrate any man, much less any Christian. But the words of Fr. Leslie Rumble ring true here: "Protestants who idealize Martin Luther urge his supposed sanctity as an argument in favor of the Protestant Reformation. To meet that argument Catholics have no choice but to produce evidence that Luther was not a holy man at all. Catholics argue that one who claims to be commissioned by God to reveal Christ to a degenerate world should himself exhibit a Christ-like life. But Luther did not; and it is inconceivable that such a type of man as he should have been chosen by God to reform the Church of Christ."

[47] John 17:21

man could adopt it in preference to Congregationalism or Greek Orthodoxy or anything else. It is more like a hall out of which doors open into several rooms. If I can bring anyone into that hall I shall have done what I attempted. But it is in the rooms, not in the hall, that there are fires and chairs and meals. The hall is a place to wait in, a place from which to try the various doors, not a place to live in. For that purpose the worst of the rooms (whichever that may be) is, I think, preferable.[48]

In other words, C.S. Lewis is saying quite frankly that even the very worst Christian denomination would be better than "non-denominationalism." For a bare-bones, loose set of beliefs (accompanied as it usually is today by people grouping around similar tastes in "Christian" rock) is not a religion. One can scarcely open up to a page of the New Testament without realizing that following Christ is anything but a mere mindset; rather, what Jesus started as clearly displayed in the pages of the New Testament is a concrete, literal institution; one with a real hierarchy, real Sacraments, real regulations, and a real need to meet regularly together in worship. In fact, **no one denies that the earliest Christians are among the greatest Christians, whom we should all strive to imitate. And these early Christians did not even have the Bible.** As the great scholar mentioned in this book's preface once pointed out, "The New Testament was a *Sacrament* long before it was a *document.*" We sin against the Bible itself by supposing that it is all we need in order to have a personal relationship with Jesus Christ.

Here, I feel I must give a brutally honest personal testimony. I have worked for years as a philosophy professor at a secular, public New York college—and not just any college, but one in the middle of what is repeatedly ranked as the most "post Christian" and "least Biblically minded" urban area in the entire country—so, to put it lightly, I am not exactly standing in front of a group of well-catechized pious nuns and seminarians when I stand up each day to teach. But there is one

observation that I wish I could avert, but simply cannot: of the hundreds of students I have had in this atmosphere, it is sometimes the zealous Protestant or non-denominational Christians who—even among the many pagans, atheists, and "nones" sitting adjacent to them—can be the most stubborn in not wanting to acknowledge sound arguments, valid logic, and good philosophy. You see, my teaching tends to focus on Goodness, Truth, and Beauty as found in the ancient Greek philosophers (e.g. Socrates, Plato, Aristotle). But many Protestants and non-denominational Christians have been fed the "faith alone" and "Scripture alone" lies for so long, and some have so readily gobbled up these lies, that (perhaps without even recognizing it) they have come to despise works, they have come to despise good moral philosophy, and they have even come to despise the serious application of reason[49] and intellect to any of the great existential questions. **And these are the fruits of Luther.**

Oh, how I wish I could count Protestants and non-denominational Christians as nothing but separated brethren who have virtually all the truth and are merely missing a few details, thus allowing me to ignore what they lack and pretend all is well. But that brand of ecumenism, though popular today, is a false one. For it is a form of hatred: it entails implicitly desiring a soul to remain in error and to remain deprived of the graces of the Sacraments which are so enormous as to be nowhere rivaled in all the world.[50] And these errors are by no means merely hypothetically dangerous, but rather have already wreaked havoc upon the entire world. For example, many academics and researchers have already shown that it is precisely those things that most Protestants accept—e.g. artificial contraception (which is allowed by *all* mainstream Protestant denominations) and divorce—things that are at the source of the total societal and familial breakdown which we have been witnessing in the West for the last several

---

[48] Preface to *Mere Christianity*. C.S. Lewis.

[49] Reason, in particular, was discounted by Luther as a "whore"

[50] Now, we mustn't go to the other extreme and categorically reject Ecumenism; for Ecumenism properly understood is a great good. Although indeed, "outside the Church there is no salvation" is a dogma (therefore it *always will be* a dogma), all moral guilt (and consequently all impediments to salvation) can only arise from that which is intentional, which in turn can only proceed from knowledge. No one but God alone knows if a certain soul actually has sufficient knowledge to understand that the Catholic Church is the true Church necessary for salvation (and only a soul with that knowledge could be condemned or deprived of grace for refusing to enter the Catholic Church). These Divine secrets will only be revealed on Judgment Day.

decades.

And so we see that not only is Catholicism clearly the Church which Jesus Himself founded, but also that even if it were not, there would be no hope of finding His Church anywhere else, for all other options prove themselves completely unworthy. Therefore, at the minimum, any soul who earnestly desires to be joined with Christ can, of the Catholic Church, say with Peter after pondering what other Church, denomination, or movement of any sort claiming to be that of Christ: "To whom would we go?"[51] *There is nowhere else to go.*

The Miraculous Paradox

Consider that **the Catholic Church is the only institution on the face of the planet with a simple, single-click built-in total-self-destruct button perpetually sitting on the desk of its leader.** For the Catholic Church claims that all *Ex Cathedra*[52] proclamations of the Pope are truly infallible: meaning it isn't even *possible* for them to be wrong. If you were to ask a serious Catholic what he would do if, tomorrow, the Pope dogmatically taught that Mary was not assumed into Heaven,[53] he should respond to you something to the effect of "I'll answer that question when you tell me what you'd do if 2+2=5."

Indeed, **all it would take is *one single contradiction* between two Ex Cathedra declarations found *anywhere* in her history to destroy the Catholic Church.** The Church has had 266 popes over the course of this 2,000-year history. Some Popes have even been downright evil, but none pressed this button. There are of course always various schismatic traditionalist groups claiming that the button has been pressed whenever their own favorite personal theological opinions are Magisterially overturned, but these groups inevitably themselves splinter and fade into oblivion,[54] for it is not difficult for any fair observer to see, quite clearly, that the button *has not* been pressed. The dogmatic (Ex Cathedra) teachings of the Church have never once contradicted themselves; nor will they ever.

Now, this "button-pressing-constraint" would be an admirable virtue even if it were only pertaining to a small institution that has only existed for a small amount of time. But that is not what we are dealing with here. **We are dealing with the largest, oldest institution in the history of the world also so happening to be, in its fundamental design, the flimsiest institution that has ever existed** (in human and worldly terms). If this consideration does not speak volumes to you about both the Divine origin and guidance of the Catholic Church, then you simply are not thinking clearly. For just as no one could deny Divine Intervention if a man strolled randomly through a densely packed minefield for miles and escaped unscathed, while many others doing the same thing were blown to bits, so too no one who looks at the history of the Catholic Church can fail to see something truly miraculous.

Of course, while it may not have stepped on any of these mines, the Catholic Church has seen its fair share of crises, so we must consider this observation.

The Truth of the Modern Crisis

There is no small bit of irony here, for I write these words in the midst of the greatest crisis in the history of the Catholic Church. Therefore, this must be addressed explicitly, lest anyone falsely suppose that something has changed, and the argument in the previous section no longer holds.

This evil in the Church, though at a now historic level, is not fundamentally new; the Church was not without evil even when Jesus was its visible head, for at that time one-twelfth of the Bishops (the "1" referring to Judas, one of the Apostles) were downright evil. That the Catholic Church has survived and thrived these 2,000 years despite such evil forces seeking to tear her apart is, again, just another proof of her Divine protection and guidance. There have been murderous Popes; God did not permit them to teach heresy and thereby lead their flock astray. There have been falsehoods believed by the majority of clergy; God did not

---

[51] John 6:68

[52] Meaning "from the chair." A papal pronouncement is "ex cathedra" when he is speaking *as* Pope to the whole Church and employing his Apostolic authority in defining a teaching on faith or morals.

[53] For it has already been dogmatically proclaimed, in 1950 by Pope Pius XII, that Mary *was* assumed into Heaven.

[54] It should be noted that most Catholic traditionalists are not of this sort; they are, rather, merely Catholics who are rightly concerned with the abuses that have entered into the *practice*, not Magisterium, of the Church.

permit these lies to become part of the Magisterium (the teaching authority of the Church). There have been large groups of evil Catholics who sought to overtake the Church; God prevented their victory. Without what we claim as true actually being so (that God sent His Holy Spirit to ensure that, as Jesus said, "the gates of hell would not prevail against [The Church]"), this Church never would have survived. We can see that the "miraculous paradox" discussed in the last section applies not only to the "button pressing constraint," but also to the Divine Protection in so many other areas enjoyed by Catholicism throughout her 2,000 year history.

Indeed, no matter how damaged her hull or how tattered her sails; the Catholic Church remains the New Ark; the safe refuge from the deluge of sin that is now flooding the whole world. Her ministers—Catholic Priests—may be imperfect, but they bring to us the One who is Perfection Himself; Jesus Christ in the Eucharist and His Blood shed for us anew in the Sacrament of Confession. She, Holy Mother Church, will bring you home soundly to God. If you would not permit the sight of tattered clothing on your own mother's back to cause you to reject her, then also do not permit the evil you see in the Catholic Church to leave her maternal love for you. She alone is the Bride of Christ as well as His body. He is the one head, and she is the one body- outside of which there is no eternal life—from which if we separate ourselves, we wither and die.

***

But oh, how little we have covered here! Look at the saints—so many thousands of them, each trampling the world under his feet, each a hero worth a thousand biographies; each page of which, in turn, could be so filled with light as to dazzle the hardest heart. Look at the constant stream of miracles, from when, 2,000 years ago, even the mere shadow of St. Peter healed the sick,[55] all the way to the present day with so many told and untold miraculous healings; Divine Interventions; Eucharistic miracles; prophecies fulfilled; celestial phenomena observed (for example the 70,000 who saw the sun dance in the sky at Fatima in 1917); incorrupt bodies remaining for centuries in the exact same material state they enjoyed at the moment of death; Divinely drawn images (e.g. the

Image of Our Lady of Guadalupe); impossible victories won (e.g. at the Battle of Lepanto through the intercession of Our Lady of the Rosary); and the list goes on. Look to the breathtaking art, the likes of which one will find nowhere else in the history of the world, drawn by devout Catholics influenced by Catholic realities. Look at the stunning Cathedrals—all built to glorify the God Whom Catholics worship in the Holy Eucharist—masterpieces to which no other buildings on earth can compare. Behold the sacred music that, when it is chanted from the mouths of religious through the great spaces of these same Cathedrals, makes the hearers forget they are still in the midst of an earthly pilgrimage. Do not take my word for any of this; investigate it yourself.

In this investigation, among the glorious things you discover will be thousands of individual instances of clear supernatural intervention; all of it pointing to the validity of the Catholic Church and her teachings. It may be that in time one or two of these individual items are shown to be hoaxes, hallucinations, or frauds. So what? For that which they testify to (the glory of the Church, the existence of God and the revelation of His Will) to be weakened on account of them—*each and every one* would need to be shown to be false; and that will simply *never* happen. Trying to prove each of these false would render easy in comparison to the efforts of a conspiracy theorist to prove every astronaut a fraud in his efforts to argue for a flat earth.

This all, dear reader, is the work of God, not the work of man. The Catholic Church is His Church. It has been for 2,000 years, and it will be until the end of time.

Our Present Duty Given These Foundations

So here we are. Our foundation as Catholics has been examined, and it is absolutely solid; absolutely bulletproof; absolutely certain.

Truly, therefore, we all must be Catholics. In case there is any room for ambiguity in that statement regarding what is meant by "we all", let us put it more clearly: every single human being on the face of the planet has a duty to become a member of the

Catholic Church.[56] It really is that simple. We must furthermore believe everything the Church teaches, and always behave in accordance with these beliefs (and if there is ever any confusion as to what these beliefs are, the Catechism of the Catholic Church should be consulted).

This response is what is required by merely wishing to be a person who takes the demands of truth seriously; for in the preceding sections we have seen clearly that this response is simply what most basic premises (which no one can reasonably deny) lead to. And no one can pretend to take any premises seriously if he refuses to heed what follows from these premises themselves.

The Truth does not care about any rationalizations that stand opposed to it; quite the contrary, with invincible strength it knocks down anything that dares to stand in its path. Nor does the Truth care if the people of a given age proclaim it to be "politically incorrect," "judgmental," "pastorally insensitive," or any other term dreamed up by those whose motives are malicious and who pretend that *means* have a right to overthrow the only *ends* for which the means themselves exist.

But we must not merely "be" Catholics, as if a passive identification as such and a baseline following of the bare-minimum precepts was sufficient. For being a lukewarm Catholic is like being a lukewarm spouse—it contradicts the very purpose of the vocation, which is supposed to be one of a love set ablaze, and any blaze is either completely dead or is burning hot. Similarly, becoming a Catholic is like entering the Olympics, which no one does without striving for the gold. But we needn't merely ponder analogies; being a Catholic certainly entails at least a firm belief in all the Catholic Church teaches, and among these

teachings is found the *Universal Call to Holiness*: that is, the dogmatic teaching that each and every Catholic is called to perfect holiness and sanctity.[57]

So, in addition to being Catholics, we must all strive to be the best Catholics possible; not merely superficially asserting belief in the teachings of the Church, but proving the same with our comportment. But this proof, in turn, does not exist if we do not take the authentically Catholic approach to *everything*, which includes the authentically Catholic approach to private revelation, which is what we will now turn to consider.

For indeed, being Catholic and certain of the truth of the Faith—as every Catholic should be—is nevertheless not an excuse to close the mind, fold the arms, and clench the fists. These very teachings about which we are certain give us a solid foundation to stand on and a sure fence guarding the edge of a cliff, not a cave to crawl into and hide in (although many unfortunately use it for just that perverse purpose).

In fact, it is precisely this same foundation; these same Three Essential Truths, which compel us (if we take them seriously) to continue and to realize that there is no way to evade the call to follow the revelations given to Luisa Piccarreta. In other words, **it is precisely because we want to be the best Catholics possible that we should want to follow Luisa's revelations.**

But before addressing the question of discerning private revelations, and discerning Luisa's in particular, we must first address the importance of private revelation in general; sadly, much misinformation abounds within Catholic circles on this question.

7) On Private Revelation in General

One unfortunately hears sentiments like the following regularly expressed in some Catholic circles:

"Private Revelation is unnecessary; the Catholic Faith

alone is enough. We have Scripture, Tradition, and Magisterium. Why would we need all this other extraneous stuff? It is all just a distraction."

I have in fact been quite generous in wording these

---

[56] This duty, of course, does not change the fact that God judges according to the individual's level of knowledge, understanding, etc.; and we can certainly hope that most people who are objectively "guilty" of being outside of the Catholic Church are nevertheless not culpable for their state. But denying this hope for diminished culpability is no more

absurd than is blindly and lukewarmly relying on this hope instead of striving with zeal to correspond with that which is objectively true – that all are indeed called to be Catholic.
[57] Cf. Matthew 5:48, *Lumen Gentium* (The <u>Dogmatic</u> Constitution on the Church), paragraph 40.

sentiments, for usually those who voice them go on to contradict themselves, as they continue their lecture to include the Rosary in their list of things that are "sufficient" and "preclude the need for private revelation." Of course, as any diligent student of Church History knows, the Rosary itself is the matter of a *private revelation* given to St. Dominic. It speaks volumes that this Rosary is usually included in the lists of things that are "enough" as opposed to "superfluous" private revelation; for indeed, **the Rosary is *necessary*;** it truly is. **The fact that it is not a constituent of the Deposit of Faith does not detract from its status as** *necessary*. And it seems we have finally reached a stage in the history of the Church where most serious Catholics are beginning to realize this fact. Every pontiff in recent memory has begged Catholics to pray the Rosary. Every saint who knew of it insisted upon it, with this insistence growing ever more fervent over the centuries. The odds of the Catholic Church ever condemning, cautioning against, or even ceasing to encourage the Rosary are about as high as the odds of a law of Gravity being successfully repealed. And more recently, we have the saintly seer of Fatima—perhaps the most clearly reliable private revelation in history, which no serious Catholic doubts—putting it perfectly bluntly:

"**All** people of good will can, and **must** say the Rosary every day ... "[58]

- Servant of God Sister Lucia (the sole Fatima seer who survived to adulthood)

Indeed, the Rosary *draws from* Scripture, Tradition, and Magisterium, and harmonizes with the same; *all* (valid) private revelations do. But in itself, the Rosary is indisputably a private revelation. **We should always remember, therefore, that whatever one categorically says about private revelation, he also says about the Rosary, which we have here shown is *necessary*, and whose eschatological importance in this Final Confrontation the Church is now facing is almost impossible to overestimate.** And whatever one says about private revelation, he thereby says not only of the Rosary, but of devotion to the Sacred and Immaculate Hearts, the Miraculous Medal, the Brown Scapular, the Divine Mercy (of St.

Faustina—e.g. the Image, the Chaplet), Our Lady of Guadalupe (and Fatima, Lourdes, etc.), and on the list goes. Furthermore, while the Eucharist and Confession are obviously not the results of private revelations, the enormous emphasis due to them (e.g. the importance of daily Communion, frequent confession—at least monthly, Eucharistic adoration, etc.) largely is.

In fact, there is no such thing as "private" revelation, if by "private" is meant "only intended to be heard and heeded by those who find themselves drawn to it." We know from Scripture, rather, that "*he who prophesies edifies the church,*"[59] and that the extraordinary charisms of the Holy Spirit, of which prophecy is one, exist not for one's own sanctification, but for the sanctification of the Church. The Catechism teaches:

> Whether extraordinary or simple and humble, charisms are graces of the Holy Spirit which directly or indirectly benefit the Church ... **Charisms are to be accepted with gratitude** by the person who receives them and by **all members of the Church** as well. They are a wonderfully rich grace for the apostolic vitality and for the holiness of the entire Body of Christ...[60]

Take note that the Catechism does not say that charisms are to be accepted by "those members of the Church who find them agreeable," but rather "by **all** members of the Church."

The Catechism itself also seems to find the prevailing terminology unfortunate, entitling its section on the topic "On so-called 'private' revelation," putting the word *private* in quotes as if to imply that such a word really should not be said of a revelation from God, even if it is not one that is itself an element of the Deposit of Faith. (Unfortunately, some Catholics treat this sentence in the Catechism as if it is the word "revelation" that is in quotation marks! This alteration, of course, completely inverts the implication.) Rather, these messages are better considered quite simply as *revelations*, so long as they are not confused with the Deposit of Faith—comprised of Scripture and Tradition, and authoritatively interpreted by the Magisterium. **This Deposit of Faith is the absolute norm for judging all other alleged revelations,**

---

[58] National Catholic Register. "Fatima's Sister Lucia Explains Why the Daily Rosary is a 'Must'" November 19, 2017. Joseph Pronechen, Citing "*Fatima in Lucia's own words, volume 1*"

[59] 1 Corinthians 14
[60] *Catechism of the Catholic Church*, paragraph 799-800.

Luisa's included, and this Deposit alone universally demands the assent of Supernatural Catholic Faith.

But that is where the limitations on private revelation stop, even though some career lay apologists in the last few decades have taken it upon themselves to radically extend these limitations and promote the lie that the only things a man must ever heed are the specific Magisterial demands of the Catholic Faith itself. Here I must ask: is it too bold for me to ponder if some outwardly zealous Catholics really, in substance, see Heaven's direct intervention in the world as competition for their own carefully strategized 'apostolates'—that is, *business endeavors and book sale royalties*? For on the Day of Judgment it will be revealed that many who now parade themselves as the day's great promoters and defenders of the Church were in fact the greatest obstacles to God's Will, doing more harm to God and to His plans for the world than is wrought even by those who explicitly dedicate themselves to that very task. For on That Terrible Day, the words of C. S. Lewis regarding it shall be vindicated: "**We shall then, for the first time, see every one as he really was. *There will be surprises.***"[61]

Against the Sowers of Discord

Nevertheless, a few popular career lay apologists are not the only guilty ones here. There are some promoters even of private revelations—including priests—who make this tragedy their own in their treatment of private revelations *other* than the ones they have dedicated themselves to. This injustice is especially common among some promoters of private revelations that have already managed to secure the highest levels of Church approval (especially the Rosary, Our Lady of Guadalupe, Our Lady of Fatima, the Miraculous Medal, the Sacred Heart, and Divine Mercy). Now, I do not merely *encourage*; no, rather, I *fervently beg* all Catholics to embrace fully each of these revelations: to pray the Rosary daily, to have and venerate the Guadalupe Image, to carry out faithfully the Fatima message (e.g. the First Five Saturday Devotion), to wear a Miraculous Medal, to accomplish continually the First Nine Friday Devotion, and to recite the Divine Mercy Chaplet daily while both having and promoting the Divine Mercy Image.

Some promoters of these revelations, however, (and some of whom in turn have built careers around them), treat their own apostolates pertaining to them as businesses, even though they clothe them in holy attire to not appear at first glance as businesses, while treating *other* apostolates and private revelations as "the competition." We see this attitude clearly displayed in the following behaviors:

- They refuse to see fruits from other revelations even if many fruits exist, for they are careful to never look at where they know the fruits would be seen. Thus, they claim that other revelations do not have fruits and should be ignored. (They themselves have built veritable empires off their own apostolates and are easily capable of distributing newsletters chock-full of stories which they can appeal to as their own fruits; but they unjustly expect this infrastructure of apostolates that are relatively minuscule and cannot afford newsletters, advertisements, paid staff, and the like.)
- They divisively attack other private revelations and then accuse them of the very "divisiveness" which they themselves caused. For in fact those whom they attack are merely justly defending themselves against baseless accusations (did not Our Lord, when the time was fitting, defend Himself against the Pharisees absurd criticisms?), and if they even had the honesty to look at the history of their own private revelation, they would have no trouble seeing the exact same things they now attack other private revelations on the basis of.
- They are always ready to claim that they suddenly have "no time" for any other private revelation whenever one is brought up (perhaps only minutes after they are done admonishing others who say they have no time for their own apostolate's revelations), even when virtually no time is asked of them (but instead only a little humility).

Sadly, I have personally observed these antics explicitly displayed (in private) from even some of the most well-known promoters of some of the most well-known private revelations. Doubtless due to the prevalence of these antics, there has still been no successful mission that combines and promotes, as one unified effort, *all* the trustworthy

---

private revelations that Heaven has blessed the Church with (particularly in the last century). But Heaven acts with one will alone: The Divine Will. Therefore, whatever is truly from Heaven never works against anything else that is truly from Heaven.

What is needed today is an army of souls willing to embrace *all* the calls made by Heaven. Perhaps a specific apostolate, with a physical headquarters, a newsletter, and employees is not called for; with due respect to the risk that it may well quickly become the very thing it was created to safeguard against. So instead, **what I earnestly beseech all reading these words is that they form this army without barracks nevertheless: an army of souls united at least by their willingness to listen to and act upon *all* the calls issued by Heaven**—always, of course, using the Church-sanctioned means of discernment (and submitting to her judgment when she does act in a binding manner) which will be delineated shortly—and refusing to succumb to ever seeing different trustworthy private revelations as competition for each other.

The Term "Private Revelation"

Returning to the issue of the very term "private revelation," I acknowledge my hesitation in even using it: although there is of course nothing wrong with the term, there is a risk that its excessive use could give the impression that the response to it is entirely a matter of personal preference. This indeed has become a common notion among some Catholics today—that private revelation is a "whatever floats your boat" matter. Their argument is essentially as follows:

"Since Private Revelation is never a matter of Catholic Faith, there can never be any moral obligation to heed it. It's entirely a matter of preference and you should respond however you feel like."

This contention ignores the simple fact that reacting to *anything* "however you feel like" is a recipe for disaster in this fallen world. The mere fact that one does not put Divine Faith in a Private Revelation does not mean that he can never have any obligation in the matter! From that same logic, one might as well assert that *"The Deposit of Faith does not hold that 2+2=4, therefore one has no obligation to*

believe that 2+2=4, and if he feels so inclined, he can demand 5 dollars in return from a debtor he loaned 2 dollars to one day and another 2 the next with due regard to his own views on the mathematics of addition."

Quite the contrary, **you and God both know what invitations He has extended to your heart, and on Judgment Day your eternal glory will be meted out by how you responded to these Divine Invitations**, and not just by whether you have faith in the Deposit of Faith. That latter assertion would be a slightly Catholicized version of the Protestant "Faith Alone" heresy. This heresy holds that the only question in salvation is whether one believed what one was required to believe with Supernatural Faith. But Catholic teaching, of course, rejects this idea. **Consider what the Catechism says:**

> **In all he says and does, man is obliged to follow faithfully what he knows to be just and right**.[62]

It does not say *"only in those matters that the Catholic Church teaches are true must man follow faithfully what he knows to be just and right."* Furthermore, **Vatican II teaches "He is not saved, however, who, though part of the body of the Church, does not persevere in charity."**[63] From these authoritative teachings, it is clear that the approach insisted upon by those who erroneously conflate "not required *as a matter of* Catholic Faith" with "never possibly an obligation of any sort for any Catholic" is not only taught nowhere by the Catholic Church, but is in fact clearly repudiated by her. I repeat: it is manifestly absurd to wager that a Catholic is always and everywhere free to hold to whatever opinion he so desires so long as it does not involve the contradiction of the Catholic Faith itself.[64]

Besides, the glorious history of the Catholic Church tells a radically different story from the "whatever floats your boat on private revelation" approach. For it is a story in which whether Catholics respond faithfully to genuine "private" revelations as determining the course of history—especially concerning **the requests at Fatima to the children, the message to St. Faustina, the requests of Jesus for the Sacred Heart devotion, the requests of Our Lady of Guadalupe through St. Juan Diego, and the list goes on**. Would God have taken no offense if the tens of thousands who witnessed the miracle

---

[62] *Ibid.* 1778.
[63] *Lumen Gentium,* paragraph 14.

[64] Remember as well, as mentioned elsewhere in this book, that the Magisterium itself now teaches that the Magisterium is insufficient. Cf. *Gaudete et Exsultate*, paragraph 170.

at Fatima turned their backs on that "unapproved nonsense?" Would St. Faustina's spiritual director have committed no sin if he ignored or opposed the promulgation of the Divine Mercy message instead of helping it, saying "this is extraneous and what we already have is enough"? Would Bishop Zumaragga have been safe in the Will of God by ignoring St. Juan Diego coming to him with the request of Our Lady of Guadalupe to have a church built? Did not King Louis XIV's failure to respond to the Sacred Heart requests of Jesus through St. Margaret Mary result in disaster for France? **Though each is now approved, and no devout Catholic doubts their validity,** *none of these revelations had already enjoyed Church approval at the time Heaven called for the corresponding response to each.* The "ignore all private revelation unless or until it is approved" approach has already been rendered absurd by the facts of history.

Considering these events and so many more like them, we can find a renewed appreciation for the advice regarding Marian apparitions of Pope Urban VIII who allegedly said:

> … cases which concern private revelations, it is better to believe than not to believe, for, if you believe, and it is proven true, you will be happy that you have believed, because our Holy Mother asked it. If you believe, and it should be proven false, you will receive all blessings as if it had been true, because you believed it to be true.[65]

The case of Our Lady of Kibeho is especially noteworthy as it is a recently approved apparition of Mary.[66] **She came to warn the people of an impending disaster with** *rivers of blood,* **and to instruct us on how to avert it. Twelve years later, the Rwandan Genocide occurred,** in which one million innocent people were slaughtered by their own neighbors. It all could have been avoided if only we had listened to Our Lady's plea in that private revelation. Now, before one responds with "Ah, but that is an approved apparition," he should bear in mind that the **full approval only came after the genocide took place.** "*The Marian dimension of the Church precedes the Petrine,*"[67] as the Catechism itself teaches (although the two must never be seen

as opposed). Similar stories and timelines exist for many now-approved apparitions. Even a cursory examination of the historical facts yields the unavoidable conclusion: **Jesus and Mary come with messages because we need to listen to them and heed them**, not because they just want to be another blog competing for our attention, which we may feel free to ignore if we wish.

Some Catholics will cite a few admonitions given by St. Teresa of Avila or St. John of the Cross in their avoidance of private revelation. In so doing, they misuse quotes of these great Doctors, for they cite quotes that apply only to one desiring one's *own personal* apparent revelations from God, or in overzealously seeking such private revelations to answer all of their specific, personal questions. And how true it is that such revelations are not something to be desired! For blessed is the one who believes without seeing.[68] We should give thanks to God that we have been given the gift of Faith despite not being among those chosen to have great visions and revelations, and we should neither desire nor ask for this situation to change. However, **this pious and true advice from these Doctors was not intended by them to have any bearing whatsoever on how we should react to the alleged private revelations of** *others*, especially those whose revelations have received many Ecclesiastical approbations and whose causes for beatification are going well (as in the case of Luisa's!).

Holy Curiosity and Love

Let us consider curiosity. It can be a negative thing, especially when it is opposed to custody of the eyes, discernment of spirits, contentment with what God has given you, and the like. But there is at least one sense in which we can indeed refer to holy curiosity. And the absence of this holy curiosity in the soul, far from proving a holy contentment (we are all pilgrims on this earth and therefore none of us has any grounds for contentment, for the perfection of our knowledge has not yet been attained), proves only the presence of spiritual sloth. Pope Benedict XVI taught:

---

[65] Though a difficult quote to verify, I include it here due to the circumstantial possibility that it referred to the revelations of Mary of Agreda, which was a very contentious issue during his Papacy. Admittedly, however, great weight should probably not be given to this quote, as it is proving a very difficult one to verify.

[66] This approval was declared by Bishop Augustin Misago on June 29, 2001.
[67] Catechism of the Catholic Church, paragraph 773, Cf. John Paul II "Mulieris Dignitatem," paragraph 27.
[68] Cf. John 20:29

The shepherds made haste. Holy curiosity and holy joy impelled them. In our case, it is probably not very often that we make haste for the things of God. God does not feature among the things that require haste. The things of God can wait, we think and we say. And yet he is the most important thing, ultimately the one truly important thing. Why should we not also be moved by curiosity to see more closely and to know what God has said to us? At this hour, let us ask him to touch our hearts with the holy curiosity and the holy joy of the shepherds, and thus let us go over joyfully to Bethlehem, to the Lord who today once more comes to meet us.[69]

These words should primarily be taken with respect to their admonishment to have that joy and holy curiosity in where we know we have Jesus: in the Eucharist, in the Gospel, and in the Church. But it can also be applied to when the Spirit seeks to bless the Church with revelations, and, indeed, it must.

"At the evening of our lives, we will be judged by our love."[70] This is not a mere pious sentiment that can be overlooked by those who do not feel drawn to it. It is an authoritative, Magisterial teaching of the Catechism of the Catholic Church, itself quoting St. John of the Cross, a Doctor of the Church. In other words, we will not be judged positively by how stubbornly we cling to a certain stage in our spiritual growth, as if the Deposit of Faith were a desk to hide under instead of a solid foundation to stand on. We will not be judged positively by insisting that, because the "old wine" is good, it is "good enough," on contradiction to the admonitions of Our Lord in the Gospel.[71] We will not be judged positively by refusing to seek earnestly and follow the Will of God because we prefer to live what we see as a comfortable or safe spiritual life.

We will be judged by our love. By our love of God, and our love of neighbor. In that order, and the latter for the sake of the former. If you do not want to listen to what your spouse says now because you wish only to consider what your spouse has said in the past, then you do not love your spouse. It is that simple. Do you wish to be a loving spouse of God? Or do you wish only to be a slave to which He imparts a set of orders and then leaves on His own?

The Rotten Fruit of Dismissing Private Revelation

Today, the Church suffers from a crisis that is, in its essence, the heresy of Modernism. For it has become fashionable in some theological circles today to ignore or contradict any teaching whatsoever that is not explicitly and clearly infallibly contained in the Magisterium or in Sacred Scripture for no other reason than the perverse desire for an autonomous and artificial "newness." Entire libraries could be filled with the nonsense that has proceeded from this methodology, so instead of attempting a comprehensive overview it, I will only present a few of its more common manifestations. After each, we will consider how private revelation guards us against these traps.

• As mentioned in other parts of this book, **today some significant theologians teach that hell might just be empty now**—and always remain that way—of all human beings (that no one ever has been or ever will be damned, and that only demons populate hell). In one detail they are right: The extraordinary Magisterium has never infallibly declared that any particular soul is in hell. These theologians carefully dodge any accusation of formal heresy by pointing this out, and by carefully couching their argument in sophistry that they are only saying it is a "reasonable hope." But no one who takes private revelation seriously falls into this error: for all of them make it clear that there are many humans in hell.

• **Moral Theology is in tatters today**, and constantly is used for evil: to pretend that commandments are mere ideals, that virtually nothing amounts to formal cooperation with evil, that just about any imaginable rationalization for a sin mitigates the culpability thereof, that condemnations of divorce and adultery are "unrealistic," that circumstances can even justify any intrinsic evil (e.g. abortion, homosexual acts) etc. Counter to this, we see private revelation always dealing very gently with sinners, while always being bold and uncompromising in addressing sin itself (for unlike moral theologians, Heaven has not forgotten to *love the sinner but hate the sin*).

---

[69] Benedict XVI. Homily at Christmas Vigil Mass. December 24th, 2012 (Libreria Editrice Vaticana).

[70] CCC 1022
[71] Cf. Luke 5:39

- Imaginative fiction regarding the biographical details of the Holy Family has become completely unrestrained lately. **The most absurd things are posited about the earthly life of Jesus, Mary, and Joseph**: that Joseph had other children, that Mary endured great pain in childbirth and was scarcely any different from a normal mother (other than the fact that she did not commit blatant sins), that Jesus misbehaved as a child and had to be rightly scolded by Joseph and Mary, and the list goes on regarding such lamentable fiction. Far from merely being relegated to the pages of novels that no one buys, these "insights" regularly find their way into homilies and popular Catholic writings, which in turn, quite tragically, form the minds and hearts of ordinary Catholics in accord with grave falsehood. But in private revelation we always see a Holy Family like the one that Catholic tradition has always envisioned.

- **A completely distorted Christology** has become popular today, wherein (for example) Christ is ignorant even of His own Divine Mission. Fr. James Martin, now infamous for his book endorsing homosexuality, announced his problematic views in public much earlier, even writing an article for CNN asserting that, on Easter Sunday, Jesus was of all people most surprised by the Resurrection. Private revelations always show us a Jesus whose Divinity is never the least bit in doubt.

- Many worldly minded theologians have adopted an **attitude of compromise and assimilation with the spirit of the age**, supposing that the various sins of the past and the fact that the Western World has progressed past a small sampling of them means that we are actually a more moral and holy world now than we ever were before. This is the opposite of the consensus of every private revelation: all of them assert, unambiguously, that the world is now shrouded in more sin, error, and darkness than ever before.

- **The Book of Genesis is often treated as a mere myth**—symbolic literature and nothing more—by many theologians today. But every private revelation that speaks of its contents affirms that Adam and Eve were real people; that they and only they really are our first parents; that they really did live in paradise but sinned and thus destroyed it; that the flood really did occur as a purification of the world from its sinfulness; and so on.

- There is a movement among some theologians to disregard completely the *sensus fidelium* regarding the Signs of the Times, and instead **entertain the notion that we are nowhere *near* the End of the Age**, and may still be in the very earliest era of Church History—that, perhaps, generations *many* thousands of years from now will look back at *us* as Fathers of the Church. While not a heresy, it is still a dangerous view, because it breeds a complacency regarding hastening the Coming of Our Lord, dispels urgency, and gives theologians a faulty sense of their own leeway (as it allows them to think of themselves as perhaps being "Fathers of the Church"). On the contrary, every Private Revelation that speaks of the times we are in makes it clear that the Cosmic, Divine Intervention spoken of in the Book of Revelation will soon be at hand.

- Today one can scarcely find anything but a **totally dismissive approach to Purgatory when the issue is broached.** Although the existence of Purgatory is a Dogma, there is not much infallible teaching on the nature of it, so the private-revelation-dismissers take this as their opportunity to pretend Purgatory is no big deal at all: that it's nothing other than perhaps a slightly less glorious Heaven, and we shouldn't concern ourselves much with praying and sacrificing for the souls there. On the contrary, we have every Private Revelation that speaks of it referring to it as a place of great suffering and emphasizing the extreme importance of praying for the souls there.

Now, these errors are not refuted only once or twice in private revelations here and there, but rather they contradict easily verifiable *consensuses* of trustworthy private revelation, and consequently, one who acknowledges the importance of private revelation is essentially invincible against the aforementioned errors; just like one who acknowledges the importance of science is invincible against flat-earth theory.

Here, one might protest: *"What does private revelation have to do with any of this? I can refute all these errors without it!"* Well, perhaps some—even most—could be addressed without private revelation. But to say confidently all can be thoroughly refuted without it is questionable, as some errors listed above are difficult to refute definitively from Scripture, Sacred Tradition, and Magisterium. It seems, rather, that if one takes stock of his rhetorical arsenal, he may discover it is lacking in its defense against Modernism without private revelation.

The Only Sure Guard Against Modernism

Here we see a tragic irony: those who are fearful and distrusting of private revelation on the grounds that it is not infallible and thus might be a risk to orthodoxy (one often hears this fear voiced in some circles), only open themselves up to the far greater danger of a deceptive worldly exegesis, masquerading as scholarship, generating far more errors in their minds than even a somewhat overzealous approach to private revelation ever could. (For indeed, willed fear never edifies.)

Most of these errors, of course, relate to tenets of the Heresy of Modernism. One may think himself safe against this broad heresy merely by virtue of his love for Catholic Tradition; but this will not suffice. We can see why from the following considerations:

- Who shall inform him as to what the consensus of Sacred Tradition even consists in? His own research? There is far too much content within Catholic Tradition for any one person to summarize on his own.
- Shall he, in fear of the subtleties of modernism, close his ears entirely to the voice of the Holy Spirit today? Catholic tradition itself repudiates this as a Godless way of life, after the manner of the Pharisees, so this is self-defeating.
- Shall he rely on this or that saint whom he believes stated well what tradition consists in and gave a sure guide to applying it to one's life as a Catholic? Perhaps St. Pius X or St. Josemaria Escriva? This also cannot work: a life cannot be well lived without addressing the issues *of the day*. By definition, these are the very issues that no canonized saint can directly confront, since these saints are no longer with us on earth.
- Shall he simply read the Magisterium and let nothing else guide him? This approach can never work either. The majority of issues that

one need confront in his life will never be directly settled by the Magisterium. Those that are addressed by the Magisterium are usually only dealt with many years after they become utterly pressing. This is all besides the fact that the Magisterium itself now assures us that, though necessary (binding), it is inadequate (failing to address everything that must be addressed), stating in paragraph 170 of the Apostolic Exhortation *Gaudete at Exsultate*: **"Nor are the Church's sound norms sufficient."**

- Shall he then find an authoritative guide, living today, to Catholic Tradition, in whom to place all of his trust? Many do precisely this: perhaps in this or that blog, apostolate, or pundit. But this is the most vain attempt of all; for where does this guide get his own guidance? We have only kicked the can down the road and, like a sloth or a coward, outsourced that discernment which should always be our own.

Only a healthy approach to private revelation will succeed in fully and assuredly safeguarding one against Modernism (at the minimum, we can say that this is true today at least, when we see that the straight-and-narrow path of Our Lord has become razor thin.)[72]

I beseech you to not take my word for this. Instead, go about and investigate it for yourself. Spend time in the many Catholic circles or "subcultures" that you can find, and still you will discover that almost all of them are full of sin and error (with some hiding it better than others). Among the only groups you will find that have had any success in building up a bulwark against this sin and error are the ones who are devoted to private revelation. I know I have found this success in Divine Will groups, Marian Movement of Priests Cenacles, Divine Mercy apostolates, and the like.

Remember that the theologians who promote the errors listed in the previous section are very intelligent and very learned. They are experts in deflecting any criticism of which they are guilty of clear heresy: namely, of contradicting any unanimous consensus of Tradition, or of violating infallible Magisterial teaching.

Consider the priest mentioned in the last section's

---

[72] I have in mind especially the heretical interpretation of *Amoris Laetitia*, wherein adultery and divorce are essentially condoned, apparently being promoted by the majority of mainstream voices who have commented on it.

list, Fr. James Martin. It is difficult to find a single voice in the Catholic world today that is causing more damage than his, as he incessantly cheers and hastens the moral decay of the Church. Despite this, he repeatedly insists that he does not contradict any Church Teaching. He often says, for example, that his book " ... *has the ecclesial approval of my Jesuit superiors and the endorsement of several cardinals, archbishops and bishops,*"[73] and he deftly refutes any arguments levied against him that he is guilty of heresy.

If you think that you are ready to take on Fr. Martin and others like him (many are more skilled than he) in a debate and, in your rhetorical conquering of them, preserve your own orthodoxy, then you are sorely mistaken and likely guilty of pride. Their rhetoric will prevail if all you have is the sealed Deposit of Faith, which the devil—who feeds the modernists their arguments—knows the contents of far better than we ever will. They will *not* beat you if you also have private revelation at your disposal. (It is no accident that virtually all modernists despise or at least ignore private revelation.) **You will easily be able to, in truth and charity, show them that they have only two options: repent of their Modernism, or categorically reject private revelation. And what has already been shown (and will continue to be shown) in this chapter suffices to refute the latter option.**

***

I hope that in these pages I have given you sufficient reason for taking private revelation very seriously, but I do not want to leave you with my own arguments; instead, we will close this chapter by deferring to a brief sample of far more authoritative voices than my own.

Great Minds on Private Revelation

It is easy to drum up a list of quotations from seemingly authoritative voices in the mainstream Catholic "blogosphere" today that pooh-pooh private revelation (not usually by explicitly and categorically rejecting it, but by downplaying the importance that we have shown private revelation in fact deserves). While we have already refuted this distorted view, let us consider the flip-side and

see what the truly authoritative modern Catholic voices have to say about the matter.

I will not here be listing saints who are known for acting on private revelations that they themselves directly received, as that would admittedly not be particularly germane to the question at hand, which concerns how a Catholic ought to approach the private revelations received by others. Additionally, it would be impossible to present such a list, as practically every saint was formed by the private revelations God gave him or her.

I will also not be presenting in this list any saints before the 20th century for one simple reason: the issue is not often broached before that century, since only upon the dawn of diabolical Modernism during the 1900s did private revelation begin to lose its rightful status of glory—considering the history of the Church, the dismissive approach to private revelation is a new phenomenon. Open up the pages of just about any traditional work of a Catholic saint and you will regularly find private revelation deferred to and respected. There never used to be a need to defend private revelation *in general* because private revelation *in general* never used to be attacked as it is today!

Pope St. John Paul II

Pope St. John Paul II, justly referred to by many as "John Paul the Great," gives us the example *par excellence* of the proper approach to Private Revelation. Consider the following, taken from a later chapter in this book:

> Pope St. John Paul II said, when speaking about his Encyclical Dives in Misericordia (which was greatly inspired by his reading of the Divine Mercy Diary): "Right from the beginning of my ministry in St. Peter's See in Rome, I consider this message ["Divine Mercy"] my special task. Providence has assigned it to me in the present situation of man, the Church and the world. It could be said that precisely this situation assigned that message to me as my task before God."[74] He also spoke of the Divine Mercy Message as "forming the image of [his] pontificate." Lest anyone be concerned he was merely speaking of Divine Mercy in general, and not intending to allude to Faustina's writings, he also said that he had a "burning desire" that this particular

---

[73] "@JamesMartinSJ" Twitter Account. November 13, 2018.
[74] Pope John Paul II, Angelus Address to Collevalenza on November 22nd, 1981.

message of St. Faustina's be proclaimed "to all the peoples of the earth."[75]

Here we see this saintly Pope bluntly stating that the entire purpose of his Pontificate was a Private Revelation. This is coming not only from a saintly Pope, but from the one who may well be the greatest man of the 20th century. When faced with this stunning example, how dare we, who are nothing compared to him, fear dedicating our small lives to private revelation? We are like poor misers afraid to invest a few dollars in a noble cause when a wise millionaire living next door sells all his possessions to invest it all in the same thing. *Nota bene*: St. Faustina's revelations were condemned at the time when John Paul II, as Karol Wojtyla, discovered them and made them his mission.

St. Mother Teresa

Mother Teresa of Calcutta, among the greatest saints of the 20th century, was also one of the most well-known supporters of the apparitions at Medjugorje. This support is testified both in a letter written by her, in which she stated, "We are all praying one Hail Mary before Holy Mass to Our Lady of Medjugorje," and also by the testimony of the eminent theologian and trustworthy source Dr. Mark Miravalle.[76]

St. Teresa's greatness and her willingness to support an unapproved apparition and pray to Our Lady under its title should speak volumes to those now fearful of approaching any private revelation that hasn't already received full Church approval of every form.

St. Padre Pio

When one reads the life of Padre Pio, one sees clearly the life of not just any saint, but rather the life of one of only a few such souls that the entire history of the Church is blessed with. A stigmatist and a mystic, he had innumerable spiritual gifts and was the originator of countless miracles. As stated elsewhere in this book, the demons were forced to reveal that they feared him more than they feared St. Michael the Archangel. We even know of cases wherein Padre Pio bilocated:

Among the most remarkable of the documented cases of bilocation was the Padre's appearance in the air over San Giovanni Rotondo during World War II. While southern Italy remained in Nazi hands American bombers were given the job of attacking the city of San Giovanni Rotondo. However, when they appeared over the city and prepared to unload their munitions a brown-robed friar appeared before their aircraft. All attempts to release the bombs failed. In this way Padre Pio kept his promise to the citizens that their town would be spared. Later on, when an American airbase was established at Foggia a few miles away, one of the pilots of this incident visited the friary and found to his surprise the little friar he had seen in the air that day over San Giovanni.[77]

Now, these and similar facts about this great saint are more or less well known, but what is not common knowledge is the love he had for private revelation, and his willingness even to endorse and promote unapproved private revelations. In addition to being a supporter of Luisa (see the section on Luisa's life for more details), he was a strong supporter of Garabandal. We see, for example, in a formal answer to an inquiry on Garabandal, a theologian at EWTN asserting:

Finally, the principal promoter of Garabandal, Joey Lomangino, testifies that it was Saint Padre Pio who told him the Blessed Virgin was appearing at Garabandal and he should go. It seems, therefore, that notwithstanding the decisions of two commissions accepted by the bishops of Santander, that there are reasonable grounds for individual Catholics to find Garabandal credible. [78]

Of course, St. Pio ran up against extraordinary opposition from some members of the Church hierarchy; for a time, he was even censured by Rome. An overly cautious Catholic might see precisely this as a reason to *not* be like the saint: that is, to avoid all the "risks" involved with private revelation—especially those that are yet to be approved ("unapproved"). But "safety first" is no way to live and is certainly no way to become the saints that all are called to be, as the story of Padre Pio and of countless others teach us.

Mother Angelica

---

[75] Homily at Mass of Dedication of the Divine Mercy Shrine on August 17th, 2002.

[76] Mark Miravalle. *Is Medjugorje Real? Facts and First-hand Accounts.* June, 2008.

[77] Voice of Padre Pio, November 1998, Friary of Our Lady of Grace.

[78] https://www.ewtn.com/expert/answers/garabandal.htm

Mother Angelica, the holy foundress of EWTN, was one of the greatest evangelists of the 20th century. After she died, Pope Francis stated bluntly "she is in Heaven!"[79] Besides being one of the greatest evangelists, she was also one of the most wholehearted and zealous promoters of private revelation in the Catholic world. This ruffled the feathers of many, but she did not care. She knew it was far too important to neglect. She even openly promoted the prophecies of Garabandal—an apparition that has not received full Church approval—on national TV.

She wrote, of Michael Brown's book *Sent to Earth* (which is chock full of private revelations and prophecies concerning the coming times),

> If you didn't buy his book, you're missing it. It's not a scary book; it's a very good book. If you haven't bought it I would buy it. I think it's a great book, just terrific. I think it's important for my future and your future. I want you to read Sent To Earth. Why? It's logical, it's truthful, it's sensible, and it's God's way of saying, 'Let's be ready.'[80]

As John Haffert says in his book, *The Great Event*, Mother Angelica was a firm believer in many prophecies given by private revelation (both approved and unapproved):

> In her first appearance on her own Eternal World Television Network, the day after the miraculous cure which enabled her to put aside the steel braces she had worn for over forty years, Mother Angelica was asked in the exuberance of the moment about the future. She answered by repeating two prophecies which had been made by saints in the past and which seem now close to fulfillment. (The Pope himself had said in his daring book, Crossing the Threshold of Hope: "It seems, as we approach the millennium, that the words of Our Lady of Fatima are nearing their fulfillment.") The first great prophecy Mother Angelica expected to see fulfilled in the near future was that, on a given day all over the world, people will see themselves as God sees them [in a reference to The Warning of Garabandal].

Fr. Rene Laurentin

Father Laurentin is a veritable giant of the Catholic world of the 20th century. He is likely the greatest

Mariologist of the same century and is a foremost expert on Lourdes in particular (writing, as he did, a many-volume scientific history of it). The author of over 100 books, he is cited and mentioned dozens of times in the authoritative New Catholic Encyclopedia. The New York Times itself even ran a story upon his death in 2017. Pope Benedict XVI named him a Prelate of His Holiness in 2009. He played a significant role as a consultant at the Second Vatican Council and was extolled by Vatican Radio as "certainly one of the last living witnesses of this great period of effervescence."[81]

The University of Dayton biography page dedicated to Fr. Laurentin says of him:

> He has received various awards and distinctions including the Marian Award of 1963 from the University of Dayton (1964), the Wlodzimierz Pietrzak Literary Award (1974), Italy's National Catholic Culture Award (1996), Officer of the Legion of Honor (2002), and many other awards for his writing and contributions to Catholicism and Mariology. Laurentin is widely recognized as an expert in the field of Mariology and is the author of over 100 works and numerous scholarly articles. His writings, translated in many languages, cover a range of topics on Marian apparitions including Lourdes and Medjugorje; visionaries and mystics including Bernadette Soubirous, Thérèse de Lisieux, Catherine Labouré, and Yvonne-Aimée de Malestroit; as well as biblical exegesis, theology, and Vatican II.[82]

We can see, now, that it would be difficult to overstate the importance of Fr. Laurentin in Mariology today—even in Catholic Theology in general—or to overestimate the degree of his trustworthiness and competence in speaking on these matters.

Therefore, it is with enormous confidence that we can heed the lesson he gave us.

> In his book, a religious bestseller when it came out, Father Laurentin expressed his view that, in the current skeptical and psychoanalytic climate, the apparitions at Lourdes would not have been recognized by the Church. [83]

A tireless advocate of private revelation, Fr.

---

[79]"'She's in heaven' – Pope Francis on Mother Angelica." CatholicNewsAgency.com. March 30, 2016

[80] Store.spiritdaily.com/product-p/mhb-116.htm

[81]"René Laurentin, Investigator of Celestial Visions, Dies at 99" New York Times. September 15, 2017.

[82] Father René Laurentin collection, 1948-2003. Marian Library, University of Dayton Libraries, Dayton, Ohio. https://archivescatalog.udayton.edu/repositories/2/resources/105

[83]Michael Brown, spiritdaily.net/Luarentinreligious.htm

Laurentin may be most well-known for defending and promoting the apparitions of Our Lady at Medjugorje which, to this day, remain unapproved. But this was no stumbling block for him. He in fact became so well known for this mission that its acknowledgement was a major part of the article ran about him in the New York Times after his death. The article ends with the paragraph:

"What strikes me in Our Lady's messages is that they are an echo of the Gospel," Father Laurentin said in 2003. "The messages from Medjugorje do not say anything new; they just repeat to our deaf ears what we have forgotten, what we do not want, or are not able to hear any more: to pray, to have a strong faith in God, to fast, to read the Gospel."[84]

Fr. Edward O'Connor

The authority of Fr. Laurentin as a voice to be fully trusted in these matters settled in the previous section, let us now look at what he himself said of another theologian, Fr. Edward O'Connor:

Edward O'Connor, former professor at the University of Notre Dame, is a classic theologian, open to apparitions and their discernment. He knows how to recognize false visionaries, and defend those who have been discredited unjustly by the mistakes that commonly occur in this domain ... we are grateful to Father O'Connor for having resolved the paradoxical contradictions between the spiritual phenomenon of apparitions and the canonical repression which sometimes broke out against the visionaries[85]

Fr. O'Connor writes:

Being cautious and discreet does not mean being closed-minded. Visions, apparitions and messages from god, while always being extraordinary, are a normal part of the Christian life. They are much more abundant than is generally recognized. Pope John Paul II himself declared: "The Church is mission! Today she also needs 'prophets' who can reawaken in the communities faith in the revealing Word of God, who is rich in mercy"[86]

Fr. Edward O'Connor is indeed an authority on these matters, and it is noteworthy that, of the many books he wrote, he only wrote *one* entirely dedicated to a specific apparition: *Living in the Divine Will*, written in 2014, in which he defends and explains Luisa's revelations. This also appears to be his last work; perhaps he even considered it the Crown and Completion of his ministry of private revelation.

Dr. Mark Miravalle

Mark Miravalle, a renowned theologian, Mariologist, and professor at the Franciscan University of Steubenville, is also among today's foremost experts on mysticism in Catholicism.

Of unassailable orthodoxy, Professor Miravalle is nevertheless unafraid of private revelation—approved or unapproved. He is a well-known defender and promoter of the apparitions of Our Lady at Medjugorje, even authoring the New Catholic Encyclopedia article on the same. Miravalle published a comprehensive and admirable anthology, *Mariology: A Guide for Priests, Deacons, Seminarians, and Consecrated Persons*, a work specifically written with the intent of being an authoritative and fully trustworthy reference for Catholic teaching. Its contributors include other authoritative theologians such as Edward Sri and Fr. Peter Fehlner, and it bears a foreword written by Cardinal Burke. In it, Miravalle himself writes:

Can an obedient member of the Catholic Church make a personal assent of belief regarding a reported revelation before the Church, local or universal, has made an official statement about its authenticity? The answer, based on the Church's repeated precedent, is in the affirmative. While respecting the need for prudence and appropriate caution regarding any reported apparition about which appropriate Church authorities have not yet made a determination, the faithful are nonetheless free to make their own personal discernment and decision of authenticity, based upon the same norms which the Church uses in its authoritative evaluation. Practically speaking, **it is oftentimes only after the faithful begin to pilgrimage privately to reported apparition sites that the local Church initiates its authoritative evaluation. The beatification of Fatima visionaries Jacinta and Francisco Marto in 2000 by John Paul II further illustrates the legitimacy of the faithful personally accepting a private**

---

[84]"René Laurentin, Investigator of Celestial Visions, Dies at 99" New York Times. September 15, 2017.
[85] *Listen to My Prophets.* Father Edward O'Connor. 2011. Preface.

[86] Ibid xii

revelation as authentic before the Church's official decision. Francisco and Jacinta died in 1919 and 1920 respectively, some ten years before the Church's official approval of the Fatima apparitions on October 13, 1930. In matter of fact, Jacinta and Francisco were beatified for the heroic living of the Fatima message, which in their lifetimes remained a reported apparition, as yet unapproved by the Church.[87]

It is not difficult to see what the history of the Church tells us regarding how we ought to approach private revelation. Thankfully, there are some scholars, Dr. Mark Miravalle among them, who (as seen above), have the courage to remind us of that. I, for one, know of no single private revelation in the history of the Church that, though now approved, consisted of a message in which Our Lady (or Jesus) was content waiting for the Church to approve it before people (and not just the visionaries themselves) needed to respond.

Miravalle has also helped to correct a rampant error, alluded to elsewhere in this book, pertaining to the teaching of a certain 18th century Pope. One sometimes hears a few apologists paraphrase Pope Benedict XIV[88] in his teaching[89] that private revelations are not matters of Divine, Catholic Faith, and thus may be disbelieved without direct affront to Catholic Faith. But they conflate this important teaching with another idea that this Pontiff never promulgated (nor did any): namely, that, because one may do something without direct and explicit affront to Catholic Faith, one may freely do it without any affront to any virtue or duty whatsoever. As pointed out elsewhere in this book: from this erroneous premise it would also follow that one may harmlessly reject that 2+2=4.

Thankfully Dr. Miravalle, a *bona fide* theologian whom the Vatican has appointed to commissions to investigate private revelations (unlike any of the aforementioned apologists) corrects the distorted understanding, writing:

> While clearly acknowledging the real possibility and danger of false prophecy, Pope Benedict's balanced examination does not leave one with an exaggerated phobia of private revelation, but rather with a cautious but open mind and heart to these supernatural "interferences" through which

God has willed, and continues to will, to assist humanity in tis search for Christian salvation and sanctification.[90]

It should also be noted that, in this same work, Dr. Miravalle points out that an otherwise valuable book by Fr. Benedict Groeschel, *A Still Small Voice*, portrays an incorrect approach to private revelation because it draws erroneous references to Benedict XIV…

> … from Poulan rather than from the original work, and with a similar overriding tenor which likewise does not reflect the sensitive balance maintained by Benedict XIV.

Bishop Paul Kim

While some Bishops inevitably will, sadly, go down in history as the ones who fought against God's intervention in the world (we think, for example, of Bishop Pierre Cauchon, who presided over the trial of St. Joan of Arc), this is usually not the case. In fact, Bishops generally have a far better track record with private revelation than most others! One Bishop who has spoken particularly powerfully on private revelation in general is the Bishop Emeritus of the Cheju Diocese in Korea, Bishop Paul Tchang-Ryeol Kim. Here are some extracts from his Pastoral Letter written on Easter Sunday of the year 1999:

> Our age is indeed an age of private revelations. However, as has always been the case, disturbing remarks are now being heard within the Church in Korea and, especially, words of apprehension are being uttered by most of the shepherds. Such apprehension, however, is groundless, caused by lack of proper understanding of private revelations … The Council [Vatican II] gave a new clarification on this subject to the pastors and theologians in the Church. The reason for the concern about private revelations despite the Council's teaching must be that, as the number of private revelations has been increasing, false revelations unavoidably have been occurring also, causing confusion. However, should we throw away money because there is counterfeit money? Because there are false private revelations, should we frown upon and ignore private revelations and inspirations themselves? All of the devotional movements and apostolates

---

[87] *Mariology: A Guide for Priests, Deacons, Seminarians, and Consecrated Persons.* Mark Miravalle. Page 840.
[88] Not to be confused with Pope Benedict XVI

[89] Cf. Heroic virtue : a portion of the treatise of Benedict XIV on the beatification and canonization of the servants of God.
[90] *Mariology: A Guide for Priests, Deacons, Seminarians, and Consecrated Persons.* Mark Miravalle. Page 831.

such as the Eucharistic devotion, the devotion to the Sacred Heart of Jesus, the devotion to the Immaculate Heart of Mary, the Stations of the Cross, the rosary, novena devotions, Legio Mariae, M.E., Cursilio, Foccolore, Knights of St. Mary, Third Orders of the Franciscans, of St. Vincent, of St. Damian, etc. could not have started in the Church without private revelations. … The Second Vatican Council, which we deem so precious, could not have started, either. That is because that Council was summoned under the inspiration of a private revelation to Pope John XXIII. … One cannot lead a life of faith with public revelations alone. That is because the life of faith is a living communion with God. A church that only has organization, dogmas and theology would be a cold, lifeless organization. … This is the very reason why our Church has untiringly defended the need for and the important role of private revelations by both explanations and actions despite the persistently recurring false private revelations and their harmful effects.[91]

As we can see, the good Bishop has spoken even more boldly in support of private revelation in general than I myself have anywhere in this book.

Fr. John Arintero

Fr. Arintero, a Dominican priest and eminent theologian of the mystical life, has very strong words for those who would discount private revelation. The New Catholic Encyclopedia, in addition to citing his works many times and in many entries, says of him in his own entry:

> As a specialist in the natural sciences … he inaugurated at Valladolid the Academía de Santo Tomás, dedicated to the study of natural science in relation to philosophy and theology. In 1903 he was recalled to Salamanca as professor of apologetics, and except for one year (1909—10), which he spent as a professor at the Angelicum in Rome, he remained for the rest of his life in that city. The title of master in sacred theology was conferred upon him in 1908. At this period, he abandoned the study of the natural sciences and apologetics in order to give himself completely to ascetical and mystical theology…As a result of **his teaching regarding the call of all Christians to perfection and the normal development of the life of grace into contemplative prayer…**

Arintero became embroiled in controversies …

Here we see that not only was he a great theologian, but also a true prophet of his age; writing as he did decades before the Second Vatican Council and its now famous Universal Call to Holiness. Sadly, Fr. Arintero is largely forgotten today and his works are hard to find. One of his works is particularly noteworthy:

> The book Evolución mística (Mystical Evolution) had positive reception at the time of its publication and probably his was one of the reasons that contributed to Arintero being required as a teacher in Rome for the recently opened Angelicum.[92]

In this book, the full title of which is *The Mystical Evolution in the Development and Vitality of the Church*, and lamenting those who, in the perverse exaltation of "reason," oppose mysticism and private revelation, he writes:

> Poor autonomous reason which attempts to deify itself and be the absolute norm of everything, but is incapable of knowing the "all" of anything or of making the least correction or modification in the divine operation. Poor foolish reason which, unable to understand the most insignificant thing or a single atom, presumes to pass judgment on the loftiest mysteries. Poor infatuated reason, blinded by the rays of the infinite light, prefers to pronounce its judgment and close its eyes and live in darkness like a nocturnal bird, rather than strengthen its vision with the virtues of faith, hope, and charity. Poor misguided reason, fleeing from the great, the noble, and the divine, which are the only things that can enrich and perfect it, cannot help but be degenerated, vitiated, and degraded. Desiring to be sufficient unto itself, it abandons itself to its own powers and busies itself with fatuities or bagatelle, if not burying itself in uncleanness which obscures and perverts it.
>
> O reason, whatever you succeed in discovering apart from God, the more it enlightens you the more it will disillusion and deceive you. Ultimately it will avail you but little when, fleeing as you do from the very source of light and life, you end in the exterior darkness. If, by following the proud banner whose theme is "I will not serve," you disown the loving God who

---

[91] Pastoral Letter by His Excellency Paul Tchang-Ryeol Kim, Bishop of the Cheju Diocese, Korea. Easter Sunday. 1999 Marys-touch.com

[92] F.M. Requena, 'ARINTERO (Juan González)', in Dictionnaire d'histoire et de géographie ecclésiastiques. Turnhout:Brepols

Publishers, 2017, vol. 32, cols 514-518, in Brepolis Encyclopaedias.

redeemed you and regenerated you with His blood and thus lose the torch of divine faith received at baptism, well can we lament over you as over the cruel prince to whom you have delivered yourself: "How art thou fallen from heaven, O Lucifer, who didst rise in the morning!... But yet thou shalt be brought down to hell, into the depth of the pit." "But we all beholding the glory of the Lord with open face, are transformed into the same image from glory to glory, as by the Spirit of the Lord."[93]

Anyone who doubts that these words of Fr. Arintero are indeed directed at those who, in the arrogance of their supposed "reason," (that is, the *rationalistic* approach to matters pertaining to Heaven) scoff at private revelation, should check the context of that quote for themselves. It was not given in a chapter condemning atheism, modernism, heresy, or anything of the like. It is, rather, the last portion of his **chapter entitled "Importance of Private Revelations,"** and is found immediately after several paragraphs in which he loftily extols the greatness of the gifts enjoyed by the mystics and the fruits of their private revelations. That being said, the unabridged quote contains multiple references to "evolution," implying that he also has in mind the proponents of evolution, which he was surrounded by in the earlier years of his studies of natural science. Therefore, while it is no doubt that the strongest words (i.e. the last few sentences) of this quote are directed to those who give a radical "*non servio*,"[94] it also seems unavoidable that he also has anyone in mind—including and perhaps especially those within the Church—who oppose private revelation.

And Fr. Arintero has hit the nail on the head. Although those ordinary Catholics who avoid private revelation generally do so merely because they have been misled into overestimating its potential danger, it is another story entirely among the scholars. Their usual motivation for rejecting private revelation has nothing to do with simply being prudent in the face of the risk of being misled by the devil, by fraud, or by the mystic's own imagination[95] (even if, as a façade, they give these reasons as their explanation). No, it is almost always an arrogant overestimation of their own

intellectual prowess that urges on these scholarly scoffers at private revelation; convinced, as they are, that they are simply "above" such "excessive piety fit only for elderly women." As a Dominican theologian and professor, Fr. Arintero was doubtless surrounded by this mentality, hence his vigor in denouncing it. And as one with a theology degree from a Catholic college and seminary myself, I can vouch that I have seen no shortage of this type of mentality.

***

For my part, I have studied no less than 300 different prophecies. Moreover, the more ancient of these prophecies describe accurately subsequent events such as the Reformation, the French Revolution, the rise of Capitalism and Democracy, and even Communism. The sceptic may say that these prophecies are nonsense, but the nonsense is in his own mind. Or again, he may say that they are only "private", but so are Lourdes and Fatima; so are the Scapular and the Rosary. It matters little, really, whether a revelation is private or public, so long as it has given reasonable evidence of being true.

- Yves Dupont. Author of *Catholic Prophecy.*

A Word of Caution and Comfort

Now that we have settled the glorious place the private revelation deserves in our lives as Catholics, we must nevertheless ensure that our pursuit of private revelation is always maintained in accordance with the virtues of prudence, justice, and wisdom. **We should have a disposition of openness to private revelation, *not* a by-default presumption of its validity, and not a willingness to contradict Church teachings because of some alleged "revelation."**

For there is no negligible number of people—today especially—who reject these virtues when it comes to private revelation and readily go head over heels in following anyone who claims to have any sort of supernatural insight. This is an extremely dangerous demeanor, and, in some circles, it is growing rapidly. All I have wished to do in the previous sections is refute the knee-jerk reaction of lukewarmness or apathy to private revelation. But perhaps even worse than exhibiting this lukewarmness would be harboring a sense of guilt

---

[93]*The Mystical Evolution in the Development and Vitality of the Church Volume II.*
[94]Rejecting submission to God

[95] Such prudence is, indeed, called for and extremely important; its details will be considered in the next chapter.

and anxiety for not reading or following any given private revelation (if you simply do not feel ready, or do not feel at peace with such a pursuit).

If you discern a spirit of disturbance in pursuing any given private revelation, then by all means, cease! We must indeed test the spirits, and *"hold fast what is good,"*[96] and there is a subjective aspect to that. Whenever private revelation feels overwhelming to you, you can and should redirect yourself and take consolation in that glorious and infallible Deposit of Faith we find in Scripture, Magisterium, and Sacred Tradition. All I have intended to do here is rid you of notions that dispel urgency and anesthetize the workings of the Holy Spirit in a *dismissive approach* to private revelation. I do not wish to err on the opposite extreme and lay a heavy burden upon your shoulders. That burden would not be Christ's, for His is easy and light.[97]

Furthermore, we should be especially careful to avoid that perverse approach to supposed "private revelation" which:

- Bears an inordinate fascination with and desire for unnecessary knowledge of spiritual secrets that does not aid in salvation or sanctification.
- Entails a willingness to contradict Church teaching just because some self-proclaimed seer, locutionist, "faith healer," Near-Death-Experiencer made a statement at odds with the Magisterium.
- In any way involves the New Age, the Occult, Gnosticism, or Esotericism (e.g. divination, sorcery, fortune-telling, hypnosis, "spirit-mediums," astrological horoscopes, "astral projecting," "remote viewing," etc.)

These errors are grave and, if succumbed to, may lead to one's spiritual destruction. Therefore, we mustn't ever become so zealous about private revelation that we fall into any of them, or into any related error!

Indeed, there are *many* false private revelations, and their true nature is not always at first obvious. The last several years before the publication of this book (leading up to 2019, that is) seemed to yield an extraordinary amount of false prophecies and revelations. They furthermore did great damage since, with the help of the internet, they spread their falsity to large amounts of people very rapidly. But perhaps the greatest damage is found in their inspiring of a cynical approach to private revelation in general which often prevails among Catholics today.

But it should surprise no one that the devil misses no opportunity; that, seeing the incredible outpouring of God's grace through the explosion of private revelation of the modern era, he has taken it upon himself to inspire many false apparitions and revelations to limit this outpouring of grace. **But, thankfully for us, the devil is no match for a proper and careful approach to discerning private revelations, which is the topic we will next consider.**

Official Church Sanctioned Norms for Discerning Private Revelation	
Criteria in support of validity	Criteria against validity
<ul><li>Psychological equilibrium</li><li>Honesty</li><li>Rectitude of moral life</li><li>Docility towards Ecclesiastical Authority</li><li>Normal regiment of faith continued following apparition</li><li>Theology and spirituality free of error</li><li>Spiritual fruit (e.g. conversion, charity)</li></ul>	<ul><li>Doctrinal errors attributed to (that is, allegedly said by) God or a saint[98]</li><li>Evidence of a search for profit connected to the revelation</li><li>Grave sins associated with the events of the revelation on the part of the seer or followers</li><li>Psychological disorder or psychopathic tendencies</li></ul>

---

[96] 1 Thessalonians 5:21

[97] Matthew 11:30

[98] The same document acknowledges, regarding this very point, that the subject of the revelation may have unconsciously added purely human elements from which error might arise without precluding it being an authentic revelation. In other words, the Church does not expect

8) Discerning Alleged Private Revelations

In a preceding chapter we grew certain (if we weren't already) that the Catholic Church has the fullness of the Truth; the Truth that we must follow with absolute certainty—without ever wavering, without ever hesitating, and with the unshakeable commitment to do whatever it takes to be the best Catholics possible. In the last chapter, we discovered how incredibly important—indeed, indispensable—private revelation is in this very commitment.

Therefore, our next step is as imperative as it is obvious: learn what the Catholic Church teaches about private revelation and follow this teaching, come what may. Now, this same Church teaches (guided by the Holy Spirit Himself, and instructed as well by 2,000 years of experience) that alleged revelations are to be judged by certain criteria.

There is no need for confusion on this question, or for appealing only to the personal criteria of individual Catholics on how one ought to discern alleged revelations. For the Church herself has already told us how to discern them, but unfortunately this teaching is almost never brought up, as those who should be deferring to and promoting this teaching instead prefer to denounce revelations according to their own personal criteria.

Official Church Sanctioned Norms

In 1978, the Congregation for the Doctrine of Faith promulgated a document entitled "Norms regarding the manner of proceeding in the discernment of presumed apparitions or revelations."[99] The document itself is short and well worth reading, but the essence of its criteria is summed up in the included table on the preceding page.

The same document instructs Ecclesiastical Authority to, after considering these criteria, give **"special regard to the fecundity of spiritual fruit generated from this new devotion,"** in expressing a judgment of authenticity. This point in particular is

at once the most important of the document (evidenced by the document's authors' choice of words), and the one most rejected by many critics who appoint themselves as the judges of private revelation. For they often insist that fruits are not valid criteria for discerning validity, even though the Church herself here teaches that fruits must be given *special regard*. This focus on the fruits, of course, aligns perfectly with the words of Our Lord Himself, Who taught that "by their fruits you shall know them."[100] But it is also perfectly in line with what Jesus said to Luisa. Let us consider what He said to Luisa on this issue and briefly consider her situation before returning to the question of discernment of private revelation in general.

> It is from the fruits that the tree is known... and I am greatly disappointed that instead of looking at the fruits, they judged the cortex of the tree... Poor ones, what can they comprehend by looking at the cortex of My ways without descending to the fruits that I have produced? They will remain more in the dark, and they can incur in the disgrace of the Pharisees who, looking in Me at the cortex of My works and words, not at the substance of the fruits of My Life, remained blind and ended up giving Me death ... Ah! my daughter, my crime is always love, and it is also the crime of those who love Me. Finding no other material on which to judge, they judge my too much love, and that of my children, who perhaps have laid down their lives even for them. And besides, now they can judge as they want, but what will their confusion not be when they come before Me and will know with clarity that I Myself have been the One who has acted in that way, condemned by them, and that their judgment has prevented for Me a great glory of mine and a great good in the midst of creatures, which is that of knowing with more clarity what it means to do my Divine Will and to let It reign? There is no graver crime than that of preventing good.[101]

Now, all these criteria and considerations given by the Church leave no room for reasonable doubt on Luisa's revelations. As we will see in a forthcoming

---

absolute infallibility even from a valid seer receiving an authentic revelation.

[99] http://www.vatican.va/roman_curia/congregations/cfaith/documents/rc_con_cfaith_doc_19780225_norme-apparizioni_en.html (Bear in mind, when reading this document, that by "the fact," it means "the alleged revelation, apparition, or locution," and by "the subject" it means "the alleged seer, visionary, or locutionist.")

[100] Matthew 7:16

[101] July 9, 1930.

section on her life, she exhibited an astounding degree of stability and psychological "equilibrium." Despite the enormous spiritual battles going on in her soul, she was always serene and peaceful. She was revered by many authoritative figures who knew her; one of whom is now a canonized saint who made the promotion of Luisa's revelations the main mission of the last years of his life. Although over seventy years have passed since her death, there still has not surfaced even the slightest indication of any moral fault in Luisa whatsoever, leaving her moral rectitude unassailable—so much so that the Church has declared her a *Servant of God*. Her obedience to all Ecclesiastical Authority was always perfect, and she truly lived, to a heroic degree, the "docility" the Church calls for in discernment. She remained a totally committed and devout Catholic until her last breath, and her teachings—although spanning thousands of pages—have not succumbed to a single doctrinal error (as has already been asserted by multiple Vatican-appointed theologians whose very job it was to examine all her writings in search of errors). Far from ever searching for any sort of profit, she remained completely poor her entire life, contributing to her own meager sustenance through working, in her bed, as a seamstress. Finally, the "normal regiment of life following apparition" criterion given by the Church in supporting the validity of the mystic is particularly noteworthy in Luisa's case, because the last 10 years of her life did not involve her writing anything of her revelations or mystical experiences (for at the end of 1938 she was relieved, by the Church, from her command to write down what Jesus told her; thus she stopped). Instead, she only continued to live, in humility and poverty, as a model Catholic in every way, even writing letters to people thus demonstrating her continued depth of wisdom and soundness of judgment as a Catholic.

In the following chapter, we will continue this examination and delineate a plethora of overwhelming reasons why no one has any grounds to doubt the validity of Luisa's revelations, but even from this merely cursory overview of what the Church requires for us to consider in discerning any alleged revelation, it is clear that no serious discerner, even if he at first felt a great aversion to Luisa, can do anything but unclench the fist. And while the above Church-sanctioned considerations in discerning alleged revelations remain paramount, we should not neglect to look at even more factors before moving on to the next chapter.

Additional Norms for Discernment

For over a decade, I have been carefully paying attention to many alleged private revelations, a good portion of which have over time simply become more clearly true, while others have been revealed to be clearly false. From these experiences, some additional positive and negative indications of validity have become clear, which are as follows.

Positive Indications

- Years having passed since the seer's death, without any revelations of moral fault.
- A demeanor of truly unassailable humility.
- A demeanor of peace and tranquility that is always maintained even in the face of a torrent of unjust personal attacks.
- A stand on issues that is at once dripping with mercy in its approach to individual sinners, but doctrinally uncompromising when dealing with the principles which pertain to the sins themselves.
- A fundamental agreement with the related contents of overlapping private revelations.

Negative Indications

- Anonymity (this is certainly not a "deal breaker," but it is a cause for extra caution).
- Refusal to reveal who his or her spiritual director is.
- Self-referentialism in subject's writings (or talks) and an excessive eagerness to share personal stories, experiences, etc.
- Evidence of a blogger mentality: running commentary on current events or the insistence upon seeing localized events (e.g. American Politics) as the major—or perhaps even sole or primary—prophetic indicators.
- Voiced opinions which align almost perfectly with one Catholic subculture, political ideology/party, or popular conspiracy theory.
- Defensiveness.
- Divergence with the prophetic consensus (whereas, on the flip side of the coin, mere reiteration of the same exact prophetic consensus already known can also be a

negative indication)

(In all of these, too, Luisa's revelations fall squarely in the "positive" category and do not exhibit anything from the "negative" category.)

Now, there are other norms that some commentators have proposed as their own personal criteria for evaluating alleged revelations, but which are utterly invalid: contradicted by reason, by Church History, and in some cases even by the Magisterium itself. **These *invalid* "negative criteria" (which should *not* weigh into one's discernment as they do not constitute *actual* negative criteria) include the following:**

- **High frequency of visits**. There is no reason even daily visits or messages from Jesus or Mary are an obstacle to recognizing the validity of the revelations. Many now-approved and doubtlessly valid private revelations have had precisely that occur; for example, St. Faustina's.

- **Great magnitude of content.** The Church has never placed a limit on the greatness of the realities that the revelation in question may speak of, so long as they revelations themselves do not claim to contradict, correct, or surpass the Deposit of Faith itself, contained in the already complete Public Revelation. But this simple limitation is completely perverted by those who wish to put God on their own leash and determine, in accord with their own feeble understanding of how the future should proceed, how God can and cannot intervene. More on this point is contained in the "Answers to Objections" chapter of this book.

- **The absence of rose-colored glasses.** Jesus and Mary often have extremely hard words for the Church, and neither priests nor bishops are exempt. It is erroneous to conflate the Church's teaching, as mentioned above, that the alleged *seer must be docile to ecclesiastical authority* with the notion that the messages themselves must treat ecclesiastical authority, in general, gently. The latter, besides never being taught by the Church, is clearly absurd on its own right, for one needn't be a Church

Historian to know that the ranks of the institutional Church have long harbored many depraved members who indeed deserve the harshest words. Failing to issue these words, if anything, would be an indication of invalidity, as it would reveal a source that is a "respecter of persons," which God is *not*, according to Acts 10:34. As you will see in a forthcoming section (entitled "Heed the Hard Words of Jesus for the Church"), Jesus gave Luisa many hard words for the Church and there is no hint of that worldly and ugly "respect of persons" in Luisa's messages.

- **Differences in circumstances from similar revelations.** One will frequently hear a given revelation or seer criticized because of the differences they have with some other revelation or seer. But Heaven never would have intervened to give messages in the first place if it wanted nothing other than the exact same message given which has already been given! Instead, Providence would simply arrange for that other revelation to receive greater exposure. So long as the difference does not clearly amount to a negative criterion for discernment, it should not be considered to act as one. Unfortunately, this unjust judgment is common; for example, since the only Fatima visionary who survived to adulthood became a religious sister, some Catholics will oppose any visionary who does not do the same. This is an affront to God's sovereign right to call whom He wills.[102]

- **Messages with "Doom and Gloom."** Anyone who has read the Book of Revelation knows that some very ugly things are going to happen on this planet in the coming times. The fact that there are some Catholics who denigrate anyone who is honest about this fact as a "doomsday preacher" proves only that these Catholics enjoy burying their heads in the sand — a perverse inclination should never be considered a valid criterion for discernment. While a "doom and gloom" message *without hope* would be a valid reason to discount an alleged revelation, the

---

[102] Cf. Romans 9

mere presence (even if it is a large presence) of stark messages for the future should not cause any hesitation in believing the revelation, as long as the stark messages themselves are embedded within an overarching message of hope and triumph. Here it must be noted that Luisa's revelations are at once the most severe (in their description of the coming Chastisements) and the most hopeful (in their description of the grace available despite the Chastisements, and the nature of the time that will come after them) of any private revelation I have ever read.

- **Lacking an immaculate record with Church authorities.** The fact that there are still some Catholics who cling to this is very sad; for permanently condemning an apparition just because it had, in the past, been temporarily restricted or even condemned, has long been proven an errant approach. This would require one to oppose St. Faustina and her writings, St. Padre Pio, St. Joan of Arc, and many others. St. Teresa of Avila, Doctor of the Church, was formally investigated five times by the Church because of her mystical experiences—at least once she was even ordered to destroy manuscripts. And yet any orthodox Catholic today knows that her writings are totally sublime and among the most important works of spiritual theology in the history of the Church. Condemnations of individuals or of revelations are not part of the Church's infallible Magisterium (which deals only with the actual contents of Faith and Morals), and thus they can be changed—and have been changed. Hesitancy in realizing that is not prudence; rather, it is obstinacy.

So let us be sure to avoid all these pitfalls in discerning private revelation; any one of them can easily lead to erroneous conclusions on the most important matters, which in turn can have tragic consequences for our individual lives and for the history of the world and God's plan in it. Approaching private revelation must be done with

great care and the same holy fear that Scripture itself insists upon in Acts 5:

> Gamaliel, a teacher of the law, held in honor by all the people, stood up and ordered [the apostles] to be put outside for a while. And he said to them … " … in the present case I tell you, keep away from these men and let them alone; for **if this plan or this undertaking is of men, it will fail; but if it is of God, you will not be able to overthrow them. You might even be found opposing God!"**

Some private revelations must indeed be opposed. But we should be very sure of ourselves before ever doing so. For when we are dealing with private revelation, we are dealing with the very real possibility of opposing God Himself. And I tremble to think of what a terrifying Judgment Day many "good Catholics" are now preparing for themselves by being the persecutors of Heaven under the guise of orthodoxy.

Luisa and The Index of Forbidden Books

The last point in the preceding section's list is especially important and must be expanded upon. Indeed, some of Luisa's own works were placed on the Index of Forbidden books! So were St. Faustina's, and so were many others now known to be good and true.

And this placement says nothing; for the Index no longer exists. Although everyone knows this, some Catholics go so far as to say that, unless a book has been explicitly lifted from the Index and formally approved, it still is condemned. This position, though patently absurd, is still promoted by a few radical traditionalists. In June 1966, the Congregation for the Doctrine of Faith issued a "Notification regarding the **abolition** of the Index of books,"[103] itself referencing an Apostolic Letter by Pope St. Paul VI given in December 1965. The notification is short and should be read by anyone interested in this question, but the most relevant excerpt is what follows:

> … the Index remains morally binding, in light of the demands of natural law, **in so far as** it admonishes the conscience of Christians to be on guard for those writings that can endanger faith and morals. But, at the same time, it no longer has

---

[103]http://www.vatican.va/roman_curia/congregations/cfaith/documents/rc_con_cfaith_doc_19660614_de-indicis-libr-prohib_en.html

the force of ecclesiastical law with the attached censure. In this matter, the Church trusts in the mature conscience of the faithful ...

For those unacquainted with the technical meaning of the bolded term above, understand that "A **in so far as** B" means that A does not contain or refer to anything beyond B. Here, that means it is *only* still morally binding to avoid what was on the Index *in just those cases which* the Index's prohibitions still — under the knowledge and facts one has access to in the present day — regard works that "endanger faith and morals." For such works obviously still remain the same danger to faith and morals; that is, they did not magically cease to be so upon the abolition of the Index, as some individuals on the opposite end of the spectrum foolishly thought and were well corrected by this Notification.

But **whether a work which was placed on the Index does, in fact, endanger faith and morals is not a question that is logically possible to settle by determining whether it was lifted from the index** — especially if that lifting would have had its opportunity to occur after 1966, when the Index was abolished. In Luisa's case, her writings were not looked at again until the 1990s, long after lifting a book from the index was even possible (once the list was abolished; lifting entries from the list also ceased).

It is clear, therefore, in pretending that prudence demands that one dismiss or avoid a revelation or writing merely because it was on the Index or otherwise once condemned in the past, it is the height of feigned religiosity. We should always remember that what the Pharisees did to Our Lord was made infinitely more evil because they murdered Him under the pretense of piety.

As stated at the beginning of this section, we recall that even the revelations given to St. Faustina were also placed on the index. Indeed, these two great and final missions from God — one, His last effort of salvation (Divine Mercy), the other, His last effort of sanctification (Divine Will) — stood side by side on this same index for seven years; both remaining

within its pages upon its abrogation by Paul VI.

One sometimes hears recognition of this placement on the Index of St. Faustina's devotion hastily dismissed with no small hint of anxiety and a pretense that it was nothing but a procedural misstep, miscommunication, or translation issue (and sources are never cited to back up these dismissive explanations). But the truth must be known: an entire page of the Vatican's annual record of its official acts (the Acta Apostolica Sedis) pertains to the prohibition of the Divine Mercy devotion of St. Faustina (found on page 271 of the 1959 edition of A.A.S.).[104] The words of the prohibition itself — which anyone is free to read — make it clear that the Supreme Sacred Congregation of the Holy Office *did indeed* carefully examine the "visions and revelations" of St. Faustina. Despite this examination, the Holy Office still chose to forbid any dissemination of the images and the writings of the Divine Mercy revelations.[105] As the veteran Vatican journalist, John Allen, points out:

> Officially, the 20-year ban is now attributed to misunderstandings created by a faulty Italian translation of the Diary, but **in fact there were serious theological reservations** — Faustina's claim that Jesus had promised a complete remission of sin for certain devotional acts that only the sacraments can offer, for example, or what Vatican evaluators felt to be an excessive focus on Faustina herself.[106]

Clericalism evidently dies hard; some Catholics cannot fathom that the men in the Vatican can ever be simply, flat-out wrong. They ignore that only the Magisterium is Divinely protected — not the (far more numerous) juridical actions of the Church. The real reason St. Faustina's revelations were prohibited clearly has little to do with translation issues, even if these were involved, but rather is indeed as Mr. Allen describes. As anyone who has read her diary (*Divine Mercy in My Soul*) knows, St. Faustina's revelations make claims of such an enormous magnitude that, whoever was of the erroneous "private revelation may only sit quietly in a corner" mindset, would inevitably

[104]http://www.vatican.va/archive/aas/documents/AAS-51-1959-ocr.pdf
[105] "Si rende noto che la Suprema Sacra Congregazione dei Sant'Offizio, prese in esame le asserite visioni e rivelazioni di Suor Faustina Kowalska, dell'Istituto di Nostra Signora della Misericordia, defunta nel 1938 presso Cracovia, ha stabilito

quanto segue ... doversi proibire la diffusione delle immagini e degli scritti chepresentano la devozione della Divina Misericordia nelle forme proposte dalla medesima Suor Faustina ... "
[106] John Allen Jr. "A saint despite Vatican reservations" August 30, 2002.

pounce to condemn them. This, indeed, is precisely what happened to both Faustina and Luisa.

And yet, this prohibition of Faustina's revelations is no longer binding and (in consideration of the immense degree of Church approval) any Catholic would be guilty of great timidity in acting as if there is any value whatsoever to the view that would ignore or dismiss St. Faustina's revelations on account of them once being on the Index of Forbidden Books. Consequently, the only way any Catholic can pretend that this same history—which Luisa's revelations share with Faustina's—is in and of itself a cause for concern is by virtue of either the aforementioned timid behavior, or the willingness to be completely intellectually dishonest and partial in judgment.

A better option than timidity or dishonesty is to simply realize that the past prohibition of Luisa's writings is no longer binding and to proceed with proper Catholic discernment in accordance with the guidelines given by the Church. Therefore, with these guidelines in mind, we will shortly apply them to Luisa's life and revelations. But before turning to that chapter, a few more words are in order regarding the past prohibition of Luisa's writings.

As Stephen Patton pointed out in the year 2000:

> The 1938 condemnation had nothing whatsoever to do with Luisa's 36 volume spiritual diary, known as "Book of Heaven," which is her most important work. This work of 40 years, containing the overwhelming weight of her spiritual doctrine on the Divine Will, was never placed on the Index. This is especially significant because in 1938 Vatican officials not only knew about this exhaustive work, they also had the actual, original volumes in the Vatican archives! If they had ever wanted to "condemn" this work of Luisa, that would have been the time. But they didn't. And so, no taint of condemnation has ever been upon the most important thing that Luisa wrote. In fact the official, Church appointed censor, gave the Nihil Obstat to the first 19 volumes of the "Book of Heaven" after examining them intently in their original Italian language over a period of 17 years, prior to his death. The archbishop who appointed this censor gave his handwritten Imprimatur directly on those original manuscripts. Regarding the three books that were placed on the Index in 1938, two of them had several other editions. The condemnation was limited only to the specific editions officially mentioned. Other editions of these same two books have been published with full ecclesiastic approval, even as late as 1997. The third work was a compilation of edited extracts from Luisa's writings, which has never been reprinted.

In addition to the important points Mr. Patton makes above, it is even more noteworthy that, in the years since he wrote those words, two of the three works of Luisa's that were placed on the index have since had their prohibition lifted *and* the Moratorium on their open publication ended. The lifting of the prohibition occurred not merely with the abrogation of the Index but also with the 1994 *Non Obstare* of Luisa's cause, which presupposes there being no condemnations in force pertaining to the potential saint's works which would inhibit the recognition of her sanctity. Not only is that true, but there also no longer exists any Moratorium whatsoever on their printing, and instead they may freely be published (the "Moratorium" currently in place on Luisa's 36 Volumes is not any sort of condemnation whatsoever; it is merely a temporarily limit on the publication as the official English translation nears completion; see the Appendix dedicated to addressing this issue). And the third work, as mentioned in the quote, has never been reprinted anyway. There are simply no excuses for even the most cautious of Catholics to suppose that the Church is asking them to be hesitant with Luisa's writings.

9) The Authenticity of Luisa and Her Revelations

Having now finished our delineation of the Church-sanctioned criteria for evaluating private revelation, it remains now to consider Luisa's case in greater detail and lay out the facts of the matter so that a proper conclusion regarding authenticity can be reached.

But first, validity aside, perhaps you struggle to even make yourself interested in the revelations given to Luisa; one who might seem to be just another obscure 20th century mystic—a person whom you would be more than happy to wait until Heaven to get to know. Sometimes it does seem that the various devotions, mystics, and private revelations vying for and at times demanding our attention are almost innumerable; and they certainly are diverse enough that it simply isn't possible to dedicate much time at all to the totality of them—even if they "generously" offer us their revelations, not for $20, but for the "much more reasonable price of $19.99!" But I believe that if you only give the following pages a brief chance, you will quickly see that not only do Luisa's revelations deserve a place in your spiritual life, but even more so, they are truly unique among all private revelations and deserve a whole-hearted response from every single human being on the face of the planet. For we mustn't allow ourselves to become slaves to whatever inclinations we happen to wake up with in the morning; we must, rather, *form* our inclinations in accord with what the intellect discovers is *best*. Now, let us put that great gift of intellect to use in so discovering.

General Overview

This brings us to the first reason why Luisa's writings are worth a chance: she did not seek out people to listen to her, much less to give her so much as one penny; quite the contrary, she wanted nothing but silence and solitude, and to be unknown and little. The greatest penance of her life was writing down the revelations Jesus gave to her, for she wanted nothing to do with worldly recognition. Her humility in this regard was so heroic that **it was only when her spiritual director, Fr. Gennaro Di Gennaro (who was appointed by the Archbishop specifically to be Luisa's director), commanded her under holy obedience to write that she in fact did so.**[107] Lest you be concerned that this moment marked the end of her humility, know that she stopped writing in the later years of her life, when she was no longer told to do so under obedience. From the very onset of these revelations, it is only thanks to the intervention of the Catholic Church that we have any record of Jesus' words to Luisa.

But the intervention of the Catholic Church in ensuring that Luisa's revelations were known did not stop there. A detailed overview of the important events will be given in the following pages, but before we proceed to that timeline,

emphasis should be given to a few facts in particular.

Pope St. John Paul II himself canonized a certain priest, Hannibal Mary Di Francia, in the year 2004. St. Hannibal was a truly great priest; a zealous worker of important apostolates, including starting a school, an orphanage, and two religious congregations dedicated to praying for vocations. In his canonization homily, St. John Paul II said that St. Hannibal had a " ... *love for the Lord [that] moved him to dedicate his entire life to the spiritual well-being of others.*"[108] What you unfortunately will not see in any popular work on the life of St. Hannibal is the fact that he was appointed by his Archbishop[109] to be Luisa's spiritual director, extraordinary confessor, and censor librorum. St. Hannibal became so utterly convinced not only of the legitimacy of Luisa's revelations but also of their dire urgency and importance. In fact, towards the end of his life, **St. Hannibal completely devoted himself to Luisa's revelations,** writing four months before his death, "*I want you to know that since I have totally dedicated myself to the great work of the Divine Will, I practically don't concern myself at all with my institutes.*"[110] He tirelessly worked to approve, publish, print, and disseminate her revelations. For he insisted, in his own personally published written word, that Luisa's revelations consist in **"... a mission so sublime that no other can be compared to it—that is, the triumph of the Divine Will upon the whole earth, in conformity with what is said in the 'Our Father'"**[111]

St. Hannibal was renowned for his gift of discernment. One of the seers of La Salette (a fully approved apparition that is sadly often overlooked, perhaps because of the extremely strong message Our Lady gave there), Melanie Calvat, was for a time a nun in the convent he started and St. Hannibal knew her well.[112] And let us recall that not only did Pope St. John Paul II choose to canonize St. Hannibal, but he even went so far as to make his own St. Hannibal's belief in the reality of this coming new holiness. Seven years after beatifying Hannibal, and seven years before

[107]Cf. Bernardino Giuseppe Bucci, OFM: *Luisa Piccarreta, A Collection of Memories* (Roma 52, San Ferdinando Di Puglia: Tipolitographia Miulli, 2000), Ch. 1.
[108] Homily given by Pope John Paul II, "Canonization of Six New Saints," May 16, 2004 (Libreria Editrice Vaticana).
[109]Archbishop Joseph Leo
[110]Letter of St. Hannibal to Luisa Piccarreta, dated February 14th, 1927.

http://www.divvol.org/luisa_piccarreta/en/hannibal_letters.html).
[111] *Hours of the Passion*. Preface.
[112] Gaetano Passarelli: *Father Annibale, A Heavenly Dream* (Transcribed into eBook format by St. Hannibal Rogate Center, 2011), Ch. 7.

canonizing him, John Paul said in an address to the order that St. Hannibal founded, the Rogationists:

"[St. Hannibal saw] the means God himself had provided to bring about that 'new and divine' holiness with which the Holy Spirit wishes to enrich Christians at the dawn of the third millennium, in order to 'make Christ the heart of the world.'"[113]

***

Now, I know what many readers are thinking at this point, for it goes something like this:

Hold on. John Paul the Great not only canonized St. Hannibal, but went so far as to explicitly endorse his most bold claim—**a claim that St. Hannibal received directly from Luisa's revelations, which he dedicated himself to spreading**—that there is an unprecedented gift of Divine Holiness now available for the Church as we have reached the dawn of the third millennium, that this gift will transform the world … **and I haven't heard of this?!**

I understand these sentiments because they were mine as well before I knew of Luisa's revelations and the history behind them. The devil's attempts now, in opposing this greatest mission of all, are restricted not to refutation—as he now sees that as impossible—but to obfuscation and silencing, hoping that he can simply prevent too many people from even discovering these truths. (Do not let him succeed!)

Also of great importance is the context of the quote given above, for it not only demonstrates Pope St. John Paul II's clear and explicit endorsement of Hannibal's promulgation of the Divine Will message of Luisa,[114] but it also touches on precisely how this will come about—namely, through priests and through the Eucharist that comes to us from their hands:

The three foundational principles of St. Hannibal, or three buds you could say, that would blossom into this new springtime are: I. To put the Blessed Eucharist at the centre of personal and community life … II. To exist as a body in unity, in the unanimity of hearts that makes prayer acceptable to God. III. Intimate association with the suffering of the Most Sacred Heart of Jesus.[115]

The order St. Hannibal founded, the Rogationists, holds *vocations to the priesthood* as its entire purpose. It is no mere happenstance that he was the priest Jesus chose to be the greatest herald of His own revelations to Luisa, for Jesus Himself said to Luisa:

My daughter, it is a great necessity to form the first Priests, they will serve me as the Apostles served me in order to form my Church; and who will occupy themselves with these writings in order to publish them, putting them out in order to print them in order to make them known, they will be the new evangelists of the kingdom of my Supreme Will.[116]

But this reference to a New and Divine Holiness was not some isolated comment spoken and then forgotten; five years later, Pope St. John Paul II became even more bold, and in an address to the youth of Rome, made an explicit encouragement to "enter into" and Live in the Divine Will.[117] (Although the English translation of the address provided by the Vatican uses the term "dwell" instead of "live," nevertheless the same thing is being referred to.)

***

Already we have the bold words of a saint, and of the Pope (also a saint!) who canonized him, in support of Luisa's writings. But this still only constitutes the tip of the iceberg of reasons why we should not be afraid of approaching her revelations (as many are due to the grandiose nature of their claims, the opposition to them by a few common names, or an incorrect understanding of the implications of the current Church regulations on her writings). Rather, we should be zealous to learn from them.

Three sets of Luisa's works—amounting to thousands of pages of revelations from Jesus, which indeed contain the essence of the Divine Will

---

[113] Address of His Holiness Pope John Paul II to the Rogationist Fathers. Paragraph 6. 16 May 1997.
[114] Although when we consider the context of this quote of Pope St. John Paul II's it is clear that a reference is being made to Luisa's revelations, this unfortunately has not been noticed much in mainstream circles, despite this particular quote of his getting much note. For example, a wonderful book written by Fr. Kosicki, *Be Holy*, bears endorsements from at least three Bishops, including the late Cardinal George of Chicago. It devotes an entire Chapter to precisely this quote of the Pope's.
[115] "The Coming New and Divine Holiness." Mark Mallett. www.markmallett.com/blog
[116] January 18, 1928.
[117] Address of John Paul II to the youth of Rome preparing for World Youth Day. March 21st, 2002 (Paragraph 5. vatican.va).

message—were given an imprimatur by Archbishop Giuseppe (Joseph) Leo.[118] For those rightly wary of how much error has been promulgated these past few decades in the name of imprimaturs by those who assume that whatever has one contains only infallible words, remember that these imprimaturs given to Luisa's works were granted almost a century ago.

When St. Hannibal took Luisa's *Hours of the Passion* to the Pope (Fr. Hannibal was well known for his holiness and among the friends of the Holy Father) and briefly read from it, the Pope—none other than the great **Pope St. Pius X himself—said**, *"Father, this book should be read while kneeling: it is Jesus Christ who is speaking!"*[119] The Pope proceeded to encourage him to have it printed and promulgated immediately.

St. Pio (Padre Pio) was known to say to pilgrims who came from Corato to see him, *"What have you come here for? You have Luisa, go to her."*[120] Although these two never met in person, they nevertheless esteemed each other highly as a result of Padre Pio sending a convert of his, a man by the name of Federico Abresch, to go meet her. When three of Luisa's writings were condemned, St. Pio even sent her consolation by way of Federico, saying *"Dear Luisa, saints serve for the good of souls, but their suffering knows no bounds."*[121] Padre Pio's canonization, despite the great opposition it encountered, is yet another reason to give credit to Luisa's revelations, for this extraordinary Capuchin is now agreed upon as being among the greatest saints of modern times.[122]

The **official, Church-sanctioned biography of Luisa published by the Vatican dedicates a section to the relationship between Luisa and Padre Pio.**[123] Some excerpts from that section are as follows:

There are countless testimonies beyond these [Frederico Abresch and Mrs. Caterina Valentina]

that talk about the mutual esteem and faith Luisa and Padre Pio had in each other, perhaps because of the deep similarities in their lives, too. A young girl recalls going on a pilgrimage to San Giovanni Rotondo with her aunt and going to Mass that Padre Pio was celebrating at 5 o'clock in the morning. When the aunt told Padre Pio that the girl had been dying, but she received a miracle through Luisa Piccarreta, Padre Pio made the sign of the cross on her head and said, "Yes, by the intercession of Luisa Piccarreta, the Lord has saved her." Obviously the whole town started talking about this event. Even the residents of San Giovanni Rotondo knew how much respect Padre Pio had for Luisa. Miss Adriana Pallotti recalls that day she asked Padre Pio, her spiritual father, if she was doing the right thing by donating money to have Luisa's books printed. Padre Pio said "yes," and, in fact, rather uncharacteristically, he had her repeat the question, astounding his spiritual daughter to no small degree. The answer again was a clear "yes."[124]

Timeline of Events Relevant to Her Cause

Above all, Luisa's revelations should be approached with confidence because Providence has abundantly blessed her cause for Beatification, as well as the canonical status of her writings. The public critics of Luisa's writings wrote the bulk of their arguments (which unfortunately are often the first things which still today pop up when one does an internet search for *Living in the Divine Will*) against Luisa and her revelations in the 1990s. Consider what has happened since then:

- November 20th, 1994: Cardinal Joseph Ratzinger nullifies the previous condemnations of Luisa's writings, allowing Archbishop Carmelo Cassati to formally open Luisa's cause on the Feast of

[118] These writings were Luisa's *Hours of the Passion*, Volumes 1-19 of her diary, and *The Virgin Mary in the Kingdom of the Divine Will.*
[119] Bernardino Giuseppe Bucci, OFM: *Luisa Piccarreta, A Collection of* Memories (Roma 52, San Ferdinando Di Puglia: Tipolitographia Miulli, 2000), Ch. 4.
[120] *Ibid.*, Ch. 3.
[121] *Ibid.*
[122] Unfortunately, some individuals attempt to dispute this *fact* of Padre Pio's endorsement of Luisa. Their arguments usually stem from a letter allegedly written by a Franciscan at San Giovani Rotondo who implies that, because he himself knows nothing of the correspondence between Luisa and Padre Pio, it could not possibly have actually happened. Sadly, many often fall into this patently fallacious line of reasoning which supposes that if they do not know of something, it cannot be. Similarly, I recall hearing of a priest who (years before it was popular) warned a penitent away from devotion to the Divine Mercy. His reasoning? "I haven't heard of it, so it cannot be acceptable."
[123] Cf. *Sun of My Will*, pages 174-175.
[124] Ibid.

Christ the King of the same year.

- **February 2nd, 1996:** Pope St. John Paul II permits the copying of Luisa's original volumes, which up until then had been strictly reserved in the Vatican Archives.
- **October 7th, 1997:** Pope St. John Paul II beatifies Hannibal Di Francia (Luisa's spiritual director and devoted promoter of Luisa's revelations)
- **June 2nd & December 18th, 1997:** Rev Antonio Resta and Rev. Cosimo Reho—**two Church appointed theologians—submit their evaluations of Luisa's writings to the Diocesan tribunal, affirming nothing contrary to Catholic Faith or Morals is contained therein.**
- **December 15th, 2001:** with the permission of the diocese, a primary school is opened in Corato named after, and dedicated to, Luisa.[125]
- **May 16th, 2004:** Pope St. John Paul II canonizes Hannibal Di Francia.
- **October 29th, 2005, the diocesan tribunal and the Archbishop of Trani, Giovanni Battista Pichierri, render a positive judgment on Luisa** after carefully examining all of her writings and testimony on her heroic virtue.
- **July 7th, 2010,** Pope Benedict XVI formally blessed and prayed next to a seventeen-foot-high statue of St. Hannibal which had just been installed within the Vatican itself, occupying a particularly prominent and honorable position.
- **July 24th, 2010, both Theological Censors (whose identities are secret) appointed by the Holy See give their approval to Luisa's writings, asserting that nothing contained therein is opposed to Faith or Morals (in addition to the 1997 Diocesan theologians' approval).**
- **April 12th, 2011,** His Excellency Bishop Luigi Negri officially **approves the Benedictine Daughters of the Divine Will** (explicitly dedicated to Luisa's Divine Will spirituality) as a Pious Association of the Faithful.[126] (*Note: More details on this are found in the following section*)
- **November 1st, 2012,** the Archbishop of Trani writes a formal notice[127] containing a rebuke of those who "*claim [Luisa's] writings contain doctrinal errors,*" stating that such people scandalize the faithful and preempt judgment reserved to the Holy See. This notice furthermore encourages the spreading of the knowledge of Luisa and her writings. (The entire notice is contained in an appendix of this book.)
- **November 22nd, 2012, the faculty of the Pontifical Gregorian University in Rome who reviewed Fr. Joseph Iannuzzi's Doctoral Dissertation defending and explaining Luisa's revelations give it unanimous approval, thereby granting its contents ecclesiastical approval authorized by the Holy See.**
- 2013, Imprimatur given to Stephen Patton's book, *A Guide to the Book of Heaven*, which defends and promotes Luisa's revelations.
- 2013-14, Fr. Iannuzzi's Dissertation received the accolades of almost fifty[128] Catholic Bishops, including Cardinal Tagle.[129]
- 2014: Fr Edward O'Connor, theologian and long-time professor of theology at Notre Dame University, publishes his book, *Living in the Divine Will: the Grace of Luisa Piccarreta*, strongly endorsing her revelations.[130]
- April 2015: Maria Margarita Chavez reveals that she was miraculously healed through the intercession of Luisa eight years earlier. The Bishop of Miami (where the healing took place) responds by approving investigation into its miraculous nature.[131]
- **April 27th, 2015, the Archbishop of Trani writes: "I wish to let you know that the Cause of Beatification is proceeding positively...** I have recommended to all that they deepen the life and the teachings of the

---

[125] En.luisapiccarretaofficial.org/news/December-15-2001/195

[126] www.benedictinesofthedivinewill.org

[127] https://danieloconnor.files.wordpress.com/2017/04/official-letter-from-archbishop-pichierri1.pdf

[128] Rev. Joseph L. Iannuzzi, STD, Ph.D. "Living in the Divine Will" Missionaries of the Most Holy Trinity (Nov. 2014-May 2015): Page 2.

[129] *Cf.* Fr. Joseph Iannuzzi, (www.ltdw.org), 2014.

[130] A renowned expert on private revelation, this nevertheless appears to be the only book Fr. O'Connor ever wrote solely dedicated to one private revelation in particular. It also appears to be his last book, as he has since died.

[131] En.luisapiccarretaofficial.org/news/the-miracle-attributed-to-luisa/44

Servant of God Luisa Piccarreta..."[132]

- January 2016, *Sun of My Will*, the official biography of Luisa Piccarreta, is **published by the Vatican's own official publishing house** (*Libraria Editrice Vaticana*). Authored by Maria Rosario Del Genio, it **contains a preface by Cardinal Jose Saraiva Martins,**[133] **Prefect Emeritus of the Congregation for the Causes of Saints, strongly endorsing Luisa *and* her revelations from Jesus.**[134] (Considering his position, if anyone alive knows what makes a saint and an authentic revelation, he does.)

- November 2016, the Vatican publishes the *Dictionary of Mysticism*, a 2,246-page volume edited by Fr. Luiggi Borriello, an Italian Carmelite, professor of theology in Rome, and "consultant to several Vatican congregations."[135] Luisa was given her own entry[136] in this authoritative document.

- June 2017: The newly appointed Postulator for Luisa's cause, Monsignor Paolo Rizzi, writes: "I appreciated the work [carried out thus far]... all this constitutes a solid base as a **strong guarantee for a positive outcome**...the Cause is now at a decisive stage along the path."[137]

- November 2018: An official Diocesan inquiry is initiated by Bishop Marchiori in Brazil, into a miraculous healing of a man named Laudir Floriano Waloski thanks to Luisa's intercession.

This timeline of events and facts relevant to Luisa's revelations could be continued and expanded upon greatly, but is that now necessary for even the most skeptical? **For one who acknowledges the proper means of discerning any alleged revelation, mystic, or seer, there is no longer any doubt.**[138] The bumps in the road which have occurred in the past prove only that there are imperfect human beings in the Church who have erred in their dealings with Luisa and her writings.

---

[132] "Final Letter by the Archbishop" www.luisapiccarretaofficial.org. Posted directly here: https://danieloconnor.files.wordpress.com/2019/02/final-letter-by-the-archbishop-giovan-battista-pichierri-1.pdf

[133] Even among Cardinals, he is highly distinguished, being one of only several" Cardinal Bishops," an honor bestowed upon him by Pope Benedict XVI

[134] Here, for example, is one excerpt from his preface: "From her continual contemplation of Jesus' passion, Luisa is led to conform herself to Christ ... This "living in the Divine Will" is the actual way in which the Son Jesus lived on earth, bringing here with him the life of Heaven."

[135] *Mystery and the World: Passion for God in Times of Unbelief*. Maria Clara Bingerner. Page 193.

[136] Page 1266.

[137] Tinyurl.com/y37rgmrr

[138] I do not think, in the entire history of the Church, one will ever find a mystic whose cause has seen a similar degree of success as Luisa's and whose life exhibited the endorsements that Luisa's did, but who has later proven to be a fraud or an agent of the devil. Those are the only two alternatives if one wishes to reject the validity of Luisa's revelations, and when one considers the history of mysticism in the Church, he will find them to be untenable alternatives, as each would entail the assertion of something entirely unprecedented and radically departing from anything we have ever seen. And if any assertion is dubious, it is that one; not the simple recognition that Luisa's revelations are valid.

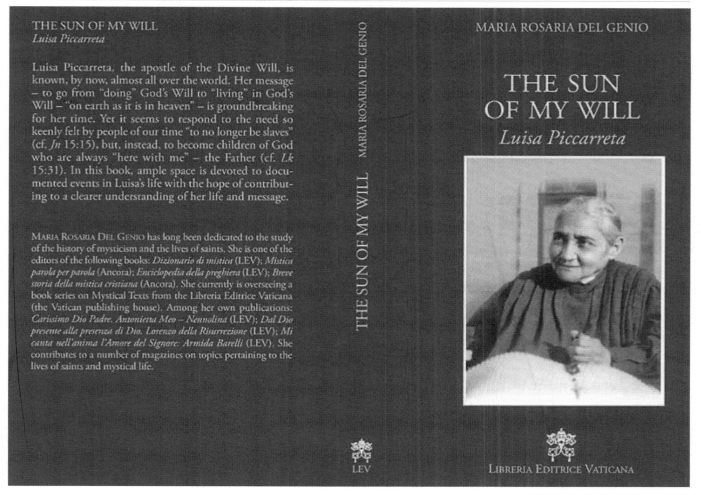

THE SUN OF MY WILL
Luisa Piccarreta

Luisa Piccarreta, the apostle of the Divine Will, is known, by now, almost all over the world. Her message – to go from "doing" God's Will to "living" in God's Will – "on earth as it is in heaven" – is groundbreaking for her time. Yet it seems to respond to the need so keenly felt by people of our time "to no longer be slaves" (cf. *Jn* 15:15), but, instead, to become children of God who are always "here with me" – the Father (cf. *Lk* 15:31). In this book, ample space is devoted to documented events in Luisa's life with the hope of contributing to a clearer understanding of her life and message.

MARIA ROSARIA DEL GENIO has long been dedicated to the study of the history of mysticism and the lives of saints. She is one of the editors of the following books: *Dizionario di mistica* (LEV); *Mistica parola per parola* (Ancora); *Enciclopedia della preghiera* (LEV); *Breve storia della mistica cristiana* (Ancora). She currently is overseeing a book series on Mystical Texts from the Libreria Editrice Vaticana (the Vatican publishing house). Among her own publications: *Carissimo Dio Padre. Antonietta Meo – Nennolina* (LEV); *Dal Dio presente alla presenza di Dio. Lorenzo della Risurrezione* (LEV); *Mi canta nell'anima l'Amore del Signore. Armida Barelli* (LEV). She contributes to a number of magazines on topics pertaining to the lives of saints and mystical life.

MARIA ROSARIA DEL GENIO

THE SUN OF MY WILL
Luisa Piccarreta

LEV

LIBRERIA EDITRICE VATICANA

Providence in the EWTN Monastery: the Story of Mother Gabrielle

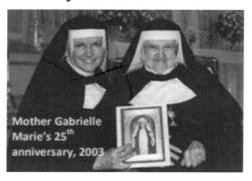

Mother Gabrielle Marie's 25th anniversary, 2003

Although not directly related to the validity of Luisa's revelations, I nevertheless find this story both inspirational and instructive, so I decided to share it within this chapter as a sort of "extended footnote" corresponding to the entry that mentions this in the section above. Indeed, Luisa's revelations have borne abundant fruit, but since they are still relatively little known, recognition of this fruit rarely make it into the "mainstream." Raymond Arroyo's recent book on, *Mother Angelica: Her Grand Silence: The Last Years and Living Legacy,* however, is an exception to this norm.

(Note: as almost all references in this section are from this book, in lieu of footnotes, I will simply be placing parenthetical notes with the relevant page numbers listed).

In this book, Arroyo shares many details of what transpired in the monastery where Mother Angelica lay, almost entirely bed-ridden, during the last years of her life. Even in this state, Mother Angelica wished to "do God's life," whether through her sacrifices or her sufferings. She was very open to doing His Will and also to the private revelations of many mystics, including the writings of Luisa Piccarreta.

In Our Lady of the Angels Monastery in Hanceville, Alabama, however, some of Mother's fellow sisters were not as open to these writings and the messages contained within them. While to the outsider the convent seemed like the perfect place, with nuns going about their day in times of prayer, times of silence, adoring Jesus in the Most Blessed Sacrament, and living in a seemingly-peaceful community with like-minded religious sisters, there were many troubling things manifesting themselves within the monastery walls. Inside of the convent, many sisters were encountering temptations of their own self-wills being placed above that of Our Lord. Because of this, there was a tremendous divide beginning to form, and it was one that would last several years.

Perhaps Mother Angelica caught a glimpse of what was to come in her final years at a much earlier point, because she often spoke to her sisters about embracing, and not questioning, God's Will, even saying at times that following their self-wills would destroy them. And maybe this is why, even before her stroke on Christmas Eve of 2001, she granted permission for her sisters to read the writings of Luisa.

Published in 2016, Arroyo's book details much of these hitherto unknown events. While I will cover some of what transpired, I encourage all who read this to see for themselves the exact details of the events. But of special interest here is the fascinating convergence of the stories of two of the Poor Clare nuns in the Hanceville convent; namely, Sr. Catherine and Sr. Margaret Mary.

Well before Mother Angelica's stroke at the end of 2001, Sr. Catherine had obtained permission from Mother Angelica to introduce the writings of Luisa Piccarreta to the nuns in the order. Arroyo states that Mother Angelica was very accepting of the Divine Will devotion being introduced to the sisters, and—so long as the nuns did not "impose it on anyone"—they were "free to read" the writings, study them, and put into practice the devotions as they saw fit in their own prayer life. As with any not-yet-approved private devotion, no one was obligated to follow it or forced to do so. (P. 67)

But the introduction of this "new devotion" was met with anger on the part of some sisters, especially the older ones who weren't comfortable with change. (P. 67) What is more, after Mother's stroke many sisters became furious about the direction of things; Sr. Catherine had been made vicar and also the "de facto superior" of the Hanceville convent. (P. 62) Although she held this high position, some sisters began to question her leadership.

Now, most of the sisters found Sr. Catherine to be

"relaxed, accessible, and very human," and in fact Arroyo states that "[a] great majority of the young sisters looked up to Sister Catherine, as did many of the older nuns." But there was a small handful of older sisters who felt differently, and they even began "ignoring Sister Catherine's authority." (P. 65) Their "main gripe" against Sr. Catherine was her adherence to and "affection for" the devotion of Living in the Divine Will. (P. 66) Some sisters were so opposed to this devotion that they wanted to do away with anything related to it—including doing away with Sr. Catherine herself. And by their side stood another nun, Sr. Margaret Mary, whom the older nuns thought could bring all the answers and even "deliver them… and provide a leadership alternative to Sister Catherine."

Sr. Margaret Mary, according to Arroyo's book, "seemed to live at Mother's side… [w]ith a devoted fussiness…" and "…often wore a wearied expression— as if she were suddenly afflicted by a pain she was too polite to share." Although sensible in many matters, she was also known for being "exacting and particular." (P. 64) Upon hearing the complaints regarding Sr. Catherine and this "new devotion," Sr. Margaret Mary learned of the many misperceptions of the strong-willed sisters who saw the devotion as "heresy" (p. 72) and even as "propaganda spread among the young sisters." (P. 67) Arroyo states that by 2006, "these suppressed resentments" began "to rise to the surface," and by 2009, when it came time for elections of vicar and chapter members in the convent, some sisters were dead set on seeing the removal of Sister Catherine and any nuns who were supporters of the Divine Will revelations. In the lead of this "resistance movement" was none other than Sr. Margaret Mary. (P. 72)

Now, Arroyo notes that these two sisters were considered to be "representatives of the two visions of Mother's spirit in the monastery," a spirit that none of the sisters wanted to be forgotten. (P. 69) He states that both Sr. Margaret Mary and Sr. Catherine were seen to be the personification of "Mother Angelica's charism and spirit," and goes on to say that:

> Sister Catherine reflected Mother's freewheeling, Spirit-driven leadership; she was not adverse to sudden moves when God took things in a new direction. In total accord with Mother Angelica's vision for community life, she craved a "family monastery" that was warm and joyous. (P. 70)

Sr. Margaret Mary, according to Arroyo, "emphasized decorum and obedience" and "was annoyed by the whimsical nature of some of Sister Catherine's decisions." (p. 70) It is important to note that Arroyo says that "it was clash of styles and approaches that divided them..." but that regarding important issues such as the Eucharist and the Liturgy, both sisters "probably agreed more than they disagreed." (P. 70)

All the same, things were getting quite ugly inside the convent walls, and when voting time came, the sisters (all except for Mother Angelica herself) cast their votes. The results were quite shocking: Sr. Margaret Mary won the election—but only by one single vote. And the answer for "deliverance?" It didn't come; in fact, matters only became far worse after Mother Margaret Mary's election.

Sr. Margaret Mary, who could (according to Arroyo) be "prone to drama," (P.78) would have emotional outbursts, "complete with tears and frequently raised voice..." and she began "chastising Sister Catherine in front of the community for perceived errors." (P. 80) What is more, she put an end to the starting of any new foundations within the order, and expelled from the Hanceville convent a few of the sisters (postulants included), "particularly those who practiced the Divine Will" (P. 79). More sisters left not long after as well.

Arroyo shares the following:

> Purging the monastery of the Divine Will books became a chief priority even though, according to several nuns interviewed, only five or six were actively reading it. Margaret Mary fumed about the devotion at length, insisting that the Divine Will "was not Eucharistic" and was "a heresy." One of the extern nuns remembers the vicar instructing her to stop selling the writings of Luisa Piccarreta in the nuns' gift shop and told her that the books should not even be on the monastery grounds. The new rules and vanishing postulants created an atmosphere of anxiety and worry. (P. 80)

Because of the many growing concerns regarding Sr. Margaret Mary's election, some of the sisters sent a letter of complaint to Rome. These sisters asked for a re-vote, and held onto the hope of invalidating— on just grounds (again, see Arroyo's book for more details)—Sr. Margaret Mary's election.

Rather than receiving the answer they were hoping for, they received the announcement that the Vatican would be performing a formal investigation of the community. This commenced on August 15th, 2009. In the lead-up to it, however, Arroyo notes:

> Sister Margaret and her supporters gathered... each night to pray a special rosary to Our Lady of Success. They prayed that the coming Vatican visitation would produce a positive outcome. On their wish list: the removal of Sister Catherine and several sisters who they thought were distorting the life of the monastery. (P. 99)

When the results of the investigation were unveiled, however, the sisters learned more shocking news: another religious sister was going to be imported "from outside the community" and serve as the new superior, and both Sr. Margaret Mary and Sr. Catherine were instructed to leave the Hanceville convent "immediately for at least a two-year sabbatical." (P. 114)

So, what came of these two sisters? Arroyo offers a couple of sentences to say that Sister Margaret Mary "now wears a Carmelite habit and is attached to a group of Carmelite monks in Wyoming. She interacts with the monks and occasionally ventures into public, though she technically lives as a hermit." (P. 119)

Regarding Sr. Catherine, however, Arroyo shares much more:

> **At the suggestion of Bishop Baker, Sister Catherine went to Rome to pursue studies at the Angelicum,** the Pontifical University of St. Thomas Aquinas. While there, the nun felt called to begin a new order. At the end of her sabbatical period, Catherine was informed that she was welcome to remain a Poor Clare of Perpetual Adoration with financial support from the community but could not return to Our Lady of the Angels Monastery. Not wanting to confuse the public by wearing the Poor Clare habit out in the world, and feeling an internal prompting to establish a new religious order, she asked to be released from her vows in 2011. Catherine would instantly take private vows in Italy.
>
> **At the invitation of Bishop Luigi Negri of the diocese of San Marino-Montefeltro on the northeastern Italian coast, Sister Catherine founded a new community. Wearing a white habit she now goes by the Name Mother Gabrielle Marie, the superior of the Benedictine Daughters of the Divine Will.**

"I was thirty-three when I entered Our Lady of the Angels, and I was there for thirty-three years," Mother Gabrielle Marie told me at the time of her departure. "Now I'm sixty-six years old, having trouble learning the language, but when God asks me to do something, I have to do it."

As of this writing the Benedictine Daughters of the Divine Will have four professed sisters and seventeen women from Italy and America interested in joining the group.

"The order has Mother Angelica's spirit," Mother Gabrielle Marie enthused. **"We have a lot of joy and peace. There is no criticism. It is a house of charity." The Benedictine Daughters practice Eucharistic adoration, study the writings of Luisa Piccarreta, and are devoted to God's will.** They are hoping to collect the necessary funds to renovate the Convent of Sant'Igne, a thirteenth-century Italian cloister reputedly built by St. Francis of Assisi. (P. 117-118)

Benedictines of the Divine Will

Now, I understand that some readers may be angry that I have here shared less than flattering facts about what transpired in Mother Angelica's Monastery. But I trust that God did inspire Raymond Arroyo—a good man and an orthodox and devout Catholic—to publish this story for a reason. And I believe the reason is this: it is a perfect illustration of a story that has repeated itself many times in general over the history of the Church, and not infrequently in the past several decades with respect to Luisa's revelations specifically.

That is, a story wherein God makes His Will clear in a situation, but those who have grown comfortable with "the way things were," and have succumbed to seeing their vocation as akin to that of a museum curator, proceed to persecute the one

through whom God desires to institute His Will. Other curators, in turn, hear of what transpired and add their own condemnations, castigating the "divisiveness" of the one who dared to rock the boat by striving to know and do God's Will.

Indeed, the biographies of the saints and the histories of all the now-approved revelations are replete with incarnations of this dynamic.

But it is a modern "pastorally correct" lie that, as soon as any sort of division is detected, everything associated with it must not be of God. Jesus Himself teaches the exact opposite in the Gospel (e.g. Matthew 10:34)—saying that He *will* be a source of division. This does not mean that division is a good thing or that we should ever desire it; of course, it is *in itself* a tragedy. But those who are *phobic* of division are simply guaranteeing that they will not hear the voice of God, for He has greater purposes in mind than merely maintaining the status quo. When God acts, He does so for a reason. There will always be those who oppose this reason, and it is from this opposition that a certain amount of division is always going to transpire.

Considering now the situation at hand, I understand that those who have already decided to oppose Luisa's writings will, upon hearing of what transpired at this Monastery, simply use this as fuel for their accusations.

Thankfully, however, most Catholics realize that our vocation is not that of a museum curator. For it is not difficult to look at what transpired with Mother Gabrielle (Sister Catherine) and realize that she was doing God's Will and being persecuted for just that. Nevertheless, God had a plan in mind in allowing it all, and Mother Gabrielle now leads a thriving and beautiful religious order dedicated to the revelations Jesus entrusted to Luisa. This is just one of so many of the beautiful fruits of Luisa's revelations now seen; but it happens to be one of the few that has received mainstream attention, thanks to Raymond Arroyo. I again recommend that anyone who wishes to know more simply purchase his book. Upon reading it, you will clearly see the hand of Providence guiding Sister Catherine/Mother Gabrielle.

But ultimately, what to "make of it all" will still be up to you. If you wish, you may choose to side with those who saw Sister Catherine as an evil heretic. But that would not be a wise choice. I close this section with a reminder that the Divine Will writings were not being forced upon anyone; Mother Angelica herself had made it clear that they were to be allowed but not required in her Monastery. Compare, therefore, the antics of Sister Margaret Mary to those of Sr. Catherine; the former relentlessly attacking the latter for merely offering this spirituality to those who wanted it. Search Church History far and wide and you will find few if any examples of Sr. Margaret Mary's antics vindicated – but you will find *Butler's Lives of the Saints* full of those of Sr. Catherine.

***

Let us now change tone and consider the validity of Luisa's revelations from an entirely different perspective.

Luisa's Own Doubts Addressed

An additional quality of Luisa and her writings should now be noted: whoever you are and however many fears you may have about the legitimacy of the source of Luisa's revelations, you probably do not have as many such concerns as Luisa herself had. **I do not believe that there has ever been a soul who was more diligent than Luisa in constantly ensuring that what she was receiving was not from either the Devil or from her own imagination.** Throughout her volumes, one constantly sees quotes like this one:

> Fearing that it might be the devil, I signed Him with the cross several times, and then I said to Him: 'If You really are Jesus, let us recite the Hail Mary to our Queen Mama together...[139]

Here Luisa's diligence is displayed in guarding against the deception of Satan. But perhaps even more than the attacks of the devil, the trap of imagination and fantasy being confused for reality was what Luisa was cognizant of regarding the need to be zealously on guard against, for we regularly see quotes like the following throughout many parts of her writings (and in this particular exchange we see Luisa mystically conversing with St. Francis of Paola as follows):

> I fear that [my state] was my fantasy ... [St Francis:] "The sure sign to know whether a state is Will of God is that the soul is ready to do otherwise, if she knew that the Will of God was no longer that state."[140]

In the introduction to the first Volume, Luisa summarizes what had transpired in her mysticism for the several years leading up to it. In this introduction, she writes:

> In this [state of desolation] I would spend sometimes two days, sometimes four, more or less, as He pleased. My only comfort was to receive Him in the Sacrament. Ah! yes, certainly I found Him there—I could not doubt; and I remember that only a few times He would not let Himself be heard, because I prayed Him and prayed Him and importuned Him so much, that He would content me. ... After I would spend those days in that state described above, especially if I had been faithful to Him, I would feel Him come back within me. He spoke to me more clearly, and since during the previous days I had not been able to conceive one word or feel anything within me, I came to know, then, that it was not my fantasy, as I would say many times before; so much so that, of what has been said up to here, I would not say anything, either to the confessor or to any other living soul.

In the beginning years of her mystical revelations, Luisa was so concerned about the risk of the messages being the result of fantasy, that she wouldn't even tell anyone about them. However, under the close care of Church-appointed spiritual directors, she (and each of her directors, who were priests) grew to understand that there was no risk of fantasy.

Indeed, the best demonstration of the validity of Luisa's revelations is perhaps found outside of the external facts listed in the sections above— demonstrative as indeed they are—**for the revelations themselves communicate their own validity to anyone with ears to hear**. Try as one might, for example, to argue that beauty is merely subjective and essentially non-existent, there simply is no one who can deny the objective and real beauty of a great symphony of Mozart well played, or a sunset over a picturesque mountainous landscape. Similarly, **no catechized Catholic in God's grace who delves into Luisa's revelations with sincerity will long find himself doubting their validity**. I encourage anyone with lingering doubts to simply do precisely that; pray to the Holy Spirit, open up her writings randomly, and read. You will not be disappointed. We close this section with the entire entry from Luisa's diary on March 7, 1922:

---

[139] February 19, 1900.

[140] April 8, 1908.

I was thinking about what has been written, and I said to myself: 'Is it really Jesus that speaks to me, or is it a trick of the enemy and of my fantasy?' And Jesus, on coming, told me: "My daughter, my words are full of truth and of light, and they carry with them the virtue of transforming the soul into truth itself, into light itself, and into the very good which they contain, in such a way that the soul does not only know the truth, but she feels within her the substance of operating according to the truth which she has known. Further, my truths are full of beauty and attraction, in such a way that the soul, taken by their beauty, lets herself be enraptured by them.

In Me everything is order, harmony and beauty. See, I created the heavens; they alone could have been enough—but no, I wanted to adorn them with stars, almost studding them with beauty, so that the human eye might enjoy more from the works of its Creator. I created the earth, and I adorned it with many plants and flowers … I created nothing which did not have its own ornament. And if this is in the order of created things, much more so in my truths, which reside within my Divinity. While it seems that they reach the soul, they are like solar rays, which hit and warm the earth without ever departing from the center of the Sun. And the soul remains so enamored with my truths, that she finds it almost impossible not to put into practice the truths she has known, even at the cost of her life.

On the other hand, when it is the enemy or the speculation of fantasy that want to speak about truths, they bring neither light, nor substance, nor beauty, nor attraction. They are empty truths, without life, and the soul does not feel the grace to sacrifice herself to put them into practice. Therefore, the truths that your Jesus tells you are full of Life and of all that my Truths contain. Why do you doubt?"

The Life of Luisa Herself

Note: This overview of Luisa's life will be kept brief; instead of presenting a complete biography here, I would rather direct you to the book entitled *Sun of My Will*, by Maria Rosaria Del Genio, published in 2016 by the *Libreria Editrice Vaticana*. This is the Vatican's official publishing house, and thus it is an authoritative and trustworthy text. Instead of presenting extensive footnotes in this chapter for each detail, I again refer you to that more complete biography, and to

the biography written by Fr. Bucci, a Capuchin priest who in his childhood knew Luisa, and whose priesthood was prophesied by her.[141] His biography is also authoritative as it contains an Imprimatur and is easy to find posted online.

On April 23rd, 1865 (in that year, this date was the Second Sunday of Easter—a day we now know as Divine Mercy Sunday), Luisa was born into the world. The wonders that God chose to work in her life (as confirmation of His message to the world through her) began from this very day. Despite being born breech—a dangerous medical condition—Luisa caused her mother no pain whatsoever during the delivery. Later, on that same day, her father took her to the parish priest to have her baptized.

Luisa's desire for hiddenness was manifest at the earliest age; as a toddler her favorite spot was a hollow in a great tree, in which she would spend hours alone in prayer. When guests arrived at her house, she could not be found; for she passed all such times hiding behind a bed in prayer. As was the case with countless saints, antics such as these concerned people around her—but when one learns of her interior life, these external habits make perfect sense. As a young child, she suffered from terrible demonic nightmares. Instead of succumbing to the horror of them, these experiences were in fact what caused her to flee with such fervor to Jesus for safety. This utter dependence on Christ was no doubt what disposed her, even before she had reached the age of reason, to be the perfect instrument in the hand of God.

From these details we can see why Jesus chose Luisa, for they demonstrate His reasoning for saying (regarding how He chose Luisa), *"I went around the earth over and over again, and beheld all souls one by one to find the lowliest of all."*[142]

At twelve years of age, Luisa began to hear Jesus speaking to her interiorly. These locutions came to her in the most precious moments of her life: the moments after receiving Holy Communion. He would instruct her, correct her, and guide her. After a year of these communications, Luisa experienced a life-changing event that invited her to become a victim soul: she received a vision of Jesus below her balcony, carrying His cross, amidst great persecutions from a throng surrounding Him. He

---

[141] Fr. Bucci relayed this in a live talk given by him at a conference I attended in 2014.

[142] Rev Joseph Iannuzzi, Doctoral Thesis., 1.1.

then stopped, looked up at her, and said "*Soul, help me!*" It was not long after this that her mystical life progressed exponentially; she was soon incapable of keeping down ordinary food, and thus began her lifelong Eucharistic fast (although it did indeed extend throughout her whole life, it took different forms at different points). Jesus was " *... training her to live exclusively on the Divine Will, which, along with the Eucharist, would constitute her daily bread.*"[143] Adding to this utter dependency upon God, another mystical phenomenon came to define her days: she was completely rigid each morning, incapable of being moved even by several strong people. It was not until a priest came to bless her that she was finally capable of moving. This obviously supernatural phenomenon is unique; we know of no other saints who were subject to such a radical dependency on the Church. Who else, in her very physical ability to move, was totally dependent upon the blessing of a priest? This sacrifice, unprecedented in history, tells discerning minds that God, in turn, is at work in some task equally unrivaled in history.

***

But this sacrifice brought along with it many other sacrifices. In the official Church sanctioned biography of Luisa published by the Vatican, we read (regarding this period of Luisa's life and this condition of hers):

> The family suffers seeing her in this condition and, making it worse, they have a hard time seeking and finding a priest willing to go to the house to bless the girl. It is highly probable that right during this period, Luisa's family makes a decision that will affect Luisa for the rest of her life. Here again is the testimony of her niece, Giuseppina, who brings the news to light: "*Poor grandmother weeps with sorrow seeing her daughter in that state and, not knowing what else to do, decides to go to the bishop and, accompanied by my father, she goes to Trani. She explains everything to the bishop, who, being interested, orders the priests to go to the sick girl; from that moment on, a priest goes to her bedside every morning and she obediently wakes up from her deep slumber.*" The archbishop of Trani is Archbishop Giuseppe de' Bianchi Dottula and, because of his intervention, he unites Luisa, in a way, with priestly authority—creating a bond that, over the years, will take shape in the official confessors' spiritual assistance. This is the

moment Father Michele De Benedittis, who has known her ever since she was a child, temporarily accepts the archbishop's invitation. He, too, is able to release her with his blessing and Luisa is quite amazed. It is then she realizes that being released from her rigid state does not depend on the holiness of the priest, but on the grace he received. **From now on, Jesus has placed her in the priests' hands. While this may seem like a great grace, they soon become the reason for a true war against her.** With the absence of Father Cosma and Father Michele who is not able to arrive, **the priests who get called in say that her condition is a complete sham; others think that only a beating will put an end to Luisa's nonsense; and there are still others who think that the girl just wants to make herself believe she is a saint or is possessed by demons ... She is thought to be arrogant, a fake, a cheat, someone who wants to grab all the attention for herself. Often, the priests whom her family members approach refuse to go and, even if they do go, they then bitterly reproach her. Once they left her in her rigid state for more than 18 days. Her mother cries. She is mortified. She does not understand ...**

The fact escapes Luisa that her dependence on priestly authority has a precise purpose within the church since Jesus manifests His works through His priests. This is how Luisa spends the next three or four years—subjected to a continual battle on the part of the priests. There is a lot of physical suffering, but the moral suffering is just as bad when she "wakes up." In fact, after a priest blesses her and brings her back to a normal state, instead of comforting her with a kind word or compassion, he reprimands her, telling her that she is capricious and disobedient.[144]

Having read the revelations given to Venerable Mary of Agreda in *The Mystical City of God*, I am reminded in reading the details of Luisa's early years of the treatment meted out to Our Lady herself once she entered the service of the Temple. As the Blessed Virgin endured horrible abuse there, so too Luisa endured similar treatment from those close to her who should have been the most compassionate. For we see in the quote above that, until it became completely impossible to ignore that her state was of supernatural origin, even many priests initially would scoff at her. Seeking to prove that she was merely pulling a stunt, she was once mercilessly left for eighteen days in this state

---

[143] Ibid, 1.5.
[144] *Sun of My Will*, Ch. IV.

of rigidity, incapable of moving, until a priest finally came to bless her, thus freeing her from the captivity. Indeed, the people around her in these early years often suffered from a "spiritual blindness"[145] which was just another sacrifice offered up by Luisa for the Coming of the Kingdom. [146]

But even these sacrifices were only the beginning. For Luisa was even deprived of the ability to eat. Regarding this condition, we read, from the same Church-sanctioned work:

> We said that when Luisa regains consciousness, she returns to normal. Well, that is not exactly right. She returns to normal in that she can move again, but what lingers is a strong revulsion for any kind of food. If sometimes she eats something, when forced by a family member, she brings it all back up again just a few minutes later. This, too, is seen as some form of mischief on her part, so that both her family and other people are after her, scolding her. And yet, they should be noticing that something unusual is happening — the food she brings back up is whole, fresh and fragrant. **But the people around her seem to have a kind of spiritual blindness.** They are not able to take a leap into seeing something miraculous. On the contrary, they keep looking for earthly cures. The priest, in fact, gets the idea of making her take quinine, which is used to simulate the appetite. At the same time, he obligates her to eat every time she vomits. So Luisa eats, but she has continual bouts of vomiting. She brings it all back up and is left feeling the same hunger as before — indeed, she is even hungrier than before, because of the medicine she took. What is happening? She feels the pangs of hunger, but she is afraid to ask for food and she wonders, what will my family say? She threw up just a little while ago and now she wants to eat again? She becomes determined to bear with the hunger and if they give her something, she will take it; otherwise it is up to the Lord! About four months go by. One day the Lord tells her to ask the priest for permission not to take the quinine anymore and not to make her eat after she has thrown up. When her confessor arrives, she makes her request — with very little hope, but then he orders her to eat just once a day and to stop taking the quinine. Luisa thinks that the problem has been solved, but when she eats just that one time a day, she still brings it all back up ... and the food is always fragrant. Once more the priest does not understand, and he tells her to accept this mortification as well. Luisa also confesses to him that the Lord sometimes tells her to ask for permission not to eat anything, but the confessor will not allow it. At first, she brings her food back up every three or four days, but after a while it happens every time she eats. ... [147]

Dear reader: please consider well what you have just learned. Do not let it go "in one ear and out the other," a habit we are all too experienced with in our modern information-overload culture. These facts about Luisa's life were always known by anyone eager enough to discover the truth (for we have always had plenty of eyewitness testimonies and documentation for verification), but now we see that they have been shared with us in the pages of an official Church-sanctioned biography published by the Vatican, and it would be wrong to doubt them. You have learned that **this lowly Italian woman, Luisa Piccarreta, experienced mystical phenomena and endured sacrifices of such magnitude that they are not rivaled anywhere in the 2,000-year history of the Church. You will proceed, shortly, to learn that these phenomena existed for a reason: because the soul experiencing them is also going to be entrusted with revelations. These revelations call for our response and are of such a magnitude that the likes of these, too, have been seen nowhere in history.** This changes everything. We mustn't forget that. There simply is no turning back.

We should also note that these mystical phenomena and sacrifices, though truly extraordinary, were carefully chosen by God to preserve Luisa's littleness and humility. Indeed, upon entering her room, one would not guess that he had just stumbled upon the main (earthly) figure

---

[145] *Sun of My Will*, P. 46.

[146] The theologian, Fr. Edward O'Connor, writes in his book on Luisa about another extraordinary account of spiritual blindness and its resolution: "In 1917, Archbishop Regime, newly appointed to the diocese of Trani, forbade priests to enter Luisa's house or to celebrate Mass there (although this privilege had been granted by Pope Leo XIII and confirmed by Pope Pius X). But as he was signing this decree, the Archbishop was suddenly afflicted by partial paralysis. When the priests who were present came to his aid, he indicated that he wanted to take them to Luisa's house. Supported by two priests, and uttering incomprehensible words, he came to the door. When he entered Luisa's room, she said "Bless me, your Excellency!" The Archbishop raised his hand in blessing, and was instantly cured. He remained for two hours in a secret conversation with Luisa, and thereafter visited her regularly for spiritual conversations. Many vocations, of both men and women, were inspired by Luisa…" *Listen to My Prophets*, P.60.

[147] Ibid.

in the turning point of history, as indeed Luisa is. Instead, the impressions one would receive would doubtless be as we see described in the Church-sanctioned biography:

> Once, a distinguished individual who came to visit her said upon leaving her room, "Luisa possesses an angelic soul! It seems like with her you are breathing in the scent of fragrant lilies! That heavenly smile and that clear smiling face speak to you of God and they let you catch a glimpse of a tiny corner of paradise. It seems like breathing an air imbued with celestial perfume! In that little room, people forget all about the bothersome things in life; they feel the soul at peace. They forget their quarrels, deceptions, jealousies and they breath the joy of God's grace."

This text finds an echo in something written by Msgr. Luigi D'Oria, another priest from Corato who knew Luisa and who, in 1961, had the task of writing a report about her life. Among the things he wrote concerning the apostolate Luisa carried out by being in bed, he states: 'When somebody loves, it is impossible not to speak about the person loved, especially if it is God, the one who—beyond His many loving titles, makes happy the person who gives his heart to Him. Luisa loved God and others. She could not then be quiet about God, because she wanted God to be known and loved by others; and that it was in this that one would find true happiness—the fruit of God's love. Naturally, her favorite topic was the Divine Will, which is very kind in itself, given what she wanted to do for our benefit and out of true love, obeying His law and conforming herself according to His dispositions. As such, every conversation, whatever it was about, was illuminated and warmed by God's love. Many people went to her to express their needs—of the spirit and body, drawn by the scent of her union with God. And everyone had, as an answer to their problems, the loving uniformity to the Divine Will, which not only eases the pain and makes it praiseworthy, it also sheds light on what to do. Those who presented themselves to Luisa in the hopes of finding a fortune-teller were not listened to and were left out[148]

Now, we return to our chronological overview of Luisa's life.

***

For the next sixty-four years, this was her life. It was perhaps the simplest life the world has ever seen, and the most dependent upon God. Neither her bodily nourishment nor even the ability to move her very own limbs came from any source but God, through the hands of a Catholic priest in beginning each day by blessing her to relieve her of her rigidity and in feeding her with the Eucharist—the only food she could always keep down.

In her early years, the basis for her religious education and formation was the Catechism of the Council of Trent, and at age 18, she became a Third Order Dominican, taking the name Sister Magdalene. The next year her Archbishop, Giuseppe Dottula, formally appointed Fr. Michael De Benedictis as her confessor, and she was visited daily by him. Thus began another defining factor of all of her remaining days: complete obedience to the Church through her priest directors (of which she had many), all of whom were appointed formally by her Bishops, with each director utterly convinced of the validity of her mystical phenomena.

At this point it is worth mentioning what was never a part of her life until its final few days: illness. Her only real illness was the bout of pneumonia that took her life at the very end; and she was not even afflicted with bed sores, despite being perpetually bedridden. This state alone is nothing short of miraculous, as anyone who is accustomed to the care of bed-ridden patients is aware.

In the year 1898, she received a new confessor, Fr. Gennaro Di Genarro, and he served in this capacity for the next 24 years. However, a mere one year into this ministry, he commanded Luisa, under holy obedience, to write down her revelations. So great was her humility that this was an enormous penance for her, but her obedience was always perfect, and so she wrote.

After Fr. Gennaro came Fr. De Benedictis, and after that, St. Hannibal Maria di Francia was appointed to be Luisa's censor librorum, a role he held until his death in 1927. More than a decade earlier, however, deeply convinced of the necessity of Luisa's revelations, he had been publishing the *Hours of the Passion*. He gave volumes 1-19 of Luisa's diary his Nihil Obstat and afterward the Archbishop, Joseph Leo, gave them his Imprimatur. Fr. Benedict Calvi was Luisa's next, and final, confessor. He too became a zealous advocate and promoter of Luisa's writings, and he

---

[148] *Sun of My Will*, P. 63-64.

documented an overview of her daily life as follows:

> Toward six o'clock in the morning the confessor was beside her small bed. Luisa was found all curled up, crouched over so tightly that when the sister or person of the house—in obedience to the confessor or the Bishop—had to sit her up in bed in her usual position, they could not move her on account of her weight. It seemed as if she were a huge piece of lead. ... Only when the confessor, or on certain occasions any priest, imparted to her his blessing by making the sign of the Cross with his thumb on the back of her hand, Luisa's body regained its senses and she began to move. ... Throughout the 64 years of being nailed [this figurative terminology likens Luisa's bed to the cross of Christ] to her small bed, Luisa never suffered any bedsores. Immediately afterwards, there followed the reading of that which Luisa had written during the night concerning the sublime truths on the Divine Will, which was read only by her confessor beside her small bed. There was yet another extraordinary event. What was her food? Everything she had eaten, after a few hours, came back up completely intact. All of these events I observed, scrupulously controlled and subjected to careful examination by many doctors and professors of dogmatic, moral, ascetic and mystical theology ... [Each morning] After having awakened Luisa in the name of holy obedience, the confessor or another priest celebrated Holy Mass in her little room before her bed. Therefore, having received Holy Communion, she would remain there as though in a trance, in ecstasy and in intimate conversation with the Lord for two to three hours, but without her body becoming petrified or experiencing the absolute loss of its senses. However, many times throughout the day she would be with the Lord in a manner that engaged her senses, and on occasion the people that were in her company would notice it.[149]

Luisa would work at sewing for the Church during her days, and altar cloths were what she mostly made. She would work on her sewing until ten thirty at night, and in the middle of the night (between midnight and 1am) she would enter into an ecstatic state like a petrified statue (even if the pillows behind her were not correctly in place), and her mystical experiences, as documented in her diary, ensued.

Such were all of her days. Intermixed with them were apparitions, locutions, introspection, bilocation, invisible stigmata, and countless other miracles, but little or nothing externally and visibly extraordinary.

On August 31st, 1938, three of her works were placed on the Index of Prohibited Books, and this placement was published on September 11th.[150] At this point in her life she was staying at a convent with the Sisters of Divine Zeal. She loved staying there, and had been living with the sisters for ten years. A mere month after her works were placed on the index, the superiors asked her to leave. This condemnation of her works (which now is in no way, shape, or form binding) was nevertheless an important element of the Divine Plan, so that Luisa could be more perfectly conformed to the image of Jesus Christ, who also was condemned by the legitimate Ecclesiastical authority of His day. Immediately after news of the condemnation reached her, Jesus told Luisa:

> My dear daughter, if you knew how much I suffer, if I let you see it, you would die of pain. ... Know that they didn't condemn you, but Me, together with you. I Myself feel as though being condemned, since condemning Good is condemning Myself. You, however, unite in My Will Our condemnation to the one I received when I was Crucified and I will give you the merit of My condemnation and all the Goods that It produces: It made me die, then It called to Life My Resurrection, in which everyone was to find Life and Resurrection of all Goods. With their sentence they believe they can kill what I said on My Divine Will, but I will allow such chastisements and sad events that I will make My Truths rise again more beautifully-more majestic, in the midst of the peoples. Therefore, from your side and Mine, let's move nothing. Let's keep doing what we have done, even if everybody should be against us.[151] This is My Divine Way: for all evils creatures may do, I never move My Works. I always preserve them with My Creative Power and Virtue. For Love of those who offend Me, I always Love them without ceasing. ... My daughter, what is not enjoyed today, will be

---

149 Rev Joseph Iannuzzi, Doctoral Thesis. , 1.8.
150 Cf. Acta Apostolica Sedis of 1938. Page 318. Vatican.va.
151 Jesus is **not** telling Luisa to be disobedient. In fact, nowhere in Luisa's 8,000 pages did Jesus ever budge in insisting to Luisa that she obey all authorities placed over her

by the Church. Here, Jesus is merely telling Luisa to stay strong in continuing to write down her revelations (she was still under obedience to write in her diary at this point!) and pray, suffer, and sacrifice according to her usual manner, which obviously was not affected by the condemnation.

enjoyed tomorrow; what now seems darkness because it finds blind minds, will turn into sun tomorrow for those who have eyes. How much Good they will do. So, let's keep doing what we've done. Let's do what is needed from our side so that nothing may be missing of help, Light, Good and Surprising Truth to make My Will known and to make It Reign. I will use every means of Love, Grace and chastisement. I will touch all sides of creatures in order to have My Will Reign. When it will seem that the True Good is about to die, then, it will Rise Again more Beautiful and Majestic.[152]

Two months after being kicked out of the convent, Luisa finished her last writing, as she was no longer bound under obedience to write upon its completion. One year later, World War II began.

Nine years later, on March 4th, 1947, she breathed her last. Regarding this moment, Father Benedetto Calvi (her confessor at that time) wrote:

> She died like the saints die, as a final act in the Divine Will. I am still recovering from the tremendous shock I experienced from the deeply distressing but sublime impression her last breath made…
>
> Her body remained rigidly upright, sitting up in bed, but her limbs completely lacked the rigidity of rigor mortis so they could be moved in any direction, even all the joints in her fingers; her eyelids were closed but could be opened and her pupils stayed crystal clear.
>
> All of that led to some doubt whether she was really dead, so we had a number of medical examinations done. Her body was viewed for a good four full days in this state without the slightest sign of decomposition…
>
> Nobody went to work [during her funeral], but everyone without exception took part… a truly rare sight, perhaps unparalleled, and whoever had the good fortune to take part will never be able to—and never know how—to express how magnificent it was.[153]

Indeed, throngs of thousands lined the streets to pay homage to "the saint of Corato." Jesus told Luisa:

> My daughter, it is My absolute Divine Will that these writings on My Divine Will be made known. Despite the many incidents that may occur, My

Will shall overcome them all. Although it may take years and years, My absolute Will knows how to dispose everything to accomplish its objective. The time in which these writings will be made known is relative to and dependent on the disposition of souls who wish to receive so great a good, as well as on the effort of those who must apply themselves in being its trumpet-bearers by offering up the sacrifice of heralding in the new era of peace, the new sun that will dispel the clouds of all evils.[154]

Forty-seven years later, all condemnations nullified, her cause for beatification and canonization was officially opened. And Luisa is not finished. Jesus told her:

> As for you, then, your mission is extremely long, nor will you be able to complete it on earth. Until all the knowledges are known and the Kingdom of the Divine Will is established upon earth, your mission can never be called finished. In Heaven you will have much to do…[155]

Invoke her intercession, and trust that you will receive it. I know I have, and I have not been disappointed.

Her Life According to St. Hannibal

St. Hannibal himself, as mentioned, was perhaps *the* most dedicated promoter of Luisa's revelations. He gave a beautiful description of Luisa in his own published words, as follows: (These words of St. Hannibal are taken directly from *Sun of My Will*.[156])

> The pious author of The Hours of the Passion… never, for any reason in the world, would have put into writing her intimate and prolonged communications with revered Jesus—communications which have been going on from her tenderest age until today, and are still continuing until who knows when—if Our Lord himself had not repeatedly obliged her to do so, both personally and through holy obedience to her directors, to whom she always surrenders with enormous duress upon herself, and also with great strength and generosity, because her concept of holy obedience would even make her refuse to enter into paradise…
>
> The purest virgin, wholly of God, who emerges to be a singular predilection of the Divine Redeemer,

---

[152] September 18, 1938.
[153] *Sun of my Will*, pages 185-186. (I have taken this quote from the official biography for the sake of ensuring no one doubts its validity; however, this letter was actually published in a parish newspaper in Brooklyn, NY in 1947.)

[154] Rev Joseph Iannuzzi, Doctoral Thesis. , 1.11.6.
[155] March 19, 1927.
[156] *Sun of My Will*, pages 122 and 123.

Jesus Our Lord, who century after century, increases ever more the wonders of His love. It seems that He wanted to form this virgin, whom He calls the littlest one He found on earth, and bereft of any education, into an instrument of a mission so sublime, that is, the triumph of the Divine Will... She receives from Our Lord Himself a recurring crucifixion... After all we have mentioned of her long and continuous permanence, rooted to a bed as victim for years and years, experiencing many spiritual and physical sufferings, it might seem that the sight of this unknown virgin would be distressing, like seeing someone on his back with all the signs of the pain endured in the past and of current sufferings and the like.

And yet, there is something admirable here. Seeing this spouse of the crucified Jesus, who spends the night in painful ecstasies and sufferings of every kind, but then seeing her in the day, sitting up in bed, working with her needle and pins—nothing, absolutely nothing shows through, nothing of someone afflicted who suffered so much during the night, no appearance of something out of the ordinary or supernatural. On the contrary, she looks entirely like someone who is healthy, happy and jovial. She talks, chats, laughs when appropriate, but she receives few friends.

Sometimes someone with a troubled heart confides in her and asks her for prayers. She listens with kindness, she comforts, but she never goes so far as to act like a prophetess, never a word that might hint at revelations. The great comfort she offers is always one thing—always the same thing—the Divine Will.

Although she does not possess any man-made knowledge, she is abundantly endowed with a wisdom that is fully celestial, the science of the saints. Her way of speaking enlightens and consoles. By nature she is not lacking intelligence. She studied up to the first grade when she was little; her writing is filled with mistakes, although she is not without the appropriate terms in conformity with the revelations, which seem instilled in her by Our Lord.

Theology too Deep for Human Origin

I begin this section by citing the words of the great Fr. John Arintero, speaking of souls who have received private revelations:

> Who would not be filled with admiration at seeing the marvel of lights and the sublimity of concepts in souls thus enriched by the divine Spirit? Who would not be amazed at the nobility of language which they spontaneously employ whenever they express the words spoken by God or the Blessed Virgin, while the things spoken on their own account are filled with simplicity and candor? Whence comes that loftiness of ideas and that elegance and purity of style in souls lacking all human culture? **What power of suggestion could infuse in them at one stroke that remarkable Science which they have never studied and those sublime concepts which they have learned from no other person?** This is a positive fact against which all human explanations are shattered, however much they may appeal to suggestion, contagion, telepathy, or any other influence which is not supernatural.[157]

Fr. Arintero's authority and expertise having been settled in a preceding chapter, we can see that in this small paragraph, he is able to show implicitly one reason Luisa's revelations must be true—the loftiness, the elegance, and the purity of Jesus' words in them could not possibly have come from Luisa herself.

For we must recall Luisa's circumstances: an uneducated lay woman who was bedridden her entire adult life. Now, one may strive to evade the clear conclusion these circumstances point to by insisting she learned profound truths of the spiritual life from her many visits with her priest spiritual directors; but this evasion immediately fails when one considers that the astonishing degree of spiritual and theological perfection in her transcriptions of Jesus' words to her is evident from the first volume, which she wrote towards the beginning of her acquaintances with priests. More importantly, we have no reason to believe that these priests were giving her theological instruction (that is not what spiritual direction consists in); in fact, that would be rather strange indeed, for this was not their mission. They were sent to bless her and thus free her from her rigidity, to celebrate Mass in her room and give her Communion each day, and to be her confessors and spiritual directors.

---

[157] *The Mystical Evolution in the Development and Vitality of the Church Volume II*. Importance of Private Revelations.

We should note, however, that the inclusion of this section is rather superfluous. One need only open to *any* page of Luisa's writings to see immediately a depth of meaning that could not be of human origin. Nevertheless, it may be useful to share just a few snippets that I've stumbled upon in my own reading of Luisa's volumes which reveal a theology too deep for an uneducated lay Catholic.

The Will Constrained by the Good

Although this remains a contested topic, the best philosophers rightly teach that the will, as the faculty of the soul directed to the good, is itself constrained by this end to which it finds its very nature affixed. This is so true that the will is not even ontologically capable of willing evil *qua* evil; that is to say, it cannot will an evil *because and as* it is evil, but only because of an in pursuit of some good attached to that evil. For indeed, nothing can consist entirely in absolute evil, inasmuch as evil is the privation of a due perfection. Now, do not misunderstand; this does not mean that there is not evil, or that evil is only apparent! It simply means that all evil acts consist in willing some lesser good in contradiction to some greater good; as, for example, a psychopathic murderer who kills for the pleasure of it is willing the good of pleasure in contradiction to the greater good of the dignity of human life.

But this, too, is a rather technical philosophical and theological issue; it is, rightly, not addressed in anything but advanced treatments of related matters. Despite its advanced nature, it is contained clearly in Jesus' words to Luisa, for we see Him say:

> My daughter, I am love and I made the creatures all love. Their nerves, bones, flesh, are woven with love; and after I wove them with love, I made blood flow in all their particles, as though covering them with a garment, in order to give them the life of love. So, the creature is nothing other than a complex of love, and she does not move other than out of love. At the most, there can be varieties of love, but it is always out of love that she moves. There can be divine love, love of self, love of creatures, evil love — but always love; nor can she do otherwise, because her life is love, created by the Eternal Love, **and therefore led to love by an irresistible force. So, after all, even in evil, in sin, there must be a love that pushed the creature to do that evil.**[158]

Jesus and Faith

Jesus had absolutely no Faith and no Hope.

One may be scandalized to read that statement, but it is perfectly orthodox and in accord with Church teaching. For Faith requires the absence of sight; and Jesus, being God, sees all — even in His human nature, He *saw* Divine Truths so clearly that Faith was not possible. Hope, too, requires not possessing that which is hoped for; but Jesus, lacking nothing that a soul in Heaven has; always had the Beatific Vision from the first moment of His conception, therefore He could not hope for what He already possessed.

These teachings are not exactly Catechism 101; in fact, they are almost never touched upon except in advanced Christology graduate courses, to which Luisa had no access. Therefore, it is unsurprising to learn that, one day, Luisa prayed to Jesus to make His own Faith her own. Innocent and understandable though this prayer was, Jesus did not hesitate to correct her, as we see in the following passage:

> I was praying according to my usual way — that whatever I do, I do it as if I were doing it with Our Lord and with His own intentions. So, I was reciting the Creed, and without realizing it myself, I was saying that I intended to have the faith of Jesus Christ to repair for so many unbeliefs, and to impetrate the gift of faith for all. At that moment, He moved in my interior, and told me: "You are wrong, I had neither faith nor hope, nor could I have them, because I was God Himself — I was only love."[159]

Here again we see an admonishment from Jesus that, all other considerations aside, is highly unlikely to have come from the imagination of an uneducated lay woman.

The Exaltation of Marriage and the Family

In the 1920s — decades before the Theology of the Body made this teaching popular — Luisa's revelations exalted Christian marriage more highly than anything I have ever come across from that time period. To speak so highly of marriage would not have been a prudent tactic of a fraudster in the 1920s who wished to have her own imaginings considered by others in the Church to be

---

[158] February 26, 1912.

[159] November 6, 1906.

revelations. In fact, we can see that these words are prophetic and, above all, certainly not demonically inspired. Jesus tells Luisa:

> **Marriage was elevated by Me to a Sacrament, in order to place in it a sacred bond, the symbol of the Sacrosanct Trinity,** the divine love which It encloses. So, the love which was to reign in the father, mother and children, the concord, the peace, was to symbolize the Celestial Family. I was to have on earth as many other families similar to the Family of the Creator, destined to populate the earth like as many terrestrial angels, to then bring them back to populate the celestial regions.[160]

To call marriage the "symbol of the Sacrosanct Trinity," goes even farther than St. Paul's famous depiction of marriage as symbolizing the bond between Christ and His Church. Theological expositions on the Trinitarian dimension of marriage and the family have become more popular recently in the works of theologians like Dr. Scott Hahn. And these are true teachings which greatly edify the Church. To this day, however, there are theologians of more rigid mindsets who take issue with such treatises, falsely claiming that it is unorthodox to see the Trinity itself in marriage and family. But here we see such statements decades before "their time" in Luisa's writings.

At one point, the Virgin Mary herself says to Luisa **"all states are holy, marriage too ..."[161]** In her letters, too, Luisa never hesitates to insist that this greatest sanctity of Living in the Divine Will is completely attainable by the married—and, indeed, is essential to be those in the married state. In fact, of all the people with whom Luisa corresponded, it seems she took most seriously her letters written to a recipient named Federico Abresch; a married man, father, and a convert to the Faith thanks to Padre Pio reading his soul (after which point, he became a daily Communicant and, along with his wife, a Third Order Franciscan). Incidentally, many of the most famous photographs that we have of Padre Pio were taken by Mr. Abresch, and his own son even became a Catholic priest who went on to work in the Vatican.

But Our Lady's words to Luisa go much farther than merely calling marriage holy. In revealing details of the Wedding Feast at Cana, Mary says:

We went there, not to celebrate, but to work great things for the good of the human generations. My Son took the place of Father and King in the families, and I took the place of Mother and Queen. With Our presence We renewed the sanctity, the beauty, the order of the marriage formed by God in the Garden of Eden—that of Adam and Eve—married by the Supreme Being in order to populate the earth, and to multiply and increase the future generations. Marriage is the substance from which the life of the generations arises; it can be called the trunk from which the earth is populated. The priests, the religious, are the branches; but if it were not for the trunk, not even the branches would have life. Therefore, through sin, by withdrawing from the Divine Will, Adam and Eve caused the family to lose sanctity, beauty and order. And I, your Mama, the new innocent Eve, together with my Son, went to reorder that which God did in Eden; I constituted Myself Queen of families, and impetrated the grace that the Divine Fiat might reign in them, to have families that would belong to Me, and I might hold the place of Queen in their midst. ...

In addition to this, my child, with my presence at this wedding, I looked at the future centuries, I saw the Kingdom of the Divine Will upon earth, I looked at families, and I impetrated for them that they might symbolize the love of the Sacrosanct Trinity, so that Its Kingdom might be in full force.

We see again Mary reiterating Jesus' own words to Luisa: that the family is indeed a symbol of the Sacrosanct Trinity. We see Our Lady being constituted by her Son as Queen of Families, restoring to them the beauty and sanctity that marriage had in the Garden.

In this section it should also be mentioned just how highly Jesus exalts the acts of even a baby or a toddler. If some people in Luisa's era were guilty of thinking of childhood as a "necessary evil" on the way to adulthood, and proceeded to adopt a perennially annoyed and grouchy approach to the things pertaining to babies, toddlers, and small children, this mindset is the opposite of what is relayed in the following words of Jesus to Luisa here (to give just one example):

> Who can say, original sin being removed, that the newborn is not Innocent and Holy? And if Baptism is given, a period of the life of the baby, even to such that actual sin does not enter into his soul, is not the baby an Act of My Will? And if he

---

[160] November 5, 1925

[161] *The Blessed Virgin Mary in the Kingdom of the Divine Will.* Day Seventeen.

moves his step, if he speaks, if he thinks, if he makes his little hands act, all these little acts wanted and disposed by My Will, are they not Tributes and Glory that We receive? Perhaps they will be unaware, but My Will receives from that little nature what It wants.[162]

To say that each little step of a baptized baby is a tribute and a glory to God is of course a lofty praise, and here, too, we see a type of wisdom and theology undergirding these revelations the origin of which cannot be explained in merely human terms.

On the Body

Continuing and broadening the theme in the previous section; we know that it is precisely because of the goodness of the body, but the concomitant failure to recognize its goodness, that Pope St. John Paul II felt the need to create the *Theology of the Body*, through his famous series of addresses on the topic. In the decades before these addresses, it was not common to see serious Catholic thinkers with such a thoroughly healthy and orthodox approach to the matter; and yet we see precisely this from Luisa's writings. For example, Jesus once said to her:

> My daughter, it is an enchantment of Beauty to see the human nature that Lives in My Divine Will covered and hidden as under a meadow of flowers, all invested by the most resplendent Light. The soul by herself could not have been able to form so many varieties of Beauty, while united she finds the little crosses, the necessities of life, the variety of circumstances, now sorrowful, now cheerful, that as seeds serve as sowing in the earth of the human nature, so as to form its flowery field. The soul does not have earth, and could not produce any flowering; on the other hand, united with the body, O! how many beautiful things it can do. Even more because this human nature was formed by Me, I molded it part by part, giving it the most beautiful form. I can say that I did as the Divine Craftsman and I placed such Mastery there, that no one else can reach Me. So I Loved him. I still see the touch of My Creative Hands Impressed on the human nature, therefore it is also Mine, it pertains to Me.[163]

But Luisa never fell into the opposite extreme, now

seen today by some theologians in the so-called "new natural law" school,[164] wherein the goods of the body are seen as so intrinsic and essential that consecrated celibacy, for example, is almost frowned upon (in stark contrast to Magisterial teachings and Sacred Tradition). Consecrated celibacy is exalted even more highly in Luisa's writings, and Luisa is often known to use somewhat extreme terms in her desire to enter Heaven, even referring in some cases to her body as a "prison." Even if such terminology is extreme, nevertheless such a balance of orthodoxy in the face of such strong pulls to one side or the other are not likely to be the result of the human ingenuity of someone of Luisa's caliber.

On Exaggeration

It is common to hear some modern "scholars," very proud of their own historical research, conclude (while sparing no expense in promoting this conclusion) that Scripture must simply be exaggerating much of the time. Here they judge God by their own human sinfulness; knowing that they themselves fall into exaggeration, they fail to (or, rather, refuse to) realize that exaggeration is nothing but a lie, and a lie is an intrinsic evil. God, Goodness Himself, can never commit an evil, thus He can never exaggerate. Luisa, more innocently than the aforementioned scholars, once supposed that Jesus must be exaggerating considering how glorious what He was telling her was, and she voiced this to Him:

> 'Jesus, my Life, it seems to me that you exaggerate a little bit in manifesting to me what extent a soul can reach who does your Will.' Knowing my ignorance and smiling, Jesus told me: "No, no, my beloved, I do not exaggerate. One who exaggerates may be deceitful. Your Jesus doesn't know how to deceive you; rather, what I have told you is nothing. You will receive more surprises."[165]

The "Scriptural claims as exaggeration" argument of the modernists was not popular until well after Luisa wrote this entry, and it is not likely that she could have herself come up with this response that Jesus gave to her own supposition.

Perfect Orthodoxy in Mariology

---

[162] July 20, 1934.
[163] April 13, 1932.

[164] More on the problems with this school of thought are found in Part Three of this book.
[165] March 21, 1914.

While the most prevalent error regarding Our Lady is to diminish her glory (and this error is not only prevalent among Protestants, but among Catholics as well), it is also the case that some fall into the opposite error. (These are most often beginners who are so blown away by the glorious Mariology given to us by the saints, that they conclude that she must be a Goddess of some sort, equal or perhaps superior to her Divine Son.) But this description of course is not true, and Jesus' words to Luisa are at once the most glorifying of Our Lady that will be found anywhere, while also being perfectly orthodox in this glorification, never falling into any sort of idolatrous approach to Mary. Jesus tells Luisa:

> And since my Humanity possessed not only the fullness of my Will as Its own virtue, but the Word Himself, as well as the Father and the Holy Spirit as a consequence of Our inseparability, It surpassed in a more perfect way both innocent Adam and my very Mama. In fact, in them it was grace, in Me it was nature; they had to draw light, grace, power, beauty from God; in Me there was the springing fount of light, beauty, grace ... So, the difference between Me, as nature, and my very Mama, as grace, was so great, that She remained eclipsed before my Humanity.[166]

Here we see that Jesus being the Divine Will by nature, and Mary having all that God has by grace, is not just some ad-hoc-afterthought-of-a-distinction that doesn't actually mean anything significant. Rather, it is an enormous distinction with enormous implications; so much so that Jesus' nature goes so far as to *eclipse* His own mother.

Passions in Jesus

The question of the nature of the passions in the humanity of Jesus, although debated by many theologians and philosophers, still lacks a completely clear answer. In Luisa's revelations, we see the straight and narrow orthodox path on this question walked perfectly—beyond anything she herself could have conceivably come up with independently. On the one hand, we have passions clearly predicated of Jesus; to cite just one example, He points out that happiness is real in Him, saying:

> And We feel twice as happy, not because We are not happy without the creature, since, in Us, happiness is Our nature, but because We see the

creature happy, who, by virtue of Our Will, comes closer to Our Likeness, loves with Our Love and glorifies Us with Our own works. We feel that the Creative Power of Our Fiat reproduces Us and forms Our Life and Our works in the creature.[167]

Things of this nature are frequent in Luisa's revelations. This is not to mention the repeated sorrow Jesus expresses to Luisa as truly experienced by Him in the face of man's sinfulness and His own need to chastise. But, on the other hand, we have entries in Luisa's writings like that of February 9th, 1908. Here we read the words "There are no passions in me." Some readers have taken this to be a blunt assertion that Jesus Christ is absolutely without any passions. But this is incorrect. Nowhere does that entire entry indicate that is Jesus Himself who is directly speaking. Instead, in that entry, we only see a certain "He" giving a response to Luisa asking the "Lord" a question. (Contrast this to the diary entry immediately after, where Luisa makes it clear that it *is Jesus Himself* directly speaking to her.) Combine this with the fact that in other places in Luisa's writings, Jesus makes it clear that He *does* have passions, for example: "When it's a question of her wanting to Love Me, I never render her discontent, because Love is **one of My Passions**,"[168] which states that Jesus does have love as one of His passions, and also clearly implies (i.e. "one of") that others exist. What this seems to say, then, is that the Divine Nature ("Lord") is completely without passions, but the person of Jesus, inasmuch as the Second Person of the Trinity is hypostatically united to a human nature, does have "passions," in a sense. And the sense is this: they are *pro*-passions.

This in fact is a thoroughly orthodox and Thomistic Christological insight. (It is also one which has not received much attention—in 2008, there was published a scholarly work entitled *The Passions of Christ's Soul*, by a theology professor, Dr. Paul Gondreau. In its description, we see this book billed as " ... *an invaluable resource for theology students and scholars. In this pioneering and unparalleled study, Paul Gondreau breaks Thomistic scholarship's silence on this particular aspect of the Angelic Doctor's thought. Illuminating the sources of Aquinas's doctrine on Christ's passions ...* "[169]). For in Aquinas' Summa Theologica, Part 3, Question 15, Article 4 (Corpus) we see that there were indeed passions in Christ,

---

[166] Mary 21, 1926.
[167] November 6, 1929.
[168] June 10, 1935.
[169] Clunymedia.com

but they were completely different from our own in three important ways:

> First, as regards the object, since in us these passions very often tend towards what is unlawful, but not so in Christ. Secondly, as regards the principle, since these passions in us frequently forestall the judgment of reason; but in Christ all movements of the sensitive appetite sprang from the disposition of the reason. ... Thirdly, as regards the effect, because in us these movements, at times, do not remain in the sensitive appetite, but deflect the reason; but not so in Christ, since by His disposition the movements that are naturally becoming to human flesh so remained in the sensitive appetite that the reason was nowise hindered in doing what was right.

In many other places throughout Luisa's writings, we see this balanced, orthodox, Thomistic approach to the passions in Christ carefully maintained to a degree that would have been impressive if seen even in the works of a theologian.

Limbo and Paradise

As all Christians know, Jesus said to the good thief being crucified next to Him: "On this day you will be with me in paradise."[170]

Upon perusing the various places Catholics and Christians discuss this incredible saying of Jesus, one finds all manner of attempts at interpreting it. (Since, indeed, it seems strange for a number of reasons; among them the fact that Heaven's gates were not opened until the Resurrection of Christ days later, and it seems odd to some that the good thief—St. Dismas—would not spend a good deal of time in Purgatory). You will find some people issuing great speculations over punctuation, wondering if perhaps the phrase "on this day," due to the absence of punctuation in the original Greek, is actually meant to be nothing but an unnecessary reminder that Jesus said what He said on the day He said what He said; not that Dismas would be with Him in paradise (that is not the case). Others wonder if by "paradise," Jesus meant "Purgatory" (He did not). Still others, noting that God is outside of time, pretend that any statements that have anything to do with time and Divine matters are somehow exempt from the constraints of logic (they are not).

Most people, however, simply confess their confusion on this point. But Jesus, with a few words, clarifies it perfectly to Luisa: **"With My presence, Limbo became Paradise…"**[171]

Dismas, along with all the just who had died up to that point, descended into limbo. Christ, too, upon His own death, "descended into hell," which of course is not a reference to the literal hell of eternal punishment inhabited by the demons and the damned souls, but rather to that same limbo into which Dismas was about to descend. But having the veil of His flesh temporarily put aside, the glory of Jesus' presence was no longer hidden, and His presence in limbo therefore immediately transfigured it entirely into paradise the very moment He entered! This makes Jesus' words to Dismas quite literally true. As usual, it is highly unlikely that Luisa grasped these matters with her intellect, thus we can clearly see Divine Light shining forth in her writings.

Free Will and Beatific Vision

Orthodox-minded Catholic theologians still debate whether free will exists for the blessed in Heaven. The conundrum is not difficult to sympathize with: Heaven must mean *absolutely guaranteed safety* for all eternity. This must be a metaphysical reality that cannot be undone anymore than a circle can be made square while still being circular. Obviously guaranteeing this safety is not difficult for the Omnipotent God; but would not, some wonder, by His granting of it mean by definition that the freedom of our will is annihilated? Wouldn't the will remaining free mean that it might, conceivably at least, someday choose to rebel and thus condemn itself to hell? Jesus answers this to Luisa:

> You are in a condition which is almost similar to the conditions of the Blessed in Heaven. **They have not lost their free will; this is a gift which I gave man, and whatever I give once, I never take back.** Slavery has never entered Heaven. I am the God of sons, not of slaves… But in Heaven the knowledge of my goods, of my Will and of my happiness, is so great and so vast that they are filled to the brim, to the point of overflowing; and so their will finds no place to act. And while they are free, the knowledge of an infinite Will and of the infinite goods in which they are immersed,

---

[170] Luke 23:43
[171] April 16, 1927.

leads them, with an irresistible force, to use their will as if they did not have it, considering this as their highest fortune and happiness, but still, in spontaneous freedom and of their own will.[172]

The mystery of how Confirmation in Grace enjoyed by the Blessed in Heaven can at once be an absolute and eternal guarantee such that falling from that grace—into hell—is not even a metaphysical possibility, while at the same time preserving the existence of their free will, is here explained beautifully by Jesus to Luisa. The elect *are* free, but the knowledge of the Goodness of God is *so* great that it *irresistibly* causes them to use their own will always in perfect accord with the Divine Will, thus absolutely guaranteeing eternal safety in that state.

Limits of the Humanity of Jesus

All Christians know that Jesus is both God and man, and that, due to this reality, we rightly worship Him even bodily due to the hypostatic union. But the details of more advanced Christology are by no means intuitive or widely known. However, Jesus' words to Luisa convey a perfect understanding that is not reasonable to see from someone of Luisa's degree of theological education (or lack thereof).

When one studies the teachings St. Thomas Aquinas, for example, he learns that not even the humanity of Christ can completely comprehend the Divinity. This is because perfect knowledge of a thing is none other than the thing itself, and the Divinity itself is infinite, whereas the humanity of Christ—though utterly supreme—is nevertheless a created thing (because it began to exist in time). But all created things are in a sense finite; incapable of containing entirely within themselves the infinite. Jesus conveys this truth to Luisa with the following words:

> Not even My Humanity could enclose, by Itself alone, all the immensity of the creative light; I was completely filled with it, inside and out, but-oh! how much of it remained outside of Me, as the circle of My Humanity did not have an equivalent magnitude in which to enclose a light so endless. The reason for this is that created powers, of whatever kind they might be, cannot exhaust the Uncreated Power, nor embrace it and restrict it within themselves.[173]

The Number of the Elect

In modern times, it has tragically become fashionable to pretend that damnation is either non-existent or is reserved only for the occasional Hitler figure. But this fad did not exist in Luisa's day and, quite the contrary, the prevailing mindset was far too stingy on the question, as a tendency continued to exist, which even minimized the Divine Mercy message. (Hence the need, discerned well by Pope St. John Paul II, to exalt St. Faustina and her writings to such an enormous degree—as will be discussed later in this book.)

Therefore, when we see words of overwhelming mercy assuring us of God's goodness and His desire to save as many souls as possible by almost any means necessary, then we can rest assured this is no invention of human art if its intent was to be well received within the various Catholic circles of its day. Therefore, we can read excerpts like the following with great confidence that, indeed, they do come from Jesus:

> In speaking with the confessor, he told me that it is difficult to be saved, for Jesus Christ Himself said it: "The door is narrow; you must strive to enter." Then, after I received Communion, Jesus told me: "Poor Me, how stingy they consider Me. Tell the confessor: from their stinginess they judge mine. They do not hold Me as the great, immense, interminable, powerful Being, infinite in all of my perfections, who can make great crowds of people pass through narrowness, more than through wideness itself."

> And as He was saying this, I seemed to see a very narrow pathway, which led to a little door, narrow, but jam-packed with people, who were competing with one another to see who could advance more and enter into it. Jesus added: "See, my daughter, what a great crowd is pushing forward; and they compete to see who arrives first. In a competition there is much gaining, while if the pathway were wide no one would bother hastening, knowing that there is room for them to walk on whenever they want. But while they are taking their time, death may come, and not finding themselves walking on the narrow pathway, they would find themselves at the threshold of the wide door of hell.

> Oh, how much good this narrowness does! This happens also among yourselves: if there is a feast or a service, and it is known that the place is small, many hurry up, and there will be more spectators enjoying that feast or service. But if it is known

---

that the place is large, nobody bothers hastening and there will be less spectators; because, knowing that there is room for everyone, everyone takes his time, and some arrive in the middle of it, some at the end, and some find everything finished, enjoying nothing. This is what would have happened if the pathway to salvation were wide—few would bother hastening, and the feast of Heaven would have been for few."[174]

Similarly, in Luisa's day it was still common to hear people murmur in response to hearing of someone's sudden death; almost assuming that this type of death precludes their salvation. Thankfully this murmuring has largely diminished, as Catholics have rightly recognized that it is absurd to conclude that someone's soul is likely damned merely because he died suddenly, without the aid of the Last Rites.[175] Nevertheless, due to the prevalence of this bad habit decades ago, Luisa was not unaffected, and therefore was distressed when her own sister was taken by a sudden death. As always, Luisa opened her heart to Jesus, and He gave her the most profound words in response:

> I felt all afflicted because of the sudden death of one of my sisters. The fear that my lovable Jesus might not have her with Himself tormented my soul, and as my Highest Good, Jesus, came, I told Him of my pain, and He, all goodness, said to me: "My daughter, do not fear…for one who is not perverted, a sudden death serves in order to prevent the diabolical action from entering the field—his temptations, and the fears which he strikes into the dying with so much art, because he feels them being snatched from him, without being able to tempt them or follow them. Therefore, what men consider to be a disgrace, many times is more than grace."[176]

(Earlier in the same quote, Jesus points out that the absence of Last Rites in a sudden death is not worth worrying about, because it is not as if the person *rejected* recourse to this Sacrament. But such rejection, indeed, would be a cause for concern).

And while some would say that fear of being lost is a good and healthy thing, as it helps us avoid damnation; at the end of the day this is simply not true wisdom, even though it superficially seems to "make sense." For the Gift of Holy Fear is not even

about damnation—that fear, too, is among those cast out by perfect love.[177] If we trust God, we should not fret about being lost. But even if such fears were to enter into your mind from time to time, know that even Luisa fell into this way of thinking, and Jesus says to you what He said to her:

> Since my always lovable Jesus had not come and I was very afflicted, while I was praying, a thought flew into my mind: 'Did the thought ever come to you that you might be lost?' I never really think about this, so I remained a bit surprised. But good Jesus, who watches over me in everything, immediately moved in my interior and told me: "My daughter, this is true strangeness, and which saddens my love very much… I would say to one who doubts about my love, and feared that she might be lost: 'How is this? I give you my Flesh for food, you live completely of my own. If you are ill, I heal you with the Sacraments; if you are stained, I wash you with my Blood. I can say that I am almost at your disposal—and you doubt? Do you want to sadden Me? Tell Me, then: do you love someone else? Do you recognize some other being as another father, since you say that you are not my daughter? And if this is not, why do you want to afflict yourself and sadden Me? Aren't the bitternesses that others give Me enough—you too want to put pains in my Heart?"[178]

Before leaving this consideration, one important point must be made: **Jesus' words to Luisa do not fall into the error of supposing that most souls will be saved because of what one often hears in left-leaning modernist theological circles today: the "mitigated subjective culpability" argument**, which holds that there is nothing to be concerned about, even though the vast majority of the world is objectively treading the path to perdition, because, as they say, "almost no one is culpable for this."

That analysis, of course, is diabolical nonsense. It is very rare that one evades culpability for grave violations of the natural law; one needn't be a catechized Catholic to know that transgressions of this law (which is written on our hearts) are wrong, for he has a conscience that tells him as much even if it isn't fully formed. On the contrary, **Jesus tells Luisa that, if most are saved, it is only due to His "daily catch,"[179] at the moment of death,** wherein He works extraordinary miracles of mercy to

---

[174] March 16, 1910.
[175] That is, Anointing of the Sick
[176] November 21, 1926.

[177] 1 John 4:18
[178] May 12, 1917.
[179] March 22, 1938.

"wrench," as it were, an act of contrition from them so long as they do not perversely and forcibly resist Him with all their might. (Needless to say, this wrenching, when successful, does not dispense the soul from Purgatory). This is doubtless a reason why the Rosary is so important; in such sorry times as our own, salvation is likely primarily attained "at the hour of death," and in each Hail Mary we intercede for precisely that intention. More on this "daily catch" is found in the "No Fear of Death" section in Part Two of this book.

Now, this "daily catch" does not dispense us from one iota of the zeal we should have in order to, as Sacred Scripture admonishes, "save souls by snatching them out of the fire" (Jude 1:23); that is, the fire of sin; for the reality of the daily catch does not change the sorry state of the souls in mortal sin before that moment. The modernists, on the other hand, who pretend that it is "mitigated subjective culpability" which causes virtually everyone to go to Heaven, can clearly be seen to have ulterior motives. These dark motives usually consist in their desire to give Communion to those who are not disposed, to formally cooperate with evil men, to make uncalled for compromises with the world, to rationalize their own unwillingness to perform the spiritual work of mercy of admonishing the sinner, etc. On the other hand, no hint of these motives is found anywhere in Luisa's revelations.

***

We must now put an end to this section; for it could easily be continued, but we would soon find ourselves simply reading the entirety of Luisa's revelations from Our Lord on these pages!

Therefore, I instead conclude this section with a simple appeal. **If you do not hear the voice of the shepherd in these writings,[180] then I humbly recommend that you strive to further develop your sense of hearing with more prayerful reading of Sacred Scripture.**

Wisdom in Her Letters

Unlike the previous section, wherein we saw a theology and a spirituality far too deep to be of human origin (even if we grant the most generous concessions to Luisa's natural abilities), what we see in her letters, unsurprisingly, is quite different. For her letters come from her own thoughts (although it is obvious in them that she draws from the holy teachings given to her by Jesus); whereas the majority of the content in her volumes come directly from Jesus Himself.

And what these letters reveal about their author is her possession of a type of wisdom that is only held by saintly souls. It is neither the wisdom of a theologian who explains everything in terms of doctrines and dogmas, nor the wisdom of a scholar who can cite many details from Scripture and the lives of the saints to demonstrate his every point. Nor is it the wisdom of a philosopher who gives precise logical arguments for each claim; rather, it is indeed the wisdom of one who has been an unflinchingly devout Catholic for decade after decade—the wisdom of one who has lived and breathed Catholicism all her life and has held nothing back from the dominion of Holy Mother Church—to the extent that the *Sensus Fidei* (the sense of the faith) has become the very mode of her own thoughts, and she always knows exactly how to fruitfully counsel souls no matter what situation they find themselves in.

All the other clear indications of the validity of these revelations aside, the odds of someone who manifests this type of wisdom being a fraud of any sort is minimal. Recall, from the previous section in which we discussed the official and Church-sanctioned norms for discerning private revelation, that these norms call for us to look for a "normal regimen of a life of faith" following the apparitions. Many of Luisa's letters were written years after her writings were placed on the Index of Forbidden Books, after she was kicked out of the convent she was staying at, and after she was no longer writing own any revelations from Jesus. And while she was not shy in sharing her pain from these events, it is equally clear that they did not have even the slightest effect on her saintly outlook and advice; in a word, on her Gift of Wisdom from the Holy Spirit.

Let us, then, look at some of this profound wisdom that Luisa shared. All her letters are well worth reading; we only highlight some miscellaneous excerpts here. Although this is included in the chapter on the authenticity of Luisa's revelations because it is indeed a beautiful demonstration of the same, what is more important now is simply that we ourselves grow spiritually from the

---

180 Cf. John 10:27

wisdom she here shares.

Ease of Living in the Divine Will

Although Luisa knew that this sanctity of Living in the Divine Will was and is the greatest sanctity of all—the greatest sanctity possible—she never hesitated to insist that it was for all people; not just for religious, or priests, or the consecrated. In letter #19 to Mrs. Antonietta Savorani (a widow), she wrote:

> Do you see, then, how easy it is? Nor does one have to be a religious to do this. The Sanctity of living in the Divine Will is for all; or rather, to tell the truth, It is for all those who want It.

And, in another letter, she pointed out that "It is not our occupations that take us away from Him, but our will…"

Similarly, in letter #74 to Mrs. Caterina Valentino from San Giovanni Rotondo, Luisa wrote:

> Therefore, let us be attentive; it takes nothing but a firm decision of wanting to live in the Holy Will. It is Jesus who wants it; He will cover us with His Love, hide us within His Light, and will reach the extent of making up for us in all that we are unable to do.

And In letter #81 to Mother Cecelia, she wrote:

> With the most tiny things, with trifles, we can form the little stones to give the Divine Fiat the material to build our sanctity. And for this, one attention, one thought, one word left unsaid, one sigh of desire for the Holy Will, is enough.

In a beautiful exposition of the Little Way of Thérèse of Lisieux, Luisa wrote, in letter #120:

> More so, since the Lord does not teach difficult things. What He wants is precisely the little things, because they are easier to do, and we cannot find an excuse and say: "I could not do it." The little things are always around us, in our hands; while the great ones come rarely. So, we cannot say that sanctity is not for us. Even our own nature is formed with many little acts—the breath, the heartbeat, the motion; yet, they form our life. And if we lacked even one breath, our life—we could say—is ended. So we can say if our little acts are not animated by the Will of God. Therefore, let us allow everything we do to flow in the Divine Will and we will feel enlivened and in possession of the Life of the Fiat. How happy and holy we will be!

Even though Luisa had gone through tremendous pains and sacrifices to make the Divine Will known and to live in it herself, she never demanded or expected this of others, but instead wished that people know how easy it was if only we desire it.

> Do not think it is difficult to obtain this great good; rather, it is very easy, as long as you want it with a firm decision to live from the Divine Volition, converting everything you do into Divine Will.
>
> Don't lose heart because of the difficulties and the circumstances of life; they are steps which make us go higher in the Divine Volition. Especially in painful circumstances, dear Jesus takes us by the hand to make us rise higher and achieve beautiful conquests—not human, but divine and of infinite value.
>
> As far as weaknesses, miseries and the like, as long as our will is not there, don't worry, since that is our ruin. They can serve as footstool on which the Divine Volition forms Its throne in order to dominate us and reign; or serve as the crushed stone and rubble serve one who wants to build himself a house, or as soil in the hands of our Celestial Farmer, Who makes out of our miseries, without our will, the most beautiful flowerings to extend His Kingdom. Everything serves His glory and our good in the divine hands of the Fiat.

On Feelings

Luisa knew well how prone people are to focus too much on feelings; supposing that within them is found sanctity. But feelings are not under our control, therefore our sanctity (or lack thereof) does not consist in them. In letter #43 to an unnamed recipient, she wrote:

> Oh, how easily we pay attention to what we feel! Feeling is not ours, it is not in our power; while Jesus, because He loves us very much, gave us our will into our power, so that, as we put it on the countertop of the Divine Will, it could turn into divine acts… Therefore, our coldness, the tears not shed, our pains, the involuntary distractions, can ask for the Kingdom of God upon earth. They will be as many sweet pledges in the hands of Jesus, which bind Him to make the Kingdom of the Divine Will come upon earth. Therefore, let us be attentive—let us live as if we had no other life, no other word, but the Divine Will…

From Letter #13 to Fr Bernardo of the Most Holy Hearts from Assisi, we read:

> Here is the means to sin no more: to be united

with Jesus, love Him, and always do His Will. Don't think about the past, this harms you a great deal; rather, even today, begin your life with Jesus and you will find out for yourself how all things change for you; you will feel like another man, born again in all that is holy.

In letter #84 to an unnamed woman, Luisa wrote:

Therefore, I recommend: in whatever state you feel, be always tranquil—do not think of cold or warm. The Divine Will is more than everything: more than prayer, more than recollection, more than fervor, more than miracles—more than everything.

In letter #120 (perhaps to Federico Abresch), she advised:

To feel pleasures, imperfections, weaknesses, is not evil. Wanting them is ugly, because the Lord does not care about what we feel, but about what we want.

On Suffering

Luisa had a special gift for encouraging others in their sufferings. From Letter #18 to Mrs. Constanza Bendetta Pettinelli from Siena:

Therefore, courage, courage. All other things are left; while sufferings are brought to Heaven, and form our most beautiful throne and never ending glory. Now I repeat my refrain: continue to promote the Divine Will. I expect a great deal from you, and so does Jesus and the Celestial Mama.

And in letter #15, to Mrs. Copparo La Scola:

Together with Jesus, pains change their look, miseries disappear; and from pains, miseries and weaknesses the most beautiful conquests, celestial riches and the strength of God arise, and the very Angels and Saints envy our lot.

And, in letter #30 to an unnamed religious superior, Luisa wrote:

Mortifications, adversities, crosses, come to us veiled and do not let us see the good which they contain; but peace removes the veil and allows us to recognize the finger of God in our sufferings…

Luisa knew nothing of the vice of respect of persons and was more than happy to correspond with anyone she could find the time to write to; whether a Bishop or a man confined to prison. To one who happened to find himself in the latter circumstance (a Mr. Vincenzo Messina), she wrote (letter #35):

Never neglect the Rosary to the Celestial Mother, and if you can, be a missionary in the prison, by making known that the Queen of Heaven wants to visit all the prisoners to give them the gift of the Divine Will.

Even amid the greatest of sufferings—which, for most people, correspond to the loss of a loved one—Luisa was firm in insisting on peace and trust. To an unnamed recipient, Luisa wrote a letter on August 14, 1934, containing the following advice:

By the same token I must tell you that it is not good for you to embitter yourself so much over the loss of your beloved son. He is certainly happier now than when he was with you; and if you really loved him, instead of crying, you would rejoice at his happiness. In grieving, you do not love your son, but yourself. Furthermore, we are just one step away from our dear departed ones; when we least expect it, we will find ourselves together with them. Therefore, I recommend to you peace, courage and true resignation, and you will see what the Lord will make of you.

Luisa's advice even sounds amazingly similar to that of St. Teresa of Calcutta, who was well known for gently reminding the sickly people she cared for that, in their sufferings, Jesus was kissing them. Luisa once wrote "… think about making yourself a saint. In every pain, give Jesus a kiss, hug Him very tightly, and force Him to let the Kingdom of the Fiat come upon earth."

To Mrs. Mazari, in letter #85, Luisa wrote the following words:

My good daughter in Jesus Christ, do not get discouraged, never lose trust. What I recommend is that you look at your crosses as many visits from Jesus, Who brings you the life of the Divine Will, to make It reign in you and to give you all His love as food… if you do the Will of God, you will feel a strength in all your sufferings…

On Peace

Perhaps what is seen most often in her letters is the exhortation to peace. From Letter #12 to Mrs. Antonietta Savorani, Luisa wrote:

Three things I recommend to you: firmness in good, perennial peace, filial trust. Trust will make you live like a little baby in the arms of her mama, and Jesus and the Celestial Mama will take care of all the things you need. They will tell you with facts: "Think about living from Our Will, and We will take care of everything, even the salvation of your brothers." Aren't you happy?

In letter #36 to Mother Cecilia from Oria, she wrote:

If there is peace, there is God. His children are as though kneaded in peace; therefore they are peacemakers, and bearers of peace. Their words, their manners, are never boisterous or sharp, but embalmed with the balm of peace, such as to sweeten the most embittered hearts; so much so, that those who are restless feel humiliated and confused in the face of a peaceful soul…When the Divine Volition wants to reign in the soul, It first sends Its message of peace. Many times it is about closing one's eyes to little bagatelles, trifles and specks, so as not to lose peace or time; in this manner, the Divine Fiat makes Its own ways in our souls, forming Its throne

In letter #56, "to a young lady," Luisa wrote:

The storm is always prelude to clear skies. Therefore, don't lose heart, wait with untiring patience for the hour of God. When it comes, its dominion will put everything into place, and maybe your very enemies will become your friends.

In a fascinating insight from this same letter, Luisa advises her that, by refusing to allow peace to reign in our hearts, we "… *let the devil laugh, because if you are not firm and always the same, the enemy will say to you: 'You wanted to do good to others, and you were unable to do it to yourself.'*" Here, Luisa identifies a common but subtle plague in the spiritual life: failing to love ourselves (in the proper sense of the term) by—in a tragic irony—supposing that our concern for others must render us without peace so long as others are in danger. This is commonly observed in parents who are worried about their straying children. And indeed, all such parents should be like St. Monica; praying continually for the conversion of their children. But God's delay in answering these prayers fully must never allow these parents to lose their peace!

To an unnamed religious woman, Luisa wrote (in letter #59):

…daughter, Jesus loves you and wants you good and holy. Do not listen to the enemy, who would want to snatch the gift from the hands of Jesus; do not pay attention to doubts or anything which is not peace. These are things of the enemy, rags of hell, not of Jesus. His things are peace; the rags of Heaven are certainties. Therefore, as a mother who loves her daughter, I beg you to no longer let

these infernal rags enter your heart; and if the enemy torments you, determined, say to him: "These are things that don't belong to me. I don't want to steal from anyone, not even from hell." And then, I repeat to you my usual refrain: unshakable firmness in good. Interest yourself in nothing but Jesus and what pertains to your office; in this way you

Luisa knew well that one of the greatest enemies of peace is the incessant tendency of some to dwell on the past, therefore she was always firm in insisting that people forget the past. Regarding this, as seen in letter #60 (to another unnamed religious), Luisa wrote:

As far as wanting to go over the past again—no, because the past has passed in God, and it would be as though stealing His rights, His own things. If there is something wrong in it, the Lord can let us know with calm. As far as the future, don't worry about it either, because it is not ours, but belongs to God. We must obey and make ourselves saints, not for our interest, but for the glory of God. So, banish every doubt, since doubt, fear and agitation do not come from God, but from the devil; rather, think of loving and doing the Will of God, because with doubts we displease the Lord much more than if we sinned… Therefore, swear, or make a solemn promise that you will never think about doubts again…

She was intent on reminding people not to dwell on their sins, their past, their weaknesses, or their miseries; but instead to simply trust in and love Jesus.

On the contrary, I tell you that when you abstain because of fear, you form firewood for Purgatory, and the Communions you do not receive on earth, you will receive with fire in Purgatory, because Jesus burns with love in the Most Holy Sacrament and wants to come into our hearts in order to pour out His flames; while if we abstain, He burns more, becoming fidgety and delirious, and with Justice He will make us burn more in Purgatory.

Oh, how good is Jesus! If we knew Him, we would die enraptured with love. And, with love, the enrapturer Jesus hides us in Love, so as not to make us die … Only the doubt that Jesus does not love us very much, saddens Jesus and embitters Him. Love calls for more love. The more we believe He loves us, the more we feel like loving Him; and Jesus, seeing Himself loved, loves us more.

Moreover, when Jesus feels loved, He forgets our sins—and why would we want to lose our minds in remembering them?

In an incredibly consoling few words regarding a soul with a sinful past, Luisa wrote in letter #132:

> And even if in the past [Jesus] was wounded by this creature, He looks at these wounds, smiles and says: "I have conquered her; she is my victory", and He shows her around to all of Heaven to make feast.

Continuing to encourage the frequent reception of Holy Communion, Luisa wrote the following in letter #100 to Francesca:

> I like to hear that you always receive Communion. Never leave it, either out of disturbance, or distress, or fears. Nothing which is not peace ever comes from God, but always from our enemy, who gains a lot when he sees us disturbed. And we lose true trust; we lose our arms to take refuge in Jesus. Therefore, in order to become saints, nothing is needed but courage, trust and peace, in order to live in the immense sea of the Divine Will.

Luisa grasped how to counsel souls for the acquisition of peace even when they are in the midst of the greatest temptation to deprive themselves of it; namely, the dark night of the soul. In letter #54, to Mother Elisabetta (a religious superior) she wrote:

> But Jesus never leaves you—He hides; and in His hiding, the ardor of His love is so great that He gives you hidden kisses and tender hugs; but He gives them slowly and quietly, so as not to be felt. However, He can't last too long with all this, and when you least expect it, He makes Himself felt in the depth of the soul in order to sustain you

Peace was not merely something Luisa advised, but something she lived. Luisa never held any grudges against her enemies but, on the contrary, prayed for them and hoped for their forgiveness. She was certainly unafraid to state bluntly the evil consequences of their actions (for Luisa was not one to wear rose-colored glasses or succumb to the error of the 'power of positive thinking'), but above all she loved her enemies in a Christlike fashion. For example, in letter #99 to Federico Abresch, she wrote:

> Dearest one in the Lord, nothing new happened here, as far as what you say about Rome. On the contrary, there has been a terrible storm against the books and against me. However, I think it was caused by some priests and religious from Corato. May the Lord bless and forgive all. It must be a diabolical rage, since, in just hearing the name of Will of God, he is consumed and becomes furious. So, let us pray.

In reading this, we must recall what Luisa suffered because of the condemnation of her writings. She suffered especially because she knew they were true (even though she submitted entirely and without hesitation to the condemnation), and Luisa thus also knew that their condemnation was a great harm to the purpose of the writings: the Reign of the Divine Will on earth. But Luisa also suffered directly in her own life; as a result of the condemnation, she was kicked out of the convent she had been living in for a decade (a place she loved), and even had daily Mass—a privilege she had had for decades thanks to the direct intervention of multiple Popes—taken away from her for a time.

***

I end this section by sharing what Luisa often noted in the end of her own letters, for it reveals a genuine humility. Although Jesus lavished spiritual gifts on her and she was made well aware of them, she was always very conscious of her littleness and her misery (similar to St. Faustina and St. Thérèse). Thus, in her letters, she earnestly beseeched the recipients of them to pray for her, insisting that she sincerely needed their prayers.

Prophecies Fulfilled

As St. Hannibal himself wrote, regarding Luisa's writings,

> In the course of these publications which we are beginning, there are chapters which foresee divine scourges of earthquakes, wars, fire, cloudbursts, devastation of lands, epidemics, famines and the like. **Everything, everything has been predicted several years before, and everything has come about, and much yet is left to come about**. [181]

Unfortunately, it is often overlooked that Luisa's writings are filled with prophecies given by Jesus Himself which have come to pass (while, of course, the majority have not yet come to pass; see Part Three of this book on the Era of Peace). Even alone, this prophetic aspect of her messages succeeds in

---

[181] *Hours of the Passion*. Preface.

demonstrating that Luisa's writings are not of human origin. Let us look at just a few of these "prophetic bullseyes" and their historical context.

World War II

Perhaps most profound among the prophecies in Luisa's writings is Jesus' repeated insistence to Luisa, in the midst of World War I and immediately following it, that an even worse war would soon come.

It seems that the earliest indication of this in Luisa's writings is found in 1904 in the following entry:

> … blessed Jesus told me: "Do you think that the triumph of the Church is far?" And I: 'Yes indeed—who can put order in so many things that are messed up?' And He: "On the contrary, I tell you that it is near. It takes a clash, but a strong one, and therefore I will permit everything together, among religious and secular, so as to shorten the time. And in the midst of this clash, all of big chaos, there will be a good and orderly clash, but in such a state of mortification, that men will see themselves as lost. **However, I will give them so much grace and light that they may recognize what is evil and embrace the truth, making you suffer also for this purpose.** If with all this they do not listen to Me, then I will take you to Heaven, and things will happen even more gravely, and will drag on a little longer before the longed-for triumph.[182]

By prophesying a clash so severe that "men will see themselves as lost," it seems Jesus is referring to World War I, which of course we know came in the following decade. But Jesus also promised "I will give them so much grace and light…," implying that this blessing would be during or after that clash. This, I believe, is precisely what He did at Fatima, sending Our Lady to give an unprecedented miracle. Of course, we know how that transpired as well; people still did not listen, and so, as Our Lady said would indeed happen, another war came. Unfortunately, it is obvious that even after World War II, people still did not listen to Heaven's messages. Shortly after its end, in 1947,

Jesus did indeed take Luisa to Heaven, and the state of the world has only continued to worsen.

But we return to the prophecies themselves, for Jesus says much more to Luisa than merely the aforementioned generalities, as His statements became more specific after World War I. In 1923, Jesus said to His little daughter:

> Ah! it is **the second general turmoil that the nations are preparing…** I have done everything to dissuade them…But everything has been in vain; the more they united together, the more discords, hatreds and injustices they fomented, to the point of forcing the oppressed to take up arms to defend themselves. And when it comes to defending the oppressed and justice, also natural, I must concur; more so, since the nations which appear to be victorious, succeeded on the basis of the most perfidious injustice. **They should have understood this by themselves, and been meeker toward the oppressed; on the contrary, they are more inexorable, wanting not only their humiliation, but also their destruction. What perfidy!** What perfidy, more than diabolical! They are not yet satiated with blood. How many poor peoples will perish! I grieve, but the earth wants to be purged—more cities will be destroyed…[183]

And later that same year:

> Last year, **France, by moving against Germany, rang the first bell. Italy, by moving against Greece, rang the second war bell. Then, another nation will come, which will ring the third,** to call them to the fight.[184]

Three years later, beginning a series of messages separated by several months, Jesus addresses the impending war.

November 1926:

> They have so blinded themselves, that they are preparing fierce wars and revolutions. This time it will not be just Europe, but other races will unite together. The circle will be more extensive; other parts of the world will participate. How much evil does the human will—it blinds man, it impoverishes him, and it makes of him the

---

[182] August 15, 1904.

[183] January 16, 1923. Nota Bene: There is also an essential teaching contained within this quote: Jesus is not categorically condemning war or insisting upon pacifism. He says clearly, "when it comes to defending the oppressed… I must concur…" It would be a perversion of Luisa's revelations to say that Jesus, in them, is condemning anyone for participating in World War II. Obviously, for example, Hitler

was an oppressor, and justice demanded that the oppressed be defended; thus, the Divine Will concurs with those who rise to this defense. War itself is horrendous; but sometimes not all parties involved in a given war bear moral blame for it.

[184] September 2, 1923.

murderer of himself. But I will use this for my highest purposes, and the reunion of so many races will serve to facilitate the communications of the truths, so that they may dispose themselves for the Kingdom of the Supreme Fiat. So, the chastisements that have occurred are nothing other than the preludes of those that will come. How many more cities will be destroyed; how many peoples buried under the ruins; how many places buried and plunged into the abyss. The elements will take the part of their Creator. My Justice can bear no more; my Will wants to triumph, and would want to triumph by means of Love in order to establish Its Kingdom. But man does not want to come to meet this Love, therefore it is necessary to use Justice…[185]

March 1927:

So, as my love sees itself being persecuted, my justice enters the field and defends my love, striking with scourges those who persecute Me, and uncovering the pretenses they make—not only with Me, but also **among themselves as nations, because, in brawling, they reveal themselves—that instead of loving one another, they hate one another fiercely**. This century can be called the century of the most awful pretenses—and among all classes; and this is why **they never come to an agreement among themselves, and while apparently it seems that they want to agree, in reality they are plotting new wars**. Pretense has never brought true good, either in the civil order or in the religious order; at the most, a few shadows of a fleeting good. And so, here is how **they are converting that peace, so praised with words, but not with deeds, into preparations for war. As you can already see, many different races have united to fight, some with one pretext, some with another—and more will unite together.** But I will use the union of these races, because for the coming of the Kingdom of my Divine Will it is necessary to have the **union of all races by means of another war, much more extensive than the last one,** in which Italy was involved financially. Through the union of these races, the peoples will come to know one another, and after the war, the diffusion of the Kingdom of my Will will be easier. Therefore, have patience in bearing my privation—this is the void that my justice wants to form in order to defend my persecuted love. You, pray and offer everything, so that the Kingdom of my Fiat may come soon.[186]

August 1927:

All the nations are taking up arms to make war, and this irritates divine justice more, and disposes the elements to take revenge against them. Therefore, the earth will pour out fire, the air will send fountains of waters, and the wars will form fountains of human blood, in which many will disappear, and cities and regions will be destroyed. **What wickedness—after so many evils of a war they have gone through, they are preparing another one, more terrible, and they are trying to move almost the entire world, as if it were one single man.** Does this not say that sin has entered deep into their bones, to the point of transforming their very nature into sin?[187]

There is much to consider in these messages. Everybody knows the great fault that Germany bears for World War II. But too many have forgotten the fault that other nations bear. France engaged in a terribly unjust military occupation of Germany in the 1920s because Germany was incapable of paying the severe reparation payments demanded of them because of World War I. There is nothing prophetic about this point in Luisa's writings, because the particular message was given in 1923, after France had already begun the occupation. But the civil unrest and hyperinflation that this occupation and these payments caused was the reason the path was paved for Hitler to seize power in Germany. Therefore, **the prophetic reality in the 1923 message is found in Jesus' calling France's move as "ringing the first bell." This makes no sense outside of understanding it as a harbinger of a coming conflict.**

We now know, in studying the buildup to World War II, that it is perfectly accurate to say that, in the 1920s, France did indeed "ring the first bell." But we can also see that Mussolini's imperial attempts in 1922 to create a "New Roman Empire" constituted the "second bell," as Jesus told Luisa. For in "moving against Greece" by formalizing control of the Greek Dodecanese Islands and ordering the invasion of Corfu (another Greek island), Mussolini created a conflict that was elevated to the League of Nations and contributed significantly to the deterioration of conditions which lead to World War II.

---

[185] November 16, 1926.
[186] March 31, 1927.

[187] August 12, 1927.

But what about this mysterious "third bell"? Remember that Luisa received this message in 1923, long before anyone knew that Germany would suddenly explode onto the world stage and invade Poland in the following decade. That was all it took for World War II to begin: one more "bell," and only one more nation was needed to "ring" it. Clearly Germany fulfilled this role. Many other nations had parts to play, but no one denies that World War II began by Britain declaring war on Germany in 1939 in response to Germany's invasion of Poland. In prophetic analysis, this is what is called a "bullseye." It is particularly noteworthy that Jesus gave Luisa this "third bell" warning in September 1923. It was only two months later that Hitler made his first major (albeit failed) move, attempting to militarily seize power in Munich.

In His messages in 1926 and 1927, we see Jesus repeatedly lamenting how the coming clash would be so much worse than the preceding one. This, too, was no doubt scarcely tenable to the ears of those who had just endured the "Great War," World War I, which was known as "the war to end all wars." But in retrospect, we of course know that His words were thoroughly accurate. World War I resulted in about 18 million people killed. World War II resulted in over 70 million killed. Also prophetic are Jesus' words on the scope of the war: while the vast majority of the combatants of World War I were European (with several million troops from the United States), in World War II huge numbers of both troops and casualties came from Asia, Africa, and the Americas.

Globalization

In the last section, we did not address one important aspect of the messages from Jesus there quoted; namely, the whole purpose of Jesus allowing the global chaos that was World War I and II. For we know from basic theology that God only allows any evil to occur if He knows a greater good will come of it. Admittedly, we have to wait until Heaven to see the greater good in most cases, but sometimes we get glimpses of it here and now; and this is certainly the case with the World Wars. And it is clear that His plan with these corresponds to His plan in allowing the rise of the Roman Empire; for just as He orchestrated the rise of this Empire in

order to facilitate the explosion of Christianity throughout the world, so too He has allowed modern Globalization (which, although it tragically often carries with it many evils, is not in and of itself an evil—and this fact is attested to by numerous Magisterial Church teachings) in order to allow for the impending Third Fiat. Jesus told Luisa:

> As you can already see, many different races have united to fight, some with one pretext, some with another—and more will unite together. **But I will use the union of these races, because for the coming of the Kingdom of my Divine Will it is necessary to have the union of all races by means of another war, much more extensive than the last one … Through the union of these races, the peoples will come to know one another, and after the war, the diffusion of the Kingdom of my Will will be easier.**[188]

The Roman Empire reached the peak of its geographic spread and political power precisely at the time that the preaching of the Apostles was ready to explode throughout the known world; and this it was, indeed, capable of doing thanks to the infrastructure which was put in place by the Empire.

But today, we see an extent of Global infrastructure which could scarcely be the matter of dreams for those Romans of earlier days. What many forget is that this globalization would not have been possible without the unification of the races and countries, the various trade deals and treaties and the like, which resulted from the second World War, its resolution, and the aftermath of cooperation.

It is scarcely tenable that Luisa could have predicted this.

Miraculous Knowledge of Current Events

In some messages, we see not so much a prophecy as a miraculous knowledge of an event transpiring that very moment. One example is contained in the following entry:

> One morning… my dear Jesus… showed me a man who had been killed by shots from a revolver, and who was then breathing his last and going to hell… If the whole world knew how

---

[188] March 31, 1927

much Jesus suffers for the loss of souls, they would use all possible means so as not to become lost eternally …at least to spare our Lord that pain.[189]

Luisa then offered herself to accept the pains he deserved and thus save his soul, and upon receiving them, she described them as so terrible that she did not know how she remained alive. The next morning, the priest came in to her room to call her to obedience as usual, and he asked her why she was in such a sorrowful state. She wrote:

> So he asked me the reason for such a state, and I told him the fact, as I have described it above, telling him the place in town where it seemed to me that it had happened. The confessor told me that it was true, but that they thought he was dead. However, then it became known that he was very ill, but little by little he recovered, and he is still alive.[190]

While the prophetic value of the previous section cannot be doubted, since no one can deny that Luisa wrote many of those words years before the events spoken of transpired, a particularly vehement critic might accuse Luisa of simply making this up in her writings. Such a critic, however, would be forgetting that all of Luisa's writings were carefully scrutinized by many in the Church *of that time,* who would have loved to have the opportunity to denounce her, and they would have immediately pounced on this series of events if it were open to such criticism (for they could have easily simply consulted the confessor referenced in the quote above). Clearly this attempt would have been fruitless, and we must instead take the entry at its word.

Mussolini's March on Rome

In an astonishing prophecy given the very day before this historical event took place, Jesus gave the following message to Luisa (on October 27, 1922):

> Ah! my daughter, you know nothing of what they want to do. They want to gamble away Rome; the foreigners, and even the Italians, want to gamble her away. The evils they will do are such and so many, that if the earth were to unleash fire to burn her to ashes, it would be a lesser evil than what they will do. See, people pop out from all sides, to join together and storm her; and, what's more,

under the guises of lambs, while they are rapacious wolves that want to devour the prey. What diabolical unions—they band together to have more strength and storm her. Pray, pray— this is the last precipice of these times, into which the creature wants to hurl herself.

What Jesus describes here to Luisa is exactly what happened the next day when fascist troops under Benito Mussolini entered Rome. Instead of defending her, the King (Victor Emmanuel III) simply handed power over to them without conflict; thus, as Jesus said, "gambling away Rome." (Jesus of course knew that in this insurrection laid in wait demonic plans for the second World War, hence His severe lamentations in this passage.)

This was particularly lamentable, of course, because it placed the Vatican itself within a political entity being ruled by Fascists. The King did not care, not seeing Fascism as a threat to the establishment, which made him willing to enter into this unholy gamble. The essence of this account being the true one is attested to by the Encyclopedia Britannica, which states:

> [the March on Rome was the] Insurrection that brought BENITO MUSSOLINI to power in Italy. Social discontent gave Fascist Party leaders the opportunity to take control of the Italian government. Assisted by the armed squads known as BLACKSHIRTS, they planned to march on Rome and force King VICTOR EMMANUEL III to call on Mussolini to form a government. **Since the king was unwilling to use the Italian army to defend Rome, the government capitulated to the Fascists' demands.** The March on Rome turned into a parade to show the Fascist Party's support for Mussolini as the new prime minister.[191]

Now, a critic would say that this is merely Luisa's imagination working on the fact that Mussolini had threatened to take Rome on October 24th. However, it is, first of all, highly unlikely that Luisa knew of this announcement; for she never knew any news of the world except what was occasionally told to her by visitors, who were anything but zealous to keep her up to date on the current political issues. But more importantly is the fact that the message she received on the 27th of October contains much more than a mere worry about Rome being taken;

---

[189] Luisa's introduction to the First Volume
[190] Ibid

[191] *Encyclopedia Britannica.* Concise Version. 2006. Page 1639.

rather, it includes a clear lamentation about Rome being *"gambled away,"* which no one but God (and perhaps King Victor) knew would happen. Even the prime minister himself (Luigi Facta) assumed this gamble would not happen, proven by his declaration of a State of Siege[192] (to allow for Rome to be defended against the march) which the King later refused to sign. Indeed, there is no reasonable explanation of this passage other than the admission of its prophetic nature.

The "Century of Pride"

Before even two months had passed after the dawn of the 20th century, Luisa did not hesitate to assert "Ah, yes, it really seemed that this century of ours will be renowned for its pride."[193]

She said this having clearly been shown by Jesus that the century which had just begun would not be a good one. In several messages during the first two decades of this century, Jesus makes it clear to Luisa that many chastisements would occur for quite some time.

Looking back at the 20th century, this seems an obvious diagnosis to us. But in the very beginning of the 1900s, it was far from apparent that the century then in its infancy would be horrendous. In fact, the opposite was true: **it *seemed* that a period of great prosperity, peace, and progress was in motion and destined to continue.** For upon the turning of the century, the world has enjoyed its 85th consecutive year of Pax Britannica; that period of "peace"[194] between the Great Powers of the world where the unprecedented imperial influence of the British Empire gave at least apparent stability to much of the world.[195] The Congress of Vienna was still in force, and the Napoleonic Wars (which included the last major European conflicts before World War I) were becoming a memory. Without a doubt, there were still conflicts; but they paled in comparison to what had previously dominated. Amazing new technologies—especially in transportation and communication—were making life easier than it ever had been and were opening

new opportunities which had never been dreamed of. It seemed that the "public mood" had never been higher. Perhaps a truly rare expert in international affairs could have discerned something awry; one of borderline prophetic skill—but not someone like lowly Luisa. And yet, it was in her writings, in this social context, that we see the following:

> February 23rd, 1900: "The time has come, the end is approaching, but the hour is uncertain."

> June 28th, 1900: "My daughter, how many masks will be unmasked in these times of chastisements! In fact, these present chastisements are nothing but the predisposition ..."

> July 3rd, 1900: "Yet, my daughter, the chastisements I am sending are still nothing compared to those which have been prepared."

> July 14th, 1900: "My daughter, the decree of chastisements is signed; there is nothing left but to decide the time of the execution."

> July 27th, 1900: [Luisa speaking] I saw the cruel torment that continues to go on in the war of China—churches knocked down, images of Our Lord thrown to the ground... And this is nothing yet. That which frightened me the most was to see that if now this is done by barbarians, by secular people, later on it will be done by false religious who, removing their masks and letting themselves be known for who they are, uniting with the open enemies of the Church, will launch such an assault as to seem incredible to the human mind.

> July 25th, 1900: [Luisa speaking] This morning my adorable Jesus came and made me see a machine in which it seemed that many human members were being crushed, as well as something like two signs of chastisements in the air, which were terrifying.[196]

> September 30th, 1900 "Console [My Mother], for She is very afflicted because of the heavier chastisements I am about to pour upon the earth."

> October 22nd, 1900: [Luisa speaking] 'If the many chastisements about which I wrote in these books should really happen, who would have the heart

---

[192] i.e. Martial Law

[193] February 19, 1900.

[194] Please note that I am not arguing that all was well during the "Pax Britannica." I am aware that there were many conflicts and many atrocities being committed. My point is merely to consider what the commentators of the day would have claimed. How legitimate "Pax Britannica" was in reality

is not germane to the issue of demonstrating how very prophetic Luisa's revelations were.

[195] not without many tragic violations of human rights, of course

[196] Note: at this time, military technology was largely as it had been for many years. But World War I, 14 years later, saw the incredible advance of horrendous and lethal new military technologies. Luisa was likely shown one of them here.

to be spectator of them?' And the blessed Lord made me comprehend with clarity that some of them will take place while I am still on this earth, some after my death, and some will be spared in part. So I was relieved a little bit, thinking that I will not have to see them all.

Later, we see messages equally prophetic regarding the continuation of the evil nature of the century. This, too, is noteworthy, because after the end of World War I and the concomitant formation of the League of Nations (a historically unprecedented international organization, explicitly established to ensure world peace), many thought lasting peace was finally at hand. Jesus made it clear to Luisa that this was not so. For example (and we will only briefly recall two quotes here; more fulfilled prophecies regarding World War II are found in the eponymous section, above, of this same chapter):

> November 20th, 1914 (in World War I's opening months):…[Jesus] keeps telling me that the wars and the scourges which are occurring now, are still nothing, while it seems that they are too much; that other nations will go to war—and not only this, but that they will wage war against the Church, attack sacred people and kill them …

> October 16th, 1918 (Close to the end of this war): "I will renew the world with the sword, with fire and with water, with sudden deaths, and with contagious diseases. I will make new things. The nations will form a sort of tower of Babel; they will reach the point of being unable to understand one another; the peoples will revolt among themselves; they will no longer want kings. All will be humiliated, and peace will come only from Me. And if you hear them say 'peace', that will not be true, but apparent. Once I have purged everything, I will place my finger in a surprising way, and I will give the true Peace … Therefore, pray—and it takes patience, **because this will not be so soon, but it will take time**."

The looming Chastisements which would increase exponentially beyond their relatively minor level at the time was a constant theme in Jesus' messages to Luisa in the year 1900 (along with Luisa repeatedly begging Jesus to let her suffer instead of chastising the people; a request Jesus would often oblige), and the fact that they would continue was a constant theme of her post-World War I writings (Luisa stopped writing a few months before World War II began, as at that point she was no longer commanded, under holy obedience, to do so).

It was, of course, Pope Pius XII who made a similar declaration about this century (albeit less prophetic, for he spoke this in 1946), saying:

"Perhaps the greatest sin in the world today is that men have begun to lose the sense of sin."

And what pride is greater than refusing to acknowledge sin itself? That, indeed, is the pinnacle of pride. That is what defined the 20th century and, tragically, continues to define the modern world. Luisa told us this would be the case in the first months of the 20th century.

St. Hannibal di Francia's Exaltation

Let us recall that Luisa had *many* confessors, spiritual directors, and bishops with authority over her (a list of each is contained in the appendices of this book). Despite the multitude of choices that Jesus had of men whom he could exalt in His words to Luisa, it was none other than "Father Di Francia" about whom he spoke most highly. Lo-and-behold, 76 years later, Fr. Di Francia was raised to the honor of the altars and made a canonized saint. So, while we have already covered just how great of an endorsement this is—to have a canonized saint be such a zealous supporter and promoter of a private revelation—the flipside is true as well; for a private revelation to so highly exalt someone who later winds up being canonized is also prophetic in its own right and serves as its own demonstration of validity.

Jesus tells Luisa:

> And do you think that the memory of Father Di Francia, his many sacrifices and desires to make my Will known, to the point of initiating the publication, will be extinguished in this great work of my Divine Fiat, only because I brought him with Me to Heaven? No, no; on the contrary, he will have the first place, because by coming from far away, he went as though in search of the most precious thing that can exist in Heaven and on earth, of the act that glorifies Me the most, or rather, will give Me complete glory on the part of creatures, and they will receive complete goods. He prepared the ground so that my Divine Will might be known; so much so, that he spared nothing, neither expenses, nor sacrifices; and even though the publication did not have its completion, by even just initiating it he prepared the ways so that one day the work of my Will in the midst of creatures can be known and have life. Who will ever be able to destroy the fact that Father Di Francia has been the first initiator in

making known the Kingdom of my Will? — and only because his life was extinguished, the publication did not have its completion? So, when this great work becomes known, his name, his memory, will be full of glory and of splendor, and he will have his prime act in a work so great, both in Heaven and on earth.[197]

And how true it is that St. Hannibal has had the "first place," as Jesus told Luisa in 1928, among those who promote these revelations on the Divine Will. His cause for canonization began in 1945, and was officially formalized in 1979, with Pope St. John Paul II declaring his heroic virtues in 1989. As promised by Jesus, Fr. Hannibal was given the first place: no promoter of Luisa's had been honored so clearly by the Church before that point.

But Luisa even goes so far as to call Fr. Di Francis a saint! Luisa said:

> I was feeling very afflicted, not only because of the privations of my sweet Jesus, but also because I had received the unexpected news of the death of Reverend **Father Di Francia**. He was the only one left to me, to whom I could open my poor soul. **How well he could understand me — it was to a saint that I would entrust myself**, who had very much comprehended all the value of what Jesus had told me about the Divine Will. He had so much interest in it that, with insistence, he had taken all the writings with himself in order to publish them. So, I was thinking to myself: 'After Jesus allowed that he would take the writings with himself, to my great sacrifice, because I did not want it, and only **because he was a saint I had to surrender**… And now, Jesus has taken him to Heaven.'[198]

Luisa wrote those words the very day of Fr. Di Francia's death. Although in many other points in Luisa's volumes (and especially in her letters), many individual people are spoken of, I do not know of any other non-canonized person being referred to in these writings as a "saint."[199] And here — perhaps the only time she does so refer — it was indeed a reference to someone who wound up being canonized 77 years later.

In a similar vein, Luisa also had her own insight into Padre Pio's holiness. While we could not go so far as to say this is prophetic, it is nevertheless significant. As was settled in the section on the life of Luisa, we know that St. Padre Pio himself spoke highly of her. But even if one insists upon unreasonably doubting that, one cannot doubt that Luisa thought highly of Padre Pio. This speaks volumes because they both lived during the same time, and unlike ourselves who have the benefit of hindsight and his canonization, Luisa could tell on her own that he was a holy man whom one should seek out for advice, although he was seen by many as controversial and had even been censured by the Church for some time, which made many question the authenticity of his holiness. In a letter to a friend of hers who knew Padre Pio, Luisa wrote:

> Dearest son in the Divine Volition, since you are near holy Padre Pio, talk to him about our things, that he may talk about them with the Lord; and if the Lord wants, let him tell you something. Entrust me to his prayers, for I need them very much. Kiss his hands for me…

The Law of Divorce (Hague Convention of 1902)

In a series of messages which span the entirety of the year 1902, Jesus repeatedly laments to Luisa about a "law of divorce" that was being promoted at the time. I know of no other specific political-cultural issue that Jesus is more displeased with in Luisa's writings than this one.

And this degree of focus is prophetic (even aside from the specifics which will presently be discussed), for it is difficult to think of a single thing (except perhaps abortion) that has wrought more havoc upon society than divorce. This tragedy of divorce has become such a diabolical epidemic that, as of this writing (in the United States, at least), a horrendous threshold has just been crossed: most children are growing up today without a married mother and father. And now, divorce is even making its way into the Church, with many priests, theologians, bishops, and even cardinals openly advocating for a heretical interpretation of *Amoris Laetitia* that essentially allows for divorce.

In hindsight, we can easily see the Divine Wisdom in Jesus directing so much focus on this issue in 1902; but at that time, it would have no doubt

---

[197] February 28, 1928.
[198] June 1, 1927 (Note that Luisa is here referring to "not wanting" her writings to be published; recall that, such was her humility, that she only wrote at all because she was commanded to, and she wanted no fame or recognition whatsoever.)
[199] Please note, however, I could certainly be forgetting instances of this happening.

seemed strange as divorce was extremely rare, and spoken of or advocated for as equally rarely. Let us now turn to look at some excerpts from some messages where Jesus speaks to Luisa about the issue.

January 11th, 1902:

He transported me outside of myself, and I found myself in the midst of many people who were saying: "If this law is confirmed, poor woman, everything will turn out bad for her." All were anxiously waiting to hear the pros and the cons, and in another separate place many people could be seen who were discussing among themselves. One of them took the floor and reduced everyone to silence; then, after much struggling, he went out the door and said: "Yes indeed, in favor of the woman." On hearing this, all those who were outside made feast, and those who were inside remained all confounded, so much so, that they did not have the courage even to go out. I believe that it is the law of divorce that they are talking about, and I understood that they did not confirm it.

January 12th, 1902:

My daughter, see now where the blindness of men has reached—to the point of wanting to make laws which are iniquitous and go against themselves and their own social welfare. My daughter, this is why I am calling you to sufferings again—so that, as you offer yourself with Me to Divine Justice, those who must fight this law of divorce may obtain light and efficacious grace in order to be victorious. **My daughter, I tolerate that they make wars and revolutions, and that the blood of the new martyrs inundate the world—this is an honor for Me and for my Church; but this brutal law is an affront to my Church, and it is abominable and intolerable to Me."** Now, while He was saying this, I saw a man who was fighting against this law—tired and exhausted in his strengths, in act of wanting to withdraw from the enterprise. So, together with the Lord, we encouraged Him, and he answered: "I see myself fighting almost alone, and unable to obtain the intent." And I said to him: 'Courage, for contradictions are as many pearls which the Lord will use to adorn you in Heaven.' And he took heart and continued the enterprise. After this, I saw someone else, all weary and worried, not knowing what to decide, and someone saying to him: "Do you know what you should do? Quit—get out of Rome." And he: "No, I cannot, this is the word given to my father; I will lay down my life, but as for quitting—

never".

February 3rd, 1902:

I, seeing the evils of society raging more, said to Him: 'My sweet Good, tell me, what will happen with this divorce that they talk about? Will they come to make this evil law, or not? ... I offer You my life to suffer any pain in order to obtain that they do not come to this. And so that my offering may not be rejected in any way, I unite it to your sacrifice in order to obtain the deed of grace with certainty.' While I was saying this, it seemed that the Lord was using my offering to present it to Divine Justice ... It seems that, at any cost, men want to confirm at least a few articles of this law, since they are unable to confirm it completely as they want and please.

February 9th, 1902:

[Luisa speaking:] I want You to operate a prodigy with your omnipotence—that the will of creatures be chained so that they may not be able to confirm this law [of divorce].' The Lord seemed to accept my proposal, telling me: " ... You want Me to operate a prodigy so that this divorce may not be confirmed, otherwise this may not happen. Well then, for love of you, I will make this prodigy, and this will be the most refulgent star that will shine on your crown—that is, having prevented my Justice, through your sufferings, after the so many wicked deeds they commit, from permitting also this evil in these sad times, which they themselves have wanted…"

February 24th, 1902:

My daughter, there are certain offenses which surpass by far the very offenses I suffered in my Passion. ..'Lord, what about this law of divorce that they talk about—is it certain that they will not confirm it?' And He: **"For now it is certain. As for five, ten or twenty years from now, if I suspend your state of victim or call you to Heaven, they may be able to do it; but the prodigy of chaining their will and of confounding them I have done for now**. If you knew the rage of the demons and of those who wanted this law, who were certain to obtain it—it is so great, that if they could, they would destroy any authority and would make a slaughter everywhere. So, in order to mitigate this rage and to prevent these slaughters in part, do you want to expose yourself to their fury a little bit?" And I: 'Yes, as long as You come with me.' So we went to a place in which there were demons and people who seemed to be furious, enraged, mad. As soon as they saw me, they ran over me like many wolfs, and some would beat me, some would tear my flesh; they would have wanted to destroy me, but did not have the power to do it. As for me, however, though I suffered very much, I did not fear them, because I had Jesus with me.

December 8th, 1902:

… I saw a priest clothed in white together with Our Lord; it seemed to me that he was the Pope, and the confessor was with him. They were praying Him to make me suffer so as to prevent the formation of this law of divorce, but Jesus would not pay attention to them. So, the confessor, heedless of the fact that he was not being given audience, with extraordinary impetus, such that it seemed it was not him, took Jesus Christ in his arms and, by force, cast Him inside of me, saying: "You will remain crucified within her, crucifying her, but this law of divorce we do not want." Jesus remained as though bound inside of me, crucified by such command, and I felt, bitterly, the pains of the cross. Then He said: "Daughter, it is the Church that wants it, and her authority, united to the power of prayer, binds Me."

From December 18th, 1902:

My daughter, come again to suffer with Me in order to conquer the obstinacy of those who want divorce. Let us try once more. You will always be ready to suffer what I want, won't you? Do you give Me your consent?" And I: 'Yes, Lord, do whatever You want.' As soon as I said yes, blessed Jesus laid Himself within me as crucified, and since my nature was smaller than His, He stretched me so much as to make me reach His very person. Then He poured — very little, yes, but so very bitter and full of sufferings, that not only did I feel the nails at the places of the crucifixion, but I felt my whole body as transfixed by many nails, in such a way that I felt all of myself being crushed. He left me in that position for a little while, and I found myself in the midst of demons who, on seeing me suffer like that, said: "*In the end this damn one is going to win again, so that we don't make the law of divorce. Curse your existence — you try to harm us and to disperse our businesses by ruining our many toils, rendering them vain. But we'll make you pay for this — we will move bishops, priests and people against you, so that next time we'll make you drop this whim of accepting sufferings*" …

In this profound series of messages, a few key points arise: First, that there was a group of people trying to pass a law permitting divorce; second, that Luisa interceded with Jesus, accepting tremendous sufferings, and prevented their success; third, that this success would (or, as Luisa was then told, might) be only temporary (i.e. no longer in effect after Jesus suspended Luisa's state of victim or called her to Heaven).

Now this is, in fact, exactly what happened. In 1902, the Hague Divorce Convention was held. (Officially, it was the "Convention on the Recognition of Divorces and Legal Separations." Note that The Hague is the city seat of government of the Netherlands and has long been recognized to be the de facto place of international deliberations. International Law conventions began there in 1893, and since then many more have been held.)

If this convention was successful in its original intent to legalize divorce, it would have proven of immense historical importance. Thanks to Luisa's intercession, however, it is now nothing but a small footnote in history books. Although the prophetic nature of Jesus' words to Luisa here is rather clear from a broad view of history, the foreknowledge becomes especially obvious upon examining the February 24, 1902 message, **wherein Jesus assured Luisa it was certain that, for now, the law of divorce would *not* pass. But the agreed articles of the Convention, in which it was made clear that indeed divorce was not being legalized, were not signed until June 12, 1902 (almost four months later).** And there was no way for anyone to know, before that point, what the outcome would be.

But the demons made good on their blasphemous rant (italicized in the last quote above). The full legalization of divorce and its concomitant entrance into the mainstream, though delayed for decades, has nevertheless now come to fruition. It is unlikely that a nuclear war would have wreaked the level of havoc on society that divorce has managed to cause.

Particularly noteworthy is Jesus' insistence to Luisa that this is a diabolical affront to His Church (the Catholic Church), which, since the beginning of the Protestant Reformation, has always distinguished itself as the bulwark against divorce; and Western Society largely followed suit by making it extremely difficult if not downright outlawing it.

The Smithsonian Magazine gives some worthwhile insights into the evolution of divorce:

Multiple studies have shown that women bear the brunt of the social and economic burdens that come with divorce. The quickest route to poverty is to become a single mother. This is awful enough, but what I find so galling is that the right to divorce was meant to be a cornerstone of liberty for women. ... The most celebrated divorce case in history remains that of Henry VIII versus Pope Clement VII. The battle began in 1527, when Henry tried to force the pope into annulling his marriage to Catherine of Aragon, who had failed to provide him with a male heir. Determined to make the younger and prettier Anne Boleyn his wife, Henry finally broke with Rome in 1533 and declared himself the head of a new church, the Church of England ... Henry's marriage to Anne led to precisely one divorce—in 1552. The term was not even used again until 1670. ... When a divorce law was finally enacted in 1857, and the "floodgates" were opened, the number of divorces in English history stood at a mere 324.Only four of the 324 cases were brought by women.[200]

As we can see here, despite the importance of divorce in the formation of Protestantism, it was nevertheless scarcely a phenomenon in Europe before the 1900s. Legalizing it and promulgating it were among the devil's top priorities, and this newly formed Hague conference on International Law was his perfect opportunity. Not only did he fail in his intent at that time, but he continued to fail for decades—as it was not until the 1970s (after Luisa was taken to Heaven—i.e., no longer a victim soul) that divorce became commonly legalized and practiced throughout the western world.

Earthquakes

On April 17th, 1906, Luisa was shown great chastisements; specifically, **earthquakes in three different cities. We read:**

> This morning I had a bad time; I was outside of myself and I could see nothing but fire. It seemed that the earth would open and threaten to swallow cities, mountains and men. It seemed that the Lord would want to destroy the earth, but in a special way three different places, distant from one another, and some of them also in Italy. They seemed to be three mouths of volcanoes—some were sending out fire which flooded the cities, and in some places the earth was opening and horrible quakes would occur. I could not understand very well whether these things were happening or will have to happen. How many ruins! Yet, the cause of this is only sin, and man

does not want to surrender; it seems that man has placed himself against God, and God will arm the elements against man—water, fire, wind and many other things, which will cause many upon many to die.[201]

The very next day, the great san Francisco earthquake struck. According to the USGS, this "ranks as one of the most significant earthquakes of all time," and it remains the deadliest earthquake in American history. 3,000 people were killed and 80% of the city of San Francisco was destroyed.

Four months later, the 1906 Valparaíso Earthquake occurred in Chile which killed even more people than the San Francisco quake.

Two years later, the great 1908 Messina Earthquake wreaked havoc in Sicily (Italy). It remains the worst and deadliest earthquake in European history. At least 80,000 people were killed (and perhaps up to 200,000), and the city of Messina (as well as Reggio Calabria) was destroyed. Luisa was also shown this earthquake the morning before it happened. Below is the entirety of the entry from the morning of the earthquake (note that Corato is about 200 miles from Messina, and reports indicate that the tremors were felt even 300 miles away):

> Finding myself in my usual state, I felt as if the earth were shaking and wanted to slip away from beneath us. I was concerned, and I said to myself: 'Lord, Lord, what is this?' And He, in my interior: "Earthquakes." And He kept silent.

> I almost paid no attention to Him, and within myself I continued my usual interior things when, all of a sudden, about five hours after that word had been spoken to me, I felt the earthquake sensibly. As soon as I felt it cease, I found myself outside of myself. Almost confused, I could see harrowing things, but this sight was immediately removed from me, and I found myself inside a church. A young man clothed in white came from the altar—I believe He was Our Lord, but I cannot tell with certainty—and drawing near me, with an imposing look He told me: "Come".

> I shrugged my shoulders, without getting up, and calculating within me that at that hour He was scourging and destroying, I said: 'Lord, You want to take me now?!', almost refusing His invitation. And the young man threw Himself into my arms, and in my interior I heard Him say: "Come, o

---

[200]"The Heartbreaking Story of Divorce." Smithsonian Magazine. February 2014.
[201] April 17, 1906.

daughter, that I may end it with the world; I will destroy a great part of it, with earthquakes, with waters and with wars."[202]

Luisa received her messages from Jesus in the middle of the night, between midnight and 1am, whereas this earthquake struck at 5:20am. Furthermore, the priest would come in to say Mass in her room early in the morning; it is not tenable that she scribbled down this passage (she was a slow writer) in the short time between her feeling the earthquake and the priest coming to say Mass. Besides, as is made clear, the extreme extent of this earthquake is evident in the tone of this message, whereas Luisa would have had no earthly means of grasping any hint of its extent for many hours, if not days, after its occurrence.[203] For all she would have physically felt 200 miles away were relatively faint trembles which, for all she knew, could have just been a small (but nearby) earthquake.

Socialism and The Italian People's Party

My daughter, **the socialists have plotted among themselves to strike the Church**. This they have done publicly in France, and in Italy in a more hidden way; and my Justice is looking for voids so as to lay hand to chastisements.[204]

While shrewd observers today are well aware of the evil motives lurking behind socialism and its dark history, this degree of understanding was rare in 1903, when Jesus spoke these words to Luisa. At that point, the Italian Socialist Party was only 11 years old, and it would be prophetic on its own right for one to recognize, at that time in its relative infancy, that its plan was to strike the Church.

Furthermore, it will soon become clear that, sadly, this particular nefarious plot by the socialists, which Jesus informed Luisa about in this message, was indeed eventually victorious. But, as with many tragedies, it began long ago with noble intentions.

Formed by the Servant of God Fr. Luigi Sturzo, the Italian *People's* Party was inspired by the teachings of Pope Leo XIII's famous encyclical, *Rerum Novarum*, and sought to put it into concrete political action. Unfortunately, and although noble in intention, the Italian People's Party only paved the way for many in it to turn to support the Socialist Fascism[205] of Mussolini and thus contribute to the persecution of the Church.

> In fact, if the party did not exist, the element against which one would want to fight would be missing. But how many from this party, which in appearance is said to be catholic, are true wolves covered with the mantle of lambs, and will give many sorrows to my Church. Many believe that with this party religion will be defended; but it will be the complete opposite, and the enemies will use it to rail more against Her.[206]

Now, it is more than safe to say that Fr. Luigi Sturzo, who we recall is now a Servant of God, and who was leader of the party for some time, is definitely not among those Jesus is referring to as wolves in sheep's clothing. In fact, the external "absurdity" of such a statement merely proves the prophetic value of the same, for no reasonable Catholic commentator at the time would have spoken in the manner Jesus here does about this party. And yet, history's development proved the words of Jesus correct. The demise of the party—essentially a direct action of the Vatican—came a mere two years after Jesus said these words to Luisa. In its entry on Fr. Luigi, the *New Catholic Encyclopedia* shares some details about the Italian People's Party:

> By 1919 [Fr Sturzo] was in the national limelight as the moving spirit behind the Partito Popolare, forerunner of the Christian Democratic party. This was his master stroke in politics, for it gave Italy a democratic mass party of Catholic orientation. Moreover, by refusing to make religion a divisive factor in politics, the Popular Party paved the way for a normal development of political life between the extremes of clericalism and anticlericalism. **Unfortunately, fascism proved too strong for it, for reasons which Sturzo treats in Italy and Fascism (New York 1927). Historians, awaiting archival evidence, attribute Sturzo's resignation from party**

---

[202] December 28, 1908.
[203] Modern readers should be reminded that Luisa did not spend her nights sitting up in bed on her iPhone, looking through real-time pictures of events being posted on Twitter.
[204] April 7, 1903.
[205] The juxtaposition of these terms is not accidental; Mussolini's "conversion" from socialism to fascism was

superficial, and "Mussolini the fascist" still maintained what was worst about "Mussolini the socialist." Recall that Mussolini only "declared war" on socialism inasmuch as it was opposed to nationalism.
[206] September 21, 1921.

leadership in 1923 to pressure from the Vatican. By 1926, when the party was dissolved by royal decree, Sturzo had been living in exile for two years. His prodigious effort to liberate democratic forces among the Catholics of Italy seemed to have come to nought, but he had laid the groundwork for the eventual triumph of Christian Democracy.

Also two years later, in a passage of similar contents in Luisa's diary, we read:

This morning my always lovable Jesus transported me outside of myself, to a place in which one could see flags being waved, and parades in which all classes of people were participating, including priests. And Jesus, as though offended by all this, wanted to clutch the creatures in His hand in order to crush them; and I, taking His hand in mine, clasped Him to myself, saying to Him: 'My Jesus, what are You doing? After all, they don't seem to be doing evil things, but rather, good things. It seems that the Church is uniting with your enemies of before, and these no longer show that aversion to dealing with people from the Church; on the contrary, they call them to bless the flags. Is this not a good sign? And You, instead of being pleased with it, seem to get offended.' And Jesus, sighing and highly afflicted, told me: "My daughter, how you deceive yourself. This is the blackest point of the present society, and their union means that they all have one color. **The enemies are no longer afraid and horrified to approach people from the Church, because since the true fount of virtue and of religion is not in them—on the contrary, some of them celebrate the Divine Sacrifice without believing in my existence; for others, if they believe at all, it is a faith without works,** and their life is a chain of enormous sacrileges— so, what good can they do if they don't have it within themselves? How can they call others to a conduct of a true Christian by making known what great evil sin is, if the life of grace is missing in them? **With all the unions that they form, there are no more men who fulfill the precept, therefore it is not the union of the triumph of religion—it is the triumph of their party; and masking themselves with it, they try to cover the evil they are plotting.** It is true revolution that is hidden under these masks, and I remain always the God offended, both by the evil, who pretend a shade of piety in order to strengthen their party and therefore do graver evil, and by people from the Church, who, having a false piety themselves, are no longer good for drawing the peoples to follow Me; on the contrary, it is the peoples that carry them away. Can there be a time sadder than this? Pretense is the ugliest sin, and the one that most wounds my Heart. Therefore, pray and repair."[207]

As of this writing, the Italian People's Party has undergone many transformations and successions, but today (as it ultimately has morphed into the Democratic Party of Italy) is nothing but another force for the socialist destruction of society. Thus Jesus' words to Luisa are again proven prophetic.

***

Before leaving aside this "prophecies fulfilled" section, I wish to remind my readers of what was said in this book's introductory notes: I am just one lowly follower of Luisa's, and I by no means consider myself an expert. What I have presented here is little more than those fulfilled prophecies which I happen to recall from my own reading of her writings. I am sure that many more exist in her volumes, and I encourage you to discover them for yourself!

10) <u>The Gift Itself</u>

If you have read the preceding chapters, then at this point it has become clear that the revelations Jesus gave to Luisa are as authentic and valid as they come, and truly call for a wholehearted response. So what is this unprecedented, enormous, astounding "Gift" of which they speak?

<u>What It Is</u>

Now that, at long last, I am ready to tell you openly and without veil just what this Gift is, I must ensure I do so very carefully, just as I would only with the greatest caution hand to another person a spectacular and most precious diamond.

And so, we ask: **what exactly *is* this Gift?**

The *Gift of Living in the Divine Will* is the best and broadest name for this new sanctity, this "New and Divine Holiness" spoken of by Pope St. John Paul II. But it has many other names. Among them are: *the continuous participation in the Trinity's one eternal*

---

[207] April 21, 1923.

operation; the *full actualization of the soul's powers*; the sharing in God's prime motion; the *Divine and Eternal Mode of holiness*; *the greatest sanctity*; and *the Real Life of Jesus in the soul.*

But what exactly does this mean? What *is* the gift? I shall answer this question by posing three questions, followed by an explanation of the proper responses to them in light of the Gift of Living in the Divine Will. I encourage you to pause after reading each question and ponder how to truly answer it in the best, most complete, possible way.

First: What four humans are unlike all others? I do not mean merely by matter of degree; e.g. who is mentioned most in Scripture, or who was the wisest Doctor, or greatest Father, or noblest Patriarch. What I mean is, what four people were so radically above all others that it is impossible to compare them to anyone else, just as it is impossible to compare a grain of sand to a mountain? There is only one way to answer such a question: Adam, Eve, Jesus, and Mary. It is these four and these four alone who were created[208] in perfection, with sin playing no part whatsoever in them; their lives were products of the Divine Will as daylight is a product of the sun.[209] There was not the slightest impediment between the Will of God and their being, and therefore, their acts, which proceed from being. The Gift of Living in the Divine Will then, open for the asking since Luisa's time to any soul in a state of grace, is that same state of sanctity as that which these four possessed (albeit with important distinctions).

Now, the Blessed Virgin Mary is truly the quintessence of Living in the Divine Will and our model for it. Her dignity far surpasses that of Adam and Eve, and, furthermore, she remains a creature unlike her Divine Son. Through Our Lady, God demonstrates just what marvels of sanctity He is capable of working in a created human being. In Luisa's revelations we learn that it is not God's Will that *only* Mary remain in such a lofty state of sanctity, merely for us to gaze upon from a nearly infinitely inferior position. On the contrary, it is His

Will that we, too, rise up to her level, so that it can even be said of us, as it has long been rightly said of her, that *one of our acts can give God more glory and surpass in merit all the acts of all other saints combined.*[210]

It is important to note that no creature can ever come close to Mary in love and in sacrifice, nor can any other creature possibly receive the singular privileges that God has bestowed upon her—privileges which raise her up to a height of truly inaccessible glory—especially the privilege of being the Sovereign Queen of all Creation, and above all, the Mother of God. For all eternity these attributes shall be hers and hers alone, and all creatures without exception will bow down before her. Nevertheless, through the Gift of Living in the Divine Will, our sanctity becomes like her own and glorifies God in a similar way; this is what Jesus is inviting us to in Luisa's revelations—not that we become the same as Our Lady or surpass her in any way (for what a blasphemy it would be to even think this!).

***

Second: what is the greatest thing that has ever happened? Such a broad and fundamental question will likely confound any Christian, for there is no shortage of great things from which to choose! But in reality, the answer is simple and there is no close second: The Incarnation. In the Incarnation, the infinite entered into the finite and in so doing exalted it to the Divine Realm. The Catechism of the Catholic Church states (quoting Athanasius and Aquinas, respectively):

> 'For the Son of God became man so that we might become God.' [and] 'The only-begotten Son of God, wanting to make us sharers in his divinity, assumed our nature, so that he, made man, might make men gods.'[211]

And indescribably great as the Incarnation was:

> The Father of Mercies willed that the Incarnation should be preceded by assent on the part of the predestined mother ... [212]

---

[208]Here I refer only to the created human nature/human soul of Christ (as opposed to His Personhood and His Divine Nature). The Person, Jesus Christ, is of course none other than the 2nd Person of the Trinity, and is uncreated.

[209]This perfection of course radically changed for Adam and Eve at the Fall

[210] *Cf.* St. Louis de Montfort: *True Devotion to Mary* (Bay Shore, NY: Montfort Publications, 2006), paragraph 63.

[211] *Catechism of the Catholic Church* 460, quoting St. Athanasius and St. Thomas Aquinas.

[212] *Ibid.*, 488, cf. *Lumen Gentium,* Ch. VIII, Section 2, paragraph 56.

By pronouncing her 'fiat' at the Annunciation and giving her consent to the Incarnation, Mary was already collaborating with the whole work her Son was to accomplish.[213]

How simple! These clear teachings from the Catechism of the Catholic Church set both the framework and the foundation for understanding Mary's Fiat in view of the Gift of Living in the Divine Will. And the understanding is this: God does not want only one "Fiat" in history to be so great and so pleasing to Him; rather, He wants all the acts of His creatures to be reflections of that perfect and quintessential Fiat of His beloved handmaid, so that, as her "Fiat" preceded the very Incarnation itself, so our "Fiats" may, as it were, cause as many incarnations as acts we undertake. If ordinary virtuous acts build up treasures of mansions and mountains in Heaven, then these acts *in the Divine Will* build up treasures of cities and continents.

But even that is not enough. Now that God has willed to bestow this Gift upon whoever desires it, He also calls us to spiritually "re-do" all the acts of creation—past, present, and future—*in the Divine Will*, to be as they would have been were the Fall to never have happened, and as He Himself did throughout His earthly life. For whatever He does as the Head, so must we follow as His body. Jesus says to Luisa,

> There is nothing—no love, greatness or power— that can compare to My conception … the immensity of My Will, enclosing all souls of the past, present and future, conceived … the lives of all souls. And as My life developed, so did all lives develop within Me.[214]

The point is not to pretend that we can change the past; objective acts of the past cannot be changed[215] for "*that which has happened*" to become "*that which has not happened*" is simply a contradiction, like a four-sided triangle.[216] However, what God is in fact calling us to do with this Gift is to repair the relation between the acts of the past and eternity, to ensure that the present has the proper relation to

eternity, and to prepare the future to have the proper relation to eternity, mystically taking it into ourselves. We do this by the intention with which we undertake all the ordinary acts which form our days. In this way, Living in the Divine Will can be seen as the full realization of the Little Way of St. Thérèse of Lisieux. We also re-do the acts of creation through special prayers given to Luisa; namely, the "Rounds of Creation" and the "Hours of the Passion," both of which will be discussed later.

***

Third: How must *"Thy will be done on earth as it is in Heaven"* be fulfilled, if it is to be fulfilled in total? For Jesus Himself prayed this prayer, and it is impossible that supplication of the Son of God not be granted. Many unfortunately assume this third petition given by Our Lord in the prayer He taught us (and which we recite at the holiest part of every Mass) merely describes an ideal at which human history should aim, as opposed to offering a request that can actually be answered. This understanding, however, doubts the power and mercy of God, Who, according to Luisa's revelations, will in fact ensure that (within the realm of time) His Will shall reign on earth as it does in Heaven. This reign is referred to as the "Third Fiat" of Sanctification (third to Creation and Redemption). It is not a subtle rewording of a modified millenarian or Joachimist heresy[217] which supposes a coming new Public Revelation, or a passing of the Age of the Church, or even a literal reign of the physical Jesus Christ on earth before His final coming. Rather, this coming age of which Jesus speaks to Luisa entails a time when, instead of this Gift only being enjoyed by a few people, it is lived universally; and just as the consequences of sin are seen in the devastation of the physical world, so, too, will be seen in the physical world the consequences of this greatest grace being lived by all. This Reign of the Divine Will on earth is the best and fullest understanding of what is also referred to in other mystical revelations as the "Triumph of

---

[213] *Catechism of the Catholic Church*, paragraph 973.
[214] Rev Joseph Iannuzzi, Doctoral Thesis. , 3.1.1.
[215] *Cf.* St. Thomas Aquinas, *Sum* I, Q25, A4
[216] This is an important point. The Christian Creed rests upon and requires the certainty of historical events having occurred in the past; e.g. The Incarnation. To entertain the possibility that the past can change is to have this certainty vanish, and thereby render the contents of our Faith merely contingent

upon no one ever acquiring the power to change the past and choosing to use this power. (Take care to note that contingent "faith" is not true Faith.)
[217] These concerns are addressed in detail in the "Era of Peace" chapter of this book

the Immaculate Heart of Mary,"[218] the "Glorious Eucharistic Reign of Peace," or the "Era of Peace." Luisa's revelations give no dates, but they do indicate that this prophesied time is to come soon. Just how soon largely depends upon our response.

The purpose of the times we are now living in is to enable certain souls to receive this Gift as individuals in preparation for the time when the entire world will receive it. Consider the decades of wonder and anticipation which preceded the Fiat of Redemption that was fully consummated at the Last Supper;[219] when word spread slowly but surely regarding the amazing things taking place, when:

> …fear came on all their neighbors. And all these things were talked about through all the hill country of Judea; and all who heard them laid them up in their hearts, saying, 'What then will this child be?' For the hand of the Lord was with him.[220]

When Simeon and Anna prophesied in the temple, when Herod knew the Savior was upon us and instituted a massacre in his demonically inspired, vain attempt to subvert the Will of God (is that not what is happening today with abortion?), and when unprecedented and unfathomable wisdom poured forth from the mouth of a 12-year-old boy in the Temple, and all were amazed. Those days are analogous to current times.

The total fulfillment of this Third Petition of the Our Father consists in this: living the very life of the Blessed in Heaven as far as holiness is concerned, while still retaining that which is intrinsic to life on earth—the absence of the Beatific Vision, the continued presence of the Veil, the ability to suffer, the need for the supernatural virtues of Faith and Hope, etc.[221]

Jesus told Luisa:

> My daughter, the first Fiat was pronounced in creation with no intervention of a human creature. The second Fiat was pronounced in Redemption […] Now, for the fulfillment of both, I want to pronounce the third Fiat […] This third Fiat will bring to completion the glory and the honor of the Fiat of Creation, and will be the confirmation and development of all the fruits of the Fiat of Redemption. These three Fiats will be the Most Holy Trinity's overshadowing of man on earth, and I will obtain My Fiat Voluntas Tua on earth as it is in heaven. These three Fiats will be inseparable, with each one constituting the life of the other.[222]

Dr. Thomas Petrisko elaborates on this, saying:

> Since Christ's ascension, the mystical body of Christ has prayed for the coming of the Kingdom of the Father, "on earth as it is in heaven." However, over the centuries some of the meaning of this divine petition to the First person of the most Holy Trinity has become somewhat removed. Contemporary theologians note that Christians say the words of the Our Father without ever contemplating what they are asking for. Likewise, few think about God's Kingdom truly coming to exist in some greater form on earth. But since the 19th century, the chosen ones of God, His prophets and visionaries, have said that there is greater meaning in this prayer than we may think and that we need to reexamine it more clearly to understand God's plans. At Fatima, Mary promised that God would bring a new era into the world. It is to be an era that honors God and gives Him the Glory He deserves. Mary says it is to be an era of peace. Most of all, experts who have studied Mary's words say it is to be an era that will more closely resemble the Father's "Kingdom on earth" than any time since the beginning—one that fulfills to a greater degree the words of the Our Father prayer—and one that finally brings to fulfillment an old prophecy, long held to be found in Judeo-Christian Scripture and Tradition…
>
> Church historians tell us that the Judeo-Christian faith functionally begins in prophecy and history. The Fathers of the Church understood that Christianity and its root, Judaism, were radically different from other religions. Prior to Judaism, religions of the world were without historical perspective. But beginning with Abraham, promises of future events were prophesied and then fulfilled in history. From Sarai's conception to the coming of Moses, the liberator, God shared His foreknowledge of the future with His chosen

---

218 Third Apparition at Fatima, July 13th, 1917. "In the end, my Immaculate Heart will triumph … "

219 Cf. St. Faustina, *Divine Mercy in my Soul*, Paragraph 684. *"At the moment of Consecration, love rested satiated — the sacrifice fully consummated. Now only the external ceremony of death will be carried out — external destruction; the essence [of it] is in the Cenacle."*

220 Luke 1:65-66

221 *Cf.* 1 Corinthians 13:12

222 Rev Joseph Iannuzzi, Doctoral Thesis. , 4.1.

people, and then proved His words were true through the unfolding of events. With the coming of the prophesied Messiah, the continuation of religion based on the hope found in fulfilled prophecy is seen again and becomes the foundation of the world's largest religion. Christianity, like Judaism, took on the form of a historic religion, as one prophesied event after another was fulfilled … [223]

If, at this point, you find yourself worried about the orthodoxy of such massive claims, I fully understand. Feel free to skip to the "Answers to Objections" chapter of this book. For now, it shall suffice to say that these assertions regarding the Divine Will can indeed be found elsewhere in good solid, orthodox Catholic spirituality, and for the next chapter we will turn our attention to examining these other sources and consider where else it has been spoken of a similar way. In so doing, we will be able to see clearly that Jesus' choice to reveal this Gift to Luisa was not some sudden proclamation of a message in an unprepared environment—like a foolish boy proposing to a girl he just met, but rather, was something perfectly called for and prepared for in how the Holy Spirit had long been guiding the Church.

Against the Most Perverse Inclination of Fallen Human Psychology

We must now address what might be the most perverse inclination of our fallen human psychology, for it is one which often rears its head when people learn of this great degree of holiness attainable with the relative ease of Living in the Divine Will. **And the inclination is this: horror at the mere suggestion that there is a better way. Hatred of good news.**

This perversion is seen everywhere, and it is in some ways related to the economic fallacy of the sunk cost, wherein one erroneously supposes that an expense already incurred should prevent financially shrewd decisions moving forward, which entail recognizing that incurring this expense was ill-advised.[224] More generally, the thought process that goes along with this perversion usually runs something like this:

> Oh, no. That can't be. I've been doing it another way for so long now; and this other way I've been doing it is much harder than this new way I am now learning about, and my old way takes much longer. If this new way is valid, then I'm going to feel so horrible about the fact that I've been doing it another way for so long… I hate feeling horrible, so I'm going to assume this new way cannot be valid, in order that I may remain feeling good about myself and how I've been hitherto going about things.

It is my hope that just this presentation of the inclination suffices in exposing its nature and revealing its absurdity. Now, I confess I've fallen into this perversion myself; even in trivial matters. I recall driving a certain route for some time in my commute to work, only for it to dawn on me one day, after years, that perhaps there was a better way. Foolishly, I allowed this realization to cause in me regret instead of excitement! For I succumbed to the usual human perversity of lamenting the past instead of and in contradiction to being open to the future. For indeed, the primary fallacy in **the Hatred of Good News Perversion** is that it concerns itself with the past instead of the present. Luddites respond in accord with this perversion to new technologies for no other reason than they want everyone to suffer from what they suffered from. And one often hears "experienced" members of religious orders likewise despising any loosening of any rules for the same reason.

It is precisely because of this perversion that many oppose the Little Way of St. Thérèse. Believe it or not, this great Doctor of the Church is still murmured against in many schools of thought in the Catholic theological world, seeing her Little Way as a mark on the ascetical tradition of Catholic spirituality.

And it is also precisely because of this perversion that many oppose the Divine Will revelations given to Luisa. They should be "overcome with joy," as we pray in the Mass, at being offered so great an invitation (an invitation which in no way

---

[223] Dr. Thomas Petrisko. *The Kingdom of Our Father*. P. 32.
[224] For example, consider the case of one who foolishly bought a fancy sports car only to have its engine fail months later. Still paying a large sum each month for the loan, the purchaser supposes *"Well, I simply must pay $7,000 to replace this engine; I am, after all, still paying off this car."* But this reasoning is ludicrous; whether one is still paying off the car has nothing to do with what, in moving forward, is the wise decision — which is to get rid of the obscene luxury of a sports car by selling it for whatever it can obtain without a working engine, and proceeding to buy a more humble vehicle, even though the sports car still must be paid off.

contradicts anything in Catholic Sacred Tradition, but rather serves as a beautiful crown for the same, as will become evident in the next section). Instead, they are overcome with anger that God dare to offer so great a Gift; supposing, illogically, that it somehow constitutes an affront to the saints of earlier ages, much like the laborers in the vineyard rebelled against the owner for generously rewarding the other laborers who arrived close to the end of the day (Cf. Matthew 20).

I will not spend much more time in these pages addressing this perversion. Those who cling to it need prayer more than argumentation. But we also must zealously adhere to the extreme importance of always staying close to our Catholic Tradition, and never accepting anything in contradiction to it, or which amounts to an artificial, inorganic development of it. So considering the Gift in more detail, we should now turn to examine the foreshadowing of this Gift throughout history—both Salvation History and Church History—so we can see clearly that it truly is the Crown of what God has given us thus far.

11) The Gift Foreshadowed

"Surely the Lord God does nothing, without revealing his secret to his servants the prophets."—Amos 3:7

The Gift of Living in the Divine Will did not pop into existence in a spiritual vacuum within the development of Catholic Tradition. On the contrary, one can see how perfectly it fits, and how this moment of Church History was the long awaited for time for God to reveal it. It is indeed the Crown and Completion of all Sanctity, and one can easily see, building over the centuries like the crescendo of a classical masterpiece, the preparations for this Coronation of All Creation.

But Jesus does certainly tell Luisa that He has chosen *her* as the one to whom this Gift has its first full revelation. For example, He once said to her, *"Go through as many books as you want, and you will see that in none of them will you find what I have told you about my Will."*[225] At the age of 24, in the year 1889, Luisa received the Gift for the first time and, ten years later, was commanded under holy obedience to write down the revelations she received from Jesus. Therefore, it would not be consistent for anyone to hold Luisa's revelations as true on the one hand, and, on the other, believe that this Gift had been either fully received or had the essence of it fully revealed before that point. [226]

Therefore, what is being proposed here is not that the Gift Itself in all its fullness and substance was already clearly revealed in Scripture, or in the Church Fathers, or in Sacred Tradition; only that it was alluded to and that the way was prepared. Another example of this distinction can be seen in the case of the Dogma of the Holy Trinity: nowhere was it explicitly taught in the Old Testament. The Catechism makes this clear, saying "…[God's] inmost Being as Holy Trinity is a mystery that is inaccessible to reason alone or even to Israel's faith before the Incarnation of God's Son and the sending of the Holy Spirit."[227] And yet, when one knows of this dogma, one can clearly see hints of it contained in Divine Revelation earlier. One can even see how there was a certain need for the Dogma of the Trinity in order to understand the full meaning of the Divine Revelation of the Old Testament; in, for

---

[225] September 12, 1913.
[226] Some followers of Luisa hold that this is not the case; that, indeed, there have always been souls who truly Lived in the Divine Will. The passage they cite is the following: "…*So, the order of Our Wisdom, the operating Life of Our externized Love, could not tolerate the failure of Our purpose; this is why, in all centuries, there has always been some soul whom God has formed as center of the whole Creation, and within her Our Love leaned and Our Life palpitated and obtained the purpose of the whole Creation. It is by means of these centers that the whole Creation is maintained, and that the world still exists; otherwise, it would have no reason to exist, because the life and the cause of everything would be missing. Therefore, there has not been one century, nor will there be, in which We will not choose souls dear to Us, more or less portentous, who will form the center of Creation, in whom We will*

have Our Life palpitating and Our Love operating. And according to the epochs, the times, the needs, the circumstances, they have been offered for the good of all, they have given themselves to all, they have defended all; they alone have been the ones who have sustained my sacrosanct rights and have given Me the field to maintain the order of my infinite Wisdom." – October 20, 1931. But a careful reading of this passage, taking it fully at its own word, does not say anything about souls actually living in the Divine Will in all centuries; only that each century had its "center" in at least one extraordinary soul. And indeed, it is only thanks to these victim souls that the world has survived. But this does not mean they lived in the Divine Will like Luisa did and like we now are called to so live.
[227] CCC 237.

example, the use of first-person plural pronouns in the creation account of Genesis ("let us make man in our own image"[228]), the distinction between "God" and the "Spirit of God" in the very first and second lines of Genesis, respectively,[229] the otherwise incomprehensible wording of Psalm 110 ("the Lord said to my Lord"), and the fascinating vision of Daniel ("… with the clouds of heaven there came one like a son of man, and he came to the Ancient of Days and was presented before him…"),[230] and in other cases as well.

That being said, foreshadowings of the Gift can be found even more clearly in the forthcoming sections. So, we now consider what these references are in the following sources. Before going through each in detail, however, a general observation is necessary.

The Four Great Invitations

In the preceding section, we spoke of the foreshadowings of the Gift "building over the centuries like the crescendo of a classical masterpiece." This crescendo can be most clearly seen in four paradigms that constitute God's Four Great Invitations that He offers in preparing the way for the Universal Reign of the Divine Will.

Each of these paradigms will be discussed in detail within forthcoming sections, but we should now take a broad look at the astonishing thing happening in the Catholic world today; for only with this broad look can we see that these are not merely separate apostolates or movements, but are rather four prongs of the same Divine Attack to win back the world for God and Restore All Things in Christ.

These four prongs, invitations, or paradigms are:

- Marian Consecration popularized by St. Louis de Montfort and many other writers after him
- The new teachings on the unification of the human and Divine Wills found in the French spirituality of the 17th and 18th centuries that found their pinnacle in the teachings of St. Thérèse of Lisieux
- The teachings on Mystical (or Spiritual) Marriage in the Doctors of the Church

- The clear teachings on human Divinization (or Deification) found in virtually all the Fathers of the Church, which is now at long last making a comeback in Catholic spirituality and theology

Providentially, in each of these four paradigms, we find in their nature a "pointing;" that is, an indication that they themselves are directed to some result beyond themselves. For "Divinization" and "Deification" are words that imply a *process* ("-tion") which calls for some culmination. Mystical marriage, or spiritual marriage, as a marriage indeed, is ordered towards the generation of children, thus it calls for a fruitfulness beyond itself. Marian consecration, if it is to reach its fulfillment, requires a likeness — a true similarity in the most important way — between the one being consecrated and the one to whom consecration is directed. And the unification of wills always calls for, just as any unification does, not just correspondence but also a total merging of the two unified things, as the water dropped into the chalice at the Mass becomes inseparable from the wine therein.

So, these four great paradigms, while each deserves enormous exaltation on its own right, are nevertheless essentially invitations. *They are invitations to Live in the Divine Will.*

Unification of Wills

As will become clear when reading the details of each listed spiritual writer in the next section, a growing understanding in Catholic theology developed throughout the centuries (beginning especially around the 11th) that the true essence, beginning, and end of the spiritual life revolved entirely around the will: specifically, the total unreserved handing over of the human will to the Divine Will. The more this fact was understood, the more forcefully the great spiritual writers promulgated the teaching and the more carefully they centralized their writings around it.

But let us briefly turn to consider a related heresy. Recall that God only allows any evil of any form to transpire in order to bring a greater good out of it. This is true with heresies as well; He allows them so that Catholics may, in understanding the flaws

---

228 Genesis 1:26
229 Cf. Genesis 1:1

230 Daniel 7:13

thereof, better refine, understand, and live by the true teachings that become aped by the heresies.

Quietism, a heresy which became popular at about the same time and place that witnessed the explosion of beautiful, profound, and orthodox teaching on the Divine and human wills, taught:

> …radical passivity and [the] doctrine of "pure love". The spiritual teaching of Quietism suggested that the believer need not avail himself of devotional practices, of religious and domestic duties, and of the Church's sacramental economy: all that truly mattered was a will lovingly passive to God.[231]

From this heresy's formal condemnation in the year 1687 by Pope Innocent XI, the teaching on the Divine Will in the great French spiritual-theological writings of the following century were guarded from Quietism and, particularly in the writings of Caussade (who died in 1751 and thus knew well— and abided by—the 1687 condemnation), we see an exposition of this teaching given so beautifully that one is tempted to wonder if Caussade himself was given a prophetic glimpse of Luisa's revelations in advance. But even Caussade's teachings are perhaps exceeded in radicality by those of the "Greatest Saint of Modern Times," that is, St. Thérèse of Lisieux, Doctor of the Church.

For if one truly understands the spiritual teachings contained in these writers, then one will have no problem whatsoever believing Jesus' revelations to Luisa and opening up one's self to the Gift contained therein.

In his own introduction to Caussade's masterpiece, *Abandonment to Divine Providence,* Dom Arnold, OSB, writes:

> The "Abandonment to Divine Providence" of Fr. de Caussade is as far removed from the false inactivity of the Quietists, as true Christian resignation is distinct from the fatalism of Mohammedans. It is a trusting, childlike, peaceful abandonment to the guidance of grace, and of the Holy Spirit: an unquestioning and undoubting submission to the holy will of God in all things that may befall us, be they due to the action of man, or to the direct permission of God. **To Fr. de Caussade, abandonment to God, the "Ita Pater" of our Divine Lord, the "Fiat" of our Blessed Lady, is the shortest, surest, and easiest way to holiness and peace**.[232]

Divinization

Dr. Scott Hahn, in his foreword to the book *Called to be the Children of God: The Catholic Theology of Human Deification,*[233] writes:

> Jesus saves us from sin and death. Rescue from sin and death is indeed a wonderful thing—but the salvation won for us by Jesus Christ is incomparably greater… Saint Basil the Great put it boldly, in A.D. 375 in his De Spiritu Sancto, when he enumerated the gifts of the Spirit: "abiding in God, being made like God—and, highest of all, being made God" (9.23). This is classic Christianity. In recent centuries, however, this primal language of salvation has fallen into disuse in the Western Church. Its decline began in the late Middle Ages, with the nominalist corruption of philosophy and then theology…[deification] vanishes entirely in subsequent [post-Calvin] generations of Protestantism. **Even in the Catholic Church, the idea of divinization got lost amid all the post-Reformation disputes over the relationship of faith, works, and justification. For four centuries, Catholic and Protestant theologians alike focused so narrowly on these controversies that they obscured the central fact of Christian salvation**…

In this astounding observation, Dr. Hahn points out that Divinization is central to Christianity but has for centuries been neglected and forgotten, and that this tragedy is another casualty of the Protestant revolt. But just as undeniable as its lamentable eclipse is its current resurgence. Daniel Lattier writes:

> Among Christians, the renewed interest in deification seems to hold ecumenical hope. For over a century, Roman Catholics have been engaged in a ressourcement—a "return to the sources" of the Christian faith represented by the writings of the Church Fathers. As the narrative goes, the West lost contact with some of these sources as time passed, and elements of their theologies went underemphasized. In particular, the West has sought a reengagement with the thought of the Eastern Church Fathers. This reengagement with the East is most famously represented in the work of Roman Catholic

---

[231] *Called to be the Children of God.* Ch. 8
[232] *Abandonment to Divine Providence.* Introduction. From the Tenth Complete French Edition by E. J. Strickland, 1921.

[233] Ignatius Press. 2016

theologians Yves Congar, Louis Bouyer, Jean Danielou, Henri de Lubac, and Hans Urs von Balthasar, and has been reiterated recently in Orientale lumens call for Catholics "to deepen their knowledge of the spiritual traditions of the Fathers and Doctors of the Christian East"... John Henry Newman was both a forerunner and catalyst of the modern ressourcement movement in the West ... His appropriation of the Eastern Fathers, and the centrality of deification in their thought, led him to the Roman Catholic Church, which he saw as "the nearest approximation in fact to the Church of the Fathers". The Eastern character of Newman's thought began to influence the shape of Catholic theology in the years leading up to the Second Vatican Council, leading some to term Newman the "Father of the Second Vatican Council". But the ecumenical value of Newman's recourse to deification goes even deeper. As he demonstrated in his own life, the indwelling of Christ was not only a doctrine for Christians to affirm, but the very principle of their life, thought, and action. [234]

Considering this equally profound observation from Dr. Lattier, we can see the hand of Providence at work in an extraordinary way in raising up the intellectual giant of Newman (and others) to have so great an impact in reviving Divinization in the post-Vatican II Catholic world. Beatified in 2010 by Pope Benedict XVI, Blessed Newman is expected to be canonized soon by Pope Francis, as in November of 2018 the Vatican approved a second miracle due to Newman's intercession.

Mystical Marriage

As stated elsewhere, mystical marriage has long been seen as the definitive triumph of the spiritual life of a saint on earth, consisting in the highest degree of sanctity possible for a wayfarer, but given only to extremely few saints throughout Church History.

In his masterpiece entitled, simply, *Spiritual Theology*, Fr. Jordan Aumann—Dominican priest, theologian, and highly respected author in matters pertaining to the spiritual life—gives a comprehensive overview of the topic. Although lengthy, it is well worth including here, in its only slightly abridged entirety:

> The last grade of prayer is the transforming union, identified by many mystics as the spiritual

marriage. It constitutes the seventh mansions of *The Interior Castle* of St. Teresa and is the highest degree of perfection that one can attain in this life. It is, therefore, a prelude to the beatific life of glory. **This state is nothing less than a transformation into God, and St. John of the Cross does not hesitate to use such expressions as "transformed into God by love," "God of God by participation," and "more divine than human." Such expressions may seem daring and even excessive when applied to the spiritual life of the soul, but they are fully justified by a usage that goes back to St. John, St. Paul, and the Fathers of the Church, especially the Eastern Church...**

In this grade of prayer there is a total transformation of the soul into the Beloved. The soul has entered into its very center, so to speak, which is the throne room of the interior castle where the Trinity dwells through grace. There God and the soul give themselves to each other in the consummation of divine love, so far as is possible in the present life. There is no more ecstasy, for the soul has now been strengthened to receive the full power of love, but in the brightness of an intellectual vision the soul experiences the Trinity with vivid awareness. ...

We can distinguish three elements in this loftiest degree of the prayer of union: transformation in God, mutual surrender, and the permanent union of love. As St. John of the Cross states:

"The soul becomes brilliant and transformed in God, and God communicates to the soul his supernatural being to such an extent that the soul appears to be God and to have all that God has. Such a union is effected when God grants to the soul this supernatural mercy; as a result of which all the things of God and the soul are one in a participated transformation. The soul seems to be more God than soul and is truly God by participation, although it is true that its being, so distinct by nature, is possessed by the soul as something distinct from the being of God, as it was formerly, even though transformed, just as the window is distinct from the ray of light which illumines it."

As to the mutual surrender, it is a natural consequence of the transforming union just described. Between God and the soul there are a perfect communication and the mutual gift of self, for which reason the prayer of transforming union is called a spiritual marriage. Lastly, St.

---

[234] *Called to be the Children of God: the Catholic Theology of Human Deification.* Forward. Ignatius Press. 2016.

Teresa teaches that in this grade of prayer, unlike the grades that preceded it, there is a permanency of union and love.

Concomitant with the permanent union of love is the soul's *confirmation in grace.* St. John of the Cross maintains that the transforming union never falters and the soul is confirmed in grace, but St. Teresa warns that as long as we are in this world we must walk with caution, lest we offend God. However, the apparent contradiction is readily resolved when we say that confirmation in grace does not mean intrinsic impeccability, for the Church teaches that it is an impossibility in this life. Nor is it a question of avoiding all venial sins in this life, for that would require a special privilege of grace as was bestowed on the Virgin Mary. Consequently, confirmation in grace must be understood as the special grace and assistance from God to avoid all mortal sins and thus have moral certitude of salvation.

Effects of Transforming Union

Perhaps no one has described as clearly as St. Teresa the marvelous effects produced in the soul by the transforming union or mystical marriage. We shall summarize her description of these effects as given in her *Interior Castle,* Seventh Mansions, Chapter 3:

1. *A forgetfulness of self* **so complete that it seems as if the soul no longer existed.** There is no longer any knowledge or remembrance of heaven or life or honor as regards the soul, so completely is it absorbed in seeking the honor of God. The soul lives in a state of forgetfulness so that it has no desire whatever in regard to self, but desires only to do what it can do to promote the glory of God, and for this it would gladly lay down its life.

2. *A great desire to suffer*, but now the desire does not disturb the soul as it did previously. **So great is the soul's longing that the will of God be done in it that it accepts whatever God wills as the best for it.** If he sends suffering, well and good; if not, the soul does not worry or fret about it as it did previously.

3. *Joy in persecution.* When the soul is persecuted, it experiences great interior joy and much more peace than formerly. It bears no enmity toward those who treat it badly or desire to do so. Rather, it conceives a special love for such persons, and if it were to see them in some affliction it would be deeply grieved and would do all in its power to relieve them. It loves to commend such persons to God, and would rejoice at relinquishing some of the favors it receives from God if it could bestow them on its enemies, and thus perhaps prevent them from offending God.

4. *Desire to serve God.* Whereas the soul formerly suffered because of its longing to die and to be with God, it now experiences a strong desire to serve God and to help any soul that it can. Indeed, it now desires not to die but to live for many years and to suffer the most severe trials if in this way it can be a means whereby God is praised. Its conception of glory is now connected in some way with helping Christ, especially when it sees how often people offend him and how few there are who are truly concerned about his honor.

5. *Detachment from everything created.* The desires of the soul are no longer for consolations because the soul realizes that now the Lord himself dwells within it. **As a result, the soul experiences a marked detachment from everything, and a desire to be alone or to be occupied with something that will be beneficial to the soul.** There is no more aridity or interior trial, but only a constant recollection in God and a tender love for him. There is no fear that this period of tranquility may be caused by the devil, because the soul has an unwavering certitude that it comes from God. This experience takes place in the very center of the soul and in the highest faculty, into which the devil cannot enter.

6. *Absence of ecstasies.* Upon reaching this state, the soul has no more raptures, or very seldom. The great weakness that formerly was the occasion for raptures has now given place to a great strength granted by God. Nevertheless, the soul walks with great care and still does all in its power to strengthen itself with the help of God's grace. Indeed, the more it is favored by God, the more cautious it becomes and the more aware of its own littleness and humility.

Ideal of Christian Perfection

Such is the bittersweet path that leads to the heights of contemplative prayer and the transforming union. It is the sublime ideal of Christian perfection, and it is offered to all souls in grace. When Jesus pronounced the precept: "You must be made perfect as your heavenly Father is perfect" (Matt. 5:48), he was speaking to all souls without exception. The Christian life, if it is developed according to the supernatural powers that are inherent in it, will lead to the transforming union of charity, which is in turn the prelude to the beatific vision.

The highest perfection consists not in interior favors or in great raptures or in visions or in the spirit of prophecy, but in the bringing of our wills so closely into conformity with the will of God that, as soon as we realize he wills anything, we desire it ourselves with all our might, and take the bitter with the sweet, knowing that to be His Majesty's will.[235]

From this beautiful overview of mystical marriage, we should bear in mind—and this is from St. John of the Cross and St. Teresa of Avila as well—that it was indeed considered the highest state of sanctity possible *on earth*, **but not the highest state of sanctity *possible*.** It is rather undeniable, in all these writings on mystical and spiritual theology, that the state of sanctity of the blessed in Heaven is nevertheless superior. And Jesus makes it equally clear to Luisa and to other mystics of the 20th century that it is precisely this Heavenly sanctity which He is now freely giving to those who yearn for it.

***

Here we must pause to address a conundrum which may now have presented itself to the minds of some readers. It goes something like this:

> Hold on. What I've just read about the nature of spiritual marriage is so extreme that in many ways it seems to surpass what is said about the Gift of Living in the Divine Will, not vice versa! The effects of this spiritual marriage on the recipient are so great that I doubt there is more than a soul or two alive at a given time on the face of the planet who enjoys such a state. How could we possibly speak of a higher degree of sanctity even than this—and for the masses!?

This is a perfectly understandable response, but it arises from a confusion of what is being described in different cases. Living in the Divine Will is pure grace; it does not override the ordinary theology of the spiritual life, and it completely flees the senses. Even with this Gift, one must strive to attain what is described by St. John of the Cross, St. Teresa of Avila, etc., regarding spiritual marriage. In much of their analysis, these great Doctors are describing not the intrinsic nature of the grace of spiritual marriage itself, but the manifestations and effects of this invisible grace on the life of the soul. And these manifestations are indeed often superior to the manifestations of one who may have an intrinsically greater gift (i.e. Living in the Divine Will), but who has not yet enjoyed sufficient "accidental" (in the philosophical sense of the

word) spiritual growth to exhibit anything like the glorious manifestations of the "lesser" gift (i.e. spiritual marriage).

Therefore, we can see that this is one of many reasons why we should never speak of someone who has the Gift of Living in the Divine Will (even if we somehow knew he had the Gift) as "greater" than someone else who did not (due to living in the time before the Gift was offered). **When we speak of the "greatness" of a saint, we often (perhaps always) intend to refer to the greatness of the manifestations of God's grace in their lives, or the correspondence to God's grace that the saint exhibited—not merely to the intrinsic nature of the grace itself within the depths of their souls, which is hidden from our sight.**

Let us briefly consider an analogous situation. In the Sacrament of Confession, a Catholic receives an ontologically[236] superior gift—even if his contrition is quite imperfect—than a Protestant does when he asks God for forgiveness in his own personal prayer. But let us say this Protestant is truly remorseful and contrite to a far greater degree than the Catholic. Although nothing changes the fact that the Catholic, through the Sacrament of Reconciliation, has received an intrinsically greater gift, it remains true that this Catholic should nevertheless admit that this particular Protestant's contrition (which would be a manifestation of grace) is superior to his own, and the Catholic should strive to imitate this superior contrition. Similarly, in the Eucharist, a Catholic receives an infinitely greater gift than the Protestant does by "inviting Jesus into his heart" as a part of their "personal relationship." Nevertheless, the Protestant may show more manifestations of grace which should indeed be zealously imitated by a Catholic; perhaps the Catholic is lukewarm and does little to correspond to the infinite graces of the Eucharist he receives, and perhaps the Protestant is zealous and strives mightily to be virtuous, evangelize, love God and neighbor, etc. This does not change the fact that the Eucharist is an intrinsically greater gift, even though the Protestant has done a better job corresponding to the lesser gifts he himself has received.

It seems that virtually all those critics of Luisa who take offense at the "greatness" of the Gift of Living

---

[235] Fr. Jordan Aumann. *Spiritual Theology.* "Prayer of Transforming Union." Chapter 12.

[236] That is, relating to the being itself

in the Divine Will simply do not understand this simple distinction (maybe through no fault of their own, because perhaps they have only heard distorted interpretations of Luisa's revelations).

***

Returning from this aside, we must bear in mind that the spiritual writers who gave this teaching (e.g. St. John of the Cross, St. Teresa of Avila) were correct. Indeed, in their times, spiritual (mystical) marriage *was* the greatest sanctity possible on earth, since the time had not yet arrived in which God deemed to give His Will to creatures.

But it is equally true that this reality of mystical marriage itself clearly points to something outside of itself. For those who preach its ultimate nature are perhaps forgetting that marriage is ordered toward something beyond itself; the marriage itself is not definitive. Moreover, it is not even an ontologically indissoluble union until it has been consummated, and beyond this, it is expected that the marriage bear children. In fact, though it is often forgotten today, we must remember that the **"primary end of marriage is the procreation and the education of children."**[237] In other words, **the good of the spouses is a secondary and subordinate end** to this primary end. It should be clear, then, that mystical marriage too—inasmuch as the mystical life is an authentic reflection of earthly realities, which indeed it is—is ordered towards something beyond itself. A critic might say I am taking an analogy too far; but it would be strange for so essential an analogy as spiritual marriage (an analogy chosen by God Himself in describing what He has wrought in the lives of the saints who experienced it) to fail to remain analogous on such an important property.

Now, this consideration which I here present is by no means my own innovation; rather, even before Jesus revealed The Gift clearly to the mystics of the 20th century, there was a sense that perhaps there is something higher still, theoretically attainable on earth, exceeding the "third stage" (the illuminative way) of the spiritual life, which finds its own height in mystical marriage. Hugh Owen writes:

> In his spiritual biography of Archbishop Luis Maria Martinez, spiritual director of Venerable Conchita Cabrera, Fr. Joseph Trevino of the Missionaries of the Holy Spirit observed that the traditional division of the spiritual life into three stages—the purgative, illuminative, and unitive—had obscured the existence of a fourth stage where the transforming union of the soul and God produced its supernatural fruit. According to Fr. Trevino: "It would be absurd actually, if, when the soul reaches the highest union on earth, its life would stagnate, that it would remain permanently inactive. Just the contrary happens; that is the time when the action of the soul, under the motion of the Holy Spirit, reaches its maximum. This is the fourth stage [after the purgative, illuminative, and unitive stages of mystical theology.] ... In the transforming union, the soul is united with the Word. But this union is spiritually fecund; its fruit is Jesus, Jesus reproduced in the soul itself and, through its ministry, Jesus reproduced in the souls of others (apostolic life)....
>
> In his treatise on "the four degrees of violent love," Richard of St. Victor wrote: In the first degree the betrothals take place, in the second the wedding, in the third the marriage is consummated, in the fourth the childbirth occurs ... In the first degree, the soul receives frequent visits; in the second, she is betrothed; in the third, she is made one with her beloved; in the fourth, she becomes a mother." The Seraphic Doctor, St. Bonaventure, seems to have hinted at something similar in his famous *Itinerarium mentis in Deum*, The Soul's Journey into God. In order to describe the three stages of the spiritual life, the Seraphic Doctor uses the symbol of the "Six-winged Seraph" who effected the Stigmata in St. Francis of Assisi. This Seraph somehow surrounded or identified itself with the "One Crucified" from whose wounds rays came forth to form the wounds in Francis' body. St. Bonaventure uses the image of the "Six Wings" as symbols of the stages of the spiritual life. Each pair of wings corresponds to the contemplations proper to each of the three stages of the spiritual life. By trying to describe something above and beyond the three levels of the three pairs of wings, Bonaventure obscurely pointed to something more than the three usually understood stages. The language is somewhat difficult, but definitely points to a Fourth Stage.[238]

From all these considerations, a profound picture emerges: Mystical Marriage—the pinnacle of the

---

[238] Hugh Owen. *New and Divine: The holiness of the third Christian millennium.* John Paul II Institute of Christian Spirituality. 2001. p.44-45. (**Henceforth "*New and Divine*"**)

third stage of the spiritual life—though truly Deifying in its own right and hitherto considered the highest degree of sanctity possible on earth, nevertheless on closer consideration seems ordered to something else superior to itself. Giving a hint as to where this superior 'something" resides, St. John of the Cross himself—the one most known and regarded for his teachings on mystical union—writes:

> The entire matter of reaching union with God consists in purging the will of its appetites and emotions so that from a human and lowly will it may be changed into the divine will, made identical with the will of God.[239]

Marian Consecration

Of the Four Great Invitations spoken of in this section, Marian Consecration is the final and definitive blow to the human (self) will; thus, making straight the way for the reign of the Divine Will both in individuals and, soon, over the whole world. The other three of the Great Invitations have long been more or less popular in the spiritual theology of the Church, but Marian Consecration has exploded in popularity only recently. This explosion itself has been caused by God in order to serve as the immediate precursor to the Gift of Living in the Divine Will, which too shall soon "explode" throughout the world. The Father of Marian Consecration himself was aware of the fact that when this spirituality would spread among Catholics, it would form the saints of the end of the Era and usher in the Reign of Peace; in fact, he prophesied exactly this, as we shall soon see.

One who consecrates Himself to Our Lady, and consequently becomes clothed in her very own virtues—as the aforementioned Father of Marian Consecration, St. Louis de Montfort, promised such a soul would be so clothed—cannot but live in the Divine Will. For it is precisely this type of life that is the essence of her sanctity and is therefore also the Gift she earnestly desires to mediate to all of her children. This great 17th century apostle of Marian Consecration so revered by Pope St. John Paul II and who is now making a great comeback in Catholic theology, issued famous prophecies about the future of the Church and the World—prophecies that are at once indications of the Gift of

Living in the Divine Will and of the Era of Peace. St. Louis rightly recognized that this great sanctity will be mediated by the hands of Mary, who will clothe us with *her very own holiness*, which is none other than the Gift of Living in the Divine Will.

> This will happen especially towards the end of the world, and indeed soon, because Almighty God and his holy Mother are to raise up great saints who will surpass in holiness most other saints as much as the cedars of Lebanon tower above little shrubs ... These great souls filled with grace and zeal will be chosen to oppose the enemies of God who are raging on all sides. They will be exceptionally devoted to the Blessed Virgin. Illumined by her light, strengthened by her food, guided by her spirit ...
>
> ... Mary has produced, together with the Holy Ghost, the greatest thing which has been or ever will be—a God-man; and **she will consequently produce the greatest saints that there will be in the end of time.** The formation and education of the great saints who shall come at the end of the world are reserved for her. For it is only that singular and miraculous Virgin who can produce, in union with the Holy Ghost, singular and extraordinary things. They shall be great and exalted before God in sanctity, superior to all other creatures by their lively zeal, and so well sustained with God's assistance that, with the humility of their heel, in union with Mary, they shall crush the head of the devil and **cause Jesus Christ to triumph.**[240]

But St. Louis teaches that this is all thanks to our Consecration to Mary. A beautiful description of the essence of Marian Consecration is given by the Franciscans of the Immaculate:

> By this consecration, one offers himself wholly to Our Lady, so that in all he does and undergoes, he depends on her. If it is made as it should be, this consecration achieves a complete surrender of self into Our Lady's hands. From the moment of consecration, she is to enter the life of the person in order to completely Marianize it—to transform it according to her ways. The consecrated person ought to succeed in "living with Mary, for Mary, in Mary," as St. Louis Montfort teaches...
>
> The consecration of oneself as a slave is taught by St. Louis de Montfort, and it expresses principally the sacrifice of one's liberty in order to live fettered and ruled by love for Our Lady.

---

[239] St. John of the Cross: *Ascent of Mt Carmel. Book III*, Ch. 16, Paragraph 3.

[240] St. Louis de Montfort, *True Devotion to Mary* (Bay Shore, NY: Montfort Publications, 2006), paragraphs 46-48.

Consecration of oneself as her property was taught by St. Maximilian M. Kolbe, and this principally expresses an unconditional surrender of oneself into Mary's immaculate hands as her instrument or property.

The other form of consecration is inspired by the Little Flower's offering of herself as a victim of Jesus' merciful love, and it expresses principally the total immolation, the complete sacrifice, of oneself to God, to become like Mary when she totally sacrificed herself in the exercise of generous, merciful love.

Identical in substance, each of these forms of consecration is intended to make us carry out a filial devotion to Our Lady in the most deep-rooted, radical way. They mean to make us sink our roots into Mary's Heart with the happy certainty that "he who plants his roots in Mary becomes holy" (St. Bonaventure).

The experience the saints have had assures us that this is quite true.[241]

And although St. Louis de Montfort died in 1716, his legacy has lived on and his impact has only continued to grow. In the past several years especially, Marian Consecration has deservedly begun to dominate the scene of Catholic spirituality. We have seen St. Maximilian Kolbe's efforts in his Militia Immaculata blessed abundantly by providence, and more recently, millions of Catholics around the world have taken that enormous step to consecrate themselves to Mary; many in response to the "My Consecration" apostolate of the late hero of Our Lady's causes, Anthony Mullen, as well as Fr. Michael Gaitley's *33 Days to Morning Glory.*

***

Understanding these Four Great Invitations is necessary, first, for one's personal benefit in receiving the Gift. You are more than ready to receive the Gift of Living in the Divine Will if you take all four invitations seriously and obey their instructions. It is also necessary in order to see how perfectly the Gift fits in to the organic development of spirituality within the Church; it shows how this moment is the opportune time for God to make haste in giving it.

These Four Paradigms do easily refute the various attacks made against the orthodoxy of the Gift; for almost all these attacks against the loftiness of The

Gift could be just as easily levied against any of the Four Great Invitations, each of which is of unassailable orthodoxy. Consequently, any argument which accuses them of unorthodoxy is thereby revealed to as a fallacious argument.

The Old Testament

Although a modern Jew may respond rather emphatically in the negative if asked whether Judaism allows for the concept of the Divinization or Deification of Man, one can only wonder if this response is inspired by a lurking defensiveness against Christianity. So instead of consulting individual Jews from the Christian era, we must turn to the fundamental sources; above all, the Hebrew Scriptures.

Psalm 8 reads differently depending upon the translation. The King James version, for example, reads, "For thou hast made [man] a little lower than **the angels**, and hast crowned him with glory and honour." But this is, in fact, not an accurate translation. The Revised Standard Version (Catholic Edition) gets it much better: "**Thou hast made him little less than *God*.**"

Of this translation issue, the scholar Huston Smith wrote:

That last word is a straight mistranslation, for the original Hebrew plainly reads "a little lower than the gods [or God]"—the number of the Hebrew word 'elohim is indeterminate. Why did the translators reduce deity to angels? The answer seems obvious: It was not erudition that they lacked, but rather the boldness—one is tempted to say nerve—of the Hebrews. We can respect their reserve. It is one thing to write a Hollywood script in which everyone seems wonderful; it is another thing to make such characters seem real. The one charge that has never been leveled against the Bible is that its characters are not real people. Even its greatest heroes, like David, are presented so unvarnished, so "warts and all," that the Book of Samuel has been called the most honest historical writing of the ancient world. Yet no amount of realism could dampen the aspiration of the Jews. Human beings who on occasion so justly deserve the epithets "maggot and worm" (Job 25:6) are equally the beings whom God has "crowned with glory and honor" (Psalm 8:6). There is a rabbinic saying to the effect that whenever a man or woman walks down the street

---

he or she is preceded by an invisible choir of angels crying, "Make way, make way! Make way for the image of God."[242]

Already in the Old Testament—before the Sacraments even existed—we see the Divinization of Man taken for granted. In fact, Jesus Himself, in the Gospels, rebukes those who fail to see this:

> The Jews took up stones again to stone him. Jesus answered them, "I have shown you many good works from the Father; for which of these do you stone me?" The Jews answered him, "We stone you for no good work but for blasphemy; because you, being a man, make yourself God." Jesus answered them, "Is it not written in your law, 'I said, you are gods'?"[243]

While Jesus is here making an important reference to a Psalm which calls the vengeance of God down upon unworthy shepherds of Israel, it is also clear that He is rebuking the Pharisees for their implicit categorical condemnation of the notion of the Divinization of Man.

And indeed, Our Lord's rebuke was well placed, for the Pharisees should have known that this was not blasphemy. As Huston Smith points out in the excerpt above, pious Jews had always acknowledged this reality. Unfortunately, today one often hears promoted a misconception about the relative spiritual position of men and angels—namely, the assumption that all angels are categorically higher than man because they are pure spirits. But this assumes the erroneous premise that there is something "low" about matter (a premise which, if it ever had any value, was refuted by the Incarnation and should not be held by any Christian). While an angel obviously has more power than a man's physical body does (which is why we have Guardian Angels, and why we should frequently pray for the intercession of the Angels), this says little. This view of the angels is also refuted by what we already know: the position of Our Lady, who no Catholic denies is immeasurably above all angels. But it is not only Our Lady who can be said to be higher than angels. Consider the well-known words the demons were forced to say of St. John Vianney,; namely, "If only there were three others like him, our Kingdom would be destroyed," and, later, the demons were

also forced to reveal that they feared St. Padre Pio more than they feared even St. Michael the Archangel. Of course, more authoritative still is Sacred Scripture, which refers to the knowledge we can have as humans as "things into which angels long to look."[244], and furthermore asserts, "Do you not know that we are to judge angels?"[245]

Of course, ancient Jews had access to none of this knowledge contained in the New Testament, and yet they still knew that the loftiness of man's potential holiness was almost impossible to overstate. This all comes from the very first chapter of the very first book of the Bible shared by Jews and Christians, and all know well that it states:

Then God said, "Let us make man in our image, after our likeness ..." Genesis 1:26

What is unclear here? In making man, God made a being like Himself. We have no Scriptural evidence that He said this even of the angels in creating them. How, then, shall we differentiate between God and man to avoid pagan pantheism? In this: The Divinization of Man erases the distance, but not the difference.

Any artist, in painting a self-portrait, will create an imperfect one with many differences between himself and his work of art; but these differences arise from the fact that the artist himself is not perfectly skilled in his own craft. We cannot, however, ascribe any similar manner of imperfection to God, and therefore we are left with the conclusion that He did succeed with His intent of creating man in His own image and likeness. He had to put everything that He Himself had into man; thus, man becomes by grace what God is by nature.

> What would be said of a mother who generated, not a child who had eyes, mouth, hands, feet, and would be similar to her in all members—at most, smaller than her in all members, but lacking nothing of all the organs of the mother—but generated a plant, a bird, a stone, things which are dissimilar from her? It would be incredible—things against nature and unworthy of a mother, who was not able to infuse her image and all of her members in her newborn. Now, if all things generate and form things similar to themselves,

242 Huston Smith. *The World's Religions*. Pages306-307.
243 John 10:31-34
244 1 Peter 1:12

245 1 Corinthians 6:3

much more so does God, first Generator, whose honor and glory in forming the creatures was to form them as similar to Himself.[246]

The New Testament

With good reason, the foreshadowing of the Gift increased dramatically with the coming of Our Lord in the flesh. The New Testament is full of indications of this spiritual reality. While there is perhaps only one instance in which it is bluntly stated (the climax of the Our Father prayer, "*Thy Will be done on earth as it is in Heaven*"), it is seen elsewhere in many places in proximate or implicit form. We will only consider a few here.

St. Peter

Where better to start than the Catechism itself? In answering the question "Why Did the Word Become Flesh?", it teaches us:

> The Word became flesh to make us "partakers of the divine nature": "For this is why the Word became man, and the Son of God became the Son of man: so that man, by entering into communion with the Word and thus receiving divine sonship, might become a son of God." "For the Son of God became man so that we might become God." "The only-begotten Son of God, wanting to make us sharers in his divinity, assumed our nature, so that he, made man, might make men gods."[247]

Here, it quotes Scripture (2 Peter 1:4), as well as St. Irenaeus, St. Athanasius, and St. Thomas Aquinas, respectively. Due to this diversity of sources, the quote will be referred to again in upcoming sections, but let us now focus on its New Testament reference. The unabridged Scriptural verse it cites, along with the one preceding it, reads:

> His divine power has granted to us all things that pertain to life and godliness, through the knowledge of him who called us to his own glory and excellence, by which he has granted to us his precious and very great promises, that through these you may escape from the corruption that is in the world because of passion, and become partakers of the divine nature.[248]

The amount of literature that exists merely for the sake of meditating on the implications of just those few words "partakers of the divine nature," could fill volumes. Suffice it to say that it is no mere modern innovation to recognize that contained within it is a great mystery which requires our understanding and our response. Of this verse, authors Fr. David Meconi and Carl Olson wrote:

> On one hand, this text is certainly unique, for the phrase "partakers of the divine nature" appears nowhere else in Scripture, prompting one commentator to venture that "with that remark [the author] seemingly took a step that no other writer of the New Testament dared take." On the other hand, without downplaying its uniqueness, it is notable that First Peter not only contains ten references to "glory"; it contains this oft-overlooked verse: "So I exhort the elders among you, as a fellow elder and a witness of the sufferings of Christ as well as a partaker [koinonos] in the glory that is to be revealed" (1 Pet 5:1). This passage points to the glory to be revealed at the return of Christ, but indicates a real and current participation, "for while its full manifestation belongs to the future, he holds (cf. esp. iv. 14) that, with the End so close at hand, those who suffer for Christ already enjoy a foretaste of it.[249]

There is no exegetical evasion technique to escape the acknowledgement that St. Peter here—and thus the Holy Spirit Himself Who is inspiring these words of Scripture—is teaching something radical about the degree to which God wills to transform us. Since all Christians must be grounded in Scripture above all, we can see that **to be a Christian is to refuse to be content until one has found the best and fullest understanding of partaking of the Divine nature.** (And that understanding is this: Living in the Divine Will.)

St. Paul

" ... it is no longer I who live, but Christ who lives in me ... "—Galatians 2:20

Here, St. Paul makes it clear that he has totally renounced his self-will; so much so that it can even be said to have been crucified with Christ (as the beginning of this same verse indicates). This is so true that He asserts, with the inerrancy of the Holy Spirit inspiring his words, that Christ lives in him.

For reasons previously stated, we cannot say that

---

[246] Jesus to Luisa. December 8, 1926.
[247] CCC Paragraph 460.
[248] 2 Peter 1:3,4

[249] Fr. David Meconi, and Carl Olson. *Called to be the Children of God: the Catholic Theology of Human Deification*. Ignatius Press. 2016. Chapter 1. **(Henceforth "*Called to be the Children of God*")**

St. Paul truly had the Gift of Living in the Divine Will, but we can clearly see that he had all the prerequisites for receiving it and certainly would have, had he been privileged enough to live in our times. (To be sure, the Gift of Living in the Divine Will, as its very name makes clear, is about even more than God living in us; it is about us living in God. If there were any doubts that there is indeed a distinction between these two graces, or any question as to which is greater, Pope Francis Magisterially settled the matter, teaching: "So often we say that God dwells in us, but it is better to say that we dwell in him, that he enables us to dwell in his light and love."[250])

It is safe to say that St. Paul did not include this verse in his letter to the Galatians to be praised for the height of his sanctity. He did so in order to instruct all of us to likewise no longer live for ourselves, but rather to allow Christ to live in us.

This, too, is utterly radical. It is not achieved simply by a "personal relationship" with Jesus Christ, which is about all one hears spoken of in many Protestant circles (and sadly, many Catholic ones as well). It is certainly not achieved merely by believing what one must believe for the sake of orthodoxy. It is not achieved merely by obeying the moral law. Nor is it achieved merely by passively receiving the Sacraments. It is achieved only by a total, holding-*nothing*-back death to self. (This type of death to self is spoken of in more detail in the "Abnegation" section of the "Foundational Virtues for the Gift" chapter of this book.)

Another passage in St. Paul where we find the Gift foreshadowed is found in his letter to the Philippians:

"Let the same mind be in you that was in Christ Jesus" — Philippians 2:5

If St. Paul meant only that we ought to submit intellectually to all the teachings of Jesus and strive to imitate in our daily endeavors the actions of Jesus, then he could have chosen a much more accurate way of saying this than by insisting the "**same mind**" be in us! As a teacher, I would rightly be called insane if I told my students that, to pass the test I am about to give them, they must have *my same mind* in them. At best, this would be a silly

exaggeration — but Scripture never exaggerates, notwithstanding the desperate attempts of the modernists to insist that it does just that. For exaggeration is a lie, and God — Who cannot lie — is the author of every word of Sacred Scripture, as is made clear not only by the older Magisterial documents but also by Vatican II itself (in "Dei Verbum"), which in turn is promulgated by the Catechism.

Instead, St. Paul teaches that our own mind truly can (and must) be absorbed into Jesus' mind — and, thus, the Divine Mind — so truly that it cannot even be said we operate with separate minds.

The poignancy of this foreshadowing is also due to the faculty to which it refers: our mind, or our intellect. For there are two steps in a human act: the intellect directing and the will executing; therefore, as the act of the intellect precedes the act of the will, one can easily see that if we truly have the same mind as Christ Jesus, it is only natural that the next step is to have the same will; which is precisely what Jesus' revelations to Luisa are all about.

St. John

In his first letter, St. John — the beloved Apostle of Jesus, who also wrote the Gospel bearing his name as well as the Book of Revelation — writes:

"See what love the Father has given us, that we should be called children of God; and so we are."[251]

This adoption as true children of God is seen elsewhere in Scripture as well, for example, St. Paul's letter to the Galatians states:

> God sent forth his Son, born of woman ... so that we might receive adoption as sons. And because you are sons, God has sent the Spirit of his Son into our hearts, crying, "Abba! Father!" So through God you are no longer a slave but a son. [252]

There are similarly profound verses speaking of this adoption as God's true children in Romans, Ephesians, and Corinthians. But the proper understanding of sonship is necessary in order to grasp what God is teaching us in these verses. Many throughout the history of the Church have written this teaching off as only a use of

---

[250]*Gaudete et Exsultate.* Apostolic Exhortation. Paragraph 51.
[251] 1 John 3:1

[252] Galatians 4:4-7

metaphorical language. They are, however, wrong; **it is not *metaphorical*, but is, rather, *literal*, that we are made into children of God** (through His grace)!

Commenting on this notion as taught by the great 19th century theologian and mystic Fr. Matthias Scheeben (who was proclaimed by Pope Pius XI as a man of genius), Timothy Kelly writes:

> According to Scheeben, the Christian sonship of which Scripture speaks, and which the Fathers expound, is not meant, he says, "by simple analogy or resemblance" with the eternal Sonship of the second Person of the Trinity, but in "literal truth". This is an astonishing claim. By "literal truth", Scheeben does not mean to abolish the personal distinction between the natural Son of the Father and the adoptive sons of God, but rather to emphasise the point that the predication "son of God" for the Christian is, somehow, warranted ontologically. Our sonship is not meant, he insists, "in some vague way", but insofar as "the most important relations existing between a son and a father are present in our relations of sonship to God."[253]

Obviously, none of us are or ever can be the Uncreated Second Person of the Blessed Trinity, as Jesus Christ alone is. Nevertheless, our sonship is not a mere metaphor; rather it is an assertion of our possession—by grace, not by nature—of all of that which is essential to sonship. And just as any good father who adopted a child would rightly rebuke another for claiming that the sonship of this child was a metaphor, so too we mustn't detract from the glory and truth of our own Divine sonship with such a reductionistic approach unworthy of the reality at hand.

The Church Fathers

> Constituted in a state of holiness, **man was destined to be fully "divinized" by God in glory**. Seduced by the devil, he wanted to "be like God", but "without God, before God, and not in accordance with God."[254]

-The Catechism of the Catholic Church.

Early in Church History, the concept of the **Divinization, Deification, or Theosis**[255] **of Man,** long spoken of especially in Eastern Catholic Mysticism, speaks in a way that beautifully foreshadows Luisa's revelations.

The New Catholic Encyclopedia, writing about several major Fathers of the Church in its entry on the History of Theology, says:

> [They emphasized] the mystical and ontological side of the Christian mystery, on man's divinization rather than on his liberation from sin … on the Incarnation as the root of man's divinization more than on his Redemption from sin through Christ's passion, death, and resurrection. Their speculation kept close to life; it meant faith and morality, theology and mysticism all in one.[256]

This brings up a key point; namely, the lack of finality in man's redemption from sin. Unfortunately, looking at redemption from sin as final or quasi-final has become a dominant view, and this is no doubt at least in part due to the Protestantization of Catholic theology. One expects to hear, in Protestant circles, an almost exclusive focus on "being saved," after which point one is "all set" and is just waiting for Heaven. It is not even uncommon to see a few particularly zealous Evangelicals walking around city streets, asking strangers if they are saved, and then supposing that all must be well as long as an affirmative answer is given to their question. The traditional hymn, *Amazing Grace*, comes to mind here: although beautiful, its spirituality is not very rich, for it seems to imply that the entirety of the spiritual life is contained within the transition from being "lost" to being "found."

This is in no way to detract from the immense importance, which cannot possibly be overstated, of the Redemption and of the application of the graces of Redemption to individuals for their salvation. This remains the foundation, and the Church Fathers knew that: but they also knew this was (as all foundations are) the beginning, not the end, of the spiritual life. The end was Divinization. The same Encyclopedia article puts it bluntly:

> The Son of God became man so that the sons of men might become sons of God (cf. St. Augustine…). The Word was made flesh so that

---

[253]*Called to be the Children of God.* Chapter 11.
[254] CCC, paragraph 398.

[255] *Apotheosis*, on the other hand, is usually a reference to the blasphemous Pagan practice of worshipping men – perhaps rulers of cities.
[256] New Catholic Encyclopedia, page 902.

men might be deified (St. Athanasius, Inc. 54). These words express Christ's mission: He came for men's salvation **and** divinization.

Another solid overview of Divinization in the Fathers is given by Daniel Keating, who writes:

[In Maximus' view of Divinization] "The whole of the human being is interpenetrated by the whole of God and becomes all that God is, excluding identity of essence. The human being receives to itself the whole of God" ... Deification for the Greek Fathers is not a separate and exotic path off on its own, but the culmination of all that the Father has done for the human race through the Son and in the Spirit ... For the Greek Fathers, our deification is "by grace and not by nature". They are concerned to avoid any sense of pantheism, any confusion of human nature with the being and nature of the triune God. Paradoxically, though deification raises us to a participation in God that is above our nature, it does not bring about a change in our nature. Rather, through deification our nature is exalted, glorified, and brought to the goal for which we were made. Andrew Louth sums this up: "Deification, then, is not a transcending of what it means to be human, but the fulfillment of what it is to be human."[257]

Let us, then, examine in more detail what these Fathers of the Church settled about the matter.

St. Maximus the Confessor

Fourteen years after Pope Benedict XVI (as Cardinal Ratzinger) nullified the condemnation of Luisa's writings, he taught this about Maximus:

St. Maximus tells us that, and we know that this is true, Adam (and we ourselves are Adam) thought that the "no" was the peak of freedom. He thought that only a person who can say "no" is truly free; that if he is truly to achieve his freedom, man must say "no" to God; only in this way he believed he could at last be himself, that he had reached the heights of freedom. This tendency also carried within it the human nature of Christ, but went beyond it, for Jesus saw that it was not the "no" that was the height of freedom. The height of freedom is the "yes", in conformity with

God's will. **It is only in the "yes" that man truly becomes himself; only in the great openness of the "yes", in the unification of his will with the divine, that man becomes immensely open, becomes "divine".** What Adam wanted was to be like God, that is, to be completely free. But the person who withdraws into himself is not divine, is not completely free; he is freed by emerging from himself, it is in the "yes" that he becomes free; and this is the drama of Gethsemane: not my will but yours. It is by transferring the human will to the divine will that the real person is born, it is in this way that we are redeemed.[258]

As you can see, the overlap is astonishing—to the point where one wonders if Pope Benedict here explicitly intends to guide us to Luisa's Divine Will spirituality through his commentary on Maximus. The overlap with Divine Will spirituality continues in other teachings from Maximus:

Nothing in theosis is the product of human nature ... It is only the mercy of God that has the capacity ... In theosis man (the image of God) becomes likened to God, he rejoices in all the plenitude that does not belong to him by nature, because the grace of the Spirit triumphs within him, and because God acts in him. [259]

The nature of the will of man (as exemplified in Christ) was also not lost on Maximus, who lived during the time of the Church Council that dealt with the question, and this brings up yet another major overlap. The Third Council of Constantinople (which was the Sixth Council of the Church), settled that Jesus truly did have two Wills: one human, one Divine.[260] Thus it condemned the heresy of Monothelitism. Understanding the orthodox teaching of the Church here is important in understanding the Gift of Living in the Divine Will (for the operation of the Human and Divine Will of Christ gives the model for understanding the Gift).

Maximus… had first been disarmed in front of the novelty of the problem posed by the prayer of Jesus at Gethsemane: his human will appeared to be contrary to the divine will, and Sergius had

---

[257] *Called to Be the Children of God.* Chapter 2. (Note that in referring to the "Greek" Fathers, Dr. Keating is not implying that Deification is absent from the Latin Fathers; rather, these words of his are contained in a chapter specifically dedicated to the Greek fathers. In fact, Dr. Keating clearly points out, in preceding paragraphs, that Deification *is* found in the writings of the Latin Fathers as well.)

[258] Benedict XVI. General Audience. June 25th, 2008 (Libreria Editrice Vaticana).

[259] Letter 22.

[260] This fact Jesus also makes clear to Luisa, thus revealing the slanderous nature of the accusation one may stumble upon on the internet which accuses Jesus' words to Luisa of the heresy of Monothelitism.

concluded in favor of the negation of that will. Maximus subsequently highlighted the reality of that human will and showed its soteriological [pertaining to salvation] importance.[261]

Although we see the foreshadowing of the gift perhaps most clearly among the Fathers in Maximus, a much earlier Church Father (St. Athanasius—also a Doctor of the Church) is the one most well-known for the same. In fact, the teaching of the two are deeply related, as recently noted by a scholar contributing to the *Blackwell Companion to Christian Mysticism*:

> Similarly, it is because Christ became human— that he possessed a human body—that our bodies have the possibility of healing and of returning to their pre—lapsarian condition. Though post— lapsarian bodies are broken and broken in diverse ways, the mystery of Christ's incarnation enables the brokenness of human bodies to be made whole once again (cf. Ambiguum 8). **Embellishing the Athanasian insight** that God became human so that humans could become gods, Maximus notes: "By his gracious condescension God became man and is called man for the sake of man and by exchanging his condition for ours revealed the power that elevates man to God through his love for God and brings God down to man because of his love for man. By this blessed inversion, man is made God by divinization and God is made man by hominization. For the Word of God and God wills always and in all things to accomplish the mystery of his embodiment (Ambiguum 7)."[262]

Let us now turn to consider this "Athanasian insight" from which Maximus drew.

St. Athanasius

The Great Exchange, "God was made man that we might be made God,"[263] comes to us most explicitly from St. Athanasius, although St. Irenaeus gave a similar version even earlier. Lest anyone be concerned about the orthodoxy of such a bold saying, remember that the Catechism of the Catholic Church explicitly quotes, and therefore itself promulgates as Magisterium, this very

teaching (in the previously quoted paragraph 460).[264]

St. Athanasius, that great Father and Doctor of the Church most fondly remembered as the heroic defender of the Divinity of Christ against the onslaught of the Arian heresy, is rightly growing in popularity today in consideration of the crisis of Faith now facing the Church; a crisis that matches or perhaps exceeds the crisis with which he dealt. Sadly, however, his mysticism is often forgotten. The Catechism's revival of this quote from Athanasius to the mainstream, therefore, was no doubt Providential. As orthodox-minded Catholics continue to turn to his intercession and example in order to confront the crisis in the Church today, let us ensure that we do not lose sight of **the entire purpose of the Christological orthodoxy which Athanasius fought for; namely, that we too become "other Christs,"** just as Luisa prayed:

> Having received Holy Communion, I was saying to my beloved Jesus: "My Love and my Life, Your Will has the virtue of multiplying Your Life for as many beings as exist and will exist on earth. And I, in Your Will, want to form as many Jesuses in order to give the whole of You to each soul of Purgatory, to each Blessed of Heaven, and to each being living on earth." [265]

Many more quotes on the deification of man exist in the writings of Athanasius, but there is not as much depth of explanation regarding what this entails as there is in the writings of other Fathers of the Church, to which we will now turn.

Sts. Augustine, Ambrose, and Gregory of Nazianzus

Some teachings of the Fathers of the Church are so important that they are additionally exalted through their incorporation in the Magisterium (as in the cases of the Catechism quotes previously provided) or in the Liturgy. Such is the case with Augustine's teaching on Divinization, which is found in the Divine Office as follows:

> Beloved, our Lord Jesus Christ, the eternal creator

---

[261] Jean-Yves Lacoste. *Routledge Encyclopedia of Christian Theology*. (2004) Page 348.

[262] George E Demacopoulos, *The Blackwell Companion to Christian Mysticism*. 2012. Page 272.

[263] *Nicene and Post-Nicene Fathers. Series II, Volume 4*. Philip Schaff. Athanasius: Select Works and Letters 54.3

[264] I still recall when, many years ago, I first came upon this Catechism quote. It was printed out from a Microsoft Word

document, and I thought that Word must have erroneously auto-corrected the second "God" in the sentence to be capital, even though it should have been lower-case. I, however, was the one who erred: that second capital "G" is in fact intended, and is in the CCC. Divinization is no mere metaphor.

[265] February 23, 1927.

of all things, today became our Savior by being born of a mother. Of his own will he was born for us today, in time, so that he could lead us to his Father's eternity. **God became man so that man might become God.** The Lord of the angels became man today so that man could eat the bread of angels.[266]

Elsewhere, we find these words of Augustine:

But he himself that justifies also deifies, for by justifying he makes sons of God. 'For he has given them power to become the sons of God' [Cf. John 1:12]. If then we have been made sons of god, we have also been made gods...To make human beings gods, He was made man who was God. (sermon 192.1.1).

Fr. David Meconi, S.J., writes:

Among academic theologians, Augustine is normally not associated with those Church Fathers who expounded the glorious transformation of the human person in Christ. Yet, more and more studies are showing how he did in fact understand Christianity in terms of deification ... [Augustine] is never afraid to call this adoption our "becoming gods" as long as he (1) stresses how this is the result of union with Christ and no other supposed "deity" who claims to make its adherents into gods, and (2) highlights how this process of deification is achieved not through the abolishing of our human nature but by its perfection in and through grace ... participation in God is no mere metaphor for Augustine but proves to be the heart of the Christian life. In many beautiful ways Augustine presents Christianity as mankind's mirrored response to the Incarnation ... [Augustine says] "The Lord makes those whom he wishes devout so that they have recourse to the Lord and desire to be ruled by him and make their will dependent upon his will and, by constantly clinging to him, become one spirit with him." ... **Augustine taught a sacramental realism, never wavering that what the priest celebrated on the altar at every Mass is in fact the sacred Body and Blood of Jesus Christ. Yet, establishing this Real Presence is rarely his aim when preaching about the Eucharist. He instead stresses the recipients' role in receiving and thus becoming this Christ**.[267]

It is also important to recall Augustine's teachings on the matter because of an error spread in some circles today wherein Divinization is referred to as a "merely Eastern phenomenon." But Divinization

is certainly found in the Latin Fathers, and not only in the quote above from Augustine. Writing on the matter, Jared Ortiz teaches:

Indeed, it has become something of a commonplace to say that the Latin Fathers did not really hold a doctrine of deification, that the few exceptions to this learned it from the Greeks, and that the Latins are generally guilty of losing sight of the big picture of salvation (becoming God) by reducing it to a narrow conception of redemption (overcoming sin) ... [but] many Latin Fathers are reticent to use the word "deification", though by drawing on a range of complementary terms—ascent, adoption, grace, contemplation, vision, knowledge, likeness to God, imitation, perfection, sanctification, participation, union, angelic life, immortality—they all, to greater or lesser degrees, point to the same reality of deification ...

The Transfiguration, Tertullian says, proves that this glorification will not destroy our nature, for Christ himself retained both his human and divine nature intact when transfigured, while Moses and Elias were shown still to be fully human in their glorified state. Highlighting the related moral and ontological dimensions of deification, Tertullian eloquently sums up the hope Christ has given us: "God held converse with man, that man might learn to act as God ...

"Then a Virgin conceived," Ambrose says, "and the Word became flesh that flesh might become God." In a number of treatises, Ambrose develops a spiritual itinerary of the soul espoused to God, which he develops in surprising ways. Not only does the espoused soul ascend so as to delight in God himself, but because the soul is transformed by deifying virtue, Christ himself delights and even feeds on the soul.

... One of the great synthesizers of the Latin tradition—and therefore an important witness to the Latin patristic understanding of deification—Pope Leo the Great preached the content of deification in a variety of contexts. ... [in his teaching] The noncompetition of the two natures inseparably united in Christ brings about our divinization without violating our human nature.

... God, by loving us, restores us to His image, and, in order that He may find in us the form of His goodness, He gives us that whereby we ourselves too may do the work that He does, kindling that is the lamps of our minds, and inflaming us with the fire of His love, that we may love not only

266 Office of Readings. Saturday before the Epiphany.
267 *Called to Be the Children of God*. Chapter 4.

Himself, but also whatever He loves. From this arises a unity of will that makes us friends with God—that is, a kind of "equal" because we have attained "the dignity of the Divine Majesty", not, of course, by nature, but by the grace of the Incarnation and the sacraments, which makes us like God.[268]

Only a few excerpts are included here. Elsewhere in the work (which I highly recommend purchasing), Dr. Ortiz goes on to list many other clear teachings on Divinization found within the Latin Christian tradition, including the writings of Boethius, Benedict, Peter Chrysologus, and others. He has even produced an entire 300-plus page volume, published by the Catholic University of America Press in January of 2019, in which he examines many more. Entitled *Deification in the Latin Patristic Tradition*, it hopefully will settle once and for all that the Divinization of Man is a unanimous consensus of the Fathers, and **whatever is a unanimous consensus of the Fathers is by that very fact a Dogma of the Catholic Church**.[269]

Gregory of Nazianzus

Gregory, an early Church Father (also a saint and Doctor of the Church), admired greatly by St. Augustine, was no less forceful in his insistence upon Divinization; teaching, for example, in his Orations:

> Let us become God's for His sake, since He for ours became Man.[270]

> For He still pleads even now as Man for my salvation; for He continues to wear the Body which He assumed, until He make me God by the power of His Incarnation.[271]

> While His inferior Nature, the Humanity, became God, because it was united to God, and became One Person because the Higher Nature prevailed in order that I too might be made God so far as He is made Man.[272]

Justin Martyr, Irenaeus, Clement, Theophilus, Hippolytus, Gregory

In explaining the theology of Justin Martyr, the New Catholic Encyclopedia states:

Justin explains that because of His redemptive work, Christ has become the source of a new humanity that He has regenerated through water, faith, and the cross (cf. Dial. 40). It is this profoundly biblical perspective that Irenaeus takes up from Justin and develops into a comprehensive theory of recapitulation: "He recapitulated in Himself the long history of man, summing up and giving us salvation in order that we might receive again in Christ Jesus what we had lost in Adam, that is, the image and likeness of God" ...This runs through from Irenaeus (cf. Adversus haereses 3.19.1) to Cyril of Alexandria [cf. Jo. 1.9 (on Jn 1.13)]. Into this notion of divinization is assumed the understanding of 2 Pt 1.4, "sharers of the divine nature." This is understood as a participation in and a communion with the Triune life itself.[273]

It would be vastly beyond the scope of this text to present a detailed examination of the many teachings on Divinization found in all the Church Fathers. Therefore, in closing this section, I will only briefly cite the words of five more Fathers of the Church.

Irenaeus

> [T]he Word of God, our Lord Jesus Christ, who did, through His transcendent love, become what we are, that He might bring us to be even what He is Himself.[274]

> 'For we cast blame upon [God], because we have not been made gods from the beginning, but at first merely men, then at length gods; although God has adopted this course out of His pure benevolence, that no one may impute to Him invidiousness or grudgingness he declares, "I have said, Ye are gods; and all of you are sons of the Most High.[275]

> For it was necessary, at first, that nature should be exhibited; then, after that, that what was mortal should be conquered and swallowed up by immortality, and the corruptible by incorruptibility, and that man should be made after the image and likeness of God.[276]

Clement of Alexandria

> [T]he Word of God became man, that thou mayest learn from man how man may become God.[277]

---

268 *Ibid.* Chapter 3.
269 *unanimis consensus Patrum*, DS 1507, 3007
270 Oration 1. Paragraph V.
271 Orations 30 Paragraph XIV
272 Oration 29. Chapter XIX.
273 *New Catholic Encyclopedia*. Grace (Theology of). P. 385.

274 Philip Schaff. *Ante-Nicene Fathers*. Volume 1.IX.VII.I.
275 Ibid. Volume 1. IX. VI. XXXIX.
276 Ibid.
277 Ibid. Volume 2. VI. II. I.

For if one knows himself, he will know God; and knowing God, he will be made like God[278]

[H]is is beauty, the true beauty, for it is God; and that man becomes God, since God so wills ... For the Word Himself is the manifest mystery: God in man, and man God[279]

[H]e who listens to the Lord, and follows the prophecy given by Him, will be formed perfectly in the likeness of the teacher—made a god going about in flesh.[280]

Theophilus of Antioch

For if He had made him immortal from the beginning, He would have made him God. Again, if He had made him mortal, God would seem to be the cause of his death. Neither, then, immortal nor yet mortal did He make him, but, as we have said above, capable of both; so that if he should incline to the things of immortality, keeping the commandment of God, he should receive as reward from Him immortality, and should become God ... [281]

Hippolytus of Rome

And you shall be a companion of the Deity, and a co-heir with Christ, no longer enslaved by lusts or passions, and never again wasted by disease. For you have become God: for whatever sufferings you underwent while being a man, these He gave to you, because you were of mortal mould, but whatever it is consistent with God to impart, these God has promised to bestow upon you, because you have been deified, and begotten unto immortality.[282]

If, therefore, man has become immortal, he will also be God. And if he is made God by water and the Holy Spirit after the regeneration of the laver he is found to be also joint-heir with Christ after the resurrection from the dead.[283]

Gregory of Nyssa[284]

...since the God who was manifested infused Himself into perishable humanity for this purpose, viz. that by this communion with Deity mankind might at the same time be deified, for this end it is that, by dispensation of His grace, He

disseminates Himself in every believer through that flesh, whose substance comes from bread and wine, blending Himself with the bodies of believers, to secure that, by this union with the immortal, man, too, may be a sharer in incorruption.[285]

For just as He in Himself assimilated His own human nature to the power of the Godhead, being a part of the common nature, but not being subject to the inclination to sin which is in that nature... so, also, will He lead each person to union with the Godhead ... [286]

The Great Spiritual Writers

The following spiritual writers listed here in chronological order (of birth) are mentioned so that one can clearly see the action of the Holy Spirit as the architect of this profound development of the spirituality of the Divine Will. Some of these writers are saints, some are Doctors of the Church, some mystics or theologians who, though not canonized, are nevertheless widely recognized by orthodox Catholics for their spiritual insight.

St. Bernard of Clairvaux

St. Bernard, the great monastic, Doctor of the Church, founder of the Cistercians, and transitional figure between the Fathers and the saints thereafter, is a veritable giant of Catholic spiritual theology. Often forgotten is the fact that he may even be an originator of the notion of Our Lady as the Mediatrix of All Grace; for it was he who said, long before many others were ready to accept this tenet of Mariology, "God has willed that we should have nothing that did not pass through the hands of Mary"[287]

Bernard, as the "last of the Fathers,"[288] did not fail to incorporate divinization into his teachings:

O pure and cleansed purpose, thoroughly washed and purged from any admixture of selfishness, and sweetened by contact with the divine will! To reach this state is to become deified. [289]

---

[278] Ibid. Volume 2. VI. III. III. I.
[279] Ibid.
[280] Ibid. Volume 2. VI. IV. VII. XVI.
[281] To Autolycus. Book II. Chapter 27.
[282] Refutation of All Heresies. Book X. Chapter 30.
[283] Philip Schaff. *Ante-Nicene Fathers*. Volume 5. III. IV. II. VI.
[284] not to be confused with his friend, Gregory of Nazianzus, already quoted in this section
[285] The Great Catechism. Part III. Chapter 37.

[286] Ascetical Works (The Fathers of the Church, Volume 58). P. 116.
[287] *New Catholic Encyclopedia*. P. 262.
[288] Pope Pius XII. Encyclical *Doctor Mellifluus*. Nota bene: This reference does not mean Bernard literally was a Father of the Church, but rather that he ensured that their legacy did not die in the centuries after the close of the age of the Fathers in the 8th century.
[289] St Bernard of Clairvaux "On loving God" Ch. 10

Venerable Pope Pius XII highly exalted St. Bernard, writing:

> Of [Divine Charity], possibly nobody has spoken more excellently, more profoundly, or more earnestly than Bernard: "The reason for loving God," as he says, "is God; the measure of this love is to love without measure. ... O holy and chaste love! O sweet and soothing affection! ... It is the more soothing and more sweet, the more the whole of that which is experienced is divine. **To have such love, means being made like God.**"

We see that St. Bernard, and likewise Pope Pius XII, speaks of love not merely as the supreme virtue, but as having the power of transforming one into the very likeness of God. This is precisely the transformation that Living in the Divine Will completes — that is, the restoration of the likeness of God lost at the Fall of Man.

Richard of Saint Victor

Richard of Saint Victor was a highly esteemed Scottish theologian and abbot who lived in the 12th century. The New Catholic Encyclopedia refers to him as a *"remarkable theologian… above all a mystic, [and] the greatest theoretician of mysticism in the Middle Ages."*[290] Richard taught that the highest level of union with God involves the following:

> ... an ecstatic 'passing over into the divine glory' ... like iron in a fire, the mind becomes liquefied ... and 'incandescent ... and becomes one spirit with God,' its will having become fully identified with the divine will[291]

In this great mystic and theologian, we already find clear intimations of the Gift of Living in the Divine Will, almost a thousand years before its time. Most importantly, he clearly indicates that there is in fact possible a higher (fourth) degree of union with God beyond the three usually spoken of in mystical theology.

In his introduction to Richard's treatise of "the Four Degrees of Violent Love", Dr. Andrew Kraebel, a theologian, writes that Richard's previous descriptions of the earlier Degrees ...

> …lead Richard into his final account of the fourth degree — for the experience of union with God enjoyed in the third degree can only be fleeting,"

and the contemplative thereafter returns to his community as a transformed human being. His absolute conformation to the Will of God makes the contemplative Christ-like. No longer interested in achieving temporary experiences of vision or union, he is now intent only upon seeing to the salvation of his fellow human … Thus, again, the insatiability of the general metaphor for the fourth degree returns here, as the contemplative is relentless in seeking new ways to achieve his desired ends.[292]

This has a fascinating overlap with Jesus' words to Luisa, in which He encourages her to not so much think about her own sanctity, but rather to be concerned entirely with the salvation of souls and the consolation of His Heart. Dr. Kraebel continues:

> Richard's account indicates that, as one progresses through the degrees, one's own agency becomes less important, while God's agency becomes ever more so. For example, the proper ordering of one's life in the first degree, described as the soul's own quitting of Egypt and journey through the Red Sea, gives way to the soul passively being "snatched away into the abyss of divine love". By this point, Richard suggests, **the will of the contemplative and the will of God become the same thing, and so the question of agency becomes redundant**.

Kraebel presents a translation of the work itself from Richard, in which we read:

> In the first degree the soul thirsts for God. In the second it thirsts toward God. In the third the soul thirsts into God. In the fourth it thirsts in accordance with God… The soul thirsts in accordance with God when concerning its own will — not just in fleshly things, but also indeed in spiritual things — the mind relinquishes everything from its own judgment and commits itself wholly to the Lord, never thinking "of things that are its own, but of the things of Jesus Christ," so that the soul itself may also be able to say, "I did not come to do my will, but the will of my Father who is in heaven." … when the soul has in this manner been melted away in the divine fire, inwardly softened and thoroughly liquefied, what then will remain except that "the good will of God, pleasing and perfect" be displayed to the soul, as if that divine will were a certain mold of consummate virtue to which it might be shaped? For when metals have been liquefied and the

---

[290] THEOLOGY, HISTORY OF. New Catholic Encyclopedia. P. 905-906.

[291] Boyd Taylor Coolman. *The Blackwell Companion to Christian Mysticism.* 2012 page 258.
[292] Andrew Kraebel. Introduction to *On the Four Degrees of Violent Love.*

molds have been set up, the metalworkers shape any image through a decision of their will and produce whatever vessels they wish in accordance with the proper shape and intended form. So, too, does the soul in this state easily adapt itself to every wish of the divine will, nay, rather it adapts itself with spontaneous desire to each of God's decisions and forms its every wish in accordance with the measure of divine benevolence. And just as a liquefied metal easily flows down into whatever passage is open to it, running toward the things that lie below, thus the soul in this state voluntarily humbles itself to every act of obedience and bends itself freely to every humiliation according to the divine arrangement…And so this type of man becomes a new creature: "the old things have passed away and, behold, all things have been made new." For in the third degree he has been killed; in the fourth, as it were, rising from the dead, "he dies no more; death no longer has dominion over him, for insofar as he lives, he lives for God. Therefore, in this degree the soul is made in some way immortal and impassible ... He who ascends to this degree of love without a doubt exists in a state of love (amoris) wherein he is truly able to say, "I have become all things to all men, so that I might bring about salvation for all…[293]

Hugh Owen, in his book, *New and Divine*, quotes this same treatise in which Richard teaches, rather boldly, that:

> In the first degree the betrothals take place, in the second the wedding, in the third the marriage is consummated, in the fourth the childbirth occurs ... In the first degree, the soul receives frequent visits; in the second, she is betrothed; in the third, she is made one with her beloved; in the fourth, she becomes a mother.[294]

Here we see profound intimations of the Gift. These intimations are so powerful and accurate in their description that, no doubt, one who reads these words (venerated rightly by Catholic tradition) and opens himself up to the light contained therein, will in so doing open himself up to the Gift of Living in the Divine Will.

St. Thomas Aquinas

St. Thomas Aquinas, the Angelic Doctor of the Church, was a 13th century Dominican theologian whose *Summa Theologica* is also the greatest theological work in Church history. The first formal scholastic treatment of tension between the Divine Will and the human will occurred during the 12th century in the writings of Peter Lombard, who himself commented on a passage from St. Augustine. This observation set the stage for further development.[295] Later, **St. Albert the Great taught that conformity to the Divine Will was the highest rule of moral action.**[296] Finally, Thomas Aquinas definitively summed up what had been said on the matter by using the words of Our Lord: *"Not as I will, but as Thou wilt,"*[297] to build his case. He stated:

> The goodness of the will depends on the intention of the end. Now the last end of the human will is the Sovereign Good, namely, God ... Therefore the goodness of the human will requires it to be ordained to the Sovereign Good, that is, to God. Now this Good is primarily and essentially compared to the Divine Will, as its proper object.[298]

Later in this same article, Aquinas speaks of conformity to the Divine Will on our part being limited in scope to mere imitation; in other words, *doing* the Divine Will. Incidentally, this limitation is precisely what Luisa's revelations change,[299] and **Aquinas' teaching here is extremely useful in proving that there is such a thing as a higher degree of the Union of Wills than is found in simple imitation (even if it is perfect).**

Nevertheless, from the issuance of this teaching and moving forward chronologically, conformity — or uniformity — to the Divine Will was prevalent in the spirituality of the saints, and grew to be seen (as the following sections will make clear) as the ultimate reality to which the entire spiritual life was directed. From this growth, one can clearly see how Luisa's revelations are the

---

[293] Ibid.

[294] Hugh Owen, *New and Divine*.

[295] Peter Lombard: *Sentences Book 1*, Distinction XLVIII. (Peter Lombard, Bishop of Paris, was a theologian who, though rarely spoken of today, was an enormous influence on western theology. He is referred to by Aquinas in the Summa simply as "the Master.")

[296] *New Catholic Encyclopedia; Conformity to the Will of God.*

[297] Matthew 26:39

[298] St. Thomas Aquinas, *Sum* I-II. Q19, A9.

[299] Luisa's revelations build beautifully on the foundation laid by 2,000 years of Catholic Tradition, and in no way do they contradict a single Church teaching. Needless to say, however, they are not simply identical to all that came before. The entire point of them is that they reveal a new sanctity. More on this distinction is contained in the "Answers to Objections" chapter.

perfectly fitting crown.

St Catherine of Siena

St. Catherine of Siena is another Dominican Doctor of the Church who, in addition to being an extraordinary mystic, gave profound teachings on the sanctity of transformation via the Divine Will. On Catherine and her teachings, Fr. Andrew Hofer, O.P., writes:

> Catherine expresses this transformation in various letters ... [for example] "The soul who has fallen in love with God, she who is a servant and slave ransomed by the blood of God's Son, attains such great dignity that she cannot be called a servant now, but an empress, spouse of the eternal emperor!" **Just as a maid becomes an empress through marital union with the emperor, so a creature becomes deified through a union with God** made possible by the Passion of Christ. Catherine loves to speak of fire. In a striking phrase, she prays to God about how her nature is that of the Creator: "In your nature, eternal Godhead, I shall come to know my nature. And what is my nature, boundless Love? It is fire, because you are nothing but a fire of love. And you have given humankind a share in this nature, for by the fire of love you created us ... **The will, now completely transformed by God's love, has no selfishness in it, but is completely divinized.**"[300]

In her *Dialogue*, St. Catherine herself writes that a divinized soul is...

> ... like the burning coal that no one can put out once it is completely consumed in the furnace, because it has itself been turned into fire. So it is with these souls cast into the furnace of [God's] charity, who keep nothing at all, not a bit of their own will ... They have been made one with [God] and [God] with them.[301]

Here we see clearly displayed both the necessary predisposition for the Gift and its effects; the predisposition being keeping *"nothing at all, not even a bit of one's own will,"* and the effect being *oneness with God.*

St. Francis de Sales

St. Francis de Sales, 16th century bishop and one of the greatest Doctors of the Church, is often rightly held up as the ultimate teacher on the spiritual life for the laity. He strongly insisted upon the need

for—and ability of—all to become holy, relaying clearly in his own writings what was not taught as clearly in the Magisterium for hundreds of years after his death (until the Second Vatican Council).

His most famous work is the *Introduction to the Devout Life*, but he gives a wealth of spiritual teachings in other works as well. Worth noting is that he was also perhaps the first Apostle of the "New Evangelization," (hundreds of years before it was called this), as he made great use of what was then new technology—the printing press. He would print thousands of leaflets defending the Faith and slip them under the doors of those who refused to listen to him. He *personally* converted tens of thousands of souls (many of whom were previously caught up in the newly formed Protestant Reformation), and an innumerable amount have been deeply edified by his writings since his death.

Of his spiritual teaching in general, Michon Matthiesen writes:

> [St. Francis de Sales] urges a preference for experiencing an "ecstasy of life", by which he means a life no longer lived by the natural, old self, but a self-sacrificing life devoted to God, a hidden life in Christ. This new life is a "supernatural ecstatic" existence of love; it brings with it newfound vigor. The devout life, which is the way to union with God, largely focused on the will. Spiritual perfection comprised a practical doctrine of intimacy with Jesus that reaches beyond simple imitation to a union of wills and life. The possibility of deification is largely embedded in the language of the soul or will "going beyond" the limits of its natural life. Francis' profound teaching about this union of wills and about living in the permissive will of God establishes a keystone in the French School of Spirituality ... Through such a self-obliteration, the will "departs" from the "limits" of its natural life, thereby being transformed into "the divine". **The believer's will can so participate in the divine will that those "tiny, ordinary things of life" done with love are, as it were, done by God.** Francis brings his Treatise on the Love of God to a close with passionate words that identify his call to all believers to live Jesus, and to live him with immense love.[302]

In Dr. Matthiesen's accurate and helpful overview

300 *Called to be the Children of God.* Chapter 5.
301 St. Catherine of Siena: *The Dialogue*, p. 147.
302 *Called to be the Children of God.* Chapter 8.

of de Sales' spirituality here, we see something so close to what Jesus reveals to Luisa that it would be nearly identical if only the words "as it were" were removed from the penultimate sentence of the quote above. And although the preceding quote is peppered with words from de Sales himself, let us turn now to a lengthier quote directly from one of this great Doctor's works; his *Treatise on the Love of God*, in which we see St. Francis de Sales write:

> So the soul that loves God is **so transformed into the divine will**, that it merits rather to be called, God's will, than to be called, obedient and subject to his will. Whence God says by Isaias, that he will call the Christian church by a new name, which the mouth of the Lord will pronounce, imprint, and engrave, in the hearts of his faithful; and then, explaining this name, he says it shall be: My will in her: as though he had said, that among such as are not Christians every one has his own will in the midst of his heart, but **among the true children of our Saviour, every one shall forsake his own will, and shall have only one master-will, dominant and universal, which shall animate, govern and direct all souls, all hearts and all wills: and the name of honour amongst Christians shall be no other than God's will in them, a will which shall rule over all wills, and transform them all into itself; so that the will of Christians and the will of Our Lord may be but one single will.** This was perfectly verified in the primitive Church, when, as says the glorious S. Luke: In the multitude of the faithful there was but one heart and one soul: for he means not there to speak of the heart that keeps alive our bodies, nor of the soul which animates hearts with a human life, but he speaks of the heart which gives our souls heavenly life, and of the soul that animates our hearts with the supernatural life; the one, the singularly one heart and soul of true Christians, which is no other thing than the will of God. Life, says the Psalmist, is in the will of God, not only because our temporal life depends on the divine pleasure, but also because our spiritual life consists in the execution of it, by which God lives and reigns in us, making us live and subsist in him ... Yes, we are in this world not to do our own will, but the will of thy goodness which has placed us here. It was written of thee, O Saviour of my soul, that thou didst the will of thy Eternal Father, and by the first act of the will of thy human soul, at the instant of thy conception, thou didst lovingly embrace this law of the divine will, and didst

place it in the midst of thy heart there to reign and have dominion for ever. **Ah! who will give my soul the grace of having no will save the will of her God!**[303]

Here we see, with the utmost clarity, the boldest of Jesus' words to Luisa (i.e. that we must have *no will but the Will of God*) clearly taught by a 16th century saint and Doctor of the Church. De Sales even gives a beautiful description of what the Reign of the Divine Will on earth will look like; all having the same will operating in them (the Divine), and thus all grounds for conflict are eradicated. Perhaps most importantly, **de Sales draws a sharp contrast (in the first sentence of the quote) between being transformed into the Divine Will and merely being obedient and subject to the Divine Will—a distinction Jesus emphasizes to Luisa. In so doing, de Sales is contradicting the opinion of Aquinas, quoted above, wherein the conformity to the Divine Will is limited to imitation.** This is noteworthy because de Sales undoubtedly was well acquainted with this opinion of Aquinas and would not contradict lightly any opinion of his.[304]

Of St. Francis de Sales in general, and of this quoted work in particular, Pope Benedict XVI taught:

> Francis found peace in the radical and liberating love of God: loving him without asking anything in return and trusting in divine love ... he simply loved God and abandoned himself to his goodness. And this was to be the secret of his life which would shine out in his main work: *The Treatise on the Love of God*... **In an intensely flourishing season of *mysticism The Treatise on the Love of God* was a true and proper summa ... [in it] we find a profound meditation on the human will** and the description of its flowing, passing and dying in order to live (cf. ibid. Book IX, chapter XIII) in complete surrender not only to God's will but also to what pleases him, to his "bon plaisir", his good pleasure (cf. ibid., Book IX, chapter I) ...It is not for nothing that we rediscover traces precisely of this teacher at the origin of many contemporary paths of pedagogy and spirituality; without him neither St John Bosco nor the heroic "Little Way" of St Thérèse of Lisieux would have come into being. Dear brothers and sisters, in an age such as ours that seeks freedom, even with violence and unrest, the timeliness of this great teacher of spirituality and peace who

[303]St. Francis de Sales. *Treatise on the Love of God.* Ch. VIII.
[304]De Sales went through his seminary formation in the late 16th century- after the Council of Trent- wherein Aquinas'

Summa was honored more than ever, and was insisted upon as the primary text for the formation of priests.

gave his followers the "spirit of freedom", the true spirit. St Francis de Sales is an exemplary witness of Christian humanism; with his familiar style, with words which at times have a poetic touch, he reminds us that human beings have planted in their innermost depths the longing for God and that in him alone can they find true joy and the most complete fulfilment.[305]

Pope Benedict's efforts to revive this work of de Sales here quoted (which is often eclipsed by his more popular—but also wonderful—book formerly mentioned, *Introduction to the Devout Life*), as well as the Pontiff's insistence on the spirituality of St. Maximus the Confessor depicted in a previous section, should inspire all Catholics to pursue zealously Divine Will spirituality as the ultimate key to sanctity, even aside from considerations of Luisa's revelations.

We should also note that Pope Pius XI dedicated an entire encyclical to St. Francis de Sales, strongly exhorting the faithful to heed this Doctor's teachings. Entitled *Rerum Omnium Pertubationem*, a paragraph found within it illustrates to us beautifully that this spirituality of total submission to the Divine Will does not in the least mean a quietistic or passive life:

> He was accustomed to repeat to himself, as a source of inspiration, that well known phrase, "Apostles battle by their sufferings and triumph only in death." It is almost unbelievable with what vigor and constancy he defended the cause of Jesus Christ among the people of La Chablais. In order to bring them the light of faith and the comforts of the Christian religion, he was known to have traveled through deep valleys and to have climbed steep mountains. If they fled him, he pursued, calling after them loudly. Repulsed brutally, he never gave up the struggle; when threatened he only renewed his efforts. He was often put out of lodgings, at which times he passed the night asleep on the snow under the canopy of heaven. He would celebrate Mass though no one would attend. When, during a sermon, almost the entire audience one after another left the Church, he would continue preaching. At no time did he ever lose his mental poise or his spirit of kindness toward these ungrateful hearers. It was by such means as these

that he finally overcame the resistance of his most formidable adversaries.[306]

Let us, therefore, imitate St. Francis both in his profound understanding of the renunciation of the self-will for the sake of living in the Divine Will, and in his overwhelming zeal for the salvation of souls.

Pierre de Bérulle

Pierre de Bérulle, a 17th century Cardinal and founder of the French Congregation of the Oratory, was especially noteworthy in the spiritual power of his writings. Of him, the old Catholic Encyclopedia states:

> Cardinal de Bérulle's writings exhibit a robust and vigorous doctrine full of unction and piety ... One of his biographers, Father Cloysenet, has said: 'He wrote the books at his leisure and weighed each word,' and the biographer adds very justly that the reader is rewarded for his trouble, for 'it is impossible to read them without feeling oneself filled with love for our Saviour Jesus Christ.'[307]

Considering the unassailable orthodoxy of the old Catholic Encyclopedia, and its insistence that this holy writer and Cardinal *weighed each word* that he wrote, we can approach his spiritual theology with confidence. For in Bérulle we see an amazing and even prophetic approximation of Luisa's revelations regarding Jesus "re-doing" of our lives Himself, which renders them ready for us to claim in His Will. Of Berulle's teaching, scholars have recently written:

> Bérulle takes the daring position that, because divinity and humanity co—exist in the Word, all the states of the interior of Jesus' human life have been divinized and made available to those who conform themselves to Him, thus enabling humankind to be divinized. The process of conformity is explicitly Pauline and must take place through a profound adherence of the will to the divine Will.[308]

And, also in this same anthology, we read:

> Benet of Canfield's Rule of Perfection (1593) **defined the spiritual life with a maxim: the will of God is God himself.** Bérulle was consistent

---

[305]Benedict XVI. General Audience. March 2, 2011.

[306]*Rerum Omnium Perturbationem*. Encyclical Of Pope Pius XI On St. Francis De Sales. Paragraph 8.

[307]Ingold, A. (1907). Pierre de Bérulle. *The Catholic Encyclopedia*.

[308] Wendy M. Wright. *The Blackwell Companion to Christian Mysticism*. 2012 page 445

with this tradition. According to him, in fact, the possession of God happens through knowledge of his will, and knowledge of the divine will is carried out in the renunciation of self will. Henceforth, the Incarnation, that "divine invention" whereby God has mysteriously joined the created and the uncreated, reveals the ultimate meaning of such a renunciation. ... (Grandeurs II, X). So the logic of nothingness and abnegation is not nihilistic. On the contrary, it is the logic of a greater real intimacy between Creator and creature.[309]

Even St. Louis de Montfort, in his famous treatise entitled *True Devotion to Mary*, strongly defended Bérulle and spoke highly of him, writing:

> Cardinal de Berulle, whose memory is venerated throughout France, was outstandingly zealous in furthering the devotion in France, despite the calumnies and persecutions he suffered at the hands of critics and evil men. They accused him of introducing novelty and superstition. ... But this eminent and saintly man responded to their calumnies with calm patience. He wrote a little book in reply and forcefully refuted the objections contained in it. He pointed out that this devotion is founded on the example given by Jesus Christ, on the obligations we have towards him and on the promises we made in holy baptism. It was mainly this last reason which silenced his enemies. He made clear to them that this consecration to the Blessed Virgin, and through her to Jesus, is nothing less than a perfect renewal of the promises and vows of baptism. **He said many beautiful things concerning this devotion which can be read in his works.**[310]

What we should be most careful to remember from Bérulle is his incredible insight—only made clear centuries later in Luisa's writings—that all of Jesus' earthly life consisted in His own divinizing of all human acts, through His own Divine acts in His human nature, and that these divinized states remain open for us to claim. This is precisely what we do through the Gift of Living in the Divine Will. Since this is among the more abstract (and for some quite difficult to grasp) of the teachings found in Luisa's writings, it is particularly important to recognize that it has long existed in orthodox Catholic spiritual theology.

St. John Eudes

St. John Eudes was a 17th century French priest who founded multiple congregations. A zealous promoter of devotion to the Sacred Heart of Jesus, he was also a strong critic of Jansenism. Regarding St. John Eudes' spiritual teachings, Dr. Matthiesen writes:

> Jesus in turn tells the Christian believer that "you are also in me living my life and I am in you, communicating that very life to you." Such mutual indwelling indicates the actual continuation of Jesus' holy life in his followers. Eudes points to several other New Testament passages (for example, Col 3:3-4; Eph 2:5; 2 Cor 4:10-11; Gal 2:20; 2 Thess 2:11-12) that insist upon this intimacy between Christ and his disciples: this scriptural witness leaves believers no choice but to conclude that **"Jesus Christ should be living in us and that we should live only in him... that our life should be a continuation and expression of his life." In fact, we have "no right" to live any other life on earth but his. In short, the baptized Christian should aim for nothing short of being "other Jesus Christs on earth". This "basic truth" of Christianity reflects the will of Jesus, whose union to us makes such an existence possible** ... Eudes stipulates that this divinized vision grants a twofold knowledge: we know the infinite worth of God, and we are aware keenly of the world's smoky "vanity" and of our own "nothingness, sin and abomination" ... John Eudes, in particular, shows himself to be quite ahead of his time, **anticipating by three centuries the Second Vatican Council teaching on the common priesthood of all the baptized**, and on the active participation of the laity in the offering of the Eucharistic sacrifice. Eudes articulates that the laity are not simply to attend Mass in order "to assist or to see". Rather, the Christian worshipper at Mass performs an action—"the most important thing you have to do in the world"[311]

Here we see that this saint's teachings continue to pave the way for the Gift of Living in the Divine Will, for he goes farther than offering this great union of wills, and instead insists that this ultimate form of sanctity is a veritable requirement for all Christians. *The Blackwell Companion to Christian Mysticism* says of Eudes:

> Eudes' spirituality was heart-centered. He combined Berulle's mystical Christocentrism with the spirit of devotion preached by the Savoyard. Longing to live in constant intimacy with Jesus

---

[309] Jean-Yves Lacoste. Routledge Encyclopedia of Christian Theology. 2004. Page 202

[310] *True Devotion to Mary*. Paragraph 162.
[311] *Called to be the Children of God*. Chapter 8.

and his mother Mary, the unity of whose hearts he insisted on, he composed liturgical and poetic works that gave expression to his vision. He taught that Mary's heart, composed of bodily, spiritual and divine (fine point) dimensions, was perfectly conjoined to that of her son. As exemplar of the human person, Mary shows the way in which divinization takes place: loving incorporation into the mystery of the Christ life...[312]

This explanation also demonstrates Eudes' insight into the superior means of acquiring this Divinizing grace of union of wills: the Sacred and Immaculate Hearts of Jesus and Mary, which he again anticipated devotion to by many years. Indeed, it is largely thanks to him that today we can benefit from our devotion to the Heart of Mary. He was formally declared, by Pope St. Pius X at his beatification, to be the "father, doctor, and apostle of the liturgical cultus of the Sacred Hearts." There is even a significant movement underway in consideration of his being declared a Doctor of the Church, with the head of this effort, Bishop Luc Crepy, already having met with Pope Francis to discuss it. Considering all of this and much more left unsaid, we should take care to heed the admonitions of this great saint for the good of our spiritual life, **not neglecting to remember his bold insistence that we have no right, as Christians, to fail to live *in* Christ.**

Jean-Jacques Olier

Jean-Jacques Olier, founder of the Sulspicians, was a 17th century French priest and a great reformer of the spirituality of diocesan priests. His writings give another major impetus to the development of Catholic spirituality on unification of wills. Regarding Olier's spiritual teachings, Dr. Matthiesen writes:

Most directly, the demands of authentic religion are met by becoming a host-victim to the Father, joining one's own sacrifice to that perfect oblation of Jesus. This oblative act of the Christian depends upon a prior abnegation, which serves to clear a path to union with Jesus in his own kenosis ... Olier's language is most austere on this point of abnegation or annihilation (aneatissement). This **abnegation, however, is a requisite preparation**

to the believer's gradual consummation into the very life of God ... no one participates in the ascension of Christ who does not first pass through Jesus' abnegation, suffering, humiliation, Cross, and his "death to everything". After this spiritual death, the Christian may participate in the resurrected life of Christ. This risen life, effected by the Spirit, is a life hidden in God, in which the soul is engulfed, absorbed, and annihilated by God, who hides the soul in himself. **... [The soul] is in such a breathless pursuit of God that only a very small part of it actually enlivens the flesh ... since the soul has been caught up in God and only lives for him.** The soul borrows the qualities of God and his being. It is much more appropriate that God should consume us than enliven us, since he is ablaze in himself. This remarkable description of divinization, here considered as a "resurrection" in the Spirit, asserts **that the soul can borrow divine power, and, more, that such a state is somehow fitting—given the nature of God and the capacity of the soul for intimate union with him.**[313]

We should not let Olier's status of not yet being a canonized saint dissuade us from taking his writings seriously. In the highly regarded masterpiece written by Fr. Faber, *Growth in Holiness*, we find the following said of Olier:

I have observed elsewhere that of all the uncanonized servants of God whose lives I have read, [Olier] most resembles a canonized saint.[314]

St. Vincent de Paul even considered Olier a saint, going so far as to pray for his intercession. This was shared in the Vincentian Heritage Journal, which states:

It is clear that Vincent regarded Olier as a saint. Writing to Mademoiselle d' Aubrai on 26 July 1660, just two months before his own death, Vincent stated that he had "asked God for great graces through the intercession of M. Olier."[315]

Jean Pierre de Caussade

Jean Pierre de Caussade was an 18th century French Jesuit priest who is greatly revered as one of the giants of Catholic spirituality. In 2011, Dr. Jeff Mirus wrote a piece strongly encouraging Caussade's spirituality and his work *Abandonment*

---

[312] *Blackwell Companion to Christian Mysticism*. Page. 446
[313] *Called to be the Children of God*. Chapter 8.
[314] Fr. Frederick William Faber: *Growth in Holiness*. 1856 Edition. P. 376.

[315] Robert P. Maloney C.M.: "Vincentian Heritage Journal." Volume 28. Issue 1. Article 1. P. 13.

to Divine Providence in particular, in which we read:

> This book is at once extraordinarily deep and wonderfully practical. It is superbly organized — subdivided into titled sections which generally run from just one to three pages, making the presentation perfect for daily spiritual reading ... r. de Caussade's work is one of the great classics of spiritual direction, holding a place in Catholic spiritual literature which is about as high as one can go without having been canonized and declared a doctor of the Church ... Catholic spiritual directors around the world have been recommending the book regularly now for some two hundred and fifty years. It has stood the test of time. There are some concepts which, under whatever name, are fundamental to the spiritual life. Practicing the presence of God, for example, is one of these. And so is abandonment to Divine Providence — a simple yet profound idea which beckons all souls who love God. Not for nothing, for example, did Bishop R. Walter Nickless of Sioux City recently conclude a stirring pastoral letter on Church renewal by urging Fr. de Caussade's insights upon all the priests, religious and laity of his diocese.[316]

As mentioned in the section on "Unification of Wills" in this book, in Caussade we find writings so sublime and so resembling Luisa's that one cannot help but wonder if somehow Caussade was miraculously given a prophetic glimpse of her Volumes. Although considered one of the greatest spiritual works in the history of the Church, his *Abandonment to Divine Providence* is nevertheless known to cause consternation in beginners who stumble upon it, for they understandably wonder if his teachings are orthodox, considering the astonishing magnitude of their claims. One such person contacted EWTN with precisely this concern, and was given the following response from one of EWTN's theologians, Dr. David Gregson. In his response, he first gives his own opinion and then goes on to quote an authoritative source:

> <u>**Abandonment to Divine Providence** is a spiritual classic, and Jean Pierre de Caussade's orthodoxy is unimpeachable</u>. From the New Catholic Encyclopedia (1967), "Caussade's doctrine is dominated by the idea of peace. A disciple of St. Francis de Sales and of Fenelon, he remained faithful to Ignatian spirituality as interpreted by Louis Lallemant. He relates all spiritualty [sic] to interior peace, obtained by fidelity to the order of God, by faith in the universal and ever actual working of the Creator, by accepting one's cross, and by a confidence in God's fatherly goodness. This is the Salesian ideal of evangelical simplicity and of absolute docitilty [sic] to the will and pleasure of God."[317]

Let us now turn to the teachings themselves as found in his own words. Summing up the importance and the effects of the renunciation of the self-will is a beautiful soliloquy written by him, which gives us everything we need to know in becoming disposed to receive the Gift of Living in the Divine Will:

> If, besides, [souls that tend towards sanctity] understood that to attain the utmost height of perfection, the safest and surest way is to accept the crosses sent them by Providence at every moment, that the true philosopher's stone is submission to the will of God which changes into divine gold all their occupations, troubles, and sufferings, what consolation would be theirs! What courage would they not derive from the thought that to acquire the friendship of God, and to arrive at eternal glory, they had but to do what they were doing, but to suffer what they were suffering, and that what they wasted and counted as nothing would suffice to enable them to arrive at eminent sanctity: far more so than extraordinary states and wonderful works. O my God! how much I long to be the missionary of Your holy will, and to teach all men that there is nothing more easy, more attainable, more within reach, and in the power of everyone, than sanctity. How I wish that I could make them understand that just as the good and the bad thief had the same things to do and to suffer; so also two persons, one of whom is worldly and the other leading an interior and wholly spiritual life have, neither of them, anything different to do or to suffer; but that one is sanctified and attains eternal happiness by submission to Your holy will in those very things by which the other is damned because he does them to please himself, or endures them with reluctance and rebellion. This proves that it is only the heart that is different. **Oh! All you that read this, it will cost you no more than to do what you are doing, to suffer what you are suffering, only act and suffer in a holy**

---

[316]https://www.catholicculture.org/commentary/otc.cfm?id=879.

[317]http://www.ewtn.com/v/experts/showmessage.asp?number=481328.

manner. It is the heart that must be changed. When I say heart, I mean will. Sanctity, then, consists in willing all that God wills for us. Yes! Sanctity of heart is a simple "fiat," a conformity of will with the will of God.[318]

Regarding the teachings of both Caussade and St. Thérèse of Lisieux two centuries later, Dr. Matthiesen says the following:

> Both of these later figures discover the possibility of deification in loving abandonment to the providential will of the Father. De Caussade and Thérèse understand that this abandonment—simple and complete—means that Jesus Christ becomes the source of action within the believer … Thérèse speaks of God entirely taking over one's desire, will, and actions. For both of these spiritual writers, the universality of their spiritual teaching—its hidden, sacrificial way—epitomizes the *vive Jesus* … [319]

Turning her focus specifically to Caussade, Dr. Matthiesen writes:

> De Caussade puts it this way: "God desires to be the unique cause of all that is holy in us, so all that comes from us is very little. In God's sight there can be nothing great in us—with one exception: our total receptivity to his will." While it is true that de Caussade's thought on the abandonment of the will depends largely on Francis de Sales, whom he quotes frequently in his letters of spiritual direction to the Visitation Sisters at Nancy, it is likewise the case that Berulle's influence emerges in de Caussade's depiction of abandon as a permanent state or disposition. De Caussade does speak of many discreet punctual acts of sacrifice that manifest self-abandonment; but he also addresses abandonment as a kind of continuous or habitual act. Formal acts of turning one's will over to God are gradually replaced by a steady disposition of heart, a readiness to will what God wills in every moment and circumstance. **This surrender thus becomes a kind of perpetual state, one that shares in Jesus' continual fiat voluntas tua (thy will be done).** Perhaps most accurately, we could say that abandonment is a more general fiat that contains a multiplicity of individual acts of surrender. De Caussade speaks of these acts as more or less unconscious; that is to say, they may leave little or no "trace" upon the spirit, so that the will does not recognize the act as its own—which is, in fact, the

ideal, for then it is God acting through the human will without resistance of any kind. At this point, what God wills and what the believer desires is one. **When such a unity of wills obtains, the believer is participating not only in God's design, but in God's life** … De Caussade eloquently articulates the vive Jesus and Eudes' firm assertion that Christians continue in their daily lives that holy and divine life of Jesus. His particular contribution is to locate this participation in **a union (by way of surrender) of the human will to the divine will.**[320]

St. Alphonsus Liguori

St. Alphonsus Liguori was an Italian Bishop and theologian who is also a Doctor of the Church. A prolific writer, he is especially known for his incredible insights into Mariology, long before such a deep understanding of the Glories of Mary (the title of one of his books) was common. He is also known for his profound teachings on the spiritual and moral life and, like most of the greatest Catholic writers of his day, he was despised by the Jansenists. Of St. Alphonsus' teachings, the great Fr. Aumann writes:

> If love is the essence of Christian holiness and if love is friendship, then the love that constitutes perfection will necessarily imply conformity to God's will; this, in turn, requires detachment from all that is an obstacle to union with the divine will. The goal, then, is to will only what God wills and thus attain a state of holy indifference to everything but God. Such conformity bears fruit in obedience to God's laws, which are the expression of his will for us…

> It has been said that the spiritual doctrine of St. Alphonsus is oriented to the ascetical life, and that is true, but it is an asceticism which serves as an excellent preparation for the mystical state. He places great stress on total renunciation, complete conformity to the divine will, and an intense life of prayer, all of which are favorable predispositions in mysticism. Like no other theologian of his time, St. Alphonsus made the traditional doctrine on the spiritual life practical and popular, yet he was well within the tradition of the great masters such as St. Augustine, St. Thomas Aquinas, St. Teresa of Avila, St. John of the Cross and St. Francis de Sales.[321]

---

[318]Jean-Pierre de Caussade, *Abandonment to Divine Providence* (also known as "The Sacrament of the Present Moment"). Section IX.

[319]*Called to be the Children of God.* Chapter 8.

[320]*Ibid.*

[321]Jordan Aumann. Christian Spirituality in the Catholic Tradition. P. 215-6

Though not so much regarded as a mystic, St. Alphonsus nevertheless presents beautiful, practical, and powerful norms on the application of Divine Will spirituality to one's life as a Catholic. For it was he who dedicated one of his greatest works to this very theme, entitling it *Uniformity With God's Will*. In this work, he begins by reminding us that the essence of our faith is nothing but this fact of God's Will:

> Perfection is founded entirely on the love of God: "Charity is the bond of perfection;" and **perfect love of God means the complete union of our will with God's**: "The principal effect of love is so to unite the wills of those who love each other as to make them will the same things." It follows then, that the more one unites his will with the divine will, the greater will be his love of God. Mortification, meditation, receiving Holy Communion, acts of fraternal charity are all certainly pleasing to God—but only when they are in accordance with his will. When they do not accord with God's will, he not only finds no pleasure in them, but he even rejects them utterly and punishes them. ... The greatest glory we can give to God is to do his will in everything. Our Redeemer came on earth to glorify his heavenly Father and to teach us by his example how to do the same ... Our Lord frequently declared that he had come on earth not to do his own will, but solely that of his Father: "I came down from heaven, not to do my own will, but the will of him that sent me." ... Furthermore, he said he would recognize as his brother, him who would do his will: "Whosoever shall do the will of my Father who is in heaven, he is my brother."[322]

He moves on to demonstrate that this is not some new insight of his, but is in fact the essence of the lives of the saints as well:

> To do God's will—this was the goal upon which the saints constantly fixed their gaze. They were fully persuaded that in this consists the entire perfection of the soul. Blessed Henry Suso used to say: "It is not God's will that we should abound in spiritual delights, but that in all things we should submit to his holy will." "Those who give themselves to prayer," says St. Teresa, "should concentrate solely on this: the conformity of their wills with the divine will. They should be convinced that this constitutes their highest perfection. The more fully they practice this, the greater the gifts they will receive from God, and the greater the progress they will make in the interior life." ... During our sojourn in this world, we should learn from the saints now in heaven, how to love God. The pure and perfect love of God they enjoy there, consists in uniting themselves perfectly to his will. It would be the greatest delight of the seraphs to pile up sand on the seashore or to pull weeds in a garden for all eternity, if they found out such was God's will. **Our Lord himself teaches us to ask to do the will of God on earth as the saints do it in heaven: "Thy will be done on earth as it is in heaven."**[323]

And he reminds us that this Divine Will was the essence of sanctity also in the times of the Old Testament, saying:

> Because David fulfilled all his wishes, God called him a man after his own heart: "I have found David ... a man according to my own heart, who shall do all my wills." David was always ready to embrace the divine will, as he frequently protested: "My heart is ready, O God, my heart is ready." He asked God for one thing alone—to teach him to do his will: "Teach me to do thy will."[324]

Next, Alphonsus speaks to the extraordinary power of the Divine Will:

> A single act of uniformity with the divine will suffices to make a saint. Behold while Saul was persecuting the Church, God enlightened him and converted him. What does Saul do? What does he say? Nothing else but to offer himself to do God's will: "Lord, what wilt thou have me to do?" In return the Lord calls him a vessel of election and an apostle of the gentiles: "This man is to me a vessel of election, to carry my name before the gentiles." Absolutely true—because he who gives his will to God, gives him everything. He who gives his goods in alms, his blood in scourgings, his food in fasting, gives God what he has. But he who gives God his will, gives himself, gives everything he is. ... St. Augustine's comment is: "There is nothing more pleasing we can offer God than to say to him: 'Possess thyself of us'." We cannot offer God anything more pleasing than to say: Take us, Lord, we give thee our entire will. Only let us know thy will and we will carry it out. If we would completely rejoice the heart of God, let us strive in all things to conform ourselves to his divine will. Let us not only strive to conform ourselves, but also to unite ourselves to whatever dispositions God makes of us. **Conformity**

---

[322]St. Alphonsus Liguori. *Uniformity With God's Will.*
[323]*Ibid.*

[324]*Ibid.*

signifies that we join our wills to the will of God. Uniformity means more — it means that we make one will of God's will and ours, so that we will only what God wills; that God's will alone, is our will. This is the summit of perfection and to it we should always aspire; this should be the goal of all our works, desires, meditations and prayers. To this end we should always invoke the aid of our holy patrons, our guardian angels, and **above all, of our mother Mary, the most perfect of all the saints because she most perfectly embraced the divine will.**[325]

Lest anyone be concerned that this Uniformity is any sort of a depressing task, Alphonsus reminds us that the greatest happiness and perfect peace is found in the Divine Will and in It alone. He writes:

If souls resigned to God's will are humiliated, says Salvian, they want to be humiliated; if they are poor, they want to be poor; in short, whatever happens is acceptable to them, hence they are truly at peace in this life. In cold and heat, in rain and wind, the soul united to God says: "I want it to be warm, to be cold, windy, to rain, because God wills it." **This is the beautiful freedom of the sons of God, and it is worth vastly more than all the rank and distinction of blood and birth, more than all the kingdoms in the world. This is the abiding peace which, in the experience of the saints, "surpasseth all understanding."** It surpasses all pleasures rising from gratification of the senses, from social gatherings, banquets and other worldly amusements; vain and deceiving as they are, they captivate the senses for the time being, but bring no lasting contentment; rather they afflict man in the depth of his soul where alone true peace can reside. ... By uniting themselves to the divine will, the saints have enjoyed paradise by anticipation in this life. ... **Our Lord assured his apostles: "Your joy no man shall take from you ... Your joy shall be full." He who unites his will to God's experiences a full and lasting joy:** full, because he has what he wants, as was explained above; lasting, because no one can take his joy from him, since no one can prevent what God wills from happening.[326]

Finally, the single key to all of this is nothing but the very thing that every Christian knows by heart. For in yet another work, St. Alphonsus (quoting another saint when he gave advice on what to meditate on from the Our Father prayer), once wrote:

The Lord recommended to St. Catherine of Genoa, every time she said the Our Father, to pay particular attention to these words: "Thy will be done," and to beg for the grace to fulfill the Will of God as perfectly as the Saints in heaven.[327]

"Thy Will be Done." In that, is everything.

As we have seen even in this brief treatment, this great Doctor of the Church gives us nothing short of a treasure chest of teachings on the theology of the Divine Will and of our response to it, all of unassailable orthodoxy by even the most tepid of Catholics. These teachings will — if believed and followed — enable us to receive the Gift of Living in the Divine Will.

St. Thérèse of Lisieux

And now we have arrived at "the Greatest Saint of Modern Times,"[328] the little flower, St. Thérèse of Lisieux, Doctor of the Church.

Here we have something unprecedented. Before relaying it, I will first share my own dilemma. There is some debate among experts on Luisa's writings whether Luisa received the Gift of Living in the Divine Will in 1888, 1889, 1900, or some time in between. I am not worthy of contributing to this debate, so I leave it up to better men than myself to figure that out; even though the date I often cite is 1889. How exactly this debate is cleared up determines whether it is possible that Thérèse herself received (and thus spoke *directly* about) the Gift itself (Thérèse died in 1897 and wrote her famous *Story of a Soul* in the years leading up to her death). I include her in this chapter on the Gift's "foreshadowing" simply because I wish to emphasize how the teachings of St. Thérèse serve as the completion of this profound development of the spirituality of Union of Wills found in the preceding sections, each dedicated — chronologically — to the earlier writers on the same topic. But it may very well be that Thérèse more appropriately belongs in the section on "The Gift Elsewhere in Private Revelation;" for although Thérèse did not specifically receive clear messages or direct apparitions from Jesus, it is undeniable that she received clear light from Him and that He

---

[325]*Ibid.*
[326]St. Alphonsus Liguori. *Uniformity With God's Will.*

[327]St. Alphonsus Liguori, *The Twelve Steps to Holiness and Salvation.*
[328]Pope St. Pius X on Therese

inspired her words.

What is perhaps most important in the writings of Thérèse is the "ease" of receiving this great gift of unprecedented heights of sanctity from God. She wrote in her autobiography:

> How can a soul so imperfect as mine aspire to the plenitude of Love? ... Alas! I am but a poor little unfledged bird. I am not an eagle, I have but the eagle's eyes and heart! Yet, notwithstanding my exceeding littleness, I dare to gaze upon the Divine Sun of Love, and I burn to dart upwards unto Him! I would fly, I would imitate the eagles; but all that I can do is to lift up my little wings-it is beyond my feeble power to soar. ... With daring self-abandonment there will I remain until death, my gaze fixed upon that Divine Sun. Nothing shall affright me ... [329]

The necessity for "littleness" of the soul constitutes a great overlap between Thérèse and Luisa's writings, and this littleness is the key to being open to receiving the Gift of Living in the Divine Will. In demonstrating that the heights of perfection can be reached not only through the same long and arduous journey taken by many great saints we read about, but can also be achieved in a much easier and quicker way, Thérèse teaches the following:

> You know it has ever been my desire to become a Saint, but I have always felt, in comparing myself with the Saints, that I am as far removed from them as the grain of sand, which the passer-by tramples underfoot, is remote from the mountain whose summit is lost in the clouds. Instead of being discouraged, I concluded that God would not inspire desires which could not be realised, and that I may aspire to sanctity in spite of my littleness. For me to become great is impossible. I must bear with myself and my many imperfections; but I will seek out a means of getting to Heaven by a little way-very short and very straight, a little way that is wholly new. We live in an age of inventions; nowadays the rich need not trouble to climb the stairs, they have lifts instead. Well, I mean to try and find a lift by which I may be raised unto God, for I am too tiny to climb the steep stairway of perfection. I have sought to find in Holy Scripture some suggestion as to what this lift might be which I so much desired, and I read these words uttered by the

Eternal Wisdom Itself: "Whosoever is a little one, let him come to Me." Then I drew near to God, feeling sure that I had discovered what I sought; but wishing to know further what He would do to the little one, I continued my search and this is what I found: "You shall be carried at the breasts and upon the knees; as one whom the mother caresseth, so will I comfort you." Never have I been consoled by words more tender and sweet. Thine Arms, then, O Jesus, are the lift which must raise me up even unto Heaven. To get there I need not grow; on the contrary, I must remain little ... [330]

A religious sister once wrote in order to Thérèse, telling her that her "little way" was truly a "great way"—that although Thérèse says she is just a fledgling little bird with a broken wing who cannot hope to rise up to the heights of the eagles (the great saints), she is in reality just another eagle soaring in the Heavens. This view is likely shared by many Catholics when they are introduced to the Little Way of St. Thérèse—Catholics who say to themselves; "*Ah! Interesting thing for a canonized saint who never committed a mortal sin to say! And a cloistered nun, no less! This couldn't possibly be less applicable to me.*" Thérèse rebuked this sister. It was no doubt arranged by God so that Thérèse could answer this same concern for us all. She said to this sister it was not so—that she truly did not have the greatness of the saints she spoke of. Thérèse insisted that it was confidence and **blind confidence alone** in God, and nothing else. No greatness of the eagle, not even of a subtle type. In relaying the heart of Thérèse's spirituality, Dr. Matthiesen writes:

> Thérèse petitions to be so transformed by Jesus' divine substance in the Eucharist that she might ascend to the very Furnace of Love in the Trinity. It is the work of divinization to lift up and consume the soul, but Thérèse avers that such divine operation is effective only in one who becomes nothing: the smaller one is, the wider the vessel one presents to God to fill with himself. **Abandonment of the self, abandonment of the will to God's desire, should be the Christian's only "compass". Such abnegation allows God to be working through the soul so that every act is love** ...Thérèse, in a manner more strikingly **direct than Francis de Sales and John Eudes, teaches that the believer who lovingly makes**

---

[329] St. Therese of Lisieux, *The Story of a Soul* (New York: An Image Book, Doubleday, Inc. 1989). Ch. XI.
[330] Ibid, Ch. IX.

herself nothing before the will of God does indeed become a continuation of the life of Christ and a daring sharer in his divine powers. The divine and prodigal excess of the Father finds a receptacle in the soul's abandon.[331]

Here we see that **Thérèse's admonition that we become nothing before God goes so far as to allow Christ to continue His very own Life within us. That is, to live in the Divine Will.** Explicitly pointing out this truth as a rather unavoidable conclusion, Hugh Owen writes:

> … the comments of the popes who promoted her cause of canonization take on even greater significance. Indeed, what could the Holy Spirit have intended when He inspired Pope St. Pius X to call Therese "the greatest saint of modern times"? What could have moved Pope Pius XI to confess that he expected the Little Flower to work "a spiritual revolution"? Superlatives like these from the lips of the Vicars of Christ suggest that we are not mistaken in seeing her as the patroness of a "'new and divine' holiness" which would grow exponentially and help the Blessed Virgin to "crush the head of Satan completely."[332]

Certainly, we would be foolish to not realize that there is something *new* here. Mr. Owen is correct: we cannot simply discount multiple Popes speaking with such superlative emphasis on Thérèse' spirituality. We are left to conclude that it marks a turning point. This turning point brings us to Luisa.

In the official Church-sanctioned biography of Luisa, published by the Vatican, we read:

> The young Carmelite is known as St. Therese of Lisieux and is today a Doctor of the Church. Luisa has a great devotion to this woman, who teaches with her life the trusting abandonment into God's hands and a "new' way of uniting with him. In her teachings, people can talk with God at any moment of the day. When the first translation of her "Story of a Soul," a sort of autobiography, is published in Italy at the beginning of the 1900s, it becomes understood that everyone, not just priests and nuns, can live a mystical life built on the awareness of a love that is already present in the heart of every person created in the image of God. But this mystical life is to be expressed by each person in the way most appropriate to the life one leads. That way, many people learn that

they can always be united to God, even in their daily tasks, through the union of will. So often mothers who go running to Luisa for advice end up hearing the same thing![333]

It is no accident that Luisa herself was deeply devoted to Thérèse (long before the latter's canonization). Indeed, Thérèse' *Little Way* is what prepares us to receive the Gift as revealed to Lusia.

I conclude this section with a few quotes from Thérèse which she shares in her autobiography.

> My heart is full of the Will of Jesus. Ah, if my soul were not already filled with His Will, if it had to be filled by the feelings of joy and sadness which follow each other so quickly, it would be a tide of very bitter sorrow. But these alternatives do nothing but brush across my soul. I always remain in a profound peace which nothing can trouble. If the Lord offered me the choice, I would not choose anything: I want nothing but what He wants. It is what He does that I love. I acknowledge that it took me a long time to bring myself to this degree of abandonment. Now I have reached it, for the Lord took me and put me there.

> "Holiness consists simply in doing God's Will, and being just what God wants us to be…"

> "In Heaven, God will do all I desire, because on earth I have never done my own will."

Various Teachings

The preceding sections paint a clear picture: one in which union with the Divine Will is the ultimate standard of the spiritual life; serving as its origin, its end, and the life breath that sustains it in every moment in-between. Of course, for the sake of space, I sadly had to leave many worthy saints and other writers out of this consideration.

Therefore, as much as I would like to give dozens more saints their own sections in this chapter, I must restrain myself and instead end the chapter with a collection of quotes on the Divine Will from an assortment of saints. First, we will a number of excerpts I have selected from *A Year with the Saints*,[334] a wonderful book published in English in 1891. Bearing an Imprimatur from the (then) Archbishop of New York, Michael Corrigan, it gives many beautiful snippets of inspiration from

---

[331] *Called to be the Children of God.* Chapter 8.
[332] Hugh Owen, *New and Divine: the Holiness of the Third Christian Millennium*. Page 70.

[333] *Sun of My Will.* Page 30.
[334] *A Year with the Saints.* (New York: P.J. Kenedy & Sons, 1891).

the lives of the saints. An overarching theme in it is the Divine Will.

"One act of resignation to the Divine will, when it ordains what is repugnant to us, is worth more than a hundred thousand successes according to our own will and pleasure." -*St. Vincent de Paul*

How much, in the midst of all his disasters, did holy Job merit before God, by his *Dominus dedit, Dominus abstulit*—The Lord hath given, and the Lord hath taken away!

"Perfect resignation is nothing else than a complete moral annihilation of thoughts and affections, when one renounces himself totally in God, that He may guide him as He wills and pleases, as if one no longer knew or cared for either himself or anything else except God. It is thus that the soul, so to speak, loses itself in God, not, indeed as to its nature, but as to the appropriation of its powers." — Bl. Enrico Susone.

St. Catherine of Genoa was one of those happy souls who attained to a share in this holy annihilation, in which, as she herself attests, she had no longer thoughts, affections, or desires as to anything, except to leave God to do with her, and in her, all that He might will, without any choice or resistance on her part, and that this gave her in all circumstances and occasions, a delight like that of the blessed, who have no will but that of their God. And so she was able to say: " If I eat, if I drink, if I speak, if I am silent, if I sleep, if I wake, if I see, if I hear, if I meditate, if I am in the church, if I am in the house, if I am in the street, if I am sick or well, in every hour and moment of my life, I would do only God's will, and my neighbor's for His sake; or rather, I would not wish to be able to do, to speak, or to think anything apart from the will of God; and if anything in me should oppose itself to this, I would wish that it might instantly become dust and be scattered to the winds."[335]…

"When shall it be that we shall **taste the sweetness of the Divine will in all that happens to us**, considering in everything only His good pleasure, by whom it is certain that adversity is sent with as much love as prosperity, and as much for our good? When shall we cast ourselves unreservedly into the arms of our most loving Father in heaven, leaving to Him the care of ourselves and of our affairs, and reserving only the desire of pleasing Him, and of serving Him well in all that we can? —St. J. F. de Chantal[336]…

We ought to submit to the will of God, and be content in whatever state it may please Him to put us; nor should we ever desire to change it for another, until we know that such is His pleasure. **This is the most excellent and the most useful practice that can be adopted upon earth. -*St. Vincent de Paul***

The venerable Father Daponte told an intimate friend that he was glad of all his natural defects of appearance and speech, since it had pleased the Lord to mark him with them; that he was glad also of all his temptations and miseries, both interior and exterior, since God so willed it, and that if it were the will of God that he should live a thousand years, oppressed by far greater trials, and in the deepest darkness, provided that he should not offend Him, he would be quite content.

When the news of her husband's death in the war was brought to St. Elizabeth, she instantly raised her heart to God, and said: "O Lord, Thou knowest well that I preferred his presence to all the delights of the world! But since it has pleased Thee to take him from me, I assent so fully to Thy holy will, that if I could bring him back by plucking out a single hair from my head, I would not do it, except at Thy will."[337]…

So great is the delight which the angels take in executing the will of God, that, if it were His will that one of them should come upon earth to pull up weeds and root out nettles from a field, he would leave Paradise immediately, and set himself to work with all his heart, and with infinite pleasure.— Bl. Enrico Susone

[Blessed Jacopone] was so satisfied with the will of God, so completely attached and submissive to it, that he said, "I would rather be a bat at the Divine will, than a seraph at my own."

So great was the love and tenderness which St. Mary Magdalen di Pazzi entertained for the Divine will, that at the mere mention of it, she would be lost in an ocean of spiritual joy, and sometimes rapt into ecstasies.[338] …

Conformity to the Divine will is a most powerful means to overcome every temptation, to eradicate every imperfection, and to preserve peace of heart. It is a most efficacious remedy for all ills, and the treasure of the Christian. It includes in itself in an eminent degree mortification, abnegation, indifference, imitation of Christ,

---

[335]*A Year with the Saints.* (New York: P.J. Kenedy & Sons, 1891). Pages 374-375.
[336]Ibid, P. 376

[337]Ibid, Pages 373-374.
[338]Ibid, P. 371.

union with God, and **in general all the virtues, which are not virtues at all, except as they are in conformity with the will of God, the origin and rule of all perfection."** -*St. Vincent de Paul*

St. Vincent de Paul was himself so much attached to this virtue, that it might be called his characteristic and principal one, or a kind of general virtue which spreads its influence over all the rest, which aroused all his feelings and all his powers of mind and body, and was the mainspring of all his actions. If he placed himself in the presence of God in his prayers or other exercises, his first impulse was to say with St. Paul, "Lord, what wilt Thou have me to do?" If he was very attentive in consulting and hearkening to God, and showed great circumspection in distinguishing between true inspirations proceeding from the Holy Spirit, and false ones which come from the devil or from nature, this was in order to recognize the will of God with greater certainty, and be in a better position to execute it. And, finally, if he rejected so resolutely the maxims of the world, and attached himself solely to those of the Gospel, if he renounced himself so perfectly; if he embraced crosses with so much affection, and gave himself up to do and suffer all for God, — this, too, was to conform himself more perfectly to the whole will of his divine Lord.

The blessed Jacopone being astonished that he no longer felt any disturbances and evil impulses, as he did at first, heard an interior voice saying: "This comes from your having wholly abandoned yourself to the Divine will, and being content with all it does."[339]…

"Perfection consists in one thing alone, which is, doing the will of God. For, according to our Lord's words, it suffices for perfection deny self, to take up the cross and to follow Him. Now, who denies himself and takes up his cross and follows Christ better than he who seeks not to do his own will, but always that of God? **Behold, now, how little is needed to become a Saint! Nothing more than to acquire the habit of willing, on every occasion, what God wills."— St. Vincent de Paul**.

More than in anything else the Saint just quoted showed the purity and solidity of his virtue, in always aiming to follow and obey the will of God. This was the great principle on which all his resolutions were founded, and by which he faithfully and firmly carried them into practice,

trampling under foot his own interest, and preferring the Divine will and the glory and service of God to anything else, without exception.

The Lord said of David, that he was a man after His own heart; and the foundation for such high praise is given in these words, " for in all things he will do My will."

St. Mary Magdalen di Pazzi was so much attached to this practice that she often said that she would never determine upon anything, however trivial, such as going from one room to another, if she thought it not in conformity with the Divine will, nor would she omit to do anything she believed in conformity with it. And she added, that if it came into her mind while she was in the midst of an action, that such an act was contrary to the will of God, she would abandon it on the instant, though to do so might cost her life.

Taulerus relates of a certain holy and learned man, that when his friends entreated him, on his death-bed, to leave them some good precept, he said : **The sum and substance of all instruction is to take all that comes as from the hand of God, and to wish for nothing different, but to do in all things His divine will** … [340]…

St. Mary Magdalen di Pazzi knew this most important truth; and, with the guidance of so clear a light, she knew how to submit her will to that of God so perfectly, that she was always contented with what came to her day by day, nor did she ever desire anything extraordinary. She was even accustomed to say that she would consider it a marked defect to ask of the Lord any grace for herself or others, with any greater importunity than simple prayers, and that it was her joy and glory to do His will, not that He should do hers. Even as to the sanctity and perfection of her own soul, she wished that it might be not according to her own desire, but to the will of God. And so, we find among her writings this resolution: To offer myself to God, and to seek all that perfection and only that perfection which He is pleased that I should have, and in the time and way that He shall wish, and not otherwise. In conversation with an intimate friend, she once said: "The good which does not come to me by this way of the Divine will, does not seem to me good. **I would prefer having no gift at all except that of leaving all my will and all my desires in God, to having any gift through desire and will. Yes, yes, *in me sint, Deus, vota tua, et non vota mea* — Thy will,**

---

[339]*A Year with the Saints*, Pages 370-371.
[340]*Ibid*, Pages 16-17.

not mine, be done." The grace which she asked most frequently and most earnestly of the Lord was this, that He would make her remain till death entirely subject and submissive to His divine will and pleasure; thus it is no wonder that she became so holy.[341]

The following quotes are taken from various other sources. (Due to the popularity of all these quotes and the ease of verifying each, I will not burden you with a deluge of individual footnotes. Many, however, were taken from the "White Lily of the Trinity" website[342].)

But above all preserve peace of heart. This is more valuable than any treasure. In order to preserve it there is nothing more useful than renouncing your own will and substituting for it the will of the divine heart. In this way his will can carry out for us whatever contributes to his glory, and we will be happy to be his subjects and to trust entirely in him

—St. Margaret Mary Alacoque

Lord what wilt Thou have me do? Behold the true sign of a totally perfect soul: when one has reached the point of giving up his will so completely that he no longer seeks , expects or desires to do ought but that which God wills.

—St. Bernard

There could not be a surer sign of God's love for you than this pain which He has sent you. Adore the divine will.

—St. Paul of the Cross

'All that the beginner in prayer has to do—and you must not forget this, for it is very important— is to labour and be resolute and prepare himself with all possible diligence to bring his will into conformity with the will of God. As I shall say later, you may be quite sure that this comprises the very greatest perfection which can be attained on the spiritual road.'

—St. Teresa of Jesus

No one will have any other desire in heaven than what God wills; and the desire of one will be the desire of all; and the desire of all and of each one will also be the desire of God.

—St. Anselm of Canterbury

'More determination is required to subdue the interior man than to mortify the body; and to break one's will than to break one's bones.'

—St. Ignatius of Loyola

I desire to suffer always and not to die. I should add: this is not my will, it is my inclination. It is sweet to think of Jesus; but it is sweeter to do His will.

—Bl Mary of Jesus Crucified "The Little Arab"

I will attempt day by day to break my will into pieces. I want to do God's Holy Will, not my own!

—Saint Gabriel of the Sorrowful Mother

The first end I propose in our daily work is to do the will of God; secondly, to do it in the manner he wills it; and thirdly to do it because it is his will.

—Saint Elizabeth Ann Seton

"Every creature, whether it will or not, is subject to the one God and Lord; but a warning is given to us, to serve the Lord with our whole will, because the just man serves Him willingly, but the unjust serves Him as a slave."

—Saint Augustine

12) The Gift Elsewhere in Private Revelation

If indeed, as has already been mentioned, Jesus did give Luisa the Gift of Living in the Divine Will in 1889, thus opening the door for others to receive it and know it,[343] then it should be no surprise that we begin to see hints of this same spiritual reality exhibited in the works of the great mystics of the 20th century.

So, unlike the previous sections, in which we spoke of premonitions of the Gift (even though in many cases these premonitions are amazingly accurate), here in this section we can speak of the actual Gift itself. Unfortunately, there are some promoters of Luisa's writings today who reject that the Gift can be found anywhere but in Luisa's own writings, but in my opinion Our Lord has the same

---

[341]*Ibid*, Page 26.

[342]Whitelilyoftrinity.com

[343]Although we can say this *opened the door*, it is only in the promulgation of the knowledges in Luisa's Revelations that the way will truly be made straight and clear

rebuke for them as He had for His own disciples:

> "Teacher, we saw a man casting out demons in your name, and we forbade him, because he was not following us." But Jesus said, "Do not forbid him… he that is not against us is for us."[344]

Nowhere in Luisa's revelations does Jesus clearly tell her anything to the effect of Luisa being the *only* one to whom He *would ever* reveal anything about this Gift, but only that she *was* the only person to whom He *had* revealed this Gift. Beyond merely reading their own interpretation into Luisa's writings, those who insist that the Gift cannot possibly be found explained anywhere outside of Luisa's writings are not even being logically consistent. For they themselves write of (or at least speak of) the Gift! "*Yes, but we do so only by way of talking about Luisa's writings,*" they may respond. But what an absurd constraint this is when we are speaking of mysticism.[345] These people have seen Luisa's writings as physical ink on paper and thus are able to speak of them; but what of a mystic who has seen their essence revealed to him or her by God? Is God incapable of such mystical action? As you will see, this is clearly precisely what has happened in the case of the following mystics; though knowing nothing of Luisa or her revelations, they nevertheless relayed the essence of the same. **Here, indeed, we simply have another profound validation of Luisa's revelations as truly being from God**; we see this Gift nowhere before the 20th century, and suddenly upon its dawn we see its explication exploding onto the scene of private revelation in the writings of mystics who had no knowledge whatsoever of each other.

Before delving into these examples, I wish to refer you to two works: *The Splendor of Creation*, **by Fr. Joseph Iannuzzi, and** *"New and Divine: The Holiness of the Third Christian Millennium,"* **by Hugh Owen.** I will only briefly present some key points here, whereas those two books treat the matter much more thoroughly, and I heartily recommend purchasing both. The highly respected

Fatima promoter and co-founder of the Blue army, John Haffert, wrote a forward for Mr. Owen's book, resoundingly endorsing not only the book in particular, but going so far as to say:

> It is faith in the promises of Fatima, faith in the triumph of God's Will on earth as in Heaven. And we can dare to believe that it can begin now, in each of us, if we believe enough to say "Yes" to the great gift that God now offers to the world, the gift of the "new and divine" holiness.[346]

St. Faustina

St. Faustina's revelations are especially noteworthy and they are included first in this list for two reasons. First, **the overlap they share with Luisa's writings is both profound and pervasive**. But we could go even farther, I wager, and say that Faustina's and Luisa's revelations represent the two prongs of God's Final Effort in the world: the former of salvation, and the latter of sanctification. For in a word, the essence of the Divine Mercy devotion is this: *Jesus, I Trust in You*. And the essence of the Divine Will devotion is this: *Thy Will be Done*. The former disposes us for the greatest possible result of the latter.

Second, **St. Faustina's revelations can be approached with an enormous degree of confidence, for they have been approved by the Church in the greatest possible ways**. A brief discussion is in order to demonstrate the grounds for this confidence so that you can truly feel this conviction in your heart and allow it to inspire also the same conviction in Luisa's revelations with due regard to the undeniable concurrence of the revelations (which will presently be demonstrated).

Pope St. John Paul II said, when speaking about his Encyclical *Dives in Misericordia* (which was greatly inspired by his reading of the Divine Mercy Diary):

> Right from the beginning of my ministry in St. Peter's See in Rome, I consider this message [Divine Mercy] my special task. Providence has assigned it to me in the present situation of man,

---

[344] Mark 9:38-40

[345] If we are going to here criticize those who err on one side of this issue, we should do the same for those who err on the other side. For there are also those who, taking such a 'flexible' approach to Luisa's writings, have decided that they need only assert that Luisa was merely the "one whose mission" the Gift was, and anyone could have had it any time before her. This is flatly contradicted numerous times in

Luisa's writings, and it simply is not honest to hold that Luisa's revelations are genuine and to hold that the saints have always had this Gift.

[346] John Haffert. From the Foreword of *New and Divine*, by Hugh Owen.

the Church and the world. It could be said that precisely this situation assigned that message to me as my task before God.[347]

He also spoke of the Divine Mercy Message as *"forming the image of [his] pontificate."* Lest anyone be concerned he was just speaking of Divine Mercy in general, and not intending to allude to Faustina's revelations on the same in particular, he also said that he had a *"burning desire"* that this message of St. Faustina's be proclaimed *"to all the peoples of the earth."*[348] On Divine Mercy Sunday of 1993, he beatified Faustina; on Divine Mercy Sunday of 2000, he canonized St. Faustina and declared that day a Feast of the Universal Church; on the vigil of Divine Mercy Sunday of 2005, John Paul entered into his eternal reward; and on Divine Mercy Sunday of 2014, he was declared a saint. Pope St. John Paul II's insistence upon St. Faustina's Divine Mercy revelations could be the topic of a book of its own; in this section we will review only a small morsel.

John Paul's successor, Pope Benedict XVI, said in his very first message as the Vicar of Christ:

> Dear friends, this deep gratitude for a gift of Divine Mercy is uppermost in my heart in spite of all. And I consider it a special grace which my Venerable Predecessor, John Paul II, has obtained for me. I seem to feel his strong hand clasping mine; I seem to see his smiling eyes and hear his words, at this moment addressed specifically to me, 'Do not be afraid!'[349]

The following Divine Mercy Sunday, he said:

> The words [John Paul II] pronounced on that last occasion [Dedication of the Divine Mercy Shrine] were as a synthesis of his Magisterium, evidencing that devotion to Divine Mercy is not a secondary devotion, but an integral dimension of a Christian's faith and prayer.[350]

The next month he said the following:

> Sr Faustina Kowalska, contemplating the shining wounds of the Risen Christ, received a message of trust for humanity which John Paul II echoed and interpreted and which really is a central message

precisely for our time.[351]

And later, during the homily at Mass on the third anniversary of the death of John Paul II, he said,

> God's mercy, as [John Paul II] himself said, is a privileged key to the interpretation of his Pontificate. He wanted the message of God's merciful love to be made known to all and urged the faithful to witness to it. This is why he desired to raise to the honor of the altars Sr Faustina Kowalska, a humble Sister who, through a mysterious divine plan, became a prophetic messenger of Divine Mercy.[352]

Pope Francis' words are no less supportive of precisely this message of Divine Mercy from St. Faustina. He said to a gathering of the priests of Rome:

> [We are here] to hear the voice of the Spirit speaking to the whole Church of our time, which is the time of mercy. I am sure of this. It is not only Lent; we are living in a time of mercy, and have been for 30 years or more, up to today. [St. John Paul II] sensed that this was the time of mercy, [he said] ' ... the light of Divine Mercy, which the Lord in a way wished to return to the world through Sr Faustina's charism, will illumine the way for the men and women of the third millennium' It is clear. Here it is explicit ... Today we forget everything far too quickly, even the Magisterium of the Church! ... we cannot forget the great content, the great intuitions and gifts that have been left to the People of God. And Divine Mercy is one of these. It is a gift which he [JPII] gave to us, but which comes from above. It is up to us, as ministers of the Church, to keep this message alive.[353]

Later, Pope Francis took the enormous step of declaring an Extraordinary Jubilee—a Holy Year of Mercy—taking its inspiration from none other than St. Faustina. In formally proclaiming the Holy Year, Pope Francis wrote:

> I am especially thinking of the great apostle of mercy, Saint Faustina Kowalska. May she, who was called to enter the depths of divine mercy, intercede for us and obtain for us the grace of living and walking always according to the mercy

---

[347] Pope John Paul II, Angelus Address to Collevalenza on November 22nd, 1981.

[348] Homily at the Mass of Dedication of the Divine Mercy Shrine on August 17th, 2002.

[349] First Message of His Holiness Pope Benedict XVI. Wednesday, April 20th, 2005.

[350] Pope Benedict XVI. Regina Coeli Address at St. Peter's Square. April 23rd, 2006.

[351] Benedict XVI. General Audience. May 31st, 2006.

[352] Benedict XVI. Homily. St. Peter's Square. April 2nd, 2008.

[353] Pope Francis. Address to the Priests of Rome. March 6, 2014.

of God and with an unwavering trust in his love[354]

More amazing still, it appears Pope Francis chose to structure the Holy Year in a way that prophetically emanates from Jesus' words to St. Faustina. For Jesus said to Faustina:

> …before I come as a just Judge, I first open wide the **door of My mercy**. He who refuses to pass through the **door of My mercy** must pass through the **door of My justice** …[355]

In the Holy Year of Mercy, Pope Francis called for a literal, physical, "Door of Mercy" to be opened at each Cathedral in the world. He said, "*I will have the joy of opening the Holy Door on the Solemnity of the Immaculate Conception. On that day, the Holy Door will become a Door of Mercy…*"[356]

Three Popes in a row now have expressed their most heartfelt, zealous, and unflinching support for this message of St. Faustina. They have unabashedly asserted that she is indeed a prophet, bringing God's own message to us. Her diary, of course, remains a private revelation; it is not the inerrant Word of God that Scripture contains, nor can it be approached as an infallible guide to Faith and Morals like the Magisterium. But consider what you have just read—you can see that it is, nevertheless, absolutely trustworthy. It is simply beyond question that whatever St. Faustina's revelations teach us consists in a true and undeniable call from Heaven, which is why her writings serve as a most powerful means of enkindling our desire for the Gift of Living in the Divine Will.

***

Therefore, we can now delve into the treasure chest of overlap of *Divine Mercy in My Soul* with Luisa's own revelations on the Divine Will. Let us approach what follows without the slightest hint of doubt, and from that absence of doubt let proceed a blazing fire of desire for what is described.

Thankfully, these private revelations given to St. Faustina have enjoyed immense popularity recently, and they deserve no less. But the most profound and radical elements of her revelations are almost entirely ignored in virtually all the well-known books, talks, etc. on the same. Here I wish to give you, not a comprehensive and thorough

overview, but merely a glimpse and an introduction to this usually neglected aspect of Faustina's writings.

The following section will take quotes from Faustina's diary and contain added emphasis to draw special attention to the references to the Gift of Living in the Divine Will.

Living Hosts: The "Unprecedented" Grace of Union with God

In St. Faustina's revelations, we read:

> However, the soul receiving this **unprecedented grace of union with God** cannot say that it sees God face to face, because even here there is a very thin veil of faith, but so very thin that the soul can say that it sees God and talks with Him. **It is "divinized."** God allows the soul to know how much He loves it, and the soul sees that **better and holier souls than itself have not received this grace.** Therefore, it is filled with holy amazement, which maintains it in deep humility, and it steeps itself in its own nothingness and holy astonishment; and the more it humbles itself, the more closely God unites himself with it and descends to it … **in one moment, [the soul] knows God and drowns in Him. It knows the whole depth of the Unfathomable One**, and the deeper this knowledge, the more ardently the soul desires Him.[357]

St. Faustina describes Living in the Divine Will here with the term "unprecedented grace." Despite knowing nothing of Luisa and not herself being the one instructed by God on the Gift, Faustina here in fact answers the first concern that most people have about the Gift of Living in the Divine Will, namely *"How could I, who am so unworthy, receive a gift so much greater than what was received by the saints of days past who dwarf me in virtue?"* Indeed, we must be amazed at the offer God extends to us. The more we learn, the more amazed and desirous we must become, for what is known more can be loved more. The more we receive, the more humble we must become; for we recognize that, despite being unworthy servants,[358] and far inferior in ourselves to the saints of ages past, we have been given such a greater Gift, as St. Faustina here points out.

Later in St. Faustina's revelations, we read the words of Jesus:

---

[354]*Misericordiae Vultus*. Bull of Indiction. Paragraph 24.
[355]St. Faustina, *Divine Mercy in My Soul*, Paragraph 1146.
[356]*Misericordiae Vultus*. Paragraph 3.

[357]St. Faustina, *Divine Mercy in my Soul*, Paragraph 771.
[358]*Cf.* Luke 17:10

My beloved child, delight of My Heart, your words are dearer and **more pleasing to me than the angelic chorus**. All the treasures of My Heart are open to you. Take from this Heart all that you need for yourself and for the whole world. For the sake of your love, I withhold the just chastisements, which mankind has deserved. A single act of pure love pleases Me more than a thousand imperfect prayers. One of your sighs of love atones for many offenses with which the godless overwhelm Me. **The smallest act of virtue has unlimited value** in My eyes because of your great love for Me. **In a soul that lives on My love alone, I reign as in heaven.** I watch over it day and night. In it I find My happiness; My ear is attentive to each request of its heart; often I anticipate its requests. O child, especially beloved by Me, apple of My eye, rest a moment near My Heart and taste of **the love in which you will delight for all eternity.**[359]

And similarly, Faustina herself said to Jesus "**The veils of mystery hinder me not at all; I love You as do Your chosen ones in heaven,**"[360] and later, "**I live Your divine life as do the elect in heaven…**"[361]

Here we see Jesus revealing to Faustina that her acts are more meritorious—more pleasing to Him—than all the angels are in themselves. By referring to the "angelic chorus," He refers to all Nine Choirs; not merely to "an" angelic chorus, which one could argue only refers to the lowest of the nine choirs. This is what the Gift of Living in the Divine Will does—it makes our acts truly unlimited in their value, as Faustina here says, which means that even the angels cannot hope to please God as we can. It allows God to reign in our souls just as He reigns in the souls of the blessed in Heaven. But it still gives us the benefit of the veil,[362] so that we can continue to build up merit as we suffer in Faith and in union with His passion.

> When a reluctance and a monotony as regards my duties begins to take possession of me, I remind myself that I am in the house of the Lord, where nothing is small and where the glory of the Church and the progress of many a soul depend on this **small deed of mine, accomplished in a divinized way.** Therefore there is nothing small

in a religious congregation.[363]

In this excerpt, we are reminded that the most mundane, boring, and seemingly unimportant duties can (and must!) be *Divinized*. How great a thought—and how true—that the "glory of the Church" and "the progress of many a soul" depend upon doing the laundry in the Divine Will (that is, becoming Divinized)! St. Faustina ends this paragraph by saying that nothing is small "in a religious congregation." This is because in those settings, it is expected that everything is done as a prayer. Sadly outside such places, we tend to see our duties as mere "necessary evils" which we rush through with no peace, so that we can get to what we like. But it does not have to be that way. The life of prayer and work which is the expected norm in a religious congregation can, and should, be lived everywhere, especially now that we are offered this incredible gift of *Divinizing* even the smallest acts— doing them *in the Divine Will*. St. Faustina prayed:

> O Divine Will, You are the delight of my heart, the food of my soul, the light of my intellect, the omnipotent strength of my will; for when I unite myself with Your will, O Lord, **Your power works through me and takes the place of my feeble will.** Each day, I seek to carry out God's wishes.[364]

Although it may at first glance appear that this is an ordinary meditation on the importance and the glory of doing God's Will, it is in fact more. For **here St. Faustina insists that the Divine Will** *"takes the place of [her] feeble will."* **It is this Divine Substitution we receive in the Gift of Living in the Divine Will. Before Luisa, this union with God's Will was limited to imitation, as Aquinas' teaches in the Summa (cited in the previous chapter); now, taught clearly in St. Faustina's revelations, we see that the union can become far greater than that.**

> Neither graces,[365] nor revelations, nor raptures, nor gifts granted to a soul make it perfect, but rather the intimate union of the soul with God. These gifts are merely ornaments of the soul, but constitute neither its essence nor its perfection. My sanctity and perfection consist in the close

---

[359]St. Faustina, *Divine Mercy in My Soul*, Paragraph 1489.
[360]*Ibid.*, 1324.
[361]*Ibid.*, 1393.
[362]In and of itself, the veil is not good; but in so far as God permits it temporarily so that we may use it to build up treasures in Heaven, it is indeed a benefit.
[363]St. Faustina, *Divine Mercy in my Soul*, Paragraph 508.

[364]*Ibid.* Paragraph 650
[365]Here, "graces" must not be understood in the common sense of the word (which refers broadly to God's action in a soul), but rather as a reference specifically to charismatic graces.

union of my will with the will of God.[366]

St. Faustina was always conscious of her nothingness and misery, but she was not one to succumb to false humility. She was aware of the sanctity and perfection of her soul, and yet she attributed it all to the union of her will with God's Will. That union, which finds its epitome in the Gift of Living in the Divine Will, is the most complete response to Our Lord's insistence that we "be perfect, as our Father in Heaven is perfect."[367]

Transconsecration of Self

Early in the *Diary*, St. Faustina describes a profound turning point in her life. While at the convent, she was asked by Jesus to give her consent to become a victim soul. A profound exchange follows:

> And the Lord gave me to know that the whole mystery depended on me, on my free consent to the sacrifice given with full use of my faculties. In this free and conscious act lies the whole power and value before His Majesty. Even if none of these things for which I offered myself would ever happen to me, before the Lord everything was as though it had already been consummated. At that moment, I realized I was entering into communion with the incomprehensible Majesty. I felt that God was waiting for my word, for my consent. Then my spirit immersed itself in the Lord, and I said, "Do with me as You please. I subject myself to Your will. As of today, Your holy will shall be my nourishment" ... Suddenly, when I had consented to the sacrifice with all my heart and all my will, God's presence pervaded me. My soul became immersed in God and was inundated with such happiness that I cannot put in writing even the smallest part of it. I felt that His Majesty was enveloping me. I was **extraordinarily fused with God** ...A great mystery took place during that adoration, a mystery between the Lord and myself. ... And the Lord said to me, You are the delight of My Heart; from today on, every one of your acts, even the very smallest, will be a delight to My eyes, whatever you do. At that moment I felt **transconsecrated. My earthly body was the same, but my soul was different; God was now living in it with the totality of His delight**. This is not a feeling, but a conscious reality that nothing can obscure.[368]

"Transconsecration" is not a word you will often

hear! And yet it is a wonderful name for the Gift of Living in the Divine Will. By using this word (and it appears she may have been the first), St. Faustina dares to say that what occurs to the host during the Mass, has indeed occurred in her soul as well. Jesus tells Luisa the same. This particular passage from St. Faustina's Diary gives a powerful instruction on receiving the Gift because of the buildup to it: I heartily recommend opening her diary to this passage. In it we learn how pleasing and necessary offering one's self as a victim is to God, and how, so long as this offering is truly free and entire, it is infinitely meritorious even if the openness does not wind up resulting in anything at all happening.

Faustina's "Great Secret"

But now we turn to perhaps the most perfect reference of all to the Gift of Living in the Divine Will in these revelations. St. Faustina refers to a "great secret" in her writings. This great secret is referred to most clearly here:

> In this seclusion, Jesus himself is my Master. He himself educates and instructs me. I feel that I am the object of His special action. For His inscrutable purposes and unfathomable decrees, He unites me to Himself in a special way and allows me to penetrate His incomprehensible mysteries. There is **one mystery which unites me with the Lord, of which no one-not even angels-may know.** And even if I wanted to tell of it, I would not know how to express it. And yet, I live by it and will live by it for ever. This mystery distinguishes me from every other soul here on earth or in eternity.[369]

Great scholars of St. Faustina's writings puzzle over this passage and others like it in her Diary.[370] In my opinion, **this is a *direct* reference to the Gift of Living in the Divine Will.** I am not thereby imputing deceit to St. Faustina because she said no one will ever know of this great union; she knew nothing of Luisa Piccarreta, and therefore Faustina could only have thought that what was uniting her to the Lord was so utterly great and mysterious that it would not be possible for anyone to ever know of. Now, the whole point of this section has been to present instances in St. Faustina's writings which do in fact refer to the Gift of Luisa's; I am not here implicitly denying that the other references in Faustina's book are valid! I am simply saying that

[366]St. Faustina, *Divine Mercy in My Soul*, Paragraph 1107.
[367]Matthew 5:48
[368]St. Faustina, *Divine Mercy in My Soul*, Paragraph 136-7.
[369]Ibid., paragraph 824.

[370]For example, see *"What Was St. Faustina's Big, Mysterious Secret?"* Dr. Robert Stackpole. www.thedivinemercy.org. Nov. 16th, 2011.

the full reality of the Gift of Living in the Divine Will hit her in such a profound way when she wrote this entry (and similar ones) that she felt compelled to portray its utter mysterious transcendence of words, as indeed Luisa herself would often do.

If nothing else, this passage should make it clear that St. Faustina was given a far greater sanctity than even the greatest sanctity commonly known of in her time (namely, Spiritual Marriage), otherwise she would not have asserted that *"no one- not even angels- may know [it]."* Knowing that what she had was simply not expressed in any commonly known mystical writing to date, she was forced to say that this union "distinguishes" her from every other soul, and that it was a "secret." This is perfectly compatible with Luisa's revelations, which refer to the same essential thing—but explicitly. For in them, Jesus tells Luisa that *not even the angels* are permitted to comprehend what glory is bestowed upon acts performed in the Divine Will by humans here on earth.

But the treasure chest that is Faustina's revelations is far from exhausted, for we also see clear indications from Jesus as to how this "secret" is obtained, which we will cover in the next section.

Cancellation of the Self-Will: Exclusively Living by the Will of God

Even more poignantly than the spiritual writers described in the previous chapter, St. Faustina's revelations reveal the necessary approach to the self-will and the Divine Will in order to receive the great Gift. In her diary, we read the words of Jesus:

'Host pleasing to My Father, know, My daughter, that the entire Holy Trinity finds Its special delight in you, because you live exclusively by the will of God. No sacrifice can compare with this.' After these words, the knowledge of God's will came to me; that is to say, I now see everything from a higher point of view and accept all events and things, pleasant and unpleasant, with love, as tokens of the heavenly Father's special affection. The pure offering of my will will burn on the altar of love. That my sacrifice may be perfect, I unite myself closely with the sacrifice of Jesus on the cross. When great sufferings will cause my nature to tremble, and my physical and spiritual strength will diminish, then will I hide myself deep in the

open wound of the Heart of Jesus, silent as a dove, without complaint. Let all my desires, even the holiest, noblest and most beautiful, take always the last place and Your holy will, the very first. The least of Your desires, O Lord, is more precious to me than heaven, with all its treasures. I know very well that people will not understand me; that is why my sacrifice will be purer in Your eyes.[371]

If you were to quickly leaf through St. Faustina's Diary, one thing specifically would strike you: an entire page with a large "X" over it, along with the words:

"From today on, my own will does not exist."[372]

She wrote this in her own diary—reproduced faithfully in the printings of it—because Jesus had specifically directed her to do precisely that. This direction occurred after she had prayed:

I beg You, by all the love with which Your Heart burns, to destroy completely within me my self-love and, on the other hand, to enkindle in my heart the fire of Your purest love ... [373] [Jesus responded], **"you will cancel out your will absolutely in this retreat** and, instead, My complete will shall be accomplished in you."[374]

This, of course, is exactly what Jesus asks of Luisa and of us all: the total cancellation of our self-will in order that His Divine Will may become the true life principle of our souls, just as our souls are the true life-principle of our bodies. For if our body were to have a principle of its own, and refuse to be animated only by the soul that God infused into it, then this would rightly be called paralysis (or perhaps, possession). And yet, that is exactly what we do when we allow our souls to be governed, to any degree, by the self-will instead of the Divine.

***

Faustina also wrote:

The Lord gave me knowledge of the graces which He has been constantly lavishing on me. The light pierced me through and through, and I came to understand the inconceivable favors that God has been bestowing on me ... As His child, I felt that everything the heavenly Father possessed was equally mine. He Himself lifted me from the ground up to His Heart. **I felt that everything that existed was exclusively mine**, but I had no desire for it all, because God alone is enough for me[375]

[371]*Divine Mercy in My Soul*, paragraph 955-957.
[372]*Ibid.*, paragraph 374.
[373]*Ibid.*, paragraph 371.

[374]*Ibid.*, paragraph 372.
[375]*Ibid.* paragraph 1279.

This correlates well to what Jesus tells Luisa: that one who lives in His Will possesses all things just as He Himself possesses all things.

> My Jesus, **penetrate me through and through so that I might be able to reflect You in my whole life. Divinize me so that my deeds may have supernatural value**. Grant that I may have love, compassion and mercy for every soul without exception.[376]

Faustina here does not hesitate to ask for Divinization; but this is not new in Catholic spirituality. What is profound, and new, is her request that even her deeds be rendered supernatural; for this had long been said only of Jesus' own deeds on earth. St. Faustina also once prayed:

> Everlasting love, pure flame, burn in my heart ceaselessly and **deify my whole being**.[377]

As if to imply that merely asking for deification alone was not enough, she wanted to append this request with "… my whole being," as a reminder that we may leave nothing out. We must have the boldness which St. Faustina here demonstrates; the boldness to ask Jesus to *Divinize* us and our deeds; to deify our *whole being*. (And this is precisely what the Gift of Living in the Divine Will does.)

***

There are many more references to the Divine Will, which also overlap with Luisa's revelations, found throughout St. Faustina's own revelations. My goal here was only to examine a relative few. For those interested in learning more about this overlap, I recommend above all reading St. Faustina's Diary itself, in its entirety; every page is full of edifying material. I also recommend the pamphlet entitled *References to God's Divine Will in the Diary of Saint Maria Faustina Kowalska of the Blessed Sacrament*, written by Barbara Mary Canning Martin.

Servant of God Archbishop Luis Martinez

The Servant of God Archbishop Luis Martinez was the archbishop of Mexico City in the mid-20th century. Considered both spiritual father and spiritual son of Venerable Conchita (whom we will discuss in the next section), he was greatly revered for holiness in his own day, with tens of thousands turning out for his funeral, and his cause for beatification has been opened.

In a manuscript that was not published during his lifetime, the Archbishop wrote:

> In the afternoon, God brought me before the Tabernacle, He aroused in me generosity, and with profound emotion I made the following act:

> "Oh Holy Father, oh Adorable Father, through the immaculate hands of Mary, the Most Holy Virgin, my Mother, under the impulse of the Holy Spirit, and intimately united to Jesus, your Son, Immortal Victim, I give to You today the total gift, and the absolute oblation of myself, abandoning all to your sovereign Will, in order that this Divine Will, without asking my opinion, without taking me into account, might do with me and with all that is mine, whatever it pleases … My only support in making this oblation is your strength, upon which my nothingness rests … I give You that which I can now give You: my will, sincere and complete … and I cast myself into your sovereign Will."

> I experienced something most profound, most strange, as if for my soul there began a new stage; as if in those moments I was given to the Holy Spirit, that He might ravish my soul and give it to Jesus. I understood that by this union, the Holy Spirit, as an impetuous wind, was to carry away my soul, stripping it of everything and plunging it into the bosom of God….

> **The perfect transformation** gives the perfect priesthood, since it makes perfect the sacrifice of every moment, of the two victims united, Jesus and I, so that I may be able truly to say: "This is my Body, This is my Blood."

> The official priesthood is a transformation into Christ, realized by ordination, and which makes it possible to say the divine words in the Mass. But since it is not total transformation of itself, by the sacramental character only the Eucharistic sacrifice can be offered.

> When the "marvelous exchange" is realized, through the perfect transformation in which we give to Christ a passible body, and blood which He can pour out in a bloody manner, and Christ gives Himself to us, divinizing our being, making it his, making us Him, assuming our humanity through a union which is the image of the Hypostatic Union, then in every moment we can offer the two victims united in one same

[376] *Divine Mercy in My Soul*, paragraph 1242.
[377] Ibid, 1523.

immolation; we can renew unceasingly the sacrifice of Christ ... [378]

We can see that this is a reference to the Gift of Living in the Divine Will, first, because of the nature of the prayer ("act") he offered to God, asking that His Sovereign Will may "do with me and with all that is mine, whatever it pleases." But most of all, we see in what follows a clear exposition of a radical change that is almost like the Hypostatic Union itself. This indeed is the "fourth stage" of the spiritual life, beyond the traditional three, wherein we receive the Gift. Hugh Owen writes:

> In his spiritual biography of Archbishop Luis Maria Martinez, spiritual director of Venerable Conchita Cabrera, Fr. Joseph Trevino of the Missionaries of the Holy Spirit observed that the traditional division of the spiritual life into three stages—the purgative, illuminative, and unitive—had obscured the existence of a **fourth stage** where the transforming union of the soul and God produced its supernatural fruit. According to Fr. Trevino:

> It would be absurd actually, if, when the soul reaches the highest union on earth, its life would stagnate, that it would remain permanently inactive. Just the contrary happens; that is the time when the action of the soul, under the motion of the Holy Spirit, reaches its maximum. This is the *fourth stage* ... In the transforming union, the soul is united with the Word. But this union is spiritually fecund; its fruit is Jesus, Jesus reproduced in the soul itself and, through its ministry, Jesus reproduced in the souls of others (apostolic life)

> This stage, in which the Holy Spirit produces a complete humanity of Jesus in the soul and in which the soul enters into the bosom of the Trinity and participates in the divine activity, appears to correspond to the Mystical Incarnation in the writings of Venerable Conchita and to the Divine Substitution in the writings of the Canadian nun Blessed Dina Belanger (1897-1928). [379]

We now turn to his spiritual daughter, Venerable Conchita, whose teachings give more specificity on this same reality about which Servant of God Luis Martinez wrote.

Venerable Conchita

Venerable Conchita (whose full name is Concepción Cabrera de Armida), was born on the Feast of the Immaculate Conception in the year 1862; a wife and mother to nine children, she was widowed at the age of 39. She died exactly ten years and one day before Luisa herself passed, and **she is set to be beatified in May 2019. Conchita is well known for her mystical revelations; therefore, this beatification lends great weight to the orthodoxy of this new Sanctity of Sanctities, which Jesus reveals to Conchita so explicitly that there is no doubt He is revealing precisely the same thing that He reveals to Luisa** (though of course in less detail).

Of Venerable Conchita, the theologian Monsignor Arthur Calkins[380] writes:

> By any measure, Conchita was an extraordinary woman. ... [she was] the foundress of five Works or Apostolates of the Cross (Obras de la Cruz) and an awe-inspiring mystic and spiritual writer—still not well known, unfortunately, in the English-speaking world. My hope is that this article may help to introduce her to a larger English-speaking public, at least in some small way.

> I first made her acquaintance, so to speak, in 1978, when I came across a book written about her by a spiritual author whom I respected, Père Marie-Michel Philipon, O.P. (1898-1972). He had written an impressive work on Saint Elizabeth of the Trinity (1880-1906), and so I reasoned that this book, too, should be a good spiritual resource. I was not disappointed. In that book he recounted the story of an extraordinary soul who, nonetheless, wrote about profound spiritual realities in language that could be understood by ordinary people. He went so far as to compare her to the first two great women to be recognized as doctors of the Church: Saint Catherine of Siena and Saint Teresa of Avila.

> ... A huge part of Conchita's writing, in fact, is made up of the sixty-six volumes of her spiritual diary (in Spanish, Cuenta de Conciencia, or Account of Conscience), which she wrote in obedience to her spiritual directors, most of them bishops, several of whose causes have been opened in view of their possible beatification. Saints not infrequently appear in constellations, each supporting and enriching the others ...

---

[378] *New and Divine,* Pages 25, 33.
[379] *Ibid.,* P. 44.

[380] Monsignor Calkins, whom I know personally, is a trustworthy voice in the Catholic scholarly world today and is a great warrior for the Fifth Marian Dogma.

Conchita had a profound ecclesial and Marian vocation. Not only did she have an intense devotion to the Mother of God, but she also lived in constant union with Mary. This became especially manifest in the great crowning grace of her life, received on March 25, 1906, and known as the "mystical incarnation." The late Bishop Joseph J. Madera, M.Sp.S., strove to explain this extraordinary grace in this way:

"The mystical incarnation may be compared to the indwelling of Jesus in Mary from the moment of His conception in her womb. The Lord had raised Mary to a level of holiness never to be equaled by any other human being. Nonetheless, the specific grace granted to Conchita on March 25, 1906, as far as we know, has been granted to only a limited number of souls. The fundamental rule is that, even though God grants extraordinary graces to chosen souls, what he confers on them is eventually intended for the up-building of the entire Body of Christ. Since the mystical incarnation which Conchita experienced is rooted in the sacrament of baptism, this grace also constitutes for all of us an invitation to live our baptismal commitment at an ever-deeper level. This is precisely what the Fathers of the Second Vatican Council wanted to emphasize in the fifth chapter of Lumen Gentium on the universal call to holiness."

Although Conchita received this extraordinary grace in 1906, she would effectively spend the rest of her life trying to fathom what had been done in her and how to respond to it. The second to last retreat of her life in 1935, directed by her great spiritual father and friend, the Servant of God, Archbishop Luís María Martínez (1881-1956), Archbishop of Mexico City and Primate of Mexico, was still a matter of striving to penetrate more deeply into this singular grace, which was (1) a share in the priesthood and victimhood of Jesus, (2) Eucharistic and (3) Marian.[381]

At this point, it is clear there is no room for doubt or hesitation in heeding the teachings of Ven. Conchita.

The Mystical Incarnation: "Much More" than Spiritual Marriage

Let us consider the following encounter between Jesus and Conchita, which took place on none other than the Solemnity of the Annunciation (March 25th), in the year 1906: seventeen years after Luisa was given the Gift of Living in the Divine Will.

> ... before Mass, prostrate before the Tabernacle, I humbled myself as much as possible. I begged the Lord's pardon, I renewed my vows, I promised Him that I would never let my heart be taken over by the things of the world as I had done up to now. Thus, my soul empty of all else, I received Him in Communion ... I was taken over by the presence of my Jesus, quite close to me, hearing His divine voice which said to me:
>
> —Jesus:"Here I am, I want to incarnate Myself mystically in your heart ... "
>
> —Conchita:...Would it be, my Jesus, spiritual marriage?
>
> —Jesus: "Much more than that ... [it is, rather] the grace of incarnating Me, of living and growing in your soul, never to leave it, to possess you and to be possessed by you as in one and the same substance ... in a compenetration which cannot be comprehended: it is the grace of graces ... It is a union of the same nature as that of the union of heaven, except that in paradise the veil which conceals the Divinity disappears ... For you [now] keep ever in your soul my real and effective presence."
>
> ...Conchita: 'Behold the handmaid of the Lord. Be it done unto me according to Thy Word'"[382]

To speak of something "much more" than spiritual marriage, as Jesus does here to Venerable Conchita, never would have been accepted in traditional works of spiritual theology: and for good reason—as was already settled in the previous section, there *wasn't* any sanctity higher than spiritual marriage since the Assumption of the Blessed Virgin Mary, up until Luisa received the Gift of Living in the Divine Will in 1889. This hitherto supremacy of spiritual (or "mystical") marriage is not difficult to discover. The New Catholic Encyclopedia states:

> Mystical marriage or spiritual marriage ... refers to what is recognized in mystical theology as a 'transforming'' union between a soul and God, requiring extraordinary graces, and to which God calls only a few particularly privileged persons, e.g., SS. John of the Cross and Teresa of Avila.[383]

The old Catholic Encyclopedia makes this fact even

---

[381] Arthur Calkins. Missio Magazine. "The Venerable Conchita (Concepción Cabrera de Armida)—Part 1"

[382] Fr. Marie-Michel Philipon, O.P. *CONCHITA: A Mother's Spiritual Diary*. Pages 57-58.

[383] *New Catholic Encyclopedia*. Mystical Marriage.

clearer, stating:

> …the term mystical marriage is employed by St. Teresa and St. John of the Cross to designate that mystical union with God which **is the most exalted condition attainable by the soul in this life**.[384]

And yet, Jesus clearly tells Conchita—leaving no possibility of any other interpretation—that He is now giving something much greater.[385]

Father Marie-Michel Philipon was a Dominican priest and highly respected theologian whose works are cited multiple times in the New Catholic Encyclopedia. He also wrote on the spirituality of none other than St. Elizabeth of the Trinity, strongly promoting and endorsing this new sanctity as found in the French saint's writings, and doing so decades before Elizabeth was even declared a Servant of God (his own work on them did, however, receive an Imprimatur in 1941). It is clear that Fr. Philipon had the gift of discernment and knew a revelation from God when he saw it. He also strongly endorsed Venerable Conchita's revelations, and wrote a work on Conchita and her spirituality, entitled *Conchita: A Mother's Spiritual Diary*. Towards the end of this work, he sums up Conchita's spirituality, writing:

> On finishing these pages in which we have wished to present, though incompletely and imperfectly, Conchita's person and doctrine, a synthetic view, an overall view is demanded. A theologian must above all pose this question to himself: "What then did God intend to bring about through His humble servant for the benefit of His entire Church?"
>
> **The greatest degree of Holiness is attainable for everyone.**
>
> "Being a wife and a mother was never an obstacle to my spiritual life," she asserted. Speaking as a woman to one of her daughters-in-law, she stated: "I have been very happy with my husband." In the last conversation with her husband when he was gravely ill, she asked him: "What is your last wish in regard to me?" He replied: *"That you be wholly given over to God and wholly devoted to your children."*
>
> **The Lord Himself told her one day: "You**

married in view of My great designs for your personal holiness, and to be an *example* **for many souls who think that marriage is** *incompatible* **with holiness."**

> The most sublime mystical graces described by spiritual masters are not privileges confined to souls consecrated to God, priestly and religious life. They are offered to all Christians no matter what their state of life. It seems that God wanted to give us through Conchita living historical proof of this truth. Vatican II clearly and forcibly testifies to it (cf. Ch. V, especially # 40, Lumen Gentium): "Thus it is evident to everyone that all the faithful in Christ of whatever rank or status are called to the fullness of the Christian life and to the perfection of charity." There are no second class Christians. We are all called to seek the greatest holiness. Conchita received the eminent graces of nuptials and of the spiritual marriage described by the great mystics, in her state of "poor wife," as she called herself. An instrument of God, Conchita, as she was familiarly called, has a prophetic mission for today's world.
>
> The Lord Himself has announced to her that she would be a model wife and mother, but that her mission would extend far beyond to make shine the sanctifying might of Christ and of the Holy Spirit "in all states of life." Yes, indeed, she is a model wife, mother, teacher, but she is also one of the greatest mystics of the Church, leading souls to consummation in the Unity of the Trinity. Her message calls the entire laity, married men and women, to the highest sanctity.
>
> **A new type of Holiness**
>
> There is no question here of a type of holiness departing from the Gospel, but rather of a resource taken in view of a new application of this same Gospel. To depart from the spirit of the Gospel and from the teachings of the Cross would be to deny Christ. We are speaking in the same sense Therese of Lisieux spoke of a "wholly new way." <u>**We are incontestably in a new era of spirituality.**</u>
>
> What constitutes its newness is:
>
> **1) A calling of** *all*, **even of the laity, even of married people, to the** *greatest holiness*.
>
> 2) Through *transfiguration of daily life*, the sanctification of the profane, divinization by faith,

---

384 Poulain, A. (1910). On Mystical Marriage in "The Catholic Encyclopedia."

385 Perhaps the most common objection one hears to Luisa's revelations is that they speak of a sanctity– available to everyone—that is greater than spiritual marriage. Conchita's Beatification should, therefore, put a definitive end to this objection.

by love and by the spirit of sacrifice *in ordinary life.*

3) The *greatest holiness.* Transcendence of the message of the Cross. Even the most banal actions are made of value to the infinite by the offering of love in union with Christ, in imitation of the last years on earth of the Mother of God, in the service of the nascent Church.

In the evening of her life the Lord asked her to begin a new work on behalf of the sanctity of homes. "I am going to ask you one thing: a *Crusade of victim souls* to the glory of My Father, following the spirit of the Cross."

"I want many acts of expiation for the DIVORCES which are the source of so many evils in homes, harmful to spouses, children in society. "I ask expiation for so many hidden sins and for so many sins of omission in the Christian formation of children." "I want a *"Crusade of victim souls"* for the sanctification of homes" (Diary, Oct. 31, 1935).

Who does not see how providentially opportune is this work? [386]

Fr. Philipon, also, has left no room for doubt or confusion: a new holiness is indeed upon us. It is the *greatest* holiness possible, and it is offered to *all.*

Describing in more detail the teachings she received on how this new sanctity is attained, Conchita herself says:

"God's will is a bouquet which is made up of all virtues practiced in an ordinary manner or in a perfect state. His will divinizes them and makes them shine with splendor in His presence. It gives to each a new value on the divine scale and, in the purified soul, it vests them with a special color pleasing to the Holy Spirit. This total and perfect submission to the most holy will of its God and Lord is the greatest of all the virtues a soul can possess. This sublime virtue implies the integral practice of all the other virtues... it is the culminating point."

"The Lord adds. 'I have no other food... from the first moment of my Incarnation than this divine will. It is through it I came into this world, through it I was raised above the earth to consummate my life in the cruelest of martyrdoms, ...it then soothed My agony. It was My sole solace, while on earth. I would have suffered death a thousand times to fulfill it. Divine and active Love burned in my heart, had

as its main motive to carry out the divine will on behalf of man. The Redemption was naught but the faithful accomplishment of this divine will. Its echo sounds constantly in the depths of My most loving heart, causing it to throb for the salvation of souls and the glorification of My Father.'

"There is a still higher stage in this divine will. It is total self-surrender interiorly to this same will of God. This self-surrender leads to the highest summit of perfection: it is the supreme stage of all virtue" [387]

And communicating this sanctity under the title of Mystical Incarnation, she says:

"In the concrete, the mystical incarnation is nothing other than a most powerful grace of transformation which simplifies and unites to Jesus by purity and by immolation, rendering the being in its entirety, as much as possible, like to Him. Because of this likeness of the soul to the Incarnate Word, the eternal Father finds pleasure in it, and the role of Priest and Victim which Jesus had on earth is communicated to it, in order that it obtain graces from heaven for the whole world. That is why, the more a soul is like Me, the more the Eternal Father hears it, not due to its worth but due to its likeness and its union with Me and in virtue of My merits which constitute what counts for obtaining graces" (Diary, Dec. 11, 1913).

[Fr. Philipon adds] Briefly, the mystical incarnation is a grace of identification which Christ, Priest and Host, a grace which makes Him continue on in the Members of His Mystical Body, His mission of glorifier of the Father and Savior of men. It is a special grace of transformation in the priestly soul of Christ.

Fr. Iannuzzi points out that this entails God taking total possession of Conchita's will, writing:

That this new, continuously eternal activity brings with it a deeper participation in the activity of the three divine Persons of the Blessed Trinity, is evident in Jesus' words to the Servant of God Luisa and to Venerable Conchita de Armida:

"All three Divine Persons descended from Heaven; and then, after a few days, we took possession of your heart and took our perpetual residence there. We took the reins of your intelligence, your heart, all of you. Everything you did was an outlet of our creative Will in you. It was a confirmation that your will was animated by an Eternal Will. Living in my Will is the apex

---

[386]Fr. Marie Michel Philipon. *Conchita: A Mother's Spiritual Diary.*

[387]Ibid. Page 117.

of sanctity, and it bestows continuous growth in Grace. Do not think that in the mystical incarnation of the Word it is I who act, but the Trinity of the Divine Persons do so, each one of them operating according to His attributes, the Father, as Father, engendering: the Word as Son, being born; the Holy Spirit making fertile this divine action in the soul."[388]

In Venerable Conchita's writings, we see the Gift of Living in the Divine Will revealed with such clarity that whoever approaches her teachings with confidence will unquestionably receive the Gift.

Blessed Dina Belanger

Dina Belanger was a Canadian nun who died in 1929 and was beatified, along with Blessed Duns Scotus, by Pope St. John Paul II in 1993. In the homily of the Beatification Mass, John Paul said:

> Separated from each other by time, these two extraordinary personalities … gave testimony of prompt and generous correspondence to divine grace, [actualizing in their lives…] celestial gifts that awaken our admiration.[389]

In teaching about Blessed Dina during this homily, the Pope made specific reference to her "such high degree of intimacy with God," and mentioned the "life of the Most Holy Trinity in her," and in particular her "**desire to correspond fully to the Divine Will.**"

Let us look in more detail at this "Divine Substitution" about which Blessed Dina wrote.

Divine Substitution: The Same State as the Elect in Heaven

The theologian Fr. Edward O'Connor writes:

> … Jesus told Blessed Dina Belanger of a gift of "Divine Substitution," that He would bring about. He explained it thus: … the greatest joy a soul can give Me is to let Me raise it to the Divinity. Yes, my little spouse, I feel an immense pleasure in transforming a soul into Myself, in deifying it, in absorbing it entirely in the Divinity … I wish to absorb you, my little spouse, to such a degree that I shall exist in your place with all the Attributes and Perfection of my Divinity … I wish to deify you in the same manner that I united my Humanity to my Divinity in the Incarnation … The degree of holiness that I desire for you is my own Holiness, in its infinite plenitude, the Holiness of My Father realized in you by Me. (ST, vol. & no.1, p. 36)[390]

Making it even clearer that this Divine Substation is indeed the Gift of Living in the Divine Will, Dina writes:

> "Events take place, succeed one another, around my physical being, but my soul is no longer involved with them. Jesus is in control of these events: he sees to everything, he takes care of everything. It is as if my soul no longer had any connection with my body. This grace which the Trinity of my God grants me with so much love is a foretaste of my participation in the divine life; I say a foretaste, because **it is the state of the elect in heaven, yet I, in bodily form, am still on earth**."[391]

Fr. Joseph Iannuzzi, commenting on and quoting Blessed Dina's biography, writes:

> [Blessed Dina says} "During my thanksgiving after Communion, I was concentrating on remaining closely united with him… I was taken by surprise… He said: "**I want to deify you in the same way as I united My humanity with My divinity**… The degree of holiness that I want for you, is the infinite plentitude of my own holiness, it is the holiness of my Father brought about in you through me.…

> …I need a perpetual and very powerful grace to maintain me in this blessed state: I am enjoying perfect beatitude… It is truly eternity!"

> "This morning, I received a special grace that I find difficult to describe. I felt taken up into God, as if in the "eternal mode," that is in a permanent, unchanging state… I feel I am continually in the presence of the adorable Trinity. My soul, annihilated in the Heart of the Indivisible unity, contemplates it with greater suavity, in a purer light, and I am more aware of the power that pervades me… **Beginning with the grace of last January 25, my soul can dwell in heaven, live there without any backward glance toward earth, and yet continue to animate my material being.** My offering is far more active than in the

[388] *The Splendor of Creation*. Ch. 3.5
[389] https://w2.vatican.va/content/john-paul-ii/es/homilies/1993/documents/hf_jp-ii_hom_19930320_scoto-belanger.html
[390] *Listen to My Prophets*. P. 134

[391] Blessed Dina Belanger, *The Autobiography of Dina Belanger*, translated by Mary St. Stephen, R.J.M. (Sillery: Religious of Jesus and Mary, 3rd edition, 1997), P. 219. (February 22, 1925). Cited in *New and Divine*.

preceding dwellings where the love of my sovereign Substitute led me… In this new divine indwelling, what strikes me… is the power, the greatness, the immensity of God's attributes."

[*Fr. Iannuzzi writes]: To illustrate that God's eternal mode of activity in the soul of the human creature is the same interior state enjoyed by the blessed in heaven—and which St. John of the Cross "experienced in passing" only—Jesus tells Blessed Dina: "You will not possess me any more completely in heaven… because I have absorbed you totally."[392]

Relating Blessed Dina's mysticism with other exemplars of the Gift, and expounding upon the nature of her teachings, Hugh Owen shares the following:

In the years immediately following Archbishop Martinez's reception of the gift of the Mystical Incarnation, several souls who have either been beatified or canonized by the Church, described similar experiences to those described by Venerable Conchita. One of the most striking of these souls was the Canadian Blessed Dina Belanger …

[on February 1, 1925, Blessed Dina writes]"The Trinity of love is seeking souls on whom it can bestow its divine treasures. Infinite Goodness needs to give, to give itself. Few are those souls who abandon themselves totally to the sovereign will. If God is to pour a profusion of graces on a human soul, he must find Jesus living there. A soul is too finite to contain the ocean of infinite favors; but Jesus, the Illimitable, taking the place of what is limited, can satisfy in some way the immense desire of the heavenly Father. If a soul is to become an abyss, fit to be taken possession of by the Infinite, complete annihilation, in the spiritual sense, of what is human is essential; then, the substitution of Jesus for this human being and perfect continuing self-abandonment to the divine Agent. The adorable Trinity desires to pour out its treasures of mercy and love on Jesus substituted for my being. My gentle Master, taking my place, says to his Father, (still in silence, I find no other way to express it): Father, here I am to do your will. Father, the hour has come, let what you will be done in me." …

On February 7, 1925 … Jesus told her: "**You will not possess me any more completely in heaven … because I have absorbed you totally**" … [two weeks later, Blessed Dina wrote] " … This grace which the Trinity of my God grants me with so much love is a foretaste of my participation in the divine life; I say a foretaste, because it is the state of the elect in heaven, yet I, in bodily form, am still on earth. It is a participation in the divine life in the sense that, for the eternal and supreme Being, nothing comes to an end: for him everything is present, since he himself does not come to an end and will never come to an end…

On June 16, Blessed Dina testified to the likeness between the presence of God in her state of "living host" and the same presence in the Eucharist. She wrote:

"I am still aware of, and even have a clearer understanding of the presence of the adorable Trinity in which I am submerged, and of the same grace concerning the presence of Our Lord in the sacred Host."

As a "living host," Blessed Dina no longer experienced the sufferings of Jesus as a compassionate observer. Instead, she identified completely with the interior sufferings of Jesus by sharing in the "chalice of his agony." …

Blessed Dina compared these sufferings to the "real presence" of Jesus in Holy Communion. She wrote:

"My union with the Heart of Jesus has been like his real presence after holy communion, while the consecrated Host is still with me. This morning, Our Lord gave me to understand that it is just as easy for him to give himself to me—through his blessed chalice—and to extend his sensible presence over two days—through an interior and invisible act—as it is for a quarter of an hour, more or less, under the appearance of the sacred Host… He gave me to understand that, in Gethsemane, in the angel who came to console him, he saw all the souls—specially consecrated souls—who throughout the centuries would want to share in his agony" … [393]

The spiritual teachings of Blessed Dina are a veritable treasure trove, and what is presented here is only a small fraction of their overlap with Luisa's.

St. Elizabeth of the Trinity

St. Elizabeth of the Trinity was a French Carmelite mystic, canonized by Pope Francis in 2016. Her writings on the Indwelling of the Trinity give a great exposition of the Gift of Living in the Divine Will.

---

[392]*The Splendor of Creation.* Ch. 3

[393]*New and Divine.* P. 85-91. Misc. excerpts.

Personal Possession of the Trinity

In an article for the National Catholic Register, the theologian Dr. Anthony Lilles writes:

> Elizabeth regarded the Trinity as the furnace of an *excessive* love. When her prayer evokes "My God, My Three," **she invites us to take personal possession of the Trinity**. The Trinity is, for her, an interpersonal and dynamic mystery: the Father beholding the Son in the fire of the Holy Spirit. She insisted that, in silent stillness before God, the loving gaze of the Father shines within our hearts until God contemplates the likeness of his Son in the soul. **Through the creative action of the Holy Spirit, the more the soul accepts the Father's gaze of love, the more it is transformed into the likeness of the Word made flesh.**
>
> … Elizabeth roots this in adoration and recollection and advocates its fruitfulness. Through this prayer, we gain access to our true home, the dwelling place of love for which we are created—and this is not in some future moment, but already in the present moment of time, which Elizabeth calls **"eternity begun and still in progress."**
>
> Such prayer not only sets the soul apart and makes it holy, but it glorifies the Father and even extends the saving work of Christ in the world. She called this "the praise of Glory" and understood this to be her great vocation. **By canonizing Elizabeth of the Trinity, the Church has not only validated her mission,** but re-proposed the importance of silent prayer for our time… Through the witness of St. Elizabeth, the Carmelites and her friends chose to allow God to establish them "immovable" in his presence.

Even here we see intimations of something new and glorious; **a real sort of personal *possession* of the Trinity.** Previously, sanctification was only described as *participation* in the Trinity and nothing more. Indeed, a response one hears often after bringing up the heights of sanctity revealed in the exemplars listed in this chapter is precisely this limitation; namely, *"we can participate in but cannot possess the Divine Nature."* Now, there was nothing wrong with this saying in its day—but the time has now come in which we may indeed, in a real (albeit qualified) sense, *possess* (only by grace, not by nature—along with other important distinctions) the Divine Nature as Gift, as St. Elizabeth herself says.

Describing her spirituality and most important teachings in greater depth than what is shown above, Hugh Owen writes:

> Shortly after entering Carmel, Elizabeth was asked several questions: "What name would you like to have in Heaven?" "The Will of God," she replied. "What is your motto?" she was asked. "God in me and I in Him," she answered…

From the beginning of her entry into religious life, Blessed Elizabeth expressed her love for God in terms that anticipated the language of Blessed Dina Belanger and others who would describe living in God, or in the heart of the Holy Trinity, in contrast to merely doing the Will of God. Blessed **Elizabeth believed that the Holy Spirit would transform her into another humanity of Jesus**. She wrote: "O consuming fire! Spirit of love! Descend within me and reproduce within me, as it were, an incarnation of the Word that I may be to him another humanity wherein He renews his mystery! O my Christ, Whom I love, … I beseech Thee to clothe me with Thyself, to identify my soul with all the movements of Thine own. Immerse me in Thyself; possess me wholly; substitute Thyself for me, that my life may be but a radiance of Thine own…"

Blessed Elizabeth [also] wrote: **"How can one glorify God? It is not difficult. Our Lord gives us the secret, when he tells us, "My meat and drink is to do the will of him who sent me"** (John 4:34). Hold fast to every expression of the adorable Master's will. Look on every suffering and joy as sent directly by him, and your life will be an uninterrupted communion, because everything will be a sacrament sent by God. This is absolute reality, for God is not divided; his will is his whole being…Our Lord was the first to say this, and the soul in communion with him enters into the movement of his divine soul. His whole aim is to do the will of the Father who "loved us with an everlasting love" (Jer 31:3). During his thirty-three years, this will was so much his daily bread that at his death he could say, "It is consummated."…"

Interpreting Blessed Elizabeth's spiritual doctrine, Hans Urs Von Balthasar wrote: **"The human will has to be 'enclosed' in the will of God**, for otherwise it remains without focus or direction. [as St. Elizabeth wrote,]'**Our will only becomes free when we enclose it in the will of God'**…

Through abandonment to the Holy Spirit, Blessed **Elizabeth aspired to be consecrated by Him into a "living host."** She wrote to a priest: "I ask you, as a child its father, to consecrate and sacrifice me in the Holy Mass a host of praise to the glory of God. Consecrate me so well that I may be no longer myself but he, that the Father, looking on me, may recognize him."…

According to Von Balthasar: "What ultimately occupied her was the moment at which this world, conformed with the Son by that work of the Spirit, becomes a praise of the grace that brings all to its perfection. It was said, in fact, of the Spirit that he would glorify the Son (John 16:11), that he would finally accomplish in the world the glorification of the Father through the Son…"[394]

As is evident in the passage above, the most profound (and even controversial) elements of Living in the Divine Will are seen in the clear teachings of Elizabeth of the Trinity, who has had her mission fully confirmed by the Church by being raised to the altars as a canonized saint.

St. Maximilian Kolbe

St. Maximilian Kolbe is most often recalled as the heroic martyr of charity, killed at the infamous concentration camp at Auschwitz, as he willingly volunteered himself to take the place of another man. He is next best known for his amazingly successful apostolates: running the largest Franciscan friary in history (with hundreds of brothers under the same roof), and printing leaflets that reached an enormous monthly circulation. **Fewer know of his zealous promotion of Marian Consecration; and fewer still know of his profound and groundbreaking teachings on the same.**

Struck by Our Lady's words at Lourdes "I am *the* Immaculate Conception," and at first perplexed by them (for indeed, they almost seem grammatically incorrect; many who first hear these words wonder why she did not say "I was immaculately conceived"), Kolbe came to the recognition that this was no mistake. He realized that they in fact said something essential about Mary herself: that she *is the* Immaculate Conception, and truly a mirror of The *Uncreated* Immaculate Conception, Who is none other than the Holy Spirit. He furthermore realized that Mary is simply the *Created* Immaculate Conception—the perfect creature contained within the mind of God before the dawn of time, destined before all ages to be the Mother of the Word. But Kolbe did not stop there; he insisted that through Mary, this reality must define our

sanctity as well.

Transubstantiation of the Self into the Created Immaculate Conception

St. Maximilian Kolbe, although well known for his promotion of St. Louis de Montfort's same fundamental mission, did not merely repeat what he learned from this saint and others. He presented many new teachings of his own; including the "Transubstantiation into the Immaculate." Regarding this, St. Maximilian wrote:

We belong to her, to the Immaculate. We are hers without limits, most perfectly hers; we are, as it were, herself. Through our mediation she loves the good God. With our poor heart she loves her divine Son. We become the mediators through whom the Immaculate loves Jesus. And Jesus, considering us her property and, as it were, a part of his beloved Mother, loves her in us and through us. What a lovely mystery! We have heard of persons who are obsessed, possessed by the devil, through whom the devil thought, spoke, and acted. We want to be possessed in this way, and even more, without limits, by her: may she herself think, speak, and act through us. **We want to belong to such an extent to the Immaculate that not only nothing else remains in us that isn't hers, but that we become, as it were, annihilated in her, changed into her, transubstantiated into her, that she alone remains**, so that we may be as much hers as she is God's. She belongs to God, having become his Mother. And we want to become the mother who would give the life of the Immaculate to every heart that exists and to those who will still come into existence. That is the M.I.—to bring her into every heart, to give her life to every heart. Thus entering these hearts and taking full possession of them, she may give birth to sweet Jesus, who is God, that he might grow in them in age and perfection. **What a magnificent mission! … Divinizing man to the God-Man through the Mother of the God-Man.**[395]

Here, St. Maximilian renders more explicit what already existed in St. Louis de Montfort's Mariology: that **the object of Marian consecration is not a simple "be totally devoted *to* her," but rather, to "*become* her;" with the only differences which remain being somewhat superficial, or in other words (and to continue with the "transubstantiation" teaching), the differences**

---

[394]*New and Divine.* P. 74-77. Misc. excerpts.

[395]Saintmaximiliankolbe.com

are mere accidents. And, indeed, while we of course cannot use the term "transubstantiation" here in exactly the same way as we apply it to the Blessed Sacrament itself—wherein the former substance of the thing in question is completely *replaced* by an entirely new and different substance—we nevertheless cannot write this off as an exaggeration or hyperbole.

We must recall that the paradigm of Marian Consecration—as explained by St. Louis de Montfort and even more boldly by St. Maximilian Kolbe—is to acquire Mary's exalted sanctity as our own. In explaining St. Maximilian's teachings on this matter, Fr. Fehlner writes:

> … for St. Maximilian the title Spouse of the Holy Spirit also connotes: not only a functional relation to one aspect of the mission of the Holy Spirit, but to the very person of the Holy Spirit… This he does in a general way describing the Immaculate as a "quasi-part" of the Trinity, thereby succinctly indicating the point of departure for discussing the trinitarian aspects of mariology, so strongly stressed by Paul VI in *Marialis Cultus*. More specifically the Saint refers to the Immaculate as the Holy Spirit "quasi-incarnate"": not to explain the grace of the Immaculate Conception as a second grace of "hypostatic union", but to indicate how this grace is related to and differs from the "grace of union" in her Son…

> This relation he explains in precise, dogmatic detail, as an intimate union or communion of two persons and two natures, the persons and natures remaining really distinct, yet so intimate that the whole being and person of the Immaculate is permeated through and through by that characteristic of the Spirit qua complement or pleroma of Father and **Son as to be herself "transubstantiated" into the Holy Spirit and to share his name'**. In turn, this "transubstantiation" into the Spirit makes possible not only the Incarnation of the Word, but also the incorporation of the baptized into His body, the Church. This relation, finally, is best termed not a" *proprium*" but an "*appropriatum*", so as to distinguish two modes of possession of a human being by a divine person: one related to the dimension of subsistence, selfhood or firstness (*esse* or incommunicable existence); the other to the dimension of personal realization in freedom (*esse in actu secundo*). The first pertains to the Incarnation, the second to the indwelling of the

Trinity in the life of grace whose distinctive feature is the communion or fellowship of Father and Son in the Holy Spirit (cf. Jn 17, 22-23; I Jn 1, 1-3, which is eternal life (cf. Jn 17, 3; I Jn 1, 2), or perfect charity.[396]

Continuing in the same strand later in the book, he goes on to say that:

> This usage, to many curious, of a term from Eucharistic dogma … far from being the dangerous formula some see in it, is an original, yet deeply traditional insights of St. Maximilian… Being [Mary's] property [Kolbe] defines as our being annihilated in Her, changed into Her, transubstantiated into Her, so as it were to be Her

> …To promote this Marian presence in the Church is to "incorporate" the mystery of the Immaculate into the Church and into the whole of creation." To come under the influence of that presence is to be "transubstantiated" into the Immaculate, as by her Immaculate Conception She was "transubstantiated" into the Holy Spirit, becoming as it were one "personality" with that divine Person, so in relation to the Father enjoying the privilege of being Mother of God, with the Son Handmaid and Coredemptress, Instrument of the Father for the redemption of the world, effected in the Church by the sanctificatory mission of the Holy Spirit-Immaculate Conception. … **Another word to describe this promotion of the cause of the Immaculate is marianization, or the Fiat, which with that of the Creator effects the recreation or new creation**. In this context Mary Immaculate qua Immaculate is the new creature, the measure of every new creation made "in the sanctity and justice of truth" (Eph. 4, 24)." [397]

St. Maximilian was able to give the Church these beautiful and urgently needed teachings because he understood that theology cannot allow itself to be chained to the opinions of a few theologians; instead, it must be allowed to be guided by the Holy Spirit and given growth. Hugh Owen writes:

> In his Apostolic Exhortation Marialis Cultus, Pope Paul VI "insistently begged the 'entire people of God, especially the pastors and the theologians, to deepen their reflections on the action of the Holy Spirit in the history of salvation, and to strive so that the formulas employed by Christian piety should duly illustrate his life-giving influence. Such a deepened understanding should provide a better grasp of the mysterious relationship between the Spirit of God and the

---

[396]Fr. Peter Fehlner. *St. Maximilian Kolbe: Martyr of Charity–Pneumatologist: His Theology of the Holy Spirit*. P. 37-9.

[397]*Ibid.* P. 146-8.

Virgin of Nazareth, and their common action in the Church. **From these deeper meditations on these truths of faith there arise a piety that will be lived more intensely'"**

In retrospect, one can see that St. Maximilian's insights into the sanctity of Our Lady represented a definite development beyond the insights recorded in the writings of St. Louis De Montfort. And yet, St. Maximilian was able to reconcile the insights of St. Louis with the new and deeper insights that the Holy Spirit revealed to him. For example, St. Louis conceived of the union between Our Lady and the Holy Spirit as a moral union. But St. Maximilian realized that this concept did not do justice to their relationship. According to theologian Manteau-Bonamy: "**Father Kolbe ... knew that de Montfort, who never heard of the apparitions of the Rue du Bac or of Lourdes, had remained limited** to the consideration of a moral bond between Mary and the Holy Spirit. But since it is perfectly possible to understand the union which St. de Montfort writes about, in the meaning it acquired at Lourdes, Father Kolbe does not hesitate to interpret it so."[398]

It is safe to say that, from its beginning, Marian Consecration was always ordered to this. But with the advent of the Gift of Living in the Divine Will, its full potential can now at last be attained. This most avowedly does not mean that Marian Consecration should be "moved on from;" on the contrary, it means quite the opposite: we should now approach Marian Consecration with even more love and more zeal, knowing that it can truly deliver on all of its promises!

Servant of God Sr. Mary of the Holy Trinity

Sr. Mary of the Holy Trinity (her Baptismal name was Luisa) was a Poor Clare nun who received messages from Jesus. This mystic and her messages were the topic of a book published by TAN and written by Fr. Alain Marie Duboin, entitled *The Life and Message of Sr. Mary of the Holy Trinity: Poor Clare of Jerusalem (1901-1942)*. Although her revelations did not reveal the nature of the Gift as explicitly as did those of the other mystics listed in this chapter, there is nevertheless sufficient overlap to justify her

inclusion. We also see intimations of the Era of Peace in Sr. Mary's messages.

Fusion of Wills: Apostolate of Jesus' Eucharistic Life

Particularly noteworthy in Sr. Mary's writings is the insistence on a "fusion" of wills—the human and the Divine. It is precisely this term which, although not unprecedented in mystical theology, causes anger in some of Luisa's critics, who insist that no notion of "fusion" with God be entertained in the spiritual life. But these critics are misled. In Fr. Duboin's book on Sr. Mary, we read the following revelations she received from Jesus:

"Ah, if you understood! How happy each soul could be in My intimacy!... I give Myself to all souls; but I have secrets to give each one that are for her alone, with her mission which is hers alone … **The soul that understands this lives in complete contentment in doing My will** and in receiving My Word with My confidence. Write that, perhaps one or other soul will read it and will understand it."[399]

"It is thus that the light that has been entrusted to you will shine before men." If every soul would take these words to heart, each fulfilling her destined role, **then the glory of God would be visible upon earth!** "If each soul thus made that portion of the light which has been entrusted to her 'shine before men,' the House of Light, which is **the Church, would become irresistibly resplendent.**"[400]

I seek a heart whose love for Me is boundless, **"a will fused in My Will,"** a spirit so devoid of selfishness that My Spirit can take possession of it, and reign there as King… "Will you be that heart, that will, that spirit?"[401]

"My little daughter, **I live in souls as I lived on earth**. If you wish to know what fosters My life in you, see how I lived …"[402]

"… The soul that makes reparation gives Me two joys: she re-establishes order—and above all: she erases from My Heart the pain caused by the unfaithful soul, because by making reparation she arouses repentance—and nothing consoles Me so much as a repentant soul. She becomes My beloved… **The interior union of hearts that love one another and of wills that wish the good of**

---

[398]*New and Divine*, P. 101.
[399]Fr. Alain Marie Duboin, *The Life and Message of Sr. Mary of the Holy Trinity*, Part 2, Ch 1.
[400]*Ibid.*

[401]*Ibid.* Part 2, Ch 3.
[402]Ibid. Part 2, Ch 4.

others—that is your strength, an invincible power even over the Heart of God ... "[403]

"... And the most favored souls? Oh, there are many! They are those whom I call to join Me in the **Apostolate of My Eucharistic Life**. They are the richest in grace because I give them the strength they need to respond to what I ask of them. **And it is as if I hide them in the deepest depths of My Heart: their life is all in Me.**"[404]

In this same work, we find a collection of prayers composed by Sr. Mary herself, which give great insights into her revelations:

O Father, who are God, here I hold out my hands to accept sufferings and to receive them as a gift from You: may Your Reign come! O Son, who are God, here I raise my hands to offer my sufferings as a sacrifice through You: may Your Reign come! O Holy Spirit, who are God, here I raise my hands to offer my sufferings as a sacrifice through You: may Your Reign come!

Grant me, Lord, to enter fully into this vocation of suffering: make me worthy of suffering! You have given me a weak and frail body. O Father, here I am to fulfill Your Holy [Will].[405]

Reflecting upon the entirety of this book in its epilogue, Raphael Brown writes:

Dante's profoundly perceptive capsule of Poor Clare spirituality is found in the third canto of the Paradiso (verses 97-102), when his Poor Clare friend Piccarda Donati evokes St. Clare, without naming her: "'Perfect life and high merit enheaven a lady farther above,' she said to me, 'by whose Rule in your world below they take the habit and veil in order that until they die they may watch and sleep with that Spouse who accepts every vow which Charity conforms to His pleasure.'" That Spouse is Jesus Christ, in whose "will," as Dante wrote, "is our peace," because God's "Love moves the sun and the other stars." It is He who speaks to us again in our times through His Poor Clare of Jerusalem, Sister Mary of the Trinity. He is the center of the mystic world of the Poor Clares, as He was of their Father St. Francis and their Mother St. Clare. And that is their "spiritual legacy," their message, and their challenge to us. St. Clare expressed that message in this unforgettable formula in her Letter to Sister Ermentrude: "Never let the thought of Him leave your mind."[406]

Delving more deeply into Sr. Mary's teachings. Fr. Iannuzzi offers the following insight:

We find the continuous state of union with the Divine Will in the writings of God's chosen instrument Sr. Mary of the Holy Trinity.

Jesus tells Sister Mary: "To let Me live within you is to fill your heart with the utter surrender of little children… to apply all your intelligence to understanding My ways of working and to imitate them…It is to keep in the truth with all the strength of your will, cost what it may, at every instant and on every occasion."

… A few days later, Jesus defined the supernatural character of Sr. Mary's obedience that enabled his will to truly "live" and "reign" in her: "Silence, respect for all creatures… Stripping oneself in the joy of giving. Patience. Love which obeys the Voice of God, not in appearance, but from the depths of one's being, in complete adhesion to the divine will… I need all of that to live in a soul, to grow there and to reign there… Obedience is a state of the soul, a permanent state which makes the soul cling perseveringly to the will of God… You must be firmly united to Me, and to the will of God alone, and detached from all else… in order to help Me to penetrate everywhere… I live in you with a continuous and progressive life."

Overjoyed with Jesus' words of confirmation on the new state of union she presently enjoyed, Sr. Mary cried out: "My Lord, yes, to all you desire, with your help, with all my will… it is Your will that I desire… my immense desires for union among souls of goodwill for Your glory! I will intercede until the end of the world…"

…Hence Jesus' words to Sr. Mary of the Holy Trinity: "I desire a great army of victim souls who will join Me in the apostolate of My Eucharistic Life… I desire an army of victim souls who will confine their efforts to imitating My Apostolate… so that my Spirit may spread… I desire these victim souls to be everywhere: in the world and in the cloisters…"[407]

Let us now turn to the last mystic in this section; like Luisa Piccarreta, she was another 20th century Italian mystic, and she received revelations which

---

[403]Ibid.
[404]Ibid.
[405]Fr. Alain Marie Duboin, *The Life and Message of Sr. Mary of the Holy Trinity*, Part 2, Ch 5.
[406]Ibid. Epilogue.
[407]The Splendor of Creation.

again overlap with the messages given to Luisa.

Vera Grita

Vera Grita was a 20th century Italian mystic who wrote a work entitled *The Living Tabernacles*, bearing a nihil obstat. Born in Rome in 1923, she was a Salesian cooperator and her cause for beatification is under consideration.[408] Father François Marie Léthel, O.C.D, wrote that Grita was:

> …a humble consecrated lay person in whom I joyfully discovered a great mysticism of the Eucharist, perhaps one of the greatest, with a truly prophetic message for the Church of today and tomorrow[409]

(Fr. François was the preacher of Lenten spiritual exercises for Pope Benedict XVI in 2011, to whom the Holy Father wrote: *"I would truly like to express to you my deep gratitude for the precious service you have offered me and my colleagues in the Roman Curia by preaching the Spiritual Exercises in these past few days."*[410])

Living Tabernacles

Regarding her mysticism, Fr. Iannuzzi writes:

> On November 6th, 1969, Jesus told Vera that in order to enter more deeply into the mystery of his "real presence," she must offer to God her Fiat:

> "I desire that My work be diffused among priests… They will know how to prepare other souls that live in the world but are not of the world to receive Me. These will bring Me to the streets, into homes and families that I may live close to souls that are far from Me so that they may feel My continuous Eucharistic presence. The rebellious will fall… My daughter, I know where to lead you! But I cannot if you do not adhere completely to My Will. I need your Fiat… so that My Design of Love may be accomplished in its fullness in your soul and in the souls of others.

> Jesus later assured Vera that her Fiat helped actualize in her soul the new mystical union: I am already a living tabernacle in this soul and she does not realize it. She must realize it because I want her to assent to My eucharistic presence in her soul. Have you not already given your soul to Me completely? Wherefore I, Jesus, am the Master of your soul. And the Master is free to give as

much as he likes… If souls learned to at least seek Me in humility… they would discover My human-divine real presence: Me, Jesus.

Mary relates to Vera the future era of peace that is characterized by the Eucharistic reign of Jesus in souls: "Jesus comes to you with immense grace, that which has never been given before to mankind. Your Eucharistic Jesus will descend upon you so that you may seek and save those that are lost. Then the world will be purified by a "visit" from God, and also I, your Mother, will be with you and with My Son, the Eucharistic Jesus, to receive together with you, God the Creator in the revelation of his love and of his justice…"

Jesus tells Vera: "Behold, I will return to the world, I will return in the midst of souls to speak to them, to draw closer to them, to address them directly until the veils fall and they recognize Me in every brother… **Prepare the [Living] Tabernacles for this gift so that from this mystical union My coming in your midst may be revealed to the good … My Will will be done on earth as in heaven**. Months before Vera's departure for heaven, Jesus prophesied an immanent [sic] era of peace when the human race would experience the new reality of "Living Tabernacles."

As a woman who spent her life in Italy, Vera must have rejoiced on hearing Jesus speak of a future house in Rome, from which the new spirituality he had been dictating to her would set the earth ablaze: "I want a home all to Myself. It must stand in Rome as a light that will light up the whole world. My home will accept all who are called to become bearers of the eucharistic Jesus. This house will be a place that will shelter the Living Tabernacles for shifts of spiritual exercises all year long… Here the spirituality of the Living Tabernacles will be strengthened under the light of the gospel… This will be the Mother House … Others will blossom in Italy, then in Europe and then everywhere; and they will have the same purpose: to prepare the souls called to take Me in their soul…and bring Me to all your brothers."[411]

While there is not much literature currently available on Vera Grita written in English, Fr. Iannuzzi has done the English-speaking world a great service by here expounding upon her mysticism.

---

[408] Cf. The Hagiography Circle. Newsaints.faithweb.com.
[409] http://www.infoans.org/en/sezioni-eventi/item/5274-italy-the-light-of-christ-in-the-heart-of-the-church-the-theology-of-saints

[410] http://w2.vatican.va/content/benedict-xvi/en/letters/2011/documents/hf_ben-xvi_let_20110319_lethel.html
[411] *The Splendor of Creation*. Ch. 2.

***

What was true at the end of the last chapter rings true here as well: many more mystics could easily be given their own sections here, but for the sake of space, must instead be left for your own discovery. What the great theologian Fr. Marie Michel Philipon wrote in 1978 (quoted earlier), **"We are incontestably in a new era of spirituality,"** has only grown more overwhelming and undeniable than it already was when he published that observation over 40 years ago.

God is not going to let anyone stop Him. So let us put aside our own prejudices and preconceived opinions on how we think God should fashion the remainder of history and instead submit to how He will, in fact, go about it—in accordance with what He has repeatedly and clearly revealed to us.

There is simply no turning back from the unanimous consensus of trustworthy Catholic mysticism of the 20th century, and there is now no way to deny what that consensus consists in, either.

13) The Gift in Today's Catholic Voices

Here we will consider miscellaneous teachings given to us by trustworthy voices in the Catholic world today who speak of the Gift or of spirituality similar to it. I am not even attempting a systematic or comprehensive overview here; I am only presenting some "tidbits" which I have stumbled upon in my own reading and wish to share for my readers' edification. Anyone who exposes himself to good Catholic spiritual reading of the day will himself regularly find insights into the Gift—for this is the Holy Spirit's greatest desire and He regularly inspires intimations of it in the hearts of the faithful, even if they have heard nothing of Luisa. I sincerely encourage everyone to keep their minds attentive to this task.

First, I will share an assortment of brief quotes, then I will turn to dedicate separate sections to a few voices in particular.

Saint Mother Teresa of Calcutta:

"To be a saint means ... I will renounce my will, my inclinations, my whims and fancies, and make myself a willing slave to the will of God."

"There are some people who, in order not to pray, use as an excuse the fact that life is so hectic that it prevents them from praying. This cannot be. Prayer does not demand that we interrupt our work, but that we continue working as if it were a prayer. It is not necessary to always be meditating… **What matters is being with him, living with him, in his will.** To love with a pure heart, to love everybody, especially to love the poor, is a twenty-four-hours prayer."[412]

Mother Angelica:

Many ask the question, "How do I know this is God's Will for me?" The answer is simply, "If it is happening, it is God's will." It is not relevant whether it is His ordaining or permitting Will, nothing happens to us that He has not seen beforehand, pondered the good we would derive from it and put upon it His stamp of approval.[413]

Fr. Ottavio Michelini (about whom more will be said in the Era of Peace section of this book),20th century priest and mystic admired by Pope Paul VI, wrote the following meditation:

"Hallowed be thy name." We should hallow, that is, glorify, the holy name of God, uniting ourselves to the chorus of all voices (for all creatures have voices), fulfilling thus the finality of creation, which is the glorification of God. "Thy kingdom come." He who truly loves forgets himself, for his thought runs toward the person loved, from whom he desires happiness. "Thy will be done (FIAT) on earth, as it is in heaven." To seek our own desires and wishes is to place ourselves before others, and this is egotism; **to place the Divine Will before our will, so that God may work his will in us, as he does it in heaven-this is love. If he who prays does so with these sentiments, and if he places himself in God's presence, preoccupied only with his glory, with the desire that his kingdom may come and that his Will may be done, operating in him, he will see un-thought of and marvelous effects produced in his prayer; everything will be given to him and in a superabundant measure**

…Man should place himself before Me, not to ask material things, preoccupied with himself and his

---

[412]Mother Teresa, *In My Own Words*. Ch. 3
[413]Excerpt from "Two Wills – His and Mine" ewtn.com/library/mother/ma28e.htm

egotism, but rather he should recollect himself before Me, adoring and praying for the glorification of the Holy Name of my Father, in order to ask for the coming of my Kingdom now, and so that my Will may be done in him and in everyone, as I do it in heaven. To the man of faith who does this, this and all the rest will be given unto him … [414]

St. Padre Pio:

Let us adore it [divine providence] and be ready to conform our will in all things and at all times with the will of God… The total offering of our will is unfortunately very difficult. We must remember, though, that when our divine Master addressed to His Father on our behalf those words of the Lord's prayer "thy will be done," his divine mind showed Him very clearly how difficult it would be for us to do what He had promised the Father for us…Well, then, His immense love… found an admirable means… What means was this? … He asked Him also: "Give us this day, Father, our daily bread" …But what bread is this? … I recognize primarily the Eucharist… How could I fulfill that petition made by Your Son in our name: Thy will be done on earth as it is in heaven, if I did not receive strength from this immaculate flesh?… Yes, give Him to us and we shall be sure to fulfill the request that Jesus Himself addressed to You on our behalf: "Thy will be done on earth as it is in heaven."[415]

Fr. William Doyle (an Irish Jesuit priest killed in action during World War I who is widely remembered for his sanctity and his profound writings. Dr. Jeff Mirus compiled a few quotes from him as follows.):

"We do not mind what God does with us so long as it more or less fits in with our own wishes; but when his will clashes with ours, we begin to see the difficulty of the prayer, 'Not my will but thine be done.'"

"Going against self! Not in one thing or in two, but in all things where a free choice is left us. These little words contain the life-story of the saints, as they are the weapon that gained the victory which gave them heaven."

"… the Holy Spirit of God…is ever whispering what we ought to do and what we ought not to do. When we are deliberately deaf to his voice…we grieve instead of honouring the Holy Spirit of God. So let us often say: 'Come, O Holy Ghost, into my heart and make me holy…'."

Making my meditation before the picture of the Curé of Ars, he seemed to say to me with an interior voice: "The secret of my life was that I lived for the moment. I did not say, 'I must pray here for the next hour', but only 'for this moment'. I did not say, 'I have a hundred confessions to hear', but looked upon this one as the first and last. I did not say, 'I must deny myself everything and always', but only 'just this once'. By this means I was able always to do everything perfectly, quietly, and in great peace. Try and live this life of the present moment."[416]

Venerable Fulton Sheen:

"To do God's Will until death, that is the inner heart of all holiness."

"Whenever man attempts to do what he knows to be the Master's will, a power will be given him equal to the duty."

Dr. Peter Kreeft:

"Thy will be done" is the essential prayer of the saint; "my will be done" is the essential demand of the sinner. C S. Lewis says that "there are only two kinds of people, in the end: those who say to God, 'Thy will be done' and those to whom God says, in the end, 'Thy will be done.' " By giving us free will, God says to all of us "Thy will be done," but only some of us return to Him this compliment. [417]

Pope St. John Paul II:

[St. Hannibal] saw in the "Rogate" the means God himself had provided to bring about that "new and divine" holiness with which the Holy Spirit wishes to enrich Christians at the dawn of the third millennium, in order to "make Christ the heart of the world".

Pope Benedict XVI:

The love-story between God and man consists in the very fact that this communion of will increases in a communion of thought and sentiment, and thus our will and God's will increasingly coincide: God's will is no longer for me an alien will, something imposed on me from without by the commandments, but it is now my own will, based on the realization that God is in fact more deeply

---

[414] From his diary. February 5th, and 19th 1976.
[415] The Splendor of Creation
[416] https://www.catholicculture.org/commentary/otc.cfm?id=1601

[417] Peter Kreeft. *Practical Theology: Spiritual Direction from Saint Thomas Aquinas.* P. 194

present to me than I am to myself. Then self-abandonment to God increases and God becomes our joy (cf. Ps 73 [72]:23-28).[418]

…every day in the prayer of the Our Father we ask the Lord: "Thy will be done, on earth as it is in heaven" (Matt 6:10)… we recognize that "heaven" is where the will of God is done, and that "earth" becomes "heaven" – i.e., the place of the presence of love, of goodness, of truth and of divine beauty – only if on earth the will of God is done.[419]

Pope Francis:

"The one who listens attentively to the Word of God and truly prays, always asks the Lord: what is your will for me?"

[From his Apostolic Exhortation, Gaudete et Exsultate]: A Christian cannot think of his or her mission on earth without seeing it as a path of holiness, for "this is the will of God, your sanctification" (1 Thess 4:3). Each saint is a mission, planned by the Father to reflect and embody, at a specific moment in history, a certain aspect of the Gospel… reproducing in our own lives various aspects of Jesus' earthly life…Your identification with Christ and his will involves a commitment to build with him that kingdom of love, justice and universal peace… o often we say that God dwells in us, but it is better to say that we dwell in him, that he enables us to dwell in his light and love.

***

"We often refer glibly and most thoughtlessly to the Fiat of Mary, by which the "Word was made flesh and dwelt amongst us." Let us not forget that we, her children, must say Amen to our Mother's prayer. We must echo her Fiat. Christ also taught us to say Fiat to God: *Fiat voluntas tua*, "Thy Will be done on earth as it is in Heaven…"we ought to translate this prayer into living words, into our actions. If we do so the Holy Ghost will come upon us, and the Might of the Most High will overshadow us, and cause to be reproduced in us the likeness of the Son of God Himself."[420]

"The *Pater Noster*, the family prayer of the Church, has an arc like the rainbow, which springs up from the earth, touches the clouds, and then sweeps down to earth. We lift our hearts to God in its mounting petitions: "Hallowed be Thy Name: Thy Kingdom come", until we reach the

apex of the arc in: "Thy Will be done on earth as it is in Heaven…"[421]

Fr. George Kosicki

Fr. George W. Kosicki, a Basilian Father (C.S.B.), was a hermit, former biochemist, and zealous promoter of Divine Mercy whose legacy is greatly loved by the Catholic world today. One of his greatest works is a simple booklet entitled, *Be Holy! The Legacy of John Paul the Great*, and subtitled *A "Living Eucharist."*

Published in 2005, this booklet contains many ringing endorsements, including several from Cardinals (Maida, Belivacqua, George). Of note is the encouragement from Cardinal George (then the Archbishop of Chicago), which reads:

If Vatican II has not yet borne its fullest fruit in the Church, it is because we have not taken sufficiently to heart its essential teaching – the call to holiness for every member of the Church. **Father Kosicki's book brings us the good news that, for those who have good will and a desire for holiness, intimate union with Christ is available and possible**.

Finally, it contains a preface written by Fr. Benedict Groeschel, from which we read "**Fr. Kosicki has identified the principal themes of the writings of St. Faustina** as trust, thanksgiving, "being a living Eucharist" …" Indeed, thanks to the efforts of Fr. Kosicki and others, this "principal theme" in the writings of this holy nun will not be lost; for as important as Jesus' words on mercy for great sinners are in St. Faustina's revelations, it must not be forgotten that an equally important theme is this great new sanctity that Jesus speaks of multiple times to Faustina. Below are a few excerpts from this booklet:

The bottom line of why Jesus instituted the Holy Eucharist is not just to be present under the appearance (accidents) of bread and wine as a remembrance of Him, but also in order that He may transform us by His presence into His living presence, into temples of the Holy Spirit radiating His merciful love. In offering a votive Mass, #7 "For Religious," I found the Prayer over the Gifts especially meaningful: God of all mercy, you transformed [St. Faustina] and made her a new creature in your image. Renew us in the same way

[418] Deus Caritas Est 17
[419] General Audience. February 1, 2012
[420] Fr. William O'Keefe
[421] Fr. John McMahon

by making our gifts of peace acceptable to you. We ask this in the name of Jesus, the Lord. **The Lord is waiting for our freely given "yes" to His will in order the He may transform us into a "Living Eucharist"**—Note that: the bread and wine never say "no!"[422]

Fr. Kosicki was not afraid to be completely explicit about the nature of this holiness: that it truly does entail living in the Divine Will!

> **Q. What is this "new and eternal holiness" that John Paul II calls us to? A.** Pope John Paul II recently wrote of a "'new and divine' holiness with which the Holy Spirit wishes to enrich Christians at the dawn of the third millennium ... to make Christ the heart of the world" ... The new and eternal holiness is a maturing of the holiness of Jesus revealed in the Gospels. It is living the fullness of the Lord's Prayer—His kingdom come—that the Lord reign in our hearts now by the Holy Spirit to the glory of God the Father"—that His will be done on earth now as it is in heaven. Q. How can I live the fullness of the Our Father? A. We do so by becoming holy through the Holy Spirit and by doing and living in God's will on earth as in heaven. The will of the Father is His kingdom where Jesus reigns by the Holy Spirit. This is God's master plan for His grand family of saints. Where each saint is a unique, unrepeatable, precious gem in His great mosaic.[423]

Reading this quote, we can see that there is no room for doubt. Giving a "wrap up" summary of what we should do to follow this call, Fr. Kosicki writes:

> Trust in Jesus even more! • Be a "Living Eucharist." • Radiate His Presence: His Holiness, His Humility, His Mercy, to all. In this way live the Magnificat of Mary. • Rejoice in the Lord always. Pray without ceasing. In all things give thanks, For this is the will of God in Christ Jesus regarding you all! (1 Thess 5:16-19). • Live the Lord's Prayer—on earth as in heaven: "Thy will be done." • Make frequent spiritual Communions. • Give thanks for everything, always, and everywhere—all is gift! Thanksgiving is the KEY that opens up the Holiness of the Holy Trinity to us. Thanksgiving is the key to humility; humility is the key to transparency; transparency is the key to the presence of the holy Lord; presence of the Holy One, Jesus Christ in our hearts is to be a "Living

Eucharist"—a holy, humble, merciful presence of Jesus. Thus, holiness is becoming a "Living Eucharist." • Invoke the Holy Spirit unceasingly: desire and ask for more! • To please the Lord, be present to Him with your heart, in the Heart of Mary, trusting, rejoicing and giving thanks. • Love the Lord with His love, with your whole heart, your whole mind and your whole strength—and your neighbor as another self. • Don't waste your sufferings: with love, entrust them to the merciful Heart of Jesus. • Be merciful with the mercy of the heavenly Father—in deed, word and prayer. • Desire more of God. Ask for more of the Holy Spirit. Allow Him to work more in you and transform you.[424]

Servant of God Fr. Walter Ciszek

Fr. Walter Ciszek was a Polish-American Jesuit priest who was imprisoned for decades in a Soviet Gulag. His cause for beatification has been underway since 1990, six years after his death. Fr. Ciszek teaches that:

> Ultimately, the only absolute freedom we have resides in a man's free will. And that freedom was given us by our Creator, essentially, so that we might freely choose to love and serve him... It is in choosing to serve God, to do his will, that man achieves his highest and fullest freedom. It may seem paradoxical to say that our highest and fullest freedom comes when we follow to the least detail the will of another, but it is true nonetheless when that other is God[425]

> Each day, every day of our lives, God presents to us the people and opportunities upon which he expects us to act. He expects no more of us, but he will accept nothing less of us; and we fail in our promise and commitment if we do not see in the situations of every moment of every day his divine will... The kingdom of God will not be brought to fulfillment on earth by one great, sword-swinging battle against the powers of darkness. But only by each of us laboring and suffering day after day as Christ labored and suffered, until all things at last have been transformed...[426]

Commenting on Fr. Ciszek's writings and then quoting them, Fr. Iannuzzi writes:

> A more recent exemplar of total abandonment to the Divine Will is Rev. Walter ... Before his cause

---

[422]Fr. George Kosicki. C.S.B. *Be Holy! The Legacy of John Paul the Great.* pages 147-148.
[423]Fr. George Kosicki. C.S.B. *Be Holy! The Legacy of John Paul the Great.* P. 161.

[424]*Ibid*, P. 175-176.
[425]http://www.ciszek.org/Freedom_And_Gods_Will_For_Yo u.pdf
[426]Fr. Walter Ciszek, *He Leadeth Me.* Page 139.

of beatification was introduced, several of his writings were examined by theologians in Rome who found them to be both inspired and prophetic. In one of his works, **Fr. Ciszek describes how creation is transformed and set free from its slavery to corruption through the activity of God's will in man's will:**

"Christ's life and suffering were redemptive; his "apostolate" in the scheme of salvation was to restore the original order and harmony in all creation that had been destroyed by sin. His perfect obedience to the Father's will redeemed man's first and continuing disobedience to that will. "All creation," said St. Paul, "groans and labors up till now," awaiting Christ's redemptive efforts to restore the proper relationship between God and his creation. But Christ's redemptive act did not of itself restore all things, it simply made the work of redemption possible, it began our redemption. Just as all men share in the disobedience of Adam, so all men must share in the obedience of Christ to the Father's will. Redemption will be complete only when all men share his obedience… This simple truth, that the sole purpose of man's life on earth is to do the will of God, contains in it riches and resources enough for a lifetime… **The notion that the human will, when united with the divine will, can play a part in Christ's work of redeeming all mankind is overpowering.** The wonder of God's grace transforming worthless human actions into efficient means for spreading the kingdom of God here on earth astounds the mind and humbles it to the utmost, yet brings a peace and joy unknown to those who have never experienced it, unexplainable to those who will not believe."

The aforementioned writings reveal how creation is transformed under the influence of God. It is not through one individual, but through mankind's obedience to God's will manifested in the humanity of Jesus Christ that creation emerges from its slavery to corruption and enters what St. Paul calls 'the glorious freedom of the sons of God.'[427]

John Haffert

John Haffert was one of the greatest lay leaders in the Church of the 20th century. Early in his life of work for the Church, he started the Scapular

Society to promote the Brown Scapular of the Carmelites, and later dedicated himself to the messages of Our Lady of Fatima. He founded the Blue Army, whose shrine today hosts 50,000 pilgrims every year. Now officially known as the World Apostolate of Fatima, it is an officially Vatican-recognized Public International Association of the Faithful.

Mr. Haffert was a firm believer in Luisa's revelations.[428] He published at least 30 books, many of which have become well known. In one of them, entitled *Now the Woman Shall Conquer*, he wrote:

Cardinal Gagnon said at the 1996 Rome conference: "It is not enough to believe that Our Lady is Co- Redemptrix and Mediatrix. We must proclaim it." And the Pope affirmed this in his message to the International Mariological Congress later that same year. Is not the Holy Spirit urging this upon the Church at this time? Are we not speaking of **the reality of the triumph of the Immaculate Heart of Mary promised at Fatima ("My Immaculate Heart will triumph") … the reality of the forming of Jesus in the Mystical Body and in each of its members to a degree never before attained? This is the stunning message of the Venerable [sic] Luisa Picaretta** [sic] whose message was confirmed by sixty years of living solely on the Blessed Sacrament. What else could the final triumph be of Her who alone of all humanity was the first to live in the Divine Will? Does it not mean there will be saints as never before, living in the Divine Will, as Mary did, and bringing the Holy Spirit to live in the hearts of men of all nations?

As mentioned, Mr. Haffert also wrote the Foreword to Hugh Owen's book, *New and Divine: the Holiness of the Third Christian Millennium*. In this foreword, we read:

For those who have never heard of the "'new and divine' holiness," it may seem like an impossible dream—like the lifting of the veil upon the already approaching glorious time when the prayer of two thousand years will be fulfilled: **"Thy Will be done on earth as it is in Heaven." Mr. Owen clearly reveals this new "era of peace for mankind," promised at Fatima, as the era of the outpouring of the Holy Spirit and the**

---

427 *The Splendor of Creation*. Chapter 1.
428 *Nota Bene:* A certain "publishing company" devoted to attacking "false apparitions" (among which it counts Fr. Gobbi's, Garabandal, Medjugorje, Matthew Kelley's, Our Lady of All Nations, Servant of God Maria Esperanza's, and many others) claims, without any evidence or citations, that

Mr. Haffert "repented" of supporting some unnamed "false apparitions" before his death. Whatever this allegedly refers to, it should certainly be dismissed given the untrustworthiness of the source and the lack of any supporting evidence.

diffusion of the gift of living in perfect abandonment to the Divine Will…

It is faith in the promises of Fatima, faith in the triumph of God's Will on earth as in Heaven. And we can dare to believe that it can begin now, in each of us, if we believe enough to say "Yes" to the great gift that God now offers to the world, the gift of the "new and divine" holiness.

Clearly, Mr. Haffert had no reservations about the Gift, and instead recognized and boldly taught that it is indeed the fulfillment of the Lord's Prayer for our time.

14) The Gift and the Entire History of the World

Therefore, my daughter, if you remain attentive to live always of my Will, It will entrust to you all the secrets of the history of Creation … [429]

Six thousand years ago, a man ate a fruit. The millennia that followed have largely been the story of the consequences of this decision.

Here I wish to sum up the essence and meaning of what fills millions of pages of history books around the world. In reading this, you will truly have more wisdom about the whole point of history than most of the world's historians. (It seems today that few historians understand the true *form* of history, even if they know many details about its matter, like an atheistic psychologist who knows many facts about human behavior but does not know that which makes us human.)

"In the beginning God created the heavens and the earth." — Genesis 1:1. The first verse of Sacred Scripture.

The Universe does predate man chronologically, but it takes a low second place to him in order of importance. Regarding this, Jesus tells Luisa:

> The purpose of Creation was man, yet I did not create man as first; had I done it I would not have been orderly. [430]

Yes, all things were created for man. We should all, therefore, be unabashedly anthropocentric when considering creation. Jesus puts it even more clearly elsewhere, saying:

> **Everything was made for man**… [431]

So what was man's creation directed toward with respect to material things?

> Creation was made for man — in it he was to be the king of all created things. [432]

God made creation for man, and God made man to be the King of All Creation. And this, indeed, Adam was. Let us now consider this glorious state.

The Original Glory

The state of "prelapsarian" (that is, "before the fall") Adam is mostly one of speculation among the theologians of the Church, as Scripture itself gives relatively few details. Nevertheless, the clear consensus among all the Fathers of the Church and the saints is certainly that, before the Fall, Adam and Eve enjoyed a state of incredible glory, so much so that in our sorry state today we can scarcely comprehend it, notwithstanding the graces we now have access to thanks to the Redemption.

The Catechism of the Catholic Church teaches that Adam and Eve shared in the Divine Life, and that "by the **radiance** of this grace all dimensions of man's life were confirmed." [433] The term is not accidental: Jesus tells Luisa that this was not merely symbolic, but that the grace in them was so great that they were literally clothed in light.

Jesus tells Luisa:

> Now, you must know that Adam possessed such sanctity when he was created by God, and his acts, even the slightest, had such value, that no Saint, either before or after my coming upon earth, can be compared to his sanctity; and all of their acts together do not reach the value of one single act of Adam, because, in my Divine Will, he possessed the fullness of sanctity, the totality of all the divine goods. [434]

> …before sinning, Adam possessed the complete life of my Divine Will in his soul; one can say that it was filled to the brim, to the extent of

---

[429] August 22, 1931.
[430] November 20, 1929.
[431] January 9, 1920.
[432] July 29, 1926.

[433] CCC 376.
[434] October 2, 1927.

overflowing outside. So, by virtue of my Will, the human will transfused light outside, and emitted the fragrances of its Creator—fragrances of beauty, of sanctity and of full health; fragrances of purity, of strength, which were such as to come out from within his will like many luminous clouds. And the body was so embellished by these exhalations, that it was a delight to see him beautiful, vigorous, luminous, so very healthy, with an enrapturing grace.[435]

Of course, Adam and Eve enjoyed complete happiness in the terrestrial paradise that was the Garden of Eden. But as Jesus reveals to Luisa, what was most important was their holiness: because they were created directly by a deliberate act of God, justice demanded that He create them with all perfections due in the nature of man; that He create them truly similar to Himself. This He did by giving them the Gift of Living in the Divine Will. The Divine Will was immediately placed within Adam's human will from the moment of his creation, therefore Adam gave God perfect glory. And the first thing that Adam did after he was created was to say, *"I love you my God, my Father, the Author of my life."*[436]

Jesus tells Luisa that He made physical creation to house man, but he made the soul of man to house God. This was so deeply true that the Divine Will was the very principle of the life and action of Adam. Jesus tells Luisa:

> When God created Adam, he possessed such sanctity that the slightest one of his acts had such value that no [sanctity of any] saint either before or after My coming to earth can compare to his sanctity ... For in My Divine Will Adam possessed the fullness of sanctity and the totality of all divine blessings. And do you know what fullness means? It means to be filled to the brim, to the point of overflowing with light, sanctity, love and all the divine qualities, whereby he was able to fill heaven and earth, over which he exercised dominion and through which he extended his kingdom ... For by the power of My Will, within which alone all such acts may be found, Adam was able to give Me the fullness and totality of all goods, whereas outside of My Will such acts do not exist. Thus Adam possessed all the riches and acts of infinite value that My Eternal Will

communicated to him before the divinity.[437]

In the case of Adam, this grace even meant all infused knowledge:

> What others learn with so many efforts, he possessed as gift in a surprising way. So, he possessed the knowledge of all the things of this earth; he had the science of all plants, of all herbs and of the virtue which each of them contained; he had the science of all species of animals and of how he should use them; he had the science of music, of singing, of writing, of medicine—in sum, of everything. And if the generations possessed each one its special science, Adam possessed them all. [438]

> Each sense was a communication that I left between Me and her. Her thought was a communication between my Intelligence and hers; her eye was communication between her light and Mine; her speech was a channel of communication between her Fiat and Mine...[439]

Work existed, but it was not "by the sweat of our brow," for that is a result of the Fall. Jesus describes to Luisa what work was like before that abysmal moment:

> Indeed, wherever my Will reigns, all things, even the most little and natural, convert into delight for Me and for the creature, because they are the effect of a Divine Will reigning in her, which cannot issue from Itself even a shadow of unhappiness. Even more, you must know that, in Creation, Our Supreme Fiat established all the human acts, investing them with delight, with joy and with happiness. So, work itself was to be of no burden for man, nor give him a shadow of tiredness, because, by possessing my Will, he possessed the strength that never tires and never fails.[440]

But everyone must be tried; no creature with a free will is exempt from a test before eternal and absolute confirmation in grace. It would be blasphemous to accuse God of so testing Adam and Eve without His wanted Will being that they pass the test; indeed, this was what God desired (even though, of course, in His all-knowingness, He was aware that they would not in fact pass it), and He knew exactly what to do if they passed. Jesus tells Luisa:

---

435 July 7, 1928.
436 December 10, 1933.
437 Fr. Iannuzzi Doctoral Dissertation. 2.1.2.7 (quoting Luisa's diary).

438 November 12, 1925.
439 October 11, 1924.
440 March 3, 1927.

My daughter, indeed there is no certainty without a test, and when the soul passes the test, she receives the confirmation of my designs and everything that is necessary to her and befits her in order to carry out the state to which she has been called by Me. This is why I wanted to test Adam—to confirm his happy state and his right of kingship over the whole Creation; and since he was not faithful in the test, by justice he could not receive the confirmation of the goods which his Creator wanted to give him. In fact, through the test man acquires the seal of faithfulness, which gives him the right to receive the goods that God had established to give him in the state to which his soul had been called by Him. It can be said that one who is not tested has no value—neither before God nor before men, nor before himself. God cannot trust a man without a test, and man himself does not know what strength he possesses.

If Adam had passed the test, all human generations would have been confirmed in his state of happiness and of royalty. In the same way, I Myself, loving these children of my Divine Will with a love all special, wanted to go through the test for all of them in my Humanity, reserving for them the one test of never letting them do their will, but only and always my Will, so as to reconfirm for them all the goods needed in order to live in the Kingdom of my Divine Fiat. With this, I closed all exit doors for them; I anointed them with an invincible strength, in such a way that nothing else will be able to enter the so very high fences of my Kingdom. In fact, when I command that something should not be done, it is a door that I leave, through which the human will can make its exit; it is an occasion that the creature always has, by which she can go out of my Will. But when I say: 'from here there is no exit', all doors remain closed, weakness is fortified, and the only thing that is left to her is the decision to enter, never to go out again—or not to enter at all. Therefore, in order to live in the Kingdom of my Will there will only be the decision—the decision will carry the accomplished act. [441]

If Adam had not sinned, the Eternal Word, who is the very Will of the Celestial Father, was to come upon earth glorious, triumphant and dominator, accompanied visibly by His angelic army, which all were to see; and with the splendor of His glory, He was to charm everyone and draw everyone to Himself with His beauty; crowned as king and with the scepter of command, so as to be king and head of the human family, in such a way

as to give creatures the great honor of being able to say: 'We have a King who is Man and God.' More so, since your Jesus was not coming from Heaven to find man infirm, because, had he not withdrawn from my Divine Will, no illnesses, either of soul or of body, were to exist; in fact, it was the human will that almost drowned the poor creature with pains. The Divine Fiat was untouchable by any pain, and so was man to be. Therefore, I was to come to find man happy, holy, and with the fullness of the goods with which I had created him. But, because he wanted to do his will, he changed Our destiny, and since it was decreed that I was to descend upon earth—and when the Divinity decrees, no one can move It—I only changed the manner and the appearance, but I did descend, though under most humble guises: poor, with no apparatus of glory, suffering and crying, and loaded with all the miseries and pains of man. The human will made Me come to find man unhappy, blind, deaf and mute, full of all miseries; and I, in order to heal him, was to take them upon Myself; and so as not to strike fear in them, I was to show Myself as one of them, become their brother and give them the medicines and the remedies which were needed. So, the human will has the power to render man happy or unhappy, a saint or a sinner, healthy or sick. [442]

Thankfully, we need not waste any time lamenting that Adam failed the test. Glorious as it would have been if he passed, we must recall that God, in His infinite Goodness and perfect Omnipotence, never even *allows* an evil to occur unless He knows He will bring a *greater* good out of it. We should also remind ourselves of the *felix culpa* (the "happy fault"), of which we sing in the Exsultet at Easter, and in which we remember that in a sense Adam's fault was "happy," for now God was on the move to enact an even *greater* plan than He would have if Adam had passed the test. But before moving on to consider that plan, we must first understand more about the tragic Fall itself.

The Fall (~ 4000 BC)

Why did Adam sin? The answer is simple, and Jesus reveals it to Luisa:

…**do you want to know why Adam sinned? Because he forgot that I loved him,** and he forgot to love Me … So, **love ceased first, and then sin began**; and as he ceased to love his God, true love towards himself also ceased … This is why, in

---

coming upon earth, the thing on which I placed greatest importance was that they love one another as they were loved by Me, in order to give them my first love, to let the love of the Most Holy Trinity hover over the earth… never forget that I love you very much, so as to never forget to love Me…In this way, you will remain in the order, and will fear nothing.[443]

So we can see that the seed of the Fall can perhaps be found in the memory—in forgetting the works of God—for such forgetfulness neglects Scripture's admonition "do not forget the works of the Lord" (Psalm 78). And how often, even now, do we sin because we allow ourselves to forget?

But this forgetfulness of God's love had disastrous consequences. Jesus explains this in a revelation to Luisa, saying:

My daughter, terrible indeed was the moment of the fall of Adam. As he rejected Our Divine Will to do his own, Our Fiat was in act of withdrawing from the heavens, from the sun and from all Creation to reduce It to nothing … **If it wasn't that the Eternal Word offered His foreseen merits of the future Redeemer, as He offered them to preserve the Immaculate Virgin from original sin, everything would had gone to ruin**: the heavens, the sun, would have withdrawn into Our source; and as Our Divine Will withdraws, all created things would lose life. But the Word [foreseen Incarnate] presented Himself before the Divinity, and making present all of His foreseen merits, all things remained in their place, and my Fiat continued His creating and preserving work, waiting for my Humanity in order to give it as legitimate gift, which I deserved; so much so, that the solemn promise was given to man, after his fall, that the future Redeemer would descend to save him, so that he would pray and dispose himself to receive Him … **If it wasn't for my Humanity, everything was lost for man.** Therefore, not doing my Divine Will encloses all evils and is to lose all rights, of Heaven and of the earth; while doing It encloses all goods and acquires all rights, human and divine.[444]

Yes, the Fall of Man was so great that, were it not for the foreseen merits of the incarnate Christ, the Universe would have been annihilated; resolving into the chaos whence it was called by God in the beginning. So greatly exalted is man's dignity above created things that the destiny of all created things is inextricably linked to that of man's.

But we must now consider what the Fall did not mean. God hastened to act immediately with His own promise; but its fulfillment did not mean Adam's damnation. Jesus tells Luisa:

…in creating him, God had left nothing empty within him, but everything was divine fullness, as much as a creature could contain. And when he fell into sin, these acts, these riches of his, this glory and perfect love which he had given to his Creator, were not destroyed; on the contrary, it is by virtue of them and of his operating done in my Divine Fiat that he earned the Redemption. No, one who had possessed the Kingdom of my Will, even for a short time, could not remain without Redemption. One who possesses this Kingdom enters into such bonds and rights with God, that God Himself feels with him the strength of His own chains that bind Him, and He cannot get rid of him… Now, in seeing him fallen into poverty, how could Our love bear not having compassion on him, if Our Divine Will Itself lovingly waged war on Us and pleaded for the one who had lived in It? Do you see, then, what living in my Divine Will means—its great importance? In It there is fullness of all divine goods and totality of all possible and imaginable acts…if Adam deserved compassion, it was because the first period of his life was in the Kingdom of the Divine Will.[445]

Adam was invincible. He lived in the Divine Will for a time, and God can never forget, or allow to be lost, one who has lived in His Will even briefly. Furthermore, God cannot forget His love for such a soul for even a moment, and this love immediately compelled God to issue the promise of the future Redeemer, which harkens the next stage of history.

The Protoevangelium

"I will put enmities between thee and the woman, and thy seed and her seed: she shall crush thy head, and thou shalt lie in wait for her heel." —Genesis 3:15

Jesus expounds upon this to Luisa:

My daughter, my Love was not extinguished because of the fall of man, but became more ignited; and even though my Justice justly punished him and condemned him, **my Love, kissing my Justice, without delay promised the future Redeemer, and said to the deceitful**

---

[445]October 2, 1927.

serpent, with the empire of my Power: 'You have made use of a woman to snatch man from my Divine Will, and I, by means of another woman, who will have in Her power the Power of my Fiat, will knock down your pride, and with Her immaculate foot, She will crush your head.' These words burned the infernal serpent more than hell itself, and he stored so much rage in his heart, that he could no longer stay still—he would do nothing but go round and round the earth, to discover She who was to crush his head—not in order to let it be crushed, but so as to be able, with his infernal arts, with his diabolical tricks, to make fall She who was to defeat him, debilitate him and bind him in the dark abysses. So, for four thousand years he kept always wandering; and when he would see women who were more virtuous and good, he would arm his battle, he would tempt them in every way, and only then would he leave them, when he would be assured, by means of some weakness or defects, that they were not the One through whom he was to be defeated. And he would continue his wandering.[446]

God does not waste time. **As soon as the Fall had occurred, He was on the move not only to restore what was lost, but to reorder things in a greater way than would have been possible if the fall had never occurred. But the world was not ready to receive this effort. Another 6,000 years of suffering and praying—with 4,000 for the coming of the Redeemer, then 2,000 for the coming of His Kingdom—would first have to pass.**

Up to the Flood (~ 2000 BC)

All Christians know what happened after the Fall. Adam and Eve were banished from the Garden. Their children inherited the consequences of this sin. Death and suffering entered the world. But the world did not descend overnight into the degree of chaos which it exhibits now; nor to the degree of chaos it had immediately before the Flood. Only the seed—only the seminal beginnings—of these evils existed immediately. It took much time for these evils to grow so grave and numerous that the world needed to be purged. Regarding the time before the Flood, Jesus tells Luisa:

My daughter, as long as he remained in the terrestrial Eden, living in the Kingdom of the Supreme Will, Adam knew all the knowledges, as much as it is possible for a creature, of that which belonged to the Kingdom he possessed. But as

soon as he went out of It, his intellect was obscured; he lost the light of his Kingdom, and could not find the fitting words in order to manifest the knowledges he had acquired on the Supreme Will, because that very Divine Volition which would hand to him the necessary terms to manifest to others what he had known, was missing in him. This, on his part; more so, since every time he remembered his withdrawal from my Will, and the highest good which he had lost, he felt such a grip of sorrow as to become taciturn, engrossed in the sorrow of the loss of a Kingdom so great, and of the irreparable evils which, as much as Adam might do, it was not given to him to repair. Indeed, that very God whom he had offended was needed in order to remedy them. On the part of his Creator, he received no order, and therefore he was not given enough capacity to manifest it. Why manifest a knowledge if it would not give him the good it contained? **I only make a good known when I want to give it. However, even though Adam did not speak extensively about the Kingdom of my Will, he taught many important things on what regarded It; so much so, that during the first times of the history of the world, up to Noah, the generations had no need of laws, nor were there idolatries … but all recognized their one God … because they cared more about my Will. But as they kept moving away from It, idolatries arose and degenerated into worse evils. And this is why God saw the necessity of giving His laws as a preserver for the human generations.**[447]

Although the Edenic graces were removed upon the Fall, its effects lingered for some time, and Adam carried many graces with him still. But as time went on, and as more and more centuries passed after the death of Adam, the world grew farther and farther away from its origin. Thankfully, there was still at least one righteous man left. Jesus tells Luisa:

And only the acts determine the coming of a good—not the time. More so, since they were forcing Our Justice to exterminate them from the face of the earth, as it happened in the Flood, in which only **Noah, by obeying Our Will and through the prolixity of his long sacrifice of building the ark, deserved to be saved with his family, and to find in his acts the continuation of the long generation in which the promised Messiah was to come**. A prolonged and continuous sacrifice possesses such attraction and enrapturing force before the Supreme Being, as to

---

[446]May 19, 1931.

[447]September 17, 1926.

make Him decide to give great goods and continuation of life to the human kind. **If Noah had not obeyed and had not sacrificed himself in carrying out a work so long, he himself would have been swept away in the Flood, and since he would not have saved himself, the world, the new generation, would have ended.**[448]

Up to Redemption (~ 0 AD)

Knowing that man now needed to be treated like a servant, even though he was in fact a son, God prepared the way for the introduction of His Law, which was never before needed, as man (before the pre-flood corruption of the world) was intent on the Will of God. In discussing the need for the Law, Jesus tells Luisa:

> Now Our Paternal Goodness, seeing that man always goes falling more, in order to give him a support, a help, It gave him the Law as the norm for his life, because in the Creation It gave him neither laws, nor other things, except that of My Divine Will, that by continuously giving him Life, gave him Our Divine Law naturally, in a way that he would feel to it in himself, as his own life, without having the need that We would tell and command him. Even more, because where My Will Reigns, there are neither laws, nor commands. Laws are for the servants, for the rebels, not for the children. Between Us and those who Live in Our Volition, everything is resolved in Love. But with all the law, man did not remake himself, and since Our Ideal for Creation had been Man, and only for him was everything done, therefore I wanted to come on earth into their midst… [449]

The Law—great and necessary as it is—was of course preparatory for the coming of the Redeemer in the flesh. But much more was needed before that time in which God was wedded to earth; and even though God is now wed to an unfaithful spouse, He Himself always remains perfectly faithful. Continuing with the analogy of marriage, Jesus tells Luisa:

> My daughter, it is indeed true that the Supreme Being made Its marriage with humanity at the beginning of Creation; and it happened as to a husband, when his wicked wife induces him to separate in court. But, in spite of this, an affection remains in his heart, and he thinks and yearns that, if his chosen one should change, "who knows… I may once again be able to unite and bind myself with her with the bond of marriage"; and therefore he often lets news reach her ear through messengers—that he loves her.

> So God did: even though the marriage with humanity was unbound in the divine court, He kept an affection and, though far away, he longed for the new bond of marriage with humanity; so much so, that He did not destroy the palace which He had formed with so much sumptuousness and magnificence, nor did He take away from her the good of the sun that formed the day, but He left everything, so that the very one who had offended Him might make use of it. Even more, He maintained the correspondence by choosing, from the very beginning of the world, now one of the good, now another, who were like messengers. And like many postmen, some brought the little letters, some the telegrams, some the phone calls from Heaven, in which it was announced that the far away spouse had not forgotten her, that he loved her, and that he wanted the return of the ungrateful spouse.

> So, in the Old Testament, the more I multiplied the good, the patriarchs and the prophets, the more pressing were the invitations and the mail that ran between Heaven and earth, through which God was sending news—that He desired the new union. This is so true that, **unable to contain the ardor of His love any longer, and since decayed humanity was not yet disposed at that time, He made an exception, espousing the Virgin Queen and the Humanity of the Word with bond of true marriage, so that, by virtue of them, decayed humanity might be lifted up again and I might form the marriage with the entire humanity. So, my Humanity formed the new engagement with her on the Cross, and everything I did and suffered, up to dying on the Cross, were all preparations in order to carry out the desired marriage in the Kingdom of my Divine Will.** Now, after the engagement, there are pledges and gifts left to be exchanged, and these are the knowledges about my Divine Fiat. Through them, humanity is given back the great gift which man rejected in Eden—the eternal, infinite and endless gift of my Will. And this gift will attract decayed humanity so much, that she will give Us, in exchange, the gift of her poor will, which will be the confirmation and the seal of the union of the spouses, after such a long chain of correspondence, of faithfulness on the part of God, and of inconstancy, ingratitude and coldness on the part of creatures.[450]

---

[448]March 12, 1930.
[449]May 30, 1932.

[450]June 16, 1928.

This "new union" desired by God, although it was truly thanks to Our Lady most of all, was earlier enabled by the sacrifice of Abraham.

So let us at this point consider another excerpt in which Jesus gives Luisa another broad look at history and explains the place of Abraham, Noah, and relates those pivotal moments to the state of the world today. **The entry in Luisa's diary from June 26th, 1932, gives this profound overview, and I present it in its near entirety here:**

My daughter, all the Good of the history of the world is founded upon the sacrifice that is wanted of creatures by My Supreme Will; and the greater the sacrifice that We ask of her, the more Good We enclose in it. And We ask for these great sacrifices when, because of their sins, they deserve that the world be destroyed-making the new life of creatures come out from within the sacrifice, in place of the destruction. Now, you must know that at that point of the history of the world creatures deserved to exist no more-all should have perished. Noah, by accepting Our Mandate and by exposing himself to the great sacrifice, and for so many years, of building the ark, bought back the world and all the future generations.

As he went on sacrificing himself for so prolixious a time, of hardships, of toils, of sweat, so did he pour out the coins, not of gold or silver, but of his whole being in act of following Our Volition. In this way he put in enough coins to be able to buy back what was about to be destroyed. So, if the world still exists, they owe it to Noah who, with his sacrifices and by doing Our Will the Way We wanted him to do it, saved man and everything that was to serve man. A prolixious sacrifice, wanted by God, says great things-Universal Good, sweet chain that binds God and men. We Ourselves don't feel like escaping from the maze of this chain so long that the creature forms for Us by a prolixious sacrifice. On the contrary, it is so sweet and dear to Us, that We let Ourselves be bound by her, as she herself best pleases. Now, by his prolixious sacrifice, Noah bought back the continuation of the human generations.

After another length of time of the history of the world, Abraham came, and Our Volition commanded him to sacrifice his own son. This was a hard sacrifice for a poor father; it can be said that God put the man to the test and demanded a proof that was inhuman and almost impossible to execute. But God has the Right to ask whatever He wants and any sacrifice He wants. Poor Abraham-he was put in such constraints that his heart bled, and he felt death within himself, and the fatal blow that he was to strike over his only son. The sacrifice was exuberant; so much so, that Our Paternal Goodness wanted the execution of it, but not the completion, knowing that he could not have lived-he would have died of grief after an act so harrowing, of killing his own son, because it was an act that surpassed the strengths of his nature.

But Abraham accepted everything-he was heedless of everything, either of his son or of his very self, while feeling consumed with sorrow in his own son. If Our Volition, just as It commanded it, had not prevented the fatal act, even though he would have died together with his beloved son, he would still have accomplished the sacrifice wanted by Us. Now, this sacrifice, wanted by Us, was great, exuberant and **unique in the history of the world.**[451] Well then, this very sacrifice elevated him so high, that he was constituted by Us head and father of the human generations; and by the sacrifice of sacrificing his son, he poured out coins of blood and of intense sorrow to buy back the future Messiah, for the Jewish people and for all. In fact, after the sacrifice of Abraham, We made Ourselves heard often in the midst of creatures, that which We did not do before. The sacrifice had the virtue of drawing Us closer to them; and We formed the Prophets, up to the time when the longed-for Messiah came.

Now, after another most extensive length of time, wanting to give the Kingdom of Our Will, We wanted the sacrifice on which to set It, such that, while **the earth is flooded by sins and deserves to be destroyed, the sacrifice of the creature buys it back for Us, and with her sacrifice-and in her sacrifice, she calls back the Divine Will to Reign, and makes the New Life of My Volition be Reborn in the world in the midst of creatures. Here, then, I asked for the prolixious sacrifice of your life, sacrificed in a bed.** And this was nothing, because other souls have remained in a bed of pain; but it was the New Cross, which I have not asked of and given to anyone, that was to form your daily martyrdom-and you know what it is, since many times you have lamented to Me about it.

---

[451]We should here note that, contrary to the exaggerations of Kierkegaard (who, though insightful, also has dangers in his messages), the test of Abraham should not be seen as an example of the need to reduce the absolute nature of the moral norms. Jesus tells Luisa that what He asked of Abraham was "**unique** in the *history of the world*" which clearly tells us that God never had before, never has since, and never again will command someone to kill his own child.

Daughter, when I want to give a Great Good, a New Good to creatures, I give New Crosses and I want a New and Unique sacrifice-a cross for which the human can give itself no reason; but **there is My Divine Reason, that man is obliged to not investigate, but to lower his forehead and adore it.** And besides, this was about the Kingdom of My Will, and My Love had to invent and want New Crosses and sacrifices never before received, to be able to find pretexts, the prop, the strength, sufficient coins, and an extremely long chain to let Itself be bound by the creature. And the sure sign, when We want to give a Great and Universal Good in the world, is to ask of a creature a great sacrifice, and prolixity in it; these are the assurances and certainties of the Good that We want to give. And when We find one who accepts, We make him a portent of Grace, and in his sacrifice We form the Life of that Good that We want to give.

… nor should you be concerned because you do not see and hear in others the effects of your sacrifice. It is necessary that with your sacrifice you make the deed of purchase with Our Divinity; and once you have settled with God, the purchase is assured: in due time, with certainty, the Kingdom of the Divine Volition will have Life, because the purchase of It was made by the sacrifice of one who belongs to the human family.

With this message of a sure and certain hope of the coming of the Kingdom, we turn now to the Redemption itself. Just as in the last hundred years there has been an explosion of prophecy, apparitions, and revelations (more on this will be relayed in a forthcoming section), so too, in the years before the coming of God in the Flesh, there was a building expectation that is not lost even on secular scholars, one of whom pointed out:

…from the time of the Babylonian Captivity, there has been the expectation that a messianic figure would appear who would bring about the culmination of Jewish hopes. In the subsequent centuries, as Palestine came under Greek, Syrian and then Roman control, **the messianic expectation grew stronger and stronger. The Dead Sea Scrolls suggest that a great ferment and fervor existed in the period just before the beginning of Christianity**.[452]

And this prophetic explosion was not in vain; it culminated in the ardent and unprecedented prayers of a certain lowly virgin named Mary.

Redemption Itself (26 AD)

(*Many details on the life of the Holy Family and on the Passion of Jesus are contained in the "Grow in the Gift through Mary" and the "Hours of the Passion" chapters, respectively. For the sake of brevity, what is quoted in those chapters will not be repeated here, although it is quite relevant and edifying, and will hopefully be read by those who read this section*).

Now the fullness of time has come. Now the hour has arrived for God to fulfill His promise He made 4,000 years earlier. And where does it all begin? In the womb.

Of the Immaculate Conception, Jesus tells Luisa:

I want to Honor My Celestial Mother. I want to narrate the story of Her Immaculate Conception. Only I can speak of it, being Author of so Great a Prodigy. Now, My daughter, the First Act of this Conception was one Fiat of Ours, pronounced with such Solemnity and with such Fullness of Grace, as to enclose everything and everyone. We centralized everything in this Conception of the Virgin. In Our Divine Fiat, in which past and future do not exist, the Incarnation of the Word was held present, and It made Her Conceived and incarnated in the same Incarnation of Me, future Redeemer. My Blood that was in act as if I Myself were shedding it, continually sprinkled Her, embellished Her, Confirmed Her, and fortified Her in a Divine Way…

And I found in Her My Heaven, the Sanctity of My Life, My own Blood that had Generated Her and watered Her so many times. I found My own Will, that communicating Its Divine Fecundity to Her, formed the Life of Her and the Son of God. My Divine Fiat, in order to make Her Worthy of being able to Conceive Me, held Her Invested and under Its continuous Empire that possesses all acts as if they were One Single Act. In order to give Her everything, It called into act My foreseen Merits, My Whole Life, and It continuously poured it within Her Beautiful Soul. Therefore I alone can tell the true story of the Immaculate Conception and of Her whole Life, because I Conceived Her in Me and I am aware of everything. And if the Holy Church speaks about the Celestial Queen, they can say only the first letters of the alphabet about Her Sanctity, Greatness, and Gifts with which She was

---

[452]S. Ákerman (auth.), John Christian Laursen, Richard H. Popkin (eds.)-Millenarianism and Messianism.

enriched. If you knew the Contentment that I feel when I speak about My Celestial Mother, who knows how many demands you would make Me in order to give Me the Joy of letting Me speak about the One whom I Love so much, and who has Loved Me.[453]

But the true fullness of time was recognized not in the womb of Anne, but in the womb of Mary.

> Listen then: **my conception in the womb of a Virgin was the greatest work of the whole history of the world.** By Our Fiat just wanting it so, It incarnated Itself, without anyone one forcing Us, or deserving it, and with no need on Our part. The need was Our love, and only because it wanted it so. It was an act so great as to enclose and embrace all, and it contained so much love as to seem incredible, so much so, that Heaven and earth are still astounded and enraptured, and all felt invaded by so much love as to be able to feel my Life conceived within all.[454]

In the Annunciation—the Incarnation of the Word—that which is scarcely even possible to imagine transpired in reality. The infinite entered into the finite. The Creator entered into His own creation. The One who made the Universe became a child in the womb of one of His own creations. It is as if you, in authoring a story, literally jumped into the very page on which you set your pen and proceeded to interact with the characters you created out of nothing. But what no human author can ever do, the Divine Author can, and did.

God and man were no longer foreign to each other; for there was now a God-man Who would proceed to call all of His children into Himself for their own Divinization by partaking of His same nature.

Finally, after 4,000 long years, the Divine Will had its place of reigning: the home of Nazareth. But He did not yet have His Kingdom. Jesus tells Luisa:

> My daughter, indeed my Divine Will reigned in this house of Nazareth on earth as It does in Heaven. My Celestial Mama and I knew no other will, and Saint Joseph lived in the reflections of Our Will. But I was like a king without a people, isolated, without cortege, without army, and my Mama was like a queen without children, because She was not surrounded by other children worthy of Her to whom She could entrust Her crown of queen, so as to have the offspring of Her noble children, all kings and queens. And I had the sorrow of being a king without a people; and if those who surrounded Me could be called a people, it was a sick people—some were blind, some mute, some deaf, some crippled, some covered with wounds. It was a people that gave Me dishonor—not honor; even more, it did not even know Me, nor did it want to know Me. So, I was King only for Myself, and my Mama was Queen without the long generation of Her offspring of Her royal children. But in order to be able to say that I had my Kingdom, and to rule, I had to have ministers; and even though I had Saint Joseph as prime minister, one minister only does not constitute a ministry. I had to have a great army, all intent on fighting to defend the rights of the Kingdom of my Divine Will; and a faithful people that would have, as law, only the law of my Will. This was not so, my daughter; therefore I cannot say that, on coming upon earth, I had the Kingdom of my Fiat at that time. Our Kingdom was for Us only, because the order of Creation, the royalty of man, was not restored. However, by the Celestial Mother and I living wholly of Divine Will, the seed was sown, the yeast was formed, so as to make Our Kingdom arise and grow upon earth. Therefore, all the preparations were made, all the graces impetrated, all the pains suffered, so that the Kingdom of my Fiat might come to reign upon earth. **This is why Nazareth can be called the point of recall of the Kingdom of Our Will**.[455]

The work had begun. In Nazareth, there was the point of recall of the Kingdom. So much work, however, was left to be done. We should take a moment to pause here to understand that creation was never unaware of the fact that its creator was in its midst. Jesus, indeed, was like us in all things but sin—but the truth contained in this teaching is all but inaccessible to those who are so mired in sin and error that, even though they are Catholics, they have no concept of the dignity of human nature.

Jesus tells Luisa:

> My daughter, when I was on earth, My Divine Will that reigned in Me by nature and that same Divine Will that was present and reigned in all created things, kissed each other at each encounter, and longing for their encounter, they would make feast; and all created things would compete in order to meet with Me and give Me the homages that befitted Me. As the earth would hear My steps, it would become green again and flower under My feet to give Me homage. As I

---

[453]December 8, 1936.
[454]September 28, 1935.
[455]July 7, 1928.

passed by, it wanted to release from its bosom all the beauties it possessed, the enchantment of the most beautiful flowerings; so much so, that many times I had to command it not to make these demonstrations; and the earth, to give Me honor, would obey, just as, to give Me honor, it would flower.

The sun always tried to meet with Me to give Me the homages of its light, unleashing all the varieties of beauties and colors from its solar bosom before My eyes, to give Me the honors I deserved. Everything and everyone tried to encounter Me in order to make their feast for Me: the wind, the water, and even the little bird, to give Me the honors of its trilling, warbling and singing; all created things recognized Me and competed among themselves to see which one could honor Me and make feast for Me the most.

One who possesses My Divine Will has the eyesight to be able to recognize what belongs to My Will Itself. Man alone did not recognize Me, because he did not possess the eyesight and the fine sense of smell of My Will. I had to tell him in order to make Myself recognized; but with all My telling, many did not even believe Me, because one who does not possess My Divine Will is blind and deaf and without the sense of smell to be able to recognize what belongs to It. [456]

Yes—all creation lives in the Divine Will; for, having neither reason nor a free will of its own, it has no other choice. Man, however, is another story. Regarding His public ministry, Jesus tells Luisa:

… I went to the desert to call back that same Divine Will of Mine which, for forty centuries, creatures had deserted from their midst; and I, for forty days, wanted to remain alone, to repair for the forty centuries of human will during which Mine had not possessed Its Kingdom in the midst of the human family; and with my very Divine Will I wanted to call It back again into their midst, so that It might reign … My daughter, the number of forty days is symbolic and significant in my life down here. When I was born, for forty days I wanted to remain in the grotto of Bethlehem—symbol of my Divine Will which, while being present in the midst of creatures, was as though hidden and outside of the city of their souls. And I, in order to repair for the forty centuries of human will, wanted to remain outside of the city for forty days, in a miserable hut, crying, moaning

and praying, to call back my Divine Will into the city of souls, so as to give It Its dominion. And after forty days I went out to present Myself to the temple, and reveal Myself to the holy old Simeon… Forty days I spent in the desert, and then, immediately, I did my public life, to give them the remedies and the means in order to reach the Kingdom of my Will. For forty days I wanted to remain on earth after my Resurrection, to confirm the Kingdom of the Divine Fiat and Its forty centuries of Kingdom which It was to possess. So, in everything I did down here, the first act was the restoration of the Kingdom; all other things entered into the secondary order, but the first link of connection between Me and creatures was the Kingdom of my Will. [457]

My descent upon earth, taking on human flesh, was precisely this—to lift up humanity again and give to my Divine Will the rights to reign in this humanity, because by reigning in my Humanity, the rights of both sides, human and divine, were placed in force again. Yet, it can be said that I said nothing about it, or just a few words, making it understood that I had come into the world only to do the Will of the Celestial Father, so as to make Its great importance be comprehended. And in another circumstance I said: 'Those who do the Will of my Father are my mother, my sisters, and belong to Me.' As for the rest, I kept silent, while the purpose was precisely this, of constituting the Kingdom of my Divine Will in the midst of creatures. In fact, it was right that I not only was to place creatures in safety, but I also was to place my Divine Will in safety, by giving back to It Its rights over all flesh, as I had given It over mine; otherwise, there would have been a disorder in the work of Redemption. How could I come to place creatures in safety, and let Our divine rights, those of Our Fiat, go to rack and ruin? This could not be. But even though the first purpose was to balance all the accounts of my Divine Will, as Celestial Doctor I complied with giving medicines, remedies, I spoke about forgiveness, about detachment, I instituted Sacraments, I suffered atrocious pains, even unto death. It can be said that this was the new creation I prepared so that creatures might receive my Divine Will as King in the midst of His people, in order to let It reign. [458]

… Oh! how much better it would have been for [the critics] to say: 'This is not food for us, nor do we have the will to eat it', rather than giving

---

[456] October 6, 1927.
[457] September 8, 1927.
[458] November 20, 1029.

judgments. But, it is known how my truths find a place more in the simple hearts than in the learned. This happened in my Redemption; to my sorrow, no learned man followed Me, but all poor, ignorant and simple.[459]

The learned, indeed, largely wanted nothing to do with Jesus (just as they largely want nothing to do with Luisa). And once Jesus had said all He needed to say, a silence covered His public ministry. In regard to this, Jesus tells Luisa:

> My very silence says that I am about to complete the great manifestations of the Gospel of the Kingdom of my Divine Will. So I did in the Kingdom of Redemption: during the last days of my life, I did not add anything else; on the contrary, I hid Myself; and if I said anything it was a repetition, in order to confirm what I had already said, because what I had said was sufficient so that all might receive the goods of being redeemed—it was up to them to take advantage of it. So it will be for the Kingdom of my Divine Will: once I have said everything, in such a way that nothing may be lacking in order to be able to receive the good of knowing It, and to be able to possess all of Its goods, then I will have no more interest in keeping you on earth—it will be up to them to take advantage of it.[460]

And we of course know the rest of the story.

> When I am lifted up from the earth, will draw all men to myself (John 12:32)

Indeed, He was lifted up. Condemned and killed by the very people who should have received Him as King, He won the salvation of the world through His Passion. I beg you to read *the Hours of the Passion*; in this work given by Jesus to Luisa, you will find a more powerful prayer than perhaps you have ever prayed. I have included some highlights from this work in the chapter dedicated to it, so I will leave out the details from this chapter.

As He hung on this cross, the Church was born from His own Sacred Side which gushed forth blood and water "as a fountain of mercy for us."[461] This Church—the Catholic Church—was destined to serve as the New Ark for the whole world, even until the end of time. But her main task was the salvation and sanctification of souls; the Coming of the Kingdom. And while the Kingdom has come in some senses, and in other senses will only receive its definitive perfection in Heaven, there is another important sense in which it still shall come more fully—the sense relayed in the primary petition of the *Our Father* prayer, faithfully recited billions of times each day by the Church.

The Church

With the incarnation, passion, death, and resurrection of Jesus, and the institution of the Sacraments and the establishment of the Catholic Church, the evils that had multiplied and grown for thousands of years began to diminish. The fruits of Christianity and Catholicism are astounding. But they have not yet attained their full intent, which is to call down the Kingdom upon earth. Jesus tells Luisa:

> At the beginning, a graft can produce neither great goods nor great evils, but only the beginning of evil or of good. When I came upon earth, with my Conception I formed the opposite graft with the tree of humanity, and the evils began to stop, the bad humors to be destroyed; so, there is all the hope that the Kingdom of my Divine Will be formed in the midst of the human generations. The many truths I have manifested to you about my Divine Fiat are sips of life, some of which water, some cultivate, some increase the humors for the tree of humanity grafted by Me. Therefore, if the Life of my Divine Fiat has entered into the tree of my Humanity and has formed the graft, there is all the reason to hope that my Kingdom will have Its scepter, Its just dominion and Its command in the midst of creatures. Therefore, pray and do not doubt.[462]

Jesus assures Luisa that the four thousand years required to implore the coming of the Redeemer will not be necessary to implore the coming of the Redeemer's Kingdom:

> The knocks of my Church have been continuous, and I Myself was knocking in those knocks, but I used them to knock at the doors of the Divine Fiat which, tired of hearing them knocking at Its divine doors, has used you to be knocked more strongly; and opening the doors to you, It made you share in Its knowledges. And for as many truths as It made known to you, so many means has It given you to form the loving chains, to let Itself be bound to come to reign upon earth. And all the times It calls you to live in Its Divine Volition, making known to you Its qualities, Its

---

[459]February 24, 1933.
[460]February 22, 1929.
[461]*Divine Mercy in My Soul*. 84.
[462]October 27, 1929.

power, Its joys, Its immense riches, are as many pledges It gives you, with which It assures you of Its coming upon earth. In fact, in Us there is this prerogative: if We make known a good of Ours, a truth, a knowledge that belongs to Us, it is because We want to give it to the creature as gift. See then, how many gifts my Will has given you; how many of Its knowledges It has made known to you. They are such and so many, that you yourself cannot count them…

… in order for Redemption to come it took four thousand years, because the people that prayed and longed for the future Redeemer was the smallest one, of limited number. But those which belong to my Church are more peoples and—oh! how much greater in number than that one. Therefore, the number will shorten the time; more so, since religion is making its way everywhere, and this is nothing but the preparation for the Kingdom of my Divine Will.[463]

Jesus describes to Luisa about what Rome owes to Jerusalem: that is, Redemption. He tells her that Rome will return the favor; giving to Jerusalem the Kingdom:

My daughter, if Rome has the primacy of my Church, she owes it to Jerusalem, because the beginning of Redemption was precisely in Jerusalem… the first people who received the good of It, were from this city. The first criers of the Gospel, those who established Catholicism in Rome, were my Apostles, all from Jerusalem— that is, from this fatherland. Now there will be an exchange: if Jerusalem gave to Rome the life of religion and therefore of Redemption, Rome will give to Jerusalem the Kingdom of the Divine Will. And this is so true, that just as I chose a Virgin from the little town of Nazareth for the Redemption, so I have chosen another virgin in a little town of Italy belonging to Rome, to whom the mission of the Kingdom of the Divine Fiat has been entrusted. And since It must be known in Rome, just as my coming upon earth was known in Jerusalem, Rome will have the great honor of requiting Jerusalem for the great gift received from her, which is Redemption, by making known to her the Kingdom of my Will. Then will Jerusalem repent of her ingratitude, and will embrace the life of the religion which she gave to Rome; and, grateful, she will receive from Rome the life and the great gift of the Kingdom of my Divine Will. And not only Jerusalem, but all the other nations will receive from Rome the great gift

of the Kingdom of my Fiat…[464]

Indeed, no one can deny that God's Will still does not reign upon earth, and two thousand more years have passed. Jesus tells Luisa:

My daughter, when Adam sinned God gave him the promise of the future Redeemer. Centuries passed and the promise did not fail, therefore human generations enjoyed the blessings of the Redemption. **Now, by My coming from heaven to form the Kingdom of Redemption, I made another more solemn promise before departing for heaven: The Kingdom of My Will on earth, which is contained in the 'Our Father' prayer… So after I formed this prayer in the presence of My heavenly Father, certain that he would grant Me the Kingdom of My Divine Will on earth, I taught it to My apostles so that they might teach it to the whole world, and that one might be the cry of all: 'Your Will be done on earth as it is in heaven.' A promise more sure and solemn I could not make** […] My very prayer to the heavenly Father, 'May it come, may your kingdom come and your Will be done on earth as it is in heaven,' meant that with My coming to earth the Kingdom of My Will was not established among creatures, otherwise I would have said, 'My Father, may Our kingdom that I have already established on earth be confirmed, and let Our Will dominate and reign.' Instead I said, 'May it come.' This means that it must come and souls must await it with the same certainty with which they awaited the future Redeemer. For My Divine Will is bound and committed to the words of the 'Our Father.' And when My Divine Will binds itself, whatever it promises is more than certain to come to pass. Furthermore, since everything was prepared by Me, nothing else is needed but the manifestation of My Kingdom, which is what I am doing."[465]

It is this Third Fiat that He now ardently desires to give to the world, but He is waiting for our response. He is waiting for us to strive sufficiently for it, pray for it, and yearn for it. He is waiting for us to live in His Will even now, and perform as many acts in His Will as we can, in order to prepare the ground for its universal Reign. He is waiting for us to sufficiently form and spread the Kingdom of His Will upon earth now, before its true triumph. But this true triumph, Jesus tells Luisa, will not come without chastisements preceding it—chastisements, Jesus says, which will amount to the world turning

[463]May 26, 1928.
[464]October 3, 1928.

[465]Fr. Joseph Iannuzzi, Doctoral Dissertation, 4.1.1

upside down. These are also the events of which we now stand on the cusp. Nevertheless, preparation for them is still best made in the same way: Living in the Divine Will, doing all your acts in the Divine Will, and proclaiming the Divine Mercy.

We must remember that "The greatest story ever told" is not over and done with just because the Apostle John has already died and the Deposit of Faith is sealed! Public revelation is indeed already complete, but that does not mean God is now simply waiting for the time to come to put an end to our misery and commence the consummation of the world (and otherwise finished with His cosmic interventions!). Beautifully and powerfully describing this dynamic, Jesus explains to Luisa:

> …**two links connected together-the Redemption and the Kingdom of My Divine Will [are] inse**parable from each other. The Redemption was to prepare, suffer, do; the Kingdom of the Fiat was to fulfill and possess-both of them of highest importance. Therefore, My gazes were fixed on the chosen ones to whom both one and the other were entrusted… Why do you fear, then, if you have the gaze of your Jesus always looking at you, defending you, protecting you? If you knew what it means to be looked upon by Me, you would no longer fear anything."[466]

Indeed, far from being over, this Great Story now nears its fulfillment in the Coming of the Kingdom. If we wish to compare "His Story" (God's story — history) to the dramatic structure of a great tale of old, then we can say that the drama of the Garden of Eden contains the Exposition, Salvation History (the Rising Action), Redemption (the Climax), The Age of the Church (the Falling Action), the coming Chastisements and Triumph of the Divine Will to follow the Dénouement (resolution), with Heaven being our "happily ever after."

That we are now in the Dénouement has become completely undeniable considering the Prophetic Explosion of the 20th Century which we will consider in the next section. But in the following passages of Luisa's writings, Jesus' words make clear that we are indeed precisely at this moment:

> …all of My works hold hands, and this is the sign that they are My works-that one does not oppose the other… having to form My chosen people, from which and within which the future Messiah

was to be born, from that same people I formed the Priesthood, that instructed the people and prepared them for the great good of Redemption. I gave them laws, manifestations and inspirations, upon which the Sacred Scriptures were formed, called the Bible; and all were intent on the study of It. Then, with My coming upon earth, I did not destroy Sacred Scriptures; on the contrary, I supported them; and My Gospel, that I announced, opposed them in nothing; on the contrary, they sustained each other in [an] admirable way. And in forming the new nascent Church, I formed the new Priesthood, that does not detach itself either from Sacred Scriptures or from the Gospel. Now, what I manifest on My Divine Will, and that you write, can be called 'The Gospel of the Kingdom of the Divine Will.' In nothing does It oppose either Sacred Scriptures or the Gospel that I announced while being on earth; on the contrary, It can be called the support of one and of the other[467]

There is much analogy between the way in which Redemption unfolded and the way in which the Kingdom of my Divine Will will unfold. See, in my Redemption I chose a Virgin, in appearance She had no importance according to the world…I chose Her from Nazareth, [but] I wanted for it to belong to the capital city, Jerusalem, in which there was the body of the pontiffs and priests who then represented Me … For the Kingdom of my Divine Will I have chosen another virgin who, in appearance, has no importance, either of great riches or of height of dignity; the very city of Corato is not an important city, but it belongs to Rome, in which resides my representative on earth, the Roman Pontiff, from whom come my divine laws; and just as he makes it his duty to make my Redemption known to the peoples, so will he make it his duty to make known the Kingdom of my Divine Will. It can be said that one and the other will proceed in the same way and manner, as the Kingdom of my Supreme Fiat must unfold.[468]

This happened in the Redemption, **every Manifestation that was made by Us about the descent of the Word on earth, was one step that We made toward mankind. And as they yearned and prayed for It, and Our Manifestations, Prophecies, and Revelations, were manifested to the people, so they made so many steps toward the Supreme Being, such that they remained on a walk toward Us, and We toward them. And as the time of having to descend from Heaven to**

---

[466]December 25, 1927.
[467]January 18, 1928.

[468]January 30, 1930.

earth drew near, so We increased the Prophets in order to be able to make more Revelations, in order to hasten the walk on both parts.

This is so true, that in the first times of the world there was no Prophet, and Our Manifestations were so few, that one can say that one step a century was made. This slowness of walk cast coldness on the part of creatures, and a way of saying was held by almost everyone: that My descent on earth was an absurd thing, not a reality-like one thinks today about the Kingdom of My Will: a way of saying, and almost a thing that can not be. Therefore the Prophets came after Moses, almost in the last times, near to My descent on earth, such that after Our Manifestations, the walk of both parties was hastened. And then came the Sovereign of Heaven who not only walked, but ran in order to hasten the meeting with Her Creator so as to make Him descend and complete the Redemption.

See, therefore, how My Manifestations on My Divine Will are certain proofs that It walks in order to come to Reign on earth, and that the creature to whom they have been made, with an iron constancy, walks and runs in order to receive the First Meeting so as to give It to her soul in order to let It Reign, and so give It the step to let It Reign in the midst of creatures. Therefore, let your acts be continuous, because only continuous Acts are what hasten the walk, overcome every obstacle, and are the only Conquerors who conquer God and the creature.[469]

The Prophetic Explosion of the Modern Era (1900s)

More than any other century, the last one stands out in the history of the Church. One could say that Heaven has been pounding us with incessant pleas for our attention regarding what is about to come. It has reached the point that no one who actually looks at what is happening can dismiss it. Although some Catholics today, lamentably, try to pretend that everything is just business as usual and there is nothing particularly special about the age in which we live (as far as Heaven's end-of-the-age plans are concerned), even the worldly have not failed to take notice that something incredible is happening.

National Geographic ran a lengthy article in 2015 on this worldwide phenomenon, discussing the details of many apparitions and producing a helpful graph which gives a visual representation of their geographic spread, as well as a timeline of apparitions which clearly shows an exponential increase in the 1900s. The late theologian, Fr. Edward O'Connor, wrote:

> In our age, apparitions and messages of the Blessed Virgin Mary are being reported far more frequently than at any time in the past. According to the list compiled by Gottfried Hierzenberger and Otto Nedomansky, there were very few during the first ten centuries. After that they increased moderately, reaching 105 in the nineteenth century. But during the twentieth century … [there were reported] a total of 1,045 apparitions of the Blessed Mother … [470]

The vast majority of apparitions are unapproved. But to say "vast majority" is quite an understatement; of the thousands of apparitions to devout Catholics which are alleged to have occurred in the last hundred years, only a handful (nine, as far as I can tell) have been fully Vatican approved.

Now, it is not for me to say whether *most* alleged apparitions are authentic or inauthentic. But one thing I (and any Catholic) should easily be able to say is this: **the overwhelming majority of *authentic* revelations are not approved** (by which I mean *not-yet-approved*; I do not mean *condemned*). To say otherwise, which is implicit in the attitude of some Catholics who take a dismissive approach to any apparition not yet fully approved, is to tragically misunderstand God Himself—Who, in His Goodness and Omnipotence, would not allow over 99% of Heaven's alleged manifestations to devout souls to be fraudulent, demonic, or products of hallucination.

If, perhaps, any thoughts are lingering in your mind to the effect of *"ah, well, I really needn't bother much with this; it's just private revelation. I already have the Catholic Faith and beyond that I have no spiritual obligations. It would be much easier for me to simply ignore whatever is going on with this 'prophetic explosion,' so that's exactly what I'm going to do,"* then I beseech you to turn back to the "On Private Revelation in General" chapter in this book and read it again.

---

[469] May 30, 1932.

[470] *Listen to my Prophets.* Fr. Edward O'Connor. 2011. Introduction ix.

But now that the proper place of private revelation in our lives as Catholics is settled, let us proceed to take a bird's-eye look at the nature of what has been transpiring, to glean from it a "main thrust," or perhaps even a "prophetic consensus." For while indeed private revelation ought not be considered of the same authority as the inerrant and Divinely Inspired Sacred Scripture, it would nevertheless be downright absurd to reject that which is shown to be an agreed upon tenet of the same.

In the book previously quoted, Fr. O'Connor spends hundreds of pages analyzing dozens of the most important revelations, messages, apparitions, and locutions of the modern Era, and says the following about their prophetic consensus:

> The basic message is that of St. Faustina: we are in an age of mercy, which will soon give way to an age of justice. The reason for this is the immorality of today's world, which surpasses that of any past age. Things are so bad that Satan is reigning over the world. Even the life of the Church itself has been badly affected. Apostasy, heresy and compromise challenge the faith of the people. Not only the laity, but also priests and religious are grievously at fault. A hidden form of Masonry has entered into the Church. Because of all this, God has been sending prophets as never before to call us to repentance. Most often, it is the Blessed Mother who speaks through them. She warns of an unprecedented tribulation that lies in the very near future. The Church will be torn apart. **The Antichrist, already alive in the world, will manifest himself. Up to now, Mary has been holding back the punishment due to us. The time will come, however, when she will no longer be able to do so.** Not only the Church, but the whole world will experience tribulation. There will be natural disasters, such as earthquakes, floods, fierce storms and strange weather patterns. Economic ruin will plunge the whole world into poverty. There will be warfare, perhaps even a Third World War. There will also be cosmic disasters in the form of devastating meteors striking the earth or other heavenly bodies passing close enough to wreak havoc. Finally, a mysterious fire from heaven will wipe out the greater part of mankind, and plunge the world in utter darkness for three days. Before these terrible events take place, we will be prepared, first by a "Warning" in which everyone on earth will see his or her soul as it appears before God, and secondly by a miraculous sign. **The disasters to come will purify the world and leave it as God intended it to be. The Holy Spirit will be poured out as never before and renew the hearts of all mankind.** Most of the visionaries insist that the time left before these things take place is very short. Some indicate that the fulfillment has begun already. To protect us against the dangers predicted, we are urged to frequent the sacraments, pray and do penance. The proclamation of Mary as Mediatrix, Coredemptrix and Advocate is called for and predicted.[471]

As Fr. O'Connor says, the main thrust of the revelations in the last century has usually been that grave chastisements are coming, but we can mitigate these through our prayer and sacrifice. *Many* of these revelations also speak of the Era of Peace (bolded in the quote above), although this is not as overwhelming a theme as the former. (The distinction is unsurprising; the Chastisements chronologically proceed the Era and are a much easier notion to grasp.)

Before going forward to look at a selection of individual apparitions, revelations, and locutions, let us again give space to Bishop Paul Kim's powerful words on the nature of the age in which we now live, and how it relates to private revelation:

> That the present age of the Holy Spirit is also the age of private revelations is evidenced by the fact that, within thirty years after the Second Vatican Council, three women were awarded the title of Doctor of the Church, which was unprecedented in Church history. ... Before then, all of the 30 Doctors of the Church had been men. To qualify for the title of Doctor of the Church, one must have both profound holiness and outstanding knowledge. These three women were declared Doctors of the Church, because it was recognized that they met both criteria. However, even though they had profound holiness, they did not study theology; nor had they much scholarly learning. Rather the opposite was true ... The outstanding knowledge that the three women possessed was acquired solely from private revelations.[472] That they were awarded the title of Doctor of the Church was based on private revelations. Thus, the conferment of the title of Doctor of the Church on them changed the concept of knowledge and

---

[471]*Listen to My Prophets*, P. 189-190
[472]Obviously, Bishop Kim is not using "private revelation" in the strictest sense of the term here (i.e. formal apparitions with messages for the world), but in the more general use of an openness to the voice of God speaking to the soul above and beyond merely the Deposit of Faith.

was a coronation of private revelations with a golden crown. Again, these women became Doctors of the Church not by their profound theological knowledge but by the books they wrote under the inspiration of private revelations ... Therefore, to view private revelations as taboo is to turn one's face away from the graces of the age of the Holy Spirit, which is the climax of the history of salvation. Looking back at Church history, we see that those ages when private revelations were despised were also the ages of ignoring the Holy Spirit and the ages of darkness. Examples are the ages of St. Joan of Arc and St. Teresa of Jesus ...[473]

One final note is essential before delving into the specifics regarding these: **Some of the following private revelations may wind up being condemned or proven false.** (Please understand that I am not necessarily standing wholeheartedly behind an apparition or revelation just because it is in this list.) **But this changes nothing.** *All* of them would have to be proven false for their consensus to be affected; and that will never happen. And their consensus is this: **the pivotal moment of all history is fast approaching. The definitive events spoken of in the Book of Revelation are about to begin—great Chastisements, followed by a great Triumph. These events cannot be averted, but the Chastisements can be mitigated, and the Triumph can be hastened**—and above all, the salvation and sanctification of souls can be achieved more powerfully than ever in the midst of these events—by the prayer and action of the Faithful who must devote themselves wholeheartedly to this task.

For the sake of brevity and to emphasize the truly modern nature of this explosion, I am only mentioning here apparitions or revelations which occurred in the 20th century. This of course leaves out extremely important apparitions (e.g. Lourdes, Rue-du-Bac, La Salette, and many others) which are also essential to understanding this prophetic explosion; but much has been written elsewhere on them and I encourage any reader who is not already acquainted with them to research them.

In order to learn more than what I offer in my meager list below, I recommend **Mark Mallett's blog,[474] and his book** *The Final Confrontation*; **as well as the works of Fr. Joseph Iannuzzi, the books of Michael Brown, the website "Miracle Hunter," the books of Fr. Edward O'Connor, the books of John Haffert, the books of Thomas Fahy, the apostolates of Dan Lynch, and so many others**. For French speakers, a great resource exists thanks to the world-renowned theologian, Fr. Rene Laurentin. Entitled *Dictionnaire des Apparitions de la Vierge Marie*, and published in 2008, it provides over 1,400 pages of summaries of thousands of apparitions which have occurred (the vast majority from the last century).

Let us now turn to the brief list, which I include merely in order to give a small peak into this unprecedented explosion of Heavenly intervention the world has been receiving the past century:

- Most noteworthy, of course, are the apparitions of Our Lady at Fatima, Portugal, in 1917. Here, 100,000 people witnessed an unprecedented miracle in which the sun danced in the sky and all of their clothes were miraculously made dry (it had been pouring rain when everyone gathered at the Cova). Prophecies were issued (and fulfilled), and promises were given—above all, that Mary's Immaculate Heart would triumph and an Era of Peace would be given to the entire world.

- Less known but also historically unprecedented were the apparitions of Our Lady at Zeitoun, Egypt, in 1968. Our Lady appeared over an Orthodox Church and, though she did not give messages, was seen by **millions** of people (even the lowest estimates admit it was at least hundreds of thousands) over the course of three years.

- Padre Pio (1887-1968), displayed an extraordinary amount of mystical phenomenon, much of which had never before been witnessed in Church history.

- Our Lady appeared in Kibeho a decade before the Rwandan genocide (which took place in 1994), warning of rivers of blood and giving messages on how to avert the disaster. Tragically, her messages were not heeded, and the genocide occurred with an estimated one million people killed.

- At Medjugorje, Our Lady has been

---

[473]Pastoral Letter by His Excellency Paul Tchang-Ryeol Kim, Bishop of the Cheju Diocese, Korea. Easter Sunday, 1999. (Marys-touch.com)

[474]www.MarkMallett.com/blog

appearing for almost 40 years to several seers. Tens of millions of pilgrims have visited the site, with countless miracles being regularly reported and more Confessions being heard than anywhere else in history.

- The Shower of Roses: Through the intercession of St. Thérèse of Lisieux (who promised she would spend her Heaven doing good on earth), more miracles have been reported than have been by any other saint's intercession in history other than the Blessed Virgin Mary. It has reached the point where it is common knowledge among devout Catholics that any time guidance is needed and sincerely sought, Thérèse will give it through a rose upon doing a simple novena to her.
- Our Lady of All Nations appeared to Ida Peerdeman in Amsterdam, Netherlands, in 1945, imploring the Church to recognize the Fifth Marian Dogma. This apparition enjoys the approval of the local bishop.
- At Betania, Venezuela, in 1976 and for 15 years after, Our Lady appeared to the Servant of God Maria Esperanza, with dozens of other people witnessing the apparitions and many healings occurring. This apparition is approved.
- At Akita, Japan, in 1973, Our Lady appeared to Sr. Agnes, warning of impending enormous Chastisements for the world and imploring our prayers to avert them. This, too, enjoys Church approval.
- At Garabandal, Spain, in 1961, Our Lady appeared to four young girls warning of impending Chastisements, a coming Illumination of Conscience, and great worldwide miracles to follow.
- Our Lady of America appeared to Sr. Mildred Mary in 1956, asking for her enthronement in the National Basilica and prophesying also a coming time of peace.
- Our Lady, under the title of Rosa Mystica, appeared in 1947 to Pierina Gilli in Montichiari, Italy, asking for the 13th of each month to be a Marian day, and especially asking for prayers on December 8th at noon.
- Our Lady appeared in Cuapa, Nicaragua, in 1980, with messages against atheistic communism and requesting devotion to the

shoulder wound of Christ. This apparition is approved.

- Our Lady of the Rosary began appearing in 1983 to Gladys Quiroga de Motta of San Nicolas, Argentina. This apparition is also approved (for more information, see the Era of Peace section of this book).
- Our Lady has been appearing to Edson Glauber in Itapiranga, Brazil, for many years, and this, too, bears Church approval.
- Fr. Stefano Gobbi received numerous profound messages from Heaven in the late 20th century. He shares these messages in a book (*To the Priests: Our Lady's Beloved Sons*) which has been well received by thousands of priests around the world, in addition to receiving imprimaturs.

(Many other apparitions, including some lesser known ones, are listed in Part Three of this book on the Era of peace.)

My goal here, again, was only to give a small taste of this prophetic explosion, and to give a reminder that the explosion cannot be denied. Now, a certain "apparent prevalence" of some previously only locally discussed events in the modern world is not surprising, with due regard to our superior means of communications technology granting access to more knowledge. But these explanations can only go so far, and they stop short of what is needed to understand the prophetic explosion of the modern era, in which we see *orders of magnitude more* revelations, apparitions, etc., than ever before in Church History.

We are living in unprecedented times. Heaven is on the move like never before. *This means something.* And it means this: the Kingdom is at hand. Jesus tells Luisa:

My daughter, each prophecy I gave to my prophets about my coming upon earth was like a commitment I made to creatures of my coming into their midst. And the prophets, by manifesting them, disposed the peoples to desire and to want a good so great; and these, in receiving these prophecies, received the deposit of the commitment. And as I kept manifesting the time and the place of my birth, I kept increasing the pledge of the commitment. So I am doing with the Kingdom of my Will. Each manifestation I make concerning my Divine Fiat, is a commitment that

I make…[475]

But the devil is also aware of what is happening, and he will not miss his opportunity to strike. As the book of Revelation says:

> The serpent poured water like a river out of his mouth after the woman, to sweep her away with the flood.[476]

This is precisely what we see today in the flood of false apparitions that have done so much damage on their own right. But their greatest damage done is found in entirely dissuading some Catholics from heeding private revelation. We should not, however, be surprised that this is happening. The Devil always apes the things of God. As followers of Christ, we must have the courage to trust that God will give us the grace to discern the difference between the Good Shepherd (Whose voice we know) and the "liar and murderer from the beginning."[477] Rejecting this trust means closing our ears to Heaven, which is far too great a price to pay merely for the supposed "safety" of not succumbing to a trap set by the devil.

Therefore, false apparitions aside (see the section on discerning private revelation for more details on how to identify those), let us consider some other ways the devil has targeted the Divine Will revelations to Luisa with his own diabolical ploys.

The Gift Attacked by Satan (1900s)

Rash and overzealous ideologues inevitably succumb to identifying any similarity, even if superficial, between two things as a sure proof that, if one is evil, so is the other. It is precisely this perverse form of "discernment" which resulted in the phrase "hocus pocus." Most people know that phrase as a reference to absurd magical practices; and indeed, it is. But the origin of that phrase is found in the slanderous stunts of zealous anti-Catholic Protestants who believed that the Catholic Mass was idolatrous. They took the holiest words of the Mass—when the priest says, "This is my body," which, in Latin, is "Hoc Est Corpus…"—and made it sound ridiculous, changing it to "hocus pocus." Thus, they demean the Mass and taunt Catholics who go to Mass by alleging that Catholics are just engaging in magical practices like any

Pagan, whose rituals do indeed bear at least a superficial resemblance to the Catholic Liturgy.

Discerning minds and hearts know better. They indeed know that the fits of demons can be informative regarding the hidden workings of grace (the unclean spirits were in fact among the first to recognize Jesus). Those who prayerfully discern know that, as we discussed above, the devil always wishes to ape the things of God, and that the absence of such mockery proves only that the devil doesn't particularly care about the thing in question because it *isn't* too dangerous to him! To continue with the same example; the devil—in his inspiring of the various Satanic and occultist practices throughout the world—does not much bother making a mockery of the practices of Scientologists; for he clearly does not see that as much of a threat to his kingdom.

Indeed, this mission of making known the Divine Will is so great and so holy that the devil has spared no expense to try and wash it away with a torrent of sin, error, and ugliness directed towards it. And while he has not succeeded in his aims, he has wrought much destruction through his efforts; some of which can be seen in the following realms.

Voluntaristic Existential Nihilism

Perhaps the most twisted form of philosophy to ever enter mainstream thought is that of Friedrich Nietzsche. This German philosopher died at the onset of the 20th century and provided the ideological inspiration for its massacres (above all those undertaken by the Nazis), which continue more silently to this day—in the scourges of abortion[478] and euthanasia. He taught the diametric opposite of Luisa's revelations: the will to power. *"This world is the will to power-and nothing besides! And you yourselves are also this will to power-and nothing besides!"*[479] was his mantra. It was precisely the same decade when Nietzsche had descended into insanity and was on death's doorstep—having proclaimed God as dead and he himself the Antichrist—that lowly Luisa, under the obedience of her spiritual director, began to write. Luisa's writings both resemble and contradict Nietzsche's, as does the Holy Sacrifice of the Mass a Satanic

---

[475] December 18, 1927.
[476] Revelation 12:15
[477] John 8:44

[478] To Luisa it is revealed that abortion is the sin that cries out most to God. It was in the 1920s that abortion really started entering into the mainstream of the world stage.
[479] Friedrich Nietzsche: *The Will to Power*, final paragraph.

ritual.

Distorted Teachings on "Divinization" in Mormonism

Let it be clear from the onset: I am not accusing individual Mormons of being agents of Satan! Quite the contrary, it seems obvious that most of them are good people who are sincerely trying to be good Christians.

It is not individual Mormons whom I am addressing with this section, but rather Mormonism itself, which holds strange and heretical views on what "Divinization" entails. (For the proper view of Divinization, see the section in the same part of this book, entitled "the Gift Foreshadowed.")

What is most noteworthy is the fact that it may precisely be the modern Catholic world's failure to emphasize Divinization properly that has enabled the Church to lose so many members to Mormonism. As quoted in the aforementioned section, many Catholic scholars today (including Dr. Scott Hahn), deeply lament this failure of the Church to recognize that being saved from sin is only the starting point of God's ultimate plan of sanctification.

Most noteworthy among this tragedy is the case of a man named Jordan Vajda. Once a Dominican priest, he left the Church to become a Mormon. Although I know little of the man, I have secured a copy of his Master's Thesis which he wrote while still Catholic (and Dominican), and from this thesis, it is easy to see why he left: he had many orthodox and profound understandings of Divinization, and (I can only guess) had them pooh-poohed by his "experienced Catholic" friends who foolishly castigated it as a heresy found only among some Eastern Church Fathers. (This is much like what happens with critics of the Era of Peace today in the way they treat the teachings of the Fathers of the Church regarding the millennium).

As long as Catholics neglect the orthodox teaching on Divinization, we will continue to lose members to quasi Christian denominations like Mormonism who do take it seriously (and, unfortunately, pervert it significantly). Let us look at one brief quote from the Thesis of Jordan Vajda:

> The doctrine of Divinization could not survive in the church's theology proper … today defenders of orthodoxy cringe at the full implications of Paul's hope for the saints to come 'unto the measure of the fullness of Christ.' (Eph. 4:13)"

Likewise the following from Peterson and Ricks: "Indeed, if the Latter-day Saints were inclined to do so, they could point out that they alone, among contemporary followers of Jesus, seem to possess the ancient Christian doctrine of theosis …

He is, I am afraid, correct. Too many Catholic theological writers in the West reacted with fear to the Protestant revolt and simply stopped speaking of Divinization. Thus, the devil has certainly succeeded in his intent to attack this great sanctity of Living in the Divine Will and its impending Universal Reign. He has done so here by inspiring great distortions of these teachings to become popular in non-Catholic realms; thus drawing countless souls away from the One True Church—the very souls who should be devoting themselves to hastening the Coming of the Kingdom *within* Catholicism.

The New Age Movement and "Gender Theory"

The New Age Movement is the devil's mockery of God's revelations to the Church of the coming New Era of Peace—the coming of His Kingdom on earth; for indeed, it bears the similarity necessary to ape the things of God, as "new agers" hold that "humanity is on the threshold of a radical spiritual transformation."[480] Often, they identify this as the so-called "Age of Aquarius."

Most self-proclaimed "new agers" are probably good people who have been misled. They may even be inspired by perfectly valid intuitions that there are indeed major changes impending on a worldwide scale (see Part Three of this book on the Era for more on that point), but they follow these inspirations in dark, dangerous, and erroneous directions.

The Church, aware of the grave problems presented by this movement, promulgated a document entitled "*Jesus Christ the Bearer of the Water of Life.*" I strongly encourage any Catholic who has any concerns about any practice they may

---

480 NEW AGE MOVEMENT. New Catholic Encyclopedia. Page 273.

be engaged in to check that document for references to it, and to have nothing to do with any practice listed being associated with the New Age. Similarly, the highly informative article on the New Age Movement in the New Catholic Encyclopedia tells us:

> Cultural critics also asserted that exotic NA [New Age] interests such as crystal gazing and "harmonic convergence" are contrived, artificial … From a psychological perspective, some NA devotees manifest narcissistic and obsessive self-fixation traits that mirror the powerlessness, alienation, and atomistic individualism endemic in society.

The deeper danger in the New Age movement, however, is not that it is pervaded by fraud, but that it is pervaded by demons. Many New Age practices explicitly open up one's soul to demonic spiritual activity, and the spread of this movement is no doubt in part to blame for the skyrocketing need for exorcisms in the Church today.

Its aping of the Era is not the only way the New Age movement is an attack on the Divine Will; it is also through its promotion of diabolical "gender theory." The aforementioned Church document also teaches:

> The *New Age* which is dawning will be peopled by perfect, androgynous … Christianity has to be eliminated and give way to a global religion and a new world order.[481]

"Androgynous" is the operative term here, for it refers to a human nature deprived of masculinity or femininity. Perhaps nowhere is the Divine Will revealed more clearly than in one's sex. Today, one of the most zealously promoted lies of modernism is the notion that one's sex is one's choice, or that one's "sexual orientation" may be followed even if it entails a grave perversion (and now, this perversion is governmentally blessed and institutionalized by way of "same-sex marriage," which is increasingly becoming the law of the land throughout the entire western world).

This diabolical "gender theory" has rightly been condemned repeatedly and forcefully by Pope Francis, who doubtless sees it for what it is: a

fundamental assault on the Sovereign Will of God in the very material reality wherein this Divine Will is made most clear. Often ostensibly promoted under the innocent guise of "bullying prevention," gender theory will not stop until it has subverted the entire natural order to the ends of the Antichrist, who wishes to subvert and destroy everything laid down by God in the Garden of Eden in the souls and bodies of Adam and Eve.

The Culture of Death

As destructive as all the attacks listed above have been, it is impossible to deny that Satan's most destructive work is found in his turning the entire world into one massive Culture of Death. As mentioned in the preface of this book (regarding Dr. Scott Han's observation), when the devil's ferocity reaches a superlative level, he murders innocent children in a desperate attempt to prevent God's plans from being realized. The devil's ultimate attack against the Divine Will is not so much on the ideological level but is seen in his desire to destroy as many lives as possible—lives which God has destined to live in the Era of the Divine Will or hasten its Reign. The devil did this through the wars and genocides of the 20th century, but he now does this through abortion, which dwarfs all the genocides of history combined and is, by far, the leading cause of death in almost every country in our world.

In his book, *Demonic Abortion*, the exorcist Fr. Euteneuer[482] explains how the whole abortion movement is diabolical to its core. Below is an excerpt from that book in which he illustrates the parallels, writing:

> The spiritual dimension of this grisly "business," [abortion] however, is it's systematizing of ritual blood sacrifice to the god of child murder, who, in the Old Testament, is called Moloch. This demon of child sacrifice appears in many forms and cultures through his. tory (Phoenician, Carthaginian, Canaanite, Celtic, Indian, A and others), but it is always the same bloodthirsty beast that demands the killing of children as a form of worship. This demon also seeks public endorsement and ever-new forms of expression to increase his "worship." In some of the ancient

---

[481]Section 4
[482]I understand that Fr. Euteneuer had a fall from grace. He repented and has since resigned from all his positions and has remained in silence and obscurity. I see no reason why this

fall should preclude us benefitting from his teachings. It is unsurprising that a priest like him would be the object of many attacks of Satan, and I for one will not let Satan win in his attempts to silence the good things Fr. Euteneuer said.

images of these evil practices, we see huge drums being used beside the places of sacrifice as the rituals proceed. These drums were used to drown out the screams of the victims who were being sacrificed on their altars and deaden the consciences of those who participated in such evil.' ...The systematic destruction of the human body, which St. Paul calls "the temple of the Holy Spirit" is also a sacrilege. In short, abortion is a perfect demonic system that offers a perverse form of worship to the devil. If the abortion business is not truly diabolical, nothing is...[483]

Religions of Human Sacrifice	Religion of Abortion
Worship of Moloch	Worship of Moloch
Temples	Free-standing "clinics"
Altars	Abortion surgical tables
Sacrificing Priests	Medical doctors
Ritual blood sacrifice to obtain favors from the demons	Ritual blood sacrifice to obtain profit and political power
Victims are adults of conquered tribes or children	Victims are innocent babies and secondarily women who abort
Religion based upon pagan creeds	Religion based upon dogma of "choice"
Beating of drums drowns out screams	Sound of the suction ma-chine drowns out "silent screams"
Drums used for killing ritual	Drums used to carry dead bodies
Victims are "passed through the fire"	Victims are burnt as medical waste
Parishioners and congregations	Private donors and foundations
Tribal approval or acquiescence	Public approval or acquiescence

But Satan's plans will not work. In his diabolical rage, he cannot help but relentlessly spew venom at God's works, even though he knows that God has already been and will continue to be victorious. In fact, so many of the devil's ploys have already failed (although many have temporarily succeeded), and the time is now ripe for the Coronation of All Creation.

The Time for the Coronation (~ 2000 AD)

And here we are now.

We are still in the Age of the Church—we always will be until the end of time, for with Christ's birth we have seen the Dawn of the End of the Ages. (This is contrary to the various dispensationalist heresies or movements in the spiritual legacy of Joachim of Fiore). We have now arrived at the moment when the Church is almost ready for her crown; the moment when the prayer she has been praying more fervently than all others—the Our Father— is ready to be fulfilled.

Recall that Redemption occurred under the dominion of the Roman Empire, in order that the unification achieved by this secular rule might, despite the many evil rulers thereof, serve the dissemination of knowledge of Redemption; that is, the evangelization of the world. What we are witnessing today, in the Globalization following the unification of races from WWII, dwarfs any unification that the world had ever previously known. It is precisely for the end of the spread of the Kingdom of the Divine Will that God has allowed this to occur. Jesus says as much to Luisa:

> But I will use this [World War II] for My highest purposes, and the reunion of so many races will serve to facilitate the communications of the truths, so that they may dispose themselves for the Kingdom of the Supreme Fiat. So, the chastisements that have occurred are nothing other than the preludes of those that will come. How many more cities will be destroyed; how many peoples buried under the ruins; how many places buried and plunged into the abyss. The elements will take the part of their Creator. My Justice can bear no more; My Will wants to triumph, and would want to triumph by means of love in order to establish Its Kingdom. But man does not want to come to meet this love, therefore it is necessary to use justice.[484]

God has spent 6,000 years preparing us for this moment. Jesus tells Luisa:

> Those who think that Our highest goodness and infinite wisdom would have left man with only the goods of Redemption, without raising him again to the original state in which he was created by Us, deceive themselves. In that case Our Creation would have remained without Its purpose, and therefore without Its full effect, which cannot be in the works of a God. At the most, We might let centuries pass and turn, giving now one surprise, now another; entrusting now one little good to the creature, now a greater

---

one…

Now, this is how the paternal goodness is acting. In Creation I placed man in the opulence of goods, with no restriction at all; but only because I wanted to test him in something that did not cost him much, with an act of his will contrary to mine he wasted all these goods. But my love did not stop; more than a father, I began to give him a little at a time—and before that, to heal him. Many times one uses more attention with the little than when he possesses great things. In fact, if one possesses great properties and they are wasted, there is always something from which to take; but if the little is wasted, he remains on an empty stomach. However, the decision of giving the Kingdom of my Will to man I have not changed; man changes, God does not change. Now things are easier, because the goods of Redemption have made their way, they have made known many surprises of my love for man—how I have loved him, not by the Fiat alone, but by giving him my very Life, though my Fiat costs Me more than my very Humanity, because the Fiat is divine, immense, eternal, while my Humanity is human, limited and has its beginning in time. However, not knowing in depth what the Fiat means—Its value, Its power and what It can do—the human minds let themselves be conquered more by all that I did and suffered in coming to redeem them, not knowing that under my pains and my death there was my Fiat, hidden, which gave life to my pains.

Now, had I wanted to manifest the Kingdom of my Will, either when I came upon earth or before the goods of Redemption would be recognized and, for the most part, possessed by creatures, my greatest Saints would have been frightened; all would have thought and said: 'Adam, innocent and holy, was unable to live nor to persevere in this Kingdom of endless light and of divine sanctity—how can we do it?' And you yourself—how many times have you not become frightened? … Therefore my more than paternal goodness acted with you as with a second Mother of mine: from Her I hid my conception in Her womb; first I prepared Her, I formed Her, so as not to frighten Her; and when the appropriate time came, in the very act in which I was to be conceived, then I made it known to Her through the Angel; and even though at first She trembled and was troubled, immediately She became serene again, because She was used to living with Her God, in the midst of His light and before His sanctity…My daughter, do not fear, you have more help than Adam did—you have the help of a God [made man], and all His works and pains as your defense, as your support, as your cortege, which he did not have. Why, then, do you want to fear?[485]

Jesus reiterates this in one of the most well-known quotes from all of Luisa's writings, saying:

My beloved daughter, I want to make known to you the order of my Providence. Every course of two thousand years I have renewed the world. In the first two thousand years I renewed it with the Flood; in the second two thousand I renewed it with my coming upon earth, in which I manifested my Humanity, from which, as though from many fissures, my Divinity shone forth. And the good and the very Saints of the following two thousand years have lived of the fruits of my Humanity, and, in drops, they have enjoyed my Divinity. Now we are at the turn of the third two thousand years, and there will be a third renewal. This is the reason for the general confusion—it is nothing other than the preparation for the third renewal; and if in the second renewal I manifested what my Humanity did and suffered, and very little of what the Divinity was operating, now, in this third renewal, after the earth has been purged and the current generation destroyed for the most part, I will be even more generous with creatures, and I will accomplish the renewal by manifesting what my Divinity did within my Humanity; how my Divine Will acted with my human will; how everything remained linked within Me; how I did and redid everything, and even one thought of each creature was redone by Me and sealed with my Divine Volition. My love wants its outpouring, and wants to make known the excesses which my Divinity operated in my Humanity for the good of creatures, which surpass by far the excesses that my Humanity operated externally. This is also why I often speak to you about the living in my Will, which I have not manifested to anyone until now.[486]

As many triumphs as the Church has seen—and there have been so many which are so glorious they are almost difficult to believe—the common temptation is nevertheless one of despairing of the Kingdom ever coming. Jesus addresses this temptation to Luisa as follows:

[Luisa said]: How can this Kingdom of the Divine Will ever come? Sin abounds, evil worsens, creatures seem indisposed to me to receive a good so great, so much so that there is no soul, for how

---

[485] June 18, 1926.

[486] January 29, 1919.

many good ones there might be, who truly wants to occupy themselves to make known that which regards the Divine Will…

[and Jesus said] My daughter, everything is possible to us. Impossibilities, difficulties, insurmountable cliffs of creatures melt before our Supreme Majesty, as snow now opposite to an ardent Sun…Didn't it happen thus in the Redemption? Sin abounded more than ever, (there was) hardly a little nucleus of people that longed for the Messiah, and in the midst of this nucleus how many hypocrisies, how many sins of all kinds, often idolatry. But it was decreed that I should come upon the earth. Before our decrees all the evils cannot impede that which we want to do…

Now as my coming upon the earth was our decree, thus is decreed our Kingdom of our Will upon the earth. Rather it can be said that the one and the other are one single decree, [and] that having completed the first act of this decree, there remains the second to complete…

It is true that the times are sad, the people themselves are tired. They see all the ways closed, they don't find a way of exit even for the necessary natural means. The oppressions, the demands from the heads are unbearable, just suffering that they have elected for heads men without God, of evil life, without just right to be heads, that they merit a jail more than the law of the regime. Many thrones and empires have been upset and those few that have remained are all shaky ones and in the act of being overthrown, so that the earth will remain almost without king, in the hand of iniquitous men. Poor people, my poor children, under the regime of men without pity, without heart and without graces to be able to act as guide to their dependents. The epoch of the Jewish people is already being repeated, that when I was near coming upon the earth they were without king, and were under the dominion of a foreign empire (of) barbaric and idolatrous men, that didn't even know their Creator. And yet this was the sign of my imminent coming in the midst of them. Between that epoch and this—19—in many things they give each other a hand, and the disappearance of the thrones and empires is the announcement that the Kingdom of my Divine Will is not far off…Indeed the nations will continue to struggle between themselves, some for war, some for revolution, between themselves and against my Church. They have a fire that devours them in the midst of them, that doesn't give them peace, and they don't know how to give

peace; it is the fire of sin and the fire of doing without God that gives them no peace, and they will never have peace if they don't call God in the midst of them as regime and bond of union and peace. And I allow them to do it, and I will make them touch with (their) hand what it means to do without God. But this doesn't impede that the Kingdom of my Supreme Fiat comes… First we will deal with one single creature, forming the first kingdom in her, then with a few, and then making use of our omnipotence we will spread it everywhere.[487]

Jesus is never shy in revealing to Luisa that this Coronation of Creation will be preceded by great Chastisements (spoken of more in Part Three of this book). He says:

Do you think that things will always be as they are today? Ah! no. My Will will overwhelm everything; It will cause confusion everywhere—all things will be turned upside down. Many new phenomena will occur, such as to confound the pride of man; wars, revolutions, casualties of every kind will not be spared, in order to knock man down, and to dispose him to receive the regeneration of the Divine Will in the human will. And everything I manifest to you about my Will, as well as everything you do in It, is nothing other than preparing the way, the means, the teachings, the light, the graces, so that my Will may be regenerated in the human will…

'Be attentive, for this is about something too great, and about the most important thing that exists in Heaven and on earth: this is about placing the rights of Our Will in safety, about giving back to Us the purpose of Creation, about returning to Us all the glory for which all things were made, and about making Us give all the graces which Our Will had established to give to creatures, had they fulfilled Our Will in everything.[488]

As the life of the Church must follow the life of her Head; that is, Christ Himself, she too will have a time in her glorious history that corresponds to the three years of public ministry of Jesus, a time (that we are now entering) which corresponds to His passion, and also a time that corresponds to the period of His resurrected presence on earth (the Era of Peace; the Reign of the Divine Will) before His Ascension into Heaven (which, in turn, corresponds to the End of Time and the Church's definitive perfection in the Heavenly Wedding Feast). This, in fact, is precisely the description

---

[487] January 3, 1932.

[488] June 18, 1925.

Jesus uses with Luisa:

> The Saints of the past centuries symbolize my Humanity… they did not receive the mark of the sun of my Resurrection, but the mark of the works of my Humanity before my Resurrection … Therefore, they will be many; almost like stars, they will form a beautiful ornament to the Heaven of my Humanity … But the Saints of the living in my Will, who will symbolize my Resurrected Humanity, will be few… my Resurrection symbolizes the Saints of the living in my Will— and this with reason, since each act, word, step, etc. done in my Will is a divine resurrection that the soul receives…[489]

So now we, the Church, are about to be ready to follow Christ in His resurrected humanity on earth. **This Coronation is the Coming of the Kingdom: The Reign of the Divine Will on earth as in Heaven. Because I do not wish to repeat what is written in Part Three of this book on the Era, I will simply encourage you to turn to that section if you wish to now learn more about it.**

---

[489] April 15, 1919.

Part II: Receiving and Growing in the Gift

"...the whole of Heaven prays and anxiously awaits the Divine Will to be known and to reign. Then will the Great Queen do to the children of my Will what She did for Her Jesus, and Her Maternity will have life in Her children. I will surrender my own place in Her Maternal Heart to those who live in my Will. She will raise them for Me, She will guide their steps, She will hide them within Her Maternity and Sanctity…

Oh! how I would love for everyone to know that if they want to live in my Will, they have a powerful Queen and Mother who will make up for whatever they lack. She will raise them on Her maternal lap, and in everything they do She will be together with them, to shape their acts after Her own; so much so, that they will be known as the children raised, kept and instructed by the Love of the Maternity of my Mama. And these will be the children who will make Her happy, and will be Her glory and Her honor."

-Jesus to Luisa. The very last lines of the very last entry in her diary. December 28, 1938.

15) Preliminary Necessities

As noted in the introduction of this book, it is necessary to strive after all the virtues that all the saints have striven towards in this journey of Living in the Divine Will. We are dispensed from nothing that our Fathers in the Faith were required to perform.

Therefore, one should be sure to be well versed in the great spiritual masterpieces the Church has been blessed with over the millennia. Especially noteworthy are the *Introduction to the Devout Life* by St. Francis de Sales, *True Devotion to Mary* by St. Louis de Montfort, the *Story of a Soul* by St. Thérèse of Lisieux, the *Imitation of Christ* by Thomas a Kempis. Furthermore, the writing and preaching of modern-day saints such as St. Josemaría Escriva and Pope St. John Paul II are significant, for the proximity of these saints to our times means they were capable of addressing the issues of which the older saints did not know. And of course, Sacred Scripture primarily, with the Catechism of the Catholic Church following closely behind, must always remain one's foundation. **In a word: the ultimate "preliminary necessity" for living in the Divine Will is being a devout Catholic.**

But all the sources in the last paragraph teach that the first step to all sanctity is *repentance*. **Jesus' first public pronouncement was simple: "Repent, for the Kingdom of God is at hand"**[490] Therefore, for one who wishes to live in the Divine Will, there is no escaping a thorough Examination of Conscience.

Examine your Conscience

Sin and the Will of God cannot coexist; one must go. Be sure to examine your conscience with a few different thorough, detailed, and traditional Examinations of Conscience. It is advisable to enter specifically the term "traditional" if doing an internet search for examinations; many of the more modern examinations are good, but they are geared more toward evangelization than toward the sanctification of one who is already fully committed to the goal of becoming a saint. (Incidentally, this is a general dichotomy which a soul striving to become a saint must always be aware of: remembering that what suffices for evangelization may not be advisable for edification.)

The following criteria should guide a particularly thorough examination before confession (which should be at least once a month), but a brief examination of conscience should also be undertaken each night. This has always been the tradition of the Church, and has been included in the Papal Magisterium as recently as the year 2018, when Pope Francis wrote, in an Apostolic Exhortation **" ... I ask all Christians not to omit, in dialogue with the Lord, a sincere daily "examination of conscience"**[491]

Before proceeding to the criteria for the examination, let us consider a few words of Jesus to Luisa on the nature of sin, in order to encourage holding nothing back in eradicating sin:

> My beloved daughter, look well at Me, that you may know my pains in depth. My Body is the true portrait of the man who commits sin. Sin strips him of the garments of my grace; and I let Myself be stripped of my garments so as to give grace back to him once again. Sin deforms him, and while he is the most beautiful creature that came out of my hands, he becomes the ugliest one — disgusting and repugnant. I was the most beautiful of men, and I can say that, in order to give beauty back to man, my Humanity took on the ugliest form. Look at Me — how horrid I am. I let my skin be torn off by dint of lashes, to the point that I could no longer recognize Myself. Not only does sin take beauty away, but it forms deep wounds, rotten and gangrenous, which corrode the most interior parts; they consume his vital humors, so everything he does are dead — skeletal works. They snatch from him the nobility of his origin, the light of his reason — and he becomes blind. And I, in order to fill the depth of his wounds, let my Flesh be torn to shreds; I reduced all of Myself to a wound, and by shedding my Blood in rivers, I made the vital humors flow in his soul, so as to give life back to him once again. Ah! Had I not had the fount of the life of my Divinity within Me, which, since my Humanity died at each pain they gave Me, substituted for my life — I would have died from the very

---

[490]Matthew 3:2
[491]*Gaudete et Exsultate*. Paragraph 169.

beginning of my Passion. Now, my pains, my Blood, my Flesh which fell off in shreds, are always in the act of giving life to man; but man rejects my Blood so as not to receive life; he tramples upon my Flesh so as to remain wounded. Oh, how I feel the weight of ingratitude![492]

Let the Passion of Christ—which was the result of our sins—stand as a perennial reminder of what we do to Jesus when we neglect repentance.

Broadly, one should Examine his Conscience by imploring the aid of the Holy Spirit and then carefully considering how he has succeeded or failed to live rightly, in light of the following *Formulas of Catholic Doctrine*. (These particular delineations are found in the Appendix of the Vatican's own Compendium of the Catechism of the Catholic Church.)

The two commandments of love:
1. You shall love the Lord your God with all your heart, with all your soul, and with all your mind.
2. You shall love your neighbor as yourself.

The Golden Rule (Matthew 7:12):
Do to others as you would have them do to you.

The Ten Commandments:[493]

I. I Am the Lord Your God, You Shall Not Have Other Gods Before Me
II. You Shall Not Take the Name of the Lord Your God in Vain
III. Remember to Keep Holy the Lord's Day
IV. Honour Your Father and Your Mother
V. You Shall Not Kill
VI. You Shall Not Commit Adultery
VII. You Shall Not Steal
VIII. You Shall Not Bear False Witness Against Your Neighbour
IX. You Shall Not Covet Your Neighbour's Wife
X. You Shall Not Covet Your Neighbour's Possessions

The Seven Deadly Sins:
1. Pride
2. Covetousness
3. Lust
4. Anger
5. Gluttony
6. Envy
7. Sloth

The Three Supernatural Virtues:
1. Faith
2. Hope
3. Charity

The Four Moral Virtues:
1. Prudence
2. Justice
3. Fortitude
4. Temperance

The Five Precepts of the Church:
1. You shall attend Mass on Sundays and on holy days of obligation and remain free from work or activity that could impede the sanctification of such days.
2. You shall confess your sins at least once a year.
3. You shall receive the sacrament of the Eucharist at least during the Easter season.
4. You shall observe the days of fasting and abstinence established by the Church.
5. You shall help to provide for the needs of the Church.

The Seven Corporal Works of Mercy:
1. Feed the hungry.
2. Give drink to the thirsty.
3. Clothe the naked.
4. Shelter the homeless.
5. Visit the sick.
6. Visit the imprisoned.
7. Bury the dead.

The Seven Spiritual Works of Mercy:
1. Counsel the doubtful.
2. Instruct the ignorant.
3. Admonish sinners.
4. Comfort the afflicted.
5. Forgive offenses.
6. Bear wrongs patiently.
7. Pray for the living and the dead.

The Seven Capital Sins:
1. Pride
2. Covetousness

---

[492] February 9, 1922.

[493] These are taken from Section Two of the Compendium, not the Appendix

3. Lust
4. Anger
5. Gluttony
6. Envy
7. Sloth

The Gifts of the Holy Spirit:

1. Wisdom
2. Understanding
3. Counsel
4. Fortitude
5. Knowledge
6. Piety
7. Fear of the Lord

The Fruits of the Holy Spirit:

1. Charity
2. Joy
3. Peace
4. Patience
5. Kindness
6. Goodness
7. Generosity
8. Gentleness
9. Faithfulness
10. Modesty
11. Self-control
12. Chastity

The Beatitudes:

1. Blessed are the poor in spirit, for theirs is the kingdom of heaven.
2. Blessed are they who mourn, for they will be comforted.
3. Blessed are the meek, for they will inherit the earth.
4. Blessed are they who hunger and thirst for righteousness, for they will be satisfied.
5. Blessed are the merciful, for they will be shown mercy.
6. Blessed are the pure of heart, for they will see God.
7. Blessed are the peacemakers, for they will be called children of God.
8. Blessed are those who are persecuted for righteousness' sake, for theirs is the kingdom of heaven. Blessed are you when people revile you and persecute you and utter all kinds of evil against you falsely on my account. Rejoice and be glad, for your reward will be great in heaven.

Presenting a detailed, comprehensive Examination

of Conscience is outside of the scope of this book, but I again implore: do not neglect to consult the many freely available quality ones online.

***

Leaving aside, therefore, a thorough examination, let us consider some details of the major inhibitors of God's grace in the "looming issues" of our lives.

Address the Looming Issue

Simply reading the title of this section may well be enough (at least for those whom it is intended) to achieve the purpose of its inclusion in this book. Many would-be great Athletes for Christ unfortunately have one big "pink elephant" sitting in the proverbial living room of their spiritual lives, blocking grace, and they know this full well. Nevertheless, it is the one thing they do not want to address, so they are always searching for some way to evade this duty. Exasperated, they stop at nothing to find a corner to cut, a dishonest shortcut to take. Some will pile on all manner of devotions and pieties in a vain effort to compensate—for indeed, no matter how objectively holy these activities are in themselves, there simply is nothing but vanity outside the Will of God.

The looming issue must be addressed. Luisa's revelations are not a way around that; rather, they constitute just another insistence that we address it.

Only a small sample of such "looming issues" will be presented here; for ultimately, it is up to the honesty of the individual to recognize such an issue in his life—whether or not it is present in the forthcoming list of questions—and work to address it. Now, the issue needn't be entirely conquered as a prerequisite to Divine Will spirituality, but one must at least sincerely begin addressing it.

The following are just a few of the more common "looming issues":

Some have walked out on a spouse they know they are validly married to, but who, for whatever reason, has become a cross. Some have done so on the hope that a canonical slip will give an annulment that they know they do not in justice deserve. Such people must strive for reconciliation if it is reasonably possible and, above all, *remain faithful to the vows they made, even if there is no contact whatsoever between the spouses.*

Some have left the Catholic Church. Perhaps they were wounded by a corrupt member of the Church. Perhaps they desired an opportunity for ministry that the Catholic Church does not provide to someone in their state of life. Perhaps they found that they were "fed" more at some other Church. Perhaps they found what they deem a "better" liturgy elsewhere. Or perhaps even they have decided that their disagreements with the personal opinions and non-Magisterial teachings of the Pope justify entering into de facto or even explicit schism. Whatever the rationalization for leaving, such people must return. *There is no such thing as a good reason for leaving the One, Holy, Catholic, and Apostolic Church—the only Church founded by God Himself, which is necessary for our salvation.*

Some have a career that is itself immoral in a fundamental or pervasive way. Unfortunately, in these days of growing persecution of the faithful, the number of careers belonging to this list continues to increase. Some are health care professionals who formally cooperate with abortion, contraception, euthanasia, or any research or practice that violates the dignity of the embryo. Some are media workers who formally cooperate with the production or dissemination of pornography (remember that *any* display of a real or simulated sex act is, by that fact alone, pornographic).[494] The job of some involves formal cooperation with same-sex "marriage" or transgenderism. Some work in politics and support "pro-choice" policies. Some who work in the business world partake of the common practice of lying in their work activities. We must recall that lying is condemned *by nature* by the Magisterium,[495] meaning there are no circumstances and no intentions that render it licit. In short: *does a job in any way formally cooperate with any of the evils that have become so commonplace today? Whoever answered "yes" must find a way to make their careers moral, or else leave their careers.*

Some live in contradiction to a vow. Clerics who refuse to say their office; consecrated religious who refuse to render obedience and observe the rule; priests who have modified the liturgy; married people who cheat on their spouses (either gravely through formal adultery or through a more subtle contradiction of marital fidelity) or refuse to be open to life (whether through the intrinsic evil of artificial contraception, or through using NFP to avoid conception without any serious reason to do so[496]), or fail to raise their children as practicing Catholics (for these promises, too, are a part of marriage vows). Some are civilly married to another who is not their true spouse while refusing to live as brother and sister until they can be validly married (perhaps through annulment and convalidation). Some refuse to love and honor their spouse—husbands who choose not to be the head (with the wife as the heart), or wives who refuse to be the heart (allowing for the husband to be the head) of the family. *One may not live in contradiction to a vow and suppose that he can live in the Divine Will.*

Some are subtle criminals—perhaps not formal members of the mafia, but nevertheless living a lifestyle in which they regularly, gravely, break the law. To obey the civil laws which pertain to us is a serious duty not only as citizens, but as Christians. There are of course exceptions to this norm—but the exceptions are far fewer than many pretend them to be. Just because a law is bad does not mean it may be disobeyed. Some flagrantly cheat on their taxes. Some employers flout state and federal labor laws (sometimes Catholic employers in Catholic apostolates are the worst offenders here; supposing that because they themselves see the apostolate as their 'mission,' their employees must also see it as such, and therefore put in drastically more work than they are paid for). Some employees only pretend to work but actually spend all day on social media—thereby stealing from their employers in accepting payment. The driving habits of some are dangerous and illegal (and they certainly are if one is always on the lookout for a police officer, ready to adopt a totally different driving manner when

---

[494] CCC2354: "Pornography consists in removing real or simulated sexual acts from the intimacy of the partners, in order to display them deliberately to third parties." As we can see from this Magisterial definition, any sex scene whatsoever is automatically the intrinsic grave evil of pornography— completely irrespective of whether or not it is graphic, intended to inspire lust, or intended to glorify evil.

[495] CCC 2458

[496] The Magisterium has repeatedly made clear that NFP, while good and moral in itself, requires that spouses have a serious reason for it to be licitly used to avoid conception. While the details necessitate sincere discernment, the abuses are clear: suffice it to say that ensuring one can continue to afford Disney World vacations and a separate bedroom for each child does *not* constitute a serious reason to use NFP to avoid conception. More on this point can be found in the "Virtues" section of this book.

one is nearby), which not only breaks the law but is an injustice to one's neighbor whose safety is thereby flippantly disregarded. Some fraudulently benefit from insurance claims, government programs, or financial strategies—or are now living off of the fruits of these deceptive and criminal tactics. *We must obey all legitimate authority—for there is no such thing as living in the Divine Will without submitting to its earthly parallel; obedience.*

The New Age Movement or the Occult has become part of the daily routine of some. They read or watch—or allow their children to read or watch—books or media that exalt and glamorize the intrinsic grave evil of sorcery or witchcraft, erroneously supposing that they are somehow immune to this objectively disordered influence simply because they are "good Catholics." Some daily engage in fundamentally Hindu forms of worship under the guise of "stretching." Some use a selection of the so-called "alternative" medicines or treatments that are really only thinly veiled superstitious magical charms bedecked in pseudo-scientific language. Some consult horoscopes, hypnotists, "fortune tellers," mediums, psychics, etc. Some engage in or support activities that presume to heal, diagnose, or help people via "chi" or "energy" or "chakras." *These things are not indifferent: they are spiritually damaging, and they block God's grace. They must be abandoned, repented of, and the damage done by them healed.*

Some neglect the Precepts of the Church. That is—they fail to go to confession at least once a year or fail to receive Communion worthily at least during the Easter Season. They skip Sunday Mass for reasons other than truly serious and necessary ones (perhaps wrongly supposing that not wanting to "interfere with vacation," or not feeling "tops"—even though they feel well enough to go shopping!—excuses them from the Sunday Obligation). They refuse to keep Sunday holy (perhaps by erroneously supposing that, so long as they have gone to Mass, they are within their rights to treat Sunday like any other day—using it as the shopping, cleaning, sports, and housework day). They skip Mass on Holy Days of Obligation. They refuse to contribute to the Church. Or, they refuse to keep the (incredibly minimal) fasting and abstinence norms that they fall under. *The precepts of the Church are not suggestions; they are requirements—they are minimal, and one cannot pretend that he takes the Divine Will seriously if he does not follow these precepts.*

Some allow personal ties to drag them down. "*He who loves father or mother more than me is not worthy of me; and he who loves son or daughter more than me is not worthy of me,*" says Our Lord.[497] Some endorse, condone, or otherwise serve as an accessory to sinful lifestyles adopted by family members (perhaps cohabitation, homosexuality, or transgenderism), erroneously supposing that "love" mandates this behavior, which in truth is nothing but hatred. Some daily engage in evil conversation merely because it's what their coworkers do. Some watch evil media (and *no one* has the right to tell another that something is okay to watch if their own conscience says otherwise) merely because it's what those with whom they live want to watch. Some scarcely ever in their lives stand up publicly for what is good and true because they are afraid family, friends, or coworkers will find out and be displeased. Some are so terrified of even the slightest risk of problems at work, that in every way they strive to blend in perfectly with their apathetic-towards-God coworkers—having no evangelizing sign of faith on their person, their desk, their car, etc. Some have gone even farther than culpable silence, subtly adopting heretical or sinful attitudes merely because having certain mindsets makes life easier among those with whom they spend their time. Some forget that *all* worldly authority has after it one essential caveat—" *... we must obey in all things **but sin**.*" Even a great love (of a fellow human being—even a relative) is nothing but an evil if it acquires a form that contradicts the greatest love—the Love of God.

Some are rejecting a calling (that is, a genuine calling that they have carefully discerned, received spiritual direction on, taken sufficient time to consider, and consequently grown truly convicted that they have). Some are called to the priesthood but refusing to enter seminary or are called to the religious life but refusing to enter an order. One cannot refuse to follow what he knows to be God's Will for him and then pretend that any apparent progress in the spiritual life is meaningful. Rejecting such a calling is rejecting the Will of God—outside of which there is nothing good—and

---

[497] Matthew 10:37

it cannot be safely done on the pretense that such callings are "never required" or are "only ideals, not commands." Nor can any Christian—so long as he is over the age of eighteen[498]—reject a calling on the pretense that his parents disapprove. For obedience to parents ceases upon emancipation.[499]

Some, finally, have a grave sin still on their conscience that they have refused to ever confess, even though they have long since amended their lives. *This sin must be absolved.* One can drive somewhere far away from home, wear large sunglasses and a hood, and even change his voice when confessing (though all these measures are of course unnecessary)—but confess this sin he must.

***

But merely addressing the looming issue and repenting of blatant sin does not make us ready to live in the Divine Will. For that, we must continue to the next element of Living in the Divine Will.

Desire Sanctity Above All things

Recall, from Part One of this book, that we already demonstrated that all truly *must be Catholic*—that all must believe and obey each doctrine taught by the Catholic Church. One of those doctrines is the **Universal Call to Holiness**. The Church has always taught, dogmatically, that each of the faithful is called to become a saint; but recently a special emphasis has been placed on this necessity.

Consider the following teaching found in *Lumen Gentium* (the Dogmatic Constitution on the Church), itself one of the sixteen documents of the Second Vatican Council:

"...all the faithful, whatever their condition or state, are called by the Lord, each in his own way, to that perfect holiness whereby the Father Himself is perfect."[500]

This teaching, in turn, draws from none other than the words of Our Lord Himself, who said "Be perfect, as your heavenly Father is perfect."[501] **Satisfaction with just being a "decent Catholic" never sufficed at any point in the history of the Church, but at this moment it is more impossible than ever to pretend that it could suffice.**

Important as it was that we settled the dogmatic,

unquestionable necessity for every single Catholic to strive for sanctity (and to strive for sanctity by definition also means to strive for it above all things, for if "holiness" is sought second to anything, then it is not true holiness that is sought), what good is merely setting this out as a doctrine to be acknowledged and assented to in dry obedience? Perhaps little good.

We must instead now turn to inspiration, and not leave to a formal command what is better achieved by a glorious invitation—in this case, **an invitation to invincibility.**

Do you wish to be invincible from tragedy? There is only one way to achieve this state. For, in the words of Leon Bloy, that zealous 19th century French poet, novelist, and promoter of Our Lady of La Salette, who gave us the following quote promoted by Pope Francis in his Apostolic Exhortation *Gaudete et Exsultate*:

"There is only one tragedy, ultimately: not to have been a saint"

Ponder your life thus far. So often, no doubt, it has been assailed by temptations to dwell on regret. An opportunity for more money, recognition, worldly memories, possessions, security, travels, comfort, pleasure—or whatever other vanity—sails on by. Another year passes and so too (we lament), does one more notch in the likelihood of the realization of our dreams. A loved one dies, and we lament what seems to be a lost future with him. Forgiven sins come to mind to haunt us and accuse us and tempt us to despair because of their mere existence.

But all of that is nothing. Nothing is lost if, despite it all, one strives for sanctity. So long as one does this, it can truly be said that all is gain.

If only we realized that fact and comported ourselves in accord with it, we would always have perfect peace. **Therefore consider: What now robs you of the unbroken peace and joy to which you have a right as a Christian who trusts in Jesus and desires that His Will be done?**

...That there is suffering in your life? You have all eternity—which will scarcely have begun once countless trillions of centuries have passed—to

---

[498]Or whatever age is decided upon for adulthood to have begun within one's own culture.
[499]CCC 2217.

[500]Paragraph 11.
[501]Matthew 5:48

enjoy permanent ecstatic joy and the absence of any and all pain. You have a brief few moments before your death to suffer redemptively in union with Christ, grow from it, merit from it, contribute to the salvation and sanctification of souls with it. Far from a curse to lament over, it is a gift to rejoice at the bestowal of; for as St. Padre Pio said, "suffering is the one thing the angels envy us for." **Desire sanctity above all, and physical suffering vanishes as a "tragedy."**

…That you aren't working your dream job and pursuing your dream career, like others you envy are, and like the daydreams you entertained in earlier years? All those who work such jobs will, in the twinkling of an eye, find themselves old and decrepit, with the mere faint memory of their former endeavors proving radically incapable of giving even one ounce of joy. Go about the job and duties that God has called you to here and now with prayer and submission to the Divine Will, and you are achieving infinitely more than one who works the supposedly "perfect and best" job. **Desire sanctity above all, and career disappointments vanish as a "tragedy."**

…That your marriage is not what you always dreamed it would be, or that you cannot marry whom you desire, or perhaps that you've missed the opportunity for marriage entirely? Great and glorious as marriage is, it too is a passing thing, designed by God for the procreation and education of children (with even the union and good of the spouses as a subordinate end to that),[502] and it will no longer exist in eternity; which will be upon us in a flash. Do not misunderstand: if you *are* married, then you should spare no expense in working towards making your marriage beautiful, peaceful, joyful, and above all, holy. But ultimately, the fulfillment of those goals is up to two people (both spouses); yet when all is said and done, you answer only for yourself on the Day of Judgment. Therefore, the deepest joy of your soul cannot ever depend upon another earthly creature—not even your spouse. **Desire sanctity above all, and all marital problems vanish as a "tragedy."**

…Or perhaps even that your life lacks the outwardly holy things that you wish it had? So long as it is not a slothful indifference to the pursuit of holy things, but rather the Will of God, that has deprived you of them, then even the absence of these things is no

harm whatsoever to you. If your life's circumstances prevent you from going on those great pilgrimages you perhaps envy your friends for, being a part of those wonderful Catholic groups and communities that others so seem to enjoy, attending those amazing Catholic events that you now only read of, or whatever else; this is nothing to lament. Heaven will infinitely surpass all these essentially temporal blessings, and when you are there, not having had these temporal things will seem to you then as it now seems to you when you see a child missing one extra cookie during one day's dessert. Remember that all treasures in Heaven are built up solely by the Will of God; and this Divine Will can be submitted to and lived in anywhere, by anyone, at any instant. **Desire sanctity above all, and all missed opportunities for externally holy things vanish as a "tragedy."**

Many things are hard: acquiring advanced degrees, making large sums of money, gaining recognition for ourselves, trying to have people like us, securing our legacy, trying to guarantee our safety and security, acquiring and maintaining possessions, looking for promotions and new jobs, striving to order all things to our comfort and pleasure… and oh, how much we pour ourselves out in the pursuit of all of this vain garbage which seems so pressing and direly important now, and yet the next day is barely even a memory. But avoiding the only tragedy—acquiring a veritable invincibility—is comparatively easy. Acquire it! Desire *sanctity* above all else. To do otherwise would be to climb out on a long, feeble, shaky limb in pursuit of a vile copper coin when a shining gold ingot sits directly above you, easily within reach.

If only we considered the fact that Judgment Day is speeding towards us like a freight train, we would have no confusion. For on the Day of Judgment, you shall not regret missing out on that copper coin. You won't regret missing the extra $100,000 on your salary that you could have had—but you would regret foregoing the daily family Rosary in order to have more time to secure this salary. On the Day of Judgment, you won't regret a few people disliking you or thinking you odd—but you would regret keeping your Faith hidden in order to ensure you blend in well with modern society. On the Day of Judgment, you won't regret

---

[502]Cf. Decree of the Holy Office under Pope Pius XII, April 1, 1944.

"missing out" on this or that questionable movie, book, TV show, or other entertainment that is popularly praised by your friends, neighbors, and coworkers—but you would regret the decay of the soul that you risk by exposing yourself to such things. On the Day of Judgment, you won't regret "missing out" on this or that college degree, sports tournament, worldly spotlight, honor or recognition which simply requires too much of you—but you would regret having spent a life waking up each morning with your primary motivation for getting out of bed being the pursuit of such utter vanity instead of the pursuit of eternal glory. On the Day of Judgment, you won't regret not having lived in a beautiful remote paradise with hundreds of acres to yourself—but you would regret the thousands of Communions—every single one of which is incomprehensibly powerful—you could have made but didn't, due to your insistence upon living in a utopia on earth too far a drive from a Catholic Church to make it there each day. On the Day of Judgment, you won't regret having had health problems—but you would regret having spent your life expending all of your time and energy experimenting with the various health and diet fads which inundate us daily, instead of simply doing what is prudent for the sake of health and then accepting whatever suffering remains as the Will of God for your salvation and sanctification and that of the whole world. On the Day of Judgment, you won't regret not having sent your children to the "best" schools and ensured that they have the "best" opportunities—but you would regret letting the world's values seep into their minds and hearts. On the Day of Judgment, you won't regret failing to ensure you and your family members can pursue every hobby, vacation, sport, etc., that the world insists you must engage in—but you would regret neglecting significant daily prayer time that you need to forego to pursue and enable these interests.

This analysis is not a presentation of my own opinion. The infinitely surpassing value of sanctity to even the greatest of the goods of the world and the consequent need for us all to consider that which is temporal as garbage when compared to the eternal, which in turn alone deserves our primary focus, is the clear admonition of Sacred Scripture:

Indeed I count everything as loss because of the surpassing worth of knowing Christ Jesus my Lord. For his sake I have suffered the loss of all things, and count them as refuse, in order that I may gain Christ.[503]

Considering these stunning realities, what analogy suffices? In this book and elsewhere, this desire that we must have is likened to a blazing fire as the only comparison that comes close; yet even those words utterly fail unless you happen to be near one, to be reminded of its intensity. With Sanctifying Grace, the Almighty, Eternal, Uncreated, Perfect God of the Universe offers His very own Life to you, who are nothing. He promises that this life, which can be formed in you here and now, is what shall then sensibly constitute your existence when, in the twinkling of an eye, this fleeting world passes, and you embark upon the life of eternity.

And when you find yourself in that eternity, the breadth of your joy, your glory, and your closeness to God is no accident: it is decided by (and indeed proceeds from) the holiness you attain to *here and now*. In building a house, how zealously do you attend to the details of its construction to ensure it is tailored to your needs for the short few decades you will reside in it? And yet, the holiness you will enjoy in Heaven will scarcely have begun after countless trillions of centuries have passed. There, the love you now expand your soul to accommodate will be the food you eat, the water you drink, and the splendor of the Kingdom you find yourself in. There, the degree of union with God you now arrive at will be the garment you wear forever. "*There*" might be "*here*" for you in a decade, a year, a month, a day, or a minute. There is no time to waste.

"The kingdom of heaven is like a merchant in search of fine pearls, who, on finding one pearl of great value, went and sold all that he had and bought it."[504]

Spare no expense. Go all in. Hold nothing back. Put all of your eggs in one basket.

> *Lord, teach me to serve you as you deserve;*
> *to give and not to count the cost,*
> *to fight and not to heed the wounds,*
> *to toil and not to seek for rest,*
> *to labor and not to ask for reward,*
> *save that of knowing that I do your will.*

---

[503]Philippians 3:8

[504]Matthew 13:45-6

-St. Ignatius of Loyola

A Desire for Sanctity Examen

Look back at the past week; consider how you spent that time. Ask yourself if an objective onlooker could ascertain from those days that you believe these following facts, for they are inherent in the faith you profess with your lips on Sunday:

- That your every thought, word, and deed will be recalled on the Last Day in the presence of all Creation for it to be judged by its love ... (or do you think, speak, and act in ways you won't be proud of on That Day?)
- That God so highly regards your prayers and sacrifices that He has deigned to hinge, upon their being said and made, the very salvation of souls created by Him and for whom He died ... (or do you spend little time in prayer, muster up little fervency in your heart during it, and put little effort into sacrifice?)
- That every interaction, no matter how mundane, you have with any soul will help to determine if she becomes "a creature you would now be strongly tempted to worship or else a horror and a corruption you could now see only in a nightmare."[505] ... (or do you prefer vain conversation, frivolous activities, and worldly endeavors to that which benefits eternity?)
- That if you are ashamed of Christ before men—embarrassed of, cowardly about, or indifferent to Him and His teachings—then He will be ashamed of you before His Father on Judgment Day ... (or do you limit your conversation to the weather when you are with those who might not share your Faith in Christ?)
- That love is measured by sacrifice, and ever seeks to pour itself out without any expectation of repayment—and "*at the evening of our lives, we will be judged on our love*"[506] ... (or do you expect your bare-minimum following of the precepts to save you, while living a self-centered life?)
- That Our Lord takes any deed done to one of His children as done to Himself, and whenever we find ourselves in the presence of others, we are given the same opportunity to love Him, in

them, just as Veronica or Simon had on the Way of the Cross? ... (or do those around whom you live your daily life get treated by you as means to your own ends, as obstacles to your own goals, or as annoyances to be dealt with; instead of beloved children of God to be shown mercy, love, generosity, forgiveness, and compassion?)

- That the smallest sufferings of Purgatory far exceed the worst possible in this world, and yet need not be endured if you now choose to pursue perfection, and that you must prefer to suffer the greatest pains until the end of time than to commit even the smallest venial sin ... (or do you slothfully take no measures to examine your conscience and perform interior mortifications to purge from your life anything that might offend Our Lord?)

There are starving souls; starving physically and starving spiritually. Christ's very own presence dwells in each of them. How many personal enjoyments to which you have grown accustomed are you open to abandoning in order to serve them? They need you now. The women going in to have abortions need to see you on your knees outside the Planned Parenthoods. The forgotten elderly in nursing homes need your loving and prayerful presence as a consolation in their last days. The sick in hospitals need the channels of grace you can bring them as they endure suffering during which they are tempted to think God has abandoned them. The urban youth need good mentors as they are growing up in what more resembles pagan anarchy than Christian civilization. The men and women in prison need you to show them that they are loved; by you and by God, no matter what they have done and no matter what society says about them. The list goes on, but the lesson is short: unless you are a rare soul, your life needs fewer vanities (fewer hobbies, less uncalled-for effort in your job or personal projects, less time spent on activities motivated by love of comfort and pleasure, etc.) and more spiritual and corporal works of mercy.

You likely live within a short drive of a Church. Our Lord has given us Himself; Body, Blood, Soul, and Divinity; invisibly—but truly, literally, physically[507] present in the Eucharist. How much

---

[505] C.S. Lewis, the *Weight of Glory.*
[506] St. John of the Cross, Cf. *Catechism of the Catholic Church,* paragraph 1022.

[507] Not physical by quantitative extension in space, but inasmuch as physicality involves the substance of the thing in question (and, indeed, it does), then yes: The Blessed Sacrament *is, physically*, Jesus Christ Himself.

are you willing to alter your daily routine in order to center it around receiving Him? How strong is your faith in the Real Presence and how important, in relation to that, do you deem your secular endeavors? The Mass is not a symbolic remembrance of Calvary; it is an actual presentation of it in its full reality. Your eyes see only a small sanctuary, but your being stands before the Paschal Mysteries no less so than did Our Lady 2,000 years ago. Arrive early, and until you leave (which ideally is no sooner than 15 minutes after receiving Holy Communion) comport yourself with the holy fear and reverence that befits standing in the physical presence of the Almighty, stirring up fervent prayer of the heart as you cry out to God.

We live in a world of unprecedented sin, error, and corruption. How zealously do you fight this darkness; rooting out vigorously all vice, sin, imperfection, needless occasions of sin, bad influences (through bad media, harmful friendships, etc.) from your own life and from your family and household? Truly this sin, error, and darkness is so pervasive that merely avoiding the blatantly immoral influences is far insufficient—the faithful who live in the most depraved of ages must not fall victim to supporting that which simply appears good next to a great evil but is really not good at all on its own right. It is impossible to live an upright life with a mentality of compromise with the culture; for today's culture is none other than the Culture of Death. You will have to be a sign of contradiction, and therefore, you must examine your conscience critically if you find

yourself failing to be so; blending in imperceptibly with secular family, friends, and coworkers, and society at large; and allowing into your life without careful consideration the popular creations of modern culture. Never let this be the pride of a Pharisee; rather, let it be the love of a mother for even her straying children.

Lest you be discouraged, recall that what is essential is not so much our current level of virtue, holiness, piety, and the like. What is essential is that we yearn and strive for a heroic degree of all these things. Our own strength will not itself advance us one degree towards sanctity; God, in seeing our lowliness, weakness, and yet despite it all, our absolute trust in Him, will be the one Who does this work in us. If you can check off every spiritual regimen in the book from your list of accomplishments and exhibit all the externalities of an advanced monk, yet lack the inner disposition of the heart of pure love, humility (and that means truly seeing yourself as below every single other soul), and trust, then you have simply wasted your time and effort. But this fact should not be discouraging; it should be encouraging. For what even such an advanced monk longs for is itself within your reach even now: absolute trust in God despite everything—including the lowliness and misery of your current spiritual state.

***

Once we sincerely desire sanctity above all things, as the saints throughout the history of the Church always have, then we are ready to receive its crown by renouncing the self-will, desiring the Divine Will, and asking for the Divine Will.

16) <u>Renounce the Self Will</u>

Before turning to Jesus' words to Luisa, we should recall that the renouncing of the self-will is not a new teaching. Rather, as has already been shown in the previous "The Gift Foreshadowed in the Great Spiritual Writers" section, this renunciation is not only a familiar theme in the advice of the saints, but also could easily be seen as the perfect summation of what they held to be most essential and powerful component to the spiritual life.

So, we must consider first what is contrary to a proper understanding of this renunciation (even though it may superficially appear similar); namely, Quietism and eastern philosophical or

religious notions of the extinguishing of the self (or "nirvana"). For the sake of those who may have theological concerns, this issue is treated in more detail in the "Answers to Objections" chapter; for now, we will only treat it to the degree necessary for the alleviation of any potential danger.

> Beyond this, to give you My Divine Will, it is necessary that you give yours, because two wills can not **reign** inside of one heart, they would war with each other, and yours would be an obstacle to Mine, and therefore It would not be free to do what It wants, and I, in order make Mine free,

with so many instances I ask you for yours.[508]

Jesus wants to reign in your will, but there cannot be two kings. Jesus did not say that two wills cannot **exist** in one heart, but that two wills cannot **reign**. In this and in many other passages, it is clear that Jesus' words to Luisa have nothing to do with the heresy of Quietism.

Jesus tells Luisa that He wants her will *little*, not annihilated (in this He is merely reiterating to Luisa what He already subtly revealed to St. Thérèse of Lisieux in "The Little Way"), **and that he wants its *operation*, not its substance, sacrificed continually to the Divine Will,** just as Jesus Himself, and His most holy Mother, always sacrificed their human wills to the Divine Will, while they both truly had human wills which never disappeared. Jesus tells Luisa:

> **Before Us, there is no greater sacrifice than a human will that, while having life, does not exercise it** in order to give free life to My Fiat. This, however, to great profit for the soul, because she gives a will that is human, and receives a Divine one; she gives a will that is finite and limited, and receives one that is infinite and without limit.[509]

The renunciation of the self-will can be either the hardest thing or the easiest thing to accomplish. The hardest, because renouncing it is simply renouncing yourself, as the will is the greatest faculty of the soul, which in turn is our truest self. But the easiest, in accordance with what Jesus tells Luisa as follows:

> …the Divine Will and the human are two spiritual powers. The Divine, Immense with an Unreachable Power. The human, little power, but for however little, it has its power. And both being spiritual, the one can pour itself into the other and form one single Life. All the power is in the volition, and being spiritual power, it has the space of being able to place inside of its will the good that she wants, and also the evil. In fact, what the will wants, that is what one finds inside of herself: If she wants self-esteem, glory, love of pleasures, of riches, she will find inside of her volition the life of self-esteem, of glory, the life of pleasures, of riches, and, if she wants, sin-even sin

will form its life.

Even more, if she wants the Life of Our Will in hers, wanted, commanded by Us with so many sighs, if she truly wants It, she will have the Great Good of possessing Our Will as Life. And if this could not be, the Sanctity of Living in My Volition would be a difficult and almost impossible sanctity, and **I do not know how to neither teach difficult things, nor do I want impossible things. Rather it is My usual Way to make easy, for as much as it is possible for the creature, the most arduous things and hardest sacrifice**…

The human will possesses, with indelible characters, everything it does and wants to do; and if the memory forgets, the will loses nothing, it contains the deposit of all of its acts, unable to disperse anything. Therefore it can be said that the whole of man is in his will: if the will is holy, even the most indifferent things are holy for him; but if it is evil, maybe even good itself changes for him into a perverted act. [510]

Jesus here assures Luisa (and all of us, through her) that it is not difficult to renounce the self-will—even that He makes it "easy"! **And, indeed, this renunciation also makes life in general so much easier in the best of ways and that it need not be any harder than we make it be.** Consider the opposite: as a parent, I can attest from experience that the most severe screaming and crying fits which a toddler throws usually have nothing to do with anything serious; but rather, arise from simply not having some minor thing that his self-will happened to want at a given moment. My 2-year-old has dealt with running falls or painful cuts to the head with admirable grace and peace, only to the next day tantrum with all the violence of a hurricane if he cannot wear the shirt he decided he wanted to wear at that moment.

But how, specifically, do we go about effecting this renunciation? **The most important thing to know from the onset, and to continue to remind yourself throughout the process of growth in the Gift, is that there are no special formulas, no magical procedures, and no Gnostic[511] secrets. Jesus Himself says precisely this to Luisa in her revelations, and He insists that what matters is simply the soul's desire for the Gift.[512]** The Gift of

---

[508] January 22, 1933.
[509] July 19, 1928.
[510] March 19,1935.
[511] Gnosticism essentially is the heresy of the "doctrine of salvation by knowledge," whereby those who are privileged

enough to have these certain bits of knowledge are superior, and the only elect.
[512] Then why am I writing this book? Because specific knowledge of what is desired is a great benefit. This is why

Living in the Divine Will is a grace, and it is given in the same manner as is all grace: based upon the humble, pure, sincere receptivity of the one who desires it. If all you are left with once you are finished with this book is the reminder to give God all of yourself without reserve and ask earnestly, with trust, that He bestow upon you the greatest union with Him possible, then that is enough. Such a prayer is not only clearly permissible to speak, but it would even be lamentable to forego such a prayer.

Renunciation via Crosses

(Note: this point is also treated in the "Love of the Cross" and "Mortification" sections in the chapter of this book dedicated to growing in the foundational virtues for the Gift).

We should now consider how we respond to those crosses that are already a part of our lives. Jesus tells Luisa that this response is what differentiates the elect from the reprobate. St. Faustina said,

> I often felt the Passion of the Lord Jesus in my body, although this was imperceptible [to others], and I rejoiced in it because Jesus wanted it so. But this lasted for only a short time. These sufferings set my soul afire with love for God and for immortal souls. Love endures everything, love is stronger than death, love fears nothing ...[513]

Whether or not you pursue mortification of the flesh and a life of penance, you will suffer. But the question is: what will you do with this suffering? Dwell on how annoyed you are at it and whatever or whomever caused it? Lament it and complain about it? Endlessly ponder how you could have avoided it to try to ensure you won't have to feel it again? Stop at nothing to try to be rid of it? These attitudes do not conform to God's Will or the necessary trust we must have in it. Therefore, we must take stock of how we react to suffering

If, however, you unite with Christ's Passion all suffering that God's Will permits you to undergo and meditate upon His own sufferings, then this achievement can powerfully inflame your love and desire and dispose you to receive the Gift.

We must believe—for it is certainly true—that, in allowing us to suffer, God gives us the greatest gift. Remember, our ability to suffer for Him is the one thing for which the angels envy us. Luisa said:

> While Jesus was resting, I comprehended many things about the words spoken by Jesus, especially about suffering for love of Him. Oh! what a coin of inestimable value! If we all knew it, we would compete with one another to suffer more. But I believe we are all shortsighted in knowing this coin so precious, and this is why one does not come to having knowledge of it.[514]

But how is it practical to look at suffering as a gift? Because it makes the necessary thing—renunciation—so much easier. It allows us to see this passing world for what it is, and it detaches us from the trivial garbage that we have foolishly attached ourselves to and which prevent us from being open to the Gift of God's Will. If you reflect upon your life thus far, you will easily realize this is true. It has usually been our crosses which have enabled us to be free of our true chains, just as a necessary surgery—though painful—removes from our bodies that which causes far more pain than the surgery itself.

***

Remember that Renunciation should also be seen as an essential aspect of the Imitation of Christ, for He *"emptied himself, taking the form of a slave…becoming obedient even unto death; death on a cross."*[515] In its commentary on French Spirituality, the New Catholic Encyclopedia says the following:

> In the complete possession of Christ's humanity by the divinity wherein the humanity of Christ lacks its own subsistence, its own personality, they saw the absolute condition of self-renunciation and clinging to God. From this state of 'infinite servitude' they drew the most fundamental characteristic of their spirituality—the deep, total renunciation of self that is at the same time total adherence to Christ and being possessed by Him.[516]

Earlier we settled that the Incarnation was the greatest event in history. But let us now consider how much of a self-renunciation it was for the

---

missionaries preach Christ; not because it is objectively impossible to be saved without explicit Faith in Him while on earth (for more on this, see *Lumen Gentium*, Paragraph 16), but because that clear, explicit Faith is an enormous benefit to salvation.
[513] St. Faustina, *Divine Mercy in My Soul*, Paragraph 46.

[514] September 16, 1899.
[515] Philippians 2:7
[516] *New Catholic Encyclopedia*, "Spirituality, French School of." Page 450.

Second Person of the Thrice Holy God to so infinitely empty Himself as to be born in the likeness of sinful flesh. He, the almighty and eternal God, *"infinitely perfect and blessed in himself,"*[517] Who needs nothing and from Whom all good things proceed, deigned to descend a greater distance than you would if you were to become an ant, or rather, a speck of dust. This is not to mention the unimaginable emptying of self through the scandal of the Cross that this omnipotent Son of God undertook. He Who could have unmade the universe with a thought, instead submitted Himself to an unheard of torturous, public, humiliating death. Confronted with such an unspeakable and indescribable renunciation of self, how could we—who are nothing—dare hold onto even the smallest morsel of our own puny and pathetic self-wills?

***

There is so much more that can be said on the renunciation of the self-will, but the bottom line is that it is a battle that must be continually fought. There is no difference between the renunciation of the self-will in Luisa's writings and those of the saints **(referred to also as abandonment,[518] surrender, abnegation, or emptying), so I again encourage you to feel free to pursue this end by means of whatever orthodox Catholic spirituality you feel drawn to. St. Francis de Sales, often known as the doctor of the spiritual life for the laity, is also referred to as the "Doctor of Self-Abandonment,"[519] and his works are much worth reading in pursuing this.**[520] We now conclude this discussion with a quote from Bl. John of Ruysbroeck, a concrete piece of advice to act on, and a brief list of potential next steps.

> By renouncing self-will in doing, in leaving undone, and in suffering, the material and occasion of pride are wholly cast out, and humility is made perfect in the highest degree. And God becomes the Lord of the man's whole will; and the man's will is so united with the will of God that he can neither will nor desire in any

other way. This man has put off the old man, and has put on the new man, who is renewed and made according to the dearest will of God. Of all such Christ says: Blessed are the poor in spirit—that is to say, those who have renounced self-will—for theirs is the Kingdom of Heaven.[521]

Perhaps, then, you could attempt the simple spiritual exercise which follows. Place yourself, sitting or kneeling, in front of Our Lord in the Blessed Sacrament. Strive to be as close to Him as possible; at least ensuring that no one is in-between you and Him. Remain there for a time with arms at your side or resting on your lap, and with palms facing up toward the Tabernacle or Monstrance.[522] In this posture, meditate upon everything you hold dear; not just possessions, not just friends, not just family, but even your intentions, your plans for the future, your desire to avoid certain things and pursue other things, your temporal hopes, your good works, your very self, *everything*—meditate on simply dumping it all out in front of the Tabernacle for Jesus to do with as He wishes. Envision this being like casting the small pebble of your will into the immense sea of Christ's Divinity which dwells in all its fullness mere feet in front of you. Tell Him that you do this with all of your freedom, with all of your love, and with all of your desire to be filled with nothing but His Divine Will. Most important in this act, converse with Him in your own words, as you would with a trusted friend. You could also use words to the effect of:

> "Jesus, I am nothing, You are everything. Take all that I am and all that I have. Give, in return, all that You are and all that You have. For I wish to have no will but Yours." And "The Lord giveth, and the Lord taketh away. Blessed be the Name of the Lord."[523]

Miscellaneous Ways to Renounce the Self-Will

- Obeying even when we can get away with disobeying (for example, submitting to non-

---

[517] The First Paragraph of the Catechism of the Catholic Church.
[518] In another sense of the word, "Abandonment" can also refer to the feeling that one is forsaken by God, as in the Dark Night of the Soul. Additionally, beware of false notions of abandonment that entail an act of surrender to things which are intrinsically contrary to His Will; e.g. sacrificing your very salvation for the sake of abandonment. That is a contradiction, the very opposite of true renunciation of the self-will, and is a form of Quietism.

[519] Cf. *New Catholic Encyclopedia*, Self-abandonment, Spiritual Page 884.
[520] Particularly noteworthy among his works are: *Introduction to the Devout Life* and *Finding God's Will for You*.
[521] *Adornment of the Spiritual Marriage.* 14
[522] This same exercise is efficacious in front of a Divine Mercy image, a crucifix, or a statue or image of Our Lady.
[523] Job 1:21

infallible but nevertheless Magisterial statements[524] that we feel like opposing).

- Bearing insults and all manner of persecution with complete silence and praying for whomever they come from.
- Giving alms generously and taking care to not be noticed.
- Performing works of mercy.
- Meditating each day on the Four Last Things[525] — especially as we fall asleep.
- Confessing our sins regularly in the Sacrament of Penance in a heartfelt and open manner after a thorough and prayerful examination of conscience.
- Clearing worldly clutter (that breeds attachment) from our homes, cars, daily routines, etc., and instead living frugally and simply.
- Praying each day with our families at home (especially the Rosary) to help ensure these relationships are grounded in God and lead us toward God, instead of causing inordinate attachment to creatures.
- Remaining silent in the midst of discord even when another contradicts us although we are right.
- Taking measures to not be noticed or thanked for good deeds and pious practices.
- *Trying to ensure we enjoy prayer* more than anything else we do: going on Rosary walks in a beautiful place in God's creation; taking time to say our prayers slowly enough to relish them; seeking out Masses that are said

reverently; having always at hand a favorite holy hymn, Scripture passage, Psalm, etc., to recite when we find ourselves slothful; and other such measures.[526]

Holy Indifference to Circumstances

Also (and without succumbing to a form of Providentialism that amounts to neglect of duties and commitments), we should strive eagerly to develop a preferential option for both the opinions and partialities of those around us, and for the direction given by the circumstances we find ourselves in — over and above the plans we may have made — to guide our days.

This "Holy Indifference to Circumstances" can be a great means to renounce the self-will and open ourselves up to the Divine Will. To this end, ponder specific ways you can make yourself more docile to the workings of the Holy Spirit through the people and circumstances around you. Perhaps you simply need to add some serenity to your days. Constantly being in a rush is one of the most effective ways of making this docility impossible. There is no time to relish the moment, no time to respond to the needs of those you pass, no time to evangelize, and no time to pray carefully, if you are rushing. Try leaving for things earlier and spacing out your events more prudently, and you can watch all the opportunities for grace that Providence has wanted to shower upon your life open up before you; and see things — for which you used to have to strive with such difficulty to achieve — happen naturally.

17) Desire the Gift

"My daughter, you must know that as soon as the creature truly decides that she wants to live in my Divine Will, and at any cost never to do her own, my Fiat, with an unspeakable love, forms the seed of Its life in the depth of the soul."[527]

"…**one who possesses My Will possesses everything** as Gifts and Property that My Divine Volition brings with Itself."[528]

- *Jesus to Luisa*

To receive the Gift of Living in the Divine Will, we must fan the flames of our desire for it into a

---

[524] Whatever teachings are contained in Encyclicals, Apostolic Exhortations, Council Documents, etc. are necessarily Magisterial; even if not every statement in them qualifies as an infallible proclamation on Faith or Morals.

[525] Death, Judgment, Hell, Heaven

[526] Just do not let this become an insistence on *always* enjoying yourself with prayer. We must remain faithful to our prayer and other spiritual commitments and regimens whether or not we're in the mood on any given day. We should also do works of mercy that are in no way enjoyable in and of

themselves; for example, praying outside a Planned Parenthood despite being heckled for it, or visiting those in nursing homes despite overwhelmingly bad odors. It is right and just to enjoy that which is objectively good; the danger only lies in being attached to the sensation of enjoyment, and doing things only because they feel good at the moment.

[527] October 27, 1935.

[528] April 28, 1934

roaring fire. This will naturally happen if we understand that we really can receive it—that receiving it is no way unrealistic—and if we understand just how glorious it is. Therefore, while you preserve the quote above clearly before your mind's eye, serving as a reminder of just how closely within reach this Gift is, proceed to read the promises contained in the next section. These are promises which come with the Gift of Living in the Divine Will.

> Now, you must know that **the first indispensable thing in order to enter into my Fiat is wanting and yearning with all firmness to live in It**… The second thing is to take the first step … See then, how easy it is, but it is necessary to want it… I hold nothing back when it comes to making the creature live in my Will. [529]

In Its Granting of All your Wishes

What do you want? Assuming that the worldly have not made it thus far in their reading—and that those who read these words recognize that sin ought not be desired—**everything you want is contained in the Gift of God's Will.**

Perfect Happiness

Above all, we desire happiness. There is no shame in this. We are not capable of desiring anything else as an *ultimate* end but our beatitude; such desire is human nature in its integral sense, not in its fallen sense. Even the ancient philosophers—Aristotle above all—were capable of proving this.[530]

Perfect Happiness is in the Gift. Jesus tells Luisa:

> …in the Divine Will one can have not even the memory of evil, otherwise the happiness would no longer be full; and in the other current the abyss of the human will, which casts the soul into all miseries, and brings her almost into the arms of the devil, that he may tyrannize her as he pleases. …

> …as the soul enters into my Volition, with Its empire It says to her: 'Forget everything, even the home of your mother earth—here one lives of Heaven, nor is there any room for miseries and for unhappinesses. My light destroys everything, and it transforms evils into good.'[531]

> Even more, my own Divine Will, as It sees that she wants to live in It, caresses her, puts her in feast,

and helps her to suppress the outlets; It closes the doors to her evils, because We neither want, nor do We love for the creature to be unhappy—it dishonors Us and forms her sorrow and Ours. Therefore, We want to see her happy—and of Our own happiness. Oh! how painful it is for Our Paternal Heart to possess immense riches, infinite joys, and to see Our children in Our own House—that is, in Our own Will—poor, starving and unhappy."[532]

And do you know what it means to possess these knowledges on my Will? It is as if one possessed a coin which has the virtue of making arise as many coins as one wants; and if one possesses a springing good, poverty is over. In the same way, these knowledges of mine possess light, sanctity, strength, beauty and riches, which arise continuously. So, those who will possess them will have the source of light, of sanctity; therefore, darkness, weaknesses, the ugliness of sin, poverty in divine goods, will end for them. All evils will end, and they will possess the source of Sanctity.[533]

But is this happiness perhaps destroyed when the great crises come upon us? Certainly not. Jesus tells Luisa, regarding His own happiness and that of His mother:

> Just as the nature of the sun is to give light, and that of water to quench one's thirst, that of fire to warm and to turn everything into fire—and if they did not do so, they would lose their nature—**so it is the nature of my Will to make happiness, joy and Paradise arise, wherever It reigns. Will of God and unhappiness does not exist, nor can exist;** or, Its complete fullness does not exist, and this is why the rivulets of the human will form bitternesses for the poor creature. For Us, because the human will had no access into Us, happiness was always at its peak, the seas of joys were inseparable from Us. Even when I was on the Cross, and my Mama was crucified at my divine feet, perfect happiness never disassociated from Us; and if this could happen, I would have had to go out of the Divine Will, disassociate Myself from the divine nature, and act only with the human will and nature. Therefore, our pains were all voluntary, chosen by our very selves as the office which We came to fulfill—they were not fruits of the human nature, of fragility, or of the imposition of a degraded nature. [534]

---

[529] May 6, 1938.
[530] Cf. Nicomachean Ethics Book I.
[531] May 7, 1933.

[532] September 21, 1931.
[533] October 19, 1926.
[534] January 30, 1927.

More Power than a Saint in Heaven

Do you want to remain a weakling for the rest of your life, or do you want to rise up and accept from God the spiritual power He has destined for you? In the Gift is that power. Jesus tells Luisa:

> My delighting and Beatifying Will that is in Heaven, and My Conquering Will that is on earth, plunge together and flood the Celestial Regions with the New Joys that My Conquering Divine Will possesses. In fact, you must know that the Joys of My Conquering Will are quite distinct and different from those of My Delighting Will. The Conquering Joys are not in the power of the Blessed, but in the power of the creature, who must send Them from the earth, and They are formed in the middle of the stake of pain and of love, and over the annihilation of her own volition. On the other hand, the Delighting Joys are in their power, and are fruits and effects of the Celestial Dwelling in which they find themselves.
>
> There is great difference between the Joys of My Conquering Will and those of My Delighting Will. I can say that My Conquering Joys do not exist in Heaven, but only on earth, and-O! how beautiful it is to see the creature who, for as many times as she does her acts in My Volition, so many times makes herself the conqueror of It, and makes It set out for Heaven, for Purgatory, into the midst of terrestrial creatures-wherever she wants. More so since, My Will being everywhere and in every place, It has to do nothing other than Bilocate Itself to give the Fruit, the Joys of the New Conquest that the creature has made of It. My daughter, there is no scene more moving, more delightful, more useful, than to see the littleness of the creature come into Our Divine Will, do her little acts and make her sweet conquest of an Immense, Holy, Powerful, Eternal Will that encloses everything, can do anything and possesses everything. [535]

In a letter, Luisa wrote:

> To love in the Divine Will astonishes Heaven and earth; the very Saints yearn to have within their hearts this conquering Love of one who lives in exile.

Do you want infinite strength? So much strength, in fact, that no pain and no burden can trouble you in the least?

> My daughter, the creature without my Will is like a child who has no strength to be able to sustain a weight, or to do works so useful as to allow him to support, himself, his little existence. And if one wanted to force him to lift a heavy object or to sustain a work, the child, seeing himself impotent and without strength, maybe would try, but in seeing that he cannot even move that object, nor sustain that work, the poor little one would burst into tears and would do nothing about it; and in order to put him in feast it would be enough to give him a candy. On the other hand, one who possesses my Divine Will has the strength of an adult man—or rather, the divine strength; and if he were told to lift the heavy object, without becoming troubled, he takes it as if it were nothing; while the poor little one would remain crushed under it. If one wants him to sustain a work, he will put himself in feast because of the gain and the profit he will be given; and if one wanted to give him a candy, he would despise it and would say: 'Give me the just profit for my work, for I must live from it.' See then, one who has my Divine Will has sufficient strength for anything; so, everything is easy for her; even suffering, as she feels strong, she looks at it as a new gain. Why are many unable to bear anything, and it seems that a child's weakness follows them? It is the strength of my Divine Will that is missing—this is the cause of all evils. Therefore, be attentive, my daughter, never to go out of my Divine Will. [536]

Unmatched Treasures in Heaven

Do you wish to build up as many treasures in Heaven as possible? This, indeed, is the purpose of our earthly pilgrimage: to populate Heaven and to build as many treasures up there, while meriting down here below, as we possibly can. For only in Heaven are there treasures which may be enjoyed for all eternity. These treasures are built up predominantly by living in the Divine Will. Jesus tells Luisa:

> In fact, everything that is done in my Divine Will is sown, germinates, grows in an admirable way on earth, while one is living, but the completion will be formed in Heaven; the final development, the variety of the beauties, the shades, the most beautiful and striking tints, will be given to her in the Celestial Fatherland. So, each act done on earth will be like taking more room in Heaven, one additional right, and an advanced possession of the celestial dwelling. For each additional act that she has done, the creature will bring with herself new beatitudes, new joys, communicated

---

[535]June 29, 1932.

[536]July 30, 1929.

to her by my Will. My Divine Fiat never says 'enough' to the creature; It wants to make her grow in sanctity, in grace, in beauty, unto her last breath of life down here, and therefore It reserves for Itself to give the final brush stroke and completion, as Its full triumph, in the celestial regions… in Heaven nothing begins, but everything begins on earth—and Heaven completes.[537]

Jesus goes even further, telling Luisa that He will even "owe us" through our acts in His Will inasmuch as we must wait for the fulfillment of what we ask (as, for example, we must wait in imploring Him for the Coming of the Kingdom—which He is bound to give us if we ask it of Him in His Will—and yet will not be given immediately):

But when I have you wait for some time and then I come, I become your debtor—and do you think it is trivial that a God gives you the occasion to make Him your debtor?"… In addition to the 'spontaneous gifts' that I give to souls, there are the 'gifts of bond'. To the souls of the 'spontaneous gifts', I may give or may not—it is my choice, because no bond binds Me; but with the souls of the 'gifts of bond', as in your case, I am bound and forced to give them what they want, and to grant them my gifts. Imagine a gentleman and two persons; one of these two persons keeps his money in the hands of the gentleman, while the other does not. That gentleman may give to both one and the other; but which one is more sure to obtain in a circumstance of need—the one who has money in the hands of the gentleman, or the one who does not? Certainly the one who has the money will have all the good dispositions, the courage, the confidence to go and ask for what is deposited in the hands of that gentleman. And if he sees him hesitant in giving, he will say to him, frankly: 'You better give it to me, and quickly, because indeed I am not asking you for what is yours, but for what is mine.' On the other hand, if the other one goes, who has nothing deposited in the hands of that gentleman, he will go timidly, without confidence, and it will be up to the gentleman, whether he wants to give him some help or not. This is the difference that passes between when I am the debtor, and when I am not. If you could understand what immense goods are produced by having a credit with Me!"…I desire to be the debtor more than to have you as my debtor. In fact, these debts which I make with you, while being debts for Me, will be

pledges and treasures which I will keep in my Heart for eternity, and which will give you the right to be loved by Me more than others. This will be one more joy and glory for Me, and you will be repaid for even a breath, a minute, a desire, a heartbeat; and the more pressing and greedy you will be in demanding, the more pleasure you will give Me, and the more I will give you. [538]

It should go without saying that Jesus is not encouraging the vice of greed—but rather, Jesus is speaking here in the same way He was during His teaching in the Gospel itself, wherein He admonishes us to be like the widow who incessantly pesters the judge for a just judgment. Jesus continues:

Now, by living in my Will and by making It her own, the soul comes to take part in all the joys and goods that my Will contains, and she becomes the owner of them. And even though while being on earth she does not feel all those joys and goods, by keeping them in deposit within her will by virtue of my Will done on earth, when she dies and finds herself up there in Heaven, she will feel all those joys and goods which my Will delivered in Heaven while she was living on earth. Nothing will be taken away from her; on the contrary, it will be multiplied. In fact, if the saints enjoy my Will in Heaven because they live in It, it is always enjoying that they live in glory; while the soul who lives in my Will on earth, lives suffering, and it is not appropriate for her to have that joy and those goods which are reserved for her in Heaven, with greater abundance, because of the works she has done and her living in my Divine Will. So, how many immense riches does one who live in my Will on earth not take in Heaven?[539]

Nothing is lost in the Divine Will; even a single thought is sealed with "indelible characters," and will be the bearer of untold joys in Heaven:

…each thought, word, pain suffered, everything, remains written and Sealed with Indelible characters. Perhaps the memory does not keep track of everything, it has forgotten many things, but the will hides everything and loses nothing such that it is the depositary of all of her acts. Therefore the Divine Volition is Depositary and Bearer of everything and everyone; the human volition is individual depositary and bearer of itself.

What Eternal Triumph it will be, what Honor and

---

[537] June 8, 1931.
[538] January 22, 1909.

[539] September 11, 1924.

Glory, for the one who has thought and operated in a holy way. And what confusion for the one who has deposited in the human volition sins, passions, unworthy works, and will render himself bearer of his own evils! And if the evils are very grave, he will be pasture of the infernal flames, and if less grave, he will be pasture of the purging flames, such that they will purify that soiled human will by way of fire and of pains, but it will not be able to restore to him the good, the holy works that he has not done. Therefore be attentive because everything is numbered and written. You do not lose, neither you, nor Us, anything; even one thought, one word will have its Perennial Life, and they will be as faithful and inseparable friends of the creature. Therefore it is necessary that you form holy and good friends, so that they can give you Peace, Happiness and Perennial Glory.[540]

Jesus tells Luisa that every single act begun down here on earth in the Divine Will may indeed have a beginning; but it will have no end, because in Heaven it will be given its final brush stroke of completion.

Good daughter, the great good of living of a Divine Volition is amazing and almost incomprehensible for the human creature. You must know that everything good, holy, that is done in my Divine Will is nothing other than seeds that germinate in the field of the soul, placing as though many seeds of divine light, which set a beginning that will have no end. In fact, everything that is done in my Divine Will is sown, germinates, grows in an admirable way on earth, while one is living, but the completion will be formed in Heaven; the final development, the variety of the beauties, the shades, the most beautiful and striking tints, will be given to her in the Celestial Fatherland. So, each act done on earth will be like taking more room in Heaven, one additional right, and an advanced possession of the celestial dwelling. For each additional act that she has done, the creature will bring with herself new beatitudes, new joys, communicated to her by my Will. My Divine Fiat never says 'enough' to the creature; It wants to make her grow in sanctity, in grace, in beauty, unto her last breath of life down here, and therefore It reserves for Itself to give the final brush stroke and completion, as Its full triumph, in the celestial regions…[541]

But alas! for those who do not live in Our Will, how many of Our acts broken, without fulfillment; how many of Our Divine Lives only conceived or, at most, born without growing. They break the continuation of Our work and bind Our arms, unable to go forward; they put Us in the impotence of a master who has his land, and is prevented by his ungrateful servants from doing the work that is needed in his land, from sowing it, from planting the plants that he wants. Poor master, keeping the land sterile, without the fruit that he could receive, because of his iniquitous servants. Our land is the creatures, and the ungrateful servant is the human will, which, opposing Our own, puts Us in the impotence of forming Our Divine Life in them. Now, you must know that in Heaven one does not enter if he does not possess Our Divine Life, either conceived at least, or born; and for as much growth as each Blessed has formed of Our Life within himself, such will be his glory, his beatitude. Now, what will be the difference between one in whom It was only conceived, born or grown in small proportion, and one who has let Us form fulfilled Life? The difference will be so great as to be incomprehensible to the human creature. The first will be like the people of the Celestial Kingdom, while Our facsimiles will be princes, ministers, the noble court, the royal army of the great King. Therefore, one who does my Divine Will and lives in It can say: 'I do everything, and I belong, even from this earth, to the Family of my Celestial Father'.[542]

Although it should be love which motivates us, it would be foolish to ignore the fact that there is also a reward to be had. In fact, Jesus promises Luisa that He "keeps track of" and "rewards" everything—even the smallest act:

My daughter, what the soul cannot always do with her immediate acts in Me, she can make up for with the attitude of her good will. And I will be so pleased with it as to make Myself the vigilant sentry of each thought, of each word, of each heartbeat, etc.; and I will place them inside and outside of Me as my cortege, looking at them with such love, as the fruit of the good will of the creature. When the soul, then, fusing herself in Me, does her immediate acts with Me, then I feel so drawn toward her that I do what she does together with her, and I transmute the operating of the creature into divine. **I take everything into account, and I reward everything**, even the

---

[540] March 19, 1933.
[541] June 8, 1931.
[542] October 12, 1931.

smallest things; and even just one good act of the will does not remain defrauded in the creature.[543]

Assurance of Salvation

Do you wish to have your eternal salvation sealed? Live in the Divine Will. Jesus tells Luisa:

No, one who had possessed the Kingdom of my Will, even for a short time, could not remain without Redemption. One who possesses this Kingdom enters into such bonds and rights with God, that God Himself feels with him the strength of His own chains that bind Him, and He cannot get rid of him.[544]

Furthermore, the acts that you accomplish while living in the Divine Will are themselves divinized, are invincible, and are permanent anchors between your soul and its Heavenly homeland. Jesus says:

My daughter, you must know that the acts done in my Divine Will are everlasting and inseparable from God, and they leave the continuous memory that the soul had the good of operating together with a Divine Will, and that God had the creature with Himself to let her operate with His own Divine Will. This happy, operative and holy memory makes us always keep our eyes over each other—God and the soul; in such a way that we remain unforgettable—one to the other; so much so, that if the creature had the misfortune of going out of Our Will, she will go wandering, she will wander far, but will feel the eye of her God over her, calling her sweetly, and her own eye toward the One who is watching her continuously. And even if she goes wandering, she feels the irresistible need, the strong chains that pull her into the arms of her Creator.

This happened to Adam, because the beginning of his life was lived in my Divine Will. Even though he sinned, was cast out of Eden, went wandering for all his life—yet, was he perhaps lost? Ah no! because he felt over himself the power of Our Will in which he had operated; he felt Our eye watching him and drawing his eye to watch Us, as well as the dear memory that the first fruits of his acts had had life in Our Will. You cannot comprehend all the good and what it means to operate in Our Will. By operating in It, the soul acquires as many pledges of infinite value for as many acts as she does in Our Fiat; and these pledges remain in God Himself, because the creature does not have the capacity or the place in which to keep them, so great is the value they

contain. And can you ever think that while We have these pledges of infinite value of the creature, We would permit that she to whom these pledges so precious belong, be lost? Ah no! no! ... Therefore, do not fear, the acts done in Our Will are eternal bonds, chains not subject to breaking. And suppose you went out of Our Divine Will—which will not be: you can go out, but your acts remain, nor can they go out, because they were done in Our house, and the creature has her rights for as long as she remains in Our house—that is, in Our Will. As soon as she goes out of It, she loses her rights; however, these acts will have such power as to call back the one who was their possessor. Therefore, do not want to trouble the peace of your heart; abandon yourself in Me, and do not fear.[545]

Deliverance from Aridity, Temptation, Restlessness, and the Like

The usual dark nights of the soul that are often written of in various treatises of spiritual theology may indeed transpire in the soul of one journeying to live in the Divine Will. But these states are temporary in this conquest. See the entirety of the entry in Luisa's writings from July 19th, 1907:

Having spoken to someone about the Will of God, it had slipped from my mouth that if one is in the Will of God and feels aridity, one would still be at peace. Now, as I was in my usual state, blessed Jesus corrected me, telling me: "My daughter, be very careful when you speak about my Will, because my Will is so happy that It forms Our very beatitude, while the human will is so unhappy, that if it could enter Ours, it would destroy Our happiness and would wage war against Us. Therefore, neither aridities, nor temptations, nor defects, nor restlessness, nor coldness enter my Will, because my Will is light and contains all possible tastes. The human will is nothing but a little drop of darkness, all full of disgusts. So, if the soul is already inside my Will, before she enters—at the contact with my Will, Its light dissolved the little drop of darkness in order to be able to have it within Itself; Its heat dissolved coldness and aridities; Its divine tastes removed the disgusts, and my happiness freed her from all unhappinesses."

Deliverance from Any Purgatory

Do you want deliverance from Purgatory? In case you do not, I present a quote on the same from

---

[543]March 28, 1917.
[544]October 2, 1927.

[545]April 16, 1931.

Luisa's writings, and then also a teaching from Jesus to Luisa.

> [Luisa writes:] He transported me outside of myself, close to a deep place, full of liquid fire, and dark—the mere sight of it struck horror and fright. Jesus said to me: "Here is Purgatory, and many souls are crammed in this fire. You will go to this place to suffer in order to free the souls I choose, and you will do this for love of Me." ... As I arrived down there ... who can describe the pains that those souls suffered? They are certainly unutterable for people clothed with human flesh.[546]

I hope that now you have decided that you do not want to go to Purgatory. Yes, deliverance from that is within the Gift as well; one who dies after even only a single act in God's Will need not fear Purgatory. In His teaching, Jesus tells Luisa:

> ... the first thing that my Will does is to get Purgatory out of the way, making the creature go through It in advance, so as to be more free to let her live in It and to form Its life as It best pleases. **So, if the creature dies after an act, determined and wanted, of wanting to live in my Volition, she will take flight toward Heaven**; even more, my Will Itself will carry her in Its arms of light as Its triumph, as a birth from Itself, and as Its dear child. And if it were not so, one could not say: 'Your Will be done on earth as It is in Heaven.' It would be a way of speaking, not a reality. In Heaven, because my Will reigns in It, there can be neither sins nor Purgatory; so on earth, if It reigns in the soul, there can be neither sin nor fear of Purgatory. My Will knows how to rid Itself of everything, because It wants to be alone in Its place, ruling and dominating.[547]

Transformation of Your Past

Do you want your entire past to be transformed? Objective acts of the past cannot change—but their relation to eternity can change, and Jesus wishes to give even this unfathomable privilege to the children of His Will. He tells Luisa:

> Therefore, listen to the Greatest Excess of the Love of My Volition. As the creature decides with immutable firmness to want to Live of My Will, letting It Reign and Dominate in her, Our Infinite Goodness is so much, Our Love that does not know how to resist a true decision of the creature—more so because It does not want to see acts

dissimilar from Ours in her-listen to what It does. **It covers everything that she has done up to then with My Will. It molds them, It Transforms them into Its Light in a way that everyone sees, with the Prodigy of Its Transforming Love, that everything is Its Will in the creature.** And with Love all Divine, It continues to form Its Life and Its Acts in the creature. Is this not an Excessive and Amazing Love of My Volition? And together with this, of letting everyone decide, even the most ungrateful, of letting My Will Live in them, knowing that It wants to set everything aside, and cover and supply for what is lacking of My Will in them? This also absolutely says that Our Will wants to Reign in the midst of creatures, that It does not want to pay attention to anything, nor to what is lacking in them, wanting to give to them not as pay that It goes finding out if it is merited or not, but as Gratuitous Gift of Our Great Liberality, and as Completion of Our own Will. And the Completing of Our Will, is everything for Us.[548]

***

I could easily continue this section for many more pages; but that would be unnecessary. Just dive into Luisa's writings and you will not leave them without a burning desire in your heart for the Gift of Living in the Divine Will. From our renunciation, and this desire, we are completely prepared to receive the Gift. But before turning to how we ought to—finally—ask for the Gift, the Blessed Sacrament deserves a section of Its own in fostering our ardent desire to receive this incredible Gift.

In the Eucharist

We must spare no expense to ensure that the Eucharist is (and not only in theory, but also in practice) truly the source and summit of our lives as Christians, as both the Catechism and the Second Vatican Council teach it is *in fact*. This means attending Mass as often as possible (preferably every day—if this can be done without neglecting the duties of your state in life) and taking each Mass as seriously as if it were the last Mass ever to be said. It means approaching Mass not as an errand, not as a mere stop on the itinerary, but rather, it means approaching each Mass with a true sense of pilgrimage; coming early to prepare, and staying late to give thanks. It means focusing every morsel of our attention upon it and fighting off mercilessly any and all distractions in our minds, whether they

---

[546]November 28, 1899.
[547]October 27, 1935.

[548]November 3, 1936.

be from other things or people in the Church, or merely from the drifting of our thoughts.

We should spend much time with Him in the Eucharist; whether in the Tabernacle, or exposed in the Monstrance—to whichever we have access. Today more than ever there is a plethora of worldly needs and distractions ever demanding our immediate attention. Jesus has the answer to that: *"But seek first his kingdom and his righteousness, and all these things shall be yours as well."*[549]

We must receive Jesus well. He tells Luisa:

> In order to cling more tightly to Me, to the point of dissolving your being in Mine, just as I transfuse Mine into yours, you must take what is Mine in everything, and in everything leave what is yours; in such a way that if you always think of things which are holy and regard only what is good, and the honor and glory of God, you leave your mind and take the divine … If the soul reaches the point of no longer recognizing herself, but the Divine Being within her, these are the fruits of good Communions, and this is the divine purpose in wanting to communicate Himself to souls. But, how frustrated my love remains, and how few are the fruits that souls gather from this Sacrament, to the point that the majority of them remains indifferent, and even nauseated by this divine food.[550]

Let us turn to St. Faustina—whose full religious name was Maria Faustina Kowalska of the Blessed Sacrament—and learn from her sublime teachings on the Eucharist. In these teachings we see both an overlap with Luisa's on the Gift of Living in the Divine Will, and an encouragement to inflame our desire for the same.

St. Faustina's Revelations

St. Faustina often referred to the Blessed Sacrament as a "living host," until one day when her desire for union with Christ became so great, she wrote in her diary,

> When I had received Jesus in Holy Communion, my heart cried out with all its might, 'Jesus, transform me into another host! I want to be a living host for You. You are a great and all-powerful Lord; You can grant me this favor.'

As soon as she made this request, He responded that she was indeed, at that moment, a living host.[551]

In other words, she had received the Gift of Living in the Divine Will. Here then is the vital disposition in receiving the Gift: a burning desire for the greatest possible union with God imbued with a firm trust that—in His omnipotence and mercy—He can and will grant it. Faustina displayed this perfectly, and therefore He readily gave her that Gift, despite her not having specific knowledge of it through Luisa's writings. But specific knowledge of this Gift's precise and complete explication (which is only found in Luisa's revelations) is extraordinarily helpful nevertheless, and can partially make up for (though *never* dispense from the wholehearted pursuit of) what an ordinary soul may lack in the heroic virtue which Faustina possessed. **In either case, the grace flows from the Eucharist, and this is how we, too, should enkindle our desire for the Gift**.

In another excerpt from Faustina's diary, which emphasizes the beauty of the desire for the Gift of Living in the Divine Will, we see more evidence of the primacy of the Eucharist:

> Most sweet Jesus, set on fire my love for You and transform me into Yourself. Divinize me that my deeds may be pleasing to You. May this be accomplished by the power of the Holy Communion which I receive daily. Oh, how greatly I desire to be wholly transformed into You, O Lord![552]

As stated in Vatican II, reiterated by the Catechism, and emphasized by countless great men and women of the Faith, the Eucharist is the Source and Summit of the life of a Christian. In a real way, the Eucharist is the Divine Will—for the Divine Will is God, and the Eucharist is God. In enkindling our desire for the Gift, preparing ourselves to receive the Gift, and growing in the Gift of Living in the Divine Will, there is no alternative to Eucharistic devotion. Luisa's entire life demonstrated this, and St. Faustina recognized it, as evidenced by this excerpt from her diary. Lengthy Eucharistic adoration and frequent Communion, approached with unbounded reverence, fervency, trust, and love, will be the sure means of calling down the

---

[549] Matthew 6:33
[550] January 8, 1909.
[551] St. Faustina, *Divine Mercy in My Soul*, Paragraph 1826.

[552] Ibid., 1289.

Divine Will upon your soul.[553] Pope St. John Paul II himself agreed, saying:

> This **sublime and demanding reality [following God's will]** can only be grasped and lived in a spirit of constant prayer. This is the secret, if we are to enter into and **dwell in God's will.** Thus what are extremely helpful are the initiatives of prayer—especially **Eucharistic adoration**—that young people are spreading in the Diocese of Rome as a result of your work.[554]

Concluding this section with an excerpt from Luisa's writings, we see Jesus telling her, too, of the centrality of the Eucharist:

> And when I find a heart that keeps Me company [in the Blessed Sacrament], I place My Life in communication with her, leaving her the deposit of My Virtues, the fruit of My Sacrifices, the participation of My Life, and I chose her for My Residence, for the hiding place of My Pains, and as a place of My Refuge. **And I feel as though reciprocated for the Sacrifice of My Eucharistic Life, because I find one who breaks My loneliness for Me,** who dries My tears, who gives Me the freedom of letting Me pour out My Love and My Sorrows. **It is they who serve Me as Living Species,** not like the Sacramental Species that gives Me nothing, that only hides Me, the rest I do by Myself, all alone, they do not tell Me a word that breaks My loneliness; they are mute Species.

> On the other hand, in souls who use Me as Living Species, our Life develops together, we beat with one single heartbeat, and if I see her disposed, I communicate to her My Pains and I continue My Passion in her. I can say that from the Sacramental Species, I pass to the Living Species in order to continue My Life on earth, not alone, but together with her. You must know that pains are no longer in My Power, and I go asking for Love from these Living Species of souls, who make up for what is lacking to Me. Therefore, My daughter, when I find a heart who Loves Me and keeps Me company, giving Me the Freedom to do what I want, I arrive at Excesses, and I do not care about anything else, I give everything, so that the poor creature feels drowned by My Love and by My Graces, and then My Sacramental Life does not remain sterile anymore when It descends into hearts, no, It reproduces Me, Bilocating and continuing My Life in her. And these are My Conquerors who administer their life to this poor indigent Man of Sufferings, and they say to Me: 'My Love, you had Your turn at sufferings, and it is ended, now it is my turn, therefore let me make up for You and suffer in Your place.' And O! how Content I am! My Sacramental Life remains at Its place of Honor, because It reproduces other Lives of Itself in creatures. Therefore, I want you always together with Me, so that We Live together, and you take to heart My Life, and I yours.[555]

Here we see clearly, in Jesus own words, that He will proceed from "Sacramental Species" (that is, the Blessed Sacrament, in which His Body, Blood, Soul, and Divinity exist in substance under the accidents of Bread) into "Living Species" (that is, a soul who lives in the Divine Will).

18) Ask for the Gift

The next step is simple. Ask God for the Gift of Living in the Divine Will. Have we perhaps forgotten that God hears each thing we say, every moment of every day? No special strategies are needed to "reach Him." He is right next to you. Ask Him for what you desire. Jesus tells Luisa:

> How many Gifts do We want to give! But because they are not asked for, We retain Them within Ourselves, waiting to give Them when they are asked for. By asking, it is as if commerce were opened between Creator and creature. If one does not ask, the commerce is closed, and Our Celestial Gifts do not descend in order to put themselves in circulation on the face of the earth.[556]

Every day we must explicitly ask God for the Gift of Living in the Divine Will. This request should at least be made upon rising, along with your usual morning prayers. In Luisa's writings, this is referred to as the "Prevenient Act."[557] With this short prayer, we make a morning offering in the Divine Will, where we state our intention to live and act only in His will, and likewise firmly affix

---

[553]Confusions regarding comparisons between the Eucharist and the Gift of Living in the Divine Will are discussed in the "Answers to Objections" chapter.
[554]Address of John Paul II to the youth of Rome preparing for World Youth Day. March 21st, 2002. Paragraph 5. vatican.va

[555]January 18, 1933.
[556] March 20, 1932.
[557] "Prevenient" simply means "coming before."

our purpose on the same. There are many ways to do this, and you may feel free to search online for one that best suits your preferences. Here is one that I like to use:

> Good morning, Blessed Mother, I love you. Come, help me to offer my first act of the day as an act of love in the Divine Will of God.
>
> Most Holy Trinity, setting my will in Yours, I affirm I want only to live and act in Your Will, and I set all of my acts of the day in order in You. O Jesus, through, with, and in the Immaculate Heart of Mary, I consecrate and give my will to You in exchange for Your Divine Will. I truly want Your Divine Will to generate Its Divine Life in me this day—to think in all my thoughts, to speak in all my words, and operate in all my actions for the glory of our Heavenly Father and to fulfill the purpose of Creation. Abandoned in Your arms, my Jesus, I invite all the angels and saints, especially Mary Most Holy, to join in all the Divine Will does in me today, and I am confident that You will not fail to give me the grace to be always faithful and attentive to Your action within me so that my own will dare not interfere with Your freedom to form Your Real Life in me. O my Jesus, I love You with Your own Will and thank You profoundly for the knowledge and Gift of the Divine Will.
>
> Saint Joseph, be my protector, the guardian of my heart, and keep the keys of my will in your hands. Keep my heart jealously, and never give it to me again, that I may be sure of never leaving the Will of God.
>
> My Guardian angel, guard me; defend me; help me in everything so that I may be an instrument to draw all people into the Kingdom of the Divine Will. Amen.

After the "Prevenient act" above come the "present acts" throughout the day. As the "righteous man falls seven times"[558] so we, until we are very advanced in the Divine Will, likely will not succeed at remaining perfectly and continuously anchored in it.[559] Because of this fluctuation, we must reaffirm our desire to enter into the Divine Will continuously throughout the day; and we do this through our "present acts," which are just spontaneous prayers which we should offer up regularly. How exactly this is done is not important; but you can feel free to use pieces of your Prevenient act, or words of your choosing, or any other prayer.

While the Gift is indeed a "new" sanctity, these methods here listed do not constitute new spiritualities. In the New Catholic Encyclopedia, we read:

> Purity of intention is aided by joining it with acts of conformity to God's will. **To say often "Thy will be done" in union with the good intention helps one to act from a more pure love** (ibid. 604). Pope John XXIII granted a plenary indulgence to be gained once each day under the usual conditions by the faithful who in the morning offer to God their labor of the whole day, whether intellectual or manual, using any formula of prayer, and a partial indulgence of 500 days as often as with contrite heart they offer the work at hand, using any formula of prayer [Acta Apostolicae Sedis 53 (1961) 827].[560]

Indeed, something so simple as a repetition of the fundamental petition of the Our Father prayer does, in these days in which God has deigned to give the Gift, constitute a request for the Gift. Let this prayer, then, be your Mantra:

"Jesus, I Trust in You. Thy Will be Done."

In Marian Consecration

Spoken of in the previous section of this book wherein we examined the Gift's foreshadowings, we consider this again now because by totally consecrating ourselves to Mary, we are more or less explicitly asking for the Gift of Living in the Divine Will. Therefore, I heartily recommend that all children of the Divine Will—all followers of Luisa—consecrate themselves to Mary.

Total Consecration as taught by St. Louis de Montfort as well as St. Maximilian Kolbe is an especially powerful means to renounce the self-will and open oneself to the Gift of Living in the Divine Will. For by way of this devotion as given to us by these saints, we give all that we have—not merely physical and temporal, but even all of our intentions and all of our good works—to our Heavenly Mother. She, like her Divine Son, is never outdone in generosity, and she will exchange our

---

558 Proverbs 24:16
559 Bear in mind that nothing in these revelations dispense a soul from the ordinary means of grace for Catholics. Serious sin must always be confessed to a priest, and indeed regular confession is an invaluable means for receiving and growing in the Gift.
560 Prayer (theology of). New Catholic Encyclopedia p. 600.

meager merits with her own perfect merits, and clothe us with her own splendor.

We must remember that the Blessed Virgin Mary is the Mediatrix of All Grace, and that the Gift of Living in the Divine Will is a grace! Therefore, if we desire this gift, we should consecrate ourselves to Mary, from whom we will receive it, and ask her for it. Those well versed in St. Louis' True Devotion will find Living in the Divine Will the logical extension of what is promised therein; for indeed, St. Louis rightly tells us that when we consecrate ourselves to Our Lady, she gives us her own virtues and merits. Now, few have any trouble realizing that her virtues and merits are precisely those described as proceeding *from the Divine Will*, and therefore it follows that we ourselves must also be given the grace of living and acting *in the Divine Will*, if Our Lady is to be fully true to her promise as St. Louis describes it (which she of, course, will be):

> Once this good Mother has received our complete offering ... She clothes us in the clean, new, precious and fragrant garments of [her Son Jesus Christ] ... she is the treasurer and universal dispenser of the merits and virtues of Jesus her Son. She gives and distributes them to whom she pleases, when she pleases, as she pleases, and as much as she pleases ... She imparts new perfume and fresh grace to those garments and adornments by adding to them the garments of her own wardrobe of merits and virtues. ... Thus all her domestics, that is, all her servants and slaves, are clothed with double garments, her own and those of her Son.[561]

In Putting It to Use as a Divine Will Missionary of Mercy

I would like to suggest another way you may ask for the Gift of Living in the Divine Will: as a means to the end of spreading God's grace to others. Consider how readily God dispenses grace to those whom He sees will put it at the service of others. When Jesus healed Peter's mother-in-law, she arose to wait on them.[562] When He "*called to him his twelve disciples and gave them authority*,"[563] He did so immediately before sending them out, and in order to grant their ministry success. When He "*breathed on them*"[564] (and in so doing gave them the Holy Spirit), it was in order to allow them to forgive the sins of others.

This is the approach of the apostolate mentioned previously, the Divine Will Missionaries of Mercy[565]—to take the grace received through the Eucharist at Mass out on to the streets, by way of the Gift of Living in the Divine Will. Before setting out, the following prayer is said after Mass. I believe it is a powerful means of asking God for the Gift.

> Most Holy Trinity, You Who now dwell inside my body in all of Your Divinity, I come before you and say *Fiat Voluntas Tua*. I renounce my self-will, and instead desire to do and live in only Your Will.
>
> I ask You to miraculously preserve the Real Presence of Jesus in the Eucharist within me, so that You may make of me a living Monstrance, that my walk today may be a true Procession through this city's streets. Make of me a living Host, that all who see me truly gaze upon Your face.
>
> Let the Transubstantiation of the Host within me effect the Transconsecration of my very self, that I may receive the Gift of Living in the Divine Will, so that Jesus may walk in my walking, speak in my speaking, pray in my praying, and indeed substitute His Divine and Eternal operations for all of my acts, and through me re-do all of the acts of Creation, past, present, and future—in the Will of God, offering them back to the Father with the seal of my Fiat, which I pray may become an echo of Jesus and Mary's perfect Fiat.
>
> Dear Jesus, let all of my sufferings console Your Sacred Heart, atone for my sins and those of the whole world, and be perfectly united with Yours in Your Passion.
>
> Let all who see me that lack Faith be as Longinus, and acknowledge You are the Son of God. Let all who see me that lack works be as Dismas, and receive the grace of perfect contrition, hope, and trust. Let all who see me that live in sin be as Magdalene, and amend their ways. Let all who see me that suffer from wounds of spirit be healed of them, and in place of any darkness or despair, be filled with peace and joy, as You preached the good news to the poor. Let all who see the image of Your Mercy that I wear venerate it and therefore receive the promise You entrusted to

[561] St. Louis de Montfort. *True Devotion to the Blessed Virgin Mary*. Paragraph 206.
[562] Cf. Matthew 8:15
[563] Matthew 10:1
[564] John 20:22
[565] www.DWMoM.org

Faustina, so they may not perish. Let all who see the weapon of Your Mother that I carry receive grace through her intercession, that she may crush the head of the serpent in their lives.

Do not restrict these graces to only those few who see me, but let them be extended to all the friends and family of these, and continue in this manner until they reach the furthest ends of Earth, Heaven, and Purgatory; past, present, and future.

And if, Dear Lord, You see fit to bless this work with success, to Your Name give all the glory, for You alone are good, and I am an unworthy servant.

As I depart from this Church, do not depart from me, Lord. Let my adoration remain unbroken, fixated upon Your Eucharistic Presence within me. I firmly trust and believe that You can do all of these things, for I ask in the name of the Father, and of the Son, and of the Holy Spirit. Amen.

Whether or not you feel called to be a Divine Will Missionary of Mercy, you can still strive to approach all of your endeavors with this demeanor and this intention, and you can modify the above prayer however you so like, in order to apply it to whatever endeavors you will be engaged in after Mass.

More suggestions can be found on the apostolate's website, but I conclude our treatment here with a final encouragement. Now that you have at least read this Divine Will Missionary of Mercy prayer once, you can from now on—whenever you are walking or driving anywhere; or doing anything at all that will involve many people seeing you— invoke it. That is, you can simply make an *Act of Spiritual Communion* (below, from St. Alphonsus Liguori) if you have not just literally received Communion, and then, before beginning your Rosary, Chaplet, or whatever other prayer you will be saying, simply invoke the petitions in the prayer above by saying **"In the Divine Will, I pray for all of the intentions in the Divine Will Missionary of Mercy prayer applied to this ___drive, walk, errand, etc.___"** and then proceed to recite your ordinary prayers as usual.

My Jesus, I believe that Thou art present in the Blessed Sacrament. I love Thee above all things and I desire Thee in my soul. Since I cannot now receive Thee sacramentally, come at least spiritually into my heart. As though thou wert already there, I embrace Thee and unite myself wholly to Thee; permit not that I should ever be separated from Thee.

In Your Current Spiritual Regimen

While we should take concrete and new measures to live in the Divine Will, we also must not ever neglect how God has hitherto worked in our spiritual lives; for **God's Will is not to supplant and replace the spiritual life we have thus far developed as devout Catholics.**

Keep on doing what you are doing, for God desires this of you. Therefore, a key to asking for the Gift will be learning how to integrate it into your current spiritual regimen. Here are just a few thoughts in that regard:

- Strive vigorously to ensure that your first act of the will each day is made captive for Christ; that is to say, an act in the Divine Will. Do not lament the buzzing of the alarm, and do not immediately engage your mind in the worries the day will bring. Rather, say—out loud or mentally—words to this effect: "*Good morning Jesus and Mary; I love you. Thank you for this new day. Setting my will in Yours, O Lord, I affirm I wish only to Live and Act in the Divine Will.*"

- Before each ordinary prayer of your day (whether it be the Rosary, the Divine Mercy Chaplet, the Divine Office, the Holy Mass, *Lectio Divina*, or whatever else) at least let your intention be known to God that you desire to pray in the Divine Will. For example, your Rosary could begin with "*In the name of the Father, and of the Son, and of the Holy Spirit. Amen. In the Divine Will, I pray: I believe in God…*"

- In the Communion line as you walk up to receive Jesus, offer Him the following prayer: "Lord, remove my self-will and give me Thine in return, that You may receive Yourself in me, and receive perfect and infinite consolation."

- In the minutes after you receive Holy Communion, beseech Jesus in the Eucharist within you to make the Transubstantiation of the Host you consumed effect the Transconsecration of your very self. Meditate upon the substance inside you—the Real Presence of Jesus—transforming you into Himself, with the accidents of bread and wine, which dissolve, being taken over by your own acts made in the Divine Will.

- Wear or carry a crucifix to help you remain continually conscious of and uniting yourself to the Passion of Jesus, remembering especially Jesus' words in *The Hours of the Passion*.

- When you behold the beauty of creation (whether out your window, in a park, at a cemetery, on a walk outside, in the night sky, or even just remotely in media), strive not to merely appreciate it, but to (through your intention) bi-locate your soul within it and impress your Fiat—*your I love you, I adore you, I glorify you, God*—upon it and offer it back to the Father from Whom it came.

- **Do not neglect the devotions God has asked of us through other private revelations. The Rosary, The Brown Scapular, the First Saturdays (and most importantly the at-least-monthly confession this implies) and First Fridays Devotion, the Divine Mercy Chaplet, weekly fasting, the Miraculous Medal, daily prayerful Scripture reading, etc.—all remain vital for our present day. Far from eclipsing these devotions, Luisa's revelations on the Divine Will only increase their importance.**

Ask Again

But what if you leave the Divine Will once in it? Is all then lost for you—have you just succumbed to a fate similar to that of Adam's?

Absolutely not. God never tires of forgiving—we tire of asking for the forgiveness. Similarly, God never tires of giving us His Will again, even if we have left it many times. Jesus tells Luisa:

> My daughter, all the good of the creature is tied to my Divine Will. If she unties herself from It, all her goods are ended. You must know that every single time she does her human will, she gambles away the Divine with all Its goods; hence, she loses all that is beautiful, all that is holy and good. This is an incalculable loss. The poor creature is thrown into the most squalid misery; she loses the rights to all goods, and she is invested by such unhappiness that gives her no peace; and even if it seems that she has something good, it is apparent, and it ends up torturing her completely.

On the other hand, each time she decides with total firmness to do my Divine Will, she gambles away the human will, the miseries, the passions; she loses all evils, the miserable rags, the filthy clothes that the human will had formed for her. What a happy loss! To lose evils and miseries is glory, it is victory, it is honor. But to lose the goods is cowardice and dishonor. **See then: if the creature wants it, she can recover from the great loss of my Will that she suffered by doing her own; more so, since she will have the help of Our Power, of Our Love and of Our Will Itself. By acquiring again the rights to all goods, all will defend her in order for her to recover from the lost game.**[566]

You must never allow discouragement or anxiety to enter into your heart in your quest to live in the Divine Will. As you will see in a forthcoming section, discouragement is always a tactic of the devil who is incessantly striving to make us forget the infinite mercy of our loving Father. In fact, when we begin to falter, Jesus only steps up the graces, and we can always count on Him to so respond to our times of need:

> I do not break the life [of the Divine Will in the soul] because of involuntary indisposition or weakness, but I continue it; and it may be that in those very indispositions there is also my Will, allowing those weaknesses, therefore the will of the creature is already flowing within Mine. Besides, amid everything I look at the agreement made together—the firm decision that was taken—against which there has been no other contrary decision, and in the light of this I continue my commitment of making up for anything she may lack. Even more, I double the graces, I surround her with new love, with new loving stratagems, to render her more attentive; and I kindle in her heart an extreme need to live in my Will. This need serves in a way that, as soon as she feels the weaknesses, she flings herself into the arms of my Will, and begs It to hold her so tight, that she may always live together with It.[567]

19) Do All of Your Acts in the Divine Will

Just as important as asking for the Gift, we should always ask Jesus to do with us, through us, and *in* us whatever we are doing at the moment. This is God's plan with the Gift; not that it be passively enjoyed, but that it be used to become the principle of all our acts—which, previously merely human, now become divinized.

This first serves as a continual examination of conscience throughout the day; for Jesus cannot sin, and therefore whatever you do that is sinful cannot possibly be done in the Divine Will. The "practice

---

[566]September 6, 1937.

[567]September 5, 1938.

of the presence of God" is a great way of understanding this reality. *Doing your acts in the Divine Will* also bears a great resemblance to, and serves as a beautiful development of, the sanctification of the ordinary, as taught in the "Little Way" of St. Thérèse of Lisieux as well as the spirituality of St. Josemaría Escrivá and Opus Dei.

But we should not let our consideration of Jesus acting in us stop at simply asking, *"is this sinful? If so, I better not do it, since Jesus then could not do it in me."* Let this consideration instead permeate even those behaviors which may have been hitherto subtly dismissed as irrelevant to the spiritual life; for truly, *nothing* is irrelevant to the spiritual life. We should apply it to posture, tone, comportment, dress, conversations, recreation, demeanor, attitude—everything. *"Put on the Lord Jesus Christ."*[568] More on this point will be considered in the "Demeanor" section in the virtues chapter of this book.

To develop this way of life, we must consider practical ways of turning the ordinary acts of our day into prayer. Jesus asks us to pray constantly, as St. Paul instructs, in order to live in the Divine Will. Jesus tells Luisa:

> **What I ask of you is a spirit of continuous prayer. The continuous effort of the soul to converse with Me—with its heart or with its mind, with its mouth or with a simple intention—renders it so beautiful in My sight that the notes of its heart harmonize with the notes of My heart**. I feel so drawn to converse with this soul that I manifest to it not only the operation ad extra of My humanity, but I keep manifesting to it something of the operation ad intra, which My divinity accomplished in My humanity.[569]

So, ask yourself: what is your mind usually doing? Is it reciting a worldly song that is stuck in your head, strategizing about finances, or pondering the To-Do list? Is it indulging in the anticipation of some upcoming physical enjoyment (e.g. the next meal, the next social gathering, getting home from work, going to bed); or is plotting out the next career move, worrying about loved ones, etc.?

We must say *"no"* to such thoughts constantly invading our minds and hearts. Instead of letting these thoughts invade our minds we must, rather, implement practical ways of ensuring that we are constantly in a state of recollection, peace, and prayer. Keeping good company is a first and obvious step. Turning off the worldly vanity is essential as well. In all things, say *"Jesus, I trust in You. Thy Will be Done."* Whenever you find yourself with a free moment, start praying a Rosary or Divine Mercy Chaplet. Constantly ponder (with great joy!) the Truths of our Faith as you slowly recite the Creed, dwelling on and relishing each statement. Try praying the Divine Office—you will find that the Psalms are always on your lips and in your mind throughout the day as a result. Simply converse with God continually, speaking to Him each moment about anything whatsoever. Strive to slip into contemplation and meditation frequently. These are just a few suggestions; you must find your own ways to ensure that you are truly in a state of continual prayer, for it is an essential disposition to receive the Gift of Living in the Divine Will, to grow in the Gift, and to perform all of your acts truly *in* the Divine Will.

With respect to continuous prayer, we must also ensure that we truly give thanks to God in all things. Scripture insists upon this: *"Rejoice always, pray constantly, give thanks in all circumstances; for this is the will of God in Christ Jesus for you."*[570]

First, you can try to do a better job of offering up (perhaps for the salvation of souls and the deliverance of the holy souls in Purgatory) every single suffering, irritation, and dislike you experience throughout the day. Do so without making any excuses or exceptions, and with the gratitude of being given the opportunity to exercise that one ability of ours which, again, the angels envy us for: our potential to suffer for Christ. God loves a cheerful giver. Do a better job of giving thanks to God not only for every good thing that happens to you, but also every bad thing, in so far as it is a means to grow and is part of His permissive, perfect Will. Make these things into such habits that they become second nature, and each night before bed examine your conscience and ask yourself if you have achieved them throughout the preceding day.

---

[568] Romans 13:14
[569] Fr. Joseph Iannuzzi, Doctoral Dissertation 4.1.10
[570] 1 Thessalonians 5:18

***

With the Gift, Jesus is inviting us to have the operation within His very own Self *always* be our *primary* endeavor. He is inviting us to have it *always* be our very *reason* for doing *everything* that we do. Once we are praying continually in all that we do, this even greater dignity can be ours as well.

Jesus tells Luisa that He re-did each of our lives during His thirty years of hidden life on earth; this "re-done" version of our life, in the Divine Will, remains suspended in God, awaiting our entrance into the Divine Will to claim these acts for our own by doing all that we do truly in His Will. Fr. Iannuzzi explains:

> Because Adam's withdrawal from the Divine Will interrupted within his humanity and that of other humans the formation of God's aforesaid kingdom, Jesus assumed a humanity like that of Adam and, within himself, enclosed a kingdom for each creature. This kingdom was made up of all the divine acts that all humans were to have accomplished if Adam had not sinned. These divine acts were formed within Jesus' humanity, whose human will took possession of the Divine Will and vice-versa… For Jesus' divine acts were ordered to the divinization of human nature and to empowering souls to accomplish the same divine acts that he accomplished. Indeed, from the time of man's creation, the divine acts that God had prepared for all souls, and that await their actualization, were already present to the Son of God and their number established.[571]

When we perform these acts in the Divine Will, we form suns that, though small in themselves, nevertheless invest all creation with the light and heat of their splendor; just as the sun, which appears small in relation to the sky it inhabits, gives life to all the earth.

These suns are formed by Jesus truly doing in us whatever "we" are doing. Therefore, as many times as you can remember throughout the day, in whatever you find yourself doing, simply ask Jesus to do it in, with, and through you, to accomplish in you what He accomplished in the thirty years of His hidden life in Nazareth. Ask yourself, *"would Jesus do what I am doing, in the manner I am doing it?"* If not—change what you are doing! Perhaps at this moment you can simply choose one specific activity you frequently do: whether changing diapers, hammering in nails, scanning items at a cash register, doing the dishes, or whatever else, and commit to do it from now on *in the Divine Will*. This can be done by saying or thinking, before said activity, *"Jesus wishes to do ____, therefore we will do ____ together,"* and proceeding with deliberateness and a spirit of prayer, recollection, and consciousness of God's presence.[572] The more acts you do in the Divine Will, the deeper into It you enter and the more you restore creation.

Jesus explains to Luisa:

> My daughter, in order to forget herself, the soul should make it in such a way that everything she does, and which is necessary to her, she does as if I Myself wanted to do it in her. If she prays, she should say: 'It is Jesus who wants to pray'; and I pray together with her. If she has to work: 'It is Jesus who wants to work'. 'It is Jesus who wants to walk; it is Jesus who wants to take food, who wants to sleep, who wants to get up, who wants to enjoy Himself … ', and so with all the other things of life. Only in this way can the soul forget herself, because she will do everything, not only because I want it, but because I Myself want to do it—it is necessary precisely to Me."
>
> Now, one day I was working and I thought to myself: 'How can it be that, while I am working, it is Jesus who works in me and He Himself wants to do this work?' And Jesus: "I Myself—and my fingers, which are in yours, are working. My daughter, when I was on earth, did my hands not lower themselves to work the wood, to hammer the nails, and to help my foster father Joseph? While I was doing that, with those very hands, with those fingers, I created souls and called other souls back to the next life; I divinized all human actions; I sanctified them, giving a divine merit to each one of them. In the movements of my fingers I called in sequence all the movements of your fingers and those of others; and if I saw that they were doing them for Me, or because I wanted to do them within them, I continued my life of Nazareth in them, and I felt as though cheered by them for the sacrifices and the humiliations of my hidden life, giving them the merit of my very life.
>
> Daughter, the hidden life that I conducted in Nazareth is not taken into consideration by men,

---

[571] Fr. Joseph Iannuzzi, Doctoral Dissertation 3.1, 3.1.1.1

[572] And hopefully this will serve as a beginning to doing each one of your acts in the Divine Will, so that all you do, even unconsciously, might give God infinite glory. *"O Most Holy Trinity! As many times as I breathe, as many times as my heart beats, as many times as my blood pulsates through my body, so many thousand times do I want to glorify Your mercy."* – St. Faustina's Diary, paragraph 163.

when in fact, after my Passion, I could not have done a greater good for them. By lowering Myself to all those acts, little and lowly—those acts which men do in their daily lives, such as eating, sleeping, drinking, working, starting the fire, sweeping, etc.—all acts which no one can do without—I made a divine little coin of incalculable value flow in their hands. So, if my Passion redeemed them, my hidden life provided each human action, even the most insignificant one, with divine merit and with infinite value.[573]

As glorious as this reality is of Jesus operating within your acts—and, perhaps, as abstract as it might sound to some—the Gift of Living in the Divine Will does make it possible. As we have discussed, the Gift consists in the Will of God becoming the life principle of your soul just as your soul even now is the life principle of your body.

When, for example, a man is building a chair and fastening the bolts together, he could honestly say "my hands did that," but it would be better for him to say, "*I* did that." For when multiple powers concur in a single act, the greater receives more recognition. While the soul of man is designed to enliven the flesh and command its acts, the Will of God can do much more: it can become the life of the acts of another free will that is distinct from Itself. **Although a great mystery, it becomes a reality through the Gift, so that just as the soul truly does what the body it gives life to does, the Divine Will does what the soul living in it does.**

Recall that our model for doing our acts in the Divine Will is none other than Jesus Himself. How often do we pause to consider that the Gospel which speaks so beautifully of Our Lord only really details the final 3 years of his 33-year life on earth? Not often enough! And yet, He could have easily simply come to earth miraculously as a fully grown man and achieved all He needed to very quickly. But instead, He spent decades doing what we all must do—*working*. And this was not in vain (for what a blasphemy it would be to attribute vanity to God Incarnate!). Jesus reveals to Luisa:

> If I walked, I had the virtue of being able to go from one city to another without making use of My steps, but I wanted to walk in order to place My Love in every step so that in every step it would run… if I worked with St. Joseph in order to procure the necessities of life, it was Love that

ran. They were Conquests and Triumphs that I made, because one Fiat was enough for Me to have everything at My Disposal. And making use of My Hands for a little profit, the Heavens were amazed; the Angels remained enraptured and mute in seeing Me abase Myself to the humblest actions of life. But My Love had its outlet, it filled, overflowed, in My Acts, and I was always the Divine Conqueror and Triumpher… Taking food was not necessary for Me, but I took it in order to make Love run more and to make New Conquests and Triumphs. In fact I gave course to the most humble and base things of life that were not necessary for Me, but I did in order to form as many distinct ways in order to let My Love run, and to form New Conquests and Triumphs over My Humanity in order to make a Gift of them to those I Loved so much…[574]

In all these acts, we should have the intention of fusing ourselves to God's Will. As we have seen, Jesus is the one Who completed these acts in the Divine Will for us during His own earthly life, and in fusing ourselves with His Will, we make possible claiming these acts as our own. Jesus tells Luisa:

> My daughter, fusing yourself in my Will is the most solemn, the greatest, the most important act of your whole life. To fuse yourself in my Will is to enter the sphere of eternity, to embrace It, to kiss It, and to receive the deposit of the goods which the Eternal Will contains.[575]

Various Helps

There are many more helps for achieving this. I will give just a few more suggestions in list form:

- **Try to be more deliberate (less sloppy) even in your physical comportment.** Think, for example, about the last time you looked up at the Communion line in front of you. Most people will be waddling back and forth like ducks. It is, of course, not that such a method of walking is required (human anatomy is not of a "waddling" sort); it's simply that this is what we fall into in sloppiness if we do not think about what we are doing. Fidgeting, slouching in chairs or sitting in absurd postures, incessant shaking of the leg, dragging feet or stomping like elephants whenever walking, clumsiness, speaking sloppily without any concern for enunciation, and various nervous ticks can at

---

[573] August 14, 1912
[574] April 16, 1933.

[575] January 4, 1925.

times also be symptoms of a comportment which lacks deliberateness. (Of course, deliberateness can become excessive, at which point it is merely a self-defeating distraction from the very thing it should be oriented toward, so clearly a happy medium of naturalness is needed here.)

- If you are easily startled, try to work on that. You aren't a wild animal living in the jungle, therefore there is no need for you to be so prone to severely reacting to external stimuli such as sudden noises, items dropping, doors opening, etc. This growth of course is not something that can happen overnight, but the **calming of your nerves** is a skill you can develop over time.

- As will be discussed in greater depth in the Foundational Virtues section of this book, one should strive to develop **a general demeanor of silence, prayer, and peace**. Jesus cannot act in and through a demeanor radically at odds with His own—that is, a demeanor of giddiness, chattiness, worry, moodiness, and the like.

- As much as it is in your power, **strive to ensure your surroundings are dignified** and uncluttered. There is always sufficient grace available to overcome any external distractions when we are in an environment that is not up to us; but when we are in our own homes, rooms, offices, etc., God expects us to treat them with respect and with an approach that is in accord with our calling to live simple, dignified, prayerful lives.[576]

- **Strive for greater peace in social situations.** Instead of being ever anxious about what to say in them, simply cultivate an attitude wherein you do not fear some silence. For it is often the fear of silence which compels us to blurt out absurd things that never should have been said; and, obviously, such folly cannot be done in the Divine Will. Silence needn't be awkward; and there is no shame in having a particular strategy for dealing with it. Perhaps in silent moments where you are not inspired with any edifying words, you could make a habit of simply reaching into your pocket, thumbing your Rosary beads, and offering some silent prayers. To be sure, you should develop your own

methods—but if you do not come up with some strategies, then you will likely just succumb to doing what most people do: blurting out pointless comments about the weather, or some sports team, or perhaps harmful gossip, every time there is a second or two of a lull in a conversation. The peace which must permeate all of our conduct can also be greatly aided by our remembering that God has a perfect plan for our life; and this does not merely concern itself with the grand scheme of things. No, rather, this perfect plan applies to each "minor" situation we find ourselves in.

- **Try adding more formality to your days.** When we schlep about in flip-flops and sweatpants for everything we do, only putting on more formal attire for those "big" events like weddings, we forget that life is not about the "big" events. Life is about each day; it is about the ordinary—doing the ordinary in the Divine Will. The modern world disdains formality precisely because it knows formality is so helpful in reminding us of how we ought to behave, and modernism would prefer us all acting like animals. Bear in mind that by "formality," I do not mean ostentatiousness or obsession with appearance; these vices would be far worse than informality itself. A proper approach to formality need add little more than a few seconds to your morning routine: perhaps buttoning up an oxford shirt instead of merely slapping on a sweatshirt, or lacing up some more formal shoes instead of only slipping on flip-flops.

- We should also **partake of wholesome enjoyments.** Yes, Jesus wants to enjoy Himself in our enjoyment! It is of course important that we do not allow our lives to revolve around enjoying ourselves, but it is also important that we do not become miserable pseudo-ascetics. As a newly re-awakened Catholic, I remember subtly falling into some dualistic views; thinking that this life was *nothing* but a test for eternity, and all that matters is whether you pass that test. Although there is some merit in that mindset inasmuch as it is helpful to rid oneself of laxity and lukewarmness (which are

---

[576] For example, we should not clutter up our walls with pointless images (and numerous family portraits can make a house appear as a shrine to one's own family), our counters and desktops with needless trinkets, and above all we should not pollute the air with vain sounds from radio, television, etc. If we haven't used something in a year, it should probably go in a box of items that we will be donating to a local thrift store.

worse and more widespread traps than rigorism and overzealousness), that is nevertheless *not* the incarnational view of life which Catholicism provides. Nor is it the view we need to adopt to live in the Divine Will. We ought to enjoy ourselves, so long as this enjoyment is put in its proper place by right reason—that is, after the pursuit of holiness and the undertaking of the duties of our state in life. Wholesome enjoyment energizes you for the more zealous undertaking of the pursuit of holiness, and whether it achieves that is largely how you can gauge whether any given activity is a *wholesome* enjoyment. Make small enjoyments part of the daily routine, and lengthier enjoyments part of the weekly routine. Focus on enjoyments that are free or inexpensive, easy to plan, and edifying. Perhaps you could take regular walks in places of quiet, natural beauty (cemeteries are excellent, underused opportunities for this—they are among the few places today not inundated with noise, advertisements, and ugly, artificial materials and lighting), or go on hikes in nearby mountains or trails (in such a manner and at such a pace that you are doing them in order to truly soak in the incredible beauty of the unsullied creation of God surrounding you—not in a rushed-through manner in order for you to brag about how many peaks you've climbed).

- **Have something easily accessible on your person—an item which, merely touching, serves as a prayer** (which is, of all the things we must do, the one that is most conducive to being an act in the Divine Will). How often the moment surprises us with a pressing need for prayer! There is usually not enough time to kneel down formally and pray a Rosary, and perhaps our surroundings make it so that we cannot even audibly pray anything. Needless to say, in such situations, pray mentally. But our prayer is greatly benefited if there is a physical accompaniment to it; embodied creatures that we are. Rosary beads in your pocket work very well. Perhaps you can wear a Marian consecration chain as a bracelet. Inside my wife's and my wedding rings is engraved "To Jesus, through Mary," that—along with the fact that it is a sign of our sacrament of Matrimony,

blessed at our Nuptial Mass—helps me to feel I am truly praying simply by subtly touching it with my thumb. A crucifix or a scapular that can be easily grasped at any moment, or some holy medals (e.g. a Miraculous Medal and a St. Benedict medal) in your pocket can well serve this purpose.

Now, if you still find yourself confused as to what it means to do your acts in the Divine Will, do not fret. Above all else, simply strive to live in His Will; and the rest is essentially done. Jesus tells Luisa as much:

> As soon as the creature will possess Our Volition, all her acts-small and great, human and spiritual-will be animated by My Will, so as to rise between Heaven and earth, investing and braiding together the sky, the sun, the stars and the whole Creation.[577]

> Just like the sun, which animates everything with its light, but does not destroy or change things; rather, it places from its own and communicates the variety of colors, the diversity of sweetnesses, making them acquire a virtue and a beauty which they did not possess. **So my Divine Will is—without destroying anything of what the creature does; on the contrary, It animates them with Its light, It embellishes them, and communicates to them Its Divine Power.**[578]

Manual Labor

While explicitly holy endeavors are ideal materials to serve as acts done in the Divine Will, and indeed all (morally licit and willed by God) activities can, and should, be undertaken in the Divine Will, some are particularly noteworthy in how conducive they are to this great dignity. In my opinion, manual labor seems chief among them. The reason is clear: Jesus Himself spent the majority of His own earthly life doing just that.

Pope St. John Paul II pointed this out in the Papal Encyclical *Laborem Exercens*, writing " **... the one who, while being God, became like us in all things devoted most of the years of his life on earth to manual work at the carpenter's bench.**"

We must recall that labor is not a result of the Fall—only the suffering involved in it is—on the contrary, work would have still been one of the many joys of Original Holiness. Pope Leo XIII

---

[577]October 3, 1937.   [578]September 16, 1931.

affirmed this, saying:

> As regards bodily labor, even had man never fallen from the state of innocence, he would not have remained wholly idle; but that which would then have been his free choice and his delight became afterwards compulsory...[579]

And since manual labor has long been a big part of my own life, I would like to impart some personal advice on it. Contrary to what we are inclined to think, *that* **you are working is usually more important than** *what* **you are working on or towards**. Strive, therefore, to recognize this fact when you go about setting up your work day; optimize it more for quality of the experience than for the quantified results (while not neglecting whatever of the latter is necessary to ensure you are fulfilling well the duties of your state in life).

- Must you do much driving? There is nothing wrong with taking a route which, though a few miles longer, allows you to drive with greater peace and prayer; perhaps one with fewer billboards, less chaotic traffic, more beautiful scenery, etc.
- Do you have a task in front of you well suited to a noisy power tool? If you could achieve the same thing with a hand tool without sacrificing too much practicality, go for the latter. You needn't always forsake the power tool, but at least some of the time perhaps you could: Instead of chop saws and circular saws, use a hand saw; instead of nail guns, use a hammer; instead of lawn mowers, use a manual mower; instead of snowblowers, use a shovel; instead of leaf blowers, use a rake; instead of power washers, use a brush and cloth.
- Go about your tasks with sufficient deliberateness that you can truly pray in them

and during them, which in turn enables them to be done as acts in the Divine Will. This will at times mean a slightly slower pace than some would like. This is okay; set aside the time for it if at all possible, while of course not dragging your feet or neglecting your duties. Doing a task quickly is not necessarily at odds with doing it in the Divine Will; in fact, I can attest that it is precisely those times I am most conscious of the need to do my work in the Divine Will that I've found I have accomplished by far the most in the least amount of time.

Incidentally, reacquiring a respect for the dignity of manual labor is central to the general revival of society. The modern world snubs its nose at manual labor, demanding that each person acquire an advanced degree in order to be taken seriously, while supposing that we must zealously pursue technological advancement to finally rid the world of the "burden" of manual labor. These are lies from hell. For man is a working being; and in practice, those who disdain manual labor only wind up transferring labor away from manual work and towards something much less fulfilling— perhaps clicking away all day on a spreadsheet while sitting in a cubicle under buzzing tube-fluorescent lights. While those who are genuinely called to such a task will indeed be able to accomplish it in the Divine Will, most are not called to this as a way of life, and they will struggle to do these acts in the Divine Will. Reacquiring a love of manual labor—which involves a revival of genuine masculinity (especially in more men wanting to work with their hands) and femininity (especially in more women wanting to have children and raise them) is vital for the *Restoration of All Things in Christ*.

20) Grow in Knowledge of the Truths

Luisa's revelations span thousands of pages, and not one letter of them is in vain. But you will only come across a small percentage of them in this book. This deficiency, of course, means that you ought to dive into Luisa's writings themselves and benefit from them directly. Such a task is essential not merely so that you can memorize facts in order to inform action; rather, **the knowledge** of the truths of the Divine Will that Jesus entrusts to Luisa

is in and of itself **a powerful means for Living in the Divine Will** and hastening the Coming of the Kingdom.

Do you ever feel the burden of your human will is so great? Do you ever lament, with St. Faustina, "Oh, how everything drags man down to the

---

[579]Pope Leo XIII, *Rerum Novarum* 17.

earth"?[580] Do you ever lament, with St. Paul "who will free me from this body of death?"[581] The remedy to these ills is closer at hand than you may think: it is found in simply reading the truths that Jesus revels to Luisa. He told her, "**each knowledge I manifest to you on My Divine Fiat is a blow that I give to the human will...**"[582]

Your human will (self-will) is the cause of your misery. You have never had any actual problem transpire in your entire life that was not somehow a consequence of it. If, therefore, you wish to resolve any issue, the resolution will only be found in giving sufficient "blows" to the self-will that it bows to the Divine. This necessary task is ordinarily difficult but, as you can see, **Jesus promises that *merely acquiring* these knowledges that He reveals to Luisa is itself—upon each successive acquisition—a blow to the human will!** To pass up on these "free blows to the human will" would be folly, for this would be more lamentable than would be a man dying of an infection passing up on a simple cure.

Yes, in Heaven we will learn of these truths, anyway. But Jesus tells Luisa:

> If you knew what difference will pass between those who bring My knowledges from the earth and those who will acquire them in Heaven ... The first will have them as their own endowments and one will see in them the nature of the Divine Beauty, and will hear the same sounds of the joys and happinesses that their Creator makes one hear and forms. On the other hand, in the second, these will be neither their own nature nor their own endowments, but they will receive them as the effect of the communication of others, almost as the earth receives the effects of the sun, but does not possess the nature of the sun. **Therefore, those who will possess all the knowledges will form the highest choir, and according to their knowledge, so will the different choirs be formed**...However, all those who have acquired these knowledges, whether in full or in part, will have the noble title of children of My Kingdom...[583]

By reading thus far, you have already secured for yourself the "noble title of children of My Kingdom," promised by Jesus in the last portion of the quote above (assuming, of course, you correspond to grace). But by delving more deeply into the truths themselves, Jesus promises that you will form the highest choirs in Heaven, according to the knowledge of the Divine Will which you have attained here on earth.

Indeed, work is needed to appropriate the grace contained in these truths. But not much is needed; rather, the grace is waiting behind an ever-so-thin veil, waiting to burst forth at the touch, but it will not do so without that touch, which requires human effort. We are not in Heaven yet, and until we arrive at our Celestial Fatherland, we will have to work to acquire anything of value. Jesus tells Luisa:

> In sum, all things down here have the veil that covers them, to give to man the work and the will, the love to possess them and enjoy them. Now, My Truths surpass natural things by far, and they present themselves to the creature like noble queens, veiled, in the act of giving themselves to them. But they want their work; they want them to draw near them by the steps of their will, in order to know them, possess them and love them- necessary conditions in order to tear the veil that hides them. Once the veil is torn, with their light, of their own they make their way, giving themselves in possession to those who have searched for them ... This is the reason for those who read the truths on My Divine Will and show that they do not comprehend what they read-even more, they are confused: because the true will of wanting to know them is lacking.[584]

If we had the faintest idea of just how valuable these truths on the Divine Will are, then we would all bury ourselves in them. Do not misunderstand: we wouldn't neglect the duties of our state in life (Jesus insists to Luisa, strongly, upon meeting these well), or any of our current spiritual practices— daily Mass, daily Scripture reading, daily Rosary, etc. (Jesus tells Luisa that one ought to not neglect one's practices!). We would, however, be zealous in learning more and more about the Divine Will as revealed to Luisa. Jesus tells Luisa:

> **See then, what it means to know <u>one</u> truth more, or <u>one</u> truth less—if all knew what great goods they miss, they would compete in order to acquire truths.**[585]

We can see that Jesus gives to Luisa great promises

---

[580] *Divine Mercy in My Soul.* 210
[581] Romans 7:24
[582] December 14, 1927.

[583] February 28, 1928.
[584] August 2, 1930.
[585] January 25, 1922.

for **each** new truth one learns regarding His Divine Will; promises so great that all of Heaven rejoices upon the entrance of a soul into it simply due to each piece of knowledge of this great Gift that soul brings along to paradise.

Remember that what you have read here is nothing but a very unworthy work written by a very unworthy author. It is a desperately inadequate overview of Luisa's writings; hence my insistence that I only present an *introduction* (or, rather, an *invitation*) to the Gift of Living in the Divine Will. So please continue this good work you have begun of learning more and more of these most sublime truths of His Divine Will! Dive into her writings, seek out true experts, seek out Divine Will prayer groups, conferences, etc. I cannot encourage this enough!

But let us now consider more insights Jesus gives to Luisa about the power of the knowledges:

> My daughter, don't you know that these writings of Ours come from the depth of my Heart, and in them I make flow the tenderness of my Heart, to touch those who will read them, and the firmness of my divine speech, to strengthen them in the truths of my Will? In all the sayings, truths, examples, which I make you write on paper, I make flow the dignity of my celestial wisdom, in such a way **that those who read them, or will read them, if they are in grace, will feel within themselves my tenderness, the firmness of my speech and the light of my wisdom, and, as though in between magnets, they will be drawn into the knowledge of my Will.**[586]

> In it the creature will no longer feel alone; between her and my Will there will be no more separation; whatever my Will does, she will do as well, operating together. Everything will be hers by right—Heaven, earth, and God Himself. See then, how noble, divine and precious will be the scope of these truths which I made you write on my Divine Will—to form Its day. And for some they will form the dawn; for others the beginning of the day; for some others the full daylight and, lastly, the full midday. **These truths, according to one's knowledge of them, will form the different categories of the souls who will live in my Will. One more knowledge, or one less, will make them ascend or remain in the different categories.** Knowledge will be the hand to make them go up to superior categories; it will be the

very life of the fullness of my Will in them. Therefore, I can say that with these truths I have formed the day for whoever wants to live in my Divine Will—a day of Heaven, greater than Creation Itself; not made of sun or stars, because each truth has the virtue of creating Our Life in the creature, and—oh! how this surpasses the whole of Creation! Hence, Our Love has surpassed everything in manifesting so many truths on my Divine Will. Our glory on the part of creatures will be full, because they will have Our Life in their power, to glorify Us and love Us.[587]

As we can see, each new knowledge we acquire of the Truths makes our acts more powerful. Are you confused about how to do all your acts in the Divine Will? Soak up more of the knowledges. Regarding this, Jesus tells Luisa:

> Every time I speak to you about my Will and you acquire new cognitions and knowledges, your act in my Will has more value and you acquire more immense riches. It happens as to a man who possesses a gem, and knows that this gem has the value of a penny: he is rich one penny. Now, it happens that he shows his gem to a competent expert, who tells him that his gem has a value of five thousand lira. That man no longer possesses one penny, but he is rich five thousand lira. Now, after some time he has the opportunity to show his gem to another expert, even more competent, and this one assures him that his gem contains the value of one hundred thousand lira, and is ready to buy it if he wants to sell it. Now that man is rich one hundred thousand lira. According to his knowledge of the value of his gem, he becomes richer, and feels greater love and appreciation for the gem; he keeps it in custody more jealously, knowing that it is all his fortune, while before he held it as a trifle. Yet, the gem has not changed—as it was, so it is; he is the one who went through the change, by understanding the value that the gem contains. Now, the same happens with my Will, as well as with virtues. According to how the soul understands their value and acquires knowledge of them, she comes to acquire new values and new riches in her acts. So, the more you get to know about my Will, the more your act will acquire Its value. Oh! if you knew what seas of graces I open between you and Me every time I speak to you about the effects of my Will, you would die of joy, and would make feast, as if you had acquired new kingdoms to dominate.[588]

A true model of humility, Luisa nevertheless could

---

[586] December 8, 1926.
[587] November 7, 1937.
[588] August 25, 1921.

not hide the power of these words (for that would be a false humility) which she received from Jesus. In a letter after the prohibition of her books, Luisa wrote:

> Allow me, Father, to open my heart to you like a baby. Even the Heavens put themselves in mourning because of the prohibition of the books. The evil spirits of the earth and of hell make feast, because the Divine Will has such strength that even a single piece of knowledge of It, one word about It, or one action done with It, makes the spirits of darkness feel such torture as to feel their power paralyzed, and their torments in hell increased. Therefore, we should take to heart making this Kingdom of the Divine Will known, and living in It.

Although more will be included on this point in Part Three of this book, we should still note here that it is precisely these knowledges of the Divine Will that will both hasten and enable the Era of Peace. Jesus tells Luisa:

> Here is, then, the necessity of the knowledges about It: if a good is not known, it is neither wanted nor loved. Therefore, the knowledges will be the messengers, the heralds, which will announce my Kingdom. My knowledges about my Fiat will take the attitude now of suns, now of thunders, now of bolts of light, now of mighty winds, which will call the attention of the learned and of the ignorant, of the good and also of the evil, falling into their hearts like lightnings, and knocking them down with irresistible strength, to make them rise again in the good of the knowledges acquired. They will form the true renewal of the world; they will assume all attitudes in order to attract and win the creatures, taking the attitude now of peacemakers, who want the kiss of the creatures to give them their own, so as to forget about all the past and remember only to love each other and make each other happy; now of warriors, sure of their victory, to render sure the conquest they want to make of those who come to know them; now of incessant prayers, which will cease to supplicate only when creatures, conquered by the knowledges of my Divine Will, will say: 'You have won — we are now prey to your Kingdom'; now of king, dominating and inspiring love, such that they will lower their foreheads to let themselves be dominated. What will my Will not do?[589]

We will now conclude this chapter with perhaps the most profound point about the knowledges in general. It is indeed true that the glory of the saints in Heaven is fixed — their merit is stable and cannot be added to; nor can they experience sorrow due to any deficiency down here on earth. Nevertheless, their accidental glory (which is no trifle) may be contributed to even now, and they are anything but indifferent to what transpires on earth, even though their happiness is already perfect. Each knowledge we acquire of the Divine Will on earth **creates a distinct beatitude in Heaven itself.** Jesus tells Luisa:

> Each truth contains within itself a distinct beatitude, happiness, joy and beauty; so, each additional truth you know brings beatitude, happiness, joy, beauty into yourself, with which you remain enriched. These are divine seeds that the soul receives, and by manifesting them to others, she communicates these seeds and enriches whomever receives them. Now, since the truths that one has known on earth are divine seeds which sprout with beatitudes, joy, etc. in Heaven, when the soul is in her Fatherland they will be electric wires of communication through which the Divinity will unleash from Its womb so many acts of beatitude for as many truths as she has known… One who does not have the seed, who has not known a truth while on earth, lacks the void in order to be able to receive these beatitudes… Now, the truths are the secretaries of my beatitudes, and if I do not manifest them to souls, they do not crack the secret which they contain. They swim within my Divinity, waiting for their turn to act as divine agents, and make Me known — how many more beatitudes I contain. And the longer they have remained hidden in my womb, the more uproariously and majestically they come out to inundate the creatures and manifest my glory. **Do you think that all of Heaven is aware of all my goods? No, no! Oh! how much remains for It to enjoy, which It does not enjoy today. Each creature who enters into Heaven having known one more truth, unknown to others, will bring within herself the seed so as to have new contentments, new joys and new beauty unleashed from Me**, of which that soul will be as though the cause and fount, while others will take part in them. The last day will not come if I do not find souls who are disposed, in order for Me to reveal all my truths, so that the Celestial Jerusalem may resound with my complete glory, and all the Blessed may take part in all my beatitudes — some as direct cause,

---

[589] October 30, 1927.

for having known that truth, and some as indirect cause, through the one who has known it... I want to tell you which ones are the truths that glorify Me the most: they are those which regard my Will, primary cause with which I created man—that his will be one with his Creator ... In fact, so that the soul may open the doors and render herself disposed to knowing the truths that my Will contains, the first thing is wanting to live of my Will, the second is wanting to know It, the third is to appreciate It.[590]

21) Grow in the Foundational Virtues for the Gift

Having received the Gift of Living in the Divine Will thanks to our renunciation of the self-will, as well our desire for the Gift and our asking for It, it naturally follows that we should strive to do whatever it takes to remain anchored in this Gift, so as to grow more deeply into It and never lose It. This is achieved in part by growing in all the virtues; especially those most closely related to the Gift.

Now, the inclusion of this chapter is, admittedly, redundant: **the foundational virtues for the Gift are quite simply what the great Catholic spiritual writers (above all, the saints and Doctors of the Church previously mentioned) have always taught.** Nevertheless, I include this chapter because Jesus draws special attention to some virtues in particular, and has very powerful words pertaining to them which can educate and inspire us further.

(*I would also like to note that the virtues I list here are presented—as with everything else in this book—as merely what I have personally found to be inspiring, predominant, etc. in my own reading of Luisa's revelations. I repeat: I do not have Luisa's revelations memorized and I do not even consider myself an expert in them. What I list may be incomplete and even missing very important things, and I do not wish my meager and unworthy efforts here to ever be referred to by anyone as any sort of definitive and comprehensive summary of Luisa's revelations. Please, seek out better men than myself for that task and, above all, read Luisa's writings for yourself.*)

What will presently follow is a hefty list of virtues; perhaps some individuals might be discouraged at the mere sight of it. But I remind you again of what I have said many times: **Christ's burden is light. His yoke is easy. Living in the Divine Will is not difficult. Virtue, too, is not difficult, and Jesus reiterates this to Luisa, saying:**

> **My daughter, they say that the path of virtue is difficult. False**. It is difficult for one who does not move, because knowing neither the graces nor the consolations she would receive from God, nor the help for her to move, it seems difficult to her; and without moving she feels all the weight of the journey. But **for one who moves, it is extremely easy, because the grace that inundates her fortifies her**, the beauty of the virtues attracts her, the Divine Spouse of souls carries her cleaving to His arm, accompanying her along the journey. And the soul, instead of feeling the weight, the difficulty of moving, wants to hasten her way in order to reach, more quickly, the end of the path and of her very center.[591]

And haven't we all found this to be true? When we sit down to merely think about a task, it seems tremendous, and too often we cower in our rooms trembling at the sheer thought of it. But when we ignore these thoughts and simply get to work, we find things proceeding much more smoothly than we would have imagined. This is not so much because our intellectual consideration of the challenges was factually wrong, but rather it was because in these considerations, we always lean too heavily on ourselves and underestimate God, Who is never outdone in generosity and Who always inundates us with His grace—making easy anything we need to do in order to carry out His Will.

Therefore, set out! Get to work! Engage in your mission. You know what it is. The grace to be virtuous will come in the midst of your faithful undertaking of the Will of God for your life.

In a word, as Jesus says: *move*! Do not even spend much time dwelling on these pages here. Feel free to simply refer to them when necessary.

Perfect Love

If you've read this book so far, you at least have some idea of the incredible magnitude of the Divine Will and its importance in our lives. So you may now be surprised to hear that Jesus also told Luisa

---

[590] January 25, 1922.

[591] May 15, 1905.

the following:

> My daughter, **Love and Will of God are on par** with each other, they never separate, and they form one single Life... if you do my Will, you will love, and if you love you place my Will in safety within you.[592]

> **My daughter, there is nothing that can surpass Love**—neither doctrine nor dignity, and much less nobility... So, Love makes up for doctrine and surpasses it; It makes up for dignity and surpasses all dignities, providing one with divine dignity. It makes up for everything and surpasses everything.[593]

> **The most essential and necessary thing in a soul is charity.** If there is no charity, it happens as to those families or kingdoms which have no rulers: everything is upset, the most beautiful things remain obscured, one can see no harmony...[594]

> My Divine Will is light, love is heat. Light and heat are inseparable from each other, and form the same life...[595]

It is, therefore, quite true to say that it is impossible to overemphasize the importance of love. "God is love,"[596] as Scripture teaches, and, as Jesus said in the Gospel, the whole law is summed up in loving God and neighbor.[597] Needless to say, Luisa's revelations do not change that: if anything, they simply draw even **more** attention to the centrality of these truths.

The first step in acquiring the love we must have to live in the Divine Will is to recognize that we lack it. These words of Jesus to Luisa will succeed in helping just about anyone in this first step:

> My daughter, one who really loves Me never gets annoyed about anything, but tries to convert all things into love... The weight of any action, be it even an indifferent one, increases according to the dose of love it contains, because I do not look at the work, but at the intensity of love that the working contains. Therefore I want no annoyance in you, but always peace; because in annoyances, in disturbances, it is always the love of self that wants to come out to reign, or the enemy to do harm.[598]

And so we must strive more zealously to attain this love we now lack. Practically speaking, most people can probably most readily gauge their love by their relation to others; that is, by observing how this virtue plays out in those relations. Jesus gives Luisa the standard for this, too. He says:

> My daughter, true charity is when, in doing good to his neighbor, one does it because he is my image. All the charity that goes out of this sphere cannot be called charity.[599]

Simple pity is not true love. Simple pity can be a good start; that is, letting our hearts break over the suffering of others—but it only becomes true charity when this love takes the form of a recognition that God is the Supreme Good and that He truly resides in all His children, and when we will their good we are indeed willing His good. Now, do not worry if you fear that your intention may not yet be fully purified to the extent that all the good you do for others is inspired by your recognition of the image of God in them. Do not let this concern you or in any way limit your deeds of love. Simply keep doing what you are doing—or, rather, step it up!—and keep trying to fix your intention into the proper place.

In this regard, we must recall that love is an act of the will—not an emotion. You cannot control how you feel, but you can control what you *will*. In Luisa's writings, we see the following entry:

> I was thinking to myself: 'How miserable I am. I feel like I haven't done anything for Jesus... I should be all on fire—and I'm not.' But while I was thinking this, He came back, and scolding me sweetly, told me: "My daughter, what are you doing? Do you want to waste time? Don't you know that all you should care about is to do my Will and know whether you are in It? ... **Your Jesus never looks at what the creature feels**; many times feelings can deceive her. But rather, I look at her will and what she really wants—and that is what I take. How many things are felt, but one does not do them; on the other hand, if one wants something, all is done. Besides, in my Will nothing gets lost."[600]

Here we see that Jesus is giving a teaching reiterated by the *Catechism of the Catholic Church,*

---

[592] October 20, 1935.
[593] May 20, 1909.
[594] October 29, 1900.
[595] May 21, 1929.
[596] 1 John 4:8
[597] Cf. Matthew 22:37-40

[598] July 22, 1905.
[599] September 8, 1905.
[600] May 15, 1938.

which states:

> Strong feelings are not decisive for the morality or the holiness of persons; they are simply the inexhaustible reservoir of images and affections in which the moral life is expressed.[601]

Your feelings do not determine your love. Think of all the greatest saints of the modern era. Who, of them, seems to stand out in love? Doubtless, most would rightly respond "St. Mother Teresa." And yet, upon the release of her diaries, we now know that she scarcely *felt* any love at all; that, rather, almost her whole life was one giant and extreme dark night of the soul. But that did not stop her. She simply kept doing good; she kept loving. And her love was never that of a mere activist or a merely compassionate soul who pitied others. No, **Mother Teresa's love was all about quenching the thirst of Jesus on the cross: His thirst for souls. Let us, like Mother Teresa, live our lives to lovingly quench the thirst of Jesus** on the cross. And if you ever need strength to do this better, just do the *Hours of the Passion* (see the corresponding chapter in this book), and you will acquire that strength.

If we *will* charity in all our acts (which is indeed possible, since charity is the *form* of all virtues), then we have purity of intention. Without purity of intention, all works are utterly useless. Jesus tells Luisa:

> My Person is surrounded by all the works that souls do, as by a garment; and the more purity of intention and intensity of love they have, the more splendor they give Me, and I will give them more glory; so much so, that on the Day of Judgment I will show them to the whole world, to let the whole world know how my children have honored Me, and how I honor them…My daughter, what will happen to so many works, even good, done without purity of intention, out of habit and self-interest? What shame will not fall upon them on the Day of Judgment, in seeing so many works, good in themselves, but made rotten by their intention, such that, their very actions, instead of rendering honor to them, as they would to many others, will give them shame? In fact, I do not look at the greatness of the works, but at the intention with which they are done. Here is all my attention.[602]

***

Jesus tells Luisa that it is through love, and only through love, that we enter into the Infinite. He says:

> We know that the creature has nothing to give Us, …**Though she has nothing, she has her little love, unleashed by Our Own in the Act of Creating her, therefore she has a particle of the Infinite Love of God**…[603]

Jesus also tells Luisa that our loving Him binds Him to love us:

> My daughter, not loving one who loves Me is impossible for Me. Rather, I feel so drawn toward her, that at the littlest act of love she does for Me, I respond with triple love…[604]

Furthermore, loving God *transforms* us into Him. Jesus says:

> My daughter, the other virtues, although high and sublime, always cause the creature to be distinguished from her Creator. **Only love transforms the soul in God**. But no one can give true love if love does not receive life and food by my Will. Therefore, it is my Will that, united with Love, forms the true transformation into Me… therefore, one can say that she is another Me… even her breath or the contact with the ground that she treads is precious and holy…[605]

Love is also our greatest glory in Heaven; not the great works. Jesus tells Luisa the following:

> But who were the fortunate ones who cried out more loudly, who made this note, 'Love', resound in everything, and who brought great happiness into Heaven Itself? They were the ones who had loved the Lord more when they lived on earth. Ah, they were not the ones who had done great things, penances, miracles… Ah, no—never! **Love alone is what surpasses everything, and leaves everything behind. So, it is one who loves much, not one who does much, that will be more pleasing to the Lord**.[606]

And, in fact, it was precisely because Adam forgot love that the Fall of Man occurred, and the entire world was disfigured. Jesus tells Luisa:

> …do you want to know why Adam sinned? Because he forgot that I loved him, and he forgot to love Me … So, love ceased first, and then sin

---

[601] CCC 1768.
[602] May 7, 1899.
[603] January 12, 1932.
[604] November 15, 1916.

[605] August 28, 1912.
[606] October 16, 1906.

began; and as he ceased to love his God, true love towards himself also ceased ... This is why, in coming upon earth, the thing on which I placed greatest importance was that they love one another as they were loved by Me, in order to give them my first love, to let the love of the Most Holy Trinity hover over the earth... never forget that I love you very much, so as to never forget to love Me...In this way, you will remain in the order, and will fear nothing.[607]

***

Now, I recognize that in this age of "God is love" platitudes often being the only thing one hears in Sunday homilies—where anything that smacks of "Old Testament" or even so-called "pre-conciliar"[608] theology is scoffed at and ignored—it is unfortunately (even if understandably) becoming common for some Catholics to react too strongly in the other direction; categorically rejecting the tenderness that necessarily comes with genuine charity. While false charity that is nothing other than "mercy" without truth and amiability at all costs is light years away from what Jesus is saying to Luisa, He also will never allow us to become coarse, hardened rigorists who neglect tenderness. He tells Luisa:

> A love, when it is not tender, is like a food without condiment, like a beauty that is aged, incapable of attracting anyone to make itself loved; it is like a flower without fragrance, like a dry fruit without humor and sweetness. A love that is hard, without tenderness, is unacceptable and would have no virtue of making itself loved by anyone. Therefore, My Heart suffers so much in seeing the hardness of creatures, that they reach the point of changing My graces into scourges.[609]

Considering the unsurpassable importance of love, we must examine our lives to see if they have this virtue.

It has been said, rightly so, that "... *your love for God is measured by your love for the one in this world whom you love least.*" What a waste (and worse) this book on Luisa's revelations has been if it shifts your focus away from Our Lord's command to love one another as He has loved us, and towards simply asking God for a certain grace of union (even if it is the highest one). Consider your life carefully. Charity begins in the home. How do those with whom you live, work, and pray, feel about your

demeanor towards them? Of course, there will always be slander, misunderstanding, and the like; but generally, if you hold charity in your heart and in your deeds towards others, many will recognize it and acknowledge it. If you cannot recall them doing so recently, then you likely need to reevaluate your behavior towards them. Do you go beyond this, though, and regularly perform works of mercy; not in the hopes of being repaid or noticed, but out of the pure desire to serve the needy in whom Christ dwells? Do you have a disposition of openness to whatever needs of others Providence might present to you throughout the day, or are you dead set in following—no matter what—the plan you have in your head for the next ten minutes of your life, wherever you find yourself? Have you ever sensed a fear in others of approaching you? If you truly had charity, no one would fear to approach you. Jesus Christ, the Almighty Creator of the Universe Who could have leveled all of Jerusalem with a thought, was the most approachable person who ever lived, and no one feared to come to Him.

Self-forgetfulness and Humility

Although I have used two terms in the title of this section, there is little difference between them, for it can be said that each is contained within the other. This is clear from the following: humility is "nothing but the truth,"[610] as St. Faustina says. (She pointed this out upon realizing that, in her earlier years, she had been overzealous in pursuing humility and thus had succumbed to distorting it; even accusing herself of things she really wasn't guilty of and seeking humiliations beyond those the Will of God had given her.) **But the truth is that, compared to God, we are nothing**.

Perhaps that is too abstract, so let us attempt a brief mental exercise. Compare yourself to mankind (which is nothing compared to God). You likely have a hard time even remembering the names of the tiny circle of people with which you semi-regularly interact. This circle, in turn, is a minuscule fraction of the town in which you live. That town is joined by hundreds of others just in your own state, which in turn (if you live in America), is one of fifty. That entire Union of 50 states, then, composes only one country among

---

[607] September 6, 1923.
[608] That is, before the Second Vatican Council

[609] March 30, 1931.
[610] *Divine Mercy in My Soul.* 1502

hundreds of others and houses a mere 4% of the world's population. That entire population represents only a few generations of out of more than a hundred generations of mankind's existence on earth. And what of this earthly life of yours that is so dwarfed by the race of men? In the twinkling of an eye, your earthly existence will be reduced to a rotting corpse, and in one more twinkling, your entire legacy will probably be forgotten (on earth), and a future historian may even struggle to prove you ever existed. Will becoming famous change this? Not at all. Shortly after your death, dear famous person, someone will change the "is" following your name on your Wikipedia page to "was," and that page will scarcely be visited by anyone; for no matter what you achieved, the masses will be far too busy watching the next viral YouTube video to care about what you did.

That is you. That is I. (As far as this earthly life is concerned). Forgive the brutality of the exposition, but pride must be dealt with mercilessly.

It is clear that we are nothing. And if only we can recognize that, receiving the Gift of Living in the Divine Will shall prove a smooth path. For **we will then forget ourselves (why remember a nothing?),** and once we have forgotten ourselves, we have attained the perfection of humility. So, if you simply forget yourself, you will be humble, for pride will find itself without the necessary matter with which to form its diabolical life. But nothingness is a fundamental concept in the spiritual life, and important for receiving the Gift, so let us now consider it in more detail in a section of its own.

The Need for Nothingness

The consciousness of one's own nothingness is neither a Quietest heresy nor is it an innovation of Luisa's. The *Quietistic* prayer of nothingness is directed at a state wherein the soul can no longer *act*, for its faculties are annihilated. The proper prayer of nothingness—the one advocated by Luisa and many others—is directed at the soul never acting *independently of the Divine Will*; its faculties are absorbed in God, not annihilated. Remember that Jesus said to Luisa:

...So my Divine Will is—without destroying

anything of what the creature does; on the contrary, It animates them with Its light, It embellishes them, and communicates to them Its Divine Power.[611]

And so we can see that nothingness refers to the independence of the soul. Within this understanding, St. Faustina prayed: "*reduce me to nothingness in my own eyes that I may find grace in Yours.*"[612]

The Servant of God John of St. Samson, a 17th century Carmelite mystic, taught that:

The queen of the spiritual life is love, which is directed to Christ ... Love brings with it as an inseparable partner, detachment ... Love looks to the All of God, detachment to the nothingness of the creature. Love makes the soul steadily more contemplative; detachment causes it to turn steadily further away from the nondivine. Thus the spiritual life looks to nothingness and to the All at the same time.[613]

Consider this beautiful prayer as well from the Precious Blood Devotional (which bears a Nihil Obstat):

Merciful Savior, conscious of my nothingness and of Thy sublimity, I cast myself at Thy feet and thank Thee for the many proofs of Thy grace. I thank Thee especially for Your Cross and Precious Blood by which you revealed your infinite love, forgave our sins and gave us a share in your eternal life.

Fr. Caussade, the great spiritual master who was covered at length in Part One of this book, wrote:

To surrender ourselves to God by a total abandonment of self, and to lose ourselves in the abyss of nothingness so as to find ourselves again only in God, is to perform the most excellent act of which we are capable. O the richness of nothingness! Why do people not know you? The more a soul reduces itself to nothingness, the more precious it becomes in God's sight. To lose oneself in one's nothingness is the surest means to finding one's self again in God.

Fr. Peter Cameron, the eminent Dominican theologian who was the first editor of the *Magnificat* devotional magazine, often speaks of nothingness and laments that, when he does so, some people complain. To address the issue, he wrote an article for the *Magnificat* publication on what he means by

---

[611] September 16, 1931.
[612] St. Faustina, *Divine Mercy in My Soul*, 1436.

[613] New Catholic Encyclopedia on "John of St. Samson."

"nothingness." In the article, he stated:

> To say we are "nothing" is not a moral judgment; it is not a statement about how we are but about who we are. As Saint Paul challenges, "What do you possess that you have not received" (1 Cor 4:7). Beginning with our very existence. God revealed to Doctor of the Church Saint Catherine of Siena: "Do you know, daughter, who you are and who I am? If you know there two things you have beatitude in your grasp. You are she who is not; I am he who is."

> Saint John Eudes tells us ... "Beg [Jesus] to give you a share in his divine knowledge, that you may realize your nothingness: to imprint upon your souls a lively perception of your nothingness; and to grant you the grace to think, say, and do nothing for yourself, but all for him." Jesus proclaims the poor in spirit blessed precisely because they embrace their nothingness as a fact and a grace.[614]

St. Thérèse of Lisieux, Doctor of the Church, settles the matter and assures us that there is not only nothing unorthodox about recognizing our nothingness, but rather, it is a key to sanctity. She shares:

> This enlightenment on my nothingness does me more good, in fact, than enlightenment on matters of faith.[615]

> Marie, though you are nothing, do not forget that Jesus is All. You have only to lose your own nothingness in that Infinite All, and thenceforth to think only of that All who alone is worthy of your love.[616]

> ... perfection appears easy, and I see that it is enough to acknowledge our nothingness, and like children surrender ourselves into the Arms of the Good God.[617]

> Verily the Divine Heart's Goodness and Merciful Love are little known! It is true that to enjoy these treasures we must humble ourselves, must confess our nothingness ... and here is where many a soul draws back.[618]

Returning to Jesus' revelations to Luisa, we can see His insistence on nothingness as well:

> My daughter, the sun is symbol of grace. When it finds a void, be it even a cave, a vault, a fissure, a hole, as long as there is empty space and a little opening through which to penetrate, it enters and fills everything with light; nor with this does it diminish its light in the other spaces. And if its light does not illuminate more, it is not because it lacks light, but rather, because of the lack of space in which to be able to diffuse its light more. So is my grace: more than majestic sun, it envelops all creatures with its beneficial influence; however, it does not enter but into empty hearts—as much empty space as it finds, so much light does it let penetrate into the hearts. These voids, then—how are they formed? Humility is the hoe which digs and forms the void. Detachment from everything and also from oneself is the void itself. The window in order to let the grace of light enter into this void, is trust in God and distrust of ourselves. Therefore, as much trust as one has, so much does he enlarge the door in order to let the light in, and to take more grace. The custodian which keeps the light and expands it, is peace.[619]

Do not Think About Yourself

Jesus tells Luisa:

> Thinking of oneself is the same as going out of God and returning to live in oneself. Moreover, thinking of oneself is never virtue, but always vice, be it even under the aspect of good.[620]

The title of this section is, of course, the opposite of what the world insists upon. For worldly advice often amounts to nothing less than incessant navel gazing:

- The world expects us to be well versed on all our various personality quirks and psychological diagnoses; knowing what letter our personality type is, what our Myers-Briggs classification is, what character we are most like in all our favorite works of fiction—and on the list goes. Some take the additional step of expecting others to cater to their own self-classifications. Usually, this amounts to little more than a perverse obsession with analyzing the very thing we need to renounce—the self-will—, much like a cancer-ridden man growing fixated upon his tumor instead of allowing a surgeon to remove it.
- The "power of positive thinking" movement insists that we make "daily affirmations," each morning saying out loud how wonderful we

---

[614] Father Peter John Cameron, O.P. "Loving our nothingness." lead editorial from Magnificat (February, 2018).
[615] *Story of a Soul*. Chapter 9.
[616] Letter II to her cousin Marie

[617] Letter VI
[618] Letter VII
[619] May 16, 1909.
[620] August 23, 1905.

think we are. This—continuing the last point's analogy—is akin to not merely being fixated upon the tumor, but deliberately feeding it.

- We are surrounded by billboards, advertisements, and all manner of noise demanding that we constantly turn our thoughts to the self and compare ourselves to others; constantly insisting that we consider our "image" and make sure that we own all the products and patronize all the businesses that are conducive to generating this "image."
- The modern social media craze (Facebook, Instagram, Twitter, etc.) is also almost always a serious harm to this necessary virtue of self-forgetfulness. Having social media accounts incessantly foists the temptation into one's mind to be constantly gauging what he is doing by how more or less "cool" it would look if he shared it on his profile.

Indeed, one of the favorite "Gospels" of the modern world is the false gospel of self-esteem psychobabble. **But this navel gazing must stop.**

We must stop thinking about ourselves. There are always so much greater things we could be doing with our thoughts, words, and deeds, than directing them towards ourselves. Is there not an Omnipotent, All-Powerful, God Who is always closer to us than our skin; begging us to acknowledge Him, think of Him, and converse with Him?

One damaging but perhaps superficially holy thing some Catholics do which makes self-forgetfulness difficult is to turn their homes into shrines of themselves, their friends, and their family, by plastering all the walls with pictures of the same. To do this while at the same time realizing the importance of self-forgetfulness makes about as much sense as a man who struggles with the virtue of purity (or anyone, for that matter) filling up his room with pornographic materials.

"The sons of this world are wiser in their own generation than the sons of light."[621] Oh, if only we put some thought, effort, and strategy into becoming saints as we do to the various worldly endeavors we must engage in, we'd all be saints in no time!

But we should not only stop thinking about ourselves; we should stop, also, talking about ourselves. Self-forgetfulness is impossible to attain while engaging in self-talk. We should stop being so eager and willing to share stories about ourselves or about things we've experienced (unless, of course, they are stories that are directly and entirely concerned with evangelization or edification). We should stop updating everyone on our lives *needlessly*. Jesus tells Luisa:

> Therefore, I recommend that you not leave my Will, and that you continue not to think about yourself, but about others; otherwise you would impoverish yourself and would feel the need for everything.[622]

We should live our lives like a tiger in the pursuit of its prey; so fixated upon its mission that a war could be raging on all sides of it and it would scarcely notice. Our mission is the salvation of souls (as Jesus says here, think "about **others,**" and by that He means their *salvation*), as well as the consolation of the Sacred Heart of Jesus, and the hastening of the Coming of the Kingdom of the Divine Will. Our calling is the greatest calling in history. For us to spend time thinking about and talking about ourselves is more lamentable than a marine who, upon being sent on a mission of utmost importance to help end a war, instead stops for sightseeing in the city into which he was sent.

Self-forgetfulness, however, cannot be achieved without an appropriate forgetfulness of others as well. (That is, forgetfulness of their vices.) It is amazing how much gossip is passed around in Catholic circles under the guise of "prayer requests." If *anyone* has fallen victim to *anything* that is not particularly flattering for others to know about, then it must always be left to that person alone to decide whether to allow others to know of it for the sake of receiving their prayers. This is not a decision to be taken out of their hands—if you for whatever reason come to know of such a situation, then you should use it to guide your own prayers for that person, but you must not decide to go sharing that prayer need with others without that person's permission.

Self-forgetfulness also cannot be achieved without forgetting what, in the past, ought to be forgotten. Jesus tells Luisa:

---

[621] Luke 16:8
[622] November 1, 1912.

In fact, the creature who lets herself be carried and possessed by It can make such changes that she no longer recognizes herself, if she even retains a distant memory of her past life…[623]

…one who lives in my Will is already sanctified, and enjoys, nourishes herself with, and thinks of all that my Will contains. And even though she has committed sins in the past, finding herself in the beauty, in the sanctity, in the immensity of goods that my Will contains, she forgets the ugliness of her past and remembers only the present…[624]

…the thought of the past is truly absurd—it is like wanting to claim the divine rights.[625]

Elsewhere, Jesus refers to the thought of lost things in the past as an affront to His mercy, like wanting to "roll in the past mud." In her letters, Luisa herself wrote:

Don't think about the past, this harms you a great deal; rather, even today, begin your life with Jesus and you will find out for yourself how all things change for you; you will feel like another man, born again in all that is holy.[626]

Listen to the Celestial Mama and to sweet Jesus. They want you to not think of the past—to place a sepulchral stone on it, so that you may forget everything and say: "My life will start today; I am born again together with my Queen Mama, with Jesus, and with the Divine Will… courage! Those who think of the past lose the present. The Lord has disposed everything: crosses, illness, state of marriage; in a word—everything. The Lord had to prepare the material in order to make of you a saint; and He has prepared enough of it. So, all you have to say and do is this: "The Heart of Jesus wants me a saint: I must become a saint!" Have we understood each other?[627]

As far as wanting to go over the past again—no, because the past has passed in God, and it would be as though stealing His rights, His own things.[628]

It is more than safe to say that, whatever it is about the past that you now dwell on—your sins or the sins of others, missed opportunities, wounds, better times now gone, etc.—whatever it is that now comes back to haunt you, that you waste time regretting or lamenting: it needs to be eliminated

from your mind. You need to say "no" to these thoughts firmly, for entertaining them is destroying your spiritual life and distancing you from God. Besides, everything in the past can be repaired—and is repaired—by living in the Divine Will. The objectives acts of the past won't change, but their relation to eternity (which is all that matters) will.

**

Now, forgetting the self does not preclude the need for a nightly examination of conscience. But it does mean that we should avoid going much past that—nor should we allow even our necessary examinations of conscience to grow too long (although if we are preparing for a general confession, a much lengthier examination is, of course, called for). A good examination of conscience will always render us more humble, for in it we will recognize just how much more room for growth we have; and if it is a healthy examination, it will not contradict self-forgetfulness. Jesus tells Luisa:

The more the soul humiliates herself and knows herself, the closer she draws to the truth; and being in the truth, she tries to push herself along the path of virtues, from which she sees herself very far away. And if she sees herself on the path of virtues, immediately she realizes how much there is left for her to do, because virtues have no end—they are infinite, as I am. So, being in the truth, the soul always tries to perfect herself, but she will never arrive at seeing herself perfect. And this serves her, and it will make her work continuously, striving to perfect herself more, without wasting time in idleness. And I, pleased with this work, keep retouching her little by little, in order to portray my likeness in her.[629]

On the other hand, when we do much more than this, and start analyzing our own sanctification like a foolish businessman who spends all his time perusing his company's financial statements, we will work against the very thing we are superficially working towards. For just as a good businessman is dedicated to the product his business makes or the service it renders, as he understands that the financial minutiae, though important, is secondary; so, too, one who truly

---

[623] November 13, 1938.
[624] July 1, 1907.
[625] March 6, 1938.
[626] Letter #13 to Fr Bernardo of the Most Holy Hearts from Assisi.
[627] Letter #17 to an unnamed recipient.
[628] Letter #60 to an unnamed religious.
[629] January 1, 1900.

wishes to become a saint is dedicated to the salvation of souls and the consolation of Jesus, instead of the endless pondering of the current state of his sanctification and the strategizing of the next step in that process. For as the good businessman understands that healthy finances are best assured by doing well what the business exists for the sake of, so, too, the wise man who desires to be a saint will recognize that his sanctification is best assured by his zeal for the salvation of souls and his love of Jesus. Jesus tells Luisa:

> …I would like that you too would not occupy yourself with your weaknesses, your evils and your troubles. In fact, the more the creature thinks about those, the weaker she feels, and the more the poor one feels drowned by evils, while her miseries press round her more tightly. By thinking about it, weakness feeds more weakness, and the poor creature keeps falling even more; evils acquire more strength, miseries make her die of hunger. On the other hand, by not thinking about them, they disappear of their own. The complete opposite happens with what is good. A good feeds another good; one act of love calls for more love; one abandonment in my Will makes her feel the new Divine Life within herself. Hence, the thought of what is good forms the nourishment and the strength in order to do more good. This is why I want your thoughts to be occupied by nothing other than loving Me and living in my Will. My Love will burn up all your miseries and all your evils, and my Divine Volition will become your Life, making use of your miseries as the footstool on which to raise Its throne.[630]

> [Luisa said]: I was thinking: 'What would be better: to think about sanctifying oneself, or to occupy oneself, only before Jesus, with repairing Him, and to seek at any cost, together with Jesus, the salvation of souls?' And blessed Jesus told me: "My daughter, one who thinks only of repairing Me and of saving souls, lives at the expense of my Sanctity. In seeing that the soul wants nothing other than to repair Me, and echoing my enflamed heartbeat, she asks Me for souls, I see in her the characteristics of my Humanity; and taken by folly toward her, I make her live at the expense of my Sanctity, of my desires, of my love, at the expense of my strength, of my Blood, of my wounds, etc. I can say that I place my Sanctity at her disposal, knowing that she wants nothing other than what I want. On the other hand, one

who thinks about sanctifying only herself, lives at the expense of her sanctity, of her strength, of her love. Oh! how miserable will she grow. She will feel all the weight of her misery, and will live in continuous struggle with herself. Instead, for one who lives at the expense of my Sanctity, her path will flow placid; she will live in peace with herself and with Me."[631]

Let us conclude this section by directly addressing the diabolical vice of pride—a topic that we have dealt with in a much more general manner in the preceding pages.

Against Pride

The Gift of Living in the Divine Will is the greatest gift that God can give. He will not give it to the proud. He will, rather, *scatter the proud in their conceit.*[632] If you desire that people think of you as having the Gift, you will not receive it. If, in having the Gift, you would think yourself as above any other soul, you will not be given it

A desire for and pursuit of hiddenness is among the most powerful means to destroy pride. This hiddenness was a defining factor of Luisa's own life. In like manner, you should be careful where you permit your thoughts to wander. In doing good, do you daydream about people finding out? Or better yet, finding out while still thinking you wanted no one to find out? Cease such thinking and remember that your thoughts are not your own any more than your actions are your own; God must be sovereign over them all. Foster in your heart a sense of holy embarrassment at the thought of anyone admiring you, for you know how weak and miserable you are. Perhaps only you, your confessors, and God alone know just the extent of it.

Is growth in holiness for you really a means to some vain end, perhaps getting this or that person to respect you more, or rising in the ranks of your parish, order, school, diocese, or other institution? Plot out practical ways to ensure that other people are thanked for your efforts. Have in mind a way of responding to any compliment that will give the credit where it is due; namely, to God, and to others. Ponder how to do so in a way that you are not just making sure you get the credit for the good deed, and for the apparent humility in crediting

---

[630] December 25, 1937.
[631] November 15, 1918.

[632] *The Magnificat; Cf.* Luke 1:51

God! Remember that humility is nothing other than truth—when you see God, you will be humbled before Him, no matter how great your virtue becomes. It is best you prepare yourself for that now.

On the Feast of the Immaculate Conception, Our Lady said to St. Faustina:

> I desire, My dearly beloved daughter, that you practice the three virtues that are dearest to Me-and most pleasing to God. The first is humility, humility, and once again humility…[633]

Although humility is neither a moral virtue,[634] supernatural virtue, gift of the Holy Spirit, nor fruit of the Holy Spirit, it is nevertheless a shortcut—an elevator, almost—to all of them. It is the key to receiving grace. Of all perfections of the soul one can pursue, humility will yield the greatest results the most quickly. St. Faustina later refers to humility as *the most precious of the virtues."*

Having settled the place that humility deserves in our lives, I propose the following four-word norm to guide our every thought, word, and deed, whenever the virtue of humility is in question: **if in doubt, humility.**

Moving on, then, from our full-frontal attack on Pride, let us consider the next foundational virtue.

Attentiveness

(*Note: as there are a number of exhortations included here which fall under the banner of "attentiveness," but which are quite distinct from each other, I have simply included them all here, and have separated the different points with the triple asterisk.)*

God does not waste one second. He understands much better than we do just how incredibly precious is this very short amount of time we spend as pilgrims on earth. Therefore, He is always trying to make us into great saints, but this cannot be successful if we refuse to be attentive to this endeavor. Jesus tells Luisa:

> …**what I wanted from Adam-the little sacrifice of depriving himself of a fruit-and it was not granted to Me.** How could I trust him and ask of him a greater sacrifice? … The same happens in all creatures. It is My usual way to ask for small sacrifices-depriving oneself of a pleasure, of a

desire, of a small interest, of a vanity, or detaching oneself from something that seems to do one no harm. These small tests serve as little shelves on which to place the great capital of My Grace in order to dispose them to accept greater sacrifices … How many sanctities begin from a small sacrifice; and how many, after denying Me a small sacrifice, as it seemed to them that it was something of no importance, have remained scrawny in good, cretinous in comprehending it, weak in walking on the way that leads to Heaven. ..Therefore, My daughter, it takes greater attention to small sacrifices than to great ones, because the small ones are the strength of the great…[635]

Oh, how tragically often Christians jump to defensiveness at the smallest hint of a suggestion (whether it be interior- within their own hearts and minds; or exterior -from the word of another) that something (which is not intrinsically evil) nevertheless should be abandoned and moved on from, simply because it is not helping, and is perhaps even hampering, spiritual growth.

But it is God Himself Who makes these suggestions (either by doing so directly within one's own heart, or by using another person as a messenger), and woe to those who stop at nothing to defend whatever the status quo happens to be. These people know exactly who they are, and so do their friends and relatives. They are proud of all their vanities—their entertainment preferences, their music and dancing habits, their concern for fashion, their questionable tastes in literature, their love of this or that expensive hobby, etc.—and they have become experts in defending these vanities against any encroachment by God's grace. They often even have a whole slew of blog posts they are ready to cite, from "good Catholic authors," insisting that there is nothing wrong with what they are doing!

Alas, they miss the point entirely. **Even if there is nothing intrinsically wrong with what they are doing (which itself is often dubious), that does not change the fact that what they are doing is not conducive to their spiritual growth; if they were only attentive, they would realize this.** In continuing with these habits which they are so quick to defend, they are rejecting these little requests from Jesus for small sacrifices, just as

---

[633] St. Faustina, *Divine Mercy in My Soul*, Paragraph 1415.
[634] Although it is considered to be annexed to the moral virtue of temperance.

[635] August 15, 1927.

Adam refused the sacrifice of a simple fruit. How, then, can they pretend to be surprised if God does not trust them with anything significant? How can they pretend to be surprised when they remain mired — day after day, month after month, year after year — in exactly the same vices, when they are not even open to the smallest sacrifice? (For abandoning that which is intrinsically evil is justice, not sacrifice). How can they pretend to be surprised when God does not bless any of their efforts, any of their discernment, any of their apostolates, with any significant degree of success, when they have proven that they are misers with Him?

Indeed, if only we remain attentive (as Jesus is constantly reminding Luisa), there would be no more mystery for us in the spiritual life. For attentiveness is the simple understanding that God desires our sanctification even more than we do, and He is not lacking in initiative or ideas for how to bring it about.

***

Now, attentiveness is largely a virtue that corresponds to the memory, which in turn is the most neglected faculty of the soul. Jesus tells Luisa:

> The memory is the beginning of a good ... And not only does this memory produce the origin of every good in life, but after one's death also it produces the origin of glory... the more the soul remembers what belongs to Me, my graces, the lessons I have given her, the more the fount of my goods grows within her, to the point that, unable to contain them, they overflow for the good of others.[636]

Thankfully, we can give aid to our memory in this task! For example, we can place holy reminders — whatever individual quotes, images, etc., touch us the most — in places we will often see them: our desk, our car's dashboard, our nightstand, across from our bed, next to the bathroom mirror, etc. We can develop habits; the momentum they generate will serve as a great aid to the memory. We can be sure to put the things needed for our sanctification on our calendars; not merely the things needed to attend to our duties in the world.

***

Attentiveness also means not letting any ignoble acts force their way into our lives chronologically in between our coming to know God's Will and our

execution of the same; for these two events should always be simultaneous. Jesus tells Luisa of how *cosmically* tragic even a small hesitation in doing the Divine Will is once this Will is known; how even a *sigh* of complaint causes all Heaven to lament. But don't we do this all the time?

- Do we allow ourselves even a brief — exterior or interior — roll of the eyes before proceeding to do what we already know is God's Will, because circumstances have revealed it to be such? This is rebellion.
- Do we do what we know we must, but only after making sure it is known to those around us (or, if we are alone, at least to the empty air around us) how annoyed and irritated we are that we must do this? This is rebellion.
- Have we concocted little rules for ourselves that allow a period of "venting," complaining, or stomping about when something doesn't go how we had expected it or wanted it to go? This is rebellion.
- And, when no one else can see or hear, do we allow ourselves to curse our circumstances — perhaps with exclamations along the lines of "unbelievable!" or "ridiculous!"? This is rebellion.

***

Those who, according to their state in life, have the duty of being attentive for the sake of others, must exercise this duty diligently. In Jesus' words to Luisa we do not see that laxity which is always willing to write off every sin as mere "weakness;" instead, we see His words:

> My daughter, that which is said to be human weakness, most of the time is lack of vigilance and of attention on the part of leaders — that is, parents and superiors. [637]

Dear parents: you have a task in front of you, the importance of which cannot be overstated. By failing to be attentive in your parenting; by letting vices, bad influences, impure media, disobedience, etc., creep in here and there in your children's lives — you are setting them up for disaster. Dear Fathers: it is your duty especially to never allow any of this in your home.

***

Another vital aspect of attentiveness is exercising it in the midst of good works instead of letting these

---

[636] June 1, 1924.

[637] December 29, 1904.

works become merely dry, habitual, reluctant, "check-off-the-box" type activities. Jesus tells Luisa:

> My daughter, the works which most exacerbate my hands, and which most embitter and enlarge my wounds, are the good works done without attention. In fact, lack of attention takes life away from the good work, and things which have no life are always near to rotting; therefore they nauseate Me, and for the human eye a good work done without attention is a greater scandal than sin itself.[638]

It is doubtful that this lack of attention to good works pains Our Lord anywhere more than in the Holy Mass said hastily and as a matter of routine. Tragically, one sees this everywhere today: priests who would clearly rather be doing just about anything else, and who race through a bare-bones minimum of the prayers simply to get them done with. But I do not say these words to foment annoyance at priests: most of us are not priests, and Jesus still says these words to us. Rather, we consider the image of the Mass said poorly, and how clearly lamentable this is, in order to remind ourselves how lamentable it is when we ourselves do the good works of our own state in life with a similar element of hasty and inattentive dissatisfaction. For all the baptized share in the common priesthood, and in the Divine Will especially we are called to offer all our acts to Him and accomplish them in Him.

Remaining attentive does not mean we have to do everything slowly. But it does mean that we must resist the temptation to become like robots; especially when doing good.

Discernment

A frequent theme in Luisa's revelations is Jesus' insistence that what is good and holy only objectively and externally is nothing but utter trash if it is outside of His Will. Readers today should be more inclined to receive this message well, as this matter has been well articulated by great saints like Thérèse of Lisieux, and in the Ignatian *Discernment of Spirits* which is thankfully making a comeback today.

Despite these great works, some Catholics unfortunately have succumbed to a mindset that

goes something like this: "*One needn't concern himself with trying to know God's Will on individual matters so as to accomplish it. One need only know the commandments and other teachings of the Church and obey them; so long as the clear Magisterial teachings are being obeyed, that is all that is ever truly expected of a Catholic.*" This is, to be frank, a diabolical lie from the depths of hell. Incidentally, the approach some take to private revelation in general is in part a consequence of this mentality (see the chapter "On Private Revelation in General" in Part One of this book for more details on that point). Merely avoiding mortal sin—merely refraining from those behaviors which are infallibly condemned by the Church as intrinsic evils—is radically inadequate for any believer in God, much less for any Christian, and much less still for any Catholic. God is not like some referee at a sports game whose only job is to call out fouls or other violations when they occur; He is closer to each of us than our own skin, and He desires to be wedded to our souls. What a crime when we treat Him as a mere referee! About those who take and promote this approach, Jesus tells Luisa:

> They think that not doing my Will is something trivial, but instead, it is the total ruin of the creature; and as many more acts of her own will as she does, so many times does she increase her evils, her ruin, and she digs for herself the most profound abyss in which to fall.[639]

What follows, therefore, is the extreme importance of trying to discern—so that we may both know and do—the Will of God in all things, instead of erroneously supposing that, so long as we are choosing between objectively good options, God has no Will in the matter. This discernment is an essential dimension of our attentiveness.

In the same passage quoted above, Jesus treats this matter carefully, knowing how inclined His children can be, on the one hand, to scrupulosity, and on the other hand, to flippantly moving forward without concern for God's Will. He continues:

> My daughter, Adam fell so low, because he withdrew from an expressed Will of his Creator, that enclosed the test in order to prove his faithfulness toward He who had given him life and all the goods he possessed. More so, since after the so many goods He had given to him for

---

free, God asked of him to deprive himself of one fruit alone of the many fruits He had given him, for love of He who had given him everything.

And in this little sacrifice that God wanted from him, He had let him know that it was for nothing else but to be sure of his love and of his faithfulness. Adam should have felt honored that his Creator wanted to be sure of the love of His creature…

See, then: when My Will is expressed, wanted and commanded, the sin is graver and the consequences are irreparable; and only My Divine Will Itself can make up for such great evil, as it happened with Adam. On the other hand, when It is not expressed, even though the creature has the duty to pray to Me in order to know My Will in her operating, if there is some good in her act, it is My pure Glory, while-if My Will is not expressed-the evil is not so grave, and it is easier to find a remedy.

And I do this with each creature, in order to test their faithfulness, and also to secure the love that they say they have for Me… in order to be sure, I let them know that I want some little sacrifices, that will bring all goods and sanctity to them, and they will fulfill the purpose for which they were created. But if they are reluctant, everything will be upset in them, and all evils will swoop down upon them. Therefore, not doing My Will is always an evil-more or less grave, depending on the knowledge of It that one possesses.[640]

While it is indeed true that the evil of neglecting God's Will, as Jesus says here, is proportional to the degree to which He has expressed it, this does not change the fact that, when we develop a habit of carelessness and inattentiveness to what God desires of us (even in those things which are technically not objective matters that the Faith itself decides for us), we will cause "all evils" to "swoop down" upon us. This, of course, is a terrible fate; but it is exactly what we do to ourselves when we pretend that, so long as we aren't objectively sinning, we can "do whatever we want." No. We must always discern.

Therefore, these words of Jesus should not cause in us a sort of paralysis whereby we fear making decisions unless we know with clarity God's Will (considering the earlier parts of the quote above). And it should equally remind us to not neglect both including God in all of our decisions and sincerely desiring to do all that He Wills—and only that which He Wills—even in our "indifferent" decisions.

The virtue of discernment is of course most important when it comes to discerning one's vocation in life. But presenting an exposition on that would be far too long for these pages. Instead, I recommend St. Francis de Sales great work, *Finding God's Will for You*, and, in general the Discernment of Spirits approach of St. Ignatius of Loyola.

But discernment must always be the theme of our decisions; we are not "done" with it after we have settled into a vocation. We should pray every day to know and do God's will in everything. When discernment seems to lead us to an impasse in a given decision, we should do a novena to know God's Will in it (I recommend a novena to St. Thérèse of Lisieux, who has always told me what to do in such situations by sending a rose). There is not always time for a Novena, nor should we even strive to do a Novena over every little decision we must make. But at least a "Hail Mary" said sincerely before making a small decision can change everything. Do not be afraid, either, to ask God for signs to indicate His Will for you (while not supposing that the lack of these signs indicates anything in particular; for it is not always His Will to give signs to make His Will clear—sometimes a temporary lack of clarity regarding His Will can be a great tool in His hands for your sanctification).

Remember as well that successful discernment can only proceed from the foundation of the principles of orthodox Catholic teaching, so be sure to never give "discernment" sufficient leeway to contradict these—it never can do so. Finally, we should note that discernment essentially amounts to hearing (and heeding) the voice of the Holy Spirit within you—but that quiet voice can be drowned out by two things which will destroy discernment: undisciplined flesh and worldly attachments. These impediments to discernment will be addressed in their own sections later (sections entitled *Mortification and Sacrifice*, and *Detachment*, respectively).

Constant Prayer and a Preference for Silence

"Rejoice always, <u>pray constantly,</u> give thanks in all circumstances; for this is the will of God in Christ Jesus for you. " —1 Thessalonians 5:16-18

Scripture, we can see, admonishes to pray not sometimes, not often, and not *almost* always... but rather, it admonishes us to pray **constantly**. Therefore, this constancy is not optional for any Christian. While the best way to pray constantly is to do all your acts in the Divine Will (as discussed in an earlier chapter), we should also consider simple conversational prayer with God as a continuous occurrence; whether on one's mind or on one's lips. Instead of seeing this as a burden, we should see this as a joy. The Almighty Creator of the Universe desires to always be in conversation with you! And if we acquiesce to this loving desire of His, the Gift is ours. It is that simple. Jesus tells Luisa:

> What I recommend to you is a spirit of continuous prayer. **This continuous effort of the soul to converse with Me, whether with her heart, or with her mind, with her mouth, or even with a simple intention—renders her so beautiful in my sight**, that the notes of her heart harmonize with the notes of my Heart... the beauty that a spirit of continuous prayer makes her acquire is so great, that the devil is as though struck by lightning, and remains frustrated in the snares he lays in order to harm this soul.[641]

Jesus assures Luisa that this continuous desire of the creature to speak with Him "wrenches" the Gift out of His hands, and He cannot help but give it to such a soul.

Does not every child know this? If a child is in loving conversation with his father, he knows that no ill can befall him; he knows that he is exactly where the father wants him and he does not fear, in the midst of a loving conversation, that there may be any offenses—small or large—that he is committing against the father. He furthermore knows that his father will give him everything he needs—everything that is good for him—in this conversation, for how could the father neglect to do so? It is only when conversation ceases, and perhaps a distance arises, that fears enter, and the child may succumb to wondering what his own state is in relation to his father.

What a child cannot do with his earthly father—

remain in continuous loving conversation, certain that his father *always* hears and responds with even more love—we can all do with God, our Heavenly Father. If only we remained constantly speaking to Him—even if this speech is purely mental and subtle and simple, perhaps even scattered among the pauses in our work—then we would have nothing to fear. We would know that the Gift is ours, we would know that our salvation and sanctification is assured, and we would rest always in the peace of knowing that God's Will is done in us.

But what is one thing that makes this constant conversation with God impossible? A failure to respect the virtue of silence. A talkative mind, a talkative mouth, or talkative surroundings. Considering the enormous good that is damaged by these factors, we should proceed to deal rather sternly with them. Jesus tells Luisa:

> ...**one who talks much shows that he is empty** in his interior, while one who is filled with God, finding more taste in his interior, does not want to lose that taste; he hardly speaks and only out of necessity. And even while speaking, he never departs from his interior, and he tries, as much as he can, to impress in others that which he feels within himself. On the other hand, **one who talks much is not only empty of God, but with his much talking, he tries to empty others of God**.[642]

St. Faustina put it even more bluntly, writing in her diary: "A talkative soul will never attain sanctity."[643]

Let us proceed to examine our consciences thoroughly to ensure that talkativeness has no place in our lives.

- Do we waste away the days in idle conversation? Families can be such an incredibly powerful path to sanctity (just read about the family life of St. Thérèse of Lisieux or St. Thomas More—the latter would have Scripture read during dinner—for perfect examples), or they can drag us down to the earth and all the vanities thereof with relentless persistence. Therefore, we should ensure that our homes are not dominated by chatter, gossip, worldly television and music, etc. It can help to have an audio Bible (or Book of Heaven) playing during times that otherwise tend to be

---

[641] July 28, 1902.
[642] May 8, 1909.

[643] *Divine Mercy in My Soul.* 477

dominated by idle chatter: perhaps when doing dishes or preparing food, and to have a good evening prayer regimen such as the Rosary, spiritual reading, and the daily reading of the family's book of intentions, instead of simply "hanging out" until it is time to go to bed.

- Do we turn on secular music or talk radio (and even Catholic stations play plenty of material that is anything but edifying) every time we drive, work, walk, etc.? Or do we fool ourselves into thinking that "Christian" rock or similarly degraded forms of music are edifying just because edifying lyrics are attached to the fundamentally tribal, sexual (and sometimes demonic) beat?
- Do we spend large amounts of time on the telephone?
- Do we feel the need to constantly make comments about our surroundings, or give a voice to every trivial thought that enters our mind or feeling that enters our body—needing to let everyone in the room know whenever we are tired, hungry, hot, cold, have a headache, etc.?

Let us also consider that, on the Day of Judgment, we are going to see what percentage of the time, among all the conversations we found ourselves in, we spent talking vs. the time we spent listening. Many people are in for a rude awakening. O talkative soul, why do you feel the need to tell everybody you come in contact with every detail about news, worldly facts, and stories regarding yourself that even you have a hard time caring about? Are you afraid of silence? It does not take advanced theology or mystical spirituality to diagnose this disease; for even the great philosopher Aristotle saw it full well for what it was:

> And wicked men seek for people with whom to spend their days, and shun themselves; for they remember many a grievous deed, and anticipate others like them, when they are by themselves, but when they are with others they forget.[644]

Indeed, the constant need for noise sometimes arises from our desire to distract ourselves from ourselves. What used to be done with the constant company of others, as Aristotle mentions above, is today more often done by always having a television, radio, computer, or smartphone telling us what to think.

Incessant long stories, soliloquies, rants, gossip, and idle chatting destroy not only the individual, but also the community. Sometimes all it takes is one such person to ruin the social cohesion of an entire group. So many Catholic apostolates have been torn apart by symptoms that all boil down to talkativeness and a neglect of proper silence. Meanwhile, even many worldly endeavors plod along well next to these dying apostolates, because their members at least exercise the restraint to control the tongue and do not feel the need to share their every thought, opinion, criticism, and defense.

This is why good religious orders are so careful in enforcing the Rule as it pertains to silence. The rule of silence is, among other things, a guard against motormouths, gossips, opinionated and defensive individuals destroying the community's atmosphere. Furthermore, the Church (especially the Magisterium of Pope Francis) is careful to even insist that homilies be brief! Yes, a homily too can easily become nothing but a drawn-out talking session by the preacher. And if this goes on for long, it will destroy the Parish. Indeed, talkativeness can turn even seemingly holy things into vanity (for another example, by carrying on a holy conversation long after it should have ended and turned to holy *action*).

***

Cardinal Robert Sarah recently wrote an excellent book, *The Power of Silence: Against the Dictatorship of Noise*, and in it he provides many gems of wisdom, a few of which we consider here:

> "Words often bring with them the illusion of transparency, as though they allowed us to understand everything, control everything, put everything in order. Modernity is talkative because it is proud, unless the converse is true. Is our incessant talking perhaps what makes us proud?"

> "Superficial and vain, the talkative person is a dangerous being. The now widespread habit of testifying in public to the divine graces granted in the innermost depths of a man's soul exposes him to the dangers of superficiality, the self-betrayal of his interior friendship with God, and vanity."

---

[644]Nicomachean Ethics Book IX. Section 4.

"It is necessary to leave our interior turmoil in order to find God. Despite the agitations, the busyness, the easy pleasures, God remains silently present. He is in us like a thought, a word, and a presence whose secret sources are buried in God himself, inaccessible to human inspection. Solitude is the best state in which to hear God's silence."

"Without silence, God disappears in the noise. And this noise becomes all the more obsessive because God is absent. Unless the world rediscovers silence, it is lost. The earth then rushes into nothingness"

"If our "interior cell phone" is always busy because we are "having a conversation" with other creatures, how can the Creator reach us, how can he "call us"?"

As the Cardinal aptly demonstrates, the issue is far too pressing to approach with lukewarmness. Let us not make excuses; even so-called "therapeutic talking," or "venting" is not okay, and is not something we have a right to simply because we have decided that we "need it." In fact, whenever we feel inclined to rationalize something with the words "I need this," it is most likely not God's Will. Unfortunately, we all fall into pretending our needs are thousands of times larger than they actually are.

For what we *really* need is silence. This silence will also dispose us for the next Foundational Virtue — detachment — for it is often due to the lack of silence that we grow attached to things.

***

But external silence guarantees nothing; for it is possible that this will do nothing but further enable the operations of a talkative mind. The ultimate battle, therefore, lies within. Because of how radically divergent the nature of a talkative mind will be from person to person, we cannot go over many details here. But one common theme is thinking about the past. Jesus tells Luisa:

> My daughter, do not look at the past, because the past is already in Me and can be of distraction for you, and it can make you mistake that little bit of path that is left for you to cover. In fact, your turning to the past makes you slow your pace on the present journey, and so you lose time and do not advance on your way. On the other hand, by looking only at the present, you will have more courage, you will remain more closely united

with Me, you will advance more on your path, and there will be no danger of your being mistaken.[645]

Occasionally, thinking about the past can be edifying: if, for example, this thinking involves the recollection of the guidance, blessings, etc., God has given you when so recalling becomes helpful. But usually, thinking about the past is little more than useless nostalgia or, worse, ungodly dwelling on wounds or otherwise "living in the past." This behavior must be left behind.

Thinking about the future is equally harmful (although it, too, of course also has times when it is called for — such as anticipating the Coming of the Kingdom, praying for a holy death, etc.). Usually, harmful thinking about the future arises from mistrust, which will be dealt with in its own section shortly.

Another common object of a "talkative mind" is the endless pondering of those things to which one is attached. Detachment, therefore, is the next virtue we shall consider.

Detachment

It only takes one tiny thread tied to a bird to prevent its flight. So it is with us in the spiritual life; particularly with regard to the Gift of Living in the Divine Will. Jesus tells Luisa:

> [the life of the soul] must be a life more of Heaven than of earth — more divine than human! Even one shadow, one little thing, is enough to prevent the soul from feeling the strength, the harmonies, the sanctity of my heartbeat; and so she does not echo my heartbeat, she does not harmonize together with Me, and I am forced to remain alone in my sorrow or in my joys.[646]

> My daughter, courage, the beginning of eternal beatitude is to lose every taste of one's own…Not one soul that enters the port of eternal beatitude can be exempted from this point — painful, yes, but necessary; nor can she do without it. Generally they do it at the point of death, and Purgatory does the last job; this is why, if creatures are asked what God's taste is like, what divine beatitude means, these are things unknown to them and they are unable to articulate a word. But with the souls who are my beloved, since they have given themselves completely to Me, I do not want their beatitude to

645 November 2, 1909.

646 April 1, 1916.

have its beginning up there in Heaven, but to start down here on earth. I want to fill them not only with the happiness, with the glory of Heaven, but I want to fill them with the goods, with the sufferings, with the virtues that my Humanity had upon earth; therefore I strip them, not only of material tastes, which the soul considers as dung, but also of spiritual tastes, in order to fill them completely with my goods and give them the beginning of true beatitude.[647]

Attachments cannot enter Heaven. But, as we see here, Jesus does not want us to go to Purgatory (and nor should we want to go there), where we will be detached from everything, but with far greater pain than would be required on earth to achieve the same detachment. Furthermore, in Purgatory there is no merit or eternal glory from the detachment there achieved.

In this teaching, Jesus is expanding upon attachment in general, saying that even tastes must be done away with. However, I have named this section "detachment" instead of "absence of tastes" simply because the latter would, I think, be confusing to those perusing the Table of Contents. But there is also indeed a difference: one can be *attached* to worldly things, but one can have a *taste* even for holy things. All of that must go and be replaced with the Will of God. Let us first consider the lower attachments to worldliness.

…From Worldliness

It should go without saying—but unfortunately it does not—that worldliness and living in the Divine Will are mutually exclusive.

There are always a million excuses available for one to justify worldliness. Saying *yes* to the Divine Will requires saying *no* to all these excuses. And we should be rigorous in dealing with these excuses; few will come out unscathed after reading the following paragraphs (least of all I, who wrote them!).

Some dedicate their lives to amassing possessions and financial investments or savings, buying fancy cars, and endlessly perfecting their houses. They simply defer to that catch-all rationalization used any time a Christian wants to justify doing something of this sort that he knows is not in accord

with his call to sanctification: "prudence." Prudence of course is a virtue, and we must have and pursue it. But here is what Jesus tells Luisa about *human* prudence:

> Ah! **how many divine works the human prudence has caused to fail in the midst of creatures. Like sluggards, they have reached the point of withdrawing from the holiest works.** But my Will will know how to triumph of everything and make a mockery of them; however, I cannot hide the sorrow for such great human ingratitude …[648]

We ought to remember that *there is no such thing as worldly safety, and there is no such thing as worldly security*. These are both illusions. Find the man who, in all the world, seems to have the most of both and anyone can easily show just how precarious his real position is. Recall what God said to the man who amassed grain in Jesus' parable:

> Fool! This night your soul is required of you; and the things you have prepared, whose will they be?[649]

Some want to justify questionable choices in music, movies, and media in general. Sadly, many Catholics just cannot bear not being lock-step with the times when it comes to what the media presents to us. Such an approach, far from constituting "meeting people where they're at," or "being an ordinary person in a good way," is really a thinly veiled worldliness and is incompatible with sanctity.

Some are attached to travel. They bring up the "quote from St. Augustine" (he never said it): "The World is a book, and those who do not travel read only a page." (The quote comes from an 18th century French author of erotic and anti-clerical novels.[650]) Indeed, aside from a pilgrimage or mission when it was called for, most saints felt no need to travel, for they all knew that the Will of God was perfectly accessible to them where God had placed them. But affixing a pious looking sticker to a worldly desire for travel changes little.

Some obsess over appearance. Ignoring the admonitions in Sacred Scripture (for example, St. Peter's admonitions to women: "*Let not yours be the outward adorning with braiding of hair, decoration of*

---

[647] December 6, 1904.
[648] August 23, 1928.
[649] Luke 12:20

[650] Louis-Chalres Fougeret de Monbron

gold ... "[651]), they pretend that they have a right and even duty to do everything possible to look like the pictures of models on the front covers of worldly magazines. Pretending further, they assert this is really "glorifying the God Who gave them their bodies," and they conclude from this premise that He also wishes them to fixate themselves upon picking away at its superficial, fleeting perfection. In this category, women go about putting on pounds of makeup every morning, and men (and some women) spend hours in the gym every day.

But alas, we still have not mentioned the appearance-obsession epidemic today: social media. Some practically live for the glorification of their Facebook profile. Everything they do is judged solely on the criteria of *"Will posting about this and getting pictures of myself doing this make me look cooler on my profile?"*

Here the matter of old age should be addressed; for **old age is God's invitation to a life more directly focused on Him and to take more care to move on from the worldly attachments that may have been too great an influence in earlier years.** And if this invitation is heeded, then old age can be the greatest era of one's days on earth, and thus become the true "Monastery of Life." But so many reject this invitation from their loving Father; turning old age into nothing but an opportunity to increase and explore vanities that they could not find the time for when they worked full-time or raised children. How tragic this is: precisely at the time when the external frivolities of life start to fade in a glorious way, thus inviting the soul to fix itself upon that which remains eternally, the soul instead turns to frantically striving to maintain these frivolities and expand them.

***

Please understand that none of the things referenced above are evils. One who objects to this section by pointing out this fact, therefore, is missing the point. Indeed—travel, movies, caring for one's appearance, and other things can be licit so long as we are careful to observe moderation, implore and follow the Will of God in all of them, "make no provisions for the flesh"[652] (e.g. never *follow* the passions), and be ready in an instant to abandon our current approach completely if we discern that God is calling us out of it.

And what is one sure way of knowing we are not approaching these things with moderation and in accord with the Will of God? *That we think about them when not directly occupied with them.* St. Francis de Sales, the great Doctor of the Spiritual Life for the Laity, teaches that in this we know we have developed an unholy affection for a thing.

"Whatever you think about most ... that might be your God."[653]

...From Our Time Wasters

Jesus repeatedly implores Luisa not to *waste time.* Luisa too, in her letters, implored their recipients to not *waste time.* In one diary entry, Jesus even sums up all the teachings He gave in it in one sentence to Luisa:

So, I recommend to you—do not waste time, because by wasting time you come to hamper my real Life, which I am forming in you.[654]

And the first line of one of Luisa's letters was simple:

I beg you not to waste time.[655]

Most people, tragically, have more or less deliberately filled their lives up with utterly vain time wasters to the point that they've decided they simply "don't have time" for more prayer, works of mercy, spiritual reading, etc. Perhaps this, above all, is why most who reject Luisa's revelations do so: they've decided they just "don't have time" for "another private revelation." (Perhaps such people should be handed this book with a bookmark placed on this page!)

Ignoring for now the most obvious of time wasters, let us consider what remains. So many allow their lives to be dominated by constant needless visits to doctors, dentists, and various other health care professionals (contra Our Lord's own words, "those who are well do not need a physician"[656]); having hair stylist appointments and barber visits; getting car washes (not to mention the incessant "necessary" maintenance that many people believe is necessary merely because those who profit off of

---

[651] 1 Peter 3:3
[652] Romans 13:14
[653] Cf. The First Commandment: Thou Shalt Have No Gods Before Me
[654] November 5, 1923.
[655] Letter #99 to Sister Remigia
[656] Luke 5:31

giving it say so); having needlessly long exercise routines each day; having every single afternoon filled up with the kids' sports (and the concomitant need for incessant chauffeuring); treating pets like children; getting pedicures and manicures; having daily makeup and hair routines, and general self-pampering rituals; incessant self-photographing or family-photographing; visiting the dry cleaner for things that could easily be tossed in the laundry without the world ending; washing clothes long before they are dirty and showering after even the faintest hint of sweat has become visible; obsessing over the perfection of the home's cleanliness; mowing the lawn five times as often as necessary (along with innumerable other pointless self-imposed lawn and garden duties); shopping for unneeded things, "window shopping," and having enormous amounts of time spent grocery shopping due to how finicky they've allowed their tastes to become (along with huge amounts of time spent cooking gourmet meals each day); and having countless hours researching product purchases, or "shopping around" when it at best saves a few dollars.

And all these items are just the various chores and "To Dos" which people fill up their days with; it is not even to mention that, despite this lamentable busy-body way of life, there is somehow oodles of time each day to waste on utter nonsense. Social media, web browsing, television, movies, video games and computer games, oversleeping, lazing about, entire afternoons spent "vegging out," endless "hanging out," hours spent on the phone in unimportant conversations, etc.

So many people's days are chock full of things that make us stressed, consume our time and money, do not make us happy, and are completely pointless. If we even were rid of half of these things (although we ought to be rid of them all) and chose to replace them with prayer, we would quickly become saints (not to mention very happy people!).

For all of this garbage with which we fill our days flies in the face of the truth of how incredibly precious these few moments on earth are—moments that God has graciously given us. When we squander it on vanity, we behave like Esau who gave away his inheritance for a bowl of soup.[657] We

cannot live in the Divine Will if we do not recognize the gifts that the Will of God has already bestowed upon us: especially the most precious gift of time. And we prove with our deeds that we do not recognize the preciousness of this gift when we waste it; just as no one who, upon handing a beautiful present to another, would believe the latter's voiced gratitude if he immediately tossed it into a garbage can.

…From Other People

It matters not how good and holy the object of our attachment is: all attachments must go. Is anything holier than the humanity of Jesus? And yet, even that "had to go" in order for the Apostles to fulfill their mission; as Jesus said in the Gospel, "do not cling to me, for I have not yet ascended to the Father."[658] Jesus tells Luisa:

> Do you not remember that this was said to my very Apostles—that it was necessary for them to detach themselves from my Humanity, which they loved very much, and could not be without It? This is so true that, as long as I lived on earth, they did not depart from Me in order to go throughout the whole world to preach the Gospel and make my coming upon earth known. But after my departure for Heaven, invested by the Divine Spirit, they received this strength to leave their region in order to make known the goods of Redemption, and to lay down even their lives for love of Me. So, my Humanity would have been a hindrance to the mission of my Apostles.[659]

Even devout souls are sometimes unfortunately known to dispense themselves from this virtue of detachment so long as they feel they are justified in being attached to something sufficiently good in itself. But Jesus' words are clear:

> He who loves father or mother more than me is not worthy of me; and he who loves son or daughter more than me is not worthy of me; and he who does not take his cross and follow me is not worthy of me. He who finds his life will lose it, and he who loses his life for my sake will find it.[660]

- Young adults today are known to be so attached to their parents that one wonders if they think they are still in elementary school; vocations, even, are often lost because of this degree of attachment.

---

657 Cf. Genesis 25:33
658 John 20:17

659 December 3, 1926.
660 Matthew 10:37-39.

- The Will of God, clearly expressed, is often rejected because it would entail moving on from a good parish or a good circle of Catholic friends who have become the object of attachment.
- People accumulate so many possessions that have "sentimental value" or "holy value" that their house is a perpetually cluttered mess. Some parents treat toddlers like infants and school-aged children like toddlers. Even good Catholic parents spend all their time worrying about their grown-up children and catering to their every superficial need.
- Catholics called to higher degrees of sanctity nevertheless remain stuck in the early stages of the spiritual life only because their good Catholic friends are stuck there, and they are too attached to move on from the past.
- "Family traditions" become so numerous and expansive that they bog down the spiritual life and defeat their own purpose. People spend copious amounts of time watching old home videos and leafing through pictures of days gone by.

The list goes on. As painful as it might be at first to hear that we must be detached from everything—even the holiest things—it is not difficult to see how necessary this type of detachment is.

Abnegation

Abnegation, or abandonment, while related to the detachment discussed in the previous section, is nevertheless sufficiently distinct that it deserves its own section. Jesus tells Luisa:

> The virtue of abandonment is the greatest virtue, it is a pledge to God that he takes care of the abandoned one in his arms, abandonment says to God: 'I don't want to know anything of myself, this life of mine is yours…[661]

This abnegation must be complete; for it must be such a renunciation that we give up even our "spiritual rights" to Jesus. Here we see nothing other than exactly what St. Louis de Montfort taught that Marian Consecration consists in, where **all** our intentions and spiritual "rights" are given entirely to the Blessed Mother. Jesus tells Luisa:

> … there are souls who, when they reach the point

of losing all the rights over their own will, draw back and content themselves with conducting a life in the middle. In fact, losing one's rights is the greatest sacrifice that a creature could do; but it is the one which disposes my goodness to open the doors of my Will for her, and, letting her live in It, to give her my divine rights in exchange.[662]

Why do we need "rights"? We know that our Father is all powerful and loves us infinitely and perfectly. We know that He wants to give us His own Will. We do not need rights any more. Rights are for those who have some degree of distrust for the one in power. God gives us spiritual rights so that even those who are weak in trust have something to cling to; but this is a stage in the spiritual life in which we ought not linger. We must, instead, cast **everything** into the loving hands of God.

"Thy Will, not mine, be done."[663]

If those blessed words of our Blessed Lord are always on our lips, and if we always strive with our whole heart to mean it more and more each day, then we are well on the way to living the total abnegation—the total surrender—that Jesus wishes of us in order to live in His Will.

Remember, as discussed in the renunciation section which deals with this virtue more broadly, that Jesus does not want our wills destroyed or annihilated like the darkness disappears upon illumination. He simply wants them small and continually sacrificed to His. Nor does He want our wills weak and fluid like a jellyfish or an ephemeral wisp of smoke. He wants them like diamonds. Though inevitably small, these souls are constant and indestructible, certain of God's Will where God has revealed it and with face set like flint with great strength to proceed in that path; come what may, whether this entails heroic exertion, epic conquests, appearing foolish and ridiculous in the eyes of the world, the shedding of every drop of blood, or anything else—even being content with a life far less "great" than one initially wanted. Sometimes, ironically, that last abnegation can be the hardest of all, so we turn now to consider abnegation even in our pursuit of sanctity.

Even in Our Pursuit of Sanctity

---

[661] April 23, 1933.
[662] September 22, 1924.

[663] Luke 22:42

Dr. Peter Kreeft, a Catholic Philosopher, shared great wisdom in a talk he once gave, saying "becoming a saint requires abandoning all of our own plans, including those we have on how to become a saint." Indeed, we should regularly ask all the following questions, and answer them with our lives as best we can:

- How can I most effectively aid in the salvation of souls?
- How can I most effectively aid in the sanctification of souls?
- How can I most effectively oppose the nefarious plans of the enemies of Christianity?
- How can I most effectively defend the Truth?

These and other questions are important to ask ourselves regularly —with due regard to Our Lord's admonition to be wise as serpents,[664] and not only innocent as doves; and also with due regard to His lamentation that the worldly are more zealous in their own affairs than are the children of light.[665]

However, it is equally important to ensure that how we answer those questions is always subservient to the answer to the question infinitely superior to them all, which is:

What is God's Will; that I may know it, do it, and live it, no matter what?

All that matters is God's Will. There are always only two options: God's Will, or straw.

Jesus' words to Luisa make this clear. For example, He says:

> My daughter, true charity must be disinterested on the part of one who does it, and on the part of one who receives it. If there is interest, that mud produces a smoke which blinds the mind, and prevents one from receiving the influence and the effects of divine charity. This is why in many works that are done, even holy, in many charitable cares that are performed, one feels as though a void, and they do not receive the fruit of the charity that they do."[666]

> This is why I keep taking everything else away from you, be they even good and holy things: to be able to give you the best and the holiest—which is I; and to be able to make of you another Myself, as much as it is possible for a creature.[667]

...the acts that are not done in My Will, be they even good, do not set out on the Royal Road; they set out through winding roads, and make a long stop to go to Purgatory, and there wait for the creature, so as to be purified together by dint of fire. And when they are done with being purified, then do they set out for Heaven, to take their place-not in places of Prime Order, but in secondary places. Do you see the great difference?[668]

[Luisa laments]: "And if one hears of some awakening of religion, of works of Catholic Actions—some of them seem to be masquerades; others seem to have only the mark of good, but deep inside, in the substance, there are some with vices and passions such as to be wept over, more than before."[669]

And many other passages could easily be quoted which give the same essential teaching: that which is objectively good and holy is not necessarily the Will of God at any given moment for any given person. On Judgment Day we will see how many seemingly good and holy works were thoroughly tainted by the human will, but even now it is not difficult to see examples:

- Many Catholic apostolates become worldly; for shortly after they become well known they change to become operated with a purely temporal mindset instead of an eternal mindset.
- Many Catholic parishes operate more like businesses than what they should be: saint factories.
- Many Catholic authors seem more concerned with book royalties than with disseminating the Truth.
- Many ambitious Catholics, desiring notoriety, neglect the infinitely more important duties of their state in life for the sake of pursuing this notoriety.

In all the above, Jesus Himself is often entirely forgotten, ignored, and neglected despite these works being nominally directed to His ends. And these are all the fruits of being fixated upon the external and objective goodness or holiness of a work and neglecting the one thing that ultimately matters: The Will of God. The last point in particular is addressed in Luisa's writings. Jesus

---

[664] Cf. Matthew 10:16
[665] Cf. Luke 16:8
[666] July 31, 1902.

[667] June 12, 1913.
[668] February 16, 1932.
[669] June 18, 1925.

tells Luisa:

> Even in Heaven there are diversity of choirs of Angels, diversity of Saints: one is Martyr, one is Virgin, one is Confessor. On earth My Providence maintains so many diverse Offices: one is king, one is judge, one is priest, one is people, one commands, one is dependent. If all were doing one single Office, what would become of the earth? A complete disorder. **O! if everyone knew that only My Divine Will knows how to do the Greatest Things, and although they would be little and insignificant, O! how they would be all content and each one would love his little place, the Office in which God has placed him.** But since they let themselves be lorded over by the human volition, they would want to give of themselves, to make the great actions. That they cannot do, therefore they are always discontent with the conditions or the place in which Divine Providence has placed them for their Good. [670]

So many want a "clearer" path to the goal than the Will of God. So many want something more "tangible." And indeed, there are many clear and tangible helps to arrive at the end of sanctity; but none of them are sanctity itself—not even the holiest of them. And what happens if we nevertheless still insist on casting this truth aside? Jesus answers this, saying:

> The thing which [the devil] abhors the most is that the creature do my Will. He does not care whether the soul prays, goes to Confession, goes to Communion, does penance or makes miracles; but the thing which harms him the most is that the soul do my Will, because as he rebelled against my Will, then was hell created in him…[671]

What strategy shall we concoct to stave off the need to practice abnegation even in holy things and thus allow the Will of God to be our beginning, our end, and even our constant and sole true companion along the way? What objectively good and holy thing shall we grab from the list to ascribe as our ultimate end to "simplify" (that is, transform into self-will) our spiritual lives and our endeavors to become saints? Let us consider a few in order of ascending degree of objective holiness, and recognize how each could easily prove divergent from the Will of God and thus do nothing but destroy His works:

- Shall we devote ourselves to apologetics?

How easily one could spend a life in apologetics and only at the end of it realize that he has done nothing but push people away.

- Shall we devote ourselves to being examples to others in an effort to draw them in to our way of life—our faith? Without this being the Will of God, it becomes little more than an exercise in vanity and a prideful love of self.

- Shall we pour ourselves out in works of mercy? It may well be that even a dedicated undertaking of the same will be received by all with nothing but scorn.

- Can we simply then leave it all to the Sacraments—with daily Mass and weekly confession guaranteeing our sanctity? This can easily become nothing but a thoughtless routine, turned into mere opportunities for chatting.

- Will countless hours in prayer at least make us saints with certainty? What good is such prayer if it is a one-way conversation? You may well find that, even with your days filled with prayers that are objectively good, you are still doing nothing but what Jesus lamented, namely, "babbling like the pagans."[672]

Can we then at least be certain of our sanctity if we spend all day in Eucharistic Adoration? Here we come so close to the ultimate good; but still, even this is an externality, and no externality guarantees anything. On Judgment Day, your motives may be revealed as little other than wanting others to see your "holiness" and appreciate the same, while when in adoration your mind and heart are far from God. Furthermore, it is even possible that you could forget that the Eucharist will not exist in Heaven and Jesus does not Will to forever remain hidden under veils. Doubtless, the Eucharist is the greatest source of sanctification for us; in receiving it daily at Holy Mass, and in spending as much time as possible with Jesus in the Eucharist in adoration. So, while never neglecting the superlative importance of these things, let us see what Jesus says to Luisa about them. Contrasting a certain mother to certain bad priests and so-called "devout" souls who receive the Eucharist daily, Jesus says, of this mother:

---

[670] October 4, 1935.
[671] September 9, 1923.

[672] Matthew 6:7

...there may be a mother who does my Will and who, because of her situation, not because she does not want to, cannot receive Me every day; and one sees that she is patient, charitable, and carries the fragrance of my Eucharistic virtues within herself. Ah, is it perhaps the Sacrament or, rather, my Will to which she is submitted, that keeps her subdued and makes up for the Most Holy Sacrament? Even more, I tell you that the Sacraments themselves produce fruits according to how souls are submitted to my Will. They produce effects according to the connection that souls have with my Volition. And if there is no connection with my Will, they may receive Communion, but will remain on an empty stomach; they may go to Confession, but will remain always dirty; they may come before my Sacramental Presence, but if our wills do not meet, I will be as though dead for them, because my Will alone produces all goods and gives life to the very Sacraments in the soul who lets herself be subdued by It. And those who do not understand this—it means that they are babies in religion.[673]

It was only with much trepidation that I even included the previous list in this book; I have done something dangerous here. For indeed, I would be devastated to learn that any of my words ever had the slightest effect of lessening anyone's zeal for works of mercy, prayer, the Sacraments, daily Mass, adoration, etc. So please, I implore you, do not slacken in zeal for these holy things. **My point, rather, is simply this: God's Will, and God's Will alone is wherein sanctity is found, and the Will of God is already perfectly simple, therefore it cannot be reduced to anything simpler,** notwithstanding our human desires for a clear formula which defines the attainment of all our ends.

Now, while it may at first be painful to hear that none of those exceedingly holy *things* can guarantee *your holiness* (but that only the Will of God can), this truth should in fact do nothing but allow a great peace to permeate your entire soul: for **the Will of God is pure love, and it is always with you. It is never inaccessible; nothing can separate you from it.** Through no fault of your own, you may be deprived of the Eucharist, Confession, the ability to perform works of mercy, or even the ability to pray. But no matter what has transpired

thus far with respect to these things, the greatest sanctity is nevertheless knocking at your door this very moment, and always will be—and all you need to do is say "yes" to it. *Fiat.*

This Fiat will, in fact, inundate you with peace. So let us turn now to peace as a Foundational Virtue.

Perennial Peace and Trust

Although "peace" is indeed more a fruit than a strict virtue, it is nevertheless not unwarranted to include it in this section, inasmuch as nothing in the spiritual life is merely passive, but rather requires our cooperation. Let us, therefore, ensure we always cooperate with God's Will for our perennial peace.

What is the greatest obstacle to holiness?

A response close at hand would, no doubt, be "sin." But that response would be wrong. Jesus tells St. Faustina:

> My child, know that the greatest obstacles to holiness are discouragement and an exaggerated anxiety. These will deprive you of the ability to practice virtue.[674]

Sin, therefore, is not the greatest obstacle to holiness. Though this may at first seem heretical or groundbreaking, it is, in fact, neither. Consider that if sin was the greatest obstacle to holiness, then any serious Catholic would be utterly insane to do anything but find a good monastery (utterly devoid of any occasion of sin) and join it. That is indeed a great calling, but it is truly not the genuine calling of most. So, let us heed the words of Pope Benedict XVI:

> Dear friends, may no adversity paralyze you. Be afraid neither of the world, nor of the future, nor of your weakness. The Lord has allowed you to live in this moment of history so that, by your faith, his name will continue to resound throughout the world.[675]

In Luisa's letters, what she perhaps exhorted their recipients to most frequently was peace. Luisa knew—from her own wisdom as a devout Catholic and from the revelations she received from Jesus—that the perennial temptation in our lives is to deprive ourselves of peace as if this were somehow called for, when in fact this deprivation is always

---

[673] September 25, 1913.
[674] St. Faustina, *Divine Mercy in My Soul*, Paragraph 1488.

[675] Benedict XVI. Homily at World Youth Day. August 20, 2011.

an affront to the goodness of God, Who never desires that we be without peace.

But in order to have a true and deep peace, we should, as our first step, consider how we view God's mercy; for only trust in this mercy can bring about peace. Do you truly trust in God's mercy, knowing that it will be there for you no matter how great or numerous your falls, or do you really view it as just a safety net for you if your own human efforts prove insufficient? Know well that God's mercy is the only hope for any of us, even the greatest of saints. St. Faustina was known to respond genuinely to anyone who mentioned her as being saintly with: *"if it were not for God's mercy, I would perish just like any sinner."* Our attitude should be the same, no matter how virtuous we become, and no matter how highly others view us.

In pursuing this attitude, strive to remind yourself, whenever you meet a poor soul mired in the dissolution and a life of mortal sin, *"there but for the grace of God go I."* Your own efforts were not the cause of your current state, nor will they be the cause of your preservation in grace; God is sovereign over both. Have no fear of evil news, for the same God who now nourishes you with everything you need will still be there no matter what happens to you. As Jesus said in the Gospel:

> Therefore I tell you, do not be anxious about your life ... Consider the lilies of the field, how they grow; they neither toil nor spin; yet I tell you, even Solomon in all his glory was not arrayed like one of these. But if God so clothes the grass of the field, which today is alive and tomorrow is thrown into the oven, will he not much more clothe you, O men of little faith?[676]

God wants to pour His grace into our lives; we prevent Him by preferring anxiety and fretfulness to peace and trust. Jesus tells Luisa:

> See, I love so much that souls be with Me in full trust, that many times I hide some defect or imperfection of theirs, or some lack of correspondence to my grace, so as not to give them any occasion to not be with Me in full trust…distrust blocks the development of virtues, and puts freezing cold into the most ardent love. Oh! how many times, because of lack of trust, my designs and the greatest sanctities are blocked.

This is why I tolerate some defects rather than distrust—because those can never be so harmful.[677]

In this amazing passage, we see that Jesus is so intent on receiving our trust, that sometimes he takes the step of even temporarily hiding from us our very own faults, not wanting to risk any harm to trust! It is of course not that Jesus is content with any imperfections; but He knows that, if we succumb to mistrust, that itself will be a greater obstacle to our growth in perfection than anything else, for it is precisely by this trust that we "shine the most," as He here says to Luisa:

> My daughter, the souls who will shine the most, like bright gems in the crown of my divine mercy, are the souls who have more trust…I deal more with those souls who trust than with the others.[678]

Elsewhere, Jesus tells Luisa:

> You must know that one of the purest joys that the creature can give Me is trust in Me. I feel her as My daughter, and I do what I want with her. I can say that trust makes Me known for who I am-that I am the Immense Being; My Goodness, without end; My Mercy, without limits. And when I find more trust, I Love her more, and I abound more toward creatures.[679]

But the opposite demeanor on our part also gives the opposite of this joy to God. Jesus also tells Luisa, *"My daughter, do not increase my pains by worrying,"*[680] wherein we are reminded that Jesus has everything figured out for us, and we add to His pains by doubting that.

Some people will lose peace in the very pursuit of sanctity itself. This is perhaps the most dangerous trap of all. Here we must understand that **God's design for the perfection of our sanctity never begins anywhere other than *where we already are at that moment*.** At this moment, I am sure we can all say that we face many difficulties and other issues and problems. We must never suppose that these need to be resolved *before* this perfect plan is put to work. God's perfect plan is *already* at work, and we must believe that.

> And my sweet Jesus, moving in my interior, told me: **"My daughter, why do you afflict yourself? The teachings of your Jesus will never serve to**

---

[676] Matthew 6:25,30
[677] September 2, 1924.
[678] April 10, 1912.
[679] May 26, 1935.

[680] December 9, 1916.

condemn you. Even if you did only once what I have taught you, you would still place a star in the heaven of your soul. ... "[681]

But alas, in encouraging peace and trust, I cannot simply leave you with a batch of inspirational quotes. Too much is at stake here.

Choose Peace

Although this might appear paradoxical, in fact we should not be lax with ourselves in ascertaining whether peace reigns in our lives. As mentioned, when one reads Luisa's letters (and it is safe to say that no one grasps the essence of Jesus' revelations to Luisa better than the recipient of them!), a few constant themes are easily discernible; the need for peace being the principle one. Therefore, we must conclude that peace is not merely some prize that we await as a result of our yet-to-be-attained perfection; as if living it could be guiltlessly "put off" until that undetermined point in time. No; as far as we are concerned, it is a veritable command. Indeed, it is a fruit of the Holy Spirit—a gift from God. But, mysteriously, as with all the fruits, it must also be directly willed, and no excuse suffices in evading this requirement.

Now, I say this as a father of three young children, a college professor who teaches at a secular, public, New York (read: chaotic) institution, and a homeowner who lives on a busy street. I am, therefore, aware of the various objective contraventions of the theme of peace that exist in the world. But none of it excuses us from our duty to choose peace. Peace is a demeanor that anyone can choose, at any time, in any place, without exception. **And while peace is an interior virtue; the external realities associated with it must not be neglected.**

Let us get specific with some examples. Consider the case of parents with small children. Two-year-old children in particular do not much care about the various teachings of the saints on the virtue of peace, therefore most parents (no matter how well they raise their children) can reliably depend upon having multiple opportunities, every single day, of witnessing (first hand) behavior that is about as contrary to peace as a Category 5 hurricane is to a calm, sunny day. Are, then, such parents exempt

from the Command of peace? Absolutely not.

Toddlers *cannot* destroy peace; it is not within their power to do so. The peace of a family can only be destroyed by how the parents choose to *react* to such occurrences. Whether the family enjoys peace is entirely in the hands of the parents. If they choose—as many parents sadly do—to descend to the level of their children's behavior when the latter throw tantrums, then, indeed, peace will die. That is, if the parents allow themselves to respond to their child's behavior by getting moody, emotional, snappy, frustrated, annoyed—or, Heaven forbid, abusive.

If, on the other hand, parents realize that this is what they "signed up for" in choosing to get married, and if they set their faces like flint to always respond to such events with grace,[682] then nothing whatsoever the children do can cause the smallest dent in the peace of the home.

But the example of parents and their young children is only one of countless: indeed, unless we are hermits, we will all constantly find ourselves in *situations* which are not peaceful. **These situations do not justify our own comportment, demeanor, thoughts, words, or choices contradicting the virtue of peace.** There was never a situation more objectively and externally contrary to peace than the passion and death of Jesus—and yet, He maintained perfect peace in the midst of it all. Do not write this off as the behavior of a God that cannot be demanded of us mere creatures: it was He, in the Gospel, Who said we must be perfect just as He is.

So, simply *choose* to not fear, choose to not worry, choose to not fret, choose to not react emotionally to circumstances, choose to remember always that a perfect plan for your good is in the works—all by the grace of God, but not without your effort and cooperation—and you will then have peace.

Sins against Trust

While, as previously stated, the most important dimensions of peace and trust are the interior ones of calmness of soul and resting in God's Will, we also should not neglect to consider what concrete actions constitute external violations of this peace

---

[681] June 4, 1919.

[682] Which does not necessarily mean effusive gentleness or loquaciousness—often times graceful conduct with a

tantruming child will mean firmness in correction and punishment as a consequence; but done completely under the direction of reason and never emotion and trust commanded of us by God.

One of the most common ways married Catholics sin against trust is when they avoid conception due to trifles (that they use NFP instead of artificial contraception does not make everything okay). A few words on this are necessary, for it is common today, even in "orthodox Catholic" circles, to hear a fashionable perversion of Catholic teaching promoted, wherein couples are advised to "practice NFP" *by default* (by which they mean "avoid conception using methods that are over 99% effective").[683]

One will not find this view anywhere in the Magisterium of the Church. For the Magisterium is in no way unclear: **avoiding conception by way of NFP can indeed be morally licit, but it may only be undertaken for serious reasons;** if such reasons exist, then couples may (and even should) take advantage of NFP in order to avoid conception. But if such serious reasons do not exist, then spouses are sinning against their vocation by refusing to be open to life and, instead, choosing to wait for an unspecified "right time" to have the next child. For example, we see the following Magisterium:

> *Catechism of the Catholic Church,* paragraph number 2368: "…For **just reasons**, spouses may wish to space the births of their children. **It is their duty to make certain that their desire is not motivated by selfishness but is in conformity with the generosity** appropriate to responsible parenthood. Moreover, they should conform their behavior to the objective criteria of morality…"

> *Humanae Vitae* 16: "**If** therefore **there are well-grounded reasons** for spacing births, arising from the physical or psychological condition of husband or wife, or from external circumstances, the Church teaches that married people **may then** take advantage of the natural cycles immanent in the reproductive system and engage in marital intercourse only during those times that are infertile"

> *Casti Connubii* 53: "…virtuous continence (which Christian law *permits* in matrimony *when* both parties consent)…" [In other words, both spouses must agree in order to use NFP to avoid conception. One spouse cannot simply decide this on his or her own.]

> Venerable Pope Pius XII Address to Midwives:

"… If, however, according to a reasonable and equitable judgment, there are no such grave reasons either personal or deriving from exterior circumstances, the will to avoid the fecundity of their union, while continuing to satisfy to the full their sensuality, can only be the result of a false appreciation of life and of motives foreign to sound ethical principles."

Generosity in one's vocation is not optional; it is the only path to sanctity. Just as no priest will grow holy if he avoids being in the confessional and saying Mass, so too no parent will become holy if he needlessly avoids having another child.

I will not give a treatise here on what exactly constitutes a "serious" reason that justifies avoiding conception, and besides, that is not a question I deem myself worthy to answer for others. **I wish here only to lay down the principle**: that, indeed, a serious reason *is* needed.

I will at least note that, if our ancestors were as stingy with their vocations as some Catholics are today—using any inconvenience as a reason to justify not having more children—then few of us would exist. But I am not some rigorist who is saying that NFP may only licitly be used if the wife has cancer and is receiving chemotherapy (nor am I some laxist saying that NFP may be licitly used to ensure Disney World Vacations can continue uninterrupted and each child can still have his own separate bedroom). Clearly the truth lies somewhere between these two mistaken extremes, and discerning that golden mean is something I will leave to worthier minds than my own. Again, I see my job merely as to remind people of forgotten principles; for discernment can never be successful if it does not begin with the right principles.

***

The excessive (unnecessary) use of NFP is of course only one of the many ways we can sin against trust. Others include:

- Accumulating excessive savings or financial investments.
- Refusing to do what God has clearly called us to out of safety concerns.
- Being so overzealous to avoid the occasion of sin that, in so doing, we paradoxically neglect the Will of God. (This is not to

---

[683] If, on the other hand, by "use NFP" one simply means "use charting, etc., so that fertile times can be better known in order to *aid* in conception," then obviously the admonishment here presented is irrelevant.

detract from the great importance of avoiding the occasion of sin).

- Willingly succumbing to scrupulosity.
- Insisting upon having a plethora of expensive insurance plans to the extent that it adversely affects charitable giving and other more important things we could be doing with that money.
- Insisting upon constant unnecessary text-updates from loved ones, caring more about encouraging their safe driving than encouraging their holy living.
- Spending an inordinate amount of time planning for the future and strategizing contingencies if "Plan A, B, and C" don't work out—whether these plans are formal and written, or only daydreams.
- Being overly concerned about possessions being damaged, stolen, or lost (and much concern at all indeed counts as "overly").
- Priests locking the doors of their Churches because their fear of theft outweighs their love of letting parishioners pray with Jesus in the Blessed Sacrament.
- Taking so many precautions to try to procure or secure one's own health that it adversely affects the duties of one's state in life, prayer, spiritual reading, works of mercy, etc.

I only present this list to "get the ball rolling," in the consideration of what concrete behaviors may contravene trust; I encourage each reader to continue this consideration on his own. For we mustn't be slothful in this consideration; too much is at stake. If necessary, re-read the beginning of this section to remind yourself just how loftily Our Lord exalts the virtue of trust, and with what magnanimity He rewards it.

Obedience

Whoever reads the Book of Heaven will doubtless be struck by the enormous degree of importance Our Lord puts on obedience; more importance than any mere moral virtue, and more importance than any heroic act. Luisa's own life, of course, was defined by holy obedience to such an extraordinary degree that no precedent is found in the history of the Church.

Just as grace builds upon nature, no one can hope to live in the Divine Will if he refuses to exercise the human and earthly obedience to which he is called. Therefore, reading what follows might hurt; but it is necessary.

> My daughter, if one reasons over obedience, by merely reasoning over it he dishonors it, and one who dishonors obedience, dishonors God.[684]

Jesus furthermore teaches that our obedience be constant; not an occasional virtue that we exercise when it is convenient for us. In this exhortation, He points out that He—the almighty God—obeyed His very executioners:

> Someone else is obedient to someone, submitted, humble; he makes himself a rag, in such a way that the other can do with him whatever he wants. But with another he is disobedient, recalcitrant, proud. Is this the obedience that comes from my Heart; as I obeyed everyone, even my very executioners? Certainly not.[685]

But this is not some horrendous burden; it is, rather, *freeing*. For when obedience dictates some path to us, it frees us from the greater difficulty of discernment. And even if what obedience requires is little, in our exercise of the virtue of obedience, it becomes great. Jesus tells Luisa:

> I do not look so much at the multiplicity and greatness of the works, but at the connection they have, either directly with divine obedience, or indirectly with obedience to one who represents Me.[686]

Both in the world and in the Church, obedience is today thoroughly mocked or, at best, neglected and forgotten. But a true Christian—and certainly one who wishes to live in the Divine Will—must not partake of this folly. And while relatively few of us are consecrated religious who have the opportunity to exercise obedience in a perfect way—by seeing in religious superiors' decisions the Will of God revealed in clarity—we all can, and must, nevertheless live obedience in the ways in which our own lives stand in relation to it.

Above all, we must of course obey God and the Church. This means believing everything that the Church teaches and obeying all the

---

[684] January 21, 1905.
[685] August 25, 1905.
[686] August 9, 1904.

commandments and precepts. But the obedience of a Christian does not stop there.

Most people reading these words likely live in a family; with siblings, or a spouse, or parents in the house. Children, of course, have a duty before God to obey their parents—a duty so supremely important that it is found in the Ten Commandments themselves. But obedience in the family does not consist only in children obeying their parents.

The Father as the head of a Christian family is not an optional role. Jesus laments to Luisa how mankind rejects His Will, and compares this scenario to one in which the father is not treated as he ought to be; the commander of the family:

> How sorrowful it was to see that …not letting themselves be dominated by Our Will, so many places would Our Will lose upon earth. It happened as in a family in which, instead of the father being the one who commands and dominates, all the children command and dominate.[687]

There are no ways out of this teaching. Scripture makes it clear, as does Magisterium. The husband is the head, and the wife is the heart of the family. This is not a mere optional configuration for traditionally minded families. It is a commandment of God and a teaching of the Church; taught clearly, for example, in 1 Corinthians 11:3, Ephesians 5:22, 1 Peter 3:1, Pope Leo XII's *Immortale Dei* 17 (i.e. "… authority of the husband…"), Pope Pius XI's *Casti Connubii* 26 (e.g. "… subjection of the wife and her willing obedience [to the husband]… the man is the ruler of the family…," etc.). Any Catholic should know that a teaching repeated several times in Scripture and in the Magisterium can never- and will never- change.

Pope St. John Paul II indeed gave important qualifications and specifications to this teaching in his writings on the dignity and vocation of women. For example, a wife's call to submissiveness does not mean she is relegated to the same status as a child under her husband or is a servant of her husband—not in the least! She is an equal. Nor does her call to submissiveness mean that the husband is the sole decision maker who runs the family autonomously—far from it! Head and heart act together in guiding, even though head must have

the final say and their relations must be properly understood.

Many who understand the importance of the respective roles of husband and wife will, I think wisely, decide that the wife should be a stay-at-home mom and the husband the breadwinner. But it must be remembered that this arrangement does not imply that the money is the husband's own just because he "earns it." All money is just as much the wife's as it is the husband's (even though the ultimate authority on its use rests with the husband). The husband is only able to make that money because of the great toil and sacrifices made by the wife in being a homemaker and caring for the children. He should never suppose that he can take that money and make large unnecessary purchases with it, without discussing it first with his wife. And the wife should be able to use that money just as freely as the husband; in fact, just as in the body, a good approach to its health calls for the needs of the heart to be considered more important to address and fulfill than those of the head, so too in marriage, the heart of the family—the wife—is really its essential element.

We should also recall that the husband's authority does not give him any right to demand that the wife contradict her vocation and dignity. A mother's very vocation is to raise her children—to raise them as faithful Catholics—to nurse her babies, to stay at home with her young children if she deems that necessary (no man can demand his wife get a career if she has young children), etc. These are certainly her rights. And it goes without saying that no one—husband and head of the family included—has any right whatsoever to tell anyone to sin; to contradict their consciences.

But, returning to the teachings of the Pope, John Paul did not alter or deny the infallible teaching on the headship of the husband. The teaching on the necessity of submissiveness of the wife to the husband always has been and always will be. And this teaching is not the same thing as the teaching on the subjection of a husband to his wife; as if one could merely say that spouses "must obey and submit to each other," and pretend he has thus done justice to the full truth. It is not only theologically impossible (contrary to the clear teachings of Scripture, Tradition, and

---

[687] March 26, 1927

Magisterium), but it is philosophically impossible that two independent minds and wills can equally submit to each other in exactly the same way; for this is nothing but a pretense that seeks to wish away the existence of conflict and contradiction.

Indeed, John Paul preferred to focus on the mutual subjection aspect of St. Paul's teaching in his letter to the Ephesians; but this focus of the Pope changes no Church teachings. Mutual spousal subjection is taught in Ephesians 5:21, but Ephesians 5:22-24 teaches *how* a wife subjects herself to her husband (via obedience), and Ephesians 5:25-29 teaches *how* a husband subjects himself to his wife (via laying down his life for her).

As with earlier controversial points in this chapter, recall that my only desire here is to settle the simple principle itself, so that discernment of the particulars can successfully follow. Different families will live this teaching in somewhat different ways. That is not only acceptable, but important. And circumstances also affect how to live this teaching. **The important thing is to accept the principle** and pray about how to put it into practice. In this effort, it must be remembered that whatever is done for the sake of one's vocation is done for God. Jesus assures Luisa as much, telling her:

> This **[fulfillment of the duties of one's office] may not appear to be such a great thing—but rather, it is everything. In fact, when one is called to an office and fulfills the duties pertaining to that office, it means that he does it for God**; and in the fulfillment of one's duty there is sanctity. [688]

We should also remember that, for children, obedience ceases upon emancipation. It has often rightly been pointed out that the Fourth Commandment—Honor thy father and mother—has no expiration date. Indeed, we must always have great love, respect, and honor for our parents, no matter our age. But once a child has become an adult, it is ridiculous to pretend that he still has an absolute duty to obey his parents. The Catechism makes this clear:

> Obedience toward parents ceases with the emancipation of the children [689]

Many vocations and missions are lost—and what could be good and holy marriages are never entered into—because adult children make the mistake of thinking they can or should merely do what their parents want and suppose that is automatically the Will of God.

Turning from obedience in the family to other forms of obedience, we should also consider the exercise of this virtue with respect to Civil Authority. Unfortunately, a certain argument has become popular among good Catholics by which, considering how corrupt the world and our government has become, we no longer need to take the civil law particularly seriously. This is not only absurd, but it is a heresy and living it out is a sin. Scripture makes it clear that we have a duty to obey civil authority even if the men who hold the authority are evil and even if their demands are stupid. We are only justified in breaking the civil law if it contradicts our conscience; that is, if it asks us to sin (by commission or omission).

But let us say you are not underneath anyone to obey, you already obey the law and the precepts of the Church, and you aren't sure what else to do to live out this virtue more excellently. Well, I have a suggestion that will be challenging for just about anyone: submit to all the Social Teachings of the Church, as found in the *Compendium of the Social Doctrine* and the Social Magisterium promulgated since this Compendium was written (that is, *Caritas in Veritate, Evangelii Gaudium*, and *Laudato Si*).[690] Since it seems almost everyone these days has had their political opinions formed by worldly pundits, it is equally true that almost everyone has a multitude of views at odds with Church Teaching. Learning about—and submitting to—this area of Church Teaching will be a glorious death to self, a beautiful exercise of the virtue of obedience, and will help open up your soul to the Gift of Living in the Divine Will.

Some Catholics are rather stubborn on this point, so we must expand upon it; but in doing so, let us back

---

[688] May 13, 1926.

[689] CCC 2217.

[690] Pope Francis does not teach, in *Laudato Si*, that man-made "global warming" definitely is happening, nor does he even talk much about it, despite mainstream media conveniently labeling *Laudato Si*, according to their own narrative, to be "the global warming encyclical." He merely points out that there is a consensus among scientists that it is happening; but everybody already knew that. And scientific consensuses are often wrong. As for me: I do not know if there is in fact man-made global warming.

up in time for a moment. The Creator and Ruler of the universe entered into it 2,000 years ago. He founded a Church with the authority to teach all the nations, and that very Church which He founded persists to this day under the vicarious headship of Pope Francis. Whether one likes it or not, this Church does have a whole treasury of Magisterial teachings on politics. Is every word of it strictly infallible? Of course not. But there is simply no way to be a loyal child of Holy Mother Church while dismissing an entire category of Church Teaching, as many Catholics in fact do (whether they are "left wing" or "right wing").

Letting the world form us on something as important as fundamental political issues is a vice. It is something that needs to be repented of, not something that should be defended. If, in an honest analysis of our lives, we realize that this is precisely what we have done, then we should repent and make amends. Amends can be made by reading, and choosing to submit to, the Church's Social Magisterium, and deciding beforehand that this Magisterium matters more than our own opinions.

Too often, the same Catholics who will (rightly) lambaste other Catholics who prefer the Cafeteria approach by saying, *"I'm against abortion, but I can't advocate imposing that view on others through law"* will nevertheless turn around and themselves say that they refuse to submit to clear teachings in a Papal Encyclical. How are we any different from Pagans if we read the Social Magisterium with the mindset of purely allowing it to educate us and give us food for thought, instead of actually handing ourselves over to it in order to be formed by it? Anybody can read the Social Magisterium if they do so in the comfort of the self-will armchair, knowing they need not worry about having to abandon their own opinions for the sake of a greater truth. As Catholics, our calling is much higher than this "comfort-zone-at-all-costs" ideology.

"...the Church's social doctrine has the same dignity and authority as her moral teaching. It is authentic Magisterium, which obligates the faithful to adhere to it." (*Compendium of the Social Doctrine of the Church*, paragraph 80.)

If, therefore, you find yourself in need of an exercise of the virtue of obedience, I believe you will find sufficient material for this exercise in the Social Doctrine.

Courage and Fearlessness

One of the most prevalent exhortations found in all of Luisa's revelations is Jesus' repeated admonition to Luisa to the virtue of courage. When God has such great plans at work—and there is no greater plan than this mission of the Divine Will—timidity, fear, and lukewarmness destroy everything. Jesus tells Luisa:

> My daughter, timidity represses Grace and hampers the soul. A timid soul will never be good at operating great things, either for God, or for her neighbor, or for herself…she always has her eyes fixed on herself, and on the effort she makes in order to walk. Timidity makes her keep her eyes low, never high…On the other hand, in one day a courageous soul does more than a timid one does in one year.[691]

With courage and conviction come zeal; for, as stated elsewhere in this book, no one who approaches the spiritual life like a Quietist will receive the Gift. Jesus tells Luisa:

> In the order of grace it happens as in the natural order: the sun gives light to all, yet not everyone enjoys the same effects; however, this is not because of the sun, but because of creatures. One uses the light of the sun in order to work, to be industrious, to learn, to appreciate things; this one makes herself rich, she constitutes herself, and does not go around begging for bread from others. Someone else, then, keeps lazing about, she does not want to meddle in anything, the light of the sun inundates her everywhere but for her it is useless, she wants to do nothing with it. This one is poor and sickly because sloth produces many evils, physical and moral… grace which, more than light, inundates souls…and impregnates [them] completely. But who is attentive on receiving all these flows of grace—who corresponds to Me? Ah, too few! And **then some dare to say that to these I give grace for them to make themselves saints, and to others I do not, almost wanting to hold Me responsible, while they content themselves with conducting their lives lazing about,** as if the light of grace were not there for them.[692]

Courage will allow us to respond with zeal to the invitations God gives us instead of, as Jesus

---

laments here, "lazing about."

Remember that courage is not some feeling which we are miraculously given before we set ourselves to work; rather, it is a grace which emboldens our steps when they are made in accord with God's Will. Do not, therefore, sit there idly wondering why you lack the courage to do God's Will; simply do God's Will, and trust that you will have the courage to persevere in it—and, as Jesus assures you, you will do so, saying:

> My daughter, only in the act in which the creature sets herself to do what I want, then am I drawn to give her the strength necessary, or rather, superabundant—not before. I cannot give things uselessly, because they would be held more responsible before Me if they felt the strength but would still not do what I want. How many, before doing an action, feel so helpless, but as soon as they set to work they feel invested by new strength, by new light. I am the One who invests them, as I never fail in providing the necessary strength that is needed in order to do some good. Necessity binds Me and forces Me, if necessary, to do together with the creature whatever she does. Therefore, I Myself am the true necessities, it is I Who want them, and I am always together with the creatures in the necessities. But if what they do is not necessary, then I put Myself aside and let them act by themselves.[693]

In fact, it is precisely when we do not feel courage that we can be most courageous. Jesus tells Luisa:

> My daughter, don't you know that discouragement kills souls more than all other vices? Therefore, courage, courage, because just as discouragement kills, courage revives, and is the most praiseworthy act that the soul can do, because while feeling discouraged, from that very discouragement she plucks up courage, undoes herself and hopes; and by undoing herself, she already finds herself redone in God.[694]

And when we pluck up this courage, we must not be fickle in following through with our good intentions; for courage also means never giving up in doing the Will of God. Jesus tells Luisa:

> It is said: man proposes, God disposes. As soon as the soul proposes to do some good—to be holy—I immediately dispose the things that are needed around her: light, graces, knowledge of Me,

detachments. And if I do not achieve the purpose with these, then by means of mortifications I do not deny anything to that soul, in order to grant her what she had proposed. But, oh, how many forcefully escape from this crafting that my Love has woven around them! Few are those who do not give up and let Me accomplish my work.[695]

Fuel for the inflaming of our courage can be found in the simple reminder that, for all eternity, we will not ever again have the opportunity that we now have in these short few moments before our death. Jesus tells Luisa:

> Now in Heaven, in my Celestial Country there are no works, neither on my behalf, nor on the part of creatures, one who enters in those Celestial regions, puts there her enough, and says to herself: 'my work is finished, that which I have done is done, nor can I add on not even one more comma to my work, to my sanctity; and I can not make new conquests in their souls, because death says confirmation, nor can they make one more step ahead, therefore there are no works in the Celestial Country, but everything is triumph and glory, I can say that I show off (in) everything because I give new joys, new happiness and continuous beatitudes, that I hold all Heaven enraptured, everything is on my part, but in them it is not given to me to acquire anything more. Behold therefore they please me more, because the conquests, the works, the tastes that I find in these terrestrial Heavens of the human volition, they can not be there where everything is triumph and glory, even in the regions of my Divine Country. Therefore be attentive and never go out from my Will, and I promise you to never stop my Divine works in your soul."[696]

Courage also means the willingness to approach the spiritual life with intentionality, and not passivity. It is amazing how many rationalizations are given for laziness! Even Catholics will contort the Little Way of St. Thérèse to justify it. They will claim that they have "rights" to "vegging out," entire afternoons spent in front of the television, a constant barrage of needless naps, hours more sleep every single night than is at all necessary for their health. Jesus laments to Luisa that this indeed is the prevailing reality:

> And yet, **most souls are indolent and lazy**, and not only do they not become saints, but they make

---

[693] May 15, 1938.
[694] September 8, 1904.
[695] August 20, 1912.

[696] April 29, 1933.

of their own state in life either a purgatory or a hell.[697]

Do not be like "most souls." Do not ever rationalize laziness in your own conduct merely because others are lazy. You are a member of the Church Militant—the most elite fighting force on the face of the planet. Act like it. Jesus tells Luisa:

> What is sacrifice? It is to empty oneself out in the love and in the being of the beloved; and the more one sacrifices himself, the more he is consumed in the being of the beloved, losing his own, and acquiring all the features and the nobility of the Divine Being. See, it is so also in the natural world, though very imperfect: who acquires a name, nobility, heroism?—a soldier who sacrifices himself, who exposes himself in battle, who lays down his life for love of the king, or another who stands arms akimbo [with arms hanging down at the waist]? Certainly the first one.[698]

Now, courage entails no *willed* fear. As already discussed, courage is not a feeling, and similarly it does not consist in an absence of the feeling of fear; but it does require the absence of deliberately willing fear. So, let us turn now to consider the general question of fear.

No Fear of Anything

In Jesus' revelations to Luisa, we see a full-frontal attack on fear. Scripture indeed is clear enough on the matter: fear is not okay. It is always a temptation, and we ought never succumb to it. But, time and time again, Christians find ways to rationalize themselves into it. They say, perhaps:

- *"Even Jesus was afraid in the Garden."*
- *"I know Jesus condemns fear, worry, and anxiety in the Gospels, but the world is so different today, anyway: there's so much more to be afraid of, I can certainly justify it now."*
- *"Fear of death and hell, at least, is certainly important; and I should try and remind myself every day to be afraid of it so I can use this fear as a path to sanctity."*
- *"God understands that human suffering and pain is so great that we really cannot help but fear it, and act in accord with this fear."*

All the preceding statements are false. Jesus makes this clear to Luisa. He says:

> My daughter, do not fear; **fear is the scourge of the poor nothing**, in such a way that the nothing which is beaten by the whips of fear, feels itself lacking life and losing it. On the other hand, love is the surge of the nothing into the All, such that, as the All fills it with Divine Life, the nothing feels true life, which is not subject to be lacking, but to always living.[699]

> … fear is from your human will… **My Will excludes <u>every</u> fear**, because it has nothing to fear; on the contrary, It is sure of Itself and unshakeable… Therefore, banish **every** fear, if you do not want to displease Me.[700]

> Therefore, My gazes were fixed on the chosen ones to whom both one and the other were entrusted [those who occupy themselves with the Fiats of Redemption and Sanctification] … Why do you fear, then, if you have the gaze of your Jesus always looking at you, defending you, protecting you? **If you knew what it means *to be looked upon by Me*, you would no longer fear anything.**[701]

What amazing words; both consoling and overwhelming in the best way. That even to be *looked at* by God is something so profound that, if we grasped it, we would be immune from all fear.

We must understand that **Jesus was not afraid in the Garden.** His cry to His Father, "let this chalice pass," was not a prayer of fear, it was a prayer on behalf of His body, the Church. It furthermore had nothing to do with the fear of the pains of His passion, but the chalice He was referring to was the chalice of lost souls: the chalice of knowing that, despite all He would do, many would reject His love and choose damnation. Dear reader, if you think that Jesus was afraid of pain, then you have much to learn about our Blessed Lord.

> …in the Garden I cried out to the Father: 'If it be possible, let this chalice pass from Me'. Do you think it was I? Ah, no!—**you deceive yourself. I loved suffering to folly; I loved death to give life to my children.** It was the cry of the whole human family that echoed in my Humanity; and I, crying out together with them to give them strength, repeated as many as three times: 'If it be possible, let this chalice pass from Me'[702]

---

[697] *Blessed Virgin Mary in the Kingdom of the Divine Will*, Day 17.
[698] October 29, 1907.
[699] October 12, 1930.
[700] July 29, 1924.
[701] December 25, 1927.
[702] July 28, 1922.

My daughter, do you think it was because of the chalice of my Passion that I said to the Father: 'Father, if it be possible, let this chalice pass from Me'? Not at all; it was the chalice of the human will which contained such bitterness and fullness of vices… in the name of all I cried out to the Father: 'May the human will be done on earth no more—but the Divine. May the human will be banished, and may Yours reign.' …[703]

I never said: 'If it be possible, let this pain pass'. On the contrary, on the cross I cried out: 'I thirst'—**I thirst for pains**.[704]

Yes, Jesus thirsted for *more* pains, not as a masochist, but rather knowing that, by pains, He won the salvation of souls, and therefore He loved the most horrendous pains possible both as means to the ends of salvation and sanctification, and as outlets for His burning love for us. Jesus, Who carried the cross of the entire world on His shoulders, had no fear of anything. How can we, who will barely have to carry the most minuscule splinter of that cross, justify ever fearing?

But I know that many will refuse to banish fear from their lives just by hearing that, in general, we must not allow it. So let us consider several specific ways we must say "no" to fear.

No Fear of the Devil

One often hears the following words of Jesus in the Gospel appealed to in order to justify fear of the devil:

I tell you, my friends, do not fear those who kill the body, and after that have no more that they can do. But I will warn you whom to fear: fear him who, after he has killed, has power to cast into hell; yes, I tell you, fear him!

But such an appeal requires an erroneous interpretation of this verse. **The devil does not have the power to cast us into hell**. Only God can do that—and God never *would* do that by external imposition; for, as Scripture says, He "wills that all men be saved."[705] What then, in truth, does this verse mean? **It means fear the self-will: the only thing that can cast us into hell**. If we are ever to fear anything, it should only be the self-will. But since this is not even sensible in accord with what most people mean by the word "fear," which in the

ordinary usage is directed to things external to ourselves, it is perhaps more accurate to simply say that we must fear nothing.

Do not misunderstand: we must indeed zealously oppose the devil, despise him, and recognize that, as Scripture says, he "prowls around like a roaring lion, seeking someone to devour."[706]

This does not mean, however, that we should fear him. Jesus tells Luisa:

Daughter, temptations can be conquered easily, because **the devil is the most cowardly creature that can exist**, and a contrary act, a contempt, a prayer, are enough to make him flee. In fact, these acts render him even more cowardly than he is, and in order not to bear that confusion, as soon as he sees the soul resolute in not wanting to pay attention to his cowardice, he flees terrified.[707]

No Fear of Death

Jesus speaks the most consoling words imaginable to Luisa about the moment of death; so much so that anyone who realizes that these words are genuinely from Our Lord (as, indeed, anyone who has read the chapter on the authenticity of Luisa's revelations should!) will, upon reading them, lose all fear of that moment.

My daughter, the moment of death is the hour of the loss of illusion. In that point all things present themselves, one after the other, to say to the creature: 'Good-bye, the earth is ended for you; now begins eternity for you.' It happens to the creature as when she is locked inside a room and someone says to her: 'Behind this room there is another room, in which there is God, Paradise, Purgatory, Hell; in sum—Eternity. But she can see none of these. She hears them being asserted by others, but since those who speak about them cannot see them either, they speak in a way that is almost not credible, not giving great importance to making their words believed as reality—as something certain. Now, **one day the walls fall down, and she can see with her own eyes what they had told her before. She sees her God and Father, Who has loved her with great love.** One by one, she sees the benefits that He has done to her, and how she has broken all the rights of love that she owed Him. She sees how her life belonged to God, not to herself. Everything passes before her: Eternity, Paradise, Purgatory, Hell.

---

[703] January 4, 1924.
[704] November 19, 1926.
[705] 1 Timothy 2:4

[706] 1 Peter 5:8
[707] March 25, 1908.

The earth runs away from her; pleasures turn their back on her—everything disappears; the only thing that remains present to her is in that room whose walls have fallen down—that is, Eternity. What a change for the poor creature! **My Goodness is such, wanting everyone to be saved, that I allow the falling of these walls when the creatures find themselves between life and death—at the moment in which the soul exits the body to enter eternity—so that they may make at least one act of contrition and of love for Me, recognizing my adorable Will over them**. I can say that I give them one hour of truth, in order to rescue them. **Oh! if all knew my industries of love, which I perform in the last moment of their lives, so that they might not escape from my hands, more than paternal—they would not wait for that moment, but they would love Me all their lives**.[708]

Elsewhere, Jesus puts it plainly: **"...what fear can the soul have, in her dying, of coming to Me, if she is already in Me?"**[709] When one lives in God's Will, death is not even much of a change!

Never have I read in any writing of a saint or in any mystical revelation a description so beautiful of the moment of death as is contained in Luisa's writings. Jesus says to Luisa that this is His great daily catch; that moment when at long last He can show Himself to the creature. At that moment so many souls are saved (even though a lengthy Purgatory will be required of many of them). In it, Jesus goes so far as to wrench, as it were, an act of repentance and love from them, and this He achieves successfully in all but those most obstinate souls who choose to condemn themselves. This daily catch occurs, Jesus says, at the instant which separates a soul from time and eternity, and therefore is not dependent upon any external, earthly observation of repentance. He speaks of finally being able to allow His creatures to see His irresistible face, which, if they only accept it, will inundate them with love and save them from the perdition that they have been walking the path of for so many years.

The only revelation I know of that comes close to this is St. Faustina's, which bears an enormous similarity in this regard (as with all others!) to Luisa's. To St. Faustina, Jesus reveals this encounter He has with despairing souls at the point of death:

O soul steeped in darkness, do not despair. All is not yet lost. Come and confide in your God, who is love and mercy. But the soul, deaf even to this appeal, wraps itself in darkness. Jesus calls out again: My child, listen to the voice of your merciful Father. In the soul arises this reply: "For me there is no mercy," and it falls into greater darkness, a despair which is a foretaste of hell and makes it unable to draw near to God. Jesus calls to the soul a third time, but the soul remains deaf and blind, hardened and despairing. Then the mercy of God begins to exert itself, and, without any co-operation from the soul, God grants it final grace. If this too is spurned, God will leave the soul in this self-chosen disposition for eternity. This grace emerges from the merciful Heart of Jesus and gives the soul a special light by means of which the soul begins to understand God's effort; but conversion depends on its own will. The soul knows that this, for her, is final grace and, should it show even a flicker of good will, the mercy of God will accomplish the rest.[710]

These revelations to Faustina should also give us great hope in praying for the salvation of even the most seemingly lost souls—for no one with breath is lost to God. They should furthermore encourage us to pray for the deliverance from Purgatory of those whom we might be tempted to assume went to hell; for this is never a fair assumption to make. Similarly, Jesus tells Luisa:

So, as evil and bad as a creature might be, if she has the fortune of letting one act of my Will enter into herself, even at the point of death, since my Will is life, It sows the seed of life in the soul. And as she possesses this seed of life, there is great hope that the soul may be saved, because the power of my Will will be careful so that this act of life of Its own, which has entered the soul, may not perish and turn into death.[711]

***

One may protest that it is not death that he fears, per se, but *hell*.

Perhaps you feel confident that you are in grace now, but you fear what might happen at the end of your life. But do you really think God will abandon you at the final moments of your life? That is to doubt His goodness, which pains Him much. Trust in Him, and trust in His promises, for He has issued you so many salvation-ensuring ones. Remember that hope, being a supernatural virtue, has no

[708] March 22, 1938.
[709] June 23, 1905.
[710] St. Faustina, *Divine Mercy in My Soul*, Paragraph 1485.
[711] May 23, 1926.

corresponding vice of excess. What I mean is that it is possible to be "too courageous," in a sense; for you could become reckless. You can likewise be "too prudent" in a sense; for you could become paralyzed. You cannot, however, be too hopeful. You cannot have too much confidence in God. That is impossible. Therefore, await your salvation with the joy that a faithful bride has as she awaits the return of her bridegroom who is on a long journey; not wondering if this return will be joyful or miserable, but *knowing* it will be the former. Now, every worldly bridegroom is imperfect, and from that imperfection proceeds at least some lack of perfection of the trust in him that his bride has. But you await your Heavenly reunion with the perfect Bridegroom, the Lamb of God, Who is perfectly faithful so long as God is God.

I do not mean to coax you into laxity. Quite the contrary, we must continue to work and pray with the same degree of fervor, ardency, and zeal as if you could indeed lose your salvation in those final moments (for you pray on behalf of the whole Church, and there are many who may indeed be lost, but many of those will be saved depending upon your prayer). Here and now, I mean only to help rid you of that servile fear that is not compatible with the perfectly pure love of God that you must have.

Perhaps you fear the assaults of the devil in your final agony. This threat, too, is nothing to fear. All is permitted by the most holy and perfect Will of God for your good.[712] These final assaults of the demons are only permitted (if they are permitted at all in your case) because the last moments of your life are the last moments you will ever have to earn merit for Heaven, and God wants to give you as many chances for that as possible—and little is more meritorious than direct combat with the devil. That is the sole reason this occurs, not because your salvation might be lost in that strife.[713]

Likewise, St. Faustina, the authority of whose revelations has already been well established in preceding pages, was given a vision of hell and observed, " ... *I noticed one thing: that most of the souls there [in hell] are those who disbelieved that there is a hell.*"[714] In other words, at least simply believing in hell's existence is itself a good indication that you will not be there, and there cannot be more than double the amount of souls in hell than souls who, on earth, did not believe in it. Later in the Diary, Jesus speaks of those about to die in states of despair and darkness—who, by all external appearances, already have died—nevertheless being saved by His mercy if they show so much as *"even a flicker of good will."*[715]

Recall that in Luisa's own revelations, Jesus has nothing but rebukes for those who insist that His words in the Gospel that *"many are called, few are chosen"*[716] indicate that most will wind up in hell and only a small number will go to Heaven. He explains that people who say such things are just exposing their own miserliness.

Now, make no mistake: many, many souls are in hell, many are falling into hell as you read this sentence, and many more will continue to fall into it. There is no greater tragedy imaginable. All I wish to do is to help you abandon the notion that only a scarce few will wind up in Heaven. Though it appears to be a rigorous stance, it only ironically breeds its own form of laxity. Consider what the devil said to St. Faustina: *"Do not pray for sinners, but for yourself, for you will be damned,"*[717] and likewise what Our Lord said to her, previously quoted, *"My child, know that the greatest obstacles to holiness are discouragement and an exaggerated anxiety. These will deprive you of the ability to practice virtue."*[718] If you think that only a scarce few will make it to Heaven, then you will indeed have exaggerated anxiety. Your pursuit of virtue will be seriously hampered, and you will be too afraid to pray for the world like Jesus wants you to. You will do *nothing* but beg God for mercy for yourself, which God indeed wants us to do, but which (as we see above) the devil wants us to do *exclusively.* Your servile fear of God will result in a servile fear of sin, which will keep you from your missions and calling—callings which God desires of you, and which are the very things that will be your means of sanctification.

No Fear of Pain

---

[712] *Cf.* Romans 8:28
[713] *Cf.* Sister M. De L.C., "An Unpublished Manuscript on Purgatory" (e.g. "God never allows a soul that has been devoted to Him during life to perish at the last moment.")
[714] St. Faustina, *Divine Mercy in My Soul*, Paragraph 741.
[715] *Ibid.*, Paragraph 486.
[716] Matthew 22:14
[717] St. Faustina, *Divine Mercy in My Soul*, Paragraph 1465.
[718] *Ibid.*, Paragraph 1488.

Seeing all that Luisa suffered (or at least, the small portion of what she suffered that is visible in her writings), one may be tempted to despair of ever receiving the Gift of Living in the Divine Will himself. Speaking for myself, I can say that Luisa suffered and sacrificed so much more than I—in my miserable weakness—could ever even dream of suffering and sacrificing. In speaking of Luisa's sufferings, Jesus says:

> Therefore, it is necessary to make known how much this Kingdom of my Will costs Me; that I had to sacrifice the littlest of all creatures—so that man might enter once again into the Kingdom he had lost—keeping her nailed to a bed for forty years and more, without air, without the fullness of the light of the sun that everyone enjoys; how her little heart has been the refuge of my pains and of those of creatures; how she has loved all, prayed for all, defended all; how many times she has exposed herself to the blows of Divine Justice to defend all of her brothers; and then, her intimate pains, and the very privations of Me that martyred her little heart, giving her continuous death. In fact, since she has known no other life but mine, no other Will but mine, all of these pains laid the foundations of the Kingdom of my Will, and, like solar rays, matured the fruits of the Supreme Fiat. So, it is necessary to make known how much this Kingdom cost you and Me, so that, from Its cost, they may know how much I yearn for them to acquire It; and from Its cost they may appreciate It, love It and aspire to enter, to live in the Kingdom of my Supreme Will.[719]

But this, too, is no cause for fear. **For we have a gift that Luisa did not have: Luisa herself.** She did for us things that we need not all do. One day, Luisa was thinking:

> If living in the supreme Kingdom of the Divine Will requires so much attention, so many sacrifices, very few will be those who will want to live in a Kingdom so holy.

Jesus responded to this, saying:

> My daughter…one who is called to be the head of a mission… [suffers] more than anyone ... That which is necessary for you, who must form the tree with all the fullness of its branches and the multiplicity of its fruits, will not be necessary for one who must only be branch or fruit. Their task will be to remain incorporated in the tree, in order to receive the vital humors it contains—that is, to let themselves be dominated by my Will…[720]

Similarly, Jesus said:

> My daughter, there is an immense difference between one who must form a good, a kingdom, and one who must receive it in order to enjoy it. I came upon earth to expiate, to redeem, to save man; and in order to do this I had to receive the pains of creatures, and take them upon Myself as if they were my own. My Divine Mama, who was to be Co-Redemptrix, was not to be dissimilar from Me; rather, the five drops of blood which She gave Me from Her most pure Heart in order to form my little Humanity, came out of Her crucified Heart. For Us the pains were offices which We came to fulfill, therefore they were all voluntary pains, not impositions of a fragile nature. [721]

We must remember that Jesus and Mary suffered nothing that was not entirely from their free will; their explicit, intended choice to suffer it.

Speaking of pain more generally, one who lives in the Divine Will is not exempt from this pain, but pain does become something glorious and never feared. Jesus tells Luisa:

> So, one who does my Will and lives in It has no need of miracles—she lives under the rain of the miracles of my Volition, and possesses within herself the fount, the source, which transforms the creature into the miraculous virtue of my Divine Will, in such a way that in her appear the miracle of invincible patience, the miracle of perennial love toward God, the miracle of continuous prayer without ever tiring. And if pains appear, they are miracles of conquests, of triumphs, of glory, which It encloses in her pains. For one who lives in my Will, It wants to give to the soul the miracle of divine heroism, and in the pains It puts the weight and the infinite value—It puts the imprint, the seal, of the pains of your Jesus.[722]

And furthermore, there is a limit to what even this pain can do. Jesus says:

> …for one who lives in my Will pain cannot enter her soul;, pain remains outside of the soul—that is, in the human nature—and while the soul feels all the spasm of my privation and the weight of an infinite pain, which is the privation of Me, because she is invested by the Divine Fiat she

---

[719] July 11, 1926.
[720] August 22, 1926.
[721] January 30, 1927.

[722] May 25, 1933.

seems incapable of grieving. And so she feels pain without pain, sorrow without sorrow, because **pain and sorrows cannot enter the sacrarium of my Will—they are forced to remain outside. The soul feels them, sees them, touches them, but they do not enter into her center.**[723]

We all know what Jesus means by referring to a pain "entering into one's center," for we have all seen it. A sheer physical pain is always bearable with God's grace; but for those who reject God's grace, their extreme sufferings become almost identifiable with their nature itself. Their pain mingles with their despair, their lack of faith, and even their hatred of God, to create a true foretaste of hell and a sight of extreme horror. Such a sight should certainly inspire us to be ever more zealous in praying, sacrificing, and working for the salvation of souls. But such a sight should also remind us of what can never happen in God's Will.

But perhaps you are among those who have read about the great chastisements that are looming on the horizon and bound to inundate the world any moment now. Should you perhaps fear the pain of these? Certainly not; that is all in Our Lady's hands. Jesus says to Luisa:

> You must know that I always love my children, my beloved creatures, I would turn Myself inside out so as not to see them struck; so much so, that in the gloomy times that are coming, I have placed them all in the hands of my Celestial Mama—to Her have I entrusted them, that She may keep them for Me under Her safe mantle. I will give Her all those whom She will want; even death will have no power over those who will be in the custody of my Mama."

> Now, while He was saying this, my dear Jesus showed me, with facts, how the Sovereign Queen descended from Heaven with an unspeakable majesty, and a tenderness fully maternal; and She went around in the midst of creatures, throughout all nations, and She marked Her dear children and those who were not to be touched by the scourges. Whomever my Celestial Mama touched, the scourges had no power to touch those creatures. Sweet Jesus gave to His Mama the right to bring to safety whomever She pleased.[724]

Understanding this teaching, Luisa wrote in a letter:

> Even more, I want to tell you a secret which has been promised by the Divine Fiat: It will take to heart the destiny of all those who will live from It, and will provide them with everything they need, both for the soul and the body. It will make them lack nothing, and if necessary, even by miraculous means.

So let us now turn to the next thing we must not fear.

No Fear of Purgatory

St. Thérèse, Doctor of the Church, once said to one of her fellow religious:

> You are not sufficiently trusting, you fear God too much. I assure you that this grieves Him. Do not be afraid of going to purgatory because of its pain, but rather long not to go there because this pleases God who imposes this expiation so regretfully. From the moment that you try to please Him in all things, if you have the unshakable confidence that He will purify you at every instant in His love and will leave in you no trace of sin, be very sure that you will not go to purgatory.[725]

I begin this section with such authoritative words because, in some Catholic circles, it has become practically expected that each person acknowledge that he will be spending much time in Purgatory (and sometimes this unfortunately even becomes a sort of flippant joke). This is un-Catholic and it pains Jesus much, as St. Thérèse said. We should all *plan* firmly on not going to Purgatory, and since we know that Jesus does not want us to go there (but rather, to go directly to Heaven), we can remain confident that this "plan" of ours pleases Him much.

If it winds up that you will have to go to Purgatory (and again, dare not resign yourself to this), then it will be out of desire. God will not push you in there kicking and screaming; you will dive head-first into it when you see it because you ardently desire to receive this purification before seeing the Lord face-to-face, just as a bride would not think twice about showering before her wedding, even if the temperature of the water was not to her liking. But as Thérèse has said, we can be sure even of

---

[723] May 10, 1928.
[724] June 6, 1935.
[725] *Annales de Sainte Therese, Lisieux.* Nr. 610, February, 1982. (Citation from Father Hubert van Dijk, ORC. Translated from German.)

bypassing Purgatory so long as we strive to please God in all things and have absolute confidence in His love. Furthermore, we have that incredible gift of the Plenary Indulgence, which we may (and should) receive each day, to put an Ecclesiastical seal upon this confidence of avoiding Purgatory.[726]

And this is all not to mention that, with the Gift of Living in the Divine Will, we cannot go to Purgatory. We consider again here what was previously quoted in the "Desire the Gift" chapter:

> The first thing that my Will does is to get Purgatory out of the way, making the creature go through It in advance, so as to be more free to let her live in It and to form Its life as It best pleases. So, if the creature dies after an act, determined and wanted, of wanting to live in my Volition, she will take flight toward Heaven; even more, my Will Itself will carry her in Its arms of light as Its triumph, as a birth from Itself, and as Its dear child. And if it were not so, one could not say: 'Your Will be done on earth as It is in Heaven.' It would be a way of speaking, not a reality. In Heaven, because my Will reigns in It, there can be neither sins nor Purgatory; so on earth, if It reigns in the soul, there can be neither sin nor fear of Purgatory. My Will knows how to rid Itself of everything, because It wants to be alone in Its place, ruling and dominating.[727]

We can see, therefore, that there is nothing for us to fear regarding Purgatory. But what about fearing God Himself?

No Fear of Jesus

Do not be scandalized by the title of this section: as is emphasized throughout this book, we must never slacken in our *Holy* **Fear** (the filial fear that is a genuine Gift of the Holy Spirit and can also be described as awe and reverence), nor may we ever let our reverence fade. But we also must never forget that perfect love casts out all fear,[728] and Living in the Divine Will requires perfect love. Now, I am speaking here of servile fear: the fear of punishment. This is the type of fear that must be cast out by perfect love.

Surely you do not love God *enough*—we all have

room to love Him more! But do not bother fretting and being anxious over whether you love Him. One of Luisa's harshest rebukes from Jesus occurred when—likely thinking she was being humble—she complained to Jesus that she did not love Him. He told her, in the strongest of terms, that *of course* she did love Him. So, you *do* love Jesus. Just keep trying to love Him *more*, never being satisfied with where you are. And since you do love Him, this love of yours **forces** Him to love you in return and grant you His salvation (of course, He loved you first anyway, but that is another matter!). Jesus cannot fail to love one who loves Him. It is an ontological impossibility.

Now consider an illustration. On a walk in the park, my wife has no fear of me. She loves me and she knows that I love her. That fact does not mean she is thereby asserting that no pain could come to her from my hands. She knows full well that if a truck came hurtling towards her, I would push her out of the way with all of my might—to such a degree that it would certainly cause her pain. But she knows that I would only do so out of love—and if it were necessary and for her good—and therefore when we are together, again, she would have nothing but complete comfort, and an absence of fear. This is how we must be with God, but to a much greater degree, of course.

In His messages to Luisa, Jesus confirms everything He told Faustina about His merciful love, and how He is begging us not to be afraid of Him, but rather to approach Him with unfaltering trust, knowing that no matter how numerous or heinous our sins, He will not turn us away. He tells Luisa:

> **I feel sad when they think that I am severe**, and that I make more use of Justice than of Mercy. They act with Me as if I were to strike them at each circumstance. Oh! how dishonored I feel by these ones. In fact, this leads them to remain at due distance from Me, and one who is distant cannot receive all the fusion of my love. And while they are the ones who do not love Me, they think that I am severe and almost a Being that strikes fear; while by just taking a look at my life, they can but notice that I did only one act of Justice—when, in order to defend the house of my Father, I took the

---

[726] One plenary indulgence may be received for one's self (or offered for a soul in Purgatory) for each Communion received within 8-20 days of Confession, along with detachment from all sin and, of course, the indulgenced act: such as Stations of the Cross, a Rosary prayed in Church or as a family, 30 minutes of adoration, or 30 minutes of Scripture reading.

[727] October 27, 1935
[728] Cf. 1 John 4:18

ropes and snapped them to the right and to the left, to drive out the profaners. Everything else, then, was all Mercy: Mercy my conception, my birth, my words, my works, my steps, the Blood I shed, my pains—everything in Me was merciful love. Yet, they fear Me, while they should fear themselves more than Me.[729]

How could you fear Him? He has been closer to you than your mother, closer to you than your spouse, closer to you than your very self—for your entire life—and, for the rest of your life, He will remain closer to you than anyone, 'til the moment your body is called forth from the depths of the earth at the General Judgment. Jesus tells Luisa:

> Even more, you must know that as soon as a baby is conceived, My Conception goes around the conception of the baby, to form him and keep him defended. And as he is born, My Birth places itself around the newborn, to go around him and give him the helps of My Birth, of My tears, of My wailings; and even My Breath goes around him to warm him. **The newborn does not love Me, though unconsciously, and I Love him to folly;** I Love his innocence, My Image in him, I Love what he must be. My Steps go around his first vacillating steps in order to strengthen them, and they continue to go around unto the last step of his life, to keep his steps safe within the round of My Steps. In sum, My Works go around his works, My Words around his, My Pains around his pains; and when he is about to breathe the last breath of his life, My Agony goes around him as support of his own, and My Death, with Unconquerable Strength, goes around to give him unexpected helps, and with Jealousy, all Divine, it presses itself around him so that his death may not be death, but True Life for Heaven. And I can say that even My Resurrection goes around his sepulcher, waiting for the propitious time in order to call, by the Empire of My Resurrection, his Resurrection of the body to Immortal Life.[730]

Nothing can separate you from the love of God. Do not fear Him.

Mortification and Sacrifice

Jesus tells Luisa:

> The cross is my flowery bed, not because I did not suffer harrowing spasms, but because by means of the cross I delivered many souls to grace, and I could see many beautiful flowers bloom, which would produce many celestial fruits. So, in seeing

so much good, I held that bed of suffering as my delight, and I delighted in the cross and in suffering. You too, my daughter—take pains as delights, and delight in being crucified on my cross. No, no, I do not want you to fear suffering, almost wanting to act like a sluggard. **Up, courage, be brave, and, of your own, expose yourself to suffering**.[731]

The beginning of Luisa's writings especially is full of invitations from Jesus to mortify her inclinations; in food, in comforts, in conversation, in amusements and enjoyments, etc. There is no use looking to Divine Will Spirituality as a shortcut around the ascetical life. If anything, it is an ever-deeper invitation into it! For Jesus reveals to Luisa just how tremendously powerful voluntary pains (e.g. mortifications) are before the throne of God:

> If I wanted pains without will, there is such an abundance of them in the world, that I could take as much as I want; but since the gold thread of their will is missing, they are not for Me… A quarter of an hour of voluntary pains is enough to make up for and surpass all the most atrocious pains that exist in the world; because these are in the human order, while voluntary ones are in the Divine Order.[732]

So we can see that these pains we undertake with the full consent and cooperation of our will have such spiritual strength as to surpass all else.

But why, on a more basic level, do we need mortification? Because a spiritual cream puff will always do the self-will. Laxity and leniency in the spiritual life will never succeed. The fallen aspect of our nature, which hates growth in the spiritual life, makes sure we always have plenty of excuses if it is not overcome by discipline. Please do not think you have this area of the spiritual life covered just because you have two small meals and one big meal on Ash Wednesday and Good Friday! St. Josemaría Escrivá said that the day you have eaten a meal without at some point, during it, mortifying the flesh by holding back from completely indulging the appetite is the day you have eaten like a pagan. St. Faustina said it is so important to undertake small sufferings willingly each day so that we are prepared for the big ones when they come. Of course, only God's grace will get us through difficulties, but let us not forget that grace also builds upon nature, and we are not thereby

---

[729] June 9, 1922.
[730] March 6, 1932.

[731] May 1, 1900.
[732] April 2, 1931.

dispensed from doing our part. God understands, yes—He is well aware of the weakness of our flesh. He is also well aware of the strength of the spirit He has put in us! We should not presumptuously suppose He will be pleased by the refusal to exercise it.

Fasting from food is perhaps the most important form of mortification. This discipline is largely frowned upon today by those who say that "fasting" from other things will suffice. That is a not true! Fasting, in the most literal possible terms, is more direly needed today than ever before; **in so many apparitions Our Lady is begging us to fast. This should be a part of our weekly routine in whatever form and to whatever extent we discern we are called.**

Some will say that mortification should only occur under the close supervision of a spiritual director, but that is not always realistic. Spiritual direction is good, and you should indeed pray that God sends you a spiritual director, as well as seek one out (one who ideally will be a holy and orthodox priest). But even with that diligence, some will take years to find a spiritual director, and mortification should not be put off for years. Try small but consistent mortifications (and tell no one, lest they merely become bragging points). In this way we work, slowly but surely (which is often the best way), at canceling the self-will. I am not advocating for a stoic approach to life. Remember that God wants us to be happy and partake in wholesome enjoyments as well! But mortification should be a regular—daily—part of our lives. Just be sure to be constantly on guard against pride, and keep the mortifications small enough that you are not at all tempted to brag (even to yourself) about them.

When it comes to the larger mortifications, penances, and sacrifices, great care must be taken. God needs victim souls, yes, and we should indeed offer ourselves as these. But consider that a sacrifice which is holy and pleasing in God's sight is in fact one that causes less suffering than would its absence. This simple truth was demonstrated all throughout Luisa's life. When she was deprived of the sufferings that she wished to undertake for Jesus (perhaps because holy obedience, to which all in her life was submitted, directed otherwise), it was this deprivation which caused her more anguish than the suffering itself! We should apply this understanding to our own lives as well. For example, if you feel called to take on a daily holy hour at nocturnal adoration from 3am-4am as a sacrifice, then you may indeed well be. But pause to **ensure that you do so not out of a sense of external imposition, but out of a sense of internal attraction (incidentally, this is a key to discernment in general).** For if such a sacrifice is to be pleasing in God's sight, then it is a response to a desire He has put on your heart, and the refusal of that desire causes you more suffering (often in the form of restlessness, anxiety, and frustration) than would dragging yourself out of bed at 2:30am each day.

To illustrate the same concept in more human terms, imagine your closest loved one stuck in her car in a snowbank on the side of the road many miles away from any sign of life. It will be a long time until help can come, and she will be cold, hungry, and thirsty. Wouldn't you rather be with her than merely be comfortable at home? Wouldn't partaking in the cold, hunger, and thirst along with her be better than bearing the sorrow of knowing that your loved one suffers alone?

And now consider an everyday example. You arrived at a busy event early enough to reserve for yourself a nice comfortable seat. As the event begins, you recognize an elderly woman struggling to remain standing in the aisle. Wouldn't your choice to take her place and bear the discomfort of a long duration of standing, actually itself involve less suffering for you than would seeing her in pain as you sit comfortably?

This is how we should suffer redemptively. If we have no desire to suffer redemptively (or, in other words, to offer ourselves as victim souls) then we have a problem that we should work to resolve, and not a mere convenient lack of a calling to be victim souls! A healthy young man really *must* give up his seat for that struggling elderly woman. It is not a matter of discernment, but as you can see, it does require love.

I will discuss this in more detail in the section on the *Hours of the Passion*. In those particular writings of Luisa, we learn a profound truth about redemptive suffering on our part; in other words, about being victim souls. We learn that it is really about simply being close to Jesus, and not primarily about experiencing a certain degree of pain. We are not supposed to go about intentionally making our lives miserable in an effort to be victim souls! That would amount to masochism, or at best a misguided stoicism. Rather, we are to be unconditionally close to Jesus, to meditate upon His sufferings, to be with Him in them (especially by being with Him in adoration of the Eucharist, in which all of His Acts—including those of His passion—are present), and to be completely open to whatever He may give us. So long as this openness is genuine and sincere, it can itself be just as meritorious as the suffering of one with miraculous visible stigmata, even if this openness has only so far resulted in smaller sufferings (which none of us are free from), nevertheless borne with gratitude, joy, love, and patience.

We know that the beautiful and still urgently necessary Sacred Heart devotion given to St. Margaret Mary Alacoque has its Scriptural basis in St. John resting his head on Jesus' chest at the Last Supper. In Luisa's *Hours of the Passion*, we learn that Jesus (after observing Judas choosing damnation) was so devastated, that He was in need of consolation from a soul that would let Him save him. Jesus therefore took the beloved apostle and placed his head on His own Most Sacred Heart. **Herein lies the essence of the consolation of the Sacred Heart of Jesus, and therefore of redemptive suffering in general: being close enough to Him that He—and you—can delight in the fact that you have said, and firmly intend to say, "yes" to Him—*Fiat*.** It is good that you are willing to carry Christ's cross with Him, and carry it you must, to whatever extent He permits. But in reality, you could not carry one microscopic splinter of that cross. He does it all; and Living in the Divine Will makes that even truer.

Your duty is simply to be near Him, even in your imperfection, and to be unafraid of His wounds, for that means the world (and more) to Him. In addition to the Eucharist, it is also essential to find this closeness to Him through His Word: Sacred Scripture (by way of Lectio Divina), and through His mystical body, the Church—especially in her suffering and poor members. By constantly being among these three presences of Christ, we develop the openness needed in order to be victim souls and help bring to fruition God's plan for our times.

In the early 20th century, God told Sr. Mary of the Holy Trinity (whose writings also exhibit the same fundamental sanctity as Luisa's Gift of Living in the Divine Will):[733]

> I desire an army of apostolic souls… not to expiate the sins of others by extraordinary trials; no… I desire a great army of victim souls who will join me in the apostolate of My Eucharistic Life… I desire these victims to be everywhere: in the world and in the cloisters; in every occupation… in families… everywhere… I want souls to know that by the Vow of Victim they enter into a life of union with Me… It is thus that society will be reconstituted.[734]

I conclude this section by reiterating that, in understanding the value of mortification, we must not allow ourselves to feel guilty in wholesome enjoyment, nor should we develop an unhealthy focus on mortification. As always, what matters above all is doing all things in the Will of God, for the love of Him. Jesus tells Luisa:

> For what reason did you want to mortify yourself? Certainly for love of Me. And I say to you: 'For love of Me mortify yourself, and for love of Me take the reliefs; and both one and the other will have the same weight before Me.'[735]

Therefore, while those mortifications, sacrifices, and penances which we choose to take upon ourselves are one question, the proper approach to those crosses that come our way whether we like it or not are another. We turn now to consider the latter.

Love of the Cross

> …upon looking at the Cross—at Its length and breadth—I rejoiced, because I saw in It sufficient dowries for all my spouses, and none of them could fear not being able to marry Me, because I held in my own hands—in the Cross—the price of their dowry. But with this condition alone: that if the soul accepts the little gifts I send to her— which are the crosses—as the pledge of her acceptance of Me as her Spouse, the marriage is formed and I give her the gift of the dowry. If then she does not accept the gifts—that is, if she is not resigned to my Will—everything is undone…[736]

The clearest indication of how we stand before God is none other than how we stand before the Cross.

---

[733] Cf. Fr. Iannuzzi. *Splendor of Creation.* Page 113
[734] Sr. Mary of the Holy Trinity, excerpted from *They Bore the Wounds of the Christ: The Mystery of the Sacred Stigmata,* by Michael Freze. Pages 66-67.

[735] July 22, 1905.
[736] July 27, 1906.

In one entry in Luisa's diary, we read:

> Finding myself in my usual state, I found myself outside of myself; I seemed to see a soul in Purgatory, whom I knew... And she told me: **"It takes nothing to know whether you are doing well or badly: if you appreciate suffering, you are doing well; if you don't, you are doing badly.** In fact, one who appreciates suffering, appreciates God; and by appreciating Him, one can never displease Him."[737]

Later in that same entry, Jesus Himself takes this teaching further, telling Luisa:

> My daughter, in almost all of the events that occur, creatures keep repeating, over and over again: 'And why? And why? And why? Why this illness? Why this interior state? Why this scourge?' And many other why's. The explanation of 'why' is not written on earth, but in Heaven, and there everyone will read it. Do you know what 'why' is? It is egoism, which gives continuous food to love of self. **Do you know where 'why' was created? In hell. Who was the first one that pronounced it? A demon.** The effects produced by the first 'why' were the loss of innocence in Eden Itself, the war of untamable passions, the ruin of many souls, the evils of life. The story of 'why' is long; it is enough to tell you that there is no evil in the world which does not carry the mark of 'why'. 'Why' is destruction of divine wisdom in souls. And do you know where 'why' will be buried? In hell, to make them restless for eternity, without ever giving them peace. The art of 'why' is to wage war against souls, without ever giving them respite.[738]

Obviously, by repudiating the "why," Jesus is not condemning innocent inquiry into matters; He is, rather, insisting that we not ask the accusatory "why" every time something goes the way our self-wills did not want it to go. We must, instead, understand that, as St. Alphonsus Liguori said, **"it is certain and of faith that, whatever happens, happens by the Will of God."**

It is that simple. If it happened, it was God's Will. By lamenting what has happened, we lament God's Will. How are we supposed to submit to— much less *live in*—God's Will if we lament that very thing? Instead, any complaining of any sort has no place in the life of any Christian, and must be repudiated by one who wishes to live in the Divine Will. But we must go farther than merely refuse to complain of crosses; we must *love* them.

But how can we love the cross? If a cross is by definition that which we suffer in receiving, and if suffering is needing to endure that which we do not want, then is this not a fundamental contradiction? No, it is not a contradiction. "Folly to the gentiles,"[739] indeed, but not a contradiction.

There are many ways to strive to love the cross. We should be particularly zealous to read the *Hours of the Passion* in order to foster the growth of this virtue within us.

Let us also consider, regarding this Way of the Cross, what it tells us about our own approach to our life's crosses in the distinction between Simon and Veronica. For indeed, what is needed is not more Simons, but more Veronicas. And how ironic this is; for Simon's sacrifice, in physical and absolute terms, was so much greater than Veronica's. Simon actually bore, on his own shoulders, so heavy a cross and did so in the midst of such horrendous persecution by the crowds and the soldiers. On the other hand, all Veronica did was hand Jesus a simple cloth and wipe His face. But Veronica is infinitely more exalted than Simon. One Veronica does for God what a thousand Simons do not. What, then, could an army of Veronicas not do? Nothing would be beyond their power—or rather, the power of the Divine Will operating in them. The devil's Kingdom would swiftly be brought to naught if only we had today in the Church an army of Veronica's—even if, like Veronica herself, their sacrifices didn't appear great from the outside, nevertheless the spontaneity, trust, and love with which they are undertaken would win over the heart of God.

But there are other methods of ensuring that we love the cross. **Consider the fact that the crosses that life sends your way are nothing other than God (in His infinite Goodness) taking direct control of the mortification necessary for your spiritual growth.** For indeed, we are such weak creatures. I know I am; I more than anyone need the very advice I gave in the preceding section. And yet, I can say truly, as did Jesus in the Gospel, "the spirit is willing, but the flesh is weak."[740]

When God allows a suffering to come our way, it is

---

[737] January 30, 1909.
[738] Ibid.

[739] 1 Corinthians 1:23
[740] Matthew 26:41

only because He carefully hand-picked it from eternity as the precisely perfect thing for us to have at the moment when we receive it. It is as if the greatest spiritual director who ever lived devoted his entire career to carefully examining our whole life and carefully picking out exactly what mortifications were perfect for our advancement in sanctity. Truly, this is an enormous gift. If we had the faintest concept of how glorious a thing God is giving us in any suffering of any sort, we would have no problem loving the cross.

Let us now ensure that we are thinking clearly about the cross.

Against Distorted Views

On Disorder. A subtly perverse view of the cross, stemming from a distorted philosophy and theology, has crept into the minds of even some orthodox Catholics. In its essence, it is a strategy for the evasion of the cross. And it sometimes rears its head in the cases of good Catholics striving to approach the question of disability with grace. They often speak of how individual disabilities are gifts from God. So far, so good; this is a beautiful response to such a situation. But, unfortunately, some take it a dangerous step further, and insist this particular cross actually constitutes *who* the disabled person *is* in his *essence*. But this is simply not true, and frankly, it is an assault on the goodness of God, Who does not directly want any deformation of any sort; for none of these disabilities will exist in Heaven (e.g. a person born without hands will nevertheless have hands in Heaven), nor do any of them correspond to the deepest and truest realities of the person.

Sometimes those who succumb to this view are the first to criticize "liberal" Catholics for speaking of the homosexual inclination (same-sex attraction) as a blessing that constitutes who the person actually is in his essence. And, indeed, criticizing such speech is right and necessary, for it is a diabolical lie to say that a person is, in his essence, his cross; that the ontological reality of the person is inseparable from this sexual temptation to disorder that he happens to bear. This error is certainly more dangerous than the one we are here touching on,

for it pertains to an inclination to *moral* evil, and not a mere physical "evil." But it still arises from the same flawed philosophy and theology; supposing that God can and does *directly* will deformation and disorder (which can never be—and which, if it is supposed of Him, inevitably distorts one's view of God, His plan for creation, and what He has prepared for us in Heaven).

So, we should not attempt to have our response to the cross being a mere act of pretending that it doesn't exist, or that it's an intrinsically good thing by itself. This diminishes the value of our carrying it. Jesus wants us to carry our crosses with joy, love, and resignation—not by employing some psychological trick and pretending our crosses are lazy boy sofa chairs.

On Unholy Crosses. Another distorted view of the cross arises when we needlessly pile on cross after cross, filling up our days with burdens, stresses, and anxieties that are not God's Will (a fact we would easily realize if we simply paused to pray sincerely). It is not difficult to discern the difference between these unholy crosses and the genuine crosses that God Himself has fashioned for us. Here are a few indications that a cross is a perverse one which we ought to discard. **In addition to damaging our peace, these unholy "crosses":**

- Are borne primarily to impress others. (For example, pursuits of physical perfection or impressive feats, or constantly attending events we dread only in hopes of others seeing us at them.)
- Proceed from a desire to live a more expensive life than we ought. (For example, working a job we hate because its salary is necessary to enable the luxurious life we have crafted for ourselves.)
- Consist in striving to conform ourselves perfectly to Pharisaical standards—even in holy matters. (For example, supposing that the newborn, the 1-year-old, and the 2-year-old all need to be dragged to a 2 hour long Latin Mass each Sunday—which not only is a great cross for the family who does so, but also makes the Mass a great cross for everyone else in attendance![741] Or, similarly, supposing that one

---

[741] It is not without reason that the Church, in her wisdom, only requires Mass attendance of children once they turn seven! Of course, younger children should be brought to Mass also; but individual Catholics mustn't pretend a strict obligation exists to bring toddlers and babies to Mass, when the Church specifically teaches that no such obligation exists..

absolutely must hold himself to all the fasting requirements—and other Canonical strictures— which the Church promulgated in earlier ages and has since abrogated.) [742]

- Are involved in helping someone whom you primarily wish to help because of his or her wealth, popularity, looks (or because of some other vain motive); or, similarly, are involved in helping someone who has unjustly forced himself into your life and demanded too much of you, beyond your proper boundaries. (For example, when adult children still demand that their parents serve all their children's' wants, and, so often, the latter relentlessly oblige.)

- Are exacerbated—or perhaps primarily exist only due to—the anticipation of future pain. For this contradicts the virtue of simply living in the present moment and dealing gracefully with the suffering at hand in that moment. This anticipation consists in brooding over what is likely to come in the minutes, hours, days— or even years—ahead, and in so doing psychologically (and needlessly) taking into one's soul all these potential future sufferings, thus (by our self-will) making our crosses far heavier than God intended them to be. (It is precisely this that often motivates suicide: living in the future instead of the present.) Many will find the grace to bear their crosses with grace simply by putting an end to this attitude of assumption wherein fretting about the anticipated future sufferings is always automatically added to the present sufferings.

- Only exist because of our pursuit of some vain or overly ambitious goal that we arbitrarily decided we must have, even if it has nothing to do directly with the salvation or sanctification of souls. (For example, finishing reading some large volume which a friend referred to us, even though its content is not important.)

- Consist in the adoption of some absurdly demanding health, diet and exercise regimen that a friend or family member "swears by" and won't stop bothering you to adopt as a supposed panacea.

It is so important that we not pile these types of crosses onto our lives because **they will deprive us of the strength needed to bear those crosses that God has chosen for us,** and they will also destroy in us the peace which must permeate every moment of our lives if we wish to live in His Will.

On Ailments

I do not believe that, in insisting we love the Cross, Jesus is asking us to always passively accept any and all suffering that comes our way. For He is not asking us to dispense of prudence (a virtue he exalts greatly in His revelations to Luisa), which directs us to address physical suffering when it arises to see if there is a reasonable way to eliminate it.

I will give a personal example only because I think it illustrates well a distinction that must be made. I suffer from two bodily pains: heartburn, and something I recently discovered is called "nutcracker esophagus." The former is so easy to address that I do not believe God Wills that I simply sit down and accept it in a situation where I could easily swallow a gulp of water mixed with baking soda; thereby cheaply, easily, and safely "curing" the heartburn in mere seconds. "Nutcracker esophagus," on the other hand, is significantly more painful than the heartburn, comes less frequently, and has no correspondingly convenient method of treatment. Upon briefly researching it, I discovered that there is not much to be done about it, and it is not something to be worried about, anyway. It is, rather, just something one should deal with.

I could of course bend over backward to combat this suffering; but why? It does not make me incapable of fulfilling the duties of my state in life, and the time, expense, and risk that combating it would entail would most likely be an exercise in futility. But this defeat-is-not-an-option combat, unfortunately, is the approach of many individuals to every ailment—real or imagined—with which they find their bodies afflicted. **They seem to think they have a right to a pain-free life, so most of their free time is spent researching new ways of combating their health issues,** trying out new drastic approaches, adopting radically new diets every few months, and making sure everyone they live with is aware of each new pain they feel. Each week they discover—through their relentless

---

[742] If these are undertaken with love and willingness, then they can be very spiritually powerful; not so, however, if they are undertaken with a sense of external imposition, since the truth is that these strictures no longer carry the power of external imposition.

research—the existence of some new chemical, which they grow convinced is the cause of all their ills, and they proceed to ensure it is eliminated from their household and never purchased again; then they quickly forget they did this, and when nothing changes, they blame everything on some other chemical. Then they turn to every "alternative" medicine they can find through Google searches, not caring that many of these "alternative" methods are actually new age or occult and are condemned by the Church, and almost all of them are pseudoscientific garbage at best. After this endless pursuit of the panacea, they proceed to spend down their savings patronizing the snake-oil salesmen who practice these approaches.

This cross-rejection-mentality has become common today; seeping into the minds of even good Catholics who have been fooled into believing that there is guilt in all their pains and they must not cease their efforts in pursuit of physical cures until all pains are gone. Thus, the devil has a victory—this cross, willed by God, is no longer a meaningful part of the lives of the Church Militant—not because the pains thereof have been eliminated, but because it is no longer borne with resignation to the Divine Will, wherein alone lies an efficaciously borne Cross.

I end my treatment of this issue by again asserting that prudence is a good thing and that we should follow whatever it tells us in dealing with our various pains (generally, a certified medical doctor will be the best person to consult in this regard, and generally, his advice should be taken). But understand that there is a legitimate outlet to those who feel overwhelmed with zeal to end pain. Hasten the coming of the Kingdom of the Divine Will! This alone will radically reduce the pains you so despise. Feel free to turn now to the section of this book on precisely that, if you feel so compelled!

Our Reaction to Pain

Having considered ailments in the last section, let us now briefly consider the various other pains which life sends our way. Our pre-rational-thought reactions to things (that is, whatever we say or do almost automatically in the first second or two of our reaction) speak to how we have succeeded—or failed—to make the virtue of Love of the Cross an anchor of our lives.

Some think of the virtue of Love of the Cross as being concerned only with how one reacts to those large, overarching, enormous sufferings of our lives—the loss of a loved one, a cancer diagnosis, etc. These situations are of course important to approach well, but what about the small crosses of which each day is full? Let us not fail to consider how we react to those, as our reaction to them is anything but irrelevant to the virtue presently being discussed:

- Upon a bump to the head or after stubbing the toe, does a curse—or any other vain, needless exclamation—immediately exit our mouth, or do we instead immediately offer up this pain and suffer silently, not needing to display our small cross to everyone in the room?

- When we have to briefly endure a cold temperature that our rational reflection can easily ascertain is no potential threat to our health (when we consider its expected duration), do we nevertheless make sure we vigorously shiver, behave frantically, complain of the temperature, and act like we are dying of hypothermia? Or do we, instead, serenely accept this circumstance and use it for the salvation of souls?

- When we have a headache, stomach ache, feel tired, etc., do we make sure everyone in the house knows about it in hopes that they will pour out their sympathies upon us, or is Divine Consolation sufficient for us?

- When minor circumstances become stressful for whatever reason (perhaps small children misbehaving, running late for an appointment, the day not going according to plan, or simply any unfortunate thought that won't seem to leave our head), do we miss no opportunity to sigh, snap, and otherwise display moodiness to all around us? Or do we, instead, remind ourselves that *nothing but God's Will can happen*, and proceed with a graceful comportment?

This ties in closely with the virtue of attentiveness that we discussed earlier in this chapter. Being attentive means realizing that God is always at work in our sanctification; He is not simply waiting for the "right time" to come to generate some enormous leap in our spiritual life. Instead, He wishes us to grow holier and more virtuous every minute of every day. This growth in holiness often coincides with and even is determined by our reaction to the small crosses of which each day is full.

Demeanor

Having already settled that Living in the Divine Will (not to mention Christianity in general!) requires recognizing that nothing (other than our sins) are our own—but rather, everything we are and everything we have is God's—we can easily see that we are not entitled even to a given demeanor that we happen to prefer or find ourselves inclined to, if it is contrary to the one that Jesus expects of us. Jesus tells Luisa:

> **One who lives in my Will loses her temperament and acquires mine**. So, in the soul who lives in my Will one finds a pleasant, attractive, penetrating, dignified temperament, and simple at the same time—of a childlike simplicity; in sum, she looks like Me in everything. Even more, she keeps her temperament within her power as she wants and as is needed. Since she lives in my Will, she takes part in my power, so she has all things, and herself, at her disposal, and according to the circumstances and the people she deals with, she takes my temperament and applies it.[743]

Yes, we even must look like Jesus in His demeanor and temperament. Critics will say that this section is too restrictive; too specific; too traditional; too harsh. But I have no choice other than to follow the words of Jesus which He has chosen to entrust to Luisa. Therefore, this section must exist, because **Jesus insists not just upon the virtues themselves, but also because He goes much farther and teaches that nothing whatsoever in our lives is free from the requirement of being completely subjected to the Divine Will.**

Before continuing on to discuss a few aspects of the demeanor we must strive to acquire, let us leave it to the great Doctor, St. Francis de Sales, to demonstrate the importance and necessity of this quest for all Christians:

> There are some persons who are naturally light and frivolous; others sharp and waspish; others tenacious of their own opinions; others inclined to anger and indignation; in fact, there are very few persons in whom we do not find some kind of imperfections. But though such faults may appear to be natural to each one, yet they may be corrected and moderated, and with great care and by cultivating the opposite virtue we may free ourselves from them altogether. And I tell you, Philothea, that **this must be done**. Means have

been found to change bitter almonds into sweet, merely by piercing the foot of the tree so as to let the juice run out. Why can we not expel our perverse inclinations and so become better? There is no natural character so good that it cannot be made bad by vicious habits: there is none so forward [difficult to deal with] that it cannot be subdued, first, by the grace of God, then by industry and diligence.[744]

(Now, **above all, we must have a demeanor of peace**, but as this virtue has its own section, I will leave out quotes and teachings specifically concerning it from here and instead remind readers to review that section, if necessary.)

Gentleness

Gentleness is a fruit of the Holy Spirit; and this fact is often forgotten by some Catholics who seem to think that gentleness is a mere consequence of effeminacy making its way into the Church. Not so; no one laments effeminacy as much as Jesus (as we will see shortly), but gentleness is not effeminacy; it is a demeanor of Our Lord and it is required of us all. A simple illustration may clarify any confusion. Consider the least gentle people who exist: babies. Their lack of gentleness has nothing to do with strength of any sort; for in addition to being the least gentle of all, they are also the weakest of all. Indeed, despite having almost no strength, they will immediately destroy any fragile thing they are handed, since what little strength they do have is (as is fine and natural for a baby!) always flailing about haphazardly and unrestrainedly. Conversely; gentleness and strength can go hand-in-hand, for gentleness is strength which is carefully exercised in accordance with reason. Jesus tells Luisa:

> I do not want this restless heart. Everything in you must be sweetness and peace… I love this sweetness and peace so much, that even if it were about something great concerning my honor and glory, I do not want, I never approve, resentful, violent, fiery manners, but rather, sweet and peaceful manners…If one speaks about or deals with things, even of God, with manners that are not sweet and peaceful, it is a sign that he does not have his passions in order; and one who does not keep himself in order, cannot order others. Therefore, be careful with anything which is not sweetness and peace, if you do not want to

---

[743] February 24, 1912.
[744] Devout Life, part I. Ch. 24.

dishonor Me.[745]

In carefully reading these words of Jesus, two things are clear. First, that His teaching that we have a peaceful, gentle, sweet demeanor is not an optional way of life which He presents to those who feel so inclined, but that these virtues are universal requirements for all His children. Second, that He is not categorically condemning severity and sternness, but He is saying that we must be careful with them; for they these approaches are very rarely called for. One, therefore, who regularly finds himself succumbing to them, is not living in accord with God's Will, much less living *in* it.

Too many justify acquiring a temperament foreign to any saint in response to the depravity of the times. This is unacceptable; no matter how heinous the times, God's standards for our demeanor do not change. Discord that is not up to us—but which is foisted upon us by others as a result of our virtuous deeds—is not only acceptable, but rather is highly meritorious (as Our Lord promises in the last Beatitude[746]); but it is equally true that if discord follows us everywhere we go, then this does not bode well for our spiritual state. Jesus also tells Luisa:

> The sign that the soul is perfectly clasped and united with Me, is that she is united with all neighbors. Just as no clashing or disordered notes must exist with those who are visible on earth, so can no clashing note of disunion exist with the invisible God.[747]

The times indeed are disordered and often the righteous will be persecuted precisely because of their righteousness. But this does not change the fact that if you are largely disliked by those who are in your physical presence regularly, this usually means that you do have spiritual problems that need to be addressed.

Joy

Let us recall that joy is a Scripturally[748] and Doctrinally[749] defined Fruit of the Holy Spirit. In a sense, therefore, it is also a command. To be depressed is simply not an option for a Christian, it is definitely not an option for a Catholic, and it is categorically impossible for one who lives in the

Divine Will. To reject joy, therefore, is not only masochistic and foolish; it is also heretical.

And in hundreds of separate instances, Jesus exalts joy and happiness in His words to Luisa. For example, He says:

> My daughter, why this melancholy? Don't you know that melancholy is to the soul as winter to the plants… it strips her of divine freshness, which is like rain that makes the virtues turn all green again; it renders her incapable of doing good, and if she does good, she does it with difficulty and almost out of necessity, not out of virtue.[750]

> Don't you know that cheerfulness for the soul is like fragrance for flowers, like condiment for foods, like the skin tone for people, like maturation for fruits, like the sun for plants?[751]

> The Supreme Fiat is more than father, for It contains the fount of all goods, and therefore, wherever It is present, happiness reigns and It makes one abound with everything.[752]

While it is indeed important to remember that joy "is a must," it is of course more so a fruit than a command; that is, it is a result of other goods. These other goods themselves are an understanding of and belief in God's love for us, and an understanding of and belief in the glories of His promises, the promise of our salvation, the certainty of the coming of the Kingdom, and so many other things. Our joy will be guaranteed if we take the time necessary to remind ourselves regularly of these truths in prayer and in spiritual reading. If we allow ourselves to become detached from this foundation of prayer and spiritual reading, then as sure as the sun sets at a certain time, joy will recede from our hearts and we will acquire the depression that always accompanies a life absorbed in busy-ness, amusements, hobbies, laziness, etc.

We should also ensure that we do nothing which contradicts the existence of joy in our demeanor and engage in that which is objectively associated with joy. For example, here are a few "helps" to holy joy:

- Without supposing that you can "power of positive think" hard realities out of existence,

---

[745] December 3, 1906.
[746] Cf. Matthew 5:11
[747] October 10, 1905.
[748] Cf. Galatians 5:22-23

[749] Cf. CCC 1832
[750] August 15, 1904.
[751] February 5, 1924.
[752] January 28, 1927.

do not either needlessly dwell on thoughts which depress you; instead, consider such topics only as long as is needed to do your duty in addressing them and not one moment longer. Learn to say "no" to needless negative thoughts knocking on the door of your mind.

- Think often of Heaven.
- Have the lyrics of good holy hymns ready in your mind for singing (or tunes for whistling or humming) at times when doing this would not bother anyone around you.
- Give enthusiastic greetings, hugs, or handshakes.
- Greet cashiers and the various other employees of companies you receive services from joyfully and charitably, instead of treating them as obstacles to your day's progress by dismissing them with a scarcely alive salutation.
- Smile at others.
- Do not go about your days sighing out loud about those things that disappoint you.
- Do not "vent." You are not a balloon. Depression and anger are fought by prayer and virtue, not by letting these vices seep into our behavior even moderately in "appropriate" times (there are no appropriate times for vice).
- Be of good cheer in all of your giving. "God loves a cheerful giver."[753]
- Without becoming obsessive about it, do not neglect your health. Enough sleep, eating well, and exercising will help your body cooperate with the virtue of joy.
- Laugh when it is appropriate to do so.
- Ensure that wholesome enjoyments are a part of your life (while not becoming focused on enjoying yourself).
- Beautify your surroundings (again, without too much fixation upon this): declutter your house, turn off the buzzing tube fluorescent light, and do what it takes to make nightly dinner an occasion to look forward to.
- Enjoy some beer or wine (or other enjoyable beverage of your liking) in moderation.

Dignity

Jesus expects a dignified demeanor from all of us. Recall the words of Jesus quoted at the beginning of this section, wherein He speaks of His "dignified temperament" which He expects us to acquire. Elsewhere, Jesus says to Luisa:

> My daughter, in all my pains I was always the same—I never changed. My gaze was always sweet, my face always **serene**, my words always **calm** and **dignified**. In my whole person I had such equality of manners, that if they had wanted to recognize Me as their Redeemer, merely by my way, always the same, in everything and for everything, they would have recognized Me.[754]

But what does "dignified" even mean as it pertains to one's temperament? We are perhaps more used to hearing this word attributed to living conditions or human rights; and indeed, that is one legitimate usage of the word. But it also entails behaving in a *serious and respectable* manner.

First, **the opposite of this temperament of a serious manner of behavior would be giddiness. Having just covered joy in the previous section, it is now essential that we discuss avoiding giddiness, which is the *perversion and excess of joy.*** Some will doubtless be offended to hear that giddiness is a demeanor that must go, but, indeed, go it must. To Luisa, Jesus is simply reiterating Scripture's own admonitions against this demeanor (e.g. 2 Timothy 3:6, Titus 2:3).

Avoiding giddiness does not mean rejecting having a good sense of humor. It does, however, mean that our humor should itself be built upon a foundation of seriousness and dignified manners; not vice versa. We should not go about our social interactions always ready to pounce on any opportunity to tease, joke, or offer a sarcastic or facetious remark in response to things said or done around us. One observes such giddy antics to the extreme in many groups of youth, whose social gatherings are often nothing but non-stop cackle-fests wherein each clique member does nothing but laugh unrestrainedly and wait for the chance to add his own attempted witticism to the raucous cacophony. Sometimes it seems this Godless comportment is no less rare in "good Catholic" schools, Universities, and youth events than in the world in general. There is nothing holy or healthy about this approach to "humor" and "joy." Whether or not it is accompanied by chemical drunkenness, it is in itself a form of spiritual drunkenness.

---

753 2 Corinthians 9:7

754 September 16, 1925.

Lamentable as this behavior is even for youth, there is unfortunately no small number of older people—including some who fashion themselves devout—whose behavior is not much different. The prevalence of such an unbecoming demeanor is thanks in part to the media that saturates the world today. Virtually every television sitcom and morning news talk show (and radio show) currently in existence berates all those unwise enough to watch or listen to them with incessant incitements to this ridiculous, giddy behavior, wherein the hosts do nothing but flirt, tease each other, effeminately drone on about superficial and pointless topics, laugh raucously, and relentlessly force attempts at humor upon everything. There is nothing innocent in this. We must remember that our souls are always being formed by whatever we choose to expose ourselves to, and we will never have the demeanor necessary for living in Jesus if we adopt this giddiness as our own.

Finally, we should remember that, as important as joy is, it is not the supreme virtue. One often hears it said in Catholic circles that the absolutely supreme way to evangelize is with our joy. This is not true, and it is contrary to Our Lord's own words; for He said that it is "by your love" that they will know you, not by your joy.[755] Joy is easy to parade the appearance of without having its substance; not so with true, sacrificial love. Furthermore, joy is not the first fruit of the Holy Spirit; charity (love) is. This is not to diminish joy (just re read the previous section to remind yourself of its importance!), it is only to put it in its proper place; whenever we exalt any good even slightly above its proper place, we are setting ourselves up for succumbing to a perversion of that very good.

Masculinity and Femininity

Behaving in accordance with one's own gender is also essential for a dignified demeanor. **For men, this means masculinity, and for women, this means femininity. There are no other options.** Effeminacy in particular is strongly lamented by Jesus. He once said to Luisa:

> In these times **everything is effeminate**; priests themselves seem to have lost the masculine characteristic and acquired the feminine characteristic. So, only rarely can a masculine priest be found; the rest—all effeminate. **Ah, in**

what a deplorable state poor humanity is!"[756]

Effeminacy, we see, is such a damaging vice as to be able to render the world *deplorable*. Now, Jesus said this to Luisa in 1906, and obviously effeminacy has become an exponentially larger problem since that time. Christians and Catholics, therefore, should be especially on guard against it.

This does not mean that men should resort to a so-called "toxic masculinity," nor does it mean we should in any way detract from the virtues of gentleness (which is a virtue men must have as well as women, even though how it is practiced will be different). The mere fact that modern minds succumb to supposing that one must choose between effeminacy and "toxic masculinity" demonstrates just how lost many have become. Indeed, this false dichotomy reigns: today, many men who see that effeminacy is a problem tend to react in terrible ways by merely adopting many other sins which in no way combat the vice of effeminacy. They become sexualized, obsessed with sports and lifting weights, competitive and argumentative, obsessed with gratuitously violent themes in media and music, willing to take absurd risks just for a thrill; they become impure and vulgar in their conversations, crude in their conduct, and perhaps even physically abusive. This is all utterly tragic and only makes the problem far worse.

Instead, **we need a return to *true* masculinity,** which is found in men reacquiring a willingness to sacrifice, lead, protect, and defend what is good, true, and beautiful, without any care for what it costs, how much it hurts, or how much risk is involved. It is found in fathers returning to the place of head of their households; ensuring, no matter what, that these are households of holiness, and preventing—no matter what—the invasion of any evil into them. It is found in husbands laying down their lives for their wives. It is found in more men becoming priests, and those priests becoming models of true manliness. It is found in manual labor being exalted as it deserves, and men no longer fearing dirtying their hands. It is found in men stepping up to the plate and accepting those missions that are particularly difficult or dangerous so that women don't have to (e.g. being police officers, soldiers, fire fighters, construction

[755] John 13:35   [756] October 23, 1906.

workers, security guards, etc.), and this stepping up should exist not merely in career choices, but in everyday life. (E.g. is there a disturbance in the room? Men: step up and address it. Are there not enough seats at an event? Men: be the ones to stand. Does anything difficult in the home need to be taken care of? Men: take care of whatever it is, no matter how much you dislike the thought. Do circumstances ever demand that someone endure cold, heat, risk, hunger, etc.? Men: be the ones to so endure.) It is found in a return to chivalry. It is found in men *being* physically strenuous instead of sitting on their couches watching *other* men being physically strenuous (who in turn are being paid millions of dollars to play games in front of cameras).

Just as direly, we need a return to true femininity, which is found in women reacquiring a willingness to be nurturing, domestic, reserved, and modest. It is found in women wanting to be mothers again — and mothers of many children, at that — instead of succumbing to the lies of modernism that their worth is found only in degrees and careers, and that one or two children is enough. It is found in mothers wanting to raise their own children instead of paying daycare centers to do it for them. It is found in wives submitting to their husbands. It is found in more women becoming religious sisters in traditional orders. It is found in women's chaste and reverent behavior inspiring men to themselves be pure and pious. It is found in women exhibiting their femininity with their virtue instead of succumbing to that false and sinful "femininity" of immodest dress, excessive makeup and jewelry, prissiness, ditziness, flirtatiousness, excessive shopping, expensive shoes, squeamishness, obsession with appearances in general, etc.

Perhaps the most important arena in which true masculinity and femininity are fundamental for success is in marriage; with each spouse readily undertaking the role proper to him or her.

Dear wives: your family needs the love, warmth, peace, and joy that only its heart (you) can give. Dear husbands: your family needs the leadership, strength, consistency, and protection that only its head (you) can give. It goes without saying that husbands should strive manfully to provide a dignified living for their families, and wives should take seriously the importance of being homemakers. But we mustn't ever allow the secondary duties of a vocation to eclipse its primary duties. Many Catholics are more than willing to speak of how sad it is to see a pastor approach this vocation like a businessman who cares more about parish finances than about the Holy Sacrifice of the Mass — but this trap is the same one which Catholic spouses fall into when they neglect the advice above.

And we should not neglect the externalities; although obviously secondary in importance to the interior realities of genuine masculinity and femininity, they are important, nevertheless. **Women should dress and comport themselves like women, and men should dress and comport themselves like men.** Androgynous dress and hairstyles have become so popular today, even in the Catholic world, that one can sometimes scarcely distinguish between the sexes of those sitting in the pews. This is historically unprecedented and unavoidably damaging to society, which depends for its proper functioning on the complementarity of the sexes, and the living out of this complementarity even in the "superficial" things of everyday life. Unfortunately, it sometimes is the case that with the increase of age comes the increase of this androgynous approach to hair, dress, and comportment; even though the opposite should be true, and the older one gets, the more he or she should exhibit behavior in accordance with his or her gender and so inspire younger people to do likewise.

While women acting like men is lamentable, it seems that the plague of men acting like women is worse and is in fact what Jesus focuses His lamentations on. Before leaving this question, therefore, we should define effeminacy. Aquinas defines it as a man being "ready to forsake a good on account of difficulties."[757] Limp wrists, deliberate lisps, womanly tones of voice, excessive concern for appearance, feminine styles in clothing, etc., are involved in effeminacy, and all men should shun such behaviors that are unbecoming of their manhood. But none of this gets to the heart of effeminacy, which is cowardliness and willed weakness in the face of sacrifice and suffering. A large man with a deep voice, huge biceps, and who stomps about only in work boots may well be

---

[757] Summa Theologica. II-II. Question 138. Article 1.

effeminate. For a deeply effeminate man is one who seeks to ensure his love of comfort, rest, pleasure, safety, and security is not intruded upon by duty or by higher callings.

***

Related to the issue of masculinity and femininity are the issues of modesty and purity. But these require a lengthy enough treatment that they are in need of their own section, to which we will presently turn.

Modesty and Purity

Jesus minces no words on these virtues to Luisa—neither on the importance of them, nor in rebuking us (modern culture) for the horrendous disregard we have shown them:

> Look, even the plants, by being covered with leaves, flowers and fruits, teach you honesty and the modesty you must have with your body; but you, having lost any modesty and even the natural reserve you should have, have become worse than the animals, so much so, that I have nothing else to which to compare you. You were my image, but now I no longer recognize you; even more, I am so horrified at your impurities, that the mere sight of you nauseates Me, and you yourself force Me to flee from you.[758]

If you checked the footnote, you realized that Jesus spoke these words around the turn of the century. Bikinis and miniskirts did not even exist then, nor was there any attire even remotely close to these extremely impure modern innovations. Jesus is rebuking mankind, in the strongest of terms, for beginning (as indeed was done in the early 20th century) to turn away from the guidelines of modesty that had always been agreed upon for thousands of years by civilized people throughout the entire world—Christian and Pagan alike.

It is from this framework given by Jesus Himself to Luisa that we should understand the virtues of modesty and purity. Too many Christians and Catholics reduce these virtues to nothing more than the avoidance of a few particularly grave or obvious contradictions of them—which is an absurd approach to any virtue, just as prone to failure as would be defining "charity" as "simply not punching people in the nose" in the effort to live a genuinely loving life.

Therefore, whenever we seek out advice on how to live these virtues, we should be very cautious (more so here, perhaps, than anywhere else) in choosing those from whom we seek it. For it is sadly so that many who today parade themselves as experts on Theology of the Body, or Catholic modesty, or anything related, are precisely the most inept in giving a solid and holy understanding of the same. And unfortunately, this diagnosis does not exclude some of the most well-known and highly promoted speakers and writers on these topics (even in "orthodox" Catholic circles).

My Wife at Our Wedding

When it comes to the proper understanding of Theology of the Body, I recommend, first of all, the *Theology of the Body* itself (that is, the actual text of the series of addresses given by Pope St. John Paul II, the entirety of which can easily be found online). Secondly, I recommend the works of Alice von Hildebrand, the wife of the great theologian, Dietrich von Hildebrand.

For modesty, I recommend the book *Dressing with Dignity*, by Colleen Hammond. (My wife heartily endorses this book, and she encourages any woman to read it for both a thorough history of, and wonderful suggestions for, modest dress as well as dignified comportment.) If one wants specific guidelines for modesty, I recommend looking up the clear guidelines on the same directly from the Vatican from the 1920s through the 1950s. As of this writing, Judie Brown has a helpful post on the matter on EWTN from July 14th, 2006. Venerable Pope Pius XII gave many relevant teachings on the matter, and Cardinal Pompili, the Cardinal-Vicar of Pope Pius XI, gave good and clear standards on September 24th, 1928. [759]

---

[758] August 1, 1899.

[759] I also recommend researching the movement in support of "Mary-like" dress, which has specific modesty standards pertaining to it and is very much in need of a comeback today.

In all these norms, one can easily discover what modesty *really* means; not how it is distorted by those voices and authors today who ignore thousands of years of tradition pertaining to how each sex should cover the body.

Now, if one is tempted to condemn this approach as "living in the past" (a condemnation, incidentally, of no worth), then I would remind this person that the Vatican still enforces a dress code to this day; such that many Catholic women would not even be allowed to set foot in this holy place — the earthly center of their Faith — in the ways they usually dress themselves. This, of course, in turn, has its own response: "*Yes, but that's the Vatican; a holy place full of priests and bishops. I'm just about my daily endeavors; obviously I can't be expected to dress as modestly in these cases as I would have to in the Vatican!*"

This response, which one hears often, is the *opposite* of the truth. When one is around priests and bishops, she is around people who are generally (not always, of course!) more advanced in the moral and spiritual life than ordinary folk, and are thus less prone to succumbing to the base temptations of lust. A woman should be *more* careful about modesty in her ordinary daily endeavors than she would be in the Vatican. This care should proceed from respect for herself and charity to the people she will invariably be in the presence of; for we are all our brother's keeper, and this means not exposing others to occasions of sin.

But we will not go into specifics here. Those unwilling to discover on their own what the aforementioned modesty standards entail as specific criteria, will likely only react with anger if I were to present them here; and those who have the humility to resist such a reaction will be better served by doing their own research, which is bound to be eye opening and edifying.

Aside from that research into the specifics, let us look generally at almost any culture, from any time, in any place, in any nation, under any religion; and we will see the women especially covering the same parts of their bodies in essentially the same manner. This incredibly unanimous consensus of human civilization only really crumbled with the dawn of the 20th century (particularly the 1920s — and in America, at least; it happened later in other countries); and every decade since then has seen further deterioration.

We should now ask ourselves a dangerously honest question:

"If I see that all of Christian culture — and virtually all culture in general — unanimously insisted upon a certain behavior as truly essential and virtuous ... and if I furthermore see that this behavior only began to be abandoned at the same time the world was breaking from its Judeo-Christian foundation like never before ... am I really safe in concluding that this abandonment was a just and holy thing, condoned by God, that I ought to go along with in my own comportment?"

That is not a difficult question to answer.

I am of course not advocating for an adoption of the styles themselves of previous centuries; I am merely encouraging a return to the *virtue* of modesty that was displayed during them. I hasten to add, as Colleen Hammond also emphasizes in her book, that modesty does not mean ugliness or frumpiness; there is nothing wrong with a woman caring for her appearance (in moderation), and dressing in a way that is beautiful.

Recall that it was Jesus Who chose to — mere months before the dawn of the 20th century — lament to Luisa that society was abandoning modesty and purity. If we are to take Him seriously, I believe we should look to what trends were beginning at that time to see just what it is in our dress and comportment that displeases Him, and then be rid of it once we have discovered what it is. And this teaching is far from unique to Luisa's revelations; in many others, Jesus and Mary lament how much the fashions of the day offend God (e.g. Our Lady's words to Lucia at Fatima in 1917).[760]

I could have presented here page after page of quotations from Papal Magisterium of the 20th century insisting upon the importance of enormous care for modesty and purity, and rejecting the notion that Catholics have a right to simply go along with the culture of their day — but these documents are easy to discover for one's self and I did not want to expand this section's length any further. I only recommend that, in perusing these

---

[760] https://www.americaneedsfatima.org/ANF-Articles/private-revelations.html

documents, you not remain content with commentaries and summaries given by the popular apologists of the day (whose writings are usually the first results that pop up on Google). Instead, read the Magisterial documents themselves, and remember: **once Magisterium, always Magisterium**. Nothing in those documents was changed by the more modern Popes; the latter simply have not focused on the issue as much. Remember as well that the Popes who wrote these documents' condemnations of immodesty obviously had in mind the prevailing cultural trends *of the years they wrote them* — the 1920s through the 1950s — which are the very trends that some Catholics wrongly look to as the pinnacle of modesty. (And it is supremely ironic to defer to a condemnation of an innovation of the 1950s in the very attempt to promote an innovation of the 1950s!)

***

We must now expand our consideration to the virtue of purity in general; for modest dress is just one part of this broader virtue of purity that Jesus lamented the abandonment of at the turn of the century.

Just a few decades after the above quoted words of Jesus to Luisa, the Popes themselves started particularly zealously reproving society for its impurity, in Magisterial texts that are just as authoritative today as the day they were published (and which are even more pressing now, since we have only become exponentially more impure since the days they were promulgated). The veritable flood of diabolical impurity that has today swept over the whole world and, increasingly, the Church, can scarcely be overstated.

But I do not need to spend time here castigating blatant pornography or so-called "pride parades," wherein the most perverse obscenity is openly flaunted, as I highly doubt anyone who has picked up this book has anything but disdain for such evil, and my goal here is not to preach to the choir. My goal here is to edify the devout and prepare them to be more open to receiving the Gift of Living in the Divine Will. **Ignoring that which is most obviously impure, then, let us turn to consider how impurity has flooded the lives of many in the Church who are likely oblivious to its infiltration:**

- Most movies, television shows, etc., are to one degree or another pornographic, including many recommended by good Catholic sources whose standards have sunk incredibly low. We should, therefore, always check for ourselves to discover what content some media item contains before exposing ourselves — or our children — to it. We can check the "Parents Guide Content Advisory" on imdb.com, ParentPreviews.com, or CommonSenseMedia.org. We should not assume that the approval of an "authoritative voice" renders a movie or tv show acceptable for viewing.[761]

- Many people are openly flirtatious in their interactions with members of the opposite sex — including many good Catholics — ignoring that this, too, is a sin against purity. We mustn't allow this behavior into our own conduct.

- Beaches and other public swimming areas are full of women who are completely naked, save a few square inches of material, and so many seem to think this is okay due to "situational appropriateness," as if there is no such thing as more modest bathing suits. But for a man to expose himself to that is spiritual insanity.

- Most music produced during the last several decades — including "Christian" rock — has a tribal and sexual beat which makes it spiritually damaging (particularly to the virtue of purity) even if it has superficially holy lyrics. The so-called "oldies," largely endorsed even by the devout, often partake of this same fundamental problem of sexualized rhythms, which exploded in popularity in the 1920s with jazz or swing music.

- Some Catholic spouses seem to forget that lust does not cease being a deadly sin merely because it is practiced by a married couple. In truth, over 99% of the time, spousal conduct should be as "un-sexual" as any two people's conduct (with distinctions, of course, since the problem is unnecessary arousal here, whereas the risk with the unmarried is the intrinsic grave evil of sexual acts outside of marriage).

---

[761] One of the most obscene movies (which I sadly had the misfortune to watch) made within the past 5 years, was publicly recommended by an Archbishop who is known for his orthodoxy.

Pope St. John Paul II reminded us that whoever lusts after *his own wife* has thereby committed adultery (the Pope was there expanding Jesus' admonition in the Gospel that whoever lusts after a woman has already committed adultery with her in his heart). And it should go without saying (but unfortunately does not) that sexually perverse acts do not become licit merely because they are practiced by spouses.

- Modern coeducational institutions—including Catholic schools—tend to be completely oblivious to the dictates the virtue of purity makes on how to deal with the sexes; hence, boys and girls are sometimes even made to play contact sports together and are placed in the same room for certain discussions that should only be had with single-sex groups.
- Similarly, Catholic couples who are engaged or courting are not reminded of how important it is to avoid the occasion of sin by not being alone (behind closed doors—in absolute privacy) together before marriage. They are also told that all sorts of behaviors are okay when, in fact, the dogmatic truth is that *any* deliberate following of the sexual appetite *whatsoever* outside of marriage is always an intrinsic, grave evil (i.e. a mortal sin, if committed with full knowledge and consent).
- Even the best of the good Catholic media producers often include material for youth that is patently contrary to purity, with this inclusion rationalized by appealing to the need to "reach the youth where they're at," which, in turn, is as absurd as giving an alcoholic more alcohol. Therefore, we can never "turn off" our discernment of media and suppose that simply because it is from a given source, it is safe.
- Some of those who promote the Theology of the Body often do so with complete disregard for prudence, and suppose that any conversation whatsoever can be licitly held any time, irrespective of audience, just because Pope St. John Paul II (perhaps earlier as Father, Bishop, or Cardinal Wojtyla) once wrote of it or mentioned it. They proceed to discuss things in mixed settings that should only be carefully and rarely dealt with in single-sex groups, and they create an enormous occasion of sin for their whole audience.
- Others who promote the Theology of the Body only ultimately contribute to the pornification of culture by speaking and writing in ways that our Grandparents would have rightly smacked them for. These "good Catholic" authors are known to publish books *the very titles* of which are so obscene that I will not even mention them here. They foolishly reject the careful reservation Catholics have always rightly had with these topics as an outdated relic when, in fact, it is an essential element of Christian Tradition (and cultural tradition in general) which helps to safeguard purity.
- Still others who promote the Theology of the Body do so without carefully giving the clarification that John Paul himself gave; namely, that consecrated celibacy for the Kingdom is superior to marriage—great and exalted as marriage is—and consequently many vocations are lost because young men and women are falsely led to believe that marriage and (moral) sexuality are such great goods that basically they cannot be done without.

Purity is a virtue so roundly rejected today that just being a good Catholic is no longer enough, for many of these have succumbed to worldly impurity to a degree that they do not recognize. Therefore, without an attitude of judgment or any hint of an air of superiority, we must nevertheless be careful to ensure that our own lives are completely free of this impurity that so saturates both the world and the Church today, and we should strive by our humble example to inspire others to renew their understanding of and living of the virtue of purity.

Constancy

Remember that Jesus is asking we be like Him in everything. And Jesus, as God, never changed.

One of the clearest proofs that one is devoid of grace—and, certainly, does not live in God—is a moody, unstable, unpredictable demeanor, or having tastes, intentions, and goals that are constantly changing. Jesus tells Luisa:

> …**the soul who is not completely mine is empty**… she is in a continuous alternation of tastes and disgusts; and since any taste which did

not come from Me is not lasting, many times tastes turn into disgusts, and this is why many variations of character can be noticed: **now too sad, now too cheerful, now all irascible, another time all affable. It is the void of Me which she has in her soul that gives her so many variations of character**—in nothing similar to mine, as I am always equal and I never change. [762]

Elsewhere, Jesus says:

Unequal things are always bothersome, defective; and if one wants to place something on them, there is the danger that the unequal part may let it fall to the ground. A soul who is not always the same, one day wants to do good—she wants to bear everything; another day she can no longer be recognized—indolent, impatient. So, one can place no reliance on her. [763]

Constancy also requires diligence and persistence in our commitments and spiritual practices. Jesus tells Luisa:

One who feels downhearted, dry and deprived of my presence, and remains yet firm and faithful to her usual practices—even more, she takes the opportunity to love Me and to search for Me more, without tiring—comes to participate in the merits and goods which my Mother acquired when I was lost.[764]

Firmness produces heroism, and it is almost impossible that one not be a great saint. Even more, as she keeps repeating her acts, she forms two bars—one to the right, and the other to the left—which serve her as support and defense; and as she reiterates her acts, a fount forms within her, of new and increasing love. Firmness strengthens grace and places on it the seal of final perseverance. Your Jesus does not fear that His graces may remain without effects, and therefore I pour them in torrents over the constant soul. From a soul who today operates and tomorrow does not, who now does one good, now another, there is not much to expect.[765]

Here, we see how **much is lost when we so readily abandon our commitments merely because we are no longer in the mood, or no longer enjoy them like we used to, or find our lives busy and, rather than getting rid of vanities, instead get rid of holy practices.** Instead, we must stick to those practices that God has placed on our hearts in the

development of our spiritual lives.

Constancy is so important that Jesus frequently returns to this virtue in His revelations to Luisa. He also says:

…[others] feel an unlimited charity for someone, that is, at one time they are all fire, they make true sacrifices, they would want to lay down their lives; but then someone else comes, perhaps more in need than the first one, and in one moment the scene changes: they become icy, they don't even want to make the sacrifice of listening or saying a word… [this] is a vicious charity, all human and according to one's liking, which seems to flourish at one moment, and it withers and disappears at another. Someone else is obedient to someone, submitted, humble; he makes himself a rag, in such a way that the other can do with him whatever he wants. But with another he is disobedient, recalcitrant, proud. Is this the obedience that comes from my Heart; as I obeyed everyone, even my very executioners? Certainly not. Someone else is patient on certain occasions; be they even serious sufferings, he looks like a lamb that does not even open its mouth to lament. But with another suffering, maybe smaller, he loses his temper, he gets irritated, he swears. Is this perhaps the patience whose root is fixed inside my Heart? Certainly not. Someone else one day is all fervent, he prays always, to the point of transgressing the duties of his state; but another day he has had an encounter a little disappointing, he feels cold, and he abandons prayer completely, to the point of transgressing the duties of a Christian—the prayers of obligation. Is this perhaps my spirit of prayer, as I reached the point of sweating blood, of feeling the agony of death, and yet I never neglected prayer for one single moment? Certainly not. And so with all the other virtues. Only the virtues which are rooted inside my Heart and grafted into the soul are stable and lasting, and shine as full of light. The others, while they appear to be virtues, are vices; they appear to be light, but they are darkness.[766]

Constancy also means persevering, no matter how we feel. Jesus tells Luisa:

But my love is not content with just flowers—it wants fruits. So it begins to make the flowers fall—that is, it strips her of the sensible love, of fervor and of everything else—in order to make

---

[762] June 6, 1923.
[763] February 2, 1922.
[764] September 17, 1905.

[765] March 4, 1918.
[766] August 25, 1905.

the fruits be born. If the soul is faithful, she continues her pious practices, her virtues, she takes no pleasure in any other human thing, she does not think about herself, but only of Me. Through trust in Me, she will give flavor to the fruits; through faithfulness, she will make the fruits mature; and through courage, tolerance and tranquility, they will grow and become rich fruits. And I, the Celestial Farmer, will pick these fruits and make of them my food, and I will plant another field, more flowery and beautiful, in which heroic fruits will grow, such as to snatch unheard-of graces from my Heart. But if she is unfaithful and mistrustful, becomes restless, takes pleasure in human things, etc., these fruits will be unripe, insipid, bitter, covered with mud, and will serve to embitter Me and to make Me withdraw from the soul.[767]

Not even great trials excuse us from this need for constancy. Expanding on a quote provided earlier, Jesus says:

> My daughter, in all my pains I was always the same—I never changed. My gaze was always sweet, my face always serene, my words always calm and dignified. In my whole person I had such equality of manners, that if they had wanted to recognize Me as their Redeemer, merely by my way, always the same, in everything and for everything, they would have recognized Me. It is true that my pains were so many as to eclipse Me and surround Me like many clouds, but this says nothing: after the heat of the pains, I would reappear in the midst of my enemies like majestic sun, with my usual serenity, and with my same manners, always equal and peaceful. To be always the same is only of God, and of the true children of God ... On the other hand, a changing character is of creatures, and it is a sign of passions that roar within the human heart...[768]

Yes, even in the midst of His bitter Passion, Jesus did not allow Himself to change His demeanor.

Another virtue annexed to constancy is patience. This virtue neither knows nor cares how whether a given trial just began, or whether it is in its 90th year; it simply keeps doing what must be done for no other reason than it is God's Will.

Indeed, that of the soul which pleases Me the most

is perseverance, because perseverance is seal of eternal life and development of divine life. In fact, just as God is ever old and ever new and immutable, in the same way, through perseverance, by having exercised it always, the soul is old, and by her attitude of exercising it, she is ever new...[769]

We should defer to the life of Luisa, for she is the example par excellence of the form of patience we must have, even with respect to the very thing we are desiring: the Gift of Living in the Divine Will. Though it may appear superficially that desire and patience are in competition, they truly are not. We must ardently desire the Gift, as already discussed. But how exactly we progress in this is not up to us. It is up to God. And so, we must strive to exercise patience to a heroic degree. St. Padre Pio is often quoted as saying that the greatest and most difficult application of patience (but likewise the most necessary for a devout soul) is its application **with respect to one's own growth in holiness**. As you are not the cause of your growth in holiness, you do not answer for its pace; you only answer for your openness and your response. It is the same with pursuing the Gift of Living in the Divine Will.

Do you find that you are frustrated with your pace of growth in the spiritual life? That is a true martyrdom of love! For not loving Jesus as much as you want to love Him is indeed a martyrdom, and a greatly meritorious one so long as you never give up striving to love Him more.[770] Or are you merely tempted to annoyance at the pace of traffic during your morning commute? Either way, hand it all over to God and say: *"Nothing but your Will can happen, O Lord. I trust in You. Thy Will be done."*

Finally, recall from the section on love Jesus' admonition to Luisa, in which He says:

> My daughter, **one who really loves Me never gets annoyed about anything**, but tries to convert all things into love.[771]

Indeed, *ever* allowing ourselves to grow annoyed is a display of the self-will; a display of impatience; a display of lacking constancy; a proof that we do not live in His Will.

This does not mean that one who wishes to live in

---

[767] May 25, 1916.
[768] September 16, 1925.
[769] April 11, 1905.
[770] Cf. Sister M. De L.C., "An Unpublished Manuscript on Purgatory" "...love is a true martyrdom. The soul that really tries

to love Jesus finds that notwithstanding all its efforts it does not love Him as much as it wants to, and that is for that soul a perpetual martyrdom..." (Undergoing this type of martyrdom on Earth can itself dispose one to forego Purgatory entirely.)
[771] July 22, 1905.

the Divine Will should be a doormat, a quietist, or a "power of positive thinking" or "law of attraction" new ager—far from it! One who lives in the Divine Will might wind up confronting issues just as frequently and firmly as one who does not; perhaps standing up and walking out of a talk that becomes blasphemous, issuing a fraternal correction when it is called for, defending the innocent against unjust attacks, etc. **The point is, we should do all these things without ever succumbing to the emotion of annoyance, agitation, irritation, moodiness, snappiness, etc.** We must address issues in response to the impetus of our *reason*, not as a consequence of the emotions continuing to rise and rise until, finally, they are boiling over the power of our will to restrain them—which is how many people "address issues." That is; by silently stewing over them in annoyance until, finally, they are so annoyed that they no longer even have either the willpower or the grace to restrain themselves, and they snap with a rude remark, an angry outburst, or even, Heaven forbid, actual violence.

Allowing ourselves to behave this way is a terrible way to live, and Jesus is cautioning Luisa—and, through her, all of us—to not even let this way of life b*egin;* for indeed, we have begun it each time we allow annoyance to enter into our souls. I recommend, therefore, that you ponder carefully what things in your life cause annoyance most often:

- Is it your computer? Take each time it freezes as opportunities to pray a few Hail Mary's while it restarts.
- Is it any other product? Your printer, heating system, car, zipper, or anything else? Remind yourself that it is a collection of molecules with no soul which bears you no ill will, and proceed to act in accordance with reason regarding it: throwing it out if it is useless, fixing it if that is called for, and in general, having a mature attitude and behavior with it.
- Is it slow drivers on the road? Grab your Rosary and start praying a Divine Mercy Chaplet if you cannot safely pass them.
- Is it some annoying thing that some other person does? If it is something that should be addressed, then do so quickly and with enormous care for gentleness and charity (always giving every benefit of the doubt), without spending time stewing. If not, offer up the temptation to annoyance for the salvation of his or her soul, and thank God for the opportunity for that sacrifice.
- Is it anything at all that makes you want to respond immediately with the exclamation "unbelievable!" or "ridiculous!"? Needless to say, you are probably just succumbing to temptation in so responding, and you should consider the situation calmly and react with grace.

Of course, I cannot address every annoyance; but it is important that you try to plan ahead how you will react when your own more common temptations to annoyance knock at the door of your heart.

Daily Invocation for the Virtues

What many people unfortunately forget, regarding virtue, is to pray for it! Catholics tend to read so many books on how to be virtuous, but if this learning is not accompanied by prayer for the grace to put the learning into practice, then it will remain factual knowledge in the head and little more. It is important, therefore, that we explicitly pray—out loud, every day—for the most essential of the virtues. I recommend something like the following, which may be modified, added to, or subtracted from, however you deem appropriate:

- Please enlighten our minds and hearts and give us a true knowledge of self, so that we may be rid of all sin, attachment to sin, darkness, malice, pride, vice, and imperfection of *any* sort; and instead truly love God with all our heart, soul, mind, and strength, and love our neighbor as ourselves.
- We pray for the grace of bearing all of our crosses and sufferings with patience, humility, love, and joy. Please let them all be united with the sufferings of Jesus and Mary in atonement for our sins and those of the whole world.
- We ask that You accept all of our acts of this day, especially our sufferings, as acts done in the Divine Will, and that You accept them through the mediation of Your most holy mother.
- We ask for the grace of praying constantly.
- May the Precious Blood of Jesus protect us from all the attacks of evil spirits, and guard us from all temptation.

- We pray for an outpouring of the Holy Spirit into our hearts, that He may bestow upon us all the virtues, gifts, and fruits.
- -We pray especially for perfect Trust in Jesus, perfect humility, and perfect love.
- We pray for the grace to live out our vocations as [spouses, parents, children, siblings] as saints, and for perfect and selfless love for one another.
- We pray for discernment in all of our endeavors and apostolates, and for great fruit borne in those endeavors you do call us to, especially:_____

- And that we may properly discern, know, and do Your will in all of our decisions, especially concerning: _____

This list of prayer intentions for the virtues is, as with other lists I present, only here to "get the ball rolling." You certainly know better than anyone what virtues you are in most need of praying for growth in; I recommend, therefore, taking some time before the Blessed Sacrament to compose a list of your own invocations that you can pray each day to ask God for the grace to live out the virtues in whatever areas you are in most need.

Before closing this chapter on the Virtues, I wish to remind everyone to read, in the beginning of Part One of this book, "The Essence of the Message in One Page." Remember that the Gift is simple and receiving it is not difficult! (Even if a lengthy exposition on some of the virtues particularly associated with It belies that fact.) No matter how much you may think you now lack virtue (and no matter how much you do in fact lack virtue!), there is no reason to feel the slightest discouragement, and you will be reminded of this by re-reading that single page.

22) <u>Heed the Hard Words of Jesus for the Church</u>

Perhaps a reason why Luisa's revelations were not approved earlier can be found in just how strongly Jesus rebukes some priests, as well rebuking some aspects of the institutional Church and the by-and-large failure of Catholics. If these rebukes seemed too strong (at least to those who only saw outward appearances) in Luisa's day, they can now be seen as not only correct, but even prophetic. In this chapter, we will consider a few of Jesus' hard words, and shed light on the sorry state of the Church today to further emphasize the accurate and prophetic nature of His words to Luisa.

First, we consider how Jesus laments to Luisa that too often even good priests are unwilling to take any risk for the sake of what they know is good, but instead go about their ministries like cowards with tails between their legs. In one entry, Luisa says:

It seemed that it was not only the secular that were moving away from the Pope, but also priests, and these gave greater sorrow to the Holy Father. How pitiful it was to see the Pope in this position! After this, I saw Jesus who echoed the laments of the Holy Father, and added: **"Few are those who have remained faithful, and these few live like foxes withdrawn inside their dens.**

They are afraid to expose themselves in order to pull their children away from the mouths of the wolves. They speak, they propose, but those are all words cast to the wind—they never come to deeds." Having said this, He disappeared.[772]

Jesus also laments:

... in the religious, in the clergy, in those who call themselves Catholics, my Will not only agonizes, but is kept in a state of lethargy, as if It had no life. Oh! how much harder this is. In fact, in the agony, at least I writhe, I have an outlet, I make Myself heard as existing in them, even though agonizing. But in the state of lethargy there is total immobility—it is the continuous state of death. And so, only the appearances—the clothing of religious life can be seen, because they keep my Will in lethargy; and because they keep It in lethargy, their interior is drowsy, as if the light, the good, were not for them. And if they do anything externally, it is empty of Divine Life and it resolves into the smoke of vainglory, of self-esteem, of pleasing other creatures; and I, and my Supreme Volition, while being inside, go out of their works.[773]

One of the things that displeases Our Lord the most is this "lethargy," that is, lukewarmness,

willed fatigue, spiritual drowsiness, etc. **And Jesus does not lament what is not a choice**, therefore it is clear that lethargy is often a choice. We know this is true because of how many old priests, full of physical ailments and other crosses, nevertheless approach their ministry with all the love and enthusiasm that physical possibility allows; whereas we see many far younger priests—even those in the prime of their ministry—who, though their obligations seem enormous to them, actually have relatively light burdens and yet are always tired and looking for a break. And oh, how many breaks they are able to find! Has one inch of snow fallen on the ground? Daily Mass is canceled despite every single business owner in town having enough zeal for his own endeavors to realize that this is no reason to halt ordinary operations. Is it a national holiday? Mass is canceled.[774] Is anything at all recommended (even strongly) by the Church, but not strictly required? It is ignored. Homilies at daily Mass are neglected, any optional prayer omitted, never are any devotions hosted: pre- or post- Mass with Rosaries, Chaplets, Adoration, Benedictions, etc. Are few, if any, coming to Confession? The already pathetic hours it is offered are reduced even further.

Pope Francis, in his Magisterium, has strongly condemned lethargy of the faithful in general—particularly those who think they are "all set" because they think they are in a state of grace. Pope Francis teaches:

> The path of holiness is a source of peace and joy, given to us by the Spirit. At the same time, it demands that we keep "our lamps lit" (Lk 12:35) and be attentive. "Abstain from every form of evil" (1 Thess 5:22). "Keep awake" (Mt 24:42; Mk 13:35). "Let us not fall asleep" (1 Thess 5:6). <u>Those who think they commit no grievous sins against God's law can fall into a state of dull lethargy. Since they see nothing serious to reproach themselves with, they fail to realize that their spiritual life has gradually turned lukewarm. They end up weakened and corrupted.</u>
>
> <u>Spiritual corruption is worse than the fall of a sinner,</u> for it is a comfortable and self-satisfied form of blindness. Everything then appears acceptable: deception, slander, egotism and other subtle forms of self-centredness ...[775]

Now, this lethargy does not overwhelm any priest (or anyone, for that matter) overnight; I am not proposing that is a clear choice that one simply makes at one point. Lethargy is, rather, the cumulative result of so many choices directed towards it. One night a TV show seems like a better idea than praying the office. The next, a family barbeque seems more inviting than ministering to the sick in the hospital. Still another, snoozing the alarm sounds like a better idea than getting up early enough to review the Mass readings and prepare a brief homily. On movie night, choosing to watch a superficial comedy proves more attractive than instead watching something that might edify. Each of these decisions pushes the soul toward spiritual lethargy.

Lethargy must be exorcised from the soul. One way to accomplish this is through great devotion to the Passion of Jesus. And it is precisely that which is so neglected in modern Churches today. Jesus says to Luisa:

> All the remedies needed for the whole of humanity are in my Life and Passion. But the creature despises the medicine and does not care about the remedies; and so one can see, in spite of all my Redemption, the state of man perishing, as though affected by an incurable consumption. But that which grieves Me the most is to see religious **people who tire themselves out in order to acquire doctrines, speculations, stories—but about my Passion, nothing. So, many times my Passion is banished from churches, from the mouths of priests; therefore, their speech is without light, and the peoples remain more starved than before**[776]

***

Jesus also laments to Luisa that, instead of giving the truth, all that people receive is human and worldly intents from the clergy who are so afraid of being disliked that they are content seeing their

---

[774]This is not to say that priests shouldn't have days off – they certainly should. But these days off should not have to always be precisely the same days off that the world takes. Are not priests called *out* of the world? Did they not sacrifice the very right to have a family of their own so they *wouldn't* be constrained by the same limits as the laity? Why then, after such great sacrifice – which could be so powerful before God – do they so readily accept the very restraints and obligations that this sacrifice was supposed to free them from? Police officers and emergency room nurses also need days off – but, unlike many priests (whose job is even more important), they realize the importance of their jobs and therefore do not arbitrarily decide they all need the same days off, which would throw society into peril.

[775] *Gaudete et Exsultate*. paragraphs 164-165.
[776] October 21, 1921.

flock mired in sin, error, and ugliness.

> Ah, my daughter, in these sad times, how hard it is to find someone who would manifest this naked truth, even among the clergy, the religious, and devout people! Their speaking and operating always nurses something human, of interest or other things, and the truth is manifested as though covered or veiled. So, the person who receives is not touched by the naked truth, but by the interest or the other human purpose in which the truth has been wrapped, and he does not receive the Grace and the influence which the truth contains. This is why so many sacraments, so many confessions, are wasted, profaned and without fruit, even though I do not abstain from giving them light. But they do not listen to Me, because they think to themselves that if they did so, they would lose their prestige, their being well liked, their nature would no longer find satisfaction, and they would go against their own interests. But—oh, how they deceive themselves! In fact, one who leaves everything for love of the truth will superabound in everything more profusely than others. Therefore, as much as you can, do not neglect to manifest this naked and simple truth—it is understood, always complying to the obedience of the one who directs you; but as the opportunity arises, manifest the truth.[777]

Before presenting more of Jesus' hard words for the Church—and indeed, there are many more—it is time now to reflect upon some details of the prevailing state of the Church today in order to realize just how right He was. I am going to be completely honest in this following assessment—one which will come across as brutal, but which is necessary to be clear in diagnosing the disease, otherwise it will never be cured. For if these words of Jesus were difficult for some Catholics to swallow in the early 20th century, they should not be difficult to see the truth of now, as will become clear through this forthcoming honest analysis.

The Story of Joe

Consider what an average Catholic today, we will call him Joe, must endure from his parish. For the sake of this illustration, we will consider this parish to be a somewhat liberal, suburban parish built in the 1970s and run by a Pastor in his 60s. This is not about *a* parish; it is about *any* parish. (It is, of course, doubtful that any one parish exhibits all the faults that will be illustrated here.)

If Joe goes to Mass early in order to prayerfully prepare, as he ought, he is subjected to a veritable circus; the raucous conversation more resembling a child's birthday party than a place of prayer in preparation for the presentation of the Eternal Sacrifice on Calvary.

Often the pastor himself is the instigator, chumming it up with everyone who passes by before Mass as he stands in the vestibule or even strolls about the pews. Even if not the instigator, he has never said or done anything to try to change this sorry state of affairs.

Joe, a grown man, must then endure a processional hymn that sounds like it was taken out of a low-budget children's television show. (Later, the Gloria itself is destroyed by being set to a similarly absurd tune).

Once the time for the homily arrives, things only worsen. A seeming eternity is then spent listening to the pastor drone on and on with an incoherent blend of usually all the following:

- Remarks on how the first reading from the Old Testament was mere myth and needn't be bothered with.
- Patronizing explanations of the Pauline theology in the Epistle as a mere misunderstanding which Saint Paul had because St. Paul simply lacked the psychological studies we have today.
- A long talk on "what the Gospel means to me." At best, this amounts to a little power-of-positive-thinking encouragement to have more self-esteem and consider doing a random act of kindness now and then instead of taking Jesus' words in the Gospel seriously and at face-value. Equally often, however, it descends into a mix of lamentable theological confusion, heresy, and even blasphemy.
- All of this is presented by way of lengthy stories about himself or his experiences, mixed in with terrible jokes.

After an eternity has been spent listening to this homily—which, despite its length, did not succeed in quoting a single saint, relaying a single Church teaching, or inspiring a single soul to holiness or conversion—the Creed is then rushed through so quickly as to resemble the fine print of a radio ad.

---

[777] September 16, 1906.

The prayers of the faithful are little more than an extension of the homily's lukewarmness, entirely human and temporal in nature, with virtually no concern for any of the issues that Our Lady has requested prayers for in her many apparitions.

And the Liturgy of the Eucharist, which one would hope would finally be treated with some degree of solemnity and reverence, is now rushed through just like the Creed. Much of the glorious prayers of the New English Translation are ignored, and those that are said are again raced through. Worse still, often the prayers as found in the Missal are even changed or ad-libbed by the pastor—a more lamentable flippancy than a physicist making up his own Gravitational Constant in his calculations.

Then, the consecration displays no hint of Faith in the Real Presence, with virtually no time spent elevating the host or genuflecting after the consecration. Communion is distributed to everyone—including all the congregants openly living lives of mortal sin—and there is never the slightest hint from the pulpit regarding who may licitly receive Communion. (Unless Joe wishes to exercise his right[778] to receive Communion on the tongue whilst kneeling, then and only then, might the pastor consider denying Communion to someone.)

The moment Mass (or the 10 minutes of secular announcements) ends, the circus returns, and the atmosphere of the Church cannot be distinguished from that of a coffee shop. Whoever wishes to pray in thanksgiving for the Almighty God literally and substantially dwelling within his very body (as indeed He does for 15 minutes after receiving Communion) is thought insane or at least "anti-social."

***

So much for Sunday Mass. Perhaps Joe, heeding both natural and Divine law, actually wants to pray more often than one hour of each week's 168. But every time he tries do to so at his parish—perhaps on a lunch break or before or after work—**he is met by a locked door**. The safety of the gold candlesticks and pleasing the insurers at all costs is far more important in the pastor's mind than the sanctification of his flock and the consolation of

Jesus in the Blessed Sacrament.[779]

Joe then wants to go to **Confession**, as is his solemn duty. Only 30 minutes a week of this most essential Sacrament are offered (if the pastor even makes it on time as scheduled), in the middle of the only day of the week Joe has to get his house work and errands done (since, as he is striving to be a good Catholic, he does not do these things on Sunday).

Perhaps Joe wants to go to **daily Mass**, as all Catholics who can really should. Only a 9am Mass is offered, which only retirees can attend due to how late in the morning it is held. If he ever is able to make it, he immediately realizes that this daily Mass, which should be regarded as both the backbone and the foundation of the life of a Parish (for it is precisely that), is instead considered a nuisance to be offered due to expectations from the Chancery, or at best is considered on-par with some inconvenient parish group that is never given too much thought.

Noisy events are carried on without inhibition in adjacent rooms, and he is subject to all the lights being turned off within approximately three seconds of the final blessing, with the Sacristan impatiently pacing back and forth expecting him to leave the Church after 30 seconds of prayer of Thanksgiving. Joe sees that, like a poor child neglected by derelict parents who prefer instead catering to the needs of the family dog, daily Mass is given last place over virtually everything else the parish undertakes.

Suppose Joe wants to get involved with his parish and meet other Catholics; understanding the need for community among the Faithful. Upon doing so, he realizes that virtually all his fellow parishioners:

- Do not have the faintest clue what the Church teaches on anything even remotely "controversial" (they are never instructed on these matters from the pulpit).
- Are almost all mired in objective grave sin: using artificial contraception, viewing pornography, skipping Mass on Sundays or Holy Days, cohabiting, etc.
- Have patently heretical and even blasphemous

---

[778] Cf. The 2011 update to the USCCB's 2003 Guidelines on GIRM 160

[779] Pope Francis calls the many reasons parishes give for locking their doors "excuses," and insists that the doors should be open - literally. (See also *Evangelii Gaudium*, paragraph 47.)

beliefs regarding Jesus and Mary, the nature of the Church, the Bible, etc.

- Do not even know, much less believe, that the Eucharist is really, substantially, Jesus Christ's Body, Blood, Soul, and Divinity.
- Do not pray at all outside of Church.

Perhaps one day Joe takes his concerns from all these experiences to the Bishop. He then discovers that his parish operates without the slightest friction with this Successor of the Apostles who reigns over it—it is, after all, a very *"successful"* parish! The marketing, finance, legal, and communications experts who work in the Chancery can easily verify that diagnosis by running the numbers. Perhaps there aren't many vocations coming out of it… but there are many first Communions, a successful parochial school, relatively full pews, dozens of groups and clubs, and the list goes on! "What is there to be concerned with?" is the only response Joe gets.

Joe leaves this meeting realizing he just met with a group of businessmen and nothing more; the same sorry conclusion Jesus relayed in His words to Luisa:

> …Oh! if you saw how few [priests] who are disposed to separate from their families with their hearts also, and to throw-up this poison of interest—you would cry with Me…
>
> … so many modernists, so many priests empty of true piety, so many of them given to pleasures, so many to intemperance, many others who look at souls being lost as if it were nothing, without the slightest bitterness, and all the other absurdities they do…
>
> My daughter—to the leaders, **to the bishops? The poison of interest has invaded everyone**, and since almost all of them are taken by this pestilential fever, **they lack the courage to correct** and to check those who depend on them. And then, I am not understood by those who are not stripped of everything and of everyone. My voice resounds very badly to their hearing; even more, it seems an absurdity to them—something that is not appropriate for the human condition. If I speak with you, we understand each other well enough, and if nothing else, I find a vent for my sorrow, and You will love Me more, because you know that I am embittered.[780]

And what is the source of all of this—that is, this whole tragedy of the Story of Joe? **Interest. Priests and bishops who do not undertake their vocation in accordance with their vows, but rather in accordance with the opportunities it provides for their own interest: comfort, pleasure, enjoyments, popularity, security, etc.** Jesus tells Luisa:

> … Faith is almost extinguished among the peoples, and if there is any spark left, it is as though hidden under ashes. **The life of priests, which is almost completely secularized, and maybe worse than that, as well as their examples, which are not good, lend a hand to extinguish this spark**.…Ah! my daughter, do you know what the most insurmountable stumbling block and the strongest lace is? It is mere self-interest. Self-interest is the wood worm of the priest, which renders him like rotten wood, that is fit only for burning in hell. Interest makes the priest the laughing stock of the devil, the mockery of the people, and the idol of their families. Therefore, the devil will put many obstacles to hinder their work, because he sees that the net in which he has kept them chained and enslaved to his dominion is being broken [in freeing priests of self-interest]…[781]

> And the priests? Ah! my daughter—that is even worse. They do good to all?! You deceive yourself. They do good to the rich; they have time for the rich. By them also the poor are almost excluded; for the poor they have no time; for the poor they have not a word of comfort or help to tell them; they send them away, reaching the point of pretending they are ill. I could say that if the poor have moved away from the Sacraments, the priests have contributed to this, because they have always taken their time to confess them, and the poor grew tired and no longer came back. But then, if a rich person would show up, it is all the opposite: they would not hesitate one instant; time, words, comforts, help…, they would find anything for the rich. [782]

So, **what should Joe do? That is, what should *we all* do?**

How exactly do we fight this battle? In short, **we must do so by choosing the path of Mary, not the path of Peter in the garden.** Peter reacted with violence and anger at His Lord being disrespected, and he became consumed by this anger. As the path he chose was devoid of grace, since it was not God's Will, Peter did not even have the strength to remain

---

[780] January 15, 1911.
[781] January 8, 1910.
[782] June 31, 1908.

close to Jesus, and instead denied Him. This is the path chosen by no small number of Catholics today who, seeing the sorry state of the Church and especially how the Eucharist is treated, become increasingly caustic in their language, wrathful in their hearts, accusatory in their speech, ready to spread gossip, enclosed in their circles, joyless in their demeanor, rigid on what is optional, and in a word, completely lacking the doctrinally defined Twelve Fruits of the Holy Spirit, which are the sure evidence of God's presence in the heart.

Peter was not there for Jesus — not in the way that Jesus wanted. Jesus wanted prayer, and Peter wanted sleep, and we know whose will prevailed in that case. Peter was, however, ready and willing to throw a fit when things started going wrong. Is that what we are like? Are we doing what Jesus is clearly asking of us now — that is, what He is asking us through Scripture, through the Magisterium, through apparitions of His mother, and through His Vicar, the Pope? Are we adoring the Eucharist and receiving it as often as possible with love and reverence, performing works of mercy, going out to the peripheries, evangelizing, living and spreading the Divine Mercy, fulfilling Our Lady's requests at Fatima, fasting and sacrificing, etc.? Or are we, like Peter, sleeping through all these clear calls from Heaven, even though we are quite ready to complain, criticize, and gossip about the sins and bad decisions of individual priests, bishops, and others in the Church?

Do not follow that path. If you do, then you will fall like Peter did, because Jesus loves you far too much to see you go along that path for long. In your fall, you will be humbled, and you will need to start anew. But why not recognize that, and start anew right now?

Take heart, and let us not be like Peter but rather like Mary, at the foot of the cross, enduring not only the passion of her Son, but also the raucous debauchery of the drunken soldiers around her. She did not judge even them, and they did not feel judged by her. But, even while on earth, not one of them forgot her witness, for it was emblazoned upon their memories like a flash of lightning illuminating a landscape. Similarly, the cowardly apostles no doubt felt no judgment from Mary, even though they felt ashamed of their own

cowardice due to her example of strength and trust.

We must therefore, first, pray earnestly and frequently for our priests, without judgment on them. I have been strong in my own words in this chapter, but bear in mind that I am not speaking of any one priest in particular; only general issues that must be addressed.

Remember that the demons, knowing that their most lethal strategy is to strike the shepherds, focus far more of their attention on tempting them than upon tempting lay people. Remember also that priests gave up their lives to bring you the Sacraments. We must never be critical or gossipy, but instead persevere as silent, strong, humble witnesses to love of, and reverence for, the Eucharist. Remember that Mary, Mother of the Eucharist, is ever our patroness and intercessor in this struggle.

On the "Devout"

Jesus' hard words for the Church are not reserved for clergy; He often includes those who like to call themselves "devout" in these very same rebukes. For these "devout" souls who can check-off all the boxes in the "holiness To-Do lists" are often experts at neglecting the source of holiness itself: the Will of God. Jesus tells Luisa:

> My daughter, I had to make it in such a way that sanctity might be easy and accessible to all — unless they did not want it — in all conditions, in all circumstances and in every place. It is true that the Most Holy Sacrament is center; but who instituted It? Who subdued my Humanity to enclose Itself within the small circle of a Host? Wasn't that my Will? Therefore my Will will always have primacy over everything. Besides, if everything is in the Eucharist, the priests who call Me from Heaven into their hands, and who are in contact with my Sacramental Flesh more than anyone, should be the holiest and the most good; but instead, many of them are the worst. Poor Me, how they treat Me in the Most Holy Sacrament! And **the many devout souls who receive Me, perhaps every day, should be as many saints** if the center of the Eucharist were sufficient. **But instead — and it is something to be cried over — they remain always at the same point: vain, irascible, punctilious, etc. Poor center of the Most Holy Sacrament, how dishonored It remains!**[783]

---

[783] September 25, 1913.

And who can fail to see how called for these rebukes are? Restricting our consideration now to only that minority of Catholics who appear to receive Communion worthily, they often (if not usually) nevertheless treat Him as a dead object,[784] approaching reception of Communion as just another chore to accomplish. They have less reverence than they would have at any serious secular event, and less love than they have in pursuing their hobbies.

Even at daily Mass, many parishes seem to be not places of prayer, but rather places of socialization, where discussing the details of the day's errands seems far more important than prayerfully preparing for, or giving thanks for, receiving the Almighty and Eternal God in the Eucharist (and this is not to mention the far worse utter disregard for reverence and silence at many Sunday Masses). More emphasis is placed on the fellowship aspect than on the fact that here, creatures gather to worship their Creator in His Real Presence. If there is any significant amount of true Faith in the Real Presence of Jesus in the Eucharist, then this is not evidenced in the deeds and demeanors of average daily Massgoers, many of whom are evidently above all intent on talking about their doctor appointments, their grandchildren, the weather, the sports show they watched last night, etc. For they burst into discussions on these topics the moment Mass ends, thus demonstrating these things are exactly what they were thinking about before it ended. This, of course, is not to mention that virtually nobody stays more than a few moments after daily Mass ends—rushing out the door, immediately forgetting what they just did, even while the physical presence of Jesus in the Eucharist still remains in their stomachs.

Meanwhile, the "devout" will easily turn out in droves for sports games, secular-themed events, and barbeques at the parish, while scarcely anyone can be found to fill slots for perpetual adoration or pray and sidewalk counsel outside Planned Parenthood.

"God is able from these stones to raise up children of Abraham" (Matthew 3:9).

That is what John the Baptist said to the Pharisees, who supposed their status as children of Abraham

sufficed to determine their holiness. And Jesus and Mary say essentially the same thing to us in all their apparitions. What is needed is not more superficially "devout" Catholics who merely can check-off-the-box that they externally do all the right things. Indeed, these external "right things" are essential, but just as essential is approaching them with the correct interior disposition. This interior disposition, while invisible, is nevertheless easy to determine the absence of in many who do all the externals. We must, therefore, not be lax with ourselves merely because we do those things which are expected of the devout, lest we render ourselves the very objects of Jesus' lamentations to Luisa.

The Abuse Crisis

In His revelations to Luisa, Jesus goes so far as to say that it is the enemies of the Church who are necessary in order to purge and purify her. It is difficult to think of stronger words; but it's becoming increasingly impossible to ignore them. Today, it is sadly the Church's enemies—Godless, secular people who have long hated her—who are doing what the Bishops should have done long ago: dealing with the sin of sexual abuse as strongly as it should be dealt with and exposing the perpetrators.

In this passage, Jesus prophesies today's crisis to Luisa 100 years before it began; although He does not explicitly refer to the crisis as involving sexual abuse, I think it is safe to say that this is one of the major things (if not *the* major thing) He intended when He said to Luisa:

> I was praying blessed Jesus to confound the enemies of the Church, and my always lovable Jesus, in coming, told me: "My daughter, **I could confound the enemies of the Holy Church**, but I don't want to. **If I did so, who would purge my Church?** The members of the Church, and especially **those who occupy positions and heights of dignity, have their eyes dazzled, and they blunder a great deal, reaching the point of protecting the false virtuous and oppressing and condemning the true good**. This grieves Me so much—to see those few true children of mine under the weight of injustice; those children from whom my Church must rise again and to whom I am giving much grace to dispose them to this… I see them placed with their backs to the wall, and bound to prevent their step. This grieves Me so

[784] Jesus complains of this to St. Faustina, Cf. *Divine Mercy in My Soul*, paragraph 447, 1385.

much, that I feel I am all fury for their sake! Listen my daughter, I am all sweetness, benign, clement and merciful; so much so, that because of my sweetness I enrapture hearts. But I am also strong, as to be able to crush and reduce to ashes those who not only oppress the good, but reach the point of preventing the good which they want to do. Ah! you cry over the secular, and I cry over the painful wounds which are in the body of the Church. These grieve Me so much as to surpass the wounds of the secular, because they come from the side from which I did not expect it, and induce Me to make the secular rail against them."[785]

Here, Jesus says clearly what it has taken until now for the boldest of voices in the Church to acknowledge: The enemies of the Church, paradoxically, have now proven necessary for the Church in order to purge it. For the leaders of the Church—the Bishops—go so far as to "protect the false virtuous" (predator priests) and "condemn the true good" (traditional, orthodox-minded priests).

On Sacrilege Against the Sacraments

In Luisa's revelations we find an explication from Jesus on the Sacraments that, at the same time, both glorifies them more perfectly than any treatise you will find elsewhere, and also more strongly reproves the abuses of them—which, tragically, seem to be more common than the licit receptions thereof. In a word, we see here the opposite of the Modernist view of the Sacraments, which says that, *"they don't matter that much, they certainly aren't necessary for salvation, but so long as you at least half-heartedly approach them, this puts you in good enough shape."* Though lengthy, this whole quote is necessary to include here:

The Sacraments were instituted in order to continue my Life on earth in the midst of my children. But, alas!, how many sorrows…

While through Baptism I restore his innocence, I find my child again, I give back to him the rights over Creation which he had lost… soon my smile turns into sorrow, the feast into mourning. I see that the one who is baptized will be an enemy of mine, a new Adam, and maybe even a lost soul. Oh! how my love moans in each Baptism; especially, then, if one adds that the minister who is baptizing does not do it with that respect,

dignity and decorum which befit a Sacrament that contains the new regeneration. Ah! many times they pay more attention to a bagatelle [small trifle], to whatever show, than to administering a Sacrament

…Move on to the Sacrament of Confirmation. Ah! how many bitter sighs. While, through Confirmation, I restore his courage, I give back to him the lost strengths, rendering him invincible to all enemies and to his passions, and he is admitted to the ranks of the militia of his Creator… yet, many times He feels Himself being requited with the kiss of a traitor

… in the Sacrament of Penance. How much ingratitude, how many abuses and profanations, on the part of those who administer it and on the part of those who receive it… souls approaching this Sacrament of Penance without sorrow, out of habit, almost as a vent of the human heart… So, the Sacrament is reduced to a mockery, to a nice chat; and my Blood, instead of descending as a bath, descends as fire, which withers them even more …

The Sacrament of the Eucharist is my very Life that gives Itself to them … and each Communion serves to make my Life grow… in such a way that one may be able to say: 'I am another Christ'. But, alas!, how few take advantage of it. Even more, how many times I descend into hearts and they find the weapons to wound Me, and repeat for Me the tragedy of my Passion…

The Ordination constitutes man to a supreme height, to a divine character—the repeater of my Life… the peacemaker between Heaven and earth, the bearer of Jesus to souls … But, alas!, how many times We see, in the ordained one, how he will be a Judas for Us… Each act of this ordained one, not done according to the character impressed, will be a cry of sorrow … The Ordination is the Sacrament which encloses all other Sacraments together … [the Priest can be] the defender and the savior of Jesus Himself … But, not seeing this in the ordained one, Our sorrows are sharpened more…

How many disorders in [marriage]! Marriage was elevated by Me to a Sacrament, in order to place in it a sacred bond, the symbol of the Sacrosanct Trinity, the divine love which It encloses. So, the love which was to reign in the father, mother and children, the concord, the peace, was to symbolize the Celestial Family. I was to have on earth as many other families similar to the Family of the Creator, destined to

---

[785] May 16, 1911.

populate the earth like as many terrestrial angels, to then bring them back to populate the celestial regions. But, ah! how many moans in seeing families of sin being formed in the Marriage, which symbolize hell, with discord, with lack of love, with hatred, and which populate the earth like many rebellious angels, who will serve to populate hell…

When the Sacrament of the Extreme Unction is administered … This Sacrament has the virtue of placing the dying sinner in safety at any cost… it is the final brush stroke which the Holy Spirit gives her in order to dispose her to depart from the earth, so as to make her appear before her Creator. In sum, the Extreme Unction is the final display of Our love… But, alas!, how many moans, , how many negligences … How many losses of souls; how few the sanctities it finds to be confirmed; how scarce the good works to be reordered and rearranged.[786]

Jesus' most ardent pains in the Sacraments, however, are in the Blessed Sacrament. He says to Luisa:

[Regarding] the Eucharistic Sacrament which I left as food in order to give them perfect health — many eat It over and over again, but they appear always sick. Poor food of my very Life, hidden under the veils of the accidents of the bread — how many corrupted palates, how many undigesting stomachs, which prevent creatures from enjoying the taste of my food, and from digesting all the strength of my Sacramental Life. And so they remain infirm; and because they are members feverish in evil, they take it with no appetite. **This is why I long so much for the coming of the Kingdom of the Supreme Fiat — because, then, everything I did in coming upon earth will serve as food for those who enjoy perfect health**.[787]

… there is not one day in which ungrateful souls do not offend Me and receive Me sacrilegiously, … Ah! sacrilege is the most ruthless death that I receive in this Sacrament of love. So, in this Tabernacle I do my day by carrying out everything I carried out in the thirty-three years of my mortal life.[788]

Tragically, Jesus' pains in the Blessed Sacrament are no doubt infinitely greater today than ever before; most who receive Him have no Faith in His presence whatsoever and, furthermore, are leading lives full of objective grave sins. **If we are to take Jesus' words to Luisa seriously, this must stop. But only the Third Fiat can truly succeed in making it stop; so now let us turn our attention from Jesus' hard words to Jesus' inspiring words, which are far more common in Luisa's revelations and on which He focuses far more attention.**

23) Be a New Evangelist of the Third Fiat

Now that you know these most sublime mysteries of the Divine Will, it is imperative that you not keep them to yourself!

One should not cast pearls before swine. If you know that a certain person always struts about with a theological chip on his shoulder, ready to denounce any private revelation that has the slightest abrasion with any of his own opinions and preferences, then do not bother presenting this to him. It is also important to never present Luisa's spirituality to a non-Catholic (or lapsed, or lukewarm Catholic) as an alternative to Catholicism. But there is no reason not to share Luisa's spirituality with any practicing Catholic who has an openness to mysticism and private revelation. Even if someone you know is not a practicing Catholic, or perhaps not even a Christian, but you nevertheless sense a strong openness in him and spirit of true seeking, you could carefully share Luisa's spirituality with him, in such a way that he realizes it goes along with and presupposes being a devoutly practicing Catholic.

To Luisa, Jesus likens those who now spread knowledge of this Third Fiat to the very Evangelists who wrote the Gospels. There are indeed ways in which our duty now is even more exciting and privileged; for what they longed for, we are now truly on the cusp of attaining. At what time that is attained, and who shares in its attainment, is dependent upon our response.

What sacrifice, then, is too great to spread this Kingdom of His on earth? What vanity, now clung to, is not worth casting aside for the sake of the Reign of His Will? What risk, now feared, is not worth taking to be able to participate in the initiation of the Third Fiat of the Eternal One? Patriarchs, Prophets, Martyrs, Fathers, Doctors,

---

[786] November 5th, 1925
[787] November 2, 1926.

[788] September 12, 1931.

and yes, even the Angels, envy you for the invitation that God now extends freely to you. Take it.

Our Lady, too, harbors a special love for those who promote the Divine Will; which she shares with her Divine Son as her own greatest interest as well. In a letter, Luisa wrote:

> Their desire that the Kingdom of God come upon the earth is so great that our Celestial Mama Herself wants to descend from Heaven; She wants to enter the families and the whole world, to become leader, teacher and example of a Kingdom so holy. Therefore, She loves in a special way those who are interested in it, She will give them the first place and hold them as first children of this Supreme Will ... She will give you the peace that you so much long for…[789]

Too often we try to remedy our spiritual, psychological, moral, familial, and other such problems with incessant navel-gazing: self-evaluation, psychologists, self-help books, etc. This approach is doomed to failure because most of our problems will be solved only by forgetting ourselves and refocusing our efforts on our mission. And this is *the* mission. Is it not true that we all long for peace? Here we see that Our Lady will give us that peace if only we interest ourselves in this mission.

Although this chapter is placed immediately after one in which we saw the many hard words of Jesus for the Church—especially for priests and Bishops—we must remember that He only issues these strong rebukes because He loves the clergy, knows how vital they are, and knows how glorious a place and central a position they hold in this Greatest Mission of History. For it is precisely these men whom Jesus is begging to be the primary heralds of the Coming of His Kingdom:

> How necessary it is that the knowledges about my Fiat be known; not only this, but that it be made known that my Divine Will already wants to come to reign on earth as It does in Heaven into the midst of creatures. **And it is to the priests, as to new prophets, both through the word and through writing and through works, that the task is given of acting as trumpeters in order to make known what regards my Divine Fiat;** nor would their crime be lesser than that of the prophets, had these hidden my Redemption, if

they do not occupy themselves as much as they can with what regards my Divine Will.[790]

In a letter written to a Monsignor, Luisa beseeched its recipient:

> "This is my wish for the new year—that you may live always in the Divine Will, and that Jesus may **make of you a missionary of the Divine Will**."

Dear Priests: the Coming of the Kingdom is in your hands.

Nevertheless, whoever you are, priest or lay, there is so much you can do to hasten its coming. Jesus is begging for souls willing to be the trumpeters of these knowledges, but He finds so few. He says to Luisa:

> …I find no one who has true enthusiasm, genuine desire and the will to make my work his life in order to make it known, so as to give to others the life of the good of my work, which he feels within himself. And when I see these dispositions in one who must occupy himself with it, whom I call and choose, with so much love, for the works that belong to Me, I feel so drawn to him, that so that he may do well what I want, I lower Myself, I descend into him and I give him my mind, my mouth, my hands and even my feet, that he may feel the life of my work in everything, and, as life that is felt, not as something extraneous to him, he may feel the need to give it to others… Therefore, I am not the impotent God, but rather, that patient God who wants His works to be done with decorum and by people who are willing, not forced; because the thing I abhor the most in my works is the unwillingness of the creature, as if I did not deserve their little sacrifices.[791]

If only you set yourself to work in spreading these knowledges of the Divine Will; in making the Will of God known and loved so that it may reign on earth, then Jesus, as He promised here, will truly descend into you and give you His very Self for the task. Do you want, therefore, an utter outpouring of grace into your life, the likes of which you have never previously experienced? Spread the knowledges. Make the Divine Will known and loved.

Let us now see what else Jesus tells Luisa about those who occupy themselves with this glorious task:

---

[789] Letter #14 to Mrs. Constanza Benedetta Pettinelli from Siena.

[790] January 13, 1929.
[791] October 2, 1929.

Oh! how happy they will feel-those who, with yearning, will drink in large gulps from these founts of My knowledges; because they contain the virtue of bringing the life of Heaven, and of banishing any unhappiness...the ones who will occupy themselves with these Writings in order to publish them, putting them out to print them-to make them known, will **be the new evangelists of the Kingdom of My Supreme Will.** And just as the ones who are most mentioned in My Gospel are the four Evangelists who wrote It, to their highest honor and My Glory, so it will be for those who will occupy themselves with writing the knowledges on My Will in order to publish them. Like new evangelists, there will be greater mention of them in the Kingdom of My Will, to their highest honor and My great Glory in seeing the order of the creature, the life of Heaven on earth-the only purpose of Creation-return into My bosom.[792]

...if creatures possessed my Divine Will as life, they would know many beautiful things about It; and knowing It **and not speaking about It would be impossible for them**; therefore they would do nothing else but speak of It, love It and lay down their lives in order not to lose It."[793]

Therefore, my daughter, my goodness is so great that I reward justly and superabundantly the good that the creature does, especially in this work of my Will, which I so much care for. What will I not give to those who occupy and sacrifice themselves in order to place in safety the rights of my Eternal Fiat? I will exceed so much in giving, as to make Heaven and earth astonished."[794]

Jesus will give so much to you if you work to live in and promote the Divine Will, that He will astonish Heaven and earth in this giving.

We can see an example of this in the quote which follows, regarding St. Hannibal di Francia. Recall, from Part One of this book, that Fr. Di Francia was a spiritual director of Luisa Piccarreta's, and was the most zealous promoter of her revelations. Jesus tells Luisa:

Oh! if mortals knew the great good they acquire by knowing a true good, a truth, and by making it their own blood in order to absorb it in their own lives, they would compete among themselves, they would forget about everything in order to know one truth—and would lay down their lives to put it into practice...

While Jesus was saying this, I saw the blessed soul of father [di Francia—who had just died the day of this diary entry] before me, near my bed, invested with light, suspended from the earth, fixing on me, but without telling me one word. I too felt mute before him, and Jesus added: "Look at him, how transformed he is. My Will is light, and has transformed that soul into light; It is beautiful, and has given him all the tints of perfect beauty; It is holy, and he has been sanctified. My Will possesses all sciences, and his soul has been invested by divine science. There is nothing which my Will has not given to him. Oh! if all understood what Divine Will means, they would put everything aside, they would care about doing nothing else, and their whole commitment would be to do my Will alone."[795]

***

Now, one might be tempted, like Luisa, to think that, given how long Jesus is waiting (it has, after all, been over 70 years since Luisa died), He is not particularly eager to give this Gift of the Divine Will to all souls. Nothing could be farther from the truth, however. In Luisa's writings, we see the following exchange between Luisa and Jesus:

... I thought to myself: "If Living in the Divine Volition is a Gift that He must make to the human generations, and Jesus so much Loves, wants, yearns, that this Divine Will is known in order to let It Reign, then why is He not in a hurry to give this Gift?"

And my highest Good Jesus, visiting my little soul, all Goodness, said to me: "My daughter, you must know that although I Burn with the Desire of seeing My Divine Will Reign, yet I can not give this Gift before I have Manifested the Truths... as the creatures will know these Truths of Mine, so they will form the sphere for where to place the pupil inside, and animate it with sufficient Light in order to be able to look at and comprehend the Gift, that more than sun will be given and entrusted to them...So, giving the great Gift of My Divine Will-which more than sun will change the lot of the human generations-today, would be to give It to the blind. And giving It to the blind would be giving them useless gifts, and I do not know how to give useless things. Therefore, **I await with Divine and delirious Patience that My Truths will make their way, prepare souls, enter into them and form the eye animated with sufficient Light such that they can not only look at the Gift of My Fiat, but have the capacity in**

---

order to enclose It in themselves so that It forms Its Kingdom and extends Its Dominion in them…More than father **We yearn to give the Great Gift of Our Will to Our children, but We want that they know what they are receiving.** The Knowledges about It mature Our children and make them capable of receiving such a Good.[796]

Jesus is dying to give us His Kingdom, but it is first necessary for the Knowledges of the Divine Will to prepare its way; and it is up to us to spread these knowledges! Jesus also has strong words to those who, in cowardice, laziness, or human "prudence," neglect this mission. He says to Luisa:

> Now, since these little visits of Mine are bearers of Celestial Things, you will bring them with you into the Celestial Fatherland as Triumph of My Will and as guarantee that Its Kingdom not only will come upon earth, but has established Its beginning of Its Reigning. Those that will remain on paper will leave the Perennial Memory that My Will wants to Reign in the midst of the human generations; and they will be spurs, incitements, Divine Supplications, Irresistible Strength, Celestial Messengers, Captains of the Kingdom of My Divine Fiat, and also **Powerful Reproaches to** <u>**those who should**</u> **occupy themselves with making known a Good so Great, and who, out of indolence and vain fears, will not let them go around through the whole world, so that they may bring the Good News of the Happy Era of the Kingdom of My Will.** Therefore, abandon yourself in Me, and let Me do.[797]

But who are "those who should occupy themselves"? *You.* **That is, whoever has read these words**—Jesus' words to Luisa—which have been read by such a minuscule percentage of the devout (much less of practicing Catholics in general, much less of the Church in general, much less of the world at large, to which God will give this Gift). **You are utterly precious and pivotal in God's plan by the mere fact that you have been exposed to this.** In "stumbling upon" you by these words, God is more fortunate than is a beggar who has stumbled upon a millionaire willing to part with his fortunes. For God has found in you someone who can help hasten His greatest plan: that His Will be done on earth as it is done in Heaven.

So, what are some concrete things we can do in this

extraordinary task? I offer just a few thoughts:

- Above all, never forget that you must *live* in the Divine Will. We cannot promote the Divine Will with the human will.
- Start an apostolate (or even a blog) promoting these revelations.
- Start a Divine Will prayer group.
- Be a Divine Will Missionary of Mercy (<u>www.DWMoM.org</u>)
- Pray for Luisa's intercession and carefully document any potential miracles.
- If you are multilingual, consider working to translate Luisa's works or books on Luisa's works.
- Pray for and contribute to Luisa's cause for Beatification.
- If you are on social media, promote it on all your accounts.
- Give out books on the Divine Will to people who may be interested. Place them (if this is permitted) in perpetual adoration chapels.
- Defend Luisa's revelations against attacks that come up regularly online.

Regarding the last point: unfortunately, there are certain articles criticizing—with some downright attacking—Luisa and her writings. But please take note that these articles were written in the 1990s, before the flood of demonstrations of the validity of Luisa's revelations came to light. Sadly, however, they tend to resurface on blogs, forums, etc. every few months. You can automatically be alerted as to when this happens by setting up a "Google Alert" for the phrase "living in the Divine Will" and "Luisa Piccarreta."[798]

Those who recirculate these articles are usually sincere Catholics who are zealous for orthodoxy. But I beg you: approach this task of defending Luisa's with enormous gentleness, charity, and benefit-of-the-doubt-giving. We will only damage Luisa's cause if we ever comport ourselves in any other manner while promoting and defending her cause and her revelations. Furthermore, we should avoid going down rabbit-holes of endless back-and-forths over the intricate details of the criticisms.

Just get the truth out there: briefly, succinctly, and

---

[796] Mary 15, 1932.
[797] January 24, 1932

[798] Most alerts you receive will be auto-generated spam postings that merely re-post random material on random web pages; but some of the alerts will be of genuine postings.

poignantly. Even if the truth only gets 1% of the exposure as does the error opposed to it, the truth will nevertheless prevail. You could link to or quote from this book or others defending Luisa's revelations. You could point out that the only currently in force Church stricture is from Archbishop Pichierri's 2012 notification, which explicitly encourages reading and promoting Luisa's writings and rebukes those who claim that her writings contain doctrinal errors. You could point out that the Church-approved biography of Luisa Piccarreta, *Sun of My Will*, was published in 2015 by the Vatican itself and it strongly endorses both Luisa and her revelations.

***

These are just a few suggestions; it is important that, in this task of promoting the Divine Will—the greatest mission in history—,we be neither lazy nor stupid. Jesus' admonition in the Gospels to be cunning as serpents and innocent as doves applies here more than anywhere—therefore, apply yourself zealously to considering new and more powerful ways to promote and spread these knowledges. My few suggestions are no replacement for your own brainstorming!

Remember to go about all of this with cheerfulness, for again, "God loves a cheerful giver,"[799] and our duty here should not be seen as one of imposition, but one of joyful invitation. Jesus tells Luisa:

> Therefore, I am not the impotent God, but rather, that patient God who wants His works to be done with decorum and by people who are willing, not forced; because the thing I abhor the most in my works is the unwillingness of the creature, as if I did not deserve their little sacrifices. And for the decorum of a work so great, which is that of making my Divine Will known, I do not want to use poor cripples—in fact, when one who does not have the genuine will to do a good, it is always a mutilation that he does to his soul—but I want to use people who, as I provide them with my divine members, would do it with decorum, as a work which must bring so much good to creatures, and great glory to my Majesty, deserves."[800]

And it will be easy to approach this joyful duty with the right attitude if we recognize the nature of the message we are sharing. For one great thing about being a New Evangelist of the Third Fiat is

that you needn't have any fear of merely repeating a message which your audience has already heard a thousand times to the point that it has become nothing but a platitude. This is new. This will not bore anyone (although it will scandalize many a Pharisee; but, as St. Padre Pio said, "we must keep doing good, even though it scandalizes the Pharisees."). Jesus tells Luisa:

> Many times, My daughter, novelties bring new life, new goods, and creatures are very much drawn to novelties, and let themselves be as though carried by the novelty. More so, since the novelties of the new manifestations about My Divine Will, that have a Divine Strength and a sweet enchantment, and that will rain down like celestial dew upon souls burnt by the human will, will be bearers of happiness, of light and of infinite goods. There are no threats in these manifestations, nor any fright; and if there is anything about fear, it is for those who want to remain in the maze of the human will. But then, in all the rest, one can see nothing but the echo, the language of the Celestial Fatherland, the balm from on high that sanctifies, divinizes and makes the down payment of the happiness that reigns only in the Blessed Fatherland.[801]

Consider with what zeal an electrician can run wire in a new house; knowing, as he does, that this relatively simple act will enable such an enormous amount of effects to transpire in each room, as soon as he is done, thanks to his efforts. Jesus likens the truths on His Will contained in Luisa's revelations to precisely this: electric wires. All it takes is that they be laid, then the electricity—which He likens to the Fiat Itself—can run through them with incomprehensible rapidity and achieve all the necessary effects.[802] But the great good of the electrical current is useless without an infrastructure to carry it. And the industriousness of the laborers is needed to give this infrastructure; Jesus is begging us to be the ones to lay it out. In Luisa's diary, we see the following passage:

> … I was concerned about the publication of the writings… and, all afflicted, [Jesus] told me, "My daughter, how sorrowful I feel. They should have considered themselves honored—**they should have boasted about and gloried in making themselves known as the ones who had this great honor to publish the truths about my Holy Will. I could not have given them a greater honor**

---

[799] 2 Corinthians 9:7
[800] October 2, 1929.

[801] January 30, 1927.
[802] Cf. August 4, 1926.

and glory than calling them to an office so high but instead, they want to hide. How my Heart aches; I feel so much sorrow that I cannot contain it… Oh, how they should have yearned to receive and to make known a good so great! But instead … all the opposite. In Redemption, the Evangelists considered themselves honored to make themselves known as the ones who were putting out the Gospel, so that It might be known by the whole world; and they signed their names with glory, so much so, that when the Gospel is preached, first they state the name of the one who wrote It, and then they speak the Gospel. So I want to be done with the truths about my Will, that everyone may know who the ones are that brought so much good into the world. But what do you think this is? All human prudence. **Ah, how many divine works the human prudence has caused to fail in the midst of creatures! Like sluggards, they have reached the point of withdrawing from the holiest works**. But my Will will know how to triumph over all and mock them; however, I cannot hide my sorrow for such a great human ingratitude at a good so great."[803]

You yourself, dear reader, if only you apply yourself to this task, may well be the one who tips the balance and allows the Kingdom to come. Jesus tells Luisa:

"In addition to this, on this day of My Ascension I had a Double Crown: the Crown of My children whom I brought with Me into the Celestial Fatherland, **and the Crown of My children whom I left on earth, <u>symbol of the few who will begin the Kingdom of My Divine Will</u>**. All those who saw Me Ascend to Heaven received so many Graces, that everyone gave his life in order to make the Kingdom of the Redemption known, and they cast the foundations in order to form My Church so as to gather all the human generations into Her Maternal Womb. **The same for the first children of the Kingdom of My Will; they will be few, but the Graces with which they will be invested will be such and so many, that they will give their lives in order to call everyone to Live in this Holy Kingdom**…Such and so much will be the Light that will invest Its first children that they will carry the Beauty, the Enchantment, the Peace of the Divine Fiat, in a way that they will easily surrender themselves to wanting to know and to love a Good so Great.[804]

It truly does depend on us.

The time in which they will come to light is

relative and conditional upon when the creatures dispose themselves to receive a good so great, and upon those who must occupy themselves with being its criers, and make the sacrifice so as to bring the new era of peace, the new Sun which will dispel all the clouds of evils. If you knew how many graces and lights I keep prepared for those whom I see disposed to occupy themselves with them! … But I am looking to see who the true disposed ones are, so as to invest them with the prerogatives that are needed for a work so holy, which I so much love and want them to do. However, I must also say to you: 'Woe to those who are opposed or might place obstacles!'[805]

I hope these words inspire you and cause to well up inside you an overpowering holy desire to be the one to hasten the coming of this Kingdom. But let us turn now to a sub-section for a brief word of caution.

***

For, knowing what you now know—having read thus far in this book—just by virtue of that knowledge and your concomitant desire to spread this knowledge of the Divine Will and become a New Evangelist of the Third Fiat, you are already potentially among the most elite soldiers in the Church Militant of God. As you read these words, the devil is already likely working on a new strategy for you. I wish to circumvent these nefarious plans he has for you by warning you in advance of them.

The devil will go into damage control mode—he will try to distract you. He is utterly terrified of what you can do if you simply order your days, your goals, your priorities, and your endeavors in such a way as to optimize their eternal value and the proclamation of the truths of the Divine Will.

The devil is more afraid of you now than a deer is of a hunter. Knowing your immense power over him and his minions and his plan (only through God's grace, of course), he strives to divert you to things so far below your calling; so that even if he cannot make you his own by causing you to descend into a life of grave sin, you at least will not so greatly damage his plan in the world. (He never fully loses his desire for luring you to grave sin, but he does recognize that at a certain point it is rather unlikely, hence his redirecting of his efforts to

---

[803] August 23, 1928.
[804] May 20, 1936.

[805] August 2, 1928.

"damage control mode".) How does he distract? In so many ways:

He distracts you from your prayers. He makes you feel busy, and he makes you believe the lie that you don't have time for an intense and lengthy daily prayer routine. He fires up your passion for worldly debates. He entangles you in factiousness within the Church on issues that, even if important to be dealt with, are nowhere near as effective in the glorification of God and the salvation of souls as are evangelization, prayer, works of mercy, and the like. He makes you think your primary vocation (e.g. your duties as a provider) supersedes or replaces your universal vocation (your call to holiness). He tries to distract you from his own hideousness by compelling you to focus primarily upon the hideousness of those people who follow some of his ways. (Imagine how useless a U.S. Marine would be who, upon being sent into a foreign country to take out a terrorist cell, focused only upon eliminating the cockroach infestations there. Do not be like such a Marine, for you are in a far more elite, far more essential army: the Church Militant. Those who, tragically, follow some of the devil's ways are not themselves the devil.[806]) He eases you away from those who embolden you, and towards those who placate you. (Some Catholic groups often start out as great salvation-aiding apostolates, but before long they are just cliques. The time spent actually saying the prayers and doing the works of mercy they were founded upon becomes perhaps one hastily prayed Rosary, if even that—then hours are spent having coffee afterward engaging in mundane worldly conversation. Family gatherings sometimes become grace prayed before the meal, and then excessive "hanging out," with one worldly thing after another happening until an entire day is gone.)

Meanwhile, as the devil distracts you with everything under the sun, he will seek to convince you that the urgency and calls to conversion of private revelation (which is the one thing that actually will spiritually awaken some people) are themselves distractions, and are best avoided.

> Therefore I tell you, do not be anxious about your life, what you shall eat or what you shall drink, nor about your body, what you shall put on. Is not life more than food, and the body more than clothing? … Therefore do not be anxious, saying, 'What shall we eat?' or 'What shall we drink?' or 'What shall we wear?' For the Gentiles seek all these things; and your heavenly Father knows that you need them all. But **seek first his kingdom and his righteousness, and all these things shall be yours as well**.[807]

Don't let the devil succeed. In all four Gospels, Christ said that He came "to destroy the works of the devil." **Being a member of the Church Militant is not primarily about being on the defensive—it is first about being on the offensive**. That fact is perhaps what we forget most when we discuss spiritual warfare. Spiritual warfare should not primarily be about loading your life up with so many defenses against the devil that, once you are swimming in holy water, scapulars, crucifixes, and various other medals and sacramentals (great and necessary as these things are), you finally feel you are safe from his attacks. No, rather, it is primarily about recognizing that, through God's grace, you can devastate the devil's kingdom, and then proceeding with zeal and the fire of Divine Love in that task.

Rest when you die, not now. Proclaim the Kingdom. Be a New Evangelist of the Third Fiat.

"And Jesus said to him: Let the dead bury their dead: but go thou, and preach the kingdom of God."[808]

24) Pray the Hours of the Passion and Fuse with Jesus in His Sufferings

In the *Hours of the Passion*, which corresponds loosely to the middle years of Luisa's writings, we go with Jesus and Mary through each hour of the Passion of Jesus Christ; from its beginning, when He was last with His mother and departed from her after their exchange of blessings, to His burial. In detail we meditate upon each of the important

---

[806] My inspiration for this point is Peter Kreeft's excellent talk—"the Culture War."

[807] Matthew 6:31-33 (only several verses after Jesus gave the Our Father prayer)
[808] Luke 9:60

aspects of this act of redemption.

Even if this were not a revelation from God and were simply made up by Luisa, it would at the very least be the greatest meditation on the Passion that I have ever come across. But recall that Pope St. Pius X himself, when presented with these Hours by St. Hannibal, said that they should be read "while kneeling," because "it is Jesus Christ who is speaking" in them.

In the *Hours*, we learn astounding things (things which, incidentally, line up well with what is taught in Bl. Anne Catherine Emmerich's revelations on the Passion). In this chapter—which, should not substitute for the *Hours* themselves, but should only serve as an invitation to do the *Hours* by giving a few glimpses of them—I would like to walk through a small portion of the revelations Jesus gives Luisa about His passion.

There is, however, one noteworthy observation before walking through the *Hours*. In them, we learn that Jesus' words in the garden, "*If it be possible, let this chalice pass ...* "[809] were not regarding His apprehension at the physical sufferings. No, those words had nothing to do with that. Unspeakably dreadful as the physical sufferings were, Jesus was about as afraid of them as you would be afraid of getting wet to go and rescue your drowning child from a pool. These words of His referred, rather, to souls that, despite His love, would choose to condemn themselves to Hell.

Jesus knew it was metaphysically possible for the Father to exercise such dominion that He could simply override even the most deformed will in order to force it into Heaven. But this would contradict the greatest gift God gave to the soul— its free will. Therefore, in the ultimate act of submission to the Divine Will and as a model for us all, Jesus appended His petition with "*nevertheless not My Will, but Thine be done,*" even knowing what He was about to suffer beyond any measure for them. That is the extent of His love; that blood would burst forth from His pores in agony over the loss of His children. It was the damnation of souls that caused Him to sweat blood, and to undergo His most horrible Passion there in the garden. Any suffering the soldiers could hope to inflict upon Him with their devices of torture amounted to nothing close to it; the external passion and pain

was absolutely nothing compared to the internal passion and sorrow as He took upon Himself all the evil that had ever been done or would ever be done. He truly desired to empty out every drop of His blood, to offer every square inch of His flesh for laceration, and to feel every imaginable pain. His burning love knew no bounds, and the more He suffered, the more superabundant grace He won for His beloved creatures.

Because of this, we see throughout His passion, Jesus actually burning with desire to suffer more and more. This desire was not like that of some crazed man in love with pain, but as one so unspeakably inflamed with love that nothing—not even the greatest sufferings imaginable—could stand in His way.

> In order to form the Redemption, one Tear of Mine, one Sigh, was enough, but My Love would not have remained content. Being able to give and to do even more, My Love would have remained blocked in itself, and would not have been able to boast by saying: 'I have done everything, I have suffered everything, I have Given you everything.[810]

This love welled up as a consuming fire within Him that caused more suffering than the Passion itself, in its superabundance and in its need to expend and pour out itself entirely. And whenever His soul cried out in sorrow, it was not due to the internal or external pain, but due to seeing souls—past, present, and future—utterly refusing Him, hating Him, and choosing hell simply to spurn Him. In the *Hours* we read that He saw these souls as He looked down upon chunks of His own flesh torn off by the scourging, and it was that sight that caused Him in anguish to cry out. We read that at the height of agony, at His abandonment upon the cross, He entered into a conversation with these souls begging them not to choose Hell, begging them to go so far as to let Him suffer more and more if only they would permit Him to save them.

Nowhere else will you come across so brutal a description of His passion as you will in Luisa's *Hours of the Passion*, and yet you will not come across a truer and more accurate one, either. Throughout these *Hours*, you will say, along with Luisa, with the angels, and with the saints, "*Is such great love possible?*" It is possible—not for man, but

---

[809] Matthew 26:39   [810] April 16, 1933

for God. And in Jesus, it is a reality.

Furthermore, you will never come across another writing that so powerfully demonstrates God's love for His children as does the *Hours of the Passion*. In reading, praying, and meditating upon these *Hours*, we act as victim souls, suffer redemptively with Jesus, and foster our desire to give over our whole lives to Jesus as victims.

But in the *Hours of the Passion* we do far more than simply recall; we enter, rather, into each moment through the same bilocation of soul which occurs in the Rounds. We fuse each of our members with Jesus', kissing Him as we strive to endure His passion with Him, thus offering Him consolation and assuming the role of quasi-co-redemptrix along with Our Lady, the true Co-Redemptrix.

Jesus tells Luisa:

> These hours are the most precious of all because they are the reenactment of what I did in the course of My mortal life, and what I continue to do in the Most Blessed Sacrament. When I hear these Hours of My Passion, I hear My own voice and My own prayers. In the soul I behold My Will, that is, My Will desiring the good of all and making reparation for all, whence I feel drawn to dwell in this soul to be able to do within it what the soul itself does. Oh, with what love I desire that at least one soul in each town meditate upon these Hours of My Passion! I would hear My own voice in each town, and My justice, greatly indignant in these times, would be placated in part.[811]

Jesus gave enormous promises to Luisa with these *Hours*, promises that extend to whoever recites them. He promised that through them, the saint would become holier still, the tempted would find victory, the ill would find strength, and that, *for each word read*, **the salvation of a soul would be granted.** He said that an entire city could be spared chastisements if only one soul in it would continually pray these Hours—and this can be equally satisfied by a group of people together taking on a continual recitation of all 24 Hours of the Passion. This is known as "living clocks." Luisa also affirms that the same angels that ministered to Jesus in the garden assist the soul who now meditates upon these Hours.

The *24 Hours of the Passion* given by Jesus to Luisa speak, as the title implies, of the events of Holy Thursday and Good Friday. But we must understand that the true Passion of Jesus was not a mere 24 hours, but rather constituted His whole life, even from the womb of Mary.

> My little Jesus, just newly conceived, enclosed within Himself the great birth of all generations…Then, my tender Jesus, in the middle of that chasm of flames, so very little, told me: "Look at Me and listen to Me. My daughter, in the middle of this chasm of flames I breathe nothing but flames; and in my breath I feel that the flames of my devouring Love bring Me the breath of all creatures… oh! how vividly I feel the sins, the miseries, the pains of all. I am still little, yet, I am spared nothing… And in the midst of these devouring flames, loaded with so many pains, I look at everyone and, crying, I exclaim: 'My Love has given Me everyone back as gift; It gave them to Me in Creation, and they escaped from Me; It gives them to Me again in conceiving Me in the womb of my Mama. But, am I sure that they will not escape from Me? Will they be mine forever? Oh! how happy I would be if all would not escape from Me… And, crying and sobbing, I looked each one in the face to move them with my tears; and I repeated: 'My dear children, do not leave Me, don't go away from Me any more; I am your Father, do not abandon Me. O please! recognize Me, have pity at least on the fire that devours Me, on my ardent tears—and all because of you, because I love you too much, I love you as God, I love you as most passionate Father, I love you as my Life."[812]

Therefore, we can now turn to consider some excerpts from the *Hours* themselves, remembering that what we are learning applies not only to those 24 hours, but to the entire life of Jesus Christ.

***

(As all the following quotes are taken from the Hours of the Passion, and are furthermore laid out chronologically, they are easy to find within this work and thus footnotes will be foregone in this section.)

Before Jesus went to celebrate the last supper and institute the Holy Eucharist, He bid farewell to His mother:

> But to fulfill the Will of the Father, with your Hearts fused into each other, **You submit Yourselves to everything, wanting to repair for those who, unwilling to overcome the tendernesses of relatives and friends, and bonds**

---

[811] October 1914 (no day given)

[812] December 18, 1929

and attachments, do not care about fulfilling the Holy Will of God and corresponding to the state of sanctity to which God calls them. What sorrow do these souls not give You, in rejecting from their hearts the love You want to give them, contenting themselves with the love of creatures!

From the beginning, then, we see the theme that will play out throughout the Passion: Jesus and Mary repairing for all the evil that has been done and will be done by humans. They do so precisely at those times during the course of the Passion when circumstances give the opportunity for their human wills submit to the Divine Will in those very acts that others reject and thereby commit evil. In this passage, for example, we see that even though there never was and never shall be any greater love than the love that reigned between Jesus and Mary, they nevertheless immediately submitted even this love to the Divine Will, thus they accomplished reparation for those who, due to human loves, neglect to follow the Divine Will (e.g. refusing to follow a genuine vocational calling to the religious life because of attachment to family).

Afterward, to His own Apostles, Jesus said:

> My life down here is about to set, just as the sun is now setting, and tomorrow at this hour I will no longer be here! But, like sun, I will rise again on the third day!" At your words, the Apostles become sad and taciturn, not knowing what to answer. But You add: "Courage, do not lose heart; I will not leave you, I will be always with you. But it is necessary that I die for the good of you all.

At the last supper itself, Jesus' sorrow was above all due to Judas, whom He loved, but whom He knew would reject His love:

> And while You grieve for Judas, your Heart is filled with joy in seeing, on your left, your beloved disciple John; so much so, that unable to contain your love any longer, drawing him sweetly to Yourself, You let him place his head upon your Heart, letting him experience paradise in advance. It is in this solemn hour that the two peoples, the reprobate and the elect, are portrayed by the two disciples: the reprobate in Judas, who already feels hell in his heart; the elect in John, who rests and delights in You.

Throughout the *Hours*, Luisa prays—and we do with her—for many intentions which relate to the specific Hour being prayed:

> Jesus, o please, do not allow any more souls to be lost. Let your heartbeat, flowing through them,

make them feel the heartbeats of the life of Heaven, just as your beloved disciple John felt them; so that, attracted by the gentleness and sweetness of your love, they may all surrender to You.

Jesus gives thanks at this supper, repairing for all the good that creatures take without any thought to thanking the Origin of all good:

> You raise the hymn of thanksgiving to the Father for having given you food, wanting to repair for all the lack of thanksgiving of creatures, and for all the means He gives us for the preservation of corporal life. This is why, O Jesus, in anything You do, touch or see, You always have on your lips the words, "Thanks be to You, O Father". I too, Jesus, united with You, take the words from your very lips, and I will say, always and in everything: "Thank You for myself and for all", in order to continue the reparations for the lack of thanksgiving.

And then follows the washing of the feet, about which Jesus tells Luisa:

> Ah, my child, I want all souls, and prostrate at their feet like a poor beggar, I ask for them, I importune them and, crying, I plot love traps around them in order to obtain them! Prostrate at their feet, with this bucket of water mixed with my tears, I want to wash them of any imperfection and prepare them to receive Me in the Sacrament.

Jesus did not neglect to wash the feet even of Judas:

> But, sweet Love of mine, as You continue to wash the feet of the Apostles, I see that You are now at Judas' feet. I hear your labored breath. I see that You not only cry, but sob, and as You wash those feet, You kiss them, You press them to your Heart; and unable to speak with your voice because it is suffocated by crying, You look at him with eyes swollen with tears, and say to him with your Heart: "My child, O please, I beg you with the voices of my tears—do not go to hell! Give Me your soul, which I ask of you, prostrate at your feet. Tell Me, what do you want? What do you demand? I will give you everything, provided that you do not lose yourself. O please, spare this sorrow to Me, your God!"

Now the time has come for the climax of the Last Supper: the Institution of the Holy Eucharist.

> You stand up, sorrowful as You are, and You almost run to the altar where there is bread and wine ready for the Consecration. I see You, my Heart, assuming a look wholly new and never seen before: your Divine Person acquires a tender,

loving, affectionate appearance; your eyes blaze with light, more than if they were suns; your rosy face is radiant; your lips are smiling and burning with love; your creative hands assume the attitude of creating. I see You, my Love, all transformed: your Divinity seems to overflow from your Humanity. My Heart and my Life, Jesus, this appearance of yours, never before seen, draws the attention of all the Apostles. They are caught by a sweet enchantment and do not dare even to breathe. Your sweet Mama runs in spirit to the foot of the altar, to admire the portents of your love. The Angels descend from Heaven, asking themselves: "What is this? What is this? These are true follies, true excesses! A God who creates, not heaven or earth, but Himself. And where? In the most wretched matter of a little bread and a little wine."

Now, ready to consecrate His own Self in the bread and wine, Jesus enters into a conversation with His Father; part of which includes:

Now, allow Me to be incarnated in each Host, to continue their salvation and be life of each one of my children. Do You see, O Father? Few hours of my life are left: who would have the heart to leave my children orphaned and alone? Many are their enemies—the obscurities, the passions, the weaknesses to which they are subject. Who will help them? O please, I supplicate You to let Me stay in each Host, to be life of each one, and therefore put to flight their enemies; to be their light, strength and help in everything. Otherwise, where shall they go? Who will help them? Our works are eternal my love is irresistible—I cannot leave my children, nor do I want to.

The Father is moved at the tender and affectionate voice of the Son. He descends from Heaven; He is already on the altar, and united with the Holy Spirit, concurs with the Son. And Jesus, with sonorous and moving voice, pronounces the words of the words of the Consecration, and without leaving Himself, creates Himself in that bread and wine. Then You communicate your Apostles, and I believe that our celestial Mama did not remain without receiving You. Ah, Jesus, the heavens bow down and all send to You an act of adoration in your new state of profound annihilation.

At this, we offer more reparation along with Luisa:

Oh Jesus, I kiss your right hand, and I intend to repair for all the sacrileges, especially the Masses badly celebrated! How many times, my Love, You are forced to descend from Heaven into unworthy hands and breasts; and even though You feel nausea for being in those hands, Love forces You to stay. Even more, in some of your ministers, You find the ones who renew your Passion, because, with their enormous crimes and sacrileges, they renew the Deicide! Jesus, I am frightened at this thought! But, alas, just as in the Passion You were in the hands of the Jews, You are in those unworthy hands, like a meek lamb, waiting, again, for your death and also for their conversion…

And so, my Love, my prison will be your Heart, my chains will be made of love; your flames will be my food, your breath will be mine, the fences preventing me from going out will be your Most Holy Will. So I will see nothing but flames, I will touch nothing but fire; and while they give me life, they will give me death, like that You suffer in the Holy Host. **I will give You my life, and so, while I remain imprisoned in You, You will be released in me. Is this not your intent in imprisoning Yourself in the Host, in order to be released by the souls who receive You, becoming alive in them?**

(Here we see clearly Jesus' call, through Luisa, for us to be living hosts: another name for Living in the Divine Will; a title seen in the writings of many other mystics of the 20th century.)

I see You, O Jesus, as You administer Yourself to your Apostles, and then You add that they too must do what You have done, giving them authority to consecrate; so You ordain them priests and institute the other Sacraments. You take care of everything, and You repair for everything: the sermons badly given, the Sacraments administered and received without disposition, and therefore without effects; the mistaken vocations of priests, on their part and on the part of those who ordain them, not using all means in order to discern the true vocations.

After the Last Supper, Jesus and the Apostles proceed to the Garden, at which time the Agony ensues. Coming to Jesus in the Divine Will in this Agony, He says to Luisa and to us:

Child, are you here? I was waiting for you. This was the sadness which oppressed Me the most: the total abandonment of all. And I was waiting for you, to let you be the spectator of my pains, and to let you drink, together with Me, the chalice of bitternesses which, in a little while, my Celestial Father will send Me through the Angel. We will sip from it together, because it will not be a chalice of comfort, but of intense bitternesses, and I feel the need of a few loving souls who would drink at least a few drops of it. This is why

I called you—that you may accept it, share with Me the pains, and assure Me that you will not leave Me alone in such great abandonment.

At this point, Jesus is ready to reveal to Luisa what truly constituted the essence of His Passion:

My child, do you want to know what it is that torments Me more than the very executioners? Rather, those are nothing compared to this! It is the Eternal Love, which, wanting primacy in everything, is making Me suffer, all at once and in the most intimate parts, what the executioners will make Me suffer little by little. Ah, my child, it is Love which prevails in everything, over Me and within Me. Love is nail for Me, Love is scourge, Love is crown of thorns—Love is everything for Me. Love is my perennial passion, while that of men is in time. Ah, my child, enter into my Heart, come to be dissolved in my love, and only in my love will you comprehend how much I suffered and how much I loved you, and you will learn to love Me and to suffer only out of love.

The Passion of Jesus is His Divine Love for us, His beloved children. This burning love—this burning thirst for souls—infinitely outweighs the torments of the Passion itself even if they were somehow to be multiplied a thousand-fold.

In the *Hours*, Luisa goes on to repair for the lukewarmness of consecrated souls, which is a greater pain for Jesus than the greatest of secular sinners:

But, O my Jesus, another bitterness for your Heart: they are already sleeping. And You, always compassionate, call them, wake them up, and with love all paternal, admonish them and recommend to them vigil and prayer. Then You return to the Garden, but You carry another wound in your Heart. In that wound I see, Oh my Love, all the piercings of the consecrated souls who, because of temptation, mood, or lack of mortification, instead of clinging to You, keeping vigil and praying, abandon themselves to themselves and, sleepy, instead of making progress in love and in the union with You, draw back.

And then, in reparation for the general rebellion of creatures against the Divine Will, Jesus asks that the "chalice pass" from Him—only in order to give the fitting preface for His ultimate Fiat:

O Jesus, all the rebellions of creatures advance toward You; You see that "Fiat Voluntas Tua", that "Your Will be done", which was to be the life of each creature, being rejected by almost all of them, and instead of finding life, they find death. And wanting to give life to all, and make a solemn reparation to the Father for the rebellions of creatures, as many as three times, You repeat: **"Father, if it be possible, let this chalice pass from Me: that souls, withdrawing from Our Will, become lost. This chalice is very bitter for Me; however, not my will, but Yours be done."** But while You say this, your bitterness is so intense and so great, that You reach the extreme—You agonize, and are about to breathe your last.

Indeed, Jesus' agony in the garden was so great that He should have died from this pain alone. But He had not yet given everything, so His mission had to continue. We move on in the *Hours* to see Jesus' finding His Apostles sleeping:

And almost staggering, You are about to fall near them, while John extends his arms to sustain You. You are so unrecognizable that, if it wasn't for the tenderness and sweetness of your voice, they would not have recognized You. Then, recommending vigil and prayer to them, You return to the Garden, but with a second piercing to your Heart. In this piercing, my Good, I see all the sins of those souls who, in spite of the manifestations of your favors, in gifts, kisses and caresses, in the nights of trial, forgetting about your love and your gifts, have remained as though drowsy and sleepy, therefore losing the spirit of continuous prayer and of vigil. My Jesus, it is yet true that after having seen You, after having enjoyed your gifts, when one is deprived of them, it takes great strength in order to persist. Only a miracle can allow these souls to endure the trial. Therefore, as I compassionate You for these souls, whose negligences, fickleness and offenses are the most bitter for your Heart, I pray that, if they came to taking one single step which might slightly displease You, You will surround them with so much Grace as to stop them, so as not to lose the spirit of continuous prayer!

Having now done reparation for those who refuse to correspond to outpourings of graces, Luisa—with us and with Our Lady—moves to do reparation for and intercede for those who have fallen into grave sin:

Let us give them the Blood of Jesus, that they may find the hand which raises them up again. See O Mama, these are souls who need this Blood—souls who are dead to grace. Oh, how deplorable is their state! Heaven looks at them and cries with sorrow; the earth fixes on them with disgust; all the elements are against them and would want to destroy them, because they are enemies of the

Creator. Please, O Mama, the Blood of Jesus contains life, so let us give It to them, so that, at Its touch, these souls may rise again—and may rise again more beautiful, so as to make all Heaven and all earth smile.

Afterward, we intercede for those groups of people and some geographic regions who have not even been evangelized:

> But, listen, O Mama, this Blood cries out and wants yet more souls. Let us run together, and let us go to the regions of the heretics and of the unbelievers. How much sorrow does Jesus not feel in these regions. He, who is the life of all, receives not even a tiny act of love in return; He is not known by His very creatures. Please, O Mama, let us give them this Blood, that It may cast away the darkness of ignorance and of heresy. Let them comprehend that they have a soul, and open the Heavens for them. Then, let us place them all in the Blood of Jesus; let us lead them around Him, like many orphaned and exiled children, who find their Father; and so Jesus will feel comforted in His most bitter agony.

For those at the point of death in these regions, we implore Our lady…

> … make Yourself seen. On your face shines the beauty of Jesus; your manners are all similar to His; and so, in seeing You, they will certainly be able to know Jesus. Then, press them to your maternal Heart; infuse in them the life of Jesus, which You possess; tell them that, as their Mother, You want them to be happy forever, with You in Heaven; and as they breathe their last, receive them into your arms, and let them pass from yours into those of Jesus. And if Jesus, according to the rights of Justice, will show He does not want to receive them, remind Him of the love with which He entrusted them to You at the foot of the Cross. Claim your rights as mother, so that He will not be able to resist your love and prayers, and while making your Heart content, He will also content His ardent desires.

Moving to Purgatory, we administer the Blood of Jesus to the souls therein:

> Don't You hear, O Mama, their moans, the fidgets of love, the tortures, and how they feel continuously drawn to the Highest Good? See how Jesus Himself wants to purge them more quickly in order to have them with Himself. He attracts them with His love, and they requite Him with continuous surges toward Him. But as they find themselves in His presence, unable to yet sustain the purity of His divine gaze, they are forced to draw back and to plunge again into the flames!

The gravest task stands before us now: consoling Jesus for His most agonizing sorrow: the eternal loss of souls.

> "O child, how many souls escape Me by force, and fall into eternal ruin! So, how can my sorrow ever be soothed, if I love one single soul so much—as much as I love all souls together?" Agonizing Jesus, it seems that your life is extinguishing. I already hear the rattle of agony, your beautiful eyes eclipsed by the nearness of death, all of your limbs abandoned; and often it seems that You no longer breathe. I feel my heart burst with pain. I hug You and I feel You ice-cold … [Jesus says] **"Know that in these three hours of most bitter agony in the Garden, I enclosed in Myself all the lives of creatures, and I suffered all of their pains, and their very death, giving my own life to each one of them. My agonies will sustain theirs; my bitternesses and my death will turn into a fount of sweetness and life for them. How much souls cost Me!** Were I at least requited! You have seen that while I was dying, I would return to breathe again: those were the deaths of the creatures that I felt within Me!"

Indeed, Jesus felt the loss of each soul as His Own death; and the sorrow of each one should have killed Him—for it was a sorrow so great that, if we were to feel one sliver of it, it would alone have been sufficient to make us die a thousand times over. But each time, He returned to life to finish His mission. And now the time has come for the arrest:

> My Jesus, it is already midnight. You feel that your enemies are drawing near; tidying Yourself up and drying up your Blood, strengthened by the comforts received, You go to your disciples again. You call them, You admonish them, and You take them with You, as You go to meet your enemies, wanting to repair, with your promptness, my slowness, indolence and laziness in working and suffering for love of You. But, O sweet Jesus, my Good, what a touching scene I see! You first meet **the perfidious Judas, who, drawing near You and throwing his arms around your neck, greets You and kisses You. And You, most passionate Love, do not disdain to kiss those infernal lips; You embrace him and press him to your Heart, wanting to snatch him from hell, and giving him signs of new love. My Jesus, how is it possible not to love You?** The tenderness of your love is such that it should snatch every heart to love You; yet, they do not love You! And You, O my Jesus, in bearing this

kiss of Judas, repair for the betrayals, the pretenses, the deceptions under the aspect of friendship and sanctity, especially of priests. Your kiss, then, shows that, not to one sinner, provided that he comes humbled before You, would You refuse your forgiveness.

In this astounding passage, we have seen that Jesus never gave up on Judas; even as He was being arrested thanks to the betrayal of Judas, Jesus was still pouring Himself out to snatch him from hell. In this, we must find the strength to never give up on any sinner, no matter how hopeless the case might seem. For Jesus will refuse no one His mercy if only they come humbly before Him. In expounding upon Jesus' question to Judas asking, "Why have you come?", we see:

> But how many, to your "Why have you come?", answer: "I come to offend You!" Others, pretending not to hear You, give themselves to all kinds of sins, and answer your "Why have you come?", by going to hell! How much compassion I feel for You, O my Jesus! I would like to take the very ropes with which your enemies are about to bind You, in order to bind these souls and spare You this sorrow.

Here we see another incredible teaching. While we should indeed be ever burning with zeal to aid in the salvation of souls because of the torments of the damned souls themselves for all eternity, it is even more true that we should devote ourselves wholeheartedly to this most noble task because of the consolation it gives to Jesus. Add up all the torments that all the souls in hell feel and will feel for all eternity—add them together and you have scarcely even one iota of the agony which Jesus feels at the loss of a single soul. And yet, with our prayer and sacrifice, we can spare our loving God that agony.

But the Jews who have come to arrest Jesus are now here, so the *Hours* continue on:

> …as You go to meet your enemies: "Who are you looking for?" And they answer: "Jesus the Nazarene". And You, to them: "It is I". With only this word You say everything, and You let Yourself be known for who You are; so much so, that the enemies tremble and fall to the ground, as though dead. And You, Love which has no equal, repeating again, "It is I", call them back to life and You give Yourself, on your own, into the power of the enemies. Perfidious and ungrateful, instead of falling to your feet, humbled and palpitating, to ask for your forgiveness, taking advantage of

your goodness and despising your graces and prodigies, they lay hands on You, they bind You with ropes and chains, they grip You, they cast You to the ground, they trample upon You, they tear your hair. And You, with unheard-of patience, remain silent, suffering and repairing for the offenses of those who, in spite of miracles, do not surrender to your Grace, and become more obstinate.

> …

> And, lovingly, You correct Peter, who wants to defend You to the point of cutting off the ear of Malchus. With this, You intend to repair for the good works, which are not done with holy prudence, or which fall into sin because of excessive zeal.

Jesus here begins His formal and exterior Passion with a solemn reminder to all that He is utterly in charge—and this is seen in the Gospel itself, wherein we read the mysterious statement that the soldiers "fell to the ground" (John 18:6) after Jesus said "I am He." But in His words to Luisa, Jesus gives even more detail, and we see that the God-man pronouncing His sovereign name as The One Who Is results in the soldiers (who have come to arrest Him) essentially dying from the sheer magnitude of being exposed to this, only to be miraculously recalled to life afterward by the same words from Jesus.

And now, with the ropes and chains placed upon His Divine shoulders, Jesus embarks formally upon His exterior Passion—that for which He had so yearned—and the effects were overwhelming:

> My most patient Jesus, it seems that these ropes and chains give something more beautiful to your Divine Person: your forehead becomes more majestic, so much so, as to draw the attention of your enemies themselves; your eyes blaze with more light; your Divine Face assumes a supreme peace and sweetness, such as to enamor your very executioners. With your sweet and penetrating accents, though few, You make them tremble; so much so, that if they dare to offend You, it is because You Yourself allow them to do so.

Although they should have been emboldened, all the Apostles fled. This, again, causes Jesus more pain than the soldiers could have ever inflicted:

> You feel more pain for the abandonment of your most faithful ones, than for what the very enemies are doing to You. My Jesus, do not cry; or rather, let me cry together with You. And lovable Jesus

seems to say: "Ah, child, let us cry together over the lot of so many souls consecrated to Me, who, over little trials, over incidents of life, no longer take care of Me and leave Me alone; for many others, timid and cowardly, who, for lack of courage and trust, abandon Me; for many upon many who, not finding their own advantage in holy things, do not care about Me; for many priests who preach, who celebrate, who confess for love of interest and of self-glory.

After many atrocities Jesus endured on the way, He finally stands before Annas, at which point He says:

"I have spoken in public, and all those here present have heard Me." At your dignified accents, all feel trembling, but their perfidy is such that a servant, wanting to honor Annas, comes close to You and with a fierce hand gives You a slap, but so violent as to make You stagger, and to bruise your most holy Face…Your enemies burst into satanic laughter, whistling and clapping, applauding an act so unjust. And You, staggering, have no one to lean on. My Jesus, I hug You; even more, I want to form a wall with my being and I offer You my cheek with courage, ready to bear any suffering for love of You. I compassionate You for this outrage, and together with You I repair for the fearfulness of many souls, who get easily discouraged. I repair for all those who, out of fear, do not speak the truth; for the lack of respect due to priests, and for murmuring. But, my afflicted Jesus, I see that Annas sends You to Caiaphas. Your enemies hurl You down the stairs, and You, my Love, in this painful fall repair for those who at nighttime fall into sin under the favor of darkness, and You call the heretics and the unbelievers to the light of Faith. I too want to follow You in these reparations…

Before Caiaphas, we see similar outrages, but we also see the power of Jesus' glance in the midst of these horrendous persecutions:

As they accuse You, the soldiers who are near You tear your hair, and unload horrible slaps on your most holy Face, such as to resound through the whole room; they twist your lips, they hit You, while You remain silent and suffer. And if You look at them, the light of your eyes descends into their hearts, and unable to sustain it, they move away from You. But others take their place, to make of You a greater slaughter.…

Caiaphas says to You: "I beseech You, for the sake of the living God, tell me—are You really the true Son of God?" And You, my Love, having the word of truth always on your lips, with supreme Majesty, and with sonorous and gentle voice, such that all are struck, and the very demons plunge themselves into the abyss, answer: "You say so. Yes, I am the true Son of God, and one day I will descend on the clouds of Heaven to judge all nations." At your creative words, all remain silent—they shudder and feel frightened. But Caiaphas, recovering after a few moments of fright, full of rage, more than a fierce animal, says to all: "What need do we have of more witnesses? He has already uttered a great blasphemy! What more are we waiting for to condemn him? He is already guilty to death!" And to give more strength to his words, he tears his clothes with such rage and fury that all, as though one, hurl themselves at You, my Good; some punch your head, some tear your hair, some slap You, some spit on your Face, some trample upon You. The torments that they give You are so intense and so many that the earth trembles and the Heavens are shaken…I now see that they are making fun of You. They cover your Face with thick spit; the light of your beautiful eyes is covered by the spit; and You, pouring rivers of tears for our salvation, push that spit away from your eyes, and your enemies, with hearts incapable of seeing the light of your eyes, cover them with spit again. Others, becoming more brave in evil, open your most sweet mouth and fill it with disgusting spit, to the point that they themselves feel nausea. And since some of that spit flows away, revealing, in part, the majesty of your Face and your superhuman sweetness, they shudder and feel ashamed of themselves. In order to feel more free, they blindfold You with a miserable rag, to be able to hurl themselves, unrestrained, at your adorable Person. And so they beat You up without pity; they drag You; they trample You under their feet; they repeat blows and slaps to your Face and over your head, scratching You, tearing your hair, and pushing You from one point to another.

To even read of these torments suffered by Our Lord is a great difficulty; but the One Who was experiencing them was not concerned with Himself:

To my amazement, I now see that instead of occupying Yourself with your pains, with an indescribable love, You think about glorifying the Father, to compensate Him for all that we owe; and You call all souls around You, to take all of their evils upon Yourself and give to them all goods. And since the day is dawning, I hear your most sweet voice say: "Holy Father, I give You thanks for all I have suffered and for all that is left for Me to suffer. And just as this dawn calls the day and the day makes the sun rise, so may the dawn of Grace arise in all hearts; and as daylight rises, may I, Divine Sun, rise in all hearts and reign over all. Do you see these souls, O Father? I want to answer You for all of them, for their thoughts, words, works and steps—at the cost of blood and death." …

But I also see, my sweet Jesus, that You repair for all the very first thoughts, affections and words, which, at the rising of the day, are not offered to You to honor You; and that You call to Yourself, as though in custody, the thoughts, the affections and the words of the creatures, in order to repair for them and give to the Father the glory they owe Him…

Jesus is then presented to Pilate:

Caiaphas confirms the sentence to death, and sends You to Pilate. And You, my condemned Jesus, accept this sentence with so much love and resignation, as to almost snatch it from the iniquitous Pontiff. You repair for all the sins committed deliberately and with all malice, and for those who, instead of afflicting themselves because of evil, rejoice and exult over sin itself, and this leads them to blindness and to suffocating any enlightenment and grace…

My bound Good, Jesus, your enemies, together with the priests, present You to Pilate; and faking sanctity and scrupulousness, because they have to celebrate the Passover, they remain outside the lobby. And You, my Love, seeing the depth of their malice, repair for all the hypocrisies of the religious body.

The Judge of the Universe is next sent to stand before yet another iniquitous judge, worse than Pilate; Herod:

So, they make You arrive before Herod, who, swelling up, asks You many questions. You do not answer him and do not even look at him. And Herod, irritated because he does not see his curiosity satisfied, and feeling humiliated by your long silence, declares to all that You are crazy and mindless, and he orders that You be treated as such. And to mock You, he has You clothed with a white garment, and he delivers You into the hands of the soldiers, that they may do with You the worst they can…

My crazy Jesus, I too want to call You crazy—but crazy with love. And your folly of love is such that, instead of becoming upset, You pray and repair for the ambitions of the kings and of the leaders, who aspire to kingdoms for the ruin of the peoples; for the many slaughters they cause, and the so much blood they cause to be shed for their whims; for the sins committed in the courts…

Now that Jesus is again before Pilate, the latter seeks to free Jesus through another means: presenting Barabbas to the Jews. In even this attempt failing to placate them, Jesus does reparation for all who place Him after anything else, saying:

… some place Us after a vile interest, some after honors, some after vanities, some after pleasures, some after their own attachments, some after dignities, some after gluttonies, and even after sin. All creatures unanimously place Us after even a tiny little trifle. And I am ready to accept being placed after Barabbas, in order to repair for the misplacements the creatures make with Us.

And then, in being stripped of His garments before the scourging, Jesus says:

Be silent, O child—it was necessary that I be stripped, in order to repair for many who strip themselves of every modesty, of purity and of innocence; who strip themselves of every good and virtue, and of my Grace, clothing themselves with every brutality, and living like brutes. With my virginal blush I wanted to repair for so many dishonesties, luxuries and brutal pleasures. Therefore, be attentive to everything I do; pray and repair with Me, and calm yourself.

If you have seen the movie *The Passion of the Christ* (released in 2004), then you have a small idea of the brutality of the scourging at the pillar. But Jesus reveals more about it to Luisa than even that powerful movie shows:

But this is not all; two more take their turn, and with hooked iron chains, they continue the excruciating massacre. At the first blows, that flesh, beaten and wounded, rips open even more, and falls to the ground, torn into pieces. The bones are uncovered, the Blood pours down—so much, as to form a pool of Blood around the pillar.

… You say: "All of you who love Me, come to learn the heroism of true love! Come to dampen in my Blood the thirst of your passions, your thirst for so many ambitions, for so many intoxications and pleasures, for so much sensuality! In this Blood of Mine you will find the remedy for all of your evils.

Jesus continues His conversation with the Father during His scourging:

"Look at Me, O Father, all wounded under this

storm of blows. But this is not enough; I want to form so many wounds in my Body as to give enough rooms to all souls within the Heaven of my Humanity, in such a way as to form their salvation within Myself, and then let them pass into the Heaven of the Divinity. **My Father, may each blow of these scourges repair before You for each kind of sin—one by one. And as they strike Me, let them justify those who commit them. May these blows strike the hearts of creatures, and speak to them about my love, to the point of forcing[813] them to surrender to Me."**
And as You say this, your love is so great, though great is the pain, that You almost incite the executioners to beat You more. My Jesus, stripped of your own flesh, your love crushes me—I feel I am going mad. Your love is not tired, while the executioners are exhausted and cannot continue your painful massacre. They now cut the ropes, and You, almost dead, fall into your own Blood. And in seeing the shreds of your flesh, You feel like dying grief, because in those detached pieces of flesh You see the reprobate souls. And your sorrow is such, that You gasp in your own Blood…

My Jesus, infinite Love, the more I look at You, the more I comprehend how much You suffer. You are already completely lacerated—there is not one point left whole in You. The executioners, enraged in seeing that, in so many pains, You look at them with so much love; and in seeing that your loving gaze, forming a sweet enchantment, almost like many voices, prays and supplicates for more pains and new pains—though inhuman, yet forced by your love, make You stand on your feet. Unable to stand Yourself, You fall again into your own Blood, and, irritated, with kicks and shoves, they make You reach the place where they will crown You with thorns.

Standing once again before Pilate who asks Jesus if He is a king, Jesus tells Luisa:

By remaining so humiliated before this unjust judge, I want to make everyone understand that only virtue is that which constitutes man king of himself; and I teach to those who command, that virtue alone, united to upright knowledge, is worthy and capable of governing and ruling others, while all other dignities, without virtue, are dangerous and deplorable things. My child, echo my reparations, and continue to be attentive

to my pains.

And now, back out before the crowds, we see the condemnation itself transpire:

Not knowing what else to do, for fear of being deposed, Pilate has a bucket of water brought to him, and washing his hands, he says: "I am not responsible for the blood of this just one." And he condemns You to death. But the Jews cry out: "May His Blood fall upon us and upon our children!" And in seeing You condemned, they make feast, they clap their hands, they whistle and shout; while You, O Jesus, repair for those who, finding themselves in high positions, out of vain fear and in order not to lose their places, break the most sacred laws, not caring about the ruin of entire peoples, favoring the evil and condemning the innocent. You repair also for those who, after sin, provoke the divine wrath to punish them. But while You repair for this, your Heart bleeds with sorrow in seeing your chosen people, struck by the malediction of Heaven, which they themselves, with full will, have wanted, sealing it with your Blood which they cursed! Ah, your Heart faints; allow me to sustain It in my hands, making your reparations and your pains my own. But your love pushes You higher and, impatient, You already look for the Cross!

In His invincible and infinite love, Jesus only burns with even more desire to bear His cross upon hearing the condemnation. And after the most terrible crowning with thorns, Jesus is given His cross.

My tortured Good, with You I repair, with You I suffer. But I see that your enemies hurl You down the stairs; the people await You with fury and eagerness; **they make You find the Cross ready, which You long for with many sighs. And You— with love You gaze on It, and with firm step You approach It and embrace It. But, before that, You kiss It, and as a shiver of joy runs through your Most Holy Humanity, with highest contentment You gaze on It again, measuring Its length and breadth. In It, already, You establish the portion for each creature. You dower them all, enough to bind them to the Divinity with a bond of marriage, and make them heirs of the Kingdom of Heaven**. Then, unable to contain the love with which You love them, You kiss the Cross again, and say: "Adored Cross, finally I embrace you. You were the longing of my Heart, the

---

[813]Jesus repeatedly tells Luisa that He never forces anyone, and that our wills always remain free – this is clearly not a reference, therefore, to literal "forcing," but rather to Jesus doing everything He possibly can to beg and implore us to accept His loving mercy, such that for one who does not choose to be insane and perverted, it will "force" Him to acquiesce to this Divine Love.

martyrdom of my love. But you, O Cross, have delayed until now, while my steps were always toward you. Holy Cross, you were the goal of my desires, the purpose of my existence down here. In you I concentrate my whole being, in you I place all my children, and you will be their life, their light, defense, custody and strength. You will assist them in everything, and will bring them gloriously to Me in Heaven. Oh Cross, Pulpit of Wisdom, you alone will teach true sanctity; you alone will form the heroes, the athletes, the martyrs, the Saints. Beautiful Cross, you are my Throne, and since I have to leave the earth, you will remain in my place. To you I give all souls as dowry—keep them, save them; I entrust them to you!"

In this ode to His cross, we see the ultimate example of how we must all respond to our own minuscule crosses; each of which are nothing but a microscopic splinter of His. And after so responding, we must shoulder it as He did:

My most patient Jesus, I see You take the first steps under the enormous weight of the Cross. I unite my steps to yours, and when You, weak, bled dry and staggering, are about to fall, I will be at your side to sustain You; I will place my shoulders beneath It, so as to share Its weight with You. Do not disdain me, but accept me as your faithful companion. Oh Jesus, You look at me, and I see that You repair for those who do not carry their crosses with resignation, but rather, they swear, get irritated, commit suicide, and commit murders. And for all You impetrate love and resignation to their crosses. But your pain is such that You feel crushed under the Cross. You have taken only the first steps, and You already fall under It. As You fall, You knock against the stones; the thorns are driven more into your head, while all your wounds are embittered, and pour out new Blood. And since You do not have the strength to get up, your enemies, irritated, try to make You stand with kicks and shoves. My fallen Love, let me help You to stand, let me kiss You, dry your Blood, and repair together with You for those who sin out of ignorance, fragility and weakness. I pray You to give help to these souls.

…

The Cross, with its heavy weight, digs into your shoulder, to the extent of forming a wound so deep that the bones are exposed. At every step, it seems that You are dying, and unable to move any further. But your love, which can do everything, gives You strength, and as You feel the Cross penetrate into your shoulder, You repair for the hidden sins; those which, not being repaired, increase the bitterness of your spasms. My Jesus, let me place my shoulder under the Cross to relieve You and repair with You for all hidden sins. But your enemies, for fear that You may die under It, force the Cyrenean to help You carry the Cross. Unwilling and complaining, he helps You—not out of love, but by force. Then all the complaints of those who suffer, the lack of resignation, the rebellions, the anger and despising in suffering, echo in your Heart. But You remain even more pierced in seeing that souls consecrated to You, whom You call to be your help and companions in your suffering, escape You; and if You hug them to Yourself through suffering—ah, they wriggle free from your arms to look for pleasures, and so they leave You alone, suffering! My Jesus, while I repair with You, I pray You to hold me in your arms, but so tightly that there may be no pain that You suffer in which I do not take part, so as to be transformed in them and make up for the abandonment of all creatures.

Thankfully not all are as unwilling as Simon; Veronica, though the magnitude of her physical aid rendered to Jesus was far smaller than Simon's, nevertheless consoles Him infinitely more because of her spontaneity, courage, and love:

Ah, it is Veronica, who, fearless and courageous, with a cloth dries your Face all covered with blood, and You leave your Face impressed on it, as sign of gratitude. My generous Jesus, I too want to dry You, but not with a cloth; I want to expose all of myself to relieve You, I want to enter into your interior and give You, O Jesus, heartbeat for heartbeat, breath for breath, affection for affection, desire for desire.

Luisa then prays:

O my Jesus, I want to diffuse myself in everything, and in those wounds embittered by the many misbeliefs, I desire that the shreds of my body tell You, always: "I believe—I believe in You, O my Jesus, my God, and in your Holy Church, and I intend to give my life to prove my Faith to You!**" O my Jesus, I plunge myself into the immensity of your Will, and making It my own, I want to compensate for all, and enclose the souls of all in the power of your Most Holy Will**. O Jesus, I still have my blood left, which I want to pour over your wounds…

(*Here we should recall that this particular work of Luisa's from which we are now quoting, the "Hours of the Passion," is fully approved—bearing an imprimatur* *from a canonized saint — and has no Moratorium that applies to it [it is licitly published and may be easily downloaded by anyone], and furthermore, each section ["hour"] contained within it is followed by a meditation written by this same canonized saint [Fr. Hannibal]. Not only that, but when this work was brought to Pope St. Pius X, the saintly Pontiff said that it should be read while **kneeling**, since it is truly Jesus speaking. And within this work, we see the spirituality of the Divine Will clearly displayed; in other words, it would be impossible to "separate" this work from the entire corpus of Luisa's revelations. If this work is valid then Luisa's revelations are valid.)*

Now at the top of Mount Calvary, Jesus is stripped and crowned yet again, as His cross is prepared:

> But new sufferings await You here. They strip You again, tearing off both garment and crown of thorns. Ah, You groan in feeling the thorns being torn from inside your head. And as they pull your garment, they tear also the lacerated flesh attached to it. The wounds rip open, your Blood flows to the ground in torrents; the pain is such that, almost dead, You fall…

> with bestial fury they put the crown of thorns on You again. They beat it on well, and the torture they cause You because of the lacerations and the tearing of your hair clotted in the coagulated blood, is such that only the Angels could tell what You suffer, while, horrified, they turn their celestial gaze away, and weep! …

> In the meantime, barely looking at me with His languishing and dying eyes, Jesus seems to tell me: "My child, how much souls cost Me! This is the place where I wait for everyone in order to save them, where I want to repair for the sins of those who arrive at degrading themselves lower than beasts, and are so obstinate in offending Me as to reach the point of not being able to live without committing sins. Their minds remain blinded, and they sin wildly. This is why they crown Me with thorns for the third time. And by being stripped, I repair for those who wear luxurious and indecent clothing, for the sins against modesty, and for those who are so bound to riches, honors and pleasures, as to make of them a god for their hearts.

Despite only having unimaginable torture after unimaginable torture heaped upon Him, Jesus still has nothing but the most ardent yearning for His cross:

> Meanwhile, my Jesus, You look at the Cross that your enemies are preparing for You. You hear the

blows of the hammer with which your executioners are forming the holes into which they will drive the nails that will hold You crucified. And your Heart beats, more and more strongly, jumping with divine inebriation, yearning to lay Yourself upon that bed of pain, to seal with your death the salvation of our souls. And I hear You say: "Please, O Cross, receive Me soon into your arms, I am impatient of waiting! Holy Cross, upon You I shall come to give completion to all. Hurry, O Cross, fulfill the burning desire that consumes Me, to give life to souls. Delay no more; I anxiously yearn to lay Myself upon You in order to open the Heavens to all my children. Oh Cross, it is true that You are my martyrdom, but in a little while You will also be my victory and my most complete triumph; and through You I will give abundant inheritances, victories, triumphs and crowns to my children." As Jesus is saying this, His enemies command Him to lay Himself upon It; and promptly He obeys, to repair for our disobedience.

And then, in Luisa's response, we see the essence of true sacrifice, and how we must all love our own crosses, mortify our flesh, do penance, and in a word: be completely fused with Jesus in His Passion:

> Hear me, O Jesus, I do not want to leave You; I want to come with You, to lay myself on the Cross and remain nailed to It with You. True love does not tolerate separation, and You will forgive the daring of my love. Concede that I be crucified with You. See, my tender Love, I am not the only one to ask this of You, but also your sorrowful Mama, inseparable Magdalene, faithful John: we all say to You that it would be more bearable to be nailed with You to Your Cross, than to see You crucified alone!

True love suffers more by not suffering what the beloved suffers. It is thus that we must love our cross: seeing the suffering of Jesus and wishing to be with Him in this suffering.

> And now, my sweet Good, You lay Yourself on the Cross, looking with so much love and with so much sweetness at your executioners — who already hold nails and hammers in their hands ready to pierce You — as to make a sweet invitation to hasten the crucifixion. Indeed, with inhuman fury, they grab your right hand, hold the nail on your palm, and with blows of the hammer, make it come out the opposite side of the Cross. The pain You suffer is so great that You shiver, O my Jesus; the light of your beautiful eyes is

eclipsed, and your most holy Face turns pale and looks like death…

Your enemies are not yet content. With diabolical fury, they grab your most holy feet, contracted by the great pain suffered in the tearing of your arms, and they pull them so much that your knees, your ribs and all the bones of your chest, are dislocated. My heart cannot sustain this, my dear Good; I see your beautiful eyes eclipsed and veiled with Blood, for the intensity of the pain…

Jesus is now nailed to His cross—"—"not a bone broken," as the Scriptures prophesied (Psalm 34:20, John 19:36), and yet, not one portion of His Holy Humanity spared the most atrocious torments. But even after all this—even now nailed to a cross like the basest of criminals—He still has nothing but an overwhelming desire to suffer more for His children, as He still has more to give:

Oh Jesus, I come close to your tortured Heart; I see that You cannot take any more, but Love cries out more loudly: "Pains, pains, more pains"…Ah, if it were not already decreed that a lance would rip your Heart, the flames of your love would open their way, and would make It explode! These flames call loving souls to find a happy dwelling in your Heart, and I, O Jesus, for the sake of your most precious Blood, ask You for sanctity for these souls.

Jesus again enters into conversation with His Father:

… no longer unload the scourges of your Divine Justice upon man, but upon Me, your Son. O Father, allow Me to bind all souls to this Cross, and to plead forgiveness for them with the voices of my Blood and of my wounds. O Father, do You not see how I have reduced Myself? By this Cross, by virtue of these pains, concede true conversion, peace, forgiveness and sanctity to all. Arrest your fury against poor humanity, against my children. They are blind, and know not what they are doing. Look well at Me, how I have reduced Myself because of them; if You are not moved to compassion for them, may You at least be softened by this Face of mine, dirtied with spit, covered with Blood, bruised and swollen by the so many slaps and blows received. Have pity, my Father! I was the most beautiful of all, and now I am all disfigured, to the point that I no longer recognize Myself. I have become the abject of all; and so, at any cost, I want to save the poor creature!"

And Luisa comments:

My Jesus, how is it possible that You love us so much? Your love crushes my poor heart. Oh, I would want to go into the midst of all creatures to show this Face of Yours, so disfigured because of them, to move them to compassion for their own souls and for your love; and with the light which emanates from your Face, and with the enrapturing power of your love, make them understand who You are, and who they are, who dare to offend You, so that they may prostrate themselves before You, to adore You and glorify You…My Crucified Jesus, at so much love and pain of yours, the creature does not yet surrender; on the contrary, she despises You and adds sins to sins, committing enormous sacrileges, murders, suicides, duels, frauds, deceits, cruelties and betrayals. Ah, all these evil works weigh on the arms of your Celestial Father; so much so, that unable to sustain their weight, He is about to lower them and pour fury and destruction upon the earth.

Immediately at this moment, Jesus continues conversing with His Father:

And You, O my Jesus, to snatch the creature from the divine fury, fearing to see her destroyed—You stretch out your arms to the Father, You disarm Him, and prevent Divine Justice from taking Its course. And to move Him to compassion for miserable Humanity and to soften Him, You say to Him with the most persuasive voice: "My Father, look at these hands, ripped open, and the nails that pierce them, which nail them together with all these evil works. Ah, in these hands I feel all the spasms that these evil works give to Me. Are You not content, O my Father, with my pains? Am I perhaps not capable of satisfying You? Yes, these dislocated arms of mine will always be chains to hold the poor creatures tightly, so that they may not escape from Me, except for those who wanted to struggle free by sheer force. These arms of mine will be loving chains that will bind You, my Father, to prevent You from destroying the poor creature. Even more, I will draw You closer and closer to her, that You may pour your graces and mercies upon her!"

Following this conversation with the Father, the pains continue, and Jesus implores the Father for Divine aid—not to lessen the pain, but in order to experience *more* pain:

My Jesus, Crucified Lover, I see that You can take no more. The terrible tension that You suffer on the Cross, the continual creaking of your bones that dislocate more and more at each slightest movement, your flesh that rips more and more, the ardent thirst that consumes You, the interior pains that suffocate You with bitterness, pain and love—and, in the face of so many martyrdoms, the human ingratitude that insults You and penetrates, like a mighty wave, into your pierced Heart—oppress You so much that your Most Holy Humanity, unable to bear the weight of so many martyrdoms, is about to end, and raving with love and suffering, cries out for help and pity! Crucified Jesus, is it possible that You, who rule everything and give life to all, ask for help? Ah, how I wish to penetrate into each drop of your most precious Blood, and to pour my own in order to soothe each one of your wounds, to lessen and render less painful the pricks of each thorn, and into every interior pain of your Heart to relieve the intensity of your bitternesses. I wish I could give You life for life. If it were possible, I would want to unnail You from the Cross and put myself in your place; but I see that I am nothing and can do nothing—I am too insignificant. Therefore, give me Yourself; I will take life in You, and in You, I will give You Yourself. In this way You will satisfy my yearnings. Tortured Jesus, I see that your Most Holy Humanity is ending, not because of You, but to fulfill our Redemption in everything. You need divine aid, and so You throw Yourself into the Paternal arms and ask for help and assistance. Oh, how moved is the Divine Father in looking at the horrible torture of your Most Holy Humanity, the terrible crafting that sin has made upon your most holy members! And to satisfy your yearnings of love, He holds You to His Paternal Heart, and gives You the necessary helps to accomplish our Redemption; and as He holds You tightly, You feel again in your Heart, more intensely, the blows of the nails, the lashes of the scourging, the tearing of the wounds, the pricking of the thorns. Oh, how the Father is struck! How indignant He becomes in seeing that all these pains are given to You, up into your inmost Heart, even by souls consecrated to You! And in His sorrow, He says to You: "Is it possible, my Son, that not even the part chosen by You is wholly with You? On the contrary, it seems that these souls ask for refuge and a hiding place in your Heart in order to embitter You and give You a more painful death. And even more, all these pains they give to You, are hidden and covered by hypocrisy. Ah, Son, I can no longer contain my indignation at the ingratitude of these souls, who grieve Me more than all the other creatures together!" But You, O my Jesus, triumphing of everything, defend also these souls, and with the immense love of your Heart, form a shield to the waves of bitternesses and piercings that these souls give You.

Then, nature itself, horrified at the sight, prostrates before Jesus. And even His persecutors are reduced to silence, as something that no one present (except Our Lady) could have predicted transpires:

> My Crucified Good, I see You on the Cross, as on the Throne of your triumph, in act of conquering everything and all hearts, and of drawing them so closely to You, that all may feel your superhuman power. Horrified at such great crime, nature prostrates itself before You, and waits in silence for a word from You, to pay You honor and let your dominion be recognized. The sun, crying, withdraws its light, unable to sustain your sight, too sorrowful. Hell is terrified and waits in silence. Everything is silence. Your pierced Mama, your faithful ones, are all mute…

> What more? Even the perfidious Jews and the ruthless executioners who, up to a little while ago, were offending You, mocking You, calling You impostor, criminal; even the thieves who were cursing You—everyone is silent, mute. Remorse invades them, and if they try to launch an insult against You, it dies on their lips.

> But as I penetrate into your interior, I see that love overflows; it suffocates You and You cannot contain it. And forced by your love that torments You more than the pains themselves, with strong and moving voice, You speak as the God You are; You raise your dying eyes to Heaven, and exclaim: "Father, forgive them, for they know not what they are doing!" And, again, You close Yourself in silence, immersed in unheard-of pains.

"Is such love possible?" This Luisa asks. This the angels asks. This all creation asks at the sight.

> Crucified Jesus, how can so much love be possible? Ah, after so many pains and insults, your first word is of forgiveness; and You excuse us before the Father for so many sins! Ah, You make this word descend into each heart after sin, and You are the first to offer forgiveness. But how many reject it and do not accept it; your love is then taken by follies, because You anxiously desire to give your forgiveness and the kiss of peace to all!

> At this word, hell trembles and recognizes You as God; nature and everyone remain astonished; they recognize your Divinity, your inextinguishable love, and silently wait to see where it reaches. And not only your voice, but also your Blood and your wounds, cry out to every heart after sin: "Come into my arms, for I forgive you, and the seal of forgiveness is the price

of my Blood." O my lovable Jesus, repeat this word again to all the sinners which are in the world. Beseech mercy for all; apply the infinite merits of your most precious Blood for all. O good Jesus, continue to placate Divine Justice for all, and concede your grace to those who, finding themselves in the act of having to forgive, do not feel the strength to do it.

In these three hours on the cross, Jesus did everything.

> My Jesus, adored Crucified, in these three hours of most bitter agony, You want to give fulfillment to everything; and while, silent, You remain on this Cross, I see that in your interior You want to satisfy the Father in everything. You thank Him for all, You satisfy Him for all, You beseech forgiveness for all, and for all You impetrate the grace that they may never again offend You. In order to impetrate this from the Father You go through all of your life, from the first instant of your conception, up to your last breath. My Jesus, endless Love, let me go through all your life together with You, with the inconsolable Mama, with Saint John, and with the pious women.

At this point in the *Hours*, we pause to, along with Jesus, go through and offer everything to the Father, kissing all of Jesus' Sacred Wounds and doing reparation, in the Divine Will, for it all—asking for forgiveness in the name of all.

After these Rounds, the *Hours* continue, and we read Jesus' words to Dismas:

> You agonize with love and with pain, and the flames that burn your Heart rise so high as to be in the act of reducing You to ashes. Your constrained love is stronger than death itself; and wanting to pour it out, looking at the thief on your right, You steal him from Hell. With your grace You touch his heart, and that thief is completely changed; he recognizes You; he professes You God, and all contrite, says: "Lord, remember me when You are in your Kingdom." And You do not hesitate to answer: "Today you will be with Me in Paradise", making of him the first triumph of your love. But I see that, in your love, You are not stealing the heart of that thief alone, but also that of many who are dying! Ah, You place your Blood, your love, your merits at their disposal, and You use all divine devices and stratagems in order to touch their hearts and steal them all for Yourself

Luisa implores:

> O my Jesus, I intend to repair for those who

despair of the Divine Mercy at the point of death. My sweet Love, inspire trust and unlimited confidence in You for all, especially for those who find themselves in the grips of agony; and by virtue of your word, concede to them light, strength and help, to be able to die in a saintly way, and fly from this earth up to Heaven. O Jesus, enclose all souls—all of them, in your Most Holy Body, in your Blood, in your wounds. And by the merits of this most precious Blood of Yours, do not allow even one soul to be lost! Together with your voice, may your Blood cry out for all, again: "Today you will be with Me in Paradise."

Jesus then gives His mother to us all. Luisa observes:

> You turn your languid gaze to your Mama. She too is more than dying because of your pains; and the love that tortures Her is so great as to render Her crucified like You. Mother and Son—You understand each other, and You sigh with satisfaction and feel comforted in seeing that You can give your Mama to the creature; and considering the whole Mankind in John, with a voice so sweet as to move all hearts, You say: "Woman, behold your son"; and to John: "Behold your Mother." Your voice descends into Her maternal Heart, and united to the voices of your Blood, it keeps saying: "My Mother, I entrust all of my children to You; feel for them all the love that You feel for Me. May all your maternal cares and tendernesses be for my children. You will save them all for Me." Your Mama accepts.

And then, amidst the agony of the loss of souls, Jesus cries out to His Father in the words we all know well:

> … I see that a convulsive trembling invades your Most Holy Humanity. Your limbs are shaking, as if one wanted to detach from the other; and amid contortions, because of the atrocious spasms, You cry out loudly: **"My God, my God, why have You abandoned Me?" At this cry, everyone trembles; the darkness becomes thicker; your Mama, petrified, turns pale and faints!** My Life! My All! My Jesus, what do I see? Ah, You are about to die; your very pains, so faithful to You, are about to leave You. And at the same time, <u>after so much suffering, with immense sorrow You see that not all souls are incorporated in You. Rather, You see that many will be lost, and You feel the painful separation of them, as they detach themselves from your limbs. And You, having to satisfy Divine Justice also for them, feel the death of each one of them, and the very pains they will suffer in hell</u>. And You cry out loudly,

to all hearts: "Do not abandon Me. If you want more pains, I am ready—but do not separate yourselves from my Humanity. **This is the sorrow of sorrows—it is the death of deaths; everything else would be nothing, if I did not have to suffer your separation from Me! O please, have pity on my Blood, on my wounds, on my death! This cry will be continuous to your hearts. O please, do not abandon Me!"**

… This cry of yours, O my Jesus is, alas, painful; more than the abandonment of the Father, it is the loss of the souls who move far away from You that makes this painful lament escape from your Heart! O my Jesus, increase grace in everyone, that no one may be lost; and may my reparation be for the good of those souls who should be lost, that they may not be lost. I also pray You, O my Jesus, for the sake of this extreme abandonment, to give help to so many loving souls, whom You seem to deprive of Yourself, leaving them in the dark, to have them as companions in your abandonment. O Jesus, may their pains be like prayers that call souls near to You, and relieve You in your pain.

If it were not for the loss of souls, everything else— all the unheard of tortures we have hitherto read about—would be *nothing* for Jesus.

It is for souls that He thirsts:

The love that enflames your Heart withers You and burns You completely; and You, unable to contain it, feel the intense torment, not only of the corporal thirst, but of the shedding of all your Blood—and even more, of the ardent thirst for the salvation of our souls. You would want to drink us like water, in order to place us all in safety within Yourself; therefore, gathering your weakened strengths, You cry out: <u>**"I thirst". Ah, You repeat this voice to every heart: "I thirst for your will, for your affections, for your desires, for your love. A water fresher and sweeter than your soul you could not give Me**</u>. O please, do not let Me burn. My thirst is ardent, such that I not only feel my tongue and my throat burn, to the point that I can no longer utter a word, but I also feel my Heart and bowels wither. Have pity on my thirst—have pity!" And as though delirious from the great thirst, You abandon Yourself to the Will of the Father.

Ah, my heart can no longer live in seeing the evil of your enemies who, instead of water, give You gall and vinegar; and You do not refuse them! Ah, I understand—it is the gall of the many sins, it is the vinegar of our untamed passions that they want to give You, which, instead of refreshing You, burn You even more. O my Jesus, here is my heart, my thoughts, my affections—here is all of my being, to quench your thirst and give a relief to your mouth, dried and embittered. Everything I have, everything I am—everything is for You, O my Jesus. Should my pains be necessary in order to save even one soul alone—here I am, I am ready to suffer everything. I offer myself wholly to You—do with me whatever You best please. I intend to repair for the sorrow You suffer for all the souls who are lost, and for the pain You receive from those who, while You allow sadnesses and abandonments, instead of offering them to You as relief for the burning thirst that devours You, abandon themselves to themselves, and make You suffer even more.

Having achieved Redemption and giving everything of Himself, Jesus hands over His spirit:

Meanwhile, O Jesus, I see that You open your dying eyes again, and You look around from the Cross, as though wanting to give the last good-bye to all. You look at your dying Mama, who no longer has motion or voice, so many are the pains She feels; and You say: "Good-bye Mama, I am leaving, but I will keep You in my Heart. You, take care of my children and yours." You look at crying Magdalene, faithful John and your very enemies, and with your gazes You say to them: "I forgive you; I give you the kiss of peace." Nothing escapes your gaze; You take leave of everyone and forgive everyone. Then, You gather all your strengths, and with a loud and thundering voice, You cry out: "Father, into your hands I commend my spirit". And bowing your head, You breathe your last. My Jesus, at this cry all nature is shaken and cries over your death—the death of its Creator! The earth trembles strongly; and with its trembling, it seems to be crying and wanting to shake up souls to recognize You as true God. The veil of the Temple is torn, the dead are risen; the sun, which until now had cried over your pains, has withdrawn its light with horror. At this cry, your enemies fall on their knees, and beating their breasts, they say: "Truly He is the Son of God." And your Mother, petrified and dying, suffers pains harder than death. My dead Jesus, with this cry You also place all of us into the hands of the Father, because You do not reject us. Therefore You cry out loudly, not only with your voice, but with all your pains and with the voices of your Blood: "Father, into your hands I commend my spirit and all souls." My Jesus, I too abandon myself in You; give me the grace to die completely in your love—in your Will, and I pray that You never permit me, either in life or in death, to go out of your Most Holy Will. Meanwhile I intend to repair for all those who do not abandon themselves perfectly to your Most Holy Will, therefore losing or maiming the precious gift of your Redemption.

Jesus is now in Limbo; bringing paradise to the countless souls there who have been waiting for Him for many centuries. But his Sacred Body still hangs on that cross, and Providence is not done using this Body as the savior of mankind:

O my Jesus, even after your death You want to show me that You love me, prove your love for me, and give me a refuge, a shelter, in your Sacred Heart. Therefore, pushed by a supreme force, to be assured of your death, a soldier rips your Heart open with a lance, opening a profound wound. And You, my Love, shed the last drops of Blood and water contained in your enflamed Heart. Ah, how many things does this wound, opened by love, tell me! And if your mouth is mute, your Heart speaks to me, and I hear It say: "My child, after I gave everything, **I wanted this lance to open a shelter for all souls inside this Heart of Mine. Opened, It will cry out to all, continuously: Come into Me if you want to be saved. In this Heart you will find sanctity and you will make yourselves saints; you will find relief in afflictions, strength in weakness, peace in doubts, company in abandonments. O souls who love Me, if you really want to love Me, come to dwell in this Heart forever.** Here you will find true love in order to love Me, and ardent flames for you to be burned and consumed completely in love. Everything is centered in this Heart: here are the Sacraments, here my Church, here the life of my Church and the life of all souls. In It I also feel the profanations made against my Church, the plots of the enemies, the arrows they send, and my oppressed children—there is no offense which my Heart does not feel. Therefore, my child, may your life be in this Heart—defend Me, repair Me, bring Me everyone into It." My Love, if a lance has wounded your Heart for me, I pray that You too, with your own hands, wound my heart, my affections, my desires—all of myself. Let there be nothing in me which is not wounded by your love. I unite everything to the harrowing pains of our dear Mama, who, for the pain of seeing your Heart being ripped open, falls into a swoon of sorrow and love; and like a dove, She flies in It to take the first place—to be the first Repairer, the Queen of your very Heart, the Mediatrix between You and the creatures.

In the last of these *Hours of the Passion*, we go with Luisa to follow Our Lady in her most sorrowful departure from her Son; laying Him in the tomb, and then walking back to Jerusalem.

Desolate Mama, how much compassion I feel for You! Allow me to dry your face, wet with tears and with blood. But I feel like drawing back on seeing it now covered with bruises, unrecognizable and pale with mortal paleness. I understand—these are the mistreatments against Jesus which You have taken upon Yourself, and which make You suffer so much that, as You move your lips in prayer or as your enflamed breast sighs, You feel your breath embittered and your lips burned by the thirst of Jesus. Poor Mama, how much compassion I feel for You! Your sorrows increase ever more, and as I take your hands in mine, I see them pierced by nails. It is in your hands that You feel the pain and see the murders, the betrayals, the sacrileges and all the evil works, repeating the blows, widening the wounds and embittering them more and more. How much compassion I feel for You! You are the true crucified Mother, so much so, that not even your feet remain without nails; even more, You feel them not only being pierced, but torn by many iniquitous steps, and by the souls who go to hell. And You run after them, that they may not fall into the infernal flames. But this is not all, pierced Mama. All of your pains, uniting together, echo in your Heart and pierce It—not with seven swords, but with thousands and thousands of swords. More so, since You have the Divine Heart of Jesus within You, which contains all hearts, and whose heartbeat encloses the heartbeats of all; and in beating, It says: "Souls! Love!". And from the heartbeat "Souls!", You feel all sins flow in your heartbeat, and death being inflicted on You; while in the heartbeat "Love!", You feel life being given to You. Therefore, You are in a continuous act of death and of life. Crucified Mama, as I look at You, I compassionate your sorrows—they are unspeakable. I would like to transform my being into tongue and voice in order to compassionate You; but before so much pain, my compassion is nothing. Therefore I call the Angels, the very Sacrosanct Trinity, and I pray Them to place their harmonies, their contentments and their beauty around You, to soothe and compassionate your intense sorrows; to sustain You in their arms, and to requite all of your pains with love.

And now, desolate Mama, I thank You in the name of all for everything You have suffered; and I ask You, for the sake of your bitter desolation, to come to my assistance at the moment of my death. When I find myself alone and abandoned by all, in the midst of a thousand anxieties and fears—come then, to return to me the company which I have given You many times in life. Come to my assistance; place Yourself beside me, and put the enemy to flight. Wash my soul with your tears, cover me with the Blood of Jesus, clothe me with His merits, embellish me and heal me with your sorrows and with all the pains and works of Jesus; and by virtue of them, let all my sins disappear, giving me total forgiveness. And as I breathe my last, receive me into your arms, place me under your mantle, hide me from the gaze of the enemy, take me straight to Heaven, and place me in the arms of Jesus. Let us make this agreement, my dear Mama! And now, I pray You to return the company I have given You to all those who are agonizing. Be the Mama of all; these are extreme moments, and great aids are needed. Therefore, do not deny your maternal office to anyone. One last word: as I leave You, I pray You to enclose me in the Most Sacred Heart of Jesus; and You, my sorrowful Mama, be my sentry, so that Jesus may not put me out of It; and I, even if I wanted, may not be able to leave. So I kiss your maternal hand; and You, bless me.

Our Lady, Queen and Mother of Sorrows, pray for us.

25) Grow in the Gift Through Mary

As many great saints in recent times have discovered, Mary is the key to sanctity; she is the key to her Son, and this is true as well with her Son's greatest gift: His Divine Will.

The last entry in all of Luisa's volumes is from December 28th, 1938. Although Luisa likely did not know it was to be the last; Jesus did, and the majority of that entry is dedicated to Our Lady. We know, indeed, that Jesus' *modus operandi* is to save the best for last; therefore, I believe we can trust that, if we remember nothing else, remembering that Mary is our Mother in everything will bring us to the Gift. In Luisa's last passage, we read:

> Who can tell you how much [my Mother] loved Me and how much I loved Her? My Love was such that, in everything I did, I could not be without feeling Her Maternity together with Me. I can say that She would run even in my breathing, never to leave Me alone; and I called Her. Her Maternity was for Me a need, a relief, a support for my Life down here.
>
> … You must know that as my inseparable Mama laid Her Maternity inside and outside of my Humanity, so did I constitute Her and confirm Her Mother of each thought of creature, of each breath, of each heartbeat, of each word, and I made Her lay Her Maternity in their works, in their steps and in all their pains. Her Maternity runs everywhere. If creatures are in danger of falling into sin, She covers them with Her Maternity so that they may not fall; and if they have fallen, She leaves Her Maternity as help and defense, to make them stand up again. Her Maternity runs and extends over the souls who want to be good and holy, as if She found Her Jesus in them. She operates as Mother to their intellects, She guides their words, She covers them and hides them in Her Maternal Love, so as to raise as many other Jesuses. Her Maternity is displayed on the beds of the dying, and using the rights of authority of Mother, given by Me, She says to Me in such a tender tone that I cannot refuse her anything: 'My Son, I am Mother, and they are my children—I must rescue them. If You don't grant this to Me, my Maternity would be compromised.' And while saying this, She covers them with Her Love, She hides them with Her Maternity to rescue them.
>
> My Love was such that I said to Her: 'Mother of Mine, I want You to be the Mother of all, and what You have done for Me, You will do for all creatures. Your Maternity extends in all of their acts, in such a way that I will see them all covered and hidden inside your Maternal Love.' My Mama accepted, and it was confirmed that not only would She be the Mother of all, but that She would invest each of their acts with Her Maternal Love. This was one of the greatest graces I gave to all human generations. But how many sorrows does my Mother not receive? They reach the point of not wanting to receive Her Maternity, and of denying It. Therefore the whole of Heaven prays and anxiously awaits the Divine Will to be known and to reign. Then will the Great Queen do to the children of my Will what She did for Her Jesus, and Her Maternity will have life in Her children.
>
> I will surrender my own place in Her Maternal Heart to those who live in my Will. She will raise them for Me, She will guide their steps, She will hide them within Her Maternity and Sanctity. Her Maternal Love and Her Sanctity will be seen, impressed in all their acts; they will be Her true children, who will look like Me in everything. Oh! how I would love for everyone to know that if they want to live in my Will, they have a powerful Queen and Mother who will make up for whatever they lack. She will raise them on Her maternal lap, and in everything they do She will

be together with them, to shape their acts after Her own; so much so, that they will be known as the children raised, kept and instructed by the Love of the Maternity of my Mama. And these will be the children who will make Her happy, and will be Her glory and Her honor."

Have more beautiful, consoling, inspiring, and powerful words on Our Lady's motherhood ever been spoken? Indeed, we see here in the clearest terms that Mary is the Mediatrix of All Grace, and that we can and will receive everything from her hands. Therefore, with this understanding of our Heavenly Mother's power and love, let us proceed to learn more about her and her love for us as revealed to Luisa.

Truths About Mary Revealed to Luisa by Jesus

Perhaps best summing up His many words that He gave to Luisa on His mother, Jesus says:

> … [Mary] received the unique mission as the Mother of a God Son, and the office of Co-Redemptrix of mankind… all other creatures combined, both celestial and terrestrial, would never be able to equal Her.[814]

Time and time again throughout Luisa's 36 volumes, we see Jesus glorifying His mother, insisting that she is the way to the Gift of His Will, and encouraging our love of and devotion to her. Here we will cover only a small portion of these revelations to whet our appetite for learning more about the Glories of Mary as revealed by Jesus to Luisa.

The Enmity Between the Woman and the Serpent

Giving a profound discourse on the enmity between the Woman and the Serpent, Jesus says to Luisa:

> Then came, indeed, the Celestial Creature who crushed his head, and the enemy felt such power in Her, that it knocked him down, and he did not have the strength to go near Her. This consumed him with rage, and he employed all his infernal weapons to fight Her. But—no! He would try to go near Her, he would feel himself being worn down, his legs being broken, and would be forced to draw back; and from afar he would spy on Her admirable virtues, Her power and sanctity. And I,

in order to confound him and make him doubtful, would let him see the Celestial Sovereign, Her human things, like taking food, crying, sleeping and other things; and he would persuade himself that it was not She, because, being so powerful and holy, She was not to be subject to the natural needs of life. But then he would go back to doubts, and wanted to return to assault—but in vain. My Will is power that debilitates all evils and all the infernal powers; It is light that makes Itself known by all, and wherever It reigns, It makes Its power felt, which not even the very demons can get themselves to deny. **Therefore, the Queen of Heaven was, and is, the terror of all hell.**

> Now the infernal serpent feels over his head my immediate word spoken to him in Eden—my irrevocable condemnation that a woman would crush his head. Therefore he knows that, by his head being crushed, his kingdom on earth will be overturned, he will lose his prestige, and all the evil he did in Eden by means of a woman will be made up for by another woman…

> My daughter, the Celestial Creature was poor, Her natural qualities were apparently common, nothing extraordinary appeared on the outside. She takes a poor artisan as Her spouse, who earns his daily bread with his humble work. Suppose that it had become known before, to the great ones of the world, to the doctors and the priests, that She was the Mother of the Word—that She was the One who was the Mother of the future Messiah; they would have waged a fierce war against Her—no one would have believed Her. They would have said: 'Is it possible that there have not been, and that there aren't women in Israel, such that this poor one was to be the Mother of the Eternal Word? There has been a Judith, an Esther, and many others…

> … since the Celestial Lady is the true Queen of the Kingdom of my Will, it is Her task to help and teach the fortunate creatures who want to enter, to live in It.'[815]

If there was ever any doubt that Satan will lose, that doubt is hereby annihilated. He is terrified of Our Lady, knowing that she already has crushed his head and will soon do so even more definitively through the Triumph of her Immaculate Heart.

Our Lady, The Mother of Sorrows

Central to understanding the love Our Lady has for us and for all, is understanding the degree to which she has suffered for our salvation and

---

sanctification. Jesus tells Luisa:

> Now, you must know that in order to form the Kingdom of Redemption, those who distinguished themselves the most in suffering were my Mama and I…And even though apparently She suffered none of the pains that the other creatures knew, except for my death which was known by all… since She possessed the unity of the light of my Will, this light brought to Her pierced Heart, not only the seven swords told by the Church, but all swords, spears and pricks of all sins and pains of creatures, which martyred Her maternal Heart in a harrowing way. But this is nothing. This light brought Her all my pains… the Church knows so very little of the pains of the Celestial Sovereign Queen… This is why, by right, She was constituted Queen of martyrs and of all sorrows… since She had no sin, the inheritance of pains was not for Her—Her inheritance was the Kingdom of my Will. But in order to give the Kingdom of Redemption to creatures, She had to submit Herself to so many pains. So, the fruits of Redemption were matured in the Kingdom of my Will possessed by Me and by my Mama. There is nothing beautiful, good or useful, which does not come from my Will. [816]

No human being has ever suffered or will ever suffer anything close to what Our Lady suffered for every single soul who ever has lived and ever will live; including you. If you call to mind, this moment, the sacrifices of the one who has sacrificed most for you—likely your own earthly mother; but perhaps your earthly father, or some other family member or friend—you can rest assured that Mary, your Heavenly Mother, has suffered incomparably more *for you* specifically. And to this day, although her happiness is perfect and uninterruptable in the Beatific Vision, she still suffers mystically on behalf of her Son, whose body is the Church; evidenced in part by the so many statues in her honor now weeping tears of blood for her children so mired in sin. We must, therefore, understand what sin does to our loving Mother, and we must understand that, next to her Divine Son, she has sacrificed more for each one of us than anybody else ever has.

We must also remember that, although conceived Immaculately, this does not mean she was excused from the same crosses that all pilgrims must endure. Jesus tells Luisa:

…it is not true that the Sovereign Queen was never without Me; separated—never; but without Me—yes. But this did not prejudice the height of Her sanctity; on the contrary, it increased it. **How many times I left Her in the state of pure faith**…This pain of being left in pure faith prepared Her to receive the deposit of my doctrines, the treasure of the Sacraments and all the goods of my Redemption. In fact, since the privation of Me is the greatest pain … Had She not possessed this gift of faith, how could She give it to Her children?[817]

Seeing the Glories of Our Lady depicted in Luisa's writings, many will no doubt feel the temptation to attribute gifts to her that she in fact did not always have. On earth, she was still a pilgrim—like us. And like us, she did not know everything, but instead had to operate by pure Faith (as opposed to her Divine Son, Who did always know everything from the first moment of His conception, and therefore could not possibly have Faith). I state this in the "Mother of Sorrows" section to serve as a reminder that Mary's sacrifices cannot be discounted as the acts of one who sees God face-to-face and knows everything, which would alter the nature of the sacrifices. Instead, like us, she did not have perfect knowledge of the future, but this "deficiency" did not diminish her sanctity: it only increased it because, despite operating by Faith, she operated with all the perfection of sanctity that a Blessed in Heaven now operates even with the Beatific Vision.

Similarly, we should remember that, despite being the Queen of All Creation (with such power that, upon her mere command, the Universe would have readily annihilated itself), she appeared to be no different from any of us. Jesus tells Luisa:

> I had to hide from Her outward appearance anything that might be called miracle, except for Her perfect virtue… What would be greater: that the Celestial Queen had given sight to the blind and speech to the mute, and so forth, or the miracle of making the Eternal Word descend upon earth? … the first would have been as though nothing compared to the second… But, as Sun, She produced goods and miracles without letting Herself be seen or pointed at as the primary cause of everything. In fact, all the good I did upon earth, I did because the Empress of Heaven reached the point of holding Her empire

---

[816] July 11, 1926.
[817] August 22, 1926.

in the Divinity; and by Her empire She drew Me from Heaven, to give Me to creatures. [818]

Our Lady could have snapped her fingers and thereby cured every disease and raised all the dead throughout the entire planet (such was the Omnipotent God at her beck and call). But she was so perfectly living in the Divine Will that she had not the slightest inclination to do anything but this Will of God. Thus, here as well we can regard her as Mother of Sorrows: for she is the one who knows that she possesses a quasi-Omnipotence, but will never exercise it outside of perfect conformity to the Will of her Son.

Never at Odds with Christocentric Piety

Mary herself told Luisa the following, which addresses perfectly any concern that a focus on Mary diminishes from a focus on Jesus:

> My daughter, I am always with Jesus, but sometimes I hide within Him, and it seems that He does everything as if He did it without Me; while I am inside of Him, I concur with Him, and I am aware of what He is doing. Other times He hides within His Mama and lets Me operate, but He is always concurring along. Other times both of Us reveal Ourselves together, and the souls see the Mother and the Son who love them so much, according to the circumstances and the good needed for them; and many times it is the love that We cannot contain, that makes Us reach excesses toward them. But be sure that if my Son is there, there I am as well; and that if I am there, there is my Son. This is a task that was given to Me by the Supreme Being, from which I cannot, nor do I want to withdraw. More so, since these are the joys of my Maternity, the fruits of my sorrows, the glory of the Kingdom which I possess—the Will and the fulfillment of the Sacrosanct Trinity.[819]

Furthermore, we see that it is precisely through Mary that Jesus, to this day, receives protection. Mary reveals to Luisa that she (Mary) is often Jesus' sole consolation when He is received unworthily in Communion, and that she is also His safeguard in the hands of the priest:

> Now, this Son is Mine, He is my gift, and because He is Mine I know His loving secrets, His yearnings, His longing, such that He reaches the point of crying, telling Me with repeated sobs: 'My Mama, give Me to souls—I want souls.' And I want what He wants; I can say that I sigh and cry together with Him, because I want everyone to possess my Son; but I must keep His Life safe—the great gift that God entrusted to Me. This is why, if He descends sacramentally into the hearts, I descend together with Him for the security of my gift—I cannot leave Him alone. Poor Son of Mine, if He did not have His Mama who descends together with Him … How poorly they treat Him! Some don't even say to Him an 'I love You' from the heart, and I must love Him; some receive Him in a distracted way, without thinking of the great gift they are receiving, and I pour Myself upon Him so as not to let Him feel their distractedness and coldness; some reach the point of making Him cry, and I must calm His crying, and give sweet reproaches to the creature, that she would not make Him cry. How many touching scenes take place in the hearts that receive Him sacramentally. There are souls who are never satiated with loving Him, and I give them my love, and even His own love, to let them love Him. These are scenes of Heaven, and the very Angels remain enraptured, and We feel restored from the pains that other creatures have given Us.

> But who can tell you everything? I am the bearer of Jesus, nor does He want to go without Me; so much so, that when the priest is about to pronounce the words of the consecration over the holy host, I make wings with my maternal hands, that He may descends in-between my hands to be consecrated, so that, if unworthy hands touch Him, I let Him feel my own that defend Him and cover Him with my love. But this is not enough. I am always on guard, to see if they want my Son; so much so, that if a sinner repents of his grave sins and the light of grace dawns in his heart, immediately I bring him Jesus as confirmation of the forgiveness, and I take care of everything that is needed to make Him stay inside that converted heart. I am the bearer of Jesus, and I am so because I possess in Me the Kingdom of His Divine Will. The Divine Will reveals to Me who it is that wants Him, and I run, I fly to bring Him, but without ever leaving Him. And not only am I the bearer, but the spectator and listener of what He does and says to souls. Do you think that I was not present, listening to the many lessons that my dear Son gave You on His Divine Will? I was present, I listened, word by word, to what He was telling You, and in each word I thanked my Son, and I felt glorified twice as much for He was speaking

---

[818] October 22, 1926.
[819] May 28, 1937.

of the Kingdom[820]

After reading these words, can there possibly remain any doubt that Marian devotion is never a detraction from the Christocentrism of our Faith? Similarly, Jesus tells Luisa:

> Her faithfulness was the sweet chain that bound Me and captured Me from Heaven to earth. Here is why, then, what creatures did not obtain in many centuries, they obtained by means of the Sovereign Queen. Ah! yes, She alone was the worthy One who merited that the Divine Word would descend from Heaven to earth, and that She receive the great good of Redemption, in such a way that, if they want to, all can receive the good of being redeemed.[821]

Although the entirety of Salvation History was leading up to, preparing for, and "storing up merit" for the Incarnation and Redemption, Jesus here reminds us that it was Mary *alone* who truly merited the Incarnation. Because it is thanks to her *alone* (among creatures) that we have Jesus in the flesh, she can never be a distraction from the same.

Our Lady, Queen of the Church

As all trustworthy private revelations that touch on the matter affirm, Our Lady was the true Queen of the Church even in her earthly life; and it was only thanks to her physical presence, around which the Church gathered, that the Apostles and disciples were able to form the nascent Church after the Ascension of Jesus. But she remains the Queen of the Church to this day; her Assumption to Heaven changed that not one iota. Jesus tells Luisa:

> Now, in the midst of the disciples there was My Mama, who assisted at My Departure for Heaven. This is the most Beautiful symbol. Just as She is the Queen of My Church, She assists it, She protects It, She defends It, so She will sit in the midst of the Children of My Will. She will always be the engine, the Life, the Guide, the perfect Model, the Teacher of the Kingdom of the Divine Fiat that remains so close to Her Heart. They are Her anxieties, Her ardent desires, Her deliriums of Maternal Love because **She wants Her children on earth in the Kingdom where She Lived**. She is not content that She has Her children in Heaven in the Kingdom of the Divine Will, but She wants them also on earth. She feels that **She has not completed the task given to Her by God as Mother and Queen. As long as the Divine Will does not Reign on earth in the midst of creatures, Her Mission is not finished**. She wants Her children who are like Her and who possess the Inheritance of their Mama. So the Great Lady is all eye in order to look, all heart in order to Love, so as to help the one whom She sees in some way disposed, that they want to Live of Divine Will. Therefore in the difficulties, think that She is around you, She sustains you, She fortifies you, She takes your volition in Her Maternal Hands in order to make it receive the Life of the Supreme Fiat.[822]

Our Lady's mission is not finished. With no less conviction, then, we can say with the Apostles themselves, as they said 2,000 years ago, that they have the Queen of All Creation in their midst who will ensure that the Will of her Son is done.

Jesus continues on this same thread, describing why—among many other reasons, of course—it is that Our Lady desires for this Gift to reign on earth:

> My daughter, the Queen of Heaven, in Her glory and greatness, is as though isolated…She is the isolated Queen; She does not have the cortege of other queens who surround Her and match Her in the glory and greatness that She possesses. She finds Herself in the conditions of a queen who is surrounded by damsels, by pageboys, by faithful friends who give Her honor and keep Her company; however, no other queen, equal to Her, gives Her the great honor of surrounding Her and of keeping Her company. What would be a greater honor for a queen of the earth: to be surrounded by other queens equal to Her, or by people inferior in condition, in glory, in greatness and in beauty? There is such distance in honor and in glory between one who is surrounded by queens and one who is surrounded only by other people, that no parallel can be compared to it… the Celestial Mama wants, desires-awaits the Kingdom of the Divine Will upon earth…[823]

The Sovereign Queen of Heaven wishes to be surrounded by other queens. This simple sentence could well encapsulate the essence of the Divine Will message. For in it we see that no one can ever exceed or even have the same position as Mary—that will always be hers alone. But no one wants only to be surrounded by inferiors; they want equals. Just as Adam, looking upon all the beasts and saw no companion equal to himself, felt

---

[820] May 28, 1937.
[821] October 7, 1930.

[822] May 20, 1936.
[823] January 18, 1928.

grieved by this absence and thus God fashioned Eve out of the side of Adam—indicating equality in dignity—so, too, Our Lady wishes to have her own children live on the same spiritual plane of which she herself reigns as Queen.

The Immaculate Conception: The Greatest Feast

On the Feast of the Immaculate Conception in the year 1928, Jesus told Luisa:

… since this celestial little girl, from Her very Immaculate Conception, began Her life in the Divine Fiat, and since She was from the human stock, with my Will She acquired the Divine Life, and with Her humanity She possessed the human origin. So, **She had the power to unite the divine and the human**, and She gave to God what man had not given Him and had denied to Him, which was his will; and She gave men the right to be able to ascend to the embraces of Her Creator. With the power of Our Fiat which She had in Her power, She bound God and men. **So, all Creation— Heaven and earth, and even hell—felt in the Immaculate Conception of this Virgin little girl**, just newly born [conceived] in the womb of Her mama **… Today is the greatest feast, because the Divine Will had life in the Queen of Heaven**; it was the feast of all feasts, it was the first kiss, the first divine embrace that the creature gave to her Creator by virtue of Our Fiat, which the Sovereign little girl possessed—the creature sitting at table with her Creator. Therefore, today is also your feast, in a special way because of the mission given to you by my Divine Will…My daughter, how content I am; today it can be said that my Sovereign Mama receives from the Church the divine honors, as She honors in Her, as the first act of Her life, the Life of the Divine Will. These are the greatest honors that can be given—that the human will never had life in Her, but always, always the Divine Will. This was the whole secret of Her sanctity, of Her height, power, beauty, greatness and so on; it was my Fiat that, with Its heat, extinguished the stain of original sin and conceived Her immaculate and pure. … Therefore, today, by making known that everything in Her was the prodigy of my Will, and that all of Her other prerogatives and privileges were in the secondary order and as consequence of the effects of that Divine Will which dominated Her, it can be said that, today, it is with decorum, divine glory and magnificence that the Feast of the Immaculate Conception is celebrated; a Feast which, more truly, can be called: 'The conception of the Divine Will in the Sovereign Queen of Heaven.' And this conception was the consequence of everything It is and It did, and of the great prodigies of this Celestial Little Girl."… Oh! if creatures knew what it means to live of Will of God, they would lay down their lives to know It and live in It.

Jesus, we see, does not hesitate to name the Feast of the Immaculate Conception as the "greatest feast." (While not detracting from His assertions elsewhere that it was the Incarnation—His Own conception—that was the greatest *event* or *work*). And with good reason: aside from a brief period of time in the beginning, Creation lacked its ultimate purpose until Our Lady was conceived in the womb of Saint Anne—and even the Original Glory of Adam and Eve was utterly dwarfed by the glory of Our Lady immediately upon her Immaculate Conception.

***

Now that we have considered a small selection of excerpts from Luisa's volumes that speak of the Glories of Mary, we turn now to consider what Mary herself revealed to Luisa in the work entitled *The Blessed Virgin Mary in the Kingdom of the Divine Will.*

The Blessed Virgin Mary in the Kingdom of the Divine Will

In this work, our Blessed Mother takes us on her lap and teaches us lessons on how to live continuously in the Divine Will. This is the real design for the Gift; not that it be a passing thing, but that it define the entire life of the creature without the exception of a single moment. While *The Hours of the Passion* contain an entire 24-hour period, these lessons consist in meditations for each day over the course of a month—namely, the month of May. Each day contains three lessons: one for morning, one for noon, and one for evening. Mary tells Luisa that her guidance in this book serves to train souls to remain continuously anchored in the Divine Will, as opposed to entering and leaving the Gift (as Luisa herself did in the beginning, and as most will do as they grow in the Gift). As previously mentioned, St. Louis de Montfort taught that Mary is the quickest, surest, and easiest way to Jesus. It is the same way with the Gift of Living in the Divine Will. In this book, Mary also promises strength for the weak, victory for the tempted, a hand to raise up those who have fallen into sin, comfort for the afflicted, a path to hope for the dejected, and, in sum, the bread of the Divine Will for those who are famished. She promises her company and even promises to commit to bringing us happiness with her maternal presence.

Over the next several pages, we will walk through a selection of teachings given by Our Lady to Luisa in this work. (Since it is a fairly short work and all the quotes in this section are taken from it, easy to find, and presented in the same order that the book itself presents them, I will refrain from giving individual footnotes.)

**

Mary begins by promising Luisa that she will do whatever it takes to form her children in the Divine Will: even if she has to go to every family, nation, religious community, etc.

In order that we may have some small idea of what a tremendous privilege it is to hear these lessons, Our Lady reminds us:

> Look at Me, dear child: thousands of Angels surround Me and, reverent, are all in waiting, to hear Me speak of that Divine Fiat whose fount I possess, more than anyone; I know Its admirable secrets, Its infinite joys, Its indescribable happiness and Its incalculable value.

With Joachim and Anne

About her Immaculate Conception, Mary reveals to Luisa:

> … as soon as the Divinity smiled and celebrated my Conception, the Supreme Fiat took the third step over my little humanity. Tiny, tiny as I was, It endowed Me with divine reason; and moving all Creation in feast, It made Me be recognized by all created things as their Queen. They recognized in Me the life of the Divine Will, and the whole universe prostrated itself at my feet, though I was tiny and not yet born…there was not one created thing that did not unite itself to the smile and to the feast of the Sacrosanct Trinity. All accepted my dominion, my rule, my command, and they felt honored because, after so many centuries from the time in which Adam had lost the command and the dominion of king by withdrawing from the Divine Will, they found in Me their Queen; and all Creation proclaimed Me Queen of Heaven and earth. My dear child, you must know

Upon her conception, Our Lady could feel that all things were within her dominion. Nevertheless, a test was needed; Mary herself saw the necessity of the test, and she herself desired eagerly to submit to it as proof of her love of God:

> I remained so identified with my Creator, that I felt Myself as the owner in the divine dominions. I did not know what separation from my Creator was; that same Divine Will which reigned in Me, reigned in Them, and rendered Us inseparable. And while everything was smile and feast between Me and Them, I could see that They could not trust Me if They did not receive a proof. My child, the test is the flag that says victory; the test places all the goods that God wants to give us in safekeeping; the test matures and disposes the soul for gains of great conquests. And I too saw the necessity of this test, because I wanted to give proof to my Creator, in exchange for the so many seas of graces He had given Me, with an act of my faithfulness which would cost Me the sacrifice of my whole life. How beautiful it is to be able to say: "You have loved me, I have loved You"—but without the test, it can never be said.

Seeing that Adam had failed this same test, Our Lady became the Lady of Sorrows while she was still in the womb of St. Anne:

> Now know, child of my Heart, that in knowing the grave evils of the human will in Adam and in all his progeny, I, your Celestial Mother, though newly conceived, cried bitterly and with hot tears over fallen man. And the Divine Will, in seeing Me cry, asked Me, as proof, to surrender my human will to It. The Divine Fiat said to Me: "I do not ask of you a fruit, as with Adam; no, no—but I ask you for your will. You will keep it as if you did not have it, under the empire of my Divine Will, which will be your life, and will feel confident to make of you whatever It wants." So, the Supreme Fiat took the fourth step in my soul, asking Me for my will as proof, waiting for my Fiat…

In describing the sacrifice God asked of her in the womb of Anne, Our Lady says:

> To sacrifice oneself for one day—now yes, now no—is easy; but to sacrifice oneself in each instant, in each act, in the very good that one wants to do, for one's entire life, without ever giving life to one's own will, is the sacrifice of sacrifices; This sacrifice is so great, that God cannot ask anything more of the creature, nor can she find how to sacrifice more for her Creator…

> My child, you must know that the Divinity was assured about Me through the test It wanted—while everyone believes that I did not have any test, and that it was enough for God to make the

great portent He made of Me, of conceiving Me without original sin. Oh, how they deceive themselves. On the contrary, He asked of Me a proof which He has asked of no one. And He did this with justice and with highest wisdom, because, since the Eternal Word was to descend into Me, not only was it not decorous that He find in Me the original sin, but it was also not decorous for Him to find in Me a human will operating. It would have been too unseemly for God to descend into a creature in whom reigned the human will. And this is why He wanted from Me, as proof, and for my whole life, my will, in order to secure the Kingdom of the Divine Will within my soul. Once He secured this in Me, God could do with Me whatever He wanted; He could give Me anything, and I can say that He could deny Me nothing.

Needless to say, Our Lady passed this Test of All Tests—even though it immeasurably outweighed the size of Adam's test and was given to her at the first moment of her conception. And because of passing this test, Our Lady immediately could feel herself the mother of all:

With Its Power, Immensity and All-seeingness, the Divine Will enclosed all creatures in my soul, and I felt a little place in my maternal Heart for each one of them. From the moment I was conceived, I carried you in my Heart, and—oh, how much I loved you, and I love you…

As I took possession of the Kingdom of the Divine Will, Its steps within Me ended; more so, since these six steps symbolized the six days of Creation: each day, by pronouncing a Fiat, God took as though a step, passing from the creation of one thing to another. On the sixth day, He took the final step, saying: "Fiat—let Us make man in Our image and likeness." And on the seventh day He rested in His works, as though wanting to enjoy everything He had created with such magnificence…Now, my creation surpassed all the prodigies of Creation…The heavens could neither reach Me nor contain Me; the light of the sun was small before my light. No created thing could reach Me. I crossed the divine seas as if they were my own; my Celestial Father, the Son and the Holy Spirit, longed for Me to be in Their arms, to enjoy Their little daughter.

Having shared such glorious truths about herself with Luisa, it is time for Our Lady to give us the most surprising truth of all: that these Glories of Mary, though she will always have them above all others in a sovereign and superior way for all of eternity, are nevertheless offered to us:

Now, my child, listen to your Mama: I saw you surprised in hearing Me narrate the story of the possession in the Kingdom of the Divine Will. Now know that this destiny is given also to you: if you decide never to do your will, the Divine Will will form Its Heaven in your soul; you will feel the divine inseparability; the scepter of command over yourself, over your passions, will be given to you…

Therefore, We give to You the mandate to place in safety the destiny of mankind. You will be Our Agent in their midst. To You do We entrust their souls; You will defend Our rights, prejudiced by their sins; You will be in the middle, between them and Us, to restore the balance on both sides. We feel in You the invincible strength of Our Divine Will which, through You, prays and cries. Who can resist You? Your prayers are commands, your tears rule over Our Divine Being.

This does not mean that Mary lacked faith as her Divine Son did (for He always saw all things) or that she had perfect knowledge of the future. Far from it; Our Lady was often left—like us—in a state of pure faith, because by this faith she could merit. Indeed, she knew immediately that a Mother of the Redeemer would be necessary; but in her humility she did not assume she was to be the one, even though she was assured by God—still in the womb of Anne—that the destiny of all mankind was in her little unborn, yet maternal, hands:

And without knowing then that I was to be the Mother of the Divine Word, I felt in Me the double Maternity: Maternity toward God, to defend His just rights; Maternity toward creatures, to bring them to safety. I felt Myself Mother of all. The Divine Will which reigned in Me, and which knows not how to do isolated works, brought God and all creatures from all centuries into Me…

Now, in the middle of our loving stratagems, I remembered the painful state of my human family upon earth, for I too was of their offspring—and how I grieved and prayed that the Eternal Word would descend and put a remedy to it. And I would say this with such tenderness as to reach the point of changing smile and feast into crying. The Most High was so moved by my tears, more so, since they were the tears of a little one; and pressing Me to the divine bosom, They dried my tears and said to Me: "Daughter, do not cry, pluck up courage. Into your hands We have placed the destiny of mankind…

And then Our Lady dictates to Luisa about her birth:

My cradle was surrounded by Angels, who competed among themselves in singing lullabies to Me, as to their sovereign Queen. And since I was endowed with reason and with science, infused in Me by my Creator, I did my first duty to adore, with my intelligence, and also with my babbling little voice of a baby, the Most Holy Adorable Trinity. ...

And so the Angels, for whom my desires were commands, picked Me up, and carrying Me on their wings, brought Me into the loving arms of my Celestial Father ...[I said to the Trinity:]I will not come down off of your paternal knees if You do not give Me the deed of grace, that I may bring to my children the good news of their Redemption." The Divinity was moved at my prayers, and filling Me with new gifts, They said to Me: "Return to the exile and continue your prayers. Extend the Kingdom of Our Will in all your acts, for at the appropriate time We will make You content." But They did not tell Me either when or where He would descend. So I would depart from Heaven only to do the Divine Will. This was the most heroic sacrifice for Me, but I did it gladly, so that the Divine Will alone might have full dominion over Me.

In this passage we see revealed that, as a newborn baby, Our Lady was continually mystically ascending to Heaven and pleading before the Trinity for the coming of the Incarnate Redeemer.

She then shares a teaching for us to live by:

Now, my child, continue to listen to Me: in each one of your acts, may your first duty be to adore your Creator, to know Him and to love Him. This places you in the order of Creation, and you come to recognize the One who created you. This is the holiest duty of each creature: to recognize her origin.

Our Lady moves on to discuss her own entrance into the service of the Temple at a mere three years of age. In case this is shocking to hear, know well that this biographical fact about Our Lady is confirmed by every trustworthy private revelation that speaks of it; not excluding Venerable Agreda's *Mystical City of God*. In speaking of how great a sacrifice this was for the two "great saints," Joachim and Anne, Our Lady shares a teaching for us all: that love *in the order of God* (that is, "loving God in all things and above all things,"[824] as the prayer of

the Mass says) disposes us for any sacrifice:

I had just turned three years old when my parents made known to Me that they wanted to consecrate Me to the Lord in the Temple. My heart rejoiced in hearing this—that is, consecrating Myself and spending my years in the house of God. But beneath my joy there was a sorrow—a privation of the dearest persons one can have on earth, which were my dear parents. I was little, I needed their maternal cares; I was depriving Myself of the presence of two great saints. Moreover, I saw that as the day approached on which they were to deprive themselves of Me, who rendered their lives full of joy and of happiness, they felt such bitterness as to feel themselves dying. But, though suffering, they were disposed to make the heroic act of taking Me to the Lord. My parents loved Me in the order of God, and considered Me a great gift, given to them by the Lord; and this gave them the strength to make the painful sacrifice.

Mary then shares how she left this home and so teaches us all how to say goodbye to those things in our lives which, though good, have come time to let go of for the sake of the Will of God: thanking Him, and then placing everything in His Hands.

Now, pay attention to Me, and listen. I left the house of Nazareth accompanied by my holy parents. Upon leaving it, I wanted to give one last glance to that little house in which I was born, to thank my Creator for having given Me a place in which to be born, and to leave it in the Divine Will, so that my childhood and so many dear memories—since, being full of reason, I comprehended everything—might all be kept in the Divine Will and deposited in It as pledges of my love toward the One who had created Me. My child, thanking the Lord and placing our acts into His hands as pledges of our love causes new channels of graces and communications to be opened between God and the soul, and it is the most beautiful homage that one can render to the One who loves us so much. Therefore, learn from Me to thank the Lord for all that He disposes for you, and in anything you are about to do, may your word be: "Thank You, O Lord; I place everything in your hands."

Her Service in the Temple

Upon traveling to the temple, as a mere 3-year-old girl, Mary recognized her dominion over all

[824]*Collect* for the Twentieth Sunday of Ordinary Time. Third English Edition of the Roman Missal.

creation, for it all bowed before its Queen. In fact, to prevent outward signs from appearing to others before the proper time, she usually had to command creation to follow the ordinary course of nature:

> Now, my child, I departed from my paternal house with courage and detachment, because I looked only at the Divine Will, in which I kept my Heart fixed; and this was enough for Me in everything. But while I was walking to go to the Temple, I looked at all Creation, and—oh! marvel—I felt the heartbeat of the Divine Will in the sun, in the wind, in the stars, in the heavens; even under my steps I felt It palpitating. And the Divine Fiat that reigned in Me commanded all Creation, which concealed It like a veil, to all bow and pay to Me the honor of Queen. And all bowed, giving Me signs of subjection. Even the tiny little flower of the field did not spare itself from giving Me its little homage.

> ... when, out of necessity, I would go out of the house, the Creation would place Itself in the act of giving Me signs of honor, and I was forced to command them to remain in their place, and to follow the order of our Creator.

Finally, upon arriving at the temple, she bid her parents farewell:

> Afterwards, with courage, I said good-bye to my dear and holy parents; I kissed their right hands, and I thanked them for the care they took of my childhood, and for having consecrated Me to the Lord with so much love and sacrifice. My peaceful presence, without crying and courageous, infused so much courage in them, that they had the strength to leave Me and to depart from Me. The Divine Will ruled over Me and extended Its Kingdom in all those acts of mine. Oh! power of the Fiat—You alone could give Me the heroism, though I was so little, to have the strength to detach Myself from those who loved Me so much, and whom I saw feeling their hearts break in separating from Me.

In the temple, she—the Queen of All Creation—gladly undertook the lowliest of duties, knowing that in all of them she was fulfilling the Divine Will:

> Lord. I was most attentive to all the duties which were usually done in that holy place. I was peaceful with everyone, nor did I ever cause any bitterness or bother to anyone. I submitted Myself to the most humble tasks; I found no difficulty in anything, either in sweeping or in doing dishes. Any sacrifice was an honor—a triumph for Me. But do you want to know why? I looked at

nothing—everything was Will of God for Me.

In accordance with this, she gives instructions to religious communities:

> Ah! if all the souls consecrated to the Lord in holy places would make everything disappear in the Divine Will, how happy they would be, converting the communities into many celestial families, and populating the earth with many holy souls. But, alas, with the sorrow of Mother, I must say: how many bitternesses, disturbances and discords are not there?—while sanctity is not in the office given to them, but in doing the Divine Will in whatever office that might be entrusted to them…

Mary would constantly ascend to Heaven to implore, before the Divine Persons, to let the Word descend upon earth:

> I continued my life in the Temple, but Heaven was not closed for Me; I could go there as many times as I wanted—I had free passage to ascend and descend. In Heaven I had my Divine Family, and I burned and longed to be with Them…

> They loved to be won by Their little daughter, and to hear Me repeat to Them: "Descend—let the Word descend upon earth." I can say that the very Divinity would call Me; and I would run—I would fly into Their midst. Since I had never done my human will, my presence requited Them of the love and the glory of the great work of all Creation, and therefore They entrusted to Me the secret of the history of mankind. And I prayed and prayed again for peace to come between God and man.

Our Lady takes this opportunity to instruct us on how strange our lot as sinful creatures is, fearing the very things we should be rulers of:

> As soon as man withdrew from the Divine Will, he became fearful, timid; he lost the dominion of himself and of the whole Creation. All the elements, because they were dominated by the Fiat, had remained superior to him and could do harm to him. Man was afraid of everything; and do you think it is trivial, my child, that the one who had been created as king, dominator of everything, reached the point of being afraid of the One who had created him? It is strange, my child, and I would say almost against nature, that a child would be afraid of his father…

The Marriage to Joseph

Then, Mary tells us of how God sent Joseph to her, and in so doing teaches us that marriage is holy, as are all states in life, but unfortunately most people do not use their state to become holy:

> ... But what was not my surprise when in one of these visits of mine [to Heaven] They [Persons of the Trinity] made known to Me that it was Their Will for Me to leave the Temple; first, to unite Myself in bond of marriage, according to the custom of those times, to a holy man called Joseph; and to withdraw together with him to live in the house of Nazareth.

> ... God used [my life] in an admirable way in order to fulfill His designs, and to grant Me the grace which I so much longed for—that is, the descent of the Word upon earth. God gave Me the safeguard, the defense, the help, so that no one could talk about Me—about my honesty. Saint Joseph was to be the cooperator, the tutor, who was to take care of that bit of the human which We needed; as well as the shadow of the Celestial Paternity, in which our little Celestial Family on earth was to be formed ...

> ... So, in spite of my surprise, immediately I said: "Fiat", knowing that the Divine Will would not harm Me, or prejudice my sanctity. Oh! had I wanted to place one act of my human will, even in the aspect of wanting to know no man, I would have sent to ruin the plans of the coming of the Word upon earth. Therefore, it is not the diversity of states that prejudices sanctity, but the lack of Divine Will, and of the fulfillment of one's duties to which God calls the creature. All states are holy, marriage too, as long as the Divine Will is present in them, as well as the exact sacrifice of one's duties. But the great part are indolent and lazy, and not only do they not make themselves saints, but they make of their state, some a purgatory, and some a hell.

> So, as I learned that I was to leave the Temple, I did not say a word to anyone, waiting for God Himself to move the external circumstances to make Me fulfill His adorable Will, as indeed it happened. The superiors of the Temple called Me and said to Me that it was their will, and also the custom of those times, that I prepare Myself for marriage. I accepted. Miraculously, among many, the choice fell upon Saint Joseph; and so the marriage was formed and I left the Temple.

Mary's revelation to Luisa that Joseph was *miraculously* chosen is expounded upon in the revelations to Venerable Mary of Agreda. In Agreda's *Mystical City of God*, we see revealed the following:

> The appointed day [to choose a spouse for Mary] having arrived, all the young men of the family of David assembled together, and Joseph, whose birthplace was Nazareth, yet who at that time dwelt in Jerusalem, was among the number. He was thirty-three years old, of comely figure and pleasing countenance, very modest and incomparably graceful in appearance. At the age of twelve years he had made a vow of chastity ... The Lord inspired Simeon to place a dry rod in the hand of each of the young men, telling them at the same time to pray for the manifestation of the Divine Will. While all were engaged in prayer, they beheld the rod of Joseph blossom, and at that same moment a white dove, most pure and brilliant, hovered above his head. St. Joseph heard an interior voice which said, 'Joseph, My servant, Mary is to be thy spouse ... " Beholding this manifestation of the Will of God, the priests gave the most holy Virgin to be the spouse of St. Joseph.[825]

Returning to Mary's revelations to Luisa, we see Our Lady now telling us how she left the temple, and how in St. Joseph she saw her "good angel given to her by God." But there is another overlap with Agreda's revelations just cited: the fact that, since childhood, they had both vowed their virginity to God:

> I departed from the Temple with the same courage with which I entered It, and only to do the Divine Will. I went to Nazareth and I no longer found my dear and holy parents. I went accompanied only by Saint Joseph, and in him I saw my my good angel whom God had given Me for my custody ...

> Now, you must know that Saint Joseph and I looked at each other with modesty, and we felt our hearts swollen, because each one wanted to let the other know that we were bound to God with a vow of perennial virginity. Finally, silence was broken, and we both manifested our vow. Oh! how happy we felt; and thanking the Lord, we protested to live together as brother and sister. I was most attentive in serving him; we looked at each other with veneration, and the dawn of peace reigned in our midst.

The Incarnation and Nativity

Mary then shares that, after leaving the temple, and

---

[825]Venerable Mary of Agreda. *The Divine Life of the Most Holy Virgin*. From *the Mystical City of God*. Pages 40-41.

in the home of Nazareth, she felt "more ignited than ever" with longing for the descent of the Word upon earth. In this time of ardent prayer, Mary reveals to Luisa what transpired between she and God:

I felt Heaven lowering Itself down to Me, and the earth of my humanity rising; and Heaven and earth embraced, reconciled, to exchange the kiss of peace and of love. The earth disposed itself to produce the seed in order to form the Just One, the Holy One; and Heaven opened to let the Word descend into this seed.

I would do nothing but descend and ascend to my Celestial Fatherland, and throw Myself into the paternal arms of my Celestial Father, saying to Him with the heart: "Holy Father, I cannot endure any longer—I feel enflamed; and while I burn, I feel a powerful strength within Me that wants to conquer You. With the chains of my love I want to bind You in order to disarm You, that You may delay no more; but upon the wings of my love I want to carry the Divine Word from Heaven to earth." And I prayed and cried that He would listen to Me.

And the Divinity, conquered by my tears and prayers, assured Me by saying to Me: "Daughter, who can resist You? You have won; the divine hour is near. Return to the earth and continue your acts in the power of my Volition, and by these, all will be shaken, and Heaven and earth will exchange the kiss of peace." But in spite of this, I did not yet know that I was to be the Mother of the Eternal Word.

Here we see clearly that, at this moment, Our Lady has conquered God Himself and He has become ready to allow His Son to descend upon earth. Nevertheless, Mary still did not assume that she would be the Mother of the Son; so great was her humility that, until God made it unavoidably clear, she would never presume this dignity would be her own. But the time had come. Nothing remained but Gabriel's salutation:

... while I was praying in my little room, an Angel came, sent from Heaven as messenger of the great King. He came before Me, and bowing, he hailed Me:

"Hail, O Mary, our Queen; the Divine Fiat has filled You with grace. He has already pronounced His Fiat—that He wants to descend; He is already behind my shoulders, but He wants your Fiat to form the fulfillment of His Fiat." At such a great announcement, so much desired by Me—

although I had never thought I would be the chosen one—I was stupefied and hesitated one instant. But the Angel of the Lord told Me: "Do not fear, our Queen, for You have found grace before God. You have conquered your Creator; therefore, to complete the victory—pronounce your Fiat." I pronounced my Fiat, and—oh! marvel—the two Fiat fused together and the Divine Word descended into Me. ... and the Sun of the Eternal Word, blazing with inaccessible light, came to take His place within this Heaven [of mine], hidden in His little Humanity. And since His little Humanity could not contain Him, the center of this Sun remained in It, but Its light overflowed outside, and investing Heaven and earth, It reached every heart. And with Its pounding of light, It knocked at each creature, and with voices of penetrating light, It said to them: "My children, open to Me; give Me a place in your hearts. I have descended from Heaven to earth in order to form my life in each one of you. My Mother is the center in which I reside, and all my children will be the circumference, in which I want to form so many of my lives for as many as are my children."

Now that the Incarnation had occurred—what Jesus tells Luisa in the volumes was the "greatest event in history "—there were no more secrets. Mary explains to Luisa:

... you must know that from the moment I was conceived, I loved you as Mother, I felt you in my Heart, I burned with love for you, but I did not understand why. The Divine Fiat made me do facts, but would keep the secret hidden from Me. But as He incarnated Himself, He revealed the secret to Me, and I comprehended the fecundity of my Maternity—that I was to be not only Mother of Jesus, but Mother of all...

Therefore, we can see that the correct answer to the questions *"When did Mary become the Queen of the Universe? When did she become the Mother of All?"* **is simple: at the moment she was Immaculately Conceived in the womb of St. Anne.** And although she always mysteriously felt this motherhood, she recognized it openly and without veil upon the Incarnation of her Divine Son. Mary returns now to revealing to Luisa more about the life of Jesus in her womb:

My dearest child, who can tell you what my little Jesus suffered in my womb? Unheard-of and indescribable pains. He was endowed with full reason—He was God and Man; and His love was so great that He put as though aside the infinite seas of joys, of happiness, of light, and plunged His tiny Humanity into the seas of darkness, of bitternesses, of unhappiness, of miseries, which creatures had prepared for Him. And little Jesus took them all upon His shoulders, as if they were His own. My child, true love never says 'enough'.

... In fact, you must know that as His little Humanity was conceived, He conceived all the pains He was to suffer, up to the last day of His life. He enclosed all souls within Himself ...

Yes, even in the womb, Jesus was King of Sorrows; even from the first moment of His existence in the womb of the Virgin, He took upon Himself all sufferings and enclosed within Himself all souls. Having Jesus in her womb, Our Lady reveals to Luisa that she felt the burning desire to give Him to souls, and it was precisely this burning desire that inspired the Mystery of the Visitation:

My child, give Me your hand now, and follow Me, because I will continue to give you my lessons. So I departed from Nazareth, accompanied by Saint Joseph, facing a long journey, and crossing mountains to go visit Elisabeth in Judea, who, in her advanced age, had miraculously become a mother. I went to her, not to make her a simple visit, but because I burned with the desire to bring her Jesus. The fullness of grace, of love, of light that I felt within Me, pushed Me to bring, to multiply—to increase a hundredfold the life of my Son in creatures ...I felt the extreme need to give my dear Jesus to all, so that all might possess Him and love Him ...

My little Jesus exulted in my womb, and fixing on little John in the womb of his mother with the rays of His Divinity, He sanctified him, gave him the use of reason, and made known to him that He was the Son of God. And John leaped so vigorously with love and with joy that Elisabeth felt shaken. She too, touched by the light of the Divinity of my Son, recognized that I had become the Mother of God; and in the emphasis of her love, trembling with gratitude, she exclaimed: "Whence comes to me so much honor, that the Mother of my Lord should come to me?" I did not deny the highest mystery; rather, I humbly confirmed it. Praising God with the song of the Magnificat—sublime canticle, through which the Church continuously honors Me ...

But now Mary continues, revealing to Luisa what transpired at the birth of Jesus:

... it was midnight when the little newborn King came out of my maternal womb. But the night turned into day; He who was the Lord of light put to flight the night of the human will, the night of sin, the night of all evils; and as the sign of what He was doing in the order of souls, with His usual Omnipotent Fiat the midnight turned into most refulgent daylight. All created things ran to sing praise to their Creator in that little Humanity. ... In sum, all created things recognized that their Creator was now in their midst, and they all competed in singing His praises…

... offering Him my breast, I gave Him abundant milk—milk formed in my person by the Divine Fiat Itself, in order to nourish little King Jesus. But who can tell you what I experienced in doing this; and the seas of grace, of love, of sanctity, that my Son gave to Me in return? Then I wrapped Him in poor but clean little clothes, and I placed Him in the manger. This was His Will, and I could not do without executing It. But before doing this, I shared Him with dear Saint Joseph, placing Him in his arms; and—oh! how he rejoiced. He pressed Him to his heart, and the sweet little Baby poured torrents of grace into his soul. Then, together with Saint Joseph, we arranged a little hay in the manger, and detaching Him from my maternal arms, I laid Him in it. And your Mama, enraptured by the beauty of the Divine Infant, remained kneeling before Him most of the time.

Our Lady tells Luisa about an important lesson for us all in this act in which she placed Jesus in the manger: how radical detachment, even from holy things, is necessary; but how in the Divine Will there is perfect happiness, nevertheless.

Now, my child, a little word to you: you must know that all my joy was to hold my dear Son Jesus on my lap, but the Divine Will made Me understand that I should place Him in the manger, at everyone's disposal, so that whoever wanted to, could caress Him, kiss Him, and take Him in his arms, as if He were his own. ... My child, the Divine Will is demanding and wants everything, even the sacrifice of the holiest things.

... How happy we were. Because of the presence of the Divine Infant and of the Divine Will operating in us, that little grotto had changed into Paradise. It is true that pains and tears were not lacking, but compared to the immense seas of joy, of happiness, of light, which the Divine Fiat made arise in each of our acts, they were just little drops plunged into these seas.

She proceeds to share great lessons in the journey of the Three Kings:

Now, my child, another surprise: a new star shines under the vault of the heavens, and with its light, it goes in search of adorers, to lead them to recognize and adore Baby Jesus. Three individuals, each distant from the other, are struck by it, and invested by supreme light, they follow the star, which leads them to the grotto of Bethlehem, to the feet of Baby Jesus. What was not the astonishment of these Magi Kings, in recognizing in that Divine Infant the King of Heaven and earth—the One who had come to love and save all? In fact, in the act in which the Magi were adoring Him, enraptured by that celestial beauty, the newborn Baby made His Divinity shine forth from His little Humanity, and the grotto changed into Paradise; so much so, that they were no longer able to detach themselves from the feet of the Divine Infant—not until He again withdrew the light of the Divinity within His Humanity. And I, putting in exercise the office of Mother, spoke at length of the descent of the Word, and fortified them in faith, hope and charity, symbolized by their gifts offered to Jesus; and, full of joy, they withdrew into their regions, to be the first propagators ...

Elsewhere, however, Mary shares her lament that there were only three, saying:

> My dearest child, my Heart of Mother rejoiced at the faithfulness, correspondence and sacrifice of these Magi Kings, to come to know and adore my Son. But I cannot hide from you a secret sorrow of mine: among many, only three ...

> But my love of Mother was not yet content; I wanted to place the sweet Baby in their arms, and—oh! with how much love they kissed Him and pressed Him to their breasts. They felt paradise in advance within them. With this, my Son bound all the gentile nations to the knowledge of the true God, and placed the goods of Redemption, the return to faith of all peoples, in common for all. He constituted Himself King of the rulers; and with the weapons of His love, of His pains and of His tears, ruling over everything, He called the Kingdom of His Will upon earth.

And in the volumes, Luisa is given more insight by Jesus into the wise men's journey:

> My daughter, see the order of my Divine Providence: for the great portent of my Incarnation, I chose and made use of a Virgin, humble and poor; and, as my custodian, who acted as father to Me, the virgin Saint Joseph, who was so poor that he needed to work in order to support our lives. See how, in the greatest works—and the mystery of the Incarnation could not be greater—We make use of people whose outward appearance attracts no one's attention, because dignities, scepters, riches, are always fumes which blind the soul and prevent her from penetrating into the celestial mysteries in order to receive a great act of God, and God Himself. But in order to manifest to the peoples the coming of Myself, Word of the Father, upon earth, I wanted and made use of royal authority, of learned and erudite men, so that, by their authority, they might diffuse the knowledges of the God now born and, eventually, also impose themselves on the peoples. But, in spite of this, the star was seen by everyone, yet only three of them move, pay attention and follow it. This says that, among all, these alone possessed a certain dominion of themselves, such that, as it formed a little empty space within their interior, beyond the appearance of the star, they felt my call echoing in their interior. And heedless of sacrifices, of gossip, of mockeries—because they were leaving for an unknown place and they had to hear much talking—disregarding everything and dominating themselves, they followed the star that was united to my call which, more than speaking star, resounded in their interior, enlightened them, attracted them, and spoke many things about the One whom they were to visit; and, drunk with joy, they followed the star... But what was not their surprise in seeing the star stop, not above a royal palace, but above a vile hovel? They did not know what to think, and were persuaded that there was a mystery—not human, but Divine. When they animated themselves with faith, and entered the grotto and, kneeling, adored Me, as they bent their knees, I revealed Myself, and I let my Divinity shine forth from my little Humanity, and they recognized Me as the King of kings—the One who was coming to save them; and, promptly, they offered themselves to serve Me and to lay down their lives for love of Me. But my Will made Itself known, and sent them again into their region, to let them be, in the midst of those peoples, the criers of my coming upon earth. See then, how necessary are the dominion of oneself and the empty space in one's heart, in order to let my call resound, and to be fit for knowing the truth and for manifesting it to others.[826]

The Circumcision and the Prophecy of Simeon

Returning to Mary's revelations to Luisa, we see that the joy of the days spent with Jesus in the cave

---

[826] January 6, 1927.

turn to great sorrow with the circumcision and with the prophecy of Simeon.

> My child, what an example the Celestial Baby gives: He, who is the Author of the law, obeys the law. He is born only eight days ago, and He makes it a duty for Himself, and submits Himself to the harsh cut of circumcision; an indelible cut — as indelible as the union He came to form with degraded humanity. This says that sanctity is in doing one's own duty, in the observance of the laws, and in fulfilling the Divine Will. Sanctity without duty does not exist. It is duty that places order, harmony, and the seal on sanctity ...

> As He was circumcised, we gave Him the Most Holy Name of Jesus, wanted by the Angel. In pronouncing this Most Holy Name, the joy, the contentment, was such as to sweeten our sorrow. This Most Holy Name of Jesus makes hell tremble; the Angels revere It, and It sounds sweet to the ear of the Celestial Father. Before this Name, all bow down and adore. Powerful Name, holy Name, great Name; whoever invokes It with faith will feel the marvels, the miraculous secret of the virtue of this Most Holy Name. Now, my child, I recommend to you: pronounce this Name, "Jesus", always. When you see that your human will, weak, vacillating, hesitates in doing the Divine, the Name of Jesus will make it rise again for you in the Divine Fiat. If you are oppressed, call upon Jesus; if you work, call upon Jesus; if you sleep, call upon Jesus; and when you wake up, may your first word be "Jesus". Call Him always; it is a Name that contains seas of grace, but which He gives to those who call Him and love Him.

In hearing of the prophecy given by Simeon, Mary reveals to Luisa:

> Now, my child, you must know that in the light of the Divine Will I already knew all the sorrows I was to suffer — and even more than that which the holy prophet told Me. But in that act, so solemn, of offering my Son, in hearing it being repeated to Me, I felt so pierced that my Heart bled, and deep gashes opened in my soul.

But this sorrow — greater than any person other than her own Son can ever or will ever experience — never has the last word. Mary continues, now speaking of their journey into Egypt:

> Now, dear child, in the midst of the sorrow for human ingratitude, and amid the immense joys and happinesses that the Divine Fiat gave Us, and the feast that all Creation made for the sweet Baby, the earth became green again and flowery under our steps, to give homage to its Creator. The sun fixed on Him, and singing His praises with its light, it felt honored to give Him its light and heat. The wind caressed Him; the birds, almost like clouds, alighted around Us, and with their trills and songs, made the most beautiful lullabies for the dear Baby, to calm His crying and favor His sleep. My child, since the Divine Will was in Us, We had power over everything. So we arrived in Egypt, and after a long period of time, the Angel of the Lord told Saint Joseph that we should return to the house of Nazareth, because the cruel tyrant had died. So we repatriated to our native lands. Now, Egypt symbolizes the human will — a land full of idols; and wherever the little Child Jesus passed, He knocked down these idols and cast them into hell.

(This is yet another stunning overlap with other private revelations on the life of the Holy Family, wherein we see that the presence of the Child Jesus in Egypt miraculously demolished the idols therein).

Although not in this particular work, we do find in Luisa's volumes an amazing account of Jesus' own acts in Egypt, which should not here be left out:

> Now, you must know that My exile in Egypt was not without Conquests. When I was about three years old, from our little hovel I could hear the children playing and shouting in the street; and as little as I was, I went out in their midst. As soon as they saw Me, they ran around Me, competing with themselves for who could get the closest to Me, because My Beauty, the Enchantment of My Gaze and the Sweetness of My Voice were such that they felt enraptured for love of Me. So, they would throng around Me, loving Me so much that they could not detach themselves from Me. I too Loved these children, so I gave My first little sermon to these little ones, adapting Myself to their tiny capacity-since when Love is True, It not only tries to make Itself known, but also to give all that may render one Happy in time and Eternity; more so, since, possessing innocence, they could easily understand Me.

> And would you like to know what My Sermon was about? I said to them: 'My children, listen to Me. I Love you very much and I want to make you know about your Origin. Look up at Heaven. Up there you have a Celestial Father who Loves you very much, and who was not satisfied to be your Father only from Heaven-to guide you, to Create for you a sun, a sea, a flowery earth to make you happy; but, Loving you with Exuberant Love, He

wanted to descend inside your hearts, to form His Royal Residence in the depth of your souls, making Himself sweet Prisoner of each one of you. But, to do what? To give Life to your heartbeat, breath and motion. So, as you walk, He walks in your steps; He moves in your little hands; He speaks in your voice ... and because He Loves you very much, as you walk or move-now He kisses you, now He squeezes you, now He hugs you and carries you Triumphantly as His own dear children. How many hidden kisses and hugs Our Celestial Father does not give you! But since, being inattentive, you didn't let your kiss meet His kiss, and your hugs meet His Paternal Embrace, He remained with the Pain that His children neither hugged Him nor kissed Him.

'My dear children, do you know what this Celestial Father wants from you? He wants to be recognized within you, as having His own place in the center of your souls; and since He gives you everything-there is nothing He does not give to you-He wants your love in everything you do. Love Him! Let love be always in your little hearts, your lips, your works-in everything-and this will be the delicious food that you will give to His Paternity. "', "And, getting more excited, I told them: 'Give Me your word that you will always, always love Him! Say together with Me: "We love You, our Father who are in the Heavens. We love You, our Father who dwells in our hearts! ...

My daughter, at My Words some children remained moved, some enraptured; some squeezed themselves to Me so much that they wouldn't let Me go. I made them feel the Palpitating Life of My Celestial Father inside their little hearts, and they rejoiced and made feast, because they no longer had a Father who was far away from them, but inside their own hearts. And to make them firm and give them the strength to depart from Me, I Blessed those children, Renewing upon them Our Creative Power-invoking the Power of the Father, the Wisdom of Myself, the Son, and the Virtue of the Holy Spirit; and I told them: 'Go-you will return.' So they left ...

But they would come back the following days, almost in a crowd-a throng-of children. They set themselves to spy when I was about to go out, and to see what I was doing in our hovel. And when I went out they would clap their hands, making feast and shouting so much that My Mother would come out the door to see what was happening. O, how enraptured She would remain, in seeing her Son speaking to those

children with so much Grace. She felt Her Heart bursting with Love, and could see the first fruits of My Life down here, since none of these children who listened to Me-not a single one of them-was lost.[827]

The Holy Home of Nazareth

After leaving Egypt, Mary describes the Holy Family's time in Nazareth, wherein the Kingdom of the Divine Will was in full force, and wherein the way was prepared for its universal reign:

Dear child, in this house of Nazareth, the Kingdom of the Divine Will was in full force. Every little act of ours—that is, working, starting the fire, preparing the food—were all animated by the Supreme Volition, and were formed on the solidity of the sanctity of pure love. Therefore, from the littlest to the greatest of our acts, immense joys, happinesses and beatitudes were unleashed. And we remained so inundated as to feel ourselves as though under a pouring rain of new joys and indescribable contentments ...

Everything was peace, highest union, and each of us felt honored in obeying the other. My dear Son also competed in wanting to be commanded by Me and by dear Saint Joseph in the little jobs. Oh! how beautiful it was to see Him in the act of helping His foster father in the smith-work, or to see Him take food. But how many seas of grace did He let flow in those acts for the good of creatures? ... So, our hidden life of so many years served to prepare the Kingdom of the Divine Will for creatures. And this is why I want to make known to you what this Supreme Fiat operated in Me, so that you may forget your will, and as you hold the hand of your Mama, I may lead you into the goods which, with so much love, I have prepared for you.

In this home, Jesus entrusted to His mother the entirety of His Gospel, depositing all His goods in her, in which we see clearly (in the bolded words) that she was constituted Mediatrix of All Grace:

My dear Son placed in Me His works, His words, His pains—everything. He deposited even His breath into His Mama. And when, withdrawn in our little room, He would speak sweetly and narrate to Me all the Gospels He was to preach to the public, the Sacraments He was to institute, He entrusted everything to Me; and **depositing everything in Me, He constituted Me perennial channel and source**, because His life and all His goods were to come from Me for the good of all creatures.

Insight for the whole Church is seen in the pilgrimage of the Holy Family to Jerusalem, the loss of Jesus, and His being found:

> Once in Jerusalem, we went directly to the Temple, and as we arrived, we prostrated ourselves with our faces to the ground, we adored God profoundly, and prayed for a long time. Our prayer was so fervent and recollected as to open the Heavens, draw and bind the Celestial Father, and therefore hasten the reconciliation between Him and men. Now, my child, I want to confide to you a pain that tortures Me. Unfortunately, there are many who go to church to pray, but the prayer that they direct to God remains on their lips, because their hearts and minds flee far away from Him. How many go to church out of pure habit, or to spend time uselessly. They close Heaven, instead of opening It. And how numerous are the irreverences committed in the house of God! How many scourges would be spared in the world, and how many chastisements would convert into graces, if all souls strived to imitate our example ...
>
> [When they found Jesus ...] Upon merely seeing Him, I felt life come back to Me, and immediately I comprehended the secret reason of His being lost. And now, a little word to you, dearest child. In this mystery, my Son wanted to give to Me and to you, a sublime teaching. Could you perhaps assume that He was ignoring what I was suffering? On the contrary, my tears, my searching, and my sharp and intense sorrow, resounded in His Heart. Yet, during those hours, so painful, He sacrificed to the Divine Will His own Mama—She whom He loves so much—in order to show Me how I too, one day, was to sacrifice His very Life to the Supreme Will. In this unspeakable pain, I did not forget you, my beloved one. Thinking that it would serve as an example for you, I kept it at your disposal, so that you too, at the appropriate time, might have the strength to sacrifice everything to the Divine Will. As Jesus finished speaking, we approached Him reverently, and addressed Him with a sweet reproach: "Son, why have You done this to us?" And He, with divine dignity, answered us: "Why were you looking for Me? Did you not know that I have come into the world to glorify my Father?" Having comprehended the high meaning of such answer, and adored in it the Divine Will, we returned to Nazareth.

Her Son's Public Life

Our Lady continues to narrate to Luisa the initiation of Jesus' public life:

> His hidden life is ended, and He feels the irresistible need of love to go out in public, to make Himself known, and to go in search of man, lost in the maze of his will, and prey to all evils. Dear Saint Joseph had already died; Jesus was leaving, and I remained alone in the little house. When my beloved Jesus asked Me for the obedience to leave—because He did nothing without first telling Me—I felt a blow in my Heart, but knowing that that was the Supreme Will, immediately I pronounced my Fiat—I did not hesitate one instant; and between my Fiat and the Fiat of my Son, We separated. In the ardor of our love, He blessed Me, and He left Me ...Dear child, I had received my Son from the Divine Will, and whatever this Holy Will gives, is not subject either to ending or to suffering separation—Its gifts are permanent and eternal. Therefore, my Son was mine; no one could take Him away from Me—neither death, nor sorrow, nor separation—because the Divine Will had given Him to Me. So, our separation was the appearance, but in reality We were fused together; more so, since one was the Will that animated Us. How could We separate?

Indeed, we can see that, living in His Will, Our Lady could never truly be separated from her Son; she was, rather, always with Him and observed all of His deeds; some of which she shares with Luisa:

> His first visit was to the holy Temple, in which He began the series of His preachings. But—ah! sorrow—His word, full of life, bearer of peace, of love and of order, was misinterpreted and badly listened to—especially by the erudite and the learned of those times ...
>
> Oh! how many times, after imparting His word, I saw Him forgotten by all, without anyone who would offer Him a refreshment; alone—alone, outside of the city walls; outside, under the vault of the starry heavens, leaning on a tree, crying and praying for the salvation of all. And I, your Mama, dear child, cried with Him from my little house ...
>
> But in seeing Himself rejected by the great, the learned, my beloved Son did not stop, nor could He stop—His love ran, because He wanted souls. So He surrounded Himself with the poor, the afflicted, the sick, the lame, the blind, the mute, and with many other maladies by which the poor creatures were oppressed—all of them images of the many evils which the human will had produced in them. And dear Jesus healed everyone; He consoled and instructed everyone. So He became the friend, the father, the doctor,

the teacher of the poor ...

In fact, the poor, the ignorant, are more simple, less attached to their own judgment, and therefore they are more favored, more blessed, and preferred by my dear Son; so much so, that He chose poor fishermen as Apostles, as pillars of the future Church.

Mary also has special lessons to share with Luisa about the wedding feast at Cana:

> We went there, not to celebrate, but to work great things for the good of the human generations. My Son took the place of Father and King in the families, and I took the place of Mother and Queen. With Our presence We renewed the sanctity, the beauty, the order of the marriage formed by God in the Garden of Eden—that of Adam and Eve—married by the Supreme Being in order to populate the earth, and to multiply and increase the future generations. Marriage is the substance from which the life of the generations arises; it can be called the trunk from which the earth is populated. The priests, the religious, are the branches; but if it were not for the trunk, not even the branches would have life. Therefore, through sin, by withdrawing from the Divine Will, Adam and Eve caused the family to lose sanctity, beauty and order. And I, your Mama, the new innocent Eve, together with my Son, went to reorder that which God did in Eden; I constituted Myself Queen of families, and impetrated the grace that the Divine Fiat might reign in them, to have families that would belong to Me, and I might hold the place of Queen in their midst. ...

In addition to this, my child, with my presence at this wedding, I looked at the future centuries, I saw the Kingdom of the Divine Will upon earth, I looked at families, and I impetrated for them that they might symbolize the love of the Sacrosanct Trinity, so that Its Kingdom might be in full force.

But this earthly ministry was of course only a temporary mission, and when the time came for its end, Jesus did not hesitate to return to His mother and ask her obedience again, before entering His passion:

> "Good-bye Mama. Bless your Son, and give Me the obedience to die. My Divine Fiat and Yours made Me be conceived, and my Divine Fiat and Yours must make Me die. Hurry, Oh dear Mama, pronounce your Fiat, and tell Me: 'I bless You and I give You the obedience to die crucified. So does the Eternal Will want, and so I too want'." My child, what a blow to my pierced Heart. Yet, I had to say it, because there were no forced pains in Us, but all voluntary ...

> I was inseparable from my Son; His pains were reflected in my Heart, liquefied by sorrow and by love, and I felt them more than if they were my own. So I followed Him the whole night; there was not one pain or accusation they gave Him, which did not resound in my Heart. But, at the dawn of the morning, unable to endure any longer, accompanied by the disciple John, by Magdalene and other pious women, I wanted to follow Him ...

26) Do the Rounds

A major theme in Luisa's revelations is the "Rounds." While puzzling to some at first, the Rounds in fact—like the rest of Luisa's revelations—are a Crown that fits perfectly on Catholic Tradition and spirituality as they have hitherto developed.

Before going into more detail on these, I would like to defer to Fr. Iannuzzi, who gives the following beautiful exposition of the Rounds (as well as some background on the same) in his book, *The Splendor of Creation*:

> St. Faustina's prayer to God encompasses the whole of creation, intercedes on its behalf, and restores it to its original splendor: "O my Creator and Lord, I see on all sides the trace of Your hand and the seal of Your mercy, which embraces all created things. O my most compassionate Creator, I want to give You worship on behalf of all created things and all inanimate creation; I call on the whole universe to glorify Your mercy. Oh, how great is Your goodness, O God!"

The opening chapter described how creation is transformed and set free from its slavery to corruption. We now see it unfolding specifically through God's activity in the will of the human creature, who by praying and acting in it, reunites and restores the rights of creation. As man makes his "rounds" in creation by mystically penetrating, transforming and sublimating all creatures in God, there awakens in him a deep respect and awe for the world around him. He acquires a new set of eyes, as it were, with which he beholds all created things as a sacred extension of God's divine being and beauty.

Because man in his desire to better the earth has taken from it without replenishing it, and has managed to disfigure it to the point of extinction, God reawakens within him the first impulse of love for the earth from which he came. Man was created for God through his relation to the earth, to its creatures and the cosmos. Thus the more he learns to respect the world around him, the more its resources and potencies are available to him in his service to God and to all creatures. Once man grasps this fundamental truth, God opens his eyes to a reality that stood before him in the days of Adam, where he beholds the Creator's handiwork in every creature, where he cultivates and shepherds the earth as God intended, and where he gives back to the earth for that which he received. Indeed it is in gaining respect for the earth that man gains respect for all life around him. For God fashioned nature in such a way that it takes very good care of man, it provides for him both physically and spiritually, and by its example, trains him to care for all other creatures.

And so as the soul progresses in its love for God through the world around it, its vision of God extends not only to all created things, but to all events and all circumstances of life as well. St. Paul affirms, "all things work for good for those who love God, who are called according to his purpose," and the Servant of God Luisa Piccarreta, Blessed Dina and St. Padre Pio add, "even sin." Here God reveals to the soul his omnipotence to precede, accompany and follow all of its past, present and future acts. He precedes its good acts by performing them before the soul was yet conceived, in order that the soul might repeat his actions with him in time and space through the use of its free will: He accompanies its actions that they might perfectly conform in intention and objectivity to the Divine Will, and he follows every act by applying its beneficent effects to all other creatures.[828]

In short: **Jesus wishes to find, in our own souls living in His Will, everything that He has done — in Creation, in Redemption, and in Sanctification.** How could it be otherwise? The whole point of Living in the Divine Will is that by way of this Gift, we become by grace what God has by nature. But all is in God; therefore, all must be in us. Jesus tells Luisa:

Now, my daughter, one who does my Will and lives in It, when she does her acts, draws into herself all the acts of my Fiat, which It has done and continues to do; and my Will draws the creature and her act into Its act. So, by virtue of Its one Will, It draws her into the heavens, into the sun, into the air — in everything. And do you know what happens then? No longer does one single Divine Reason and Will fill Heaven and earth, but another reason and will, human, which, dissolving within the Divine Reason and Will, remains — one can say — as the veil of the created things, but a veil that has reason and will, though sacrificed and identified with the Divine Reason and Will. And then it happens that my Fiat is no longer alone in loving, honoring and glorifying Itself in the created things, but there is another will, human, that loves It, adores It, glorifies It, as heavens, as sun, as air. In sum, it is present everywhere and in each distinct thing in which my Will reigns.[829]

This applies not only to Creation, but even more importantly to Redemption:

My daughter, just **as all Creation is veil which hides my Will,** in the same way, my Humanity and all of my works, tears and pains are as many veils which hide my Supreme Fiat. It reigned in my acts, triumphant and dominating, and It laid the foundations in order to come to reign in the human acts of creatures. But do you know who tears these veils to let It come out to dominate in her own heart? One who recognizes It in each one of my acts, and invites It to come out. She **tears the veil of my works, she enters into them, she recognizes the noble Queen, and she prays It — she presses It to no longer remain hidden; and opening her heart to It, she invites It to enter.**[830]

In other words, the Gospel is not a mere history lesson. It is a presentation of living acts which await our own Fiat.

Do not be frightened if this seems like a task ill-suited to your meager talents (though I confess I have had the same reaction). Like the Gift itself, the Rounds are operated by way of desire and asking: it is that simple. Jesus tells Luisa:

Furthermore, Our Divine Will is present everywhere, and Heaven and earth, and everything, are filled with It up to the brim. So, all are veils that hide It, but mute veils; and if in their muteness they eloquently speak of their Creator, it is not them, but my very Divine Will, hidden in the created things, speaks by way of signs, as if It did not have speech. It speaks in the sun by way

---

[828] *The Splendor of Creation*. Ch. 4.
[829] November 30, 1930.

[830] December 8, 1926.

of signs of light and of heat; in the wind, giving penetrating and ruling signs; in the air It gives mute signs, such as to make Itself breath of all creatures. Oh! if the sun, the wind, the air and all other created things had the good of the word, how many things they would say to their Creator. But, who is the speaking work of the Supreme Being? It is the [human] creature.[831]

All creation is a revelation, but it lacks the ability to glorify its Creator *explicitly*. That task is left to us, the aforementioned "speaking work" of the Supreme Being.

One of my favorite prayers has always been the Nicene Creed. Some might say "that is not a prayer; it is merely a statement of Faith." I disagree! It is a prayer—a statement of Faith, yes, but so much more, if approached with the awe that is due to it. I have always felt like I am, in spirit, standing before the realities I affirm with my lips; gazing with wonder upon them and relishing the fact that I know of their validity with absolute certainty, impressing my own love and adoration upon them and offering them back to the God Who gave them.

This approach to the Creed can inform our approach to the Rounds, in which we spiritually "re-do" all the acts of creation—past, present, and future—in the Will of God; approaching all that has transpired as a "Creed" of sorts—for we must recall from St. Alphonsus that nothing happens but the Will of God.

With the Gift of Living in the Divine Will we can do this by visiting (in a true bilocation of the soul, through our intention) all acts that have been done or will be done, and imprinting upon them our *Fiat Voluntas Tua*; that is, our "I love you, I adore you, I glorify you, God." In this, we subject all creation to the Divine Will, as is both our right and our duty as members of the common priesthood of the baptized, in this era in which God is unleashing His greatest Gift. In this, we cooperate with God in setting "*creation free from its slavery to corruption.*"[832]

Let us turn to other sources now in order to recognize that this spirituality is not essentially new (in the sense of it being an artificial development in Church history), but truly is the Crown of what has already been given to us.

"Man is nature's priest"—John Scotus Eriugena

Consider as well, the Old Testament canticle of Daniel's companions who were thrown into the fire by Nebuchadnezzar:

> So let our sacrifice be in your presence today
> and find favor before you;
> for those who trust in you cannot be put to shame.
> And now we follow you with our whole heart,
> we fear you and we seek your face.
> Do not put us to shame,
> but deal with us in your kindness and great mercy.
> ...
> "Blessed are you, O Lord, the God of our ancestors,
> praiseworthy and exalted above all forever;
> And blessed is your holy and glorious name,
> praiseworthy and exalted above all for all ages.
> ...
> Blessed are you in the firmament of heaven,
> praiseworthy and glorious forever.
> Bless the Lord, all you works of the Lord,
> praise and exalt him above all forever.
> Angels of the Lord, bless the Lord,
>
> praise and exalt him above all forever.
>
> You heavens, bless the Lord,
> praise and exalt him above all forever.
> All you waters above the heavens, bless the Lord,
> praise and exalt him above all forever.
> All you powers, bless the Lord;
> praise and exalt him above all forever.
> Sun and moon, bless the Lord;
> praise and exalt him above all forever.
> Stars of heaven, bless the Lord;
> praise and exalt him above all forever.
> Every shower and dew, bless the Lord;
> praise and exalt him above all forever.
> All you winds, bless the Lord;
> praise and exalt him above all forever.
> Fire and heat, bless the Lord;
> praise and exalt him above all forever.
> Cold and chill, bless the Lord;
> praise and exalt him above all forever.
> Dew and rain, bless the Lord;
> praise and exalt him above all forever.
> Frost and chill, bless the Lord;
> praise and exalt him above all forever.
> Hoarfrost and snow, bless the Lord;
> praise and exalt him above all forever.
> Nights and days, bless the Lord;
> praise and exalt him above all forever.
> Light and darkness, bless the Lord;
> praise and exalt him above all forever.
> Lightnings and clouds, bless the Lord;

---

[831] February 13, 1931.

[832] Romans 8:21

praise and exalt him above all forever.
Let the earth bless the Lord,
praise and exalt him above all forever.
Mountains and hills, bless the Lord;
praise and exalt him above all forever.
Everything growing on earth, bless the Lord;
praise and exalt him above all forever.
You springs, bless the Lord;
praise and exalt him above all forever.
Seas and rivers, bless the Lord;
praise and exalt him above all forever.
You sea monsters and all water creatures, bless the Lord;
praise and exalt him above all forever.
All you birds of the air, bless the Lord;
praise and exalt him above all forever.
All you beasts, wild and tame, bless the Lord;
praise and exalt him above all forever.
All you mortals, bless the Lord;
praise and exalt him above all forever."[833]

This is still in the public (official) Prayer of the Church in the Divine Office, the recitation of which is required of all clergy and religious. This particular canticle is proclaimed every Sunday, and it is therefore still an extremely important prayer. For God desires that nothing be left out. Consider the wonder of physical creation; it is, of course, nothing compared to the wonder of the human soul, but it is nevertheless a reflection of God. In fact, each created thing reflects some aspect or attribute of God, and it is our duty to recognize this and love Him with, in, and through that reflection.

Now, the reaction of some to this canticle goes like this: *"Okay, I get it! Creation is glorious and we should bless the Lord through it. But why such repetitiveness? Why such length of this going around Creation and blessing the Lord with it? We got the point after a couple of verses!"*

But this reaction actually *misses* the point entirely. **God's purpose in inspiring these verses and in guiding the Church Universal to pray them constantly is not about intellectually recognizing the fact; it is about, with one's will, going about all created things and operating this reality! In other words, this is real work to be done (albeit a work of pure joy), not mere data to be memorized.**

Would anyone who lives in a house on a mountaintop with breathtaking views always keep his blinds shut under the premise "I already know the view is beautiful, I needn't bask in it all the time"? Certainly not. One could almost say such a resident has a "duty" to bless God constantly for the beauty he is so fortunate to be able to enjoy visually each day.

What worldly constraints prevent most of us from doing, is nevertheless always accessible in spirit, through God's grace: by living in His Will and doing the Rounds. For in His Will, we do live on a mountaintop; but one more lofty and with a greater view—a view of past, present, and future; of all things in Creation, Redemption, and Sanctification—thus, we have a far greater duty than a millionaire blessed with a mountaintop villa.

***

We see Pope Francis continuing in this same thread in the Magisterial teaching from his Encyclical *Laudato Si*:

> The universe unfolds in God, who fills it completely. Hence, there is a mystical meaning to be found in a leaf, in a mountain trail, in a dewdrop, in a poor person's face …
>
> … not because the finite things of this world are really divine, but because the mystic experiences the intimate connection between God and all beings … Standing awestruck before a mountain, he or she cannot separate this experience from God, and perceives that the interior awe being lived has to be entrusted to the Lord …
>
> … Through our worship of God, we are invited to embrace the world on a different plane. … all the creatures of the material universe find their true meaning in the incarnate Word, for the Son of God has incorporated in his person part of the material world, planting in it a seed of definitive transformation …
>
> It is in the Eucharist that all that has been created finds its greatest exaltation. Grace, which tends to manifest itself tangibly, found unsurpassable expression when God himself became man and gave himself as food for his creatures. … In the Eucharist, fullness is already achieved; it is the living centre of the universe … The Eucharist joins heaven and earth; it embraces and penetrates all creation. **The world which came forth from God's hands returns to him in blessed and undivided adoration: in the bread of the Eucharist, "creation is projected towards divinization, towards the holy wedding feast, towards unification with the Creator himself"** …
>
> … The world was created by the three Persons

---

[833] Daniel 3. Excerpts.

acting as a single divine principle, but each one of them performed this common work in accordance with his own personal property. Consequently, "when we contemplate with wonder the universe in all its grandeur and beauty, we must praise the whole Trinity."… the Trinity has left its mark on all creation. Saint Bonaventure went so far as to say that human beings, before sin, were able to see how each creature "testifies that God is three". The reflection of the Trinity was there to be recognized in nature "when that book was open to man and our eyes had not yet become darkened". The Franciscan saint teaches us that *each creature bears in itself a specifically Trinitarian structure*, so real that it could be readily contemplated if only the human gaze were not so partial, dark and fragile. In this way, he points out to us the challenge of trying to read reality in a Trinitarian key.[834]

At the end of the same Encyclical, Pope Francis offers a prayer that contains within it many intimations of the Rounds:

Father, we praise you with all your creatures.
They came forth from your all-powerful hand;
they are yours, filled with your presence and your tender love.
Praise be to you!
Son of God, Jesus,
through you all things were made.
You were formed in the womb of Mary our Mother,
you became part of this earth,
and you gazed upon this world with human eyes.
Today you are alive in every creature
in your risen glory.
Praise be to you!
Holy Spirit, by your light
you guide this world towards the Father's love
and accompany creation as it groans in travail.
You also dwell in our hearts
and you inspire us to do what is good.
Praise be to you!
Triune Lord, wondrous community of infinite love,
teach us to contemplate you
in the beauty of the universe,
for all things speak of you.
Awaken our praise and thankfulness
for every being that you have made.
Give us the grace to feel profoundly joined
to everything that is.
God of love, show us our place in this world
as channels of your love

for all the creatures of this earth,
for not one of them is forgotten in your sight.
Enlighten those who possess power and money
that they may avoid the sin of indifference,
that they may love the common good, advance the weak,
and care for this world in which we live.
The poor and the earth are crying out.
O Lord, seize us with your power and light,
help us to protect all life,
to prepare for a better future,
for the coming of your Kingdom
of justice, peace, love and beauty.
Praise be to you!
Amen.[835]

The Pope himself is essentially here showing us how to do the Rounds and is telling us clearly that the Kingdom of God will come upon earth.

***

St. Faustina was also keenly aware regarding the importance of this task of glorifying God on behalf of all creation, even though she obviously did not see it through the lens of Luisa's revelations. Nevertheless, the same God inspired both mystic's writings, and how He wishes for us to respond is thereby clear. Consider this form of the Rounds of Creation which **Faustina composed**:

O my Creator and Lord, I see on all sides the trace of Your hand and the seal of Your mercy, which embraces all created things. O my most compassionate Creator, I want to give You worship on behalf of all creatures and all inanimate creation; **I call on the whole universe to glorify Your mercy. Oh, how great is Your goodness, O God!**[836]

Be adored, O our Creator and Lord.
O universe, humbly glorify your God;
Thank your Creator to the best of your powers
And praise God's incomprehensible mercy.
Come, O earth, in all your fine greenery;
Come, you too, O fathomless sea.
Let your gratitude become a loving song,
And sing the greatness of God's mercy.
Come, beautiful, radiant sun.
Come, bright dawn which precedes it.
Join in one hymn, and let your clear voices
Sing in one accord God's great mercy.
Come, hills and valleys, sighing woods and thickets,
Come, lovely flowers of morningtide;
Let your unique scent

---

[834] Pope Francis. *Laudato Si'*. May 24th, 2015. Excerpts from Paragraphs 233-238.

[835] Pope Francis. *Laudato Si'*. May 24th, 2015. Paragraph 246.
[836] St. Faustina, *Divine Mercy in My Soul*, Paragraph 1749.

Adore and glorify God's mercy.
Come, all you lovely things of earth,
Which man does not cease to wonder at.
Come, adore God in your harmony,
Glorifying God's inconceivable mercy.
Come, indelible beauty of all the earth,
And, with great humility, adore your Creator,
For all things are locked in His mercy,
With one mighty voice all things cry out;
how great is the mercy of God.
But above all these beauties,
A more pleasing praise to God
Is a soul innocent and filled with childlike trust,
Which, through grace, is closely bound to Him.[837]

This is the Rounds! Revealed clearly in the fully approved revelations to St. Faustina, we see her praying on behalf of all created things; even, as it were, commanding them to glorify and adore their Creator.

***

An edifying account of creation, the proper approach to it, and how we have lost that proper approach today, was written by Dr. Anthony Lilles in his book, *Hidden Mountain, Secret Garden*, which dovetails well with the Rounds, and in which we read:

> The first kind of messenger the Lord sends are all the different kinds of creatures and works that compose the beauty of visible reality. Our contemporary gaze is too dull and banal. We do not see the multiplicity of creation signifying the excessiveness of God's love for us. The only meaning of material things we often entertain is exhausted by our ability to manipulate or consume them. The vast multitude of messengers bursting into the present moment remains impenetrable to eyes blinded by such opportunism. For our own lack of wonder, the divine love letter, which visible creation tries to share with us in spectacularly tangible ways, is often left unread. Ignorance concerning the sacred purpose of creation, however, does not completely prevent the beauty of nature from conveying the message entrusted to it. Even souls furthest from God are occasionally enchanted: the glowing embers of a sunset, the crashing surf against coastline, the gentle whisper of the wind rolling across the plains, the magical starlight that from time to time twinkles on even the most polluted of cities. As we begin to pray, the Lord helps us to become more sensitive to such beauty
>
> … The reality is that, from the beauty of the smallest insect to the faint shining lights of the furthest stars of the furthest galaxy, the whole visible cosmos constitutes God's declaration of love to the whole of humanity, and His particular affection for each person individually. This radiant form of creation as a whole confirms Fyodor Dostoevsky's observation that beauty will save the world.
>
> How do we vigilantly attend to such a message? St. Augustine suggests a method for listening to what visible creation has to tell us. Question these things with our heart as we behold them and they say something to us. In other words, our natural sense of wonder at what is visibly manifest before us disposes us to something God wants to communicate. He suggests that when we gaze on the things God has made, their beauty speaks to us:
>
> "I spoke to all the things that are about me, all that can be admitted by the door of the senses, and I said, 'Since you are not my God, tell me about Him. Tell me something of my God.' Clear and loud they answered, 'God is He who made us.' I asked these questions simply by gazing at these things, and their beauty was all the answer they gave."
>
> God's visible creatures communicate to us spiritual realities all the time because visible creation is a gift to humanity and this gift is designed to point to the Giver. The message of visible creation, when we are open, produces a longing for God in us, a natural religious sense of things. **Blessed [now Saint] Elisabeth of the Trinity shared this conviction. For her, all of creation is a kind of sacrament, something that gives us God. Consider one's own heartbeat: drawing all the body's blood to itself and then sending it out to the body's furthest reaches. In this sense, each heartbeat is an incredible gift for which to praise God on many different levels. Through the heartbeat, we begin to see that God is the Author of Life, all life.**
>
> At the same time, the heartbeat spiritually signifies what God continually does for those He loves. By a movement of His heart He draws us close to Him in the deepest kind of friendship and communion. By another movement He sends us out into the world so that everyone (our friends, yes even our enemies) might not perish, but that they might have eternal life. A mind searching for God in prayerful silence often finds itself caught in the wonder of the things He has made. **Everything, even in a beat of the heart, is like a**

---

sacrament that communicates the love of God. Sometimes the mind awash in wonder discovers itself submerged in adoration, and astounded by the splendor of the Lord, it bows in humble silence.[838]

Here we can see it becoming even more clear that, just as God has clearly revealed hints of the Gift itself to the mystics of the 20th century all throughout the Church, so too has He done so with the Rounds.

***

Returning now to Luisa's revelations, we read Jesus telling Luisa that the stars manifest His Divinity and steadfastness, the sun His majesty, the wind His sovereignty, the sea His purity and refreshment, and the waves His continuous love. These are just some examples of how all of Creation speaks of its Creator and demands that its king—man—who alone among material creation has reason, impresses his own Fiat upon it.

All men have an intuitive understanding of the beauty of natural things and how each of them seems to contain within itself a pearl of mysterious and subtle wisdom. This is why all are drawn to the beauty of creation. The great St. Bernard of Clairvaux, Doctor of the Church, taught:

> Believe me, you will find more lessons in the woods than in books. Trees and stones will teach you what you cannot learn from masters.[839]

Jesus also gives Luisa many explicit lessons we can use to encourage this intuition along and claim the full glory of the reality to which it points. So let us now consider just a few of the many teachings Jesus entrusted to Luisa which expound upon this truth:

The Book of Creation

> Now, when the soul has her interior book full, she will know very well the external book of the Divine Will. **All of Creation is nothing other than a book** of It; each created thing is a page that forms an immense book, and of many volumes. So, having formed her interior book and read it thoroughly, she will be able to read very well the external book of all Creation, and in all things she will find my Divine Will in act of giving her Its Life, Its lessons, most high and sublime, and Its

delicious and holy food. [840]

> My daughter, each created thing calls the creature to do the Divine Will ... In fact, each created thing carries out a distinct act of Divine Will, and with that act it calls the creature to do Its Divine Will. Each created thing has received from God, for this purpose, a special delight, in order to attract the creature in a mysterious way to do His Divine Will. This is the reason for the order, the harmony of all Creation around the creature; in such a way that the sun calls with its light, and unleashing its heat, it calls her to do the Will of her Creator. [841]

The Sea

> [the Divine Will] makes Its exposition in the sea; and while, in the sun, symbol of the Eucharist, It gives Its light, Its heat, It gives innumerable goods—but always in silence: It never says a word, It never gives a reproach, no matter how many horrendous evils It may see—in the sea instead, in the veils of the water, It makes Its exposition in a different way. It seems to speak while forming its murmuring within the veils of the water; It strikes fear in its tumultuous billows and in the roaring waves; such that, if It invests ships and people, It buries them in the depth of the sea, and no one can resist it. My Will in the sea makes the exposition of Its power, and speaks in the murmuring; It speaks in the billows, It speaks in the gigantic waves, calling man to love It and to fear It. And in seeing Itself not listened to, It makes the exposition of divine justice, and changing those veils into storm, It hurls Itself at man, inexorably. "[842]

Fields and Trees

> Oh! if creatures paid attention to all the expositions that my Will makes in the whole Creation, they should remain always in act of adoration—to adore my Will exposed in the flowery fields, in which It spreads Its fragrances; in the trees loaded with fruits, in which It spreads the variety of Its sweetnesses. There is not one created thing in which It does not make Its divine and special exposition; and since creatures do not pay to It the due honors, it is your task to maintain the perpetual adoration of the expositions which the Supreme Fiat makes in the whole Creation. You, my daughter, are the one who offers herself as the perpetual adorer of this Will with no adorer and no requital of love on the part of creatures."[843]

---

[838] Anthony Lilles. *Hiden Mountain, Secret Garden*. Ch 4. "The Beauty of Creation"
[839] Epistola CVI, sect. 2
[840] July 6, 1931.

[841] June 18, 1930.
[842] February 26, 1927.
[843] February 26, 1927.

The Heavens

Among all created things, only the heavens are always fixed and never die-symbol of the stable goods of the Celestial Fatherland, that are not subject to changes.[844]

Water

It is symbolized by water: while it appears abundant in the seas, in the rivers, in the wells, the rest of the earth appears as if there were no water. Yet, there is not one point of the earth which is not soaked with water; there are no buildings in which water has not been the first element in order to build them; there is no food in which water does not hold its primary place; otherwise it would be arid food, which man could not even swallow. The strength that water contains is such and so great, that if it had free field to go out of the bounds of the sea, it would devastate and terrify the entire earth.

My Will is more than water. It is true that in certain points, epochs and circumstances, It is as though embounded within most extensive seas, rivers and wells; but there is not one thing, from the greatest to the smallest, in which my Will does not run and does not hold Its primary place—but as though hidden, just as the water is hidden in the earth, such that, although it does not appear, it is the one that makes the plants vegetate and gives life to the roots. However, when my love will make the Era of my Will arise—the New Era of the maximum benefit toward creatures—then will the seas, the rivers of my Volition overflow; and as Its gigantic waves come out, they will overwhelm everything into my Will—but no longer as hidden; rather, Its roaring waves will make themselves seen by all and will touch all. And those who want to resist the current, will run the risk of losing their lives. [845]

The Sun: perhaps the ultimate symbol of the Divine Will is the sun, which Jesus repeatedly appeals to in order to give an illustration for His Will itself.

The sun is the symbol of my Will. As It rises over the soul, It vivifies her, It bejewels her with graces, It gives her the most beautiful shades of the divine colors, It transforms her in God. And It does this all at once—it is enough to let It rise for It to operate wonderful things. By giving, my Will loses nothing, just as the sun loses nothing by doing so much good to the earth; on the contrary,

It remains glorified in the work of the creature. Our Being is always in perfect balance; It neither increases, nor can It decrease. But do you know how this happens? Imagine a sea full to the brim; a wind invests its surface and forms the waves, which overflow outside of the sea. In swelling, this sea has lost nothing, and just as the waters have overflowed outside, so have they immediately risen, and they appear at the same level as before.[846]

…you have seen how beautiful and enchanting is [the sun's] rising over the earth; how many effects it produces, how many different colors, how many beauties, how many transformations its light can produce, and how this sun has been placed there by its Creator in order to give life, growth and beauty to all nature. So, if this is what the sun does in order to fulfill its office given to it by God, much more does the Sun of my Will, which was given to man to infuse in him the Life of his Creator. Oh! how much more enchanting and beautiful is the rising of the Sun of my Will over the creature. By pounding on her, Its light transforms her, and gives her the different colors of the beauty of her Creator. By investing her and molding her, It penetrates into her and gives her sips of Divine Life, that she may grow and produce the effects of the goods which the Life of her Creator contains. Now, what would happen to the earth without the sun? Much more ugly and frightening would the soul be without my Will. How she decays from her origin! How the nightmare of passions and vices, more than darkness, makes her die, and prepares the tomb in which to bury her. But you have seen that the light of the sun can do good insofar as the plants, the flowers and the other things let themselves be touched and invested by the light, remaining with their mouths open in order to receive the sips of life which the sun gives to them. So it is with my Will. It can do so much good, it can infuse so much beauty and Divine Life, for as much as the soul lets herself be touched, invested, molded by the hands of light of my Will. If the soul gives herself prey to this light, abandoning herself completely in it, my Supreme Will will perform the greatest prodigy of Creation—the Divine Life in the creature.[847]

Among the glorious effects of doing the Rounds of Creation—so as to cause all things to be mystically contained within yourself—is, as Jesus reveals to Luisa, the impossibility of going to Purgatory:

---

[844] March 13, 1927.
[845] July 20, 1921.
[846] April 9, 192.
[847] May 10, 1926.

And if she could go to Purgatory, they would all feel offended, the entire universe would rebel, and they would not let her go alone to Purgatory. The heavens, the sun, the wind, the sea ... —all would follow her, moving from their places and, offended, they would say to their Creator: 'She is Yours and ours—the life that animates all of us animates her. How is this—in Purgatory?!' The heavens would claim her with their love; the sun would speak up with its light, the wind with its lamenting voices, the sea with its tumultuous waves—all would have a word to defend the one who has lived a common life with them. But since one who lives in my Will absolutely cannot go to Purgatory, the universe will remain in its place, and my Will will have the triumph of bringing to Heaven the one who has lived in It on this earth of exile. Therefore, continue to live in my Will, and do not want to darken your mind and oppress yourself with things that do not belong to you.[848]

***

But what, precisely, does "doing the rounds" entail? How do we begin? In one excerpt, Luisa describes the Rounds in Creation as such:

> As that immense void presents itself before my mind, I fuse myself in the Supreme Will and, as the little child, I begin my round again and, rising up on high, I desire to requite my God for all the love he offered all creatures at the moment of their creation. I want to honor him as the Creator of all things and so, going around the stars and in each glimmer of light, I impress my "I love you" and "glory to my Creator"; in every atom of sunlight that descends, again I impress my "I love you" and "glory"; throughout the entire expanse of the heavens, ... I impress my "love" and "glory"; on the mountains' peaks and in the depths of the valleys, I impress my "love" and "glory"; I wander throughout the hearts of every creature and, wanting to enclose myself within each heart, from within them I cry out, "I love you" and "glory to my Creator". Then, as if I had united every act in such a way that everything returns love and glory to God for everything he did in creation, I go to his throne and say to him: "Supreme Majesty and Creator of all things, this little child comes into your arms in the name of all creatures to tell you that all creation gives you not only a return of love, but also the just glory for the so many things you created for love of us. In your Will, in this immense empty space, everywhere I journeyed, so that all things may glorify you, love you and bless you. And now that I have rejoined

the bonds of love between you, our Creator, and all creatures that the human will had broken, as well as restituted the glory that everyone owed you, let your Will descend to earth that it may bind and strengthen all bonds between you, our Creator, and all creatures so that all things may return to the original order you had established."[849]

In a word, the purpose of the Rounds—which should not be seen merely as a stand-alone prayer, but rather as incorporated into the essence of the Gift itself—is to give God *perfect glory* on behalf of the whole human family and the whole world; past, present, and future. And it is to do so with each one of our acts—even our heartbeat and breath. How? *By asking to and intending to.*

***

We now conclude this chapter by again looking to the tradition of the Church, which will reveal just how beautifully the Rounds given to Luisa complete the development of this tradition that God has been guiding for centuries.

The Mystical Flora of St. Francis de Sales

Of all the saints, it is Francis of Assisi who is most known for his love of God's creation and his glorification of God by way of the beauty of this creation. But there is another Francis who perhaps exceeds him in this regard: St. Francis de Sales. This great Doctor of the Spiritual Life was unparalleled in his ability to see the glory of God displayed in each created thing; and not only to see it, but to use the Divine Reflections contained within them for the edification of the faithful.

In a work entitled *The Mystical Flora* (or, *Christian life under the emblem of plants*), many of these teachings of de Sales are compiled into one volume. Written in 1877, it bears an introduction from Bishop George Conroy, which reads in part:

> Men have forgotten that God's thoughts find expression in the visible, as well as in the invisible, world, and that inner and secret harmonies bind the natural and the supernatural together. The things of beauty which God has bidden arise on the earth lose half their grace, because men do not mount by them to the better understanding of the supernal beauty of the operations of that world which Faith reveals to our gaze...
>
> And when the line of the prophets was ended, and

[God's] Son had come to reveal His Father's will, He, too, loved to employ the objects belonging to the visible world He Himself had made to describe the secret things He beheld in the bosom of His Father. The spiritual edifice of His Church was as a city built upon a rock; His apostles were the salt of the earth and the light of the world; His faithful were sheep whose Shepherd He was; the history of man's soul was the history of the seed that is sown; His followers were to learn confidence in His Providence from the bird that lives in the air, and from the lilies that neither toil nor spin. And so was it also with the teachers whom He appointed to continue his work. In the writings of the Fathers and Doctors of the Church the eternal truths are continually presented to the mind imaged in comparisons borrowed from natural objects. St. Gregory the Great speaks of the visible creation as bearing upon it traces of the footprints of God, and he describes the world's beauty as a glad smile lighted by its conscious knowledge of its Maker s secrets, and nature's voices as the murmur of Divine truth rising upon the soul from all that lives and moves within the universe. It is the sense of this harmony between the natural and the spiritual worlds that gives its clearness and freshness to the language of the Catholic liturgy; it is the key to the pregnant symbolism of the sacraments. This it is which forms the " right heart," which the author of the "Imitation" [likely Thomas Kempis' *Imitation of Christ*] tells us " finds in every creature a mirror of life and a book of holy doctrine. To it no creature is so small and vile that it does not show forth the goodness of God," Few among the Church's writers surpass St. Francis de Sales in the skilful use of comparisons drawn from nature to illustrate the operations of grace in the spiritual life. In this he holds a place peculiarly his own.

In this, we see Bishop George beautifully refuting what is just another tragic casualty of a convergence of Protestant filthy rags doctrine, Darwinian evolution, and materialism. For he refutes the notion that the material world is an ugly thing, a bad thing, or a thing displeasing to God. And the works of St. Francis de Sales presuppose a healthy and proper approach to creation.

Although it would not be correct to say that de Sales is, in these passages, literally "doing the Rounds" — for he is primarily seeking to simply use the wisdom in created things for our instruction, inspiration, and edification — let us nevertheless use this wisdom in our undertaking of Luisa's Rounds of Creation. (All of these quotes are from the same aforementioned book; therefore, in lieu of footnotes I will simply state the page number from which each is taken.)

Look at the bees upon the thyme; they find therein a bitter juice, but in sucking it they convert it into honey, because this is their special power. O worldling! devout souls find much bitterness, it is true, in their exercises of mortification, but in performing them they convert them into sweetness and joy. Fire, flames, wheels, swords, were as flowers and perfumes to the martyrs, because they were truly devout. If devotion can sweeten the most cruel tortures, and even death itself, what will it not do for acts of true virtue? Sugar sweetens unripe fruit, and corrects whatever is harsh or hurtful in that which is quite ripe. Now, devotion is the true spiritual sugar which takes from mortifications their bitterness, and all danger from consolations; it cheers the poor and restrains the rich, it mitigates the misery of the oppressed and the insolence of favourites, the sadness of those in solitude and the dissensions of those who live together. It is like the fire in winter and the dew in summer. It knows how to abound and how to want, it makes honour and contempt equally useful; it bears, with even mind, pleasure as well as pain, and fills us with a wonderful sweetness. (Page 7)

How does it happen, think you, dear Theotime, that in the spring dogs lose the scent and track of an animal more easily than at any other time of the year? Hunts men and philosophers say that it is because at that time the herbs and flowers are in their full bloom, and the variety of their perfumes so deadens the dogs senses, that they cannot distinguish between the scent of the flowers and the scent of their prey. Certainly those souls who are continually filled with worldly desires, designs, and projects, never long for Divine and celestial love, nor can they follow the loving footsteps of the Divine Love who is compared to the roe or the young hart (Cant. ii. 9). (Page 17)

I say to you about dances, Philothea, what physicians say about mushrooms; even the best are good for nothing… if you are obliged occasionally to go to a ball, take care that your dancing be well seasoned. But how is this to be done? By observing due modesty, dignity, and a good intention. Eat very few, and that not often (the doctors say in speaking of mushrooms), for no matter how well prepared they may be, too many are dangerous. Dance little, then, and very seldom, Philothea, for, if you do otherwise, you are in great danger of becoming fond of it. Pliny says that mushrooms, being spongy and porous, draw towards them whatever is near them, and being near serpents, they are supposed to imbibe their poison. Balls, dances, and such nightly assemblies, draw towards them sin and vice, and excite quarrels, envy, jealousy, and foolish love-affairs, And as these exercises open the pores of the body, so in like manner they open the pores of the heart. By this means, then, if a serpent approaching whispers a lascivious word, or some basilisk casts an unholy glance upon us, our hearts are more easily caught by the poison. Oh, Philothea, these recreations are generally dangerous; they dissipate the spirit of devotion, weaken our strength, cool our charity, and waken a thousand bad affections within us…[850] (Pages 30-31)

We are apt to imitate the cravings of sickly women who long for fresh cherries in autumn and fresh grapes in spring. I do not approve of any person, who has a particular duty or vocation, desiring any kind of life but that which agrees with his obligations, or any exercises incompatible with his present condition. For, if so, he is sure to be dissipated and careless in performing his necessary duties. (Page 16)

They abstain from sin as a sick man abstains from melons, when told by the physician that if he eats them he will die; but still he longs for them, and bargains for them, and wishes at least to smell them, and envies those who are permitted to eat them. So, weak and feeble penitents abstain from sin for some time, but it is with regret, and they would be glad to sin if they could do so without being damned. They speak of sin with feeling and zest, and think those happy who commit it. (P. 13)

Nearly all the plants with yellow flowers, and even wild chicory, which has blue flowers, turn themselves always towards the sun, and follow his course. But the heliotrope turns not only its flowers, but even all its leaves, according to the course of this great luminary. In like manner, all the elect turn the flowers of their hearts, which is obedience to the commandments, towards the Divine will. But souls that are greatly possessed by holy love do not only keep their gaze fixed on the Divine goodness by obedience to the commandments, but also by the union of all their affections, following the course of this Divine sun in all that He commands, counsels, or inspires, without any reserve or exception whatsoever.

(Page 101)

As the olive tree, planted close to the vine, gives it its flavour, so charity communicates her perfection to the other virtues with which she comes in contact. But it is also true, that if the olive is grafted on the vine, it not only flavours it, but also gives it some of its juice. Do not then content yourself with having charity and the exercise of the different virtues along with it, but take care that it may be by it and through it that you practise those virtues, so that they may be justly attributed to it. (Page 102)

The fruit of a grafted tree is always according to what has been grafted upon it. If the graft is from an apple tree, it will produce apples; if from a cherry tree, it will produce cherries; but, nevertheless, the fruit always keeps the flavour of the trunk. In the same way, Theotime, our actions take their name and their species from the particular virtues from which they spring; but from holy charity they take the flavour of their holiness, for charity is the root and source of all holiness in man. And as the stock communicates its flavour to the fruit produced by the engrafting in such a manner that each fruit still preserves the natural quality of the graft from which it springs, thus also charity infuses its own excellence and dignity into the acts of all other virtues ; but, nevertheless, it leaves to each of them the special value and goodness which it has of its own nature. (Page 105)

As the rainbow, touching the aspalathus [a type of flower], deprives it of its own peculiar perfume, but gives it a more exquisite one, so when Divine love touches our passions, it takes away their earthly object, and gives them one that is heavenly. **Our appetites may be made spiritual if, before eating, we thus excite a motive of love**: "Ah! no, Lord; it is not to please this wretched creature, nor to appease this appetite, that I now seat myself at table, but in order, according to thy providence, to maintain this body, which Thou hast Driven to me, subject to this misery; yes, Lord, for so it hath seemed good to Thee" (Mat. xi. 26). If I hope for a friend's assistance, may I not say, " Thou hast so arranged our lives, O Lord, that we must ask for help and comfort from one another; and because it pleases Thee, I will apply to this man whose friendship Thou hast given me for this purpose." Is there any just subject of fear: "You wish me to be afraid, O Lord, so that I may take all proper means of avoiding this

---

[850] Please note that St. Francis de Sales wrote these words about the culturally prevailing dance of the 1500s and 1600s. Considering how extremely hesitant he is about even these, I think it is more than safe to say he would condemn the forms of dancing that became popular beginning in the 1920s.

inconvenience. I will do so, Lord, because such is thy good pleasure." If the fear is excessive: "O God, Eternal Father, what need we, thy children, fear? What danger could come upon the little chickens sheltered under thy wing? Come, then, I will do what is right to avoid this evil, of which I stand in such dread; but after that, Lord, 'I am thine, save thou me' (Ps. cxviii. 94); and no matter what may happen, I will accept it willingly, because such is thy good will." Oh, holy and sacred alchemy! O Divine solvent, by which all the metals of our passions, affections, and actions are converted into the pure gold of heavenly love. (Page 109)

There is a certain herb, which, if chewed, imparts so great a sweetness, that they who keep it in their mouth cannot hunger or thirst. Even so, those to whom God gives his heavenly manna of interior sweetness and consolation, can neither desire nor accept worldly consolations with any real zest or satisfaction. It is a little foretaste of eternal blessedness, which God gives to those who seek Him; it is the sugar-plum which He gives to his little children to attract them; it is the cordial which He presents to them to strengthen their hearts ; it is sometimes also the pledge and earnest of the eternal rewards. (Page 119)

If the most delicate fruit and those most easily spoilt, such as cherries, apricots, and strawberries, can be kept for a whole year by being preserved in sugar or honey, it is no wonder that our hearts, although weak and foolish, are saved from the corruption of sin, when they are preserved by the incorruptible body and blood of the Son of God, who is "sweeter than honey and the honeycomb." (Page 86)

Nothing makes one find chamomile so bitter as to take honey beforehand. When we come to relish Divine things, it will be no longer possible for the things of this world to excite our appetite. (P. 120)

Basil, rosemary, marjoram, hyssop, cloves, cinnamon, lemons, and musk, joined together unbroken, form a very agreeable perfume by the mingling of their various scents, but not nearly so good as the [liquid] distilled from them, in which the sweetness of all these ingredients combines more perfectly into a very exquisite perfume, that penetrates the sense with a much keener delight than when their fragrance is inhaled in the other way. Even thus love may be fostered in unions in which both corporal and spiritual affections are mingled together, but never in such perfection as when minds and hearts alone, separated from all sensual affections, are joined together in pure spiritual love. For the fragrance of affections thus commingled is not only sweeter and better, but more vivid, more active, and more solid. (Page 97)

Just as several grains of wheat, pounded and worked together, are made into a single loaf, which is composed of all these grains, which, though they were before quite separate from one another, are afterwards so joined and united that they can never be separated again, or distinguished apart, in the same manner the Christians of the early Church were so united, and had such fervent love for one another, that their hearts and wills were all mingled and confounded, but yet this holy fusion and commingling were not any hindrance to them ; and this made this bread, that was kneaded out of all these hearts, extremely agreeable to the Divine majesty. And again, as we see that out of many grapes, all pressed together, one wine is formed, so that it is impossible afterwards to tell which portion of the wine is formed out of such and such bunches of grapes ; even so the hearts of these first Christians, in which holy charity and affection reigned, were all one mystical wine, composed of many hearts, like so many different grapes. But that which caused so great a union amongst them all was nothing else than frequent communion, and this coming to cease or to be rarely used, holy love has come thereby to grow cold amongst Christians, and has lost much of its force and sweetness. (Page 86)

Part III: The Era of Peace

Mass of Our Lord Jesus Christ, King of the Universe:

Collect:
Almighty ever-living God,
whose will is to restore all things
in your beloved Son, the King of the
universe, grant, we pray,
that the whole creation, set free from slavery,
may render your majesty service
and ceaselessly proclaim your praise…

Preface:
… making all created things subject to his
rule,
he might present to the immensity of your
majesty
an eternal and universal kingdom,
a kingdom of truth and life,
a kingdom of holiness and grace,
a kingdom of justice, love and peace…

"This is our great hope and our petition: "Your Kingdom come" — a kingdom of peace, justice, and serenity, that will re-establish the original harmony of creation."

—Pope St. John Paul II

27) Why the Era?

As the cover of this book states—the greatest petition of the greatest prayer will not go unanswered.

When the Son of God walked on earth physically 2,000 years ago, He only taught one prayer. The climax of that one prayer which He taught is a petition that some have hitherto assumed is too good to be true:

THY WILL BE DONE ON EARTH AS IT IS IN HEAVEN.

Jesus has told Luisa—and through her, He has told the whole Church and the whole world—that it is *not* too good to be true. Too good for us to fathom, perhaps, but its fulfillment is a guarantee. The time will come when His Will is done on earth as it is done in Heaven.

Our own lives can and must live that reality even now by way of the Gift of Living in the Divine Will. But God always has His eye not only on an individual but on a people; and this revelation is the ultimate application of that principle.

The entire world is going to live in the Divine Will.

The Glorious Era of Peace that God will produce for the world through this holiness is radically beyond anything the world has ever seen; for all evil—ugliness, sickness, decay, destitution, everything—is the result of sin. When the cause is removed, the effect disappears.

In the Mass, the priest prays:

> "You are indeed Holy, O Lord,
> and from the world's beginning
> are ceaselessly at work,
> so that the human race may become holy,
> just as you yourself are holy."[851]

This is an official Liturgical Prayer of the Church, and it refers not to "some humans," but *"the human race."* This, indeed, is our destiny: to return to God at the end of time in a manner worthy of Him.

Just as Creation came forth from God's hand in the beginning as noble, beautiful, and holy, so too it

will return to Him at the end of time in a similar state. Thus, the words of Revelation will be fulfilled, and the Church, the Bride of Christ, will ascend to the altar of God for the Great Wedding that commences upon the consummation of history; not dirty, sick, and stained as she now is, but bejeweled and fully prepared "as a bride adorned for her husband,"[852] thanks to the Era of Peace.

Jesus tells Luisa:

> And if it were impossible that My Will could Reign on earth as in Heaven, My all Paternal Goodness would not have taught the Prayer of the Our Father, because to make impossible things prayed for, I would not have done; nor would I have recited it with so much Love as first, placing Myself at the Head of all; nor would I have taught it to the Apostles so that they could teach it to the whole world as the most Beautiful and most Substantial Prayer of My Church.
>
> I do not want impossible things, nor do I demand from the creature, nor do I Myself do, impossible things. Therefore, if it would have been impossible that My Divine Will come to Reign on earth as It does in Heaven, I would have taught a prayer useless and without effect, and I do not know how to do useless things. At the most I wait even centuries, but I must make the fruit of My taught Prayer arise, even more because Gratuitously, without anyone having told Me, I gave this Great Good that My Will would be done on earth as It is in Heaven ... Therefore, **everything I have manifested about My Will, is enclosed in these words alone: 'May Your Will be done on earth as It is in Heaven.'**[853]

Unfortunately, a few reactions are heard among some Catholics who have grown used to a certain set of assumptions regarding what the remainder of the history of time will look like. For when this glorious Era is described to them, they initially respond with one of the following rejections:

- *"No. We don't get to Heaven until we get to Heaven—this world will never really resemble it, by and large, in any meaningful way."*
- *"No. This side of Heaven will always be a miserable*

---

[851] Eucharistic Prayer for Reconciliation I
[852] Revelation 21:2
[853] February 24, 1933.

place full of sinners—full of war, crime, error, ugliness, corruption, murder, and the like—that is our nature and it will always be that way."

- *"No. Until Heaven, we and the world will always be stuck with original sin, and all the consequences of it, precisely in the same manner that we have always endured them since the Fall."*

These responses are perhaps understandable as an initial reaction. The problem arises when one clings to them even when they are proven incorrect. It is amazing how attached some people can become to an arbitrary habit! For all one needs to do in response to these rejections is ask:

"Where, in her 2,000 years of glorious history, has the Church's Magisterium taught a single one of these claims that you use to reject the Era of Peace?"

That question will, of course, always be met by nothing but a blank stare. For indeed, none of that ever has been taught by the Church.

Of course, these rhetorical questions simply reveal the absurdity of the habitual assumptions which some Catholics have acquired regarding what the remainder of history must consist in—the assumption that the world must always be essentially the same as it is now, and the Kingdom cannot come on earth in any more powerful form than it already has come by way of the Church as it is now, and that His Will cannot be done on earth as it is done in Heaven except perhaps in the lives of a few great saints.

The New Catholic Encyclopedia article on the Kingdom of God teaches that:

> The kingdom is also to be the main message of the preaching of Jesus' disciples… The prayer Jesus taught his disciples has as its center the petition that "thy kingdom come ... to earth, as it [already] is in heaven" (Mt 6:20; Lk 11:2… **This prayer implies that the kingdom is *not yet* fully realized on earth; it is to come in its fullness in the near future, as a divine gift.** The parallel clause "thy will be done" suggest that the kingdom means that God's will be done…The petition also implies that the kingdom already exists in its fullness in heaven, even if not yet on earth. Still, in the healing and exorcizing ministry of Jesus the kingdom is already present (Matthew 12:28; Luke 11:20 [Q]), in sign, by anticipation, in

germ.[854]

And Jesus tells Luisa:

> My daughter, when Adam sinned God gave him the promise of the future Redeemer. Centuries passed and the promise did not fail, therefore human generations enjoyed the blessings of the Redemption. Now, by My coming from heaven to form the Kingdom of Redemption, I made another more solemn promise before departing for heaven: The Kingdom of My Will on earth, which is contained in the 'Our Father' prayer… So after I formed this prayer in the presence of My heavenly Father, certain that he would grant Me the Kingdom of My Divine Will on earth, I taught it to My apostles so that they might teach it to the whole world, and that one might be the cry of all: 'Your Will be done on earth as it is in heaven.' A promise more sure and solemn I could not make […] My very prayer to the heavenly Father, 'May it come, may your kingdom come and your Will be done on earth as it is in heaven,' meant that with My coming to earth the Kingdom of My Will was not established among creatures, otherwise I would have said, 'My Father, may Our kingdom that I have already established on earth be confirmed, and let Our Will dominate and reign.' Instead I said, 'May it come.' This means that it must come and souls must await it with the same certainty with which they awaited the future Redeemer. For My Divine Will is bound and committed to the words of the 'Our Father.' And when My Divine Will binds itself, whatever it promises is more than certain to come to pass. Furthermore, since everything was prepared by Me, nothing else is needed but the manifestation of My Kingdom, which is what I am doing.[855]

Indeed, the Greatest Petition of the Greatest Prayer—uttered by the lips of the Son of God Himself and which He commanded all Christians to pray—will not go unanswered.

***

Now, we must remember a few things (and these also will be addressed in more detail in the next section). Sin remains an ontological possibility when the Divine Will Reigns on earth, even if not always a practical likelihood. In other words, it is "possible," but not feared. Just as even now, as you read these words, it is possible that you might jump out the nearest window; yet neither you nor anyone around you has the slightest fear that you will do so. More importantly, far from eclipsing or duplicating Heaven, **the Era has as its entire**

---

[854] *The New Catholic Encyclopedia*, Page 173.

[855] Fr. Joseph Iannuzzi, Doctoral Dissertation, 4.1.1

purpose our Heavenly Fatherland. While the Church will be rendered beautiful and glorious in the Era, its full perfection is only in Heaven; which we will await with more eager longing during the Era than we do even now. For although during the Era the glory of the Church will far outshine its present glory, we will then be more cognizant of our ultimate destiny (the Beatific Vision), thus our longing for it will increase in stride and far exceed its current degree, just as the closer a magnet is placed to a piece of steel, the stronger is the pull.

For we must recall that Jesus tells Luisa that His plan is to restore—to man and to the world—what was lost in the Fall. But the original glory of the Garden was not the ultimate destiny of man or the world; it was a preparation for this destiny (God's Original Plan—had Adam not sinned—was to, at the proper time, once the world had sufficiently prepared, become incarnate and receive the Kingship from Adam and thus initiate the Heavenly Wedding Feast for all eternity). So even with this restoration, we are not "finished." Quite the contrary, after the restoration we will still be in an epic struggle towards our ultimate destiny in Heaven; but it will be a beautiful, victorious, glorious struggle instead of an ugly, despairing, miserable one we often observe in the world today (not, of course, that it has to be that way even now!).

One day, Jesus told Luisa the following:

> Now the nations want to fight against one other, and those which believe themselves to be the most powerful are taking up arms to their teeth in order to destroy the weak nations. This is about total destruction, my daughter…
>
> … **the whole world is upside down, and everyone is awaiting changes, peace, new things**. They themselves gather to discuss about it, and are surprised at not being able to conclude anything and to come to serious decisions. So, true peace does not arise, and everything resolves into words, but no facts. And **they hope that more conferences may serve to make serious decisions, but they wait in vain. In the meantime, in this waiting, they are in fear**, and some prepare themselves for new wars, some hope for new conquests. But, with this, **the peoples are impoverished, are stripped alive, and while they are waiting, tired of the sad present era, dark and bloody, which enwraps**

them, they wait and hope for a new era of peace and of light. <u>The world is exactly at the same point as when I was about to come upon earth</u>. All were awaiting a great event, a new era, as indeed occurred. The same now; since the great event, the new era in which the Will of God may be done on earth as It is in Heaven, is coming—**everyone is awaiting this new era, tired of the present one, but without knowing what this new thing, this change is about, just as they did not know it when I came upon earth. This expectation is a sure sign that the hour is near**. But the surest sign is that I am manifesting what I want to do, and that turning to a soul, just as I turned to my Mama in descending from Heaven to earth, I communicate to her my Will and the goods and effects It contains, to make of them a gift for the whole of humanity.[856]

Although these words were spoken by Jesus to Luisa in the early 20th century, their truth has only grown more obvious. Everyone seems to realize—across religions, nations, cultures; and even in the secular arena—that the world is on some manner of great cusp. Every day more articles come out wherein the great minds of the world acknowledge that the end of an Era is upon us.

But only the few who read trustworthy private revelation have a notion of what comes next. Nevertheless, the expectation alone (as Jesus tells Luisa) is the sure sign of the impending transformation—and this expectation has reached a veritable fever pitch today.

Jesus also tells Luisa:

> So, my daughter, man degraded himself and lost all goods because he went out of my Divine Will. In order to ennoble himself, to reacquire everything and receive the rehabilitation of the marriage with his Creator, he must enter once again the Divine Fiat from which he came. There are no ways in the middle; not even my very Redemption is sufficient to make man return to the beginning of the happy era of his creation. Redemption is means, way, light, help—but not the end. **The end is my Will, because my Will was the beginning and, by justice, one who is the beginning must also be the end. Therefore, humanity must be enclosed in my Divine Volition to be given back her noble origin, her happiness, and to place the marriage with her Creator in force once again**. Therefore, the great good that my Redemption did to man is not

---
856 July 14, 1923.

enough for Our love, but it yearns for more. True love never contents itself; only then is it content, when it can say: 'I have nothing else to give him.' And knowing that man can return to be happy, victorious, glorious, in the noble state in which he was created by God—and this, by means of my Will reigning in their midst—this is why all the divine yearnings, the sighs, the manifestations, are directed toward making Our Will known in order to make It reign, so as to be able to say to Our love: 'Calm yourself, for Our beloved son has reached his destiny. He is now in possession of Our inheritance that was given to him in Creation, which is Our Fiat! And while he possesses what is Ours, We possess him. Therefore, the marriage is fulfilled once again, the spouses have returned to their place of honor; there is nothing left but to celebrate and enjoy a good so great, after so long a sorrow'.[857]

The profoundness of the truth contained in these words is so great that merely upon reading them, a soul in grace will doubtless have their light inundate his mind. For although many have long forgotten this fact (and God permitted it perhaps because the time was not sufficiently close at hand), it is of course true: **humanity must return to God in a similar state to that in which we came forth from Him**. If we were to say this will not be so, then we blaspheme God by considering Him to be like ourselves; we who begin a task only to give up later with the end result being worse than that with which we started, like a worthless contractor who completes the demolition and brings in the new raw materials only to leave them all in a few piles around the house he was supposed to completely renovate.

As Mark Mallett put it bluntly and quite accurately: **at the end of time, God's final words will not be "Oh well, I tried."**

> Somehow, after thousands of years of salvation history, the suffering, death and Resurrection of the Son of God, the arduous journey of the Church and her saints through the centuries… I doubt those will be the Lord's words in the end…God's Word will be vindicated. His promises will be fulfilled: creation will be renewed, although not perfectly until the end of human history. But

within time, the Scriptures speak of a triumph of Christ in which His peace and Gospel will reach the ends of the earth…Wisdom will be vindicated.[858]

***

But at this point, perhaps the greatest obstacle is not so much a rational argument but instead the simple vague temptation to doubt that so great a thing will come to be; for we are so used to disappointments.

Luisa herself was not at all unlike those who today are tempted to doubt that the Divine Will could ever triumph on earth. One day she was thinking to herself that "Nothing new, which is good, can be seen in the world. Sins have remained as they were; or, rather, they are worse… how can it ever be that, all of a sudden, man would give death to all vices, in order to give life to all virtues?" Jesus responded to her, saying:

> My daughter, yet, it will be so…Our Will will have Its return; It will have Its divine generations in the human will; more so, since this was Our Prime Act, through which all things were created—that Our Will would transform and regenerate the human will into Divine. Will is what came out from Ourselves—will is what we want. All other things were done in the secondary order, while this was done, established, in the primary order of Creation. At the most, it may take time; but the centuries will not end, until my Will does not obtain Its purpose. If It has obtained the purpose of regeneration in secondary things, more so must It obtain it in the primary purpose. Our Will would never have departed from Our Womb, if It had known that It would not have obtained Its complete effects—that is, that the human will would be regenerated in the Divine Will.[859]

It *will* come. This is a guarantee. We will speak more of the absolutely assured nature of its coming in a following section. But for now we must turn our attention to demonstrating beyond any doubt the orthodoxy of the Era, for there are a few who do not understand Jesus' teachings on the Era and they proceed, from their own misunderstandings by which they confuse it with the heresy of millenarianism, to denounce the Era.

[857] June 16, 1928.
[858] Mark Mallett. "Vindication and Glory." December 14, 2016. https://www.markmallett.com/blog/2016/12/14/vindication-and-glory/

[859] June 18, 1925.

28) On the Heresy of Millenarianism

Millenarianism, the heretical teaching that Jesus will soon come to literally reign on earth for a thousand years, thus instituting temporally the definitive perfection of the Church, is an enormous and growing problem today. It is essential that no follower of Luisa succumb to this diabolical trap, which seeks to replace our hope in the Heavenly eschaton with a worldly Kingdom of Christ.

Of course, Luisa's writings themselves nowhere teach anything like this heresy, but they do teach that a more complete coming of the Kingdom is in store for the world in the Reign of the Divine Will on earth that we pray for in each Our Father. Combine this true and orthodox teaching with the fact that heretical millenarian teachings are rampant today—especially among Evangelicals and quasi-Christian sects (e.g. Jehovah's Witnesses and Mormons)—and there is a potential for danger. It is a danger wherein one may be tempted to erroneously conflate these teachings entrusted to Luisa by Jesus with other—perhaps superficially similar, but in truth completely divergent (and heretical)— teachings that sometimes employ overlapping terminology.

But the reality is that this potential for danger seems largely unrecognized in Catholic circles. One *does*, however, regularly come across Catholics who, not understanding what the Church teaches on millenarianism (though quite convinced they are experts on the matter), proceed to denounce as heresy any expectation of a fuller coming of the Kingdom of God on earth and any temporal Glorious Era of Peace.

Continuing a tragically repeated pattern throughout Church history, some Catholics today are so overzealous in their condemnation of a given heresy that they wind up drastically expanding the nature of the heresy in their own minds, and they proceed to denounce many orthodox teachings. Thus, ironically, all they do is push people away from the very orthodox truths of the Church which they fashion themselves the champions of, and push people towards the various schismatic, heretical, or even apostate movements that embrace the teaching which these overzealous Catholics condemn.

This happens with certain traditionalists' condemnations of the Charismatic Movement; thus they push souls to Pentecostalism. It happens with the modern ultramontanists' insistence upon blind agreement with every mere opinion of the reigning Pope, thus they push souls to Eastern Orthodoxy. It happens with many well-meaning Catholics' knee-jerk opposition to anything new in the spiritual life, thus they push souls to the New Age movement. It happens with "professional" Catholics in their vociferous condemnation of traditionalism, thus they push souls who would be good Catholics to Sedevacantism. But it happens especially with teachings on the millennium.

All the aforementioned "condemners" have good points, and the essence of their concerns are valid. But they inflate their concerns to the point that they condemn what the Church never has condemned, seeing themselves as the heroes of a new inquisition, and accordingly they incessantly charge at windmills.[860]

One reason the Catholic Church has lost so many souls to Evangelical movements, the Mormon church, the Jehovah's Witnesses, etc., over the past few decades is because these denominations and sects allow for an outlet of the growing understanding among Christians that there *is* indeed a glorious Era about to dawn upon the world.

Since this almost universal—and correct—intuition is often met with nothing but scorn and denunciation in some Catholic circles, people tragically seek this outlet in these movements outside of the One True Church, where the genuine intuition is almost always mixed with the aforementioned dangerous (and even diabolical) errors. Thus, history repeats itself, and the Catholics who are ostensibly most concerned for the defense against a certain error themselves become the causes of the spread of the error they so fear and oppose.

Because many have been beguiled by the arguments of these overzealous writers, we must turn now to address the fallacies and falsehoods

---

[860] Cf. Don Quixote; imagined, but non-existent, threats.

which they promote.

Refutations of the Anti-Era Inquisitors

(Since this entire section deals only with refutations of a small group of critics, I recommend that those readers who are fortunate enough to never have stumbled upon their works simply skip it and move on to the next section.)

***

Although there is an enormous amount of support for the Era of Peace (the Reign of the Divine Will; the Coming of the Kingdom of God on earth) among those whose viewpoint is most authoritative and trustworthy (so much so that *dozens* of Catholic theologians, philosophers, priests, and even Bishops *and Popes*; and not merely in their opinions, but also in their Magisterium — could be cited as open supporters of it, as indeed they are in the next chapter of this book) — this veritable consensus is unfortunately not *entirely* unanimous among the public voices on the matter of instructing the faithful regarding what prophecy tells us is to come.

For there is a small group of laymen (they could be counted on one hand with fingers to spare) now throwing quite a fit about the anticipation, among followers of Luisa and countless other revelations, of the Coming of the Kingdom. Although none of them have the requisite qualifications to be deemed authorities on the matter (as far as I know, none of them even have advanced degrees in Theology, Philosophy, or Scripture, and none of them are professors on these matters),[861] they are nevertheless quite noisy on social media and the

"blogosphere," and they have written books on the matter, with some of them even having managed to secure connections at high levels in the Church — so they get quite a hearing.

The details of their methods differ,[862] but they all try in one way or another to accuse anyone who anticipates the coming of the Kingdom on earth to be a millenarian or "mitigated millenarian" heretic in order to have these "heretics" formally condemned by the Church and those who promote these "heresies" silenced.[863] **Hence, my reference to them as self-appointed "inquisitors." I understand this may appear polemical, but I do it in order to protect them.** Anyone who for whatever reason really needs to discover who these men are will be able to do so from what I provide in these pages, but **by including their names in this book I would be unnecessarily exposing them to shame in the future when, I hope and pray, they will realize the truth (for I do believe they are sincere Catholics who are simply misled at the moment),** and I frankly can think of no better anonymous title for them than "inquisitors," as their antics have rendered that title more accurate than any other.

There are seven errors into which these men most often fall:

1. Above all, they pervasively beg the question (commit the fallacy of circular reasoning) by *assuming* that anticipation of the Era amounts to millenarianism in their very attempts to argue that anticipation of the Era amounts to millenarianism.

2. They find the opinions of a few prelates and saints which reference their own speculations and then claim they have thereby identified a veritable tenet of Sacred Tradition that must be held by all Catholics on pain of heresy. [864]

---

[861] Nota Bene: I suppose I can think of one such writer, at least, who could be considered a theologian (due to being a Jesuit priest — all of whom are at least somewhat highly trained in theology): Fr. Antonio Spadaro. Most famous for his teaching that, in theology, "2+2 can make 5," he more recently (August 31, 2018) wrote: **"No, we don't need to think about a general purification** of the cliques of shady powers (God promised that there would not be another universal flood after the first one …). **It's not possible to eradicate the evil of the divisions of the Church**, moreover, as long as it remains human. A pure and **sinless Church would be an unreal abstraction**. Where there is man or woman there is always a shadow." Here and elsewhere, Fr. Spadaro discounts the very possibility of a glorious Era of the Church. He has even incorporated his views on Millenarianism as an essential component of his infamous

condemnation of Catholic-Protestant cooperation in America on the pro-life cause as an "ecumenism of hate." (La Civilta Cattolica . July 13, 2017.)

[862] More than one of them prefer personal attacks, slander, or petty attempts to silence their opponents through manipulative complaints to superiors instead of any serious attempt at theological engagement – one can only guess at what stunts they will pull to try and force this book which you are now reading to be pulled off the shelves.

[863] One of them has openly admitted to me that this is precisely his goal.

[864] Being oblivious as to how the development of doctrine works within the history of the Church, they suppose that an opinion being common or prevailing among theologians in

3. They erroneously conflate one opinion of Augustine's with Church Dogma, supposing that once he has spoken an opinion on a matter, no other Father of the Church need be even considered if he gives a differing view, and no new understanding may ever be added to his analysis for the remainder of Church History.

4. They read their own interpretations into Magisterial statements, ignoring what the text of the statements themselves teach.

5. They wrongly interpret a relatively small amount of definitive and clear references to a Glorious Reign of Peace in fully Vatican approved Marian apparitions as a support of their own opinions which hold that no such Reign shall occur.[865]

6. They suppose that a particular verse or passage of Sacred Scripture having one valid interpretation or meaning necessarily implies that it cannot also have additional meanings beyond the one they have discovered, or further building on the one they have discovered.

7. They take the various references—whether in Scripture, Magisterium, or elsewhere—that speak of the unfortunate qualities of this world, and dramatically inflate them, treating them as nothing short of dogmatic declarations that the world is guaranteed to be, until its last moment, just as terrible as it is now and long has been.

So, read on to see the details of how each one of their arguments fails; and how, on the contrary, many veritable facts each succeed in independently defending the Era and disproving the entirety of the claims of these self-appointed inquisitors.

Promotion of an Eschatology of Despair

Lurking behind all their arguments, to an extent that varies from one to another, is a subtle form of despair. Some insist the end of time is nigh and that

any vestige of a period of peace can only possibly refer to what has already transpired, and others will grant a certain "peace" yet to come on earth that is scarcely worthy of the name. And still others insist that the Era of Peace cannot be anything but a veiled reference to Heaven itself. They will at once counter that they are not succumbing to despair but are purely insisting that all hopes be directed towards Heaven alone, and not earth. But this approach, while superficially noble, is in fact fatally flawed and is not Catholic.

Both Faith and Love have a temporal aspect. Hope does so in the sense that we can indeed sin against it even if our obstinacy in believing is nevertheless directed towards a truth that is not an Ex Cathedra proclamation (e.g. one who refuses to believe any Catholic Social Teaching that is not perfectly in line with his own political party's platform), and Love has a temporal aspect in the following sense: "*If any one says, "I love God," and hates his brother, he is a liar; for he who does not love his brother whom he has seen, cannot love God whom he has not seen.*"[866] So, too, does Hope have a temporal aspect, and whoever would reject that is not giving the full virtue of hope its due. **Whoever would be obstinate and refuse to believe that God can and will Triumph even on earth** *in the ways He promised that He would* **is sinning against hope, and deserves the admonishment given by the Archangel Gabriel to Zechariah** after the latter refused to respond with hope to the "unrealistic" and "unlikely" prophecy sent to him from God.

In his Encyclical *Spe Salvi*, which was dedicated to the topic of hope, Pope Benedict XVI wrote:

Saint Augustine, in the extended letter on prayer which he addressed to Proba, a wealthy Roman widow and mother of three consuls, once wrote this: ultimately we want only one thing—"the blessed life", the life which is simply life, simply "happiness". In the final analysis, there is nothing else that we ask for in prayer. Our journey has no other goal—it is about this alone … While this

---

the Church for a certain amount of time automatically elevates it to the level of infallible Magisterium – even though they cannot find a single Magisterial text that have wrought such an elevation.

[865] They ignore the fact that *no* Marian apparitions say there will not be a Glorious Reign of Peace, while **many** trustworthy apparitions insist there will be; some of which are already approved and others doubtless will be soon (the inquisitors love to pretend that all private revelations that prophecy the Era are entirely unapproved; which is nothing

short of slander, as you will see in a following section . Indeed, striving to interpret a silence one way or another is always doomed to failure – reminiscent of those who, after seeing that Vatican II did not explicitly condemn artificial contraception and thus assuming it was thereby rendered legitimate due to the "spirit of the Council" – were sorely disappointed upon the promulgation of Pope St. Paul VI's *Humanae Vitae*.

[866] 1 John 4:20

community-oriented vision of the "blessed life" is certainly directed beyond the present world, as such it **also has to do with the building up of this world ...**

[In the Middle Ages] It was commonly thought that monasteries were places of flight from the world (*contemptus mundi*) and of withdrawal from responsibility for the world, in search of private salvation. Bernard of Clairvaux, who inspired a multitude of young people to enter the monasteries of his reformed Order, had quite a different perspective on this. In his view, monks perform a task for the whole Church and hence also for the world. ... Contemplatives—*contemplantes*—must become agricultural labourers—*laborantes*—he says. The nobility of work, which Christianity inherited from Judaism, had already been expressed in the monastic rules of Augustine and Benedict. Bernard takes up this idea again. The young noblemen who flocked to his monasteries had to engage in manual labour. **In fact Bernard explicitly states that not even the monastery can restore Paradise, but he maintains that, as a place of practical and spiritual "tilling the soil", it must prepare the new Paradise.** A wild plot of forest land is rendered fertile—and in the process, the trees of pride are felled, whatever weeds may be growing inside souls are pulled up, and the ground is thereby prepared so that bread for body and soul can flourish. Are we not perhaps seeing once again, in the light of current history, that no positive world order can prosper where souls are overgrown?

In another section of the same Encyclical, Benedict calls out another problem with the form of hope that cares only about one's own self attaining Heaven: its Protestant excessive focus on individualism:

Drawing upon the vast range of patristic theology, de Lubac was able to demonstrate that salvation has always been considered a "social" reality. Indeed, the Letter to the Hebrews speaks of a "city" (cf. 11:10, 16; 12:22; 13:14) and therefore of communal salvation. Consistently with this view, sin is understood by the Fathers as the destruction of the unity of the human race, as fragmentation and division. Babel, the place where languages were confused, the place of separation, is seen to be an expression of what sin fundamentally is. Hence "redemption" appears as the reestablishment of unity, in which we come

together once more in a union that begins to take shape in the world community of believers ...

Benedict makes clear that redemption—for which we hope—is not merely about ensuring that one's own soul winds up in Heaven instead of hell. It is about "**reestablishment**," here and now, of the "**unity**" that was "fragmented" by sin, and this redemption "**begins to take shape in the world.**"

The old Catholic Encyclopedia article on hope refutes this "*Sola Coelum*" (Heaven Alone) view on hope even more bluntly:

Hence according to the generally followed teaching, not only supernatural helps, particularly such as are necessary for our salvation, but also **things in the temporal order, inasmuch as they can be means to reach the supreme end of human life, may be the material objects of supernatural hope**.

And this, indeed, is the entire reason we desire the Coming of the Kingdom; this is why we incessantly and fervently beg God in prayer—above all in the Our Father prayer—to "let His Kingdom come." The Coming of this Kingdom brings with it the greatest conditions on earth to serve as means to reach the supreme end of human life (Heaven), so that it can be the saint-making factory which God desires it be.

Now, the irony is that the ones most zealous in the condemnation of the Era of Peace are also zealous about eschatology in general; they usually agree that the end of an era is upon us and they rightly see many signs revealing the imminence of the transition. **But they are dead set in convincing everyone that this simply means the end of the world is here. They are, thus, the quintessential "doom and gloom" preachers**.

The obliviousness they display in promoting this view is baffling. One of them has taken Pope St. John Paul II's prophecy of an impending springtime of Christianity in the Third Millennium "of Christian Reunification" (John Paul II's own words), and, seemingly admitting that this Papal teaching naturally lends itself to the recognition that John Paul is prophesying a glorious renewal of the Faith on earth in the Third Millennium, the author proceeds to say this clear meaning of the Pope's words is not "likely."[867] With that, he

---

[867]This is a foreshadowing of how this unnamed author, years later, would in fact levy the accusation of "unrealistic" at this same Pope's Magisterial teaching (in *Familiaris Consortio*) that unrepentant adulterers cannot receive Communion.

encourages his readers to instead conclude, along with him, that John Paul was actually referring to the end of the world. Of course, this is absurd; **no Christian in his right mind would obliquely refer to the end of the world as a "springtime of Christianity" and a "millennium of Christian reunion" (and we can rest assured that Pope St. John Paul II was in his right mind). Rather, this is clearly a reference to a triumph of the Faith here on earth.**

Acknowledging that John Paul also taught that God has prepared a "new and Divine holiness," (John Paul II's own words once again), this author continues his argument that all these prophecies are references simply to the end of the world and Heaven thereafter. The irony is particularly poignant because that author was likely entirely ignorant of the context of the very words he cited (which we considered in Part One of this book on the authenticity of Luisa's revelations), in which we see that this saintly Pontiff was specifically and deliberately referring to the grace of Living in the Divine Will as both revealed to Luisa and promoted by St. Hannibal (on whom John Paul was preaching when he said those words). This is the same St. Hannibal who was Luisa's most zealous promoter, insisting as he did that in Luisa's writings we find **"...a mission so sublime that no other can be compared to it—that is, the triumph of the Divine Will upon the whole earth, in conformity with what is said in the 'Our Father'."**[868]

Nevertheless, **it is interesting that the author rightly concludes that this "new and Divine" holiness must be something held only by Jesus, Mary, Adam, and Eve (before the Fall)!** He proceeds to conclude that, due to this type of holiness coming for the Church, it must mean simply that the end of the world is coming. I suppose we should give him some credit: if one is indeed completely ignorant of the context of that quote from Pope St. John Paul II (and ignorant of many other things spoken of in modern trustworthy private revelations), it would make sense to think that a coming "new and Divine" holiness would entail the end of the world. Followers of Luisa and many others, however, know that it does not in fact mean the end of the world, but rather the dawn of a new Era of holiness in the history of the Church.

The author goes on to speak of the springtime of the Church as analogous to the Resurrection of Christ, which the Church must indeed follow. And the author is right on this, too. But during the whole discussion, **he forgets that the Resurrection took place on earth, and was followed by a significant period (40 days) of the continued earthly presence of Jesus.** If (as the author takes great pains to prove) the Church must follow the entire life of Christ—her head—then the Church, too, must have a period of earthly existence —post-Resurrection, pre-Ascension. This is the Era of Peace.

***

But why wander about in merely abstract theological considerations? Let us, rather, look concretely at what the inquisitors demand by insisting that all hope be only eternally oriented, by insisting that we dare not pray for the Coming of the Kingdom on earth. It is necessary now to ask the inquisitors a few questions:

- How many children must continue to die horrendous deaths until the end of time—in the midst of starvation, neglect, trafficking, war—to ensure that the world doesn't get 'too much like Heaven,' for you to feel that your opinion on the Era is vindicated?
- How many unborn babies must we continue to allow to be torn from limb to limb and vacuumed out of their mother's wombs so that we are not "millenarian heretics"?
- How many souls—masterpieces of God's creation, each far outweighing the glory of the entire material universe—must we remain content with being damned to hell for all eternity so that you can rest assured that we are still a sufficiently sinful world in accordance with your own Eschatological speculations?
- How many saints, eternally envisioned in their glory by God, must we stay content with never being made—instead remaining sin-and-error-mired worldlings—so that the Church, until the end of time, can linger sufficiently full of "weeds" in order for your insistences to be vindicated?

In brief: those who would put on airs of sophistication and glibly assert that the world must be essentially as it now is until the end of time should pause to consider the horrendous

---

[868] St. Hannibal's preface to the *Hours of the Passion*.

implications of such a view—instead of condemning others who pray for a better Era.

Heresies Implicit in Accusing the Era of a Messianic Duplication of Heaven

There is also a grave problem that the inquisitors reveal about their own beliefs regarding human destiny, and this revelation is given within their very condemnation of the Era; namely, the erroneous implicit assertion that the *end of man* is a terrestrial paradise. For this assertion is a necessary premise, albeit an unstated one, in the argument which condemns the Era on the grounds that the Era (by anticipating a glorious time on earth that is largely a restoration of what was lost at the Fall) places man's messianic, ultimate, and definitive hope within history.

Contrary to this error, Jesus makes clear to Luisa, in no uncertain terms, that:

"THE END OF MAN IS HEAVEN"—Jesus to Luisa. April 4, 1931

Here Jesus reiterates St. Augustine's most famous teaching in his *Confessions:*

> Thou hast made us for Thyself, Lord, and our hearts are restless 'till they rest in Thee.

But **a major school of theological thought today (within Catholicism) names this Augustine's "restless heart blunder."** Called the "New Natural Law" school, it seeks to define the End of Man (that is, the ultimate purpose or destiny of man) not as God Himself (i.e. the Beatific Vision of Heaven), but rather as the totality of natural goods. They are not claiming there will not be a Beatific Vision; only that it is not the proper end of human nature. And this is no far-left theological comedy generated by some "Catholic" college full of dissenters. No, it was founded by none other than Germain Grisez, who is considered a generally orthodox-minded theologian.

In 2005, Grisez gave a lecture entitled "The Restless Heart Blunder," in which he expounded upon his thesis. In the lecture, he states his wish to demonstrate that " ... classical restless-heart thesis was a theological blunder." In arguing that the Beatific Vision is *not* the end of man (contra Augustine, Aquinas, and Jesus' words to Luisa), he says:

> [The Beatific Vision; that is, Heaven,] is not itself a human good. It does not fulfill any capacity of human nature; it is not attained by a human act of intellect, will, or any other power. It is beyond anything human beings could ask or imagine.

Grisez is right in at least one rarely understood point: the Beatific Vision cannot be a human good *per se*; that is, it cannot be a due perfection in the very nature of man (Living in the Divine Will is the due perfection of man's nature); otherwise, God would have created an evil in creating Adam without it—which is a quite absurd notion. But what Grisez misses is that the Beatific Vision *is* nevertheless a **call** man finds within himself even once all his natural goods are perfectly fulfilled; a call of sufficient strength that one could even go so far as saying that man will experience a certain "restlessness" without it, as he longs for it earnestly. For it is rightly said that we are "*called* by nature to an end we cannot attain by nature."[869] It is precisely this yearning that Our Lady felt with such overwhelming power, even martyring power, that it snatched her from the earth and thus heralded her Assumption into Heaven.

Now, when the inquisitors attack the Era on the premise that the Era must be a lie because it would make Heaven obsolete, for "*we don't get Heaven until we get to Heaven*," as they say, they simply reveal that they are in lock-step with Grisez's error (and I am inclined to go so far as to say it may be a heresy). For this erroneous thesis of Grisez—though not articulated by the inquisitors or other critics of the Era—is nevertheless a necessary and unavoidable premise for their own accusations against the Era. But this is no small error and no minor problem. It is, rather, lethal to the entire Catholic spiritual tradition.

By insisting that the End of Man consists entirely in natural goods alone and is not ultimately ordered towards the supernatural Beatific Vision, Grisez is essentially reducing sanctity to merely the "good life" that any Pagan before Christ could have discovered without Divine Revelation (as Aristotle, in fact, did). This, for example, renders consecrated celibacy a defect, for it entails the sacrifice of a natural good (whereas Scripture, Tradition, and Magisterium all exalt consecrated celibacy as the

---

[869] I do not know the original source of this quote; I recall it from memory as taught in my graduate school theology lectures given by the Dominican theologian Fr. Brian Mullady.

greatest state in life); it makes fasting or any penance look ridiculous; it renders vain any prayer beyond a "small, healthy" dose of a "daily mind calming" exercise; and frankly, it makes the biography of just about any saint look comedic.

In fact, when one reads between the lines only a little in Grisez's arguments, one discerns no small hint of disdain in his mind for traditional Catholic asceticism and spirituality, which he seems to think is just "Neoplatonism" in disguise.[870] All these tragedies naturally flow from the mindset that refuses to see the Beatific Vision as the proper End of Man, which is the same mindset which refuses to acknowledge the utterly enormous and unfathomable difference between terrestrial paradise and Heaven. Yet, recall that this mindset is implicit (and sometimes even explicit) in condemning the Era on any grounds that it is Messianic or interferes with Heaven's sovereign dignity. And how ironic it is that, in a superficial attempt to defend one obscure view of Augustine's, the inquisitors succeed only in contradicting his most important teaching of all.

For even if the Era were to be a complete restoration of the Edenic Paradise across the whole world (and Jesus says to Luisa it won't be entirely, even though it will indeed *largely* consist in that), this still would not be the proper object of messianic hope. Our nature calls us to the Beatific Vision, which the Era does not give us. Compared to the Beatific Vision, Eden itself—in all its glory—is like the small flame of a candle next to the sun.

Consequently, when the Era comes, we will have even *more* longing for Heaven than we do now; for without sin so darkening our intellects as it does today, we will more readily understand just what we are missing in lacking the Beatific Vision, and we will almost impatiently, eagerly await the day when we depart from our earthly pilgrimage to go to our Heavenly Fatherland, even though our earthly pilgrimage will at long last be as God originally intended it to be.

Erroneous Extrapolations of Statements About the World's

Imperfections

Another common approach the inquisitors employ is the citation of various quotes—and we can find them scattered about Scripture and Magisterium—which reference the sorry state of the world or the Church, their nature as a struggle, or the full perfection thereof being found only in Heaven. The inquisitors then radically expand these references to pretend they serve as downright dogmatic declarations that the world is guaranteed to always be—until the bitter end of time—a rather terrible place which can never enjoy a more blessed existence than it now does and can never receive a more complete coming of the Kingdom. For example, we have:

1. In Matthew 13:24-30, Jesus gives the parable of the wheat and the weeds, in which He teaches that the weeds will exist until "the harvest time"
2. In Matthew 26:11, Jesus says "you will always have the poor with you"
3. In John 16:33, Jesus says, "In the world you have tribulation; but be of good cheer, I have overcome the world"
4. *Lumen Gentium*, paragraph 48 (also quoted in CCC 671) teaches that "The Church… will attain its full perfection only in the glory of heaven…already the final age of the world has come upon us…however, until there shall be new heavens and a new earth in which justice dwells, the pilgrim Church in her sacraments and institutions… dwells among creatures who groan and travail in pain until now and await the revelation of the sons of God"
5. *Gaudium et Spes*, paragraph 37, teaches: "For a monumental struggle against the powers of darkness pervades the whole history of man. The battle was joined from the very origins of the world and will continue until the last day, as the Lord has attested."

Other quotes are often cited as well, but since the others cited either manifestly have nothing to do with contradicting the Era or are of no authoritative weight (are not from Scripture or Magisterium), and merely relay the opinion of a prelate, we will

---

[870] In the same work of Grisez here cited, he implies that we may be in the very beginning of Church History, which may continue for "millions" more years. This may explain his willingness to play fast and loose with Tradition, for in such a scenario he might see himself as a potential Father of the Church. But even granting this as a possibility is harmful and contrary to the Prophetic Consensus. I treated this matter in the "On Private Revelation in General" Chapter of this book.

not bother to needlessly expand the length of this chapter by considering each one here. **It should go without saying that, in a matter as difficult as this (the details of what shall transpire for the remainder of history), some saints, Cardinals, and yes, even Popes (when they speak non-Magisterially) will err.** This should surprise no one, nor should anyone be so foolish as to cite such non-authoritative quotations as definitive refutations of the consensus of trustworthy private revelations or the best understanding of the Fathers and Scripture, or clearly Magisterial Papal Teachings of the 20th century, etc.

But we should certainly consider the quotes from Scripture and Church Councils listed above, since they are indeed authoritative and therefore they must be submitted to by all Catholics.

The first point we must settle pertains to the Vatican II references above. Beginning with item #4 in the list, we see that **"The Church… will attain its full perfection only in the glory of heaven", etc. No one who anticipates the Era denies that.** As we discussed in detail in the preceding section, the Church and all its members will long for its full perfection even more fervently during the Era than they do now. The full perfection of the Church is attained via the Last Judgment, the End of Time, the wedding of the Bridegroom (Christ) and the Bride (the Church), and the Beatific Vision. **The entire purpose of the Era is to prepare for this perfection of the Church in Heaven; and it is ridiculous to accuse these very preparations for the goal to themselves be contraventions of that goal.** Just as a bride prepares for the perfection of her engagement not by approaching the altar dirty (physically and spiritually), but rather prepared — beautiful both in soul and in body — so the Church must approach her definitive Heavenly perfection with the height of glory due to her on this earth. The glory of the bride approaching the bridegroom who awaits her at the altar is no obstacle to recognizing that this approach is nevertheless far from the full perfection of the purpose of the nuptials.

So, we can clearly see that there is no contradiction between the anticipation of the Era and this teaching on the attainment of the Church's full and definitive perfection (or any teaching related or similar to it). Nothing else in the quote from *Lumen Gentium* — nor from the entire Document — presents even any nominal issue for the Era.

We now turn to item #5, the quote from *Gaudium et Spes*. This quote says nothing about the form this "monumental struggle" will take; it only teaches that this struggle **exists** and will continue until the last day. This, again, is not a teaching anywhere contradicted by the anticipation of the Era nor is it something rejected by anyone who anticipates the Era. **The Era entails a transformation of the nature of this struggle; not an elimination of it.** The elimination of struggle is, of course, not until Heaven. **It is imperative that we merit through struggle as long as we are on this earth — even in the Era. For that is the purpose of earth, and to fail to have an opportunity for merit is to defeat the purpose of life on earth.** Jesus emphasizes this fact to Luisa in His revelations to her. Indeed, merit requires struggles; we could even say that merit requires "monumental struggle." But during the Era, the nature of this struggle will be completely different: permeated by victory, never detracting from peace, always beautiful and never ugly, never with temptations to contradict Faith, Hope, or Charity, etc.

If our struggles against evil in the world today too often look like a gruesome cage-fight, horrendous to even observe, and wherein one is tempted to be uncertain of the victor, our struggles against evil during the Era will be more like the many glorious victories won by Catholic armies aided by Heaven throughout the history of the Church; some of which entailed not a single life lost on the Christian side. Or perhaps even more like Pope Leo the Great calmly riding out to meet Attila the Hun and turning the latter with his whole army back with the mere power of his words (joined by the apparition of an Angel).

It is also possible (but I am merely speaking speculatively now) that the Era itself will largely consist in the spreading of the Era throughout the globe; that is, that it will dawn upon the earth in some regions before others, and it will be a great and glorious struggle for those who enjoy the Era to spread it across all regions of the earth. Alternatively, perhaps the struggle could consist in spiritual combat with demons alone — not with humans who have handed themselves over to demons, which is all too often the case today.

Whatever interpretation winds up being true, the important thing to remember is that there is no reason to suppose that there are any obstacles to recognizing the validity of the Era which can be found in these quotes from Vatican II, or any other Magisterial texts.

But before turning to the next objection (pertaining to points #1-3 above), we should observe how clearly mistaken the inquisitors and critics of the Era are regarding the Era itself; and, indeed, how much they reveal their own confusion about the purpose of life on earth and the nature of Heaven. It seems they have dreamed up an idea of the Era on their own—perhaps one consisting in naked saints teleporting around the clouds and gorging themselves on grapes while they play harps—and, since this dream of theirs is ridiculous and contradicts the Magisterium, they proceed to conclude that the Era itself must do so as well. That this is perhaps what they have done will become clearer still as we continue considering the remainder of their objections.

***

We now turn to consider the objections which cite the Scriptural verses listed above; objections that "sin always" will exist on earth and "suffering always" will as well.

The first potential answer to these objections is that, unless the teaching itself whence they arise makes it clear (whether in Scripture or in Magisterium), **in its own wording,** (not in how it has been hitherto non-authoritatively interpreted) that it is deliberately intending to refer to the entire remainder of history, there is no need to interpret it as anything but a statement of how the world **is;** not of how the world necessarily always **will be.**

Jesus knows how to make it clear when He is teaching that something will always be a certain way until the absolute end; for example, before He ascended to Heaven, He said, "I am with you always, **to the very end of the age.**"[871] Jesus' parable of the wheat and the weeds, on the other hand, only indicates that these two will grow together until "the harvest;" He did not say "until the end of time." The Harvest could easily refer to the Chastisements that will wipe out most evil men from the earth, as countless private revelations and prophecies throughout Church history indicate, as this will truly involve a Judgment of its own right, even though it is not the definitive Final Judgment at the end of time.

When Jesus says, "the poor you will always have with you," this also needn't necessarily refer to the absolute end of time, but could easily refer to the close of the Era in which they lived and until the commencement of the more complete chaining of Satan. In fact, a simple and honest reading of this passage (the *clear sense* of Scripture) is unlikely to cause one to conclude that Jesus is here issuing a prophecy that, until the very end of time, there will always be those living in poverty. If we examine the context of the passage itself, it is instead quite clear that Jesus is merely rebuking those who wrongly insist that service of the poor is at odds with the direct service of God (recall that Jesus was rebuking Judas for complaining about Magdalene anointing Him with costly perfume).

Time and time again over the past 150 years, Popes have issued Magisterial declarations insisting that peace and prosperity will indeed come to the world (see the forthcoming section in this Chapter on the Era on Papal Teaching & Magisterium), and that we must even now fight for the elimination of poverty, hunger, war, etc., which exists as a consequence of the world lacking this peace. Each time, the naysayers respond with condemnation, accusing the Popes of contradicting Jesus' words here in the Gospel of Matthew. What a tragedy that there are Catholics who wish to read their own hopeless interpretation into Jesus' words!

Now, rigor in following the words of Our Lord with precision is indeed an admirable virtue. But let us be impartial with that admirable rigor and see where it leads us. For this rigor must be taken to its logical completion if it is to have any merit whatsoever: and this completion in turn tells us that always means *always.* **If Jesus intended this as an absolute prophecy to be taken at its literal face-value, then it would be an insistence that we will have the poor with us in Heaven as well.** This is, however, obviously ridiculous, so clearly we can tell from the onset that this verse and others like it are not intended to be taken in an absolute and literalistic sense; instead, Jesus is leaving it to us to figure out the chronological extent of His "always," which, as we have seen, **cannot be an absolute "always."**

Magisterial statements, too, find no difficulty in making it clear what they mean by "always," as in

---

[871] Matthew 28:20

the case noted above where, in *Lumen Gentium,* the document specifically says "… only in the glory of heaven…" (which, as we have settled, presents no obstacle to the Era). We can see, then, that those who jump on the Magisterium's recognition of the world's problems (during the time the document is written) as a definitive declaration that the world will always be as it now is until the end of time, are guilty of manipulation.

However, I will readily grant that the proper interpretation of these teachings *may indeed* **be that they refer until the end of time.** In this case the Era simply consists in a radical reduction of sin, error, suffering, etc.; to the point where they largely lie dormant, even though they still exist in the world. For indeed, the mere possibility of sin (and suffering, etc.) is itself a tragedy (which is why, for example, Aquinas teaches that the human soul of Christ could not even have the *fomes*[872] of sin, contra the modernists who assert that Jesus *was* interiorly tempted to sin), and **Jesus tells Luisa that this possibility of sin goes away not during the Era, but only with the Beatific Vision in Heaven itself,** wherein absolute, ontological confirmation in grace occurs. Jesus also acknowledges to her the existence of sin in some form throughout even the Glorious Era. Furthermore, Jesus does tell Luisa that there will still be death in the Era (albeit of a much less horrendous nature than it tends to acquire now; it will be more like sleep), and that all suffering in the Era will be "full of triumph," as opposed to now, where so often it is full of misery and without any peace. This, of course, implies that there will be some suffering in the Era. He said to Luisa:

> … [in the Kingdom of the Supreme Fiat] fears and condemnations will have neither force nor life; and if there will be some suffering, it will be full of triumph and of glory.[873]

So **there simply is no reason to suppose that the truth of the Era is marred by the various statements, found in Scripture and Magisterium, about the unfortunate things of the world (sin, suffering, etc.) always existing, even if one does wish to interpret the "always" as indeed referring to the "end of time."** At the minimum, this does not mean that these things will always exist in the explosive, horrendous, world-dominating manner

that they do today! In fact, they could all be reduced to minuscule proportions, while still preserving the validity of all these statements and any others like them, even if the statements do refer to "until the end of time."

That I have presented several possible explanations and interpretations in this section should not raise any eyebrows. Unlike critics of the Era, I am not pretending to have the remainder of history figured out; nor do I have the slightest interest in presenting to my readers a precise eschatological timeline. I simply know that God is Faithful, and I know that He has promised a Glorious Era of Peace on earth during which His Will shall reign as it does in Heaven. I know this with certainty, as will anyone who sincerely educates himself regarding the facts.

Ignorance of the History of Millenarianism

Most of the inquisitors seem convinced that millenarianism is a mostly new issue; that is, a modern resurgence of an ancient heresy which only was problematic in the early Church and perhaps one or two other times. Thus, they feel that the time in which we live today is one of those unfortunate and temporary gray areas in between the revival of an old heresy and its formal Vatican condemnation (for indeed, a gap of time usually exists in such scenarios).

However, there is an enormous body of scholarly literature on millenarianism, and upon its perusal, one learns of just how many millenarian movements there have been throughout history, and how today is anything but unique in this regard. In other words, one learns how the Church has never been short on opportunities to expand its condemnation of millenarianism **to condemn** *any* **glorious Era of Peace, and it has never done so.** A brief overview of just a small sample of millenarian revivals follows:

- There were, of course, many millennial beliefs among the Fathers of the Church (more on this is found in the section dedicated to the topic in this book), and indeed, no one denies this.
- There were the carnal millenarians,

---

[872]Etymologically, "fomes" refers to tinder wood; something which could take flame from a spark. In other words, the

"fomes of sin" are the potency of sin– sin that lies dormant in the soul even though it's not acted upon.
[873] August 22, 1926.

condemned by Augustine and many others, who looked forward to a thousand-year reign of sense-indulgence on earth, inspired by the first century gnostic heretic, Cerinthus.

- In the 2nd century, there was Montanus and his "new prophecy" movement. Montanus taught an impending Era of the Paraclete, with new Public Revelations (coined 'prophecies') and said the Church would become purely spiritual, with his own disciples conveniently outranking the entire Catholic hierarchy.

- There was a relative calm in millenarian movements for several centuries after Constantine legalized Christianity; they likely still existed but just didn't make it into history books.

- There was the great millenarian anticipation (all throughout Christendom) around the year 1000, that looked forward to the physical Reign of Christ on earth commencing at what they saw as the final millennium.

- In the 13th Century, there were the Amaurians of France who preached the coming millennium of the Spirit—saying that they themselves were Christ reincarnated, and soon all would recognize their own Oneness with the Spirit. The 13th century also saw the effects of Joachim of Fiore (discussed in his own section in this book) and the "Spiritual Franciscans."

- In the 14th and 15th centuries, there were the Taborites and the Hussites, who preached millenarianism, adopting so called "Free Spirituality," and denouncing the Pope as the antichrist.

- In the 16th century, concurrent with the Protestant Revolt, there was an explosion of millenarianism. Among other places, this explosion was found in the Peasant's War (lead by Thomas Munzer, this rebellion held that the poor must inherit the millennial kingdom), the Anabaptist movement (wherein adherents sought to radically live in accord with Scriptural guidelines to prepare for the millennial reign), and elsewhere.

- In the 17th century, there were the Fifth Monarchy Men and the communities of "seekers" who believed, in their interpretation of certain Old Testament prophecies, that the four ancient monarchies described in Scripture handed on their power to the Hapsburgs, who would reign along with Christ's physical reign on earth. The "seekers" in particular, left wing Puritans in England, began to disdain formal religion and instead awaited God's manifestation through new public revelation.

- In the 18th century, there was the Chilean Jesuit, Manuel De Lacunza, who became famous for his book, *The Coming of Messiah in Glory and Majesty*, in which he posited a literal reign of Christ on earth, with the saints. His book became very popular in its own day, with many supporters and opponents throughout the Church. This work continues to inspire many Protestants to this day, and even in its own day, it inspired Edward Irving, founder of the so-called "Catholic Apostolic Church."

- In the 19th century, in China, there was the (amazingly, often forgotten) Taiping Rebellion, led by Hong Xiuquan, who regarded himself as Jesus' brother, divinely mandated to institute a Millenarian Kingdom known as the Taiping Heavenly Kingdom. This rebellion caused the deaths of tens of millions of people.

- In the 19th century, in America, there was William Miller who gathered a large following, claiming that Christ would "come again to this earth, cleanse, purify, and take possession of the same, with all the saints, sometime between March 21, 1843 and March 21, 1844." When this did not transpire, his "Millerism" nevertheless did not die, for it inspired the Seventh-day Adventist movement, with the Mormons adapting much similar theology (and both of these movements continue today).

- And of course, in the 20th and into the 21st centuries, we have the explosion of Evangelical Christians anticipating the coming "Rapture" and literal millennial Reign of Christ on earth in the flesh. Even simply listing the various movements that hold these beliefs would require its own chapter, and this exposition has been presented in many other works, so here I will leave it unexplored.

As is evident, millenarianism makes a comeback almost every century. The Church has had no shortage of opportunities to condemn in clear terms the teaching that a Glorious Era will dawn upon the earth, in the future, thanks to the intervention (or "coming") of Christ *in grace.* **But the Church *never has issued this condemnation.* Repeatedly—century after century—all that has been condemned are the notions of the following: a literal, physical reign of Christ**; the notion of an age in which the Church passes away for the sake of a coming "Age of the Spirit" in which there are new public revelations and no Sacraments or Dogmas; and the notion that this coming Era is truly Messianic (not distinct from the Beatitude of Heaven; the ultimate and definitive object of our hope). But nothing else has been condemned; only these notions—which are also radically unlike the Era as revealed by Jesus to Luisa (and in so many other trustworthy Catholic private revelations).

Ignorance of "Modified" or "Mitigated" Millenarianism

Recall that the most common and deceptive tactic of the inquisitors is to pretend that by condemning "modified" or "mitigated" millenarianism, the Church is thereby condemning *anything* which bears *any* resemblance whatsoever to millenarianism, which in turn—they erroneously argue—means that the Kingdom cannot come on earth in any more full way than it already reigns. But a seeker of the truth will, of course, desire to know the hard facts concerning what the Church means by these terms "modified" and "mitigated," and thus will endeavor to discover their origin.

Among the entries in the list presented in the previous section (and countless others which, for the sake of space, were left untreated), special attention must be given to the work of Fr. Manuel De Lacunza. For it is precisely here that we find the origins of the terms "modified" or "mitigated" millenarianism.

Fr. Manuel, in his work, *The Coming of Messiah in Glory and Majesty* (which in its time was published under the pseudonym Juan Josafat Ben-Ezra and became popular in the early 1800s), develops a new, *modified* millenarianism. He spends much of the book trying in vain to prove that the **only** heresies associated with millenarianism are the carnal view of it put forth by Cerinthus, and the "Judaizing" view (demanding universal circumcision), put forth by Nepos and Apollinarius, who wished for a "new Alexander" to impose Mosaic Law over the whole world. **Fr. Manuel wanted at all costs to maintain the literal reign of Christ on earth with the saints after the "first resurrection," and it was out of this desire that he invented "moderate" millenarianism** (which was almost certainly the inspiration for the language contained in the often-cited 1944 condemnation of mitigated millenarianism).

For example, in this book, Fr. Manuel writes:

> We know **no other error** of the Millenarians, than that which these same doctors have impugned, and with good reason condemned, in Cerinthus, Nepos, Apollinarius, and all their followers.[874]

We must bear in mind that whether it is historically accurate to say that the errors of Nepos and Apollinarius were in fact as Fr Manuel listed them to be, is immaterial; the only point here is to demonstrate that Fr. Manuel was indeed trying to argue for a "modified" or a "mitigated" millenarianism, in which Christ would still literally reign, but it would not be a hedonistic era or a "Judaizing" era.

While the inquisitors are quick to quote the 1944 condemnation of mitigated millenarianism, they seem unaware of the action of the Holy Office three years earlier, which is the first time we see a related term used in conjunction with millenarianism. For on July 11, 1941, the Holy Office condemned this book of Fr. Lacunza's, **"with specific reference to the book's _moderate_ Millenarianism."**[875]

So we can see that, while almost the entirety of the inquisitors' arguments rests on the false assumption that the condemnation of "modified" millenarianism necessarily entails the condemnation of any form of anticipation of a more full coming of the Kingdom of God on earth than we now enjoy, every single piece of relevant evidence points to the conclusion that **even**

---

[874]*The Coming of Messiah in Glory and Majesty.* Volume 1 p. 86.

[875]LACUNZA Y DÍAZ, MANUEL DE. New Catholic Encyclopedia. Page 274.

"modified" millenarianism entails a view wherein Christ literally reigns on earth in the visible flesh.

Misuse of Ratzinger's Works

Cardinal Ratzinger (Pope Benedict XVI) has been one of the most prolific theologians of the 20th century, and he wrote an enormous amount of material both before and during his Papacy. As he even made clear in the forwards to books he published *while he was Pope,* he never wanted his own theological published opinions to be taken as Magisterium. For example, in his foreword to *Jesus of Nazareth* (which he wrote while he was Pope, and which was published during his Papacy), he states:

> It goes without saying that this book is in no way an exercise of the magisterium, but is solely an expression of my personal search "for the face of the Lord" (cf. Ps 27:8). **Everyone is free, then, to contradict me**.[876]

To respect his own words, therefore, we must acknowledge that even if it can be shown that Ratzinger favored an Era-free eschatology, there is no one we offend more than Benedict himself when we pretend that citing his *opinion* on some theological matter should shut down discussion on the same. We must recall that Benedict is a humble and holy man; so humble, in fact, that in 2010 he openly admitted that he has harbored mindsets that might interfere with a full understanding of what God has in store for the times to come. For in his 2010 interview with Peter Seewald (published in the book, *Light of the World*)—given while he was Pope and also given long after he wrote all the Eschatological works cited by critics of the Era—we see the following exchange:

> **Seewald:** The homily you delivered on May 13, 2010, in Fatima struck a rather dramatic note. "Mankind has succeeded in unleashing a cycle of death and terror", you proclaimed, "but failed in bringing it to an end." On that day, before half a million of the faithful, you expressed a wish that is actually quite spectacular: "May the seven years which separate us from the centenary of the apparitions'; you said, "hasten the fulfillment of the prophecy of the triumph of the Immaculate Heart of Mary, to the glory of the Most Holy Trinity." Do these words mean that the Pope, who, after all, is the holder of a prophetic office, thinks that within the coming seven years the Mother of God could actually appear in a manner that would be tantamount to a triumph?

> **Benedict:** I said that the "triumph" will draw closer. This is equivalent in meaning to our praying for the coming of God's Kingdom. This statement was not intended—**I may be too rationalistic for that**—to express any expectation on my part that there is going to be a huge turnaround and that history will suddenly take a totally different course.[877]

There is no use trying to argue that Benedict is praising his own reason here; never once has the "rationalistic" attitude been deemed a good one in Catholic teaching. Instead, it is clear that Benedict is here admitting his own faults. Not only that, but the context of this quote leads us to the same conclusion; for in the question immediately before the one quoted above (recall that this exchange was an interview, and the response he gave to the last question would have been perfectly fresh in Benedict's mind), Benedict refers *negatively* to "rationalism," contrasting it to the theme of Our Lady's apparitions. And we also find in that quotation that Benedict, while answering the interlocutor's observation that he (Benedict) was less Marian than his predecessor, admits that he "grew up with a primarily Christocentric piety," almost, it seems, apologizing for not being as Marian as John Paul II (not that such an apology would be necessary!).

Context aside, there is simply no denying that admitting to a "rationalistic" approach is a humble admission to a fault. For rationalism, simply put, is the wrongful exaltation of reason alone to be the sole source of truth (and not faith). Fr John Hardon's "Modern Catholic Dictionary" defines it as "*A system of thought or attitude of mind which holds that human reason is self-sufficient and does not need the help of divine revelation to know all that is necessary ...*" There is nothing praiseworthy in that. Even though Benedict is here clearly speaking diminutively of his own eschatological assessments, it is unsurprising that critics of the Era have cited this exact quote as a demonstration of their own thesis, although it only succeeds in having the opposite effect they wish.

It is certainly true that a rationalistic look at the

---

[876] Pope Benedict XVI. *Jesus of Nazareth: From the Baptism in the Jordan to the Transfiguration.* Foreword.

[877] Peter Seewald and Pope Benedict XVI. *Light of the World.* Section 16.

world makes a huge change in history look impossible. But it *will* happen, nevertheless. We should be very understanding of Pope Benedict's predicament here: Luisa Piccarreta herself had exactly the same concerns; but unlike Luisa, Benedict did not have Jesus' sensible words immediately at hand. Luisa would often voice her concern that the coming of the Kingdom just did not seem likely. Time and time again, Jesus would remind her that she was using merely human analysis to look at the situation when such doubts arose in her mind, and that in those moments she was forgetting God's omnipotence and promises.

"With men this is impossible, but with God all things are possible."

-the Son of God. Matthew 19:26

We should acknowledge, however, that this whole point regarding Pope Benedict's words here quoted is not strictly necessary. By indicating that he did not believe a "huge turnaround" would occur, it is almost certainly the case that Benedict intended this diagnosis only from the perspective of rationally predicting whether worldly events themselves, upon examining their present nature, seemed likely to generate such a turnaround. **And no one who anticipates the Era supposes that it will come by way of a *turnaround*.**[878]

It would, in fact, be quite irrational to suppose that efforts aimed at promoting peace, dialogue, social justice, etc., will themselves generate a turnaround (if we are honest about their fruits and trends thus far, at least). That would be blind optimism. These efforts are still noble and necessary, as they are good in themselves and they help prepare the ground for the Era; but they simply will not generate some "huge turnaround" in which the Era itself consists. In sum, we can see that, **even if one does *not* believe that Benedict was humbly acknowledging a fault in admitting to rationalistic tendencies, it is still easy to see that**

Benedict's words are no affront to the Era, since all that these words do is dismiss the notion of the Era coming about by way of a *turnaround*—a way by which no one who anticipates the Era thinks it will come about.

***

But even with these considerations set aside, the fact remains that Ratzinger's works have been distorted to contradict the Era to a degree that Ratzinger himself never intended, even in the midst of his own admitted rationalism. We turn now to consider a specific book that twists Ratzinger's words to use them for an argument they do not entail.

In one large book that considers a multitude of eschatology-related questions and speculations and which was popular in the late 1990s, a section exists entitled '*THE "MILLENIUM"?*' [sic]. In this section, the author[879] seems to claim that "Catholic Tradition" teaches "absolutely" that any form of expectation of the Kingdom to come on earth is the heresy of millenarianism. (It is difficult to ascertain from his text exactly what the author is arguing. In some places, it seems he is only condemning as heretical the anticipation of a physical reign of Christ—and in this condemnation he is certainly correct; whereas in other points it seems he is erroneously condemning *any* millennial teaching and *any* expectation of a fuller coming of the Kingdom before the end of time). Despite his repeated claims that "Tradition" is the grounds for his thesis, he cites only *one* source from tradition: a single quote from St. Robert Bellarmine. This one quote has nothing to do with his thesis, and the only other sources he cites are the Catechism (which, as you will see in the next section, in no way denounces the Era), and one quote from a *commentary*, written by Cardinal Ratzinger, entitled *The Theology of History in St. Bonaventure*.[880]

The quote which he provides is from the following

---

[878] In none of the dozens of prophecies that speak of it – nor, indeed, in Luisa's – do we see the Era referred to as the result of a "huge turnaround" of events that changes the course of history. We see, rather, that the unanimous consensus of trustworthy private revelation indicates that the Era will come as a gift from God after the global Chastisements essentially demolish the entire world order as it now stands. This is not, by any stretch, a "turnaround," which implies a primarily human effort.

[879] I would not count this author – at least, not in accordance with anything I know thus far about his antics – among those

I have referred to as "inquisitors," as he seems to be a more serious and respectable individual than they, but it is nevertheless fitting to address his argument at this point.

[880] This commentary, in turn—in addition to in no way serving by itself as a definitive or Magisterial conveyance of Sacred Tradition, as it consists in the personal opinions of pre-Papacy Ratzinger, which Benedict himself has said we are free to contradict—only has any merit relative to his thesis if one already presupposes his thesis. In other words, we again see the logical fallacy of begging the question, or circular reasoning.

excerpt from Ratzinger's book:

> **Christ is the end of the ages; His birth coincides with the "end of the times:" On the basis of this axiom,** both Chiliasm and Montanism were declared heretical and were excluded from the universal church; for they both denied this vision and awaited still another period of more definitive salvation to follow after the age of Jesus Christ.

The author, however, does not include the bolded and underlined portion above from Ratzinger, which gives the necessary context for understanding the quote. The author's condemnation is fallacious because it assumes without demonstration that what he is condemning is, in fact, Chiliasm or Montanism. But **nowhere** has the Church defined these heresies as *consisting in* a position that anticipates the Coming of the Kingdom on earth in the future.

Indeed, the entire motivation of those who seek the Coming of the Kingdom is merely that they are praying the prayer that Jesus taught us—the central petition of the Our Father—with utmost Faith and confidence. They are **not** saying that this Coming of the Kingdom is a separate reality from Christ's birth: rather, they assert (as Jesus said to Luisa) that Redemption and Sanctification are one and the same; as He phrased it, "*two decrees of the same act.*" **No followers of Luisa await a new public revelation, a new Church, new Sacraments, a new form of salvation, a physical reign of Jesus, or anything of the sort.** The Chiliast and Montanist heresies both do await precisely these things; from which (and only from which) arises their heretical nature.

All followers of Luisa believe that Christ *is* indeed the end of the ages, and that His birth *does* coincide with the end of the times; whereas Ratzinger's rebuke here is directed only towards those who reject these claims. Furthermore, even during the Era, we will continue to pray "Thy Kingdom Come"! For during the Era, we will await more eagerly than we do even now the definitive perfection of the Kingdom found in Heaven alone.

It should also be noted that in this unnamed book, **the author inserts his own misleading bracketed remark into Ratzinger's quote after the word "Chiliasm,"** by way of which the author seeks to define Chiliasm subtly on his own terms that are in fact contrary to the Church sanctioned definitions. For in his bracketed comment, **he wrongly claims that Chiliasm consists in *any* millennial teaching; when, in fact, Chiliasm is a specific *type* of millennial belief, namely, millenarian*ism*.** According to the "New Catholic Encyclopedia" article on this heresy, **Chiliasm "** ... *teaches the visible personal rule of Christ on earth for a millennium before the end of the world.*"[881] **Nowhere has Chiliasm ever been authoritatively defined as *any* millennial teaching.** The author's entire argument rests upon this one erroneous definition.

***

But turning now to another work of Ratzinger, *Joseph Ratzinger in Communio: Volume 1: The Unity of the Church*, cited in a book written by one of the inquisitors, we see Ratzinger saying that Chiliasm…

> …refers to a conception which is indeed based in eschatology, that is, the expectation of a new world of God's making, but is not satisfied with the eschaton beyond the end of the world. Instead it virtually duplicates eschatology by expecting God to achieve his purpose with man and history in this world as well as the next, so that even within history there must be an end time in which everything will be as it should have been all along.

In a book he wrote, one of the other chief unnamed inquisitors even declared that this quote from Ratzinger was "prophetic," in that it describes exactly what those who anticipate the Era do. Here he simply assumes that the anticipation of the Era does in fact consist in the duplication of the Heavenly eschaton, condemned here by Ratzinger, in striving to prove that very thing.

He goes on to slanderously accuse all private revelations which prophesy the Era of being "unapproved"[882] (the slanderous nature of this accusation will become obvious in a following

---

[881] Page 488.

[882] Earlier in the same work, he implies that the only approved private revelation which speaks of the End Times are those of St. Hildegard. He proceeds to quote a couple small snippets (which actually in no way support his own erroneous Era-free eschatology) of her prophecies and

pretends he has thus succeeded in dismissing an entire body of dozens of trustworthy private revelations – many of which are approved – that speak in absolutely clear terms about the Era of Peace.

section of this book).[883] And he then continues, lamenting[884] that people "...*place themselves as some sort of authority on eschatological matters*," clearly implying that this is done by Fr. Joseph Iannuzzi.[885]

The irony only continues here because Luisa's revelations—and the many overlapping ones— are precisely the best remedies to correct those who would otherwise be misguided into duplicating the Heavenly eschaton in the earthly Era. Page after page of Luisa's writings make it abundantly clear that Heaven is a radically superior thing than the Era, and that *the entire reason for the Era is for the sake of Heaven.* **Through Luisa, Jesus is begging us to have Heaven be our focus, our love, our longing, and our concern.** He told Luisa that the very title of His revelations to her should be the "Book of Heaven."

Indeed, in the writings of Cardinal Ratzinger, there is a theme of perfectly valid—and very important—caution against any sort of immanentizing of the eschaton or temporalizing of salvation. It is easy to see that this concern gives the inspiration for his firm and commendable stand against millenarianism. Being keenly aware of Church history, **Ratzinger rightly sees grave problems arise whenever Heaven is neglected for the sake of earth. Jesus' words to Luisa are in full agreement.** (e.g., "*My daughter, man has forgotten Heaven for the earth.*"[886])

In this regard, Benedict is often contrasted to his successor, Pope Francis, who (some have said) is much friendlier to movements like Liberation Theology. But Ratzinger rightly sees how gravely problematic these movements are. He is also able to see similar problems in other movements.[887] He is aware of the grave traps in any brand of secular messianism and in even any apparently "Catholic" movement that has the net effect of distracting our concerns from Heaven and instead towards earth.

But it is equally easy to see that Ratzinger's concern has nothing to do with the contents of Jesus' revelations to Luisa, or with the main thrust of private revelation's consensus today on the Era, in which we see that the glory of the Era in no way substitutes for or eclipses that sovereign dignity that Heaven holds, and must always hold, in the minds and hearts of Christians; rather, it *enhances* it. **In the Era, we will long for Heaven even more fervently than we do now.**

To further understand Ratzinger's views, consider this excerpt from his 1988 book, simply entitled *Eschatology*:

> As early as the patristic Church, steps were taken to eliminate chiliasm through an effort to preserve biblical tradition in its proper form. The Joachimist dispute filled the thirteenth century and, in part, the fourteenth also, ending with a renewed rejection of this particular form of hope for the future. The present-day theologies of liberation belong in this context. But just why did the Church reject that chiliasm which would allow one to take up the practical task of realizing on earth parousia-like conditions? The rejection of chiliasm meant that the Church repudiated the idea of a definitive intra-historical fulfilment, an inner, intrinsic perfectibility of history. The Christian hope knows no idea of an inner fulfilment of history. On the contrary, it affirms the impossibility of an inner fulfilment of the world. This is, indeed, the common content shared by the various fragmentary pictures of the end of the world offered us by Scripture... In the last resort, such neo-chiliasm expresses a profound anthropological perversion. Human salvation is not to be expected from the moral dignity of man, from the deepest level of his moral personality... The values which sustain the world are turned upside down. A planned salvation would be the salvation proper to a concentration camp and so the end of humanity.[888]

Within the same work, Ratzinger powerfully condemns the various secular versions of this intra-historical fulfillment of man's ultimate destiny found in Hegelianism, Marxism, and elsewhere;

---

[883] While it may seem strange for me to call this "slander," since it is no sin to be "unapproved," I nevertheless maintain that this is what's being done, since so many of these revelations are approved, and it is essentially slanderous to accuse those who promote them of basing their expectations only on that which is unapproved.

[884] Thus achieving the very height of irony since he himself has zero qualifications in anything remotely related to theology in general (much less eschatology in particular).

[885] Which is particularly ironic, as Fr. Iannuzzi actually **is** an authority on these matters – being a Vatican educated Doctor of Sacred Theology whose professional focus is precisely these matters.

[886] April 6, 1922.

[887] for I am certainly not denying that Ratzinger's concerns in this realm are not limited to merely their implications for Liberation Theology

[888] Joseph Ratzinger. *Eschatology*. Ch. VI. Section2. b.

this, indeed, is the primary focus of his critique of the general problem of seeking to build within history that which only God can give outside of history. But I will not deny that Ratzinger also intends to condemn any supposed "Christianization" of this same problem.

We should, in fact, go even further than the inquisitors and critics themselves, and assert that there is a dire need today for a *revival* of Ratzinger's very concern which the inquisitors use against the Era; we must take it *more* seriously and conquer its object *more* zealously than do the very inquisitors and critics! For most Christians do indeed, as Jesus laments to Luisa, forget Heaven for the sake of earthly considerations; not merely as a sin fallen into and then repented of, but rather as a formal approach to Christianity itself that, in modern times, has replaced traditional Heaven-focused Christianity. This is what the Catechism condemns as the "deception of the antichrist."[889]

In accordance with this deception and Ratzinger's condemnations, the only thing some preachers talk about is social justice. Spiritual works of mercy are neglected for the sake of the corporal works of mercy. Heaven is discussed so rarely that one wonders if many priests even believe in it any more. "Building up the Kingdom" by "random acts of kindness" replaces the Scriptural admonishment to "work out your salvation with fear and trembling."[890] Every new parish Church that is built has bigger and bigger meeting rooms and smaller and smaller (not to mention uglier) sanctuaries. Holy, Heaven-focused events are not put onto the parish calendar, which in turn is chock-full of barbeques, bingo, and sports events. In the Church's political efforts, conquering the world for Christ by enthroning Him as King is replaced by advocating for more federal government welfare programs. Far more emphasis is placed on social activities than on Liturgy. The Liturgy itself begins to mimic worldly events or Protestant services, instead of giving a foretaste of the Heavenly Wedding Feast. Crucifixes disappear and felt banners take their place.

These attempts to replace messianic hope with worldly realities are nothing short of diabolical. They do, indeed, as the Catechism teaches so powerfully, form the "antichrist's deception."

The fact that the critics of the Era cannot see that this deception lies in what we have considered in the previous paragraph (and other related problems), and instead insist that it lies in trustworthy private revelation's insistence on the Era of Peace, is a testimony to their own spiritual blindness.

For these problems are so foreign to Luisa's revelations (and the general anticipations in private revelation on the Era); so diametrically opposite to them and repeatedly contradicted by them—that, were it not such destructive slander, it would be laughable to them attributed to her revelations. **In the just cause of fighting the temporalizing and immanentizing of the Eschaton and Salvation, there is no greater ally than Luisa's revelations.**

Abuse of The CDF Notification on Vassula Ryden

The next most cited work of Ratzinger in this realm is a CDF notification issued by him on October 6th, 1995, regarding Vassula Ryden, a Greek Orthodox mystic. The entire relevant portion of the notification is as follows:

> In addition to pointing out the suspect nature of the ways in which these alleged revelations have occurred, it is necessary to underscore several doctrinal errors they contain.
>
> Among other things, ambiguous language is used in speaking of the Persons of the Holy Trinity, to the point of confusing the specific names and functions of the Divine Persons. These alleged revelations predict an imminent period when the Antichrist will prevail in the Church. **In millenarian style,** **it is prophesied that God is going to make a final glorious intervention which will initiate on earth, even before Christ's definitive coming, an era of peace and universal prosperity**. Furthermore, the proximate arrival is foretold of a Church which would be a kind of pan-Christian community, contrary to Catholic doctrine.

This notification, in turn, is sometimes cited by critics of the Era as a definitive denunciation of it, and a total vindication of their own position. We should note, first of all, that it is not acceptable theological form to conclude that debate is ended and discussion is silenced on a question *even if it were* denounced tangentially in a juridical, non-

---

[889] Cf. CCC 675.

[890] Philippians 2:12

Papal action by the CDF (this notification was promulgated by Cardinal Bertone, and not Pope St. John Paul II, who was the Pope at that time), whose only purpose was to place a warning on a particular person (Vassula, in this case).[891]

But, as usual, the critics are gravely mistaken even in their more basic conclusion of what the text itself indicates; for they employ two fallacies. First, they treat the entire second quoted paragraph as if it were a list of anathemas from a traditional Magisterial Document; when, in fact, it demonstrably is not. Case in point, multiple assertions listed in that paragraph are obviously not doctrinal errors—it is not erroneous to wish for a pan-Christian Community (so long as one so wishes by virtue of praying that all currently non-Catholic Christians convert to Catholicism!), and it is equally obviously not erroneous to predict the imminent arrival of the Antichrist (Pope St. Pius X himself did so in an Encyclical, *E Supremi*, in paragraph 5).

Worse, **they pretend that the underlined portion of the bolded sentence doesn't exist, and that this notification condemns *any* notion of a "glorious intervention"** initiating on earth an Era of Peace. In fact, **that sentence only condemns the version of such a prophecy that are in *millenarian style*.**[892] (If, for example, one Catholic admonishes another, saying, "*Do not, in irreverent style, receive Communion,*" this does not mean "*do not receive Communion,*" it simply means "*do not do so irreverently.*")

Now, I am not acquainted with Vassula's writings, so I cannot speak on them in detail. But whether her writings succumb to *bona fide* millenarianism has nothing to do with whether or not Luisa's do the same,[893] as all Luisa's writings can easily be shown

to be free of that heresy, and furthermore they enjoy many Ecclesiastical Approbations (see Part One of this book).

Note, as well, that there are not any specific propositions, quotes, or teachings condemned in this CDF notification; therefore, we cannot ascertain what exactly is being condemned beyond millenarianism itself (and this of course tells us nothing new, for millenarianism was already condemned long before this notification). Finally, without *accusing* Ratzinger of error here, we must nevertheless *acknowledge that it is possible* he erred in supposing millenarianism existed in Vassula's writings. One can easily acknowledge that real possibility without in the least disrespecting the authority of the Church. A few years after writing this notification, **Ratzinger himself openly and specifically acknowledged that this CDF document and action was nothing but a warning.** He furthermore did not claim that the apocalyptic elements of her writings were heretical, but that they were *debatable*, **and he says he simply wasn't clear** on them. In his own words, we read:

> No, the Notification is a warning, not a condemnation. ... What we say is that there are many things which are not clear. There are some debateable apocalytpic [sic] elements and ecclesiological aspects which are not clear. Her writings contain many good things but the grain and the chaff are mixed up. That is why we invited Catholic faithful to view it all with a prudent eye ... [894]

An authoritative condemnation of a theological position cannot be extracted from a warning any more than dogma can be extracted from solely the authority of a private revelation.[895] To make the attempt is not only completely theologically confused, but is also philosophically flawed;

---

[891] In fact, the critics' zealous promotion of a procedural notification as one of their supposed strongest arguments to support what they say is venerable Catholic Tradition only demonstrates the weakness of their overall case and the lack of any demonstration that Tradition holds what they claim it holds.

[892] Of course, it is also possible that the author of this sentence does intend to imply that what follows the clause "in millenarian style" is in itself millenarian. But the wording of the notification itself does not indicate that this interpretation is the correct one and does not at all preclude the interpretation I have given above, therefore it cannot be simply assumed to be the correct meaning. But even if it were the correct meaning, and even if it did refer to any "final, glorious intervention" as Millenarianism, this still would not

suffice in achieving what the inquisitors wish to achieve through it, as the following paragraphs demonstrate.

[893] Recall that the majority of Luisa's writings have already received official Church approval via multiple Imprimaturs, and that all of Luisa's writings have been declared free of doctrinal error by multiple Vatican-appointed theologians. Remember, also, that for several years, her cause of Beatification has been proceeding smoothly.

[894] Interview with Cardinal Joseph Ratzinger by Niels Christian Hvidt. 1999. "The Problem of Christian Prophecy." https://www.catholicculture.org/culture/library/view.cfm?recnum=6439

[895] Inasmuch as private revelation does not bind as a matter of supernatural Catholic Faith, and dogma always does.

succumbing to the error that an effect can exceed its cause.

Fallacies Regarding the Antichrist and the Conversion of the Jews

Returning to the inquisitor's work which we began addressing several pages ago, we must address the conclusion of its attack on Fr. Iannuzzi with two more arguments—which deserve brief refutations.

First, the inquisitor begins with a point that is understandable: it seems strange, he says, that at the end of the Era, the Church's last moments before the General Judgment would entail a falling away of worldwide apostasy, with due regard to the fact that Christians will be more or less universally living in the Divine Will. But he ignores the fact that under this scenario, there *might well not* be such a falling away!

The explosive rise of Gog and Magog at the end of time, spoken of in the Book of Revelation, is not like the Antichrist's reign; for the latter's reign is lead up to by a Great Apostasy and is enabled by a population mired in sin and error, thus is open to his diabolical message, and they willfully and culpably receive his mark. The Antichrist's reign could be likened to the miserable death of a drug addict who, growing more mired in evil day by day, caps off these sorry days of his life with a lethal overdose. It is not difficult to see that this is the fitting analogy for the world today. The Antichrist, in other words, is the natural consequence of the sinfulness of the modern world. Gog and Magog, on the other hand, whom the Book of Revelation specifically says will come after the "thousand year" reign, will initiate an event more like the holy death of a martyr, wherein the chop of the blade of the executioner (that is, Gog and Magog), is really a beautiful act of the permissive Will of God—even though, directly, it is a sudden outpouring of Satan's explosive rage.

So, I think, it will be at the end of time; the world will be populated by holy Christians living in God's Will and eagerly awaiting their Heavenly Fatherland, longing earnestly to depart from their earthly pilgrimage (and even though this pilgrimage will consist in the Glorious Era, it is still

a mere nothing compared to Heaven). These Christians will not join sides with Satan, as he is briefly unchained from the pit, merely to act through this mysterious "Gog and Magog," in order to bring this Age to its ultimate and definitive end. It would not be fitting for the merciful God to directly "demolish" this beautiful world He made in the midst of the Great Conflagration that is prophesied for the End of Time, at which point we know from Scripture:

> … the elements will be dissolved with fire, and the earth and the works that are upon it will be burned up.[896]

Consequently, God allows Satan to explode, along with his legions of demons, out of the pit for a moment so as to envelop the world briefly with his evil and so justify the Wrath of God bringing an end to it.

There is no use trying to argue that this interpretation (taught by the clear sense of the Book of Revelation—see more on this point in its eponymous section in this book) is impossible by virtue of being contradicted by the Catechism: **the Catechism does not contradict this interpretation, for it never teaches that the Antichrist must *immediately* precede the end of the world.** It only teaches (paragraph 675-676) that the Antichrist must come "**before** Christ's second coming" and that his reign will constitute, for the Church, "**a final trial,**"[897] thereby clearly not intending to teach that the Antichrist will necessarily be the absolute last trial of the Church. We can see, then, that it is disingenuous to pretend this Catechetical teaching demands that we hold that the end of time follows the Antichrist immediately. But one could just as easily say that, considering the differences between the reign of the Antichrist and the explosion of Gog and Magog, the latter is scarcely even something that can be considered a "trial" for the Church, thus allowing one to, if he so pleases, continue considering the Antichrist's reign as "the" final trial.

Similarly, there is no use arguing that this interpretation contradicts Revelation 20 itself, for Scripture only says that Satan is loosed from his prison after the thousand years "*to deceive the*

---

896 2 Peter 3:10
897 Note that the inquisitor emphasized the word "final" in his own quote to draw the reader's attention away from the fact

that the Catechism was careful to use the indefinite article, not the definite article (that is, "a" instead of "the")

nations which are at the four corners of the earth"; but it says nothing about whether Satan actually succeeds in this deception. Deception is Satan's nature,[898] and to say that he is "coming out to deceive" simply says that he is emerging to strive to do what he does when he is not restrained by God. It could well be that the legions he "gathers for battle" to "surround the camp of the saints" consist simply in demons and damned souls. Unlike where the Book of Revelation speaks of the Antichrist and the Great Apostasy, this whole passage in Revelation 20 on the ultimate defeat of Satan says nothing whatsoever about any sort of falling away; in fact, the whole matter is treated in a mere few verses, implying that indeed this whole affair will be a swift phenomenon immediately before the end of time.

But if one wishes to hold fast to the interpretation which says that Satan, through Gog and Magog, will succeed in so deceiving the people at the end, then that, too, is fine, and presents no problem for the Era. The "four corners" of the earth refer to its extremities, which could easily be the geographic locations to which those who refuse to acknowledge the reign of the Divine Will flee. For perhaps relatively small portions of the world will reject Christ's dominion until the bitter end. Satan, naturally, will go to those portions of the world and deceive them, and under this interpretation it is those people he would "gather for battle" to "surround the camp of the saints."

Does even that not satisfy? Then feel free to hold that even the whole world—including those under the reign of the Divine Will—are indeed deceived by Satan through Gog and Magog. This, also, is no harm whatsoever to the Era! For as usual, this inquisitor in question—and the critics of the Era in general—makes an erroneous assumption and proceeds to build his whole argument on it alone. For the fact is that the Gift of Living in the Divine Will does **not** entail confirmation in grace. As Jesus tells Luisa:

> … for as long as the soul is a pilgrim one [that is, on earth], the doors do not close behind the Gift, but remain open…"[899]

It is therefore also possible that, even with the world's inhabitants living in the Will of God, there will be one last falling away, that God permits briefly—merely as one final reminder, for all eternity, of His unfathomable mercy. Perhaps He simply wants to—in his permissive Will—allow His children to fall into sin and error one last brief time, so that He can exercise His "greatest attribute," Divine Mercy, as this will essentially be His last opportunity to do so.

As is now clear, there is no way to use the Catechism, the Bible, or any attempt at a cunning mixture of the two, to condemn the anticipation of the Era. I have presented multiple possible interpretations of Revelation in this section because I do not feel strongly attached to any single one—nor, I think, should any of us. Although we should favor the clear sense of Scripture whenever possible, it is certainly also true that the Book of Revelation is quite mysterious, and if God wanted us to understand all the details clearly, He would have given them to us. The important thing is to remember that it is perfectly orthodox and perfectly safe in every other way to anticipate the Reign of the Divine Will on earth as in Heaven—that is, the Glorious Era of Peace.

I repeat what I stated a few sections above: that I have presented several possible explanations and interpretations here should not raise any eyebrows. Unlike critics of the Era, I am not pretending to have the remainder of history figured out. I simply know that God is Faithful, and I know that He has promised a Glorious Era of Peace on earth during which His Will shall reign as it does in Heaven.

***

But we should also take note that, in this same argument, the inquisitor furthermore reveals his own erroneous views on the nature of human free will; views perhaps shared by many critics of the Era. **He claims a "golden age" within history would "nullify" the essence of free will and therefore would consist in "bringing about conditions of human life resembling those to be found in eternity." In so arguing, he reveals he believes free will is nullified in Heaven, which is erroneous.**[900] But even if this erroneous view of his were correct, he would still be doing nothing but

---

[898] " … the devil … was a murderer from the beginning, not holding to the truth, for there is no truth in him. When he lies, he speaks his native language, for he is a liar and the father of lies." - John 8:44

[899] September 29, 1931.
[900] Heaven's confirmation in grace does not consist in the abrogation of free will, but in the glory of the Beatific Vision giving only one ontological possibility to its operation.

fallaciously begging the question; assuming without any demonstration or even reasonable argument that a Golden Age within history is somehow a duplication of Heaven (it is not) and therefore guilty of immanentizing the Heavenly eschaton.

Finally, he makes an argument about the conversion of the Jews, indicating that he has again surreptitiously inserted the word "immediately" into teachings that neither contain this word nor imply it. He rightly concludes that the Jews would be converted during the Era. He wrongly concludes that this implies that the end of the world must *immediately* follow this conversion. All he cites is the Catechism, paragraph 574, the relevant portion of which tells us that:

> The glorious Messiah's coming is suspended at every moment of history until his recognition by "all Israel", for "a hardening has come upon part of Israel" in their "unbelief" toward Jesus... The "full inclusion" of the Jews in the Messiah's salvation, in the wake of "the full number of the Gentiles", will enable the People of God to achieve "the measure of the stature of the fullness of Christ", in which "God may be all in all."

Clearly, there is no indication in this teaching that the General Resurrection, Final Judgment, and concomitant end of time must immediately follow the conversion of the Jews; there is only the teaching that the conversion of the Jews will "enable" the People of God to achieve what is there mentioned.[901]

In the same work, and immediately following his point on the Jews, he also completely dismisses the promise of the Era of Peace promised by Our Lady at Fatima, and so we now turn to address this error in its own section.

Absurd Teachings on Fatima's Promised Peace

No one denies—not even the inquisitors and critics of the Era—that Our Lady promised at Fatima that her "Immaculate Heart" would "triumph" and a "period of peace will be granted **to the world**."

Knowing they cannot deny this promise or its trustworthiness, and insisting (as most of them do) that the end is near, they are left to perform a spectacle of sophistical acrobatics to try to prove this "Period" or "Era" of peace is actually what we are witnessing now and have been witnessing for many years (either since the end of World War II or the fall of the Berlin Wall). It is primarily this notion that we will be addressing in this section, but first we must briefly consider the other method employed by one inquisitor to evade Our Lady's promise: pretending it applies only to Heaven.

We recall that Fatima is a fully Vatican approved apparition and that this prophecy of an Era (or "period") of peace is contained within the fully approved portion of its message. Anyone can, for himself, read the promise itself on the Vatican's own website regarding the apparitions at Fatima:

> In the end, my Immaculate Heart will triumph. The Holy Father will consecrate Russia to me, and she shall be converted, **and a period of peace will be granted to the world**"[902]

Now, the inquisitor we dealt with in the preceding section did indeed quote from this in his attempt to refute Our Lady's promise—**but he only quoted the first sentence**. Nowhere in the entire book in which he presents this argument against Our Lady's promise of peace *in the world* did he quote the bolded portion of the quote, wherein Our Lady promises a **period** of peace (meaning it cannot be a reference to eternity) **to the world**.

Perhaps it is difficult to believe that, in striving to prove there will be no temporal Era of peace, a Catholic author would go so far as to simply omit and completely ignore Our Lady's clear indication that there will be one—given by her a mere moment after her words which he *did* choose to quote. Difficult as it is to believe, these are precisely the kinds of tactics that critics of the Era rely on in a desperate attempt to have their eschatological

---

[901] Additionally, this passage itself, although cited by the inquisitor in opposition to the Era, actually refutes his own eschatological predictions. For the passage clearly implies that "all Israel" will, in fact, one day recognize Jesus, whereas the Eschatology of Despair, which the inquisitors promote, leaves no room for such a recognition. There is no use arguing that this recognition of Jesus by "all Israel" refers only to Heaven or the last Judgment; much of Israel will continue to reject Him until their dying breaths and,

tragically, choose hell. "All Israel," therefore, can only be licitly understood as the time on earth wherein all living Israelites confess that Jesus Christ is Lord. For it is already true—and always has been—that "all Israel" in Heaven recognizes Him as Lord, therefore eternity cannot be that to which the Catechism refers in this teaching.
[902] http://www.vatican.va/roman_curia/congregations/cfaith/documents/rc_con_cfaith_doc_20000626_message-fatima_en.html

speculations taken seriously for a little longer.

Having completely omitted what is essential to understanding Our Lady's message, he proceeds to argue that the phrase "In the end" is really just a reference to the end of the world. Now, Our Lady said "In the end" *directly after* describing many trials the Church and the world will suffer (wars, persecutions, etc.). But no honest reader would have any problem realizing that **by "the end," Our Lady is referring to the end of the trials that she just finished discussing immediately before saying that**; not randomly throwing in a veiled and awkward reference to the end of time.

***

We can now return to the more common argument among critics of the Era; namely, that we already have been enjoying the promised Era of Peace for some decades now.

Now, the suggestion that we are at "peace" in the modern world is a claim one would expect to hear from the most secular of sources (who perhaps have a vested financial interest in maintaining the status quo); not from a Catholic who should know that, as St. Mother Teresa said, "**abortion is the greatest destroyer of peace**,"[903] that billions of children have been killed by it in this "period of peace," and that it continues to kill millions more every year. Here we benefit from a famous and beautiful speech given by Dr. Peter Kreeft, in which he essentially recites an article he wrote for Crisis Magazine in June 1998:

> **If you don't know that our entire civilization is in crisis, I hope you had a nice vacation on the moon.** Many minds do seem moonstruck, however, blissfully unaware of the crisis—especially the "intellectuals," who are supposed to be the most on top of current events. I was dumbfounded to read a cover article in Time devoted to the question: Why is everything getting better? Why is life so good today? Why does everybody feel so satisfied about the quality of life? Time never questioned the assumption, it just wondered why the music on the Titanic sounded so nice.
>
> It turned out, on reading the article, that every single aspect of life that was mentioned, every single reason for life getting better, was economic.

> People are richer. End of discussion.
>
> Perhaps Time is just Playboy with clothes on. For one kind of playboy, the world is one great big whorehouse. For another kind, it's one great big piggy bank. For both, things are getting better and better …
>
> Night is falling. What Chuck Colson has labeled "a new Dark Ages" is looming. And its Brave New World proved to be only a Cowardly Old Dream. We can see this now, at the end of "the century of genocide" that was christened "the Christian century" at its birth.
>
> We've had prophets who warned us: Kierkegaard, 150 years ago, in The Present Age; and Spengler, 100 years ago, in The Decline of the West; and Aldous Huxley, seventy years ago, in Brave New World; and C. S. Lewis, forty years ago, in The Abolition of Man; and above all our popes: Leo XIII and Pius IX and Pius X and above all John Paul the Great, the greatest man in the world, the greatest man of the worst century. He had even more chutzpah than Ronald Reagan, who dared to call Them "the evil empire": He called Us "the culture of death." That's our culture, and his, including Italy, with the lowest birth rate in the world, and Poland, which now wants to share in the rest of the West's abortion holocaust.[904]

Meanwhile, entire swaths of continents—especially regions in Africa, Asia, the Middle East, and South America—are literal war zones. One of the greatest migration crises in history has been ongoing for many years now. Starvation is at levels never before seen in history, and easily curable diseases kill countless millions while billions of dollars are spent in richer nations on cosmetics. The Rwandan Genocide brought with it the wholesale cold-blooded murder of almost a million innocent civilians by their fellow civilians, and to this day, there are many ongoing genocides (while none of the world powers who could stop them seem to care), and even after the end of World War II there have been over a dozen more genocides. Warring drug cartels have managed to turn entire geographic areas into de facto war zones (even though they lack the legal qualification as such), and this is not to mention their destruction of hundreds of millions of lives throughout the world, through the addictions which they promote and off

---

[903] St. Teresa of Calcutta. National Prayer Breakfast. Washington, D.C. 1994. https://www.ewtn.com/library/issues/prbkmter.txt

[904] http://www.peterkreeft.com/topics-more/how-to-win.htm

of which they profit. Terrorism is raging throughout the world, and the deadliest such attack in history occurred on September 11th, 2001. ISIS, Boko Haram, Al Qaeda, the Fulani Herdsmen, and many other such entities have been continually committing atrocities of such grotesque evil that they can scarcely be described. Billions of people throughout the world live under tyrannies—over a billion still under Communism—in which their most basic human rights are regularly violated. **Global persecution of Christians has been far worse for the last century than ever before in history.**

And let us not forget that the vast majority of humanity is, objectively, treading the path to hell by living a life full of objective grave sins. Virtually the entire western world has completely succumbed to the Culture of Death and the Dictatorship of Relativism in ways our grandparents could barely have imagined. The family is in such crisis that most children (of whom there are incredibly few, since most Western nations' birth rates have plummeted to civilization-destroying levels) are raised in broken homes without a married mother and father. Suicide—the ultimate indication of an absence of peace in a society—has exploded to historically unprecedented levels and has become a leading cause of death; *the* leading cause among the youth, who are the bellwethers of society. And now, suicide is becoming institutionalized through Euthanasia. Pope Francis put it more bluntly than perhaps anyone else when he said, on February 19th, 2019: **"I don't think our times are better than those of the flood..."**[905] He also said that we are already in a piecemeal World War III, expressing:

> Even today, after the second failure of another world war, perhaps one can speak of a third war, one fought piecemeal, with crimes, massacres, destruction ...[906]

This is what the critics of the Era call "peace." But one who calls what this world has had the last several decades *"the worldwide period of peace and Triumph of her Heart promised by Our Lady at Fatima,"* has done great injustice to Our Lady.

***

Let us end this section by considering that, throughout the whole history of the Church, the Holy Spirit has always been at work in her; molding her, forming her, and sometimes leading her on to new understandings, even if it means moving on from old ones that worked well in their time but which are no longer adequate.

In such times of transition, there are always those who choose to see this leading—which the Holy Spirit always does in a sufficiently gentle way that any earnest seeker will recognize is not an artificial or heretical movement—as an affront, and then proceed to dedicate themselves to opposing it. In their opposition, they conflate common opinions with Church Dogmas and then persecute the development God is leading the Church to with every weapon they can find. One thinks, for example, of the many theologians who saw the Immaculate Conception as an affront to Catholic Teaching before it was formally declared *Ex Cathedra*; or of the Lefebvrists who today condemn the Second Vatican Council as heretical; or of the rigorists who, in the 1700s condemned the works of St. Francis de Sales and St. Alphonsus Liguori as laxist (works which are now regarded by the Church as among the greatest spiritual masterpieces in history). It is no different today. I only hope and pray that those who have hitherto devoted themselves to condemning the Era as heretical will receive the grace to submit to the truth once it becomes even clearer than it already is.

But whether or not they submit, one thing is certain: they cannot stop God.

> Now, if the farmer, despite all the difficulties of the earth, can hope to receive an abundant harvest, more so I, Celestial Farmer, having put forth from My Divine Bosom the so many Seeds of Celestial Truths in order to sow them in the depth of your soul, and the whole world will be filled by the Harvest. Do you want to believe, therefore, that because of the doubts and difficulties of a few-some like earth without moisture, some like hard and calloused earth-I would not make My Superabundant Harvest? My daughter, you are mistaken![907]

"When God moves, no one can resist Him."

[905]https://www.vaticannews.va/en/pope-francis/mass-casa-santa-marta.html
[906]Celebration presided over by Pope Francis at the Military Memorial in Redipuglia on the Occasion of the 100th Anniversary of the Outbreak of First World War. Homily of His Holiness Pope Francis. 13 Sept. 2014.
[907] February 24, 1933.

-Jesus to Luisa. November 27, 1927

Millenarianism and the Catechism

The Church does indeed condemn Chiliasm (which is just another word for millenarianism) and modified (or "mitigated") millenarianism.

Therefore, indeed, a Catholic must have nothing to do with these beliefs, even if he thought he saw them in Luisa's writings. But the fact is, Luisa's revelations do not posit anything close to these condemned teachings. Luisa's writings do not contain a literal interpretation of the thousand years of Revelation 20, nor a coming age when we are dispensed from the Deposit of Faith (as authoritatively taught by the Magisterium of the Church)[908] or from the Sacramental life of the Church. Nor do her revelations speak of any sort of literal, physical coming of Jesus in the flesh to reign on earth before the end of time.

Unfortunately, however, the few Catholic writers today who condemn Luisa's followers as millenarian heretics are simply taking it upon themselves to define the sense in which the Church intends the word "modified" as stated in the *Catechism of the Catholic Church* in paragraph 676, and they go far beyond the sense in which the Church intends it (which is made clear by the Church herself). An honest, objective, and thorough consideration of the matter is therefore in order.

In the *Catechism of the Catholic Church*, we read:

> The Antichrist's deception already begins to take shape in the world every time the claim is made to realize within history that messianic hope which can only be realized beyond history through the eschatological judgment. the Church has rejected even modified forms of this falsification of the kingdom to come under the name of millenarianism, especially the "intrinsically perverse" political form of a secular messianism. The Church will enter the glory of the kingdom only through this final Passover, when she will follow her Lord in his death and Resurrection. The kingdom will be fulfilled, then, not by a historic triumph of the Church through a progressive ascendancy, but only by God's victory over the final unleashing of evil, which will cause his Bride to come down from heaven.

> God's triumph over the revolt of evil will take the form of the Last Judgment after the final cosmic upheaval of this passing world.[909]

This quote—the Catechism's **only** teaching related to millenarianism—is here presented in its **entirety** to ensure that every detail is fully respected and addressed. Church teaching deserves no less.

The first condemnation contained within this Catechism paragraph is against the Antichrist's deception: one that will present a messianic claim within history. **But the Era of Peace presents no messianic claim;** rather, it is entirely founded upon the *full realization* of the very same 2,000-year-old messianic intervention through the Incarnation and Paschal Mysteries of Jesus Christ and expects no new public revelation. Furthermore, the hope placed in the Era is radically distinct from the hope placed in Heaven, and all messianic expectations are reserved for the latter.

Unsatisfied, critics of the Era of Peace assert that any notion of the "kingdom to come" on earth is necessarily modified millenarianism, however, **when one reads the Catechism itself, it can easily be seen that only a specific aspect of this school of thought that anticipates the kingdom coming to earth is condemned as heretical. Namely, the "falsification" of the kingdom to come through a "messianic hope" which forms the "Antichrist's deception."** The first two sentences of this paragraph in the Catechism deal only with this specific case and condemn only the proposition that bears these qualities. Here, as elsewhere, we see the critics falling into the classic error of the amateur in theology: failing to identify properly the condemned (i.e. anathematized) proposition by failing to take into account all the predicates by which it is defined.

Theological mechanics aside, **it is scarcely tenable that the Antichrist's deception could consist in an encouragement to the Faithful to anticipate—and pray for the hastening of—a time in which the Catholic Faith is spread and followed throughout the whole world.** Indeed, it is the refusal to anticipate and pray for this triumph that is a deception of the Antichrist; for it entails a failure to recognize and respond to God's Will that "all men be saved,"[910] and Catholic dogma that "Whosoever,

---

[908] Quite the contrary, she insisted that her works be utterly dismissed if anything be found in them opposed to Catholic teaching.

[909] *CCC*, 676-677.
[910] 1 Timothy 2:4

therefore, knowing that the Catholic Church was made necessary by Christ, would refuse to enter or to remain in it, could not be saved."[911] In fact, this deception of the Antichrist that amounts to false and secular messianism is precisely what some movements in existence today promote, including The New Age Movement, Marxist Utopianism, and—tragically, but increasingly—many heretical movements within the Church itself.

Contradicting those who would absurdly suppose that the deception of the antichrist spoken of here in the Catechism refers to teachings on Era of Peace, Cardinal Müller, Prefect Emeritus of the Congregation of the Doctrine of Faith, says clearly:

> To keep silent about these and the other truths of the Faith and to teach people accordingly is the greatest deception against which the Catechism vigorously warns. It represents the last trial of the Church and leads man to a religious delusion, "the price of their apostasy" (CCC 675); it is the fraud of Antichrist. "He will deceive those who are lost by all means of injustice; for they have closed themselves to the love of the truth by which they should be saved" (2 Thess 2:10).[912]

Cardinal Müller wrote this teaching as part of his "Manifesto of Faith" in response to a growing apostasy within the Catholic Church, wherein her infallible moral law is ignored for the sake of a false "mercy" which condones divorce, adultery, sacrilegious Communions, homosexual acts, and in general relativizes the truth. And the good Cardinal is obviously correct: this is the desire of the antichrist, and this heresy and apostasy is that in which his deception consists. The devil gains absolutely nothing—but loses much—from Catholics anticipating and praying for the full triumph of the Faith on earth.

Returning to this paragraph in the Catechism, its next condemnation is levied against the assertion that the Kingdom will be fulfilled "...by a historic triumph of the Church through a progressive ascendancy..." Critics of the Era of Peace, again, take one aspect of the condemnation and arbitrarily expand it: for they condemn *any* belief in a historic triumph of the Church—a belief held by almost all who anticipate the Era of Peace. But this belief, in fact, is a testimony to the orthodoxy of those who await the Era of Peace; for they await not the passing of the Age of the Church in anticipation of a so-called "Age of the Spirit" that will replace it, as Joachim of Fiore did in the middle ages. No; instead, they await a time in which the Church will acquire her full vigor and fulfill the prophecies and prayers of Jesus Himself, especially "Thy will be done on earth as it is in heaven;"[913] and "So there shall be one flock, one shepherd..."[914] and "...I, when I am lifted up from the earth, will draw all men to myself."[915]

Thus, **the Era of Peace entails a strengthening of the Church, not its passing away**. Perhaps above all, the Era of Peace is clearly not condemned by the Catechism **because the achievement of this Era is not sought by a "progressive ascendancy." On the contrary, it is prayerfully awaited as a bestowal of Divine Intervention.** Progressive ascendancy is a particularly dangerous idea encouraged by some proponents of Liberation Theology who have subtly adopted a Marxist utopian vision of the future. It seems that most, if not all, of the vigor with which the Church today condemns millenarianism comes from her noble desire to protect the faithful from the fatal flaws contained within elements of the Liberation Theology and other progressive-ascendency movements.

Liberation Theology is one of the most popular and dangerous expressions of millenarianism today. One well known Liberation Theologian stated that *"a 'liberation spirituality' requires a big change in how we think about salvation and how we think about the church."*[916] Another author wrote bluntly that these "big changes" consist of liberationists seeking *"...to change the object to which theology devotes its attention. They reject, with disdain, the notion that getting people to heaven is more important than getting them tolerable living conditions."*[917] This view, in turn, reflects earlier philosophical trends, such as Immanuel Kant's sociological Pelagianism which sees the Kingdom of God as a mere working

---

[911] Second Vatican Council, Dogmatic Constitution on the Church, *Lumen Gentium*, 14.

[912] Cardinal Muller's Manifesto of Faith. Paragraph 5: Eternal Life.http://www.ncregister.com/blog/edward-pentin/cardinal-mueller-issues-manifesto-of-faith

[913] Matthew 6:10

[914] John 10:16

[915] John 12:32

[916] U.S. Catholic interview, "Do you hear the cry of the poor? Liberation theology today," at U.S Catholic (March 2010) Vol. 75, No. 3, pages 18-21. www.uscatholic.org.

[917] Edward A. Lynch, "The Retreat of Liberation Theology" Homiletic & Pastoral Review (February 1994).

towards an "ethical commonwealth under divine moral legislation," and Darwin's evolutionary theory applied outside its own domain to support the notion that society itself inescapably evolves towards a temporally perfect status. All these notions were applied to societal life in general, deluding people to suppose that humanity was destined to, step by step, progressively ascend to its ultimate destiny at some scientifically predictable point in the future. The Universalists especially took up this idea with zeal. During the 19th century, under the impact of Darwinian evolution theories, the older "individual salvation theories" gave way to personal self-development and social improvement theories. The Washington statement of faith (1935) asserted only its faith in the "authority of truth, known or to be known, and the power of men of good will and sacrificial spirit to overcome all evil and *progressively to establish* the kingdom of God."[918]

Unfortunately, the ranks of Catholic clergy are also not devoid of similar heresies. Fr. Teilhard de Chardin—a Jesuit priest whose writings were declared by the Holy Office under Pope St. John XXIII to have serious errors against Catholic doctrine—taught a similar message. His influence, sadly, both was and is significant. Among his writings, we find the following:

> What increasingly dominates my interests, is the effort to establish within myself and define around me, a new religion (call it a better Christianity, if you like) where the personal God ceases to be the great monolithic proprietor of the past to become the Soul of the World which the stage we have reached religiously and culturally calls for… [God] evolves, via "complexification" and "convergence" to his own perfection, immersed in matter… One is inseparable from the other; one is never without the other …[919]

It is therefore clear, for the preservation of the Catholic Faith, just how vital the Church's condemnation is of the notion that the arrival of the Kingdom of God on earth can come by way of progressive ascendancy. It is equally clear that this condemnation has nothing to do with the anticipation of an Era of Peace as revealed by Jesus to Luisa, for this arouses not the desire to build this Era progressively, but rather the desire to pray for its hastening and prepare the ground by way of works of mercy and evangelization.

It must be emphasized that the "progressive ascendency" heresies are usually motivated implicitly or explicitly by Darwinism, and that Darwinism finds perhaps no greater enemy than in the philosophy and theology given by Jesus to Luisa. For He reveals an outlook that is, quite literally, the exact opposite: that man was originally noble, glorious, perfect; and that over time he has only become more and more corrupt, and that only His Own Divine Intervention can save man.

Although the preceding pages suffice for demonstrating that the Church's condemnations of millenarianism (and any associated movement or teaching) has nothing to do with what is prophesied in Luisa's revelations, it is even easier to see that no problem exists when one looks to other Church Documents that vindicate the orthodoxy of the Era of Peace.

For example, the following excerpt contains another Magisterial reference to modified-millenarianism:

> In recent times on several occasions this Supreme Sacred Congregation of the Holy Office has been asked what must be thought of the system of mitigated Millenarianism, which teaches, for example, that Christ the Lord before the final judgment, whether or not preceded by the resurrection of the many just, will come visibly to rule over this world. The answer is: The system of mitigated Millenarianism cannot be taught safely.[920]

This decree of the Holy Office should immediately give pause to one who would interpret the

---

[918] "Universalists," in *New Catholic Encyclopedia*, 322.

[919] Cf. onepetervie.com/teilhard-chardin-vii-architect. It must also be noted, however, that Fr. Chardin's teachings are not entirely without wisdom. Cardinal Ratzinger, for example, praised some of Chardin's writings, describing positively his views with the words: "*Teilhard went on to give new meaning to Christian worship: the transubstantiated Host is the anticipation of the transformation and divinization of matter in the Christological "fullness." In his view, the Eucharist provided the movement of the cosmos with its direction; it anticipates its goal and at the same time urges it on*". This, indeed, is a noble vision and I firmly believe that if only Fr. Chardin was exposed to Luisa's writings, they could have directed what was good in his insights in an orthodox direction. Unfortunately, Fr. Chardin was, instead, won over by the Darwinists.

[920] Henry Denzinger, *The Sources of Catholic Dogma, A Translation of the Enchiridion Symbolorum* (St. Louis, MO: B. Herder Book Co., 1957), "Millenarianism (Chiliasm) by the Decree of the Holy Office, July 21, 1944. Page 625.

Catechism's word "modified" to mean that any sort of glorious time to come is impossible! For here, (though the word "mitigated" is used, clearly the same intent is applicable) **even "mitigated" millenarianism still refers to the notion that a time will come when Christ will come to rule over this world visibly.**

The Magisterium has also implied what is meant to be condemned by "modified millenarianism" in a document published by the Congregation for the Doctrine of Faith more recently. This document states:

> [There is a] rebirth of the tendency to establish an innerworldly eschatology. This tendency is well known in the history of theology, and beginning with the Middle Ages it constituted what came to be called "the spiritual heritage of Joachim de Fiore. This tendency is found in some theologians of liberation, who so insist on the importance of establishing the kingdom of God as something within our own history on earth that the salvation which transcends history seems to become of rather secondary interest.[921]

As we can see, this particular condemnation by the CDF is directed primarily at Liberation Theology. I will not speak much of that here, as no one accuses Luisa's revelations of this heresy; her writings are about as other-worldly as possible and never confuse the coming Reign of Peace with some form of man-made system of political justice. Even Luisa is far too busy concerning herself with the things of Heaven, and thereby urging her readers to do likewise, to think or speak much of the details of the Era of Peace. The "salvation which transcends history," which Ratzinger here is so rightly concerned with ensuring is paramount (in contradiction to the Liberation Theology movements which neglect it), is always the thing that Luisa (and Jesus, in His words to her) is utterly fixated upon. The Era is desired not so much to make the world a better place, but to make Heaven a better place by means of making the world into a better saint-making factory. Indeed, in the Era to come, the salvation of souls will be far better achieved than it is today (an age in which the gravest of evils have become cultural mainstays). Temporal transformation on the earth (justice, alleviation of poverty and war, physical changes, etc.), is of secondary interest (though not insignificant).

At this point, we have settled that nothing in the Catechism condemns the Era of Peace as revealed to Luisa.

While the preceding argument explains the critics' errors in detail, the point may in fact be sufficiently made in a simple chart (contained in the following page) comparing two things: what the Catechism actually says, on the left-hand column, and what the critics' arguments erroneously suppose the Catechism says or implies (in other words, what the Catechism *would have to say* for their arguments to be valid), on the right-hand column.

---

[921] Congregation for the Doctrine of Faith. "Some Current Questions in Eschatology." 1992. Paragraph 2.

What the Catechism Says	What the Critics Think It Says
The Antichrist's deception already begins to take shape in the world every time **the** claim is made to realize within history **that messianic hope which can only be realized beyond history through** the eschatological judgment.	The Antichrist's deception already begins to take shape in the world every time **any** claim is made to realize within history **any form of hope for worldwide Divine Intervention before** the eschatological judgment.
The **Church has rejected <u>even</u> modified forms of *this* falsification** of the kingdom to come under the name of millenarianism, especially the "intrinsically perverse" political form of a secular messianism.	The Church **has rejected <u>any</u> superficially similar forms of *any* anticipation** of the kingdom to come under the name of millenarianism, especially the "intrinsically perverse" political form of a secular messianism.
The Church will enter the glory of the kingdom only **through** this final Passover, when she will follow her Lord in His death and Resurrection.	The Church will enter the glory of the kingdom only **entirely after** this final Passover, when she will follow her Lord in His death and Resurrection.
The kingdom will be fulfilled, then, not by a historic triumph of the Church **through a progressive ascendancy**, but only by God's victory over the **final** unleashing of evil, which will cause His Bride to come down from heaven. God's **triumph** over the revolt of evil will take the form of the Last Judgment after the final cosmic upheaval of this passing world.	The kingdom will be fulfilled, then, not by a historic triumph of the Church **of any sort whatsoever,** but only by God's victory over the **end of time** unleashing of evil, which will cause His Bride to come down from heaven. God's **only triumph** over the revolt of evil will take the form of the Last Judgment after the final cosmic upheaval of this passing world.

***

Letter vs Intent

Now, I am not going to ask my readers to play dumb. Obviously, these paragraphs of the Catechism do not exactly succeed on their own in indicating that a Glorious Era of Peace will indeed dawn upon the Church and the world before the end of time thanks to the intervention of Christ in grace! I would even go so far as to say it is possible the Era's critics, who say that those who wrote these words of the Catechism had in mind an eschatology more like Augustine's Amillennialism, may be correct in this guess of theirs. But this changes nothing.

If one wishes to find a clear prophetic delineation of what is to come in the future laid out before him in the Catechism, given in such a way that it precludes any private revelation giving a fuller picture, then such a person gravely misunderstands the nature and mission of the Church herself, and has completely inverted the Catechism's own insistence that *"the Marian dimension of the Church precedes the Petrine."*[922]

Such a person furthermore behaves like a man who, desiring to discover truths about the cellular structure of a leaf, proceeds to place a beautiful painting of the same under a microscope. In other words: **one cannot glean Divinely revealed truths about what is to come for the world by trying to read between the lines and discern the opinion of the authors of a text (even a Magisterial one) when these authors are themselves men who do not know what is to come, and who readily and openly admit to that fact, and would equally readily admit that they are only faithfully transmitting what has long been the most common (non-Dogmatic) opinion in the Church** on the matter. The authors of these paragraphs of the Catechism would have a good laugh if they saw

---

922 CCC 773.

critics of the Era claiming victory for their own eschatological opinions on what is to come for the remainder of the history of the world by treating the Catechism like Sacred Scripture, wherein we are well justified in reading between the lines and discerning the intent of the authors in order to discover subtle truths.

For indeed, even if the intent in the mind of the authors in writing those paragraphs of the Catechism is more in accord with the critic's own eschatological opinions (for, as we have seen, the specific words used in the Catechism are not), **these intents behind the words are not only *not* dogmatically proposed (as will be made evident in the next section), but are not even binding in any sense whatsoever on anyone.**

To be clear: the critics of the Era who resort to this method of criticism would wager that the author of the paragraph in the Catechism which condemns millenarianism *had in mind* a broader condemnation of any expectation of a coming kingdom on earth, even though the grammatically proper way of understanding the words themselves does not yield this broader condemnation.

But even if correct in its guess at the intent of the author (which itself cannot be demonstrated), it is not a relevant argument; for it **consists in the application of an exegetical approach reserved for Sacred Scripture to a document that, even in those cases in which it is Divinely protected, is nevertheless an essentially human work.**

Regarding Scripture, the Second Vatican Council teaches that "…everything asserted by the inspired authors or sacred writers must be held to be asserted by the Holy Spirit…"[923] and that, to know what God desires to Communicate through Scripture, interpreters "…should carefully investigate what meaning the sacred writers really intended…"[924] **In Scripture, there exists a *unique* situation wherein the intention of the author is always the intention of God Himself.**

In the Church's Magisterium, this same level of guaranteed correspondence between the Will of God and the intention of the human author does not exist; instead, there is simply protection provided by God, against error on Faith and Morals, that applies only to the words themselves, and not necessarily to the intention of the author. For example, if Pope Francis, in writing *Amoris Laetitia*, had in mind an intention to condone adultery or divorce, that would be irrelevant, because the actual words as they are found in the promulgated document do not do so. Therefore, it is the errors condemned by the actual words themselves contained in Magisterial documents that a Catholic must be sure to avoid. As the "New Catholic Encyclopedia" states:

> Whatever in the Church involves in any way a human, free response to God does come under the judgment of God. The fact that the Church has authority from Christ does not mean that this authority will always be exercised in the best possible way … **The fact that the Church cannot universally err in matters of faith and morals does not mean that it will always insist on the most significant truths or interpret them to the world in the way best suited to enlighten it**. In all these ways and many more the Church as such through its leaders and its members can fail to respond properly to God's initiative within it.[925]

Church History has already taught us how dangerous it can be for a Catholic to suppose that a gleaned intent hidden behind the words of even the highest Magisterial proclamations is itself the Will of God. Consider the dogmatic teaching of *Extra Ecclesiam Nulla Salus* (Outside the Church There is No Salvation) contained in the Papal Bull of Boniface VIII, *Unam Sanctam,* the texts of the Council of Florence, and other documents.

It is certainly an infallible teaching; its various expressions of much greater authority than even the Catechism's own statements. And yet, they still are prone to gross misinterpretation, and indeed probably were misinterpreted by most who had read these various promulgations.

For it is difficult to deny that the authors of these words probably had a much more severe meaning in mind, much more heavily restricting of those who could enter Heaven, than the words themselves necessarily teach; for the words themselves are now understood to refer to *objective necessity* and to have no bearing on one's subjective ignorance. In other words, they apply only to one's

---

[923] Second Vatican Council, Dogmatic Constitution on Divine Revelation *Dei Verbum* (18 November 1965), 11.
[924] *Dei Verbum*, 12.

[925] JUDGMENT, DIVINE (IN THEOLOGY). New Catholic Encyclopedia. P. 35.

objective eligibility for being saved in justice who *knows* that the Catholic Church is the one, true, necessary Church.

Today we see a different problem: many, in seeking to read the intent behind *Amoris Laetitia*, have gone so far as to implicitly or explicitly condone divorce and adultery. The source of both problems is the same: sinning against the exclusive dignity of Sacred Scripture by taking the exegetical approach reserved to it alone and applying it to Magisterial texts.[926]

Dogmatic vs. Non-Dogmatic

The entire preceding argument we considered in the last section is all besides the fact that, even if the Catechism did mean what the critics of the Era claim it means—and it certainly does not—, this would still be of no use to their thesis: as you will see in a forthcoming section, Papal Encyclicals (which are more authoritative than the Catechism) have made it abundantly clear that the very peace that Christ came to bring **will in fact come upon the earth** in an Era yet to come. And whenever contradictions arise, that which is weightier must always be that to which we defer.

The Catechism is indeed a weighty and authoritative Church Document. But an Encyclical is weightier still. Case in point: in any realm, the mutability of a thing is always inversely proportional to the degree of its authority. Within American civil law, for example, the hardest thing to change, the Constitution, is also the weightiest. The easiest things to change (perhaps parking laws, which can easily be altered on a whim even by a local town council) are the least weighty, and carry only a small fine if violated. And the weightiest things of *all* are the Divine and Natural Laws, which can never and will never change, and thus are binding without exception on every single human. The Catechism already has witnessed dozens of changes since it was first promulgated in 1992. Encyclicals, on the other hand, do not change once they are promulgated.

The Catechism, in fact, bears many similarities to Canon Law. Both were promulgated by way of Apostolic Constitutions, without themselves being Apostolic Constitutions. Both deal with a plethora of different matters; some dogmatic, some not. Both have changed. Therefore, the mere presence of a given statement within either is itself insufficient for absolutely settling a theological question; rather, one must examine the context and references of its presence to see whether it is reiterating a dogmatic matter. For example, one may indeed licitly argue that we should have a mandated three-hour Communion fast instead of a one-hour Communion fast. A critic of this argument might respond *"but Canon Law only says one hour!"* Such a critic would be missing the point. The mere fact that something *is* a Canon Law does not necessarily entail its being a Dogmatic declaration as a *de fide* truth; nor can Canon Law settle debates about what ought to be Canon Law. On the other hand, if one were to argue for women priests, he *would* be thereby contradicting Dogma; but not because Canon Law says that only men can be priests. Of course, Canon Law does say that; but the dogmatic nature of this restriction can be gleaned (among other sources) from Pope St. John Paul II himself directly writing, in a Magisterial Document he promulgated in 1994 (*Ordinatio Sacerdotalis*):

> Wherefore, in order that all doubt may be removed regarding a matter of great importance, a matter which pertains to the Church's divine constitution itself, in virtue of my ministry of confirming the brethren (cf. Lk 22:32) I declare that the Church has no authority whatsoever to confer priestly ordination on women and that this judgment is to be definitively held by all the Church's faithful.

As you can see, the Church is good at making it clear when something must be held by all the Faithful! (I am aware that some theologians claim even this is not Dogmatic. I disagree with them. If wording that powerful, directly from the Pope himself, in a Magisterial Document, do not bind—then nothing does.)

Now, back to the Catechism section in question. In the entire article containing this excerpt (CCC 668-682), except for one specific point which we will discuss in a few paragraphs, there is little or nothing Dogmatic being relayed. Indeed the Church, in her wisdom, almost never declares that one particular interpretation of Scripture verses

---

[926] This is not a subtle re-wording of the Protestant "Sola Scriptura" heresy, which states that Scripture alone suffices. Scripture alone certainly does not suffice! But it does indeed have an exegetical approach that is *reserved* to it alone. Catholic Dogma makes clear this sovereign and exclusive dignity enjoyed by the Holy Bible.

must be definitively held by all the faithful to the exclusion of all other interpretations — consequently, almost this entire section in the Catechism is *presented* to the Faithful but *not imposed* upon them. (I continue to reiterate, however, that **despite all these qualifications we are considering,** *nothing* **in the Catechism — including this section — contradicts the Era as held by Luisa's followers, therefore our present undertaking is in a way superfluous**.) Now, I know the critics are ready to pounce, both ignoring this parenthetical reminder which I have just presented, and accusing me of heretically contradicting the Catechism and claiming that the Church does not have the authority to settle matters of Scriptural interpretation.[927] But nothing could be farther from the truth; of course the Church does have the authority to settle matters of Scriptural interpretation, and this authority must be obeyed by all Catholics — *but this authority is rarely exercised*. This is not my opinion; it is the official Magisterial teaching of Venerable Pope Pius XII (quoted elsewhere in this book):

> ...**all moreover should abhor that intemperate zeal** which imagines that whatever is new should for that very reason be opposed or suspected ... in the immense matter contained in **the Sacred Books — legislative, historical, sapiential and prophetical — there are but few texts whose sense has been defined by the authority of the Church ...** There remain therefore many things, and of the greatest importance, in the discussion and exposition of which the skill and genius of Catholic commentators may and ought to be freely exercised, so that each may contribute his part to the advantage of all, to the continued progress of the sacred doctrine and to the defense and honor of the Church.

That, dear critics of the Era, *is* Magisterium: specifically, it is from paragraph 47 of the **Encyclical** *Divino Afflante Spiritu*. An ounce of honesty would reveal to the critics that they are doing exactly what Pius XII is here demanding that

we all *abhor*.

But returning again to the Catechism section in question, it is clear that what is discussed is not among those *"few texts whose sense has been defined by the authority of the Church,"* for the Catechism itself here makes no attempt to present a definitive definition (Catechisms, in fact, never definitively define anything on their own; they only compile such declarations that already exist), nor does it reference any other Magisterium that, in turn, attempts to do so. From that entire span of sections dealing with the end times, there are 40 footnotes, but within them is found only three extra-Biblical references: *Lumen Gentium* (the only relevant thing referenced from this teaches that the "full perfection" of the Church is only in Heaven; which, again, followers of Luisa and believers in the Era do not deny), Pius XI's condemnation of Communism in *Divini Redemptoris* (and it is easy to see from reading this encyclical that it is not even remotely related to millenarianism — this, mind you, is the same Pope who, in his encyclical *Quas Primas*, blatantly prophesied the Era of Peace), and *Denzinger* (a popular compilation of Catholic teachings) in section 3839.

This section of Denzinger only contains the 1944 response from the Holy Office[928] to an inquiry already mentioned, saying that "mitigated millenarianism ... cannot be safely taught." This same decree **explicitly defines "mitigated millenarianism" as the teaching that "Christ will come... visibly to rule over this world."** And, again, as mentioned, all this succeeds in proving is that even by "mitigated" or "modified" millenarianism, the Church is referring to something that no follower of Luisa — or of Catholic private revelation in general — believes in; it condemns only the teaching of a coming physical reign of Christ on earth.

In brief: actually following the footnotes the Catechism itself presents — as is expected of a

---

[927] And the irony will be lost on no one, since the most famous of the critics of the Era, who misses no opportunity to castigate believers in it as heretics, has recently become more famous for openly admitting to his own contradiction of and disagreement with a clear teaching contained in an Apostolic Exhortation written by Pope St. John Paul II: a document of even higher authority than the Catechism.

[928] (The decree can be found on the Vatican's amazing online resource, Biblia Clerus: http://www.clerus.org/bibliaclerusonline/en/dx0.htm#dj5).

Due to the immense importance of precision in wording here, I have also double checked this Denzinger entry in the most up-to-date version; the 43rd edition published in 2012, which I have on my desk. Indeed, the same thing is contained within it. Finally, the original Latin can be verified directly on page 212 of the 1944 Acta Apostolica Sedis, posted on the Vatican's website here: http://www.vatican.va/archive/aas/documents/AAS-36-1944-ocr.pdf).

theologian but apparently never undertaken by critics of the Era—demonstrates beyond doubt that it is categorically impossible to employ its teachings to denounce the Era.

Now, the relative amount of Scriptural references versus Magisterial references, while in no way problematic or deserving of a raised eyebrow, nevertheless does tell us that—beyond the need to reject a literal thousand-year reign of Christ in the visible flesh on earth—there is nothing dogmatic being reiterated in this entire section. Contrast this section's nature to, for example, that of the section on Marian Dogmas; e.g. Mary's Immaculate Conception and Perpetual Virginity, which contains a plethora of extra-Scriptural teachings: councils, Magisterium, Church Fathers, etc.

I feel I must reassure readers now: you will not find a more zealous defender and promoter of the Catechism and its authority than myself. The very last thing I would ever want to see is this authority being in any way disrespected. But Truth is always Supreme, and what we have considered about the nature of the Catechism and its authority is, simply and unarguably, **true**.

And in conclusion, I proffer my usual reminder from the preceding page: **none of the paragraphs following the table several pages above are necessary, as the Catechism does *not* condemn the Era as Jesus reveals it to Luisa**. I only provide these paragraphs in the off chance that there are any readers who cannot seem to shrug the fear that some potential *interpretations of* some of these teachings from the Catechism may not be fully in accord with what Jesus reveals to Luisa about the Era. For although such a reader would be incorrect, I nevertheless say to him: Be not afraid. Orthodoxy first and always, but these interpretations that linger in your mind are not binding, and therefore they must be considered in relation to the overwhelming evidence—in Magisterium, Private Revelation, the Fathers of the Church, and even Scripture itself—in support of a *Glorious* Era.

Augustine & Amillennialism: No Blow to the Era, Under Any Scenario

There is no denying that the Amillennialism of Augustine (the view that Revelation 20's "thousand years" refers simply to the Age of Christianity) has long been the most popular one in Catholic eschatology. Msgr. Ralph Kuehner, in a paragraph he wrote for the New Catholic Encyclopedia, states its essence succinctly and accurately:

> The millennium is to be understood in a symbolic sense. The "first resurrection" symbolizes Baptism, by which one shares in Christ's Resurrection (see Rom 6.1—10). All the faithful, both those on earth and those in heaven, share in the 1,000-year reign of Jesus, a symbol for the entire life span of the Church considered in its glorious aspect from the Resurrection of Christ until the Last Judgment, just as three-and-a-half years symbolizes the Church's life in struggle and persecution (Rv 11.2—3; 12.14). The chaining of Satan during this same period signifies that the influence of Satan has been notably reduced, not completely removed. The lessening of Satan's influence is the result of the effectiveness of Christ's Redemption. After a final struggle near the end of time … Satan will be definitively conquered by Christ. Then follows the Last Judgment. Those who have not been faithful to Jesus will experience the "second death," the symbol of eternal punishment in hell. The faithful with resurrected bodies will enter into the bliss of heaven.

I understand that some readers may still be hesitant to do anything but proceed lock-step with St. Augustine's most popular view; fearing that failure to do so might entail some form of (albeit minor) disrespect of (lowercase "t") tradition.

But the Era as revealed to Luisa needn't necessarily have anything to do with millennial beliefs of any form. As we have seen, the coming Glorious Era of Peace does not depend upon any given interpretation of the eschatological views of the Fathers or of the Book of Revelation: its coming is a guarantee thanks to both the consensus of trustworthy private revelation and Papal Magisterium. **Therefore, whoever wishes to remain in lock-step Augustinian Amillennialism can still unreservedly believe in the Coming of the Kingdom and the assurance of the arrival of the Era as Jesus promised Luisa. For such a person can simply count the Era as one of the multitudes of extremely important realities that God chose not to reveal in the New Testament explicitly; instead reserving this task for private revelation or other forms of development later in Church history (as He so chose, for example, regarding the Assumption of Mary).**

If the Church were to dogmatically proclaim the full validity of Augustine's Amillennialism as the only permissible interpretation of the relevant portion of Revelation 20 (although we can rest assured this will never happen), this proclamation would still have no effect on the orthodoxy of the Era: one can search every letter of Augustine's writings and every single treatise ever written in Catholic tradition expounding upon the Amillennialist understanding of Revelation, and he will never find anything to the effect of: *"The remainder of history is certainly guaranteed to follow a linear path until the end of time; there will never be a Glorious Era of Peace, and by and large the Church and the world will always have to be filled with sin, error, ugliness, and evil in general in more or less the same way it does now."* (This is in fact what those who foolishly wield Amillennialism as if it were a weapon against the Era pretend it says.) Indeed, the false notion that Amillennialism (even if it were the only allowable or only correct interpretation) refutes the Era is just another sad casualty of the plague of insisting upon seeing contradictions where none exist.

Therefore, we can see that the critics of the Era, who devote themselves to attacking the spiritual millennium teaching of many of the Fathers of the Church in hopes that this attack will yield a fatal blow to the Era of Peace, are gravely misleading their readers. Their antics call to mind those of certain secular opponents of Christianity who devote themselves to attacking the validity of the Shroud of Turin. Besides the fact that the Shroud of Turin is most likely valid, these assailants neglect to consider that, even in their "best-case scenario," wherein they have fully and definitively refuted the evidence in support of its validity and proven it to be a fraud, none of this would have even the slightest effect on the certainty of Christ's Life, Death, and Resurrection. For the Shroud of Turin is a nice reminder of this certainty; a useful encouragement to Faith for those whose faith might otherwise be weak; not in any way a necessary piece of evidence for the Faith. **And so it is with the teachings of the Fathers on the millennium; it is a helpful reminder of the reality of the Era, but it is not a necessary one.**

***

Just as importantly, however, we must understand that moving on from strictly holding only Augustine's Amillennialism does not entail any disrespect whatsoever for the status it has hitherto enjoyed—in fact, one could go so far as to wager that **it is a good and Providential thing that his Amillennialism has long been the most popular eschatological opinion among theologians. It certainly does give much important truth and edification, and it is a valid (even if only partial) interpretation of Scripture**. It is a good, holy, and true meditation on the Book of Revelation. We ought not repudiate it. The "first resurrection" does in part refer to Baptism, and the "binding of Satan" and the "thousand-year reign" does in part refer to the Age of the Church we have hitherto relished.

On the other hand, **we ought not pretend that this interpretation precludes all others and renders all others heretical.** The Divine orchestration in this interpretation prevailing for much of the history of the Church is no doubt due to only this moment in history being the opportune one in which the other, fuller, interpretation has become essential. For it is only now that the coming Reign of Christ—*in grace*—on earth is sufficiently imminent that Catholics must now know of its coming to pray for it, long for it, and thereby hasten it.

We must finally consider that, even as critics of the Era have gone to great lengths to show just how common Augustine's Amillennialism was—that it even was the prevailing view for the majority of the history of the Church—nevertheless this Amillennialism has never been authoritatively taught by the Magisterium, much less has it ever come *anywhere close* to being dogmatized (save for the fact that we may not believe in a literal, physical reign of Christ in the flesh on earth). And even the critics, it seems, usually acknowledge (in their moments of honesty, at least) its non-Dogmatic nature. **Do we not see the hand of Providence in this?** Augustine's interpretation was good, and it remains good. But the time has come to (while not abandoning any of the wisdom contained within it) move on from holding his view *alone* and, instead, open ourselves up to grasping the fuller meaning of the Scriptural passages, in accord with how Heaven today is begging us.

So, I propose moving on from strict Amillennialism alone—but not as one moves on from a previously held heresy; rather, as any pilgrim moves on from one stage in the spiritual life to the next, without detracting from the importance of the previous stage. We mustn't forget: **it was good that, for the** majority of Church history, Augustine's Amillennialism was the most common view, as in those times it would have been preemptive for the whole Church to be earnestly longing for the Era; in fact, its failure to come as quickly as they had hoped would doubtless turn sour, and be more of a hurdle than an aid in its hastening. (God always has perfectly good reasons for allowing an incomplete picture of some truth to reign for some time in the minds even of those who love Him.) **But now we have come to the time where the Era is truly imminent. And it is dire and urgent that we long for and pray for its hastening; which we cannot do if we do not believe it will come.**

Now, I have a humble recommendation for those who agree it is indeed time to recognize that we must acknowledge the insight of the majority of the Fathers who taught that a glorious era would come in the final millennium. We ought not say "Augustine's Amillennialism is wrong," or anything to that effect; for such a statement would itself be misleading and only partially valid, and would cause needless discord. Instead, it would be more accurate to say something to the effect of: *"It is time to be open to a more complete understanding of eschatology instead of restricting ourselves to believing only the contents of Augustine's Amillennialism and nothing more."*

And I propose two more reasons for moving on from strict *"Sola Amillennialism"*: first, Augustine had no problem with others disagreeing with his view, which he was very careful to label as a mere opinion (so long as those who disagreed did not go so far as to believe in a carnal millennium). Augustine himself forcefully acknowledged that we cannot discover the truth regarding these eschatological speculations merely with our own reason (i.e. Scriptural investigation; treating the whole matter like some giant jigsaw puzzle, as some critics of the Era do) and arguments. Second, Augustine's opinions on the timeline of history has been contradicted by the last 500 years of history. I consider both of these reasons in the two following sections.

Augustine Himself Declared the Era Orthodox

One important teaching of Augustine, given as a caveat to all his own eschatological speculations and all his own arguments against the millennial teachings of others in his day is the following:

> …as if it were a fit thing that the saints should thus enjoy a kind of Sabbath-rest during that period [of a 'thousand years'], a holy leisure after the labors of six thousand years since man was created… [and] there should follow on the completion of six thousand years, as of six days, a kind of seventh-day Sabbath in the succeeding thousand years… And **this opinion would not be objectionable, if it were believed that the joys of the saints, in that Sabbath, shall be spiritual, and consequent on the presence of God**.[929]

As we can see, Augustine's only concern with the millenarianists of his day were the carnal and literalistic views of that time to come which some of them held thanks to the Gnostic heretic Cerinthus. It is, of course, impossible to use Augustine's words to argue against a Reign of Peace if he himself has explicitly admitted there is nothing objectionable with such a view!

Furthermore, what follows is **the systematically ignored final paragraph** in Augustine's famous treatment of eschatology, found in Book 20 of *The City of God*, in which he says,

> And at or in connection with that judgment the following events shall come to pass, as we have learned: Elias the Tishbite shall come; the Jews shall believe; Antichrist shall persecute; Christ shall judge; the dead shall rise; the good and the wicked shall be separated; the world shall be burned and renewed. **All these things, we believe, shall come to pass; but how, or in what order, human understanding cannot perfectly teach us,** but only the experience of the events themselves. **My opinion, however, is, that they will happen in the order in which I have related them** [i.e., his famous Amillennialism].[930]

This quote further demonstrates that Augustine had no intent to condemn as heretical the notion of

---

[929] St. Augustine, *City of God*, Book 20, Ch. 7. (*Nota Bene*: One critic of the Era has claimed that even this teaching of Augustine is nothing but blatantly heretical Millennarianism because, he implies, the "presence of God" on Earth cannot be anything but that heresy. Here this critic only again demonstrates how spiritually (and theologically) bankrupt his arguments are in presupposing that the "presence of God"

can only refer to the Millenarianist heresy. One wonders what he thinks of the Eucharist, the indwelling of the Holy Spirit in the soul, all the Sacraments, the charisms, etc., which we enjoy now. Are they all mere symbols to him, devoid of any presence of God?

[930] St. Augustine, *City of God*, Book 20, Chapter 30.

a Reign of Peace upon the earth before the end of time, for Augustine was not one to bashfully pretend that the orthodox truths he defended against heresies were merely "his opinions." On the contrary, if Augustine says a given teaching is his *opinion*, it is because, indeed, that teaching *is just his opinion*. These two quotes—ignored by those who use St. Augustine to condemn the Era of Peace—together make it clear that this effort is futile.

We next turn to the second reason for moving beyond strict Amillennialism.

Now Being the Complete Meaning of the "1,000-Year" Chaining is No Longer Tenable

Unbeknownst to many of those who promote his Eschatology, essential to Augustine's opinions on this realm of theology was his division of all human history into six ages.[931] As with all the Fathers of the Church, he realized that the history of the world would inevitably mirror the Six Days of Creation (and the Seventh day of rest that followed them). Unlike most of the Fathers, he did not count these six ages as sets of thousand-year periods beginning with creation itself; instead, he divided them as follows:

- The First: Adam to Noah
- The Second: Noah to Abraham
- The Third: Abraham to David
- The Fourth: David to the Babylonian Captivity
- The Fifth: Babylonian Captivity to Christ
- The Sixth: Christ to the End of Time (corresponding to Revelation 20's Binding of Satan)
- (And Eternity being the Seventh)

This chronology, while meritorious in Augustine's time, is simply no longer tenable now that 2,000 years have transpired since the time of Christ, making his delineation of the six ages lopsided. (Augustine himself likely believed the end of the world would be fairly soon after his own time, as he perhaps held the view of Eusebius—now known to be incorrect—that the Fall of Man was in 5199 BC.) It furthermore seems strange to demarcate the third and fourth stages as he did. Without

detracting from the great significance of King David's reign and of the Babylonian Captivity, it simply does not seem right to look at these two events as so transcendentally impactful that they are of universal import and define the very turning points of the entire world.

But the most significant reason why this delineation of the ages of history is no longer tenable is the nature of history from the Protestant Revolt onwards. It is not surprising that someone like Augustine—who lived during a golden Era of Christianity (what Pope St. John Paul II referred to as the "millennium of Christian unity"), *after* its legalization by Constantine and *before* its tearing asunder in the second millennium—would see his own Era as the one in which Satan is chained. But we have long passed the time in which it was realistic to hold that this chaining refers *merely* to the age of Christianity in general.

For the last 500 years, the Body of Christ has been torn apart by such rampant heresy, schism, and apostasy that it makes the Arian Crisis look like child's play. For the last 300 years since the so-called "Enlightenment," diabolical Modernism has begun dominating the world. In the last 100 years, this same diabolical modernism has largely dominated the Church.[932] Despite continual efforts, the evangelization of Asia (containing the majority of the world's population) has largely failed, save a handful of its smaller countries. **This is not what the "chaining of Satan" looks like.** Especially after the dawn of the Enlightenment, each successive passing year made the wisest of Christians realize that it was becoming less and less tenable to hold that this chaining of Satan was fully in effect to the complete extent prophesied by the Book of Revelation.

This view was essentially Magisterially condemned (albeit implicitly—I am not arguing that those who hold it are heretics) by the Popes of the 20th century who, upon seeing the deluge evil inundating the world, declared that the times had become more sinful than ever before. **It is not intellectually honest to hold this Magisterial teaching and simultaneously to hold that we are in the time of the binding of Satan** spoken of in the Book of

---

[931]Cf. St. Augustine. *On the catechizing of the uninstructed.* Chapter 22.

[932]By "Church" I do not mean the Magisterium and the Sacraments – those are protected by Christ. I mean the

majority of those who call themselves Catholics being mired in objective, grave contraventions of the natural moral law.

Revelation. One of those views must go. And it mustn't be the one which is Magisterially taught. Of course, contradicting the Popes, one may protest: *"does sin really abound today? The world, and the Church, have been in dire straits before; is today any different?"*

Make no mistake about it: **the evil of the day is unprecedented.** (Incidentally, is it any surprise, then, that God is now giving an unprecedented grace to combat it through this Gift of Living in the Divine Will? "Where sin abounds, grace abounds all the more."[933]) Over the past 100 years, billions of children have been murdered through abortion. The entire earth is physically saturated with this blood of innocents that cries out to God for vengeance.[934] Take a walk down any busy city street today and you will scarcely pass by a single person whose life is not utterly mired in objective, grave, intrinsic evil; whether it be in the form of fornication, artificial contraception, auto-eroticism, drug abuse, sodomy, intentional serious hatred and unforgiveness (especially of parents), viewing pornography, physical abuse, adultery, drunken debauchery, actual or de facto atheism, occultism, or whatever else. What I have listed here are merely a few grave contraventions of the *natural* law; meaning the law that is inscribed in each person's heart and which no one has an excuse for disobeying. In other words, the vast, vast majority of God's children in this world are walking the path to eternal damnation.[935] And on this same walk down a typical city street, you will be inundated by a thousand advertisements, announcements, monuments to man, and idols of all sorts—but you will probably not stumble upon a single mere acknowledgement of the fact that the Creator of all things became man 2,000 years ago and called us to follow Him, and that nothing has any meaning outside of Him.

And the gravest evils are not merely practiced by virtually everyone (that is, virtually everyone practices at least one of them, which is tantamount to practicing all of them[936]), but they are culturally and institutionally endorsed, promoted, and insisted upon. Now governments (and peoples,

directly, through referendums) are even universally redefining the most fundamental institution which exists—marriage—so that it incorporates and blesses perversion and disorder. Never before have we seen anything remotely similar to this, except perhaps before the Flood, but even that pales in comparison to the evil of today.

> We were terrified beyond all else by **the disastrous state of human society today.** For who can fail to see that society is at the present time, **more than in any past age,** suffering from a terrible and deeprooted malady which, developing every day and eating into its inmost being, is dragging it to destruction? You understand, Venerable Brethren, what this disease is—**apostasy from God**…[937]

Pope St. Pius X wrote that in **1903**, in an Encyclical (one of the most authoritative formal acts of the Magisterium). Have things gotten better since then? Obviously, they have gotten far, far worse. Sin is now on the verge of exhausting itself. **If there was ever a time in which Satan was not chained, that time is now.**

Remember that this does not mean we are completely rejecting Augustine's interpretation. Satan certainly was chained, to a degree, upon the birth of Christ. Jesus' own words to Luisa agree. For He said to her:

> At the beginning, a graft can produce neither great goods nor great evils, but only the beginning of evil or of good. When I came upon earth, with my Conception I formed the opposite graft with the tree of humanity, and the evils began to stop, the bad humors to be destroyed; so, there is all the hope that the Kingdom of my Divine Will be formed in the midst of the human generations. The many truths I have manifested to you about my Divine Fiat are sips of life, some of which water, some cultivate, some increase the humors for the tree of humanity grafted by Me. Therefore, if the Life of my Divine Fiat has entered into the tree of my Humanity and has formed the graft, there is all the reason to hope that my Kingdom will have Its scepter, Its just dominion and Its command in the midst of creatures. Therefore, pray and do not doubt."[938]

---

[933] Cf. Romans 5:20

[934] *Cf.* Genesis 4:10

[935] This makes no attempt to ascertain culpability, which God alone knows. Nevertheless, the sins themselves are objectively evil, and are committed by the vast majority of people. This is furthermore not to assert that the "vast, vast

majority" of people today will wind up in hell – it is simply an honest assessment of their current state.

[936] Cf. James 2:10

[937] *E Supremi* October 4th, 1903. Paragraph 3.

[938] October 27, 1929.

And even though the Queen of Heaven debilitated [Satan], crushed his head, and I Myself bound him to the cross, therefore he is no longer free to do what he wants, however, those who by disgrace draw near him, he slaughters.[939]

The point is merely that, like much if not most of Scripture, there are multiple correct interpretations of the same verse—and the Chaining of Satan seems to refer not only to the Era of Christianity in general, but to some future Era on earth as well—and the need for this additional interpretation is demonstrated by the last 500 years of history, and especially the last 100. When history demonstrates a conclusion with such clarity, it is folly to cling to one non-binding interpretation of a given Scriptural passage and reject a further developed interpretation in accordance with this historical clarity.

Indeed, while remaining firmly grounded in Tradition, a degree of healthy flexibility is also **necessary**, with due regard for Pope Francis' repeated admonition that the Lord is the "God of surprises," and we are still "a people on a journey."[940] However, it was not Pope Francis, but rather Venerable Pope Pius XII, who forcefully taught, as quoted in the previous section:

> ... all moreover should abhor that intemperate zeal which imagines that whatever is new should for that very reason be opposed or suspected ... in the immense matter contained in the Sacred Books—legislative, historical, sapiential <u>and prophetical—there are but few texts whose sense has been defined by the authority of the Church</u> ... There remain therefore many things, and of <u>the greatest importance</u>, in the discussion and exposition of which the skill and genius of Catholic commentators may and ought to be freely exercised, so that each may contribute his part to the advantage of all, to the continued progress of the sacred doctrine and to the defense and honor of the Church.[941]

Extracting what is most relevant, one can see that **Pius XII is here insisting that Catholics *abhor* the automatic reaction of suspicion to new interpretations of the prophetical elements of Scripture, lest we risk damaging positive progress of the "greatest importance."**

For it is not only the facts of history, the 20th century Papal Magisterium, and the consensus of private

revelation that invites this re-evaluation of strict-Amillennialism-alone eschatology; it is also a simple deference to the proper approach to Scripture itself, other considerations aside. We now turn to consider this often-forgotten fact.

The Clear Sense of Scripture

Critics of the Era tend to bend over backward to superimpose a rather awkward meaning upon the Book of Revelation (which, they admit, contrasts with the clear sense of the words themselves). They first give lectures on how we must not be rigid, simplistic adherents to the clear sense of Scripture, but must instead understand that it is more like a riddle that, conveniently, can only really be understood by purchasing their books, which in turn are replete with speculative connections between Revelation and the modern day, at least half of which will be proven wrong by history before finishing the reading.

But I propose something simpler: the words of the relevant Chapter of *the* Book itself, which are as follows:

> Then I saw an angel coming down from heaven, holding in his hand the key of the bottomless pit and a great chain. And he seized the dragon, that ancient serpent, who is the Devil and Satan, and bound him for a thousand years, and threw him into the pit, and shut it and sealed it over him, that he should deceive the nations no more, till the thousand years were ended. After that he must be loosed for a little while. Then I saw thrones, and seated on them were those to whom judgment was committed. Also I saw the souls of those who had been beheaded for their testimony to Jesus and for the word of God, and who had not worshiped the beast or its image and had not received its mark on their foreheads or their hands. They came to life, and reigned with Christ a thousand years. The rest of the dead did not come to life until the thousand years were ended. This is the first resurrection. Blessed and holy is he who shares in the first resurrection! Over such the second death has no power, but they shall be priests of God and of Christ, and they shall reign with him a thousand years. And when the thousand years are ended, Satan will be loosed from his prison and will come out to deceive the nations which are at the four corners of the earth, that is, Gog and Magog, to gather them for battle; their number is like the sand of the sea. And they

---

[939] May 19, 1931.
[940] Pope Francis. Morning Meditation. (13 October 2014).

[941] Pope Pius XII, Encyclical Promoting Biblical Studies *Divino Afflante Spiritu* (30 September, 1943), 47.

marched up over the broad earth and surrounded the camp of the saints and the beloved city; but fire came down from heaven and consumed them, and the devil who had deceived them was thrown into the lake of fire and brimstone where the beast and the false prophet were, and they will be tormented day and night for ever and ever. Then I saw a great white throne and him who sat upon it; from his presence earth and sky fled away, and no place was found for them. And I saw the dead, great and small, standing before the throne, and books were opened. Also another book was opened, which is the book of life. And the dead were judged by what was written in the books, by what they had done. And the sea gave up the dead in it, Death and Hades gave up the dead in them, and all were judged by what they had done. Then Death and Hades were thrown into the lake of fire. This is the second death, the lake of fire; and if any one's name was not found written in the book of life, he was thrown into the lake of fire.

That is the *unabridged entirety* of the 20th chapter of the Book of Revelation.

The vast majority of people—nearly all, I dare say—who read those words and do not already have knowledge of somebody else's interpretation, would inevitably say something like the following:

"Well, I certainly can't figure out all the mysterious details, but what does look abundantly clear is that this passage speaks of a subduing of the Devil for a "thousand years," with some manner of glorious Era of Christ's reign with the saints to come on earth during this reign. And then for a brief time after that, the Devil will be released again. God, however, will immediately destroy him with fire from Heaven as he attacks the saints, and he will then be tormented in hell forever. Then, the definitive Last Judgment and Resurrection will follow, and it will be the end of time."

And what is this response that we see? It is that which is rightly called **the "clear sense of Scripture."** It is the sense of Scripture that is open to being understood by an ordinary catechized Catholic in a state of grace without needing to consult a committee of Scripture scholars for their opinion.

As we observed, Augustine's Amillennialism had

its time, but the time has now come to acknowledge the clear sense of Scripture as it regards the passage. Do not confuse this encouragement with an admonishment to always stick only to the literal sense of Scripture: **I did not say we must return to the *literal* sense, but to the *clear* sense.** The clear sense of Scripture is almost always the correct one: and usually, when the Holy Spirit inspires a verse in Scripture that is not intended to be literal, it is clear to a catechized reader that it is not a literal statement (e.g. Jesus' words "*I am the vine, you are the branches,*"[942] are obviously not intended to declare that He is truly, literally a vine).

Interestingly, a priest who was well known for opposing Luisa's writings even himself wrote, against Augustine:

> It is tragically obvious that **Augustine completely denied the clear sense of Scripture here**… Augustine was denying the love of God, without realizing it of course. [943]

He wrote this in relation to Augustine's teaching on grace and salvation. The priest goes on to blame Augustine's "*Massa Damnata*" views (that God could have thrown the whole human race into hell because of Original Sin, and chose only a few to show His mercy to) on his "*tendency to allegorical interpretations*" of Sacred Scripture which, this priest argues, caused in Augustine **his unwillingness to adhere to the clear sense of Scripture's teaching that "God Wills all men to be saved."**[944] The priest continues, saying:

> Both St. Ambrose and St. Augustine were completely wrong in their understanding of this line of St. Paul…[945]

Here, he references the line of this Apostle wherein he says that the "letter kills, but the spirit gives life,"[946] as they both, he argues, wrongly gleaned from this verse that the *letter of Scripture* kills, when in fact St. Paul was referring to the *letter of the Old Mosaic Law* which (in contrast to the grace and spirit of the New Covenant) "kills."

Now I am being much gentler with Augustine, but the fascinating analysis that this priest gives is in fact a much more perfect description of the weaknesses that are now evident with **sola-Amillennialism: it is far too ready to reject the**

---

942 John 15:5
943 https://www.ewtn.com/library/theology/augustin.htm
944 1 Timothy 2:4

945 https://www.ewtn.com/library/theology/augustin.htm
946 2 Corinthians 3:6

clear sense of Scripture for the sake of a purely spiritual one.

Before we leave this consideration, it would behoove us to remember that the primary opponents of the clear sense of Scripture today are the Modernists; it is only by their dismissal of this clear sense that they can succeed in their nefarious plot to subvert the entire moral law, denounce the Real Presence of Christ in the Eucharist, promote Darwinism, undermine marriage and family, etc. Without reverting to a literalistic view of those verses intended only symbolically, we can nevertheless assert with conviction that a **return to the clear sense of Scripture is among the most important and indispensable tools for Catholics today who wish to fight for the restoration of the Church and the world, and the Book of Revelation should not be arbitrarily exempted from this return.**

Joachim of Fiore: Radically Divergent from Teachings on the Era

Joachim of Fiore (or Flora) was an influential 12th century Cistercian abbot who wrote a large body of eschatological, apocalyptic work that had far-reaching effects throughout the late middle ages.

He erroneously taught that the days of the Old Testament were simply the days of the Father, the time since the Incarnation were/are the days of the Son, and that we now approach the days of the Holy Spirit[947] in which **we await a new Public Revelation (just as the ancient Jews, having received a valid covenant from God, nevertheless awaited a better one), as well as a new Deposit of Faith and an end of the age of the Catholic Church.** The bulk of his followers were known as the "Spiritual Franciscans," whom St. Bonaventure wrote against.

Joachim's teaching continued, holding that the "Johannine Church of the spirit would replace the current Petrine Church."[948] In typical Protestant fashion—before there was such a thing as Protestantism—he saw only the nascent Church in the earliest centuries as worthy of the highest praise, with Constantine's great, Providential legalization of Christianity being a marked degradation.

But even a basic understanding of the facts of Joachim's legacy clearly indicate that his teachings are gravely at odds with those Jesus gives to Luisa and with the beliefs of all Catholics who anticipate the Era of Peace. **In Luisa's writings, Jesus goes so far as to say that Heaven itself is veiled within the Catholic Church, of which *the Pope* is head.** Jesus speaks to Luisa not of a time where this Church is laid aside, but where this Church, *whose head is the Roman Pontiff,* will acquire her full vigor. Luisa's own life was the example par excellence of obedience and submission to the institutional Catholic Church, and Jesus makes it clear that the life of Luisa is to be the model of those who come after her wishing to receive the Gift of Living in the Divine Will. The Sacraments and all the teachings of the Church will still exist—this is the unanimous consensus of all private revelations that speak of the Era—but they will be received not merely as medicine for the sick, like so many treat them now, but rather as food for the healthy; as saintly souls even now treat them.

Joachim is a commonly cited name among the critics of the Era because he was mentioned in the CDF's 1992 document already quoted in a previous section, *Some Current Questions in Eschatology;* another work promulgated under Cardinal Ratzinger which the critics of the Era gravely misuse. The relevant portion of the text is as follows:

> There is silence about eschatology today for other reasons, of which we single out one: that is, the rebirth of the tendency to establish an innerworldly eschatology. This tendency is well known in the history of theology, and beginning with the Middle Ages it constituted what came to be called "the spiritual heritage of Joachim de Fiore". This tendency is found in some theologians of liberation, who so insist on the importance of establishing the kingdom of God as something within our own history on earth that the salvation which transcends history seems to become of rather secondary interest. Certainly, these theologians do not deny in any way the truth of realities beyond human life and history. But since the kingdom of God is located in a society without divisions, "the third age" in which "the eternal Gospel" (Rev 14:6-7) and the kingdom of the Spirit are to flourish is introduced

---

[947] He thought this would commence in 1260, which he knew would be long after his death, as he was born in 1135.

[948] ECCLESIASTICAL HISTORIOGRAPHY. New Catholic Encyclopedia. P. 874.

in a new and secularized form. In this way a certain kind of "eschaton" is brought within historical time. This "eschaton" is not presented as the ultimate absolute, but as a relative absolute. Nonetheless, Christian praxis is directed so exclusively to the establishment of this eschaton that the Gospel is read reductively, so that whatever pertains to the eschatological realities absolutely considered is in great part passed over in silence. In this way, in a theological system of this sort, "one places oneself within the perspective of a temporal messianism, which is one of the most radical of the expressions of secularisation of the Kingdom of God and of its absorption into the immanence of human history."[949]

Obviously, this CDF document is referring primarily—if not entirely—to Liberation Theology which, as we have already discussed, is not in any way similar to what is found in Luisa's writings or what is anticipated by Catholics who anticipate the Era thanks to trustworthy private revelation.

But even if one seeks to remove this CDF admonition from its proper context to accuse the Era of error, the attempt still fails, since—as we discussed—the Era in no way detracts from the superiority of Heaven; but rather enhances it. This distinction is obvious in all the private revelations which speak of the Era and in all the fruits and practices seen in the followers of the same. In fact, **if one searches the whole Church far and wide, he will have a hard time finding a single group of Catholics who are less prone to the error of prioritizing the imminent, temporal over the transcendent, eternal than are those who devote themselves to trustworthy private revelation and prayerfully await the Era.**

Before leaving the topic of Joachim of Fiore, we should take note, for the sake of justice and truth, that he was a very pious and holy man, who was not a formal heretic because his teachings were not condemned until after his death (although, frankly, he should have known better without needing a formal Church condemnation). Dante himself declared that Joachim was "endowed with a prophetic spirit." Joachim was even admired by multiple Popes during his own lifetime.[950]

Regarding Joachim, The New Catholic Encyclopedia points out that:

> He [Joachim] publicly submitted all his works to the judgment of the Holy See but died before any judgment was passed. Contemporaries testified to his love of Christ, his fervor at Mass, his inspiring eloquence in preaching. Gentle and pure, he loved all creatures and lived in utter poverty. [951]

It should not be surprising to learn that so holy and learned a man as Joachim stumbled upon some truths! For indeed, his intuition that there would be a new Era of Peace that would dawn up the world is, of course, in and of itself absolutely correct. The fact that he mixed heresies in with this truth should not cause anyone, as the old saying goes, to "*throw the baby out with the bathwater*" and conclude that everything he taught was a heresy.

As Joachim's teachings amounted to what could be considered just one specific brand of Dispensationalism, we now turn to briefly consider that heresy more broadly.

On Dispensationalism

Dispensationalism in the broad sense is a heresy common in Protestant circles, and it is not an accusation seriously levied against many Catholic believers in the Era, because even the Era's fiercest critics recognize that would be quite a long shot.

Dispensationalists, rightly concluding that there is a marked distinction between the Old Testament and the New Testament epochs, conclude that another similar rupture will occur in the future, "dispensing" us from the requirements of the New Testament times, which will be replaced by those of a time to come. The error of the Dispensationalists is that they fail to recognize that the New Testament contains the *eternal* covenant (cf. Hebrews 13:20), the *eternal* Gospel (cf. Revelation 14:6), which will never pass away and from which we will never be dispensed.

As has been repeatedly demonstrated throughout this chapter, Luisa's revelations do not entail one hint of dispensation from either the Deposit of Faith in general or one item of its contents.

---

[949] http://www.vatican.va/roman_curia/congregations/cfaith/cti_documents/rc_cti_1990_problemi-attuali-escatologia_en.html

[950] B. McGinn , Karl A. Kottman. *Millenarianism and Messianism in Early Modern European Culture*. Volume II. Ch. 1, Page 5.

[951] JOACHIM OF FIORE. New Catholic Encyclopedia. Page 876.

29) The Era of Peace Elsewhere

Before turning to Luisa's revelations on the Era, let us take some time to see just how prevalent are prophecies pertaining to it virtually everywhere one looks within Catholicism: almost all the Fathers of the Church believed in the Era, almost all private revelations that touch on the end times do prophesy an Era, and even the Papal Magisterium of the 20th century speaks clearly of the Era.

Scripture, too, prophesies the Era. However, since much of the preceding Chapter was spent discussing the various New Testament prophecies of the Era (and, specifically, refuting erroneous interpretations of them which dismiss the Era), in order to avoid needless redundancy, these will not be included within this chapter and we will, instead, consider now the Old Testament prophecies.

The Fathers of the Church

The first thing that must be understood with the teachings of the Fathers on the Era and the millennium is what I have already stated multiple times: *even if* all the Era's critics' arguments (that reject as heresy the agreement on the millennium by most of the Fathers of the Church) were correct, these arguments would still have no bearing on the reality of the Era of Peace as described by Jesus to Luisa and so many others. Recall that this Era in no way depends upon the teachings of the Fathers of the Church on the millennium; the latter is an inspirational overlap, but it is by no means a necessary vindication which, if refuted, refutes the Era of Peace. The Era of Peace is coming: no one can stop it. This reality is not contingent upon this or that interpretation of the Fathers, or the Book of Revelation, being vindicated or condemned. Nor will Almighty God change His plans to not offend a few apologists who will be scandalized when they see creation restored to its original dignity.

That being said, it does seem clear that the millennial teachings of the Fathers of the Church, concerning which a near consensus exists among them, *do* speak of the same thing that Jesus reveals to Luisa as the Era of Peace (the *Reign of the Divine Will on Earth*).

The Fathers of the Church held that the Seven Days of Creation were analogous to the seven millennia of human history. Just as with the days of the week, and the days of Creation, the last is reserved for rest, so the last millennia of life on earth would be one of "rest."[952] In speaking against the Reign of Peace, some dispute that the Fathers held that the Days of Creation were indeed analogous to the ages of time to come, but none other than Pope Benedict XVI taught this, saying:

> The Fathers of the Church considered the six or seven days of the Creation narrative as a prophecy of the history of the world, of humanity. For them, the seven days represented seven periods of history, later also interpreted as seven millennia. With Christ we should have entered the last, that is, the sixth period of history that was to be followed by the great sabbath of God.[953]

Later in the same address, Benedict had the following to say to those who insist that history is doomed to simply become worse and worse as time goes on, until the Second Coming of Christ:

> Today too there are views that see the entire history of the Church in the second millennium as a gradual decline. Some see this decline as having already begun immediately after the New Testament. [On the contrary,] In fact, "Opera Christi non deficiunt, sed proficiunt": Christ's works do not go backwards but forwards …

We also recall, from a previous section, that St. Augustine's teachings are no impediment to the anticipation of a Glorious Reign of Peace. So now let us consider the teachings of other Fathers of the Church on this topic. As the quotes explain themselves, I will simply list a few of them here for you. Remember that the point is not to advocate for this or that precise eschatological opinion of any one Father, but just to prove that the Fathers in general were supportive of the notion of a Glorious Reign of Peace before the end of time. I am not insisting upon the literal and complete validity of any one of these prognostications.

---

[952] In this, "last" refers to the Sabbath of the Old Testament: Saturday. Hence Sunday, "the Eighth Day," is allegorical for the eternal new first day – heaven.

[953] Benedict XVI. General Audience. March 10, 2010.

St. Justin Martyr: "I and every other orthodox Christian feel certain that there will be a resurrection of the flesh[954] followed by a thousand years in a rebuilt, embellished, and enlarged city of Jerusalem, as was announced by the Prophets Ezekiel, Isaias and others… A man among us named John, one of Christ's Apostles, received and foretold that the followers of Christ would dwell in Jerusalem for a thousand years,[955] and that afterwards the universal and, in short, everlasting resurrection and judgment would take place." [956]

St. Justin could not have proposed this view with more vigor. Even if Catholic orthodoxy requires leaving behind some details of it, when a Father of the Church prefaces a teaching with "I and every other orthodox Christian feel certain…," any Christian must pay heed.

Tertullian: "But we do confess that a kingdom is promised to us upon the earth, although before heaven, only in another state of existence; inasmuch as it will be after the resurrection for a thousand years in the divinely-built city of Jerusalem…"[957]

St. Irenaeus[958]: "The predicted blessing, therefore, belongs unquestionably to the times of the kingdom, when the righteous shall bear rule upon their rising from the dead; when also the creation, having been renovated and set free, shall fructify with an abundance of all kinds of food, from the dew of heaven, and from the fertility of the earth: **as the elders who saw John, the disciple of the Lord, related that they had heard from him how the Lord used to teach in regard to these times** … and that all animals feeding [only] on the productions of the earth, should [in those days] become peaceful and harmonious among each other, and be in perfect subjection to man."[959]

It is significant that **two of these quotes from Church Fathers voice not merely their own opinions, but relate what was received from the Apostle John himself.** Besides being from Our Lord directly, one could not hope to have a greater testimony on what is to come towards the end of time than John, the author of the Book of Revelation.

Lactantius, the great fourth century apologist and Church Father who served as an advisor to Constantine, dedicated a chapter in his *Divine Institutes* to this very discussion. Entitled "Of the Renewed World," it speaks in no vague terms of a literal time on earth, after an intermediate (not physical or final) coming of Christ, during which Satan is chained and the just flourish. Describing clearly how this time will involve a sort of return to the original state of justice, Lactantius describes this Era as being one in which

…beasts shall not be nourished by blood, nor birds by prey; but all things shall be peaceful and tranquil. Lions and calves shall stand together at the manger, the wolf shall not carry off the sheep…[960]

While many more teachings of the Fathers could be cited in demonstrating the existence of this consensus on the Era of Peace, it is instead fitting to end this brief treatment by quoting Lactantius himself, who, in the next chapter, also cuts short his discourse:

These are the things which are spoken of by the prophets as about to happen hereafter: but I have not considered it necessary to bring forward their testimonies and words, since it would be an endless task; nor would the limits of my book receive so great a multitude of subjects, since so

---

[954] Not a literal reference to the actual *Eternal* Resurrection (considering the indefinite article that precedes it) that Justin refers to in the following chapter

[955] Justin understands this to be symbolic

[956] Justin Martyr, *Dialogue with Trypho*. Chapter 80.

[957] Tertullian. *Against Marcion*, Book 3. Chapter 25.

[958] His work quoted here, *Against Heresies (Adversus Haereses)*, or "On the Detection and Overthrow of So-Called Gnosis," is a large, five volume work written in the 2nd century and contains his rebuttal of Gnosticism. Irenaeus wisely saw that Gnosticism was a grave threat to the integrity of the Faith, as its proponents claimed that they had access to secretive knowledge from Jesus Himself, outside of the Public and Canonical Revelation overseen by the Bishops of the Church. Irenaeus' zeal in opposing Gnosticism helps us understand that his own views on eschatology certainly were not derived from the same fundamental error; namely, that of

surreptitiously seeking secretive "knowledge" from Jesus outside the ordinary and correct means of knowing it. We can rest assured that his belief in a coming Era of Peace truly was from the Apostle John; for it is untenable that a saint and Father of the Church would have succumbed to the very same Gnostic errors he is so famous for fighting against. Even though this is only one piece of evidence among thousands demonstrating the validity of the Era, it alone is practically sufficient to render the Era a near certainty.

[959] Irenaeus. *Against Heresies*, Book V. Chapter 33, Paragraph 3.

[960] Lactantius, *Divine Institutes*, Translated by William Fletcher. From Ante-Nicene Fathers, Vol. 7. (Buffalo, NY: Christian Literature Publishing Co., 1886.) Book VII. Chapter 24.

many with one breath speak similar things; and at the same time, lest weariness should be occasioned to the readers if I should heap together things collected and transferred from all.[961]

Having already quoted many sources demonstrating his views on a coming Era of Peace, Lactantius deems it pointless to continue. The task would be so voluminous, he writes, as the same prophecies are given by so many, that its results would be "endless."

Remember that, even if some individual teachings of a few of the Church Fathers need to be set aside, this adjustment does not undermine the general consensus of the Fathers on what is essential to this Era. Regrettably, that is precisely how the Fathers' teachings are treated by critics of the Era—in quintessential Modernist fashion, flippantly casting aside entire realms of works from the Fathers on incredibly feeble grounds—stands in stark contrast to the proper, Church-condoned approach to Patristics. For indeed, when once a teaching is found to be a unanimous consensus among the Fathers, then, by that very fact, it is automatically a dogma of the Catholic Faith. This follows from the teaching of the First Vatican Council, which states: *"It is not permissible for anyone to interpret Holy Scripture in a sense contrary to ... the unanimous consent of the fathers."*[962] Furthermore, the Council of Trent promulgated the same teaching.[963]

Admittedly, only one dissenting vote is necessary to destroy unanimity. This result may be the case with the Fathers' teaching on the Era of Peace, since, as already mentioned, one interpretation of Augustine's eschatology predicts no Era of Peace; and Jerome and Origen provide some arguments against some millennial teaching as well. **But that there is a *near* unanimous consensus on the millennial Reign among the Fathers should not be ignored. On the contrary, this near unanimity is not only extremely valuable, but should in fact be considered trustworthy in proportion to its proximity to unanimity. Pope St. Pius X even invoked a *near* unanimous consensus of the Fathers to justify what was among his greatest legacies:** the promotion of as many Catholics (who are in a state of grace) as possible becoming daily communicants. In a decree issued in the third year of his pontificate, he wrote:

> ... we are bidden in the Lord's Prayer to ask for 'our daily bread' by which words, the holy Fathers of the Church all but unanimously teach, must be understood ...as the Eucharistic bread which ought to be our daily food.[964]

Therefore, it is clear that **an "all but" unanimous consensus of the Fathers, while not automatically elevating the consensus to the status of dogma, does nevertheless present a serious obligation to the conscience of a Christian for consideration, and is highly unlikely to be in error.** Considering the teachings cited above (and there are many others like them), it is difficult to deny that there is, at least, a near unanimous consensus among the Fathers of the Church on their insistence upon the coming of the Kingdom of God on earth before the end of time.

A thorough treatment of this matter is not necessary here; I simply recommend you to the works of the theologian Fr. Joseph Iannuzzi (e.g. *The Splendor of Creation* and *Antichrist and the End Times*), as well as the blog posts of the evangelist Mark Mallett (markmallett.com/blog). Encouraging you to spend time perusing Mark's website, I present below a selection of quotes (beyond what is already presented above) which he compiled from the Fathers of the Church on the Era in an article entitled *"How the Era Was Lost"* (an article which gives a detailed examination of how teachings on the Era were largely neglected for much of Church history):

> "And God rested on the seventh day from all his works… Therefore, a sabbath rest still remains for the people of God." (Heb 4:4, 9)…when His Son will come and destroy the time of the lawless one and judge the godless, and change the sun and the moon and the stars—then He shall indeed rest on the seventh day… after giving rest to all things, I will make the beginning of the eighth day, that is, the beginning of another world. —Letter of Barnabas (70-79 A.D.), written by a second century Apostolic Father

---

961 Lactantius, *Divine Institutes*. Book VII. Chapter 25.
962 First Vatican Council, Session 3, Dogmatic Constitution on the Catholic Faith (24 April 1870), in *Decrees of the First Vatican Council*, www.papalencyclicals.net, 2.9.

963 Council of Trent, Session 4, Decree Concerning the Canonical Scriptures. (8 April 1546), *in Decree Concerning the Edition and Use of the Sacred Books*, ewtn.com.
964 Pope Pius X, On Frequent and Daily Reception of Holy Communion *Sacra Tridentina*. (20 December 1905) at ewtn.com.

We say that this city [divinely rebuilt Jerusalem] has been provided by God for receiving the saints on their resurrection, and refreshing them with the abundance of all really spiritual blessings, as a recompense for those which we have either despised or lost… —Tertullian (155—240 A.D.), Nicene Church Father; Adversus Marcion, Ante-Nicene Fathers, Henrickson Publishers, 1995, Vol. 3, pp. 342-343)

Therefore, the Son of the most high and mighty God… shall have destroyed unrighteousness, and executed His great judgment, and shall have recalled to life the righteous, who… will be engaged among men a thousand years, and will rule them with most just command… —Lactantius, The Divine Institutes, The ante-Nicene Fathers, Vol 7, p. 211

So, the blessing foretold undoubtedly refers to the time of His Kingdom, when the just will rule on rising from the dead; when creation, reborn and freed from bondage, will yield an abundance of foods of all kinds from the heaven's dew and the fertility of the earth, just as the seniors recall. Those who saw John, the Lord's disciple, [tell us] that they heard from him how the Lord taught and spoke about these times… —St. Irenaeus of Lyons, Church Father (140—202 A.D.); Adversus Haereses, Irenaeus of Lyons, V.33.3.4, The Fathers of the Church, CIMA Publishing

The earth will open its fruitfulness and bring forth most abundant fruits of its own accord; the rocky mountains shall drip with honey; streams of wine shall run down, and rivers flow with milk; in short the world itself shall rejoice, and all nature exalt, being rescued and set free from the dominion of evil and impiety, and guilt and error. —Caecilius Firmianus Lactantius, The Divine Institutes

These are the words of Isaiah concerning the millennium: 'For there will be a new heaven and a new earth, and the former will not be remembered nor come into their heart, but they will be glad and rejoice in these things, which I create… There shall no more be an infant of days there, nor an old man that shall not fill up his days; for the child shall die a hundred years old… For as the days of the tree of life, so shall be the days of My people, and the works of their hands shall be multiplied. My elect shall not labor in vain, nor bring forth children for a curse; for they shall be a righteous seed blessed by the Lord, and

their posterity with them. —St. Justin Martyr, Dialogue with Trypho, Ch. 81, The Fathers of the Church, Christian Heritage; cf. Is 54:1[965]

***

Quite unfortunately, the modern debate surrounding these teachings of the Fathers concerns itself with details that, regardless of whose stance turns out to be vindicated, do not in any way affect the underlying general consensus of the Fathers: that there will be a deep symmetry found in the history of creation, within time. Just as it emerged from God holy, glorious, and peaceful, so too it will return to Him at the end in this state. Seeing the prevalence of this view, however, does not require looking only to early Church history; it can be seen also in modern Magisterium.

Popes & The Church's Magisterium

Although there are many more writings of the Fathers on this topic, my purpose here was only to give you an introduction. But we should also consider Papal Statements regarding what is to come, for many of them have taught clearly that we should indeed hope for a coming Reign of Peace.

Beginning in the late 19th century, Papal teaching began to indicate that the Church was nearing its final confrontation and its corresponding great triumph to follow. Indeed, they have gone so far to issue, as it were, authoritative conditional prophecies. In reading these following quotes, you will see that they insist that these times of Peace not only may come, but *will indeed* come—if only we do God's will. And in all these quotes it is clear that a temporal peace is referred to; a time to come before the end of history in which God's blessings will pour out in the same abundance as He promised in Scripture.

Beginning with Pope Leo XIII in 1899, one can see a real insistence that complete Divine peace, arriving within history and on earth, is not mere dreaming.

> **Leo XIII-** "It will at length be possible that our many wounds be healed … that the splendors of peace be renewed, and swords and arms drop from the hand when all men shall acknowledge the empire of Christ and willingly obey His word…"[966]

---

[965] https://www.markmallett.com/blog/2012/03/02/how-the-era-was-lost/

[966] Pope Leo XIII, Encyclical on the Consecrated to the Sacred Heart *Annum Sacrum* (25 May 1899), 11.

To ensure the reader does not assume these words refer merely to the cessation of some specific violent conflict of his day, he ends this paragraph by referring to this very renewal as the reality described by St. Paul, when he wrote that "Every tongue shall confess that our Lord Jesus Christ is in the glory of God the Father."[967]

While it was Leo XIII who ushered in the 20th century of Christianity by consecrating the world to the Sacred Heart (by way of the Encyclical which contains the aforementioned quote), it was Pope St. Pius X, following him directly, who set the stage for the decades that would follow. On the Feast of St. Francis of Assisi, in his first Encyclical — which was his first Magisterial teaching given to the Church in which he intended to give the figure of his entire pontificate — Pius X gave this master plan. Entitled *E Supremi* (*On the Restoration of All Things in Christ*), this document stated in no uncertain terms that, as quoted previously, the world had become more degenerate than ever before. But this was not the end of the story. For what he foresaw would follow this degeneracy was none other than the ultimate restoration. Therefore, in this encyclical he also wrote:

"Oh! when in every city and village the law of the Lord is faithfully observed, when respect is shown for sacred things, when the Sacraments are frequented, and the ordinances of Christian life fulfilled, there will certainly be no more need for us to labor further to see all things restored in Christ. **Nor is it for the attainment of eternal welfare alone** that this will be of service — it will also contribute largely to temporal welfare and the advantage of human society ... when [piety] is strong and flourishing **'the people will' truly 'sit in the fullness of peace...** May God, "who is rich in mercy", benignly speed this restoration of the human race in Jesus Christ ... And let us, Venerable Brethren, "in the spirit of humility", with continuous and urgent prayer ask this of Him through the merits of Jesus Christ."[968] **(Pope St. Pius X)**

He does not say that all things "might" be restored in Christ, but that they *will* be; nor does he say that *some* humans will be restored, but that the *human race* will be. This cannot be anything but a reference to an Era of Peace far beyond anything the world has seen since the Fall. Far from being an anomaly that ended with these two Popes,

this proclamation of a glorious era to come was picked up two decades later by Pius XI—its expectation in no way dimmed by the horror of the first World War—in his proclamation of the Feast of Christ the King. In the Encyclical *Quas Primas*, he wrote:

"When once men recognize, both in private and in public life, that Christ is King, society will at last receive the great blessings of real liberty, well-ordered discipline, peace and harmony ... If the kingdom of Christ, then, receives, as it should, all nations under its way, **there seems no reason why we should despair of seeing that peace which the King of Peace came to bring on earth** ... Oh, what happiness would be Ours if all men, individuals, families, and nations, would but let themselves be governed by Christ!"[969] **(Pope Pius XI)**

And, in his Encyclical Ubi Arcano Dei Consilio, he wrote:

"'And other sheep I have, that are not of this fold: them also I must bring.' He cannot but rejoice in the wonderful prophecy which filled even the Sacred Heart of Jesus with joy. 'And they shall hear my voice, and there shall be one fold and one shepherd.' May God, and We join with you and with all the faithful in this prayer, shortly bring to fulfillment His prophecy by transforming this consoling vision of the future into a present reality." **(Pius XI)**

Pius XI, instead of backing down from the bold prophecies issued by Pius X, rather strengthens and furthers them. He even continues the above quote by referring to Leo XIII's *Annum Sacrum*, reiterating the teaching that all men shall indeed "acknowledge the empire of Christ," as if to remind the reader that this theme is a continuous one which will not be abandoned. Indeed, **the mere repetition of it, now shown in three separate Encyclicals, demonstrates that this teaching must be considered Ordinary Magisterium.**

Venerable Pope Pius XII continued this theme, teaching in his Encyclical *Le Pellerinage De Lourdes* (written in French, it is a warning against materialism on the centenary of the Apparitions at Lourdes):

But however important it may be, the conversion of the individual pilgrim is not enough. We exhort you in this jubilee year, Beloved Sons and

---

[967] Philippians 2:11
[968] Pope Pius X *E Supremi*, 14.

[969] Pope Pius XI, Encyclical on the Feast of Christ the King *Quas Primas* (11 December 1925), 19.

Venerable Brothers, to inspire among the faithful entrusted to your care a common effort **for the Christian renewal of society in answer to Mary's appeal.** "May blind spirits ... be illumined by the light of truth and justice," Pius XI asked during the Marian feasts of the Jubilee of the Redemption, "so that those who have gone astray into error may be brought back to the straight path, that a just liberty may be granted the Church everywhere, **and that an era of peace and true prosperity may come upon all the nations.**"[970]

Could the Popes be any clearer? Is anyone really worried that something is a heresy if it is clearly taught in no less than five separate Papal Encyclicals? Here, Venerable Pope Pius XII prays for an Era of Peace for the entire world. In doing so, he is quoting (thus adding further Magisterial weight) his predecessor's letter of January 10, 1935.[971] That letter speaks clearly of this worldwide peace.

Pope St. John XXIII prophesied the following:

At times we have to listen, much to our regret, to the voices of people who, though burning with zeal, lack a sense of discretion and measure. In this modern age they can see nothing but prevarication and ruin ... We feel that we must disagree with those prophets of doom who are always forecasting disaster, as though the end of the world were at hand. In our times, divine Providence is leading us to a new order of human relations which, by human effort and even beyond all expectations, are directed to the fulfilment of God's superior and inscrutable designs, in which everything, even human setbacks, leads to the greater good of the Church.[972]

And, after him, Pope St. Paul VI also made clear that the future would see a new Era on earth, saying:

The unity of the world will be. The dignity of the human person shall be recognized not only formally but effectively. The inviolability of life, from the womb to old age... Undue social inequalities will be overcome. The relations between peoples will be peaceful, reasonable and fraternal. Neither selfishness, nor arrogance, nor

poverty... [shall] prevent the establishment of a true human order, a common good, a new civilization.[973]

But these prophecies did not end upon the cessation of World War II, upon the end of the Cold War, or upon the fall of the Berlin Wall; as if one could be justified in pretending that these events heralded the "peace" spoken of in the prophecies before them. Far from it—their legacy was carried forward boldly by Pope St. John Paul II himself, who, up to his death in 2005, never abandoned his hope and his firm expectation that the Third Millennium would see this new Era dawn.

Pope St. John Paul II on the Millennium

Before becoming Pope, Karol Wojtyla visited the U.S. in 1976 and gave a talk in which he stated:

We are now standing in the face of the greatest historical confrontation humanity has gone through ... We are now facing the final confrontation between the Church and the anti-Church, of the Gospel versus the anti-Gospel ... Through your prayers and mine, it is possible to alleviate this tribulation, but it is no longer possible to avert it ... [974]

This observation cannot be taken as a reference to the end of the world, as it must be put in context with other teachings given by Pope St. John Paul II; teachings issued by him, as Pope, knowing full well that he was still widely quoted from that 1976 remark which he never rescinded or "clarified." It is this 1976 teaching that demonstrates his conviction that the Church is on the verge of the final confrontation she would face, whereas it is teachings like the following which show he did not hold that it meant the end of the world:

...the tears of this century have prepared the ground for a new springtime of the human spirit.[975]

We see that the saintly Pontiff indicated that, although he was convinced that the final confrontation was at hand, he was equally convinced that a new springtime would follow. The

---

[970]Pope Pius XII. Le Pelerinage de Lourdes. Encyclical of Pope Pius XII Warning against materialism on the centenary of the apparitions at Lourdes. Paragraph 43-44.
[971]This letter, in turn, can be found on the 27th Acta Apostolica Sedis, page 7, posted on the Vatican's website here: http://www.vatican.va/archive/aas/documents/AAS-27-1935-ocr.pdf

[972] Address for the Opening of the Second Vatican Council, October 11th, 1962.
[973] Urbi et Orbi Message, April 4th, 1971.
[974] Fr. C. John McCloskey III, *The Final Confrontation*. The Catholic Thing. (1 June 2014.)
[975] John Paul II. General Audience. January 24, 2001.

next year, in a general audience, he said:

> This is our great hope and our petition: "Your Kingdom come"—a kingdom of peace, justice, and serenity, that will re-establish the original harmony of creation.[976]

One cannot accuse John Paul II of referring only to Heaven with this statement: Heaven has never been considered to consist in a re-establishment of the original harmony of creation; rather, Heaven has always been taught by the Church to be something infinitely surpassing the original harmony of creation.[977]

As discussed in Part One of this book, John Paul made it clear that he sees this new Era, to come with the dawn of the Third Millennium, as a consequence of this "new and Divine" holiness of Living in the Divine Will. He said:

> God himself had provided to bring about that "new and divine" holiness with which the Holy Spirit wishes to enrich Christians at the dawn of the third millennium, in order to "make Christ the heart of the world." [978]

In his book-length interview with Peter Seewald entitled *Salt of the Earth: The Church at the End of the Millennium*, Cardinal Ratzinger confirmed what Pope St. John Paul II was often quoted as saying (but which was difficult to find clearly sourced), that the Third Millennium would indeed be one of a springtime of Christianity—one even of Christian Reunification:

> The Pope [John Paul] does indeed cherish a great expectation that the millennium of divisions will be followed by a millennium of unifications. He has in some sense the vision that the first Christian millennium was the millennium of Christian unity—there were schisms, as we know, but there was still the unity of East and West; the second millennium was the millennium of great divisions; and that now, precisely at the end [of the second millennium], we could rediscover a new unity through a great common reflection. His whole ecumenical effort stands in this historical-philosophical perspective…

> [Vatican II] is thus filled with the hope that the millennia have their physiognomy; that all the catastrophes of our century, all its tears, as the Pope says, will be caught up at the end and turned into a new beginning. Unity of mankind, unity of religions, unity of Christians—we ought to search for these unities again, so that a more positive epoch may really begin. We must have visions. This is a vision that inspires and that challenges us to move in this direction. The Pope's untiring activity comes precisely from his visionary power … [979]

Indeed, in the closing remarks of his address to the United Nations in 1995, John Paul II himself said:

> We must not be afraid of the future. We must not be afraid of man. It is no accident that we are here. Each and every human person has been created in the "image and likeness" of the One who is the origin of all that is… with the help of God's grace, we can build in the next century and the next millennium a civilization worthy of the human person, a true culture of freedom. We can and must do so! And in doing so, we shall see that the tears of this century have prepared the ground for a new springtime of the human spirit.[980]

What we see here is an undeniably clear picture in which John Paul II envisions that the Third Millennium will be one radically superior to the second. For **these are obviously not the words of one who sees an imminent end of the world.** And yet, we have already seen that John Paul does believe in an imminent "final confrontation." Therefore, the end of the world is precisely what he would have had to acknowledge as also being imminent if he believed that this "final confrontation" were not to be followed by a commensurate Era of Peace. The conclusion is clear: Pope St. John Paul II believed in and taught the reality of an impending Glorious Era of Peace to dawn upon the whole world; that is, as he said, the Kingdom of God itself. He also said:

> God loves all men and women on earth and gives them the hope of a new era, an era of peace. His love, fully revealed in the Incarnate Son, is the foundation of universal peace. [981]

And later, he wrote in an encyclical, *Novo Millennio Ineunte*,

---

[976] General Audience of John Paul II. November 6, 2002.

[977] More on this point can be found in the "Heresies implicit in accusing the Era…" section in the previous chapter.

[978] Address to the Rogationist Fathers. paragraph 6

[979]Peter Seewald. *Salt of the Earth: The Church at the End of the Millennium*. Pages 237-8.

[980]http://w2.vatican.va/content/john-paul-ii/en/speeches/1995/october/documents/hf_jp-ii_spe_05101995_address-to-uno.html

[981] Message of Pope John Paul II for the Celebration of the World Day of Peace, January 1, 2000.

...I did not hesitate to ask [the young] to make a radical choice of faith and life and present them with a stupendous task: to become "morning watchmen" at the dawn of the new millennium.[982]

Lest anyone be confused about what the duties are of these "morning watchmen," whom he is begging the youth to become, the Pope told us clearly two years later:

On this important occasion, I would like to renew to you the appeal I made to all **the young people** at Tor Vergata: accept the commitment to **be morning watchmen** at the dawn of the new millennium. This is a primary commitment, which keeps its validity and urgency as we begin this century with unfortunate dark clouds of violence and fear gathering on the horizon. Today, more than ever, we need people who live holy lives, watchmen who **proclaim to the world a new dawn of hope, brotherhood and peace**.[983]

The following year, he said:

After purification through trial and suffering, the dawn of a new era is about to break.[984]

Pope Francis on the Kingdom

More recently, Pope Francis has made it clear that he sees the Era coming, even **teaching that the prophecies of Isaiah of universal peace do refer to a time on this earth**:

But where are we journeying? Is there a common goal? And what is this goal? The Lord responds to us through the prophet Isaiah, saying: "*It shall come to pass in the latter days that the mountain of the house of the Lord shall be established as the highest of the mountains, and shall be raised above the hills; and all the nations shall flow to it, and many peoples shall come, and say: 'Come, let us go up to the mountain of the Lord, to the house of the God of Jacob; that he may teach us his ways and that we may walk in his paths*" (2:2-3). This is what Isaiah says regarding the goal toward which we are travelling. It is a universal pilgrimage toward a common goal, which in the Old Testament is Jerusalem, where the Temple of the Lord rises. For from there, from Jerusalem came the revelation of the Face of God and of his Law. Revelation found its fulfillment in Jesus Christ, and he, the Word made flesh,

became the "Temple of the Lord": he is both guide and goal of our pilgrimage, of the pilgrimage of the entire People of God; and in his light the **other peoples may also walk toward the Kingdom of justice, toward the Kingdom of peace**. The Prophet continues: "*They shall beat their swords into plowshares, and their spears into pruning hooks; nation shall not lift up sword against nation, neither shall they learn war any more*" (2:4). Allow me to repeat what the Prophet says; listen carefully: "*They shall beat their swords into plowshares, and their spears into pruning hooks; nation shall not lift up sword against nation, neither shall they learn war any more*". **But when will this occur? What a beautiful day it shall be, when weapons are dismantled in order to be transformed into tools for work! What a beautiful day that shall be! And this is possible! Let us bet on hope, on the hope for peace, and it will be possible!**[985]

This teaching of Pope Francis is particularly noteworthy because no one can succeed in denying the Era of Peace if indeed the prophecies of peace in Isaiah refer to a time to come on earth, not a mere reference to Heaven, and not only symbolically to the age of Christianity in general. Of course, Isaiah's most important prophecies pertain to the coming of Jesus and His Paschal mysteries. And yet, it is equally clear that beating "swords into plowshares" speaks of something which has not yet happened and yet must still happen on earth. Nevertheless, critics of the Era deny that this is a reference to a time on earth; but **Pope Francis has made it clear that this *does* refer to a temporal peace (in the underlined portion of the quote above)**. Pope Francis would not waste his breath reminding his listeners that we can hope for this—that it is possible *if* we "bet on" it, and urging us to do so—if he was only referring to Heaven, where there never have been and never will be weapons (a fact of which no one is unaware). And in 2019, Pope Francis signed a declaration which reads in part:

In conclusion, our aspiration is that...this Declaration may be a witness to the greatness of faith in God that unites divided hearts and elevates the human soul...**This is what we hope and seek to achieve with the aim of finding a**

---

[982] Novo Millennio Inuente, n.9
[983] Address to the Guanelli Youth Movement, April 20th, 2002.
[984] General Audience, September 10, 2003. Examining the context of this quote, we see that John Paul is referring to the Canticle of Ezekiel. But he makes it equally clear that he is not

making a merely historical observation about Ezekiel's own expectation of Redemption. Rather, he changes the terminology, referring to it now as "our" canticle.
[985] Pope Francis. Angelus Address. December 1, 2013.

universal peace that all can enjoy **in this life**.[986]

In a book entitled *Our Father: Reflections on the Lord's Prayer*, published on the fifth anniversary of his elevation to the Papacy,[987] Pope Francis writes:

> **The kingdom of God is here** *and* [emphasis in original] **the kingdom of God will come**. It is the treasure hidden in the field; it is the precious pearl for the sake of which the merchant sells all he has (cf. Mt 13:44-46). The kingdom of God is the good wheat that grows alongside the weeds, and you have to fight against the weeds (cf. Mt 13:24, 40). **The kingdom of God is also hope; the kingdom of God is coming now but at the same time has not yet come completely**. This is how the kingdom of God has already come: Jesus has taken flesh, he has become man like us, he walks with us, and he gives us hope for our tomorrow: "I am with you always, to the close of the age" (Mt 28:20). The kingdom of God is something that belongs to us, or rather, it is better to think of it another way: we must allow ourselves to be possessed by the certainty that it has come. This is true Christian faith. But at the same time there is also the need to cast the anchor there and to hold on to the cord because the Kingdom is still coming. We do not possess the rope fully, and there is always the risk that it will slip from our hands. This is true Christian hope. These two actions are very important: faith and hope.[988]

Old Testament References

Fr. Iannuzzi has compiled a number of Old Testament references to the Era of Peace in his book *The Splendor of Creation*, some of which I share here:

> There shall no more be an infant of days there, nor an old man that shall not fill up his days; for the child shall die a hundred years old ... For as the days of the tree of life, so shall be the days of My people, and the works of their hands shall be multiplied. My elect shall not labor in vain, nor bring forth children for a curse; for they shall be a righteous seed blessed by the Lord, and their posterity with them. Isaiah 65

> Raise a glad cry, you barren one who did not bear, break forth in jubilant song, you who were not in labor, for more numerous are the children of the deserted wife than the children of her who has a husband ... Isaiah 54

> See, I come to you ... I will settle crowds of men upon you ... cities shall be repeopled, and ruins

rebuilt. I will settle crowds of men and beasts upon you, to multiply and be fruitful. I will repeople you as in the past, and be more generous to you than in the beginning; thus you shall know that I am the Lord. Ezekiel 36

> The coast shall belong to the remnant of the house of Judah ... for the Lord their God shall visit them and bring about their restoration. Zephaniah 2

> ... that the mountains may yield their bounty for the people and the hills great abundance. Psalm 72

> Her deserts he shall make like Eden, her wasteland like the garden of the Lord. Isaiah 51

> As for you, mountains of Israel, you shall grow branches and bear fruit for my people Israel, for they shall soon return. Ezekiel 36

> "This desolate land has been made into a garden of Eden," they shall say. Ezekiel 36

> The earth shall yield its fruit, for God, our God, has blessed us. Psalm 67

> Then the wolf shall be a guest of the lamb, and the leopard shall lie down with the kid; the calf and the young lion shall browse together, with a little child to guide them. The cow and the bear shall be neighbors, together their young shall rest; the lion shall eat hay like the ox. The baby shall play by the cobra's den, and the child lay his hand on the adder's lair. There shall be no harm or ruin on my holy mountain ... Isaiah 11

> 'The wolves and lambs feed together, and the lion shall eat like the ox, and the serpent shall eat earth like bread. They shall not hurt nor destroy on my holy mountain, saith the Lord ... '. Isaiah 65

> My chosen ones shall inherit the land. Isaiah 65

> No longer shall the sound of weeping be heard there, or the sound of crying. Isaiah 65

> I will turn their mourning into joy, I will console and gladden them after their sorrows. I will lavish choice portions upon the priests, and my people shall be filled with my blessings, says the Lord. Jeremiah 31

> He [the Lord] will renew your strength and you shall be like watered gardens. Isaiah 58

> The weakling among them shall be like David on that day. Zechariah 12

> Strengthen the hands that are feeble, make firm

---

[986] Pope Francis. A Document on Human Fraternity. February 4, 2019

[987] March 13, 2018

[988] Pope Francis, *Our Father: Reflections on the Lord's Prayer*. "Thy Kingdom Come."

the knees that are weak ... Then will the eyes of the blind be opened, the ears of the deaf be cleared; Then the lame will leap like a stag, then the tongue of the dumb will sing. Isaiah 35

I will lead the blind on their journey ... I will turn darkness into light before them, and make crooked ways straight. Isaiah 42

Then the Lord's name will be declared on Zion, the praise of God in Jerusalem, when all peoples and kingdoms gather to worship the Lord. Psalm 102

I come to gather nations of every language; they shall come and see my glory. Isaiah 66

In those days ten men of every nation, speaking in different tongues, shall take hold, yes, take old of every Jew by the edge of his garment and say, "Let us go with you, for we have heard that God is with you." Zechariah 8

From one new moon to another, and from one Sabbath to another, all mankind shall come to worship before me, says the Lord. Isaiah 66

The light of the moon will be like that of the sun and the light of the sun will be seven times greater ...Isaiah 30

He will give rain for the seed that you sow in the ground, and the wheat that the soil produces shall be rich and abundant. On that Day your cattle will graze in spacious meadows; the oxen and the asses that till the ground will eat silage tossed to them with shovel and pitchfork. Upon every high mountain and lofty hill there will be streams of running water. Isaiah 30

They shall live in the houses they build, and eat the fruit of the vineyards they plant ... and my chosen ones shall long enjoy the produce of their hands. They shall not toil in vain. Isaiah 65

At that time, says the Lord, I will be the God of all the tribes of Israel, and they shall be my people. Thus says the Lord: The people that escaped the sword have found favor in the desert. As Israel comes forward to be given his rest, the Lord appears to him from afar: with age-old love I have loved you; so I have kept my mercy toward you. Again I will restore you, and you shall be rebuilt, o virgin Israel; Carrying your festive tambourines; you shall go forth dancing with the merrymakers. Again you shall plant vineyards on the mountains of Samaria; those who plant them shall enjoy the fruits. Yes, a day will come when the watchmen will call out on Mount Ephraim: 'Rise up, let us go to Zion, to the Lord, our God. Jeremiah 31

They shall rebuild and inhabit their ruined cities, plant vineyards and drink the wine, set out gardens and eat the fruits. Isaiah 61

Of course, many Old Testament prophecies refer to the coming of Christ in the flesh and the establishment of Christianity. But many other prophecies—the ones listed above—are not possible to interpret as only references to this past and present reality. We must recall that the entirety of Scripture (Old and New Testaments) is the inspired, infallible, inerrant Word of God. The intended meaning of the author is, by that fact alone and whatever this meaning may be, automatically the meaning God intended—as is taught dogmatically in *Providentissimus Deus* and *Dei Verbum*. If the author did not intend a purely symbolic meaning, then no Christian has any right to insist that a verse is purely symbolic. And it simply is not possible to argue that all the prophecies above are purely symbolic—no one has ever succeeded in presenting such an argument nor, I think it is easy enough to see, will anyone ever. **Catholic orthodoxy leaves us with no other option than to at least take their general consensus as literal truth: a glorious Era will dawn upon the earth in a time yet to come.**

Against the Neo-Marcionite Heresy

Considering the preceding section, and the fact that it only gave a glimpse at the great wealth of verses found in the Old Testament which prophecy the Era, few deny that this Testament—well over half of the Bible—does speak of such a time.

So instead, to defend their thesis, critics often resort to a subtle heresy; claiming that these Old Testament prophecies are just *"exaggerated, inaccurate, and overly temporal Jewish expectations which Jesus corrected."* (Of course, Jesus never did "correct" these prophecies: He merely pointed out that His Kingdom is not of this world.)

Here we should first acknowledge, contrary the modernist slander, that the ancient Jews did in fact believe in Heaven. Therefore, we cannot accuse these prophecies of being nothing but substitutes for the natural human hope for Heaven that the Jews could not cherish in any other way (even if such an accusation were not itself heretical). Jesus did not *reveal* the existence of Heaven in the Gospel; rather, He rebuked the Sadducees for themselves failing to see on their own how clearly Heaven was spoken of in the very Mosaic Scriptures they acknowledged (Mark 12:24-27), rightly accusing them of being wrong and of knowing neither "the Scriptures nor the power of God." Furthermore, we see Heaven taught clearly in Maccabees during the martyrdom of the heroic mother and her seven sons (in 2 Maccabees chapter 7; and many other verses could be cited as well).

Now, besides amounting to a heretical contradiction of Church Dogma on the inerrancy of Scripture (which applies to both the New Testament and the Old Testament), this dismissal of Old Testament prophecy on the Era is just another tragic fall for the ancient Marcionite heresy condemned by the Catechism in paragraph 123. Describing Marcion, the founder of this heresy, the New Catholic Encyclopedia states:

> Marcion steadfastly maintained that the Church had been mistaken in retaining the OT and in regarding Jesus as the Messiah foretold by the Prophets. He cited Luke (5.36–38 and 6.43) to show that Jesus's message was entirely new. Marcion was promptly excommunicated; he then gained many disciples among those who found the OT unconvincing or unattractive ...Marcion in his Antitheses (lost) repudiated the Demiurge or Creator God of the OT... He considered this god as legal-minded, offering material rewards, capricious, violent, vindictive, a tyrant, and a petty-minded bungler, while the absolutely perfect God, the God of pure love and mercy, was visibly embodied in Jesus ...**Able to see nothing in common between the God of the OT and the God of the NT, Marcion concluded that the Gospel must be dissociated from Judaism and Jewish apocalyptic eschatology**. He repudiated the OT as devoid of any revelation of the Christian God.[989]

(If this description sounds familiar, it's precisely because Marcionism is, tragically, making an enormous comeback in the Church today; with countless pastors and preachers resorting to it whenever the day's Mass Readings include one of those so-called "harsh" Old Testament readings.)

Marcion lived in the second century A.D., and was excommunicated during his own lifetime, but his heresies were so enticing that the movement continued on for another 300 years despite its repeated, forceful condemnation. It is not possible to hold any variant of Marcionism and still be Catholic.

For in stark contrast to Marcion's heresies, we know, as a matter of Faith, that every prophecy of the Old Testament is a true Public Divine Revelation, and is thereby guaranteed to be fulfilled in accordance with its own wording. **While critics of the Era often follow in Marcion's footsteps, and, as is shown in the article quoted above, "disassociate from... Jewish apocalyptic eschatology," this is simply not an option for any Catholic or Christian**. Our Faith leaves us no choice other than heeding all the prophecies of the Old Testament along with those of the New Testament, understanding that they are both present in the same inerrant Divine Revelation.

20th Century Private Revelations on the Era of Peace

In 2009, three anti-Catholic men—chief among them a certain Mr. Jim Tetlow—embarked upon a bold quest: to write a series of books which would show that all these Marian Apparitions which have exploded in number in recent times are really a diabolical plan to unite all religions in one anti-Christian Marian Faith. Needless to say, the books (deceptively entitled, with pro-Mary looking covers to draw in Catholics, published by the anti-Catholic Chick Publications), are worthless in their intent. As always, however, the enemies of God only wind up ultimately helping His plan—and indeed, Mr. Tetlow has done a great service by spending so much time and effort in examining so many Marian apparitions, for he has discovered well their main theme, which he describes in his book, *Queen of All*:

> **Almost all of the apparitions have stated that Mary is going to usher in a new era of peace** and unity. Under her mantle all people will gather in peace and solve the problems facing the world.

Mr. Tetlow has examined Fatima, Guadalupe, Medjugorje, Knock, Our Lady of All Nations, Czestochowa, and many other apparitions; pouring over both those that are approved and many not yet approved in his quest to discover their fundamental essence and main thrust. In fact, according to his discoveries, this theme of an impending Era of Peace (or Triumph of the Immaculate Heart) is so prevalent and so important, that Mr. Tetlow shared his plans to write a new book entirely on just this topic (though

[989]MARCION. New Catholic Encyclopedia. Page 142.

he was not able to follow through with his plan, for he died in 2014). Concerning this plan, he wrote:

> … a revival of Babylonism in the name of Christ is now underway. There are several other Scriptures that support this last days' scenario **that will be examined (Lord willing) in a future book — *The Coming Reign of the Queen of Heaven and Her Eucharistic Christ*...** this harlot's false religion will encompass the globe. Her counterfeit church will consist of people from all nations, multitudes, and tongues.

In another book (also deceptively titled in order to draw in Catholics), entitled *Messages from Heaven* (which bears an image of Our Lady of Grace on the cover), he wrote about a few main themes which he perceived in all Marian apparitions:

> 1) The apparitions themselves declare that they are appearing around the world.
>
> 2) Predictions by Catholic saints agree that Mary would manifest and reign in the end time.
>
> 3) Messages from apparitions have a consistent theme.
>
> 4) All apparitions of Mary predict her triumph and an era of peace and unity. [990]

He then observes the following:

> In addition to the apparitions declaring solidarity with one another, and the predictions by saints of Mary's end time reign, there **are common themes stated over and over by the major apparitions of the world** which indicate that all the apparitions originate from a common source. For instance, the apparitions constantly emphasize the need for prayer and conversion. They also state that Mary's purpose for coming is to bring peace and unity. So **rather than deny or contradict one another, the apparitions present a united front. Furthermore, many within the Roman Catholic Church, and the Vatican in particular, are anticipating that Mary will usher in an era of worldwide peace**. Many Catholic theologians also believe that Mary is the woman of Revelation 12, and that she will be the one who destroys Satan and the demonic forces in the last days. The apparition of Mary often portrays herself as the woman of Revelation 12, and she declares that she will destroy Satan and usher in an era of peace. Therefore, we can see that the apparitions confirm the hopes of Catholic saints who have predicted her coming and that Church leaders attest to her credibility…

Marian experts agree that the triumph of "Mary's" Immaculate heart, prophesied at Fatima, will be directly linked to perpetual adoration of the Blessed Sacrament. Father Martin Lucia, writing in the journal, Immaculata, explains that all the Marian apparitions will victoriously culminate in the eucharistic reign of Jesus. The message of all the Marian apparitions, both past and present, is that the triumph of the Immaculate Heart of Mary will culminate in the Eucharistic reign of the Sacred Heart of Jesus. The Eucharistic Reign will come through perpetual adoration of Jesus in the Blessed Sacrament." Not surprisingly, the pope himself alludes to this consummation of apparitions in his encyclical, *Mother of the Redeemer* ...[991]

I have begun this section with the strange approach of extensively quoting an anti-Catholic Evangelical who sees Marian apparitions as a diabolical scheme for one simple reason: I want to make it clear from the onset that **this reality of an impending Glorious Era of Peace proclaimed by Our Lady is not some eccentric prediction artificially foisted upon her messages by a few die-hard followers of Luisa; quite the contrary, it is a reality so obvious — a consensus so unanimous and clear — that even some of the most obstinate are able to see it plainly upon examining the matter**. Now that this has been made clear, we can turn to the sources of these prophecies themselves.

***

(One final note before diving into the prophecies: I have included many prophecies here; some fully approved, some partially approved, some not yet approved. It would not be surprising if, at some point in the future, a few of the apparitions or revelations here listed are proven false. That would affirm nothing detrimental, however, for dozens of apparitions and revelations are presented and each independently confirms the reality of the coming Era.)

Our Lady of Fatima

In the realm of approved apparitions, there is the admonition of Our Lady of Fatima to pray fervently for God to hasten the Triumph of her Immaculate Heart (which is another name given to this "Era of Peace"). For Our Lady promised at Fatima that "The Holy Father will consecrate Russia to me, and she shall be converted, and a period of peace will

---

[990]Jim Tetlow. *Messages from Heaven*. Page 99.
[991]*Ibid.* 99-100, 233-234.

be granted to the world,"[992] and asked for our prayers and sacrifices to this end. The phrase "period of peace" is often translated as "era of peace," though both refer to the same thing.

While several theories exist that insist Our Lady's words here refer merely to what transpired after the fall of the Berlin Wall, this is not tenable (see the corresponding section in the preceding chapter for more details on why).

Regarding Fatima's Prophecy of Peace, Emmett Culligan had much wisdom to share. Perhaps known by most for his water softening technology, Mr. Culligan was, more importantly, a devout Catholic who had Papal Knighthood conferred upon him by Pope Pius XII. He once said, "I was born a Roman Catholic. All my ancestors for 1,400 years have been Catholics. Not one of my forefathers gave up his Catholic faith. I believe nothing matters other than saving my own soul; and nothing is more important than helping others save their souls."[993] And regarding Fatima, he wrote:

> Our Lady of Fatima promised: 'In the end my Immaculate Heart will triumph and a period of peace will be granted humanity.' This is an absolute promise without qualification. It is certain to come. What other great news could the Mother of God bring to earth other than Peace on Earth? The first promise of her Son at Bethlehem was Peace on Earth. The coming of Triumphant Peace for the world is truly great news. Our Mother's promise of Peace is one of the most profound statements that have been given to mankind since Christ's Ascension into Heaven. This promise gives the key to what man can expect from the year 1917 to the time of the General Judgment. Most people believe that this promised peace is merely a cessation of war; but it is much more than that. It will be a peace such as the world has never known. It will be peace for all humanity. It can be nothing less than ABSOLUTE peace that she will give to mankind. The words 'end,' 'triumph, ' and 'period' in Our Lady's peace promise have much significance. It would seem that the word end should indicate the conclusion of Mother Mary's age-old struggle with Satan. The word 'triumph' should mean

complete victory over evil. If the triumph is complete, this would bring the end of man's corrupt nature.[994]

Mario Luigi Cardinal Ciappi was a Dominican theologian—**the personal theologian ("Theologian of the Pontifical Household") to five popes**—who is famous for his defense of *Humanae Vitae*. When Cardinal Ciappi died in 1996, **Pope St. John Paul II himself gave the cardinal's funeral homily**, and in it referred to…

> [Ciappi's] clear thinking, the soundness of his teaching and his undisputed fidelity to the Apostolic See, as well as his **ability to interpret the signs of the times according to God**…[995]

Recall that the Pope was very close to the Cardinal; the latter being his personal theologian, and John Paul was aware of Ciappi's teachings on the Era which you will presently read. And yet, John Paul did not hesitate to exalt Ciappi's discernment of the Signs of the Times.

This Cardinal, of unrivaled orthodoxy, fidelity, learning, and spiritual discernment for seeing the signs of the times, was completely clear on the nature of the promise of peace from Our Lady at Fatima. As quoted by Joseph Pronechen at the National Catholic Register, Cardinal Ciappi wrote:

> …a miracle was promised at Fatima. And that miracle will be an era of peace, which has never really been granted before to the world… Our Lady promised us this era of peace if we say the daily Rosary, practice the First Saturday Communion of Reparation, and live lives consecrated to the truth."[996]

He furthermore wrote:

> Only Heaven knows the depth of holiness a soul must achieve to tip the scales for world peace…The "Marian Era of Evangelization Campaign" can put into motion a chain of events to bring about that era of peace promised at Fatima.[997]

Cardinal Ciappi also became the theological director of the Apostolate for Family Consecration, which he strongly supported along with Cardinal

---

[992] Congregation for the Doctrine of Faith: *The Message of Fatima*. (13 May 2000), on www.vatican.va

[993] http://www.catholicauthors.com/culligan.html

[994] Call of the Ages. P. 453-454.

[995] The Apostolate for Family Consecration. *Preparation for Total Consecration to Jesus through Mary for Families*. Page 192. (The original Italian of the complete homily can be found

here: https://w2.vatican.va/content/john-paul-ii/it/homilies/1996/documents/hf_jp-ii_hom_19960425_esequie-card-ciappi.html)

[996] http://www.ncregister.com/site/article/5_saturdays_1_salvation/blank.htm

[997] The Apostolate for Family Consecration. *Preparation for Total Consecration to Jesus through Mary for Families*. Page 194.

Arinze, and for which Saint Teresa of Calcutta served on the advisory council. This Apostolate's guide to Total Consecration to Jesus through Mary for Families (which bears both a Nihil Obstat and an Imprimatur) states:

> Pope John Paul II was the prophet for our times and for the "Fatima Formula for Divine Mercy" — which we believe is the era of peace (civilization of love) that Our Lady promised at Fatima. We are confident that this era of peace will be granted once enough people make and sacrificially live this consecration. (p. 4)

> Once we make this consecration, Mary takes all that we have, and purifies and multiplies it. This puts into the Mystical Body of Christ a tremendous spiritual power that will repair for the sins of the world and help bring about the era of peace for which we all long. Our Lady promised this at Fatima when she said that in the end her Immaculate Heart would triumph, and an era of peace would be granted to the world. (p. 101)

> …Pope John Paul II's consecration … can bring the light of the truth into our dark world so that our families can live in the greatest era of peace and religion the world has ever known. (p. 187)

John Haffert, one of the world's most respected and prolific promoters of the message of Fatima, saw the hastening of the promised Era of Peace and Triumph of Mary's Immaculate Heart as perhaps his primary motivation to promote Our Lady's messages. He constantly referred to it in many of his books, and he never once saw this Era of Peace as some sort of relatively minor cessation from war; rather, he always saw it as nothing other than the definitive Coming of the Kingdom of God on Earth, as shown to Luisa. In his book entitled *The Great Event*, he wrote:

> Therefore, the Triumph has already begun, because many the world over have already listened to the Marian messages over the years, and have made the choices She asked. They have said "Yes" to the Lord. They have joined with Mary in prayer and sacrifice to help save us all and bring the Era of Peace. In some, this Triumph of a faith-filled "Yes" has been in their hearts for many years, even from childhood. The prayers and virtuous lives of these people have certainly brought blessing and protection to an undeserving generation. For the vast majority, the Triumph seems to have not yet begun. It is to

these children of Hers that the Blessed Mother directs Her appeals. She does not want them to be lost. They must and will turn to the Lord and be saved. In them also, the Triumph will come. By Her prophecy quoted above, the Queen of Heaven assures us that the present situation will be reversed by the intervention of God. By His great mercy, by the intercession of the Immaculate Heart and of those who join with Her in Her efforts to turn the world around, it will happen. The conversion of the world is sure to come. The world will become His by our conversion and His intervention. The Triumph of the Immaculate Heart will arrive… The Triumph will be a conversion event that will be so powerful and universal that all will be compelled to praise God for the magnificent works He has done in His creature, Mary. The awesome might that this humble handmaiden possesses as she shares in the redemption of the world will be abundantly clear before all eyes. The Triumph will be recognizable in the total conversion of the world. It will be a historical event of such magnitude that it will make all former moments of glory seem like shadows … [998]

An authoritative volume entitled *Mary Co-redemptrix: Doctrinal Issues Today* was published in 2002; the collective work of many scholars, including Dr. Scott Hahn, Msgr. Arthur Calkins, Dr. Josef Seifert, Dr. Mark Miravalle, and others, it bears an introduction written by Cardinal Édouard Gagnon (who was the President of the Pontifical Council on the Family under Pope St. John Paul II as well as the Pontifical Committee for International Congresses). In his introduction, Cardinal Gagnon says this work has a " *… wealth of ideas, principles, and outstanding theological exposition … the work of an exceptional international team of theologians and Mariologists … "* The first section of the book is authored by Cardinal Luis Aponte Martínez, and in his contribution Cardinal Martinez writes:

> The dogmatic proclamation of the Mother of all peoples, Co-redemptrix, Mediatrix, and Advocate would be the gateway to the New Evangelization. It would be the "New Cana," … Let us thereby open the new millennium and its New Evangelization with a contemporary fulfillment of the Marian scriptural prophecy: "all generations will call me blessed; for he that is mighty has done great things for me" (Lk. 1:48).

Dr. Mark Miravalle authored the fourth section of

---

this volume, in which we read:

> A significant number of contemporary Marian authors and thinkers worldwide also see in the papal proclamation of Mary Co-redemptrix, along with her subsequent spiritual roles as Mediatrix of all graces, and Advocate, what has been referred to as the definitive "initiation" or beginning of the Triumph of the Immaculate Heart of Mary, as prophesied in the 1917 Apparition of Mary at Fatima, Portugal. The particular notion of the "Triumph of the Immaculate Heart" comes from the words of the Church approved apparitions of Mary at Fatima to the young Portuguese children seers. After prophesying such upcoming events as the rise of atheistic communism, persecutions for the Church and the Holy Father, a potential second world war, and the annihilation of various nations, the Virgin Mary, under the title of "the Lady of the Rosary" then stated to the children, "In the end, my Immaculate Heart will triumph…and a period of peace will be granted to the world." The Triumph of the Immaculate Heart of Mary is hence foreseen as a dramatic influx of supernatural grace upon the world, mediated to the world by the Co-redemptrix, Mediatrix, and Advocate, and leading to a period of spiritual peace for humanity. … As explained by former Vatican Ambassador Howard Dee of the Philippines: "Two thousand years ago, during the First Advent, the Holy Spirit came upon Mary, and when the power of the Most High overshadowed her, she conceived Jesus, Son of God. Now, during this New Advent, it is the Mother of All Peoples, Co-redemptrix, Mediatrix of all graces, and Advocate, who will accompany her Spouse to descend into our hearts and our souls and recreate in each of us—if we give our fiat—into the likeness of Jesus…The proclamation of the Fifth Dogma is no longer our prerogative; it is our duty. "As such, the papal proclamation of Mary Co-redemptrix would effect a historic release of spiritual grace upon the world by the full exercise of the spiritual mother of all peoples in her most generous and complete exercise of her roles as Co-redemptrix, Mediatrix of all grace and Advocate.

As this great theologian makes clear, Mary's role in these days is to "effect a *historic* release of spiritual grace upon the world," and such a historic (that is, unprecedented) release can only transform all creation.

Dr. Thomas Petrisko writes the following in *The*

Fatima Prophecies: at the Doorstep of the World:

> The Eternal Father's role in Fatima goes beyond discernment of the symbolism of the falling sun and contemporary revelations. Rather, it is the well documented opinion of theologians that the message of Fatima was completed on a Thursday night, December 10, 1929, while Sister Lucia was alone making a holy hour from eleven to midnight in the chapel of the Dorothean convent at Pontevedra, Spain, about 20 miles north of Tuy. On that night, Sister Lucia received what is referred to as the "Last Vision" of Fatima. While Lucia would continue to receive visions and revelations from Jesus and Mary, this vision is considered the last "public" message of Fatima and from it we understand why the Eternal Father is so much a part of the significance of Fatima. On that night, Lucia was given to understand the importance of the Communion of Reparation and the Consecration of Russia. But most of all, she was shown a spectacular vision that synthesized Fatima's message in a unique way. The vision revealed the Blessed Trinity, with Jesus hanging on the Cross over an altar, the Holy Spirit (represented as a dove) above His head, and with Mary standing below on the right. Mary's Immaculate Heart was visible as was a Rosary in her right hand. From Jesus' left side came the words "grace" and "mercy". Most significantly, as so many artistic renditions of the "Last Vision" have portrayed, it is the extraordinary and powerful presence of God the Father, with arms outstretched parallel to His Son's above the cross, that dominates the "Last Vision" of Fatima. In a way that no words could have ever done, this vision, as described by Lucia, indelibly seals the reality of Our Father and His role in the message of Fatima on all who ponder it. **And now, with all that has been revealed, we perhaps can better understand why. Likewise, perhaps we can also better understand why Pope John Paul II has repeatedly stated that "we approach the millennium in the hope of the definitive coining of the kingdom." This kingdom, without a doubt, is none other than that of our heavenly Father's as recalled in the Lord's prayer.**[999]

And in 2016, the theologian Monsignor Arthur Calkins wrote:

> "In the end, my Immaculate Heart will triumph." The triumph of the Immaculate Heart of Mary is not based on any condition. It is an absolute declaration and it is based on God's infallible word about the Woman who will crush the head

---

of the serpent (Gen 3:15) and the Woman clothed with the sun (Rev 12). From all that we have seen thus far, it is clear that the triumph of the Immaculate Heart will prepare the way for the triumph of the Most Sacred Heart of Jesus. It could not be otherwise. God has ordained that the mediation of the Woman, of her Immaculate Heart, should be a fundamental component in the ultimate victory over sin and death.

There is no question, then, about the ultimate triumph of the Immaculate Heart. The only question is *when* ...

... This unconditional promise offers us a message of hope, a ray of light in a darkening world, but it remains for us to appropriate it. Our Lady's Immaculate Heart will triumph with or without us, but, if without us, it will be to our shame and possible eternal damnation. Rather, this proclamation of the victory of the Heart of Jesus through the Heart of Mary should spur us on to respond generously to Our Lady's requests with our own personal contribution of prayer, penance and sacrifice for the salvation of souls, in the confidence that our spiritual works offered through the Immaculate Heart will not fail to bear fruit, despite all that may appear to the contrary. **The Triumph of her Immaculate Heart, which will usher in a new era of peace and the spread of Christ's reign, may be much closer than any of us would imagine.** As Our Lady indicated to the three shepherd children, much depends on our response.

Finally, I am personally and profoundly convinced that there is a fundamental prerequisite for the triumph of Mary's Immaculate Heart: the recognition, celebration, proclamation in teaching and preaching and the solemn (dogmatic) definition that Mary—already acknowledged as the Immaculate, Ever-Virgin Mother of God, and gloriously Assumed into Heaven—is also the Coredemptrix, Mediatrix of all graces and Advocate for the people of God ... [1000]

I conclude this section with a beautiful exposition written by Fr. Maximilian Mary Dean, a Friar of the Immaculate Conception. After proving, in a theologically and spiritually deep article, that the Immaculate Heart of Mary has already triumphed in Heaven, he concludes this article by saying:

If the triumph of the Immaculate Heart of Mary is already realized in Heaven, what do the words of Our Lady of Fatima mean: "In the end my Immaculate Heart will triumph"? The response is simple: Our Lady is not speaking about the triumph in Heaven, but the triumph in the world, in the Church, in hearts. Obviously the Mother's Heart has not yet triumphed in this sense, and it is not Her fault, but ours alone.

It is for this reason that we pray to the Father day after day: "Thy kingdom come, Thy will be done, on earth as it is in Heaven" (Mt. 6:10). The Father's kingdom is the kingdom of Jesus and Mary. God the Father "hast given… power over all flesh" (Jn. 17:2) to Jesus, and Our Lady reigns at His side as the Queen Mother. The Father's will is clear: He wills the salvation and sanctification of all souls in His only-begotten Son. Our Lady has repeated this at Fatima, but She has made more specific the divine will, namely, that in order to save souls, "God has willed to establish devotion to my Immaculate Heart in the world." God wills devotion to Her Heart, so that it might be on earth as it is in Heaven, that is, that the most Sacred Hearts might reign supreme on earth just as They already do in Heaven.

The Saints longed for this terrestrial triumph. St. Louis Marie Grignon de Montfort sighs: "Ah! When will the happy time come when the divine Mary will be established Mistress and Queen of all hearts in order that she may subject them fully to the empire of her great and holy Jesus? When will souls breathe Mary as the body breathes air?" St. Maximilian Mary Kolbe also asked: "When will it happen that the souls of men shall love the Divine Heart of Jesus with Her Heart?" Bl. Jacinta of Fatima exclaimed to Lucia: "Oh, if I could only put into the hearts of all, the fire that is burning within my own heart, and that makes me love the Hearts of Jesus and Mary so much!" We too long for this triumph.

So it is that Our Lady has need of soldiers, of a powerful army which will advance the triumph of Her Heart in the world in this third millennium. [1001]

St. Faustina (Divine Mercy)

St. Faustina, whose revelations have received the highest degree of Church approval (see the section in Part One dedicated to her for this exposition) and

---

[1000] http://livingfatima.com/the-triumph-of-the-immaculate-heart/

[1001] https://www.motherofallpeoples.com/blog/the-triumph-of-the-immaculate-heart-of-mary

recommendation, wrote:

> In spite of Satan's anger, **The Divine Mercy will triumph over the whole world** and will be worshiped by all souls.[1002]

It seems clear that this reference indicates a time on earth during which there is a triumph of the Faith in all souls living at that time. For the Last Judgment itself at the definitive end of time is not referred to as the triumph of Mercy; rather, that is rightly referred to as the time of Universal and Absolute Justice.

Earlier, Faustina wrote that she prayed for the "triumph of the Church,"[1003] and that she desired that this triumph be "hastened."[1004] It is important to note that she would not have written this if she did not believe such a triumph was willed and planned by God.

Lady of All Nations (Ida Peerdeman)

In these approved apparitions to Ida Peerdeman, a woman living in Amsterdam, Netherlands, in the mid-20th century, we see a truly amazing case.

Although condemned multiple times, all the condemnations were overturned on May 31, 2002, when the Bishop of the diocese, Bishop Jozef Punt, fully approved the apparitions—declaring them to be of supernatural origin; doing so even in consultation with Cardinal Ratzinger. (Here we see just another example of the fact that Church condemnations of mystics and their works are not necessarily correct; e.g. Luisa, St. Faustina, Padre Pio, etc.)

Our Lady came with an important message that stands out among the various individual messages she gave: the need for the proclamation of the Fifth Marian Dogma. But she also gave prophecies.

> "When the dogma, the last dogma of the Marian mystery, will have been promulgated, it will be then that the Lady of All Peoples (Nations) will give peace to the world, true peace ... "[1005]

The following prayer was given by Our Lady as well; a prayer which she urged Catholics to pray before the cross:

> Lord Jesus Christ, Son of the Father, send now Your Spirit over the earth. Let the Holy Spirit live in the hearts of all nations, that they may be preserved from degeneration, disaster and war. May the Lady of All Nations, the Blessed Virgin Mary, be our Advocate. Amen.[1006]

This prayer makes it clear that, "now," at this moment in time, we must invoke the Holy Spirit to come over the whole earth. The same thing is made clear in message 51:

> The lady of All Nations may now come in order to expel Satan. She comes to announce the Holy Spirit. The Holy Spirit will then come over this earth. You, however, shall pray my prayer, which I gave to the world.[1007]

Our Lady gave many prophecies in these apparitions that have been fulfilled with startling accuracy, and I encourage anyone who wishes to learn more about this to look up Dr. Mark Miravalle's exposition on these. There is no room for doubt as to the validity of these apparitions, so we should take to heart Our Lady's promise here that, with the Fifth Marian Dogma, there will come **true** peace to the **world**. Perhaps Our Lady put the word "true" in this prophecy to remind those who would otherwise diminish what we all know she means by "peace" (as the critics of the Era do with her promise at Fatima).

Venerable Conchita

As Venerable Conchita is an exemplar of the Gift of Living in the Divine Will, she merited her own section in Part One of this book, and I will copy here the introduction to her section:

Venerable Conchita (whose full name is Concepción Cabrera de Armida), was born on the Feast of the Immaculate Conception in the year 1862; a wife and mother to nine children, she was widowed at the age of 39. She died exactly ten years and one day before Luisa herself passed, and **she is set to be beatified in May 2019. Conchita is well known for her mystical revelations; therefore, this beatification lends great weight to the orthodoxy of this new Sanctity of Sanctities, which Jesus reveals to Conchita so explicitly that there is no doubt that He is revealing precisely the same thing He reveals to Luisa** (though of course in much less detail).

[1002]Diary of St. Maria Faustina Kowalska, *Divine Mercy in My Soul*. (Stockbridge, MA: Marian Press, 2005), 1789.
[1003] Cf. Ibid.,240.
[1004] Cf. Ibid.,1581.

[1005]Maureen Flynn. *Fire from Heaven*. Page 208.
[1006]https://catholicexchange.com/our-lady-of-nations-the-fifth-dogma
[1007]Fr. Edward O'Connor. *Listen to My Prophets*. Page 128.

We can find very clear teachings on the Era of Peace in Venerable Conchita's revelations. For example:

"On sending to the world a new Pentecost, I want it inflamed, purified, illuminated, inflamed and purified by the light and fire of the Holy Spirit. The last stage of the world must be marked very specially by the effusion of **the Holy Spirit. He must reign in hearts and in the entire world**, not so much for the glory of His Person as for making the Father loved and bearing testimony of Me, although His glory is that of the whole Trinity"

"Tell the Pope that it is My will that in the whole Christian world the Holy Spirit be implored to bring peace and His reign into hearts. **Only this Holy Spirit will be able to renew the face of the earth. He will bring light, union and charity to hearts**.

…

"May the whole world have recourse to this Holy Spirit since **the day of His reign has arrived. This last stage of the world belongs very specially to Him that He be honored and exalted**. "May the Church preach Him, may souls love Him, may the whole world be consecrated to Him, and **peace will come along with a moral and spiritual reaction, greater than the evil by which the world is tormented**.

"May all at once this Holy Spirit begin to be called on with prayers, penances and tears, with the ardent desire of His coming. **He will come, I will send Him again clearly manifest in His effects, which will astonish the world and impel the Church to holiness**" (Diary, Sept. 27, 1918).

"Ask, supplicate heaven, that all may be restored in Me by the Holy Spirit" (Diary, Nov. 1, 1927).

"I want to return to the world in My priests. **I want to renew the world** of souls by making Myself seen in My priests. I want to give a might impulse to My Church infusing in her, as it were, a new Pentecost, the Holy Spirit, in My priests" (Diary, Jan. 5, 1928).

"One day not too far away, at the center of My Church, at Saint Peter's there will take place the consecration of the world to the Holy Spirit, and the graces of this Divine Spirit, will be showered on the blessed Pope who will make it. **It is My desire that the universe be consecrated to the Divine Spirit that He may spread Himself over the earth in a new Pentecost**." (Diary, March 11, 1928)).[1008]

Venerable Marthe Robin

Marthe Robin was a French mystic and stigmatist who died in 1981. Her cause for beatification began only 6 years after her death, and in 2014 her heroic virtues were formally recognized by the Vatican, thus honoring her with the title *Venerable*. Like Luisa, Marthe too lived on the Eucharist alone as food, and she also became bedridden at the age of 28, shortly after making an "Act of Abandonment to the Love and the Will of God;" a prayer she herself composed, and which reads in part:

O God of love! Take my memory and all its memories, take my intelligence so that it will act only for your greatest glory; take my will entirely, so that it will forever be drowned in your own; never again what I want O most sweet Jesus, but always what you want; receive me, guide me, sanctify me, direct me; to you I abandon myself.[1009]

Venerable Marthe saw clearly that a glorious Era was about to dawn upon the Church and, through her, the world. In fact, as many others have, she identified the prophecy of St. Louis de Montfort (quoted in the section dedicated to him, regarding the last days seeing the greatest saints in history who would dwarf all other saints) with our own days. About this, Hugh Owen writes:

It is important to know that Marthe identified herself and her followers as some of "the Apostles of the Latter Times" of whom St. Louis de Montfort had written in his True Devotion to Mary:

"These are the great men who are to come; but Mary is the one who, by order of the Most High, shall fashion them for the purpose of extending His empire over that of the impious, the idolaters, and the Mahometans."

On September 29, 1930, Marthe had prayed for "the mighty hour of the harvest, when Good will triumph, when faith will flourish everywhere, and when the living flame of love will be ignited in all hearts." Keeping in mind that "the living flame of love" refers unmistakably to the Holy Spirit, can Marthe have been foretelling anything less revolutionary than the Triumph of the Immaculate Heart and the Reign of the Holy Spirit in the world? Indeed, according to Fr. Finet, Marthe had predicted in 1936 that "there would be a New Pentecost of Love, that the Church

---

[1008]Philipon. *Diary of a Mother*. Page 154.
[1009]*New and Divine*, Page 120.

would be renewed by an apostolate of the laity" long before Pope John XXIII, Pope Paul VI, and Pope John Paul II would speak of a "new springtime in the Church" or a "New Pentecost of Love.[1010]

Edson Glauber (Itapiranga, Brazil)

Edson Glauber is a Brazilian man who has been the recipient of approved apparitions since the 1990s. Unfortunately, when conducting an online search for this visionary's name, the first thing one is likely to stumble upon is an article[1011] on a Catholic "news and information website,"[1012] written by a lay author with no direct experience or authority on the matter, falsely claiming in the title of his post that "these apparitions were officially declared 'fake'." (Except for one link to the Diocesan website in Portuguese, no sources are cited in the body of the article and no other substantial information is provided. This title itself is a false claim; or, at best, a deceptive and partial treatment of the matter; but this is not surprising.[1013]) A National Catholic Register article published in October 2017 gives a much better account of the matter, discussing renowned theologian Dr. Mark Miravalle's work with Edson:

> Mariology expert and author Mark Miravalle doesn't simply glean some of the messages for us. He went right to the seer himself, Edson Glauber, asking him "to select what he considered to be the 'heart' of the message of Itapiranga." ...
>
> Although there were many messages over the years, this book concentrates on those centering upon and highlighting the major themes. It's very clear that if we listen to them and put them into practice, we'll please heaven and save our souls as well as the souls of so many now hovering on the brink of eternal destruction ...
>
> Edson and Miravalle also bring to us other very specific directives from out [sic] Blessed Mother, this "Queen of the Rosary." This book also includes many related messages from her—and from Jesus—pinpointing how to put the very timely directives into actions that will unshackle

us from the wide path of the world that is leading so many astray. One such directive is to "turn off your television" ... (some of the messages were also given to his mother Maria do Carmo who received some apparitions) …

Since the message of Itapiranga continues as Edson receives the supernatural visits and messages, Miravalle rightly points out this book has no "dramatic conclusion," but encourages us to read the other inspired messages of the Three Hearts (and tells us where to find them).

And he gives us two directives: Itapiranga calls for our action for ourselves, families, and others for eternal salvation; and we're to live Itapiranga…we are again at Fatima on that apparition's 100th anniversary, which we must act on, and which Itapiranga emphasizes, with some further heavenly uplifting additions.

My children, today you are celebrating My last apparition at Fatima, to My three little shepherds," Our Lady said during an October 13 apparition. So many years ago, I spoke at Fatima, giving My message, but men remain deaf. They do not want to obey what the Lord has recommended through Me. I tell you, that now as never before, listening to my Motherly appeals has become more imperative, because difficult moments are approaching you, my children. **To not heed her this time is to face unprepared the chastisements our Blessed Mother again warns us about, instead of reaching for the hope she extends**.[1014]

The full truth is this: Bishop Carillo Gritti officially approved pilgrimages to the site of these apparitions in 2010,[1015] **and declared the apparitions themselves to be of supernatural origin**.[1016] He even publicly celebrated Mass at the apparition site and spoke highly of it. The 2017 "condemnation" was only a partial juridical action undertaken by a diocesan administrator (who was in place after the death of Bishop Gritti), but *not* the local *ordinary*. (And while I have heard a reason for why he undertook this action, I will refrain from sharing it here as I have not been able to confirm it). The CDF, in turn, apparently put a private gag

---

[1010]Ibid.

[1011]In March of 2018

[1012]The website contains little if any original journalism and is in fact more accurately described as a blog-aggregator site than anything else.

[1013]Mainstream big-business Catholic media organizations very rarely do justice to private revelation until they are certain that doing so is in their best financial interest. No

doubt thanks to Mother Angelica's example –and now intercession– EWTN is often an exception to this norm.

[1014]http://www.ncregister.com/blog/joseph-pronechen/new-book-sheds-more-light-on-recent-approved-apparitions

[1015]http://www.miraclehunter.com/marian_apparitions/unapproved_apparitions/itapiranga/

[1016]Cf. http://www.ncregister.com/blog/joseph-pronechen/major-apparitions-of-st.-joseph-are-approved

order on Edson himself, but not his mother (who was also one of the seers), hence it is not accurate (even now—and even given the CDF's action) to say that the apparitions are condemned. On the contrary, one can at most only say with complete accuracy that Edson himself has *for now* been silenced (need we again recall how many now approved apparitions had similar histories?), but not that the apparitions have been condemned or "declared fake."

There is yet another extraordinary demonstration of the authenticity of the apparitions at Itapiranga that should be mentioned. The demonstration harkens back to World War II, in Italy, where there was a then famous apparition which drew even more pilgrims than Fatima itself. Unfortunately, the young seer, a seven-year-old girl named Adelaide Roncalli, was coerced to recant. A theologian recently wrote to me about this, explaining:

> "The story is a very sad but familiar one in that Adelaide was put under psychological duress by an over-zealous and self-important priest to make an official retraction (from which she later dissociated herself) regarding her visions which led to the apparition being condemned."

The apparitions were condemned (very strongly) by the Bishop due to this priest's actions; but—we must be frank—they were likely authentic. The revelations given by Our Lady to Edson Glauber took note of this,[1017] speaking to the authenticity of Adelaide's apparitions. Lo-and-behold, on February 13, 2019, the previous condemnation and ban on Adelaide's apparition was nullified.[1018]

Considering all these circumstances—the fact that the messages have enjoyed Church approval, the fact that it is not appropriate to say that the apparitions themselves are outright condemned, and the fact that no final determination has been made by the local *ordinary*—we can still licitly proceed to consider what was revealed to Edson, while not neglecting the respect and obedience due to Ecclesiastical Authority.

Dr. Mark Miravalle, the world-renowned theologian and Mariologist, wrote an entire book specifically on these apparitions. Entitled *The Three Hearts*, it relays the results of his investigation into the matter, for which he even traveled to South America and extensively interviewed Edson himself. In this book, we read the following:

> **As the celestial messages from the Queen of the Rosary and of Peace continue into the 21st century, we see profound blending of themes which include both words of warning, but also the promise of ultimate victory with the eventual Triumph of Mary's Immaculate Heart and the restoration of world peace. As Our Lady puts it, "The world will be renewed and a new dawn of peace shall take place."[1019]**

In this same book, Dr. Miravalle chose to include the following extremely important message:

MESSAGES OF 2001

January 1, 2001

The World Will be Renewed and a New Dawn of Peace Shall Take Place

Peace be with you! Dear children, I am the Mother of God and I bless each one of you. O how I love you! Today I bless you with a blessing of peace. I am the Queen of Peace. God, Our Lord, has sent Me from Heaven to bestow upon you His holy blessings and His message of peace. I come down from Heaven because God loves you. Little children, a new year begins. How joyful I am to see that you start this new year with God. Jesus is granting a special blessing for your families. Jesus can solve even the most difficult problems, if you trust Him. My Immaculate Heart is overjoyed for seeing you here. Today I bless the whole world. It was here, dear children, at this place, that your Celestial Mother appeared for the first time. And it is right here, that I turn to tell you once more: pray, pray! I bless the entire Holy Church. I bless in a special way the local church of Amazonas. I bless all the missionaries of My Son Jesus. It is necessary to evangelize for there are many hearts that are still closed to God. The word of God must reach out to the most remote places because the word of God means life to all My children. Priests, priests, priests be faithful to God. Priests, so dear to My heart, love God. Be united to Him. Bring His love to all the faithful. I invite you to be saints. Do not be a cause of sorrow for My Heart. My beloved children who are present here today, pray with me again for the priests ... [1020]

But many more messages from Itapiranga speak of the Era. I will present just a few of them here:

[1017]https://spiritdaily.org/blog/apparitions/bergamo
[1018]https://spiritdailyblog.com/apparitions/devotion-to-apparition-approved
[1019]Page 83.
[1020]Pages 208-209.

'United with me, young people will have life in abundance which will transform this world into a kingdom of peace and true happiness. Together with those who wish to listen to this call of mine I will realize my kingdom on earth just as it is in heaven and we will be one, united to the Father, for whoever is united to me knows and is united to the Father, for the Father is with me.' — November 24, 1998

Courage, courage, courage my children. The world is already about to be renewed and a new dawn will arise for all Christians. July 6, 2000

The Lord is returning to fulfil all his promises. His kingdom on earth will be as it is in Heaven. [...] Renew your lives through prayer and thus the Lord will transform you totally, renewing everything and all things. My maternal and Royal blessing to you all. **As mother and Queen I tell you: prepare for the wedding with the Lamb, for behold, he comes** — July 8, 2000

Strive for the kingdom of heaven; **not long remains before [literally: 'not much is lacking for'] your and the world's definitive liberation from all evil.** God is sending me, your Most Holy Mother, in order to prepare you for the great final battle against all evil.[...] You are already in the times of the great transformations of the world and the Lord God is already marking his chosen ones, those who are obedient to Heaven's voice. September 29, 2003

I desire [to have] saints for my kingdom of love. The earth will yet be a great paradise. First will come the sorrows, but then will come the great transformation, when all will be renewed and all things will be made new. Humanity will be revived in love and peace. Thus my kingdom on earth will be as in heaven. March 23, 2004

I love you and I tell you that those who listen to my appeals will be blessed before the Lord when he returns in the last times/final moments, in the glory of his kingdom. Jesus is about to establish his kingdom of love in the world and all those who are prepared will receive their final reward. March 25, 2004

My Lord sends me from Heaven in order to tell you that great trials will come to the world, but also times of great peace when he will renew the world. Those who are listening to the Lord's appeals will shine like a great light when he establishes his kingdom of love in the world. There will be no more suffering. There will be no more weeping. God will wipe away the tears of all those who hope with patience and do not lose faith. Little children, take heart. Courage. A while

more and everything will be transformed. Do not fear life's trials, but accept them as a means of purification by which the Lord frees you from all your defects and weaknesses. August 7, 2005

Presented above are just a few messages; the coming of Great Chastisements followed by a Glorious Reign of Peace is a constant theme in these approved revelations.

Gladys Quiroga (San Nicolas)

Under the title of Our Lady of the Rosary, the Virgin Mary has appeared to Gladys Quiroga de Motta, a wife and mother, since 1983.

In 2016, many of the apparitions (those received up to 1990) were officially approved—declared to be "of supernatural origin" and worthy of belief by Bishop Hector Cardelli of San Nicolas de los Arroyos. Shortly after this Bishop's retirement at the end of 2016, the publication of further messages was mysteriously halted without explanation by the diocese. Nevertheless, the worthiness of these apparitions themselves is not diminished, and one can and should continue to approach all the messages with confidence (with a particularly high degree of belief given to those messages up to 1990). The world-renowned theologian Fr. Rene Laurentin wrote extensively on, and promoted, these apparitions. Hundreds of thousands of pilgrims have visited the apparition site, and the fruits have been overwhelming. There is, frankly, little room for doubt as to their authenticity. Of these apparitions, Fr. Edward O'Connor writes:

The wife of a retired metal worker in Argentina, with two daughters, Gladys began having visions on Sept. 25, 1983, when Mary silently held a rosary out to her. In the next seven years, she received nearly 1800 messages from Our Lord and Our Lady. Mary asked that a sanctuary be built in her honor. A victim soul, Gladys bleeds from the wrists on the Fridays of Lent, and experiences the other wounds of the Passion about 3:00 on Good Friday. In response to Mary's request, a basilica dedicated to "Mary of the Rosary of San Nicolas" has been erected. On the 25th of each month, in memory of Gladys first vision, huge crowds, sometimes 100,000 or more, gather for a Mass celebrated by Bishop Domingo Salvado Castagna, who declared: "Undoubtedly this event of grace will continue to grow; it has proved its authenticity by its spiritual fruits" (July 25, 1990). On November 14,1990, he gave an Imprimatur for the publication of the "Messages of Our Lady to

Gladys de Mona." His successor, Bishop Mario Luis Memnon, was likewise favorable. The present Bishop, Msgr. Cardelli, goes to the basilica from time to time to celebrate Mass and hear confessions.[1021]

As with all private revelations that touch on the matter, these too indicate that there will be a Glorious Era of the Church soon to come on earth. Although there are thousands of pages of messages, thus preventing any sort of exhaustive overview here, I will simply leave you with a few excerpts I have stumbled upon, **all taken from the fully approved portion of the apparitions**, which, though neither lengthy nor many, nevertheless refer clearly to this reality:

> If [man] desired to discover God, this would be **an earth of peace for all**, because only God can make peace reign, that peace so longed for by many! — June 7, 1985

> My daughter, the evil one is triumphant now, it is true, but it is a victory that will last briefly. — October 11, 1986

> …the Holy Church will soon come to shine like the brightest of stars. Glory be to God. Make it known. — November 9, 1986

> I am the Mother of Heaven, who wants to reach **salvation for mankind**: The Mother who gives to the children, out of Her Great Kindness. The Mother, who today cares for the Son's fold. **Nothing will prevent the victory of my Motherly Mission**. - June 3, 1988

> As Mother of the Church, I suffer the most unbearable pain; my suffering joins that of the Pope, because his sorrow is my sorrow. **The most intense Light of Christ will rise again. As at the Calvary, after the Crucifixion and death came the Resurrection, the Church will also be reborn by the strength of Love**. Amen, Amen. You must make this known! — July 10, 1988

Our Lady of Ngome

The apparitions of Our Lady of Ngome began on the Feast of the Immaculate Heart of Mary in 1955, and were received by the Servant of God Sr. Reinolda May, a Benedictine Sister of Tutzing in South Africa. The apparitions have been largely approved; in 1990, under the direction of Bishop Manuset Biyase, the diocese proclaimed that there was nothing objectionable in the apparitions, and explicitly authorized faith expression in relation to them.[1022]

There are very few messages associated with this apparition, and as such they do not speak of anything in great detail, much less the Era of Peace. However, it is clearly alluded to in the following message:

> **I want to save the world through the Host**, My Fruit. I am completely One with the Host as I was One with Jesus under the Cross … [1023]

This message is important because, in keeping with the strongly Eucharistic theme of this entire apparition, Our Lady emphasizes how the Era will indeed be a Eucharistic Reign. At Ngome, Our Lady also clearly refers to the New and Divine Holiness—that is, Living in the Divine Will—by teaching that we must truly become living hosts (see Part One of this book for more details on this theme):

> **Be hosts**. Prepare hosts for Me. Hosts who put themselves completely at My disposal. Only a flaming sea of hosts can drive back the hate of the godless world…[1024]

Pedro Regis

Pedro Regis, a seer from Anguera, Brazil, has been receiving many messages for decades and enjoys the support of his Bishop, Don Silverio Albuquerque, who, while not going so far as officially and definitively approving the apparitions, nevertheless stated:

> About the apparition that has been occurring in Angüera for a few years, I have to say that my attitude, to date, has been of prudence … There are many miracles, I would not say physical miracles, but rather miracles of conversion, even the conversion of physicians who did not believe. **I have already reached the conclusion that, from the pastoral point of view, the meeting in Angüera is valid** …[1025]

Critics, however, regularly castigate Mr. Regis and his followers due to the sheer number of prayer requests given in these messages—indeed, it is not

---

[1021]*Listen to My Prophets*. Page 230.
[1022]http://www.miraclehunter.com/marian_apparitions/statements/ngome_statement3.html
[1023]http://www.miraclehunter.com/marian_apparitions/messages/ngome_messages.html
[1024]Ibid.
[1025]Signs and Wonders Magazine. Spring/Summer 2011. Page 56.

uncommon, in any given month, to see dozens of different localities mentioned in his messages as being in need of prayer due to some impending disaster. The critics claim that this "grapeshot" approach to prophecy is sure proof that the messages are of human origin, for they levy that Mr. Regis (and other seers whose messages include a similar degree of specifics) is simply issuing as many prophecies as possible in hopes that at least some will eventually prove correct.

But this is a strange criticism, and the motivation for it is nowhere found in the Church-sanctioned norms for discernment of apparitions. Quite the contrary, it makes perfect sense that, if mentioning a specific place as in need of prayer will better help inspire people to pray, then that is exactly what Our Lady will do. Furthermore, the "grapeshot" approach is patently absurd, as anyone knows who has tried to guess another's password merely by pounding randomly at a keyboard: it just doesn't work. There are always too many possibilities for aimless guessing to produce fruit. Additionally, the bullseye prophecies which have been given in Pedro Regis' messages are so profound that not even a thousand messages a day would be capable of rendering the outcomes which Pedro's few messages a week have rendered.

While my purpose here is simply to demonstrate the prophetic consensus around the Era of Peace, I would like to draw special attention to what I think is one of the most profound of Pedro Regis' prophecies in order to encourage you to, like his Bishop, believe in their validity.

In 2005, Pedro Regis received the following message (n. 2570) from Our Lady:

> Dear children, I love you and I want you to be faithful to My Jesus. Take care of your spiritual life and don´t let material things make you stray from the way of salvation. **WK: because of this many will die. Those chosen to defend the truth will deny it.** I suffer because of what awaits you. ... Pray. Pray. Pray.[1026]

Likely out of a desire to avoid any possibility of committing calumny, the administrators of the English section of the website substituted the actual name received with the initials "WK." But the original message, which is shown in the official Brazilian section of the same website, reads clearly: **Walter Kasper.**

Most readers today will undoubtedly recall Walter Kasper as the Cardinal who is now famous for his heretical teaching on marriage, divorce, adultery, and Communion; that is, his proposal that those who are unrepentantly committing objective acts of adultery may nevertheless be validly absolved and licitly receive Holy Communion. Without delving into a theological treatise on *Amoris Laetitia*, I can at least say the following: **It is difficult to imagine a more accurate and important prophecy than one which claims that "many will die" as a result of "WK."**

This prophecy is especially astonishing because when it was issued (on March 9th, 2005), Cardinal Kasper was a relative nobody on the theological world scene. Nobody seeking to provide an accurate assessment of where the world would be a decade from then would have mentioned him. Ten years and two pontificates later, it became clear that his words would indeed mean the spiritual death of countless souls across the world; for in the name of a false and diabolical mercy, he seeks to overturn Church dogma.

Unfortunately, the spiritual death that he has caused and will continue to cause is not limited to his infamous "Kasper Proposal," but will undoubtedly seep into areas outside of the issue of divorce as well. Exactly thirteen years to the day after this prophecy from Pedro Regis, Sandro Magister published a highly circulated article on his website[1027] in which he takes note of Kasper's attempt to subvert even *Humanae Vitae* (wherein Pope St. Paul VI infallibly condemned artificial contraception as an intrinsic evil).

While there are many other "prophetic bullseyes" that can be attributed to Pedro Regis' messages in order to support their validity, presenting them would needlessly expand the length of this section, in which I merely wish to demonstrate the consensus of private revelation on the Era of Peace. So we now turn our attention to consider a few messages received by this seer which speak of the Era:

[1026] http://www.apelosurgentes.com.br/en-us/mensagens/ano/2005/

[1027] http://magister.blogautore.espresso.repubblica.it/2018/03/09/humanae-vitae-under-siege-two-new-assaults-and-a-counterattack/

My children, God invites you to be strong and firm in faith, to live in Grace and His love. I want to make your saints for the glory of the reign of God. Open your hearts! **Very soon the world will be transformed into a new world, without hate or violence. The world will be a new garden** and all will live happily. Pray and be converted. – October 8, 1988

You belong to The Lord and need fear nothing. Firmly believe that the world will be transformed, first passing through a purification, and then there will be the triumph of My Immaculate Heart. I want you to be part of My army. The moment of battle has come. – May 7, 1996

Let the Grace of My Lord transform you. I want you to be a part of the Lord´s victorious army. The Lord has reserved a great Grace for His own. He will transform humanity into a new garden. When all this happens the world will be abound with goods and man will lack nothing. It will be a time when the fruits of trees will be multiplied and there will be two crops per year. Hunger will no longer exist for humanity.- June 3, 2000

Whatever happens, stay with Jesus. He is in control of everything. **Trust in Him and you will see the transformation of the earth. Humanity will be made new by the Mercy of Jesus**. A great sign from God will appear, and mankind will be astonished. Those separated will be led to the truth and great faith will possess the elect of the Lord. – December 24, 2011

…those who remain faithful until the end will be called blessed by the Father. Do not allow the flame of faith to be extinguished within you. You still have long years of trials ahead of you, but the great day is coming. **My Jesus will give you the grace to live in complete peace. The Earth will be completely transformed and all will live joyfully**. – December 24, 2013

When the tribulation is over, the Earth will be transformed. Peace will reign and the just will live joyfully. – June 9, 2014

When everything seems lost, a miracle of God will occur and peace will reign upon the Earth. Go forward. – February 3, 2015

I know your needs and I will plead with my Jesus for you. Have trust, faith and hope. The Definitive Triumph of my Immaculate Heart will bring peace to the world and men and women of faith will experience great joy. Go forward. – December 17, 2016

…you will see the transformation of the earth with the Definitive Triumph of My Immaculate Heart" – June 2018

"The Definitive Triumph of My Immaculate Heart will be the great reward for My Devotees. Men will contemplate what human eyes have never seen." Christmas Message 2018

Do not be discouraged. In the most difficult times for you, call for Jesus. He has something marvelous for you. Courage. **My Lord will transform the earth and righteous men will live happily. After all sorrow, the Victory of God will happen**. – December 29, 2018

Elizabeth Kindelmann

The revelations to Elizabeth Kindelmann, a 20th century Hungarian wife and mother, speak primarily of the grace of the "flame of love" of the Blessed Virgin Mary. She speaks of the power of this flame of love to completely blind and bind Satan, and she also insists that this flame of love will, in fact, triumph over the whole world and usher in the true Coming of the Kingdom. Before proceeding to the revelations on the Era contained in her messages, let us first demonstrate how trustworthy they are considering the degree of approval they have received.

In 1989, the Archbishop of Guayaquil wrote his own preface to Kindelmann's diary, not only giving approval for its publication, but also expressing:

> … the most fervent wishes that it will reach numerous hands and turn itself into the instrument by which all of us can come together with God, unceasingly enlightened by this eternal Flame of Love, the Immaculate Heart of Mary.

Cardinal Bernardino Echeverria also gave his approbation to the Flame of Love movement and asked the same of the Pope Himself; and while the Vatican did not go so far as to issue its own official stamp of approval onto the revelations, the Cardinal did nevertheless receive the response: "Encouraging you to take every measure for the Association to give abundant fruits among its members and also in the whole Church, I invite you to go on with the tender task of spiritual accompaniment." More recently (in 2009), Cardinal Erdo, Primate and Archbishop of Budapest, Hungary, officially approved the Flame of Love movement dedicated to the promulgation of these revelations, and gave his imprimatur to the revelations themselves. More recently still, Archbishop Chaput gave his Imprimatur to yet another compilation of an English translation of

Kindelmann's revelations.

Even Pope Francis has taken note of the revelations, responding to an inquiry on them with the following words though a secretary, Archbishop Angelo Becciu:

> His Holiness, Pope Francis, is grateful for this gesture of kindness and affection, and asks the Lord to grant you His abundant Grace through the Blessed Virgin Mary, to serve the plan of salvation for mankind. With these wishes, His Holiness, invoking the protection of the Immaculate Heart of Mary, is pleased to impart the Apostolic Blessing, which He extends to the Movement "Flame of Love of the Immaculate Heart of Mary"[1028]

Therefore, these revelations can be approached with great confidence. In them, we read:

> Enter into the battle. We will be the winners! My Flame of Love will blind Satan in the same measure that you will propagate it in the whole world. I want that, as my name is known throughout the world, so also be known the Flame of Love of my Heart, which makes miracles in the bottom of hearts. With regard to this miracle, you don't need to begin to make investigations. The whole world will feel its genuineness in their heart. And the one who will have felt it once will communicate it to others, because my grace will act in him. This miracle doesn't need to be authentified. I am going to authentify it in every soul, so that they should know the effusion of grace of my Flame of Love."[1029]

Later, the Virgin Mary told Elizabeth that the whole "surface of the earth" will be dominated by this Flame of Love:

> The soft light of my Flame of Love will ignite and take fire on the whole surface of earth, and Satan, humiliated and reduced to impotence, will no longer be able to exercise his might. However, these pains in giving birth, don't try to prolong them !"[1030]

One day, Elizabeth was shown a vision, and wrote in her diary:

> … my heart overflowed with a huge cheerfulness … In my heart, I saw how Satan becomes blinded, and also the beneficial effects that men will reap from it, in the whole world. Under the effect of that gladness, I could hardly close my eyes during the whole night, and when a light sleep came on me, my guardian angel woke me saying: "How can you sleep like that, with such a great gladness which will shake the world?"

Immediately after her guardian angel said these words, Jesus revealed to Elizabeth more about what this blinding of Satan entails. Jesus said:

> That Satan becomes blind means the world triumph of my Sacred-Heart, the liberation of souls, and that the road of Salvation will open in all its plenitude.[1031]

In an undated entry from August 1962, Jesus said to Elizabeth:

> You know, don't you, that I invited you to my special training camp for fighters? Don't let yourself be seduced by the transitory comforts of the world, but instead, let the coming of my Kingdom be the aim of your life on earth… I know that it is not new for you, seeing that you talk of it passably. What grieves Me above all, it is that you only talk of it, and you don't do your utmost to establish among you the kingdom of God. You know more than anybody else what violence somebody has to impose on himself for my Kingdom to come to him. Don't live in a hypocritical manner! You offer the Holy Sacrifice before the faithful, but for you it remains a little superficial. So many among you celebrate it in this manner!

Continuing the same thread in the forthcoming years, we read Our Lady's words to Elizabeth:

> Yes, my little Carmelite, speak, all of you, with repentant soul, to my Divine Son and to Me when you think of the Reign of my Divine Son and you make everything for it to happen to you all. That is why I want to make overflow my Flame of Love on earth for you to see the road which leads to the Reign of my Divine Son[1032]

Our Lady of Zaro

The apparitions of Our Lady of Zaro began in 1994 to several members of a prayer group in the diocese of Ischia in Southern Italy. The apparitions have been the subject of an official Diocesan inquiry since 2014, and while no determination has yet been reached, the messages remain un-prohibited and no condemnation has been issued. Acknowledging the existence of at least alleged

---

[1028]Communication N. 16.604. June 19, 2013. Secretary of State at the Vatican.
[1029]Kindelmann Diary, October 19th, 1962.

[1030] Ibid. November 27th, 1963.
[1031] Ibid. November 13-14th, 1964.
[1032] Ibid. April 9th, 1966.

supernatural phenomena, the Bishop's Decree reads in part:

> Having been heard, through the means of social communication and the information gathered at the People of God that is in Ischia, of alleged supernatural phenomena related to the Virgin Mary, in place for two decades on the territory of the Diocese, in the area commonly referred to as "Zaro", in the municipality of Forio ... I ask the whole Church of God which is in Ischia to accompany with prayer the work of the Commission, because it can help to shed light on the phenomena mentioned above and, in this regard, be offered to the faithful the appropriate indications.[1033]

There is no hint of a negative tone in this pronouncement, and it is equally clear that many indications of validity exist. For example, in an article about the apparitions on Michael Brown's website, Spirit Daily, we read (after Mr. Brown carefully considers the matter):

> One asks: why would these young people—so preoccupied these days with other matters (not to mention smartphones)—perpetuate a "hoax" for so long? Sometimes, the explanations of naysayers exceed in unlikelihood the notion that: Mary appears, somewhat urgently, in our modern world—even very urgently, struggling to stave off chastisement for so many years now.[1034]

Finally, we should consider that, if an official Diocesan inquiry (the *vast* majority of apparitions are simply ignored by the Diocese in which they occur—only a few of the most promising, or the most obviously fraudulent are investigated—and the latter are generally swiftly condemned) into an apparition has been underway for over twenty years, and has not once resulted in any move against the site, this fact speaks volumes, and should alone be enough to allay most concerns. Let us now consider a few excerpts from the messages themselves:

> At one point, I saw something like a great sun illuminating the whole **earth** and Mother told me: "Behold, **when my heart will triumph everything will shine more than the sun.**" December 26, 2018

> Children, I want everyone to participate in the Triumph of My Immaculate Heart. December 8, 2018

In St Peter's Square [I saw] a great struggle: dead and wounded people, many priests and bishops were lying dead or badly wounded on the steps of St Peter's, then a loud roar and the dome is torn apart and thick black smoke comes out, the ground begins to shake ever more strongly. And in a corner of the square some people of different ethnic groups and religions cling to each other and hold hands and start praying forcefully, clutching the Holy Rosary in their hands **and everything stops: evil disappears, the screams and pain, the dead are gone, a great peace reigns and a single prayer is heard rising to heaven... My beloved children, learn to say to the Lord "Thy Will be done" and learn to accept it.. "** — August 8, 2018

Go forward with courage and with the weapon of the Holy Rosary in your hands, pray for the salvation of souls and for the conversion of all humanity. Hard times await you, but do not turn away, be perseverant, because with your prayer and your suffering you can save many souls. **My children, your ears will hear distant noises and clashes of war, the earth will yet tremble, but I am with you, do not be afraid; after the tribulation there will be peace and my Immaculate heart will triumph.**" May 8, 2018

I saw St Peter's Basilica; its walls were shaken as by an earthquake, however then I began to see that through the colonnade the ancient enemy was going quickly. He was like a great dragon with great paws, his steps were noisy, everything was moving. Mother said: "**The Church will be attacked, there will be a period of great doubt on men's part, many will turn away from her but then everything will shine and shine more than before.**" Finally, Our Lady took off her mantle and put it on the church. I began to see a great light, and to feel a strong sense of peace. December 8, 2016

My children, again I ask you to pray for all those people who do not know and live in peace. Pray for peace. May peace descend upon all the peoples of this world." At a certain point, the globe that Mother had beneath her feet lit up, and she told me: "See, daughter, the power of prayer: alas, if all would pray, then yes, peace would reign…December 26, 2015

Children, pray much for Pope Francis, he is very saddened by all that surrounds him; hard times await him ... Pray, pray, pray! First all these and many things will have to happen, and **finally my**

Immaculate Heart will triumph. June 26, 2014

Servant of God Maria Esperanza

Maria Esperanza was a wife, mother, mystic, and recipient of the approved apparitions at Betania, Venezuela (approved by the Bishop in 1987). She died in 2004, and her cause for beatification has already officially opened (January 31st, 2010).

The theologian Fr. Edward O'Connor writes the following about her:

> St Therese of the Child Jesus told her to go to Rome, where she would meet her future husband which she did. The two of them had seven children. Padre Pio became her spiritual director, and appeared to her on the day of his death, announcing that she would have to carry on his work. Maria had many extraordinary gifts: she could see things taking place a long distance away, as well as future events; she experienced levitation, transfiguration and the stigmata; she had the gift of healing and other mysterious gifts. From 1976 to 1984, Our Lady appeared to her several times as "Reconciler of Peoples," asking that some farmland in Betania, 45 miles from the city of Caracas, be dedicated to Mary, and a chapel be built in her honor. From 1984 on, other people (between 1000 and 2000) witnessed many of the apparitions. Maria's bishop, Pio Bello of thechocese of Los Teques, personally conducted an investigation, and in 1987 declared that the apparitions were authentic, and that the site where they occurred be considered sacred.[1035]

Michael Brown, who often spoke to her and knew her personally, wrote the following of her prophecies:

> It was Esperanza's view that Jesus would soon come in a different way than He did 2,000 years ago, that He would appear to many people, in a way that would be more private ... She speculated that the manifestation—which sounds different than the actual Second Coming, and would precede what she called an "awakening" ... and that He would come "in the same way as He resurrected, as an apparition." "That's why I have been saying to be ready, because things are starting to happen," asserted the mystic ... [1036]

If the fact that she is the recipient of approved apparitions, and that her cause for Beatification is proceeding smoothly—if that is not enough to convict you of the validity of her messages, also know this: she even issued prophecies of striking accuracy regarding the terrorist attacks of September 11, 2001, long before they occurred, with specific reference to "two towers in New York." From the same source quoted above:

> ...headline from December 2000: "In unusually strong language," said the subhead, "and citing two foreign nations' ... Seer Maria Esperanza warns U.S. and says world 'soon will be saddened.'" [In the article, she said the enemies were already on U.S. soil. Nearly a decade before, Esperanza told pilgrims she saw two large towers in New York on fire, and related to us that she had seen them collapsing]

In 1984, Mary revealed to Esperanza:

> "Behold the great triumph of a way that unifies, reestablishes, weighs the merit of the multitudes that will be arriving at my place chosen for these times. Conversion of the sinner, health of body and soul, priestly and religious vocations, holy marriages, families renewed in the faith, charisms of the Holy Spirit working in all who draw near in humility—these will happen!"[1037]

And Dr. Petrisko shares more of Esperanza's teachings regarding the Era:

> In many interviews, Maria has spoken of the coming times. She indicates somewhat that she knows what the Era of Peace may be like and what it may bring. In an interview found in the book *The Bridge To Heaven* by Michael Brown, Maria stated: "The environment will be fresh and new, and we will be happy in our world, without the feeling of tension."..."This century is purifying; after will come peace and love."..."It will be in a way never before imagined by man, because the Light of His New Rising will be evident to everyone. And of course, man is still not ready for this, to accept these profound things, which actually are so simple and so clear, just as the water which comes down from the spring."
>
> ... [The Lord told me] ... "I will come among you in a resplendent sun. My rays will reach all nations to illuminate you, to enlighten you, that you may rise and grow as plants grow, with fruits. You all have the right to receive the grace of God the Father ... "[1038]

[1035]*Listen to my Prophets*, Page 207.
[1036]"From Esperanza To St. Bernard, Questions Raised On Christ's 'Intermediate' Coming" Spiritdaily.net. (Google webcache.)
[1037] *Call of the Ages*. Page 469.
[1038]*Ibid.* 469-470.

Medjugorje

The apparitions at Medjugorje, while neither approved nor condemned, have nevertheless become among the most famous Marian Apparitions in history. One of the seers, Mirjana, recently published a book, the very title of which speaks of the Era of Peace. Entitled *My Heart Will Triumph*, we see in it clear hints that the Era is coming. For example, she ends Chapter 14 with the following statement:

> I cannot divulge much more about the secrets, but I can say this—Our Lady is planning to change **the world**. She did not come to announce our destruction; she came to save us, and with her Son, **she will triumph over evil**. If our Mother has promised to defeat evil, then what do we have to fear?

It is clear that this triumph over evil that Our Lady has prophesied at Fatima, Medjugorje, and many other places, is speaking of a triumph *in the world*, which entails its total transformation; she is not patronizing us with an obtuse reference merely to her eternal triumph in Heaven, which we all already knew was guaranteed and did not need a prophecy to tell us about. Almost all Marian Apparitions speak of *peace* incessantly. It would be odd if this peace were not to succeed in reigning on earth through the Triumph! In Chapter 26, Mirjana writes:

> In Medugorje, Our Lady continued calling for peace. In 1995, she asked people to transmit her messages to the world so that "a river of love flows to people who are full of hatred and without peace." She also invited everyone to be her "joyful carriers of peace in this troubled world," and she asked for our prayers, **"so that as soon as possible a time of peace, for which my heart waits impatiently, may reign."**

Recall, from the previous section's quotes from Papal Magisterium, that the renewal of the earth is a natural consequence of the renewal of Faith. This is made clear by Luisa as well. But from Mirjana—who was shown what will transpire—we read:

> I cannot speak about the details of the other secrets before the time comes to reveal them to the world, except to say that they will be announced before they occur. **After the events take place as predicted, it will be difficult for even the staunchest skeptics to doubt the existence of God...**

My friends, a time wherein even the "staunchest skeptics" have difficulty failing to believe in God cannot describe anything other than an Era of Peace.

In Chapter 15, we read:

> So, when Our Lady told us that Medugorje would be the fulfillment of Fátima and that her heart would triumph, it was a message of hope, not gloom... people often ask me how they should prepare for the time of the secrets. Should they stock their basements with food? Move to the countryside and live off the land? Buy a weapon to protect themselves? I tell them, "Yes, you should get a weapon, and you should use it often." I show them my rosary. "This is the only weapon you'll ever need. But it only works if you use it." In one of her earliest messages, Our Lady told us, **"Prayer and fasting can stop wars and change the laws of nature." She was not speaking figuratively;** prayer is more effective at creating change than anything we can do alone. The rosary is an especially powerful prayer.

Here Mirjana, relaying words from Our Lady, rightly reprimands those who refuse to believe in a coming Era of Peace because it is "not realistic," as at least one of the more well-known critics of the Era has written in his published works. *Prayer can change the laws of nature.* God can and will Triumph; to discount this as "unrealistic" is borderline blasphemous. Our Lady will not be mocked, and she does not lie. Further illustrating the nature of this Triumph as a reality which we will experience on this earth, Mirjana writes (in Chapter 30):

> I wish I could divulge more about what will happen in the future, but I can say one thing about how the priesthood relates to the secrets. We have this time that we are living in now, and we have the time of the triumph of Our Lady's heart. Between these two times we have a bridge, and that bridge is our priests. Our Lady continually asks us to pray for our shepherds, as she calls them, because the bridge needs to be strong enough for all of us to cross it to the time of the triumph. In her message of October 2, 2010, she said, "Only alongside your shepherds will my heart triumph."

To those who believe in an Eschatology of Despair, supposing that on this earth we have nothing but horrendous Chastisements to look forward to and no Era of Peace, Mirjana says the following:

> When people ask me gloomy questions about Biblical catastrophes and the end of the world, I feel sorry for them. Some seem to think that all the

secrets are negative. Maybe they have a guilty conscience; maybe they are afraid of how they've lived their life and so they fear God's punishment. Perhaps when we do not have enough good inside, we expect bad things. ... **The people who are concerned about the secrets have not seen Our Lady and do not know about God's complete project—why Our Lady comes here at all, or what she's preparing us for.** But if your life is in her hands, and God is in your heart, what can harm you?[1039]

Finally, Mirjana ends the book with the following exhortation:

> This is how I see all the confusion in the world today. This is how I see Our Lady's apparitions and God's plan. A truly clean house starts with a big mess. Will you be like most children who stand back while Mom cleans, or will you not be afraid to get your hands dirty and help her? Like Our Lady said in one of her messages, "I desire that, through love, our hearts may triumph together." May the triumph of her heart begin with you.

Luz de Maria

Luz de Maria De Bonilla is an Argentinian lay woman—a mother of eight children (one of whom has been a priest for almost 20 years)—who began receiving messages from Heaven in the 1990s. Her messages often speak explicitly about Living in the Divine Will and its impending Universal Reign on Earth in a Glorious Era of Peace.

Peter Bannister, a theologian whom I know personally (and trust completely), spent time with Luz de Maria, after which he wrote that she is…

> … someone of great warmth with a deep yet childlike love for Jesus and the Blessed Mother. Her way of speaking is spiritually profound and intelligent without being intellectual, and in my own mind there is no way that some of the highly sophisticated, even elliptical expressions that feature especially in the messages of Our Lord to her could have originated purely in her imagination. Of course there may be some of her own subjectivity in some of her words, visions and interpretations, so there is always a need to discern each purported heavenly communication case by case, but in general I am confident that there is a supernatural origin to her experiences.

In addition, there are many miraculous phenomena occurring in association with these revelations (including images exuding miraculous oil with full video documentation), even though, out of the seer's humility and prudence, the majority of the phenomena are not openly published.

Luz de Maria's revelations, in fact, are so significant that she was granted a meeting with Pope St. John Paul II three separate times, and twice with Pope Benedict XVI. This alone, but also combined with the fact that no action has been taken against her or her revelations, should speak volumes. Equally importantly is the approval her revelations have already received; **Bishop Mata of Esteril granted an imprimatur on all of her messages dating from 2009 to 2017. In conjunction with granting this imprimatur on the Solemnity of St. Joseph in the year 2017, he also wrote:**

> The volumes that contain "PRIVATE REVELATION" from Heaven given to Luz de María from the year 2009 to the present time have been given to me for the respective Ecclesiastic Approval. I have reviewed with faith and interest these volumes entitled: "THY KINGDOM COME", and have come to conclusion that they are a call to Humanity to return to the Path that leads to Eternal Life, and that these Messages are an explanation from Heaven in these moments in which man must remain attentive to not go astray from the Divine Word. ... I DECLARE that I have not found any Doctrinal error that attempts against the faith, morality and good habits, for which I grant these publications the IMPRIMATUR. Together with my blessing, I express my best wishes for the "Word of Heaven" contained here to resonate in every creature of good will. **I ask the Virgin Mary, Mother of God and Our Mother, to intercede for us so that the Will of God be fulfilled "…on earth as it is in Heaven."** (Mt, 6:10)

As you can see, the Bishop himself sees in these messages references to the fulfillment of the Our Father prayer for the whole world… **just as Jesus showed Luisa**. The original document containing these words and the imprimatur can easily be found online.

Let us, therefore, simply look at what those messages say about the coming Era of Peace (all of the following quotes are taken from the documents posted on the website currently hosting her messages, revelacionesmarianas.com).

THE ERA OF PEACE IS COMING FOR

[1039]Chapter 14.

MANKIND. [An] Era in which everything will be reborn; man, purified and fused with God's Will, Creation, which will then feel in harmony with mankind. Total and complete happiness. Peace and harmony are coming. In order for mankind to overcome that great transition, it must first come to be purified and eradicate such a high degree of offenses with which My Son's Most Sacred Heart is hurt. — January 30, 2011

My children trust and love My Will. My children revere and worship My Will. My love rescues souls…The new dawn will come for My children. Evil will not find a place among men and all will be peace. My children will see in all of Creation the seed of My Love. My Mother will camp with Her children; the lost gifts will be deserved by man again and I will see Myself pleased in each human being. All of the Cosmos will vibrate with the beating of My Heart to a single unique rhythm, and man will breathe My Peace in total concordance. — February 26, 2011

Come. I will guide you to enjoy my son's love, my son's peace. The days of peace will return, humanity will believe again, and on that day, you will look back and see that my calls are correct.- August 15, 2012

{In} the end, the Immaculate Heart of my mother will triumph, and my Divine Will, will reign on earth as … in Heaven.- July 7, 2014

Continue holding My Hand, that My Son's people will find Me, though they be just a few! …but the faithful, those who love My Son in spirit and in truth, who will never deny Him and remain standing, those who are firm and true, they will be the one who will give My Son the Reign of His Will.- September 21, 2014

Each one of the volumes of Luz de Maria's messages bearing the imprimatur contains the following words in its initial pages (in which Luz de Maria herself presents the volume to the readers), all in bolded, uppercase letters so that no one misses it:

WITH THE ASSURANCE THAT THE WOMAN CLOTHED WITH THE SUN WILL CRUSH THE HEAD OF SATAN AND THE CHILDREN OF GOD WILL ENJOY THE ERA OF PEACE.

Clearly, Luz de Maria herself—who knows the main thrust of the messages she was given better than anyone—sees the Era of Peace as essential to

Jesus and Mary's plan for the world.

Fr Ottavio Michelini

Fr. Ottavio Michelini, priest, mystic, and member of the Papal Court of Pope St. Paul VI (one of the highest honors bestowed by a Pope on a living person), received many private revelations which, rightly, no one has made any serious attempt to refute considering their manifestly trustworthy source. We consider a few of his revelations here:

…it will be men themselves who will provoke the imminent conflict, and it will be I Myself who will destroy the forces of evil to draw good from all this, **and it will be the Mother, most holy Mary, who will crush the head of the serpent, thus beginning a new era of peace; IT WILL BE THE ADVENT OF MY KINGDOM UPON EARTH. It will be the return of the Holy Ghost for a new Pentecost.** It will be my merciful love that will defeat Satan's hatred. It will be truth and justice that will prevail over heresy and over injustice; it will be the light that will put to flight the darkness of hell.[1040]

In another passage, Fr. Ottavio was told:

Hell will be defeated: my Church will be regenerated: MY KINGDOM, that is a kingdom of love, of justice and of peace, will give peace and justice to this humanity, subjected to the powers of hell, which my Mother will defeat. A LUMINOUS SUN WILL SHINE upon a better humanity. Courage, therefore, and do not fear anything.[1041]

Later still,

The shoots of the announced springtime are already springing up in all places, and the ADVENT OF MY KINGDOM and the victory of the Immaculate Heart of my Mother are at the doors.[1042]

And again,

In my regenerated Church, there will no longer be so many dead souls, that are numbered in my Church today. This will be my proximate coming to the earth, with the ADVENT OF MY KINGDOM IN SOULS, and it will be the Holy Ghost who, with the fire of his love and with his charisms, will maintain the new Church purified, that will be eminently charismatic, in the best sense of the word…Indescribable is its task in this intermediate time, between the first coming of

---

[1040]Ottavio Michelini, "Thou Knowest That I Love Thee." Entry from December 9, 1976.

[1041] Ibid, December 10, 1976.
[1042] Ibid, November 7, 1977.

Christ to earth, with the mystery of the Incarnation, and his second coming, at the end of time, to judge the living and the dead. Between these two comings that will manifest: the first the mercy of God, and the second, divine justice, the justice of Christ, true God and true man, as Priest, King, and universal Judge there is a third and intermediate coming, that is invisible, in contrast to the first and the last, both visible. This intermediate coming is the Kingdom of Jesus in souls, a kingdom of peace, a kingdom of justice, that will have its full and luminous splendor after the purification.[1043]

St. Dominic Savio revealed to him:

And the Church, placed in the world as a Teacher and Guide of the nations? Oh the Church! The Church of Jesus, that issued from the wound of his side she also has been contaminated and infected by the poison of Satan and of his wicked legions, but it will not perish; in the Church is present the divine Redeemer; it cannot perish, but it must suffer its tremendous passion, just like its invisible Head. Afterwards, the Church and all of humanity will be raised up from its ruins, to begin a new path of justice and of peace, in which THE KINGDOM OF GOD WILL TRULY DWELL IN ALL HEARTS, THAT INTERIOR KINGDOM THAT UPRIGHT SOULS HAVE ASKED FOR AND IMPLORED FOR SO MANY AGES.[1044]

A soul by the name of "Marisa" revealed to him that, indeed, this Era is precisely what Jesus told Luisa it consists in; namely, the fulfillment of the *Fiat Voluntas Tua* of the Our Father prayer:

In fact the immense swarming of men who cover the Earth and who are feverishly agitated, enveloped in the obscurity, aren't but a handful of dust which will soon be dispersed by the wind. The earth … will be made arid and desolate then "purified" by fire to be fertilized by the honest labor of the just escaped for the divine goodness to the tremendous hour of the divine anger. **Then … there will be the reign of God in the souls, that reign the just ask from God invoking "Thy Kingdom come."**[1045]

Particularly noteworthy regarding this holy priest's revelations is the assertion of Bishop Miguel Garcia Franco, who says, "…I find all the doctrine contained in the book [the one quoted above] 100% orthodox, more yet, in whole coincident with the writings of Mrs. Conchita Cabrera de Armida … and with the book of Father

Esteban Gobbi, books for which we have ecclesiastic approbation…"[1046]

And as noted in the section dedicated to her earlier, Conchita is now a Venerable, set to be Beatified in May of 2019.

Barnabas Nwoye (Precious Blood Revelations)

Barnabas Nwoye is a Nigerian man who has been receiving messages from Heaven since childhood, centering on the Precious Blood of Jesus. Of him and his messages, Fr. Edward O'Connor writes:

In 1995, at exactly 3:00 p.m., the hour of Divine Mercy, Our Lord Jesus Christ called for the first time Barnabas Nwoye, a teenager from Olo, Enugu state, Nigeria, and appeals to him to console Him and to adore His Precious Blood. In a vision two years later, the Lord gave him the Chaplet of the Precious Blood and twelve promises for all those who pray it. Barnabas also received from Jesus Consolation and Adoration Prayers as well as the Mystical Prayers, which had been offered by Jesus to His Father during His Passion. The messages, prayers, hymns and choruses, as well as the instructions given directly by Our Lord, His Mother Mary, the Angels and Saints, between 1997 and 2003, constitute the Precious Blood Devotion

The prayer book associated with Barnabas' revelations, *Precious Blood of Jesus Daily Devotional*, was given a nihil obstat in 1999 through his Archdiocese (Onitsha, Anambra State, Nigeria); consequently, we can approach its contents with confidence. In them, we find the revelation speaking of a Glorious Reign of Peace.

Repeatedly, the following prayer is offered, and it is one of the devotions' primary supplications to God:

"Agonizing Jesus, I offer You my heart to be united with Your Agonizing Heart as a co-bearer of Your agony. Jesus, I wish to be in agony with You so as to hasten Your Glorious Reign of Peace. Amen."

Another prayer of this devotion is the "Prayer for the Manifestation of the Divine Will," the entirety of which is as follows:

Eternal Father, You are the creator and author of life. You love the world You made. That is why

---

[1043] Ibid.
[1044] Ibid June 15, 1978.

[1045] Ibid January 2, 1979.
[1046] Jesusmariasite.org

You sent Your only-begotten Son to come for its redemption, so that Your Kingdom will come. Look upon Your Son and rise up on Your throne. Raise Your right hand and save Your people. I offer You all the sufferings, pains, and death of Your only begotten Son Whom You love, **for Your triumph and reign on earth**. May You, through the Precious Blood of Your Son, make a new covenant and bring all Your children back to Your Holy Will. Amen. Precious Blood of Jesus Christ—reign forever. Agonizing Jesus Christ—Thy Kingdom come. Amen.

In the same approved devotional, we find another prayer revealed to Barnabas. Entitled "The Prayer for the Reign of Glory on Earth," it reads as follows:

O Loving and Merciful Father, all knowing and all powerful, the Alpha and the Omega, the Eternal Father Who created all things, that You should forsake Your children, Your nature forbids. **Look kindly on Your begotten Son Jesus Christ Who came to save men and bring Your Kingdom down on earth**. We offer You all the agonies, tortures, pains, and the Precious Blood of Your Son Jesus Christ for the defeat of all the enemies of the holy Cross of salvation; the Antichrist and the Red Dragon who are fighting against the truth now and in the end of the age. May they, through the Precious Blood of our Redeemer and His last breath on earth, disappear like foam exposed under the sun, so that Your Kingdom may quickly come on earth. Amen.

Servant of God Cora Evans

Cora Evans was an American lay woman, mother, and mystic who received revelations from Jesus on the Mystical Humanity of Christ, and whose cause for Beatification has begun.

Upon examining her writings, it becomes clear that they refer to the Gift of Living in the Divine Will. An *Our Sunday Visitor* article written about her states:

[A former Mormon], Cora converted to Catholicism in 1935. Mack and their two daughters converted as well (their son died from an infection while he was a toddler). Dorothy remembers how her mother would school her in the Catholic faith, encouraging her to invite Jesus into her heart whenever she received Communion.

The anti-Catholic sentiment in Ogden ran deep, and Cora paid a heavy price for her conversion, … Yet despite the persecution, Cora's example drew many converts from the Latter Day Saints, Dorothy said. Cora's mystical experiences began with an apparition of Mary at age 3. After an experience of ecstasy in 1938, she resolved to serve God for the remainder of her life. She wrote, "It was necessary for me to live my chosen vocation with him as my companion. **By loaning Jesus my humanity for him to govern as well as dwell within would make my life a living prayer, for he was life, living life within me, and my body now dead to me was his living cross**, his cross to take to Calvary—Calvary, the door to eternal life." The way of prayer entrusted to Cora is known as the Mystical Humanity of Christ, a Eucharistic spirituality encouraging the faithful to live each day with a heightened awareness of the living, indwelling presence of Jesus in their lives …

"The Mystical Humanity of Christ focuses on the human state of the divine," said Father Gary Thomas, pastor of Sacred Heart Church in Saratoga, California, in the Diocese of Monterey. **"The Mystical Humanity makes Christ a real and tangible human person but retaining his divinity**. It expresses the imminent nature of God who is both transcendent (the Creator) and imminent (the Savior/Redeemer)." …

She has been declared a Servant of God as her cause for canonization is considered, and the Diocese of Monterey is investigating her life and writings. **Monterey Bishop Richard Garcia is "100 percent" behind** the investigation, McDevitt said, and has done much to assist the process … **"Cora was a laywoman whose life centered on doing the will of God,"** McDevitt said. "The choices she made, we can make; like the saints, there are many aspects of her life we can emulate." Father Thomas noted: "It amazes me that this woman touched so many people in her short life through her faith and miraculous visions, yet her humility covered over her notoriety until so recently." Dorothy added: "I have so many good memories of my mother. She loved God so much and helped me to know and to love God, too."[1047]

Although I do not know of any extensive revelations from Cora that speak of the Era (which does not imply such a thing does not exist), she

---

[1047]"Cora Evans: Mystic, wife and mother Monterey diocese backs sainthood cause of woman who proclaimed 'Mystical Humanity of Christ,'" Jim Graves. July 26, 2017.

does nevertheless refer to it. Jesus told her:

> I am giving this gift through you, better to establish My Kingdom of love within souls. I desire all souls to know I am real, alive, and the same today as after My Resurrection. **For My kingdom in souls to be better known is another step in the golden age,** golden because souls in sanctifying grace resemble the light of the golden, noonday sun. In that golden kingdom, I may personally dwell if I am invited, for I have said, "The kingdom of God is within you." Through this knowledge many souls still loan Me their bodies. Thus they actually become My Mystical Humanity, and in them I relive My life on earth as I did after My Resurrection.'[1048]

In speaking of her and her revelations, Michael Brown writes:

> Intriguingly, the mystic/housewife added, *"The center of the imaginary monstrance appeared to be above the nations of China and India.* Thin vapors, like bead-like fire, rained upon the earth from the center of the golden light.
>
> "Millions of people saw that apparition, yet none were harmed or frightened."
>
> That apparition—which obviously has not yet come to pass—would represent, she claimed, a "glorious age" of faith and peace, one that would last "several hundred years." This is in line with latter revelations of a period or era of peace.[1049]

Our Lady of America

Our Lady of America is a Marian apparition that has many associated Church approvals (including approbation from Archbishop Leibold) and consists in visitations from the Blessed Virgin to a religious, Sister Mary Ephrem (also often referred to by her baptismal name, Mildred Mary Neuzil), in Indiana in the year 1956. **In a letter to the Bishops of the USCCB, Cardinal Raymond Burke (then Archbishop Burke of the diocese of St. Louis) wrote, regarding these apparitions**:

> Having reviewed the correspondence between Sister Mary Ephrem and her spiritual director of many years, Monsignor Paul F. Leibold, Vicar General of the Archdiocese of Cincinnati, who later became the Bishop of Evansville and, then, Archbishop of Cincinnati, **it is clear that the devotion, as proposed by Sister Mary Ephrem, received his approbation...**The contents of **the**

> private revelation received by Sister Mary Ephrem were published in a booklet, first in 1960, and, again, in 1971. Both of these editions were published with the Imprimatur of Archbishop Leibold...A specific request of Our Lady of America was that her statue be placed in the Basilica of the National Shrine of the Immaculate Conception... While the National Shrine is the largest shrine in the world at which there was not a previous apparition, the private revelation to Sister Mary Ephrem very much confirms the mission of the National Shrine....What can be concluded canonically is that **the devotion was both approved by Archbishop Leibold and, what is more, was actively promoted by him**. In addition, over the years, other Bishops have approved the devotion and have participated in public devotion to the Mother of God, under the title of Our Lady of America. Although the devotion to Our Lady of America has remained constant over the years, in recent years the devotion has spread very much and has been embraced by many with special fervor. Seemingly, as has been suggested by Father Peter Damian Mary Fehlner, F.I., in his homily of August 5, 2006, at the Shrine of the Most Blessed Sacrament in Hanceville, the moral crisis of our time, which demands a new teaching and living of the virtue of purity, has found an especially fitting response of loving care from the Mother of God in her message to Sister Mary Ephrem ...As one deeply devoted to fostering the devotion to Our Lady of Guadalupe in our nation, I have wondered about the relationship of the devotion to Our Lady of America to the devotion to Our Lady of Guadalupe. Archbishop Leibold, in fact, raised the question with Sister Mary Ephrem. Sister Mary Ephrem responded that Our Lady of Guadalupe is Empress of all the Americas, whereas "Our Lady of America, The Immaculate Virgin," is the patroness of our nation, the United States of America. The two devotions are, in fact, completely harmonious. As our late and most beloved Pope John Paul II reminded us, Our Lady of Guadalupe, Mother of America and Star of the New Evangelization, draws all of the nations of America into unity in carrying out the new evangelization. Our Lady of America calls the people of our nation to the new evangelization through a renewed dedication to purity in love...[1050]

The trustworthiness of this apparition being settled, we turn to consider some of its prophecies.

[1048]Cora Evans in "Golden Detachment of the Soul."
[1049]https://spiritdaily.org/blog/apparitions/cora-apparitions

[1050]http://www.ewtn.com/library/BISHOPS/burkeolamer.htm

What happens to the world depends upon those who are living in it. There must be much more good than evil prevailing in order to prevent the holocaust that is so near approaching. Yet I tell you, My daughter, that even should such a destruction happen because there were not enough souls who took My warnings seriously, **there will remain a remnant untouched by the chaos who, having been faithful in following Me and spreading My warnings, will gradually inhabit the earth again with their dedicated and holy lives. These souls will renew the earth in the power and light of the Holy Spirit**, and these faithful children of Mine will be under My protection, and that of the Holy Angels, **and they will partake of the life of the Divine Trinity in a most remarkable way**. Let my dear children know this, precious daughter, so that the will have no excuse if they fail to heed my warnings.[1051]

This was Our Lady of America's last message to Sister Mary. It is quite profound not only in its clarity that, after the purging of the earth through the chastisements, the faithful will renew the earth, but also in that these faithful will "partake of the life of the Divine Trinity in a most remarkable way." This is, no doubt, a reference to living in the Divine Will when one considers other messages to Sr. Mary, including the following from the Blessed Virgin:

It is the wish of My Son that fathers and mothers strive to imitate me and my chaste spouse in our holy life at Nazareth. We practiced the simple virtues of family life, Jesus our Son being the center of all our love and activity. The Holy Trinity dwelt with us in a manner far surpassing anything that can ever be imagined. For ours was the earthly paradise where God walked among me ... The Divine Trinity will dwell in your midst only if you are faithful in practicing the virtues of our life at Nazareth. Then, you also my children, you also will become another paradise. God will then walk among you and you will have peace.[1052]

Alicja Lenczewska

Alicja was a Polish mystic and an incredibly saintly woman who lived from 1934 to 2012 and received mystical revelations from Jesus. In 2017, Bishop Henryk Wejman, the Bishop of her native diocese of Szczecin, Poland, authorized the publication of

these messages, giving his Imprimatur to two separate books compiling them.[1053]

Below is a small selection of her messages from Jesus which prophesy a Glorious Era of Peace:

"Yes, and My Church will give away in pain what it took from the world. And it will seem that it has died. And Satan and his servants will rejoice—as they rejoiced then in Jerusalem. But the time of their apparent victory will be short, **for the morning will come of the Resurrection of the Holy Church, immortal, giving birth to new life on earth—the holiness of My children**." (November 11, 2000).

"**The Immaculate Heart of My Mother will triumph**. She is the mother of the Church, which is always holy regardless of the sins and betrayal of many children of the Church…My Church suffers as I suffered, it is wounded and bleeds, as I was wounded and marked the way to Golgotha with My Blood. And it is spat upon, and defiled, as My body was spat upon and abused. And it succumbs, and falls, as I under the burden of the Cross, because it also carries the Cross of My children through the years and ages. And it gets up and walks towards Resurrection through Golgotha and Crucifixion, also that of many saints…And **the dawn and spring of the Holy Church is coming**, although there is an anti-Church and its founder, the Antichrist…

A purification will be given that will bring the sons of darkness to the light of God's Truth, and every person will according to their own will in the light of that Truth will have to choose the **Kingdom of My Father** or give themselves over eternally to the father of **lies. And the world will be freed from the spider's web of the Great Harlot of the Church of the Antichrist and those who served him from among My children**.

Mary is the one through whom will come the rebirth of My Church, so that it would shine with the full splendor of God's Holiness. The present time requires of the children of Truth heroic faith, hope and love. It is necessary to recognize the signs of the times in the light of prayer and the word of God and to fulfill the appeal of My Mother and the appeal of my beloved servant John Paul II, and to pray and do penance for the intention of saving My lost children." (June 8, 2002).

"Christians and the Church must be crucified, in

order that My Sacrifice be completed and so that the resurrection of humanity would occur in the Holy Spirit. I will die again in My people, so that the Holy Spirit would give new birth to humanity. It is the time of the Church's sacrifice—the time of the sacrifice of Christians. The time of the Crucifixion of My Body, which is the Church. Therefore the testimony of faith, prayer and mortification are necessary for the intention of rescuing humanity and the world from being lost in Satan. The Church must die away in order to be reborn through resurrection in the full power of God and to shine with the radiance of the Holy Spirit" (February 15, 2000).

"The escalation of evil must be completed. Just as it was completed for Me two thousand years ago, so now it strives for fullness with regard to My Church and to many of My faithful children. Then there will be the miracle of the resurrection of faith and love when I come in with power in order to put an end to the rule of Satan and his servants "(April 29, 2006).

In Alicja's messages especially we see an emphasis on a recurring theme in trustworthy revelations: that the Church on earth will follow the same path her Lord took on earth. Just as Jesus had a time of his resurrected humanity on earth after His passion, so too will the Church have a time of glorious triumph and peace which corresponds to Jesus' resurrected life on earth before His Ascension into Heaven (with the Ascension corresponding to the Final Judgment, General Resurrection, End of Time, and Heavenly Wedding).

Fr. Adam Skwarczynski

Fr. Adam Skwarczynski is a Polish priest and recipient of mystical revelations and prophecies.

He was interviewed on his revelations on July 27, 2012, and the video of this dialogue was posted online, being entitled "Conversation about Christ's Parousia with Fr. Adam Skwarczynski from Poland." In other places, it is posted with the title "I Have Seen the New World." Below, I present a partial personal transcription of an English translation narration provided by Tom Karol on the video interview. Please note that since this 2012 interview, Fr. Adam has continued his ministry and his mission, ever insisting on the impending arrival of these events he was shown. He was also interviewed as part of the major Polish project, "Proroctwo," ("prophet") and which can be found online.[1054] Fr. Adam also maintains his own website.[1055]

Fr. Artur: Even though these apocalyptic visions fill one with dread, fear, and horror, still there is a horizon of light behind them, and it's about the new world, about the visions of the new world emerging as if from conflagration of the old world, which I would like to ask you about now, father Adam.

Fr. Adam: I described it as best as I could in the novel "Into the New World with an Angel", here my language is too inadequate to describe it, because we can do it only in categories known to us; categories of the world that surrounds us. So, how to describe, for instance, new clothes, which have not yet been seen by anyone having only at one's disposal the old clothing which is falling apart, after having been previously patched up. I am dressed in the old patched-up clothing and say: "imagine that I am wearing beautiful clothes"… now, how can I describe it? It is not easy because it will be the Spirit, not matter which will fill the cleansed, renewed world. So, the transformation of Spirit, and that was what Our Lord Jesus saw when he spoke of the coming of His Kingdom, and not in the way the Jews awaited it, but He had in mind the kingdom of the Spirit. "If anyone loves me," He said, "he will keep my word and my father will love him, I will come to him and make our home with him," that will be the Kingdom of God in souls. When He reigns in people's souls, he will also rain in the surrounding world. **The whole of nature will thus be transformed; it will not only become friendly to man who up to now has been surrounded by pests, worms, various diseases, microbes, which have been destroying him, but when faithful to God the new Israel will receive a similar promise to the one the old Israel did—"If you obey me I will bless you" this very blessing will be made manifest in the whole world surrounding us, in our physical state and in the state of nature being transformed all around us.** In order to somehow visualize it to people, at least from the point of view of nature, I will gladly describe the case of transformation which took place in the South American town called Almolonga, Guatemala, where people have been so deprived that in that small place several over crowded prisons existed—incredible moral decline of the people. It all started when some bandits threatened to kill a Protestant pastor and when they were just about to do it, by pointing a gun into his mouth, it did not fire: the bandits left him in peace, and the pastor out of gratitude to God for having been saved, began to gather together a small group of people; there was nobody there to pray—Protestant communities were either non-existent or virtually empty; people began to pray together with him for the transformation of the whole town. They were joined by those who previously had been indifferent, distant, churches began to fill up, people started meeting together in families and eventually after some years the prisons were no longer needed. The last prison closed in 1998 and changed into a wedding parlor. The people changed so much, prayed so much, got so close to God, that they acknowledged Him even in public life, and God replied with the showering of His blessings upon them. If at the time of their moral decline just a few lorries a year loaded with vegetables left their fields, so after the conversion several dozen lorries a week drove way carrying the crops of the field, so enormous, that it was unequaled anywhere in America or in the whole world. They write on the internet that a cabbage could be so huge that the head of a woman holding the cabbage disappears behind it… or carrots as massive as a forearm: huge vegetables, so abundant that the small town has become a provider for neighboring countries (with no microorganisms or any additional fertilizers). As for my childhood visions, I can say that I saw my own garden in which we are sitting in three stages: first it appeared just as it was during my father's time, I did not know it yet as a child, it was all filled with beehives—thirty something beehives—beautifully tended with plants for the bees; later I saw it in a state of total neglect, just as it is now: overgrown, dying trees, new branches eaten out by cancer—disintegrating, ailing. Finally, the third stage of the garden's existence, that is in a new world: it was so beautiful, with little alley ways, all around, full of flowers, people working there with joy, filled with fruits completely unknown to me; foreign to our climate, more typical of the Mediterranean climate; several kinds of palms growing here—the climate is to change in Poland, and it is to be a temperate climate all over the world. Well, first and foremost, the essence of this new world is what would describe as matter illuminated by spirit; I've seen it many times—suddenly I was startled at how it could be in other words: such a powerful spirit radiates out of matter, so luminescent, so colorful, raising us up to God, filling us with joy**… It's difficult to describe, there's nothing to compare it with, it's as if the whole of nature that surrounds us was shining with a new brilliance. I imagine it to be a piece of heaven,** because it's also supposed to be illuminated by the spirit of love; the sun won't be needed there. People should strive toward such a kind of world, even if they stand before God at the warning time when they are at His judgment seat, they should hold onto this wonderful perspective of the world which they are to enter with joy , praising God with hymns for the great things He's done for them. Thus, a [magnificent] world, a world worshipping God. If they don't have this perspective, then what will happen when Christ comes suddenly like a lightning and his judgment falls on them? They will find themselves in terrifying panic, unable to raise their hearts up. And as Christ said to Saint Faustina that Poland was to prepare the world for His second coming, it's more or less the same from her, […]from Poland would come forth to prepare the spark. It's something extremely important, and I suppose that's why we are here talking about it right now… I would very much like for this filmed interview to spread around the world, so that the suffering I have to go through, and will still have to go through by offering my final sacrifice will bear the fruits of hope; perhaps there is someone out there who will translate all this, not just into Spanish but also into English or into other languages and send it out into the world, since I have discovered my calling at the end of my life. It seems that God has been showing me all that so that I become a witness to a reality not yet known to people. I am a witness ready to give up my life to testify that what I am saying here and now is true. I take God for my witness, the God in whom we live and move and have our being, the one who creates this world for us, which is temporarily polluted by us, the God who will later create it anew as a beautiful world. I take God for my witness that what I am saying is true to the extent that I was able to come to know it, to ascertain. When people are prepared to cross over onto the other shore, over the footbridge of The Warning—El Aviso—, that terrifying judgment followed by chastisements encompassing the whole Earth, along with earthquakes, volcanic eruptions, then, they will go through those experiences having been prepared for it. This calling of mine, of even the last few months, is a sort of an offshoot of what I've called powerful spark that God wanted to come out of Poland and to prepare people; maybe will be added to that flame whose name is John Paul II who entrusted the world to God's Divine Mercy after having entrusted it to the Immaculate Heart of Mary. Maybe, but I ardently desire for its having a practical meaning, the rest will happen from the other side: when my persecutors throw themselves upon me, those Satanists will take my earthly life away in accordance with God's will, I promise to help everybody to cross that footbridge to new world from the other side.

Although lengthy, I provided this excerpt from Fr. Adam's messages due to how inspiring and profound they are. We should also remember that, without ever knowing about the prophecies of Garabandal or the locutions received by Fr. Gobbi, Fr. Adam had long received almost identical messages himself, further demonstrating the reality of a "prophetic consensus" that is today undeniable.

On his website, in one of the few English-language publications he has made, Fr. Adam wrote the following:

Well, those disasters, predicted by Jesus in the Gospels would be pointless at the end of the world, since the world would be destroyed soon during The Last Judgment … It is so evident in the Gospels, in the Apocalypse, in some Psalms and in the prophets' books, especially in Isaiah, not to mention the Marian apparitions from last centuries, which Church acknowledges but does not realize the relevance of the Parousia in them. If seen at the end of the world, Mary's massages in Fatima, in Amsterdam, in Akita in Japan, in Kibeho in Rwanda and so many others are misunderstood. If Church itself has this kind of attitude, no wonder it doesn't give the importance to the apparitions in Garabandal in Spain, in Naju in Korea nor in Medjugorie with ten "mysteries" related precisely to the Second Coming! … Although John Paul II predicted that after the year 2000 the Church will enter in a new stage of its history, that there would be a new spring and a new Day of Pentecost, he did not reveal anything more. He hasn't been heard nor understood. And today, those who want to stick to the apostolic tradition could ask "Where is that spring? Isn't it winter actually?", while the liberals, preachers of false mercy for everybody who doubt in the existence of hell would answer: "It has already come!". However, both of them don't know the answer for the question "what next?". … There is hope that many of you will remain on the earth to recreate the world with God on evangelical principles, to build a new, happy world on the ruins, a world my spirit have been moved to, and which I miss profoundly. It's a much more beautiful world than anyone could dream of. It's a world, which, like a huge surprise, will be God's gift at the end of times. Before the earth will come to an end, humanity will be given a special time … to realize how was the life on earth supposed to be, if everybody had obeyed God and his commandments. …

In Sinu Jesu

The book, *In Sinu Jesu: When Heart Speaks to Heart — The Journal of a Priest at Prayer*, contains the locutions received by an anonymous Benedictine monk beginning in the year 2007, and is considered authentic by the monk's spiritual director. It contains both an Imprimatur and a Nihil Obstat and is strongly endorsed by Cardinal Raymond Burke. In it, Jesus tells this priest-monk:

I am about to sanctify My priests by a new outpouring of the Holy Spirit upon them. They will be sanctified as were My Apostles on the morning of Pentecost. Their hearts will be set ablaze with the divine fire of charity and their zeal will know no bounds. They will assemble around My Immaculate Mother, who will instruct them and, by her all-powerful intercession, obtain for them all **the charisms necessary to prepare the world—this sleeping world—for My return in glory**. I tell you this not to alarm you or to frighten anyone, but to give you cause for an immense hope and for pure spiritual joy. **The renewal of My priests will be the beginning of the renewal of My Church**, but it must begin as it did at Pentecost, with an outpouring of the Holy Spirit on the men whom I have chosen to be My other selves in the world, to make present My Sacrifice and to apply My Blood to the souls of poor sinners in need of forgiveness and healing…

The attack on My priesthood that appears to be spreading and growing is, in fact, in its final stages. It is a satanic and diabolical onslaught against My Bride the Church, an attempt to destroy her by attacking the most wounded of her ministers in their carnal weaknesses; but I will undo the destruction they have wrought and **I will cause My priests and My Spouse the Church to recover a glorious holiness that will confound My enemies and be the beginning of a new era of saints**, of martyrs, and of prophets. This springtime of holiness in My priests and in My Church was obtained by the intercession of My sweet Mother's Sorrowful and Immaculate Heart. She intercedes ceaselessly for her priest sons, and her intercession has obtained a victory over the powers of darkness that will confound unbelievers and bring joy to all My saints.[1056]

The day is coming, and it is not far off, when I will intervene to show My Face in a priesthood completely renewed and sanctified; **when I will intervene to triumph in My Eucharistic Heart by the conquering power of sacrificial love alone; when I will intervene to defend the poor and vindicate the innocents whose blood has marked this nation** and so many others as did the blood of Abel in the beginning.[1057]

Profound as the above locutions are, the locution he received on January 8, 2010, is especially powerful, and merits to be relayed here in full:

This is the prayer I want you to say in all circumstances of life:

My Jesus, only as Thou willest,
when Thou willest,
and in the way Thou willest.
To Thee be all glory and thanksgiving,
Who rulest all things mightily and sweetly,
and Who fillest the earth with Thy manifold mercies. Amen.

Pray in this way, and so you will allow Me to deploy My grace and manifest My munificence in all places and in all the circumstances of your life. I desire to heap blessings upon you. I ask only that you give Me the freedom to act upon you, and around you, and through you, as I will.

If more souls would give Me this freedom to act as I will, My Church would begin to know the springtime of holiness that is My burning desire for her. **These souls, by their entire submission to all the dispositions of My providence, will be the ones to usher in My kingdom of peace and holiness on earth.**

Look at My most pure Mother; this was her way and this was her life— nothing but My will and the will of My Father, in complete submission to the Holy Spirit. Imitate her, and so will you too bring My presence into a world that waits for Me.

Here, we see not only a confirmation of the Era of Peace, but also a confirmation that this Era will indeed consist in the coming of the Kingdom of God on earth. And not only do we see this reality confirmed, but we see confirmed how it will come about: through souls living in the Will of God.

Apostolate of Holy Motherhood

An anonymous young mother ("Mariamante")

received messages from Jesus and Mary in 1987 and these locutions are compiled in a book entitled *The Apostolate of Holy Motherhood*, which received both a nihil obstat and an imprimatur, so we can approach the content of the messages without fear of unorthodoxy. Furthermore, the book was compiled and edited by Dr. Mark Miravalle, the world-renowned theologian whose discernment of private revelation is unrivaled.

So, it is with great confidence and joy that we should read these words given as part of these revelations:

The Triumph of My Mother's Immaculate Heart has already begun. Rejoice and be glad that you are part of it. The reign of My Sacred Heart is the fulfillment of the promises of Fatima, that is, the reign of peace which was foretold. This Era of Peace which will encompass the world will be the result of the Triumph of the Immaculate Heart of Mary, My Mother. **The deplorable conditions in which the world now finds itself will be transformed into the likeness of My Father's Kingdom for a time, and there will be peace.** I say again, **rejoice that you are privileged to live in this era.** Many are unaware of the importance of the times in which they are living. This will all soon change as it will become apparent that something unique and supernatural is about to begin on the face of the earth. I am heartened by your response and hope that others will fulfill their calls so that all may be accomplished quickly and for the greater glory of My Father. You will be given many opportunities to fulfill the will of My Father, but do not hesitate in your call. The salvation of many souls is at stake. This is why so many **extraordinary graces are being poured forth**. The Era of My Mercy has come. It will **unite Heaven and earth in one hymn of love to the Blessed Trinity**. I call you to rejoicing. The time has come. So be it. Amen.[1058]

Sr. Natalia of Hungary

Sr. Maria Natalia of the Sisters of St. Mary Magdalene was a 20th century nun and mystic whose revelations bear a Nihil Obstat (from Fr. Antonio Gonzalez, Ecclesiastic censor) and an Imprimatur (from Jesús Garibay B., General Vicar) in 1999. Regarding Sr. Natalia herself, we read the following, taken from the Introduction of the book dedicated to her revelations, entitled *Victorious*

[1056] Locution on March 2, 2010.
[1057] Locution on November 12, 2008.

[1058] Thomas Petrisko. *Call of the Ages*. P. 441

Queen of the World:

Her life is full of historical and political events, since she lived during most of the 20th century. She died on April 24, 1992, in the odor of sanctity. From an early age she clearly perceived her religious vocation and at seventeen she entered the convent of Pozsony ...[her] messages are a call to atonement for sin, for amendment and the devotion to the Immaculate Heart of Mary as the Victorious Queen of the World. Most of these messages were written between 1939 and 1943. During World War II, Sister Natalia advised Pope Pius XII not to go to Castelgandolfo, his summer retreat, because it would be bombed, as it was in fact. Sister Natalia had to transmit some very severe messages to the Catholic hierarchy of Hungary: that they distribute their wealth to the poor, abandon their palaces and do penance. For many this call was not only madness but absurd. Only a few paid attention to the call to the "Apostolate of Amendment." Only after the war, in 1945, when cardinal Mindszenty was elected Primate of Hungary, did the movement of amendment seriously begin. He wanted a chapel built in Budapest and granted permission for the foundation of a new order of nuns, whose only purpose would be to make reparation and penance for the sins of the nation. But unfortunately it was too late and the chapel was never finished. The communist authorities not only prohibited the foundation of the new order, but dispersed the existing ones. The terror against the Hungarian people was three times more severe than in the neighboring satellite countries. ... Sister Natalia offered her life for priests when she entered the convent. The Lord accepted her offering: she supported incredible sufferings, in her body and in her soul, because Jesus shared with her his cross, his pain that He feels for the lukewarm priests and also his joy for the good and loyal ones. She completely identified herself with Jesus. Jesus rejoiced and suffered in her, as He himself said: "For my beloved sons, the Priests."

The first messages given to Sr. Natalia that speak of the Era occur early on in her diary, when she writes:

When somebody asked the Lord about the end of the world, He answered: "The end of sin is close, but not the end of the world. Soon no more souls will be lost. My words will be fulfilled, and there will only be one flock and one Shepherd." (Jn. 10:16) I saw people of other denominations enter the Church, purified and sanctified, but only after sin is defeated and Satan is chained.

And later:

Jesus said to me: —I am telling you again: "Pray, so that before the holy peace, and the great mercy for the world arrives, sinners may be converted and accept my mercy, amending their lives. Otherwise those that have not converted before or during this period of grace will die eternally. You, who are just, should not be scared. Pray and trust in the power of holy prayer. Rejoice, because they have found mercy with my celestial Father. Do not be afraid, rather rejoice, because my Immaculate Mother with her power of Queen, full of grace, along with the celestial legions of angels, will annihilate the forces of hell.

"Why is the promised world peace coming so slowly?" A priest asked [this] question of me, and I received the following answer from the Most Holy Virgin: "The age of world peace is not delayed. The Heavenly Father only wants to give time to those who are able to be converted and find refuge with God. Many will be converted, even those that deny the existence of God. The world has received the grace by this extension of time before the punishment, because the celestial Father has received with affability reparation and the sacrifices of the victim souls for everyone. For those that are converted before, the doors of hell will be closed and they will not be condemned. The power of their conversion will prevent them from falling into sin. Reparation has power, because I am praying with you and consoling the greatly offended God with you. My daughter, even your breathing and respiration should be an expiating prayer before God."...

A priest requested me to ask the Most Holy Virgin what we must do to hasten the victory. The answer came from the Most Holy Virgin: —"If you want to hasten the great miracle of victory of your Queen, with which I will save the world, you must trust me and my Son, as children trust their mothers, in addition performing reparation, offering your lives and praying. Your trust so far has not been sufficient, and yet the effectiveness of your prayer depends on your trust! If you pray with full confidence, the victory that you are eagerly awaiting will bring the joy of world-wide peace in a cleansed environment. Trust me! Trust me always, my children!"

Jesus also gave Sr. Natalia a direct vision of the Era itself, which she describes in the following diary entry:

Jesus showed me in a vision, that after the purification, mankind will live a pure and angelical life. There will be an end to the sins against the sixth commandment, adultery, and an end to lies. The Savior showed me that unceasing love, happiness and divine joy will signify this future clean world. I saw the blessing of God abundantly poured out upon the earth. Satan and sin were completely defeated. After the great purification, the life of the monks and the laypeople will be full of love and purity. The purified world will enjoy the peace of the Lord through the Most Holy Virgin Mary. But the Lord never told me when all this would take place

… Jesus also told me that the Church, purified and renewed by such great sufferings, will be clothed again in humility and simplicity, and will be poor as at her beginning. There will not be titles, given or bought, or ranks to distinguish the one from the other. Instead of this the spirit of holiness will penetrate all the members of the Church and all will live according to the spirit of the Sermon on the Mount. As we get closer to the fulfillment of the end of the world, this simplicity and poverty will receive wider and wider acceptance. After the chastisement, it will be meaningless to have plush homes or extravagant attire. Everyone will know his duties and for that reason titles will not be necessary. The title of the priest will be: brother priest and even the Pope will be called Brother Pope…[Jesus said] "I brought peace when I was born, but the world has still not enjoyed it. The world has a right to this peace. Men are children of God. God instills His own Spirit in them. God cannot let Himself be put to shame, and that is why the children of God are entitled to enjoy the peace that I promised."

In a vision in which Sr. Natalia was shown the Chastisements themselves and the reign of Satan transformed into the Era of Peace, she writes:

God in Three Persons acted on the Immaculate Mother, as if the Holy Spirit had overshadowed Her again, that She might give Jesus to the world again. The celestial Father filled Her with graces. From the Son, unspeakable happiness and love radiated towards Her, as if He wanted to congratulate Her, while He said:

"My Immaculate Mother, Victorious Queen of the World, show Your power! Now You will be the savior of humanity. As you were part of My saving work as Co-Redemptrix according to My will, so I want to share with you My power as King. With this I entrust you with the work of rescuing sinning humanity; You can do it with your power as Queen. It is necessary that I share everything with you. You are the Co-Redemptrix of humanity."

Then I saw that Her mantle was impregnated with the blood of Jesus, and this gave it a scarlet tinge.

My attention soon went to the angels, who surrounded their Queen with great reverence. The angels dressed in white, red, and black. I understood that the white symbolized the future purity of the world, the red the martyrdom of the saints, and the black the mourning for condemned souls. Then the Virgin Mary began to walk softly and majestically towards the world. I saw the world as a giant sphere covered with a crown of thorns that was full of sin, and Satan, in the form of a coiled serpent around the sphere and all kinds of sin and dirt came out of him.

The Virgin Mother rose above the globe as the Victorious Queen of the World. Her first act as Queen was to cover the world with her mantle, impregnated with the blood of Jesus. Then She blessed the world, and I saw that at the same time the Most Holy Trinity also blessed the world. The satanic serpent then attacked Her with terrible hatred; flames coming from its mouth. I feared that Her mantle would be reached by the fire and would burn, but the flames could not even touch it. The Virgin Mary was calm as if she was not in a fight, and calmly stepped on the neck of the serpent.

The serpent did not stop throwing flames, symbol of hatred and revenge, but it could do nothing, while the crown of thorns, made of sins, had disappeared from around the world, and from its center a lily appeared and began to bloom. I also saw that the blessing of the Virgin Mother had fallen on all the nations and people. Her voice was indescribably calm and majestic when She said: "Here I am! I will help! I will bring order and peace!"

Jesus then explained to me: "My Immaculate Mother will overcome sin by means of her power as Queen. The lily represents the purification of the world, the arrival of the era of paradise, when mankind will live as without sin. There will be a new world and a new era. It will be the era when humanity will recover what it lost in paradise. When my Immaculate Mother steps on the neck of the serpent, the doors of hell will be closed. The armies of angels will take part in the battle. I have sealed My own with My seal, so that they will not perish in this battle."

These words speak for themselves, and it is clear that they speak of exactly the same reality that was revealed to Luisa.

Fr. Stefano Gobbi (Marian Movement of Priests)

Father Stefano Gobbi, the founder of the

worldwide and incredibly fruitful Marian Movement of Priests, was an Italian priest, mystic, and theologian who died in 2011. Of him and his mysticism, Colin Donovan at EWTN writes:

> In his favor… are the opinion of his spiritual director, his own zeal to promote Consecration to the Immaculate Heart and fidelity to the Magisterium, the great numbers of lay, religious and priestly vocations strengthened, and in some cases saved, through the Marian Movement of Priests, and the good will shown him by very many members of the hierarchy, including the Pope, who has received him and encouraged him in his work on several occasions.[1059]

He is also the recipient of revelations (locutions) recorded in "the Blue Book," the actual title of which is *To the Priests, Our Lady's Beloved Sons*.

This book bears full Ecclesiastical approbation; having an Imprimatur from Bishop Donald Montrose of Stockton and Cardinal Bernardino Echeverria Ruiz. The latter did not merely give his imprimatur, but went farther, writing: "I consider it a privilege not only to be able to give the Imprimatur… But also to take this opportunity to recommend the reading of these messages. They will contribute to the spread of devotion to Our Lady." Below are some excerpts from this book, with the date on which each message was received following it.

> I have chosen you and prepared you for the triumph of my Immaculate Heart in the world, and these are the years when I will bring my plan to completion. It will be a cause of amazement even to the Angels of God; a joy to the Saints in Heaven; a consolation and great comfort for all the just on earth; mercy and salvation for a great number of my straying children; a severe and definitive condemnation of Satan and his many followers. In fact at the very moment when Satan will be enthroned as lord of the world and will think himself now the sure victor, I myself will snatch the prey from his hands. As if by magic he will find himself empty-handed and in the end the victory will be exclusively my Son's and mine: this will be the triumph of my Immaculate Heart in the world. December 1973

> Beloved sons, at this time you must become the sign of my immense sorrow. in your hearts carry, with Me, the suffering of the world and the Church, in this its new hour of agony and of redemptive passion. It will be only from this

suffering of ours that a new era of peace for all can be born. September 15, 1981

I am the Queen of all the Saints. Today you are bid to lift up your eyes to Paradise, where so many of your brothers have preceded you. They are praying for you and helping you, that that Reign of Jesus, which in Heaven is the cause of our joy and glory, may soon come also upon earth… By your prayer, your suffering and your personal immolation, I will bring my plan to completion. I will hasten the time of the triumph of my Immaculate Heart in the Reign of Jesus, who will come to you in glory. **Thus a new era of peace will begin and you will at last see new heavens and a new earth**. November 1, 1981

The Father wants to mould with His own Hands a new creation, in which His divine imprint will be more visible, welcomed, and accepted and His Fatherhood exalted and glorified by everyone. The breath of this new creation will be the breath of the Father's love … And Jesus will reign … **Jesus, Who taught you the prayer for asking for the coming of God's kingdom upon earth, will at last see this prayer of His fulfilled, for He will establish His Kingdom. And creation will return to being a new garden in which Christ will be glorified by all and His divine Kingship will be welcomed and exalted; it will be a universal Kingdom of Grace**, beauty, harmony, communion, justice and peace. July 3, 1987

In the hour of the great trial, *paradise will be joined to earth, until* the moment when the luminous door will be opened, to cause to descend upon the world the glorious presence of Christ, **who will restore his reign in which the divine Will shall be accomplished in a perfect manner, as in heaven, so also on earth** . November 1, 1990

The new era, toward which you are journeying, is bringing all creation to the perfect glorification of the Most Holy Trinity. The Father receives his greatest glory from every creature which reflects his light, his love and his divine splendor. The Son restores his reign of grace and of holiness, setting free every creature from the slavery of evil and of sin. The Holy Spirit pours out in fullness his holy gifts, leads to the understanding of the whole truth, and renews the face of the earth.

The new era, **which I announce to you, coincides with the complete fulfillment of the divine will**, so that at last there is coming about that which Jesus taught you to ask for, from the Heavenly Father: 'Your will be done on earth as it is in heaven.' This is the time when the divine will of

---

[1059] https://www.ewtn.com/expert/answers/mmp.htm

the Father, of the Son and of the Holy Spirit is being accomplished by the creatures. From the perfect fulfillment of the divine will, the whole world is becoming renewed, because God finds there, as it were, his new garden of Eden, where He can dwell in loving companionship with his creatures. August 15, 1991

Christ risen is now bringing the will of the Father to perfect fulfilment, through his second coming in glory, **to restore his reign, in which the Divine Will may be accomplished by all on earth**. April 19, 1992

These excerpts (and many more which I have left unquoted) speak for themselves; no one could pretend that they do not refer to a glorious reign of peace, *on earth*—the veritable Coming of the Kingdom in fulfillment of the Our Father prayer— *before* the end of time. Similarly, anyone who tries to accuse this book of heresy[1060] will be immediately revealing only his own obstinacy, considering the degree of Church approvals and God-sent fruits attached to it.

***

Finally, recall that Fr. Gobbi himself explicitly endorsed Luisa and her revelations, once saying:

> **There is a mystic, Luisa Piccarreta, whose cause for beatification is in progress, who wrote great works about the Divine Will.** When I was in Mexico, I was given some of these writings which relate to numerous aspects described in our book [To the Priests...]. I was impressed by them—I should read the exact text to you, but I don't have it with me today. It says that every two thousand years there has been a great renewal. Two thousand years after creation there was the deluge of water. Two thousand years after the deluge of water, there was the deluge of blood: the redemption. After two thousand years there will be the deluge of fire—a spiritual fire, I think—and finally, the Kingdom of the Divine Will will come upon earth, because every creature will fulfill the Divine Will in a perfect way.

> And so, I think that this return of Christ in glory will be able to bring the Kingdom of the Divine Will into the world, and each creature will be able to do the Will of the Father in a perfect way, and the Father will be glorified by these children of his who say 'yes' to his Will; and Christ will bring

about his Kingdom—a Kingdom of holiness and of docile obedience to the heavenly Father.[1061]

Jesus King of All Nations

The revelations of Jesus King of All Nations were given to an anonymous young American woman beginning in the 1980s. Bishop Enrique Hernandex Rivera of Caguas, Puerto Rico, granted this Ecclesial approbation, and also said of these revelations that he recognized "the need to foster more devotion [to them]." The great theologian and Mariologist, Fr. Peter Fehlner, was a zealous promoter of these revelations as well. He wrote that he believed in "the authenticity of [the revelations of the Jesus King of All Nations Devotion] as revelations directly dictated by Jesus to his Secretary [the seer] and in the truth of their content."[1062] He also wrote: "…the revelations were a remedy for the imminent chastisement under way."

Although sometimes anonymity of a seer can be a red flag, there can also be good reasons for this. In this case, I personally know Dan Lynch, the man who is entrusted with spreading the messages (and who, in turn, knows the visionary), and I can vouch for his trustworthiness. We should proceed, therefore, to consider these messages with confidence. In them, we read:[1063]

> This image is to be a sign that I rule Heaven and earth, and My Kingdom, My Reign, is near at hand. ... My Most Holy Mother is preparing the great triumph. The triumph of her Immaculate Heart ushers in the Reign of My Love and Mercy. ... I have come to entrust to you a message of great importance for the world. I tell you, My very little one, the days are coming when mankind will cry out to Me for mercy. I tell you, My child, that in these times only one thing will be given as a remedy. I Myself AM that remedy…

In another message, Jesus said to the seer:

> Therefore let it also be known that a great renewal of My Holy Church, of mankind and indeed of all creation will follow the cleansing action of My Justice. How greatly I Love My people! It is for your good O mankind that I allow My Justice to be poured out in order to awaken your conscience

---

[1060] As one is always, unavoidably, implicitly doing by condemning as Millenarianism the anticipation of such a glorious Reign
[1061] Address by by Fr. Stefano Gobbi. The Triumph, The Second Coming and The Eucharistic Reign. June 24, 1996.

[1062] Jkmi.com/jesus-king-of-all-nations
[1063] All of these quotes are taken from the website of Dan Lynch, jkmi.com.

and correct your sinful behavior. Yet you see how dearly I Love you in that I continually warn you and even seek to comfort you in the pain of the cleansing which is almost upon you.

Return to Me My people. I Love you Infinitely and Eternally for such is My very Nature as God; the One-True God, the Sovereign King of all that is.

Pray and trust in Me My Faithful ones. I will not abandon you in the dark and cloudy day which rapidly approaches. Stay close to My Immaculate Mother; cling to her Holy Rosary, invoke her Immaculate Heart.

Janie Garza

Janie Garza is a visionary from Austin, Texas, who has the support of her bishop and whose messages are only published after review and approval of her Carmelite priest spiritual director, Fr. Henry Bordeaux. Often her messages are published on the highly regarded theological website, Mother of All Peoples.[1064]

Of Janie and her messages, Fr. Edward O'Connor writes:

In 1989, when Janie was a psychiatric social worker in Austin, Texas, "Our Lady of the Rosary" began to appear to her. Janie resisted these apparitions for fear of being deluded; but when she prayed to Jesus to protect her sanity, He Himself appeared and assured her that Mary was coming to help her in her family life, and enable her to help others. Later St. Joseph, St. Philomena and other saints appeared and spoke to her.[1065]

In her messages, we see the following:

On September 5,1996 Janie Garza had a vision of the new earth. Janie said: "St. Michael showed me a vision of the world as it is in these evil times. Then he showed me a vision of the new earth. It was beautiful. There was no pollution, and the earth was impregnated with much life. The ocean was so beautiful and abundant with sea life. There was no poverty, no suffering, no violence, only true peace from Heaven. This was a vision of hope for all of God's children who keep their focus on God in these evil times"

On April 19, 1994 Janie Garza received from Jesus a vision of the New Jerusalem. Janie said: "In the seventh vision I saw new life. I saw a garden full of life. The trees were beautiful and very green. I saw flowers of all kinds. I saw beautiful springs of water in different areas of the garden. This is the most beautiful garden I have ever seen, and I knew it was like no garden on this earth. Then I heard Jesus speak Scripture to me. Jesus said: "This is the New Jerusalem. This is the new house of the people of My Father. Here there will be no more weeping, no more calling for help. Babies will no longer die in infancy and all people will live out their life span. Those who live to be a hundred will be considered young and to die before that time will be a sign that My Father had punished them. "Like trees, people will live long lives. They will build their homes and get to live in them. Their homes will not be used by someone else. The work they do will be successful and their children will not meet with disaster."[1066]

In a locution she received on January 6, 2003, we read:

When the Dogma of Mary, Co-Redemptrix, Mediatrix and Advocate is proclaimed, a new divine radiance will cover the world. The Catholic Church will be renewed and strengthened. Faith will be renewed in many fallen away priests and religious. The commandments of God will again be accepted by many. The Church will have its authority. The sacraments will be accepted once more by many, especially the true Presence in the Blessed Sacrament. Confession and all the sacramental and pious means to salvation will be renewed in many hearts…[1067]

Julka (Yugoslavian Visionary)

The messages received by "Julka," a Yugoslavian widow born in the 1920s, were the subject of several books—allegedly endorsed by Pope St. Paul VI himself—entitled *Jesus Calls Us*. As I could not verify this endorsement, I leave this visionary's messages at the end of this section and propose them for your discernment. I include these messages because a direct Papal endorsement of a message of this sort is a rare thing, and I find it somewhat unlikely that this claim would be allowed to circulate for decades without any attempt at refutation if it were not true; nevertheless, I understand that this is no sure proof. Unfortunately, it is difficult to secure copies of her books, but at least a few messages can still readily be found; and these few that I could find, given to

---

[1064] For example, here:
https://www.motherofallpeoples.com/blog/september-6-2018-message-of-saint-michael-to-janie-garza

[1065] *Listen to My Prophets*. Page 212.
[1066] *Fire from Heaven*. Pages 286-287.
[1067] http://www.pdtsigns.com/garzalatest.html

Julka by Jesus, are profound:

> The Roman Catholic faith will be the only one in the entire world. The pope will be the one true shepherd. "This will be the Little Flock and I shall hover over it. In those days there will be one Shepherd and one Faith, that of the Roman Catholic Church, which I established when I walked visibly on the earth. After the distresses, which I am now permitting to come upon My obstinate people on earth, there will arise a fair and pure race and the earth will abound with My gifts….The time is coming, when the face of the Earth will be renewed. After the great catastrophe, all regions of the world will be transformed….After a certain amount of time, Our Lord Jesus commanded the great trial to cease. Thereupon the terrible darkness receded from the earth and, along with all the demons, disappeared into the horrible abyss… Our Lord said 'I have removed the living earth from the dead earth. To the living earth I have given Grace

the Great Tribulation."[1068]

of My Wisdom that it may live in My Spirit.' God the Father and the Holy Spirit commanded that the sun should shine with renewed strength upon the Earth. The air became crystal clear and the earth appeared newborn. "I shall fashion and renew it, and it will be more beautiful than it is now. My laws will be different from what they are now, because My Divinity will be present in everything. I shall go amongst My creatures so that many will see Me and countless numbers will hear Me and they will recognize that I am the Living God from Heaven…"

Everything was beautiful. "The Earth was transformed into a most beautiful garden full of flowers. It was soaked in bright sun-beams and veiled in gleaming purity. Everything seemed transparent, orderly and pure…"

Everything is new. "I will transform the Earth and it will be new . . The people whose lives I spare will revere My Holy Name. The hearts will be shaken by My Voice, which they will hear after

**

As we can see, there is an utterly overwhelming consensus in private revelation as to the guaranteed coming of a Glorious Era of Peace, to be lived on earth (before the end of time). In fact, while writing this section, there came a point where I simply had to stop myself. It was getting too long, and I could have easily kept going for many more pages, so inescapable are these prophecies of the Era in trustworthy private revelation.

Now, as mentioned in the introduction to this section, it would not be surprising if a few of these apparitions or revelations here listed will wind up being someday proven false. This says nothing; we have considered dozens in this partial overview alone. *All* of them would have to be proven false in order to weaken the argument for the Era. And we can rest assured that there isn't even the slightest chance of that ever happening. **Dismissing the Era,**

therefore, is to simply dismiss private revelation entirely and adopt the position that the *sensus fidelium* (sense of the faithful) can err (which, in turn, is a heretical position, directly condemned by the Catechism[1069] and *Lumen Gentium*[1070]) by an entire century of prophets—trustworthy, devout Catholics, across the entire world—being systematically and radically deceived on one of their fundamental, unanimous tenets.

Traditional Prophecies About the Era

Although there has been an explosion of prophecies about the Era of Peace in more recent times, these prophecies are by no means new. On the contrary, they have existed throughout the entire history of the Church. The old Catholic Encyclopedia, of unassailable orthodoxy and great authority, makes this clear:

> The more noteworthy of the prophecies bearing

upon "latter times" seem to have **one common end**, to announce great calamities impending over mankind, **the triumph of the Church, and the renovation of the world. All the seers agree** in two leading features as outlined by E.H. Thompson … "First they all point to some terrible convulsion, to a revolution springing from most deep-rooted impiety, consisting in a formal opposition to God and His truth, and resulting in

---

1068 Compiled from *Call of the Ages*, by Dr. Petrisko, and *the Marian Messages*, by Vince Farrell.
1069 CCC 92.

1070 In paragraph 12

the most formidable persecution to which the Church has ever been subject. Secondly, **they all promise for the Church a victory more splendid than she has <u>ever</u> achieved here below.**[1071]

There is, of course, nothing ambiguous here: the authors of this Encyclopedia—authoritative scholars in their field—did not hesitate to publish (in a work of unrivaled care and precision) that **all** the prophecies and seers agree that in the "latter times," the Church would enjoy a period of triumph and victory unlike anything in history. Although the article does not list many specific prophecies, it does include one from St. Edward The Confessor:

> " ... The extreme corruption and wickedness of the English nation has provoked the just anger of God. When malice shall have reached the fullness of its measure, God will, in His wrath, send to the English people wicked spirits, who will punish and afflict them with great severity, by separating the green tree from its parent stem the length of three furlongs. But at last this same tree, through the compassionate mercy of God, and without any national (governmental) assistance, shall return to its original root, reflourish and bear abundant fruit.'

We now consider a few prophecies given before the 20th century which deserve sections of their own, and then we will turn to consider a wide array of miscellaneous trustworthy prophecies compiled from various sources.

Our Lady of Good Success (Quito)

Our Lady of Good Success is the name of an approved apparition in Quito, Ecuador to a nun, Venerable Mother Mariana de Jesus Torres, beginning at the very end of the 16th century. Although these apparitions do not speak in detail about the Era, they do make clear that a **complete restoration** will occur:

> In order to free men from the bondage to these heresies, those whom the merciful love of my most Holy Son has designated to effect the restoration, will need great strength of will, constancy, valor and confidence of the just. There will be occasions when all will seem lost and paralyzed. **This then will be the happy beginning of the complete restoration.**[1072]

Sacred Heart

In the Sacred Heart revelations of Jesus to St. Margaret Mary Alacoque in the 17th century—among the most important private revelations in history—we see the beginnings of a real worldwide understanding of an impending new Era through the Reign of Christ in grace. As Hugh Owen points out:

> In 1860, two French associations, the Apostleship of Prayer and the League of the Sacred Heart, merged and launched the first worldwide movement of prayer for the reign of the Sacred Heart of Jesus, adopting as their motto the words, "Thy Kingdom Come!" Subsequently, the Apostleship of Prayer fast became the largest prayer association in the history of the Catholic Church, an indication that the Holy Spirit stood firmly behind its mission. In addition to intensifying the prayer of the faithful for the social reign of the Sacred Heart, the Apostleship of Prayer also largely introduced and popularized one of the most powerful forms of personal prayer, the morning offering to the Sacred Heart of Jesus through the Immaculate Heart of Mary.[1073]

Although the Sacred Heart revelations do not specifically, explicitly prophesy the Era, Catholics around the world nevertheless began to recognize that such an Era would indeed dawn upon the world in accordance with the enormous promises Heaven was beginning to make. It was the Sacred Heart revelations which gave that unprecedented promise that, whoever completes the Nine First Fridays devotion *cannot be lost*. But that was not the only promise given; it was only the last of the famous twelve promises. Jesus told St. Margaret Mary that to those who practice devotion to His Sacred Heart:

> (1) "I will give them all the graces necessary in their state of life.
> (2) I will establish peace in their homes.
> (3) I will comfort them in all their afflictions.
> (4) I will be their secure refuge during life, and above all, in death.
> (5) I will bestow abundant blessings upon all their undertakings.
> (6) Sinners will find in my Heart the source and infinite ocean of mercy.
> (7) Lukewarm souls shall become fervent.

1071PROPHECY. The Catholic Encyclopedia. Newadvent.org
1072http://www.miraclehunter.com/marian_apparitions/messages/quito_messages.html

1073*New and Divine*, Page 57.

(8) Fervent souls shall quickly mount to high perfection.

(9) I will bless every place in which an image of my Heart is exposed and honored.

10) I will give to priests the gift of touching the most hardened hearts.

(11) Those who shall promote this devotion shall have their names written in my Heart.

(12) I promise you in the excessive mercy of my Heart that my all-powerful love will grant to all those who receive Holy Communion on the First Fridays in nine consecutive months the grace of final perseverance; they shall not die in my disgrace, nor without receiving their sacraments. My divine Heart shall be their safe refuge in this last moment.".[1074]

These astounding promises must be taken seriously. And to take them seriously is to realize that, in due time, they will have worldwide repercussions; hence the motto of the aforementioned League, "Thy Kingdom Come!"

Miraculous Medal (St. Catherine Labouré)

St. Catherine Labouré was the 19th century French visionary of Rue du Bac who was given the Miraculous Medal which has, as the name implies, produced countless miracles.

Just as important, this medal—in its prophetic design—portrays Our Lady crushing the serpent in the world, with rays of graces shining forth from her hands inundating this same world, therefore foreshadowing the Triumph of her Immaculate Heart.

In his book entitled *Now the Woman Shall Conquer*, John Haffert writes:

> Several explicit prophecies confirm the imminent triumph, now, of the Queen of the World who appeared in Paris at the beginning of these times with Her foot crushing the serpent's head. Most important is the prophecy She Herself made at Fatima: "Finally my Immaculate Heart will triumph. Russia will be converted and an era of peace will be granted to mankind." … In Amsterdam, in messages approved in … She said the triumph would begin when the Pope proclaimed as a dogma Her role as coredemptrix, mediatrix, and advocate. Among the saints who have prophesied what we witness now are St.

Grignion de Montfort, St. John Bosco, St. Maximilian Kolbe, and St. Catherine Labouré.

> Particularly striking is the prophecy of St. Catherine Labouré who received the first message of the Marian Age almost two hundred years ago: "O how wonderful it will be to hear Mary as Queen of the World … it will be a time of peace, joy, and prosperity that will last long; She will be carried as a banner and She will make a tour of the world." The more one thinks of this prophecy the more unusual it appears, not just because it says that we will hear Mary acclaimed Queen of the World, but that the acclaim itself will be the sign of a long-lasting era of peace. **It will be not only an era of peace, but an era of joy! It will be an era of prosperity.**[1075]

This ties in closely to other apparitions—particularly the Lady of All Nations—wherein we see clearly that Our Lady receiving the honor she is due by the Church through the dogmatic proclamation of her just titles is largely the event by way of which the Era dawns upon the world. Elsewhere in association with these apparitions, we see the need to proclaim Our Lady as Queen of the *Universe*:

> Confirming the predictions of Saint Louis Grignion de Montfort, Saint Catherine says that the Most Holy Virgin will be proclaimed Queen of the Universe: "Oh! how beautiful it will be to hear: Mary is the Queen of the Universe. **The children and everyone will cry with joy and rapture."**

> That will be a lasting era of peace and happiness. She will be displayed on standards and paraded all over the world."[1076]

La Salette

The apparitions of Our Lady at La Salette, France, are among the few apparitions that have risen to so great a stature as to receive Vatican approval. Although not all the La Salette messages are contained within the portion of the apparition that was approved, it does not follow that the remainder of the messages are to be ignored. It would be much wiser to heed the entire message; while of course remembering that the fully Vatican-approved portion deserves a particularly high level of belief. Nevertheless, we will not restrict our consideration here to only that portion. In the La

---

[1074] https://www.ewtn.com/library/CHRIST/PROMISES.TXT

[1075] Pages 23-24.

[1076] https://www.americaneedsfatima.org/Our-Blessed-Mother/novena-to-our-lady-of-the-miraculous-medal.html

Salette messages, we read:

> Behold the time; the abyss opens. Behold the king of kings of darkness. Behold the beast with his subjects, calling himself the savior of the world. He will raise himself up with pride into the air in order to go even up to heaven; he will be smothered by the breath of the holy Archangel Michael. He will fall, and the earth which for three days will be in continual evolutions, will open its bosom full of fire; he will be plunged for ever with all his own into the eternal chasms of hell. Then water and fire will purify the earth and will consume all the works of the pride of men, and all will be renewed: God will be served and glorified.'

We here recall that Melanie Calvat, one of the two seers who received this apparition, was a spiritual directee of St. Hannibal later in life, and the latter was no doubt aware that her apparitions referred to the same Era spoken of in much greater detail to Luisa, whose works he dedicated his life to promoting.

In one of the secrets published in 1871, Melanie wrote:

> … Jesus Christ, through a miracle of his justice and his great mercy for the just, will order his angels that all my enemies be put to death. Suddenly, the persecutors of the church of Jesus Christ and all the men given over to sin will perish, and the Earth will become like a desert. Then peace will be made, the reconciliation of God with men. Jesus Christ will be served, adored, and glorified. Charity will flower everywhere. The new kings will be the right arm of the Holy Church, which will be strong, humble, pious, poor, zealous, and imitate the virtues of Jesus Christ. The Gospel will be preached everywhere, and men will make great advances in faith because there will be unity among the workers of Jesus Christ and men will live in the fear of God.'[1077]

The other seer, Maximin Giraud, was also told that a "great peace" would come on earth.

Various Prophecies throughout Church History

Dr. Thomas Petrisko, in his book *Call of the Ages*, shares an assortment of Catholic prophecies that speak of the Era of Peace from various points in Church history:

As far back as the Fifth Century, **Saint Caesar of Ailes (469- 543)** reportedly left this prophecy concerning a coming time of peace: During this time, "nations that are living in error and impiety shall be converted, and an admirable peace shall reign among men during many years because the wrath of God shall be appeased through repentance, penance and good works. There will be one common law, only one faith, one baptism, one religion. All nations shall recognize the Holy See of Rome, and shall pay homage to the Pope."

Brother John of the Cleft Rock (1340) boldly predicted a future time of peace for the world: "An Era of Peace and prosperity will begin for the world…God will raise up a holy Pope over whom the angels will rejoice. Enlightened by God, this man will reconstruct almost the entire world through his holiness and lead all to the true faith, and everywhere fear of God, virtue, and good morals will be dominant. He will lead all erring sheep back to the fold, and there shall be only one faith, one law, one rule of life, one baptism on earth. All men will love each other and do good, and all quarrels and war will disappear."

Three hundred years later, **Venerable John Holzhauser (d. 1658)** outlined a coming Era of Peace: "All nations will adore God their Lord according to Catholic teaching. There will be many wise and just men. The people will love justice, and peace will reign over the whole earth."

In the Seventeenth Century **Venerable Mary of Agreda (1602- 1665)**, who wrote the classic Mystical City of God, conveyed what was told to her about an Era of Peace: "It was revealed to me that through the intercession of the Mother of God, all heresies will disappear. This victory over heresies has been reserved by Christ for His Blessed Mother. In the last times the Lord will especially spread the renown of His Mother: Mary began salvation and by Her intercession it will be concluded. Before the Second Coming of Christ, Mary must, more than ever, shine in mercy, might and grace in order to bring unbelievers into the Catholic Faith. The powers of Mary in the last times over the demons will be very conspicuous. Mary will extend the Reign of Christ over the heathens and Mohammedans, and it will be a time of great joy when Mary, as Mistress and Queen of Hearts, is enthroned."

[1077] William Christian. *Visionaries: The Spanish Republic and the Reign of Christ.* Page 352.

About 150 years after Saint Louis de Montfort [whose prophecy of the Era Dr. Petrisko also shared, but I omit so as to include it in its own section], **Pope Pius IX (1878)** prophetically proclaimed the coming era as if he could sense it was approaching: "All erring souls will return to the path of truth and justice after the darkness of their minds has been dispelled, and there will be one flock and one shepherd."

On February 23, 1882, the stigmatist of Blain, **Marie-Julie Jahenny**, reported the following message from Jesus on this prophesied era: "The Church is destined to put up with the most awful affronts. It will vanish away like the bodily life of Christians; but it will rise again in the midst of the trials, and its Triumph will be secured. Tell My children not to harbour any doubt about her forthcoming Triumph, because doubting would be offending Me." Jesus also told Marie about the reign of peace: "The world will be laid in its casket, but after being cleansed in its own blood, it will be resurrected in such glory as I was resurrected from my grave. The reign of My peace will be wonderful, and from the rising sun to the setting sun My Name will be praised and will be called on for help. This radiation will be a call to all the nations to come and find refuge in My Heart. Tell it to My children; do not doubt the coming victory. If they doubt, they hurt Me."

Around the same time, the mystic **Sister Marie Chambau**, who died in 1907, said she was told: "The Triumph of the Church will be hastened by devotion to the Five Wounds and Precious Blood of Jesus Christ." As we now know, these are two devotions that have become very popular and widespread in the last half of [the 20th] century … "[1078]

And in another book, *The Kingdom of Our Father*, written by the same author, we find more still:

St. Hildegard saw a great purification that was to be followed by a "peace" for the "world. "During this period of peace," writes the great saint, "people will be forbidden to carry weapons … and many Jews, heathens and heretics will join the Church."

St. Mechtitilde of Helfta, a highly celebrated mystic of the 13th century, whose revelations scholars suspect formed the basis of Dante's Divine Comedy, sees an age of evangelization and a new order of preachers who would cover the world during the era of peace.

Likewise, a group of celebrated prophets of this age treats the coming of the Kingdom. Werdin d' Otrante, of the 13th century, believed that after years of war "peace will reign over the earth." John of Vatiguerro (13 century) prophesied that "after many tribulations, the whole world shall venerate the Church for her sanctity, virtue and perfection."

… a prophet named Dolciano (14th century) stated that "Under a holy pope there will be a universal conversion."

In the 15th century, St. Frances of Paula mentioned of the era of peace, saying that a new order known as the Knights of the Cross would be instrumental in an evangelization process…

St. Nicholas of Flue (15th century) saw a great suffering for the Church to be followed by a great victory. "The Church will be exalted in the sight of all doubters," he wrote. In the 16th century, a prophet named Telesphorus of Cozensa described the same golden era: "After terrible wars … They (a leader and a Pope) will convert the world and bring universal peace." St. Robert Bellarmine also believed in a temporal ' 'terrestrial" kingdom of God that would come before the end of the world.

But perhaps one of the most concise versions of the prophesied coming of the Kingdom during the Medieval period came from St. Vincent Ferrer who wrote that "there would be a new reformation in the world." "This would occur," said Ferrer, "in the days of peace that are to come after the desolation, revolutions and wars, before the end of the world."

…Palma Maria (19th century): "The Triumph of the Church will make people quickly forget all evils."

Perhaps the words of Sr. Bertina Bouquillon (19th century) best summarizes the prophecies of the coming of the Kingdom in this period. Her words resound confidently that an era of peace will reign. Known as the Nursing Nun of Belay, she received the stigmata and was known for her gift of prophecy and visions. Concerning the temporal Kingdom, she wrote, "What I see is so wonderful that I am unable to express it."[1079]

Blessed Anna-Maria Taigi, a mystic who received many revelations, said the following:

After the three days of darkness, Saints Peter and Paul, having come down from heaven, will preach throughout the world and designate a new pope. A great light will flash from their bodies

---

[1078]*Call of the Ages*, pages 447-451 (misc. excerpts).

[1079]*The Kingdom of Our Father*. Pages 61-70. Misc. excerpts.

and will settle upon the cardinal, the future Pontiff. Then Christianity will spread throughout the world. Whole nations will join the Church shortly before the reign of Anti-Christ. These conversions will be amazing. Those who shall survive shall have to conduct themselves well. There shall be innumerable conversions of heretics, who will return to the bosom of the Church; all will note the edifying conduct of their lives, as well as that of all other Catholics. Russia, England, and China will come to the Church.[1080]

Venerable Elizabeth Canori-Mora was shown the following:

Then a beautiful splendor came over the earth, to announce the reconciliation of God with mankind.

The small flock of faithful Catholics who had taken refuge under the trees will be brought before Saint Peter, who will choose a new pope. All the Church will be reordered according to the true dictates of the holy Gospel. The religious orders will be reestablished and the homes of Christians will become homes imbued with religion.

So great will be the fervor and zeal for the glory of God that everything will promote love of God and neighbor. The triumph, glory and honor of the Catholic Church will be established in an instant. She will be acclaimed, venerated and esteemed by all. All will resolve to follow Her, recognizing the Vicar of Christ as the Supreme Pontiff.[1081]

Blessed Anne Catherine Emmerich, 19th century nun and one of the greatest visionaries in the history of the Church regarding the un-revealed details of Scripture, did not only see the past, but saw the future as well:

The Church will be bigger and more magnificent than ever. I saw in the distance great legions approaching. In the foreground I saw a Man on a white horse. Prisoners were set free and joined them. All the enemies were pursued. Then I saw that the Church was being promptly rebuilt, and she was more magnificent than ever before

Fr. Pere Lamy, a highly regarded French priest and mystic born in 1855 and the subject of a book, *Pere Lamy* (published by TAN in 2009), wrote the following:

Peace will be given back to the world, but I shall not see it, and other things will come to pass of which I do not personally see the end. When peace once more is established in the world, what changes shall have to come to pass! War is big business. … the exploitation of the mines, the iron works, all that will dwindle. There will be no longer those great factories where morality withers and disappears. The working class will be bound to turn back to the land. Land work will receive great impetus. Land will again be very dear… God willed to purify the faith of His people… there will be once more a splendid efflorescence of Orders and Congregations.[1082]

St. Vincent Ferrer prophesied a time of triumphant Christianity:

In conformity with this, St. Vincent Ferrer (*Vitae Spirit.*, 19) announced that the time would come when a great multitude of Christians would have no other words or tastes or affections but those of Jesus Christ..[1083]

St. John Bosco, well known for his vision of the Church as a great ship on troubled waters, navigating them with the aid of the two pillars of Mary and the Eucharist, also prophesied the Era of Peace:

There shall yet come a violent hurricane. Iniquity is at an end, sin shall cease, and before two full moons shall have shone in the month of flowers, the rainbow of peace shall appear on earth … Throughout the world a sun so bright shall shine as never seen since the flames of the Cenacle until today, nor shall it be seen again until the end of time.[1084]

In his book, *Catholic Prophecy*, Yves Dupont examines a number of traditional Catholic prophecies about the end times and concludes, about what is to come after the Chastisements, with the following:

Russia and China are converted to Catholicism, as also the Mohammedans. All non-Catholics return to Mother Church. A holy Pope is elected; he shows great firmness; and he restores all the former disciplines in the Church. All the nations of Western Europe unite and form a new Roman Empire, and accept as their emperor the great

---

1080The Three Days of Darkness and Prophecies of Latter Times. Americaneedsfatima.org
1081Ibid.
1082*Call of the Ages*, Page 479.

1083*New and Divine*, Page 17.
1084http://www.ewtn.com/library/mary/boscodrm.htm

Christian Prince, chosen by God, who works hand-in-hand with the holy Pope. The triumph of the Catholic Church is universal. The whole world enjoys a period of complete peace and unprecedented prosperity in mutual love and respect among people and nations.[1085]

He proceeds to go over many prophecies, some of which are included below (in some cases the author is speaking, in others he is quoting prophecies. The distinction is clarified by appropriate punctuation):

> Berthe Petit announces the great disaster that will cause the almost total collapse of modern civilization. Br. Louis Rocco foretells the Great King who is to rule over Europe and extend his moral influence throughout the whole world during the period of peace which will follow the great disaster…
>
> Monk Hilarion (15th century). "Before the Christian churches are reunited and renovated, God will send the Eagle who will travel to Rome and bring much happiness and good. The Holy Man will bring peace between the clergy and the Eagle, and his reign will last for four years. After his death God will send three men who are rich in wisdom and virtue. They will spread Christianity everywhere. There will be one flock, one shepherd, one faith, one law, one life, and one baptism throughout the world."…
>
> Nicholas of Fluh (15th century). "The Church will be punished because the majority of her members, high and low, will become so perverted. The Church will sink deeper and deeper until she will at last seem to be extinguished, and the succession of Peter and the other Apostles to have expired. But, after this, she will be victoriously exalted in the sight of all doubters."…
>
> Telesphorus of Cozensa (16th century). "A powerful French Monarch and French Pope will regain the Holy Land after terrible wars in Europe. They will convert the world and bring universal peace. They will overcome the German ruler."…
>
> Sr. Jeane le Royer: ""I see in God that the Church will enjoy a profound peace over a period which seems to me to be of a fairly long duration. This respite will be the longest of all that will occur between the revolutions from now till the General Judgment.

(I hasten to add that I do not recommend the book in its entirety, even though the author has done helpful research. Suffice it to say the author comes to some incorrect eschatological conclusions and furthermore peppers his works with overly traditionalist, anti-Vatican II comments, even implying that the Novus Ordo is perhaps invalid.)

In *The Christian Trumpet*, a book of prophecies on the Chastisements and the Era published by a priest in 1875, we read a prophecy from none other than the Curé of Ars himself, St. John Vianney:

> People will imagine that all is lost ; but the good God shall save all. It will be like a sign of the last judgment… God shall come -to help; the good shall triumph when the return of the king shall be announced … This shall re-establish a peace and prosperity without example. Religion shall flourish again better than ever before.[1086]

In the same book, a lesser known mystic is quoted who gave astounding prophecies:

> Magdalene Porsat is a humble, illiterate, and aged country maid… [she] has been favored with divine revelations since the year 1843… " Mary comes from Heaven. She comes accompanied by a legion of angels. The elect living upon earth should through spiritual electricity (great fervor) elevate themselves in order to go forward before the messengers of God. Behold the host of the Lord ! Many holy women, few St. Johns. Behold the armor of God ! No gun or musket, no club or truncheon, no bolt, no watch-dog, no material force, no human means. [This shows how perfect order, security, honesty, and peace will be upon earth.][1087]

Note that the bracketed remarks in the quote above were in the original text. Continuing to share more revelations from Magdalene Porsat, the following pages read:

> A grand event shall have to take place in order to terrify the wicked to their advantage. After this, Mary, all powerful, shall change all men into good wheat. All shall be good. The Pharisees (the hypocrites) will be the last (to be converted); the great brigands (great sinners) will arrive beforehand. The Jews who have refused to receive Jesus Christ in his humiliation will acknowledge him at the glorious arrival of Mary. The dove (the peace and grace of God through Mary) comes to us from heaven, wearing on her breast a white cross, sign of reconciliation, and waving a sword of fire, symbol of love. She seats herself on a

---

[1085] Yves Dupont. *Catholic Prophecy*. Introductory pages.
[1086] *The Christian Trumpet*. Page 88.
[1087] *The Christian Trumpet*. Page 194.

throne of solid gold, figure of Noah's ark; for she comes to announce the end of a deluge of evils. Behold, she comes, our Mother! The Church prepares everything for the glorious arrival of Mary. The Church forms for her a guard of honor to go before the angels. The triumphal arch is nearly accomplished. The hour is not far distant. It is Mary in person! But she has her precursors,—holy women, apostles, who shall cure the wounds of the body as well as the sins of the heart. Holy women, images of Mary, shall have power to work miracles. After them comes Mary to prepare the place for her Son in his triumphant Church. **Behold the immaculate conception of the kingdom of God that precedes the arrival of Jesus Christ! It is the mansion of God upon earth, which is going to purify and prepare itself to receive the Emmanuel. Jesus Christ cannot come into this hovel of the world. It is necessary that God should send his spirit to renew the face of the earth by means of another creation, to render it a worthy mansion for the God made man…**

the love of God comes to embrace and transfigure the world. I see the earth rendered level; its valleys are raised; its mountains are lowered; there is nothing more than gentle hills and beautiful vales (images of the Christian virtues regenerating fallen humanity). Since I am as I am, I see nothing else before us but union and universal fraternity. **All men are in reciprocal love. One helps the other. They are all happy.**[1088]

In this profound confirmation of Luisa's revelations, we see that the purpose of the Era is precisely to ensure that God's Kingdom is found in place, on earth, before His definitive and final coming.

***

Even if you only glanced through a few of the prophecies provided in the preceding pages, one thing is doubtless clear to you now: just as the reality of the coming Glorious Era of Peace on earth before the end of the world is an undeniable consensus of trustworthy 20th century private revelation, so it has been throughout the history of the Church.

Authoritative Voices

In learning of the Era, we should not limit ourselves only to considering that which was uttered in a directly prophetic manner; we should also learn from the wisdom of those most qualified to be listened to regarding their insight into spiritual matters. Many such people have spoken clearly of the times to come and the Era that we will soon enjoy. In this section we will consider just a small selection of them.

First, we should carefully consider the work of the late 19th century, the French priest Fr. Charles Arminjon, who gave a series of retreats at the Cathedral of Chambéry, which, collected into articles, has only recently been translated into English and published under the title, *The End of the Present World and the Mysteries of the Future Life*. St. Thérèse of Lisieux, the great Doctor of the Church, said of this book, "**This reading was one of the greatest graces of my life**… the impressions I received are too deep to express in human words."[1089] Among many other eschatological teachings, Fr. Arminjon presents the following:

> The most authoritative view, and the one that appears to be most in harmony with Holy Scripture, is that, after the fall of the Antichrist, the Catholic Church will once again enter upon a period of prosperity and triumph … [referencing Romans 11] These words are formal, and appear to leave no room for doubt. They are in harmony with those of St. John: 'I then saw … those who had won the victory over the beast and its image and also the number that signified its name … They sang the song of Moses, the servant of God, and the song of the Lamb.'[1090]

Here Fr. Arminjon argues forcefully—not merely as his own eschatological speculation, but as the most authoritative view most in harmony with Scripture—that there will in fact be a period of Triumph for the Catholic Church after the reign of the Antichrist.

***

Dr. Thomas Petrisko compiled an assortment of authoritative Catholic voices on the Era and shared them in his book, *Call of the Ages*. Some are included here:

> Father John Lozan in his book Mary, Model of Disciples, Mother of the Lord, [writes]… "Mary's message of peace at Fatima takes on the full

[1088] *The Christian Trumpet*. Pages 196-197.

[1089] Thérèse of Lisieux, *Story of a Soul: The Autobiography of Saint Thérèse of Lisieux* (Washington, DC: ICS Publications, 1996), 102.

[1090] Charles Arminjon, *The End of the Present World and the Mysteries of the Future Life* (Manchester, N.H: Sophia Institute Press, 2008), 57-58.

meaning of the word 'shalom, 'a state of well-being in communion with God and with our brothers and sisters."

Father Albert J. Hebert writes in his book, Prophecies! The Chastisement and Purification, concerning the Era of Peace: "The Era of Peace will come ... **There will be a freshness, something like when Adam and Eve walked in the original paradise** before their unhappy fall from grace. "

In his other book, The Tears of Mary and Fatima, Father Hebert writes: "Without a doubt, then, the eventual Triumph of the Immaculate Heart of Mary, as she also promised at Fatima, and an era of the Reign of Christ over hearts will take place. A number of reliable seers, as far as this author is concerned (including reportedly Lucy of Fatima), are credited with seeing light at the end of the tunnel and the coming victory of the Immaculate Heart of Mary and an Era of Peace."

Bishop Seamus Hegarty of Raphoe, Ireland, said in June 1989: "I believe we are going to experience a radiation of this atmosphere of peace ...extending itself over the entire world...."

On March 10, 1991, **[Pope St. John Paul II]** went to Portugal. Before arriving in Fatima, he called to mind Saint Augustine, and prophetically declared: **"Don't be afraid, dear children. This is not an old world that is ending. It is a new world that begins. A new dawn seems to be rising in the sky of history,** inviting Christians to be light and soul to the world that has enormous need for Christ, Redeemer of Man."

This was not the first time the Holy Father had spoken about a New Era. As Denis Nolan states in his book Medjugorje, A Time For Truth – A Time For Action, "John Paul II is the great prophet of the new times." Mr. Nolan argues that the Pontiff is greatly "aware of the approaching fulfillment of the promises of Fatima." Indeed, since the beginning of his Pontificate, Pope John Paul II has been pointing to a New Era, a new advent. Almost as if he were aware of God's mind, the Holy Father's words have consistently echoed the words of visionaries throughout the world over the last twenty years. In his very first encyclical, [Redemptor Hominis], John Paul II began to speak of the new millennium and invited "the Church and the whole world to look toward the year 2000. " And, as already stated, the Pope clearly writes in his new book Crossing the Threshold of Hope that "Fatima's fulfillment" is near.

In his 1992 address to The National Medjugorje Conference at Notre Dame, Father Gianni Sgreva of Italy, a founder of the new Marian community "Oasis of Peace" in 1991, reflected on the Holy Father's repeated call to a second Pentecost. Father Sgreva insisted that the present collaboration between the Holy Spirit, the Virgin Mary and Pope John Paul II clearly reflected the words and prophecies of the prophet Isaiah, especially in the following passage: "Lo, I am about to create new heavens and a new earth; The things of the past shall not be remembered or come to mind. Instead, there shall always be rejoicing and happiness in what I create; For I create Jerusalem to be a joy and its people to be a delight." (Is 65:17-19) But while the Holy Father's many declarations give us hope, the words of Mary assure this reality. For throughout the world, visionaries are reporting that Fatima's promise is about to be realized.

***

Written in 1875 by an anonymous missionary priest, The Christian Trumpet, mentioned in the preceding section, is a book that compiles a number of traditional Catholic prophecies on the latter times. But the priest-author begins by sharing great wisdom in the work's preface:

For the sake of the general good, in announcing salutary truths we should neither fear the sneer of the sceptic, the sarcasm of the infidel, nor the sickly condition of the effeminate and sensual Christian…Let us bravely and wisely act upon the maxim of the great Pope St. Gregory, Minus jacula feriunt, que previdentur, – Foreknowledge blunts the stroke. Whether we like it or not, the threatened punishment shall soon fall upon a guilty world.

Proceeding in the same preface to refute that tragic view wherein all but the Deposit of Faith itself is treated flippantly, the author writes:

Our Lord moreover desires that… all sincere and virtuous Catholics should believe those truths which his Holy Spirit vouchsafes to reveal to his favorite friends for our common good and edification. It is under this deeply seated conviction that this book has with some labor been prepared for publication.

The book's inner front page contains several subtitles, one of which is **The Universal Triumph of the Church**. In the chapter pertaining to this triumph, the author begins with his own broad-view analysis of the Era before proceeding to the individual prophecies. In this analysis, he gives several amazing observations:

It is only the supernatural power of a religion with the sanction of divine authority that is able to draw order out of human chaos, and restore hope and happiness to the desponding heart of society. It is only an infallible Church that can promptly detect and authoritatively condemn all religious and moral errors, and teach all truths to humanity. The Roman Catholic Apostolic Church alone can appeal to the present and past generations of two thousand years, to witness that she possesses these divine prerogatives, because she alone has constantly exercised them for the general welfare of mankind. **Hence all true and good men ardently desire and fervently pray for her speedy universal triumph**. Hence Catholic unions for supplications, and for the exercise of zeal and virtue and charity. Hence the universal revival of faith in the Catholic world. Hence the solemn declaration by the Ecumenical Council of the Vatican of the Pope's infallibility, which secures to Catholicity a safe, trusty, unerring, and victorious leader in the approaching spiritual conquest of the world. Unity is strength, and strength united is victory and triumph. *Magna est Veritas et prevalebit*. **The proximity of this final victory and glorious triumph of the Catholic Church is announced by the actual accomplishment of the great prophecy made two thousand and six hundred years ago by the holy Prophet Isaias, and confirmed about two thousand years hence by the greatest of all prophets.** (Luke iii. 5.) The following are their words :

"Be comforted, be comforted, my people, saith your God. Speak to the heart of Jerusalem, and call to her; for her evil is come to an end. The voice of one crying in the desert: Prepare ye the way of the Lord; make straight in the wilderness the paths of our God. Every valley shall be exalted, and every mountain and hill shall be made low, and the crooked shall become straight, and the rough ways plain. And the glory of the Lord shall be revealed, and all flesh together shall see the salvation of God. ... Behold, the Lord God shall come with strength, and his arm shall rule. Behold, his reward is with him, and hit work is before him. He shall feed his flock like a shepherd. He shall gather together the lambs with his arm, and shall take them up in his bosom." (Isa. xl. 3.)

We discover the literal realization of this remarkable prophecy in the construction of railroads in almost every direction on the surface of the earth; in the long tunnels bored through previously impassable mountains; in the deep, wide, and extensive canals dug across isthmuses to unite the Mediterranean Sea with the East Indian Ocean, and in the contemplated one between the Atlantic and Pacific. We behold the accomplishment of this prophecy in the numerous and stately **steamboats** gliding over the waters. We read it in the public press and in the **telegraph**, claimed as the most ready and powerful auxiliaries to a universal dominion. We most cordially believe that **all the principal practical inventions of this present century are by a most wise and merciful Providence intended to facilitate the approaching general triumph of the faith and religion of Jesus Christ upon earth for the conversion, sanctification, temporal and eternal happiness of mankind**. The pagan **Romans** also planned and constructed commodious roads in different countries of Europe, Asia, and Africa, and spanned deep and rapid rivers with their solid bridges to enlarge their military conquests, to facilitate the effective administration of their government, and to stimulate and encourage trade and commerce. But without their knowing it, and in opposition to their designs, **they served as instruments in the hand of God to prepare an easy way to the spiritual conquest of the Christian religion**. The large Roman roads and convenient bridges were traversed by many Christian missionaries bringing the good tidings of the gospel to the benighted idolatrous nations of the earth, and in their constant intercourse with the infallible head of Christianity in Rome. **With more effective means at our disposal in our own days, we expect soon to witness more perfect results ; and under this well-founded and cherished expectation, we pass to the perusal of the predictions which clearly and distinctly announce them to the world.**[1091]

Amazingly, in the late 19th century, this priest was able to conclude rightly that the historically unprecedented infrastructure being laid in place was part of a Providential plan to allow for the explosion of the Triumph of the Church and the Era of Peace. While he was obviously preemptive in his prognostication—not realizing that it would not be for some time longer that true worldwide dominion could be so quickly and easily achieved in the 21st century (through the internet)—he was nevertheless correct in the main thrust of his assessment. And Jesus' words to Luisa confirm this, for in them we see that World War II itself was in part allowed by God to pave the way for the Globalization that would enable the knowledges of the Divine Will to spread across the world in a short

---

[1091] *The Christian Trumpet*. Pages 146-148.

amount of time. Unfortunately, of course, it is also true that the Antichrist will take advantage of these technologies for his own dominion; and we must be on guard against that. But currently, our calling is to take full advantage of these technologies—just as the early Christians took advantage of the then historically unprecedented Roman infrastructure for the early explosion of Christianity's evangelization—to use them to lay the spiritual "infrastructure" for the Reign of the Divine Will. That spiritual infrastructure is none other than the knowledges of the Divine Will.

***

St. Louis de Montfort and St. Maximilian Kolbe

As is widely known, but largely neglected by the mainstream voices that speak of his teachings, St. Louis de Montfort prophesied in the clearest terms possible that, "towards" the end of the world, there would be a glorious Era of peace and a wave of Marian saints of such holiness that the history of the world will have never seen anything like them. Quoted partially in the Marian Consecration section of this book, the entire quote, from paragraphs 46 through 48 of his work *True Devotion to Mary*, is as follows:

> All the rich among the people, to use an expression of the Holy Spirit as explained by St. Bernard, all the rich among the people will look pleadingly upon her countenance throughout all ages and particularly as the world draws to its end. This means that **the greatest saints, those richest in grace and virtue will be the most assiduous in praying to the most Blessed Virgin, looking up to her as the perfect model to imitate and as a powerful helper to assist them.**
>
> I said that this will happen especially towards the end of the world, and indeed soon, because Almighty God and his holy Mother are to raise up great saints who will surpass in holiness most other saints as much as the cedars of Lebanon tower above little shrubs. This has been revealed to a holy soul whose life has been written by M. de Renty.
>
> These great souls filled with grace and zeal will be chosen to oppose the enemies of God who are raging on all sides. They will be exceptionally devoted to the Blessed Virgin. Illumined by her light, strengthened by her food, guided by her spirit, supported by her arm, sheltered under her

protection, they will fight with one hand and build with the other. With one hand they will give battle, overthrowing and crushing heretics and their heresies, schismatics and their schisms, idolaters and their idolatries, sinners and their wickedness. With the other hand they will build the temple of the true Solomon and the mystical city of God, namely, the Blessed Virgin, who is called by the Fathers of the Church the Temple of Solomon and the City of God. By word and example they will draw all men to a true devotion to her and though this will make many enemies, it will also bring about many victories and much glory to God alone. This is what God revealed to St. Vincent Ferrer, that outstanding apostle of his day, as he has amply shown in one of his works.

> This seems to have been foretold by the Holy Spirit in Psalm 58: "The Lord will reign in Jacob and all the ends of the earth. They will be converted towards evening and they will be as hungry as dogs and they will go around the city to find something to eat." This city around which men will roam at the end of the world seeking conversion and the appeasement of the hunger they have for justice is the most Blessed Virgin, who is called by the Holy Spirit the City of God."[1092]

From the quote above, especially the bolded portions, we can see that St. Louis de Montfort's teachings leave no room for doubt that not only will there be a glorious Era of Peace, but it will entail a new and unprecedented Gift of sanctity for the Church through Mary (which is precisely what Jesus reveals to Luisa as well). St. Louis had many other teachings that overlap Luisa's, but although we cannot address all of them here, we shall conclude treatment of this great saint by quoting a few more of his writings:

> Mary's power over the evil spirits will especially shine forth in the latter times, when Satan will lie in wait for her heel, that is, for her humble servants and her poor children whom she will rouse to fight against him. In the eyes of the world they will be little and poor and, like the heel, lowly in the eyes of all, down-trodden and crushed as is the heel by the other parts of the body. But in compensation for this they will be rich in God's graces, which will be abundantly bestowed on them by Mary. They will be great and exalted before God in holiness. They will be superior to all creatures by their great zeal and so strongly will they be supported by divine

---

[1092]St. Louis de Montfort, *True Devotion to Mary*, paragraphs 46-48.

assistance that, in union with Mary, they will crush the head of Satan with their heel, that is, their humility, and bring victory to Jesus Christ... But what will they be like, these servants, these slaves, these children of Mary? They will be ministers of the Lord who, like a flaming fire, will enkindle everywhere the fires of divine love. They will become, in Mary's powerful hands, like sharp arrows, with which she will transfix her enemies... They will be true apostles of the latter times to whom the Lord of Hosts will give eloquence and strength to work wonders and carry off glorious spoils from his enemies. They will sleep without gold or silver and, more important still, without concern in the midst of other priests, ecclesiastics and clerics. Yet they will have the silver wings of the dove enabling them to go wherever the Holy Spirit calls them, filled as they are with the resolve to seek the glory of God and the salvation of souls... They will point out the narrow way to God in pure truth according to the holy Gospel, and not according to the maxims of the world. Their hearts will not be troubled, nor will they show favour to anyone; they will not spare or heed or fear any man, however powerful he may be. They will have the two-edged sword of the word of God in their mouths and the blood-stained standard of the Cross on their shoulders. They will carry the crucifix in their right hand and the rosary in their left, and the holy names of Jesus and Mary on their heart. The simplicity and self-sacrifice of Jesus will be reflected in their whole behaviour. Such are the great men who are to come. By the will of God Mary is to prepare them to extend his rule over the impious and unbelievers.[1093]

Your divine commandments are broken, your Gospel is thrown aside, torrents of iniquity flood the whole earth carrying away even your servants... Will everything come to the same end as Sodom and Gomorrah? Will you never break your silence? Will you tolerate all this for ever**? Is it not true that your will must be done on earth as it is in heaven? Is it not true that your kingdom must come? Did you not give to some souls, dear to you, a vision of the future renewal of the Church?** [1094]

Thankfully, the greatest promoters of Marian devotion have not allowed de Montfort's prophecy to go unheeded. As Hugh Owen points out, the **reality and nature of the coming Era held by St. Louis de Montfort was also taught clearly by no less authority than St. Maximilian Kolbe:**

In his writings and conferences, St. Maximilian described a spirituality of total renunciation of the human will in favor of the "Divine Will reigning in Mary." But he did not view this spirituality as something extraordinary or necessarily reserved to a favored few. On the contrary, he confidently predicted the conversion of Russia and an era of peace through the triumph of the "Divine Will reigning in Mary" in the hearts of all mankind. He wrote:

'We [the Franciscan Order] fought for seven centuries for the recognition of the truth of the Immaculate Conception, and that battle has been won with the proclamation of the Dogma and with the apparition of the Immaculate Virgin at Lourdes. Now is the time for that history to be continued—to work for the planting of that truth in souls, so that it may bring forth fruits of sanctity. And this—in all souls—all that now exist and all that will be to the end of the world. The first seven centuries were only the preparation, the idea, the cause. Now comes the realization of that truth, the manifestation of the Immaculate Virgin to souls; her introduction to souls with all the blessed effects which follow from it. In every country there must arise Cities of Mary Immaculate ... **you will soon see tears flowing from the eyes of the most hardened sinners; prisons will be emptied; honest workers will unite; families will overflow with virtue, peace, and happiness; all discord will be banished, for it [will then be] the new era**.'[1095]

Conflicting Interpretations of Prophecies about the Antichrist and the Era

We should now briefly address an issue that sometimes arises when one tries to draw a single clear picture from the hundreds upon hundreds of prophecies given over two thousand years of Church history (not to mention those of thousands of years of salvation history before that); namely, the issue of pinning down accurately the succession of primary events in the latter times.

Catholics of a more traditionalist bent sometimes focus primarily, if not exclusively, on the pre-20th century prophecies listed in the preceding section,

---

[1093]*Ibid.* Paragraphs 54-59. Misc. excerpts.
[1094]St. Louis de Montfort. "Prayer for Missionaries." Paragraph 5.

[1095]Hugh Owen. *"New and Divine: The Holiness of the Third Christian Millennium."* Pages 21- 22

adding only Fatima on to that list.

While this approach certainly succeeds in making it clear enough that both Chastisements and an Era of Peace are coming for the world, it falls short in other regards. This failure is not due to the traditional prophecies themselves; it is due, rather, to the neglect of one's duty to read the signs of the times *in which he lives* and not suppose that his calling as an aspiring eschatologist is similar to the job description of an archeologist.

Perhaps products of this temptation of archeology, some works written in the latter half of the 20th century took a rather dim view (whether explicitly or implicitly) of the messages Heaven blessed us with in that century; or perhaps, alternatively, their authors simply were not informed of these revelations.

But in reading the prophecies given throughout salvation history, one does not expect to see the same precision or detail in Enoch as in Abraham; in Abraham as in David; in David as in Isaiah; in Isaiah as in John the Baptist. For just as in salvation history, the closer the time came to the fulfillment, the more frequent, precise, and detailed the prophecies were; so, too, today the same reality is repeated.

Those who miss this "rhyming" of history and focus only on the older prophecies **sometimes rigidly stick to the idea that the Antichrist cannot possibly come at any point other than immediately before the end of time, and that the Era of Peace can only precede him.** Furthermore, they maintain that this Era might not be that significant of a thing (in duration, at least), but might only correlate to the 25-year period spoken of at La Salette.

Some of these authors even play fast and loose with accusations of heresy, concluding that those who disagree with their own eschatological opinions and predictions are guilty of doctrinal error merely because they believe, along with Pope St. Pius X, Pope St. John Paul II, and many others (we will get to that in a moment) that the Antichrist is

imminent, and the Era will *follow* his defeat.

Three important points must be made regarding this discord.

First, and most importantly, as with questions related to Augustine and Amillennialism, **Luisa's revelations and the reality of the Glorious Era neither rise nor fall on how questions of the placement of the Antichrist and the duration of the Era are ultimately answered.** I do not know of Luisa's revelations addressing the placement of the Antichrist, nor do I know of them stating how long the Era will be.[1096] Therefore, **whatever opinion you choose to adopt on this matter, understand that it presents no obstacle to your fully embracing Luisa's revelations**.

Second, while not detracting from the preceding point, **it seems clear that the Antichrist is indeed imminent** and that the Era will *follow*, not *precede*, his defeat. Recall, as quoted elsewhere in this chapter, that Pope St. Pius X taught, in a high-level Magisterial document, his encyclical *E Supremi*, **"…there may be already in the world the "Son of Perdition" of whom the Apostle speaks (II. Thess. ii., 3) …"**[1097]

All private revelations and prophecies given before the promulgation of that document must now be read through the lens of its teaching. For citing 2 Thessalonians 2:3 (as Pius does—the citation is from the original Encyclical; I did not add it) is always a direct reference to the Antichrist, and Pius also makes it clear that is what he is doing in the very same paragraph of the Encyclical. This is a **Pope** who is a **Saint** writing a high-level act of the **Magisterium**, and teaching, in it, that the Antichrist may well be in the world already.[1098] This is also the same Pope who—in this same Encyclical— prophesies a glorious temporal Era of Peace (see preceding section for details). **Could it now[1099] be any clearer that the imminence of the Antichrist and the reality of the Era of Peace after his defeat is not only an acceptable position to hold, but is also by far the preferable one?**

But this is no mere isolated Magisterial remark

[1096] Although I admit this proves nothing, as I do not have all of Luisa's revelations memorized!

[1097] Pope St. Pius X. *E Supremi*. Paragraph 5.

[1098] Admittedly, Pius wrote this in 1903 – my point in including it is not to argue that such a supposition in his time would have been chronologically accurate. My point is

merely that, given this Magisterial admission of the possibility (or, rather, the probability) of the Antichrist being in the world means that it is now impossible for a Catholic to categorically reject the notion that the Antichrist might be imminent.

[1099] that is, since 1903

(although even if it were, that would not remove its enormous value). Rather, this saintly Pontiff was expressing what was commonly understood in his day. We see that in the late 1800s, this view was almost taken for granted among those whose voices were most authoritative. Somehow, in the 1900s, this view was lost among many of the popular Catholic authors on the topic (I can only wonder if perhaps these authors formed their own views in a vacuum; or at best in a very incomplete library). For example, as we discussed in more detail in the preceding section, we see the teachings of Fr. Charles Arminjon, which St. Thérèse of Lisieux said were among the greatest graces of her life:

> The most authoritative view, and the one that appears to be most in harmony with Holy Scripture, is that, after the fall of the Antichrist, the Catholic Church will once again enter upon a period of prosperity and triumph.[1100]

Many readers will also no doubt recall the famous words of Pope St. John Paul II (as Cardinal Wojtyla) during his visit to America in 1976:

> We are now facing the final confrontation between the Church and the anti-church, between the gospel and the anti-gospel, between Christ and the Antichrist.

Note that John Paul was careful not to omit the definite article "the," nor to replace it with the indefinite article "an" — rather, he made it clear that the Church **now** faces *the* Antichrist.

Besides these authoritative sources, the imminence of the Antichrist is the view which harmonizes best with the prophetic consensus of the most trustworthy private revelations of the 20th century. We all know that the reign of the Antichrist is enabled by an utterly apostate world, completely mired in sin an error — much like the world now stands. But this horrendous state of the world does not seem to be a likely situation to ever return after the initiation of the Era of Peace, when all will live in the Divine Will and the Church will acquire her full vigor. Furthermore, many private revelations specifically speak of the imminence of the Antichrist and the Era following his defeat: those given to Fr. Gobbi, Luz de Maria, Pedro Regis,

Barnabas Nwoye, and many others. The imminence of the antichrist is also beginning to be promoted by some highly regarded holy and orthodox prelates; for example, Cardinal Mueller has recently stated that the present explosion of heresy we are witnessing in the Church is likely related to the antichrist himself.

Third, it seems likely that some traditional prophecies do truly refer — accurately — to the Era properly, while some others refer either to only dim intimations of the Era (even at times with an admixture of error), or perhaps to a type of **"pause" in the Chastisements; a pause that will indeed be given before the reign of the Antichrist, but a pause of sufficient duration and magnitude that it is sometimes falsely identified by interpreters of these prophecies as the Era of Peace itself**. This "pause" may indeed entail the prophesied Illumination of Conscience (or "The Warning") — spoken of at Garabandal and elsewhere — and the concomitant evangelization of the world that it will generate. Mark Mallett has written well on this possibility, referring to it as the "eye of the storm."[1101] For when a city receives a direct hit from a hurricane, there is a brief period during which the eye passes over it and many will be tempted to think the storm is over, — so suddenly and completely did the wind and rain end — when, in fact, half of the storm still remains to be endured before it is ultimately passed.

This would explain why these prophecies identify the Era as preceding the Antichrist and why the Antichrist seems, in these prophecies, to be the final event of history. For in this case, we see that **the job of these prophecies was not to speak of what is to transpire after the Antichrist; hence, they are largely silent on that point — or merely speak of the end of the world "following" the Antichrist**. Repeatedly, those who wish to develop their own eschatological timelines unfortunately interpret instances of parlance like this in Scripture and private prophecy without the appropriate exegetical approach. For they constantly fall victim to the trap of assuming that one event "following" another — that is, "A happening *and then* B," — necessarily implies that there will be little or no time in between the events mentioned. But this is

---

[1100] Charles Arminjon, *The End of the Present World and the Mysteries of the Future Life* (Manchester, N.H: Sophia Institute Press, 2008), 57-58.

[1101] https://www.markmallett.com/blog/2007/05/11/eye-of-the-storm/

not the nature of God's revelation—either in His public revelation or in the private revelations He sends us even now. He is not authoring a technical instruction manual; He is telling us, rather, what we need to know to benefit our salvation and sanctification. **Whenever someone decides he is going to squeeze an eschatological timeframe out of a prophecy which does not intend to clearly reveal one is always dooming himself to failure and misleading his readers.**

We must also remember that even valid private revelations often contradict each other. We cannot treat them like inerrant Sacred Scripture! For example, I wholeheartedly support the revelations to Blessed Anne Catherine Emmerich and those to Venerable Mary of Agreda. But these two glorious revelations blatantly contradict each other on a number of points, which of course means that at least one of them is wrong on each point of contradiction.

It should not surprise us, therefore, that some older prophecies do not get all the details of the Era (and the events that will immediately precede and follow it) perfectly correct. That was not their job; as they were much farther removed from these events than we are now and have been in the 20th century.

What has emerged, however, in the modern era of private revelation, is a clear picture and a prophetic consensus (which we examined a portion of in the preceding section). And while details of private revelations can indeed be wrong, the prophetic consensus never is; for that would entail a categorical failure of the *sensus fidei*, which both the Catechism and the Second Vatican Council tells us is impossible.[1102]

Most Theologically Fitting

Finally, let us consider the theology of fittingness regarding what is to come upon the earth in its remaining days. Above all, the Era is most fitting (indeed, necessary) for reasons already discussed in other sections and chapters of this book—because it is the fulfillment of the Our Father prayer, and because it is necessary to enable creation to return to God at the end of time in a similar glory with which it issued forth from Him at the beginning of time. But there are other reasons

the Era is fitting; although they are not as definitive those aforementioned ones, they are still worth considering.

What follows, therefore, is speculative; God alone knows what is truly fitting in these regards, but that should not stop us from pondering it. Therefore, I present these considerations primarily as side-notes or addendums to the more important truths contained in the preceding sections; the Era neither rises nor falls on any of the following points.

A Time for Necessary Purgation Before the End

If, as the critics of a Reign of Peace suggest, history will simply follow a course of becoming more and more depraved until at long last, at the very depths of sin and error with only a few faithful left, Christ comes to both end and judge the world—then what becomes of those who are to be saved by Divine Mercy in those last moments?

It would be abhorrent to assume that, under such a scenario, Our Lord would simply permit the vast, vast majority of humanity to descend into hell. But it would likewise be an affront to justice for all the inhabitants of such a world—culpably mired in obstinate, blasphemous evil as they will be—to simply ascend to Heaven immediately with no ability to be purified in Purgatory. And yet this would be the only possibility, for it is a Dogma of the Faith that Purgatory ceases to exist[1103] upon the General Resurrection and the Last Judgment.

This dilemma is best resolved by a Reign of Peace, whereby the just flourish upon earth, before the end of time. In this Era, those evildoers who nevertheless died repentant in the last moment amidst the great Chastisements will have time for purification before the Beatific Vision which commences universally for the elect upon the end of time. And likewise, those upon earth, living in a universal Reign of the Divine Will, will not be in such a state as to necessarily require Purgatory after their deaths. While some medieval conceptions of Purgatory's time may have been literalistic, we must also not err in the opposite direction and say such foolish things as "in Purgatory there is no such thing as time." Time passes differently there, but some type of time is

---

[1102] Cf. CCC 92 and LG 12.
[1103] Cf. John 5:28-29

still required for its existence and for the accomplishment of its effects.[1104] Yet, there will come a true and literal *time* — a certain number (known only by God) of hours from now — when Purgatory will be no more; namely, the Last Judgment.

We must remember that the demands of Purgatory are no mere optional exercises that God imposes upon those who have sufficient time before the end of the world to accommodate it. It is an absolute decree of His justice which He cannot neglect. Even in the most merciful private revelation ever given — no doubt to remain in this place of honor until the end of time; namely, the Divine Mercy revelation given to St. Faustina — Jesus says (regarding Purgatory): "*My mercy does not want this, but justice demands it.*"[1105] We can see, therefore, that for souls who die in objective need of purification, Purgatory is a requirement of Divine justice that *nothing* can abrogate.

This same argument also supports well the fact that the end of time is not imminent (the imminence of the end of time is posited by those who recognize the signs of the times pointing to the end of an era, yet reject the Era of Peace). It also goes without saying that many (if not practically all) of those dying today seem to be in such a spiritual state as to require a rather lengthy stay in Purgatory. But this opportunity would not exist if the end of time were at hand.

"Lead All Souls to Heaven"

Hans Urs von Balthasar, and more recently Bishop Robert Barron, are well known for their bold assertion put forth in the former's book entitled *Dare we Hope*, that it is reasonable to hope that there is not now (and never will be) a single human soul in hell.

Now, Universalism — the teaching that hell will eventually be abolished, and all creatures are guaranteed reconciliation with God in eternity — is condemned as a heresy. Fr. Hardon describes it as:

The theory that hell is essentially a kind of

purgatory in which sins are expiated, so that eventually everyone will be saved. Also called apokatastasis, it was condemned by the church in A.D. 543, against the Origenists, who claimed that "the punishment of devils and wicked men is temporary and will eventually cease, that is to say, that devils or the ungodly will be completely restored to their original state" (Denzinger 411).[1106]

Barron and von Balthasar, however, insist that what they preach is not Universalism, since they are not claiming that hell will end as Purgatory will; rather, they assert that they are merely claiming that hell might be completely empty of humans. Pope St. John Paul II was aware of these subtle distinctions, nevertheless did not seem convinced by their attempt to evade the condemnation meted out to Universalism, as he responded to von Balthasar's concerns by saying:

And yet, the words of Christ are unequivocal. In Matthew's Gospel he speaks clearly of those who **will go** to eternal punishment…[1107]

John Paul II here does not say that Christ's words refer to those who "might" go to eternal punishment, but to those who "will" go to eternal punishment.

All of this has been written about many times in the years since Bishop (then Father) Barron revived Von Balthasar's hypothesis. Thankfully, the consensus of orthodox-minded Catholic writers seems to be that, **while Bishop Barron is a gifted evangelist and theologian, he is wrong on this point. It is *not* reasonable to hope that hell is and always will be completely empty of any human beings. The mere fact that the Church does not teach who exactly is in hell proves nothing, for that is not within her Divine mandate**. The Church also does not teach the laws of mathematics, which nevertheless cannot reasonably be doubted, for they are known with certainty by means outside of the Deposit of Faith.

We do know, from the Deposit of Faith, that hell is eternal and anyone residing there cannot possibly leave it (referring again to the condemnation of

---

[1104]Time, being the measure of the reduction of potency to act, clearly is necessary in some sense in Purgatory, where the perfect purity of the soul is only in potency, and the purging fires reduce it to act. This is certainly not to say that it is impossible for God to satisfy the purgation in an instant of earthly time; it is merely to say that it is more fitting if that need not be the case.

[1105]St. Faustina, *Divine Mercy in My Soul*, 20.

[1106]Hardon, John A. *Modern Catholic Dictionary*. (Bardstown, Kentucky: Eternal Life, 2004.) UNIVERSALISM, on therealpresence.org

[1107] Pope John Paul II, and Vittorio Messori. *Crossing the Threshold of Hope*. (New York: Knopf, 1994), 185.

Universalism). We also know, from the unanimous consensus of the saints, as well as the clear sense of every relevant passage of Sacred Scripture, the Sensus Fidelium, the unanimous consensus of trustworthy private revelation, the unanimous consensus of exorcists (who have experienced people being possessed by the souls of damned human beings), and a host of other sources, that many people have already gone to hell. Consequently, it is in no way reasonable to hope that all are saved.

However, there is one great shortcoming in the logic which is shared by almost every major critic of Bishop Barron, and it shows that, though technically incorrect, he is also grasping at an important truth. These critics do not address the fact that whatever is prayed for must, lest it be a deceptive and duplicitous prayer, be capable of being reasonably hoped for. No orthodox Catholic prays for blessings for a soul already in hell. No orthodox Catholic prays for God to change the past.[1108] No orthodox Catholic prays for God to love evil or hate good. No orthodox Catholic prays for God to make a square triangle.

And yet, orthodox Catholics throughout the world pray, every day, "… save us from the fires of hell; **lead all souls to Heaven, especially those in most need of thy mercy,**" as they end each decade of the Rosary with this prayer given to the children at Fatima. Therefore, only three options remain as logical possibilities:

1) Continue saying this prayer knowing that it is a lie.
2) Agree with Bishop Barron and von Balthasar and suppose that one may reasonably hope that not a single soul is lost.

3) **Recognize that this prayer is essentially forward looking and thus indeed possible for God to fulfill.**

Clearly the first option is intolerable, and the second has already been disputed, so the third option is the only reasonable choice which remains. Indeed, it is not only reasonable, but is the best approach to take regarding this question in general. **For when one prays "lead all souls to heaven…" one is referring to all souls who can be led; namely, the souls now on earth, the souls yet to be**

created by God, and the souls in Purgatory. The third category is already guaranteed salvation, and therefore praying that they be lead to Heaven amounts to praying for the hastening of their deliverance. But to pray that all the souls of the first two categories be led to Heaven is to suppose that it is reasonable to hope that all of them will be saved.

Such a hope is nothing other than the hope for the hastening of the coming of the Era of Peace. For it is simply not realistic to look at the world as it currently is (or as it ever has been since the fall) and suppose that every soul alive will be saved. But consider an age when the Gospel has been preached and accepted to the ends of the earth, when the Catholic Church triumphs in the greatest sense of the word, and the Will of God is done on earth as it is done in Heaven; that is an age where one may hope that all are saved. **And the possibility of the arrival of such an age is unavoidably annexed to this Fatima prayer which begs God for the salvation of all souls**.

In sum: Bishop Barron is wrong, but if only he reformulated his thesis to say "we may reasonably hope that, *looking forward to the Era*, all will be saved and none go to hell," it would be both correct and prophetic.

Intimations of the Era Outside of Catholicism

In the beginning of the chapter on (the heresy of) millenarianism, we briefly introduced an issue which deserves a more thorough treatment. And the issue is this: everywhere—across religions, cultures, and nations—one sees a growing understanding among the people of the day that radical changes are soon coming upon this earth.

Precise details of Augustine's Amillennialism, Magisterial proclamations against millenarianism, etc. aside, critics of the Era of Peace are sometimes known to compare its general premise to the premises of a plethora of confused movements throughout history—but especially throughout the world today—all positing, with great admixture of error, that before the world comes to its ultimate end in time, a new and glorious age will dawn upon it in which most, if not all, of the evils we now

---

[1108]Not even God can change the past. *Cf.* St. Thomas Aquinas, *ST* I, q. 25, a. 4 trans. English Dominican Province.

endure will be gone. These same critics fallaciously assert that, since these movements are clearly in error (many even expressly denying some tenet of Catholic Faith), the Catholic anticipation of the Era of Peace also must also be simply another product, albeit clothed in superficially holy attire, of whatever erroneous premise led to the other movements.

But their conclusion does not follow from its premises. The Catholic view of revelation does not hold that grace overrides nature, but rather it teaches that grace "perfects nature."[1109] Applied to what history shows are universal human intuitions, this axiom teaches that such intuitions should not be utterly discarded and replaced by Divine Revelation, but instead, they are to be adjusted and fine-tuned in accord with it.

Aristotle, the "ultimate philosopher" according to St. Thomas Aquinas, even defers to these intuitions as the starting points of philosophy itself, assuming they are first principles which philosophical investigation has no more right to contradict than a theory has a right to contradict a law.[1110] Therefore, if **religions and cultures across times and places reflect a common intuition that a great change will come upon the world entailing an eradication of evil or a return to its original glory, then this idea ought not be immediately discounted simply because various errors are attached to this essential premise wherever it is found outside of Catholic orthodoxy.**

Instead, the *grace* of Divinely protected Catholic teaching should be used to correct, reformulate, and, in a word, *perfect*, this *natural* universal intuition. An example of what traps are involved in neglecting this proper approach is found in the cynical, modernist approach to interpreting the Genesis account of the Fall of Man. In the modernist approach, it is common for scholars to dismiss this account as nothing more than mere myth.[1111] The justification given is that many other cultural

myths which existed when the Book of Genesis was written depict something fundamentally similar — that is, an original state of bliss followed by a fall; usually by human choice.[1112] From this premise they conclude that Genesis, too, must result from the same error to which these other cultural myths succumbed. Note, however, that the fallacy employed here is the same as the fallacy used in dismissing the Era of Peace on identical grounds; namely, the fallacy of asserting that an erroneous conclusion can only arise from an erroneous first premise, when in fact any erroneous conclusion can come from two sources: first, *any* single faulty premise; or second, a faulty logic applied to them. These modernists assume that the faults in pagan myths must arise from a fatal flaw in the first premise itself (that there was indeed an original state of glory which some ancient fall destroyed), when in fact those pagan errors arise from premises inserted much later, or from faulty logic applied to them.

There is no need to await the vindication of the view that rejects this modernist account, for the Church has already condemned such heretical methods of exegesis on multiple occasions. Pope Pius XII, for example, taught that Genesis does "…pertain to history in a true sense…"[1113] while also condemning the notion that Adam and Eve were not real, or were not our actual first parents.[1114] Contradicting these Magisterial teachings is required to hold the modernist view of Genesis, and consequently the view itself cannot be held.

Returning to the perfecting action of grace, however, the task must not be undertaken timidly. Outside of Catholic orthodoxy, there is great danger in espousing the view that the end of this age is imminent, to be followed by the arrival of a more glorious one. This danger exists in the movements already discussed, which promote Liberation Theology, but is even more pressing in what has come to be known as the "New Age

---

[1109]*ST*, I, q. 1, a. 8 trans. English Dominican Province.
[1110] For example, in Nicomachean Ethics Book I, Aristotle appeals to what we instinctively feel about *The Good* to justify what it cannot be.
[1111]For example, Bishop Thomas Gumbleton referred to Genesis' creation account as a "myth" in his March 9th, 2017 article on ncronline.org.
[1112] For example, in *Pagan Origins of the Christ Myth*, John G. Jackson argues that the truth of the Biblical depiction of the Fall is disproven by a similar depiction existing earlier in

"sculptured in the magnificent temple of Ipsambul in Nubia" (1941. Page 2. Accessed via archive.org.) Stories of original bliss followed by some sort of Fall by human choice exists in many creation myths.
[1113]Pope Pius XII, Encyclical Concerning some False Opinions Threatening to Undermine the Foundations of Catholic Doctrine, *Humani Generis* (12 August 1950), 38
[1114]Cf. *Humani Generis*, 37.

movement." This movement, strongly condemned by the Church, and likely one of the most perverse versions of the universal human intuition that another Era is coming, teaches of an "…imminent astrological Age of Aquarius"[1115] in which a "syncretism of esoteric and secular elements … can be described as 'a modern revival of pagan religions with a mixture of influences from both eastern religions and also from modern psychology…'"[1116] The same Vatican document here quoted proceeds to point out that the movement's inspiration comes not from God, but from disciplines such as quantum mechanics and "feelings, emotion, and experience" over reason. Distorted as this movement is, and as firmly as the Church condemns its errors, she is careful to avoid categorically condemning one of the fundamental premises that inspires it, as some overzealous and sloppy critics have done. The document states:

> The search which often leads people to the New Age is a genuine yearning: for a deeper spirituality, for something which will touch their hearts, and for a way of making sense of a confusing and often alienating world. There is a positive tone in New Age criticisms of "the materialism of daily life, of philosophy and even of medicine and psychiatry; reductionism, which refuses to take into consideration religious and supernatural experiences; the industrial culture of unrestrained individualism, which teaches egoism and pays no attention to other people, the future and the environment". Any problems there are with New Age are to be found in what it proposes as alternative answers to life's questions. [1117]

Far from condemning the fundamental premise that leads many to this movement, the Church both condones it and insists that the problems are not found in that premise, but are rather found only in the "alternative answers" it gives after following that premise down the wrong paths.

Although beyond the scope of this book, a similar analysis could easily be undertaken regarding any of the movements found in which people, throughout the world and throughout history, instinctively feel that a new and glorious age will dawn upon the world before its consummation entailing some manner of restoration of the original state it enjoyed as it came forth from its Creator. These movements include Christian or quasi-Christian examples: Mormonism, Evangelical Christian Millenarianism, the United Society of Believers in Christ's Second Appearing (Shakers), Jehovah's Witnesses, as well as non-Christian examples such as Shia Islam awaiting of a new Millennium and Mahdi, the resurgence of Messianic Judaism, and Buddhist Maitreyan worship and expectation.

Naturally, the closer one gets to Catholicism, the closer the intimations alluded to in the title of this section will be to the truth. And indeed, Evangelical Christians are well known for their firm belief and zealous insistence upon the Millennial Reign. I needn't waste space castigating them for their errors here; doing so is already pervasive in Catholic circles due to how fashionable it is to condemn overzealousness in a frantic desire to appear reasonable to the world and the worldly. Of course; their castigations are correct—there will be no rapture, no literal, physical reign of Jesus, and no definitive perfection to be found on this side of the end of time.

But just like those who, as the Magisterial document cited above laments, can only find time to castigate what is wrong in the New Age wind up forgetting that this movement is inspired by "genuine yearning"; so, too, those who can only castigate the errors found mixed in with the various millennial teachings found throughout the world and throughout history just wind up missing the whole point, and failing to see God's clear—albeit subtle—ways of working in the world.

**

Before turning to what Jesus told Luisa about this coming Era, we need to first do something difficult, and consider what must necessarily precede the coming of this Era: the purification.

30) The Chastisements

[1115]Pontifical Council for Culture, A Christian reflection on the "New Age." *Jesus Christ Bearer of the Water of Life* 1.1.

[1116]*Jesus Christ Bearer of the Water of Life*, 2.1.
[1117] *Jesus Christ Bearer of the Water of Life*, 1.5.

Most people reading this book likely already know that the times ahead will involve more suffering, disaster, persecution, war, famine, plague—and on the list goes—than has ever been seen at any time in history. Because this reality has become fairly well understood in the Catholic world today (at least among those willing to listen to private revelation and the signs of the times), we will not dedicate too much time to the matter here. But let the relative brevity of this treatment not beguile anyone into supposing that the Chastisements might not occur, or might not be that grave of a matter after all. Jesus repeatedly warns Luisa of the coming Chastisements, which will purify the world and pave the way for the Reign of the Divine Will.

Before briefly considering these Chastisements, we must understand that they do not detract one iota from the love that God has for all of us; in fact, the Chastisements themselves are great acts of Divine Love. Jesus tells Luisa:

My daughter, courage, everything will serve for the triumph of my Will. If I strike, it is because I want to restore. My love is so great, that when I cannot win by way of love and of graces, I try to win by way of terror and fright. The human weakness is such that many times it pays no heed to my graces, it plays deaf to my voice, it laughs at my love. But it is enough to touch its flesh, or take away the things necessary to the natural life, that it lowers its pride, it feels so humiliated as to become a rag; and I make of it whatever I want. Especially if they do not have a perfidious and obstinate will, a chastisement is enough—seeing themselves on the brink of the sepulcher—that they return into my arms.

You must know that **I always love my children, my beloved creatures, I would turn Myself inside out so as not to see them struck**; so much so, that in the gloomy times that are coming, I have placed them all in the hands of my Celestial Mama—to Her have I entrusted them, that She may keep them for Me under Her safe mantle. I will give Her all those whom She will want; even death will have no power over those who will be in the custody of my Mama."

Now, while He was saying this, my dear Jesus showed me, with facts, how the Sovereign Queen descended from Heaven with an unspeakable majesty, and a tenderness fully maternal; and She went around in the midst of creatures, throughout all nations, and She marked Her dear children and those who were not to be touched by the scourges.[1118]

What profound words. **Jesus tells us that *He would turn Himself inside out*** (in another translation, it says that He would *eviscerate* Himself) in order to not see any of us—His dear children—harmed by Chastisements. There is no one who comes even close to Jesus in utterly despising the thought of Chastisements and lamenting their impending arrival. He only allows them—it would not even usually be correct to say that He "imposes" or "sends" them, as most Chastisements are a natural result of mankind's sinfulness—as an utter last resort to save us from the fires of hell.

In this same diary entry, we also see Luisa describing how she saw in the Queen of Heaven, Our Blessed Lady, the sure protection from all Chastisements for her dear children. Let us, therefore, especially remember Our Lady's power over all things which are to transpire on this world in the sad days to come, and whenever we are tempted to fear, let us instead re-consecrate ourselves to her and renew our love of and devotion to her.

***

Having stated what is most important, we turn now to some details. To that end, we revisit here what was included in Part One (in the "Prophetic Explosion of the Modern Era" section); an excerpt from a work of the theologian, Fr. Edward O'Connor, in which he analyzes dozens of modern private revelations and ascertains their main thrust, which he describes as follows:

The basic message is that of St. Faustina: we are in an age of mercy, which will soon give way to an age of justice. The reason for this is the immorality of today's world, which surpasses that of any past age. Things are so bad that Satan is reigning over the world. Even the life of the Church itself has been badly affected. Apostasy, heresy and compromise challenge the faith of the people. Not only the laity, but also priests and religious are grievously at fault. A hidden form of Masonry has entered into the Church. Because of all this, God has been sending prophets as never before to call us to repentance. Most often, it is the Blessed Mother who speaks through them. She warns of an unprecedented tribulation that lies in the very near future. The Church will be torn apart. The Antichrist, already alive in the world, will manifest himself. Up to now, Mary has been holding back the punishment due to us. The time will come, however, when she will no longer be able to do so. Not only the Church, but the whole world will experience tribulation. There will be natural disasters, such as earthquakes, floods, fierce storms and strange weather patterns. Economic ruin will plunge the whole world into poverty. There will be warfare, perhaps even a Third World War. There will also be cosmic disasters in the form of devastating meteors striking the earth or other heavenly bodies passing close enough to wreak havoc. Finally, a mysterious fire from heaven will wipe out the greater part of mankind, and plunge the world in utter darkness for three days. Before these terrible events take place, we will be prepared, first by a "Warning" in which everyone on earth will see his or her soul as it appears before God, and secondly by a miraculous sign. The disasters to come will purify the world and leave it as God intended it to be. The Holy Spirit will be poured out as never before and renew the hearts of all mankind. Most of the visionaries insist that the time left before these things take place is very short. Some indicate that the fulfillment has begun already. To protect us against the dangers predicted, we are urged to frequent the sacraments, pray and do penance. The proclamation of Mary as Mediatrix, Coredemptrix and Advocate is called for and predicted. [1119]

All of this is confirmed by Jesus' words to Luisa. While presenting a comprehensive overview would require far more space than we can dedicate to the matter, a few snippets are as follows:

> This is the reason why my Divine Will is as though on the lookout from within the elements, to see whether they are disposed to receive the good of Its continuous operating; and in seeing Itself rejected, tired, It arms the elements against them. **Therefore, unforeseen chastisements and new phenomena are about to happen;** the earth, with its almost continuous tremor, warns man to come to his senses, otherwise he will sink under his own steps because it can no longer sustain him. The evils that are about to happen are grave, otherwise I would not have suspended you often from your usual state of victim. [1120]

These words of Jesus to Luisa are important

because we cannot pretend that we can even fully understand what the Chastisements will entail at this moment, before having experienced them. For there will be "new phenomena," although we can rest assured that they will be carefully chosen by Jesus to be not one ounce more heavy than necessary, and that they will be undertaken with the precision of a surgeon. Plenty of the phenomena, however, are well within our capacity to at least be informed of; therefore, it is to a few examples of these that we now turn our attention:

> It seems that one can no longer live in these sad times; yet, it seems that this is only the beginning... If I do not find my satisfactions—ah, it is over for the world! The scourges will pour down in torrents. Ah, my daughter! Ah, my daughter! [1121]

> It seemed that many thousands of people would drop dead—some from revolutions, some from earthquakes, some in the fire, some in the water. It seemed to me that these chastisements were the precursors of nearing wars. [1122]

> Almost all nations live relying on debts; if they do not make debts, they cannot live. And in spite of this they celebrate, they spare themselves nothing, and are making plans of wars, incurring enormous expenses. Do you yourself not see the great blindness and madness into which they have fallen? And you, little child, would want My Justice not to strike them, and to be lavish with temporal goods. So, you would want them to become more blind and more insane. [1123]

> This is precisely the great scourge that is preparing for the ugly vertiginous race of creatures. Nature itself is tired of so many evils, and would want to take revenge for the rights of its Creator. All natural things would want to place themselves against man; the sea, the fire, the wind, the earth, are about to go out of their boundaries to harm and strike the generations, in order to decimate them. [1124]

> But the chastisements also are necessary; this will serve to prepare the ground so that the Kingdom of the Supreme Fiat may form in the midst of the human family. **So, many lives, which will be an obstacle to the triumph of my Kingdom, will disappear from the face of the earth...** [1125]

[1119] *Listen to My Prophets.* Pages 189-190.
[1120] November 24, 1930.
[1121] December 9, 1916.
[1122] May 6, 1906.

[1123] May 26, 1927.
[1124] March 22, 1924.
[1125] September 12, 1926.

My daughter, I am not concerned about the cities, the great things of the earth—I am concerned about souls. The cities, the churches and other things, after they have been destroyed, can be rebuilt. Didn't I destroy everything in the Deluge? And wasn't everything redone again? But if souls are lost, it is forever—there is no one who can give them back to Me.[1126]

My daughter, the Kingdom of my Will is all prepared within my Humanity, and I am ready to put It out to give It to creatures. It can be said that I formed the foundations, I raised the factories; the rooms are innumerable and all adorned and illuminated—not with little lights, but with as many suns for as many truths as I have manifested about the Divine Fiat. Nothing else is needed but those who would inhabit It; there will be a place and room for everyone, because It is vast, more than the whole world. With the Kingdom of my Will everything will be renewed in Creation; things will return to their original state. This is why many scourges are necessary, and will take place—so that Divine Justice may place Itself in balance with all of my attributes, in such a way that, by balancing Itself, It may leave the Kingdom of my Will in Its peace and happiness. Therefore, do not be surprised if such a great good, which I am preparing and which I want to give, is preceded by many scourges.[1127]

Only a very small sample of messages pertaining to the Chastisements are presented here. The Chastisements are an overarching theme of Jesus' words to Luisa, and the mitigation of them is a very important calling of all who wish to live in the Divine Will.

***

But a few more words are in order on the necessity of the Chastisements. If you have read this book thus far, you have at least an idea of how incredibly glorious this Gift of His Will is that God is offering all of us. And yet, so many reject it. The contrast between what He is offering to man and how man responds is so obscene as to devastate the hardest heart. It is a more lamentable scene than one in which an unfaithful wife of a good husband, after leaving him and violating his love in every conceivable way, is herself sought out by him and offered complete reconciliation at no "cost" whatsoever, only to then throw the offer back in his face with a torrent of new insults. This is precisely what man, today, is doing to God.

We must recall that the Father of the Prodigal Son did not go out and find the latter and force him out of his debauchery. Although he is the image of love, this father nevertheless allowed the son's debauchery to produce its inevitable natural consequences of utter misery, knowing that this misery would bring the son to his senses.

Because of this response of man to God's initiative—in which He would have so much preferred to conquer us by love—there is simply no other way than to let the Chastisements run their course. The Chastisements, indeed, are guaranteed to do the job. They are not how God wanted it to happen, but they will work.

> …since this way of living [in God's Will] was to be of all creatures—this was the purpose of Our Creation, but to Our highest bitterness We see that *almost all* **live at the low level of their human will**…[1128]

> …created things feel honored when they serve a creature who is animated by that same Will which forms their very life. On the other hand, my Will takes the attitude of sorrow in those same created things when It has to serve one who does not fulfill my Will. This is why it happens that many times created things place themselves against man, they strike him, they chastise him—**because they become superior to man, as they keep intact within themselves that Divine Will by which they were animated from the very beginning of their creation, while man has descended down below, for he does not keep the Will of his Creator** within himself.[1129]

> [Luisa observes:] Yet, the cause of this is only sin, and man does not want to surrender; it seems that man has placed himself against God, and God will arm the elements against man—water, fire, wind and many other things, which will cause many upon many to die. What fright, what horror! I felt I was dying in seeing all these sorrowful scenes; I would have wanted to suffer anything to placate the Lord.[1130]

> … the Supreme Fiat wants to get out. It is tired, and at any cost It wants to get out of this agony so prolonged; and if you hear of chastisements, of cities collapsed, of destructions, this is nothing other than the strong writhing of Its agony.

[1126] November 20, 1917.
[1127] August 30, 1928.
[1128] October 30, 1932.

[1129] August 15, 1925.
[1130] April 17, 1906.

Unable to bear it any longer, It wants to make the human family feel Its painful state and how It writhes strongly within them, without anyone who has compassion for It. And making use of violence, with Its writhing, It wants them to feel that It exists in them, but It does not want to be in agony any more—It wants freedom, dominion; It wants to carry out Its life in them. What disorder in society, my daughter, because my Will does not reign! Their souls are like houses without order—everything is upside down; the stench is so horrible—more than that of a putrefied cadaver. And my Will, with Its immensity, such that it is not given to It to withdraw even from one heartbeat of creature, agonizes in the midst of so many evils. And this happens in the general order of all... **And this is why It wants to burst its banks with Its writhing, so that, if they do not want to know It and receive It by ways of Love, they may know It by way of Justice. Tired of an agony of centuries, my Will wants to get out, and therefore It prepares two ways: the triumphant way, which are Its knowledges, Its prodigies and all the good that the Kingdom of the Supreme Fiat will bring; and the way of Justice, for those who do not want to know It as triumphant**. It is up to the creatures to choose the way in which they want to receive It.[1131]

The quote immediately above is the most important to remember because it tells us clearly that the severity of the Chastisements will be proportional to the deficiency of the knowledges of the Divine Will among the people. This fact is a clear corollary of what He says, for it is the contrapositive given by Jesus in this quote. Jesus tells Luisa that either the knowledges of the Divine Will can prepare the way, or the Chastisements can. Consequently, if the knowledges do not do so (and they will not if they are not proclaimed), then the Chastisements will make up for what is found lacking. **Do you want, then, to mitigate the Chastisements? Do you want to spare this world at least some of the historically unprecedented misery that is about to deluge it? Be a New Evangelist of the Third Fiat.**

Above all, live in the Divine Will, and Jesus Himself will not be able to resist your pleas for the mitigation of the Chastisements:

> We even reach the extent of giving her the right to Judge together with Us, and if We see that she suffers because the sinner is under a rigorous Judgment, to soothe her pain We mitigate Our Just chastisements. She makes Us give the kiss of Forgiveness, and to make her Happy We say to her: 'Poor daughter, you are right. You are Ours and belong also to them. You feel in you the bonds of the human family, therefore you would want that We Forgive everybody. **We'll do as much as We can to please you, unless he despises or refuses Our Forgiveness.' This creature in Our Will is the New Esther wanting to rescue her peoples**. O! how Happy We are to keep her always with Us in Our Will because, through her, We feel more inclined to use Mercy, to concede Graces, to Forgive the most obstinate sinners, and to lessen the pains of the purging souls. Poor daughter! She has a thought for everyone, and a pain similar to Ours, seeing the human family swimming in Our Will without recognizing It-living in the middle of enemies in the most wretched misery.[1132]

***

We also recall that one who lives in the Divine Will—but truly, any soul in God's grace—has no fear of the Chastisements, for even at their most terrible, he approaches them like a person with dirt on his body approaches a shower. Jesus tells Luisa:

> Courage, my daughter—courage is of souls resolute to do good. They are imperturbable under any storm; and while they hear the roaring of the thunders and lightnings to the point of trembling, and remain under the pouring rain that pours over them, **they use the water to be washed and come out more beautiful; and <u>heedless of the storm</u>, they are more than ever resolute and courageous** in not moving from the good they have started. Discouragement is of irresolute souls, which never arrive at accomplishing a good. Courage sets the way, courage puts to flight any storm, courage is the bread of the strong, courage is the warlike one that knows how to win any battle. [1133]

What a beautiful teaching! Without ever succumbing to any form of flippancy regarding the looming Chastisements, we can nevertheless await them with a type of excitement; for we can use them, as Jesus here asks us to, in order to cleanse ourselves of what we know is filthy but which we have not yet found the strength to be rid of. I share a few suggestions on how, perhaps, we can put this advice into practice when the opportunity presents itself:

[1131] November 19, 1926.
[1132] October 30, 1938.

[1133] April 16, 1931.

- When what is impending becomes even more clear, look to what is coming with the trust which accompanies the knowledge that, despite your own misery, nothing but perfect love comes from God's hands. If He permits you to suffer, it is because that specific suffering is the greatest blessing that He can imagine for you at that moment. In this, you will never be disappointed. You are invincible. You can say, with David, "[I] have no fear of evil news" (Psalm 112). To arrive at that point does not require a long and arduous ascent of the mountain of moral virtue. It just requires that, even in this very moment, you say with all of your heart "Jesus, I Trust in You."

- When your loved ones die, trust that God knew it was the perfect time for them to go home to Him, and that you will see them soon enough, when your own time comes. And give thanks to God that He has given you an opportunity to be detached from creatures so as to become more attached to your Creator, in Whom you will find more joy and peace than in a perfect relationship with a million friends and family members combined.

- When you lose your home and all of your possessions, give thanks to God that He has deemed you worthy of living that most blessed life of St. Francis'—perfect reliance upon Providence with each moment—and that He has also given you the grace to live what He asked the wealthy young man to live without, a young man who nevertheless was not given the grace to follow through, for he "went away sad." (Matthew 19:22)

- When you are thrown into a jail cell for a crime you did not commit, or for a good deed you did indeed do, which is falsely considered, in this twisted world, to be a crime—give thanks to God that He has given you the life of a monastic—the highest vocation—, and that you can dedicate yourself entirely to prayer.

- When you are beaten or tortured, whether literally by a malicious person or simply by circumstances that are extremely painful (whether hunger, exposure, fatigue, illness, or what have you), give thanks to God that He is permitting you to suffer for Him, in Him. Such occasions, when there is no means to avoid them without sinning, amount to God Himself serving as your spiritual director, deciding that you need mortifications. And the mortifications that Providence chooses are always better than our own, and they always yield great joy and build up enormous treasures both on earth and in Heaven.

- When persecution in any form touches you, rejoice with unutterable joy because you have been deemed worthy—among the billions of Catholics who have not been—to be so dealt with. "Then they left the presence of the council, rejoicing that they were counted worthy to suffer dishonor for the name."—Acts 5:41. For the only Beatitude that Our Lord deemed so great that He needed to dwell upon it and reiterate it was the last, "Blessed are those who are persecuted for righteousness' sake, for theirs is the kingdom of heaven. Blessed are you when men revile you and persecute you and utter all kinds of evil against you falsely on My account. Rejoice and be glad, for your reward is great in heaven, for so men persecuted the prophets who were before you." (Matthew 5:10-12).

Remember that Jesus told Luisa it is quite easy to distinguish the reprobate from the elect: just as, on Day of Judgment, the Sign of the Son of Man (the cross) in the sky will cause terror in the former and ecstasy in the latter, so too now, the reaction to one's crosses in life reveal one's eternal destiny. So, In all things say, with Job, "The Lord giveth and the Lord taketh away. Blessed be the Name of the Lord." (Job 1:21)

The good thief and the bad thief found themselves in an identical situation. One praised God in the midst of it, and one cursed Him. Choose now which you will be.

***

Having addressed the looming Chastisements—their nature and their necessity—we turn now to the more joyful task of contemplating the Glorious Era of Peace to come thereafter. And let us end this chapter by deferring to the words of Jesus to Luisa, in which He reminds us that these Chastisements will serve a greater purpose:

My daughter, everything you saw [Chastisements] will serve to purify and prepare the human family. The turmoils will serve to reorder, and the destructions to build more beautiful things. If a collapsing building is not torn down, a new and more beautiful one cannot be formed upon those very ruins. **I will stir everything for the fulfillment of my Divine Will**. And besides, when I came upon earth, it was not decreed by Our Divinity that the Kingdom of My Will should come, but that of Redemption; and in spite of human ingratitude, It was accomplished. However, It has not yet covered all of Its way; many regions and peoples live as if I had not come, therefore it is necessary that It make Its way and walk everywhere, because Redemption is the preparatory way for the Kingdom of My Will… And when We decree, all is done; in Us, it is enough to decree in order to accomplish what We want. This is why what seems difficult to you will all be made easy by Our Power.[1134]

Furthermore, it is only because God – being eternal and therefore outside of time—Himself can see the times to come and the glory of the Era, that it is possible for His justice to refrain from annihilating all creation instantly. Jesus tells Luisa:

And if there was not in Us the Certainty that Our Will would Reign in the creature, in order to form Our Life in her, Our Love would Burn Creation completely, and would reduce it to nothing; and if it supports and tolerates so much, it is because We see the times to come, Our Purpose Realized.[1135]

***

31) <u>On the Era Itself</u>

Having settled the need for the Era, determined the orthodoxy of the Era, discovered the Era as seen in countless other sources (Scripture, the Fathers of the Church, Papal Magisterium, and virtually every private revelation)—it is now time to do what, perhaps, readers really were looking for in opening to Part Three of this book: that is, learning more *about* the Era itself!

The first thing to understand about the Era is that it does not exist for its own sake. This truth is so important that it must be addressed first, and it indeed needs its own section, to which we turn our attention now before considering further details about the Era.

<u>It is All About Heaven</u>

One concern that might enter the minds of some after they learn about the Era is "Might this be a distraction from Heaven itself—the *ultimate* 'Era of Peace'?"

The answer, simply, is: it ought not be!

The Era of Peace itself obviously is not definitive. It is a more or less brief,[1136] temporal period on earth, which in turn is—to put it rather bluntly—a saint-

making factory for populating Heaven. Jesus tells Luisa:

The end of man is Heaven, and for one who has my Divine Will as origin, all of her acts flow into Heaven, as the end which her soul must reach, and as the origin of her beatitude which will have no end. And if you have my Divine Will as end, you will give Me the glory and the requital of love for having prepared a Celestial Fatherland for creatures, as their happy dwelling. Therefore, be attentive, my daughter, and I seal in your soul my Divine Will as origin, means and end, which will be for you life, the safe guide, the support, and will lead you in Its arms to the Celestial Fatherland.[1137]

You must not, therefore, allow yourself to waste time pondering whether you will be alive for the Era of Peace; and, most importantly, you must not allow yourself to fret over this same question. **The height of folly would be to respond to learning of the Era by worrying about when it will come and striving to secure worldly means to live long enough to see it from earth.** The notion of a holy martyrdom should still inspire you just as much as it has always inspired all Christians. What a tragedy it would be for you to lose that inspiration

---

[1134] April 30, 1928.
[1135] May 30, 1932.
[1136] Whether several decades or several centuries makes little difference
[1137] April 4, 1931.

merely because it would "deprive you of the ability to live in the Era!" That would be ridiculous. Those in Heaven will enjoy the Era of Peace much more than those on earth will. Those who die before the Era are far more blessed than those who "make it" to the Era before their death.

Instead, we should eagerly await the Era and strive to do all that we can to hasten it—crying "continually," as Jesus tells Luisa, "let the Kingdom of your Fiat come, and let your Will be done on earth as it is in Heaven!"—because we recognize that the Era consists in none other than the ideal earthly conditions for the building up of eternal glory of Heaven. To draw a crude analogy, we should await the Era like a laborer awaits some new technology that will drastically multiply his productivity; this laborer still engages in his work not merely for its own sake, but to provide for his family; but, he will be able to provide for his family far more effectively with this new technology.

Jesus speaks clearly to Luisa of the Happiness that exists only in Heaven. Indeed, the happiness of the Era will be enormous; but it is not our ultimate destiny, it is not our end, and it is utterly dwarfed by the happiness of Heaven.

> But then, in all the rest, one can see nothing but the echo, the language of the Celestial Fatherland, the balm from on high which sanctifies, divinizes and makes the down payment of the happiness which reigns only in the Blessed Fatherland.[1138]

Living in the Divine Will—now or during the Era—merely "makes the down payment" on something that we do not receive until Heaven. Therefore, we can see even more clearly now that, indeed, one who lives in the Divine Will but dies before the Era is most blessed of all; because in so dying, he returns to His Heavenly fatherland, and spares himself the ardent longing that he would have had for Heaven, had he lived long enough to enjoy the Era from earth!

> This is the reason why We insist so much that Our Will be always done, that It be known, because We want to populate Heaven with Our beloved children.[1139]

Here we see that Jesus puts it even more bluntly: His whole plan is to populate Heaven with His beloved children. The Era is the greatest means to that end.

In the Era, the veil is thinned, but still exists; we do not see God face-to-face in the Era, thus it is not truly our ultimate and definitive destiny. Jesus tells Luisa:

> My daughter, everything here below, as much in the supernatural order as in the natural order, are all veiled. Only in Heaven are they unveiled, because in the Celestial Fatherland, veils do not exist, but things are seen as they are in themselves. So, up above, the intellect does not have to work to understand them, because by themselves, they show themselves for what they are. And, if there is work to do in the Blessed Dwelling, if one can truly call it work, it is to enjoy and be happy in the things that one openly sees.[1140]

Elsewhere, Jesus even uses man's neglect of Heaven and sole focus on the earth as the very reason for the Chastisements themselves, saying:

> My daughter, man has forgotten Heaven for the earth. It is justice that what is earth be taken away from him, and that he go wandering, unable to find a place in which to take refuge, so that he may remember that Heaven exists. Man has forgotten the soul for the body. So, everything is for the body: pleasures, comforts, sumptuousness, luxury and the like. The soul is starving, deprived of everything, and in many it is dead, as if they did not have it. Now, it is justice that their bodies be deprived, so that they may remember that they have a soul. But—oh! how hard man is. His hardness forces Me to strike him more—who knows, he might soften under the blows.[1141]

The Era is also not absolute confirmation in grace, or the definitive and final eradication of evil. Sin will largely lie dormant in the world; but its final, definitive destruction is not until the end of time—the General Judgment and the General Resurrection. Jesus makes it clear to Luisa that Living in the Divine Will is *not* confirmation in grace:

> ...*only someone who is insane* would flee from such a great good [Living in the Divine Will]. In fact, for as long as the soul is a pilgrim one, the doors do not close behind the Gift, but remain open, so that, freely, not being forced, she may

---

[1138] January 30, 1927.
[1139] June 6, 1935.
[1140] August 2, 1930.

[1141] April 6, 1922.

live in Our Gift; more so, since Our Will will not give this Gift by necessity, but because It loves her, and It is fully her own.[1142]

This should have no dampening effect on the joy of our anticipation and zeal of our efforts to hasten the Glorious Reign of Peace, however. For although (as Jesus says and Catholic orthodoxy affirms) the "doors do not close behind the Gift" so long as we are pilgrims (that is, living on earth), that does not mean we need to live in constant dread of escaping through the open door. As noted earlier; do you harbor even the slightest practical fear that you will, even this instant, sprint toward the closest window and jump through it? If you do not fear that, then you need not fear sin once you truly live in the center of the Divine Will. For no sane person fears that he may act insanely, and Jesus assures us that one who Lives in the Divine Will would have to be insane to leave it.

***

Remember, as well, that Luisa was specifically told she would not see the Era of Peace from earth. We must, then, learn from her own disposition with respect to this knowledge, for there are two things that we must especially note which this knowledge did not cause in her: first, it did not cause her to lose one iota of the zeal she previously had for hastening the Era, and secondly, it did not disappoint her in the least (for it was always Heaven, not the Era of Peace, that she was looking forward to). Jesus tells Luisa:

> After I have completed everything, I will quickly bring you into our Fatherland. Do you think that you will see the full triumph of the Kingdom of the Eternal Fiat before coming to Heaven? It is from Heaven that you will see Its full triumph… And once I have completed everything, I will entrust my Kingdom to my ministers, so that, like second apostles of the Kingdom of my Will, they may be the criers of It. Do you think that the coming of Father Di Francia, who shows so much interest and who has taken to heart the publication of what regards my Will, came by chance? No, no—I Myself disposed it. It is a providential act of the Supreme Will that wants him as first apostle of the Divine Fiat and proclaimer of It.[1143]

Now, I sincerely hope that this section has not dampened anyone's enthusiasm for the Era: please,

let us all continue to long for it with all of our hearts, to beg God for it, and to work and pray to effect the hastening thereof. My only wish with this section is to preserve, in all of Luisa's followers, every ounce of Heavenly longing they have always had as devout Catholics—or, rather, to inflame it even more.

The Glory of the Era

Let us now learn about just a few of the glorious things Jesus has told Luisa about the Era.

> I anxiously await that My Will may be known and that the creatures may Live in It. Then, I will show off so much Opulence that every soul will be like a New Creation-Beautiful but distinct from all the others. I will amuse Myself; I will be her Insuperable Architect; I will display all My Creative Art … O, how I long for this; how I want it; how I yearn for it! Creation is not finished. I have yet to do My Most Beautiful Works.[1144]

The essence of the Era is this: God's Will shall be done on earth as it is done in Heaven. If that recognition alone does not fill you with an overwhelming and holy joy, then you must not have much considered these words.

Dr. Thomas Petrisko has written extensively on Marian apparitions (especially Fatima), as well as topics regarding God the Father, Purgatory, Heaven, and Hell, and other matters found within Catholic theology. Convinced as he is of the validity of Luisa's revelations on the Gift of Living in the Divine Will and its Universal Reign, he has written at length endorsing Luisa's writings. In a preface to Dr. Petrisko's book, *Living in the Heart of the Father*, Fr. David Tourville writes:

> Yes…the Divine Paternal Heart of the Father is the Treasure of Heaven that desires to 'beat in unison' with our hearts through shared Love in order that "Your Kingdom come, Your will be done, on earth as [it is] in Heaven" (Mt 6:10). Dr. Thomas Petrisko sheds light on this infinite desire of the Father to be known, loved and honored by each of His children, now, in this Grace-filled 'era of time.' Dr. Petrisko foresees Mary, leading her children to bring about the long-awaited Triumph of her Immaculate Heart in order to usher in that promised 'Era of Peace,' **a time when the Church will know the Father intimately and live in the Kingdom of His Divine Will. This will be a time**

[1142] September 29, 1931.
[1143] November 6, 1926.

[1144] February 7, 1938.

when our Eucharistic Lord will truly be the source and summit of our spiritual lives, revealing: '(Philip) as you have seen Me, you have seen the Father;' consequently, 'as you have received Me, you have received the Father.'

And in the body text of the same book, speaking of God the Father with reference to living in the Divine Will (and its universal reign in the Era of Peace) Dr. Petrisko writes:

The Father of all Mankind, His Divine Paternal Heart overflowing with Love and Mercy, is waiting and desirous to be present to each of us in a new way…He bids us to allow Him to do His Will in and through us, especially through our hearts. He speaks to us—through the events, through the people, through the crosses of our lives…

Yes, the Spirit of change is upon us and in us, as our Father, in this time, now seeks to guide through our Mother Mary and through the mystery of the Church, His prodigal children Home to His **Kingdom … Once His Will is fulfilled, our Father has great plans for His "Kingdom on Earth." His Church is to shine brightly as a jewel in the crown of our Mother and Queen.** Mary tells us that God wills there to be **an epoch of peace, a new time of light that will not fade, will not die, and will not perish. It is to be a glorious new era with countless hearts glowing in love with their Father, sharing their love for Him, heart to Heart to heart, illuminating the world with a new radiance of God,** a new reality of the divine—the truth of the Father of All Mankind, who reveals even more His visible Plan of Love for all of humanity! Indeed, our neglected Heavenly Father needs us now to hurry to Him, to hurry to His Paternal Heart, so the new era—the new times—may begin.

…Freely inviting the world, such recognition and honor of our Father's Divine Paternal Heart by His children and by His Church, must now come, for it is to be a cry, **a shout of joy to Heaven, that will help bring forth the collapse of evil like the walls of Jericho—opening the gates to a new era of extraordinary grace, an era of peace, justice, love and complete joy in God, such as the world has never known. It is to be an era like none other, where love will heal the wounds of God's children, and the truth of who our Father is will be forever illuminated and indelibly sealed in the hearts, minds and souls of all, for God's children will have claimed their rightful** inheritance…Yes, the Triumph of Love—the long awaited reunification of Our Father with His children on earth—Heart to heart—will have finally come, bringing a new oneness with God, a preview of eternity, where we will remain in our Father's Divine Paternal Heart forever! …Most of all, we must be one in truth and spirit. This means we must be united in praying the Our Father, united in our hearts in fidelity to our Father's Heart in order to bring greater love, devotion, and honor to Him so He may pour out His Blessings—His merciful intercession upon our world, upon all mankind. This is our Father's Will for us, the Church, the world. It is the path to the Kingdom "within." It is the path which advances the Kingdom "on earth." It is the path to holiness. It is the Holy Spirit's path to peace, within us and within the world—the peace of shalom—a holy peace that is the reconciliation of the world to our Father's Divine Will. It is peace where life is lived in God and each child has a home within His Heart, for it will be true peace, one in which man abides in God and God abides in man. **Thus, for every hope there is the power to make it so, and now the hope of our Heavenly Father is that His Love for us and our Love for Him will plant the seeds of a new beginning for our world, a new era that is to see God's Peace flowing like a river. It is to be a world filled with the Light of Jesus Christ, bathed in the Love of the Holy Spirit, basking in the radiant Glory of the divine family of God, living together in the rhythm and harmony of the Divine Paternal Heart of God Our Father!**[1145]

Although lengthy, I presented this quote from Dr. Petrisko's work because it is among the best I have come across—outside of, indeed, Jesus' own words to Luisa—which speaks to the nature of the Era that will soon dawn upon the world.

All of those glorious things we fight for with such energy—devoting such time and hardship to the pursuit of; and yet, far too often see scarcely even a minuscule portion of progress in—will be poured out upon the entire world in superabundance. **The most important dimension of this superabundance is the clarity of faith which in turn will cause the salvation and sanctification of souls all across the world; for we recall that the Era is all about Heaven.**

Clarity of Faith

Faith only disappears upon the Beatific Vision;

[1145] Thomas Petrisko. *Living in the Heart of the Father.* Ch. 4

wherein Faith becomes impossible because it is replaced by the clear and perfect sight of what was once believed on the word of others. But just because Faith is intrinsic to our life on earth does not mean that, for the rest of time, it has to remain so difficult and obscure a thing as it is now! Quite the contrary, during the Reign of God's Will, Faith will reign triumphant.

A critic might object and argue that God's existence is *already* as clear as the sun on a cloudless day; that is, he might argue it is already "manifest" or "obvious." But this is not true, and there really are sincerely-seeking atheists and agnostics in the world to whom injustice is done by such statements. St. Thomas Aquinas himself, in his *Summa*, contradicts this view. He teaches that the existence of God—though indeed provable with certainty even from reason alone (that is, without needing to appeal to Faith)—is nevertheless *not* manifest. In fact, he dedicates an entire Article (Article 1, of Question 2, in the First Part of the Summa) to his teaching that the existence of God is not self-evident. But that will change during the Era. God's existence, His love, His presence, and so many of His attributes will become self-evident to us. It is almost impossible to overestimate the effects this will have on the world, on salvation, and on sanctification. Jesus tells Luisa:

> My daughter, when my Will has Its Kingdom upon earth and souls live in It, Faith will no longer have any shadow, no more enigmas, but everything will be clarity and certainty. The light of my Volition will bring in the very created things the clear vision of their Creator; creatures will touch Him with their own hands in everything He has done for love of them. The human will is now a shadow to Faith; passions are clouds that obscure the clear light of It, and it happens as to the sun, when thick clouds form in the lower air: even though the sun is there, the clouds advance against the light, and it seems it is dark as if it were nighttime; and if one had never seen the sun, he would find it hard to believe that the sun is there. But if a mighty wind dispelled the clouds, who would dare to say that the sun does not exist, as they would touch its radiant light with their own hands? Such is the condition in which Faith finds Itself because my Will does not reign. They are almost like blind people that must believe others that a God exists. But when my Divine Fiat reigns, Its light will make them touch

the existence of their Creator with their own hands; therefore, it will no longer be necessary for others to say it—the shadows, the clouds, will exist no more." And while He was saying this, Jesus made a wave of joy and of light come out of His Heart, which will give more life to creatures; and with emphasis of love, He added: "How I long for the Kingdom of my Will. It will put an end to the troubles of creatures, and to Our sorrows. Heaven and earth will smile together; Our feasts and theirs will reacquire the order of the beginning of Creation; We will place a veil over everything, so that the feasts may never again be interrupted.[1146]

In this breathtaking teaching, Jesus assures Luisa that, just as a saintly soul even now is overwhelmed with knowledge and love of God merely upon observing His handiwork in creation, in the Era this proper reaction to the works of God will be automatic and universal. The analogy He uses is particularly helpful: clouds can so obscure the sky on some days that the outline of the sun is impossible to discern, and one who was "born yesterday" might even seek to deny its existence, despite the fact that even on this cloudy day he is still inundated by the effects of the sun. But who could deny the existence of the sun on a cloudless day?

As already stated—and most importantly—error pertaining to holy things will disappear. But ignorance in general will also largely die, since it is not the Will of God that we believe error about anything whatsoever. Jesus tells Luisa:

> Now, you must know that one who Lives in the Divine Will will reacquire, among so many prerogatives, **the Gift of Infused Science**; Gift that will be her guide in order to know Our Divine Being, that will facilitate for her the carrying out of the Kingdom of the Divine Fiat in her soul. It will be as Guide for her in the order of natural things. It will be like the Hand that guides her in everything and will make known the Palpitating Life of the Divine Volition in all created things, and the Good that It continuously brings her. **This Gift was given to Adam at the beginning of his Creation. Together with Our Divine Will he possessed the Gift of Infused Science, in a way that he knew Our Divine Truths with clarity. Not only this, but he knew all the Beneficial Virtues that all created things possessed for the Good of the creature, from the greatest thing**

---

even to the littlest blade of grass.

Now, as he rejected Our Divine Will by doing his own, Our Fiat withdrew Its Life and the Gift which he had been bearer of; therefore he remained in the dark without the True and Pure Light of the Knowledge of all things. **So with the return of the Life of My Will in the creature, Its Gift of Infused Science will return.** This Gift is inseparable from My Divine Will, as light is inseparable from heat, and where It Reigns It forms in the depth of the soul the eye full of Light such that, looking with this Divine Eye, she acquires the Knowledge of God and of created things for as much as is possible for a creature. Now My Will withdrawing, the eye remains blind, because It who animated the sight departed, that is to say, It is no longer the Operating Life of the creature.[1147]

This Gift of "infused science" will doubtless almost completely extinguish error of all sorts throughout the world; and such an extinguishing will not be isolated to some mere abstract intellectual good, for error generates all sorts of harms and the absence of error is a safeguard against these very harms.

Currently, the only way we can learn anything whatsoever is through the senses. Aristotle and Aquinas demonstrated this well—even the intellectual knowledge we possess which we might be tempted to think is purely abstract, can in fact quite easily be traced back chronologically to find its origin in something we received through our senses. Consequently, overcoming all error is a monumental task that is, even among the greatest scholars and greatest geniuses, never even remotely attained.

This limitation will end during the Era, and we will be able to once again receive truths from God directly infused into our intellects.

Multiplicity of Sanctities

If there is one thing that the Era will *not* resemble, that one thing would be Communism. In that diabolical system, a bland uniformity is foisted upon everyone. This artificial and institutionalized sameness is in stark contrast to God's designs, which are always varied in a beautiful way. Jesus tells Luisa, about what would have transpired on earth had man not fallen (and thus, consequently, what He will bring about on earth during the Era):

If the creature had not withdrawn from the Supreme Will… all would have been saints, but one distinct from the other—all beautiful, but varied, one more beautiful than the other. And according to the sanctity of each one, I was to communicate a distinct science; and with this science, some would know one attribute of their Creator more, some another. You must know that as much as We can give to the creature, she only takes the little drops of her Creator, so great is the distance between Creator and creatures; and We have always new and different things to give.

And besides, since Creation was created by Us so that We might delight in It, where would Our delight be, had We formed in the creature only one sanctity, or given only one beauty and only one knowledge of Our incomprehensible, immense and infinite Being? Our wisdom would have grown bored with doing only one thing. What would be said of Our wisdom, love and power, if in creating this terrestrial globe, We had made it all sky, or all earth, or all sea? What would Our glory have been? Instead, the multiplicity of so many things created by Us, while singing the praises of wisdom, love and power, speaks also of the variety of sanctity and beauty in which creatures were to arise, for love of whom they were created. See, the sky studded with stars is beautiful, but the sun also is beautiful, though they are distinct from each other, and the sky does one office, the sun, another. The sea is beautiful, but the flowery earth, the height of the mountains, the expanse of the plains also are beautiful, though the beauties and the offices are distinct among them. A garden is beautiful, but how many varieties of plants and beauties are in it? There is the tiny little flower, beautiful in its littleness; there is the violet, the rose, the lily—all beautiful, but distinct in color, in fragrance, in size. There is the little plant and the highest tree … What enchantment is a garden guided by an experienced gardener!

Now, my daughter, in the order of human nature also there will be some who will surpass the sky in sanctity and in beauty; some the sun, some the sea, some the flowery earth, some the height of the mountains, some the tiny little flower, some the little plant, and some the highest tree. And even if man should withdraw from my Will, I will multiply the centuries so as to have, in the human nature, all the order and the multiplicity of created things and of their beauty—and to have it even surpassed in a more admirable and enchanting way.

[1147] May 22, 1932.

In this beautiful teaching from Jesus, we also see an error corrected that some may fall into regarding the Gift; namely, that the Gift is a *single* sanctity that will simply replace all others. Far from it! It is more of a *category* of sanctity that in no way obliviates the varieties of beauty in the spiritual life that God has already generated. Instead, it will only preserve and multiple these varied beauties!

Physical and Bodily Transformation

We should know that this Era is not merely a matter of holy people thinking, saying, and doing holy things. Although the holiness of the Era is far and away its most important aspect, it would be foolish to ignore that there will be many glorious physical manifestations of these spiritual realities. Jesus tells Luisa:

> …[after the fall] the body also lost its freshness, its beauty. It became debilitated and remained subject to all evils, sharing in the evils of the human will, just as it had shared in the good. **So, if the human will is healed by giving it again the life of my Divine Will, as though by magic, all the evils of the human nature will have life no more**.[1148]

Too often we forget that all degradation—including physical—is the result of sin (even if indirect). Jesus even revealed this reality to St. Gertrude the Great. As we read in *The Life and Revelations of Saint Gertrude*, Jesus told this saint that:

> You can never understand all the reciprocal sweetness which My Divinity feels towards you… this movement of grace glorifies you, as My Body was glorified on Mount Thabor in presence of My three beloved disciples; so that I can say of you, in the sweetness of my charity: 'This is My beloved daughter, in whom I am well pleased.' For it is the property of this grace to communicate to the body as well as to the mind a marvelous glory and brightness.[1149]

This property of grace, though usually largely veiled on this side of the Era, will freely flow between the physical and the spiritual upon the dawn of the same. Jesus' state of Transfiguration on Mount Tabor was natural; it was how He should have always looked. One could fairly say that Tabor was the norm; the rest of His public ministry was the exception. So too Adam, before the fall, resembled Christ Transfigured.

Duly revealing the natural connection between grace and nature even to St. Gertrude, Jesus reveals more fully to Luisa that this will indeed be the visible reality during the Era:

> Then, yes!, will the prodigies that my Volition knows how to do, and can do, be seen. Everything will be transformed… my Will will make greater display, so much so, as to form a new enchantment of prodigious beauties never before seen, for the whole of Heaven and for all the earth.[1150]

He also told her:

> So, once the Divine Will and the human are placed in harmony, giving dominion and regime to the Divine, as it is wanted by Us, **the human nature loses the sad effects and remains as beautiful as it came out of Our creative hands**. Now, in the Queen of Heaven, all Our work was on Her human will, which received with joy the dominion of Ours; and Our Will, finding no opposition on Her part, operated prodigies of graces, and by virtue of my Divine Volition, She remained sanctified and did not feel the sad effects and the evils which the other creatures feel. Therefore, **my daughter, once the cause is removed, the effects end**. Oh! if my Divine Will enters into creatures and reigns in them, It will banish all evils in them, and will communicate to them all goods—to soul and body.[1151]

> My daughter, you must know that the body did nothing evil, but all the evil was done by the human will. Before sinning, Adam possessed the complete life of my Divine Will in his soul; one can say that he was filled to the brim with It, **to the extent that It overflowed outside. So, by virtue of my Will, the human will transfused light outside, and emitted the fragrances of its Creator -fragrances of beauty, of sanctity and of full health; fragrances of purity, of strength, which came out from within his will like many luminous clouds. And the body was so embellished by these exhalations, that it was delightful to see him beautiful, vigorous, luminous, so very healthy, with an enrapturing grace…**[after the fall, the body] became debilitated and remained subject to all evils,

---

[1148]July 7, 1928.
[1149] *The Life and Revelations of Saint Gertrude*. "By a religious of the order of Poor Clares." 1865. Page 150.
[1150] June 9, 1929.

[1151] July 30, 1929.

sharing in all the evils of the human will, just as it had shared in the good… So, **if the human will is healed by receiving again the life of my Divine Will, all the evils of the human nature will have life no more, as if by, magic**.[1152]

Obviously there is no "magic" happening here; Jesus says that these physical transformations will occur "as if by" magic because of how rapid and substantial they will be, and because it will be difficult for us at first to see how they transpired, until we grow in our understanding that it is not normal or natural for such glorious spiritual goods to fail to have the physical realm correspond to them.

Audible Celestial Music

What even the ancient Greek philosophers knew intuitively—that the heavenly bodies, so beautiful and harmonious in their motion, could not merely be moving with such perfection in vain, but rather constitute in their motion a veritable symphony—will be realized openly by all; not by mere philosophy, but sensibly. This ancient intuition is referred to as the Music of the Spheres, and Jesus tells Luisa that we will hear it:

> **The Creation, echo of the Celestial Fatherland, contains music, the royal march**, the spheres, the heavens, the sun, the sea, and all possess order and perfect harmony among themselves, and they go around continuously. This order, this harmony and this going around, without ever stopping, **form such admirable symphony and music, that it could be said to be like the breath of the Supreme Fiat blowing into all created things like many musical instruments, and forming the most beautiful of all melodies, such that, if creatures could hear it, they would remain ecstatic. Now, <u>the Kingdom of the Supreme Fiat will have the echo of the music of the Celestial Fatherland and the echo of the music of Creation</u>.** The order, the harmony and their continuous going around their Creator will be such and so great, that each one of their acts, words and steps will be a distinct melody, like many different musical instruments which will receive the breath of the Divine Volition, in such a way that everything they do will be as many

distinct musical concerts which will form the joy and the continuous feast of the Kingdom of the Divine Fiat… Then Our work of Creation will sing victory and full triumph, and We will have three Kingdoms in one—symbol of the Sacrosanct Trinity, because all Our works carry the mark of the One who created them."[1153]

Death as Mere Transition

Because life in the Era is so close to Heaven (as is life for one who even now lives in the Divine Will), it is scarcely even an exile, but more of a happy pilgrimage; and the return to the Heavenly Fatherland—that is, death—is a smooth and glorious thing:

> My daughter… for one who lives in [the Divine Will], [earth is] …but one step of distance, such that, when one least expects it, once that step is made, she will find herself in the Celestial Fatherland, not like one who comes from the exile, who knows nothing about it, but like one who already knew that it belonged to her, and who knew the beauty, the sumptuousness, the happiness of the Eternal City. My Will could not tolerate keeping one who lives in It in the condition of an exiled one; in order to do this, It should change Its nature, and the regimen which exists between one who lives in It in Heaven and one who lives in It on earth—which It cannot do, nor does It want to. Is it perhaps called exile when one goes out of his home to move just one step away from it? Certainly not. Or, can it be called exile if one goes to a town within his own homeland? [1154]

Similarly, Jesus tells Luisa:

> Death will no longer have power in the soul; and if it will have it over the body, **it will not be death,[1155] but transit.** Without the nourishment of sin and a degraded human will that produced corruption in the bodies, and with the preserving nourishment of My Will, **the bodies also will not be subject to decomposing and becoming so horribly corrupted as to strike fear even into the strongest ones, as it happens now; but they will remain composed in their sepulchers, waiting for the day of the resurrection of all …** The Kingdom of the Divine Fiat will make the great

---

[1152] July 7, 1928.

[1153] January 28, 1927.

[1154] October 10, 1927.

[1155] That is, the smoothness of it will be so different from how most deaths today occur that it can scarcely be called "death" when compared – even though it still technically will entail the same result: the soul departing from the body. Luisa's

own death is no doubt the example par excellence here, where there was perfect peace, and for days they could not tell if she had even died (see the details in the chapter on Luisa's life).

miracle of banishing all evils, all miseries, all fears, because It will not perform a miracle at time and circumstance, but will keep the children of Its Kingdom with Itself with an act of continuous miracle, to preserve them from any evil, and let them be distinguished as the children of Its Kingdom. This, in the souls; but also in the body there will be many modifications, because it is always sin that is the nourishment of all evils. Once sin is removed, there will be no nourishment for evil; more so, since My Will and sin cannot exist together, therefore the human nature also will have its beneficial effects.[1156]

All Catholics know that many saints are perfectly incorrupt; their bodies lie in their tombs without showing the slightest hint of decay and giving off nothing but a pleasant aroma. This is how all death will transpire during the Era.

Abundance of All Goods

Jesus tells Luisa:

… poverty, unhappiness, needs and evils will be banished from the children of my Will. It would not be decorous for my Will, so immensely rich and happy, to have children who would lack something, and would not enjoy all the opulence of Its goods which arise continuously.

Therefore, each one will possess the fullness of goods and full happiness in the place in which the Supreme Will has placed him; whatever the condition and the office they will occupy, all will be happy of their destiny…[1157]

But the abundance of the Kingdom of the Divine Will, of course, will be nothing like the abundance now seen in the rich men of the earth. It was precisely this distortion that inspired St. Augustine to condemn the millenarians of his day who followed Cerinthus' carnal views of what was to come. Material abundance, sadly, usually corrupts souls today; inclining those who have it towards a life lived in accord with the desires of the flesh, the lust of the eyes, and the pride of life.[1158] It will not be so in the Kingdom of the Divine Will, where all will be able to say, with St. Paul:

I know how to be abased, and I know how to abound; in any and all circumstances I have learned the secret of facing plenty and hunger, abundance and want.[1159]

Reiterating and expounding upon this Pauline teaching, Jesus tells Luisa:

In fact, wherever My Divine Will reigns, there is no fear that natural means and abundance of goods might do harm; on the contrary, the more means she has and the more abundance she enjoys, the more she looks at the power, the goodness, the richness of the Supreme Fiat in them, and she converts everything into most pure gold of Divine Will. [1160]

So indeed, Jesus teaches Luisa that the Era will be full of abundance, but above all this abundance is of *people*; while not excluding also all the goods they need. Jesus compares this abundance to the joy of a family blessed with many children, as opposed to the earth today, which more resembles a miserable sterile couple:

You must know that Our adorable Majesty, in forming the Creation, established that every place was to be populated by inhabitants, and that the earth was to be extremely fertile and rich with many plants, in such a way that all would have in abundance. As man sinned, he attracted the indignation of divine justice, and the earth remained deserted, infertile, and in many places depopulated—image of those sterile families in which there is no laughter, no feast, no harmony, because they are without children, and so there is no one who breaks the monotony of the two spouses and the nightmare of isolation weighs on their hearts leading them to sadness. Such was the human family. On the other hand, where there are children, there is always something to do, something to say, and occasions to celebrate. Look at the sky—how populated with stars it is; the earth was to be the echo of the sky, crammed with inhabitants, and it was to produce so much and to render everyone rich and happy. As man withdrew from my Will, his lot changed; and I wanted to go into the desert in order to call back the blessings of my Celestial Father and, by calling my Will to reign, restore the earth, populate it everywhere and fecundate it, in such a way that the earth will produce more seeds, and more beautiful ones, such as to increase it a hundredfold, rendering it more fecund and of radiant beauty. How many great things will do the Kingdom of my Divine Fiat! So much so, that all the elements are all in waiting the Sun, the wind, the sea, the earth and the whole Creation— to deliver from their womb all the goods and

---

[1156] October 22, 1926.
[1157] January 28, 1927.
[1158] Cf. 1 John 2:16

[1159] Philippians 4:12
[1160] January 28, 1927.

effects which they contain. In fact, since the Divine Will that dominates them does not reign in the midst of creatures, they do not put out all the goods which they enclose within them, giving them only what they have to as alms, and as to servants. So, the earth has not produced all the seeds; the Sun, not finding all the seeds, does not produce all the effects and goods It contains; and so with all the rest. This is why all await the Kingdom of the Fiat—to show creatures how rich they are, and how many admirable things the Creator has placed in them for love of the ones who were to be the children of His Will.[1161]

In this particularly profound teaching, Jesus tells Luisa that the "elements are all in waiting" in order to "deliver from their womb all the goods and effects which they contain." We can only wonder at the full glory this might entail. Suffice it to say that many of the assumptions we have made about the limits of what "the elements" (that is, nature in general) can give us are doubtless incorrect.

I speculate that the sun will give us far more energy; this, in turn, will give plants what would now seem to be explosive growth. But the plants that do receive this explosive growth will be precisely the ones which most benefit us: trees that produce the highest quality wood for construction, vegetation that produces the healthiest foods in abundance, etc. The very air (as Jesus says in this quote, the "wind") will likely deliver far higher concentrations of Oxygen and Carbon Dioxide instead of the not-as-useful Nitrogen that now composes the majority of the air we breathe.

Animals—in addition to reacquiring their natural obedience to man, such that all will automatically behave like the best of domesticated dogs now act—particularly those most known for service to man, like draft horses, will be far more powerful. Natural oils (e.g. olive oil) will produce drastically more heat and light than they now do. Add all these effects together and you have a situation that renders most of our modern technology superfluous. This recognition, in turn, can answer the conundrum some face regarding technology: will we have it in the Era? Well, I suppose we will have the ability for it, but I cannot see us often bothering with it. Even now, no one would bother with a tractor or a car if oxen and horses were twice as strong, twice as fast, effort-free to raise, and perfectly obedient to man. Even now, no one would

bother with any medical technology if we already enjoyed health. Even now, we would not bother with such communication-technology-obsession if we were delivered from that subtle fear, in the back of our minds, that those with whom we wish to "keep in touch" might not make it to Heaven, where we will have all eternity to keep in touch with them.

Returning to the previous issue, some may question why animals would change so much in this coming Era—as it is not as if they themselves are sinning now and depriving the earth of the Divine Will; that is entirely man's fault. But the fact is that man, as head of all creation, determines the fate of the rest of all creation. As he fell; creation too fell even though it shared none of the guilt.

But since Jesus and Mary lived perfectly in the Divine Will, nature itself automatically wanted to serve them, as was the purpose of nature from the beginning; many today forget, especially the so-called "environmentalists," that the entire universe was made for the sake of man.

About His own earthly life, Jesus tells Luisa:

> And in fact, when it was needed, at a little wish of Ours [Jesus and Mary], even the birds served Us, bringing Us fruits, fish and other things in their beaks, making feast because they were serving their Creator and their Queen. With their trilling, singing and warbling, they played for Us the most beautiful melodies; so much so, that in order not to attract the attention of creatures with Our uniqueness, We had to command them to depart, to continue their flight under the vault of the heavens where Our Will was waiting for them; and, obedient, they would withdraw.[1162]

Although in Christ all things see their Creator, it is also true that in any soul who lives in the Divine Will, physical creation sees its master. This is the state to which nature will return.

**

Ultimately, however, it seems impossible to deny that, most generally and broadly, humans want one thing: happiness. Everything else is done for the sake of happiness, and happiness itself is not sought for the sake of anything else. Summing up, therefore, the preceding sections on the glory of the Era, we can consider more generally the happiness of the Era.

[1161] June 25, 1928.

[1162] January 28, 1927.

Universal Happiness

Jesus tells Luisa:

> My daughter, look at how beautiful is the order of the heavens. In the same way, when the Kingdom of the Divine Will will have Its dominion on earth in the midst of creatures, also on earth there will be perfect and beautiful order…Just as all created things, so will all the children of the Kingdom of the Supreme Fiat have their place of honor, of decorum and of dominion; and while possessing the order of heaven and, more than celestial spheres, being in perfect harmony among themselves, the abundance of goods which each one will possess will be such and so great, that one will never have need of the other—**each one will have within himself the source of the goods of his Creator and of His perennial happiness. Therefore, poverty, unhappiness, needs and evils will be banished from the children of my Will**. It would not be decorous for my Will, so immensely rich and happy, to have children who would lack something, and would not enjoy all the opulence of Its goods which arise continuously. [1163]

Jesus also tells Luisa:

> … [during the Era, creatures] will move on to enjoy the fruits of the "Fiat Voluntas Tua" on earth as it is in Heaven, as well as the lost happiness, the dignity and nobility, the peace all celestial, which by doing his will, man had made disappear from the face of the earth. Greater grace I could not give him, because by placing him again in relation with my Will, I give back to him all the goods with which I endowed him in creating him. [1164]

We recall from the chapter on the authenticity of Luisa's revelations, that Luisa herself had all the same doubts and difficulties that many of her critics today express. She was especially confused about how the coming Kingdom of the Divine Will could cause a universal degree of happiness that not even Redemption immediately caused. In one diary entry, we see the following exchange:

> [Luisa says:] 'My Love, if with your Redemption not all are saved, how can it be that your Will will give this happiness to all?' And Jesus: "Man will always be free, I will never take away from him the rights which I gave him in creating him; only, in Redemption I came to open many ways, small

paths and shortcuts to facilitate salvation, the sanctity of man, while with my Will I come to open the royal and straight way which leads to the sanctity of the likeness of their Creator, and which contains true happiness. But in spite of this, they will always be free to remain—some on the royal way, some on the small paths, and some completely outside; however, in the world there will be what now is not—the happiness of the Fiat Voluntas Tua on earth as It is in Heaven. [1165]

In other words, the Kingdom of the Divine Will on earth is not some type of Divinely governed communism where bland sameness is instituted across the people! Far from it. Just as even now there are many degrees of holiness within God's holy people, so, too, this will be the case during the Era. Happiness in general will reign thanks to the Divine Will; but this happiness will be enjoyed in many ways, to different degrees by the people during the Era—depending upon the response of each.

Now, this happiness will be complete in a terrestrial sense; but as we have discussed in these pages, that does not mean it has attained its final and full perfection. Happiness, during the Era, will be everything that happiness was supposed to be on earth. But this earthly happiness, in turn, was created by God to enliven our desire for the Eternal, Heavenly Beatitude, to which our relatively minor happiness now points.

Therefore, during the Era our happiness will indeed be immense, but it will also involve a triumphant longing for Heaven—a longing that will, perhaps paradoxically, be another source of joy. Even now, any serious Christian can doubtless recall that his moments of greatest happiness were precisely in the moments he most hoped for, longed for, and meditated upon Heaven. That will be doubly true during the Era: we will be much closer to Heaven, but this proximity will only make our ardent longing for it even more inflamed.

Sacramental Reign

We end this section with what is perhaps the most crucial point; a point we have broached in a number of other sections within different contexts. Contrary to the various Dispensationalist and Joachimist heresies,[1166] Jesus makes it clear to Luisa

---

[1163] January 28, 1927.
[1164] August 13, 1923.
[1165] April 25, 1923.

[1166] That is, those eschatologies which proceed from the "spiritual legacy of Joachim of Fiore"

that this Era entails the *Triumph* of the Church, not its passing away—the Sacraments being received finally with all their power realized, not the Sacraments ending or no longer being received.

Jesus tells Luisa:

> The Kingdom of my Will will be the true echo of the Celestial Fatherland, in which, while the Blessed possess their God as their own life, they receive Him into themselves also from the outside. So, inside and outside of themselves, Divine Life they possess, and Divine Life they receive. **What will not be my happiness in giving Myself sacramentally to the children of the Eternal Fiat, and in finding my own Life in them? Then will my Sacramental Life have Its complete fruit; and as the species are consumed, I will no longer have the sorrow of leaving my children** without the food of my continuous Life, because my Will, more than sacramental accidents, will maintain Its Divine Life always with Its full possession. In the Kingdom of my Will there will be neither foods nor communions that are interrupted—but perennial; and **everything I did in Redemption will serve no longer as remedy, but as delight, as joy, as happiness, and as beauty ever growing. So, the triumph of the Supreme Fiat will give complete fruit to the Kingdom of Redemption.**[1167]

Although Joachim of Fiore had some genuine insights, his primary mistake was that of supposing that the so-called "Age of the Spirit" will come and *replace* the "Age of the Son." In fact, as Jesus tells Luisa, the opposite is true: the coming Era entails the complete fruit of Redemption itself finally being borne. It entails the Faithful receiving the Sacraments not merely as medicine for the sick (as most Catholics now receive them), but as food for the healthy—as a saint even now receives them.

Hastening the Coming Reign of the Divine Will

Now that we have some faint idea of how glorious the coming Era will be—how it truly constitutes the Reign of the Divine Will on earth as in Heaven—I am hopeful that all who have read thus far are burning with a holy desire to hasten its arrival. Let us all ensure, therefore, that we never allow this desire to lie stagnant in our hearts; let us, instead, always act upon it.

Much of the effort involved in hastening this coming Era is the same as that involved in "being a New Evangelist of the Third Fiat," so I encourage anyone looking for more practical guidelines to turn again to that chapter.

In order to further ennoble this desire to hasten the coming Reign, we should consider several more teachings related to the Era that Jesus gives to Luisa.

> **Redemption and the Kingdom of my Will are one single thing, inseparable from each other.** My coming upon earth came to form the Redemption of man, and at the same time it came to form the Kingdom of my Will in order to save Myself, to take back my rights which by justice are due to Me as Creator…Now, when it seemed that everything was over and my enemies were satisfied for they had taken my life, my power which has no limits called my Humanity back to life, and by rising again, everything rose together with Me—the creatures, my pains, the goods acquired for their sake. And as my Humanity triumphed over death, so did my Will rise again and triumph in the creatures, waiting for Its Kingdom… It was my Resurrection that made Me known for Who I was, and placed the seal over all the goods that I came to bring upon earth. In the same way, my Divine Will will be the double seal, the transmission into creatures of Its Kingdom, which my Humanity possessed. More so, since it was for the creatures that I formed this Kingdom of my Divine Will within my Humanity. Why not give It then? At the most, it will be a matter of time, and for Us the times are one single point; Our power will make such prodigies, lavishing upon man new graces, new love, new light, that Our dwellings will recognize Us, and they themselves, of their own spontaneous will, will give Us dominion. So will Our life be placed in safety, with its full rights in the creature. With time you will see what my power knows how to do and can do, how it can conquer everything and knock down the most obstinate rebels. Who can ever resist my power, such that with one single breath, I knock down, I destroy and I redo everything, as I best please? **Therefore, you—pray, and let your cry be continuous: 'May the Kingdom of your Fiat come, and your Will be done on earth as It is in Heaven.'**[1168]

Jesus is asking us that our cry be continuous. We must have such longing for this Kingdom that we cannot bear to stop begging God for it. And how do we beg God for it? By the primary petition of the

---

[1167] November 2, 1926.

[1168] May 31, 1935.

Lord's Prayer. Be zealous in praying the Our Father; each one recited hastens the coming of the Kingdom. Jesus tells Luisa:

> There are those who water this seed in order to make it grow—each 'Our Father' that is recited serves to water it; there are my manifestations in order to make it known. **All that is needed are those who would offer themselves to be the criers**—and with courage, without fearing anything, facing sacrifices in order to make it known. So, the substantial part is there—the greatest is there; the minor is needed—that is, the superficial part, and your Jesus will know how to make His way in order to find the one who will accomplish the mission of making known my Divine Will in the midst of the peoples.[1169]

Jesus here say to Luisa that the only thing needed to cause the arrival of this glorious Kingdom is people who will be the unshakably courageous criers of its coming. The whole Kingdom is already formed! Jesus already did the hard part with Luisa decades ago. All we need to do is pick the fruit. But what is needed is people like you to proclaim this Kingdom.

Furthermore, hastening the coming of the Kingdom is the most noble effort one can undertake; completely immune from the various ulterior motives that so often sneak into many other holy endeavors. Jesus tells Luisa that, in so doing:

> You seek nothing for yourself, and you go round and round, asking over and over again that My Divine Will be known, and that It dominate and reign. **Not a shadow of what is human enters into this, nor any personal interest; it is the holiest and most Divine prayer and act; it is prayer of Heaven**, not of the earth, and therefore the purest, the most beautiful, the invincible one, that encloses only the interest of the Divine Glory. [1170]

We must show God that we want this Kingdom, so that His bestowal of it consists in His answering our ardent prayers. Jesus tells Luisa:

> If a king or the leader of a country must be elected, there are those who incite the people to cry out: 'We want such and such as king, or such and such as the leader of our country.' If some want a war, they make the people cry out: 'We want the war.' There is not one important thing that is done in a kingdom, for which some do not resort to the people, to make it cry out and even tumult, so as to give themselves a reason and say: 'It is the people that wants it.' And many times, while the people says it wants something, it does not know what it wants, nor the good or sad consequences that will come. If they do this in the low world, much more do I, when I must give important things, universal goods, want entire peoples to ask Me for them. And you must form these peoples—first, by making all the knowledges about my Divine Fiat known; second, by going around everywhere, moving Heaven and earth to ask for the Kingdom of my Divine Will."[1171]

Jesus will give us this Kingdom; but He is waiting for the moment that its bestowal can truly be said to be a loving response to an earnest request from His beloved children, in order for it to not be in any way an imposition. **And if you never, ever give up, Jesus will not know how to deny you what you seek:**

> Firmness, faithfulness, unshakeability in good and in asking for the good known, can be called divine virtues, not human, and therefore it would be like denying to Ourselves what the creature asks from Us.[1172]

> Firmness in asking is the assurance that the gift is yours. And asking for the Kingdom of my Divine Will for all, is the prelude that others can receive the great gift of my Supreme Fiat. Therefore, continue to repeat, and do not tire."[1173]

Jesus even describes this plea of ours to hasten the coming of the Kingdom as a noble and glorious "fight" that we engage in with Him. This is highly mystical and symbolic language: but if we approach it correctly, it is edifying and helpful. Let us then read how Jesus describes this fight to Luisa so that we may better engage in it ourselves:

> … together with you fights all the strength contained in the heavens, in the sun, in the water, in the wind, in the sea; **they all wage battle on Me. They do it with Me to make Me surrender the Kingdom of the Divine Fiat**; they do it with creatures with the weapons which each created thing has in its power, to make them surrender to recognizing my Will, so that creatures may let It reign as they themselves let It reign. And wanting to win, they all have placed themselves as though in order for battle; and seeing that creatures resist, wanting to win by all means, because they have

---

[1169] August 25, 1929.
[1170] August 12, 1927.
[1171] May 30, 1928.

[1172] October 7, 1930.
[1173] March 24, 1930.

with them the strength of that Will which animates them and dominates them, with the weapons they possess they knock down people and cities, with such empire that no one can resist them. You cannot comprehend all the strength and power that all the elements contain; it is such that, if my Will did not keep them as though restrained, the battle would be so fierce that they would make a heap of the earth.

Now, their strength is also yours; therefore, you — go around in their midst to put them in order for battle; let your acts, your continuous asking for the Kingdom of the Supreme Fiat, call all Creation to stand at attention. And my Will, moving within It, places all of Its acts in royal office in order to give and to win Its Kingdom in the midst of creatures. Therefore, it is my Volition Itself that fights — that wages battle with my very Will for the triumph of Its Kingdom. So, your fight is animated by It, which has sufficient and irresistible strength in order to win. **Therefore, go ahead and fight, for you will win; and besides, to fight in order to win the Kingdom of the Supreme Fiat is the holiest fight that can exist; it is <u>the most just and most rightful battle that can be fought.</u> This is so true, that my Will Itself began this battle and this fight as It formed the Creation; and only when It wins completely — then will It surrender.**

But do you want to know when you fight with Me and I with you? I fight when I manifest to you the knowledges about my Eternal Fiat. So, each saying, each knowledge, each simile about It is one fight and one battle that I make with you in order to win your will, put it in its place, created by Us, and call it, almost by dint of fighting, into the order of the Kingdom of my Divine Volition; and as I do it with you in order to subdue your will, I start it in the midst of creatures. I fight with you when I teach you the way which you must follow, what you must do in order to live in my Kingdom, and the happiness, the joys, which you will possess. In sum, I fight by dint of light, which my knowledges contain; I fight by dint of love and by the most touching examples, in such a way that you cannot resist my fight; I fight by means of promises of happiness and joy without end. My fight is persistent, nor do I ever become tired — but to win what? Your will, and in yours, those who will recognize Mine in order to live in my Kingdom. And you fight with Me when you receive my knowledges, and placing them in order in your soul, you form the Kingdom of my Supreme Fiat within you; and fighting with Me,

you try to win my Kingdom. Each one of your acts done in my Will is a fight that you make with Me. **In each round you do through all created things, to unite yourself to all the acts that my Will does in all Creation, you call all Creation to wage battle in order to win my Kingdom, moving my very Will dominating in all created things, so as to wage battle on my Will Itself in order to establish Its Kingdom.**

This is why, in these times, the wind, the water, the sea, the earth, the heavens, are all in motion more than ever, waging battle against creatures as new phenomena occur — and how many more will occur — destroying people and cities: because in battles it is necessary to dispose oneself to suffer losses, and many times also on the part of the winner. There have never been conquests of kingdoms without battle, and if there have been, they have not been lasting ones…Therefore, I fight with you, and you fight with Me. This fight is necessary — to you, in order to win my Kingdom; and to Me, in order to win your will and to begin the battle in the midst of creatures, so as to establish the Kingdom of my Supreme Will. I have my own Will, and all of Its very Power, Strength and Immensity in order to win; you have my Will Itself at your disposal, all Creation and all the good I did in Redemption, in order to launch a formidable army to wage battle and win the Kingdom of the Supreme Fiat. See, each word you write is also a fight that you make with Me — one more soldier that joins the army, which must win the Kingdom of my Will. Therefore, be attentive, my daughter, for these are times of fight, and it is necessary to use all means in order to win."[1174]

This amazing teaching that Jesus gives to Luisa needs no explanation, but it should be read many times, for each successive reading will cause to flourish in your heart a love for partaking in this most epic and glorious battle to win the Kingdom of the Divine Will.

Know, too, that in hastening the coming of the Kingdom, you are entering into the most holy and joyous endeavor with the very saints in Heaven. Like good friends competing in a sport, you and they are both endeavoring zealously to see who can do more to hasten the arrival of this reign on earth (for the souls in Heaven want this reign even more than the souls on earth do; due to the latter often being subject to doubts and short-sightedness). Jesus tells Luisa:

[1174] February 19, 1927.

So, the circular from earth echoes the celestial circular, and Heaven and earth move, occupying themselves with the one purpose of the Kingdom of My Divine Will… It seems that Heaven and earth hold hands and compete with each other, to see who hastens more to prepare a Kingdom so holy.[1175]

And this is not only the ardent desire of the saints in Heaven, but it was the same of Jesus Himself; both now in Heaven and in His time on earth. He tells Luisa:

> My daughter, as God there didn't exist in me any desire… however as man I had my desires… **if I prayed and cried and desired it was only for my kingdom that I wanted in the midst of creatures,** because He being the holiest thing, my Humanity could do no less (than) to want and to desire the holiest thing in order to sanctify the desires of everyone and give them that which was holy and of the greatest and perfect good for them.[1176]

He also says:

> …**the first indispensable necessity** in order to obtain the Kingdom of the Divine **Will is to ask for It with Incessant prayers**… [the] **Second necessity**, more indispensable than the first, in order to obtain this Kingdom: it is necessary **to know that one can have It**. Who can ever think of a Good, desire it, love it, if he does not know that he can obtain it? No one. If the Ancients had not known that the future Redeemer was to come, no one would have given it a thought, nor prayed, nor hoped for salvation, because the salvation, the sanctity of those times, was fixed-centralized in the future Celestial Savior. Outside of this there was no good to be hoped for. To know that one can have a Good forms the Substance, the Life, the nourishment of that Good in the creature. Here is the reason for the so many Knowledges about My Will that I have manifested to you-that it may be known that they can have the Kingdom of My Will. When it is known that a Good can be possessed, arts and industriousness are used, and the means to obtain the intent are employed…The **third necessary means is to know that God wants to give this Kingdom.** This lays the foundations, the sure Hope in order to obtain It, and forms the final preparations in order to receive the Kingdom of My Divine Will …[1177]

Yes, God wants to give this Kingdom even more than we want to receive it. Now, with all this effort put into hastening the coming of the Kingdom, it is only natural that waiting to see the fruits will be difficult. But we should remind ourselves that, in a way, **it is "harder" for Jesus—for He desires this even more than we do, and the difficulty of the wait is always proportional to the desire for the thing for which one is waiting.** Jesus tells Luisa:

> But my greatest pain is the continuous waiting. My gazes are always fixed on souls, and I see that one creature has fallen into sin, and I wait and wait for her return to my Heart, to forgive her; and not seeing her coming, I wait with the forgiveness in my hands. That waiting renews my pain and forms such torment for Me as to make Me pour out Blood and flames from my pieced Heart. The hours, the days that I wait seem like years to Me. Oh! how hard it is to wait.[1178]

How paradoxically refreshing these words are to hear! For we are all so used to being reminded that, for God, "a thousand years is like a day," and indeed that is true. But this is not the whole story! And when we only hear this partial account, we are tempted to have thoughts something like, "*Oh, how depressing it is to remember that God is timeless and thus not subject to all of my restless impatience in desiring the fulfillment of His promises. I might as well just put this on the backburner, since it clearly won't come about any time soon.*" We must perish such thoughts! If every month that passes without the Kingdom on earth seems like a year to you, then it seems like a millennium to Jesus. Perhaps there is nothing more powerful we could do, therefore, to console His Sacred Heart, than to hasten the coming of this Kingdom.

***

Let us now consider some concrete steps we can take to hasten the coming of the Kingdom. Above all, its hastening is a matter of living in the Divine Will and being a New Evangelist of the Third Fiat in general (see the chapter with that title for more ideas). But there are also some measures we can take that are directed specifically towards the coming of the Kingdom:

- Whenever confronted with sin, error, or ugliness, cry out for the coming of the Kingdom as a just lamentation over what you are witnessing. Considering the nature of the world today, simply adopting this approach alone will make your "cry be continuous," as Jesus

[1175] May 20, 1928.
[1176] January 29, 1928.
[1177] March 20, 1932.
[1178] July 21, 1935.

asks of us. Remember, as Scripture says, that righteous Lot was *"…greatly distressed by the licentiousness of the wicked (for by what that righteous man saw and heard as he lived among them, he was vexed in his righteous soul day after day with their lawless deeds)…"*[1179] The so-called "power of positive thinking" is no virtue; it is spiritual blindness. Being joyful and peaceful people—as we must be as Christians, as Catholics, and as children of the Divine Will—does not preclude being appropriately dismayed by evil when we witness it; so long as we respond to such situations with this hopeful plea for the Kingdom.

- Make a list—mental or physical—of things that you are tempted to be annoyed about in the modern world; things to which you are frequently subjected. Perhaps these will be things in your neighborhood, at your job, in your commute, or elsewhere. Firmly commit to begging God for the coming of the Kingdom every time you are so subjected.[1180]

- Whenever confronted with goodness, truth, or beauty, cry out for the Kingdom as a blessing of God's Will in what you are witnessing, and a petition that it soon come on earth in its full glory for all to see and live in.

- Turn all the crosses in your life into pleas for the coming of the Kingdom.

- Till the soil by building up the Kingdom in whatever apostolates and works of mercy God has called you to.[1181] Although (contrary to the various progressive ascendency heresies; e.g. liberation theology) these efforts will not themselves generate the Kingdom on earth, they are nevertheless important preparations, just as a farmer who tills the soil knows that his

own work, while necessary, is radically and infinitely beneath the mysterious processes created by God wherein a seed becomes a plant and bears fruit.

***

Now we turn our attention to remind ourselves of the guaranteed arrival of this Kingdom, so that our zeal in hastening it may never waver.

It's Coming is a Guarantee

Perhaps the best way to ensure we are doing everything we can to hasten the Coming of the Kingdom is to remind ourselves constantly of the certainty of victory. For many are at some point tempted to doubt this victory; all it takes is a brief look at the world under the aspect of merely human analysis. Since our physical eyes are capable of only seeing these appearances, we must be on guard against the temptation to despair of the Coming of the Kingdom that they will regularly foist upon us. Under such superficial analysis, the Reign of the Divine Will on earth appears to be a downright impossibility, and the doubt this analysis generates will in turn put a damper on our zeal in fighting for the Kingdom, which then will delay its coming. So we must not allow our zeal to slacken through discouragement.

Of course, we also do not want our reminders of the certainty of victory to breed laxity in our hearts; although it is guaranteed to come, the time of its arrival is not guaranteed, but rather depends upon our response—and **the proximity of its arrival is proportional to the number of souls which will be saved from eternal damnation by its arrival**. So indeed, we must be zealous.

[1179] 2 Peter 2:7-8

[1180] For me, one such thing is tractor-trailer engine braking (or "jake braking"); a practice that should be outlawed except where absolutely necessary (e.g. while driving down mountainous slopes). Large trucks have "engine brakes," which slow the truck down without having to wear down brake pads, but at the expense of generating a thunderous, eardrum-shattering noise, which some truck drivers seem to take pleasure in, thus destroying the peace of entire neighborhoods. Since I live near a highway intersection, I hear this all the time. Instead of allowing myself to constantly grow aggravated at this practice, I try to always remember to beg God for the coming of the Kingdom each time I have to hear it – for I am sure there will be no engine-braking in the Kingdom!

[1181] At this point, I feel the need to add that one cannot hasten the coming of the Kingdom by simply wishing it; that is, by

pretending the Fall of Man never occurred, and proceeding to act in accord with this mindset. For there is no negligible amount of people today who seem to think that if only we stop using pesticides, pasteurization, refinement, vaccines, and any agricultural technology, then the Garden of Eden will magically reappear in our midst. Now, the merits or demerits of each of these things must be determined by the qualified experts in their respective fields (not by overzealous bloggers who have done a few Google searches), and however this expert determination transpires, one thing is certain: seeking, through technology and other means, to help limit some of the tragic consequences of the Fall is not only not wrong, but is actually demanded (at least in general) by the moral law.

Let us, then, remind ourselves of the guaranteed nature of its coming by reviewing several teachings Jesus gives to Luisa:

> We never do useless things. Do you think that the many truths We have manifested to you about Our Will with so much love will not bear their fruit and will not form their lives within souls? Not at all. If We have issued them, it is because **We know with certainty that they will indeed bear their fruit and will establish the Kingdom of Our Will in the midst of creatures.** If not today—because it seems to them that it isn't food adaptable for them, and perhaps they even despise what could form Divine Life in them—the time will come when they will compete to see who can get to know these truths more. By knowing them, they will love them; love will render them food adaptable for them, and in this way my truths will form the life that they will offer to them. Therefore, do not be concerned—it is a matter of time.[1182]

Jesus also said:

> Now, if the farmer, in spite of all the difficulties of the earth, can hope and receive an abundant harvest, much more can I do it, Celestial Farmer, having issued from my divine womb many seeds of celestial truths, to sow them in the depth of your soul; and from the harvest I will fill the whole world. Would you, then, think that because of the doubts and difficulties of some—some, like earth without moisture, and some like thick and hardened earth—I would not have my superabundant harvest? My daughter, you are mistaken! Time, people, circumstances, change, and what today may appear black, tomorrow may appear white; in fact, many times they see according to the predispositions they have, and according to the long or short sight that the intellect possesses. Poor ones, one must pity them. But **everything is in the fact that I already did the sowing; the most necessary thing, the most substantial, the most interesting, was to manifest my truths. If I have done my work, the main part has been set in place, I have found your earth in order to sow my seed—the rest will come by itself.**[1183]

On another occasion in which Luisa expressed a doubt about the coming of the Kingdom, we see the following exchange between Jesus and Luisa:

> But while I thought this, I said to myself: "But who knows who will see when this Kingdom of the Divine Fiat will come? O! how difficult it seems." And my beloved Jesus, making me His brief little visit, told me: <u>"My daughter, and yet It will come</u>. <u>You measure the human</u>, the sad times that involve the present generations, and therefore it seems difficult to you. But the Supreme Being has Divine Measures that are so very long, such that what is impossible for human nature, is easy for Us…

> …And then, there is <u>**the Queen of Heaven who, with Her Empire, continuously prays that the Kingdom of the Divine Will come on earth**</u>, and when have We ever denied Her anything? For Us, Her Prayers are impetuous winds such that We cannot resist Her. And the same Strength that She possesses of Our Will is for Us Empire, Command. **She has all right to impetrate It, because She possessed It on earth, and She possesses It in Heaven. Therefore as Possessor She can give what is Hers, so much so that this Kingdom will be called the Kingdom of the Celestial Empress. She will act as Queen in the midst of Her children on earth.** She will place at their disposition Her Seas of Graces, of Sanctity, of Power. She will put to flight all the enemies. She will raise them in Her Womb. She will hide them in Her Light, covering them with Her Love, nourishing them with Her own hands with the food of the Divine Will. What will this Mother and Queen not do in the midst of this, Her Kingdom, for Her children and for Her people? **She will give Unheard-of Graces, Surprises never seen, <u>Miracles that will shake Heaven and earth.</u> We give Her the whole field free so that She will form for Us the Kingdom of Our Will on earth.** She will be the Guide, the True Model, It will also be the Kingdom of the Celestial Sovereign. Therefore, you also pray together with Her, and at Its time you will obtain the intent.[1184]

Our Lady herself is begging her Divine Son for the coming of the Kingdom on earth. As all Catholics should know, Jesus has no power to resist the pleas of His mother. Furthermore, **Jesus tells Luisa that He has handed over to His mother the power to do whatever is necessary on earth even now to secure the arrival of the Kingdom—"miracles that will shake Heaven and earth," "unheard-of graces," "surprises never seen." We have been given a taste of these interventions of Our Lady throughout the 20th century. But we can rest assured that these are only the foreshocks of what she has prepared for the world.**

[1182] May 16, 1937.
[1183] February 24, 1933.

[1184] July 14, 1935.

We should also realize that this certainty of the Coming of the Kingdom was not only a message that Jesus incessantly gave to Luisa, but is also a reality which Luisa made her own personally-held conviction. We see this conviction sincerely relayed by Luisa in her letters. For example, she once wrote to a priest:

> Reverend Father, it is the Will (decision) of God that His Kingdom come upon earth; therefore, it is most certain that It will come—either by means of love, or by chastisements. Otherwise, Creation would be a work deprived of Its crowning. God would seem to be as though impotent in the face of the other creatures who possess fecundity, because only the Divine Will would not be able to form Its divine Life within our souls. No—not this. We are convinced that the Kingdom of His Will will come.

And in a letter to Federico Abresch, Luisa wrote:

> Therefore, the prodigies of living in the Divine Will are inexhaustible, and maybe we will get to know them in Heaven. This is the reason for which the infernal enemy has closed all doors, using ecclesiastical people. **But the time will come when Jesus will triumph over all, and His kingdom on earth will certainly come**, because it is a decree of God, and He does not easily change His decrees because of the wickedness of men. However, **blessed are those who interest themselves in His Will, because the Lord will use them to open the ways which had been closed**, and will use their acts as many keys in order to open Heaven and to make It descend and reign upon earth. Therefore, dearest son, let us be attentive; let us never move from the Supreme Fiat.

Addressing the concern that man simply cannot raise to the level of meriting this Kingdom, Jesus says to Luisa:

> … what merit did man have that We Created the sky, the sun, and all the rest? He did not exist yet, he could not say anything to Us. In fact Creation was a Great Work of Marvelous Magnificence, all Gratuitous of God. And the Redemption, do you believe that man merited It? Indeed it was all Gratuitous, and if he prayed to Us, it was because We made him the Promise of the future Redeemer; he was not the first to say it to Us, but We were. It was Our all Gratuitous Decree that the Word would take human flesh, and it was completed when sin, human ingratitude,

galloped and inundated the whole earth. And if it seems that they did something, they were hardly little drops that could not be enough to merit a Work so great that gives of the incredible, that a God made Himself similar to man in order to place him in safety, and that additionally man had made Him so many offenses.

> Now the great Work of making known My Will so that It could Reign in the midst of creatures will be a Work of Ours completely Gratuitous; and this is the mistake, that they believe that it will be the merit and on the part of creatures. Ah yes! it will be there, as the little drops of the Hebrews when I came to Redeem them. But the creature is always creature, therefore it will be completely Gratuitous on Our Part because, abounding with Light, with Grace, with Love to her, We will overwhelm her in a way that she will feel Strength never felt, Love never experienced. She will feel Our Life Beating more vividly in her soul, so much so that it will be sweet for her to let Our Will Dominate.[1185]

Jesus wants us to beg for this Kingdom; to prepare the way; to announce it to the world, yes… but it does not follow from these premises that we ourselves are the ones to build this Kingdom or merit it. What anxiety that would cause! We simply do not have the power. But that is okay, because the coming of this Kingdom is completely gratuitous. We do not deserve it now nor is there anything we can do to deserve it later; God will, in His munificence, bestow it upon us nevertheless.

This fact is also an important refutation of the various "progressive ascendency" heresies condemned by the Magisterium (especially those found in liberation theology), wherein man progressively builds "the Kingdom of God" on earth through his own effort until at long last it is definitively recognized within time; or wherein man "evolves" gradually to some "omega point" in the future, in which consists the Kingdom.[1186] As discussed earlier in this book, that notion is radically contrary to the nature of the Era as Jesus reveals it to Luisa.

Of course, many who denounce the Era will not abandon their denunciation. But they cannot stop the Era. Jesus tells Luisa:

> …when [the Divine Will] decides to operate in one creature in order to fulfill Its greatest designs in the midst of the human generations, It lets no

---

[1185] March 26, 1933.

[1186] Cf. Pierre Teilhard de Chardin

one dictate to It the law—neither who it must be, nor the time, nor the way, nor the place—but It acts in an absolute way. Nor does it pay heed to **certain short minds, which are unable to elevate themselves in the divine and supernatural order, or to bow their forehead to the incomprehensible works of their Creator;** and while they want to reason with their own human reason, they lose the divine reason, and remain confounded and incredulous.'.'[1187]

So we must never be discouraged. Let us end this chapter with some words of inspiration and exhortation that Jesus entrusted to two other mystics of the 20the century with the same mission:

Go, fortified by My grace, <u>and fight for My kingdom in human souls; fight as a king's child would; and remember that the days of your exile will pass quickly,</u> and with them the possibility of earning merit for heaven. I expect from you, My child, a great number of souls who will glorify My mercy for all eternity. My child, that you may answer My call worthily, receive Me daily in Holy Communion. It will give you strength ...

-Jesus to St. Faustina

(Divine Mercy in my Soul, Paragraph 1489)

***

All are invited to join my special fighting force. <u>The coming of my Kingdom must be your only purpose in life</u>... Do not be cowards. Do not wait. Confront the Storm to save souls.

- Jesus to Elizabeth Kindelmann (approved "Flame of Love" revelations)

"When Will All of This Take Place?"

Here we have stumbled upon the "elephant in the living room." Hopefully all readers are at this point very eager for the coming of the Era, and it is only natural to wonder exactly when it will finally come.

But when this question knocks at the door of our minds, we must never fail to remember that it is ultimately a futile question, since the answer is simple: **it's up to you.**

That is not a ploy, not a trick, not an evasion. It really is true. You yourself may even be the "straw

that breaks the camel's back," if only you cast yourself upon that back—which is the present Kingdom of the prince of this world, the Devil.

Jesus was careful to not reveal in His words to Luisa when exactly the Era would come (all He said was it will be "about" 2,000 years after Redemption), so as to not mislead anyone into thinking its arrival is a matter of passive waiting. For, quite the contrary, asking when it will come is as absurd as asking somebody else when you—the one asking—will finally follow your calling. You know the answer to that, not the person you are asking!

Of course, the basic constraints of logic always hold true. Since Jesus promised the Era would come "about" 2,000 years after Redemption, it will indeed do just that. Jesus—God—knows everything, including every single detail of the entire future (human free will does not change this fact), and He never lies. He also does not exaggerate. But He does *round*. Everybody rounds; it is necessary and there is nothing dishonest about it—no one, in giving directions to another, says "take a right after 5,376.5 feet," rather, he says "take a right in a mile," even though a mile is 5,280 feet. But there has been no dishonesty in these directions, as they never proposed to be absolutely precise. One who does choose to take a right hand turn after exactly 5,280 feet and consequently drives into a ditch has only himself to blame.

The only thing, therefore, that we can say with certainty about the arrival of the Era is that it will occur by such a time that it would not be an erroneous rounding to say it is "about" 2,000 years after Redemption. Of course, that does not say much, and countless signs of the times seem to make it clear that the long-prophesied events which will precede the Era are at the very doorstep, not 500 years away.

Now, while we must recall that we "know not the day nor the hour" (Matthew 25:13), it is nevertheless also important to know that, as of the publication of this book, we are growing very near to the precise 2,000th anniversary of Redemption. If indeed the revelations to Blessed Emmerich and the consensus of most scholars is correct, then our calendar is off by several years, and Jesus was actually crucified in what our present calendar would refer to as 26 A.D.

The Era does not have to come exactly two thousand years after Redemption (2026 A.D.). But there is no denying that such a time of arrival would be very fitting, and perhaps if all who read these words truly devote themselves to hastening the Coming of the Kingdom, such a fitting fulfillment will become a reality.

Part IV: Appendices

32) The Moratorium and the Status of Luisa's Writings in the Church

When one today undertakes an internet search for Luisa Piccarreta, the status of her cause, or the nature of the moratorium on her volumes, he is most likely to first stumble upon a web page published by a large and generally very trustworthy Catholic media company. While this page strives to present all the relevant information, it unfortunately contains a few serious falsehoods that have remained uncorrected for years. In order to set the record straight, this appendix is necessary and should be read carefully by anyone who may have stumbled upon partial, or even false, information relevant to the matter.

We should first acknowledge that **no one has any right to promulgate any restrictions on Luisa's writings or cause other than the competent Church authority**, and this authority has only been exercised by the Archbishops of Trani (Luisa's own diocese). The current Archbishop of Trani is Leonardo D'Ascenzo; as of this writing (early 2019), he has neither removed anything from nor added anything to the norms promulgated by his predecessor, Archbishop Giovanni Pichierri. Pichierri, in turn, has listed all the relevant norms in his notification from November, 2012 (which adds to all the previous notifications and authoritative actions**). I include this notification, in its unabridged entirety, in the following section. Whoever claims that there are restrictions on Luisa's writings or Cause that are not found in this 2012 notification is spreading misinformation and perhaps committing slander** (of an at least implicit nature, as he would be falsely condemning promoters of Luisa; accusing them of violating Church authority by falsely claiming that this authority forbids what they are doing). Indeed, there is no shortage of slander now circulating online against promoters of Luisa and her writings.

The only official communication (that pertains to Luisa) from Archbishop Pichierri promulgated between the 2012 notification and his death in July 2017, was a letter dated April 26, 2015 which reported on an international conference that he convened for the 150th anniversary of the birth of Luisa. This letter reads in part:

> Around 650 participants arrived from [many countries listed]… I received with joy the commitment that participants declared solemnly they would take upon themselves to be more faithful to the Charism of "living in the Divine Will" according to the example of the Servant of God Luisa Piccarreta…I wish to let you know that the Cause of Beatification is proceeding positively…I have recommended to all that they deepen the life and the teachings of the Servant of God Luisa Piccarreta… I extend my appeal to the Bishops of the dioceses in which 'groups of the Divine Will" are located, to welcome and support such groups, assisting them to put into practice concretely the spirituality of the Divine Will."[1188]

Needless to say, and to put it lightly, these are not the words of one who wishes to see Luisa's revelations put under a bushel basket. If there was ever any doubt as to how his 2012 notification was to be understood (there never was any honest doubt to begin with), that doubt has been definitively ended with this 2015 update. Published within the same document as this update, the official website for the Cause of Luisa[1189] includes an official handout from the conference itself (no doubt approved by, or perhaps even written by, the Archbishop) that includes a **commitment** of the participants to:

"…invoke unceasingly with prayer and with their acts in the Divine Will the definitive coming of the Reign of God on earth as Jesus has taught us to ask in the 'Our Father.'"[1190]

In sum: in this Archbishop we have one who

[1188]https://danieloconnor.files.wordpress.com/2019/02/final-letter-by-the-archbishop-giovan-battista-pichierri-1.pdf

[1189]http://www.luisapiccarretaofficial.org/download
[1190]Ibid.

wholeheartedly gave his public support to the essence of—and even the most controversial parts of—Luisa's revelations. For anyone to dare use him or his official communications as weapons used against these revelations is the height of duplicity.

We now turn to address more specifically the errors contained on the website we mentioned above.

Error #1: "Lay people may not teach on this." The page states: "*Lay persons will no longer be permitted to teach publicly, either about the spirituality of the Divine Will, or regarding her [Luisa's] life and virtues*" This statement cites as its authority paragraph 14 of a 2007 letter written by Msgr. Savino Giannotti (the Vicar General of Trani), implying (deceptively) that this restriction is actually contained within it. In fact, **nothing even remotely similar to this restriction is found in paragraph 14 or anywhere in the letter**. Indeed, in paragraph 5 of the 2012 notification (the only currently binding document), it is made clear that no one "outside of the association" has been granted permission to speak on "life, thought and writings of the Servant of God" *in their names* **(the names of those in the official Association promoting Luisa's Cause)**. This restriction should be obvious! One can never speak in another's name without explicit permission to do so. But this web page—and many others—erroneously concludes from this simple fact that nobody whosoever can speak about Luisa and her writings except for those who are sent by the Archdiocese to officially speak in the name of the Association. Such a conclusion is in no way supported by any official communications from the competent Church authority.

Error #2: "Luisa's writings may not be circulated." The page asserts that "any" English translations of Luisa's writings now "circulating" are contrary to the will of the Archbishop. But, **as can easily be ascertained from reading the 2012 document itself instead of the interpretation of it presented on the website in question, the Archbishop is merely prohibiting the *publication* of Luisa's writings**. Sharing and reading them within prayer groups dedicated to Luisa is not only *not* prohibited, but is clearly encouraged by the Archbishop in the very same letter that the web page here wrongly summarizes.

- The webpage completely ignores that **the Archbishop himself said, in the same 2012 notification they cite, that the "ardor" of those** who **"recommend the reading of her [Luisa's] writings"** is **"not only not prohibited, [but is] rather very much desirable."** How is it possible that any "circulation" of Luisa's writings whatsoever would be automatically deemed contrary to the Archbishop's directives, considering what he himself clearly stated here?

- Whoever would like to assume—contrary to the clear statements in the document itself—that the 2012 notification condemns and prohibits even private circulation of Luisa's volumes and even the quotation of excerpts from her Volumes in other published works, should themselves remember *ei incumbit probatio qui dicit, non qui negat* ("the burden of proof is on the one who declares, not on one who denies"). Indeed, the 2012 notification does clearly prohibit the *publication* of Luisa's volumes. But to condemn the private circulation and the quotation of excerpts would entail a prohibition that extends substantially beyond the stated prohibitions in any existing official communications, and consequently would require another official act of either the Archdiocese of Trani or of the Vatican so indicating. **No such act has ever occurred**.

- This is not to mention that Luisa's writings have long been quoted, at length, fully licitly many times since the Moratorium was put in place. This book you are reading is just one example of many such cases. Other examples include Stephen Patton's 2013 *A Guide to the Book of Heaven*, which bears a Nihil Obstat and an Imprimatur from the author's Bishop; as well as Fr. Joseph Iannuzzi's 2012 Doctoral Dissertation that received unanimous approval from the faculty at the pontifical Gregorian University in Rome and thus bears the implicit approval of the Holy See, and finally, the theologian and Notre Dame professor Fr. Edward O'Connor's 2014 book, *Living in the Divine Will*. All of these works and many others similar to them remain available for purchase, fully licitly, to this day. It should also be pointed out that Luisa's critics regularly and publicly quote extensively from her writings in order to attack them.

- **Although I have indeed quoted extensively from Luisa's volumes, I have nevertheless only included a minuscule fraction of the totality of her volumes—such a small fraction, indeed, that there are no legitimate canonical or civil criteria in the world by virtue of which what I** have done here consists in the "publication" of Luisa's Volumes. Not only is the fraction of what is included a small one, but it has been undertaken in strict accord with all the norms defining Legal Fair Use in Title 17 of U.S. Copyright Law. I have _not_ "published" the volumes. Furthermore, it is precisely those works which have no Moratorium on their publication that I have quoted from most heavily (in proportion to their length): the _Hours of the Passion_, the _Blessed Virgin Mary in the Kingdom of the Divine Will_, and Luisa's letters.

Error #3: "All Divine Will conferences must be approved directly by Trani." The web page also states "_So, while unable to regulate what local bishops might allow, the Postulation is discouraging Catholics from attending conferences given by individuals without a letter of authorization from the Archbishop of Trani, Italy._" This is completely contrary to what Pichierri himself wrote in his 2015 letter quoted above: "**I extend my appeal to the Bishops of the dioceses in which 'groups of the Divine Will" are located, to welcome and support such groups, assisting them to put into practice concretely the spirituality of the Divine Will.**" These are not the words of one who wishes to discourage any conferences that lack his own specific, explicit seal of approval. The Archbishop of Trani does not have the time to personally approve every conference on the Divine Will around the world; indeed, to even posit that such a step would be called for is absurd. The 2012 notification—which this website admits is the presently binding document—only requires (in section 8) that "**"conferences, spiritual retreats, prayer meetings, etc." be authorized by** "_one's Bishop_," which is an obvious reference to the local Ordinary of the location of the conference, not to the Archbishop of Trani.

But perhaps more problematic than the errors themselves are the omissions of which this webpage is guilty. To be sure, it provides links to the documents that state the following, but it draws no attention to the following and does not even deem the following worth acknowledging; whereas the "Summary" which the web page provides of them not only excludes these teachings,

but also contradicts them:

As partially quoted above, paragraph 9 reads:

> "Necessary prudence cannot lessen the ardor of those who feel compelled to spread the knowledge of the sanctity of life of the Servant of God, or of those who recommend the reading of her writings, or of those who encourage the faithful prayer for her beatification. All this not only is not prohibited, rather very much desirable"

In other words, this official communication is above all an exhortation to be _more_ zealous in promoting Luisa and her writings.

And, in paragraph 4, we see the Archbishop's strong rebuke to critics of Luisa:

> I wish to address all those who claim that these writings contain doctrinal errors. This, to date, has never been endorsed by any pronouncement by the Holy See, nor personally by myself. I would like to note that in this way, in addition to anticipate [sic] the legitimate judgment of the Church, these persons cause scandal to the faithful who are spiritually nourished by said writings, originating also suspicion of those of us who are zealous in the pursuit of the Cause. In the anticipation of the judgment by competent Authority, I invite you to make more serious and in-depth meditations and reflections in your personal reading on these writings

As we can see clearly in the Archbishop's own words, it is actually the people who publicly criticize and impute heresy to Luisa's writings who are themselves being the scandalous and disobedient ones. Pichierri is here admonishing such people to do a better job reading Luisa's writings (incidentally, an exhortation that would be impossible if the Moratorium meant what the critics pretend it means), after which point, they will realize that they have been doing great harm to the Church.

***

The next section consists in the entire, unabridged, unedited text of the aforementioned 2012 Communication. All emphasis is from the original.

The Only Presently Binding Church Norms — Abp. Pichierri's 2012 Notification

Mons. Giovanni Battista Pichierri

ARCIVESCOVO
di TRANI - BARLETTA - BISCEGLIE
TITOLARE di NAZARETH

Prot. N. 182/12/C3

COMMUNICATION n°. 3
About the process of Beatification and Canonization
of the Servant of God LUISA PICCARRETA

Addressing the many who, in different ways in the world, are interested in the Servant of God *Luisa Piccarreta* and the spirituality of *Living in the Divine Will*, I like to [sic] update what I have previously reported on several occasions, and above all in the Communications of April 23, 2007 and of May 30, 2008. The diffusion in the world of the figure and writings of the Servant of God Luisa Piccarreta has grown considerably in recent years, reaching new nations in all continents. Letters from Bishops, priests, and lay persons alike give proof of this, as well as the record of visitors to the places related to Luisa in Corato.

The joy of witnessing the growth of this reality is accompanied by the concern to extend to all a heartfelt **appeal for unity** and the mutual esteem, rejecting "quarreling and jealousy" as one who waits for the advent of the "fullness of day" (Rm 13:11-14). If we live in the light of the Divine Will we cannot but cultivate in ourselves the fruits of mutual Charity, for "anyone who claims to be in the light but hates his brother is still in the darkness, " (1 Jn 2:9).

I still observe with sorrow that "the doctrine of the Divine Will has not always been presented in a correct and respectful way, according to the doctrine and the Magisterium of the Church, putting remarks in the mouth of Luisa that are not even implicitly found in her writings. This provokes a trauma in consciences and even confusion and rejection among the people and by some Priests and Bishops" (*Letter* of March 9, 2006).

Therefore, it is my duty to point out some directions in a way that is clear for all.

Current state of the Cause

1. Actor of the process of Beatification and Canonization is the "Association "Luisa Piccarreta — Little Children of the Divine Will" of Corato, that with its new statute dated June 13, 2010, I wanted to constitute as a Public Association of the Faithfu [sic] due to its particular ecclesial significance.

2. I have given the Association a mandate in 2006 to constitute *the Secretariat of the Cause of Beatification of the Servant of God Luisa Piccarreta*, as an organism of liaison, support and information at the service of the many who in various ways are interested in the Cause itself; with the further task of opening dialogue with other Dioceses, persons, groups, and associations. "The Archdiocese and the Association will use *exclusively* the Secretariat to receive and answer any request made to them" (*Communication* of April 23, 2007). Therefore, no person or Association in the world can issue official notice apart from this Secretariat. I forbid anyone from attempting to do so in my name.

3. In 1994, with the *non obstare* of the Holy See was opened the Diocesan Inquiry into the life, virtues and fame of sanctity. This was concluded on October 29, 2005 with the transmission of the

Proceedings to the Congregation for the Causes of Saints and the nomination of Dr. Silvia Monica Correale as Postulator and Rev. Fr. Sabino Amedeo Lattanzio as Vice-postulator. The Congregation subsequently has communicated to me that "before proceeding *any further*, an examination of the writings of the Servant of God will be done, in order to clarify difficulties of a theological nature."

4. In the prayerful anticipation of the outcome of this examination, I wish to *address all those who claim that these writings contain doctrinal errors*. This, to date, has never been endorsed by any pronouncement by the Holy See, nor personally by myself. I would like to note that in this way, in addition to anticipate [sic] the legitimate judgment of the Church, these persons cause scandal to the faithful who are spiritually nourished by said writings, originating also suspicion of those of us who are zealous in the pursuit of the Cause. In the anticipation of the judgment by competent Authority, I invite you to make more serious and in-depth meditations and reflections in your personal reading on these writings in light of Sacred Scripture, Tradition, and the Magisterium of the Church.

5. Furthermore, I wish to reiterate that if the writings of the Servant of God are read by people as to lead to the formation of one or more groups, this should not occur against the will of the Ordinary of the Place. Likewise, I recall what I have already communicated: "Neither the Archdiocese nor the Association nor the Secretariat has delegated any person, group or other association, in any way, to represent them outside of their legitimate locations, to spread knowledge about the life, thought and writings of the Servant of God or to make any decision in their names. From the moment that the Diocesan Inquiry was begun, the Archdiocese has never officially designated any Theologian or Censor for the writing of Luisa. Likewise, it has never nominated any official translator of the writings from Italian into any other language" (*Communication* of April 23, 2007).

Preparation of the typical edition of the writings

6. "As I have already expressed at the conclusion of the diocesan phase of the Cause, it is my desire, after having heard the opinion of the Congregation for the Causes of Saints, to present *a typical and critical edition of the writings* in order to provide the faithful with a trustworthy text of the writings of Luisa Piccarreta. So I repeat, the said writings are *exclusively* the property of the Archdiocese" (Letter to Bishops of October 14, 2006). To accomplish this demanding work that requires a certain kind of competence, I shall avail myself of a team of experts chosen in agreement with the Postulation.

7. Nevertheless, I must mention the growing and unchecked flood of transcriptions, translations and publications both through print and the internet. At any rate, "seeing the delicacy of the current phase of the proceedings, any and every publication of the writings is absolutely forbidden at this time. Anyone who acts against this is disobedient and greatly harms the cause of the Servant of God." (Communication of May 30, 2008). All effort must be invested in avoiding all "leaks" of publications of any kind.

Groups of the Divine Will

8. "It is with great joy that I receive the news that more and more of the groups that are inspired by the Divine Will are strengthening their community links with their diocesan Bishops, so creating that indispensable communion within the local Church and so allowing any possible tension or division to be overcome" (*Communication* of May 30, 2008). I reiterate, therefore, that "initiatives that are taken in reference with the spirituality of Luisa, for example conferences, spiritual retreats, prayer meetings, etc., must be authorized by one's Bishop in order to give serenity to the participants" (Letter of November 24, 2003).

9. Necessary prudence cannot lessen the ardor of those who feel compelled to spread the knowledge of the sanctity of life of the Servant of God, or of those who recommend the reading of her writings, or of those who encourage the faithful prayer for her beatification. All this not only is not prohibited, rather very much desirable. I also invite you to "reinforce the unity and communion among the dioceses in which individuals, groups and associations inspired by the Servant of God

Luisa Piccarreta, and who know her writings, are to be found" (Final Communication of October 28, 2005).

What is asked of those familiar with Luisa Piccarreta

1. To pray for the Beatification of the Servant of God, that the Most Holy Trinity might be glorified and be diffuse the Reign of the Divine Will.
2. To send to the Postulation, through the Secretariat the testimonies and all else that regards the Servant of God, together with the economic donations needed today more than ever, for the work of the "typical edition" of the writings of Luisa.
3. To create a network of links between the several groups united with their Bishop, and our own Archdiocese, to make visible, ever more the great family of the *Divine Will*, established in the bond of unity, of the ecclesial communion and of the commitment of the new evangelization for the tradition of faith.

With great friendship and warmth, I greet and bless you all.

Trani, November 1st, 2012

✠ *Giovan Battista Pichierri*
Archbishop

33) <u>Answers to Objections</u>

As mentioned after the chapter on the authenticity of Luisa's revelations in this book, **the vast majority of concerns, objections, criticisms, and even downright attacks that have been levied against Luisa's revelations are clearly answered—carefully, objectively, and with great orthodoxy—within Luisa's revelations themselves.** Any sincere, learned Catholic who reads Luisa's revelations will find within them virtually all of his concerns addressed. We see, in Luisa's diary, the following exchange:

> [Luisa laments:] Before I used to have no doubts about what You told me; now—no; how many doubts, how many difficulties. I myself don't know where I go fishing for them.' And Jesus: "Do not worry about this either. Many times I Myself cause these difficulties in order to answer not only you, confirming to you the truths that I tell you, but to answer all those who, in reading these truths, may find doubts and difficulties. I answer them in advance, so that they may find light, and all of their difficulties may be dissolved. Criticism will not be lacking; therefore, everything is

necessary.[1191]

I have spent enormous amounts of time reading the objections, criticisms, and attacks levied against Luisa's writings; I have found that they are almost always proffered by those who have themselves spent virtually no time reading Luisa's writings themselves—people who have only heard very partial presentations of Luisa's revelations, and then take issue with these presentations.

So, above all, one should simply pray for humility and read Luisa's writings with a sincere desire to know and submit to the Truth; whatever it may be. This will not be disappointing!

Admittedly, however, it might be some time until one stumbles upon the specific answer to his concern within he volumes, so I will address some objections in the following pages. But, before examining and answering specific objections, I must first make it clear that anyone who opens up Luisa's writings with a merely critical eye, having the sole intention of finding juicy details at which

---

[1191] December 5, 1921.

to scream "heresy!" will have no shortage of opportunities to do so. Certain internet blogs and forums are replete with those who have taken such a task upon themselves. No effort here will be made to address superficial, Pharisee-like objections. The only remedy to that malady is to unclench the fist and pray for humility. Just as Our Lord had little patience for the quibblers when He came to earth 2,000 years ago, so today His laments are the same. He tells Luisa:

> …if I had wanted to listen to what was said about Me, and to the contradictions that they made to Me about the Truths that I Manifested when I came on earth, I would not have formed the Redemption, nor Manifested My Gospel. And yet they were the most learned, the noblest part-some who had studied Scriptures, and some who taught religion to the people. I let them talk, and with Love and Invincible Patience I endured their continuous contradictions, and they served Me as wood for the pains that they gave Me, in order to burn and consume Myself on the Cross for the Love of them and of everyone. The same today, if I would want to listen to what they say about the Truths of My Divine Will, I would have put an end to the Manifestations about It, and to the designs that I want to fulfill by Manifesting them. But no, We are not subject to changeability. The human work has this weakness, and acts according to the appreciation that others make them, but Us, no-the Divine Work is Immutable. When We decide, there is no one who changes Us, neither all creatures, nor all hell. Nevertheless, with Our Inextinguishable Love We wait for times, circumstances, and people who would serve Us for what We have established.[1192]

If, perchance, you are inclined to respond with, "ah, but the days of the Pharisees are over, and we needn't concern ourselves with avoiding that trap anymore," then I implore you to open up to the "Note to Scholars" section towards the end of this book.

But do know that I am not claiming that everyone with concerns is a Pharisee! Far from it. Sometimes, when presenting Luisa's revelations to one who is unaware of them, I even say to him, "Look; you'd be a bad Catholic if you *didn't* have some hesitations and concerns here with what I'm about to tell you." Perhaps in those words I have gone too far and have underestimated the grace at work in their souls, through which God can make

it easy for a humble and sincere seeker to quickly and fully see the truth in His words to Luisa. **Nevertheless, many good Catholics will not be in that situation, and may struggle at first with these revelations. That is okay. I wish to address your concerns in this chapter as one who understands that they proceed from your genuine desire to carefully maintain Catholic orthodoxy. For that is a good and holy desire, and it is essential that we all maintain it in these days of increasing heresy and apostasy.** Indeed, we always have a duty to test and discern *any* alleged private revelation before believing.

Isn't important Catholic content missing from Luisa's writings?

Objection: Why doesn't Luisa talk more about the Rosary? About Eucharistic Adoration? About the need to do works of mercy for our neighbor, etc.?

Answer: One thing is clear: Luisa's revelations are not sufficient, and they are not comprehensive. They are "missing" important things, even essential things. The Almighty decreed this so that it is clear to us that they are intended to fit within a structure which is itself complete; that is to say, within the Roman Catholic Church. This way, no one can justify trying to start a new "Luisan" religion or denomination. It is heretics and schismatics who constantly vie for an apparent sense of totality in their movements; for drawing souls away from the One, Holy, Catholic, and Apostolic Church is precisely their aim. Those who pursue evil ends (whether by malice of will or their own deception) often reveal the cloven hoof when they seek this completion and autonomy.

Consider, therefore, how important it is to not draw any conclusions from merely what is either apparently or actually lacking in Luisa's writings. For example, there was quite some time in my own reading of her writings that I had not once (to my memory) come across an instance of Luisa mentioning the Rosary. However, when I finally did come across it, it was in a letter in which she strongly admonished the recipient to *never* neglect praying it. How easily that one single letter could have not existed! Imagine, if it had not, what folly would have been committed by a devotee of Luisa's revelations who, upon realizing he never read about the Rosary in her writings, decided that

---

February 24, 1933.

this prayer must not be important. Due to the existence of that one letter, we now know that such a devotee would not only be committing a grave error, but would even be contradicting the very wish of Luisa herself—who, above all, knows best what Jesus is asking of us in these Divine Will revelations.

Luisa wrote her many pages of revelations because she was commanded to write them by her spiritual directors. These directors instructed her to write down what she received from Jesus; they did not say to her: *"Luisa, write down a comprehensive overview of how a Catholic ought to behave in light of these revelations that Jesus is giving you."* If that was what her directors said to her, and if that was her mission, then we would have a right to criticize her writings for what they lack. But **Luisa had nothing but deference to the Catholic Church—and all of its traditions included—in all things. Her writings presuppose devout Catholicism in every way, shape, and form that it ordinarily takes, therefore it is unjust to ask of Luisa a comprehensive overview of all things Catholic, when in fact God's mission with her was very specific.**

It should also be noted that many of those things Luisa's writings are sometimes accused of lacking are actually found throughout her writings, and in such a way that it is clear there isn't the least bit of flippancy, ignorance, or dispensationalism regarding them. For example, in her writings we see confession insisted upon, the Eucharist as the source and summit of Luisa's life, "ordinary" evangelization still exalted as good and necessary, Our Lady exalted as by far the greatest creature—the Mediatrix of All Grace and the Co-Redemptrix—and on the list goes. In fact, one would have a difficult time finding *any* private revelation that is as thoroughly confirming of all that Catholic tradition and spirituality presents to us as are Luisa's.

Why, then, does the Our Father say Thy Will be "done," not "lived"?

Objection: If the universal reign on earth of the Gift of Living in the Divine Will is what Jesus referred to by saying *"Thy Will be done on earth as it is in Heaven,"* then why didn't He make it clearer? If He

intended so great a prophecy, He would have issued it in a similar fashion as, for example, that in which He issued the eschatological prophecies regarding famines, earthquakes, and the like in the Synoptic Gospels. He could have at least said, *"Thy Will be lived on earth as it is in Heaven"* instead!

Answer: It is certainly true that Our Lord could have been clearer regarding the coming fulfillment of the third petition in the prayer He taught us, but this lack of clarity was His intent for the time, for He also said in the Gospel:

> I have yet many things to say to you, but you cannot bear them now. When the Spirit of truth comes, he will guide you into all the truth…[1193]

This Scriptural ambiguity was also His intent with other great private revelations; for example, devotion to His Sacred Heart or the Immaculate Heart of His holy mother. Both of these do indeed have Scriptural basis, but only tiny glimpses that no one would be able to realize the full actualization of without a new private revelation from Heaven. We know the Apostle John rested his head on Jesus' breast at the Last Supper; we know blood and water flowed forth from it when pierced by a lance. But no one could, from those verses, conclude anything like what St. Margaret Mary Alacoque gave us in her Sacred Heart revelations. Likewise, we know that at the Presentation of Jesus in the temple and after the prophecy was given by Simeon, Mary *"kept all these things in her heart."*[1194] We do not thereby learn that, *"in the end, [her] Immaculate Heart will triumph,"*[1195] even though that revelation at Fatima is truly an explication of the former Public Revelation in Scripture, just as Luisa's revelations are an explication of the Scriptural basis for them.

The reason why He did not pray "Thy Will be lived on earth as it is in Heaven" is clear. Had He said it in this manner, it would have been largely inapplicable to the following 2,000 years of Church history to come. That would have deprived millennia of Christians the joy of knowing that they are fulfilling this petition of the Lord's Prayer. Since Living in the Divine Will rightly falls under the category of doing God's will (but the converse does not necessarily hold—doing God's Will does not always amount to Living in the Divine Will), the

---

[1193] John 16:12-13
[1194] Luke 2:19

[1195] Apparition to the children at Fatima, July 13th, 1917.

wording of the Our Father is more generally applicable. Furthermore, "doing God's will" is a far more intuitive concept than "living in God's will," as the latter requires explanation, which it was not God's plan to give until Luisa.

Nevertheless, the latter portion of this petition ("*on earth as it is in heaven*") is indeed a reference to living in the Divine Will, and for 2,000 years it has served as a reminder that what we are praying for simply has not yet come to pass. Jesus tells Luisa that it is impossible for God's will to be done on earth as it is in Heaven—that is, in the same manner the blessed in Heaven do God's will—without the Gift of Living in the Divine Will. He tells Luisa:

> Now, my daughter, listen to me; the most serious doubts, the gravest difficulties that they found in your writings are precisely these: that I told you that I was calling you to live in the Kingdom of my Divine Will, giving you the special and unique mission to make It known, so that, as I Myself said in the 'Our Father', and the Holy Church says still now, 'Thy Kingdom come'—that is, your Will be done on earth as It is in Heaven. **It does not say in the 'Our Father' that this Kingdom is on earth, but it says: 'Come'; and I would not have composed a prayer if I were not to obtain its effects**. Therefore, in order to reach this, was I not to elect another woman, whom the infernal serpent so much fears; and as he, by means of the first woman, ruined the human kind to Me, I, to confound him, make use of another woman to make up for the ruin he caused, and make the good which he tried to destroy, arise for all?[1196]

Elsewhere, Luisa herself voices this exact same objection to Jesus, and He gladly obliges her:

> [Luisa says:] 'In the 'Our Father', Our Lord teaches us to say—to pray: "Your Will be done". Now, why does He say that He wants us to live in It?' And Jesus, always benign, moving in my interior, told me: "My daughter, 'your Will be done' which I taught in the 'Our Father' meant that all were to pray that they might at least do the Will of God. And this is for all Christians and for all times; nor can anyone call himself a Christian if he does not dispose himself to the Will of his Celestial Father. But you have not thought of the other addition which comes immediately after: 'On earth as It is in Heaven'. 'On earth as It is in Heaven' means to live in the Divine Will; it means to pray that the Kingdom of my Will may come on earth in order to live in It. In Heaven, they not only do my Will, but they live in It—they possess It as their own thing, and as their own Kingdom. And if they did It, but did not possess It, their happiness would not be full, because true happiness begins in the depth of the soul. To do the Will of God does not mean to possess It, but to submit oneself to Its commands, while to live in It is possession. Therefore, in the 'Our Father', in the words 'your Will be done' is the prayer that all may do the Supreme Will, and in 'on earth as It is in Heaven', that man may return into that Will from which he came, in order to reacquire his happiness, the lost goods, and the possession of his Divine Kingdom."[1197]

Isn't this Millenarianism, modified Millenarianism, Chiliasm, Dispensationalism, or Joachimism?

Answer: Not even close. None of these heresies are even implied in Luisa's writings. Since this is perhaps the most common objection voiced today, with a few writers spilling much ink over the topic, this book contains an entire chapter dedicated to its definitive refutation. Please see the chapter on millenarianism in Part Three of this book for this complete answer.

Isn't this "new sanctity" heretical—simply too great?

Objection: This type of union with God spoken of in Luisa's revelations is simply too great, and it cannot be true. Spiritual (or "mystical") marriage, described by St. John of the Cross, is the absolute limit of sanctity. To cross that boundary is to succumb to eastern philosophical or religious traditions like those of Buddhism or Pantheism.

Answer: First, we must quickly settle that Pantheism, Hinduism, and Buddhism all teach a spirituality radically at odds with what is found in Luisa's revelations; for these religions and philosophies teach (erroneously) that one need only *recognize* the "identity or sameness of the Atman—the deepest self—with the Braham—the Godhead" (Hinduism), or the "Godhead of everything" (Pantheism), or the "extinguishment or nirvana of the self" (Buddhism). Even a superficial glance at Luisa's revelations would not fail to be struck by the enormous difference between them and eastern philosophy or religion. Luisa's revelations teach not the extinguishing of

---

the self, but the sacrificing of the will to God. They teach not the "recognition" of the divinity of the self, but the *attainment* of the divinization of the self through the ordinary Catholic spiritual life, *combined with* desiring the Gift of Living in the Divine Will and asking for it. They teach not the Divinity *of* all things, but the Divine *impression left on* all created things by their Divine Craftsman.

Recognizing that Luisa's revelations do not even bear any resemblance to these Eastern traditions, we turn to the more general objection that this sanctity of which Jesus speaks to Luisa is simply too great.

In this regard, it should first be noted that **this objection could be just as easily levied against any of the great spiritual writers discussed in the chapter of this book entitled "The Gift Elsewhere in Private Revelation," some of whom are canonized saints and whose spiritual theology should not be doubted by any serious Catholic.** I therefore encourage anyone who is inclined to this particular objection to simply re-read that chapter. But this objection could also be largely applied to the saints whose writings were discussed immediately before that chapter in the "Great Spiritual Writers" section. Indeed, one often did hear precisely that objection levied against the spiritual teachings of St. Thérèse of Lisieux before she was proclaimed a Doctor of the Church (and even still there are many rigid theologians who grumble about that).

At this point, we should revisit what was included in Part One of this book on mystical marriage (if you have already read that, you may wish to skip to the next triple asterisk).

Here, we must pause to address a conundrum that may now have appeared in the minds of some readers. It goes something like this:

> *Hold on.* What I've just read about the nature of spiritual marriage is so extreme that in many ways it seems to surpass what is said about the Gift of Living in the Divine Will, not vice versa! The effects of this spiritual marriage on the recipient are so great that I doubt there is more than a soul or two alive at a given time on the face of the planet that enjoys such a state. How could we possibly speak of a higher degree of sanctity even than this—and for the masses!?

Although an understandable response, it arises from a confusion of what is being described in different cases. Living in the Divine Will is pure grace; it does not override the ordinary theology of the spiritual life, and it completely flees the senses. Even with this Gift, one must strive to attain what is described by St. John of the Cross, St. Teresa of Avila, etc., regarding spiritual marriage. For in much of their analysis, these great Doctors are describing, not the intrinsic nature of the grace of spiritual marriage itself, but the manifestations and effects of this invisible grace on the life of the soul. And these manifestations are indeed often superior to the manifestations of one who may have an intrinsically greater gift (i.e. Living in the Divine Will), but who has not yet enjoyed sufficient "accidental" (in the philosophical sense of the word) spiritual growth to exhibit anything like the glorious manifestations of the lesser gift (i.e. spiritual marriage).

This is one of many reasons why we should never speak of someone who has the Gift of Living in the Divine Will (even if we somehow knew he had the Gift) as "greater" than someone else who did not (due to living in the time before the Gift was offered). When we speak of the "greatness" of a saint, we often (perhaps always) intend to refer to the greatness of the manifestations of God's grace in their lives, or the correspondence to God's grace that the saint exhibited—not merely to the intrinsic nature of the grace itself within the depths of their souls, which is hidden from our sight.

Let us briefly consider an analogous situation. In the Sacrament of Confession, a Catholic receives an ontologically superior gift—even if his contrition is quite imperfect—than a Protestant does when he asks God for forgiveness in his own personal prayer. But let us say this Protestant is truly remorseful and contrite to a far greater degree than the Catholic. Although nothing changes the fact that the Catholic, through the Sacrament of Reconciliation, has received an intrinsically greater gift, it remains true that this Catholic should nevertheless admit that this particular Protestant's contrition (which would be a manifestation of grace) is superior to his own, and the Catholic should strive to imitate this superior contrition. Similarly, in the Eucharist, a Catholic receives an infinitely greater gift than the Protestant does by "inviting Jesus into his heart" as a part of their "personal relationship." Nevertheless, the Protestant may show more manifestations of grace which should indeed be zealously imitated by a

Catholic; perhaps the Catholic is lukewarm and does little to correspond to the infinite graces of the Eucharist he receives, and perhaps the Protestant is zealous and strives mightily to be virtuous, evangelize, love God and neighbor, etc. This does not change the fact that the Eucharist is an intrinsically greater gift, even though the Protestant has done a better job corresponding to the lesser gifts he himself has received.

It seems that virtually all those critics of Luisa who take offense at the "greatness" of the Gift of Living in the Divine Will simply do not understand this simple distinction (maybe through no fault of their own, because perhaps they have only heard distorted interpretations of Luisa's revelations).

***

God is certainly capable (and everyone must at the least grant this hypothetically) of working the same type of holiness in anyone as He has already worked in the Blessed Virgin. We must emphasize: **The Blessed Virgin Mary is the greatest creature that will ever exist. For all eternity, she alone will be the Queen of the Universe and the Mother of God; here she is absolutely sovereign. Furthermore, she will for all eternity remain immeasurably above even the very greatest saint below her. Luisa's revelations grant all these truths more clearly than one will find anywhere else, and make no attempt to alter them.** Granting these glorious statuses that Our Lady now enjoys and always will, we must nevertheless acknowledge that Our Lady is a creature, thus whatever type of holiness she enjoys has been entirely, 100%, given to her by God, and whatever type of holiness God gave to her, He is also capable of giving to others.

There are simply no Magisterial, theological, Scriptural, philosophical, or any other grounds for denying this Divine capability. In Mary, God showed us all what He is capable of doing in a human being. **If He can give something to Mary, then He can give it to us**; we who are her children and who are no more or less human than she is. Since no one can deny this—and if one does indeed grant that Our Lady truly Lives in the Divine Will—then all one can do to oppose the Gift is to imprudently castigate God for His imprudence in being so generous with His grace in these days where "sin abounds." We needn't spend any time here refuting the absurdity of placing oneself in that position!

The Fifth Marian Dogma

At this point, the only recourse left for one who wishes to deny the Gift because it is simply "too great" is to deny *the very possibility* of this degree of sanctity; in other words, to say that not even Our Lady had such sanctity.

So it is ironic that, while some detractors of Luisa's revelations hinge their criticisms on Luisa being exalted too greatly in comparison to Our Lady, perhaps even more serious detractors will simply take issue with how much Luisa's revelations exalt Our Lady! And truly this exaltation is enormous. Jesus tells Luisa that Mary dominates Him, and that the least of her breaths and motions contained—and contain—enchanting marvels. He tells Luisa that, upon Mary's Assumption, the glories within her were so great that they filled Heaven itself and therefore burst forth to fill all of creation as well, and that her beauty is so utterly unreachable and conquering that even the angels are speechless and cannot find words to describe what they observe in Mary. We could go on and on, but if anyone wishes to be reminded of the exaltation Mary receives in Luisa's revelations—which seems to me to be unrivaled—see the chapter entitled "Grow in the Gift through Mary."

Indeed, Mary's sanctity is a vitally important truth; upon the understanding of which the fate of the world may largely hinge. Perhaps that sounds ridiculous to some, but we should recall how much depends upon whether Our Lady is dogmatically proclaimed Mediatrix of All Grace, Co-Redemptrix, and Advocate—titles by which she is already validly referred but unfortunately lack dogmatic definition. It is precisely those who think that not even Our Lady could truly live in God's Will who also oppose this proclamation of the Fifth Marian Dogma.

This question, in turn, hinges upon the proper interpretation of the Angel Gabriel's words to Mary, "*full of grace.*" The canonization of Luisa and the full approval of her writings is no doubt contingent upon the continuation of authentic, orthodox Marian theology, which in turn will require departing from one additional opinion of

Aquinas.[1198]

Aquinas asserts that this "fullness of grace" is proper to (meaning, "only held by") Christ. He compares the words of the Angelic salutation to the words Scripture uses to describe St. Stephen, who is likewise said to be "full of grace ... "[1199] In the Summa, Aquinas writes:

> The Blessed Virgin is said to be full of grace, not on the part of grace itself-since she had not grace in its greatest possible excellence ... [1200]

This particular opinion of Aquinas, that Mary "had not grace in its greatest possible excellence," must be set aside not only to heed Luisa's revelations, but also to heed the great bulk of development in good Marian theology (especially as taught by St. Louis de Montfort, St. Alphonsus Liguori, and St. Maximilian Kolbe) and make way for the proclamation of the Fifth Marian Dogma. Now Thomas' philosophy and theology remain the best and surest norm for arriving at truths of Faith, but we should not be afraid to set aside just a few opinions of his thousands! Remember as well that Luisa, being a Third Order Dominican, no doubt naturally had a great deference to and respect for Aquinas.

Most importantly, this opinion of Aquinas appears to be contradicted by Pope Pius IX, in the same Apostolic Constitution in which he defined the Dogma of the Immaculate Conception; for in that the Pope teaches:

> When ... by order of God himself, [Mary was] proclaimed full of grace by the Angel Gabriel when he announced her most sublime dignity of Mother of God, they [the Fathers of the Church] thought that this singular and solemn salutation, never heard before, showed that the Mother of God is the seat of all divine graces ... To them Mary is an almost infinite treasury ... Hence, it is the clear and unanimous opinion of the Fathers that the most glorious Virgin ... was resplendent with such an abundance of heavenly gifts, with such a fullness of grace ... that **she approaches as near to God himself as is possible for a created being** ... [1201]

Bear in mind that by saying "it is the clear and unanimous opinion of the Fathers ... " he is not merely presenting an "opinion" to Catholics that they may likewise hold if they feel so compelled. Rather, that which is unanimously held by the Fathers of the Church is, by that very fact, a dogma of the Faith. For the Word of God is not merely Scripture, but Scripture *and* Tradition; and what is unanimously held by the Fathers cannot be anything other than Sacred Tradition. The First Vatican Council taught that: "*It is not permissible for anyone to interpret Holy Scripture in a sense contrary to ... the unanimous consent of the fathers.*"[1202] The Council of Trent teaches the same thing.[1203] Interpretation of Holy Scripture here does not refer to the limited scope that this phrase might imply in common speech today; rather it applies to the entirety of Faith. Consider that Aquinas did not primarily consider himself a "theologian," but rather a "commenter on the sacred page."

Therefore, we should regard these words of Pius IX as infallible; if not explicitly by their wording, then at least implicitly due to what they represent. And with these words, he strongly supports Mary as having the fullness of grace not merely on the part of the subject, as Aquinas asserts, but rather on the part of the object as well. For if, as he says, "*she approaches as near to God himself as is possible ... ,*" then the "fullness" is attributed to the grace itself; for otherwise there would be nothing to prevent another creature from at some point in the future approaching closer to God than she, in which case he would have said merely that Mary *did approach* nearer to God than any other creature *had approached*.

To illustrate: if one were ranking the achievements of expert mountain climbers, the only justification he could reasonably present for saying that a given climber "approached as high an altitude as is possible for a climber" would require that the climber in question did in fact reach the peak of the world's tallest mountain. If it were not so, there would be no way to assert with such absolute confidence that no climber would ever ascend higher still. Of course, one who ranks mountain climbers may be in error in his assessments, but a Pope issuing a clear teaching on Faith contained in an Apostolic Constitution cannot be. We know,

---

[1198] That is, in addition to his opinion that Mary was not conceived immaculately.
[1199] Acts 6:8
[1200] St. Thomas Aquinas, *Sum* III, Q7, A10.
[1201] Pius IX. Ineffabilis Deus

[1202] Decrees of the First Vatican Council. Chapter 2.9
[1203] Council of Trent. Decree Concerning the Edition, and the Use, of the Sacred Books

rather, that what logically follows from these clearly authoritative Magisterial teachings is also certainly true.

Furthermore, if Mary is, as the Pope here teaches, *"the seat of **all** divine graces ... an almost infinite treasury ... ,"* then there is no grace that is not within her. The fact that she did not do this or that good work on earth, or receive this or that sacrament,[1204] does not anymore diminish the fullness of grace in her than it does in her Son.[1205]

A beautiful summary of the glories of Mary is given by Fr. Peter Damian Fehlner (quoting Aquinas, Thomas Cajetan, Conrad of Saxony, and Pius XII's encyclical "Ad Caeli Reginam", respectively), saying that Mary:

> ... in virtue of Her divine Maternity, enjoys a 'certain infinite dignity,' that 'touches the limits of divinity,' [and] that 'God can make a greater world, but could not make a mother more perfect than the Mother of God,' [and] that 'the dignity of the Mother of God is most singular, sublime, and quasi-divine.[1206]

One could still attempt to argue that Mary did not have the fullness of grace due to such a thing being logically incoherent, just as it is meaningless to refer to the "biggest number." But Aquinas answers this objection well in his next Article of the *Summa*, for he says that the grace in Christ is in fact not infinite (but we know that he earlier argues rightly that Christ did indeed have the fullness of grace on the part of grace itself). This is due to the simple fact that grace, being an accident, inheres in the soul. But the Soul of Christ is not eternal; it was created at the Annunciation, and whatever is created cannot be infinite. As usual, however, the proper distinctions allow the situation to be phrased either way, for one can indeed validly say that the grace in Christ (and therefore also in Mary, or in one who has the Gift of Living in the Divine Will) is infinite in so far as that refers to *"[having] whatsoever can pertain to the nature of grace."*

There are many more distinctions, qualifications, and specifications that could be made regarding fullness of grace and modes of infinitude, which would be well beyond the scope of this work. Suffice it to say that Mary indeed did, in a certain real sense (beyond the sense in which Aquinas

granted) have the fullness of grace on the part of grace itself, and in a way had infinite grace, which is likewise something that can be attributed to a soul who lives in the Divine Will, albeit with additional important qualifications that would not apply to Mary or the Soul of Christ.

The fate of Luisa's writings in the Church no doubt is largely bound up with the fate of Mary's cause in the Church. The Fifth Marian Dogma awaits proclamation; let us pray it may come soon. As if by way of a parting gift, Pope Benedict XVI—despite never (to my knowledge) having used the term before—in some of his final words to us as our Holy Father, left us with a reference to Mary as "the Mediatrix of All Grace." This is clearly the desire of the Holy Spirit. Let it be so!

***

Fear or hesitancy in accepting the Will of God when He wishes to realize great plans for His creatures is not humility. St. Faustina learned this lesson well, sharing in her diary:

> When I became aware of God's great plans for me, I was frightened at their greatness and felt myself quite incapable of fulfilling them, and I began to avoid interior conversations with Him, filling up the time with vocal prayer. I did this out of humility, but I soon recognized it was not true humility, but rather a great temptation from the devil.[1207]

This profound warning given to us by St. Faustina leads us to consider the next objection.

Isn't too much greatness ascribed to something as "easy" as living in the Divine Will?

Objection: It is simply not credible to assert that mere desire and a state of grace can be sufficient to enable the reception of a Gift greater even than Spiritual Marriage, which was enjoyed by the most venerated canonized mystics of the Church. I am no St. Francis or St. Teresa of Avila and I know it, whether or not I receive "the Gift of Living in the Divine Will."

Answer: First, there is one important sense in which this objection is completely valid: you are correct—you are no St. Francis! You will not work

---

1204 E.g. Holy Orders
1205 E.g. Matrimony
1206 *Mary at the Foot of the Cross*, VII. Page 200

1207 St. Faustina Kowalska, *Divine Mercy in My Soul*, Entry 429.

the wonders that he worked, you will not fast like he fasted, you will not inspire countless biographies, and you will not have a Pope named after you. But that does not mean you cannot receive a greater gift than St. Francis received.

A distinction must be made between the greatness of the gift and the greatness of the recipient. We likewise rightly do not say that a baptized baby, or a school girl returning from her First Communion, is greater than King David or Moses. But it would be a heresy to say that they did not receive a greater gift, and therefore whatever greater sanctity corresponds to it and is bestowed "*ex opere operato.*"[1208]

Likewise, when we speak of Living in the Divine Will as the "greatest" sanctity, we cannot fully settle the matter of what that means in a cut and dry fashion without the important distinctions. By the very limitations of our current state as wayfarers,[1209] when we refer to someone's sanctity we refer only to the external evidence of it (or at least we can at best strive to refer to its internal reality by way of inference from the external evidence), for God alone sees the heart of man.[1210]

Now the Gift of Living in the Divine Will entirely flees the senses; there is not necessarily anything external about it. So there is no reason for us, even if Luisa's revelations are fully approved, to assert that—due to the Gift—this or that saint who lived after Luisa's time is holier than this or that saint who lived before Luisa's time. When we attribute holiness to someone, we do so by way of that external evidence which neither indicates nor depends upon the Gift of Living in the Divine Will. So there is no need to alter our terminology of comparable holiness (not that comparing holiness is a particularly prudent thing to do, anyway!). **If St. Francis had lived today, we can be certain that he would indeed be Living in the Divine Will, but that does not mean that his biography would look any different. So it is utterly confused and invalid to ever look down upon saints of the Church who lived before this age of the Divine Will. They were no less virtuous, no less sacrificing, no less in love with God, and no less mystically insightful. It is simply that an entirely invisible**

grace—the Gift of Living in the Divine Will—was not bestowed upon them on top of these things for no other reason than they did not live in the time of its bestowal.

***

There is another sense, however, in which we must indeed assert that one who receives the Gift of Living in the Divine Will is "greater" than all the saints who came before insofar as he has been given an even greater gift. If we are not willing to recognize this (with the right distinctions, in the right context, and in the right sense), then there is no point in following Luisa's revelations at all.

So we must first settle that the mere fact that one's biography—if it were to be written—would not look like that of St. Francis of Assisi or St. Paul the Apostle, is itself no impediment to recognizing that this person has nevertheless been given an unfathomable gift.

Consider first what the writings of the saints teach us about the relative ease and rapidity with which one can attain the greatest degrees of sanctity. For example, St. John of the Cross taught:

> Yet I reply to all these persons [those who refuse to believe that the **habit of charity** of a certain soul in this life has become **as perfect as in the next**] that the Father of lights [Jas. 1:17], who is not closefisted but diffuses himself abundantly as the sun does its rays, without being a respecter of persons [Acts 10:34], wherever there is room—always showing himself gladly along the highways and byways—does not hesitate or consider it of little import to find his delights with the children of the earth at a common table in the world [Prv. 8:31]. It should not be held as incredible in a soul now examined, purged, and tried in the fire of tribulations, trials, and many kinds of temptations, and found faithful in love, that the promise of the Son of God be fulfilled, the promise that the Most Blessed Trinity will come and dwell in anyone who loves him [Jn. 14:23]. The Blessed Trinity inhabits the soul by divinely illumining its intellect with the wisdom of the Son, delighting its will in the Holy Spirit, and absorbing it powerfully and mightily in the unfathomed embrace of the Father's

---

[1208]Meaning "from the work performed." Defined at Trent to indicate that the sacraments are true instrumental causes of grace; that by the mere fact of them being validly administered, they do indeed confer the grace intended.

[1209] That is, as opposed to "comprehensors," or in other words, the blessed in heaven.

[1210] *Cf.* 1 Samuel 16:7

sweetness.[1211]

All that St. John has here is well-grounded rebukes for those who choose to doubt the unfathomably great levels of sanctity quickly achievable by an "ordinary" soul who has been victorious over tribulations, trials, and temptations (and what devout Catholic today hasn't?). He goes so far as to insist that not only can habitual charity—that is, sanctifying grace[1212]—become in a soul as perfect in this life as in the next, but he also insists that this can be attained with ease because God *"is not closefisted but diffuses himself abundantly."*

Similarly, St. Faustina taught:

> **How very easy it is to become holy; all that is needed is a bit of good will.** If Jesus sees this little bit of good will in the soul, He hurries to give himself to the soul, and nothing can stop Him, neither shortcomings nor falls-absolutely nothing. Jesus is anxious to help that soul, and if it is faithful to this grace from God, it can **very soon attain the highest holiness possible** for a creature here on earth. God is very generous and does not deny His grace to anyone. Indeed He gives more than what we ask of Him."[1213]

"Very soon" and "highest possible"- these phrases should give us great pause. How easy it would have been for St. Faustina to leave them out! Recall that St. Faustina was well aware that Jesus had revealed to her a new and unprecedented sanctity; her Diary itself makes this fact undeniably clear (see the section on St. Faustina in the "Gift Elsewhere in Private Revelation" chapter for an exposition of this point). Faustina knew clearly, therefore, that she was saying that it was precisely this Great and Unprecedented Sanctity which could be attained "very soon," and that its attainment was "very easy."

Relaying the same teaching, St. Thérèse of Lisieux wrote:

> How can a soul so imperfect as mine aspire to the plenitude of Love? ... Alas! I am but a poor little unfledged bird. I am not an eagle, I have but the eagle's eyes and heart! Yet, notwithstanding my exceeding littleness, I dare to gaze upon the Divine Sun of Love, and I burn to dart upwards unto Him! I would fly, I would imitate the eagles; but all that I can do is to lift up my little wings-it is beyond my feeble power to soar. ... With daring self-abandonment there will I remain until death, my gaze fixed upon that Divine Sun. Nothing shall affright me ... "[1214]

In demonstrating that the heights of perfection can be reached not only through precisely the same long and arduous journey that was taken by the great saints we read about, but can also be achieved in a much easier and quicker way, Thérèse teaches the following:

> You know it has ever been my desire to become a Saint, but I have always felt, in comparing myself with the Saints, that I am as far removed from them as the grain of sand, which the passer-by tramples underfoot, is remote from the mountain whose summit is lost in the clouds. Instead of being discouraged, I concluded that God would not inspire desires which could not be realised, and that I may aspire to sanctity in spite of my littleness. For me to become great is impossible. I must bear with myself and my many imperfections; but I will seek out a means of getting to Heaven by a little way-very short and very straight, a little way that is wholly new. We live in an age of inventions; nowadays the rich need not trouble to climb the stairs, they have lifts instead. Well, I mean to try and find a lift by which I may be raised unto God, for I am too tiny to climb the steep stairway of perfection. I have sought to find in Holy Scripture some suggestion as to what this lift might be which I so much desired, and I read these words uttered by the Eternal Wisdom Itself: "Whosoever is a little one, let him come to Me." Then I drew near to God, feeling sure that I had discovered what I sought; but wishing to know further what He would do to the little one, I continued my search and this is what I found: "You shall be carried at the breasts and upon the knees; as one whom the mother caresseth, so will I comfort you." Never have I been consoled by words more tender and sweet. Thine Arms, then, O Jesus, are the lift which must raise me up even unto Heaven. To get there I need not grow; on the contrary, I must remain little.[1215]

A religious sister once wrote to Thérèse to admonish her, saying that her "little way" was truly a "great way," and that although Thérèse says

---

[1211] John of the Cross, *The Living Flame of Love.* 1.15(2-3).

[1212] 1914 Catholic Encyclopedia, *Christian and Religious Perfection.*

[1213] St. Maria Faustina Kowalska, *Divine Mercy in My Soul,* paragraph 291.

[1214] St. Therese of Lisieux, *The Story of a Soul* (New York: An Image Book, Doubleday, a division of Bantam Doubleday Dell Publishing Group, Inc. 1989), Ch. XI.

[1215] Ibid, Chapter IX.

she is just a fledgling little bird with a broken wing who cannot hope to rise up to the heights of the eagles (the great saints), she is in reality just another eagle soaring in the heavens. This view is likely shared by many Catholics when they are introduced to the Little Way of St. Thérèse—Catholics who say to themselves: *"ah! Interesting thing for a canonized saint who never committed a mortal sin to say! And a cloistered nun, no less! This couldn't possibly be less applicable to me."* Thérèse rebuked this sister. The exchange was no doubt arranged by God so that Thérèse could answer this same concern for us all. She said to this sister it was not so—that she truly did not have the greatness of the saints she spoke of. Thérèse insisted that it was confidence and *blind confidence alone* in God, and nothing else. No greatness of the eagle, not even of a subtle type.

As you can see, it is not the saints themselves who exhibit such hesitancy and refusal to believe that the highest levels of holiness are readily within reach of anyone. It is we—ordinary Christians—those who should be the most thankful for this accessibility, who paradoxically are the hesitant ones in this regard! Let us be utterly rid of that hesitancy, for it stems from a skewed, Pelagian perspective of grace. Furthermore, it stems from a cheap humility, for true humility disposes one to look up to some virtue in each person he meets here and now, even the most difficult of souls. Cheap humility is satisfied with relegating this acknowledgement of superiority to dead saints.

Nevertheless, do not expect a mere state of grace and desire for the Gift to long suffice. That temporary state is only the invitation; becoming stable in the Gift and growing deeper into it requires the same *pursuit* of virtue in which all the saints engaged. The present availability of the Gift does not exempt us from seeking heroic virtue anymore than advanced weaponry exempts a modern soldier from the basics of boot camp. Recall that the words of Our Lord *"To whom much is given, much is expected"*[1216] remain true. Our task is to respond to love with love; and if indeed Luisa's revelations are to be believed, then how much more so now must we love God?

A final note is in order on this objection to reiterate just what Living in the Divine Will does *not* do to the soul. For although the loftiness of the claims in

Luisa's writings may at first glance seem without bound, there are of course very important limitations. The creature remains a creature; and whatever glories it participates in by way of Living in the Divine Will are purely by unmerited grace, not by nature. Furthermore, Stephen Patton explains:

> Any involvement that the creature, in the divine will, might be said to have in the eternal, universal act of creation and redemption is entirely derivative, non-essential and participatory. Everything claimed in Luisa's diary about the value of the creature's acts in the divine will, regardless of how enormous, can nevertheless be understood within the parameters of these principles.[1217]

Hugh Owen also reiterates an important distinction regarding the sanctity of a soul living in the Divine Will (one that is sometimes missed by some followers of Luisa) :

> The qualification "insofar as it is possible for a creature" [Jesus gives this distinction to Luisa when discussing the sanctity of a soul after being given the Gift of Living in the Divine Will] is essential to distinguish this concept of mystical union from the concept of Meister Eckart that was condemned as heretical in 1329 by Pope John XXII, namely, that the "Just and divine man ... operates whatever God operates" (*DS* 513). In the Divine Substitution, Blessed Dina participated in the activity of the Holy Trinity, but always within the limits inherent in her possession of a human personality, intellect, memory, and will. Pope John XXII also condemned Meister Eckart's statement that "we are transformed entirely in God, and we are changed into Him; in a similar manner as in the sacrament the bread is changed into the body of Christ; so I am changed into Him, not like (to Him); through the living God it is true that there is no distinction there" (*DS* 510). The statement "there is no distinction" at the end of the article indicates that Meister Eckart could be understood as having conceived of a transformation of the soul into God in such a way that the soul ceased to exist as a distinct created person. Thus, Eckart may have conceived of a transformation of the soul "in a similar manner as in the sacrament the bread is changed into the body of Christ" in the sense that the substance of the soul would disappear just as the substance of the bread disappears in transubstantiation. But that is not what St. Faustina, Blessed Dina, or

---

1216 Luke 12:48

1217 Stephen Patton, *A Guide to the Book of Heaven*. Page 48.

Venerable Conchita mean when they speak of a "living host." For all of them, a "living host" is one who allows Jesus to operate in her humanity so freely that her thoughts, words, and deeds become the thoughts, words, and deeds of Christ—with the full intention of Christ. But they remain the thoughts, words, and deeds of the soul nonetheless.[1218]

As Mr. Owen shows, this new sanctity as revealed to Luisa and many other mystics of the 20th century (some of which he lists in this quote) has important differences from that which the Church has condemned in Meister Eckart's writings; differences which are indeed both fundamental and substantial. Jesus does compare the transubstantiation of the Eucharist to the Gift of Living in the Divine Will in Luisa's writings (and in those of St. Faustina, Blessed Dina, and many others); but He does not say to any of these mystics that a human being with this gift of sanctity is literally himself transubstantiated. For transubstantiation entails a *replacement* of substance. St. Faustina, on the other hand, was inspired to use terminology both similar and different, and she prayed for the *transconsecration* of her very self.

In the Blessed Sacrament, absolutely no substance of bread or wine remains after the consecration; only the accidents remain. In receiving the Gift of Living in the Divine Will, one remains the exact same person he was before receiving it—**but the principle of his soul has been transformed** from the self-will into the Will of God. Furthermore, in His revelations to Luisa, Jesus refers to the Gift of Living in the Divine Will as a *grace* (albeit the greatest possible grace[1219]); but grace is (in the traditional philosophical metaphysics of Thomas— something that has largely been adopted by the Church's Magisterium) an *accident*,[1220] whereas the soul in which it inheres is a *substance* [1221] (or, at least, is the form—the essence—of the substance of the person whose matter is the body).

But this extremely important distinction, in turn, naturally leads us to the consideration of the next objection.

Isn't the Eucharist the greatest thing?

Objection: It is heretical to assert that the Gift of Living in the Divine Will is greater than the Eucharist. God cannot give a greater gift than the Eucharist, and nothing can be called greater than the Eucharist.

Answer: Which is greater: a truckload of bricks, or five miles?

That question makes as much sense as the question of whether the Eucharist or the Gift of Living in the Divine Will is greater. The Eucharist is a substance, the Gift of Living in the Divine Will is an accident (as shown in the previous section). This is not to say we cannot in any way compare the two, but from the onset we must understand that we are not making a literal comparison of greatness of one thing to the other in the same sense (as if, for example, we were comparing the heights of two buildings).

Regarding the intrinsic nature of substance of the Eucharist, it is beyond question that nothing can be greater, for in this the Eucharist is, quite simply, God. It is in this sense that it is often said of the Eucharist, rightfully so, that "God cannot give a greater gift." Of course He cannot! He cannot give more than Himself. To this end, St. John Vianney beautifully proclaimed, *"There is no reality greater than the Eucharist!"*

There are, however, two ways in which something may legitimately said to be "greater" than the Eucharist. The first way is on the part of the subjective effect on the recipient. For example, **if one is in a state of mortal sin and is not perfectly contrite (but is indeed imperfectly contrite),[1222] then the Sacrament of Reconciliation would be far greater *for him* than the Eucharist.** The Eucharist would only serve to increase his condemnation,[1223] whereas Reconciliation would restore him to sanctifying grace. Therefore, in this respect it should be clear that, as there are no doubt many souls in hell, who while on earth received the Eucharist, there can be greater things to desire *for oneself* than the reception of the Eucharist (for

---

1218 Hugh Owen, *New and Divine*. Page 40.
1219 E.g. "Greater grace I could not give" October 20, 1916.
1220 This is meant in the scholastic philosophical sense of the word —a category of being whose nature is not to exist in itself, but in another.

1221 That is, being existing in and by itself – a thing that other things are said of or inhere in. Primary existent.
1222 Cf. *Catechism of the Catholic Church*, paragraph 1453.
1223 Cf. 1 Corinthians 11:29

another example, confirmation in grace).

The second way a thing may be greater than the Eucharist is if, though similar in substance, its accidents correspond more fittingly to the substance than they do in the case of the Eucharist. The Eucharist is the sole example in the universe of a disconnect between the substance of a thing and its accidents. This disconnect enables Christ's true, substantial, physical[1224] presence to remain with us always[1225] without destroying us, thanks to the lowliness of the accidents. However, it is inherently imperfect for accidents to be so poorly conformed to the substance which underlies them, and this is why the Eucharist will cease to exist upon the consummation of the world—because of its imperfection. If the Eucharist, in its current form, was as great as possible, then the Final Coming of Christ at the end of time would be an evil, for it would directly cause the cessation of the greatest good. Such an assertion of course would be absurd. Heaven is something we eagerly await with unbounded joy, and not something we dread because the Eucharist will not exist there!

In this same sense, Christ's final coming in glory will be greater than the Eucharist; not because there is any truly *substantial* difference, but because the accidents of the former will be more properly conformed to the substance; indeed, there will be no more disconnect. Likewise, the Incarnation of the Word is substantially identical to the Eucharist. At the Annunciation, Mary's womb was changed from an empty vessel to a tabernacle for the eternal, infinite, almighty God. At the consecration, the priest's hands go from holding a piece of bread, to holding the eternal, infinite, almighty God. But we rightly say that the Incarnation was greater still than the consecration we witnessed at Mass this morning. We say this for many reasons. First, the Incarnation was preceded by the greatest act of Faith in history: the *Fiat* of the Blessed Virgin. Secondly, in the Incarnation, the Second Person of the Holy Trinity assumed accidents more pleasing to Him than the accidents of bread and wine.

Scripture also teaches us that, upon being found by His parents after being lost for three days, Jesus continued to grow *"in wisdom and stature, and in favor with God and man."*[1226] In a word, He became greater. And yet it goes without saying that He remained the same Person—the Word of God—from His conception onward. But it is far more fitting for the substance of God to be actualized in a full-grown man than in a baby, for childhood is a state of imperfection whose end is full maturity and adulthood.

In a similar sense, Jesus reveals to Luisa that He deems it more fitting to actualize His real life in the soul of a human creature than in the dead accidents of bread and wine. This revelation does not mean that the human being is literally transubstantiated in the precise same manner the Eucharist is! (See the preceding section for a more detailed explanation of this point). The creature remains a creature. The substance of the human being is not replaced with the substance of God, as is the case in the Eucharist. Hence no human other than Jesus—even if by a special revelation of God, the man or woman was known to have the Gift of Living in the Divine Will—can ever be worshipped. We worship God alone, which is why we worship Jesus in the Eucharist; for there is no *other* substance in the Eucharist along with Him,[1227] therefore it is not an idolatrous object of worship.

It is not illicit, however, to consider one respect the Gift of Living in the Divine Will can be said to be greater than the Eucharist, so long as we are careful to issue these distinctions when we speak such words around those not already aware of the distinctions. Jesus tells Luisa:

> My daughter, you too can form hosts and consecrate them. Do you know what the garment is that veils Me in the Most Blessed Sacrament? It is the accidents of the bread with which the host is formed. The life, which dwells in this Host, is My Body, Blood [,soul] and divinity. ... The unconsecrated host is material and purely human. You too have a material body and a human will. This body and this will of yours—if you keep them pure, upright and far from any shadow of sin—are the accidents, the veils that allow Me to consecrate Myself and live hidden within you. But this is not enough, lest it be like an unconsecrated host: My life is needed. My life is composed of

---

[1224] Although it is true that Christ is not in the Eucharist by way of quantitative extension in space, He nevertheless is indeed physically present in the Eucharist inasmuch as He is literally substantially present, and the substantial presence of a thing which has physicality necessarily implies that same physicality present at least qualitatively.

[1225] *Cf.* Matthew 28:20

[1226] Luke 2:52

[1227] As there is in a created person Living in the Divine Will.

sanctity, love, wisdom, power and all else, but the operation is entirely My Will. That is why, after you have prepared the host, you must make your will die within it; you must trample it asunder so that it may no longer re-emerge. Then you must let My Will permeate your entire being ... Only in these living hosts do I find compensation for the loneliness, the hunger and all else that I suffer in tabernacles ... I knew that many graces were needed since I was to operate the greatest miracle that exists in the world, namely, continuously living in My Will [...] This miracle surpasses even that of the Eucharist. Of themselves the accidents of the unconsecrated host possess no reason, will or desire that might otherwise oppose My sacramental life. So, the host contributes nothing, as the work of consecration is entirely Mine. If I so will it, I accomplish it. On the other hand, to accomplish the miracle of living in My Will, I have to bend the soul's reason, its human will, desire and love that are entirely free. And how much effort this takes! Indeed, there are many souls who receive Communion and take part in the miracle of the Eucharist while sacrificing little. Now, it requires more sacrifice to realize the miracle of My Will living in souls, and yet very few there are who dispose themselves to receive it.[1228]

If you are still unconvinced, simply recall once more that this notion is not without precedent or concurring revelations. Rejecting the Divine Will revelations based on this objection would entail the rejection of many other revelations and teachings of saints as well. For example, as was mentioned in the preceding section: **St. Faustina, after long referring to the Eucharist as a "living host," one day asked Jesus to make her very self into the same,** to which He responded: "*You are a living Host, pleasing to the Heavenly Father.*" Also mentioned previously was Venerable Conchita, to whom Jesus revealed " *... to possess [Jesus] and to be possessed by [Jesus] as in one and the same substance*"[1229] In referring to being "one and the same substance," Jesus says to Conchita precisely what Jesus is saying to Luisa in the quote above.

Isn't Christian holiness already greater than original holiness?

Objection: If the purpose of the Gift of Living in the Divine Will is to restore our souls to the same state as Adam's before the fall, then this entails a rejection of the superior dignity of Christian holiness, and it would have simply been better if Adam never sinned in the first place. But God would not have permitted the fall if He were not to bring a greater good out of it, and in the Exultet of the Easter Liturgy, we pray "*O happy fault that merited such and so great a Redeemer!*" Furthermore, the Catechism teaches that the new creation in Christ exceeds Adam's state. Therefore, any reference to a restoration of Adam's state is absurd, since ours as Christians is better.

Answer: **The Church clearly teaches that in some ways our current state is better than Adam's, and in other ways it is not.**

Not only is it not absurd to refer to a restoration of Adam's state in a positive sense as far as holiness is concerned, but even the Church herself uses such terminology in a **prayer of the Mass**:

> ... it is right to celebrate the wonders of your providence, by which **you call human nature back to its original holiness ...** [1230]

Therefore, it is clear that there is at least some aspect of Adam's holiness that even Christians must seek. We can be sure of this duty, as the prayer does not say "you *have placed* human nature back into [or above] its original holiness." Rather, it refers to a *call* – in other words, something we must try to respond to even as Christians with sanctifying grace. From this premise we can conclude that all of us today, even those Christians who have been so blessed as to have received the sacraments and thus sanctifying grace, must still strive for something that Adam had before the fall. Since no one strives for what is below, it is manifest that at least some aspect of Adam's holiness was superior to Christian holiness.[1231]

In the Catechism, however, we read that:

> ... the first man was not only created good, but was also established in friendship with his Creator and in harmony with himself and with the creation around him, in a state that would be surpassed only by the glory of the new creation in Christ.[1232]

[1228] Rev Joseph Iannuzzi, Doctoral Thesis. , 4.1.22.1.

[1229] Fr. Marie-Michel Philipon, O.P. *CONCHITA: A Mother's Spiritual Diary*. Pages 57-58.

[1230] Roman Missal. Preface of Holy Virgins.

[1231] It is obvious that Adam was superior in the senses of lacking concupiscence, having infused knowledge, etc., but that is not to what I am here referring.

[1232] *Catechism of the Catholic Church*, paragraph 375.

It is not immediately clear whether the Catechism is teaching that the new creation in Christ, *in and of itself*, is a superior state to Adam's before the fall, or if the glory of the new creation in Christ would at some point contain a greater glory than Adam's. In other words, it is not clear whether the Catechism is saying that Christian Baptism *itself* makes one holier than Adam, or merely disposes one to receive a greater holiness. Either interpretation, however, is compatible with Luisa's revelations; for even if we defer to the former interpretation, we can simply look to whatever *aspects* of Adam's holiness was superior to ours (for we have already demonstrated that the Church teaches there certainly were aspects of greater holiness in him), and understand that it is this dimension of his holiness that God wishes to restore to us with the Gift of Living in the Divine Will.

To that end, let us examine what is already taught by the Church or agreed upon by theologians about Adam's state (also called "original holiness," "original innocence," "original justice," or "integral nature."[1233])

Adam was created to be a true King over all the world. In addressing the question of whether Adam had mastership over all creatures, Aquinas says:

> Man in a certain sense contains all things; and so according as he is master of what is within himself, in the same way he can have mastership over other things.[1234]

Therefore, we can rest assured that the notion that Adam had a special priestly and kingly calling is not some strange, Gnostic premise to a new-age spirituality! Especially in Luisa's *Rounds of Creation*, we read about (and participate in) Adam's office as priest of creation whose job it is to interiorly assume all things and glorify God in, with, and through them.

We must also not fall victim to believing that, since we now have the Public Revelation of Jesus Christ, our knowledge of God is superior to what Adam had before the Fall. Although this idea may at first glance sound pious and incarnational, it is not true. Again we will defer to the Angelic Doctor, who said:

Nevertheless he **[Adam] knew God with a more perfect knowledge than we do now**. Thus in a sense his knowledge was midway between our knowledge in the present state, and the knowledge we shall have in heaven ...[1235]

The first man was established by God in such a manner as to have knowledge of all those things for which man has a natural aptitude. ... moreover ... the first man was endowed with such a knowledge of [...] supernatural truths as was necessary for the direction of human life in that state. But those things which cannot be known by merely human effort, and which are not necessary for the direction of human life, were not known by the first man; such as the thoughts of men, future contingent events, and some individual facts, as for instance the number of pebbles in a stream; and the like.[1236]

So we can see it is already established that Adam's knowledge of God was greater even than ours is today—notwithstanding the Incarnation, Redemption, Sacred Scripture, Magisterium, Sacred Tradition, etc. This reality alone speaks volumes, as we can combine this fact with the fact that "what is known more is loved more," a veritable axiom in Catholic theology; and from the combination it is evident that Adam's love of God exceeded even our own love of God. But holiness consists in the love of God; therefore Adam in a real, significant sense had a greater holiness than we do.

Of course, a given degree of knowledge does not necessarily *guarantee* a comparable degree of love—tragically there are many who know much about God but do not love Him in stride with that knowledge. We can rest assured, however, that this tragedy was not evident in prelapsarian Adam, whose love and knowledge would have never suffered this disconnect observed so frequently today; for such a disconnect would have itself been a sin, which is by definition excluded from any prelapsarian considerations. Without sin, the rupture between knowledge and love never would have existed, thus Adam's superior knowledge of God alone guaranteed his superior love of God.

Now, it must be admitted that Aquinas held that the Incarnation of Christ was a "contingent" event (that is, not an eternal decree), hence in his view

---

1233 John Paul II, *Man and Woman He Created Them, A Theology of the Body* (Boston, MA: Pauline Books & Media, 2006), Address of September 19, 1979.
1234 St. Thomas Aquinas, *Sum* I Q96, A2 Corpus.

1235 *Ibid.*, Q94, A1 Corpus.
1236 *Ibid.*, A3 Corpus.

Adam would not have known of it, but this idea is by no means Church Teaching. In Luisa's writings we learn that Jesus *would* indeed have become incarnate even had Adam never sinned;[1237] not in order to be a suffering savior, but to be a glorious King to receive the sovereignty from Adam. We learn that the Incarnation was an eternal decree that God had already planned before the dawn of time.

This particular question vindicates the opinion of Bl. Duns Scotus, who insisted that indeed Christ's Incarnation was not contingent. This is not to accuse the *Felix Culpa*[1238] of the Liturgical prayer at Easter of error! The Exultet prayer is far older than Scotus, and he would never contradict it. However, the fault of Adam was in fact—historically—*the reason why* Christ did come (even though He would have come regardless), therefore it remains correct to say that this fault of Adam did indeed *"earn for us so great a Savior."* Hence there is no contradiction between this opinion of Duns Scotus (and Luisa's revelations), and this particular prayer of the Mass.

Thankfully, recognition of the non-contingency— that is, the essential and eternal nature—of the Incarnation seems to be making a comeback in Catholic theology today. This comeback is in part thanks to a renewed love of the teachings of the Fathers of the Church and a continued growth in understanding of the immensity of the Incarnation. Indeed, man's creation—as Genesis says—*"in the image and likeness of God"* makes the most sense with respect to the foreseen Incarnation, which could not have been foreseen, in that sense, upon man's creation if it were contingent, since there had not yet been sin and the concomitant issuance of the protoevangelium. St. Hildegard of Bingen, recently proclaimed a Doctor of the Church, also argued for the eternal nature of the Incarnation, teaching that it was an "ancient counsel" (among those things God predetermined before the foundation of the world). This eternal nature of the Incarnation is also supported by many private revelations which describe the Fall of the Angels as consisting in their rebellion after being presented with the future Incarnation. Fulton Sheen famously relayed this very teaching in his talks. St. Maximilian Kolbe also held that God willed the Incarnation and Immaculate Conception of Mary in one and the same *eternal* decree.

Francisco Suarez, that great 16th century Jesuit compiler and harmonizer of Aquinas and Scotus, also taught that Adam indeed had a belief in the Trinity and in the future Incarnation of the Word of God. There is no use in arguing against this position by saying, *"Nonsense. For with that knowledge, Adam would not have sinned."* You have that knowledge: has it prevented you from sinning? *"No,"* you may reply, *"as I have concupiscence, and Adam did not."* But that, too, fails to satisfy, for it is highly unlikely that your sins are all explicable by mere weakness! Only the Beatific Vision (which indeed Adam did not have) is an absolute safeguard against the possibility of sin. Sins of pure pride or curiosity do not stem merely from concupiscence. It is utterly invalid—and un-Catholic—to assert that all of today's sins are the mere result of concupiscence and nothing else.

***

So it is clear that Adam's knowledge could rightly be considered immense; perfect, in a real way. But we may also separately consider the degree of his merit. On this question, Aquinas teaches:

> We conclude therefore that in the state of innocence man's works were more meritorious than after sin was committed, if we consider the degree of merit on the part of grace, which would have been more copious as meeting with no obstacle in human nature: and in like manner, if we consider the absolute degree of the work done; because, as man would have had greater virtue, he would have performed greater works. But if we consider the proportionate degree, a greater reason for merit exists after sin, on account of man's weakness; because a small deed is more beyond the capacity of one who works with difficulty than a great deed is beyond one who performs it easily."

As you may have already gleaned, Aquinas is by no means distinguished, among the great theologians of the Church, for the degree of exaltation he gives to prelapsarian Adam. Nevertheless, we see even him clearly teaching here that Adam not only had more knowledge of God than we do now (as was settled above), but also that even as far as merit is concerned, **there are *two* senses in which Adam merited more than we do even now as Christians with sanctifying grace, and only one sense in which we merit more now**

[1237]Hence it is not "contingent," or dependent upon some other precursor; i.e., The Fall.

[1238] "Happy Fault"

than prelapsarian Adam did.

For Aquinas here teaches that Adam merited more both in absolute terms (as a rich man can give more money than a poor man), and even on the part of God's grace (which, notwithstanding Adam lacking the Sacraments, could nevertheless be poured out more freely into him than it can be poured into a Christian in a state of grace); however, after sin man can merit more in proportional terms (as the poor widow in the Gospel, in giving two pennies, gave more than the Pharisees).[1239] This beautifully succinct teaching of the Angelic Doctor suffices almost entirely in settling the question of "Original Holiness versus Christian Holiness." Yes, Adam had a greater degree of holiness and merit than even a Christian saint could possibly attain. And yet, there is another sense in which a Christian saint has a greater degree of holiness than Adam could possibly attain.

This distinction provides the answer to the dilemma presented by the consideration that merely returning to a former unfallen state after a fall is not sufficient for God to even permit a fall in the first place. For we know that three conditions are necessary in order for God to so much as permit an evil: first, God must know that He will bring a good out of that evil; second, the good that comes must be greater than good lost; third, there must be no other way of bringing about that greater good.

Only given these three conditions can the existence of any evil possibly be consistent with two great dogmatic truths regarding God; namely, His omnipotence, and His goodness. God created Adam with the highest category of holiness. But God permitted Adam to fall because He foresaw a coming age in which Adam's highest category of holiness could be combined with Christian grace through the merits of the Incarnation and Passion of His Son. In that coming age, treasures could be built up in Heaven that could not possibly have existed without the fall—treasures that will make the blood, sweat, and tears of their attainment seem like nothing. These treasures embellish our celestial home, that which we are "called to by nature but cannot achieve by nature," whereas were Adam to have never fallen, although we would never have lost the terrestrial paradise and the perfect state of our souls, the celestial paradise would not have received the same embellishments and we would be eternally devoid of the glorious crowns which we now have the ability to merit if we so choose. These glorious crowns proceed from our willing suffering and our participation in the sufferings of Christ; which in turn could not have happened without a Fall, as Christ would have then had no cause to suffer. But without the Passion of Christ, God's infinite love for us never would have had its most perfect and beautiful exposition. Therefore we can indeed say that, "thanks to" the fall of Adam, we will have the most glorious possible and imaginable exposition of Divine Love before our eyes for all eternity in the marks that Our Lord continues to carry in His hands and feet, even in Heaven.

When one carefully observes this *Greatest Story Ever Told*, it becomes clear that there is no contradiction between—on the one hand—God's ultimate plan being the restoration of what was lost at the Fall and—on the other hand—Christian holiness being in a sense greater than original holiness. In fact, only now that Jesus has revealed this ultimate plan in detail to Luisa do mysteries which have hitherto perplexed the greatest minds in Church History now begin to become unveiled, and the most difficult of puzzle pieces begin to come together.

Although the theological concerns contained in this objection have already been adequately addressed, it is still worth considering another important realm of teaching on Adam: that given to us by the Fathers of the Church. After pointing out that it is already *defined doctrine* (implicitly at the Council of Trent) that Adam possessed sanctifying grace, Fr. John Hardon sums up the attitude of the Fathers on Adam's state of holiness as follows:

> The Fathers explicitly teach that the first man possessed [deification]… which Adam lost by the fall. … some of the Greek Fathers, like Basil and Cyril of Alexandria, believed that the supernatural sanctification of Adam is indicated in Genesis 2:7. They took spiraculum **vitae to mean the grace of the Holy Spirit as a supernatural vital principle.** Others, notably Ireneus, Gregory of Nyssa and Augustine, held that imago Dei referred to Adam's nature, while similitudo Dei described him as being in the state of sanctifying grace. Apart from their

---

[1239] Cf. Luke 21:3

interpretation of the texts, the Fathers' common belief that Adam received both natural and supernatural life is a witness to Christian tradition.[1240]

On this same topic, Cardinal Schonborn—the editor of the new official *Catechism of the Catholic Church*—recently taught "**Deification is located in the reestablishing of fallen man in his innate dignity.**"[1241]

These beliefs of the Greek Fathers (Basil, Cyril, and others)—that Adam was "deified" and that the Holy Spirit was the *very supernatural vital principle of his life*—point to a far higher degree of sanctity in Adam than even a Christian in a State of Grace necessarily enjoys. For the deification (or, alternately, the divinization or "Theosis") of man is that at which the highest sanctity aims, not that at which it begins, which is sanctifying grace. **By teaching that the Holy Spirit was the vital principle of Adam's life, the Greek Fathers are almost explicitly teaching that Adam possessed the Gift of Living in the Divine Will, and that he possessed a divinized state that is far higher than "ordinary" Christian holiness.** (Jesus explicitly describes the Gift to Luisa as a state wherein the Will of God becomes the life principle of one's soul just as the soul is the life principle of one's body).

But we should conclude this consideration with a reminder that Jesus makes it clear to Luisa that the Fall enabled man to become more glorious than he ever was before falling; and He gives Luisa this teaching while praising the Church's proclamation of Adam's "happy fault." We must never lose sight of the fact that God, as the saying goes, "had a plan" with the Fall, and that we need not waste time lamenting it, for what we now have access to in Christ's Incarnation and Paschal Mysteries is even greater (especially now that God has deigned to reveal the Gift to us through Luisa). He tells Luisa:

> My daughter, I created the creature beautiful, noble, with eternal and divine origin, full of happiness and worthy of Me. Sin ruined him from top to bottom, it disennobled him, it deformed him, and rendered him the most unhappy creature, unable to grow, because sin stopped his

growth and covered him with wounds, such as to be repugnant to the mere sight. Now, my Redemption ransomed the creature from sin, and my Humanity acted just like a tender mother with her newborn: since he can take no other food, in order to give life to her baby, she opens her breast and attaches her baby to it; and from her own blood, converted into milk, she administers to him the nourishment to give him life. More than mother, my Humanity let many holes be opened in Itself by blows of lash, almost like many breasts, which sent out rivers of blood, so that my children, by attaching themselves to them, might suckle the nourishment to receive life and develop their growth. And **with my wounds I covered their deformities, rendering them more beautiful than before; and if in creating them I made them like clearest and noble heavens, in Redemption I adorned them, studding them with the most refulgent stars of my wounds so as to cover their ugliness and render them more beautiful**. To their wounds and deformities I attached the diamonds, the pearls, the gems of my pains in order to hide all their evils and clothe them with such magnificence as to surpass the state of their origin. **This is why, with reason, the Church says: 'Happy fault'—because with sin came Redemption; and my Humanity not only nourished them with Its Blood, but clothed them with Its own Person, and adorned them with Its own beauty**… [1242]

But understanding this exaltation of Adam's state is also the key to unlocking another mystery about which Catholic theologians have debated for millennia (not to mention philosophers before Christ) but who have still failed to come to a solid conclusion regarding (and the Church still does not have a definitive teaching to settle the matter). And the mystery is: the natural end of man.

The Natural End of Man

We know that no evil can be attributed to God, and yet the proper definition of evil is "the absence of a due perfection." So the next question is: "what perfection is due in man, in his very nature?" This question is essentially identical to the question "What is the natural end of man?" For whatever perfection is due to man in his nature must itself

---

[1240]John A. Hardon, S.J., *God the Author of Nature and the Supernatural*. Thesis VIII. Part III. (Note: in the original text, Fr. Hardon indicates that the Fathers "called sanctifying grace deification;" but I have omitted this from the quote because my purpose here is to draw attention to the view of the Greek Fathers that Fr. Hardon here cites—Church Fathers who

clearly view Adam's state as consisting in much more than just sanctifying grace.
[1241] Cardinal Christoph Schonborn. *From Death to Life: The Christian Journey*. 1995. Page 50.
[1242] February 26, 1922.

also be our natural end even now, and must have been in Adam upon his creation (lest we attribute an evil to God in creating Adam without this due perfection, which would be abhorrent). Hence we arrive at the debate regarding the natural end of man. After a lengthy treatment of the various positions on this question, the New Catholic Encyclopedia states:

> "The present disagreement among Catholic thinkers concerning the natural end of man indicates that **there is not yet a completely satisfactory resolution of this problem** ... "[1243]

It will likely seem strange, to one not hitherto acquainted with this theological and philosophical conundrum, that such an important question about our very nature itself does not yet have a "satisfactory resolution." But God has a plan in allowing this delay. **Jesus' revelations to Luisa give the satisfactory resolution to this problem**, and we will presently discuss the nature of this resolution.

First, some background is needed. A catechized Catholic—or, for that matter, even any lukewarm Christian—will likely respond correctly when asked what man's purpose is: "Heaven." Indeed, Heaven is our ultimate end and our ultimate destiny. One brought up learning the Baltimore Catechism will respond even more precisely to the same question: "To know, love, and serve God in this life, and be happy with Him forever in the next."

These answers, while correct, also leave something out. Heaven—the Beatific Vision—although it truly is our destiny, is nevertheless not a due perfection in our nature itself. It is, rather, a completely gratuitous gift from God; not a "just payment" that arises from our nature. This distinction is anything but "hair splitting," for **what is due in our nature itself is also that which Adam must have enjoyed before the fall and is that to which we must return before the end of time.**

Although there are still some theologians who cling strongly to the notion that the Beatific Vision itself is not only the "end" or "destiny" of man, but also is man's *natural* end, the fact is that Venerable Pope Pius XII taught this clearly in his encyclical, *Humani Generis*, that this teaching is in error. In paragraph 26, the Pope lists a number of errors he condemns (e.g. the notion that the Eucharist is a mere symbol), and among these anathematized propositions, we read:

> Others destroy the gratuity of the supernatural order, since God, they say, cannot create intellectual beings without ordering and calling them to the beatific vision.

So, we see that the Magisterium has strongly condemned the notion that the creation of an intellectual being (i.e. man or angel) automatically demands that such beings be ordered to (in other words, "have the natural end of...") the Beatific Vision. For, as the Pope says, this contradicts the fact of the *gratuity* of the supernatural order, because a thing is gratuitous if it is given above and beyond the demands of justice, whereas God creating a thing with its *naturally due perfections* is an act of justice, not of gratuitousness.

Wrestling with this conundrum, some philosophers and theologians recently have gone too far in the opposite direction—which is indeed the greater danger—and have sided with Germain Grisez and the "new natural lawyers," who hold that the natural end of man consists merely in terrestrial goods. They do not deny that there will be a Beatific Vision, but they deny we are called to it in our nature. Here lies the subtle yet essential distinction: while God cannot create a being that lacks its due perfections (for that would be an evil), He *can* create a being that lacks the total fulfillment of all the calls that arise from that being's nature (for that is not an evil but is simply a step in a process whose ultimate goal has not yet been attained).

Between these two erroneous extremes, we have a golden mean teaching that has not yet been proposed in the mainstream theological schools of thought in the Catholic world today, and yet clearly resolves the conundrum. It is none other than the answer we find in Jesus' revelations to Luisa. For the sake of clarifying its distinction from the extremes, we consider this answer as juxtaposed to them:

[1243] *New Catholic Encyclopedia*. Second Edition. 2003. Man, Natural End Of. *Toward a Solution.*

Erroneous Extreme 1:	The natural end of man—the due perfection of man's very nature—is the Beatific Vision itself.
Golden Mean Truth:	The natural end of man consists in his greatest faculty—his will—having as its own principle the Divine Will. The Beatific Vision is a *call* that man finds within his nature even with this natural end fulfilled; thus the end of man is still Heaven.
Erroneous Extreme 2:	The natural end of man consists merely in the terrestrial goods, and even more broadly the end of man excludes the Beatific Vision (even though the Beatific Vision will indeed be given as a gift for which we do not even naturally long, and to which we are not naturally called).

As we have already shown, Erroneous Extreme 1 was clearly condemned by Pope Pius XII (although it is still promoted by some strict Thomists today), and beyond that is clearly theologically and philosophically flawed: God created Adam without the Beatific Vision, and thus we cannot say the Beatific Vision was due in the nature of man, otherwise God would have thus committed an evil. Erroneous Extreme 2 is worse; its exponents even explicitly condemn Augustine's famous teaching that *"our hearts are restless 'till they rest in Thee"* as a "blunder"(see the section entitled "Heresies Implicit in Accusing the Era of a Messianic Duplicating of Heaven" in the chapter against millenarianism for a more substantial explanation of the problem of this view).

One might still wonder what makes the "Golden Mean Truth" listed above correct; for merely placing a proposition in between erroneous extremes does not alone justify the proposition. So, we now turn to consider, positively, why the golden mean listed in the table above is indeed the truth.

The "good"—that is, the "natural end" (wherein "end" refers to purpose or goal, not to demise or cessation)—of any individual thing always consists

in the greatest power of that thing being completely dominated by the corresponding power of a being of a higher nature.

Accordingly, the "good," or "natural end," of any musical instrument is to have its musical potency (its greatest power as a physical object) actualized by an expert musician, with the instrument itself providing no impediment to the musician's skill, but rather beautifully incarnating the same. The good of a plant is to have its fruit (the generation of which is its own greatest power) be consumed and digested by a sentient being (whether man or animal), such that the matter of this fruit becomes so dominated by this sentient being that it is incorporated into the body of the latter. The good of an animal is to be perfectly obedient with its own sentience (its greatest power) to man and to serve the latter; for example, one observes most clearly the natural end of an animal in a domesticated service dog who obeys his master perfectly.

And the natural end, or good, of man is to have his own greatest faculty—his will—be completely and totally dominated by the corresponding power of a higher being: the Will of God. In other words, the natural end of man is Living in the Divine Will.

Isn't ordinary holiness enough? How could not "Living in the Divine Will" be an evil?

Objection: I heard that Jesus condemns "not living in His Will" as "the greatest crime." How absurd! With these words, He is basically condemning all the saints of Church History before the 20th century!

Answer: **This is a serious misinterpretation of Jesus' revelations to Luisa which is repeatedly contradicted in the revelations themselves.**

There are some passages in Luisa's writings that are misleading if read out of context—for they might be misinterpreted to mean that so-called "ordinary" sanctity—the type of sanctity that the Church has always had and that the Saints have always enjoyed—is a bad thing; a kind of "dung" compared to the Gift of Living in the Divine Will.

But this indeed would be a grave misinterpretation, because **whenever Jesus seems to be saying something like it to Luisa (that is, lamenting "merely doing" the Divine Will instead of "living in it"), He always is referring to one who** deliberately chooses to only do God's Will and correspondingly rejects the invitation to the even greater glory of living in It. For example, Jesus tells Luisa:

> …one who does my Divine Will and does not live in It, finds herself in the condition of being able to receive, but not to give; and since she lives outside of God, not in God, she sees the earth, feels the passions, which put her in continuous danger and give her an intermittent fever, such that they feel now healthy, now sick; now they want to do good, and now they get tired, they are bored, they become irritated and leave good. They are just like those who do not have a home in which to be safe, but live in the middle of the street, exposed to cold, to rain, to the scorching sun, to dangers, and they live of alms. **Just penalty, for one who *could* live in God, while she contents herself with living outside of God**.[1244]

We also recall that Jesus tells Luisa that, before He revealed the Gift to her, it could not be enjoyed by the saints on earth, for—through no fault of their own—they simply did not happen to live in the time of its Reign. By definition, therefore, almost all the saints of Church History were not living in the Divine Will. Despite the fact that these saints were "only" doing the Divine Will, Jesus has nothing but the greatest exaltation for them in His words to Luisa. Consider, for example, what Jesus tells Luisa about St. Aloysius—a soul who "only" did the Divine Will (he died in 1591):

> **Look at how beautiful Aloysius is**; but what was greatest in him, which distinguished him on earth, was the love with which he operated. **Everything was love in him**—love occupied his interior, love surrounded him externally; so, one can say that even his breath was love. This is why it is said of him that he never suffered distraction—because love inundated him everywhere, and with this love he will be inundated eternally, as you see. "And in fact it seemed that **the love of Saint Aloysius was so very great, as to be able to burn the whole world to ashes.** Then Jesus added: "I stroll upon the highest mountains, and there I form my delight." Since I did not understand the meaning of it, He continued, saying: "**The highest mountains are the Saints who have loved Me the most, and in them I form my delight, both when they are on earth, and when they pass into Heaven**. So,

everything is in love."[1245]

And elsewhere:

> My daughter, Aloysius is a flower and a Saint bloomed from the earth of my Humanity and made bright by the reflections of the rays of the Sun of my Will… Aloysius, more than flower, bloomed from my Humanity—pure, holy, noble, possessing the root of pure love, in such a way that in each petal of his flower one can see written, 'love'. But what renders him more beautiful and brilliant are the rays of my Will, to which he was always submitted—rays which gave such development to this flower as to render it unique on earth and in Heaven.[1246]

It would be difficult to find any private revelations that extoll the saints more than Jesus here extolls Saint Aloysius Gonzaga, and it is precisely in this exaltation that we see how to properly treat, even in light of these Divine Will revelations, those who "only" do the Divine Will—**namely, no differently at all**. For as we can see, there is simply no room for the false interpretation of Luisa's writings that would dare to look down on "only doing the Divine Will." And not only does Jesus exalt the saints who "merely did the Divine Will," but throughout Luisa's diary, Jesus regularly extols the "ordinary" virtues of "ordinary" sanctity. Indeed, St. Hannibal—who will always be the supreme interpreter of Luisa's revelations—is vindicated in his insistence that one who wishes to follow Luisa's revelations must pursue all the virtues that the saints have always pursued—not less so now that we have access to the Gift of Living in the Divine Will—but, rather, *more* so!

But what about St Joseph?

St. Joseph *is* the greatest saint after the Blessed Virgin Mary. Luisa's revelations neither change that nor attempt to change that. There are only two saints Luisa invokes in every single volume of her diary: Mary and Joseph. Jesus goes so far as to call St. Joseph the very prime minister of the Kingdom of the Divine Will (a title Jesus gives to no one else), and says that this Kingdom was in full force in the home of Nazareth. He tells Luisa that Joseph lived in the reflections of the Divine Will (some argue that Jesus here teaches that St. Joseph actually did truly live in the Divine Will; I leave that debate to

---

[1244] January 10, 1930.
[1245] June 20, 1899.

[1246] June 21, 1926.

worthier followers of Luisa than myself).

It is difficult to understand why the people who have no problem seeing that the Eucharist is a far greater gift than St. Joseph ever received (for he died before the Institution of the Eucharist)—but that this nevertheless does not detract from the reality of St. Joseph's *own* superior greatness—cannot acknowledge that the same thing could be said of the Gift of Living in the Divine Will.

One who rejects Luisa's revelations on the Gift of Living in the Divine Will—but does not fail to criticize them for a perceived inadequacy in depicting St. Joseph with respect to the Gift—is only thereby revealing his duplicity. For he apparently does not even believe in the Gift of Living in the Divine Will; saying either there is no such thing, or a human cannot have it other than Our Lady, or no human could have it on earth—while at the same time complaining of St. Joseph not having this very thing that he says no one can have anyway. It is reminiscent of the arguments of those atheists who cannot decide whether they disbelieve in God or whether they are angry at God, and proceed to castigate Him with all manner of contradictions.

***

Admittedly, we are still left with another potential confusion, for one might still say, "*Okay; I grant that distinction, but I still do not understand how not living in the Divine Will could be some sort of an evil or a crime if one is at least doing the Divine Will as the alternative; for doing the Divine Will is an intrinsically good thing; how could it ever constitute an evil?*"

But even this qualified objection itself still arises from a banal and uncatechized view of the nature of evil, which perhaps reduces it to mere physical pain and contradicting the Commandments.

For evil itself is, simply, the *absence of a due perfection*. More precisely, Aquinas teaches that evil is "the absence of the good, which is natural and due to a thing."[1247] Therefore, the greater the perfection that is lacking, the more evil is the lack thereof.

It is not an evil for a child to be born without wings, for wings are not due in the nature of man. It would be an evil for a child to be born without an index finger on his right hand, as this is due in the nature of man. But it would be a far greater evil (in the physical sense, of course, not the moral sense) for a child to be born without eyes, as this is an even greater due perfection in the nature of man.

We have already settled, countless times throughout this book (and indeed the entire purpose of Luisa's revelations is precisely this), **that Living in the Divine Will is the greatest due perfection of man. It is impossible, therefore, to come to any conclusion whatsoever other than the one that holds that its lack must be the greatest evil.**

Before God had deigned to reveal the Gift, its lack could not have been a moral evil (even though, in a sense, it was still an "ontological evil," since human nature still demanded the Gift even though it was not then accessible to us), for there can never be an "ought" without a "can." Similarly, before Christianity—even though fallen humanity still earnestly needed a savior—no Pagan before Christ was guilty for not acknowledging the One who had not yet become Incarnate. And even now, invincible ignorance safeguards from moral evil those who, although they live in the Age of Christianity, nevertheless have not been given sufficient opportunities to truly recognize the validity and necessity of Christ and His Church.

In the same way, Jesus' rebukes that are directed towards not living in His Will are only directed towards those who 1) live in the time in which He has deigned to give the Gift, 2) know about His desire to give the Gift, and 3) have acquired sufficient understanding regarding this desire of His. For such a person, indeed, rejecting this offer to live in God's Will for the sake of wishing to only do His Will is a great evil.

There is nothing novel about the diagnosis wherein a great evil is seen to have arisen from circumstances involving choosing an objective good, but in contradiction to choosing a greater good. Throughout Church History and salvation history, perhaps the greatest obstacles to God's plan for the world and for individual's lives comes not from those who directly promote evil, but rather from the rejection of greater goods that God wishes to give, ostensibly for the sake of the dignity

---

[1247] *Summa Theologica*. First Part. Question 49. Article 1. Corpus.

of lesser goods. This is a great stumbling block to Providence.

- It is why the Pharisees preferred their Mosaic Law to Christ's Law of Grace, foolishly saying to themselves "the old wine is good."[1248]
- It is why the rich young man in the Gospels "went away sad,"[1249] rejecting the great good of radically following Christ to the lesser good of merely obeying the Commandments (and why, to this day, many vocations are lost).
- It is why so many Catholics have deprived themselves of torrents of grace, preferring the Jansenism of only receiving Communion once a year to the insistence of Pope St. Pius X that Catholics should receive it every single day.
- It is why even recently many Catholics rejected the Divine Mercy revelations given to St. Faustina, seeing them as an affront to the Sacred Heart revelations given to St. Margaret Mary Alacoque.

And it is one reason why, today, some reject the revelations of the Divine Will entrusted to Luisa by Jesus Himself, and reject the invitation to *live in* God's Will because they prefer the spirituality that is only concerned with *doing* God's Will. Holiness does not consist in intellectually discovering some objectively good things and proceeding to shut one's ears to God while pursuing these specific good things alone. Holiness consists in getting out of God's way; it consists, indeed, in listening to Him and *doing* His Will—*which also means living in* His Will if this is what He asks of us.

This is a new revelation? Isn't that heretical?

Objection: Luisa herself states that she has received a "new revelation," and that can only be diabolical. We have one, public revelation, and it is closed and finished.

Answer: Luisa's writings do indeed contain a new "revelation." So did those of St. Faustina, St. Margaret Mary Alacoque, St. Bernadette, and St. Catherine Labouré, to name a few. However, none of them offered a *new public* revelation, and neither does Luisa have a *new public* revelation.

Ironically the very paragraph of the Catechism that issuers of this objection cite is likewise the answer to their objection. Great precision must be used with our language. The Catechism states:

> Throughout the ages, there have been so-called "private" revelations ... They do not belong, however, to the deposit of faith ... Guided by the Magisterium of the Church, the sensus fidelium knows how to discern and welcome in these **revelations** whatever constitutes an authentic call of Christ or his saints to the Church.[1250]

Carefully reading this passage from the Catechism shows us **that the Magisterium itself refers to these "private" revelations quite simply as *revelations***. The only thing we must be sure to avoid is any claimed *new public* revelation; meaning, any claim to modify the Deposit of Faith.[1251]

It is also important to understand that, contrary to what sadly seems to have become a common notion today among Catholics, the preceding paragraph of the Catechism does not say that public revelation is "closed, ended, and fully understood." Rather, the Catechism simply states that public revelation is "complete" and that no "new" public revelation is to be expected. When at once this is understood, it is easy to see that there is another sense in which public revelation is still unfolding—not in the sense that there will be any new public revelations, but in the sense that the public revelation we already have remains to be fully explicated, applied, and lived. To this end, God deemed it necessary to send us mystics like St. Francis, St. Dominic, St. Margaret Mary Alacoque, St. Catherine Labouré, St. Faustina, and the Servant of God Luisa Piccarreta.

The job of the Magisterium of the Church is not to convey to the faithful precisely what is coming upon the world and the Church. How easy it is to fall into the trap of yelling "heresy!" at any surprise. Against this, Pope Francis teaches that God is:

> ... the God of surprises. And God, many times, also had surprises in store for his people ... this is why Jesus scolds the members of that generation, for being closed, for being incapable of

---

[1248] Luke 5:39
[1249] Matthew 19:22
[1250] *Catechism of the Catholic Church*, paragraph 67.

[1251] *Ibid.*, paragraph 66.

recognizing the signs of the times, for not being open to the God of surprises, for not being on a journey toward the Lord's triumphant finale, to the point that when he explains it, they think it is blasphemy.[1252]

Luisa's revelations do indeed fit beautifully on the foundation of Sacred Tradition, a fact that will be covered in the answer to a forthcoming objection and which was shown in great detail in Part One of this book. On the other hand, they are not without their surprises for the Church, either. And how many there are who fall into the perennial trap of the Pharisee, thinking in fact that they have the remainder of Church history quite well figured out, and that they are perfectly disposed to reject at a whim whatever comes along which contradicts this master plan of theirs. Dr. Peter Kreeft summed it up well when he said something to the effect of "a subjectivist is one who says that knowledge cannot attain to the truth, a Pharisee is one who says that his knowledge is identical to the truth, and a Christian is one who knows Truth but stands in awe that the Truth is greater than his knowledge of it."

Novelty-Phobia and Novelty-Philia: Both are Traps

Among the more "conservative" Catholic authors, much has been written (since the Second Vatican Council) about how dangerous of a thing obsession with novelty is. And these authors are absolutely correct. But these authors are only giving half of the story; for "novelty-phobia" can be just as harmful a disease as "novelty-philia."

Consider several things that form the very backbone of the life of a Catholic: The Eucharist, Confession, Marian Devotion, and Purgatory. Each of these four things are scarcely addressed in the Bible. Catholic apologists have done an excellent job recently explaining how, in fact, these Catholic truths do indeed have a Biblical basis. But let us also not forget that this Biblical basis is nothing but seminal and minuscule.

Nevertheless, that scarcely perceptible presence is enough to radically affect the lives of Catholics for thousands of years to come. For a good Catholic realizes that one of his most important duties is to work and pray for the deliverance of the holy souls in Purgatory. A good Catholic realizes that the

"source and summit" of his life is the Eucharist; and he even lives his whole life "from Communion to Communion." A good Catholic realizes that frequent heartfelt Confession is his "tribunal of mercy" and his ultimate source of grace after sin, and of healing in general. And a good Catholic realizes that the name of Mary should constantly be on his lips; that he should consecrate himself to her as a willing slave; that he should prayer to her at length every day in the Rosary.

One can easily see a Protestant's difficulty with these things, having only the "sealed deposit of Faith" to consult. It is precisely this "novelty-phobia," and its concomitant unwillingness to recognize the hand of Providence in any development, so ingrained in the nature of Protestantism, that seals them off from the one true Church. It causes them to "reinvent the wheel" every several decades, with each new generation of Protestants seeming to think it has finally discovered how to reacquire that "original, untainted Christianity" of the first couple centuries. Thus, they run in vain on a perpetual treadmill.

The real tragedy is that some Catholics, who should know better, do the exact same thing. They almost explicitly defend novelty-phobia, supposing it is a safeguard against the heresy of Modernism—which it is not and can never be—for safety is only found in trust in the Will of God.

No one is more excited about novelty-phobia than the devil, who is well aware of its power over the faithful and who does not miss the opportunity to use it to his advantage. In the Book of Jude (Chapter 1, verse 9), we read:

> But when the archangel Michael, contending with the devil, disputed about the body of Moses, he did not presume to pronounce a reviling judgment upon him, but said, "The Lord rebuke you."

Though at first glance mysterious, the meaning of this verse is actually well understood. The devil wanted the Israelites to know where the body of Moses was laid to rest, because he knew they would idolize it. The Archangel Michael, thankfully, prevented the devil from succeeding in his aims, and to this day no one knows where the body of Moses is.

[1252]Pope Francis. Homily on October 13, 2014.

This speaks volumes: for too often we forget that idolatry remains a sin even if its object is a good and holy thing. What the devil knew the Israelites would do with Moses' body, some Catholics today do with the teachings of St. Thomas Aquinas (or St. Augustine, or whoever else they have erroneously exalted the opinions of to the status of infallibility).

Those who display this rigidity are usually only apologists or self-proclaimed "theologians," or at best amateur theologians or brand-new graduate students or seminarians, who are completely oblivious to just how many opinions of these very Doctors they themselves contradict every day. They forget that our job as Catholics is never to simply shut off our brains and do whatever one person says, and defend his views no-matter-what.

Recall the Magisterial teaching of Venerable Pope Pius XII, quoted earlier in this book:

> ... all moreover should abhor that intemperate zeal which imagines that whatever is new should for that very reason be opposed or suspected ...[1253]

As we can see, the verdict has already been given on novelty-phobia: the Church demands that we **abhor** it.

St. Thomas Aquinas is the greatest theologian in history and the greatest Doctor of the Church. St. Augustine is not far behind him. We must have enormous admiration for these great saints and a great deference to their teachings. I believe I take my own advice here: I even consider myself a Thomist, and I pray to St. Augustine every day. But we offend no one more than these very saints themselves when we develop a novelty-phobia on their accounts. Great as these men are, they are fallible men. God has reserved infallibility for His Church; not for individual members of it.

Therefore, there is nothing pious or "safe" about a rigid insistence upon each and every opinion of this or that Doctor of the Church, not even upon those of the greatest. Some Thomists seem to forget one of the most important teachings in the entire Summa, in which he quotes Aristotle, namely:

> We ought to pay as much attention to the undemonstrated sayings and opinions of persons who surpass us in experience, age and prudence, as to their demonstrations.[1254]

Accordingly, Thomas himself would never have wanted those in the scholastic school that he inspired to be so rigidly insistent upon each of his opinions.

Consider what moral of the story the historical facts convey regarding Aquinas. Indeed, that he gave us a truly perennial philosophy and theology, and we reject it at our own peril. But likewise it teaches against the opposite extreme. In the 14th century, Pope John XXII said Aquinas' teaching "*could only be miraculous.*" Pope St. Pius V declared him a Doctor of the Church in the 16th century, saying his works are "*the most certain rule of Christian doctrine.*" In that same century, the term "dunce" was coined, a take on the name of Bl. Duns Scotus; an insult whose flourishing no doubt had at least in part to thank the fact that Bl. Scotus disagreed so clearly with Aquinas on Mary's conception, with the former insisting it was completely Immaculate.

But no doubt many thought to themselves, "*How could the greatest Doctor of the Church, so exalted and insisted upon by the Roman Pontiffs, be wrong? I will advocate for his opinion on all things; it is more reliable.*" The rest is history. Consider how foolish those Catholics who insisted upon a rigid adherence to each tenet of Aquinas' must have felt when, in 1854, Pius IX proclaimed infallibly that indeed Mary was Immaculately Conceived, free from all sin from the moment of her conception. Worse still, consider how many graces they missed out on by not acknowledging Our Lady as the Immaculate Conception. They of course were not guilty of formal heresy (the Church had not yet extraordinarily defined the teaching), but that does not mean they lost nothing due to it. Let us be sure to not, in like fashion, miss out on the graces contained in Luisa's revelations.

But most Catholics already know of Thomas' error on the Immaculate Conception. This error, however, was not some strange exception to an otherwise perfect record. Whoever reads his *Summa* will regularly stumble upon opinions of Aquinas that have rightly been moved on from by the Church (although regular, this still constitutes a minuscule fraction of his teachings; he likely has a much higher percentage of correct opinions than any other theologian). And St. Augustine, great as he is and was, had far more erroneous opinions

---

[1253] Pope Pius XII, Encyclical Promoting Biblical Studies *Divino Afflante Spiritu* (30 September 1943), 47.

[1254] St. Thomas Aquinas, *Sum* I-II. 95. 2.

than St. Thomas.

I conclude this consideration by deferring to the Magisterium. The following are excerpts from *Gaudete et Exsultate*, an Apostolic Exhortation promulgated by Pope Francis. Whatever one's opinion of Pope Francis himself or of his own personal views, one thing is clear: as Catholics, we must submit to his Magisterium. Although some points in these quotes are only tangentially relevant to the question at hand, they can all nevertheless illuminate the proper approach that we as Catholics should have to what appears novel:

> There are some testimonies that may prove helpful and inspiring, but that we are not meant to copy, for that could even lead us astray from the one specific path that the Lord has in mind for us. The important thing is that each believer discern his or her own path, that they bring out the very best of themselves, the most personal gifts that God has placed in their hearts (cf. 1 Cor 12:7), rather than hopelessly trying to imitate something not meant for them…

> Each saint is a mission, planned by the Father to reflect and embody, at a specific moment in history, a certain aspect of the Gospel…Every saint is a message which the Holy Spirit takes from the riches of Jesus Christ and gives to his people…

> You too need to see the entirety of your life as a mission. Try to do so by listening to God in prayer and recognizing the signs that he gives you…

> **Nor are the Church's sound norms sufficient**. We should always remember that discernment is a grace. Even though it includes reason and prudence, it goes beyond them, for it seeks a glimpse of that unique and mysterious plan that God has for each of us, which takes shape amid so many varied situations and limitations.

> **When somebody has an answer for every question, it is a sign that they are not on the right road**. They may well be false prophets, who use religion for their own purposes, to promote their own psychological or intellectual theories. God infinitely transcends us; he is full of surprises. We are not the ones to determine when and how we will encounter him; the exact times and places of that encounter are not up to us. Someone who wants everything to be clear and sure presumes to control God's transcendence.[1255]

This is only private revelation; can't

I ignore it if I wish?

Objection: No matter what Luisa says, and no matter what this book says about Luisa, I don't care. I simply refuse to acknowledge or follow these writings, and this is my right as a Catholic. My only obligation is to submit to the Deposit of Faith, and private revelation never becomes a part of that.

Answer: One can search every single teaching, of every Magisterial Document, from every Pope and every Church Council, from every Century of the entire history of the Catholic Church, and he will not find one word of it teaching that a Catholic is never obliged to follow private revelation, or that all Catholics are only ever obliged to submit to the Deposit of Faith and nothing more. This is only a patently false opinion that has been promoted heavily by a small handful of mostly career lay apologists the past few decades (some of whom, one cannot help but wonder, perhaps see Heaven's Messages as competition for their own writings and businesses). It is nothing but a purely demonically-inspired fabrication that, instead of rightly seeing the Magisterium as a solid foundation on which to stand and a sure fence safeguarding a cliff, rather sees it as a cage to lock oneself and in which to hide. It is easy to see how frantically the devil promotes this lie, for it is precisely private revelation that is more needed today than ever to defeat the unprecedented surge of evil dominating the entire world.

Please see the "On Private Revelation in General" chapter in Part One of this book for more information on this topic and a more complete answer to this objection.

Isn't this at least an artificial development of Tradition?

Objection: Even if nothing downright-opposed to Church teaching is contained in Luisa's revelations, they should still be shunned due to how much disagreement there is in them with the writings of Doctors of the Church and other such lofty authorities on orthodox Catholic theology.

Answer: If Luisa's revelations do exhibit an artificial degree of development of Catholic

---

[1255] Pope Francis. Gaudete et Exsultate

thought (in such a way that they do not fit comfortably and beautifully on the tradition handed onto us by two thousand years of saints), then they should indeed be shunned. For any development of doctrine to be valid, it must have stability on the foundation that precedes it. But it need not be without a single difference. Perhaps this distinction is best considered by way of an illustration.

God is seeking to build a beautiful Cathedral by Sacred Tradition's growth throughout history, not a box-shaped skyscraper. Each age in the Church on earth can count many members in two camps; in the first camp are those who disregard the foundation and strive to build a wing jutting out at a dangerous angle. This new construction will fall in a short amount of time and cause the destruction of many lives. This is what occurred in the wake of the Second Vatican Council when so many priests, religious, and laity, interpreting the Council in an erroneous manner, rejected that Hermeneutic of Continuity so beautifully defended by Pope Benedict XVI, in favor of one of rupture. Modernism invaded as orders, parishes, seminaries, and Catholic schools emptied like never before seen in the history of the Church. This indeed is the greatest danger.

In the other camp are those who insist that each successive level be identical to the one on which it rests. In so doing they declare themselves the architects instead of the laborers. But it is essential that we constantly strive to ensure that we are permitting the Holy Spirit to be the architect of history—Church history especially. Any architect who hired a builder to construct a Cathedral that was his life's masterpiece and found one day that only a warehouse was being built, would fire this builder at once and demand an account. Such a builder has buried his talent in the ground, and as such has proved himself a worthless servant, worthy of only being cast into the outer darkness.[1256]

No single cut-and-dry theological answer will suffice to settle whether Luisa's revelations consist in (as her detractors levy) an unstable wing, or if they amount to a magnificent solid gold steeple to finish off the Cathedral. But I am convinced that any learned Catholic who reads Luisa's writings, so long as this is done without the clenched fist

mentioned in the beginning of this chapter, will be struck with how harmoniously they integrate with and build upon the great writings of the Church; especially those of the Fathers, Doctors, and Popes. And if anyone has trouble seeing this harmony, educating himself on the development of the most important themes in Catholic Spirituality will help him to see it clearly, perhaps partly by reading (in Part One of this book) the chapter entitled "The Gift Foreshadowed."

***

But maybe one's concern is not so much that these are an artificial development, but that the development itself is simply too great; so great, perhaps, that it claims to surpass Public Revelation. So we now turn to the next objection.

Doesn't the sheer magnitude of these revelations imply they claim to surpass Public Revelation?

Objection: A 'new and Divine' holiness hitherto practically unknown and unexperienced by Church History's greatest saints, now up for the taking? A soon coming 'Third Renewal' or 'Fiat of Sanctification,' which will in a sense be even greater than Redemption itself? This is simply unacceptable for private revelation, in accordance with paragraph 67 of the Catechism, which teaches that private revelation may not "improve or complete Christ's definitive Revelation."

Answer: The Church does not place (nor has she ever placed) a limit on the *greatness* of the *realities* private revelation is permitted to speak of.

This leashing of Heaven is merely what certain worldly people who dwell within her institutional ranks do; fearing, as the worldly always have, that they might lose personal power, profit, or prestige if God "rocks the boat" too much. Such souls have promoted themselves to the position of the architect while demoting God to the position of the menial laborer, in the process of building the great and grand Cathedral that is Church History.

Nevertheless, the Catechism of the Catholic Church certainly must always be submitted to, as it is truly authentic Magisterium. So it is not a dishonest question to ask: Do Jesus' revelations to Luisa

---

[1256] Cf. Matthew 25:25-30

constitute an effort to "surpass, improve, complete, or correct" His definitive Public Revelation—that is, the Deposit of Faith? For if they do; then, indeed, the Catechism rejects such an effort. But an honest investigation into the relative contents of these revelations quickly reveals that the answer is a resounding "no." Jesus' private revelations to Luisa in no way violate the proper relationship between private and public revelation. In seeking to illuminate this question, it is useful to compare, on the one hand, Public Revelation, and on the other hand, Luisa's Private revelation.

Public Revelation in Christ vs. Private Revelation Through Luisa

Definitive Public Revelation in Christ	**Private Revelation through Luisa**
1. God is revealed as Three Persons, not One	1. These Three Persons now wish to share Their life more fully with creatures
2. Jesus reveals Himself as Divine	2. Luisa insists she is the lowliest of all creatures, and Jesus confirms that she is just that
3. Though truly fulfilling and not contradicting The Law, nevertheless a radical shift of focus is instituted away from it, and toward the Person, Jesus Christ	3. Simply a deepening and intensifying of focus on and love of the same Person, Jesus Christ
4. New, permanent *Church* established on earth that is necessary for salvation	4. New *spirituality* introduced, intended to be obedient to and peacefully fit within this same Church, for the sake of full sanctification
5. Seven Sacraments Instituted	5. No Sacraments instituted; the same 7 Sacraments remain the path to holiness
6. New Priesthood established	6. No new priesthood: These very same (Catholic) priests are called to be the primary heralds of the Divine Will
7. Laws altered (e.g. Divorce made impermissible, juridical Mosaic precepts dispensed from, all foods declared clean, circumcision abolished)	7. Laws entirely unchanged
8. Radically new liturgy in both substance and form	8. Identical liturgy
9. Many called to a completely new and different life, even externally (e.g. the Apostles, the disciples, communities in the Book of Acts, religious orders, clergy)	9. Followers called to live their same lives[1257]
10. Total change in leadership away from the Levitical Priesthood and to the Petrine Ministry	10. All authority remains with the Successor of Peter and all his Magisterium.[1258]

[1257] e.g., Jesus' words to Luisa, "See, then, how easy it is to Live in Our Will? The creature doesn't have to do New Things, but just what she always does; that is to say, to live her life as We gave it, but in Our Will." May 17th, 1938.

[1258] e.g. "... in my Church, in which all Heaven is veiled, one is the head, which is the Pope, and the Sacrosanct Trinity is veiled even in the triple tiara that covers his head ..." May 2nd, 1899.

A clear picture emerges even from this brief consideration of the essentials of both the Definitive Public Revelation we have been given in Christ and the Private Revelations on the Divine Will given to Luisa: they are entirely and un-confusedly distinct in their essential function. The revelations given to Luisa fit squarely within the boundaries of private revelation as given by the Church (even if they do not fit in the small box that some worldly-minded Catholics have themselves fabricated and striven to force private revelation into). But this may lead one to ask:

What, then, is the purpose of these paragraphs of the Catechism, if even so bold a private revelation as Luisa's do not qualify for being condemned by them?

Even recent Church history provides no shortage of movements, "revelations," cults, and "new spiritualities" which clearly demonstrate the importance of these paragraphs of the Catechism; movements that are to this day drawing countless souls away from Christ.

Consider, for example, the tragic successes of just a few: Jehovah's Witnesses, Mormons, the New Age Movement, Dispensationalist Christian movements, heretical or schismatic movements within the Catholic Church (which often draw from alleged "private revelations"—for example, the so-called "Army of Mary," once tens-of-thousands strong, whose founder, Marie Paule Giguere, was claimed to be a person of the "Quinternity," which included herself and the Virgin Mary, replacing the Trinity; or the so-called "Palmarian Catholic Church," the "Pope" of which was directly appointed by a "private revelation").

This is only a partial list of the countless movements throughout the world today claiming to surpass, correct, or complete Public Revelation; lead, as they are, by wolves in sheep's clothing who are dragging souls away from the Catholic Church and her infallible teachings and endangering their salvation. Meanwhile, Luisa's revelations have only done the opposite; drawing souls into the Church (I personally know people who were rescued from errant spirituality by the power of Luisa's revelations and are now completely orthodox and devout Catholics), sanctifying them, and in general producing fruits the nature of which no honest observer could possibly mistake.

Unfortunately, there are some Catholics today—particularly those who have claimed for themselves the title of "Wolf Hunters"—who incessantly repeat pseudo-axioms like "the devil will gladly tolerate 99 truths for one lie," which cause them, in their paranoia, to see the devil behind every rock and to subtly fall for ancient dualistic heresies that regard the devil as a match for God Himself. For they fail to realize that, in truth, the devil cannot help but show his teeth, and that there are clear, Church-sanctioned criteria for discovering whether he is behind a movement or a "revelation" (see, in Part One of this book, the section on discerning alleged revelations). Consequently, we need not spend year after year in confusion as to whether the devil is behind something: it is not that difficult for a serious and devout Catholic to discover the truth of the matter. But these "wolf hunters" vastly overestimate the devil by supposing that he will gladly lie in wait, decade after decade, while countless souls are saved and sanctified—all the while being himself the one to thank for it. Indeed, the devil, being of angelic origin, has a degree of intelligence beyond human comprehension. But his intelligence is always surpassed by his irrational rage, which does not allow him to wait patiently so long.

The spiritual ancestors of these "wolf hunters" are the same Catholics who relentlessly oppose the recognition of the sanctity of saintly souls for years, only to see them shortly thereafter canonized (which, among other things, is an infallible decree of the sanctity of the saint). They are the same Catholics who relentlessly oppose apparitions, only to see them shortly thereafter approved. If, as it is said, the greatest trick the devil ever pulled on the world in general was convincing it that he didn't exist, then the greatest trick he has pulled on the devout is convincing them that he is immense and quasi-omnipotent, when in fact he is a coward and a weakling.

***

This still leaves one final concern that goes along with this objection:

How is it that this private revelation does not claim to surpass the Definitive Revelation in Christ if Jesus told Luisa that the coming Third Fiat will in a sense be greater than Redemption itself?

Although this is an honest question, it arises from

an elementary confusion of language and misinterpretation of what the Catechism is here condemning. The Catechism is not teaching that no private revelation can *speak of* something greater than Redemption. It is teaching that no private revelation can claim to *itself be* **greater** than Public Revelation (most of which pertains to Redemption).

Consider a hypothetical authentic private revelation with which God chose to bless the world, through a certain saint; a revelation that depicts some details of Heaven. Indeed, this has occurred many times throughout Church History. This private revelation is itself rightly subservient to, and judged by the standard of, Public Revelation—just as Luisa's revelations are. However, this revelation *speaks of* something greater than Redemption: namely, Heaven.

Now, it is clear that Heaven is greater than Redemption because ends are always greater than the corresponding means used to attain the ends. For example, health is greater than medicine. This is a basic logical first principle of rational thought. Redemption is the means; Heaven is the end. The Church even teaches that the Sacraments themselves (the very extension of Redemption throughout time) will cease when that which is superior to them, namely Heaven, begins.

From this it is clear that private revelation is well within the bounds of orthodoxy even when it speaks of something greater than the primary object of Public Revelation—namely, Redemption—and that Luisa's revelations on the superior greatness of the coming Fiat of Sanctification with respect to the greatness of the Fiat of Redemption is in no way unorthodox.

More importantly still, we must remember (as Jesus repeatedly tells Luisa), that the Fiat of Sanctification is not separate from the Fiat of Redemption; they are one in the same, and each constitutes the life of the other. It is only the sad Protestantization of Catholic Theology that seeks to place a rupture between them (see the section in Part One of this book on Divinization for more details).

For we are finite, temporal creatures looking at the Infinite, Eternal, Perfect God's actions in the world.

What we see as different, He may see as one. So it is with Redemption and the coming Fiat of Sanctification; they are one and the same. The latter is merely the full fruit and flowering of the former; separated in time, but not in essence. It is not a new and distinct Divine undertaking. When Christ was conceived in the womb of Mary, when Christ worked in St. Joseph's carpentry shop, when Christ hung on the Cross, and when Christ was raised from the dead—it was truly the Kingdom of the Divine Will on earth that He was building in all of this (albeit in a hidden an interior way). For He was waiting until today to reveal it fully and invite us to claim it as our own.

***

But perhaps one's concerns lie not so much with the greatness of the revelation or the greatness of the Fiat of Sanctification, but with the apparent greatness of Luisa herself in this grand plan.

Isn't Luisa herself too highly exalted in these writings?

Objection: These alleged revelations exalt Luisa herself far too much, going so far as to call her a "second virgin," saying that she is necessary to fulfill God's plan for the world from all eternity, and saying that her private revelation is the necessary precondition to the establishment of God's Third Fiat (that of Sanctification, which follows the first two: Creation and Redemption.)

Answer: Jesus repeatedly makes it clear to Luisa that she is no Virgin Mary—that the Blessed Virgin, *not* Luisa, is the Queen of the Divine Will, and that Luisa will never come close to Mary (nor will any of us). He only calls Luisa the "little daughter" of the Divine Will, whereas Our Lady is the "big daughter" of the same. Jesus even laments to Luisa that people had, in her own day, falsely attributed this comparison to His words:

> …they spoke as if I had told you that you were as though another Queen. How much nonsense-I did not say that you are like the Celestial Queen, but that I want you similar to Her, just as I have said to many other souls dear to Me that I wanted them similar to Me; but with this they would not become God like Me.[1259]

On the other hand, it is indeed true that Luisa is the "earthly head" of this mission of the Third Fiat of

---

Sanctification. But what is so difficult to believe about that? In this mission, Jesus needs to use a human instrument who is still a wayfarer, as He always does in His greatest works. Is it surprising that He chose a lowly, ordinary, virgin? Of course not. The strange thing would be if He chose not to do it that way.

Let us consider an analogous situation. Who is greater, the priest who consecrates the host, or the Deacon who—at a certain Liturgy—distributes it as an extraordinary minister of Holy Communion? Clearly, it is the priest; the dignity of his office is far beyond that of the Deacon's, for the latter does not share in the order of priesthood and does not act *in persona Christi*, as the priest does. Furthermore, the greatness of uttering the words of institution with efficacy is radically above the simple picking up of a host, saying, "The Body of Christ," and placing it on the communicant's tongue. Nevertheless, in this case it is the Deacon who is the proximate instrumental cause of God's ultimate design with respect to the Eucharist: that He be received by His creatures in it. This is the same way we should view Luisa and the Blessed Virgin Mary; with the Blessed Virgin as analogous to the priest, and Luisa analogous to the Deacon.

Indeed, it is with this analogous understanding of priest and deacon that we should approach any claim which might seem to impute some sort of higher greatness to Luisa and her revelations than to Jesus and His ministry through the Sacraments, and to Mary in her role as Queen, Mediatrix, Co-Redemptrix, and Advocate. Above all, know that no such claims actually exist in Luisa's revelations; we are dealing here only with a possible false appearance of this to some readers. And as already discussed in earlier chapters (and as Jesus also makes clear in His revelations to Luisa), Luisa is not comparable to Mary in any sort of fundamental way. First of all, even the greatest of all graces, the Gift of Living in the Divine Will, is still just that: *a grace*. Mary is sovereign Queen of all Creation, the sole Mother of God, and yes, the Mediatrix of All Grace, and therefore also the Mediatrix of the Gift of Living in the Divine Will itself. Luisa, on the other hand, is the one through whom we *know of* this Gift, a knowledge which disposes us to receive it (although admittedly that certainly fails to fully express Luisa's mission!). Such a dynamic is similar

to those missionaries who proclaim the Gospel, thereby serving as the instrumental efficient cause of salvation to flow through Christ's sacrifice for those who hear and believe. Jesus says to Luisa that no one can come close, in both love and sacrifice, to Himself and His Mother. *No one*, He repeats. The Gift of Living in the Divine Will does not change that in the slightest, not even for Luisa herself.

Don't these revelations espouse the heresy of Monothelitism or Quietism?

Objection: The Church clearly repudiates the notion that Jesus had only the Divine Will and no human will (and, by extension, repudiates the notion that anyone can have only the Divine Will and no human will). Furthermore, any idea annexed to this heresy (i.e. that the human will must be completely annihilated or totally passive, like in the condemned heresy of Quietism) must itself also be in error. But it seems that the teachings in Luisa's writings amount to precisely these unorthodox conclusions.

Answer: **Time and time again, Monothelitism and Quietism are specifically refuted in Luisa's writings.** For example, with respect to Monothelitism in particular, Jesus tells Luisa:

> **Don't you know that I had a human will** which had not even one breath of life, surrendering the place to my Divine Will in everything?[1260]

It is strange that one of the major criticisms one sees (lurking around on the internet, at least) of Luisa's revelations alleges that, in these revelations, Jesus espouses Monothelitism (the false doctrine that Jesus had no human will). The fact, however, is that Jesus specifically and completely contradicts this teaching in these very same revelations multiple times.

This demonstrates, among other things, that Luisa's critics know little about her and about her writings and are likely directing their attacks against a misconception of her teachings promoted by only one or two of her followers. Recall that the criticisms which espouse these objections were almost all written before the deluge of affirmations of the validity of Luisa's revelations (some of which are listed in Part One of this book), and the most popular of the criticisms were written by men who

---

[1260] July 19, 1928.

are now dead and thus lack the opportunity to retract their criticism. Instead, these outdated criticisms are doomed, it seems, to endlessly recirculate throughout the internet so that whoever wishes to be misguided by them will easily be able to find them. Were it not for this unfortunate recirculation, these objections would scarcely even be worth addressing, as few (if any) who devote themselves to Luisa's writings ever find themselves succumbing to Monothelitism, Quietism, or anything of the sort.

Please note as well that Fr. Iannuzzi's Doctoral Dissertation presents a precise and thorough theological analysis of this concern. Even a summary of this presentation, however, would go beyond the scope of this book. It is clear, however, that Luisa's revelations **do not** teach that the Gift of Living in the Divine Will implies that the free human will undergoes a literal annihilation, or ceases to operate; in her writings, a clear teaching emerges in which both the human will and the Divine Will of God operate distinctly, but nevertheless perfectly of one accord, with the latter constituting the very life and principle of the former and indeed sublimating it. Those with a further theological interest in this objection/concern would be well advised to read the Dissertation. Recall, from Part One of this book, that Fr. Iannuzzi's dissertation was given unanimous approval by the faculty of the Pontifical Gregorian University in 2012 and is vastly more authoritative than the various misguided criticisms of Luisa floating around the internet today that reference Monothelitism.

So, while above all this Dissertation should be consulted, we conclude the consideration of Monothelitism in particular (before turning to the more general concern of Quietism) by including a few more quotations from Luisa's writings which make it clear there is no Monothelitism (or any related notion applied to one living in the Divine Will) in these revelations. Jesus tells Luisa:

> The same happened to my Humanity: though It had a human will, this will was all intent on giving life to the Divine Will. It never arbitrated itself, not even to breathe on its own, but its breath also it would take and give in the Divine Will. And this is why the Eternal Will reigned in my

Humanity on earth as It does in Heaven…[1261]

And also:

> Just like the sun, which animates everything with its light, but does not destroy or change things; rather, it places from its own and communicates the variety of colors, the diversity of sweetnesses, making them acquire a virtue and a beauty which they did not possess. **So my Divine Will is— without destroying anything of what the creature does; on the contrary, It animates them with Its light, It embellishes them, and communicates to them Its Divine Power**."[1262]

He also tells Luisa:

> My daughter, **the human will _on its own_ is nauseating, _but united with Mine is the most beautiful thing I created_**. More so, since the Divinity could never issue anything created by Us that would be nauseating … Another image is the human nature. United with the soul, it is beautiful; it sees, it hears, it walks, it operates, it speaks, it does not stink; separated from the soul, it becomes putrid, it stinks in a horrible way, it is disgusting to look at; it can be said that it can no longer be recognized. Who caused such remarkable change from a body that is alive to a dead body? The lack of the murmuring of the soul, of its continuous motion that had primacy in the human nature…So, one who does not stay united with My Will, loses the life of his soul, therefore he can do nothing good, and everything he does is without life.[1263]

If anyone were to ever be beguiled (by a confused follower of Luisa) into thinking that the human will in and of itself was bad or evil, this passage completely repudiates that heresy. **Jesus assures Luisa that not only is the human will not evil; it is, rather, _the most beautiful thing that God created._** Any passages in Luisa's writings that speak negatively of the human will are **only** referring to the operation of the human will in contradiction to or separated from the Divine Will; **never is the human will itself condemned in Luisa's writings**.

And Luisa, expounding upon the teachings Jesus gave her, says the following:

> Oh! how I would love to destroy this littleness of mine, that I may feel nothing but Divine Will alone; but I comprehend that I cannot, nor does

[1261]October 16, 1923.
[1262]September 16, 1931.
[1263]January 31, 1928.

Jesus want it to be completely destroyed. **He wants it yet small, but alive, so as to be able to operate inside a living will,** not a dead one, to be able to have His small little field of action within my littleness, which, being small, incapable, weak, with reason must lend itself to receive the great operating of the Divine Fiat.[1264]

The quote above clearly contradicts both Monothelitism and Quietism, so we turn now to consider the latter specifically.

***

Quietism, condemned by Pope Innocent XI in his Apostolic Constitution *Coelestis Pastor*, involves a number of errors (forty-three condemned propositions, to be exact), including the notions that nature is an enemy of grace, that man must reduce all his powers to nothingness, that vows are contrary to perfection, that eternity ought not even be considered, that neither love nor understanding of God is necessary.

It is not surprising to hear that even a few holy and learned souls have opposed Luisa's revelations as Quietist if all they have heard is bad presentations of her writings; but when one has spent any significant amount of time reading Luisa's writings themselves, it becomes almost comical to read the condemned propositions of Quietism, all of which are radically contrary to what Jesus tells Luisa. Indeed, Living in the Divine Will is diametrically opposed to the heresy of Quietism.

Jesus said, "*The Kingdom of Heaven suffereth violence, and the violent bear it away.*"[1265] Quietism, on the other hand, teaches a simple passivity and indifference to all things; by this false teaching, the only negative thing is to exert the will whatsoever. There is not one page of Luisa's writings that fails to dispute Quietism.

The twelfth condemned proposition in Pope Innocent's aforementioned Encyclical gives a particularly good insight into what the heresy of Quietism is, as it states:

> He who gives his own free will to God should care about nothing, neither about hell, nor about heaven; neither ought he to have a desire for his own perfection, nor for virtues, nor his own sanctity, nor his own salvation-the hope of which he ought to remove.

Luisa's writings represent the opposite of this approach; for one example, when she learns of her mother's death, she incessantly begs Jesus to deliver her mother from Purgatory until He finally does so! Luisa is constantly interceding with Jesus (praying, sacrificing, etc. — in a word, exercising her will) for the salvation of souls — an intercession that Jesus demands of Luisa and of us all — and for all the other ends which Quietism repudiates.

It has long been understood that self-renunciation, or total abandonment to the Divine Will, can be misinterpreted in a quietist fashion, so it should not be surprising that some confuse the two as intrinsically linked; a confusion that would necessarily lead them to wrongly accuse Luisa's writings of Quietism. The history of Catholic spiritual theology is replete with examples (especially in 17th to 19th century France) of even good, holy, and learned theologians mistakenly condemning some of the greatest spiritual masterpieces in history as Quietistic; works later exalted by Catholic Tradition and even Magisterium as bearing enormous spiritual insight and orthodoxy (e.g. Caussade's *Abandonment to Divine Providence*, St. Alphonsus Liguori's *Conformity to the Will of God*, St. Francis de Sales' *Treatise on the Love of God*, and St. Thérèse of Lisieux's *Story of a Soul* as well as her letters.)

It is essential that anyone who feels tempted to condemn Luisa's revelations as Quietistic and yet is not well versed in these veritable cornerstones of Catholic theology listed above now hasten to educate themselves on the latter, after which he will in turn quickly discover that his temptation was precisely that and nothing more. A brief overview of some parts of these works is found in Part One of this book.

In reading these works and others like them — many of which have been written by canonized saints and are explicitly extolled even by the Magisterium — one will discover that there is not a single argument by way of which he can accuse Luisa's revelations of the heresies of Monothelitism or Quietism that could not just as easily be levied against these other works of unassailable orthodoxy.

***

While addressing Quietism, there is a certain term that also needs to be addressed; namely,

---

[1264]March 26, 1933.

[1265]Matthew 11:12

"annihilation." This word frequently arises in Luisa's writings, but the majority of the time the term is used, it consists in cases of Luisa herself simply trying—always imperfectly—to describe her *feeling* in some interior state. Jesus Himself uses the term occasionally as well. But this should not be any cause for concern. We recall that one who insists upon reading heresy into Jesus' words every chance he gets will have no shortage of apparent opportunities to do so in Luisa's writings; but he will have plenty of such opportunities when reading Scripture, Magisterium, and the writings of the Fathers and Doctors of the Church as well!

Indeed, "annihilation" need not entail the heretical quietist meaning of the term. Consider, for example, the writings of the great Blessed Jacopone da Todi, the medieval Franciscan author of the well-known and greatly-revered hymn, Stabat Mater. Of his poetry, it is said:

> 'Totally annihilated,' the soul, under Jacapone's pen, soars to the highest stages of divine union, 'one without division.' In the boldness with which he expressed his mystical experience, he ranks among the greatest medieval mystics[1266]

Here, we see that the "annihilation" of the soul, in the proper mystical sense, is not the Quietist or the eastern pagan sense—in which its will ceases to exist, or become entirely passive—but, rather, in the sense that there is "no more division" between it and God; that is to say, no more contrast between the operation of the human will and the operation of the Divine Will. In other words, "the distance" is annihilated, not "the difference."

References to this interior annihilation are by no means uncommon in orthodox Catholic spirituality, therefore it would be unjust and partial to view their presence in Luisa's writings as problematic. Let us consider, for example, the teaching of Charles de Condren. Of him, the old Catholic Encyclopedia (the unassailable orthodoxy of which is universally agreed upon) quotes St. Jeanne de Chantal, who in turn said that "it would seem that Father de Condren was capable of teaching the angels," and it also quotes Saint Vincent de Paul, who said of Father de Condren, "there had never been a man like him."[1267]

Of Father de Condren's spirituality, the New Catholic Encyclopedia writes:

> At the heart of Condren's spirituality was a strong consciousness of the fact of creation and the nothingness of man the creature, who is wholly dependent on God. This led to a great devotion to the Word Incarnate, the supreme priest and perfect victim, who in a state of interior annihilation and total immolation offered to God the only sacrifice worthy of the Creator. Man's duty is to imitate this sacrifice by reflecting continually on his own nothingness and by giving himself wholly as a victim to the service of God.[1268]

At this point it should be fairly clear that Luisa's revelations espouse neither the heresy of Monothelitism nor the heresy of Quietism.

But some critics may still find themselves irritated, even though their objections have here been refuted. The source of this irritation is clear: when one chooses any heresy and sets his heart to, at all costs, diametrically oppose it as his self-appointed "God-given mission," and throw prudence and wisdom to the wind – he is bound to fall into a trap that is perhaps more dangerous than the heresy itself. "Without knowledge, even zeal is not good." (Proverbs 19:2). Consider that all heresy is only even possible because it clings to some truth; just as a shadow can only be discerned by virtue of the illuminated region to which it "clings" (to which it is adjacent), and evil more broadly is "the absence of a due perfection." Similarly, all heresies contain some truth (if they contained no truth, they wouldn't be heresies, they would just be laughable absurdities). The problem is that heresies exaggerate *that one truth* at the expense of other truths. Jansenism is correct in that God is Just and He does punish. Arianism is correct in that Jesus is certainly distinct from the Father. Pelagianism is correct in that human moral effort is an important thing in the spiritual life, and so on. Quietism, too, like all heresies, clings to a very important truth; namely, that God alone is the source of our sanctification, and that nothing but His Will can happen. One who has decided that he is going to become a self-appointed anti-Quietism inquisitor is bound to mistake the truth to which the heresy clings as consisting in the heresy itself. As the

---

[1266]*New Catholic Encyclopedia*, Jacopone Da Todi. Page 692.
[1267]French Congregation of the Oratory. *The Catholic Encyclopedia*. Newadvent.org/cathen/11274a.htm

[1268]*New Catholic Encyclopedia*. Condren, Charles de, Page 73.

saying goes, "when all you have is a hammer, every problem seems like a nail." For one who has decided that he is, above all, a heresy-hater, everything will seem like heresy. Now, we all must hate heresy. But we will only fall just like the heretics do if our love of truth—and our virtues of humility and charity—do not supersede even our hatred of heresy.

***

We conclude the consideration of this objection with a brief aside. The great difference between the heresy of Quietism and the orthodox notion of renunciation and union of wills in one's own spiritual life has great parallels with the Liturgy; a difference beautifully described by Peter Kwasniewski as follows:

> In the liturgy, man is most active, he is most fully acting as man—and he is most receptive, most fully acted upon by God, in order to be divinized. In liturgy, the desire of man to be the master of his fate is actualized in a surprising way: by giving himself to God in the way God has determined, man denies his disordered concupiscence, overcomes his self-destructive autonomy, and draws one step closer to that immortality of bliss for which he longs. All this is truly his work, albeit not exclusively or even primarily his work, for God is the principal agent who brings us into the mystery that infinitely exceeds our created powers, and the gifts He pours into the soul are His alone to bestow and sustain. Although liturgy is the greatest act of man, it is never an act of man by himself, but the action of Christ the High Priest, true God and true man, who allows and enables us to participate in His theandric action, His all-sufficient Sacrifice for the salvation of the world. Liturgy is therefore a peculiar kind of action, one in which man is also most passive, in the sense of being utterly receptive to the gift God wishes to give him, through the hands of the Church.[1269]

Isn't asserting primacy of will (and not intellect) the error of Voluntarism?

Objection: Thomas Aquinas teaches that, of the powers of the soul, the intellect is superior and deserves primacy. In Luisa's revelations, this is inverted, and the will receives the primacy.

Answer: First, we must settle the fact that the human soul is *simple*; meaning, it is not composed of separate parts. Whatever the soul does, it does *as* the soul. The body, on the other hand (though truly one with the soul), can be considered to only do something in or with one of its parts; for example, the eye sees, the stomach does not. Therefore, of the powers of the soul, it is difficult to say, "*does the intellect do this, or does the will?*" Such questions are not wrong to ask; we simply must recognize that, at the end of the day, the important thing is that we recognize the soul is one, and it must be entirely given to God, for the great and first commandment is this: "*You shall love the Lord your God with all your heart, and with all your soul, and with all your mind ...*"[1270] And along with love of neighbor, all the law and prophets depend upon it.

Nevertheless, it is the case that Luisa's revelations emphasize the primacy of will among the powers of the soul.

Pope Benedict XVI himself implicitly endorsed this view in an Apostolic Letter on Duns Scotus, writing:

> **The primacy of the will sheds light on the fact that God is charity before all else**. This charity, this love, Duns Scotus kept present when he sought to lead theology back to a single expression, that is to practical theology. According to his thought, since God 'is formally love and formally charity,' with the greatest generosity he radiates his goodness and love beyond himself.' And in reality, it is for love that God 'chose us in him before the foundation of the world, that we should be holy and blameless before him. He predestined us in love to be his adoptive sons through Jesus Christ' (cf. Eph 1:4-5).[1271]

While we must admit that Benedict is not necessarily demanding that we all hold the primacy of will over the intellect, it is equally clear that the primacy of will cannot be said to be a heresy (even if it contradicts the opinion of St. Thomas Aquinas), given that it is so clearly endorsed here in a Magisterial document. Cardinal Schonborn also shares a great insight on the human will:

[1269]Peter Kwasniewski. *Noble Beauty, Transcendent Holiness*. Ch 4.
[1270]Matthew 22:37

[1271]Pope Benedict XVI. *Apostolic Letter for the 7th Centenary of the Death of Blessed John Duns Scotus*. October 28th, 2008.

Deification is located in the reestablishing of fallen man in his innate dignity. If it is clear that the fall was caused by a perversion of the human will, then it follows that the reestablishment must affect above all the act of human willing.[1272]

***

Now, the word "voluntarism" can mean different things, but we need not hold (nor should we) the mistaken notion that what is good is only good because God wills it, aside from any other sort of consideration of human nature itself. Even if some theologians proposed this view (e.g. William of Ockham), Catholics should thoroughly repudiate it. For the natural law—although confirmed by Divine Law and Revelation so that it may be held with the certainty of Supernatural Faith—can simply be correctly thought of as the result of right reason being applied to human nature. Supposing that natural law can be known only by revelation alone—and no other source—is essentially a tenet of the heresy of Fideism. Pope St. John Paul II taught well against both Fideism and Rationalism in his Encyclical *Fides et Ratio,* but clear, Magisterial condemnations of Fideism go back at least to the First Vatican Council (1870). Fideism is not the same as Voluntarism, but there is indeed an overlap.

We must, however, consider that one can put "-ism" after anything and make it look like a heresy; indeed, this approach can be taken just as easily to the opposite side of the question at hand.

For while it is common to hear theologians and philosophers who are dead-set on insisting upon the total superiority of the intellect accuse the contrary view of succumbing to a Nietzschean triumph-of-will voluntarism, one could just as easily accuse their own view of succumbing to a modernist supernatural-denouncing rationalism, thereby lumping the strict Thomists in with the great heretics of modernist philosophy (such as Descartes, Spinoza, and Rousseau). That, of course, would be a grave slander against the Thomists; just as lumping together the Augustinians and Franciscans who teach the superiority of the Will with the likes of Nietzsche, Ockham, etc., would be a serious injustice.

All we must accept in order to hold fast to Luisa's

revelations is that the will is, in at least some sense, the greatest power of the soul. This is taught by Bl. Duns Scotus, St. Augustine, and Franciscan theology in general; it is by no means an "unsafe" opinion for a Catholic to hold; and it is *certainly* not an unorthodox view. A thorough treatment of the matter is beyond the scope of this work, but I will present a brief excerpt of Scotus' teaching on the matter at the end of this section.

Bl. Duns Scotus' entire spirituality focused upon love; for him, the primacy of will was essential for the primacy of love, as Pope Benedict taught. He was considered the "ecstatic doctor" because, despite being such a prolific theologian of compilation (like Aquinas), he seemed to have a mystical life more like St. Joseph of Cupertino! Fr. Stefano, a biographer of Scotus, writes the following:

> St. Teresa [Avila], in fact, recounts that one day her confessor gave her a book for meditation, by Friar Minor Fr. Francis Ossuna. It was entitled 'The Third Spiritual Alphabet,' and it explained the life of prayer and meditation strictly according to the views of Blessed Scotus. And St. Teresa states: 'I so esteemed that treatise that I decided to follow the way outlined there with the greatest diligence of which I was capable … So disposed, I entered that spiritual way with this book as teacher.'[1273]

Central to the question of primacy of will or primacy of intellect is which of these powers undertakes the commanding of an act. In response to Aquinas' assertion that commanding is an act of reason that merely presupposes some act of the will, Scotus argues it is essentially the will, as follows:

> As Augustine says (De Trinit. c.3, The will unites the parent to the offspring); moreover, the will gives commands to itself … no matter what dictate of reason is in place, the will freely chooses. Therefore the will alone commands itself and the intellect; so it belongs to the will alone to command the intellect and not the reverse, since, even when the ultimate sentence of practical deduction is in place, the will is able, by its dominating power over itself, to ignore that dictate and embrace worse counsels, or at least to suspend itself and refrain from any action.— Lastly, the intellect or intellectual virtue says that a thing is true or not true, whether in matters to

---

[1272]Cardinal Christoph Schonborn. *From Death to Life: The Christian Journey.* 1995. Page 50.

[1273]Fr. Stefano M. Manelli, *Blessed John Duns Scotus: Marian Doctor.* Page 51.

be thought or in matters to be done: but the commanding will, or the will to command, says that the act which has been commanded as needing to be immediately done is to be carried into execution; therefore the act of commanding does not belong to reason dictating that this ought to be done but to the appetitive power ordering that what was intended be done.[1274]

The old Socratic and Platonic notion of the supremacy of the intellect[1275]—and even of the goodness of the contents of the intellect guaranteeing the goodness of the person—dies hard. It is as tragic as it is obvious that the will is capable of commanding an act that is completely contrary to the goodness and truth presented to it by the intellect. Indeed, if that were not possible, then the fall of man never would have happened.

***

More important than settling the debate on voluntarism one way or another is understanding that Jesus gives the intellect all the exaltation that it deserves in Luisa's writings. For example, He says:

> These three suns are the three powers: intellect, memory and will. While being distinct among themselves, they hold hands and arrive at forming one single power, symbol of Our adorable Trinity, which is such that, while We are distinct as Persons, We form one single power, one single intellect, and one single Will. Our love in creating man was so great, that only when We communicated Our likeness to him—then did Our love feel content. These three suns were placed in the depth of the human soul, just like the sun in the depth of the vault of the heavens…[1276]

Just as the Three Persons of the Trinity share in One Divine Nature, so, too, the three powers of the soul equally share in the one soul—the one person. Thus, the truly important thing with the soul (just as with the Trinity) is that each of the three receives its due.

Jesus also tells Luisa:

> My Love is that which comes closest to man— even more, It is the cradle in which he was born, although everything is in harmony in my Divinity, just as the members are in full harmony with the body. Even though the **intelligence takes on the directing role, in which the will of man resides,** if he does not want, one can say that the eye does not see, the hand does not work, the foot does not walk. On the other hand, if he wants, the eye sees, the hand works, the foot runs—all members place themselves in accord. The same with my Divinity: my Will takes on the directing role, and all the other attributes place themselves in full harmony in order to follow what my Will wants.[1277]

In this we see that, in another way, the will is not "different" from the intelligence; rather, it resides within it. Any sort of "competition" between the two, therefore—even in our theological and philosophical debates—is, ultimately, futile. Jesus says to Luisa:

> … the thought is king of the soul, the dwelling, the throne in which the soul carries out her activity, her life, her regimen.[1278]

Indeed, Jesus exalts the intellect dozens of times in His revelations to Luisa, and rarely speaks of the superiority of the will to it. Instead, He focuses almost exclusively on the exaltation of all three faculties of the soul and the importance of understanding their proper object and operation, while at the same time emphasizing the need for the human will to be completely submitted to the Divine Will. So, it is only with much hesitation that I even dwell on this question, which is rather superfluous and unnecessary. I only do so because of how very zealous those (particularly strict Thomists) are who promote the superiority of the intellect in opposing anything they see as a threat to their own published works on the question. Let us continue, therefore, and consider a few of their arguments and the weaknesses of the same.

First, we see the problem of man's definition as "rational Animal" and the conflation a philosophical definition of a thing with the assertion of its greatest aspect.

Indeed, man can be defined as "rational animal." This philosophical definition goes all the way back to Aristotle, and is well-formulated, since a philosophical definition consists in a determination of both genus (or, category of being) and species

---

[1274]Scotus. Oxon. 3 d.36; 4 d.14 q.2, d.49 q.4 (Citation *Cf.* aristotelophile.com)

[1275]Although incredibly wise teachers of wisdom, Socrates and Plato were certainly far from infallible.

[1276]June 7, 1928.

[1277] February 17, 1922.

[1278] February 25, 1928.

(or, the "specific difference" that separates it from all others within that same category). Man, of course, is an animal, but that which separates him from all the beasts is reason; hence man is "rational animal." Jesus even confirms this definition to Luisa, saying "Human reason" is the "primary endowment of man, which distinguishes him from the beast."[1279]

But it does not follow to say that intellect is the greatest faculty of man. Consider an example: how would we go about philosophically defining "convertible"? It is safe to say that this is a roof-opening-capable car. Does is it follow that the opening roof is the greatest aspect of the convertible? Of course not. The greatest aspect of the convertible is still that which it shares with all other cars: its motive force; its ability to transport its passengers for long distances.

There is another flaw in this intellectualist line of reasoning, for the definition of man could simply be switched around without detriment to its effectiveness, and we could say that man, instead of "rational animal," is actually "embodied spirit" (as indeed he is).[1280] From this it would follow that man's body is his greatest aspect, which is absurd, for—despite the ontological unity of the two—no orthodox Catholic denies the superiority of the soul to the body.

On the Intellect

The next error is supposing that those elements of precedence that are rightly said of the intellect necessarily exalt it to a generally superior status; or, similarly, supposing that acknowledging the superiority of the will would detract from those things in which the intellect is superior. But this is not the case.

For example, Catholic "voluntarists" do not deny that, indeed, "nothing can be loved (will) unless it is first known (intellect)," and that, consequently, the intellect comes first and has primacy at least with respect to chronological considerations. Furthermore, the intellect is the primary faculty in the enjoyment of man's ultimate destiny (namely, the Beatific Vision), which involves the intellectual vision of the essence of God without medium. But this fact, too, is not denied by the recognition of the will's superiority. For just as the greatest physical sense is vision, it nevertheless is not usually the primary recipient of the greatest physical satisfactions.

Head vs. Heart

Finally, we should consider the classic "competition" of head and heart—a word I place in quotation marks because of the absurdity of seeing these things as conflicting, but which nevertheless is necessary to consider the question at hand.

This consideration is far from precise; different things are meant by "head" and "heart" in different contexts—even in different places in Scripture, Tradition, and Magisterium, which do not use the terms entirely consistently. Therefore, while we should hesitate to draw any particularly strong conclusions from this consideration, it is, on the other hand, not irrelevant to consider the "competition" of head and heart, where "head" *roughly* corresponds to intellect and "heart" *roughly* corresponds to will.

The following comparisons, therefore, will not yield any demonstrative or even good argument for the primacy of the will. However, taken together, they do present a case for it.

[1279]December 7, 1902.

[1280]For if having reason distinguishes man from all animals, having a body distinguishes him from all spirits.

Head (Intellect)	Heart (Will)
Sacred Head Devotion & the Crowning with Thorns	**Sacred Heart Devotion & the Piercing with the Lance**
These are two important devotions for our time, but who can deny that it is really the Sacred Heart devotion that Heaven has mandated for our times as being preeminent between the two? And of these two great acts of the Passion here mentioned, both are essential to be regularly meditated upon. But which has Heaven asked us to give more focus to? Jesus said to St. Faustina: *"When you say this prayer, with a contrite heart and with faith on behalf of some sinner, I will give him the grace of conversion. This is the prayer: 'O Blood and Water, which gushed forth from the Heart of Jesus as a fount of Mercy for us, I trust in You.'"*[1281] Additionally, He said to Faustina, regarding the pale and red rays of the Divine Mercy image, *"These two rays issued forth from the very depths of My tender mercy when My agonized Heart was opened by a lance on the Cross. These rays shield souls from the wrath of My Father. Happy is the one who will dwell in their shelter..."*[1282]	
Faith	**Charity**
Scripture settles this matter: *"And now there remain faith, hope, and charity, these three: but the greatest of these is charity."*[1283] Furthermore, of the three supernatural virtues, only Charity remains in Heaven. (For you cannot have Faith in what you see, nor can you Hope for what you already have.)	
God is Truth	**God is Love**
God is Truth and Love. But which requires particular focus? The latter. The Catechism mentions both, but it mentions God as Love at least five times, and God as Truth only once. *"'God is Love' and love is his first gift, containing all others."*[1284]	
"Saints of Intellect"	**"Saints of Will"**
The Church is blessed with countless great saints, some of whom could (roughly and admittedly sloppily) be categorized into these two groups of "head" or "intellect" saints and "heart" or "will" saints, both of which are indispensable to the life of the Church. But which is greatest? We must conclude the latter. Great as the saints of the intellect are (e.g. Aquinas, Bonaventure, and Bellarmine), they simply have not been proven the instruments of *as much* grace as the great saints of the heart have been (e.g. Francis of Assisi, Thérèse of Lisieux, Teresa of Calcutta, and the many approved Marian visionaries).	
Jesus, Word of God	**Jesus, Son of God**
Both titles of the Second Person of the Trinity contain immense Christological value, but they are not on the same level. Jesus Himself (not to mention the Creed) prefers to refer to the Second Person of the Trinity as "Son" more than as "Word."	

Doesn't this contradict the Theory of Evolution?

Objection: Most scientists today hold that mankind began hundreds of thousands of years ago when it evolved out of apelike creatures. Aren't Luisa's revelations contradicting this by saying the Fall of Adam was only 6,000 years ago?

The short answer to this objection is: *yes.*

Luisa's revelations do contradict Darwinism; that conjecture wherein the origin of man—the very pinnacle of creation—is not God's supernatural intervention, but rather, chance emergence from the womb of an irrational apelike creature hundreds of thousands of years ago. A theory wherein this son-of-an-ape then proceeded to commit bestiality with the species from which he emerged, and thus the human generations came to be. Jesus makes it clear to Luisa that it has been **six-thousand years** since the Fall of Man—specifically,

---

[1281] St. Maria Faustina Kowalska, *Divine Mercy in My Soul*, Paragraphs 186-187.
[1282] *Ibid.*, 299.
[1283] 1 Corinthians 13:13
[1284] *Catechism of the Catholic Church*, paragraph 733.

the *real* man and woman *Adam and Eve*. There is no possible way to explain this away with theological smooth talk.

But **this aspect of Luisa's revelations does not mean you have to be a young earth creationist to believe in them** (although you certainly can be). Jesus does not explicitly settle the question of how long the first Days of Creation were in these writings. In one diary entry, we even see the following words given by Jesus to Luisa:

> …in Creation: I pronounced the 'Fiat' and then kept silent. And even though they are called 'days', in those times the day did not exist, therefore those could be even epochs in which I formed the great machine of the universe.[1285]

On the other hand, there is no intellectually honest way to both believe in Luisa's revelations and to believe that *mankind* is tens or hundreds of thousands of years old (if it eases any concerns, know that scientists themselves can scarcely agree on *any* concrete details regarding the Origins of Man. All they can seem to generally agree on is the main thrust of the fabricated narrative, like partners in crime who collude before giving testimony; and there are countless more-than-qualified scientists who utterly reject macro-evolution in its entirety, and have already succeeded in tracing the genetic origins of the entire human race to a single set of parents only several thousand years ago).

But rejecting the thesis that mankind is hundreds of thousands of years old may cause exaggerated anxiety in some Catholics who have hitherto been told that siding with the "scientific consensus" of the day is a veritable demand of evangelization. Let us, therefore, consider the issue in order to see that this anxiety is misplaced.

After spending hundreds of pages carefully examining countless scientific, philosophical, and theological documents, including Magisterial texts and the writings of Pope St. John Paul II, Pope Benedict XVI (including his earlier works as Cardinal Ratzinger), and even Pope Francis, Fr.

Michael Chaberek, a Dominican priest, writes the following in the conclusion of his book, *Catholicism and Evolution: a History from Darwin to Pope Francis*:

> All three models [creationism, and two types of theistic evolution] contain common elements, as well as elements that make them mutually exclusive. … At the same time, they are all currently allowed in Catholic theology. This means that the teaching of the Church is not specified; rather, it accepts completely different, even contradictory, ideas about creation. Pluralism of opinions has a positive influence on the development of the debate. Unfortunately, a significant number of the most influential theologians treat the issue as if evolution were already an established "dogma." … Was Eve Adam's monovular twin in the womb of the most developed hominid [ape], which had not yet passed the threshold of humanity (J. Zycinski), or did God make Adam fall asleep and take out his rib, from which He Himself formed the first woman, who is the "bone of his bones" (Gen. 2:23)? So far the natural sciences have not provided answers to these questions. What is more, it is very doubtful that the natural sciences are capable of providing such answers at all. We are thus left with theology. If we take into consideration how difficult it has sometimes been in history for the Church to establish certain truths, one may conclude that also in this case the Church, led by the unfailing inspiration of the Holy Spirit, will in future discover the whole truth and will present it in the form of a relevant dogma.[1286]

I trust that Fr. Chaberek has done his best to be fair to all sides in this debate, and he nevertheless rightly concludes that Church teaching simply does not settle the matter; therefore, no matter how many documents, Papal addresses, or Theological Commission findings we pour over in search of clarity, we will not find it there. **The Church clearly teaches—and all Catholics must believe—that Adam and Eve were real people, that they are our first parents, and that our design is intended by**

[1285] November 6, 1932. [Personal note: Those who would respond by arguing that a "day" is always, by definition, "24 hours," seem to miss the point that an hour is defined as 1/24th of a day, therefore this response is devoid of any meaning – if there is not a day, then there is not an hour. Newtonian concepts of time that treat it as some sort of an absolute quasi-substance are seriously mistaken. Time is

merely a measure (of the reduction of potency to act), not a medium.]

[1286] Catholicism and Evolution. Michael Chaberek, OP. Conclusion.

God and not a result of chance.[1287]

If you wish to proceed beyond these simple facts, you generally cannot appeal to the Magisterium. But that fact, of course, does not mean there isn't a truth of the matter: there is a truth, and we are guilty of sin if we flippantly reject a truth (about which we have sufficient knowledge to recognize its validity) merely because it is not a truth explicitly contained within the Magisterium (albeit a different category of sin than if we, for example, reject a truth that is taught by the Magisterium).

Now, in pointing out that the Magisterium has no clear teaching beyond the basics, my main purpose is to show that those who would strive to appeal to the personal opinions of Popes or documents of various theological commissions and the like in their argument that evolution is correct, are engaging in an exercise in futility. Although it is common to see those who do so appeal misrepresent their findings in these exercises as "Church teaching," the truth is that they will never succeed in presenting anything remotely as authoritative as older documents which are much more on the side of contradicting evolution.

What is needed, therefore, is a discussion about evolution, Creationism, young earth Creationism, and other such questions among Christians who take each other seriously and are willing to follow the best arguments wherever they lead—understanding that the Church is not going to walk us by the hand to an answer to the question. Unfortunately, this discussion almost never occurs, as each side is too busy throwing unjust labels at the other. But if it does ever occur in such a way that definitive answers are found, **the nature of these answers has no bearing on Luisa's revelations, which one may be a "good follower of" so long as he at least grants that the Fall of Man was indeed 6,000 years ago. Therefore, what is most important to remember is that there simply are no grounds for division or for attacking Luisa's revelations, based on Young Earth Creationism, or opposition to the same, or anything annexed to these issues.** If such division knocks, then we must sternly bid it depart. For your approach to this matter ought to correspond to that of the Church, our Mother, who, in her great

wisdom, allows her children to follow the dictates of their own intellectual conscience on this question, so long as certain basics are subscribed to.

Therefore, while we must indeed remain steadfast in avoiding any division children of the Divine Will (and among Catholics in general) due to these questions, we should nevertheless consider the issue, which we will do over the next pages with a select few points that seem to be usually neglected in the mainstream debate. My hope is that these simple considerations will help to ease any anxiety one may feel in believing in Luisa's revelations and fearing that this entails a contradiction of mainstream modern science's view on evolution.

***

Every single empirical method that has been employed to determine the age of any living thing whatsoever to allegedly be older than 6,000 years rests entirely upon a single, unproven assumption: that the radioactive decay of certain elements follows a neat and smooth exponential function *for millions or hundreds of thousands of years,* based upon the half-life of these elements as modelled by a relatively simple approach. Add all the evidence together for dating any life form to be older than 6,000 years, and you are left with an argument so weak that, if a similar one was used to prosecute a man for a speeding violation, it would fail to convict. For it would be as if the conviction rested entirely upon the use of a certain radar gun that was only known to work for speeds under 30 mph, whereas the man in question was driving on a highway and ticketed for going 70 mph. But even this analogy fails to illustrate the absurdity we are dealing with here; for at least 30 mph and 70 mph are somewhat proximate. Evolutionists, on the other hand, use methods that have *never* been demonstrated to be accurate beyond about 4,000 years, and pretend that these same methods can be trusted to date things to be hundreds of thousands (and even millions) of years old. With such willingness to blindly extrapolate the effectiveness of a method and apply it to situations that are *orders of magnitude* beyond its verified scope, one might as well seek to "eyeball" the distance of two stars from each other because he has elsewhere managed to accurately "eyeball" the distance of two buildings

---

[1287]*Nota Bene*: Those simple facts alone – just the dogmatic, Magisterial truths which no Catholic is free to deny – are sufficient to on their own cause the worldly to laugh at you;

so, what is so hard about garnering a few more laughs from them by outright rejecting macro-evolution?

from each other.

On the other hand, the one method of dating the oldest living things on earth (trees) that we *do* know is accurate (directly verifying the number of rings found in a core sample) has never once succeeded in discovering a single tree that existed more than about 4,000 to 6,000 years ago. The various reports one regularly stumbles upon which claim trees have been found that are tens of thousands of years old are always "clonal" trees which were dated using radioactive decay methods, thus their alleged ages obviously cannot be used to verify the accuracy of the method used to determine these alleged ages (that is the very matter here in question)!

Willard Libby himself, the scientist who developed radiocarbon dating, pointed out that the fundamental assumption of these dating methods—namely, that the radioactive decay occurs at a functionally constant rate—was questionable. Only over time was his fear proven legitimate. Calibrations of course followed these observations to give the appearance of the inherent problems being fully addressed (reminiscent of tobacco companies "solving" the health issues of cigarette smoking by adding filters), but as usual the hailed "scientific consensus" is incapable of taking a step back and examining itself in broader terms. For it is somehow incapable of seeing that the present-day "consensus"—despite some minor corrections it now enjoys—has little more reason to be considered free of grave foundational errors as the previous (and now-refuted) consensus had.

Already, suspicions should be arising in the minds of any honest inquirer: why has the only dating method that we have actually verified the accuracy of failed to produce a single living thing which existed more than 4,000 to 6,000 years ago? There have apparently been many trees dated using radioactive decay methods to be tens of thousands of years old; yet, we cannot find a single tree with more than 6,000 rings to count and thus confidently verify its age (although we can find many trees with 3,000-4,000 rings and possibly some with

5,000-6,000).

But this inconvenient conundrum for the evolutionists is not only evident with respect to trees. As any historian, archeologist, or anthropologist worth his salt knows, there is a veritable mountain of details available about human history up to about 4,000 years ago (recall that Genesis teaches a worldwide flood wiped out everything except Noah and whatever was on his ark, at that time), and only a relative scant few details about the 2,000 years preceding that, and also nothing about human history before 6,000 years ago (the only "evidence" of human history dating back beyond 6,000 years in the past is, unsurprisingly, only presented through radioactive decay dating methods).

Of course, one can concoct all manner of imaginative historical fiction to strive to force these facts to correlate with the evolutionism; many scientists have done precisely this, although since they have PhDs after their names, they have convinced the world to treat their conjectures as trustworthy scientific hypotheses. But all that these conjectures boil down to is nothing but a well-covered-up fundamental premise that every single piece of verifiable evidence of life on earth quasi-magically disappeared 4,000-6,000 years ago, leaving only those things from before that time—in superlative convenience—which could be dated only radiometrically.[1288] Indeed, what one cannot do is tell anyone, while maintaining a straight face, that these ponderings are anything but an awkward attempt to avoid the clear conclusion: there simply *wasn't* a human history more than 6,000 years ago.

***

Let us also consider more reasons, from Faith, to question the scientific "consensus" on evolution. While we have already settled that a Catholic has great leeway to follow his own intellectual conscience in this matter *as far as the Catholic Faith itself* is concerned (since the Magisterium currently[1289] allows for this flexibility) it does not follow that Scripture itself fails to indicate that one interpretation is better, even if a contradictory one

---

[1288]That is, using a radioactive-decay method of absolute chronological dating.

[1289]I am not trying to imply that the Magisterium may change to contradict itself; I'm simply pointing out that the Magisterium can develop in the future to no longer permit

Catholics to believe what it once did permit. For example, before the 19th century, Catholics were permitted to believe that Mary was not Immaculately Conceived. This belief is, however, no longer permitted.

is permissible. So, let us consider what is taught by the most honest and the best interpretation of our Scriptural foundation.

When addressing this question, the debate almost entirely revolves around the Book of Genesis. The Theistic evolutionists claim Genesis is not a science textbook (as if anyone had ever been unaware of this fact), and they discount much of it as mere myth—some discounting *all* its pre-Abrahamic history as only symbolic (even though there are no theological, philosophical, or exegetical reasons to come to this conclusion). But let us leave this aside for now, as there is already enough written elsewhere on the nature of the historical claims in the Book of Genesis.

For regardless of the proper literal or symbolic interpretation of certain verses of Genesis, there is no doubt that the Genealogy of Jesus found in the Gospel of Luke is literal. The various methods employed by modern exegetes to strive to evade those teachings that are clearly intended as historical statements in Genesis utterly fail when applied to the Gospels (not that they succeed when applied to Genesis—as Pius XII clearly taught, Magisterially, *"the first eleven chapters of Genesis... do nevertheless pertain to history in a true sense..."*[1290]; I am merely pointing out that even the modern exegetes lack the audacity to make similar claims about the Gospels).

As we have already settled, the Magisterium itself requires that all Catholics believe that the literal people, Adam and Eve, are our first parents. For example, in his Magisterial teaching in the encyclical *Humani Generis*, Venerable Pope Pius XII taught:

> For <u>the faithful</u> **cannot** embrace that opinion which maintains that either after Adam there existed on this earth true men who did not take their origin through natural generation from him as from the first parent of all, or that Adam represents a certain number of first parents.[1291]

Combine this belief with the fact that the Genealogy of Luke (Chapter 3, verses 23 through 38) follows Jesus' lineage all the way back to Adam, and one is left with no grounds for supposing that Adam's son Seth was born much more than 4,000 years before Christ. Even if one can argue that the phrase "the son of" in this lineage may sometimes

refer not directly to father and son but perhaps to a levirate marriage or to grandfather and grandson (and considering that argument is beyond the scope of the present work), there is no way to argue that this lineage would simply skip the tens-of-thousands of years that would be necessary to skip in order to force it to agree with the scientific "consensus" on the evolutionary heritage of man.

For this would entail the Gospel of Luke, by the words "the son of," actually meaning the "great, great, great, great, great, great, great, great ...x100... grandson of." Now, if such antics do not amount to deception, then there is no such thing as deception. But if Scripture deceives, then its Divine Author (it is Church dogma that the Holy Spirit is the author of every word of Sacred Scripture) deceives, and to claim that God deceives is blasphemy.

Let us also consider that strictly limited Theistic Evolution (the only type that a Catholic may hold) requires, at the very least, a belief that Evolution is merely the material process that God used to specifically create the various species, while in truth He was using His own Divine Intervention behind the scenes all the while; much like a puppeteer hides behind a curtain and pulls the strings, allowing one who seeks some innocent entertainment to pretend that the puppet himself is moving under his own volition. (While atheistic—materialistic or naturalistic—evolution rests entirely upon the laughable "scientific" conjecture that, given enough time, order will arise from disorder by mere chance; much like the argument that, given enough opportunities, a tornado passing through a junkyard will design and construct a large array of supercomputers, or an earthquake ravaging a city will in so doing generate a better one.)

From this simple recognition of these basic (although unstated) corollaries of their assertions, we can see that a Theistic Evolutionist believes in far more miracles of a far more outlandish nature than does a simple Creationist: for the former must believe (lest he fall into simple atheism or, at best, heretical Deism wherein the Creator merely sets the necessary processes in motion and then is absent) that God miraculously intervened—contravening the ordinary course of nature and laws of physics—

[1290]Pius XII, *Humani Generis*. Paragraph 38.

[1291]Ibid, Paragraph 37.

trillions of separate times throughout billions of years of history to evolve the single cell into modern man (and all the other species). A Creationist simply believes that God fashioned the species directly. And it would be of no use for the Theistic Evolutionist to strive to evade this observation by arguing that he regards evolution as a mere unfolding of a Divinely pre-programmed design in the first cell (what evolutionists call the "Ancestral Cell" or the "Universal Common Ancestor"), much like the growth of a tree consists purely in the unfolding of a Divinely pre-programmed order that is contained in its seed. For no evolutionary biologists hold that this is even a remotely plausible scenario. [1292]

There is simply no way for a Theistic Evolutionist to evade the fact that he is indeed positing the aforementioned scenario, wherein God supernaturally suspended the laws of nature and physics trillions of separate times, intervening from His throne in Heaven each of these times, in order to—over the course of billions of years—fashion each species by hiding His deliberate design under the guise of so-called "beneficial mutations." While not impossible for God, nor internally inconsistent, nor patently heretical, it nevertheless is difficult to even speak such a theory out loud without it seeming quite strange.

For although the modernists have convinced even Christians to save their chuckles for Genesis itself, we see now that it is far easier to simply say that the clear sense of Scripture got the Origin of Man right, than it is to posit this incredibly awkward theory of Theistic Evolution.

Now, we must admit that some aspects of evolution are obviously true. As with most worldly theories created by worldly men, Evolutionary Theory is a mix of good and bad—truth and error. Clearly species change over time. Even the most ardent Creationist must admit this, for we all are the children of Adam and Eve, and yet we can easily observe how different humans are: the difference between one of African, or Irish, or Chinese origin is significant. It furthermore seems clear that these differences exist as a consequence of environmental factors (or, one could even say, "natural selection"); for example, the light skinned

Irish need to be able to absorb sunlight more efficiently due to its scarcity in their region, whereas the dark-skinned Africans need to be able to protect against sunlight more efficiently, due to its abundance.

Furthermore, scientists have clearly empirically observed bacteria mutating in response to their environment (whereas virtually all other elements of "evolutionary biology" are conjecture and in a more honest society would be considered, at best, interesting science fiction).

But there are fundamental roadblocks which reveal the unscientific wishful-thinking extrapolation of these basic observations to suppose that the same phenomena can also explain that which is radically beyond their observed scope:

1. The entire Theory of Evolution rests upon the notion that one species can become another, over time, by mere chance (even with natural selection "helping" the process, it still is fundamentally and inescapably a mere-chance-driven process). However, a species has never once been seen in the history of human observation to become another species (nor have we ever even found evidence of such a transformation in the fossil record). Even when human intervention does its best to exponentially increase the speed of the posited species-change-process, it still fails utterly to deliver. This is demonstrated most clearly in dogs, which have perhaps the most variation found within their ranks of any species, and yet every dog remains a dog, no matter how hard the breeders try to generate a new species from the variations contained within the species.

2. The unfolding of a preexisting order is radically different from the emergence of a new order. The former is more than sufficient to explain the cases wherein scientists have observed species change by adaptation. That is to say, the variations found within these species' original genetics already allowed for the variations in the first place. It is a simple case of a potency being actualized, not a case of some previously non-existent design being bestowed by chance. Similarly, a batch of seeds having identical genetics can nevertheless produce very different looking plants depending upon environmental factors.

[1292] Indeed, the molecular structure of DNA *cannot* encode sufficient information within itself to contain the separate design of every species in the genetics of a single cell. It is, of

course, useless to propose a theory that any evolutionist would scoff at in order to appease these very evolutionists themselves.

For natural selection, as its name implies, can only mindlessly "select" among those things presented to it; much like a raging river "selects" the sharp corners and edges of the stones within it for removal by gradual abrasion in order to form the smooth stones that compose its riverbed. Indeed, it is no groundbreaking theory to say that, when a group of bacteria or other life-form is exposed to some trauma (perhaps a certain antibiotic), those individual specimens whose genetic variation is more resistant to the trauma will be less likely to die, thus they will, moving forward, be the ones whose genetics will be more likely to dominate the whole population of the group. This observed phenomenon "proves" the theory of evolution about as successfully as observing a rainstorm expose a sculpture previously covered by mud "proves" that the rainstorm itself created the sculpture.

***

Now, it is difficult to blame a good Catholic for believing in something that the Church allows belief in and the validity of which is insisted upon by the majority of scientists. So, the real and lamentable reason for so many religious people today falling hook-line-and-sinker for all the tenets of evolution is perhaps primarily due to the absence of holy aversion. For few of us can be scientists, and even though a rigorous scientific investigation would indeed succeed in uncovering the flaws of Darwinism, applying this rigor is impractical for all but a few. But we do all have discernment, a conscience, and a natural, God-given ability to "smell" truth by virtue of the beauty, or lack thereof, of a proposition. For Truth is beautiful, and all God-fearing people know that instinctively. Even though it lacks infallibility, this intuition must never be neglected.

It sadly does not disgust Christians today—as it should—to ponder the idea of the pinnacle of all creation (at the time), Adam, emerging from the womb of a mindless ape, committing bestiality with these apes, and thus generating our heritage. But of course, the abolition of holy aversion has effects far beyond evolution. It is why so many good Catholics condone hideous music. It is why so many good Catholics condone immodest dress. It is why so many good Catholics condone ugly art,

build ugly Churches, and advocate for ugly Liturgies. It is why so many good Catholics condone terrible movies. It is why so many good Catholics condone sexualized dancing. Against many of these things, no clear and fully objective theological argument or Magisterial condemnation exists; God intends, rather, for us to reject them by listening to our conscience, which should give us a clear holy aversion to them. But, alas, we have lost that today.

Similarly, too many Catholics are anxious to evade the duty to avoid anything that the Church does not clearly condemn in her extraordinary Magisterium—even if they are things worthy of the condemnation of any just person—because so condemning means a missed opportunity to blend in with the world. In so doing, they completely misunderstand the mission of the Magisterium, which is not to condemn every single sin, evil, and ugliness; but only to give the bare bones basics; condemning the most blatant and intrinsic evils, and little more. It is the job of individual Christians to be open to the Holy Spirit, discern, and only allow into their lives (or beliefs) whatever is in accord with this Spirit.

So, indeed, it seems to me that the widespread acceptance of evolutionism among Catholics today is just another casualty of our inability to blush. The disgusting no longer disgusts us. The scandalous no longer scandalizes us. The dangerous no longer reminds us to proceed with caution. The modernists—both in the world and within the ranks of the Church—have spent the last several decades lecturing us on how one's spiritual "maturity" is determined solely by the degree to which he has "grown out of the vice of prudery;" and the Church has largely gobbled up this lie.

Consequently, we refuse to listen to our God-given intuition that speaks to all of our hearts and tells us when a thing, though not an intrinsic evil or a dogmatically condemned heresy, is nevertheless contrary to the Will of God. Therefore, in contradiction to the rationalism of our modern apostate age, let us reclaim the conviction our ancestors held that God does speak to all of us, and that we must always heed His voice in everything.

34) A Few Words for Scholars

Dear Scholar,

As a scholar, you know well that whatever is to be loved must first be known. It was perhaps this fact that largely fueled your desire to dedicate yourself to studies of holy things. This is good and true. But the inverse is true as well.

> You must know that in order to know one Truth, one needs to love it. Love makes the appetite arise, the appetite gives the taste, the taste makes arise the hunger of eating to fullness and chewing very well the substance of a food, that is, My Truths. Chewing them produces easy digestion in a way that one feels the possession of the Great Good that My Truth possesses and produces, and then the doubts cease, the difficulties melt like snow before the rays of a burning sun Now, if they have hardly touched them without eating them with a profound study, with a love that generates the appetite, what wonder is it that they make doubts and difficulties? O! how it would have been better to say: 'It is not food for us, nor do we have the will to eat it,' rather then give judgments. But one knows that My Truths find a place more in simple hearts then learned. This happened in My Redemption. To My Sorrow, not one learned one followed Me, but all the poor, ignorant, simple ones.[1293]

Jesus spoke those words to Luisa.

And His words are not contradictory. *Truth* must be loved in order for *truths* to be really understood; *truths* must be known in order for *these truths* to be loved.

Therefore, dear scholar, you must ask yourself sincerely, in prayer, not holding anything back:

"Do I love Truth, or do I love the vindication of my opinions, the feeling of winning a debate, the praises of my readers, the triumph of my particular school of thought, or some other thing that is infinitely below The Truth Itself?"

If one does not love The Truth Itself, then it is no surprise if, even after the attainment of the tenth PhD, the scholar is more mired in error than even the common man.

But perhaps a given scholar has sunk so low (and from personal experience I can testify that not even "orthodox Catholic priest" scholars are exempt from this horrible fate), that not even this admonishment touches his heart. Perhaps he cares only that he has this power—philosophical, Scriptural, or theological knowledge—that he has turned into a weapon for the undertaking of his personal battles which he simply enjoys fighting or continues due to his receiving some manner of payment—literal or metaphorical—for his fighting. To such a scholar I say: No one appointed you the judge of all things. God does not have to run everything by you first.

> Daughter, when I want to give a Great Good, a New Good to creatures, I give New Crosses and I want a New and Unique sacrifice-a cross for which the human can give itself no reason; but **there is My Divine Reason, that man is obliged to not investigate, but to lower his forehead and adore it.** And besides, this was about the Kingdom of My Will, and My Love had to invent and want New Crosses and sacrifices never before received, to be able to find pretexts, the prop, the strength, sufficient coins, and an extremely long chain to let Itself be bound by the creature. [Jesus to Luisa] [1294]

There are even Catholic scholars—no negligible number—who have fallen victim to an idea so absurd that, indeed, only a scholar could buy into it. For they have supposed that, because Jesus abrogated the ceremonial precepts of the Mosaic law, He also must have thereby abrogated His condemnations of the Pharisees: as if Our Lord's repeated rebukes of them in the Gospels pertained to mere superficial matters that concerned only a small group of people living in 30 A.D. in Jerusalem. Any ordinary Christian with even one ounce of wisdom knows that it was not in order to merely treat a small and temporary issue that the Son of God rebuked the Pharisees as "blind guides" who, for example, "strain out the gnat and swallow the camel"[1295]—along with His many other rebukes of the same sort. He was condemning their approach to God and to Divine matters; an approach that is anything but extinct today.

The spiritual sons of these Pharisees exist to this day; they exist in droves. And they are not the people whom the world (or nominal and lukewarm Christians) suppose they are. Today, the title of "Pharisee" is slanderously thrown at those who insist that, for example, the Ten Commandments are binding. But those who truly deserve the title of

---

[1293]February 24, 1933.
[1294]June 26, 1932.

[1295]Matthew 23:24

"Pharisee" today rarely hear it, for it takes a more discerning eye to recognize. Today's Pharisees are those who suppose that they have acquired so much knowledge of theology, of philosophy, of Church History, of psychology, and so forth, that they have the intellectual power to condemn God's intervention into this world on their own terms; ignoring the fruits, the signs, the miracles, and supposing that they are up to the task of judging any message itself in accordance with their own theological understandings.

And they have so blinded themselves that they refuse to see that they are doing the exact same thing to Heaven's messengers today that the literal Pharisees did to God Himself 2,000 years ago.

> My beloved daughter, who came to visit me in the grotto of my birth? Only shepherds were my first visitors—the only ones who kept coming and going, offering Me gifts and their little things. They were the first to receive the knowledge of my coming into the world and, as a consequence, the first favorites to be filled with my grace. This is why I always choose poor, ignorant, abject people, and I make of them portents of grace—because they are always the ones to be more disposed, the ones who more easily listen to Me and believe Me without raising so many difficulties, so many quibbles as, on the contrary, learned people do.
>
> Then came the Magi, but no priest showed up, while they should have been the first to form my cortege. In fact, more than anyone else, according to the Scriptures which they studied, they knew the time and the place, and it was easier for them to come to visit me. But no one—no one moved; rather, while they indicated the place to the Magi, they did not move, nor did they trouble to take one step to follow the traces of my coming. This was a most bitter sorrow for Me at my birth, because in those priests the attachment to riches, to interest, to families and to exterior things was so great as to blind their sight like a glare, harden their hearts, and render their intelligence dazed to the knowledge of the most sacrosanct and most certain truths. They were so engulfed in the low things of the earth, as to never be able to believe that a God could come upon earth in the midst of so much poverty and so much humiliation. [Jesus to Luisa][1296]

Now, I say all this as… a scholar. I hold a Master's degree in Theology, I am a philosophy professor and Doctoral student and, God Willing, will soon have my PhD in Philosophy. I am well aware that these letters after my name say very little, and that they are primarily procedural necessities required in the teaching world. They do not prove anything about my wisdom or holiness, nor do others with the same letters after their names have anything proven about their own spiritual status by the same. Nor do letters before one's name prove anything; even if those letters are "Fr." or "Bp."

I implore all you scholars, therefore, to humble yourselves for once and stop supposing that private revelation is somehow beneath you.

Recall an essential teaching from the greatest work of Theology ever written; the *Summa Theologica*. In it, Aquinas—reiterating verbatim a teaching from Aristotle—(likely the two most intelligent men who ever lived) says that even the *undemonstrated* opinions of men wiser than ourselves should be regarded (that is, even opinions they have not fully "proven" should nevertheless generally be taken seriously due to the trustworthiness of the one holding them):

> Hence the Philosopher says (Ethic. vi, 11) that in such matters, "we ought to pay as much attention to the undemonstrated sayings and opinions of persons who surpass us in experience, age and prudence, as to their demonstrations."[1297]

Indeed, it is almost impossible that any professional philosopher or theologian can pick up Luisa's writings, read them from cover to cover, and find that in each one, his own scholarly opinions have been confirmed. But what fool would expect it to be so? Who could pretend to be surprised that the greatest private revelation—wherein God Himself gives the most sublime teachings to us over the course of thousands of pages—amounts to more than a mere flattering confirmation of every little opinion he had held?

Therefore, it is necessary for scholars to, above all, pray for the humility to change their opinions if

---

[1296]December 25, 1910.
[1297]*Summa Theologica.* I-II. Question 95. Article 2. (One wonders if this article is censored from the *Summa* translations that many Thomists today work from; for they show no sign of acknowledging this sage advice—supposing, as many of them do, that their relatively minor theological knowledge of Thomism enables them to dismiss out of hand anything they find abrasive with their own theological opinions, as they write articles demanding that all Catholics do likewise.)

that be God's Will; to deviate from their own theological or philosophical school somewhat (so long, of course, as this never entails deviation from Scripture, Tradition, or Magisterium!). Are you a Thomist? A Scotist? An Augustinian? A Platonist? An Aristotelian? An Existentialist? Or something else? Whatever you call yourself, you will have to set aside rigid dogmatic adherence to each tenet of these schools of thought; for as great as they may be, they are ultimately the creations of mere men.

The fruits, the miracles, the confirmations of history, the consistency, and everything else, all attest to the unavoidable conclusion that Luisa's writings come from God Himself. Therefore, it is clear that we should defer to the teachings contained therein instead of rigid adherence to every tenet of our academic schools of thought.

Though I am unworthy of the title, I consider myself a Thomist. I do so comfortably; not at all worried that I must set aside a small handful of the opinions put forth by the Angelic Doctor in order to follow Luisa's writings. For in the *Summa* and his other writings, Aquinas put forth thousands of his own opinions; almost all of which are correct and should indeed be held by any follower of Luisa (Luisa herself was a third-order Dominican!). Is it any surprise that .01% of them may be in error? If you cannot bear such a thought, you should prayerfully consider if you have exalted a mere man—even one so great as Thomas—to Divine Status, and have thereby fallen into the sin of idolatry.

I conclude this note to scholars with words from Jesus to Luisa:

> Therefore, my daughter, I know where my aims tend to, what they must serve for, what I do, great

and beautiful, when I choose a creature. What do they know? And this is why they have always something to say about my operating. And not even my short life down here was spared, when my Most Holy Humanity was in their midst and I was all love for them; and yet, if I drew too close to sinners, they had to say that it was not decorous for Me to deal with them. And I let them talk, and without giving importance to their talking, I did the facts, I drew closer to sinners, I loved them more in order to attract them to love Me. If I did miracles, they had something to say, because they believed I was the son of Saint Joseph; they had to say that the promised Messiah could not come from a carpenter, and they kept arousing doubts about my Divine Person, so much so, as to form clouds around the Sun of my Humanity. And I aroused the little breezes to get rid of the clouds, and I reappeared more blazing with light in their midst, in order to accomplish the purpose of my coming upon earth, which was Redemption… therefore it is no wonder that their intelligence has remained as though dazzled. But if they get used to looking at the light, they will see clearly that only my Love could reach such extent; and since I love so much that my Divine Will be known in order to let It reign, I wanted to be exuberant in the excess of my Love which I contained in my Heart. Even more, everything I have done with you can be called the preludes of what I will do to those who will let themselves be dominated by my Fiat! However, I tell you that all those who had something to say about my Humanity when It was on earth, and did not surrender to believing in the sanctity of my works, remained empty of the good that I came to offer to all, and remained outside of my works. So it will be with those who, in addition to talking on the how and the way of what I have said—but if they do not surrender, they too will remain on an empty stomach, and outside of the good which, with so much love, I wanted to offer to all."[1298]

35) <u>Miscellaneous Resources</u>

Above all, a copy of Luisa's writings themselves should be secured by all interested in her revelations! Although the Moratorium prevents their publication (and, as such, the volumes cannot simply be purchased), it does not prevent their dissemination within prayer groups dedicated to Luisa. If there are no prayer groups near you, fear not: there are plenty of online prayer groups dedicated to Luisa (including some

on social media; e.g. Facebook and Twitter), which you may join and thereby licitly acquire the writings. Simply do a Google search to find these groups. You can also contact the Benedictines of the Divine Will and become associated with this group (you can even officially become an Oblate if you feel so called): daughtersofdivinewill@gmail.com

---

[1298] June 2, 1930.

(Several of Luisa's writings have no Moratorium whatsoever on their publication, and may already be purchased online through the Coming of the Kingdom website:
www.ComingOfTheKingdom.org

Alternatively, they may be downloaded freely at various locations online, including the website of the approved religious order, the Benedictines of the Divine Will:

Luisa's Letters:

https://www.benedictinesofdivinewill.org/uploads/3/4/3/2/34324596/letters_of_luisa_piccarreta.pdf

The Blessed Virgin Mary in the Kingdom of the Divine Will:

https://www.benedictinesofdivinewill.org/uploads/3/4/3/2/34324596/mary_in_dw.pdf

The Hours of the Passion:

https://www.benedictinesofdivinewill.org/uploads/3/4/3/2/34324596/hours_of_passion.pdf

- The official website for Luisa Piccarreta's cause for Beatification:
http://www.luisapiccarretaofficial.org
- Fr. Iannuzzi's podcast on Living in the Divine Will found at the website:
https://radiomaria.us/learning-to-live
- Fr. Iannuzzi's website on Living in the Divine Will: http://www.ltdw.org/
- Fr. Gabriel Barrera's teachings on the Divine Will http://eternalfiat.com/will-of-god/
- Thomas Fahy's Coming of the Kingdom website with a wealth of resources on Living in the Divine Will:
http://www.comingofthekingdom.org/
- Fr. Robert Young's talks on the Divine Will:
https://divinewilllife.org/
- The Benedictines of the Divine Will:
https://www.benedictinesofdivinewill.org
- The official biography of Luisa published by the Vatican, *The Sun of My Will*. (It appears that most of the sellers who carried this book have sold out all of their stock, and that we are awaiting another printing.)
http://en.luisapiccarretaofficial.org/news/the-sun-of-my-will/66
- Secular Order of Jesus, Mary, and Joseph:

Resources on the Divine Will.
http://sojmj.com/

List of Things the Gift is NOT

- The rendering of the creature to be infinite in itself (God alone is infinite in Himself). The Gift, rather, gives a capacity for the infinite in rendering the creature capable of performing Divine Acts by the Divine Life living in us, thus these acts have a truly eternal value.
- The absolute (metaphysical) confirmation in grace (which is only a permanent, eternal guarantee in Heaven). Granted, one very advanced in the Gift, who has reached its center even on earth, arrives at the point where sin, practically speaking, simply will not happen; but even this state must be distinguished from the absolute dominion over the human will that the Beatific Vision alone exerts.
- The elimination of the human will (e.g. Quietism, Monothelitism)
- The extinguishing of the self (e.g. Buddhist "Nirvana")
- An exemption from **any** moral or theological norm, teaching, precept, or truth of the Faith (just as Jesus came not to eliminate one iota of The Law,[1299] so the Gift presupposes the entirety of Catholic teaching)
- An exemption from the "ordinary" means of becoming a saint (as St. Hannibal said, the saints in the Divine Will must do all that the saints of previous generations did). Perhaps the most common exhortation that Luisa herself gave in the many letters she wrote to others was to work to "make yourself a saint" and to not worry about anything else.
- A replacement for the devotions already in the Church (Children of the Divine Will should remain especially zealous for the Rosary, Marian Consecration, the Sacred Heart, Divine Mercy, and many others. Luisa herself insisted, for example, that one "never neglect" the Rosary.)
- A dispensation from one's duties (Jesus repudiates, to Luisa, the idea of one ever

---

[1299] *Cf.* Matthew 5:17-18

neglecting the duties of his state in life. Instead, He points out that, to Live in His Will, one does "what he always does," and that sanctity is contained in fulfilling the duties of one's office.)

- In any way pantheistic (The Gift closes the *distance* between God and man, it does not erase the *distinction*.)

The Chaplet of the Divine Will

(composed by St. Hannibal di Francia, February 23, 1927)

Prayed on ordinary Rosary Beads.

Begin with:

- 1 Our Father
- 1 Hail Mary
- 1 Glory Be

On each of the small beads:

Latin: "*Fiat, Domine, Voluntas Tua, sicut in caelo et in terra. Amen*"

or

English: "(Fiat, Lord,) Thy Will be done on earth as it is in Heaven. Amen."

On each of the large beads:

Glory Be

After 5 decades, conclude with:

"Lord Jesus, we praise Thee, we love Thee, we bless Thee and we thank Thee, with God the Father and the Holy Spirit, in your Holy and Eternal Divine Will. Amen."

Prayer for the Beatification of Luisa

Prayer for the Beatification of the Servant of God, Luisa Piccarreta

O Most Holy Trinity,

Our Lord Jesus Christ taught us that, as we pray we should ask that our Father's Name be always glorified so that his will be done on earth and that his Kingdom should come to reign among us.

In our great desire to make known this Kingdom of love, justice and peace we humbly ask that You glorify your Servant Luisa, the Little Daughter of the Divine Will who, with her constant prayer and suffering, deeply yearned for the salvation of souls and the coming of God's Kingdom in the world.

Following her example, we pray to You, Father, Son and Holy Spirit, to help us joyfully embrace the crosses of this world so that we may also glorify your Name and enter into the Kingdom of your Will.

Amen.

+ Archbishop Carmelo Cassati

Trani, Italy

Morning Offering in the Divine Will

O Immaculate Heart of Mary, Mother and Queen of the Divine Will, I entreat you, by the infinite merits of the Sacred Heart of Jesus, and by the graces God has granted to you since your Immaculate Conception, the grace of never going astray.

Most Sacred Heart of Jesus, I am a poor and unworthy sinner, and I beg of You the grace to allow our mother Mary and Luisa to form in me the divine acts You purchased for me and for everyone. These acts are the most precious of all, for they carry the Eternal Power of your Fiat and they await my "Yes, your Will be done" (Fiat Voluntas Tua). So I implore you, Jesus, Mary and Luisa to accompany me as I now pray:

I am nothing and God is all, come Divine Will. Come Heavenly Father to beat in my heart and move in my Will; come beloved Son to flow in my Blood and think in my intellect; come Holy Spirit to breathe in my lungs and recall in my memory.

I fuse myself in the Divine Will and place my I love You, I adore You and I bless You God in the Fiats of creation. With my I love You my soul bilocates in the creations of the heavens and the earth: I love You in the stars, in the sun, in the moon and in the skies; I love You in the earth, in the waters and in every living creature my Father created out of love for me, so that I may return love for love.

I now enter into Jesus' Most Holy Humanity that embraces all acts. I place my I adore You Jesus in your every breath, heartbeat, thought, word and step. I adore You in the sermons of your public life, in the miracles You performed, in the Sacraments You instituted and in the most intimate fibres of your Heart.

I bless You Jesus in your every tear, blow, wound, thorn and in each drop of Blood that unleashed light for the life of every human. I bless You in all your prayers, reparations, offerings, and in each of the interior acts and sorrows You suffered up to your last breath on the Cross. I enclose your life and all your acts, Jesus, within my I love You, I adore You and I bless You.

I now enter into the acts of my mother Mary and of Luisa. I place my I thank you in Mary and Luisa's every thought, word and action. I thank you in the embraced joys and sorrows in the work of Redemption and Sanctification. Fused in your acts I make my I thank You and I bless You God flow in the relations of every creature to fill their acts with light and life: To fill the acts of Adam and Eve; of the patriarchs and prophets; of souls of the past, present and future; of the holy souls in Purgatory; of the holy angels and saints.

I now make these acts my own, and I offer them to You, my tender and loving Father. May they increase the glory of your children, and may they glorify, satisfy and honour You on their behalf.

Let us now begin our day with our divine acts fused together. Thank You Most Holy Trinity for enabling me to enter into union with You by means of prayer. May your Kingdom come, and your will be done on earth as it is in heaven.

Fiat!

Prayer of Consecration to the Divine Will

(Composed by Luisa herself at the request of St. Hannibal)

O adorable and Divine Will, here I am, before the immensity of Your Light, that Your eternal Goodness may open to me the doors, and make me enter into It, to form my life all in You, Divine Will.

Therefore, prostrate before Your Light, I, the littlest among all creatures, come, O adorable Will, into the little group of the first children of Your Supreme Fiat. Prostrate in my nothingness, I beseech and implore Your endless Light, that It may want to invest me and eclipse everything that does not

belong to You, in such a way that I may do nothing other than look, comprehend and live in You, Divine Will.

It will be my life, the center of my intelligence, the enrapturer of my heart and of my whole being. In this heart the human will will no longer have life; I will banish it forever, and will form the new Eden of peace, of happiness and of love. With It I shall always be happy, I shall have a unique strength, and a sanctity that sanctifies everything and brings everything to God.

Here prostrate, I invoke the help of the Sacrosanct Trinity, that They admit me to live in the cloister of the Divine Will, so as to restore in me the original order of Creation, just as the creature was created.

Celestial Mother, Sovereign Queen of the Divine Fiat, take me by the hand and enclose me in the Light of the Divine Will. You will be my guide, my tender Mother; You will guard your child, and will teach me to live and to maintain myself in the order and in the bounds of the Divine Will. Celestial Sovereign, to your Heart I entrust my whole being; I will be the tiny little child of the Divine Will. You will teach me the Divine Will, and I will be attentive in listening to You. You will lay your blue mantle over me, so that the infernal serpent may not dare to penetrate into this Sacred Eden to entice me and make me fall into the maze of the human will.

Heart of my highest Good, Jesus, You will give me Your flames, that they may burn me, consume me and nourish me, to form in me the life of the Supreme Will.

Saint Joseph, You will be my Protector, the Custodian of my heart, and will keep the keys of my will in Your hands. You will keep my heart jealously, and will never give it to me again, that I may be sure never to go out of the Will of God.

Guardian Angel, guard me, defend me, help me in everything, so that my Eden may grow flourishing, and be the call of the whole world into the Will of God.

Celestial Court, come to my help, and I promise You to live always in the Divine Will.

Amen.

"Ordinary" Holiness vs. Living in the Divine Will

"Ordinary Holiness"	Living in the Divine Will
Grace and sacraments as medicine	Grace and sacraments as food, water, air
Receiving the Eucharist and having the Real Presence leave after 15 minutes when the sacred species dissolve	Receiving the Eucharist and, through this reception, being transconsecrated into a Living Host
Praying for all	Praying in, through, and on behalf of all
Divine Will as orders to discern and obey	Divine Will as animating force of one's entire life—every thought, word, and deed.
Righteousness of the saints	Glory of Mary
Growth in virtue and in imitation of Christ	Growth in the depth of and penetration into the inner life of the Trinity through the humanity of Christ

A Round in the Divine Will

(I present the following as an example of "doing the Rounds" in the Divine Will. I did not write this--and unfortunately, I have not been able to discover who did. I include here due to its beauty and power as a prayer in the Divine Will in hopes that whoever did write it is amenable to its inclusion)

If with the prayer of the Our Father we impetrate the Kingdom, with the rounds in the Divine Will we learn how to live in the Kingdom – that is, in the Divine Will on earth as It is in Heaven.

Therefore, after each of the 24 interior acts in the Divine Will (or Hours, or Steps of the Round), and as often as we can let us repeat our celestial refrain: *"Come, O Supreme Will, to reign upon earth! Invest all generations! Win and conquer all!"*

This is the prayer that allows us to give voice to all the creatures of the universe. We will hold hands with all of them in order to reach the Creator, with the purpose of loving Him, adoring Him, thanking Him and glorifying Him – of intensifying the prayer of life: *"Come, O Supreme Will…"* **[This is a] practical and most efficacious way to do the round in the Most Holy Will of God, and to impetrate the Kingdom of the Divine Fiat upon earth.**

The soul rises into the arms of her Creator and flings herself into His Divine womb, to unite herself with Him in all the acts He did in the Creation for love of her.

So she enters into **Eden,** to receive the first Fiat of God – that regenerative breath that always generates – going around throughout all centuries, to embrace them all and to make up for all. She goes around within the **seas of the Queen Mama,** in order to repeat all of Her acts and give to her God all the acts of her Mama, as if they were her own. She flies into the **Conception of the Word** and in all the **acts that He did in His Life,** to give her own act to each act, be it even a tiny act of love - a *"thank You"*; and asking for His Kingdom, she follows Him step by step, unto His **death.** She follows Him even into **Limbo;** she waits for Him in the **Sepulcher** to ask for the triumph of the Kingdom of His Divine Will by virtue and glory of His **Resurrection.** Finally, she accompanies Him in His **Ascension** into Heaven to press Him, so that the Kingdom of the Divine Fiat may return upon earth.

PRAYER As we wake up

As our eyes open to the light of day, let us make our whole being rise in the Light of the Will of God, and let us begin our **round.**

The **first act** must be an act of love in the Divine Will. Let us make this act diffuse in all intelligences of creatures, in all gazes, in the words, in the motion, in the steps, in the heartbeats, in each breath.

Then, let us bind all of these acts of ours with those done by Adam in the Holy Will of God, with those that the creatures who will live in the Divine Will will do, up to the last one that will be done on earth.

Let us rise a little higher, then, into Creation. For love of the creature God created the sun, the stars, the sea, the earth, the birds, the flowers; and we – let us take all this love spread throughout the Creation, let us make it our own, and let us offer it to our Creator like as many acts of homage, of love, of blessings and of praises.

And now, let us go higher, up there in Paradise. Let us go through all the Angels and through all the Saints; let us unite ourselves with the whole Celestial Court, and let us give an act of love to Jesus for all and for each one.

Then, let us draw near the Virgin, our dear Mama. She is ready to give us all of Her merits as gift, and we, with the confidence of children – let us take all that She has done, from the very first moment of Her Conception up to Her last breath, and let us offer it to our God as if everything were our own.

And then, let us go to the Word, and ask Him to let us take part in all of His acts: His Conception, His birth, the flight to Egypt, the thirty years of hidden life, the three years of public life, His Passion, His death, His Ascension into Heaven. He has done all this for us - let us make it our own, and let us offer it to the Sacrosanct Trinity.

Only in this way, miserable creatures as we are, can we offer the most complete and holy act, because in this way the creature gives nothing of her own, but gives back to God all the glory that comes to her from what He Himself has done.

First Hour

The soul follows the Divine Will in all of Its acts to keep It company, and to receive Its Divine Life. She follows It in the creation of the Heavens and of the Sun.

My Jesus, I come into the heavens to sing the praises of the divine firmness. I go around and I come into the sun, to give its kiss of light and love to all.

Oh! how beautiful it is to see Your Supreme Majesty pronouncing one Fiat and extending the azure heavens with billions of stars, dazzling with light. Then It pronounces another one and creates the sun; It pronounces one more and creates the wind, the air, the sea, and all the elements together, with such order and harmony as to be enrapturing.

My Jesus, my Good, oh! how I yearn to receive within myself all the love that your Divine Fiat had in creating the heavens studded with stars, so that I myself may have as much love as It had in creating them, and I may extend my heaven of love toward the Fiat. And investing all the stars with my love, I want to give my voice to the heavens and to all the stars, so that all of them may say together with me: *"I love You – may your Kingdom come soon upon earth, for the perennial glory of your Divine Will."* I come into the heavens, I fly over all the stars, to adore and sing the praises of the divine firmness, of Its unshakable Being, so that It may render creatures firm in good, and they may dispose themselves to receive the Kingdom of your Will.

My Love, I continue my round, and I come into the sun - into the act when the Fiat unleashed so much light from the womb of the Divinity, and formed this globe of light which was to embrace all the earth with all of its inhabitants, to give its kiss of light and of love to all, with which it was to embellish, fecundate, give color, enrich and bejewel everything with its light.

Don't You feel, my Love, how your Will would want to tear the veils of the light, so as to descend and reign in the midst of creatures? And I, upon the wings of the light of the sun – I pray You, I press You, that the Kingdom of your Fiat come; and from the center of this sun, I pray You that your light may descend into the hearts of creatures and form its Sun in them. Let your love descend and burn away all that does not belong to your Will.

This sun is your divine relater. O please! my Love, let it be so that, as its light touches the creatures, it may reveal to all of them the Kingdom of your Fiat and Its Sanctity.

"My daughter, enter into Me - into my Divinity, and run in my Eternal Will. In It you will find the Creative Power as though in the act of delivering the machine of the entire Universe. In each thing I created, I placed a relation, a channel of graces, a special love between the

Supreme Majesty and the creature…" (Vol.12 – Feb. 20, 1919)

"…with highest contentment, I extended the heavens, dotting them with stars, knowing that those stars would be many and varied relations, innumerable graces, rivers of love, which would flow between my Humanity and the Supreme Being.

"…with one single creative word I created the Sun, as the continuous relater of the Supreme Being, providing it with light and heat, placing it suspended between Heaven and earth, in the act of holding everything, of fecundating, warming and illuminating everything…" (Vol.12 – Feb. 20, 1919)

Second Hour

The soul follows the Divine Will in the creation of the sea and of the wind.

My Jesus, the murmuring of the sea, the darting of the fish, the tumultuous waves together with the refrigerating freshness of the wind, ask You for the Kingdom of your Fiat.

Therefore, I come into this sea to acclaim and to love your incessant motion within its murmuring; your strength and justice in its huge waves, your purity which knows no stain in its crystal clear waters, all of your grace and your immensity that envelops everything, in the sea. And I pray You to render the man who lives hidden and wrapped in your Most Holy Will, upright, strong and pure, that he may run within your own motion, from which he came.

My Life, Jesus, I go around the wind, to love, praise, acclaim and bless in it the empire of your Will, its refrigerating freshness and its vehemence and might that knocks down, raises and kidnaps away all that it invests.

How many beautiful divine qualities are hidden in the veils of the wind. Therefore I pray You that by the empire of your Supreme Will, your Kingdom may come into the midst of creatures, and may rule in such a way that none of them will be able to resist It.

"…And now, my daughter, let us descend into the lower part of the earth; let us go into the sea, in which immense masses of crystal clear waters are piled up – symbol of divine purity. These waters are always walking – they never stop. They have no voice, yet they murmur:

'…Be pure like these crystal clear waters. But if you want to be pure, walk always toward Heaven, otherwise you would putrefy, just as these waters, so pure, would become putrid if they did not always flow. Let the murmuring of your prayer be continuous…'" (Vol. 20 – Nov. 1, 1926)

Third Hour

The soul follows the Divine Will, flying over the whole earth; and, admiring all creating things - the air, the grass, the mountains, etc., she asks for the Kingdom of the Fiat.

My Jesus, I want to bless, glorify and impress my *"I love You"* in the order of the entire Creation, in order to bring the order and harmony of the Kingdom of your Divine Will to all.

I want to fly over the whole earth, to impress my *"I love You"* on the little blade of grass, on the little plants, upon the heights of the mountains as well as in the darkest abysses, to ask You, everywhere, for the Kingdom of your Fiat.

Therefore, I keep going around, impressing my *"I love You"* in the little bird that sings, trills and warbles, to ask You, together with its singing, for the Fiat of your Kingdom. I seal my *"I love You"* in the little lamb that bleats, to ask You, in its bleating, for your Kingdom; in the turtledove that moans, to moan along with it and, loving You, ask You for your Fiat. There is no being which I do not intend to invest, in order to repeat my refrain: *Fiat! Fiat!*

"…My daughter, come and do your round in my Will. See, my Will is one, but It flows in all created things, as though divided, but without being divided. Look at the stars, the blue heavens, the sun, the moon, the plants, the flowers, the fruits, the fields, the earth, the sea - everything and everyone: in each thing there is an act of my Will – and not only an act, but my Will has remained in each created thing as the preserver of my own act…" (Vol.17 – May 21, 1925)

Fourth Hour

The soul goes into Eden and unites herself to the feast of God in the creation of man.

I was doing my round in the Divine Fiat in order to follow all of Its acts; and as I arrived at Eden, I comprehended and admired the magnanimous act of God, and His exuberant and overflowing Love in the creation of man.

My Jesus, in my shiver of love, I come right into the act in which your Supreme Majesty, overflowing with love, is about to breathe upon man, and blowing on him It infuses life in him, giving him your Likeness, and the Divine Fiat as inheritance. I too want to receive your regenerative breath; I want to love You and adore You with that perfection and sanctity with which the first father Adam loved You and adored You.

I enter into the Unity of your Will – into that very Unity which your dear jewel possessed, so that my will may be one with Yours - one the Love. And in this Unity that embraces everything, may my voice resound in Heaven, invest the whole Creation, penetrate into the darkest abysses, and say and cry out loudly: *"May the Kingdom of your Divine Will come. Fiat – Fiat Voluntas Tua on earth as It is in Heaven."*

"My daughter, Our Love was so captivated in the act of creating man that We did nothing but reflect Ourselves upon him…

Our Divine Being is most pure spirit, and therefore We have no senses. In the whole of all Our Divine Being, We are most pure and inaccessible light; this light is eye, is hearing, is word, is work, is step. This light does everything, watches everything, feels everything, is everywhere.

…Therefore, as We created man, Our Love was so great that Our light, carrying Our reflections over him, molded him; and in molding him, We brought to him the effects of Our reflections.

…With how much love was man created – to the point that Our Divine Being melted in reflections over him, to communicate to him Our Image and Likeness…" (Vol.28 – Mar. 24, 1930)

Fifth Hour

The soul is present at the fall of Adam in Eden and at the Divine Sorrow, and tries to repair with her love.

My Life, Jesus, I do not want to go out of the Unity of your Divine Will so as to make up for that which the first creatures lost; to remove the mark of dishonor that was impressed on their foreheads because they did their own will; to maintain with You the joys, the happinesses, the amusements that they had in the first times of Creation. I want to place my kiss, my continuous reparation on that

sorrow, which was so great as to make You cover Yourself with the mantle of Justice.

I want to place on You the mantle of peace, of light, of the Unity of your Will, and have one single cry: *"May the Kingdom of your Fiat come. May the first times of Creation return. May the feasts, the joys, the amusements between You and the creatures be opened once again."* I will not leave You; I will not descend from your knees, if You do not give me your word that You will let the Kingdom of your Will return once again into the midst of creatures.

"I was following my round in the Supreme Fiat, and as I arrived at Eden, I said to myself: 'My Jesus, I make the Unity of your Will my own, in order to make up for that Unity that my father Adam lost when he withdrew from It, and to make up for all the acts that all of his descendants have not done in the Unity of the Divine Fiat…" (Vol.23 – Feb. 2, 1928)

Sixth Hour

The soul continues her reparation; then she goes through all the main characters of the Old Testament, and longs for Redemption.

My Jesus, I want to hover in your Divine Will in order to trace everything and everyone. Therefore I imprison my *"I love You"* in the sacrifice of Abraham and in the obedience of Isaac, to ask You, for the sake of this sacrifice and of this obedience, for the Kingdom of your Divine Will. In this Unity of your Fiat I find the sorrow of Jacob, the sorrow of Joseph and his glory, the power of the miracles of Moses, the strength of Samson, the sanctity of David, the patience of Job.

See, my Love, these are the acts of your Will that I keep tracing within all creatures to ask You, by means of Its own acts, that your Fiat be known, loved and wanted by all.

Then I continued my round in the Divine Fiat, accompanying, with my *"I love You"*, all the prodigies It had done in the Saints, Patriarchs and Prophets of the Old Testament, as well as in those after His coming upon earth, to ask for His Kingdom by virtue of all these acts.

Seventh Hour

The soul dives into the seas of Light and Sanctity and is present at the Conception of the Celestial Mama. Together with Her, the soul prays for the

coming of the Kingdom of the Divine Will upon earth.

I see You, Three Divine Persons, giving life to the little Queen by virtue of your Creative Word, creating Her pure and spotless.

My Love, I see You laying down the mantle of Justice; and assuming the attitude of new feast, maybe more than You did in the Creation of man, all Three of You, Divine Persons, release from Yourselves seas of Power, of Wisdom, of Love and of indescribable beauty. And concentrating all of these seas, from their depth and by virtue of your creative word You call to life the little Queen, creating Her pure, spotless and so graceful with beauty as to enrapture Her very Creator. At the Conception of this Immaculate Queen, feasts open between Heaven and earth, and the whole of Creation rejoices and bends Its knees, celebrating Her as Queen.

Within Her I hear Her continuous refrain: *"May the Kingdom of Redemption come. May the Word come upon earth. May peace come between Creator and creature."*

"I was doing my round in the acts of the Divine Will and, arriving at the Conception of the Most Holy Virgin, I stopped to offer to the Divinity the Power and the Love which the Divine Persons had in conceiving this Celestial Lady, in order to obtain the coming of the Kingdom upon earth…" (Vol.35 – Oct. 25, 1937)

Eighth Hour

The soul, together with the Sovereign Mama, continues to press the Celestial Father, impetrating the Kingdom of the Divine Will, just as it happened for the Kingdom of Redemption.

Holy Mama, give your hand to your little child, and You Yourself let me cross the sea of your love, that I may place my incessant *"I love You"* in your sea of love, and form in it my little sea in order to ask, with the sea of love of the Mama and of Her child, for the Kingdom of the Supreme Fiat.

My Mama, don't You want to make your little child content by saying together with me: *"Fiat Voluntas Tua on earth as It is in Heaven"*, so that there may be one single love, one single Will, one single act and one single voice?

"Sovereign Queen, I come to hide my little love in the great sea of your Love, my adoration toward God in the immense ocean of yours. I hide my thanksgivings in the sea of yours; I hide my supplications, my sighs, my tears and pains in the sea of yours, so that my sea of love and yours may be one, my adoration and yours may be one, my thanksgivings may acquire the vastness of your own boundaries; my supplications, tears and pains may become one single sea with yours, so that I too may have my seas of love, of adoration, etc. And just as your Sovereign Height impetrated the longed for Redeemer with this, I too may present myself before the Divine Majesty with all these seas, in order to ask, to beseech – to implore the Kingdom of the Supreme Fiat." (Vol.20 – Nov. 2, 1926)

Ninth Hour

The soul follows the Divine Will in the Conception of the Word; she keeps company with the Little Prisoner Jesus in the womb of His Mama, and contemplates His birth.

My Sovereign Mama, in the same Divine Fiat I follow the Conception of the Word within your Maternal womb, in order to place in your womb, as cortege, all the acts I have done in It – my continuous *"I love You"*, my little pains…; so that, as the Divine Fiat conceives Him in You, I may provide It with my acts together with yours, in order to make It conceive Him; and for the sake of the great love He had in descending from Heaven and enclosing Himself in the little prison of your womb, I may ask Him for the Kingdom of the Divine Will.

My Jesus, I want to place my kiss and my *"I love You"* in your tender limbs without motion, and ask You, for the sake of these pains of Yours, that your Divine Will may have motion in the creatures, so that It may put to flight with Its light, the night of the human will, and form in them the perennial day of your Fiat.

My tender Little Baby, the cortege I want You to find as You come out of the Maternal womb, are all of your works, like an army ordered around You. And this tiny little one makes them say: *"I love You, I love You, I love You, I bless You, I thank You, I adore You"*. With all, I want to impress my *"I love You"* and my first kiss upon those shivering lips of Yours. When You came out of the Maternal womb, shivering, You took refuge in the arms of the Celestial Mama, and She pressed You to Her womb; She kissed You, and giving You Her milk,

She warmed You and calmed your crying.

Jesus, little as I am, I too want to place myself in the arms of your Mama, and upon Her own kiss, I want to impress my own, to make it flow within your milk, so that, as dear Mama nourishes You with Her milk, I may nourish You with my love. Everything She does to You, I too want to do.

"I was doing my round in the Creation and Redemption, and my little intelligence stopped when my charming Little Baby, in the act of coming out of the Maternal womb, flung Himself into the arms of the Celestial Mama, feeling the need to make His first outpouring of love…" (Vol.28 – Sept. 28, 1929)

* * * * *

"My daughter, in my very Incarnation, when I descended from Heaven upon earth, the first purpose was the Kingdom of my Divine Will, and in the Kingdom of my Will – that is, in my Immaculate Mother who possessed It – I turned the first steps. My first dwelling was in Her most pure womb, in which my Fiat had Its absolute dominion and Its Kingdom, whole and beautiful. And in this Kingdom of my Will I began and I formed my life down here…" (Vol.26 – May 16, 1929)

Tenth Hour

The soul follows the little child Jesus in the arms of His Celestial Mama, in the pain of the Circumcision, and encloses all human wills within that painful wound.

My charming Little Baby, my *"I love You"* follows You in the crude cut of the Circumcision. With my *"I love You"*, I want to soothe the first Blood You shed. I want to seal my *"I love You"* in each drop of It, in the tears You shed because of the intensity of the pain, and in those of the Sovereign Queen and of Saint Joseph at seeing You suffer. That Blood, that pain, those tears, ask You for the triumph of your Kingdom. My dear little Jesus, I want to press You to my heart to mitigate the spasm You suffer; I want to enclose all the human wills of creatures within this wound, so that they may have life no more, and your Divine Will may come out of this wound in order to reign in their midst.

"I was thinking to myself: 'When I go around within the Supreme Will, following Its acts in the Creation and Redemption, all things seem to speak – all of them have something to say about this admirable Will; but when I am occupied with something else, all things remain silent – it seems they have nothing to say.' But while I was thinking of this, the sun penetrated into my little room, and its light pounded on my bed. I felt invested by its light and heat, and at that moment, a light came out from within my interior, and diving into the light of the sun, the two of them kissed. I was surprised, and my sweet Jesus told me: "My daughter, how beautiful is my Divine Will bilocated in you and in the sun. When It dwells in the soul and makes a sweet encounter with Its own works, It makes feast; and as It plunges into Its own acts which It exercises in created things, they kiss each other…" (Vol.21 – Mar. 26, 1927)

Eleventh Hour

The soul follows Baby Jesus in His flight to Egypt. She calls all Creation to court Him, and asks, with everyone, for the Kingdom of the Divine Will.

My lovable Little Baby, as You are fleeing I want to make You hear my *"I love You"* with my refrain: I want your Fiat – the Kingdom of your Will.

As You flee, my Love, I feel my heart being tortured in seeing You crying and sobbing bitterly; in seeing that they are looking for You, not to give You shelter, but to make You die. And I want to calm your crying with my love.

While You flee, night and day, You are always exposed to the open-air. It is right that I take care of You and call all created things in order to cheer their Creator. Therefore I call all the light of the sun which, illumining your beautiful face, says: *"I love You"*. I call all the birds of the air, that they may form lullabies of love for You with their singing and trilling. In sum, I want to take You to Egypt, accompanied by the triumph of my love; and as refrain, I ask You for the Kingdom of your Will.

"My daughter, repeat it always, if You want to make Me happy, and calm my baby crying". (Vol.25 – Dec. 25, 1928)

Twelfth Hour

The soul with Jesus in Egypt: she offers her heart as shelter, and together with the Queen of Heaven, she asks for the Kingdom of the Divine Will.

My Jesus, I follow your crying, and I offer my heart as shelter of your Eternal Fiat.

My dear Little Baby Jesus, as I follow You, You have now arrived in Egypt, and I see that sorrow, tears, oblivion, the abandonment of all, accompany You everywhere; so much so, that You are forced to enter into a little hovel, badly sheltered, exposed to winds and to rain. No one in the world offers You a little shelter. Oh! how You sob, my most tender Baby, in seeing your little Humanity suffering the same lot as your adorable Will – no one offers, freely, the dwelling of his soul to let It reign and dominate; and even though It is in their midst, It goes as though wandering.

My beloved Baby, center of my life, while You dwell in this hovel, I want to follow all your acts and those of the Celestial Sovereign; and while She rocks You, I too want to rock You and favor your sleep with the cradlesong of my *"I love You, I love You"*. While She prepares your swaddling clothes, I want to make my *"I love You, I bless You, I thank You, I adore You"* flow in the thread that flows through Her maternal fingers, so that, when our Divine Mama will clothe You, You will feel that your garment is woven together with my *"I love You"*, which asks for your Fiat.

"…Oh! Holy Will, how lovable and powerful You are! With your loveliness, You attract me, You enrapture me, You enchant me; and I, enchanted, wouldn't know how not to remain fixed in You. And with your power, You remain firm over my littleness, You pour Yourself in torrents, in such a way that I have lost the path to go out of your endless light. But, happy loss! O please! O adorable Fiat, make everyone lose their path, that they may know no other path but that which leads into your Divine Will…" (Vol.28 – Mar. 9, 1930)

Thirteenth Hour

The soul is present at the first exit of dear Baby Jesus into the midst of the children of Egypt; she sees that He blesses them, and prays Him also to seal the human wills with His blessing.

My Celestial Baby, your love pushes You to go out of the little hovel, and the children of Egypt, attracted by your beauty, throng around You; and You speak with so much love that, they listen to You, enraptured. You instruct them, and You end by blessing them; then You run to your Mama because Her love echoes in your Heart, and as She calls You, You run into Her arms. My Love, I want to follow You in everything; I want to make my *"I love You, I adore You, I bless You, I thank You"*

resound beneath your tender steps, in the gesture of your little hands, in your words, sweet, lovable, enrapturing and full of life, and in your charming gaze, to ask You for the Kingdom of your Fiat. And as You bless the children, bless this little child of your Will, by sealing with your blessing the life of your Will in my little soul.

"I was continuing my round in His adorable Will; and while following the acts He did while He was on this earth, I paused when Jesus was blessing the children, when He was blessing His Celestial Mama, the crowds and others, and I prayed Jesus to bless this little daughter of His…" (Vol.24 – Jul.29, 1928)

Fourteenth Hour

The soul follows Jesus who, after the exile, returns to Nazareth; and with the rain of her "I love You", she asks Him, with a thousand voices, for the coming of His Divine Kingdom.

My Life, Child Jesus, I see that your exile has ended, and You return to Nazareth; and I want to follow You step by step. Even more, I want to accompany You under a rain *of "I love You, I adore You, I bless You"*; and as You retreat into Nazareth, I retreat with You, continuing with the rain of my *"I love You's"*, so as to win from You, by dint of love, that which You want, what the Queen Mama wants, and what I too want – that Your Will be known and reign in the midst of creatures.

My Life, Jesus, I am now with You in the house of Nazareth, and I want to follow You step by step to impress my *"I love You, I adore You, I bless You, I thank You"* in everything You do, and to ask You for the Kingdom of your Will. As the currents of love run between You and your Mama, my *"I love You"* runs along with them, to ask You and the Celestial Mama that your Will be known.

My Divine Jesus, I would feel unhappy if I did not follow You in everything, and if I did not keep You occupied with my company, letting You hear my refrain: *"I love You, I adore You, I bless You, I thank You"*, to ask You, together with your acts, for the Kingdom of your Will. In fact, being near You, I feel your very heartbeats wanting this, and your very Divine Will wanting to be known and to dominate in the midst of creatures.

"After this, I followed my Divine Fiat, doing my round in It; and as I arrived at the house of Nazareth, I was

saying to Him: 'My Love, may there be no act You do which is not followed by my "I love You", to ask You by means of your acts, for the Kingdom of your Will…'." (Vol.23 – Mar. 11, 1928)

Fifteenth Hour

The soul follows Jesus at the Jordan; she asks for the salutary Baptism of His Divine Will, so that all may receive Its Life, and she accompanies Him into the desert.

My Life, Jesus, as You arrive at the Jordan, I want to make my *"I love You"* flow in those waters, in such a way that, as St. John pours them over your head to baptize You, You may feel that your little child does not leave You alone, but keeps You company with her *"I love You"*, making it flow in those waters to ask You for the baptismal water of your Divine Will for all creatures, so that the beginning of your Kingdom may come. My Love, in this solemn act of your Baptism, I ask You for a grace that You certainly will not deny to me: I pray You to baptize my little soul with your holy hands, with the vivifying and creative water of your Divine Will, that I may hear, see or know nothing but the Life of your Fiat.

"My daughter, I went into the desert to call again that same Divine Will of Mine, which the creatures had deserted for forty centuries. And I, for forty days, wanted to remain alone, in order to repair for the forty centuries of human will, in which Mine had not possessed Its Kingdom in the midst of the human family; and with my Divine Will Itself, I wanted to call It back, once again, into their midst, so that It might reign." (Vol.22 – Sept. 8, 1927)

Sixteenth Hour

The soul follows Jesus at the wedding of Cana, asking Him to exchange the human will with the Divine. She continues to follow Him in His public life.

My Jesus, for the sake of that love that pushed You to surrender to the supplications of the Sovereign Queen to make the miracle of changing the water into wine, I pray You, also for the sake of your love for your Celestial Mama, to make the great miracle of changing the human will into the Divine, that It may reign on earth as It does in Heaven.

Holy Mama, You who had so much care for Jesus to change the water into wine, so as to make the

spouses happy – O please, I pray You not to let Jesus leave for His public life, if He does not concede to You that His Will will come to reign upon earth.

"How many surprises in this Will, so Holy! And what is more, is that It awaits the creature in order to keep her aware of all Its works, to let her know how much It loves her, and to give her what It does as gift." (Vol.36 – Dec. 8, 1938)

"Nothing beautiful and good will be lacking to one who has lived in my Eternal Fiat." (Vol.36 – Aug. 28, 1928)

Seventeenth Hour

The soul follows Jesus in His miracles, and asks Him to perform the great miracle of making all souls rise again in the Divine Will.

My Jesus, You keep sowing miracles, and I accompany You always with my *"I love You, I bless You and I thank You"*.

My Jesus, as You pass roads and cities, a moving scene becomes present to You: blind, mute, deaf, crippled, paralyzed people, lepers, and all the human miseries that pierce your Divine Heart. Oh! how You shudder; your Heart catches upon seeing that very human nature which came out so beautiful and perfect from your creative hands, transformed into miseries and almost horrible to the sight – all the effect of the degraded human will which, overflowing with its wicked effects, rendered humanity unhappy. O please! my Love, I beg You to let your Fiat return to reign in our midst. If You want, You can; and It will put to flight the unhappinesses that the human will has produced. Therefore, I make my *"I love You"* flow in your act of giving sight to the blind, that they may acquire the sight to know your Divine Will. How many blind to your Divine Will! The earth is filled with these poor blind; therefore I pray You that everyone may have the sight to know and look at your Most Holy Will.

"It is necessary that you go around time and time again in my Will, in the midst of my works, to ask, all in chorus, for the coming of the Supreme Fiat - so that, together with all Creation and with all my works which I did in Redemption, you may be filled to the brim with all the acts that are needed before the Celestial Father to make known and to impetrate the Kingdom of my Will upon earth…." (Vol.20 – Oct. 24, 1926)

Eighteenth Hour

The soul follows Jesus in His entrance into Jerusalem, and asks Him for the victory of the Divine Will over the human. She then follows Him in the institution of the Sacraments.

Celestial Lover, my *"I love You"* follows You in the triumphant entrance You made into Jerusalem. I impress my *"I love You"* in the branches of the palm trees, in the mantles that they lay at your feet, in the cries of hosanna that the crowds make for You - to ask You for the triumph of your Will. My Divine King, your look of victorious conqueror seems to want to give me happy news. O please! make me content – tell the little child of your Will that the Kingdom of the *Fiat Voluntas Tua* on earth as It is in Heaven will come.

"Today is the Day of the Palms, in which I was acclaimed as King. Everyone must aspire to a kingdom, and in order to acquire the Eternal Kingdom, it is necessary for the creature to acquire regime over himself and the dominion of his own passions. The only means is suffering, because suffering means reigning – that is, with patience one puts himself in place, becoming King of oneself and of the Eternal Kingdom" (Vol.6 – Apr.19, 1905)

My Love, I cling to You, and as You institute the Sacraments I place my *"I love You"* in each Baptism, to ask You by virtue of It, for the Fiat Voluntas Tua for each baptized. I bring my *"I love You"* in the Sacrament of Confirmation, to ask You, in each confirmee, for the victory of your Divine Will. My *"I love You"* seals the Sacrament of Extreme Unction, to ask You, in each of the dying, for a last act of their life in your Divine Will. My Jesus, my *"I love You"* is impressed in the Sacrament of Ordination, to ask You for Priests of your Will, and for your Kingdom within them. My *"I love You"* extends in the Sacrament of Matrimony, to ask You for families formed in your Divine Fiat. My *"I love You"* rises in the Sacrament of Confession, to ask You, in each Confession, for death to sin and for the life of your Divine Will. My Life, Jesus, my *"I love You"* will never leave You – it will be eternal with You.

Nineteenth Hour

The soul follows Jesus, step by step, in Gethsemani, and is present during the three hours of agony in the Garden.

My Jesus, I want to relieve You by making my *"I love You, I adore You, I bless You"* flow in each drop of your Blood.

My afflicted Jesus, You are entering into the sea of your Passion. Your steps are directed to the Garden of Gethsemani. I see that You prostrate Yourself to the ground, and You pray; but as You pray, pant, sigh, agonize and sweat Blood, everything comes before You – all pains and all sins, each of them carrying the mark of the deadly weapon of the human will that wages war against a God. Ah! yes, it is the human will that, with its weapons, puts the Divine Will into agony; it has kept It so for many centuries, and it still does. My agonizing Jesus, my poor heart cannot bear seeing You cast to the ground and wet with your own Blood; and because of this Blood, I ask You for the Kingdom of your Divine Will upon earth. Therefore, before You leave this Garden, give me your word – content this little child of Yours, and tell me that the triumph of your Divine Will will come.

"This agony of my Will is so painful, that my Humanity, which wanted to suffer it in the garden of Gethsemani, reached the point of seeking the help of my very apostles - but not even that I obtained; and the spasm was such that I sweat living blood. Feeling like succumbing under the enormous weight of the agony of my Divine Will, so long and terrible, I invoked the help of my Celestial Father, saying to Him: 'Father, if it be possible, let this chalice pass from Me'. In all the other pains of my Passion, as atrocious as they were, I never said: 'If it be possible, let this pain pass'. On the contrary, on the cross I cried out: 'I thirst' – I thirst for pains…" (Vol.20 – Nov. 19, 1926)

Twentieth Hour

The soul follows Jesus in the pains of His Passion, up to Calvary and to His death on the Cross; and she prays for the triumph of the Divine Will.

Jesus, may my *"I love You"* seal your spasms, up to your last breath.

My Jesus, my heart cannot bear this. I would like to put You in safety with my *"I love You, I adore You, I bless You, I thank You"*, and I ask for your Fiat, reigning on the earth – the only means to make your pains cease; otherwise we will never end, and I will have the continuous sorrow of seeing You suffer.

My heart cannot bear seeing You being presented with the Cross. You embrace It, and You place It upon your shoulders. Oh! how I would want to cover the whole Cross with my *"I love You, I adore You, I bless You"*; and I ask You, by virtue of your Cross, that all the pains which your love sends to creatures may carry the virtue of your Fiat.

Oh! how I want to cry out in each pain You suffer, in each drop of your Blood: *"May your Fiat come!"*; and in each fall, in each tearing to your hair soaked with blood, in each shove You receive: *"I love You – may the Kingdom of your Will come."*

Crucified Jesus, for the sake of the harrowing pains You suffered on the Cross, I ask that You give us graces, and that we may burn with thirst for living in your Divine Will; and that by receiving your consummation within our will, our will may be consumed in Yours. With your death, give death to our will. May your Fiat live again in all hearts; may It triumph and, victorious, may It extend through all mankind and reign on earth as It does in Heaven.

"O Jesus, I unite myself to You and I cling to your Cross; I take all the drops of your Blood and I pour them into my heart. When I see your Justice irritated against sinners, I will show You this Blood in order to appease You. When I want the conversion of souls obstinate in sin, I will show You this Blood, and by virtue of It You will not reject my prayer, because I hold its pledge in my hands. And now, my Crucified Good, in the name of all generations, past, present and future, together with your Mama and with all the Angels, I prostrate myself before You and say: "We adore You, O Christ, and we bless You, because by your Holy Cross You have redeemed the world." (From "The 24 Hours of the Passion" – 19th Hour)

Twenty-first Hour

The soul encloses herself in the sepulcher with Jesus in order to bury her will with Him. She then descends into Limbo, and with all of those souls, she asks for the Kingdom of the Divine Will.

My Love, You are now dead. Oh! how I would like to die together with You. But this is not conceded to Me! Fiat Fiat!… I want to receive You in my arms to enclose your Most Holy Humanity in my *"I love You"*, so that in everything You see, You may see my *"I love You"*, You may feel my *"I love You"*, You may touch my *"I love You"*.

My dead Jesus, after I have enclosed your Humanity in my *"I love You, I adore You, I bless You, I thank You"*, as though forming a burial with my *"I love You"* to ask You to bury the human will, that it may not come back to life - together with my sorrowful Mama and Yours, I accompany You into Limbo with my *"I love You"*.

Don't You hear, my Love, many voices dear to You? And the very Queen of Sorrows that supplicates You? And I, together with Her, say to You: *"Come – may the Kingdom of your Will come upon earth. Let everyone know your adorable Will."*

"Jesus is buried. A stone seals Him and prevents His Mama from looking at Her Son any longer. And we - do we hide from the gazes of creatures; are we indifferent if everyone forgets us? In holy things, do we remain indifferent, with that holy indifference which makes us never disobey? In the total abandonment of Jesus, do we conquer everything with a holy indifference which leads us continuously to Him? And do we form with our constancy a sweet chain, so as to draw Him toward us? Is our gaze buried in the gaze of Jesus, so that we look at nothing but that which Jesus wants? Is our voice buried in the voice of Jesus, so that if we want to speak, we do not speak but with the tongue of Jesus? Are our steps buried in His, so that as we walk, we may leave the mark of the steps of Jesus, not of our own? And is our heart buried in His, in order to love and desire as His Heart loves and desires?

My Mama, when Jesus hides from me for the good of my soul, give me the grace that You had in the privation of Jesus, so that I may give Him all the glory that You gave Him, when He was placed in the Sepulcher." (From "The 24 Hours of the Passion" – Reflections and Practices, 24th Hour)

Twenty-second Hour

The soul is present as Jesus goes out of Limbo triumphantly, and together with the Queen of Sorrows and all the souls of the just, she asks for the Kingdom of the Divine Will upon earth.

My Jesus, before You leave Limbo, concede to me that your Will may reign and dominate on earth as It does in Heaven.

My Jesus, You set out for the sepulcher in order to conquer death and make your Divine Humanity rise again. What a solemn moment! I want to place my *"I love You"* on the sepulcher, in the act in which You rise again within that Light and Glory that surround You, to ask You for the resurrection of the Divine Will in the human will. May we all rise again in You. Don't You want, then, to give me that which You enclose? Therefore, I pray You, for the sake of your Resurrection – knock down the human will with your omnipotent breath, and let Yours rise again, glorious and victorious.

Twenty-third Hour

The soul follows Jesus in the Act of the Resurrection, and asks Him to knock down the human will and to make the Divine Will rise again.

My Jesus, today, the day of your death, is the day of your victories, of your triumph. Don't You want, then, to give me the triumph of your Divine Will over the human wills? Therefore, let me hear your most sweet voice, before You leave Limbo, conceding to me that your Will may reign and dominate on earth as It does in Heaven.

My conqueror, Jesus, I see that You go out of Limbo with the whole army of those just souls.

"Then, while following the acts which the Supreme Fiat had done in Redemption, I reached that point at which my sweet Jesus was in the act of rising from the dead, and I was saying: 'My Jesus, just as my "I love You" has followed You into Limbo, and investing all the inhabitants of that place, we have asked You, all together, to hasten the coming of the Kingdom of your Supreme Fiat upon earth - so do I want to impress my "I love You" upon the tomb of your Resurrection, so that, just as your Divine Will made your Most Holy Humanity rise again as fulfillment of Redemption and as the new contract with which You would restore the Kingdom of your Will on earth – so my incessant "I love You", following all the acts You did in the Resurrection, may ask You, pray You - supplicate You to make souls rise again in your Will, that your Kingdom may be established in the midst of creatures'…" (Vol.21 – Mar.26, 1927)

* * * * *

"I continued my round in all that Our Lord did on earth and I stopped in the act of the Resurrection. What triumph! What glory! Heaven poured Itself upon earth to be spectator of such a great glory…" (Vol.36 – Apr.20, 1938)

* * * * *

"My daughter, as many acts as the soul does in my Will, so many times does she rise again to Divine Life; and the more acts she does in It, the more the Divine Life grows, and the more complete becomes the glory of the Resurrection..." (Vol.21 – Mar.26, 1927)

Twenty-fourth Hour

The soul is present at the Ascension of Jesus, and asks to be able sing, always, her loving refrain: "May the Kingdom of your Divine Will come upon earth".

My risen Jesus, my *"I love You"* follows You in all the acts You did as risen, in the midst of your disciples. I call Heaven and earth to accompany You in your ascending into Heaven when, triumphant, You opened Its doors, which had been closed for many centuries to poor humanity. I place my *"I love You"* upon those eternal doors, and I ask You, for the sake of that blessing which You gave to all your disciples who were present at the feast of your Ascension into Heaven, to bless all human wills, that they may know the great good of living in your Will; and for the sake of that love with which You opened for us the doors of Heaven, let your Divine Will descend from those very doors to reign upon earth as It reigns in Heaven.

"My blessed daughter, there is no part of my life which does not symbolize the Kingdom of my Divine Will. On this day of my Ascension, I felt victorious and triumphant. My pains had already ended; or rather, I was leaving my pains, already suffered, in the midst of my children whom I was leaving on earth, as help, as strength and support… So I was leaving and yet staying. I was staying by virtue of my pains; I was staying in their hearts in order to be loved, after my Most Holy Humanity would ascend into Heaven…" (Vol.34 – May 20, 1936)

36) <u>Some Advice for Current and Prospective Followers of Luisa</u>

Be zealous!

Have you grown convicted of the truth of these writings of Luisa, but do nothing about this conviction? Or, do you feel you could grow convicted of them—but have slothfully (or perhaps duplicitously) avoided this conviction arising? Jesus has strong words for such a soul:

> Now, who is responsible for so many pains of My Divine Will? Those who must interest themselves with making It known, but do not do it. Has My purpose perhaps been to give much news about My Fiat without the desired fruit of making It known?[1300]

But zeal is only one virtue, and even in Luisa's volumes, Jesus laments those who, for the sake of zeal, neglect prudence. So let us change tone and consider what we must not allow zeal to do to us as followers of Luisa.

Above all, this zeal must never cause us to waiver even a little in what we already know pertains to being a good Catholic.

Be an Ordinary Catholic

Consider what a blessing it is to be able to go anywhere and, by and large, the same Rosary is prayed, the same Mass is said, the same grace before meals is prayed, the same Divine Office is recited, and so on. Everywhere you go, serious, devout Catholics are often zealous for the same things: the Mass, adoration, works of mercy, confession, the Rosary, Scripture, the pro-life cause, and other similar things.

Please, then, do not risk damaging this unity by insisting that, wherever you go and whomever you find yourself amongst, your prayers and discussions center on Luisa's writings, or that they only use terminology saturated with Divine Will spirituality. This would render the children of the Divine Will just another eccentric, disagreeable, and difficult-to-interact-with subgroup within Catholicism.

Be zealous, not fanatical. If fanaticism is a real danger even for the Deposit of Faith (and it certainly is),[1301] consider how much more carefully we must avoid it with respect to Luisa's private revelations.

Perhaps some modern-day Pharisees spew much venom over minor details in Luisa's writings which are easily seen to be—when simply read with the right lens and without a chip on the shoulder—not in the least contrary to sound Church Doctrine. But let us ensure that no follower of Luisa goes to the opposite extreme by adopting ridiculous habits and behaviors based on a few misinterpreted quotes here and there in Luisa's writings.

Anti-Divine Will websites are replete with testimonies from those scared away from Luisa's revelations by bad devotees. We must consider that excessive zeal is not only self-defeating, but, specifically with respect to Divine Will spirituality, it is also the utmost example of lacking even the conformity and resignation to the Divine Will that is the indispensable disposition for receiving the Gift. If Luisa herself utterly insisted upon her writings and all the revelations contained therein being absolutely submissive to the Magisterium—then how much more so should we, mere followers, ensure that we are not overzealous about details?

Remember that the Divine Mercy devotion never would have been able to reach its present glory—a glory, please God, also destined for the Divine Will message—if its early promoters had insisted upon focusing on the most potentially abrasive parts of Faustina's Diary. All private revelations have difficult parts that require much explanation; Luisa's is no exception.

So do not focus only on how Luisa's revelations are completely different from the revelations given to other mystics, but focus as well on the similarity, which is enormous. Do not focus only on the new prayers Luisa gives, but also acknowledge how beautifully Divine Will spirituality can serve as the intention of and approach to one's current prayer regimen. **A serious Catholic should never be told that he must completely supplant his spiritual life with a new approach. Instead, all growth should be organic and proceed from interior desire, not external imposition**.

Now, I am like any serious adherent of Luisa's; I believe this is the ultimate private revelation, never to be surpassed, believing that it describes what truly is the greatest Gift God can give to man, and what His final plan is for the Church and the world. That does not mean we are to go about replacing

---

[1300]March 19, 1928.
[1301]This is not to argue we must moderate our love of the Faith. I am only referring to the need to specifically moderate zeal in certain aspects of the Faith's promotion. *In medio stat virtus.*

Sacred Tradition with what is contained in Luisa's writings! That would be confused at best, and diabolical at worst.

***

If perhaps you are among those who have become inordinately centered on Luisa's writings in an unhealthily exclusive way, consider the following: not even did the New Testament—the public revelation of Jesus Christ in which God said all He has to say[1302]—do to the Old Testament what overzealous Divine Will devotees want to do with our Sacred Tradition. For the Holy Sacrifice of the Mass is an infinitely greater and more powerful prayer than all the prayers of the Old Covenant. And yet it is precisely these "inferior" prayers that still compose the bulk of the prayer life of a priest, deacon, or religious—the "inferior" prayers of the Psalms of the Divine Office.

More abstractly, consider the infinite superiority of the Supernatural Virtues to the Moral Virtues. Faith, Hope, and Charity are completely above prudence, justice, fortitude, and temperance. Does our knowledge of that fact dispense us from focusing time and attention on those latter four virtues? Of course not. Likewise, no Divine Will devotee should find his spiritual life bereft of those things that have become inarguably essential aspects of the spiritual life of a Catholic in light of Tradition: a focus on the Mass, Scripture, Confession, Fasting, as well as the Rosary and other devotions that God has gradually formed in His Church.

Similarly, do not constantly focus on the differences between the saints potentially in the Divine Will and the saints before Luisa. Is this what we do with the saints of Church History versus the Old Testament saints—even though the former have been given infinitely superior gifts (above all the Eucharist)? No. In fact, there are many ways in which the saints of the Old Testament were greater. Were any saints of the Church found so righteous as to avert the Black Death, or the Hell-On-Earth that was the first half of the 20th century, as Noah was so incredibly righteous that it is only thanks to him that God chose not to destroy the world? Were any saints of Church History great enough to be the foster Father of the Incarnate Word, as was St. Joseph?[1303] Were any saints of the Church great enough to write prayers that even now compose the largest single chunk of the vocal prayers of all the clergy and religious in the entire world, as did King David? The answer to all these questions is "no."

In sum, do not go about with a spiritual chip on your shoulder. Do not go pushing the buttons that good Catholics have for a reason; God Himself put those buttons there so that Catholics can discern the activity of cults, heresies, schisms, and the like. You push them at your own peril, and you risk one of Our Lord's strongest rebukes in the Gospel applying to you:

> Whoever receives one such child in my name receives me; 6 but whoever causes one of these little ones who believe in me to sin, it would be better for him to have a great millstone fastened round his neck and to be drowned in the depth of the sea.[1304]

Do not Compare Luisa to Jesus

I do not mean "avoid claiming that Luisa is a person of the Trinity," for not even the most overzealous of Divine Will promoters would succumb to so blatant a heresy.

What I do mean is this: do not say things like "*well Jesus' enemies said this or that thing about His revelations, so it makes perfect sense that people would say this or that thing about Luisa's revelations.*" Jesus' revelations are the Deposit of Faith. Luisa's are not. You will be confronted with Catholics who are hesitant to approach Luisa's writings, or who, even after being told about their tenants, simply refuse to have anything to do with them. Do not take a "shake the dust off your feet" attitude to their response, for it is not a response tantamount to refusing Jesus, as the rejection of the Apostles' message was. It is furthermore useless to say things like "*well, when Jesus came, things changed also, and the Pharisees were wrong in opposing these things, so people must be wrong today in being opposed to the changes that come with Luisa's revelations.*" Jesus had every right to change things, as He came with the new and eternal covenant in order to bring to fulfillment the old and imperfect covenant. Now

---

[1302] *Catechism of the Catholic Church*, paragraph 65.
[1303] St. Joseph is the "most dignified" saint after the Blessed Virgin Mary, cf. *Quamquam Pluries*, paragraph 3, Pope Leo XIII. This is Church teaching, and the Gift of Living in the Divine Will does not change it. Though obviously he is in the New Testament, he nevertheless died before the birth of Catholicism; before he could ever even receive the Eucharist.
[1304] Matthew 18:5-6

that we *have* that eternal covenant, there can *never again* be another scenario like that of Jesus' mission on earth two thousand years ago.

To argue against this fundamental incomparability by saying, "But Luisa's revelations say we are on the verge of the Third, and Greatest, Fiat of God!" is to misunderstand in what sense the term "greatest" is meant in that context. (And I must here again say that whenever there is confusion or apparent contradiction between Church Teaching and Luisa's writings, you must *always* favor Church Teaching. I am not saying there are any *actual substantial* contradictions: I am simply saying that our inadequate minds' understanding of the two will inevitably result in occasions when intellectual honesty—which can never be set aside—requires we favor one or the other. It is in such scenarios as these that we must always, without exception, favor Church teaching.) So, "greatest," in its attribution to the Third Fiat, means finally achieving the ultimate goal for which the foundation was laid, like a tree finally producing its fruit. It is not "greatest" in the sense of a new and better foundation being built, or a new species of tree being planted or grafted.

Let me offer an example of a similar concept. Consider a Catholic who, though in a state of Grace, only receives the Eucharist as a duty to be fulfilled and thinks little about it, taking no effort to appropriate the grace from the Eucharist, and not really changing his life based upon it. Finally, one day God gives him the grace to realize the full magnitude of what he has been doing for all these years and understand it as having been a mere routine. This man's whole life changes. He abandons all of his sins and even all of his imperfections, he submits himself entirely to God, and God goes so far as to impart upon him the Spiritual Marriage described by St. John of the Cross. Along with this, everything else in his life starts working out; relationships are healed, addictions disappear, and joy and peace permeate his days. You could in one sense say that these later workings of God in this man's life were greater than the workings of the Eucharist in his life during all those previous years. But in another sense, it would be utterly wrong to say that what God did for him was greater in those later years than what

God did for him by giving Himself in the Eucharist; for God gave this man His whole Self in the Eucharist. Furthermore, the seeds of all that which took place later were indeed there earlier, though not fully applied—not fully lived. But still, God desired to reign over that man's whole life, and He did not, even though that man received the Eucharist. Likewise, God now desires to reign over this whole world, and when He raises His right hand to achieve this victory by way of the Third Fiat, what is accomplished will be, in a certain real sense, even greater than what was accomplished at the Fiat of Redemption.

If you find yourself incapable of carefully explaining such distinctions, then you should simply avoid any statements comparing the greatness of this Third Fiat to the greatness of Redemption (and anything else potentially divisive), especially when speaking with people to whom you introduce Luisa's writings. **Jesus often told Luisa that one must be very careful[1305] when speaking of the Divine Will, and that if one does not understand something, one must keep silent.[1306] If Luisa, the very recipient of these revelations, deserved these admonishments of Jesus and herself often spoke incorrectly[1307] when she tried to relay these realities on her own, how much more so will we, mere followers, succumb to spreading error if we are not extremely careful, if we fail to prefer silence when we aren't sure of something, and if we fail to give clear Church Teaching the deference it will always be due?**

On Reading the volumes

Some followers of Luisa say that it is imperative that her volumes only be read from Volume 1 to Volume 36, in that order, and only in that order. I disagree.

While it is true that this order is incredibly important for many reasons, it does not follow that we are bound to only ever read them in that order (nor did Jesus ever tell Luisa that the Volumes may only be read in such a fashion). The order of Sacred Scripture is also very important, and yet it goes without saying that there is no problem in reading it in ways other than front-to-back The Mass readings themselves do not proceed "in order."

It is often pointed out that the earlier volumes focus

[1305]E.g. July 17, 1907.
[1306]E.g. December 9, 1902.

[1307]Jesus often flatly told Luisa "You are wrong." E.g. May 15, 1926.

more on the virtues and the later volumes focus more explicitly on the Gift itself. And it is true that we must indeed pursue all the virtues for the sake of the Gift. But it is also true that, while pursuing the virtues, we will need regular reminders of the glory of the Gift to inspire our desire for it; furthermore, after having been advanced in the Gift, it will still be important to remind ourselves regularly of the virtues to continue to grow in them and remain grounded in them. Therefore, we will always be reading from various points of the volumes if we truly take the best approach to Luisa's revelations. There is also nothing wrong with simply opening up randomly and reading when one feels so inclined; this is good with Sacred Scripture, and it is also good with Luisa's writings.

37) Quick Answers to The Biggest Criticisms

While I sincerely hope that anyone with concerns will read the chapter dedicated to answering them, I also understand that time is limited; so in this Appendix, I simply wish to give very brief answers (albeit inadequate—see the aforementioned chapter for more adequate answers) to the criticisms one hears most often, and the criticisms one is most likely to stumble upon online when he does a search for Luisa's spirituality.

Objection: Luisa's writings advocate for the heresy of Monothelitism and the annihilation of the human will.

This objection, like many others, simply reveals how little Luisa's critics know about what they have chosen to publicly condemn. **Luisa's revelations repeatedly teach the opposite: Jesus specifically tells Luisa that He *did* have a human will, and Jesus repeatedly tells Luisa that He wants our wills *little*—not annihilated; *active*— not passive**. This is just like what St. Thérèse of Lisieux taught.

Objection: Luisa and her writings were condemned. They were on the Index of Forbidden Books. No Catholic is allowed to have anything to do with them. Period.

By that logic, we must also have nothing to do with St. Faustina (as well as the Divine Mercy Image and the entire corpus of revelations in her diary), St. Joan of Arc, St. Teresa of Avila, the approved apparitions of Our Lady of All Nations, Blaise Pascal, Copernicus, Victor Hugo, St. Athanasius, St. Mary MacKillop and many other saints, valid revelations, edifying works, and factual treatises. Luisa is no longer condemned. The Church's juridical actions are not infallible, and, indeed, they often change and in so changing reveal how wrong they were at first. **The only voices that count on this question (that is, the Vatican and Luisa's diocese of Trani in Italy)** **have repeatedly affirmed that the older condemnations are not binding, and, quite the contrary, that they earnestly desire Luisa's writings to be read and Luisa's spirituality to be lived**.

Objection: Luisa's spirituality is just the heresy of Quietism, wherein sanctity is falsely said to consist in the elimination of the soul's powers.

Nowhere do Luisa's writings either teach or even imply a single one of the 43 propositions that the Church has condemned as the heresy of Quietism (*Coelestis Pastor*, Pope Innocent XI, 1687). **Throughout Luisa's volumes we see the opposite of Quietism relentlessly taught**: moral effort being paramount, salvation and (avoiding) Purgatory being extremely important, interceding for others encouraged, lamenting the loss of souls (and other evils), firm insistence on **all** the virtues traditionally upheld, praying for mitigation of chastisements, etc. Trying to prove Luisa's writings aren't Quietistic is like trying to prove Pope Francis' writings aren't Jansenistic; just about any page chosen at random will do. Furthermore, any allegations of Quietism could be far more easily levied against the many Catholic saints, Doctors of the Church, and other mystics quoted in Part One of this book—any allegedly "Quietistic" elements in Luisa's writings are found far more explicitly in these works of unassailable orthodoxy.

Objection: Luisa's writings say the Universe is 6,000 years old and a 1,000-year reign of Jesus on earth is coming.

False. Luisa's revelations say neither; and this again reveals only how willing her critics are to spread hearsay and gossip of which they have never bothered to confirm the accuracy.

Objection: Luisa's writings repudiate traditional

Catholic spirituality of the Purgative, Illuminative, and Unitive way spoken of by St. John of the Cross; they speak of a sanctity too great and they make it seem too "easy."

Total ignorance of Luisa's writings is displayed here as well. **The _entire first third_ of Luisa's volumes consists in a beautiful exposition of and confirmation of the traditional three stages**. They _build_ on this foundation, they do not repudiate it. This criticism makes as much sense as opening the Bible at random and, upon reading of the Incarnation, repudiating God for not first preparing well the way with prophets and a moral law.

The criticism that the sanctity of Living in the Divine Will revealed in Luisa's writing is "too great" because it is higher even than spiritual marriage, or "too easy" because it is based primarily on sincere desire for the Gift, are both illicit criticisms that could equally be levied against St. Thérèse of Lisieux and dozens of mystics of the 20th century; many of whom are now Beatified or Canonized.

Objection: The Archdiocese in charge of Luisa's cause has demanded that none of her writings be read and no more groups dedicated to her spirituality meet.

This is a simple falsehood, and the Archdiocese has repeatedly, officially, publicly declared the exact opposite. See the Appendix containing the currently in-force notification, which clearly asks that Luisa's writings continue to be read and disseminated. (The only restriction is that her volumes not be _published_).

Objection: It is absurd to say that we can now receive a new Gift of sanctity that, before the 20th century, only Jesus, Mary, Adam, and Eve had. What about St. Joseph? St. Francis? St. Augustine? St. Paul? Why _now_ for so great a gift, given such great saints in Church History?

If one does not even believe that this Gift exists, how, then, can he be offended at the notion of the saints of previous times in the Church not having it? **Having a greater Gift does not make its recipient "greater" than those who haven't received it merely because the latter did not live in the time of that Gift.** The Eucharist is an infinitely greater gift than Moses ever received — but your having received it does not make you greater than Moses.

St. Joseph always has been and always will be the greatest saint after the Blessed Virgin; Luisa's revelations make no attempt to change that. At the very minimum, Jesus tells Luisa that His Kingdom was in full force in the home of Nazareth and that Joseph fully lived in the reflections of the Divine Will in this home, and that Joseph was _the_ **prime minister of this Kingdom.** It is not clear what is meant by "reflections" — but settling that question is something I leave to worthier followers of Luisa than myself. What is obvious, however, is that the greatness of the Gift we are now offered should be no impediment to any orthodox-minded Catholic being open to its reception.

"Are you envious because I am generous?" (Matthew 20:15)

Adopting the attitude of one who is willing to complain, "_but why wouldn't God do it this other way?_" in response to what God, in His perfect plan and wisdom, has deemed fitting, is a sure way of making grace run off of you like water off of a rock. Why didn't God reveal the Sacred Heart or Divine Mercy devotions earlier, perhaps to St. Mary Magdalene? Why weren't the Desert Fathers blessed with the Holy Rosary and its corresponding promises? Why was daily Communion not broadly encouraged before the 20th century? God has predetermined His timeline, and it is not ours to question. It is only ours to ask, when an alleged revelation or development comes along, "_is this from God?_" (using the Church-sanctioned norms for discernment discussed in Part One of this book). **If it is from God, then we must bend the knee, unclench the fist, and, close the mouth.**

Objection: Public Revelation is ended and closed. Luisa's writings try to present a new revelation, a new dispensation, therefore I know they are heretical.

Nowhere in the thousands of pages of Luisa's writings is there any hint of dispensationalism, a claim to new public revelation, or a claim to surpassing of public revelation. **In each page, Luisa's writings present themselves as only a _private_ revelation (but a revelation nevertheless) entirely subservient to — within the framework of, and upon the foundation of — Public**

Revelation in Christ (the Deposit of Faith), even though they do indeed prophesy a glorious Era to soon dawn upon the earth, as do *dozens* of other trustworthy private revelations (many of which are approved). Nowhere has the Church placed limits on how grand or glorious of a claim private revelation may make—**the Church only teaches that private revelation cannot claim to surpass or correct Public Revelation. And nowhere do Luisa's private revelations make any such claims.** If the Divine Will is very rarely referred as a "sacrament," it is done so in the same analogous sense that orthodox Catholic spirituality has spoken (for example, of the "sacrament of the present moment," or the "sacramental" approach to life and creation).

If there ever was any merit to the view that private revelation has no right to do anything but sit quietly in a corner and make minor, polite suggestions here and there, that view was demolished by the historically unprecedented degree of Church approval and exaltation given to St. Faustina's revelations, which make claims of astounding magnitude (i.e. that they—Faustina's revelations—constitute **the** very preparation of the **world** for the Second Coming).

Objection: The Kingdom is already here. Any anticipation of its coming in the future is the heresy of millenarianism, Chiliasm, or something similar.

A few lay authors today systematically distort Scripture, Magisterium, and private revelation to try and conjure up a false appearance in which the Era seems to be the heresy of millenarianism. Due to the sheer quantity of their arguments (not quality—which is incredibly low), and the unfortunate fact that they have published widely-read books on the topic, I have dedicated an entire chapter to refuting their distortions in Part Three of this book.

Regarding the status of the Kingdom, Pope Francis teaches:

> **The kingdom of God is here *and* [emphasis in original] the kingdom of God will come**… **The kingdom of God is also hope; the kingdom of God is coming now but at the same time has not**

yet come completely…there is also the need to cast the anchor there and to hold on to the cord because **the Kingdom is still coming**. We do not possess the rope fully, and there is always the risk that it will slip from our hands. This is true Christian hope. These two actions are very important: faith and hope.[1308]

Three things are obvious regarding the status of God's Kingdom: 1) the Kingdom is already here (Jesus Himself said "the Kingdom of Heaven is at hand"[1309] and "the Kingdom of God is within you"[1310]). 2) The Kingdom still must come even more fully on earth in the future (Jesus above all commanded us to pray for its coming in the Our Father, and we also pray in the Mass: "Help us to work together for the coming of your Kingdom"[1311]). 3) The Kingdom's definitive perfection is found only in Heaven. Therefore, dismissing out-of-hand the notion of the Kingdom coming in a more fully extended way than it now reigns on earth—dismissing 1) and 2) for the sake of 3) alone—is just as erroneous as any other heresy regarding the status of the Kingdom. **Nowhere do Luisa's writings present any form of millenarianism or modified millenarianism. No where do they teach a literal reign of Christ on earth; nowhere do they teach a literal 1,000-year reign of any sort; nowhere do they teach a passing of the age of the Catholic Church (rather, they teach that in the Era, the Catholic Church "acquires her full vigor"); nowhere do they teach an elimination of or addition to the Sacraments; nowhere do they teach an end of the Hierarchy, etc. There isn't a hint of millenarianism, Dispensationalism, or anything related, in Luisa's revelations.** (And I again implore anyone who has any doubts about these facts to review the chapter dedicated to them in this book.)

Objection: This at least seems like an artificial, instead of an organic, development in the Church, so for that reason alone I will dismiss it.

It is unsurprising that someone who has had little exposure to the incredibly rich spiritual and mystical tradition of the Church, and instead has focused only on the *Summa Theologica* and a small selection of Magisterial documents (*which, tragically, is the approach of some Catholic colleges and*

[1308] Pope Francis, *Our Father: Reflections on the Lord's Prayer.* "Thy Kingdom Come."
[1309] E.g. Matthew 3:2.
[1310] Luke 17:21
[1311] Eucharistic Prayer for Reconciliation I

seminaries in this rationalistic age) would see Luisa's revelations as an artificial development. But when one has had exposure to this authentic Catholic tradition—and I presented an overview of some of its key developments in Part One of this book, tracing foundations in the New Testament, through the Fathers and the greatest mystics and Doctors of the Church—**one sees, on the contrary, that Luisa's revelations are the very definition and epitome of an organic development: for they speak of the moment when the flower blooms.** The bloom, of course, will surprise one who thought he was only observing the linear growth of a blade of grass, but how lamentable for this observer to turn his surprise into a castigation of the flower! Indeed, everything has been leading up to this development *perfectly* and *beautifully*. (And the main thrust of this budding is seen everywhere in 20th century mysticism). But, you will only realize this if you unclench the fist.

Objection: But some of Luisa's followers say heretical and stupid things, and they neglect important Church teachings and traditions.

Every movement—including the very holiest ones most willed by God—count among their ranks misguided members who do great damage. These members should be directed to resources that can help them live the movement correctly, not manipulatively taken advantage of as opportunities to pounce on the movement itself, like the secular do every time they find a bad Christian. But frankly, I find this objection difficult to take seriously. In fact, I rarely hear it given; **even most of Luisa's critics seem willing to admit that Luisa's followers are devout, faithful, charitable, orthodox Catholics. These same critics just seem to forget Our Lord's admonition to judge a tree by its fruit.**

Objection: But Fr. _____ and Mr. _____ have expressed disapproval of Luisa's writings; how, then, could they possibly be valid?

This is a truly strange objection. Throughout the history of the Church, **every good and holy initiative willed by God has had its critics and enemies within the Church itself;** some have ulterior motives and see the initiative as a potential risk to their own self-interest, while others are **sincere Catholics who are simply incorrect on the matter.** (It was not only Aquinas who was wrong on the Immaculate Conception. This dogma was also rejected—before its official recognition, of course—by St. Albert the Great, St. Bonaventure, and St. Bernard of Clairvaux, to name a few. Clearly these saints were sincere, but nevertheless mistaken. Others, including some rigid defenders of Thomism who saw the acknowledgement of any errors in the *Summa* as a mark on their own prestige, were of impure intent.)

Of the small handful of common names in the Catholic realm who have voiced their opposition to or criticism of Luisa's writings, only two have been particularly distinguished as trustworthy guides to Catholic matters. And neither of these two counted as his focus or expertise the Catholic mystical tradition; although theologians, their work was focused more on Catholic apologetics. Both of them are dead now (one died in the year 2000, and likely would have changed his mind if he were alive today and saw the many validations of Luisa and her revelations which transpired in the 2000s), **and both of them, although great men, have been wrong on plenty of other things. They would themselves abhor the thought of a Catholic blindly trusting an opinion of theirs even when it has been thoroughly addressed and refuted.** If you wish to condemn a revelation, appealing to the opinions of private apologists and theologians (even if they be clergy) is radically insufficient; you will, instead, need to address the issues themselves. (**This is not to mention that both the quality and quantity of authoritative voices supporting Luisa's revelations *drastically* outweighs those criticizing them—see Part One of this book.**) In this one unworthy book alone, I have fully refuted all the common objections to Luisa's writings; including all those issued by the two previously mentioned men and all the other most commonly cited online criticisms of Luisa's revelations; and others (such as Fr. Joseph Iannuzzi, Stephen Patton, and Hugh Owen) have refuted the criticisms far better than I have.

Recall that **most movements in the Church which do not garner enemies and critics are the ones carefully strategized by business and marketing experts who optimize their efforts solely for worldly success and correspondingly know exactly how to make sure they offend no one.** Offending no one and having no critics or enemies, in fact, is proof that a "revelation" or a movement or initiative of any sort is not from God, for the Almighty always has better goals in mind than merely confirming the status-quo.

Objection: But I'm just coming across so many problematic things in Luisa's writings; even if each has an answer... why so many problems?

If this is what you are finding, then **you are approaching Luisa's writings like a teacher who is tasked with grading a student's theological term paper**, when in fact Luisa's writings are a work of great Catholic mysticism. You should approach them with the humility and prayerful demeanor that Catholic mysticism is due. **Mysticism is not primarily an intellectual exercise. It must be judged above all by its fruits, and its various literary forms along with the mode of the receiver must be understood and considered, so that what the text actually *means* can be received in accordance with the God's intended purpose.** What would become of the entire 2,000-year history of Catholic mysticism if a critical, quibbling, literalistic, hair-splitting, obsessive-compulsive approach was taken to mysticism in general? (Not to mention what would happen to Scripture itself.) If I were a dishonest man, I would surreptitiously send Luisa's critics copies of selections of works by St. Francis de Sales, St. Faustina, St. Maximilian Kolbe, St. Hildegard, St. Elizabeth of the Trinity, St. Thérèse of Lisieux, and the Greek Fathers of the Church—claiming they were written by Luisa, and asking for responses. And do you know what

would happen? I would indeed receive long treatises written by these critics, detailing all sorts of "doctrinal errors" they found in these works, so exalted by the Church, which they thought were from Luisa. Thankfully for the critics, I am not dishonest.

Objection: Okay, I guess there are legitimate answers to all my concerns. But I just still really don't like this.

Then leave this be. The Church has this covered. Luisa's cause and writings are in the hands of the Vatican. **The Church will condemn this if that is necessary (don't hold your breath!) and she does not need an army of self-appointed inquisitors to render unsolicited aid in that task.** No one is knocking on your door every day demanding that you join a Divine Will prayer group; you have nothing to defend yourself against. Aren't there better battles to fight? Aren't there women getting abortions in your very state and country? Isn't God's existence, Christ's Divinity, or the authority of the Catholic Church undermined every day by the majority of the world? Aren't the vast, vast majority of people today mired in grave sin and objectively treading the path to hell—souls created and loved infinitely by God, whom you could readily "snatch out of the fire" with your prayers, sacrifices, and works of mercy? Go and fight *those* battles; battles you know you will be praised for fighting on the Day of Judgment. **But perhaps, before heading off to those glorious conquests, you can at least spare one more minute or two to read the next section.**

38) An Epilogue for the Unconvinced

What if this is all wrong?

I admit that I do not believe that is possible, but I don't think I am dishonest for considering the question. St. Paul considered what would be the case if Christ was not raised (*cf.* 1 Corinthians 15:14).

So, I will gladly consider what would follow if it were so—what would follow if I were completely wrong about my entire purpose in writing this book. And upon so pondering, my response would be simple:

So what?

So what if these revelations to Luisa are nothing but the fantastical, decades-long imaginings of a pious, old Italian woman?

(Now, I am no Church Historian, but I do know a few things about the topic and I have a hard time thinking of a single event in Church History that would come even remotely close to such a deception as Luisa and her revelations would be if they were false. That is, a Servant of God—admired by saints and popes, whose writings enjoy many Ecclesiastical approbations, who lived a life of the greatest degree of virtue, whose legacy has not been marred despite decades passing since death, and whose days were inundated with miracles—

turning out to be a fraud, lunatic, or demon-inspired false mystic.)

I admit, I'd be disappointed, but in all honesty, it wouldn't even ruin my day. I can still lay my head on my pillow at night with absolute certainty in the Deposit of Faith. I can still recite the Nicene Creed and find indescribable joy in the knowledge that it will only be proven false when someone can draw a triangular circle; a Creed which contains Sacred Mysteries of such an incredible magnitude that I will never come close to comprehending them, blessings beyond any possible human description that God Himself freely bestows upon me.

But of course, I haven't yet really answered the question: If I'm wrong, would I, however, at least regret this time and effort I have given over to Luisa's writings?

The simple answer is: *no*, **I would not even regret that.** I am sure there are many things I will regret on Judgment Day: lukewarmness, sins of omission especially, missed opportunities for grace and mercy, and many more things. But I do not think that studying, praying, and promoting Luisa's writings would be one of the things I'd regret, even if, hypothetically, these writings turned out to not be truly from Heaven.

Whether or not they are from Heaven, they have inflamed my love for the Eucharist, they have given me a greater appreciation of Jesus' Passion than anything else ever has, they have reminded me of my duty (and ability!) to pursue and reach the highest levels of holiness, they have explicated the writings of St. Faustina, they have reminded me to strive to do all that I do as a prayer (thereby empowering my devotion to Thérèse's "Little Way" and Opus Dei's spirituality), they have provided me with countless pages of objectively edifying material, and the list goes on.

Is not a tree to be judged by its fruits? If you, dear unconvinced reader, likewise dive into these writings on the Divine Will, then—no matter how well-read you already are in Catholic spirituality—you will find in them the most powerful spiritual writings you have ever come across. If they are not from God, then they are at a minimum the creation of a genius of Catholic spirituality.

So let us pretend for a moment that Luisa never existed and nothing like her revelations ever occurred. Let us now "put ourselves in God's shoes" and ponder the nature of how He might choose to act in His greatest private revelation given to the Church in her latter days.

For if God *were* to move in a final, definitive way, through a private revelation, it would be something that provides the unification and culmination of the diverse great strands of Catholic spirituality on sanctification (the four great paradigms found in Part One of this book). It would certainly not be construable as a result of human effort, although it would equally involve plenty of the same. It would be something that would at once not replace (inasmuch as it gets rid of) anything good in the Catholic tradition, but instead would perfect it all, and empower its contribution to the very reality to which it all points. It would be something that could be engaged in every single moment of the day; for it would not merely be a specific devotion, or a prayer, or an image, or a medal (even though it would involve these). It would be very deeply-Marian and devoted to the Passion. It would doubtless bear the important similarities to Redemption itself: that is, it would involve Jesus acting through a virgin to whom He entrusted everything, and it would take place near the center of the True Faith (today: Rome; then: Jerusalem). It would necessarily be a thing so grand and glorious that it would scandalize many of the learned "Pharisees" of the day. It would have to entail the greatest holiness possible (for that is the point of everything), and some manner of restoration of what was lost at the Fall. It would entail man reacquiring his rightful place as King of Creation, serving as "nature's priest," and offering all created things back to the Father with the seal of his own Fiat. It would have to be completely in line with all that Jesus did in His Incarnation—indeed, a veritable fulfillment of the central petition of His greatest prayer. It would have to be condemned, for a time, by the religious leaders of the day.

Well, it just so happens that Luisa's revelations perfectly fulfill all of that.

Why, then, are you still waiting for this new and glorious intervention when God has clearly just presented it to your own eyes?

I understand that the primary motivation of those who choose to remain "unconvinced" is simple: it is difficult, perhaps, to believe such lofty promises of Our Lord. But allow me then to ask you: How often, in salvation history and the history of the

Church, has choosing to doubt the greatness of what God can and will do proven the approach that is vindicated?

***

While you ponder that, please also do me the justice of returning the favor I just granted to you. For I have taken time to ponder the question "What if I'm wrong," now I ask you to likewise ponder the same question. That is, dear skeptic:

What if this is true?

That may seem an odd question to include here at the end, since just about this entire book (save those chapters wherein the validity was demonstrated) assumed the validity of these revelations. But still, I know human nature, and I know how hesitant some people are to believe Good News, jaded as they are from years and years of disappointments. Yes, I know that some will have read every page of this book and nevertheless reached this very paragraph unconvinced, or at least not feeling in their hearts any sort of conviction of the reality of these revelations given to Luisa. It is to such people that I address these last few paragraphs of the book:

You do not think it, I know. Or perhaps you simply do not feel it. But suspend your judgment; even if only for a moment. Forget yourself, even if only for a brief time. Allow your mind to repose now in a position you perhaps do not ordinarily allow it to assume. Become a child again, even if only while you read during the next few moments and allow your imagination a little freedom (it is certainly deserving of this); for you needn't even tell anyone you gave it this. Assuming you are not among the small group of sorry souls today who have declared that God is not allowed to intervene in a glorious way in the world He made and the Church He started (because that would somehow be the heresy of millenarianism or dispensationalism), you will doubtless be willing to engage in what follows at least in a hypothetical, but nevertheless plausible, manner.

Imagine everything you now stress about—all of your cares and concerns—melting away like wax in a burning fire; which is precisely what will occur in the very near future when the world as we know it is turned entirely upside-down and everything you thought you know changes in a flash. Imagine all the issues now being shouted over in the news being reduced to silence, like the jabbering of monkeys in the jungle disappears upon the entrance of a roaring lion.

Imagine then, shortly after these trials and Chastisements, a New World ushered in, the likes of which the greatest works of fiction can scarcely portray even a hint. Imagine you yourself—as you are now, in your same home, with your same family and friends—being on the very cusp of experiencing these realities first hand.

Imagine, next, that you were given the opportunity to be on the right side of these coming events; imagine you were invited to be among the very elite fighting force—the best of the best of the best—dedicated to mitigating these Chastisements and hastening this Glorious Era.

And imagine now that you decided to instead remain lukewarm, undecided, and unbelieving, so that your comfortable and self-centered plans would not be affected by this "burden" of being among the few souls alive entrusted with the greatest mission in history.

Allow me to close by putting it more simply: If I am wrong, and Luisa's revelations are all a farce, then there is still much to gain but nothing to lose in heeding them. If I am right, and Luisa's revelations are valid, then there is everything to gain; so much so that you risk spending the rest of your life lamenting the missed opportunity if you choose now to neglect this invitation.

The choice is yours.

39) A Brief Checklist for Living in the Divine Will and Hastening the Coming of the Kingdom

- **Above all, be a good Catholic. Believe everything the Church teaches and obey all the Commandments and Precepts.** Undertake the duties of your state in life, whatever they may be, with diligence and love, understanding that your sanctification largely consists in precisely this. Stay strong in whatever your current spiritual regimen is; for it is not the Will of God that you abandon it.

- **Strive to be in continuous conversation with Jesus: all day, every day.** Constantly pray "Jesus, I Trust in You," "Thy Will be Done," and "Thy Kingdom Come." Continually thank Him for everything and glorify and adore Him in everything. Do not neglect this constancy either in times of comfort or times of pain; times of joy or times of sorrow; times of aridity or times of zeal. Proceed to allow the peace to enter your soul that always will if only you really believe that God hears and answers you; which, in fact, He does.

- **Strive to do everything as an Act in the Divine Will** by asking that Jesus do whatever you are doing in you, and to ensure that your **every** thought, word, and deed is pure love. If you sense that anything about to emanate from you is not pure love, then *stop*, reconsider, and only proceed with it if you can re-work it to be certain it is pure love.

- **Ask God for the Gift of Living in the Divine Will every day.**

- **Grow in virtue every day. Live the beatitudes.** *Be a saint!*

- **Spread knowledge of the Divine Will!** Start a Divine Will prayer group, distribute books and talks pertaining to it, tell others about Luisa, start your own blog, share it on social media, etc. Be creative, and be zealous. The time of the Coming of the Kingdom depends largely upon the dissemination of this knowledge.

- **Consecrate yourself to Mary** using St. Louis de Montfort's 33-day approach, and live out your Consecration totally.

- **Pray the Rosary every day,** and pray it as a family. Pray from the heart; not merely out of habit, not hurriedly, and do not willfully entertain distractions during it. Pray it so much

that doing so becomes your *joy*.

- Miss no opportunity to **beg God for the Coming of the Kingdom:** every time you see or hear *anything* that simply is not the way it ideally ought to be is a reminder for you to beg for the Coming of His Kingdom (*not* a reminder to get annoyed and irritated!). Every time you see or hear anything that *is* the way it ought to be, bless God for it and beg Him for the Universal reign of this goodness.

- **Be a warrior of prayer and sacrifice** (and, when possible, work and action!) for the most important specific prayer intentions of the day: especially pro-life efforts for an end to abortion and the Culture of Death in general, a return of marriage and the family to its traditional and true definition, an increase of holy vocations to the priesthood, the protection and sanctification of all priests, the conversion of all souls to Catholicism and the sanctification of Catholics, the defense of youth and family against the evil of the culture, and end to war, hunger, poverty, etc.

- **Wear a Crucifix, Miraculous Medal, and Brown Scapular** (and ensure you are enrolled in the Brown Scapular Confraternity by a priest), and always have a rosary in your pocket (and don't forget to use it!).

- Gently, gracefully, and naturally **evangelize in every conversation;** even if you are only sowing a small seed, and even if it is very subtle — and pray each night for those seeds to be given growth. Trust that God can work a miracle through something as simple as the salutation, "God Bless." Beyond this, evangelize with zeal and joy to whatever extent you can and in whatever way you discern you are called.

- **Attend Mass daily** if at all possible for you without neglecting the duties of your state in life. Do so with great reverence, love, and zeal: arriving early and staying late to pray, striving with all of your might to appropriate the infinite graces of Jesus in the Eucharist. Receive a Daily Plenary Indulgence.

- **Pray the Divine Mercy Chaplet every day** (one great way of doing so is after Mass, as part of a DWMoM walk—www.DWMoM.org) and live the Divine Mercy revelations given to St. Faustina.

- **Go to confession at least once a month** (and, along with that, perpetually accomplish the First Saturday Devotion of Fatima). Don't let it become a mere routine. Sincerely examine your conscience, seek God's outpouring of grace in the Sacrament, and strive to amend.

- **Never waste suffering. Love every cross God sends you**, and bear it with resignation, abnegation, patience, peace, and joy. Your feelings are not under your direct control, but your words are; never fail, therefore, to at least say "Jesus, I offer this to You" in every single pain, discomfort, displeasure, disappointment, temptation, etc. Even if you pray to be delivered of a cross, always append each such prayer with a heartfelt "*Nevertheless, Thy Will, not mine, be done.*" Proceed to thank God profusely for every suffering He allows to remain, knowing that in suffering He gives you the greatest gift, and by it you contribute to the salvation of countless souls and to your own eternal glory.

- **Do not live an indulgent life.** The details of your sacrifice, mortification, discipline, penance, and asceticism are for you to discern; but it is imperative that you not neglect this dimension of your spiritual life. **You *must* become a saint**; and there is no such thing as a comfort-, pleasure-, security-, or amusement-oriented saint.

- **Make sure you are doing regular works of mercy;** ideally, at least each week. (For example, praying outside an abortion clinic, visiting a nursing home, volunteering at a soup kitchen, etc.).

- **Sign up for a weekly Holy Hour slot at your nearest Perpetual Adoration Chapel.** If you really want an outpouring of grace, sign up for a slot in the middle of the night, or for multiple slots.

- Have whatever prayer intentions are most important to you and your family written down, and pray them every night.

- **Try to set aside at least 15 minutes a day for mental prayer:** time you dedicate solely to striving after the highest forms of meditation and contemplation (as opposed to the recitation of any given pre-defined, vocal prayer mentally recited; no matter how great).

In this time, you should strive to completely renounce the self-will—promising Jesus that you never want to do your own will, but only His—and fuse yourself in the Divine Will. It is also a good idea to do the Rounds (described in the eponymous chapter of this book).

- **Do spiritual reading every day;** especially Scripture (particularly the Gospels). But also: Luisa's Volumes, the *Hours of the Passion*, and *The Blessed Virgin Mary in the Kingdom of the Divine Will*, Papal Encyclicals, saints' biographies, and any of the great spiritual masterpieces of Church History (I especially recommend the works of St. Francis de Sales and St. Alphonsus Liguori). One of the best ways of doing spiritual reading (but which is also a powerful prayer) is to recite the Liturgy of the Hours—the official prayer of the Church outside of the Mass, required to be prayed each day by all clergy and religious, and recommended for everyone else.

- **Fast on bread and water every Wednesday and Friday** (this general norm can be adjusted as needed to accommodate your particular needs and abilities).

- **Ensure that your home is a holy place** conducive to the spiritual growth of all its members. The Kingdom will come one Nazareth at a time. Imitate the example of the Holy Family.

40) <u>About the Author</u>

Daniel O'Connor is a Philosophy Professor who holds a Master's degree in Theology from a Catholic seminary. He teaches courses in general philosophy, Existentialism, and religion, and is also a doctoral student working on a PhD in Philosophy. Daniel is the founder of the Divine Will Missionaries of Mercy (DWMoM.org). He may be contacted through his personal website, **DSDOConnor.com**. Daniel teaches in and writes from New York, where he lives with his wife and three children. Together they pray daily for all who read this book and sincerely request prayers from the same.

Made in the USA
Middletown, DE
14 July 2019